I

Contemporary Authors®

Explore your options!
Gale databases offered in
a variety of formats

DISKETTE/MAGNETIC TAPE

Many Gale databases are available on diskette or magnetic tape, allowing systemwide access to your most-used information sources through existing computer systems. Data can be delivered on a variety of mediums (DOS formatted diskette, 9-track tape, 8mm data tape) and in industry-standard formats (comma-delimited, tagged, fixed-field). Retrieval software is also available with many of Gale's databases that allows you to search, display, print and download the data.

CD-ROM

A variety of Gale titles is available on CD-ROM, offering maximum flexibility and powerful search software.

The information in this Gale publication is also available in some or all of the formats described here. Your Customer Service Representative will be happy to fill you in.

Our new fax service makes it easy to advertise your products and services to a sharply defined market. Use it to fax your promotions, press releases and announcements effectively and affordably. Gale's database of over 150,000 fax numbers combined with fast and efficient fax technology is sure to boost your response rates.

ONLINE

For your convenience, many Gale databases are available through popular online services, including DIALOG, NEXIS (Mead Data Central), Data-Star, Orbit, Questel, OCLC, I/Plus and HRIN.

For information, call

GALE

Gale Research Inc.
1-800-877-GALE

ISSN 0275-7176

Contemporary Authors®

A Bio-Bibliographical Guide to
Current Writers in Fiction, General Nonfiction,
Poetry, Journalism, Drama, Motion Pictures,
Television, and Other Fields

DONNA OLENDORF
Editor

volume 143

 **Gale Research Inc.** • *DETROIT* • *WASHINGTON, D.C.* • *LONDON*

STAFF

Donna Olendorf, *Editor, Original Volumes*

Joanna Brod, Kathleen J. Edgar, Marie Ellavich, David M. Galens, Jeff Hill, Denise E. Kasinec,
Jane Kelly Kosek, Mark F. Mikula, Roger M. Valade III, and Polly A. Vedder, *Associate Editors*

Scot Peacock, Andrea Schregardus, Geri J. Speace, Aarti Dhawan Stephens,
Linda Tidrick, Brandon Trenz, and Kathleen Wilson, *Assistant Editors*

Carol A. Brennan, Mary Gillis, Nancy Gearhart Godinez, Michele Kirkum,
Jeanne M. Lesinski, Les Stone, Arlene True, and Elizabeth Wenning, *Sketchwriters*

James G. Lesniak, *Senior Editor, Contemporary Authors*

Victoria B. Cariappa, *Research Manager*

Mary Rose Bonk, *Research Supervisor*

Reginald A. Carlton, Frank Vincent Castronova, Andrew Guy Malonis,
and Norma Sawaya, *Editorial Associates*

Laurel Sprague Bowden, Dawn Marie Conzett, Eva Marie Felts, Shirley Gates,
Sharon McGilvray, Dana R. Schleiffers, and Amy B. Wieczorek, *Editorial Assistants*

∞ ™ This book is printed on acid-free paper that meets the minimum requirements
of American National Standard for Information Sciences-
Permanence Paper for Printed Library Materials, ANSI Z39.48-1984.

Library of Congress Catalog Card Number 62-52046
ISBN 0-8103-5554-X
ISSN 0010-7468

Printed in the United States of America.
Published simultaneously in the United Kingdom
by Gale Research International Limited
(An affiliated company of Gale Research, Inc.)

I(T)P™

The trademark ITP is used under license.
10 9 8 7 6 5 4 3 2 1

Contents

Indexing note: All *Contemporary Authors* entries are indexed in the *Contemporary Authors* cumulative index, which is published separately and distributed with even-numbered *Contemporary Authors* original volumes and odd-numbered *Contemporary Authors New Revision Series* volumes.

As always, the most recent *Contemporary Authors* cumulative index continues to be the user's guide to the location of an individual author's listing.

Contemporary Authors
was named an
***"Outstanding
Reference Source"*** *by
the American Library
Association Reference
and Adult Services
Division after its 1962
inception.*
*In 1985 it was listed by
the same organization
as one of the
twenty-five most
distinguished reference
titles published in the
past twenty-five years.*

Preface

Contemporary Authors (*CA*) provides information on approximately 100,000 writers in a wide range of media, including:

- Current writers of fiction, nonfiction, poetry, and drama whose works have been issued by commercial publishers, risk publishers, or university presses (authors whose books have been published only by known vanity or author-subsidized firms are ordinarily not included)

- Prominent print and broadcast journalists, editors, photojournalists, syndicated cartoonists, screenwriters, television scriptwriters, and other media people

- Authors who write in languages other than English, provided their works have been published in the United States or translated into English

- Literary greats of the early twentieth century whose works are popular in today's high school and college curriculums and continue to elicit critical attention

A *CA* listing entails no charge or obligation. Authors are included on the basis of the above criteria and their interest to *CA* users. Sources of potential listees include trade periodicals, publisher's catalogs, librarians, and other users.

How to Get the Most out of *CA*: Use the Index

The key to locating an author's most recent entry is the *CA* cumulative index, which is published separately and distributed with even-numbered original volumes and odd-numbered revision volumes. It provides access to *all* entries in *CA* and *Contemporary Authors New Revision Series* (*CANR*). Always consult the latest index to find an author's most recent entry.

For the convenience of users, the *CA* cumulative index also includes references to all entries in these Gale literary series: *Authors and Artists for Young Adults, Authors in the News, Bestsellers, Black Literature Criticism, Black Writers, Children's Literature Review, Concise Dictionary of American Literary Biography, Concise Dictionary of British Literary Biography, Contemporary Authors Autobiography Series, Contemporary Authors Bibliographical Series, Contemporary Literary Criticism, Dictionary of Literary Biography, Dictionary of Literary Biography Documentary Series, Dictionary of Literary Biography Yearbook, DISCovering Authors, Drama Criticism, Hispanic Writers, Junior DISCovering Authors, Major Authors and Illustrators for Children and Young Adults, Major 20th-Century Writers, Poetry Criticism, Short Story Criticism, Something about the Author, Something about the Author Autobiography Series, Twentieth-Century Literary Criticism, World Literature Criticism,* and *Yesterday's Authors of Books for Children.*

A Sample Index Entry:

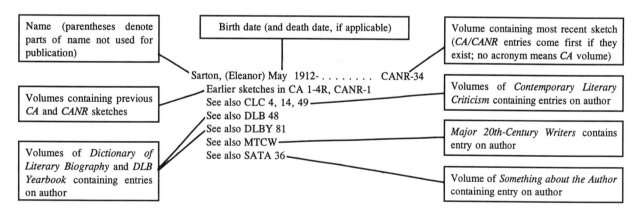

How Are Entries Compiled?

The editors make every effort to secure new information directly from the authors; listees' responses to our questionnaires and query letters provide most of the information featured in *CA*. For deceased writers, or those who fail to reply to requests for data, we consult other reliable biographical sources, such as those indexed in Gale's *Biography and Genealogy Master Index,* and bibliographical sources, including *National Union Catalog, LC MARC,* and *British National Bibliography.* Further details come from published interviews, feature stories, and book reviews, and often the authors' publishers supply material.

An asterisk (*) at the end of a sketch indicates that the listing has been compiled from secondary sources believed to be reliable but has not been personally verified for this edition by the author sketched.

What Kinds of Information Does an Entry Provide?

Sketches in *CA* contain the following biographical and bibliographical information:

- **Entry heading:** the most complete form of author's name, plus any pseudonyms or name variations used for writing

- **Personal information:** author's date and place of birth, family data, educational background, political and religious affiliations, and hobbies and leisure interests

- **Addresses:** author's home, office, or agent's addresses as available

- **Career summary:** name of employer, position, and dates held for each career post; resume of other vocational achievements; military service

- **Membership information:** professional, civic, and other association memberships and any official posts held

- **Awards and honors:** military and civic citations, major prizes and nominations, fellowships, grants, and honorary degrees

- **Writings:** a comprehensive, chronological list of titles, publishers, dates of original publication and revised editions, and production information for plays, television scripts, and screenplays

- **Adaptations:** a list of films, plays, and other media which have been adapted from the author's work

- **Work in progress:** current or planned projects, with dates of completion and/or publication, and expected publisher, when known

- **Sidelights:** a biographical portrait of the author's development; information about the critical reception of the author's works; revealing comments, often by the author, on personal interests, aspirations, motivations, and thoughts on writing

- **Biographical and critical sources:** a list of books and periodicals in which additional information on an author's life and/or writings appears

Obituary Notices in *CA* provide date and place of birth as well as death information about authors whose full-length sketches appeared in the series before their deaths. These entries also summarize the authors' careers and writings and list other sources of biographical and death information.

Related Titles in the *CA* Series

Contemporary Authors Autobiography Series complements *CA* original and revised volumes with specially commissioned autobiographical essays by important current authors, illustrated with personal photographs they provide. Common topics include their motivations for writing, the people and experiences that shaped their careers, the rewards they derive from their work, and their impressions of the current literary scene.

Contemporary Authors Bibliographical Series surveys writings by and about important American authors since World War II. Each volume concentrates on a specific genre and features approximately ten writers; entries list works written by and about the author and contain a bibliographical essay discussing the merits and deficiencies of major critical and scholarly studies in detail.

Available in Electronic Formats

CD-ROM. Full-text bio-bibliographic entries from the entire *CA* series, covering approximately 100,000 writers, are available on CD-ROM through lease and purchase plans. The disc combines entries from the *CA, CANR,* and *Contemporary Authors Permanent Series* (*CAP*) print series to provide the most recent author listing. It can be searched by name, title, subject/genre, personal data, and by using boolean logic. The disc will be updated every six months. For more information, call 1-800-877-GALE.

Online. Plans are underway to make *CA* available online.

Magnetic Tape. *CA* is available for licensing on magnetic tape in a fielded format. Either the complete database or a custom selection of entries may be ordered. The database will be available for internal data processing and nonpublishing purposes only. For more information, call 1-800-877-GALE.

Suggestions Are Welcome

The editors welcome comments and suggestions from users on any aspects of the *CA* series. If readers would like to recommend authors whose entries should appear in future volumes of the series, they are cordially invited to write: The Editors, *Contemporary Authors,* 835 Penobscot Bldg., Detroit, MI 48226-4094; call toll-free at 1-800-347-GALE; or fax to 1-313-961-6599.

CA Numbering System and Volume Update Chart

Occasionally questions arise about the *CA* numbering system and which volumes, if any, can be discarded. Despite numbers like "29-32R," "97-100" and "143," the entire *CA* print series consists of only 112 physical volumes with the publication of *CA* Volume 143. The following charts note changes in the numbering system and cover design, and indicate which volumes are essential for the most complete, up-to-date coverage.

***CA* First Revision**	● 1-4R through 41-44R (11 books) *Cover:* Brown with black and gold trim. There will be no further First Revision volumes because revised entries are now being handled exclusively through the more efficient *New Revision Series* mentioned below.
***CA* Original Volumes**	● 45-48 through 97-100 (14 books) *Cover:* Brown with black and gold trim. ● 101 through 143 (43 books) *Cover:* Blue and black with orange bands. The same as previous *CA* original volumes but with a new, simplified numbering system and new cover design.
***CA* Permanent Series**	● *CAP*-1 and *CAP*-2 (2 books) *Cover:* Brown with red and gold trim. There will be no further *Permanent Series* volumes because revised entries are now being handled exclusively through the more efficient *New Revision Series* mentioned below.
***CA* New Revision Series**	● *CANR*-1 through *CANR*-43 (43 books) *Cover:* Blue and black with green bands. Includes only sketches requiring extensive changes; **sketches are taken from any previously published *CA*, *CAP*, or *CANR* volume.**

If You Have:	You May Discard:
CA First Revision Volumes 1-4R through 41-44R **and** *CA Permanent Series* Volumes 1 and 2	*CA* Original Volumes 1, 2, 3, 4 Volumes 5-6 through 41-44
CA Original Volumes 45-48 through 97-100 **and** 101 through 143	**NONE:** These volumes will not be superseded by corresponding revised volumes. Individual entries from these and all other volumes appearing in the left column of this chart may be revised and included in the various volumes of the *New Revision Series*.
CA New Revision Series Volumes *CANR*-1 through *CANR*-43	**NONE:** The *New Revision Series* does not replace any single volume of *CA*. Instead, volumes of *CANR* include entries from many previous *CA* series volumes. All *New Revision Series* volumes must be retained for full coverage.

A Sampling of Authors and Media People
Featured in This Volume

John Charmley
Charmley's acclaimed biographies focus on British political figures, such as Winston Churchill and Alfred Duff Cooper. His conclusion that Churchill could have negotiated an earlier peace with Nazi leader Adolf Hitler stirred debate.

Roddy Doyle
An Irish novelist, Doyle is the author of several works which feature the Rabbitte family. One of his novels, *The Commitments,* was adapted into a successful film. His *Paddy Clarke Ha Ha Ha* won the Booker Prize in 1993.

Eileen Drew
Drew used her experiences as the daughter of a foreign service officer to write the tales in *Blue Taxis: Stories about Africa,* her debut collection which focuses on young, female Americans living in Africa.

Clarissa Pinkola Estes
Drawing on her Spanish, Mexican, and Hungarian ancestry, Estes developed the gift of storytelling as a healing measure. Estes—a Jungian analyst—uses fairy tales and folklore to explore psychological issues important to women in her bestselling book *Women Who Run with the Wolves: Myths and Stories of the Wild Woman Archetype.*

Harry E. Figgie, Jr.
Figgie, founder of the highly successful Figgie International Inc., predicts in his *Bankruptcy 1995: The Coming Collapse of America and How to Stop It* that U.S. fiscal policies will lead to economic disaster.

Karen Joy Fowler
Winner of the 1987 Hugo Award for best new writer, Fowler uses fantastic plotlines and characters to reveal aspects of human nature in works such as *Artificial Things* and *Sarah Canary.*

Ronald Frame
Awarded the Betty Trask prize for fiction for his debut novel, *Winter Journey,* Frame has continued to draw critical attention for his portrayals of love and intrigue in the British middle class in such works as *A Long Weekend with Marcel Proust, A Woman of Judah,* and *Bluette.*

William McCranor Henderson
In two well-received novels, *Stark Raving Elvis* and *I Killed Hemingway,* Henderson satirizes America's fixation with celebrities and other elements of popular culture.

Medbh McGuckian
An award-winning Irish poet, McGuckian is recognized for her lyrical, highly symbolic verse, which uses metaphors and evocative images to examine such themes as the feminine psyche. Among her best known works are *Venus and the Rain,* a juxtaposition of science and mythology, and *The Flower Master.*

Terry Pratchett
This fantasy novelist has received British Science Fiction Awards for his "Discworld" series, which includes *The Colour of Magic* and *Witches Abroad,* and for the biblical spoof he coauthored, *Good Omens: The Nice and Accurate Predictions of Agnes Nutter, Witch.*

Will Self
Self, a former drug addict, examines the lives of several individuals as they try to cope with insanity, substance abuse, and sexual confusion in such works as *My Idea of Fun: A Cautionary Tale, The Quantity Theory of Insanity,* and *Cock and Bull.*

Charlie Smith
Lauded for his lyrical prose, Georgian novelist and poet Smith sets much of his work in the South and embroils his characters in melodramatic situations. Smith's novels include *Canaan* and *Chimney Rock;* his poetry is compiled in books such as *The Palms,* the award-winning *Red Roads,* and *Before and After.*

Booth Tarkington
A prolific and acclaimed writer, Tarkington was known for his works describing middle-class life in the American Midwest during the early twentieth century. He is best remembered for his Pulitzer Prize-winning novels *The Magnificent Ambersons* and *Alice Adams.*

Giuseppe Tornatore
Italian film director and screenwriter Tornatore won the attention of American audiences with his *Cinema Paradiso,* which garnered the Special Jury Prize at the Cannes International Film Festival in 1989 and an Academy Award for best foreign-language film in 1990.

Donna Williams
In *Nobody Nowhere: The Extraordinary Autobiography of an Autistic* and *Somebody Somewhere,* Williams details her struggles with autism and her attempts to comprehend her world.

Contemporary Authors ®

Indicates that a listing has been compiled from secondary sources believed to be reliable, but has not been personally verified for this edition by the author sketched.

ABRAMS, Douglas Carl 1950-

PERSONAL: Born January 7, 1950, in Tarboro, NC; son of Era Glenn (a farmer) and Edna Louise (a homemaker; maiden name, Harrell) Abrams; married Linda Marie Perry (a college professor), August 2, 1980; children: Jessica Louise, Benjamin Perry. *Education:* Bob Jones University, B.A., 1972; North Carolina State University, M.A., 1974; Sorbonne, University of Paris, Certificate, 1974; University of Maryland at College Park, Ph.D., 1981. *Politics:* Republican. *Religion:* Presbyterian.

ADDRESSES: Home—22 Sewanee Ave., Greenville, SC 29609. *Office*—Department of Social Studies Education, Bob Jones University, P.O. Box 34627, Greenville, SC 29614.

CAREER: Bob Jones University, Greenville, SC, professor of history, 1974—, director of Kenya Mission Team, 1991—, head of Department of Social Studies Education, 1992—.

MEMBER: American Historical Association, Organization of American Historians, Southern Historical Association, St. George Tucker Society (fellow).

AWARDS, HONORS: Grants from National Endowment for the Humanities, 1983, 1986, American Council of Learned Societies, 1988, Southern Baptist Convention's Historical Commission, 1989, and Institute for the Study of American Evangelicals, 1992.

WRITINGS:

Conservative Constraints: North Carolina and the New Deal, University Press of Mississippi, 1992.

Work represented in anthologies. Contributor of articles and reviews to history journals.

SIDELIGHTS: Douglas Carl Abrams told *CA:* "My writing has been an important adjunct to teaching history on the university level. Just as I enjoy explaining things orally in the classroom, I enjoy the same process in written form. Driven by curiosity, I get great satisfaction from refining my thoughts in writing. I receive pleasure from both the research, which is essential for historical writing, and the actual composition stage.

"In recent years, historians have been revising their views of twentieth-century conservative or right-wing movements. My first book *Conservative Constraints* does that for business people, landowners, and southern politicians in North Carolina during the Great Depression and New Deal era. My current research, which I hope will result in another book, continues that emphasis with an examination of American fundamentalists from 1920 to 1940. This will be my first foray into social and cultural history and also will be an exercise in Christian scholarship, applying biblical values to the study of fundamentalist culture between the wars.

"My chief avocation currently is leading a team of university students biennially to Kenya. For two months in the summer, we teach, do work projects, and assist nationals and missionaries in the work of Christian missions. It is also a family affair; my wife and two children go with us. Our first trip was in the summer of 1989."

*   *   *

ABRAMSON, Edward A. 1944-

PERSONAL: Born January 14, 1944, in Brooklyn, NY; son of Arthur Aaron (a welder) and Emily (a homemaker; maiden name, Markowitz) Abramson; married Avril Nicola Brown (an artist), December 17, 1974; children:

Elise, David, Dorian. *Education:* City University of New York, B.A., 1965; University of Iowa, M.A., 1966; Victoria University of Manchester, Ph.D., 1977. *Politics:* Liberal. *Religion:* Jewish. *Avocational Interests:* Country walks, sailing, cycling, swimming.

ADDRESSES: Home—198 Park Ave., Hull HU5 3EY, England. *Office*—Department of American Studies, University of Hull, Hull HU6 7RX, England.

CAREER: East Carolina University, Greenville, NC, instructor, 1966-69; College of William and Mary, Williamsburg, VA, professor, 1986-87; University of Hull, Hull, England, lecturer, 1971—.

MEMBER: British Association for American Studies, Association of University Teachers, Amnesty International.

WRITINGS:

The Immigrant Experience in American Literature, British Association for American Studies, 1982.
Chaim Potok (monograph), Twayne, 1986.
Bernard Malamud Revisited (monograph), Twayne, 1993.

WORK IN PROGRESS: Research on Asian-American literature and Jewish-American literature.

*   *   *

ADAM, Helen (Douglas)   1909-1993

OBITUARY NOTICE—See index for *CA* sketch: Born December 2, 1909, in Glasgow, Scotland; came to the United States, 1939; died September 19, 1993, in Fort Greene, Brooklyn, NY. Actress, playwright, balladist, and poet. Remembered for her participation in the Beat poetry movement, Adam dabbled in various artistic mediums during her career. An actress in films such as *Our Corpses Speak,* she was also the subject of a documentary by filmmaker Rosa von Praunheim. Her other theatrical credits include the play *San Francisco's Burning* which she coauthored with her sister, Pat Adam. Noted as an author of Scottish ballads as well as verse, Adam first saw publication in 1923 with the book *The Elfin Pedlar and Tales Told by Pixy Pool.* Her other early works include *Charms and Dreams from the Elfin Pedlar's Pack* and *Shadow of the Moon.* Among her later volumes were *Counting-Out Rhyme, The Bells of Dis,* and *Stone Cold Gothic.*

OBITUARIES AND OTHER SOURCES:

BOOKS

The Writers Directory: 1990-1992, St. James Press, 1990, p. 5.

PERIODICALS

New York Times, October 12, 1993, p. B9.

ALEXANDER, Doris (Muriel)   1922-

PERSONAL: Born December 14, 1922, in Newark, NJ; daughter of A. J. (a physician) and Marie (a teacher; maiden name, Joachim) Alexander. *Education:* University of Missouri—Columbia, B.A., 1944; University of Pennsylvania, M.A., 1946; New York University, Ph.D., 1952. *Avocational Interests:* Music, art, cookery, window-box gardening.

ADDRESSES: Home and office—San Trovaso 1116, Dorsoduro, 30123 Venice, Italy. *Agent*—Gunther Stuhlmann, P.O. Box 276, Becket, MA 01223.

CAREER: City University of New York, New York City, head of English department, 1956-63; University of Athens, Athens, Greece, Fulbright professor, 1966-67; Pennsylvania State University, University Park, visiting professor and fellow, Institute of Humanities and Arts, 1968.

MEMBER: Dickens Society, O'Neill Society.

WRITINGS:

The Tempering of Eugene O'Neill, Harcourt, 1962.
Creating Characters With Charles Dickens, Pennsylvania State University Press, 1991.
Eugene O'Neill's Creative Struggle: The Decisive Years, 1924-1933, Pennsylvania State University Press, 1992.

Contributor to language and literature journals, including *Dickens Quarterly, Modern Drama, American Literature, Modern Language Quarterly,* and *American Quarterly.*

WORK IN PROGRESS: Looking Into Creativity, and *Ultimate Confrontations: O'Neill's Last Plays,* publication expected in 1995.

SIDELIGHTS: Doris Alexander told *CA:* "My books are all really case histories of the creative process—a new kind of biography and literary criticism."

*   *   *

ALEXANDER, Estella Conwill   1949-

PERSONAL: Born January 19, 1949, in Louisville, KY; children: Patrice Sales, Dominic. *Education:* University of Louisville, B.A., 1975, M.A., 1976; University of Iowa, Ph.D., 1984.

ADDRESSES: Office—Department of English, Hunter College of the City University of New York, 695 Park Ave., New York, NY 10021.

CAREER: University of Iowa, Iowa City, instructor and director of black poetry, 1976-79; Grinnell College, Grinnell, IA, assistant professor, 1979-80; professor of English at Kentucky State University and Hunter College of the City University of New York.

AWARDS, HONORS: Grants from Kentucky Arts Council and Kentucky Foundation for Women, both 1986.

WRITINGS:

Jiva Telling Rites: An Initiation, Third World Press, 1989.*

*   *   *

ALLEN, Bob 1961-

PERSONAL: Full name Robert L. Allen; born May 23, 1961, in Jamestown, ND; son of Eugene O. Allen and Beverly Mae (Joos) Allen. *Education:* Attended Orange Coast College, 1987. *Avocational Interests:* Cycling, skiing, travel.

ADDRESSES: Home—7919 Thorpe Rd., Bozeman, MT 59715. *Agent*—Pick Marketing, 216 North Third St., Sterling, CO 80751.

CAREER: Freelance photographer and writer. *Military service:* U.S. Navy, 1979-85, served in England and the West Pacific.

AWARDS, HONORS: Book of the year nomination, Children's Book Foundation, 1992, for *Mountain Biking.*

WRITINGS:

JUVENILE

(And photographer with Michele Dieterich) *Mountain Biking,* Wayland Publishing, 1991, Lerner Publications, 1992.
(And photographer) *Rollin' in the Dirt,* Pick Marketing, 1993.

Also photographer for *Skiing* by Michele Dieterich, Wayland Publishing, 1991, Lerner Publications, 1992.

OTHER

Contributor to periodicals, including *Bicycling, Mountain Bike Action, Velo News, Mountain Biker International, Bike, Solo Bici, Velo Tout Terrain, Tuto Mountain Bike,* and *Cycling World.*

WORK IN PROGRESS: Assembling photos and notes for a "coffee table" book featuring photography on mountain biking; printing a fine art portfolio.

SIDELIGHTS: Upon graduation from high school Bob Allen joined the Navy. "I realized that I wasn't ready to take college seriously and felt the need to travel," he told commented. While stationed in England he bought his first camera and developed a love of photography. "The

two years I spent immersed in London's rich culture provided me with a fertile environment to pursue my new-found hobby." Soon he had learned to process and print his own work and a hobby turned into a serious avocation as he visually explored the Far East and Africa during two cruises on the U.S.S. *Tarawa.*

After his discharge from the Navy in 1985, Allen spent several years racing bikes and skiing in his native Montana. He combined photography with these two sports, taking pictures especially of cycling events in which he competed. While at Orange Coast College in California, he was inspired by classes in photography and writing to begin selling photographs to cycling magazines. Allen left college before completing his degree and made a career move back to London. "I arrived [in 1989] with a bike, cameras, a handful of transparencies and . . . much enthusiasm." The London based magazine, *Mountain Biker,* began publishing his photographs and his career was launched.

In 1991 he wrote and illustrated the book, *Mountain Biking,* which is part of the "All Action" Series. In 1992 he illustrated the companion volume, *Skiing,* for the same publisher. "The 'All Action Series' is geared toward children ages 10-13 and is designed to appeal to kids who might have a reading disability and/or are intimidated by 'traditional' books," Allen told explained. "In my photography, I strive to deliver maximum image impact. My photographs capture the instant where the action and aesthetic collide. I'm fascinated with depicting motion in my work and constantly push for a fresh look."

*   *   *

ALLEN, Paula Gunn 1939-

PERSONAL: Born in 1939, in Cubero, NM. *Education:* Received B.A., M.F.A., and Ph.D.

ADDRESSES: Office—c/o University of California, Berkeley, Berkeley, CA 94720. *Agent*—Diane Cleaver Inc., 55 Fifth Ave., 15th Floor, New York, NY 10003.

CAREER: University of California, Berkeley, lecturer in Native American studies; writer. Former lecturer at San Francisco State University, University of New Mexico, and Fort Lewis College.

AWARDS, HONORS: National Endowment for the Arts award; Ford Foundation grant.

WRITINGS:

POETRY

The Blind Lion, Thorp Springs Press, 1974.
Coyote's Daylight Trip, La Confluencia, 1978.
A Cannon between My Knees, Strawberry Hill Press, 1981.

Shadow Country, University of California American Indian Studies Center, 1982.

Skins and Bones, West End, 1988.

EDITOR

From the Center: A Folio of Native American Art and Poetry, Strawberry Hill, 1981.

Studies in American Indian Literature: Critical Essays and Course Designs, Modern Language Association, 1983.

Spider Woman's Granddaughters: Traditional Tales and Contemporary Writing by Native American Women, Beacon Press, 1989.

OTHER

Sipapu: A Cultural Perspective, University of New Mexico Press, 1975.

The Woman Who Owned the Shadows (novel), Spinsters, Ink, 1983.

The Sacred Hoop: Recovering the Feminine in American Indian Traditions (essays), Beacon Press, 1986, reissued with new preface, 1992.

Grandmothers of the Light: A Medicine Woman's Sourcebook, Beacon Press, 1991.

SIDELIGHTS: Paula Gunn Allen's heritage is a mixture of various ethnicities and nationalities, but at her heart she is Native American. Branches of her family tree come from the Laguna Pueblo and Sioux cultures, and it is this American Indian past that informs and directs her work. In a 1989 telephone interview with Robin Pogrebin for the *New York Times Book Review,* Allen characterizes Native Americans as "something other than victims—mostly what we are is unrecognized." To help remedy this situation, Allen compiled *The Sacred Hoop: Recovering the Feminine in American Indian Traditions,* a collection of seventeen essays covering topics that range from the status of lesbians in Native American cultures, to literature's roots in the soil of tradition and ritual. In the *Los Angeles Times Book Review,* Quannah Karvar compliments the volume's "power and insight as a commentary on the perceptions and priorities of contemporary Native American women."

In 1989 Allen edited *Spider Woman's Granddaughters: Traditional Tales and Contemporary Writing by Native American Women,* which Karvar calls in a later essay for *Los Angeles Times Book Review* "a companion in spirit" to the author's book of essays *The Sacred Hoop.* In *Spider Woman's Granddaughters,* Allen gives space not only to contemporary authors such as Vickie L. Sears but also to legends of old deities such as the Pueblos' mother goddess of corn. She also includes the words of Pretty Shield, a Crow Indian who told her life story to ethnographer Frank B. Linderman early in the twentieth century. In the *New York Times Book Review,* Ursula K. Le Guin praises

the organization of the book, noting that Allen has arranged the pieces "so that they interact to form larger patterns, giving the book an esthetic wholeness rare in anthologies."

Allen's only novel, 1983's *The Woman Who Owned the Shadows,* received a generally favorable review from Alice Hoffman in the *New York Times Book Review.* "In those sections where the author forsakes the artifice of her style," declares the critic, "an absorbing, often fascinating world is created." The novel's heroine, Ephanie, is emotionally wounded as a young girl and struggles to mend her fractured core "guided," according to Hoffman, "by the traditional tales of spirit women."

Allen has also gained recognition as a poet. Her first published collection of poems, *The Blind Lion,* appeared in 1974. Her most recent, *Skins and Bones,* was published in 1988.

BIOGRAPHICAL/CRITICAL SOURCES:

PERIODICALS

Los Angeles Times Book Review, January 25, 1987, p. 11; July 9, 1989.

New York Times Book Review, June 3, 1984; May 14, 1989, p. 15.

*   *   *

ALLEN, Robert L.
   See ALLEN, Bob

*   *   *

ALSHAWI, Hiyan 1957-

PERSONAL: Born December 2, 1957, in Baghdad, Iraq; son of Khalid A. (a commercial law adviser) and Dorothy Elaine (a college lecturer; maiden name, Herweyer) Alshawi. *Education:* University of Warwick, B.Sc. (with first class honors), 1979; Cambridge University, postgraduate diploma in computer science, 1980, Ph.D., 1983. *Avocational Interests:* Sailing.

ADDRESSES: *Office*—American Telephone & Telegraph, Bell Laboratories, 2D-435, 600 Mountain Ave., Murray Hill, NJ 07974.

CAREER: Cambridge University, Cambridge, England, postdoctoral research fellow, 1984-85; SRI International, Cambridge, senior computer scientist, 1986-92; American Telephone & Telegraph, Bell Laboratories, Murray Hill, NJ, staff member, 1993—.

MEMBER: Association for Computational Linguistics, Trinity Hall Graduate Society (president, 1981).

WRITINGS:

Memory and Context for Language Interpretation, Cambridge University Press, 1987.
(Editor) *The Core Language Engine,* MIT Press, 1992.

Member of editorial board, *Computational Linguistics.*

WORK IN PROGRESS: Interpretation, Translation, and Reasoning, completion expected in 1995; research on the automatic translation of spoken conversation between English and Mandarin Chinese.

*   *   *

ALTMANN, Simon L(eonardo)   1924-

PERSONAL: Born January 10, 1924, in Buenos Aires, Argentina; son of Aaron (in business) and Matilde (a secretary; maiden name, Branover) Altmann; married Susana Maria Liebeschuetz (a teacher), August 6, 1948; children: Daniel Ricardo, Paul Nicholas Sebastian, Gerald Thomas Michael. *Education:* University of Buenos Aires, D.Chem., 1947; King's College, London, Ph.D., 1951; Oxford University, M.A., 1958. *Politics:* Labour. *Religion:* Agnostic.

ADDRESSES: Home—232 Woodstock Rd., Oxford OX2 7NJ, England. *Office*—Brasenose College, Oxford University, Oxford OX1 4AJ, England.

CAREER: University of Buenos Aires, Buenos Aires, Argentina, demonstrator, 1952; Oxford University, Oxford, England, research assistant at Mathematical Institute, 1953-57; University of Buenos Aires, professor of chemical physics, 1957-58; Oxford University, lecturer in theory of metals, 1959-91, fellow of Brasenose College and lecturer in mathematical physics, 1964-91, vice-principal of Brasenose College, 1990-91. University of Rome, lecturer, 1963, 1965, 1967, 1970, visiting professor, 1972, 1985; Shell Research Laboratories (Amsterdam), lecturer, 1963; United Kingdom Atomic Energy Authority (Harwell), lecturer, 1966; University of Darmstadt, lecturer, 1972; University of Stockholm, visiting professor, 1972; Technische Hochschule (Vienna), visiting professor, 1975; Instituto Rocasolano (Madrid), British Council exchange visitor, 1976; Technion-Israel Institute of Technology, visiting professor, 1978; University of Texas at Austin, distinguished lecturer, 1979; University of Zaragoza, visiting professor, 1979, visiting lecturer, 1991; University of Perugia, lecturer, 1982; Johns Hopkins University, visiting professor, 1986; Technical University of Vienna, guest professor, 1986; Catholic University of Louvain, Vlaamse Leergangen Professor, 1989-90; University of Vienna, visiting professor, 1992.

WRITINGS:

Band Theory of Metals: The Elements, Pergamon, 1970.
Induced Representations in Crystals and Molecules: Point, Space, and Nongrid Molecule Groups, Academic Press (London), 1977.
Rotations, Quaternions, and Double Groups, Clarendon Press, 1986.
Band Theory of Solids: An Introduction From the Point of View of Symmetry, Clarendon Press, 1991.
Icons and Symmetries, Clarendon Press, 1992.
(With Peter Herzig) *Point-Group Theory Tables,* Clarendon Press, 1994.

Contributor to scientific journals.

WORK IN PROGRESS: Is Nature Supernatural? A Primer on the Philosophy of Science, completion expected in 1996; research on Clifford algebra and the Euclidean group.

SIDELIGHTS: Simon L. Altmann told *CA:* "I was always interested in research (quantum mechanics, solid state, applied group theory) and I have published some sixty scientific papers. At the same time, lecturing and teaching have been a great pleasure for me and, because of this, I have tried to widen my audience by writing books. I wrote my first one in Spanish, on statistics, when I was twenty years old. It was published by the Faculty of Natural Science in Buenos Aires, and it was still selling ten years ago. Since I was in my early teens, philosophy has been underlying a lot of my reading and thinking, and now, fifty years later, I feel that I am ready to go back to it full-time; hence, the title of the new book I am writing. I am now retired and do not have to attend committee meetings, so I can sit happily at my computer from nine o'clock in the morning to six o'clock in the evening. From time to time this is done at the library, rather than my study at home; nothing is more important than a good notebook computer!"

*   *   *

AMBROSINI, Richard   1955-

PERSONAL: Born April 20, 1955, in Rome, Italy; son of Marco Valerio (a publisher) and Sara (a journalist; maiden name, Cauldwell) Ambrosini; married Claudia Marchei (a psychologist), April 26, 1986 (separated). *Education:* Attended Universita La Sapienza, 1975-81; University of Ottawa, Ph.D., 1989. *Religion:* Catholic.

ADDRESSES: Home—Via Chieti, 20-00161 Rome, Italy. *Office*—Department of English, University of Rome, Via Carlo Fea, 2-00161 Rome, Italy.

CAREER: University of Rome, Rome, Italy, English language assistant, 1986—. *Military service:* Italian Army, 1981-82; served in the Grenadier Corps.

WRITINGS:

Conrad's Fiction as Critical Discourse, Cambridge University Press, 1991.
Introduzione a Conrad, Laterza, 1991.

Translator into Italian, Joseph Conrad's *An Outcast of the Islands* and Robert Louis Stevenson's *Treasure Island.* Author of a column in *Il Messaggero.* Contributor to periodicals.

WORK IN PROGRESS: A book on Robert Louis Stevenson, publication expected in 1995; *An Italian History of the English Novel,* a comparative study of two different traditions, one evolving from popular, and the other from literary, forms.

*   *   *

AMES, Kenneth L.   1942-

PERSONAL: Born October 12, 1942, in Hartford, CT; son of Paul L. and Dorothy (Blank) Ames; married Gail J., 1965 (divorced, 1989); children: Heather A., Holly A. *Education:* Carleton College, B.A. (cum laude), 1964; University of Pennsylvania, M.A., 1966, Ph.D., 1970.

ADDRESSES: Home—846 Wright Ave., Schenectady, NY 12309. *Office*—New York State Museum, 3097 Cultural Education Center, Albany, NY 12230.

CAREER: Franklin and Marshall College, Lancaster, PA, assistant professor of art history, 1967-73, acting chair of department of art, 1971-72; Winterthur Museum, director of Winterthur Summer Institute, 1975-82, chair of Office of Advanced Studies, 1978-88, professor of Early American Culture, 1989-90; New York State Museum, Albany, chief of historical survey. University of Delaware, adjunct assistant professor, 1974-76, adjunct associate professor, 1976-88, adjunct professor, 1988-90; lecturer at Yale University, Delaware Technical and Community College, Northwestern University, Bowdoin College, University of Maryland at College Park, Boston University, Wellesley College, University of Michigan, University of Minnesota—Twin Cities, Carleton College, Smith College, State University of New York at Albany, Cornell University, Fashion Institute of America, University of Cincinnati, Miami University, Pennsylvania State University, West Chester University, Rhode Island School of Design, Utah State University, Middlebury College, and University of Virginia. Delaware Humanities Council, member, 1980-82, member of executive committee, 1981-82, chair,

1982; consultant to Franklin Mint, Tudor Place, and Theodore Roosevelt Birthplace.

MEMBER: American Association of Museums, American Association for State and Local History, American Studies Association (member of national council, 1987-90, and executive committee, 1988-89), Common Agenda for History Museums (chair of Interdisciplinary Task Force, 1988-89), Decorative Arts Society (founding member), Popular Culture Association, Society of Architectural Historians, Vernacular Architecture Forum.

AWARDS, HONORS: Grants from National Endowment for the Humanities, 1973 (for England), 1974, 1976, 1982, 1985, and 1989, and American Philosophical Society, 1974 and 1976.

WRITINGS:

Beyond Necessity: Art in the Folk Tradition, Norton, 1977.
(Editor with G. W. R. Ward) *Decorative Arts and Household Furnishings in America, 1650-1920: An Annotated Bibliography,* University Press of Virginia, 1989.
Death in the Dining Room and Other Tales of Victorian Culture, Temple University Press, 1992.
(Editor with Barbara Franco and Tom Frye) *Ideas and Images: Developing Interpretive History Exhibits,* American Association for State and Local History, 1992.

Work represented in anthologies, including *Perspectives on American Folk Art,* edited by Ian M. G. Quimby and Scott T. Swank, Norton, 1980; *Material Culture Studies in America,* edited by Thomas J. Schlereth, American Association for State and Local History, 1982; and *American Studies: An Annotated Bibliography of Works on the Civilization of the United States,* edited by Murray G. Murphey and Luther S. Luedtke, United States Information Agency, 1982. Contributor of articles and reviews to art and history journals. Newsletter editor, Decorative Arts Society, 1975-78; *Winterthur Portfolio,* book review editor, 1978-82, member of editorial board, 1979-82; editor, *Nineteenth Century,* Volume VIII, numbers 3-4, 1982; member of editorial board, *Material Culture,* 1983-86; member of board of advisory editors, *American Quarterly,* 1992-94; associate editor, *American National Biography.*

*   *   *

ANDREW, Joseph J(erald)   1960-

PERSONAL: Born March 1, 1960, in Indianapolis, IN; son of Jerald L. Andrew (a doctor) and Sylvia E. Hauselmann (a teacher; maiden name, Huss); married Anne Slaughter (an attorney), September 9, 1989; children: Meridith S. *Education:* Yale University, B.A. (magna cum laude, Scholar of the House), 1982, J.D., 1985. *Politics:* Democrat. *Avocational Interests:* Architecture, historic buildings, Democratic politics.

ADDRESSES: Home—Indianapolis, IN. *Office*—Bingham, Summers, Welsh & Spilman, 2700 Market Tower, 10 West Market, Indianapolis, IN 46204. *Agent*—Diane Cleaver, Sanford J. Greenburger Associates, 55 Fifth Ave., New York, NY 10003.

CAREER: Attorney and author. Served as a law clerk for Judge Joel Flaum of the United States Court of Appeals, Seventh Circuit, 1985-86; affiliated with law firm Baker and Daniels, 1987-88; served on the campaign of the Democratic candidate for the Indiana Senate, 1988; appointed Deputy Secretary of State for the State of Indiana, 1989; Bingham, Summers, Welsh & Spilman (law firm), Indianapolis, IN, attorney, 1991, partner, 1992—. Active in local politics, historic preservation, and pro bono legal work.

AWARDS, HONORS: Included in "New Young Writers" series, Purdue University, 1976 and 1977; received William C. Devane Prize, the Veech Prize, and the John Hubbard Curtis Prize from Yale University, for work in fiction.

WRITINGS:

The Disciples (spy thriller), Simon & Schuster, 1993.

Also editor of *Zirkus: The Yale Literary Journal,* 1980-82.

WORK IN PROGRESS: The Angels, a spy thriller.

SIDELIGHTS: Author and attorney Joseph J. Andrew has been writing since his adolescence on a tree farm near Fort Wayne, Indiana. While in high school, he was included in Purdue University's "New Young Writers" series. He continued writing as an English- and history-major at Yale University, where he won prizes for his stories. Despite this measure of success, however, Andrew decided to pursue a career as a lawyer; he also became active in Indiana Democratic politics upon graduating from law school.

While vacationing in the Bahamas in 1990, Andrew read a spy novel by acclaimed writer John LeCarre, and, as quoted by *Indiana Star* contributor Rich Gotshall, said that "this is what I should be doing." Andrew began work on what would become his 1993 espionage novel, *The Disciples.* The book is narrated by National Security Agency (NSA) operative T. C. Steele, who is investigating fellow agent Rebecca Townsend, whose family is involved in trading military secrets between nations. The plot becomes further complicated by a romance evolving between Townsend and an architect named Tommy Wood. Andrew utilizes his experience in communications and information securities law to add authenticity to his novel. A

Kirkus Reviews contributor labeled *The Disciples* "an impressive debut—and an elegantly executed conceit." Gotshall concluded in a separate *Indiana Star* review that "Andrew has crafted an exciting novel. The action is engaging, and the plot is challenging."

Andrew told *CA:* "The success of *The Disciples* exceeded my wildest expectations. I only hope I can do it again as I turn my attention to deeper, swifter waters.

BIOGRAPHICAL/CRITICAL SOURCES:

PERIODICALS

Indiana Lawyer, July 14, 1993, p. 23.
Indiana Star, July 17, 1993, pp. 1-2.
Kirkus Reviews, May 1, 1993.

*   *   *

ANDROS, Phil
See STEWARD, Samuel M(orris)

*   *   *

ANOZIE, Sunday O(gbonna) 1942-

PERSONAL: Born in 1942 in Owerri, Nigeria. *Education:* University of Nsukka, B.A., 1963; attended Sorbonne, University of Paris.

ADDRESSES: Agent—c/o Evans Brothers Ltd., 2A Portman Mansions, Chiltern St., London W1M 1LE, England.

CAREER: Conch (magazine), Paris, France, founder and managing editor, beginning 1969; critic and writer. University of Texas, Austin, visiting professor of English.

AWARDS, HONORS: Scholarship from United Nations Educational, Scientific, and Cultural Organization (UNESCO).

WRITINGS:

Sociologie du roman africaine, Aubier-Montaigne, 1970.
Christopher Okigbo: Creative Rhetoric, Africana Publishing, 1972.
Structural Models and African Poetics: Towards a Pragmatic Theory of Literature, Routledge & Kegan Paul, 1981.
(Editor) *Phenomenology in Modern African Studies,* Conch Magazine, 1982.

Contributor to *Black Literature and Literary Theory,* edited by Henry Louis Gates, Jr., Methuen, 1984. Contributor to journals, including *Presence Africaine.**

ARANOW, Edward Ross 1909-1993

OBITUARY NOTICE—See index for *CA* sketch: Born April 30, 1909, in New York, NY; died of cancer, November 7, 1993, in Scarsdale, NY. Lawyer, educator, and author. An authority on the subject of corporate takeovers, Aranow devoted parts of six decades to the legal profession. He was admitted to the New York Bar in 1933, then worked as an attorney for seven years before entering into private practice. After a stint in the U.S. Army during World War II, Aranow began a thirty year association as a founder and senior partner with the firm Aranow, Brodsky, Bohlinger, Benetar and Einhorn in New York City. In 1979 he joined the firm Botein, Hays and Sklar. Aranow also found time to lecture at the Practising Law Institute. Among his books are the standard legal texts *Proxy Contests for Corporate Control* and *Developments in Tender Offers for Corporate Control.*

OBITUARIES AND OTHER SOURCES:

BOOKS

Who's Who in American Law, 4th edition, Marquis, 1985, pp. 14-15.

PERIODICALS

New York Times, November 9, 1993, p. B10.

*   *   *

ARNAUD, Claude 1955-

PERSONAL: Born April 24, 1955, in Paris, France; son of Hubert (director of a steel manufacturing plant) and Marie-Paule (Turchini) Arnaud. *Education:* University of Paris VIII (Vincennes), maitrise (modern literature), 1983.

ADDRESSES: Home—27 rue Boissy d'Anglas, 75008 Paris, France. *Office*—13 rue de Verneuil, 75007 Paris, France.

CAREER: Worked as a printer in Paris, France, 1973-74; *Cinematographe* (cinema review magazine), journalist, 1977-83; free-lance writer, 1984—.

AWARDS, HONORS: Prix de L'Essai from the Academie Francaise, Prix Feneon, and Prix Leautaud, all 1989, all for *Chamfort; Les Histoires d'Amour finissent mal en general* received an award from the Valence Film Festival (Spain) and the Prix Jean Vigo, both 1993.

WRITINGS:

(With Bernard Minoret) *Les Salons* (play; produced at Le Theatre du Rond-Point, Paris, France, 1986-87), Editions J. C. Lattes, 1985.

Chamfort (biography), Editions Robert Laffont, 1989, translation by Deke Dusinberre published as *Chamfort,* foreword by Joseph Epstein, University of Chicago Press, 1992.
Les Histoires d'Amour finissent mal en general (screenplay), Cinea/Desmichelles Productions, 1993.
La Chasse aux Tigres (novel; title means "The Tiger Hunt"), Les Editions Grasset, 1994.
Babel, Les Editions Grasset, 1994.

Contributor to anthologies, including *Entre-Deux-Guerres* (title means "Between Two Wars"), edited by Pascal Ory and Olivier Barrot, Editions Francois Bourin, 1990, and *Gombrowicz, vingt ans apres* (title means "Gombrowicz, Twenty Years Later"), edited by Manuel Carcassonne, Christian Bourgois Editeur, 1990. Ghostwriter for Lilou Marquand's memoir, *Chanel m'a dit* (title means "Chanel Told Me"), Editions J. C. Lattes, 1990. Contributor of numerous articles to newspapers and magazines, including *Le Monde, Le Point, l'Express, Le Debat,* and *La Regle du Jeu.*

Arnaud's works have been translated into Italian, Spanish, Japanese, and German.

WORK IN PROGRESS: Perfecto, a screenplay to be directed by Anne Fontaine, with production expected to begin in late-1994.

SIDELIGHTS: Claude Arnaud told *CA:* "For a long time I dreamed of doing nothing, but doing nothing is a difficult career to pursue. You have to have talent, patience, and money, so . . .

"By chance I started writing, and I've kept writing because I enjoy it. It's a way of life that requires twice as much work as a normal job, but one that looks like a life of leisure.

"I've immersed myself in people, time periods, and various forms of writing in order to understand myself, but the more ground I gain, the more uncertain I become. I see myself as contradictory, changing, volatile. When I try to catch hold of myself, I slip between my fingers. I'm dealing with a ghost.

"In sum, I believe that we have too many identities to have only one. It would be more honest to say *we* instead of *I.* The self is a puzzle that takes years to build but can be scattered by a trifle. I write to put the pieces together again."

*   *   *

ARNOLD, Eleanor 1929-

PERSONAL: Born May 4, 1929, in Hendricks County, IN; daughter of Gilbert R. (a farmer) and Laura Maude (a homemaker; maiden name, Symmonds) Parsons; married Clarence Arnold (a farmer), December 26, 1948; children: Barbara Arnold Harcourt, Mary Arnold Roller, John Edward (deceased). *Education:* Indiana University—Bloomington, A.B., 1950. *Politics:* Independent. *Religion:* Society of Friends (Quakers).

ADDRESSES: Home—R.R.2, Box 48, Rushville, IN 46173.

CAREER: Farm homemaker, 1950—. Volunteer leader of oral history projects for Indiana Humanities Council, National Endowment for the Humanities, Indiana Extension Homemakers Association, and National Extension Homemakers Council; leader of oral history workshops; public speaker. Historic Landmarks Foundation of Indiana, member of board of directors; Indiana Rural Preservation Council, chairperson; Rush County Heritage, vice-president.

MEMBER: National Trust for Historic Preservation, Indiana Extension Homemakers Association (president), Indiana Historical Society, Indiana Covered Bridge Association, Rush County Historical Society.

AWARDS, HONORS: Community scholar of Smithsonian Institution; Commendation from American Association for State and Local History; President's Award for Volunteerism from Ronald Reagan; Jane Award for Leadership; named Homemaker of the Year.

WRITINGS:

EDITOR

Rush County Sesquicentennial History, privately printed, 1973.
Feeding Our Families, Indiana University Press, 1983.
Party Lines, Pumps, and Privies, Indiana University Press, 1984.
Buggies and Bad Times, Indiana University Press, 1985.
Voices of American Homemakers, Indiana University Press, 1985.
Girlhood Days, Indiana University Press, 1987.
Going to Club, Indiana University Press, 1988.
Living Rich Lives, Indiana University Press, 1989.

SCRIPTS

Author of the videotape *Hoosier Homemakers: The Early Years,* 1982; co-author of the plays *Rich Lives,* 1986, and *Hoosier Rich Lives,* 1988.

WORK IN PROGRESS: A history of the Arnold family.

SIDELIGHTS: Eleanor Arnold told *CA:* "I was born in the front room of an eighty-acre dairy farm in 1929, to a hard-working farm couple. I was the youngest in a family of four. The Depression years were my growing-up time, but I remember better the close community life and the loving family life I enjoyed. Since I was fourteen years younger than my next sibling, I made my own entertainment, reading constantly and spending lots of time in the woods and the fields. I always enjoyed visiting and listening to the older women in our community.

"In 1946 I graduated from high school and was given a very fine scholarship to the college of my choice. I became the first college graduate in my family. In 1948 I married a fellow student, and in 1950 we moved back to the farm background from which we both came. I settled down to farm life, had three babies in five years, and led the typical life of a farm homemaker. When the children were in school, I worked outside in the fields, helping my husband in his work by driving the tractor in the busy planting and harvest seasons. I had a big garden, which I cultivated myself, and did lots of canning and freezing. I volunteered for community work, led a 4-H club, taught Sunday school, worked for our local historical society, and worked with extension homemakers, among other things.

"All this is a typical farm homemaker's story, but I always felt that I had talents which I hadn't used. In the 1970s I became involved in an oral history project to celebrate the seventy-fifth anniversary of the Indiana Extension Homemakers Association. We soon saw that we needed to go beyond the history of our organization and decided to focus on rural women's lives, particularly their role as homemakers. With funding from the Indiana Humanities Council, we started a project in 1979 that is, in 1993, still going. This was a completely volunteer project that has yielded six books, a slide/tape program, a video, a reader's theater, and an indexed research collection of interviews.

"We were such innocents. We had no experience in publishing or book editing, but we persevered and learned as we went. We found interest and encouragement from the people we worked with, and our books became a real success. I think everyone was surprised by the degree of success which these projects attained. Certainly I had no idea when I started that we would touch such a vein of interest, or that the public would respond as it did.

"The project has been very satisfying to me personally, because I felt that the women we interviewed were of a generation whose stories had never been told. As farm homemakers, they had a whole set of skills which were essential in their day, and if they weren't documented, the knowledge would be gone. These women lived through so many changes. As one said, 'I started out in a horse and buggy, and now I've seen a man walk on the moon.' I was always impressed by the strength and good humor of these women, who worked literally from sun-up to sundown and yet didn't feel sorry for themselves. They loved their families and did their best to improve the lots of their children.

"For myself, I can really say I've had it all. I have had a rewarding personal life with my family, I stayed home with my children, I helped my husband in our farm work and, finally, I had a successful project in the area I would have chosen for a career. Everything came together at the right time."

BIOGRAPHICAL/CRITICAL SOURCES:

PERIODICALS

Christian Science Monitor, March 11, 1993, p. 14.

*   *   *

ARVENSIS, Alauda
See FURDYNA, Anna M.

*   *   *

ASHER, Ramona M.   1945-

PERSONAL: Born December 6, 1945, in Duluth, MN; daughter of William H. and Gladyce A. (Coyne) Asher; married M. C. Gorrill, 1962 (divorced, 1974); married Finn G. Jorgensen, 1988; children: (first marriage) Dawne M., Lonny J. *Education:* University of Minnesota—Duluth, B.A., 1977, B.A.S., 1978; University of Minnesota—Twin Cities, Ph.D., 1988.

ADDRESSES: Home—Minneapolis and Hovland, MN, and Copenhagen, Denmark.

CAREER: University of Minnesota—Twin Cities, Minneapolis, instructor in sociology, 1982-85 and 1987; Luther College, Decorah, IA, instructor in sociology, 1985-86; University of Wisconsin—Eau Claire, Eau Claire, assistant professor of sociology, 1988-89. *Contemporary Sociology: A Journal of Book Reviews,* editorial assistant, 1984; Eden Programs (drug treatment foundation), member of board of directors, 1990—; consultant to Hazelden Foundation.

MEMBER: American Sociological Association, Sociologists for Women in Society, National Association of Executive Women, Midwest Sociological Society, Minnesota Independent Scholars Forum (member of board of directors, 1991-93).

AWARDS, HONORS: Minnesota Book Award nomination for nonfiction, 1993.

WRITINGS:

Women with Alcoholic Husbands: Ambivalence and the Trap of Codependency, University of North Carolina Press, 1992.

Work represented in books, including *Fieldwork Experiences: Qualitative Approaches to Social Research,* second edition, edited by W. B. Shaffir and R. A. Stebbins, St. Martin's, 1990. Contributor of articles and reviews to journals in the social sciences.

WORK IN PROGRESS: Ethical Considerations in Living Related Kidney Donor Situations: Donor and Recipient Perspectives; Rethinking Social Power: A Feminist Critique; research on new developments in the field of alcoholism rehabilitation and recovery, with an emphasis on rehabilitation ideology and dynamics, especially regarding women.

SIDELIGHTS: Ramona M. Asher told *CA:* "After marrying young and spending twelve years as a rather traditional homemaker and mother, I, like many of my generation of women, struck out as a single parent, became an older college student, and discovered a more feminist self. My academic writing career took root during my graduate and doctoral work in sociology. Early retirement from my faculty position now allows ample indulgence in reading, writing, and travel, along with what is perhaps my favorite activity: reflection.

"I remain active with works in progress, such as a feminist critique of social power. Though nonfiction has always occupied my interests, and an unfolding interest in life-course transitions has me contemplating a new data collection endeavor, my writings are moving into the realm of fiction and a sort of metaphysical social psychology. I am strongly motivated to write short stories and books (two are in the making) that may help empower females of all ages and especially young girls. Rather than concentrating on one writing project at a time, I enjoy developing and returning to various projects as the mood emerges. I write out of a 'necessity of expression,' just for fun—even composing personalized verses commemorating special occasions for friends and family—but I acknowledge that my fondest desire would be to write things that would really make a huge, positive difference in people's lives and in the world."

*   *   *

ASTARITA, Tommaso 1961-

PERSONAL: Born April 6, 1961, in Naples, Italy; son of Giovanni (a university professor) and Nerina (a high school teacher; maiden name, Giuliani) Astarita. *Education:* University of Naples, Laurea in Letters, 1983; Johns Hopkins University, M.A., 1985, Ph.D., 1988. *Religion:* "No affiliation."

ADDRESSES: Home—1 Scott Circle NW, #621, Washington, DC 20036. *Office*—History Department, Georgetown University, Washington, DC 20057-1058.

CAREER: Georgetown University, Washington, DC, assistant professor of history, 1989—. Wright State University, visiting assistant professor, 1988-89.

MEMBER: American History Association, Society for Holier History Studies, Catholic History Association.

WRITINGS:

The Continuity of Feudal Power, Cambridge University Press, 1992.

WORK IN PROGRESS: Researching justice and peasant society in early modern Italy.

* * *

ATTAWAY, William (Alexander) 1911-1986

PERSONAL: Born November 19, 1911, in Greenville, MS; died of heart failure, June 17, 1986, in Los Angeles, CA; son of William S. (a physician) and Florence Parry (a schoolteacher) Attaway; married Frances Settele, December 28, 1962; children: a son and a daughter. *Education:* University of Illinois, B.A., 1936.

CAREER: Novelist, playwright, screenwriter, and songwriter. Worked briefly as a seaman, salesman, labor organizer, and actor, touring in *You Can't Take It With You.* Writer and consultant for the film industry.

WRITINGS:

Carnival (play), produced at University of Illinois, Urbana, 1935.
Let Me Breathe Thunder (novel), Doubleday, 1939.
Blood on the Forge (novel), Doubleday, 1941.
Hear America Singing, Lion, 1967.
One Hundred Years of Laughter (television script), American Broadcasting Company (ABC-TV), 1967.

Contributing editor, *Calypso Song Book,* McGraw-Hill, 1957. Contributor to periodicals, including *Challenge* and *Tiger's Eye.* Arranger of songs for Harry Belafonte.

SIDELIGHTS: Despite the versatility which he demonstrated during his career, William Attaway is remembered primarily as a chronicler of the great migration of black Americans from the South to the industrial North during the 1920s and 1930s. He displayed his knowledge of this topic in his second and last novel, *Blood on the Forge,* published in 1941. Attaway's abandonment of this promising genre at age thirty led to a distinguished career as a composer and arranger and as a television and film writer.

Attaway moved with his parents from Greenville, Mississippi, to Chicago, Illinois, when he was about ten years old and attended public schools in that city. His father and mother, a physician and schoolteacher respectively,

wanted him to enter a profession. Instead he decided to become an auto mechanic and attended a vocational high school. But his plans changed when a teacher introduced him to the work of Langston Hughes. Influenced by both Hughes's poetry and his sister, Broadway actress Ruth Attaway, he began to write plays and short stories while still in secondary school.

Attaway's parents persuaded him to enroll at the University of Illinois in Urbana, but he dropped out after the death of his father and traveled as a hobo for two years. He worked at a series of jobs—seaman, salesman and labor organizer—before returning to the university where his play *Carnival* was produced in 1935, a year before his graduation in 1936. During this time Attaway befriended Richard Wright, whose popular success with the book *Native Son* would later eclipse that of Attaway's novels.

After receiving his B.A. degree Attaway moved to New York City, where he wrote his first novel, *Let Me Breathe Thunder,* at age twenty-five. He worked at a string of odd jobs while writing and was touring in George S. Kaufman and Moss Hart's *You Can't Take It With You* when he received word that the novel would be published. Attaway abandoned acting and began his second novel with the help of a grant from the Julius Rosenwald Fund.

Let Me Breathe Thunder is the story of two white hoboes, Ed and Step, who take under their wing an innocent Mexican boy who joins the men in their wanderings. Stanley Young in the *New York Times* wrote: "All the emotions of the book are direct and primitive, and the bareness of the speech cuts the action to lean and powerful lines." Young compared the story and characters to those featured in American novelist John Steinbeck's *Of Mice and Men;* other reviewers compared Attaway's style to that of American author Ernest Hemingway.

The central event of *Let Me Breathe Thunder* is the tragic corruption of the young waif, Hi-Boy, by the two jaded older men. Although the men have a tender love for the boy, the starkness of the world they all inhabit is played out in the relationships among the trio. Step takes Hi-Boy to a prostitute and during this visit—to prove his courage to the older man— Hi-Boy stabs himself in the hand. The wound ultimately kills him, but not before his moral downfall at a ranch where he shoots animals and lies to cover up Step's seduction of a young woman. The novel is replete with Biblical metaphor, as in Hi-Boy's hand wound and the setting of apple orchards at the ranch.

Attaway's second novel, like his first, is based on personal experience. *Blood on the Forge* is the story of three black brothers, Big Mat, Chinatown, and Melody Moss, who are sharecroppers in Kentucky until Big Mat badly beats a white overseer for insulting his mother. The three men are then forced to accept an offer to travel in a sealed boxcar to a Pennsylvania steel mill, where their attempts to build new lives fail tragically. Attaway addressed not only obstacles faced by blacks in the South and North, but a tapestry of dilemmas created by the ripening industrial age: early struggles to organize labor, the uneasy mixture of Irish, Italian and Eastern European immigrants, and the spiritual damage done to men made to work like machines.

The sharply drawn characters of the brothers illustrate three aspects of the human soul, three ways of responding to the uprooting and loss of family which were common in the 1930s. Melody symbolizes the artist, with his love of blues guitar. Chinatown loves pleasure; his greatest pride is his own gold tooth. Big Mat is a man torn from the outset—he is deeply religious, an assiduous student of the Bible who hopes to become a preacher someday, but his wife Hattie's six miscarriages together with the destruction wreaked by this new, rootless life gnaw at him.

The noise of the steel mill renders mute the strings of Melody's guitar, and he falls in love with a young Mexican-American prostitute named Anna. But she is drawn instead to Mat, whose strength at a dog fight brawl saved her from harm. Mat, having learned from afar that Hattie lost her seventh baby, gives up on his dream of sending for her to join him, and he moves in with Anna. He begins to erupt in random anger, beating Anna severely, and he is arrested for the attempted murder of a man. Melody badly damages his hand in an accident, and an explosion which kills several other workers blinds Chinatown.

The town is troubled by mounting racial tensions. White union workers are threatening to strike. Steel bosses pit one man against another by preparing to bring in more southern black men, who will work for cheaper wages. In this milieu, the final tragedies of the three brothers unfold.

Attaway's second novel was even more lauded than his first. Wrote critic Milton Rugoff in the *New York Herald Tribune Books:* "[Attaway] writes of the frustration and suffering of his people and does so with crude power and naked intensity." Drake de Kay of the *New York Times Book Review* similarly praised the work of this twenty-nine-year-old author: "[*Blood on the Forge*] is a starkly realistic story involving social criticism as searching as any to be found in contemporary literature."

Literary commentators speculated on why Attaway never wrote another novel. Despite the acclaim of reviewers and their anticipation of his next book, *Blood on the Forge* did not sell many copies. In a twist of irony, Attaway's success may have been eclipsed by that of his friend Wright. Wright's novel, *Native Son*—published just one year before *Blood on the Forge*—met with both critical and popular success. Some critics suggested that mainstream Amer-

ica may have been prepared at that time for only one black novelist to burst on the scene.

When *Blood on the Forge* was reprinted in 1969, the country, now widely examining its own racist past, was perhaps more prepared to receive it. In 1987 Cynthia Hamilton wrote in *Black American Literature Forum: "Blood on the Forge* is a masterpiece of social analysis." The complexity of Attaway's characters and their story have stood up well to the passage of half a century since its initial publication.

Attaway's two later books were both about music. *Calypso Song Book* was a collection of songs and *Hear America Singing* describes for young readers the history of American popular music. In addition, Attaway composed songs and arranged tunes for his friend, Harry Belafonte.

Attaway took time out from his writing career to march for African American voting rights in Selma, Alabama, in 1965. Among other projects, he subsequently completed *One Hundred Years of Laughter,* a special on the comedy of blacks which aired on ABC-TV in 1967. Attaway was engaged by the producers of *The Man,* the film based on Irving Wallace's novel about a senator who becomes the first black president of the United States. The script, however, was deemed too rough and Attaway was released from the project; Rod Serling later received credit on the final screenplay.

After living for a decade with his family in Barbados, Attaway returned to California where he continued to write scripts for film, radio, and television. He was writing *The Atlanta Child Murders* script when he suffered a heart attack which resulted in his death in Los Angeles, California, on June 17, 1986.

BIOGRAPHICAL/CRITICAL SOURCES:

BOOKS

Black Literature Criticism, Volume 1, Gale, 1992.
Dictionary of Literary Biography, Volume 76: *Afro-American Writers, 1940-1955,* Gale, 1988.
Margolies, Edward, *Native Sons: A Critical Study of Twentieth-Century Negro American Authors,* Lippincott, 1968.
Young, James O., *Black Writers of the Thirties,* Louisiana State University Press, 1973.

PERIODICALS

Black American Literature Forum, spring-summer, 1987, pp. 147-63.
CLA Journal, June, 1972, pp. 459-64.
New York Herald Tribune Books, August 24, 1941, p. 8.
New York Times Book Review, June 25, 1939, p. 7; August 24, 1941, pp. 18, 20.
Publishers Weekly, March 30, 1970, p. 66.
Saturday Review of Literature, July, 1939, p. 20.

Studies in Black Literature, spring, 1973, pp. 1-3.*

—*Sketch by Karen Withem*

B

BAKER, Kevin (Breen) 1958-

PERSONAL: Born August 20, 1958, in Englewood, NJ; son of Charles Kenneth (an actor) and Claire (a social worker; maiden name, Slade) Baker; married Ellen J. Abrams (a writer), October 11, 1992. *Education:* Columbia University, B.A., 1980. *Politics:* Democrat. *Religion:* Quaker. *Avocational Interests:* Baseball, American history.

ADDRESSES: Home—New York, NY. *Agent*—Philip G. Spitzer Literary Agency, 50 Talmage Farm Lane, East Hampton, NY 11937.

CAREER: Gloucester Daily Times, Gloucester, MA, staff writer, 1971-80; Foundation Center, New York City, compiler of entries for reference books, 1980-85; Public Securities Association, New York City, free-lance writer on municipal bonds papers, 1986-87; letter writer for mayor's office, New York City, 1987-88; free-lance writer, 1988—.

MEMBER: American Civil Liberties Union, Amnesty International.

WRITINGS:

Sometimes You See It Coming (novel), Crown, 1993.

Contributor to *In a Word,* edited by Jack Hitt, Dell, 1992.

WORK IN PROGRESS: A book on American history with Harold Evans; another novel, a contemporary American drama set in New England.

SIDELIGHTS: Kevin Baker's first novel, *Sometimes You See It Coming,* was published in 1993. The book, which tells the story of a great baseball player's career, has met with a favorable reception from readers and critics alike, after initially impressing the people at Crown Publishing. In an article in *Publishers Weekly,* Crown editor Dick Marek explained that *Sometimes You See It Coming* "is

a book we bought for a modest advance. It's a first novel by a young writer and we bought it because we fell in love with it." *Publishers Weekly* went on to elaborate, however: "But did Marek really see *this* coming: 100,000 first printing and $100,000 in promotion budget?" These figures are impressive for a first novel, and they came about because several editors at Crown continued to read the manuscript and urge its promotion.

Reviewers have been equally supportive of Baker's work. Though it reminded many of Bernard Malamud's classic baseball novel, *The Natural, Sometimes You See It Coming* holds its own, according to critics. After noting that "this one ends the way a baseball story should: three and two, two out in the ninth, legend at bat," John Skow in *Time* urged readers to "put this one on the shelf with *The Natural.*" Kerry Luft acknowledged in the *Chicago Tribune* that *Sometimes You See It Coming* "is almost ideal for a student of baseball history. Baker is clearly a dedicated fan, and he has based many of the characters on real players."

BIOGRAPHICAL/CRITICAL SOURCES:

PERIODICALS

Chicago Tribune, April 5, 1993, section 5, p. 3.
Los Angeles Times Book Review, April 4, 1993, pp. 2, 13.
Publishers Weekly, February 1, 1993, pp. 61-62.
Time, March 22, 1993, p. 70.

*   *   *

BAKER, Mark 1950-

PERSONAL: Born October 9, 1950, in Jacksonville, FL; married; children: two sons. *Education:* University of

Florida, B.A., 1972. *Avocational Interests:* Body surfing, reading about the crusades.

ADDRESSES: Home—New York, NY. *Agent*—Esther Newberg, International Creative Management, 40 West 57th St., New York, NY 10019-4070.

CAREER: Free-lance writer, 1979—.

WRITINGS:

Nam: The Vietnam War in the Words of the Men and Women Who Fought There, Morrow, 1981.
Cops: Their Lives in Their Own Words, Simon and Schuster, 1985.
Women: American Women in Their Own Words, Simon and Schuster, 1990.
What Men Really Think about Women, Love, Sex, and Themselves, Simon and Schuster, 1991.
Sex Lives: A Sexual Self-Portrait of America, Simon and Schuster, 1994.

Contributor of articles to periodicals, including *Esquire, Men's Health, Parents, Men's Journal,* and *Cosmopolitan.*

WORK IN PROGRESS: A book of interviews with American criminals about the "life of crime."

SIDELIGHTS: Author Mark Baker has written four books using similar methods. For each, he has interviewed several individuals who belong to specialized groups and related their stories in writing. His 1981 book, *Nam: The Vietnam War in the Words of the Men and Women Who Fought There,* is perhaps his best known, and *Cops: Their Lives in Their Own Words* was also widely reviewed. Baker focused on the subject of gender for his next two titles, *Women: American Women in Their Own Words* and *What Men Really Think about Women, Love, Sex, and Themselves.* Despite their varying subjects, his books are unified by a common theme. In the words of *Time* reviewer John Skow, Baker's work, "plays the journalist's strongest card, which is his knowledge that people have a powerful urge to explain themselves."

Nam: The Vietnam War in the Words of the Men and Women Who Fought There is "the most horrifying book the war has yet produced," reported Peter S. Prescott in *Newsweek.* Assured anonymity by Baker, the book's Vietnam veterans tell stories of atrocities that some witnessed and some participated in during that conflict. Not only do Baker's interviewees reveal the horror of seeing their companions blown to pieces before their eyes, but some also admit to the pleasure they took in killing the enemy and even removing their kill's body parts as trophies. "We hear, for instance," reported Peter Marin in the *Nation,* "of various officers ordering men to commit atrocities in situations or places not yet publicly acknowledged by the government or named by the press." In addition to reveal-

ing the recollections of fighting men, Baker relates the testimony of nurses in *Nam:* "In the book's most poignant story," Prescott judged, "a nurse who hopes to relieve her patients' anxieties allows them to show her pictures of sexual atrocities they have committed." Baker also allows his interviewees to make clear the feelings of disorientation they often felt upon their return to the United States. In his *Chicago Tribune Book World* review, Jack Fuller quoted an example of one such veteran: " 'I miss the sounds of the nights in Viet Nam, with the choppers landing and the outgoing—not the incoming—fire. Although, even the incoming was exciting. The sounds are particularly vivid. The force after a large gun fires or a round lands, the feel of the gas from it on your face. Thinking about Viet Nam once in a while, in a crazy kind of way, I wish that just for an hour I could be there. And then be transported back. Maybe just to be there so I'd wish I was back here again.' " Christopher Lehmann-Haupt in the *New York Times* declared that *Nam* "constitutes a choral history, because its voices remain anonymous and are dovetailed so as to lend different shadings to every phase of the Vietnam experience." Marc Leepson in the *New York Times Book Review* concluded that *Nam* "easily stands with the best descriptive accounts of the war."

Baker's 1985 book, *Cops: Their Lives in Their Own Words,* contains its share of horror stories as well; one of his interviewees recounts the day he found the body of a dismembered child in a freezer, body parts neatly wrapped and labeled. But *Cops* also includes tales of the drudgery of policework, the everyday paperwork and handing out of parking tickets. In addition, Baker attempts to explore the inner psychology of his subjects. As Lewis J. Ellenhorn explained in the *Los Angeles Times Book Review,* "thematic chapters deal with the hardening nature of the work, the implications of deadly force, the relationships of cops to each other, the potential for brutality, the abuse of power and sadism, and the development of cynicism." Prescott praised Baker's accomplishment in *Cops* in another *Newsweek* review, noting that, "distrusting the media, their superiors and the society they serve, policemen tend to talk only among themselves." But Baker, he observed, "punched holes in the wall of reserve that paranoia built." Prescott finished by calling *Cops* "even more compelling" than *Nam. People* magazine concluded that Baker has created "a revealing portrait of the men and women who act as the blue glue that holds together our sometimes frayed social fabric."

In his 1990 book, *Women: American Women in Their Own Words,* Baker's interviewees discuss their feelings about work, men, sex, and disease. Some tell tales of rape and childhood sexual abuse; others recount stories of long-lasting, happy marriages. In *What Men Really Think about Women, Love, Sex, and Themselves,* Baker's 1991 effort, his subjects talk not only of the subtitled topics, but of others as well, including fatherhood and abortion. According to Genevieve Stuttaford in *Publishers Weekly,* many of the men in the book are "strongly anti-gay" and "exceedingly few . . . favor monogamy."

Baker told *CA:* "Even after all these years of talking to people, I am still amazed at how unpredictable and idiosyncratic human beings are. Just when you think you've got someone pegged, they tell you a story that just blows you away."

BIOGRAPHICAL/CRITICAL SOURCES:

BOOKS

Baker, Mark, *Nam: The Vietnam War in the Words of the Men and Women Who Fought There,* Morrow, 1981.

PERIODICALS

Chicago Tribune Book World, May 17, 1981, p. 3.
Globe and Mail (Toronto), October 19, 1985.
Los Angeles Times Book Review, November 10, 1985, p. 2.
Nation, June 20, 1981, pp. 765-66.
Newsweek, May 4, 1981, pp. 78, 80; August 26, 1985, p. 67.
New York Times, June 10, 1981; August 13, 1985, p. 15.
New York Times Book Review, May 17, 1981, p. 12.
People, October 27, 1986, p. 127; April 2, 1990, p. 31.
Publishers Weekly, December 20, 1991, p. 70.
Time, April 20, 1981, p. 88; August 26, 1985, p. 73.
Washington Post, September 21, 1985.
Washington Post Book World, April 26, 1981, pp. 3, 14.

—*Sketch by Elizabeth Wenning*

* * *

BAKER, (John) Roger 1934-1993

OBITUARY NOTICE—See index for *CA* sketch: Born October 15, 1934, in Edwinstowe, Nottinghamshire, England; died of complications resulting from emphysema, November 8, 1993, in Dumfries, Scotland. Journalist, critic, and author. A journalist and writer for nearly forty years, Baker is best remembered for his landmark study on theatrical cross dressing, entitled *Drag: A History of Female Impersonation on the Stage.* Beginning his career as a reporter, diarist, and music critic for the *Nottingham Evening Post,* Baker later worked for various London periodicals, including *London Life,* the *Illustrated London News,* and the *Tatler.* He also contributed to various gay publications, such as *Gay Times* and *Gay News.* As a book author, Baker explored a range of subjects, from exorcism in *Binding the Devil,* to cuisine in *Cooking for One.* Baker was revisir *Drag* at the time of his death.

OBITUARIES AND OTHER SOURCES:

PERIODICALS

Times (London), November 15, 1993, p. 17.

* * *

BALL, Joseph H(urst) 1905-1993

OBITUARY NOTICE—See index for *CA* sketch: Born November 3, 1905, in Crookston, MN; died following a stroke, December 18, 1993, in Chevy Chase, MD. Politician, journalist, and author. Ball is remembered for his outspoken advocacy concerning the creation of the United Nations (UN) while a Republican senator in the 1940s. He first covered the political world as a reporter and editor for the *St. Paul Dispatch.* Following the death of Senator Ernest Lundeen, Ball was appointed to fill the vacancy and embarked on an eight-year stint in that office. In addition to supporting UN legislation, he also drew attention for his opposition of various organized labor practices. After losing his second bid at re-election, he became vice president of the Association of American Ship Owners and later served in the same capacity at States Marine Lines. His later years were spent as a farmer in Virginia. Ball also found time to write, producing both pulp fiction for magazines and books on political issues and policies. Among his works are *Collective Security: The Why and How, The Government Subsidized Union Monopoly: A Study of Labor Practices in the Shipping Industry,* and *The Implementation of Federal Manpower Policy, 1961-1971: A Study in Bureaucratic Competition and Intergovernmental Relations.*

OBITUARIES AND OTHER SOURCES:

PERIODICALS

New York Times, December 22, 1993, p. B8.
Washington Post, December 20, 1993, p. B6.

* * *

BANI-SADR, Abolhassan 1933-

PERSONAL: Born March 22, 1933, in Hamadan, Iran; son of Nasrolah and Ashrafi Bani-Sadr; married Ozra Hosseini, August 29, 1961; children: Firouze, Zahra, Ali. *Education:* Attended the University of Teheran; received doctorate from the Sorbonne. *Religion:* Islam.

ADDRESSES: Home—5 Rue General Pershing, 78000 Versailles, France.

CAREER: Member of Iranian anti-Shah movement, 1953; wounded by police and served prison term for demonstrating against Shah's government, 1963; lived in exile, Paris, France, 1963-79; teacher at Sorbonne, Paris, until 1978; returned to Iran after revolution, 1978; Republic of Iran, acting minister of Foreign Affairs, 1979, Minister of Economy and Foreign Affairs, 1979-80, president, 1980-81. Central Bank of Iran, member of supervisory board, 1979; Constituent Assembly, member, beginning in 1979; Revolutionary Council, member of supervisory board, 1979-80, president, 1980-81. Founder of Mossadegh, Modaress, and 15 Khordad publishing houses.

WRITINGS:

(With Paul Vieille) *Petrole et violence: Terreur blanche et resistance en Iran* (title means "Oil and Violence: White Terror and Resistance in Iran"), Editions Anthropos, 1974.
Quelle revolution pour l'Iran, Fayolle, 1980.
(Translator) Mohammad R. Ghanoonparvar, *The Fundamental Principles and Precepts of Islamic Government,* Mazda Publishers, c. 1981.
L'esperance trahie, Papyrus Editions, c. 1982.
Bani Sadr racconta l'Iran, Ediesse, 1984.
Le complot des ayatollahs, Decouverte, 1989, translation published as *My Turn to Speak: Iran, the Revolution and Secret Deals with the United States,* Brassey's, 1991.
Usul-i bakim bar qazavat-i Islami: va Huquq-i bashar dar Islam, Enghelab Eslami Publications, c. 1989.
Le coran et le pouvoir, Imago, 1993.

Also author of numerous articles and books about politics and Islamic law (published primarily in Persian and French), including a six-volume diary of his time in office as president of the Republic of Iran; works from his period of exile are collected in *Iran Erupts,* edited by Ali Reza Nobari. Founder of the journal *Islamic Revolution.*

Bani-Sadr's writings have been translated into Arabic, German, Serbian, and Italian.

SIDELIGHTS: Abolhassan Bani-Sadr rose to world prominence in 1980 when he accepted the presidency of Iran shortly after the Islamic revolution that ousted the former ruler, Shah Mohammed Riza Pahlevi. In the book *My Turn to Speak: Iran, the Revolution and Secret Deals with the United States,* Bani-Sadr reflects on the chaotic days of his presidency during which he attempted to democratize a revolution controlled by authoritarian clerics. Active since 1953 in movements against the Shah's government (a regime that was supported by the United States), Bani-Sadr became a close associate of the exiled Ayatollah Ruholla Khomeini, the spiritual head of Iran's Shi'ite Muslims. After the 1979 revolution Khomeini returned to Iran from Paris, France—where Bani-Sadr had also been living in exile—and assumed the leadership of the new government. Bani-Sadr was named minister of

economic affairs in July, 1979, a post in which he attempted to revitalize Iran's economy. In 1980 he was elected president in the country's first free democratic elections.

With the real political power residing with Khomeini and other right-wing religious leaders, Bani-Sadr saw his influence as president continually weaken. For example, he was against holding American hostages from the United States embassy—an incident perpetrated by militant extremists supposedly with the blessing of Khomeini—and worked in vain to find an early solution to the crisis. After struggling to remain in office, suppressing a planned coup in 1980, Bani-Sadr was removed in 1981 by Khomeini and soon returned to life in exile in Paris. Among the charges Bani-Sadr makes in *My Turn to Speak* is the allegation that the Reagan-Bush presidential campaign secretly negotiated for the freedom of American hostages "in order to influence the 1980 election," according to R. H. Dekmejian in *Choice.* "As a historical document, this is a memoir of some importance, and Bani-Sadr's insights into the Machiavellian politics of revolutionary Iran are often absorbing," commented a critic in *Kirkus Reviews.* Dekmejian wrote in *Choice* that *My Turn to Speak* "should make interesting reading for Middle East specialists and general readers."

Bani-Sadr told *CA:* "I started to be politically active in high school. At that time, the Toudeh party (Iranian communist party) was very popular among high school and university students, and ideological debates made up most of our political activities. During my last years in high school the movement in favor of oil nationalization, led by Dr. Mossadegh (the Iranian premier from 1951 to 1953), was at its height and I became aware of the concepts of freedom and independence. These two principles still occupy the primary place in my political and scientific life; I have devoted most of my studies to these concepts, to better define them and explore their implications.

"From the 1953 coup d'etat against the Mossadegh government until the 1979 Iranian Revolution, Iranian political groups were caught in a battle of priorities: the preeminence of freedom over independence; the preeminence of independence over freedom; the preeminence of development over freedom, independence, and Islam; the preeminence of social revolution and dictatorship of the proletariat over freedom and independence; the preeminence of Islam over all these principles. . . . During these years, I attempted to free Iranian society from this war—which had paralyzed it from within for two centuries—using the basis of the zero balance, the redefined principles of independence, freedom, development, and Islam. These new definitions allowed me to terminate the war of the priorities and generated the guiding thought of the Iranian Revolution.

"In November, 1963, following a new wave of repression, I went into exile in France. I continued my studies and research in three fields: economy, sociology, and Islam. My work was published in French and Persian in books and journals. These works served as a reference to establish the guiding thought and discourse of the Iranian Revolution.

"After the final victory of the Iranian Revolution I returned to Iran with Mr. Khomeini. I urged him to organize political debates between the various political groups. This proposition was intended to prevent the various factions from settling their differences through violence, to demonstrate the need for freedom for all, and to allow the Iranian people to make a clear choice. Mr. Khomeini appointed me as the representative of Islamic philosophy during these debates despite the large number of religious leaders available.

"In the spring of 1979 I became a member of the Revolutionary Council. A week after the hostages were taken at the American embassy, I was nominated to the post of Minister of the Economy and Foreign Affairs after having been promised by Mr. Khomeini that the hostages would be released immediately once the Shah of Iran had left the United States. When it became clear that Mr. Khomeini was not going to keep his promise, I resigned as Minister of Foreign Affairs.

"I was elected to the Constituent Assembly in 1979. With a minority of elected members and despite the overwhelming majority in favor of the doctrine of sovereignty, I succeeded in passing a law that took away all executive powers from the guide. During the presidential elections Mr. Khomeini opposed my candidacy and the day before even proposed that I resign in favor of Mr. Habibi. I refused and told him: 'These elections will allow me to clarify whether the Iranian people supported the revolution because they believed in its guiding principles and were later supported by the religious leaders or whether, on the contrary, they have blindly followed the religious leaders without understanding the meaning of these principles.' On January 25, 1980, I won the presidential elections with seventy-six percent of the votes. The rout of the 'integriste' candidate, who only received four percent of the votes, clearly showed that the Iranian people were perfectly aware of the meaning of the principles for which the revolution had taken place: independence, freedom, development, and the Islam that results from these three principles.

"After the elections, proponents of the dictatorship allied. Having learned from the presidential elections, they started to limit liberties during the parliamentary elections. Mr. Khomeini gave the following order to the party of the Islamic Republic: 'Try to control the parliament.' He went further and opposed the parliament under my

leadership. Iraq's war against Iran in September, 1980, gave the proponents of despotism a golden opportunity. They concluded a secret pact with the campaigning presidential team of Reagan-Bush and enacted the final blow of their creeping coup d'etat against my government on June 15, 1981. On that day Mr. Khomeini told me, when I requested that a referendum be organized: 'If thirty-five million say yes, I will say no.'

"Following the coup d'etat, I wrote a pact based on the principles of independence, freedom, and lack of hegemony. The national council of the resistance was founded on the basis of this pact. In this way I hoped to prevent the totalitarian regime that resulted from the coup d'etat from becoming the only opposition group and thus reducing the people's choice to one between bad and worse. By referring to the guiding thought of the revolution, the resistance movement was able to propose a democratic alternative to the totalitarian regime.

"In July, 1981, I went into exile in Paris again. Upon my arrival I maintained that the purpose of this exile was to expose the relationship between Khomeinism and Reaganism and to reveal the secret agreements between the Khomeini regime and the Reagan government."

BIOGRAPHICAL/CRITICAL SOURCES:

PERIODICALS

Choice, February, 1992, p. 957.
Kirkus Reviews, March 15, 1991, pp. 367-368.
Library Journal, May 15, 1991, p. 95.
Nation, March 22, 1986, pp. 366-370.

*   *   *

BANKER, Mark T(ollie) 1951-

PERSONAL: Born February 4, 1951, in Oak Ridge, TN; son of L. Eugene (an attorney and corporate administrative assistant) and Katherine T. (a teacher) Banker; married Kathy Forbes (a teacher), July 17, 1976; children: Tollie Jean. *Education:* Attended Universidad Ibero-Americana, 1971; Warren Wilson College, B.A. (magna cum laude), 1973; University of Virginia, M.A.T., 1975; University of New Mexico, Ph.D., 1987. *Religion:* Presbyterian. *Avocational Interests:* Farming beef cattle, horses, gardening, baseball.

ADDRESSES: Home—1841 James Freeway Rd., Kingston, TN 37761. *Office*—Webb School of Knoxville, 9800 Webb School Dr., Knoxville, TN 37923.

CAREER: Teacher and head of social studies department at a school in Albuquerque, NM, 1976-81, dean of students, 1981-83; University of New Mexico, Valencia Campus, instructor in history, 1986; history teacher at a private school in Albuquerque, 1986-87; Webb School of Knoxville, Knoxville, TN, history teacher, 1987—, department head, 1990-92. Menaul Historical Library of the Southwest, archival assistant, 1981-83.

MEMBER: Organization of American Historians, Western History Association, Presbyterian Historical Society, Appalachian Studies Association.

AWARDS, HONORS: Teacher Scholar Award from National Endowment for the Humanities and *Reader's Digest,* 1993-94.

WRITINGS:

Presbyterian Missions and Cultural Interaction in the Far Southwest, 1850-1950, University of Illinois Press, 1992.

Author of the book *Toward Frontiers Yet Unknown: A Ninetieth Anniversary History of Warren Wilson College,* 1985. Work represented in anthologies, including *Religion and Society in the American West,* edited by Carl Guarneri and David Alvarez, 1987. Contributor to history journals.

WORK IN PROGRESS: Writing narration for *Warren Wilson College: A Centennial Portrait;* research on mountain peoples and mainstream America.

*   *   *

BARCLAY, Robert 1946-
(Fecit)

PERSONAL: Born July 17, 1946, in London, England; married Janet Mair Fenwick (a craftsperson), January 24, 1971; children: Anne, David, Heather, Ian. *Education:* University of Toronto, B.A. (with honors), 1975. *Politics:* "Cynic." *Religion:* "Amused bystander."

ADDRESSES: Home—3609 Downpatrick Rd., Gloucester, Ontario K1V 9P4, Canada. *Office*—Canadian Conservation Institute, 1030 Innes Rd., Ottawa, Ontario K1A 0C8, Canada.

CAREER: Canadian Conservation Institute, Ottawa, Ontario, Canada, senior conservator of ethnology, 1975—. Trumpet-maker and instructor in brass-instrument making; conservator of museum artifacts, specializing in musical instruments.

MEMBER: International Institute for Conservation, International Council of Museums, Canadian Association of Professional Conservators, Historic Brass Society.

AWARDS, HONORS: Grant from Canada Council for the Arts.

WRITINGS:

(Editor and contributor) *Anatomy of an Exhibition: The Look of Music,* International Institute for Conservation, 1983.
The Art of the Trumpet-Maker, Oxford University Press, 1992.

Author of the quarterly column "Musae Museae," under the pseudonym Fecit. Contributor to periodicals, including *Galpin Society Journal* and *Historic Brass Society Journal.*

WORK IN PROGRESS: Research on the metals of the instrument-maker and on historic musical instruments in public collections.

SIDELIGHTS: Robert Barclay told *CA:* "I work at the Canadian Conservation Institute in Ottawa, Canada, specializing in the care and preservation of musical instruments. I taught summer courses in Toronto for several years on the making of brass instruments, including trombones, trumpets, and slide trumpets. Aside from professional museum work, I have been a trumpet-maker for more than fifteen years and have made an intensive study of the traditional techniques of natural trumpet manufacture in the city of Nuremburg, Germany. I have produced more than twenty-five baroque trumpets based on a Nuremburg instrument of 1632, many of which are in the possession of trumpet players in Europe, Canada, and the United States.

"I am now researching tone formation in historic instruments made in Nuremburg to establish criteria for assessing the playing quality of the originals compared with that of accurate copies. My particular concern is in authentic instrumentation as used in performances of Baroque music. The natural trumpet of the Baroque period is particularly in need of revival as a working instrument for both live performance and recordings. Information derived from this research may result in more players finding the natural trumpet an acceptable instrument for virtuoso performance.

"I am also the contributor of a regular column on museum conservation and the editor of a journal, both of which look at the lighter side of the conservation profession."

*   *   *

BARHAM, Patte B.

PERSONAL: Born in Los Angeles, CA; daughter of Frank Barham and Princess Jessica Meskhi Gleboff; married Harris Peter Boyne, May 7, 1982. *Education:* Attended University of Southern California and the University of Arizona; received Litt.D. from Trinity Southern Bible College.

ADDRESSES: Home—100 Fremont Pl., Los Angeles, CA 90005.

CAREER: Journalist and author. Worked as a war correspondent in Korea and as a syndicated columnist; acting secretary of state in California, 1980-81; *Los Angeles Times,* entertainment reporter. President of Los Angeles Council of International Visitors; vice president of public relations and member of the international committee of the Amateur Athletic Union.

MEMBER: National League of American Pen Women, U.S. Olympic Committee (member of hospitality committee), English Speaking Union, Daughters of the American Revolution, Social Service Auxiliary, Los Angeles Orphanage Guild, various recreational clubs.

AWARDS, HONORS: Honorary doctorates from the Olympian International Sports Foundation and College, the Olympian International Sports Medicine College, (Cambridge, England), and the International Arts and Science and Cable Television; Dame Sovereign and recipient of the grand cross, Order of Alfred the Great; compagne de la Couronne d'Epines, Ancien Abbaye-Principaute de San Luigi.

WRITINGS:

Rasputin: The Man Behind the Myth, A Personal Memoir with Maria Rasputin, Prentice-Hall, 1977.
Peasant To Palace, Rasputin's Cookbook with Maria Rasputin, Romar Books, 1990.
(With Peter Harry Brown) *Marilyn: The Last Take,* Dutton, 1992.

Also author of *Pin up Poems.*

WORK IN PROGRESS: Operation Nightmare; Hearst and Me.

SIDELIGHTS: Barham is the author, with Peter Harry Brown, of *Marilyn: The Last Take.* Please refer to Brown's sketch in this volume for additional sidelights.

BIOGRAPHICAL/CRITICAL SOURCES:

PERIODICALS

Los Angeles Times Book Review, October 18, 1992.
National Review, October 5, 1992.
People, August 10, 1992.

*   *   *

BARNES, Trevor   1955-

PERSONAL: Born October 15, 1955, in Ipswich, Suffolk, England. *Education:* Corpus Christi College, Cambridge,

B.A. (with first class honors), 1978; attended Harvard University, 1978-79.

ADDRESSES: Home—12 Wingate Rd., London W6 0UR, England.

CAREER: British Broadcasting Corp., London, England, senior producer, 1979-92; Slaughter & May (law firm), London, solicitor, 1992—.

AWARDS, HONORS: Kennedy scholar, Harvard University, 1978-79.

WRITINGS:

Trial at Torun (radio play), BBC-Radio, 1986.
A Midsummer Killing (novel), Hodder & Stoughton, 1989, published as *A Midsummer Night's Killing: A Mystery Introducing Scotland Yard's Blanche Hampton,* Morrow, 1992.
Dead Meat (novel), Hodder & Stoughton, 1991, published as *A Pound of Flesh,* Morrow, 1993.
Taped (novel), Hodder & Stoughton, 1992.

WORK IN PROGRESS: An international suspense novel, completion expected in 1996.

SIDELIGHTS: Trevor Barnes told *CA:* "After a trilogy of detective novels, in which I have sought to explore what, for me, are the personal frontiers of the genre, I am now working on an international thriller—a book with a much broader canvas, but with detective elements. It is important for me to have a challenge lurking in every novel. In *A Midsummer Killing* it was combining espionage (based on personal experience of Britain's MI6) with police work. In *Dead Meat* it was the portrayal of a schizophrenic serial killer. In *Taped* it was changing the narrative perspective to that of my female detective's black assistant. In the new thriller it is setting a novel of this genre in a totally new environment."

*   *   *

BARNHART, Clarence L(ewis)   1900-1993

OBITUARY NOTICE—See index for *CA* sketch: Born December 30, 1900, near Plattsburg, MO; died of complications resulting from a fall, October 24, 1993, in Peekskill, NY. Lexicographer and editor. Keenly attuned to new words and changing usages in the English language, Barnhart oversaw the creation of a number of dictionaries and other reference works, including Random House's *American College Dictionary,* published in 1947. He also joined forces with the educational psychologist Edward L. Thorndike to produce a series of dictionaries designed for various levels of readers, from third-graders to college students. His *World Book Dictionary,* a family reference book, contained more than 250,000 entries. He began his own reference book company, Clarence L. Barnhart, Inc., in 1948, and from 1982 until his death Barnhart edited the *Barnhart Dictionary Companion* with his son Robert for Springer-Verlag.

OBITUARIES AND OTHER SOURCES:

BOOKS

Who's Who in America, 48th edition, Marquis, 1994, p. 186.

PERIODICALS

Chicago Tribune, October 31, 1993, section 2, p. 7.
New York Times, October 26, 1993, p. B10.
Washington Post, October 27, 1993, p. D5.

* * *

BARON DENNING
  See DENNING, Alfred Thompson

* * *

BARR, Nicholas 1943-

PERSONAL: Born November 23, 1943, in London, England; son of Herman (an accountant) and Edith (an art historian) Barr; married Gill Audigier, June 3, 1991. *Education:* London School of Economics and Political Science, London, B.Sc., 1965, M.Sc., 1967; University of California, Berkeley, Ph.D., 1971. *Religion:* Church of England.

ADDRESSES: Home—Endellion, Latimer Rd., New Barnet, Hertfordshire EN5 5NX, England. *Office*—London School of Economics and Political Science, University of London, Houghton St., London WC2A 2AE, England.

CAREER: University of London, London School of Economics and Political Science, London, England, began as lecturer, became senior lecturer in economics, 1971—. Consultant to World Bank.

MEMBER: Royal Economic Society, American Economic Association.

AWARDS, HONORS: Fulbright scholar, 1967-71.

WRITINGS:

(With A. R. Prest) *Public Finance in Theory and Practice,* 7th edition, Weidenfeld & Nicolson, 1985.
The Economics of the Welfare State, Stanford University Press, 1987, 2nd edition, 1993.
(With A. J. L. Barnes) *Strategies for Higher Education: The Alternative White Paper,* Aberdeen University Press, 1988.

Student Loans: The Next Steps, Aberdeen University Press, 1989.
Poland: Income Support and the Social Safety Net during the Transition, World Bank, 1993.

Contributor to economic journals.

* * *

BARRAULT, Jean-Louis 1910-1994

OBITUARY NOTICE—See index for *CA* sketch: Born September 8, 1910, in Vesinet, France; died of a heart attack, January 22, 1994, in Paris, France. Actor, mime, director, producer, playwright, and author. Known for his versatility in classical and avant-garde productions, Barrault was among the most famous personalities in contemporary French theatrical circles. He began more than sixty years in the field as a student and player at the Theatre de l'Atelier. From there, his career expanded to include work with the Comedie Francaise as well as performances as a mime, most notably in the 1944 film *Les Enfants du Paradis.* Barrault also found time to direct and produce plays, including *Rabelais,* which he also adapted for the stage. That work won him the French Drama Critics award for best show of the year. Barrault also founded theatrical troupes and companies, including Compagnie Renaud-Barrault. In the late 1950s and 1960s, he became director of France's national Theatre de l'Odeon (later known as Theatre de France). His tenure with the state-financed theatre ended, however, with his dismissal after protesting students took over and wrecked the facility. He then toured with his company before running the Theatre du Rond Point. Named commander of the French Legion of Honor, Barrault, along with his wife, Madeleine Renaud, also received the Moliere award. Barrault's writing credits include *Reflections on the Theatre, The Theatre of Jean-Louis Barrault,* and *Memories for Tomorrow: The Memoirs of Jean-Louis Barrault.* Among the plays he adapted for stage are: *Autour d'une mere, The Trial,* and *Saint-Exupery.*

OBITUARIES AND OTHER SOURCES:

BOOKS

Who's Who, 146th edition, St. Martins, 1994, p. 109.

PERIODICALS

Chicago Tribune, January 24, 1994, section 4, p. 10.
Los Angeles Times, January 23, 1994, p. A36.
New York Times, January 23, 1994, p. 30.
Times (London), January 25, 1994, p. 19.
Washington Post, January 23, 1994, p. B4.

BARRETT, (Eseoghene) Lindsay 1941-
(Eseoghene)

PERSONAL: Born in 1941, in Lucea, Jamaica; married an actor.

ADDRESSES: Agent—c/o Publicity Director, Fourth Dimension Publishing Co. Ltd., House 16, Fifth Ave., City Layout, New Haven, PMB 01164, Eunugu, Nigeria.

CAREER: Jamaica Broadcasting Corporation, Jamaica, news editor, 1961; worked variously as apprentice journalist for *Daily Gleaner* and the Jamaica *Star,* freelance worker in overseas department of British Broadcasting Corporation, lecturer for Fourah Bay College in Sierra Leone, teacher in Ghana, and worked at University of Ibadan in Ibadan, Nigeria; writer. Worked in television in Nigeria.

AWARDS, HONORS: Conrad Kent Rivers Memorial Award, *Black World,* c. 1971.

WRITINGS:

The State of Black Desire, illustrated by Larry Potter, Corbiere et Jugain, 1966.
Song for Mumu: A Novel, Longman, 1967, Howard University Press, 1974.
(Under pseudonym Eseoghene) *The Conflicting Eye* (poems), Paul Breman, 1973.
Lipskybound, Bladi House, 1977.
Agbada to Khaki: Reporting a Change of Government in Nigeria, Fourth Dimension, 1985.

Author of *Sighs of a Slave Dream* (one-act), produced in London, England; *Home Again; Blackblast; Jump Kookoo Makka;* and *After This We Heard of Fire.* Wrote radio plays for Nigerian National Radio. Work represented in anthologies, including *Black Arts,* edited by Alhamisi and Wangara, and *Black Fire,* edited by Jones and Neal. Contributor to journals, including *Black World, Black Lines,* and *Negro Digest.* Contributing editor for *Frontline* and *West Indian World.*

BIOGRAPHICAL/CRITICAL SOURCES:

PERIODICALS

New York Times Book Review, September 29, 1974, p. 40.

*   *   *

BARRY, Colman J(ames) 1921-1994

OBITUARY NOTICE—See index for *CA* sketch: Born May 29, 1921, in Lake City, MN; died of cancer, January 7, 1994, in Collegeville, MN. Cleric, educator, and writer. Barry is best known for his work as a Roman Catholic priest at St. John's University in Minnesota. Becoming a professor of history at the school in 1953, he served as the facility's president from 1964 until 1971. Continuing his pursuits as an educator, he moved on to Catholic University to serve as its dean of religious studies. Before his retirement, he returned to St. John's to head its Institute for Spirituality. Barry wrote various books concerning religion, including *Upon These Rocks: Catholics in the Bahamas, Readings in Church History,* and *A Sense of Place: Saint John's of Collegeville.*

OBITUARIES AND OTHER SOURCES:

BOOKS

Who's Who in America, 48th edition, Marquis, 1994, p. 193.

PERIODICALS

New York Times, January 11, 1994, p. B6.

*   *   *

BATES, Tom 1944-
(Timothy Lake)

PERSONAL: Born March 11, 1944, in La Jolla, CA; son of John (a merchant) and Patricia (a homemaker; maiden name, Gearin) Bates; married Eloise Schweitzer (a teacher), 1969; children: three. *Education:* University of Oregon, B.A. (with honors), 1966; University of Wisconsin—Madison, M.A., 1968, Ph.D., 1972. *Politics:* Independent. *Avocational Interests:* Travel, outdoors, history, politics.

ADDRESSES: Agent—Richard Pine, Arthur Pine Associates, 250 West 57th St., New York, NY 10019.

CAREER: Ohio University, Athens, instructor in history, 1971-72; University of Wisconsin, instructor in history, 1974; *Oregon* magazine, Portland, editor-in-chief, 1974-79; *New West* magazine, Los Angeles, CA, senior editor, 1980-81; *California* magazine, Los Angeles, executive editor, 1982-85; *Los Angeles Times,* Los Angeles, senior editor, 1986-87; writer. Member of Hosford-Abernethy Neighborhood Development Board, 1992-94; member of Peace and Justice Commission of St. Philip Neri Catholic Church, 1992-93.

MEMBER: Northwest Writers, Willamette Writers, Phi Beta Kappa.

AWARDS, HONORS: Fulbright fellowship, 1969-70; Ford Foundation fellowship, 1970-71; award for outstanding achievement from Wisconsin Literary Association, 1993, for *Rads.*

WRITINGS:

Rads: The 1970 Bombing of the Army Math Research Center at the University of Wisconsin and Its Aftermath, HarperCollins, 1992.

Contributor to periodicals, including *Journal of the History of Ideas, Los Angeles Times Magazine, Societas, Storia Contemporanea,* and *Travel and Leisure.* Also author of works under pseudonym Timothy Lake, including travel stories in various magazines.

WORK IN PROGRESS: Various articles for newspapers and magazines; research for docudramas.

SIDELIGHTS: Tom Bates is the author of *Rads: The 1970 Bombing of the Army Math Research Center at the University of Wisconsin and Its Aftermath,* which recounts events relating to the bombing that killed one man and caused six million dollars in damage at the University of Wisconsin, Madison, in 1970. Bates's book provides background on the various radicals responsible for the bombing and examines the nature of leftist concerns and activities at the time. Michael Kazin, writing in the *New York Times Book Review,* declared that in *Rads* Bates "tries to make sense of what in retrospect seems an act of political idiocy and self-destruction." Kazin added that *Rads* is "a lucid, dramatic narrative." And Elinor Langer, in her *Los Angeles Times Book Review* assessment, deemed Rads "a braided narrative that is part biography and part true crime."

Bates told *CA:* "No one ever knows what really happened."

BIOGRAPHICAL/CRITICAL SOURCES:

PERIODICALS

Los Angeles Times Book Review, December 13, 1992, pp. 1, 8.
New York Times Book Review, November 1, 1992, p. 12.

*   *   *

BEACH, Hugh   1949-

PERSONAL: Born June 7, 1949, in Key West, FL; son of Edward L. (a naval officer and writer) and Ingrid S. Beach; married Annie Norell (a consultant), June 21, 1986; children: Ellinor, Elisabeth. *Education:* Attended International School of America, 1971-72; Harvard University, B.A. (magna cum laude), 1972; Uppsala University, Ph.D., 1981.

ADDRESSES: Home—1622 29th St. N.W., Washington, DC 20007; and Herman Ygbergs Vaeg 13, 16138 Bromma, Sweden. *Office*—Department of Cultural An-

thropology, Uppsala University, Traedgaardsgatan 18, 75309 Uppsala, Sweden.

CAREER: Researcher for Swedish National Immigration Board and National Labor Market Board, 1981; Uppsala University, Uppsala, Sweden, research assistant in cultural anthropology, 1981-84, lecturer, 1984-90, associate professor of cultural anthropology, 1990—, departmental dean, 1985-86, founder and leader of Minority Interest Group, 1985-90. Umeaa University, researcher at Center for Arctic Cultural Research, 1987-90. Minority Rights Group, member of board of directors of Swedish branch, 1985—, chairperson, 1989-91. Conducted field studies at a Navaho Indian Reservation in Arizona, 1969; in Hong Kong, Bali, Sri Lanka, India, Kenya, and Tanzania, 1971-72, in Swedish Lapland, 1973-77, in Kotzebue, AK, 1982-83, in Sovkhoz Topolini, Yakutia, 1984, in Mogadishu, Somalia, 1986, to regions in Swedish Lapland impacted by contamination from the Chernobyl disaster in Russia, 1987—, and among the Saami reindeer herders of the Kola Peninsula, Lovozero, 1991.

AWARDS, HONORS: Grants from Swedish Council for Research in the Humanities and Social Sciences, 1981-84 and 1988—, Swedish Royal Academy of Science and Soviet Academy of Science, 1984, Carl-Bertel Nathhorsts Vetenskapliga och Allmaennyttiga Stiftelsen, Stiftelsen Lars Hiertas Minne, and Riksbankens Jubileumsfond, 1987; prize from Stiftelsen Torsten Janckes Minnesfond, 1990; grant from Nordic Environmental Research Program, 1993-95.

WRITINGS:

Reindeer-Herd Management in Transition: The Case of Tuorpon Saameby in Northern Sweden, Acta University, 1981.
A New Wave on a Northern Shore: The Indochinese Refugees in Sweden, Statens Invandrarverk (The Swedish Immigration Board) and Arbetsmarknadsstyrelsen (The Swedish Labor Board), 1982.
Gaest hos samerna (part of "Liv i Sverige" series), Carlsson Bokfoerlag, 1988.
A Year in Lapland: Guest of the Reindeer Herders, Smithsonian Institution Press, 1993.

Work represented in anthologies, including *The World of Pastoralism: Herding Systems in Comparative Perspective,* edited by John Galaty and Douglas Johnson, Guilford, 1990; *Mobility and Territoriality: Social and Spatial Boundaries Among Foragers, Fishers, Pastoralists, and Peripatetics,* edited by Michael Casimir and Aparna Rao, Berg (New York City), 1991; and *Readings in Saami History, Culture, and Language III,* edited by R. Kvist, Center for Arctic Cultural Research, Umeaa University, 1992. Contributor to periodicals in Europe, Scandinavia, and the United States, including *Harvard, Nomadic Peoples,* and *Cultural Survival Newsletter.*

SIDELIGHTS: Hugh Beach told *CA:* "The question of how I, an American, came to be a guest of the Saami is inescapable. In America I am often caught by it when clutching a glass at a cocktail party and, as I wind up for the long story, my conversation partner, perhaps sensing the end of light chatter, confides quickly that he has been to Stockholm and loved it. Then, throwing himself into the beckoning tide of newcomers, he disappears with hurried assurances that he will soon return to hear everything. In Sweden, the questioner frequently mixes his curiosity with self-abasement. Swedes are typically apologetic about knowing so little about the Saami native minority, just as I am ashamed concerning my ignorance of American Indians. Unfortunately, but also understandably, a touch of resentment can creep into any countryman at the thought of learning something about his own land from a foreigner, a guest. The Saami can put it quite bluntly: 'What are you doing here?'

"Sweden has always figured significantly in my family. My grandmother was Swedish and very proud of it. We were not part of any larger Swedish-American community, but the combined efforts of my grandmother and mother nonetheless secured for me and my siblings a fundamental knowledge of the Swedish language from childhood. One by one my grandmother took us to Sweden when she considered us to be of an appropriate age. Part of my introductory tour included Lapland, and since that first encounter, I have always been drawn back. It was largely through my first meeting with the Saami that I became inspired to turn from a career in biochemistry to one in anthropology.

"The study of anthropology combines well with a love of the outdoors and distant places. As a young student, I drove across the United States to the Navajo Indian Reservation in Arizona. I interrupted my college education repeatedly to travel. When bored with studies, I signed on to a Norwegian merchant ship bound for Asia and worked my way to the Philippines, Japan, Hong Kong, and Thailand where, tired of the sea, I stopped and taught English in a Buddhist temple. My return to the university was still fresh when I came upon yet a better way to leave it. This time it was as part of an anthropological study trip with a group of students led by Gregory Bateson. We visited Hawaii, Japan, Hong Kong, Bali, Sri Lanka, India, and Kenya. Bateson sowed intellectual seeds which still sprout and reseed, and the world stood before us, fresh and bursting.

"Once at night, when walking about in a crowded Asian city, I was followed by the muffled whispers of countless street vendors who, one after the other as I passed, tried to sell me whatever they could. I could have had any drug, any daughter for a wife or less, and probably my throat cut, all for only five dollars. At the end of the block a frustrated vendor shouted 'Mista, what you want?'

"What I wanted, what we all want, I am sure, is intimacy and friendship. I have found these in abundance among the Saami. *A Year in Lapland* was never conceived as simply a book about the Saami; it is also about learning to belong somewhere. The book was written when I was twenty-six years old, and I did it as much for myself, as part of the process of belonging, as for anyone else who might want to feel for these parts with the help of my pages. The manuscript was put aside and forgotten while, after many years in Lapland, I once again resumed my anthropological studies.

"My work as an anthropologist has taken me to Alaska, where I herded reindeer with the Inuit of the Seward Peninsula, to Siberia for a look at the reindeer herding program of a Soviet *sovkhoz,* and even to Somalia, where I worked briefly on a camel herding project. Currently I am leading a project, funded by the Bank of Sweden's Tercentenary Foundation, concerning the long-term social effects of the Chernobyl nuclear disaster on the Swedish Saami. The Saami and the reindeer shall always have a hold on me."

*   *   *

BEARDSELL, Peter R. 1940-

PERSONAL: Born August 11, 1940, in London, England; son of Reginald Walter (an engineer) and Iris Mary (Abbott) Beardsell; married Valerie Anne Benson (a lecturer), April 19, 1965; children: Anthony, Catherine. *Education:* Victoria University of Manchester, B.A. (with honors), 1963, M.A., 1967; University of Sheffield, Ph.D., 1974.

ADDRESSES: Office—Department of Hispanic Studies, University of Hull, Hull HU6 7RX, England.

CAREER: University of Manchester, Manchester, England, lecturer in Spanish, 1965-66; University of Sheffield, Sheffield, England, seminar lecturer in Hispanic studies, 1966-93; University of Hull, Hull, England, chair of Hispanic studies, 1993—. Society for Latin American Studies, secretary, 1993—.

MEMBER: Association of Hispanists.

WRITINGS:

Critical Edition of Ricardo Guiraldes: Don Segundo Sombra, Pergamon, 1973.
Winds of Exile: The Poetry of Jorge Carrera Andrade, Dolphin (Oxford), 1977.

Quiroga: Cuentos de amor de locura y de muerte, Thames & Grant & Cutler (London), 1986.

A Theatre for Cannibals: Rodolfo Usigli and the Mexican Stage, Fairleigh Dickinson University Press, 1992.

(Translator and author of introduction and notes) Hector Dante Cincotta, *El Pesaroso: Man of Sorrows* (poems), Sheffield Academic Press, 1992.

Critical Edition of Julio Cortazar: Siete cuentos, Manchester University Press, 1993.

General editor, "Manchester Hispanic Texts," Manchester University Press.

WORK IN PROGRESS: A book on images of Europe in the cultures of Latin America.

* * *

BECKER, Palmer (Joseph) 1936-

PERSONAL: Born May 20, 1936, in Dolton, SD; son of Joseph (a farmer) and Esther (a nurse and homemaker; maiden name, Unruh) Becker; married Ardys Preheim (a teacher and homemaker), June 27, 1958; children: Byron Weber, Jo, Sharla Becker Braun, Steve. *Education:* Freeman Junior College, A.A., 1956; Goshen College, B.A., 1958; Mennonite Biblical Seminary, M.R.E., 1965; Fuller Theological Seminary, M.Div. Equivalency, 1992, D.Min., 1995. *Politics:* Democrat. *Religion:* Mennonite Christian.

ADDRESSES: Home—1018 North Tenth St., Box 546, Mountain Lake, MN 56159. *Office*—Box 542, Mountain Lake, MN 56159.

CAREER: Relief worker in Taiwan, 1958-63; First Mennonite Church, Clinton, OK, pastor, 1965-69; Commission on Home Ministries, Newton, KS, administrative executive, 1969-79; Peace Mennonite Church, Richmond, British Columbia, founding pastor, 1979-88; Point Grey Fellowship, Vancouver, British Columbia, senior pastor, 1979-91; Bethel Mennonite Church, Mountain Lake, MN, senior pastor, 1991—. Chaplain at Mennonite Simons Center, Vancouver, 1988-91.

MEMBER: Mountain Lake Ministerial Association, Lao Ministries Task Force (president).

AWARDS, HONORS: Trophy for outstanding service from Taiwanese government; named alumnus of the year by Freeman Junior College.

WRITINGS:

Daily Thoughts (four volumes), FOMCIT [Taiwan], 1961.
Congregational Goals Discovery Plan, CHM, 1976.
You and Your Options, Faith and Life Press, 1979.
Creative Family Worship, Faith and Life Press, 1984.

Called to Care: A Training Manual for Small Group Leaders, Herald Press, 1993.
Called to Equip: A Small Group Training and Resource Manual for Pastors, Herald Press, 1993.

WORK IN PROGRESS: Focus Your Life, a "church membership preparation book and curriculum."

SIDELIGHTS: Palmer J. Becker told *CA:* "I live by the philosophy that relationships give meaning to life. My aim is to help Christian cell groups to be healthy and to help their members achieve creative thinking, feeling, and acting. Creative thinking, feeling, and acting are rooted in a person's experiences of God and in his or her relationships with significant others."

* * *

BELLIOTTI, Raymond A(ngelo) 1948-

PERSONAL: Born June 17, 1948, in Dansville, NY; son of Angelo R. (a barber) and Louise (an office worker; maiden name, Leonardo) Belliotti; married Marcia Dalby (a sculptor), May 31, 1986; children: Angelo, Vittoria. *Education:* Union College, B.A. (cum laude), 1970; University of Miami, Coral Gables, FL, M.A., 1976, Ph.D., 1977; Harvard University, J.D. (cum laude), 1982.

ADDRESSES: Home—104 Central Ave., Fredonia, NY 14063. *Office*—Department of Philosophy, State University of New York College at Fredonia, Fredonia, NY 14063.

CAREER: Miami-Dade Community College South, adjunct instructor, 1976-78; Virginia Commonwealth University, Richmond, assistant professor of philosophy, 1978-79; Phillips, Nizer, Benjamin, Krim & Ballon (law firm), New York City, summer associate, 1981; Barrett, Smith, Schapiro, Simon & Armstrong, New York City, attorney, 1982-84; State University of New York College at Fredonia, assistant professor, 1984-86, associate professor, 1986-91, professor of philosophy, 1991—, head of Faculty Council, 1989-90. Florida International University, adjunct assistant professor, 1977-78; Brooklyn Law School, adjunct associate professor, 1983-84; consultant to Committee for the Protection of Human Subjects, University of California, Berkeley. *Military service:* U.S. Army, Intelligence, 1971-74; became sergeant; received Commendation Medal.

MEMBER: International Association for Philosophy of Law and Social Philosophy, American Philosophical Association, Society for the Philosophy of Sex and Love, National Italian American Foundation, Chautauqua Italian-American Organization.

AWARDS, HONORS: Harvard University teaching fellow, 1980-82; grant from National Endowment for the

Humanities, 1986; William T. Hagen young scholar/artist award, 1991.

WRITINGS:

Justifying Law: The Debate Over Foundations, Goals, and Methods, Temple University Press, 1992.
Good Sex: Perspectives on Sexual Ethics, University Press of Kansas, 1993.

Work represented in anthologies, including *Women, Philosophy, and Sport,* edited by B. C. Postow, Scarecrow, 1983; *Philosophy for a Changing Society,* edited by Creighton Pedan, Advocate Press, 1983; and *Philosophic Inquiry in Sport,* edited by William Morgan and Klaus Meier, Human Kinetics, 1988. Contributor of articles and reviews to philosophy and sociology journals.

WORK IN PROGRESS: Morality and Politics: Italian-American Contexts, completion expected in 1995.

SIDELIGHTS: Raymond A. Belliotti told *CA:* "My books are therapeutic in that they permit me to gather and express my thoughts on a host of social, political, and legal matters. As an academic writer, my goal is not merely to exhibit technical and critical proficiency, but to infuse the work with passion and brio. Accordingly, there is a self-revelatory aspect to the work that transcends the typical critical analyses of fundamental beliefs."

*　　*　　*

BENET, Juan 1927-

PERSONAL: Full name, Juan Benet Goitia; born October 7, 1927, in Madrid, Spain; father's name, Tomas (a lawyer); mother's name, Teresa (Goitia); married Nuria Jordana, April 15, 1955; children: Ramon, Nicolas, Juana, Eugenio. *Education:* Received doctorate degree from Escuela Especial de Ingenieros de Caminos, Canales y Puertos, 1954.

ADDRESSES: Home—Pisuerga 7, Madrid 2, Spain. *Office*—CmZ, Ayala 42, Madrid 12, Spain.

CAREER: Chief director of public works in Spain, 1956-89; writer.

MEMBER: Spanish Committee on Large Dams.

AWARDS, HONORS: Seix Barral prize, Biblioteca Breve, 1969, for *Una meditacion;* prize from La Critica, 1984, for *Herrumbrosas lanzas.*

WRITINGS:

PLAYS

Max (short play), Revista Espanola, 1953.
Teatro (play collection; title means "Theatre"; includes *Anastas: O, El origen de la constitucion, Agonia confu-*

tans, and *Un caso de conciencia*), Siglo XXI de Espana Editores, 1970.

"REGION" NOVELS

Nunca llegaras a nada (short stories; title means "You Will Never Get Anywhere"), Ediciones Tebas, 1961.
Volveras a Region, Ediciones Destino, 1968, translation by Gregory Rabassa published as *Return to Region,* Columbia University Press, 1985.
Una meditacion, Seix Barral, 1969, translation by Rabassa published as *A Meditation,* Persea Books, 1982.
Un viaje de invierno (title means "A Winter Journey"), La Gaya Ciencia, 1971.
La otra casa de Mazon (novel; title means "The Mazon's Other House"), Seix Barral, 1973.
Del pozo y del Numa: Un ensayo y una leyenda (novella; title means "Of the Well and Of Numa: An Essay and a Legend"), La Gaya Ciencia, 1978.
Saul ante Samuel (novel; title means "Saul before Samuel"), La Gaya Ciencia, 1980.

OTHER FICTION

Una tumba (novella; title means "A Tomb"), Lumen, 1970.
Sub rosa (short stories), La Gaya Ciencia, 1972.
Cinco narraciones y dos fabulas (short stories; title means "Five Narratives and Two Fables"), La Gaya Ciencia, 1972.
En el estado (novel; title means "In the State"), Ediciones Alfaguara, 1977.
Cuentos completos (short stories; title means "Complete Stories"), Alianza, 1977.
El aire de un crimen (novel; title means "Air of a Crime"), Planeta, 1980.
Trece fabulas y media (short stories; title means "Thirteen and a Half Fables"), Ediciones Alfaguara, 1981.
Una tumba y otros relatos (short stories; title means "A Tomb and Other Tales"), Taurus, 1981.
Herrumbrosas lanzas (title means "Rusty Lances"), six volumes, Ediciones Alfaguara, 1983.
En la penumbra (novella; title means "In the Shadow"), Ediciones Alfaguara, 1989.
En caballero de Sajonia (novel; title means "The Knight of Saxony"), Ediciones Planeta, 1991.

ESSAYS

La inspiracion y el Estilo (essays; title means "Inspiration and Style"), Revista de Occidente, 1966.
Puerta de tierra (essays; title means "Land's Gate"), Seix Barral, 1969.
Em ciernes (essays; title means "Budding"), Taurus, 1976.
El angel del Senor abandona a Tobias (essays; title means "The Angel of the Lord Abandons Tobit"), La Gaya Ciencia, 1976.

Que fue la guerra civil? (essays; title means "What Was the Civil War?"), La Gaya Ciencia, 1976.

La moviola de Euripides (essays; title means "Euripides's Replay Machine"), Taurus, 1982.

Sobre la incertidumbre (essays; title means "On Doubt"), Ediciones Ariel, 1983.

Articulos, 1962-1977 (essays; title means "Articles, 1962-1977"), Ediciones Libertarias, 1983.

OTHER

A este lado del Paraiso (translation of F. Scott Fitzgerald's *This Side of Paradise*), Alianza, 1968.

Edad Media y literatura contemporanea (title means "Middle Age and Contemporary Literature"), Trieste, 1985.

Otono en Madrid hacia 1950 (title means "Autumn in Madrid around 1950"), Alianza, 1987.

Vistas de las obras del Canal de Isabel II fotografiadas por Clifford (title means "Views of the Works in the Canal de Isabel II, photographed by Clifford"), J. Soto, 1988.

Londres victoriano (title means "Victorian London"), Planeta, 1989.

La construccion de la torre de Babel (title means "Building the Tower of Babel"), Ediciones Struela, 1990.

El camino del Guadiana (title means "The Course of the Guadiana River"), Confederacion Hidrografica del Guadiana, 1991.

Also translator of William Shakespeare's *The Tempest, The Winter's Tale, Anthony and Cleopatra,* and *Cymbeline* into Spanish, published by Ediciones Alfaguara.

SIDELIGHTS: Juan Benet, an internationally renowned novelist and essayist, is a leading figure in the Spanish literary movement known as the "New Wave." Many of Benet's novels and short stories are set in a mythical province in rural Spain, a desolate and mysterious place that he calls Region. This fictitious area, similar to the fictional geographies of William Faulkner's Yoknapatawpha County and Garcia Marquez's Macondo, resembles in some respects northwestern Spain, where Benet served as director of public works from 1954 to 1966. It has also been interpreted as a microcosm of Spain at the time of the Spanish Civil War. During that war, which began in 1936, Benet's father was killed, and his family left Madrid for San Sebastian, in the Basque Provinces near the French frontier. It was there that Benet began his education. Returning to Madrid after the war, Benet took up the study of civil engineering and, at the same time, began reading the authors who would influence his own literary efforts, perhaps most notably William Faulkner.

While still in college, Benet published his first literary work, a short play titled *Max,* in 1953. Following his graduation he went to work as an engineer in northwestern Spain. His stay in that area inspired him to create a fictional landscape that resembled post-Civil War Spain under the rule of Francisco Franco. Benet thus created Region.

Spanish readers first encountered Region in 1961, with Benet's publication of the short story collection *Nunca llegaras a nada* ("You Will Never Get Anywhere"), which introduces many of the locale's inhabitants and much of its physiognomy. The book also set the literary style that would infuse much of Benet's subsequent work. Much like Faulkner's, Benet's style is marked by long—often multiple page—sentences, allusions to a wide range of authors, and themes of memory and time.

Benet expanded Region's literary landscape with his first novel of the series, *Return to Region.* Originally published in Spanish as *Volveras a Region* in 1967, the novel was translated by Gregory Rabassa and published in the United States in 1985. The book revolves, as much of Benet's work does, around the effects of the Spanish Civil War on modern Spain. William Herrick in the *New York Times Book Review* extolled the work as "brilliant," "lovely," and "sad." Related by an anonymous narrator, the story concerns an old doctor living a dismal life in Region with his retarded godson, whom he keeps padlocked in an upstairs room. A visitor arrives at the doctor's ramshackle house. She is a woman who was once a prostitute in Region's brothel, Muerte, which translated means "death." Returning to Region long after the war, she and the old doctor exchange haunting stories. The horror of the war permeates their tales, while details about the life and countryside gradually come to light. Alan Cheuse, in a review for the *Los Angeles Times,* finds the novelist's prose style much more difficult than Faulkner's, but commends "the slow but intense progress of the Iberian Juan Benet toward an achievement only our finest home-grown writers have equalled." Many critics consider *Return to Region* to be Benet's finest work. Despite this acclaim, the novel was not published in English until after Rabassa's translation of Benet's second novel, *A Meditation,* gained attention in 1982.

The second Region novel, *A Meditation* appeared in Spanish as *Una meditacion* in 1969. The novel was widely praised in Europe and won the Seix Barral prize in that year. *A Meditation* is an intricate, multilayered work that, in the words of *Books Abroad* contributor Ricardo Benavides (who reviewed the original Spanish edition in 1971), "reaches us through a linguistic tidal wave" that engulfs ordinary syntax, diction, paragraphing, and punctuation. Judith Applebaum, reviewing Rabassa's English translation in the *New York Times Book Review* found *A Meditation* overly ambitious and difficult. In the same review, however, Applebaum quoted critic Allen Josephs's praise for the author's "brilliant, overarching and fascinatingly difficult style."

Benet followed *A Meditation* with the ghostly novella *Una tumba* ("A Tomb") and *Un viaje de invierno* ("A Winter Journey") and *La otra casa de Mazon* ("The Mazon's Other House"), the third and fourth installments, respectively, in the Region series. Benet also gained recognition as an author of short stories and as one of Spain's foremost essayists. In 1978 he published *Del pozo y del Numa: Un ensayo y una leyenda* ("Of the Well and Of Numa: An Essay and a Legend"), which contained a sample of his essay work and also featured a novella about El Numa, one of the characters from Region. Benet returned to the setting of Region once more in 1980 with the publication of *Saul ante Samuel* ("Saul before Samuel"), the fifth book in the series. As the 1980s progressed, Benet expanded his style with the publication of *El aire de un crimen* ("Air of a Crime") and the multi-volume *Herrumbrosas lanzas* ("Rusty Lances"), both of which were praised as being more accessible than the author's earlier work. Despite the recognition for these works in Europe and Spanish-speaking countries, Benet's success in English-speaking countries has been limited, due in part to a lack of translated material. His ability to create thought-provoking and thematically challenging work in a variety of genres has endeared Benet to a number of critics and, as Janet E. Lorenz wrote in *Cyclopedia of World Authors,* earned him a ranking as "one of Spain's most important literary figures."

BIOGRAPHICAL/CRITICAL SOURCES:

BOOKS

Monteiga, Roberto C., David K. Herzberger, and Malcolm Alan Compitello, editors, *Critical Approaches to the Writings of Juan Benet,* University Press of New England, 1984.
Cyclopedia of World Authors, Harper, 1989, pp. 170-71.
Herzberger, *The Novelistic World of Juan Benet,* American Hispanist, 1976.

PERIODICALS

Books Abroad, spring, 1971.
Los Angeles Times, September 20, 1985.
New York Times, January 1, 1990.
New York Times Book Review, December 18, 1983; October 15, 1985; October 18, 1987.

*   *   *

BENNETT, Georgette 1946-

PERSONAL: Born November 12, 1946, in Budapest, Hungary; daughter of Ignatz Beitscher (a manufacturer) and Sidonie (a designer; maiden name, Horvath) Beitscher Bennett; married Warren J. Sandler, June 9, 1968 (divorced 1974); married Marc Herman Tanenbaum (an ecumenical leader and human rights activist), June 6, 1982 (died July 3, 1992); children: Joshua-Marc Bennett. *Education:* Vassar College, B.A., 1967; New York University, Ph.D., 1972; University of Delaware, diploma, 1992. *Avocational Interests:* Theater, movies, tennis.

ADDRESSES: Office—Bennett Associates, 575 Madison Ave., 3rd Floor, New York, NY 10022. *Agent*—Charlotte Sheedy, 611 Broadway, New York, NY 10012.

CAREER: City University of New York, assistant professor of sociology, 1970-77; New York City Office of Management and Budget, deputy assistant director for administration of justice, 1977-78; NBC News, New York City, network correspondent, 1978-80; Bennett Associates, New York City, owner and president, 1980-87, 1992—; First New York Bank for Business (formerly First Women's Bank), vice president and marketing director, 1987, first vice president and chief marketing officer, 1987-88, senior vice president and division executive of domestic and international and private banking, 1988-92. Rabbi Marc H. Tanenbaum Foundation, president, 1992—. Women's Advocacy Committee, New York City, member, 1971-74; Eastern Sociological Society, committee chairperson, 1972-73; member of board of American Society for Public Administration, 1976-79, Creative Arts Rehabilitation Center (publicity chairperson), 1982-89, and American Jewish World Service (treasurer), 1986—; International Rescue Committee, member of security and public affairs committees, 1992—. Host of Walter Cronkite's PBS-TV program, *Why in the World?;* host, guest, and consultant on local and national TV and radio programs.

MEMBER: Academy of Criminal Justice Sciences, American Civil Liberties Union, American Society for Criminology, American Sociological Association, American Women in Radio and Television, National Organization for Women, People for the American Way, Women's Economic Roundtable, Women's Forum.

AWARDS, HONORS: New York University Founders Day Award, 1972; American Society for Public Administration, certificate, 1975, and award, 1976, both for significant national contribution; Pulitzer Prize nomination, nonfiction book, 1987, for *Crimewarps: The Future of Crime in America.*

WRITINGS:

(With Ava Abramovitz, Catherine Milton, and Ellen Mintz) *Women in Policing: A Manual,* Washington, DC, Police Foundation, 1975.

(With Ron Waldron and others) *Law Enforcement and Criminal Justice: An Introduction,* Houghton Mifflin, 1979.

Unlocking America, two volumes, Commercial Union Insurance Companies, 1981.

Protecting Against Crime, Research Institute of America, 1982.

A Safe Place to Live, Insurance Information Institute and Crime Prevention Coalition, 1982.

Crimewarps: The Future of Crime in America, Doubleday, 1987.

Contributor of more than forty articles to professional and scholarly publications.

WORK IN PROGRESS: A Time to Love and a Time to Die: Seasons of a Life.

SIDELIGHTS: "I didn't set out to be a criminologist," Georgette Bennett revealed in an interview. "Back in 1970, I was a member of the Women's Advocacy Committee, a group mandated to explore the status of women in New York City's government agencies. We all drew assignments and, by chance, I got the police department." It was an assignment that took Bennett from a college classroom, where she taught sociology, urban demography, and research methods, to the upper reaches of the criminal justice system of New York City. From 1972 to 1974, while still on the faculty at the City University of New York, Bennett was a personal consultant to the commissioner of the New York City Police Department; in addition, she served as the department's coordinator for training and evaluation.

Bennett also pursued a parallel career as a broadcast journalist. A former network correspondent for NBC News, she also appeared frequently on Fox-TV's *Ten O'Clock News* in New York City. Off-camera, she helped to develop investigative stories for CBS-TV's *60 Minutes,* ABC-TV's *20-20,* and PBS's *MacNeil/Lehrer News Hour.* From the outset Bennett concentrated not only on crime but on American pluralism and civil liberties, citing the "haunting echoes of my roots"—her family's flight from Hungary in 1948 to escape the Iron Curtain and the relatives she had lost in the Holocaust—as the basis for these concerns.

By 1987 Bennett had developed a cautiously optimistic view on the trends she had observed in inner-city crime while maintaining a rather pessimistic outlook on the prospects for curbing white-collar criminals, and she presented her opinions in the book *Crimewarps: The Future of Crime in America.* The word *crimewarps,* Bennett explained in an interview in the *Orlando Sentinel,* "is a word I coined which means a displacement or shift in a crime pattern." Specifically, she argued that white collar crime would increase, violent crime would decrease, senior citi-

zens and women would commit more crime in the future, and cities would become safer and suburbs and rural areas more dangerous. In a review of the book in the *Los Angeles Times Book Review,* Elliott Currie suggested that Bennett had taken on too big a topic by trying to cover "both street crime and white collar crime; drug abuse and pornography; the police, courts, and prisons; homosexuality, prostitution, and gambling; even the rise of fundamentalist Christianity." Nonetheless, as Bob McKelvey pointed out in the *Detroit Free Press,* Bennett's "career in criminology . . . dispelled many of the myths we associate with crime."

Bennett told *CA:* "Most of my writing has been issue-oriented but is now becoming more personal. Indeed, I find that I get closure on the most important events in my life when I write about them or use them in a lecture. The process of self-revelation is a means of sharing and making connections. I didn't enjoy writing professionally until I started working with my agent, Charlotte Sheedy. She inspired me."

BIOGRAPHICAL/CRITICAL SOURCES:

PERIODICALS

Detroit Free Press, March 9, 1987.
Houston Chronicle, April 5, 1987, p. 21.
Los Angeles Times Book Review, April 5, 1987.
Oregonian, June 9, 1986.
Orlando Sentinel, March 15, 1987.
USA Today, March 27, 1987.
Washington Post, March 6, 1988.

*   *   *

BENTLEY, Jeffery W(estwood)   1955-

PERSONAL: Born April 5, 1955, in Heidelberg, Germany; son of Craig Burlington (a geologist) and Verlyn (a landlord; maiden name, Westwood) Bentley; divorced; children: Andrea Ruth, Samuel Martinez. *Education:* Brigham Young University, B.S., 1978; University of Arizona, Ph.D., 1986. *Politics:* "Ecologist." *Religion:* "Not Mormon." *Avocational Interests:* "Being out of doors, writing for fun."

ADDRESSES: Home—P.O. Box 93, Tegucigalpa, Honduras.

CAREER: New Mexico State University, Las Cruces, assistant professor, 1987; Zamorano, Tegucigalpa, Honduras, anthropologist, 1987—.

WRITINGS:

(With Scott R. Pearson and others) *Portuguese Agriculture in Transition,* Cornell University Press, 1987.

Today There Is No Misery, University of Arizona Press, 1992.

Co-editor, *Ceiba,* Volume XXXI, number 2, 1990.

SIDELIGHTS: Jeffery W. Bentley told *CA:* "My dad said that he and Mom had always wanted to have kids, but they had us instead. I was the oldest of six in an old Mormon family, but Mom's side had been weaving in and out of the church since wagon train days. Fortunately, we're almost all out again. Mormons believe that the Americas were peopled in the year 600 B.C. by some folks from Jerusalem. I studied archaeology in college and learned that Native Americans aren't Jewish. That's when I left the church.

"I went to graduate school in Arizona, wrote a dissertation on Portuguese peasants, taught at New Mexico State for a little while. Then I took a job at a little agricultural college in Honduras, a place called Zamorano. The school has more cows than students, more cows than [ice cream manufacturers] Ben and Jerry. I thought I'd stay two years. That was six years ago. I liked the mountains and working out of doors. The weather is perfect.

"My work is applied anthropology, creative ecology. Honduran farmers use insecticides like magic cure-alls for pest problems. My team teaches insect ecology to farmers, who then invent alternatives to pesticides. We're starting to work in El Salvador and Nicaragua, too.

"Mormons think I'm crazy for studying anthropology. Anthropologists think I'm crazy for studying bugs. But I'm happy, and that is the main idea. I work with some really fine people, which is nicer than coffee in bed."

*   *   *

BERCZELLER, Richard 1902-1994

OBITUARY NOTICE—See index for *CA* sketch: Born February 4, 1902, in Sopron, Austria-Hungary (now Sopron, Hungary); immigrated to the United States, 1941; naturalized citizen, 1948; died January 3, 1994, in New York, NY. Physician and author. In short stories penned during the course of his career, physician Berczeller recounted his experiences as a member of the Austrian Socialist movement in the 1930s. Berczeller earned his M.D. from the University of Vienna in 1926, then spent the next twelve years practicing in Austria, where he eventually specialized in internal medicine. When German forces annexed the country in 1938, Berczeller was arrested and later forced to leave any Nazi-occupied areas. He immigrated to the United States in the early 1940s and embarked on a lengthy career with New York City's Beth Israel Hospital. Among his works are *Displaced Doctor* and

Time Was, a full-length autobiography. "A Trip into the Blue and Other Stories," a selection of his autobiographical writings, appeared in the *New Yorker.*

OBITUARIES AND OTHER SOURCES:

PERIODICALS

Los Angeles Times, January 10, 1994, p. A16.

*   *   *

BERGER, Thomas R(odney) 1933-

PERSONAL: Born March 23, 1933, in Victoria, British Columbia, Canada; son of Maurice Theodore Berger and Nettie Elsie Perle (maiden name, McDonald) Berger; married Beverley Ann Crosby, November 5, 1955; children: Erin Frances, David Bruce. *Education:* University of British Columbia, B.A., 1955, LL.B., 1956.

ADDRESSES: Home—4627 West Third Ave., Vancouver, British Columbia V6R 1N5, Canada. *Office*—Number 300, 171 Water St., Vancouver, British Columbia V6B 1A7, Canada.

CAREER: Lawyer for Shulman, Tupper and Co., 1957-62, and Thomas R. Berger and Co., 1963-71; judge for Supreme Court of British Columbia, 1971-83. University of British Columbia, faculty of law, honorary lecturer, 1979-82, adjunct professor, 1983—; Simon Fraser University, adjunct professor, 1979—; University of Victoria, faculty of law, sessional lecturer, 1982-83. Served as member of Parliament for Vancouver-Burrard, 1962-63, and Legislative Assembly for Vancouver-Burrard, 1966-69; New Democratic Party of British Columbia, leader, 1969; Royal Commission on Family and Children's Law, chair, 1973-75; Commissioner for Mackenzie Valley Pipeline Inquiry, 1974-77, Indian and Inuit Health Consultation, 1979-80, and Alaska Native Review Commission, 1983-85; member of board of directors, Frontier College, 1975—, and Vanier Institute of the Family, 1977-83; International Defense and Aid Fund for Southern Africa (Canada), president, 1982—.

MEMBER: International Commission of Jurists (Canadian Section), Engineering Institute of Canada (honorary member).

AWARDS, HONORS: Distinguished Achievement Award, Sierra Club of North America, 1978; honorary degrees from numerous institutions, including University of Notre Dame and Simon Fraser University.

WRITINGS:

Northern Frontier, Northern Homeland, Queen's Printer, 1977, revised edition, Douglas and McIntyre, 1989.

Fragile Freedoms: Human Rights and Dissent in Canada, Clarke, Irwin, 1981.

Village Journey: The Report of the Alaska Native Review Commission, Hill and Wang, 1985.

A Long and Terrible Shadow: White Values, Native Rights in the Americas, 1492-1992, Douglas and McIntyre, 1992.

Contributor of articles to journals, including *Queen's Quarterly, Canadian Literature,* and *University of Toronto Law Journal.*

Berger's works have been translated into French.

SIDELIGHTS: When Thomas R. Berger was appointed to the Supreme Court of British Columbia in 1971, he was thirty-eight years old and the youngest judge in the twentieth century to sit on the province's highest court. Among the three royal commissions Berger headed during his career on the bench was the Mackenzie Valley Pipeline Inquiry, the report of which was published as *Northern Frontier, Northern Homeland.* Established in 1974 to determine the social, environmental, and economic impact of the proposed Arctic Gas pipeline—which was planned to run from Prudhoe Bay in Alaska down through the Mackenzie Valley in western Canada—the one-man commission attracted international attention. Berger recommended delaying construction of the pipeline for at least ten years; the Canadian government followed his advice. *Northern Frontier, Northern Homeland,* according to Isaac Bickerstaff in *Quill and Quire,* "quickly became the federal government's all-time bestselling publication." Bickerstaff added that, along with the hearings of the commission, the book "did much to arouse public sympathy for native land claims in the north."

Berger also headed the 1979 commission that investigated Indian and Inuit health-care programs. His 1981 demand for a statement of aboriginal rights in the new Canadian constitution helped to ensure their inclusion, although later Parliamentary provisions ended up diluting such rights. That same year, Berger's book *Fragile Freedoms: Human Rights and Dissent in Canada* was published. *Fragile Freedoms* "examines eight different episodes in which the rights, and sometimes even the existence, of a certain minority have been threatened by government indifference or hostility, usually with the tacit or open support of the majority," informed Paul Wilson in *Books in Canada.* An exploration of such topics as the expulsion and return of the Acadians, the denial of separate schools to French Canadians in Manitoba, and the persecution of Jehovah's Witnesses in Quebec, *Fragile Freedoms* stirred considerable controversy in Canada and elicited diverse opinions from critics. Wilson found the volume "timely, lucid, and humane," whereas *Saturday Night* reviewer

Robert Fulford dismissed the volume as "for the most part woolly-minded, unimaginative, and predictable."

In the *New York Review of Books,* Edgar Z. Friedenberg commented that Berger "has been perhaps the most effective and certainly the most respectable champion of the aboriginal peoples of Canada." Friedenberg also noted that, because of Berger's outspoken views, the justice became the target of attacks aimed at muzzling judicial activists. In 1983 Berger resigned from the bench, a move that enabled him to speak more freely on matters of human rights and fundamental freedoms. His 1992 book *A Long and Terrible Shadow: White Values, Native Rights in the Americas, 1492-1992* was considered by a reviewer in *Books in Canada* to be "a profoundly intelligent and thoughtful study."

BIOGRAPHICAL/CRITICAL SOURCES:

PERIODICALS

Books in Canada, January, 1982, p. 18; February, 1992, pp. 26-27.
Canadian Forum, April, 1982, pp. 28-30.
Globe and Mail (Toronto), September 14, 1985, pp. 1-2.
New York Review of Books, November 4, 1982, pp. 37-38.
Quill and Quire, December, 1981.
Saturday Night, September, 1982, pp. 2, 6.

*   *   *

BERNA, Paul   1910-1994

OBITUARY NOTICE—See index for *CA* sketch: Born Jean Sabran on February 21, 1910, in Hyeres, France; died January 21, 1994, in Paris, France. Author. A prolific author of books for juvenile readers, Berna is best remembered for his mystery and adventure stories. After a stint as a journalist, he turned to writing children's books in the 1950s, publishing regularly until the early 1970s. Some of his novels for older children that have been translated into English include *Threshold of the Stars, The Clue of the Black Cat, The Secret of the Missing Boat,* and *The Mule on the Expressway.*

OBITUARIES AND OTHER SOURCES:

BOOKS

Authors of Books for Young People, 3rd edition, Scarecrow, 1990.

PERIODICALS

New York Times, January 28, 1994, p. B7.

BERRYMAN, Jack W. 1947-

PERSONAL: Born September 25, 1947, in Lewistown, PA; son of C. William (a telephone switchboard systems installer) and Dorothy (a department store clerk; maiden name, Black) Berryman; married Elaine Headings (a homemaker), May 30, 1970; children: Andrea L. *Education:* Lock Haven State University, B.S., 1969; University of Massachusetts at Amherst, M.S., 1971, M.A., 1974; University of Maryland at College Park, Ph.D., 1976. *Avocational Interests:* All types of fishing for salmon and steelhead.

ADDRESSES: Home—12924 133rd Pl. N.E., Kirkland, WA 98034. *Office*—Department of Medical History and Ethics, School of Medicine, University of Washington, Seattle, WA 98195.

CAREER: University of Massachusetts at Amherst, instructor, 1971-72; University of Washington, Seattle, assistant professor, 1976-81, associate professor of medical history and ethics, 1981—. Ball State University, Phi Alpha Theta Lecturer, 1981; American College of Sports Medicine, D. B. Dill Historical Lecturer, 1994; consultant on environmental history, and on sport history and the history of sports medicine.

MEMBER: North American Society for Sport History (president, 1989-91), American Academy of Kinesiology (fellow), American Association for the History of Medicine, American College of Sports Medicine (historian), Outdoor Writers Association of America, Kappa Delta Pi.

WRITINGS:

(Editor with Roberta J. Park) *Sport and Exercise Science: Essays in the History of Sports Medicine,* University of Illinois Press, 1992.

Contributor to northwest fishing and travel magazines, including *British Columbia Sport Fishing.* Editor, *Journal of Sport History,* 1977-84.

WORK IN PROGRESS: "Out of Many, One": A History of the American College of Sports Medicine; research on the role of exercise in medicine, the pursuit of health in America, and the history of sports medicine.

*   *   *

BERTON, Ralph 1910-1993

OBITUARY NOTICE—See index for *CA* sketch: Born December 24, 1910, in Danville, IL; died of congestive heart failure, November 17, 1993, in Ridgewood, NJ. Educator and author. A long-time jazz enthusiast, Berton served as an instructor in the field at such institutions as the New School for Social Research, Bloomfield College, and Cooper Union. He began his career with stints in a variety of occupations, including as a boxer, truck driver, waiter, and tennis professional, then turned his focus in the late 1930s to music, originating the radio show *Jazz University of the Air* for New York City's WNYC-FM. In the mid-1970s he penned a biography of cornet player Bix Beiderbecke, titled *Remembering Bix: A Memoir of the Jazz Age,* as well as a novel entitled *Jewel City Inn.* He also authored several plays, including *Two for Tonight* and *Cassandra Kelly,* and served as executive editor of *Sounds & Fury* and as classical music editor of *Status,* both during the mid-1960s.

OBITUARIES AND OTHER SOURCES:

PERIODICALS

New York Times, November 24, 1993, p. D18.

*   *   *

BERTRAND, Cecile 1953-

PERSONAL: Born June 20, 1953, in Liege, Belgium; daughter of Andre Bertrand and Pauwen Jeannette Bertrand; married Etienne Bours (a musical adviser), October 26, 1974; children: Antoine. *Education:* Studied painting in Liege at L'Institut Saint Luc. *Avocational Interests:* Sculpture, walking in the mountains, jogging, bicycling.

ADDRESSES: Home—54 rue de la Magree, 4163 Tavier, Belgium. *Agent*—Rainbow Graphics, 32 rue de la Vallee, 1050 Brussells, Belgium.

CAREER: Contributor of cartoons to a Belgian newspaper; affiliated with a Belgian animation company. Bertrand's paintings have appeared in exhibits in several cities, including Liege, De Haan, Brussells, and Wenduine, 1975-80; participant in group exhibitions, including Mostra Internazional d'Illustrazione per l'Infanzia, Italy, 1985-90.

MEMBER: Union Professionnelle des Createurs d'Histoire en Images, d'Illustration, et de Cartoon.

AWARDS, HONORS: Prix Jeunesse du Ministere de la Communaute Francaise de Belgique, 1984.

WRITINGS:

(And illustrator) *Mr. and Mrs. Smith Have Only One Child, but What a Child!* (originally published as *Monsieur et Madame Smith n'ont qu'une fille, mais quelle fille!*), Lothrop (New York, NY), 1992.

WORK IN PROGRESS: A four-book set for children; *Le Bugs,* an animated cartoon.

SIDELIGHTS: Cecile Bertrand commented: "Many people have already explained better than I why one loves to create books for children! Simply I can say that I cannot imagine not being able to do this. This takes all my time, my energy, all my life . . . I like above all to take serious themes, very serious, and make it a funny story but one which leads into the memory of the reader."

*   *   *

BESSBOROUGH, Tenth Earl of
See PONSONBY, Frederick Edward Neuflize

*   *   *

BESSY, Maurice 1910-1993

OBITUARY NOTICE—See index for *CA* sketch: Born December 4 (one source says 10), 1910, in Nice, France; died November 15, 1993, in Paris, France. Artistic director and writer. As the artistic director of the Cannes Film Festival during the 1970s, Bessy turned over the responsibility for film selection to festival organizers (it previously had rested with a national committee), and thus is credited with providing the festival with higher quality films. Bessy began his affiliation with the film industry in the late 1920s, working for the trade periodical *Cinemonde* for a period of nearly forty years; beginning in the mid-1940s, he assumed the editorship of other motion picture magazines, such as *Une semaine de Paris* and *Film Francais.* In 1937 he co-established the Prix Louis Delluc to honor the best *film d'auteur,* or the film's "true" director, and headed the prize's jury throughout the remainder of his career. A prolific writer, Bessy penned more than twenty books about the film industry, including *Walt Disney, Orson Welles, Charlie Chaplin,* and, with Raymond Chirat, a multi-volume work entitled *Histoire du cinema francais.* He also wrote novels as well as screenplays; among the latter are *Voici le temps des assassins* ("Here Is the Time of Murderers") and *Diable et les 10 commandements* ("The Devil and the Ten Commandments").

OBITUARIES AND OTHER SOURCES:

PERIODICALS

Times (London), December 18, 1993, p. 17.

*   *   *

BIAL, Raymond 1948-

PERSONAL: Born November 5, 1948, in Danville, IL; son of Marion (an Air Force officer) and Catherine (a medical secretary) Bial; married Linda LaPuma (a librarian), August 25, 1979; children: Anna, Sarah, Luke. *Education:* University of Illinois, B.S. (with honors), 1970, M.S., 1979. *Politics:* Independent. *Religion:* Catholic. *Avocational Interests:* Gardening, fishing, hiking, travel.

ADDRESSES: Home—208 West Iowa St., Urbana, IL 61801. *Office*—Parkland College Library, 2400 West Bradley Ave., Champaign, IL 61821. *Agent*—Barbara Kouts, P.O. Box 558, Bellport, NY 11713.

CAREER: Parkland College Library, Champaign, IL, library director, 1988—.

MEMBER: Children's Reading Roundtable, Society of Children's Book Writers and Illustrators.

AWARDS, HONORS: Best Publicity of 1984, Library Public Relations Council, 1984, for "In All My Years" exhibit poster; Historian of the Year, Champaign County, Illinois, 1984; Award of Superior Achievement, Illinois State Historical Society, 1985; First Annual Staff Development Award, Parkland College, 1985, for presentation on print media and computer resources in academic libraries; Certificate of Commendation, American Association for State and Local History, 1986; Writer's Choice selection, National Endowment for the Arts and the Pushcart Foundation, 1986, for *First Frost;* Best Publicity of 1986, Library Public Relations Council, 1987, for poster advertising "Changing Image of Rural and Small Town Life" panel discussion; Staff Development Award, Parkland College, 1990, for presentation entitled "The Language of Photography"; Outstanding Science Trade Book for Children, 1991, for *Corn Belt Harvest.*

WRITINGS:

NONFICTION FOR CHILDREN; AND PHOTOGRAPHER

Corn Belt Harvest, Houghton Mifflin, 1991.
County Fair, Houghton Mifflin, 1992.
Amish Home, Houghton Mifflin, 1993.
Frontier Home, Houghton Mifflin, 1993.
Shaker Home, Houghton Mifflin, 1994.

OTHER

Ivesdale: A Photographic Essay, Champaign County Historical Archives, 1982.
In All My Years: Portraits of Older Blacks in Champaign-Urbana, Champaign County Historical Museum, 1983, revised edition, 1985.
Upon a Quiet Landscape: The Photographs of Frank Sadorus, Champaign County Historical Museum, 1983.
There Is a Season, Champaign County Nursing Home, 1984.
(With Kathryn Kerr) *First Frost,* Stormline Press, 1985.
Common Ground: Photographs of Rural and Small Town Life, Stormline Press, 1986.

Stopping By: Portraits from Small Towns, University of Illinois Press, 1988.

(With wife, Linda LaPuma Bial) *The Carnegie Library in Illinois,* University of Illinois Press, 1988.

From the Heart of the Country: Photographs of the Midwestern Sky, Sagamore Publishing, 1991.

Looking Good: A Guide to Photographing Your Library, American Library Association, 1991.

Champaign: A Pictorial History, Bradley Publishing, 1993.

Also author of introduction to *Beneath an Open Sky,* by Gary Irving, University of Illinois Press, 1990. Contributor of photoessay to *Townships,* University of Iowa Press, 1992.

SIDELIGHTS: Raymond Bial commented: "When I was growing up in the 1950s I spent several of the most joyous years of my young life in a small town in Indiana. With my friends, I bicycled around the neighborhood, went swimming at the municipal pool, stopped for ice cream at the local hotspot, and frequently visited our Carnegie public library. Some people might think that such memories are simply nostalgic, but I know that our little town was pleasant, comfortable, and safe—and I will always cherish those years.

"Later, our family moved to a farm in southern Michigan. Although I missed my old friends, as well as the charming atmosphere of my old 'hometown,' I enjoyed taking care of our livestock and running free through the woods, marsh, and fields around our new home. The moment I walked out of the house I was truly outside. The marsh, in particular, was bursting forth with wildlife—turtles, frogs, muskrats, ducks—and I delighted in my explorations and discoveries.

"Not all my childhood was wonderful. At times there were financial difficulties, family arguments, and other painful experiences. Yet for the most part I was simply thrilled to be alive, directly experiencing the world around me, especially when I could be out of doors in the light and weather.

"My work as a writer and photographer first drew upon these early moments of delight. For most of my books I have returned to rural and small town subjects. Just as when I was a child, I still love to be outside, absolutely free, making photographs. With every photograph I try to recapture that heightened sense of feeling for people, places, and things which meant so much to me as a child. I believe that adults as well as children should live not only in their minds, but through their senses.

"Ever since I was in fourth grade, I wanted to be a writer, but only as an adult in my early twenties did photography happen to me. I say 'happen to me,' because I never consciously decided to become a photographer. I simply loved the experience of making photographs. I've never received any formal training or education in either art form. Rather I have relied upon my own instincts in making photographs which matter to me personally.

"I now live in an old house in a middle-sized town in the Midwest with my wife and three children. Above all else I love being a husband and a father. For me, the only thing better than being a child oneself is to grow up and have children of one's own. In writing and making photographs, I now draw upon my experiences with my family as well as upon the memories of my childhood. I am often able to write my books at home in the midst of my family, which is just wonderful. As far as possible, I also coordinate photography assignments with family vacations so that I can make photographs and have a great time with my wife and children."

        *   *   *

BILLSON, Anne 1954-

PERSONAL: Born November 22, 1954, in Southport, Lancashire, England; daughter of Thomas Billson (a civil servant) and Ruby (Lonsdale) Billson (a civil servant). *Education:* Central School of Art and Design, B.A. (with honors), 1976.

ADDRESSES: Agent—Antony Harwood, Curtis Brown, Ltd., 162-168 Regent St., London W1R 5TB, England.

CAREER: Time Out, Ltd., London, England, literary editor, 1985-86; *Sunday Correspondent,* London, film critic, 1989-90; *New Statesman & Society,* London, film critic, 1991-92; *Sunday Telegraph,* London, film critic, 1992—. British *GQ,* contributing editor.

AWARDS, HONORS: Received Best Young British Novelists award for *Suckers.*

WRITINGS:

Screen Lovers, St. Martin's, 1988.
Dream Demon, New English Library, 1989.
My Name Is Michael Caine: A Life in Film, Muller, 1991.
Suckers (novel), Pan Books, 1993.

WORK IN PROGRESS: A ghost story and several screenplays; researching the English Civil War, skin diseases, and the music of Bernard Herrmann.

SIDELIGHTS: English writer and film critic Anne Billson is the author of a biography of Michael Caine and a novel about vampires in London. In *My Name Is Michael Caine: A Life in Film,* she attempts to prove that Caine "is the best, most important and most versatile film star that Britain has ever produced." Her 1993 novel, *Suckers,* is a dark comedy about the takeover of a London publishing empire by vampires.

BIOGRAPHICAL/CRITICAL SOURCES:

BOOKS

Billson, Anne, *My Name Is Michael Caine: A Life in Film,* Muller, 1991.

PERIODICALS

New Statesman and Society, March 27, 1992, p. 39.
Publishers Weekly, August 30, 1993, p. 67.
Times Literary Supplement, December 20, 1991, p. 18; January 24, 1993, pp. 8-9; March 5, 1993, p. 22.

*　　*　　*

BISHOP, Donald
See STEWARD, Samuel M(orris)

*　　*　　*

BITTNER, Rosanne 1945-

PERSONAL: Born January 14, 1945, in LaPorte, IN; daughter of Frank L. Reris and Ethel (Ardella) Reris Traxler; married Larry D. Bittner (a farmer and small business owner), October 2, 1965; children: Brock, Brian. *Religion:* Methodist.

ADDRESSES: Home—6013 North Coloma Rd., Coloma, MI 49038. *Office*—3219 Friday Rd., Coloma, MI 49038. *Agent*—Denise Marcil Literary Agency, 685 West End Ave., Suite 9C, New York, NY 10025.

CAREER: Worked as a secretary; full-time writer, 1984—.

MEMBER: Romance Writers of America, Council on America's Military Past, Western Outlaw-Lawman History Association, Oregon-California Trails Association, Nebraska State Historical Society.

AWARDS, HONORS: Silver Pen Awards from *Affaire de Coeur,* 1987 and 1989; Golden Certificates for best American historical romance from *Affaire de Coeur,* 1989, for *Tennessee Bride* and *Heart's Surrender,* and 1990, for *This Time Forever;* award for best western series from *Romantic Times,* 1985, for "Savage Destiny"; award for best Indian romance from *Romantic Times,* 1985, for *River of Love;* award for best fictionalized biography from *Romantic Times,* 1990, for *This Time Forever;* award for best post-Civil War romance from *Romantic Times,* 1991, for *Embers of the Heart;* Golden Pen Award for favorite historical author from *Affaire de Coeur,* 1992; Third Place Readers' Choice Award from Oklahoma chapter of Romance Writers of America, finalist for RITA Award from Romance Writers of America, and nomination for award for best Indian romance from *Romantic Times,* all 1993, all for *Song of the Wolf;* nomination for best North American historical novel from *Romantic Times,* 1994, for *Tender Betrayal.*

WRITINGS:

NOVELS PUBLISHED BY POPULAR LIBRARY

Savage Horizons, 1987.
Frontier Fires, 1987.
Destiny's Dawn, 1987.
Tennessee Bride, 1988.
Texas Bride, 1988.
This Time Forever, 1989.
Oregon Bride, 1990.

"SAVAGE DESTINY" SERIES HISTORICAL ROMANCES PUBLISHED BY ZEBRA

Sweet Prairie Passion, 1983.
Ride the Free Wind, 1984.
River of Love, 1984.
Embrace the Wild Land, 1984.
Climb the Highest Mountain, 1985.
Meet the New Dawn, 1986.

OTHER HISTORICAL ROMANCES PUBLISHED BY ZEBRA

Arizona Bride, 1985.
Lawless Love, 1985.
Rapture's Gold, 1986.
Prairie Embrace, 1987.
Heart's Surrender, 1988.
Ecstasy's Chains, 1989.
Arizona Ecstasy, 1989.
Sweet Mountain Magic, 1990.
Sioux Splendor, 1990.
Comanche Sunset, 1991.
Caress, 1992.
Shameless, 1993.
Unforgettable, 1994.
Full Circle, 1994.

HISTORICAL SAGAS PUBLISHED BY BANTAM

Montana Woman, 1990.
Embers of the Heart, 1990.
In the Shadow of the Mountains, 1991.
Song of the Wolf, 1992.
Outlaw Hearts, 1993.
Tender Betrayal, 1993.
Wildest Dreams, 1994.

OTHER HISTORICAL SAGAS

Thunder on the Plains, Doubleday, 1992.

WORK IN PROGRESS: A family saga set in northern California in the 1800s, for Bantam.

SIDELIGHTS: Rosanne Bittner is a prolific writer of novels set in the American Old West. Among her many works are *Outlaw Hearts,* about a young widow's relationship with a man wanted by the law; *Thunder on the Plains,* a love story set against the building of the Union Pacific Railroad; and *Song of the Wolf,* which chronicles the life of a Cheyenne woman and the history of her people.

Bittner told *CA:* "I always loved to write, but I was afraid to try. Once I did try, I fell in love with writing, and I wrote night and day, seven days each week. I have always loved the subject of America's Old West, and that is all I write about. I think my love for the subject shows through in my writing."

BIOGRAPHICAL/CRITICAL SOURCES:

PERIODICALS

Publishers Weekly, February 3, 1992, p. 74; February 15, 1993.

*   *   *

BJORK, Daniel W. 1940-

PERSONAL: Born August 12, 1940, in Milwaukee, WI; son of Victor Daniel (a hospital administrator) and Grace (a homemaker; maiden name, Witherbee) Bjork; married Rhonda Khae Brown (a researcher), August 31, 1968. *Education:* University of Toledo, B.Ed., 1963, M.A., 1964; University of Oklahoma, Ph.D., 1973. *Avocational Interests:* Raising pug dogs.

ADDRESSES: Home—7614 Mountain Bluff, San Antonio, TX 78240. *Office*—Department of History, St. Mary's University, San Antonio, TX 78228.

CAREER: University of Alabama, Birmingham, assistant professor of history, 1974-81; Mercy College of Detroit, Detroit, MI, professor of history, 1983-91; St. Mary's University, San Antonio, TX, professor of history, 1991—.

MEMBER: International Behaviorology Association, American Historical Association.

WRITINGS:

The Victorian Flight, University Press of America, 1978.
The Compromised Scientist, Columbia University Press, 1983.
William James: The Center of His Vision, Columbia University Press, 1988.
B. F. Skinner: A Life, Basic Books, 1993.

WORK IN PROGRESS: A biography of the "rational-emotive" psychologist Albert Ellis.

SIDELIGHTS: Daniel W. Bjork told *CA:* "My interest in B. F. Skinner began with my interest in William James.

Americans loved Jamesian psychology, and I wondered why: what did this attachment tell us about American values? Skinner, on the other hand, seemed to be disliked, even hated by Americans: what did this negativism tell us about American values? My interest in writing about famous American psychologists was, therefore, an inquiry into the American tradition. What can biography reveal about the texture of American beliefs? This remains my central concern."

*   *   *

BLEI, Norbert 1935-

PERSONAL: Born August 23, 1935, in Chicago, IL; son of George and Emily (Papp) Blei. *Education:* Illinois State University, B.S., 1957.

ADDRESSES: Home and office— P.O. Box 33, Ellison Bay, WI 54210.

CAREER: City News Bureau, Chicago, IL, reporter, 1958-59; high school English teacher, 1960-68; writer, 1969—. *Military service:* Served in the U.S. Army Reserve.

MEMBER: PEN.

AWARDS, HONORS: Cliff Dweller's Award from the Friends of Literature (Chicago); Council of Wisconsin Writers Award For Fiction and Nonfiction; Great Lakes College Association Award For Fiction; Pushcart Press Award, for outstanding collection of short stories.

WRITINGS:

POETRY

The Watercolored Word, Quixote Press, 1968.
Door Steps (prose poems), Ellis Press, 1983.
Paint Me a Picture, Make Me a Poem, introduction by Paul Schroeder, Spoon River Poetry Press, 1987.

FICTION

The Second Novel (Becoming a Writer), December Press, 1978.
The Hour of the Sunshine Now (short stories), Story Press, 1978.
Adventures in an American's Literature (novel), Ellis Press, 1982.
The Ghost of Sandburg's Phizzog and Other Stories (short stories), Ellis Press, 1986.

NONFICTION

Door Way, illustrated with own photographs, Ellis Press, 1981.
Door to Door, Ellis Press, 1985.
Neighborhood, Ellis Press, 1987.

Meditations on a Small Lake: (Requiem for a Diminishing Landscape) (essays), photographs by Mike Brisson, Ellis Press, 1987.
Chi Town, Ellis Press, 1990.
Chronicles of a Rural Journalist in America (essays), Samizdat Press, 1990.
The Watercolor Way (essays), Ox Head Press, 1990.

OTHER

Work included in *The Best American Short Stories,* edited by Martha Foley, Houghton Mifflin, 1965, and 1968. Contributor to periodicals, including *Chicago Magazine, Chicago Sun-Times, Chicago Tribune, New Yorker, StoryQuarterly, Tri-Quarterly,* and *Washington Post.*

WORK IN PROGRESS: Two collections of short stories, three novels, and three nonfiction books.

SIDELIGHTS: Norbert Blei told *CA:* "To write is the only thing that matters." So in 1969, when Blei found the cost of living too high in the Chicago suburbs, he adopted Door County—a favorite vacation retreat for summer travelers in northern Wisconsin—as his home. Since then, he has been able to write full time, producing a trilogy of books that chronicle life in Door County as well as works that draw on his knowledge of Chicago.

Typical of his Door County books is *Door Way,* comprising thirty-one profiles of area residents—among them a wood-carver, a potter, a country doctor, and a car salesman—and a group of personal essays that capture the rhythms and ambiguities of life in a rural retreat. Reviewing the book for the *Chicago Tribune Book World,* John D. Callaway described its "warm, generous, breezy, country-weekly style" and commended the "genuine, searching, feeling humanity" Blei conveys. Blei followed *Door Way* with *Door Steps,* a series of prose poems cast in the form of a daybook recording the texture of life in Door County over a calendar year. He captures images both of the northern Wisconsin landscape and the "world of nature parceled out" when he visits his parents in the suburban neighborhood of his childhood. Although the *Chicago Tribune Book World*'s Ron Grossman found the quality of the entries uneven, he praised Blei for his "poet's vision" and for showing the reader "a fresh way of looking at things, by milking words of their potential for sound and meaning."

In *The Ghost of Sandburg's Phizzog,* a collection of nine short stories, Blei returns to Chicago for his setting and themes. Many of his characters are Czechoslovakian immigrants, and the stories emphasize emotions rather than external action. In the title story, Carl Sandburg's ghost wanders around familiar locales in downtown Chicago, trying to capture "the babbling tongues of the people." "In the Secret Places of the Stairs" features the widowed

janitor of a run-down apartment building. His only pleasure is sleeping with the wife of a tenant on a cot in the boiler room while dreaming of a younger woman from the old country. The protagonist of "Skarda" is a nine-year-old boy who is left each day with his Czech grandparents while his mother works. The story records the minutiae of life in a small urban bungalow with first-generation east European immigrants. Running through these stories is a recurring loneliness. They "ring true," according to *Chicago Tribune* reviewer George Cohen, because Blei's "unimportant people are so real" that even though their lives are going nowhere, he "makes us want to take the trip along with them." Asserted Rochelle Ratner in the *New York Times Book Review,* "Blei has a rare ability to describe internal emotions as if they were earth-shattering events."

BIOGRAPHICAL/CRITICAL SOURCES:

PERIODICALS

Chicago Tribune, July 18, 1986; March 10, 1989.
Chicago Tribune Book World, October 4, 1981, section 7, p. 6; November 20, 1983, section 14, p. 34.
New York Times Book Review, October 12, 1986, p. 28.

*   *   *

BLIER, Bertrand 1939-

PERSONAL: Born in 1939 in Paris, France; son of Bernard Blier (an actor) and Gisele (Brunet) Blier; married Catherine Florin, 1973; children: one daughter.

ADDRESSES: Home—14 rue Chauveau, Neuilly-sur-Seine, France 92200. *Office*—c/o Artmedia, 10 Avenue George V, Paris, France 75008; and French Film Office, 745 Fifth Ave., New York, NY 10151.

CAREER: Screenwriter and director of motion pictures; writer. Worked as assistant director in 1950s and early 1960s.

AWARDS, HONORS: Academy Award for best foreign-language film from Academy of Motion Picture Arts and Sciences, 1977, for *Get Out Your Handkerchiefs;* Cesar Awards, 1979, for *Buffet froid;* Cesar Award for best screenplay, 1984, for *Notre histoire;* Special Jury Prize from Cannes Film Festival, 1989, for *Too Beautiful for You;* Grand Prix National du Cinema, 1989.

WRITINGS:

NOVELS

Going Places, translated from the original French edition *Les Valseuses* by Patty Southgate, Lippincott, 1974, published in England as *Making It,* J. Cape, 1975.
Beau-pere, Laffont, 1981.

SCREENPLAYS, AND DIRECTOR

(With Philippe Dumarcay) *Les Valseuses,* (adapted from Blier's novel), CAP/UPE/SN, 1974, released in the United States as *Going Places,* Cinema 5, 1974.

Calmos, 1976, released in the United States as *Femmesatales,* New Line, 1977.

Preparez vos mouchers, Les Films Ariane/CAPAC/ Belga/SODEP, 1977, released in the United States as *Get Out Your Handkerchiefs,* New Line, 1978.

Buffet froid (title means "Cold Cuts"), Parafrance, 1979, released in the United States as *Buffet froid,* Interama, 1987.

Beau-pere (adapted from Blier's novel), 1981, released in United States as *Beau Pere,* New Line, 1981.

(With Gerard Brach) *La Femme de mon pote,* 1983, released in the United States as *My Best Friend's Girl,* European International, 1984.

Notre histoire, 1984, released in the United States as *Separate Rooms,* Spectrafilm, released in England as *Our Story,* 1985.

Tenue de soiree, Hachette Premiere/DD Productions/ Cine Valse/Phillippe Dussart, Norstar, 1986, released in the United States as *Menage,* Cinecom, 1987.

Trop belle pour toi, Cine Valse/DD Productions/Orly/ SEDIF/TF1, 1988, released in the United States as *Too Beautiful for You,* Orion Classics, 1990.

Also screenwriter and director of *Hitler, connais pas,* 1963, and *Si j'etais un espion,* 1967 (released in the United States as *Breakdown*). Blier also wrote the screenplay for *C'est une valse.*

WORK IN PROGRESS: A film about women and a film about the homeless.

SIDELIGHTS: Bertrand Blier is a French filmmaker who has won considerable acclaim—and even a fair measure of notoriety—for his amoral comedies. After serving as an assistant to such directors as Georges Lautner and John Berry, Blier began his own career as a writer-director with *Hitler, connais pas,* which was released in 1963. Blier followed *Hitler* with *Si j'etais un espion,* which was eventually released in the United States as *Breakdown.* Neither of these works garnered him much success as one of France's new filmmakers.

Blier later recalled that after completing *Breakdown* he found himself at a turning point in his career. "At that time my film career was crossing the desert," he related to Paul Chutkow in a 1989 *New York Times* article. "I had done two small films, one worse than the other. . . . In desperation, I decided to try my hand at a novel."

The result of Blier's initial effort at writing fiction was *Les Valseuses* (published in English translation as *Going Places* and *Making It*), which Chutkow described in his *New York Times* article as "a stunning picaresque novel." The book, featuring a pair of whimsically unprincipled young men and their various unsavory exploits, became a major success in France, and Blier soon determined to adapt it for film. The film version, released in the United States as *Going Places,* proved to be Blier's first major success as a writer-director, although—like the novel—the movie drew strong protests from reviewers critical of its blithely amoral perspective.

Femmes fatales, Blier's next film, focused on a more unlikely duo, a gynecologist and a pimp, both of whom are endlessly troubled and pursued by violently lusty women. A *Washington Post* reviewer declared that the film, which is among Blier's lesser known productions, "is often boldly funny."

In the late 1970s, Blier completed *Get Out Your Handkerchiefs,* which ranks among his most significant, and best known, productions. This unpredictable farce—reuniting *Going Places* performers Gerard Depardieu and Patrick Dewaere—concerns two men—Raoul and Stephane— who join forces in inevitably futile attempts at enlivening Stephane's wife, Solange. The heroine, in turn, seemingly gains at least a small measure of contentment only after being impregnated by an obnoxious adolescent. With its deadpan—even misanthropic—humor, *Get Out Your Handkerchiefs* won substantial praise and was even accorded an Academy Award for best foreign-language film.

Buffet froid, Blier's next cinematic endeavor, was called "an absurdist comedy" by *New York Times* reviewer Vincent Canby. Here, a wayward accountant may, or may not have, committed a murder. What is more certain is that some time after relating the event to his wife, who dismisses it as just another mundane encounter, he begins to befriend several peculiar individuals, notably an ultra-meek murderess and a truly unfathomable police inspector. "The characters speak of having nightmares," Canby reported, "but Mr. Blier clearly believes life is such a nightmare that no one can tell the difference anymore."

Blier followed *Buffet froid* with *Beau Pere,* a comedy in which a lounge pianist resists, then submits to the sexual enticements of his adolescent stepdaughter. Janet Maslin, in her *New York Times* review, acknowledged that *Beau Pere* "would seem to have one of the more objectionable premises from [Blier]," but she added that the film is nonetheless "a tender, entertaining one," and she disclosed that Blier "depicts the romance very sweetly."

In 1983 Blier saw the release of *My Best Friend's Girl,* which he cowrote and directed. *Los Angeles Times* reviewer Sheila Benson affirmed the work as "yet another variation on his pet theme, the true-blue friendship of a pair of buddies knocked askew by a delectable and infinitely accommodating [woman]." In this film, a longtime bond is threatened by one character's infatuation for his friend's lover, who proves both resourceful and obliging. Benson observed that in this film Blier's casual, but persistent misogyny is diminished somewhat because the male protagonists are "such innocent chumps." Maslin, in her *New York Times* review of *My Best Friend's Girl*, conceded that "what it reveals about relations between sexes isn't powerfully illuminating," and she described the film as "slight but funny."

Separate Rooms (shown in England as *Our Story*), is Blier's 1984 film wherein a beleaguered husband imagines himself submitting to the sexual wiles of a rural seductress and thereupon consorting with her previous lovers. This is another of Blier's lesser-known works.

Blier won greater attention with *Menage*, a more overtly funny film about a burglar who befriends two of his victims, a husband and wife, and soon falls in love with the husband. The film was a great success in France, where it was even considered scandalous. In America, *Menage* was less favorably received, although the *New Republic*'s Stanley Kauffmann, who contended that "Blier, both as writer and director, is far above the ordinary," argued that "*Menage* is, for the most part, what [Blier] wants it to be: an ingratiating assault."

In 1989 Blier realized another of his greatest successes with *Too Beautiful for You*, in which a car dealer forsakes his spectacularly gorgeous wife for his plump, rather plain secretary. Although the plot is ripe for Blier's characteristically misanthropic humor, it is ultimately rendered in a subtle, sympathetic manner. As the *Los Angeles Times*'s Peter Rainer noted, *Too Beautiful for You* "may sound like a marital infidelity farce, but the mood is hypnotic and almost rhapsodically self-obsessed." Among the film's many supporters was Vincent Canby, who wrote in the *New York Times* that *Too Beautiful for You* is "an exceptionally rich romantic comedy." And *Nation* reviewer Stuart Klawans succinctly deemed the film a "droll fable."

Since completing *Too Beautiful for You*, Blier has mentioned plans to write and direct both a film about women and one about the homeless, but he has also vowed to the *New York Times* that he will someday write and direct another of his typically quirky male-oriented films "just for the pure, cleansing sport of it."

BIOGRAPHICAL/CRITICAL SOURCES:

PERIODICALS

Chicago Tribune, September 3, 1984.
Los Angeles Times, April 20, 1984; April 13, 1990.
Nation, April 2, 1990, p. 467.
National Review, November 21, 1986, pp. 63-64.
New Republic, November 3, 1986, pp. 26-27.
New Statesman, September 5, 1975, p. 285.
Newsweek, October 27, 1986, p. 104.
New York Times, March 25, 1984; September 4, 1987; October 9, 1987; September 17, 1989, p. B17; September 22, 1989, p. C22.
New York Times Book Review, December 22, 1974, p. 14.
Times (London), June 21, 1985.
Times Literary Supplement, November 7, 1975, p. 1338.
Washington Post, January 31, 1979, p. B1; March 9, 1979.*

—Sketch by Les Stone

*   *   *

BOLAND, Eavan (Aisling) 1944-

PERSONAL: Born September 24, 1944, in Dublin, Ireland; daughter of Frederick (a diplomat) and Frances (a painter; maiden name, Kelly) Boland; married Ken Casey (a novelist), 1969; children: Sarah Margaret, Eavan Frances. *Education:* Trinity College, first-class honors degree, 1966.

ADDRESSES: Office—c/o *Irish Times*, 13 D'Olier St., Dublin 2, Ireland.

CAREER: Trinity College, Dublin, Ireland, junior lecturer, 1967-68; School of Irish Studies, Dublin, lecturer, 1968—; writer. Worked as a housekeeper at the Gresham Hotel, Dublin, c. 1962.

MEMBER: Irish Academy of Letters.

AWARDS, HONORS: Macaulay Fellowship in Poetry, 1968; Jacobs Awards for Broadcasting, 1977; Irish American Cultural Award, 1983.

WRITINGS:

POETRY

23 Poems, Gallagher (Dublin), 1962.
New Territory, Allan Figgis (Dublin), 1967.
The War Horse, Gollancz, 1975.
In Her Own Image, illustrations by Constance Short, Arlen House (Dublin), 1980.
Introducing Eavan Boland, Ontario Review Press, 1981.
Night Feed, Marion Boyars, 1982.
The Journey, Deerfield Press, 1983.
The Journey and Other Poems, Carcanet, 1987.
Selected Poems, Carcanet, 1989.
Outside History: Selected Poems, 1980-90, Norton, 1990.

Work represented in anthologies, including *Faber Anthology of Irish Verse*, *Penguin Anthology of Irish Verse*, *Pan Anthology of Irish Verse*, and *Sphere Anthology of Irish Verse*.

OTHER

(With Micheal MacLiammoir) *W. B. Yeats and His World,* Thames and Hudson, 1971.

A Kind of Scar: The Woman Poet in a National Tradition, Attic Press (Dublin), 1989.

Regular contributor to *Irish Times.* Contributor to *Irish Press, Spectator, American Poetry Review,* and *Soundings.*

SIDELIGHTS: Contemporary poet Eavan Boland's verse has been cited by critics for its lyrical presence, a trait her work shares with that of many Irish poets. At the same time, her poems reverberate with a unique sense of her personal background and current life, reflecting her nomadic upbringing in foreign locales and her reflective, domestic existence as a wife and mother. The daughter of a diplomat father and an artist mother, Boland spent her formative years in both London and New York City. After settling in her native Ireland, she published her first book, *23 Poems,* with her own savings in 1962, when she was eighteen. Since then she has established her reputation in Irish poetry while raising two children, teaching courses, and contributing regularly to the *Irish Times.*

Boland's second collection of verse, *New Territory,* which appeared in 1967, reflects a love of language and the creative spirit, traits that have continued to serve as hallmarks of her poetry through the years. The verse in *New Territory* is often concerned with the artistic process, whether the outcome is a painting or a poem. In pieces such as the title selection and "The Poets," Boland pays homage to other lyrical poets of the past and reaffirms the necessity of the literary form to human nature, while other works draw upon Irish history and folklore. Commenting on the collection in the *Dictionary of Literary Biography,* Joseph Browne found that the historical material was less successful than other poems in the volume and appears a "dutiful response" to Boland's Irish heritage. However, Browne praised *New Territory* overall, stating that "the poems display remarkable lyrical range, verbal expertise, and technical virtuosity."

Boland's next collection of poetry, *The War Horse,* did not appear until eight years after *New Territory.* During this period Boland married novelist Ken Casey and became a mother. A common subtext of domestic routines is apparent in her writings from this point onward. Boland writes of her immediate life as a suburban housewife in such poems as "Ode to Suburbia." In "The Other Woman," she addresses the muse that guides her husband's own creative process and accepts it as a necessary part of their life together. The other twenty-four selections bring forth her own calm acceptance of her identity as a writer, and some, such as "Elegy for a Youth Changed to a Swan," delve deep into her inner thoughts. Critic Browne praised her

work in *The War Horse* as "startling poetic insights to a particular area of modern life."

In Her Own Image, Boland's fourth collection, was published in 1980 and is illustrated with drawings by Constance Short. The ten poems contrast the self-image of women with the image forced upon them from the outside. In such works as "Tirade for the Mimic Muse," "Mastectomy," and "Making Up," Boland utilizes her self-identity as a woman to question the artificial reality of the modern world, and this treatment led many critics to identify Boland's work as "feminist." Reviewing the work for the *Times Literary Supplement,* Carol Rumens criticized Boland's exploration of the subject matter as being too reminiscent of Sylvia Plath, the American poet who committed suicide in 1963. In comparing *In Her Own Image* with *The War Horse,* Rumens faulted Boland's change of style, remarking that the "strong-willed, sensuous control of language has slipped into mere stridency." Other critics, however, weren't as quick to dismiss Boland's message, arguing that the poet's ambitions are too large to allow her to be simply typecast as a feminist poet. In commenting on *Night Feed,* Boland's next collection, *Dictionary of Literary Biography* critic Browne dismissed the feminist label. He noted that "this interpretation distorts and minimizes her poetry and drastically restricts, if it does not actually preclude, the reader's capacity to experience the poems." Boland herself has stated, as quoted in *Dictionary of Literary Biography,* that "the only person I wish to represent is myself. I happen to live in one place. I happen to be a woman. But my sex and my home are just transient states to what I have to say."

The twenty-eight poems of 1982's *Night Feed* further reflect on Boland's existence as a parent and a member of a family. "Domestic Interior," for example, contemplates her emotional response to the day-to-day experiences of being part of a family household. Rather than emphasizing a sense of isolation and despair at her domestic life, Boland relates her experiences to larger patterns of existence. Michael O'Neill, reviewing the work for the *Times Literary Supplement,* praised Boland's poems, remarking that "the click with which they come together is almost audible, and yet they manage not to seem merely contrived." Critic Browne commented that *Night Feed* is Boland's "most artistic volume" and that the selections "are written with greater certainty than any previous poems."

In her poem "The Journey," first published in 1983, Boland travels to a mythological netherworld. Led by the ancient female poet Sappho, the writer finds the souls of women and children lost in plagues throughout the ages and meditates on their fate. The poem was combined with others to make up the 1987 collection *The Journey and Other Poems.* In pieces such as "I Remember," Boland again calls forth elements of domesticity, often emphasizing shades of colors and textures of fabric. In a longer piece, "Envoi," Boland explores the muse that drives her to comment on what she observes and to which she gives voice. Noting the diversity in the structures of her poems, Lachlan Mackinnon criticized such examples as "Envoi" in the *Times Literary Supplement,* describing these poems as "willed effort." He went on to note, however, that "when she conceals her art, Eavan Boland can be memorable and unnervingly honed." Anthony Libby, reviewing *The Journey and Other Poems* for the *New York Times Book Review,* noted that Boland's "language has a tranquil control . . . for which it sacrifices nothing in grace or expressive power." Singling out the title poem, Libby wrote that "the sense of history here is appropriate; I have a feeling that this moving poem may be one for the ages."

Boland's subsequent volumes are 1989's *Selected Poems* and *Outside History: Selected Poems, 1980-1990,* both collections of previously-published work. Poems such as "Woman in Kitchen" and "The Journey" appear in these editions, and critical writing on them offers an overview of Boland's body of work. Michael O'Neill, commenting on *Selected Poems* for the *Times Literary Supplement,* noted that "though resourceful, Boland can overstate her concern to bear witness to womanly experience." William Logan of the *New York Times Book Review* faulted Boland for her emphasis on home and hearth as subject matter in *Outside History,* remarking that she "is expert in the passionless household poem . . . so drawn to the realms she despises." Logan went on to suggest that when Boland ceases to emphasize the minutiae of domestic life, "she is truest to her own culture," and also conceded that Boland has "a gift for the graven phrase . . . or the poetic tremor of a single word." Other reviewers of *Outside History* commented on Boland's interior dialogues and use of language to evoke memory and emotion. Sara Berkeley of the *Times Literary Supplement* observed that "the poems swing swiftly and effortlessly from light to shadow." The critic summed up the collection by noting that "the Boland of *Outside History* is a woman and a mother, with a strong awareness of pain, the past and her own move 'out of myth into history'."

BIOGRAPHICAL/CRITICAL SOURCES:

BOOKS

Dictionary of Literary Biography, Volume 40, Gale, 1985.

PERIODICALS

New York Times Book Review, March 22, 1987, p. 23; April 21, 1991, p. 22.
Times Literary Supplement, October 17, 1980, p. 1180; May 11, 1984, p. 516; August 21, 1987, p. 904; July 7, 1989, p. 737; July 5, 1991, p. 22.*

—*Sketch by Carol A. Brennan*

BONTE, Pierre 1942-

PERSONAL: Born August 25, 1942, in Annoeullin, France. *Education:* Sorbonne, University of Paris, certificats de psychologie, 1963 and 1964, licence sociologie, 1964, doctorat d'ethnologie, 1971.

ADDRESSES: Home—1-3 rue des Fosses Saint-Marcel, 75005 Paris, France. *Office*—Laboratoire d'Anthropologie Sociale, 52 rue du Cardinal Lemoine, 75005 Paris, France.

CAREER: Affiliated with the Centre National de Recherche Scientifique, Paris, France, beginning in 1973, research director, second class, 1985—.

MEMBER: Laboratoire d'Anthropologie Sociale du College de France, l'EHESS.

WRITINGS:

(With S. Bernus, L. Brock, and H. Claudot) *Le Fils et le neveu: Jeux et enjeux de la parente touaregue,* Cambridge University Press et Maison des Sciences de l'Homme, 1986.
(Editor with M. Izard) *Dictionnaire de l'ethnologie et de l'anthropologie,* French and European Publications, 1991.
(With E. Conte, C. Hames, and Abd el Wedoud Ould Cheikh) *Al-Ansab: La Quete des origines: Anthropologie historique de la societe tribale arabe,* Cambridge University Press and Editions de la Maison des Sciences de l'Homme, 1991.
(Editor with J. G. Galaty) *Herders, Warriors and Traders: Pastoralism in Africa,* Westview Press, 1991.

WORK IN PROGRESS: Editing *Epouser au plus proche. Inceste, prohibitions et strategies matrimoniales autour de la Mediterranee,* to be published by Gallimard-Seuil.

SIDELIGHTS: Pierre Bonte told *CA:* "I have carved out my career in anthropology among the pastoral societies of northern Africa (the Sahara and the Sahel). After completing my doctoral dissertation on the Tuareg Kel Gress in Niger, I went to work for the Centre National de Recherche Scientifique (CNRS) in Paris, which is part of the Laboratoire d'Anthropologie Sociale directed by Professor Claude Levi-Strauss. My next study, which involved the Moors of Mauritania, focused on the emirate Adrar, particularly its kinship and social organization systems. I also specialize in societies of nomadic herders in Africa and am often consulted by the World Bank about development questions concerning these societies."

BOOTH, Brian 1936-

PERSONAL: Born May 30, 1936, in Roseburg, OR; son of Harrie W. (a banker and orchardist) and Lois M. (a community activist) Booth; married Gwyneth Gamble (a television producer and corporate director), October 4, 1984; children: Thomas Scott, Jennifer Susan. *Education:* University of Oregon, B.S., 1958; Stanford University, LL.B., 1962. *Avocational Interests:* Tennis, hiking, reading.

ADDRESSES: Home—Portland, OR. *Office*—Tonkon, Torp, Galen, Marmaduke & Booth, 1600 Pioneer Tower, 888 Southwest Fifth Ave., Portland, OR 97204. *Agent*—Far Corner Books, P.O. Box 82157, Portland, OR 97282.

CAREER: Stoel Rives Boley Jones & Grey (law firm), began as associate, became partner, 1962-74; Tonkon, Torp, Galen, Marmaduke & Booth, Portland, OR, partner and corporate attorney, 1974—. Oregon State Bar, past chair of Securities Section; Portland Art Museum, chair, 1976-78; Oregon Institute of Literary Arts, founder, 1986, chair, 1986—; Oregon Health Sciences University Foundation, chair, 1986-89; Oregon State Parks and Recreation Commission, chair, 1989—. *Military service:* U.S. Army, 1958-59; became captain.

MEMBER: Oregon Securities Law Association (past chair), Phi Beta Kappa, Phi Delta Theta, Coif.

WRITINGS:

Wildmen, Wobblies, and Whistle Punks: Stewart Holbrook's Lowbrow Northwest, Oregon State University Press, 1992.

* * *

BORG, Dorothy 1902-1993

OBITUARY NOTICE—See index for *CA* sketch: Born September 4, 1902, in Elberone, NJ; died following a brief illness, October 21, 1993, in Manhattan, NY. Educator and author. A historian specializing in relations between East Asia and the United States, Borg served lengthy affiliations with both the American Institute of Pacific Relations and Columbia University's East Asian Institute. Borg joined the staff of the American Institute of Pacific Relations in 1938, and during her more than twenty-year tenure with the Institute, she conducted numerous scholarly conferences and lectures and also traveled to Shanghai and Beijing. In the 1960s she transferred to Columbia, where she accepted the posts of lecturer in the department of public law and government, and senior research associate at the East Asian Institute, where she remained until her retirement. During the course of her career, she authored or edited several accounts of foreign policy. Her publications include *United States and the Far Eastern Crisis of 1933-1938,* which garnered the 1965 Bancroft Prize. She coedited *Pearl Harbor as History: Japanese-American Relations, 1931-1941* and *Uncertain Years: Chinese-American Relations, 1947-1950.* In 1986 Borg received the Graebner Prize from the Society for Historians of Foreign Relations.

OBITUARIES AND OTHER SOURCES:

BOOKS

Who's Who in America, 46th edition, Marquis, 1990, p. 339.

PERIODICALS

New York Times, October 28, 1993, p. D27.

* * *

BOTHWELL, Robert (Selkirk) 1944-

PERSONAL: Born August 17, 1944, in Ottawa, Ontario, Canada; son of John Robert (a civil servant) and Pauline (a civil servant; maiden name, Rutherford) Bothwell; married Heather Lawson (a personnel coordinator), June 25, 1976 (divorced); married Gail Alexander Corbett, August 20, 1993; children: (first marriage) Eleanor Myfanwy, Alice Pauline. *Education:* University of Toronto, A.B., 1966; Harvard University, A.M., 1967, Ph.D., 1972. *Politics:* Liberal. *Avocational Interests:* Walking, reading.

ADDRESSES: Office—Department of History, Trinity College, University of Toronto, Toronto, Ontario M5S 1H8, Canada.

CAREER: University of Toronto, Toronto, Ontario, Canada, lecturer, 1970-72, assistant professor, 1972-75, associate professor, 1975-81, professor of history, 1981—, member of executive committee of Trinity College, 1988-90; CJRT-FM, Toronto, academic broadcaster, 1989-94. Branksome Hall School, member of board of governors, 1989—.

MEMBER: Canadian Committee for the History of the Second World War, Canadian Institute of International Affairs, Ontario Heritage Foundation (member of board, 1987-93; chair of archeology committee, 1988-93; secretary, 1992-93), C. D. Howe Foundation (member of program committee, 1991—).

AWARDS, HONORS: Corey Prize, Canadian and American Historical Associations, 1980, for *C. D. Howe: A Biography;* named fellow of Royal Society of Canada, 1989.

WRITINGS:

(With Barbara Alexandrin) *A Bibliography of the Material Culture of New France,* National Museums of Canada, 1970.

(Coeditor with Michael Cross) *Policy by Other Means,* Clarke, Irwin, 1972.

(Coeditor with Norman Hillmer) *The In-Between Time,* Copp Clark, 1975.

(With Hillmer) *Canada's Foreign Policy, 1919-1939,* National Museum of Man and National Film Board, 1978.

Pearson: His Life and World (biography), McGraw-Hill Ryerson, 1978.

(With William Kilbourn) *C. D. Howe: A Biography,* McClelland & Stewart, 1979.

(With Ian Drummond and John English) *Canada since 1945: Power, Politics, and Provincialism,* University of Toronto Press, 1981, revised edition, 1989.

Eldorado: Canada's National Uranium Company, University of Toronto Press, 1984.

(With David J. Bercuson and J. L. Granatstein) *The Great Brain Robbery: The Decline of Canada's Universities,* McClelland & Stewart, 1984.

A Short History of Ontario, Hurtig, 1986.

(With Drummond and English) *Canada, 1900-1945,* University of Toronto Press, 1987.

Loring Christie: The Failure of Bureaucratic Imperialism, Garland Publishing, 1988.

Nucleus: This History of Atomic Energy of Canada Limited, University of Toronto Press, 1988.

(With Granatstein) *Pirouette: Pierre Trudeau and Canadian Foreign Policy,* University of Toronto Press, 1990.

Laying the Foundations, University of Toronto Department of History, 1991.

Canada and the United States: The Politics of Partnership, Twayne, 1992.

Also author of *Years of Victory,* 1987. *Canadian Historical Review,* associate editor, 1972-77, editor, 1977-80.

WORK IN PROGRESS: Canadian Foreign Policy, 1945-1995, University of Toronto Press, 1996; *Dean Acheson,* Twayne, 1996; *A History of Toronto,* University of Toronto Press, c. 1997.

SIDELIGHTS: For nearly a quarter of a century, Robert Bothwell has enjoyed a distinguished career as a professor of history at the University of Toronto. The focus of his research has been the political and economic history of Canada, with emphasis on some of the key figures and institutions that have shaped that history during the twentieth century. While many of his books are academic treatises, several have found a broader audience. With Ian Drummond and John English, for instance, he wrote *Can-

ada since 1945: Power, Politics, and Provincialism;* in tandem with a later volume, *Canada, 1900-1945,* it explores "the links among economics, society and politics" that were forged during Canada's expansion and development during the twentieth century. The books offer portraits of Canada's prime ministers, along with accounts of the nation's leading provincial premiers and party leaders. Additionally, both books stress economic history; *Canada since 1945,* for instance, demonstrates the authors' thesis that, during the post-World War II period, the Canadian government became overblown and exhausted its resources as the political bureaucracy tried to perpetuate itself. Writing in the Toronto *Globe and Mail,* Michiel Horn faults *Canada, 1900-1945* for its "class bias"—that is, for offering "a safe, middle-class view of Canadian history." Nonetheless, he praises the book as "crisply written" and "clear . . . and sprightly."

In *The Great Brain Robbery: The Decline of Canada's Universities,* Bothwell teamed with two other prominent historians, David J. Bercuson and J. L. Granatstein, to offer a stinging indictment of Canada's system of higher education. The book takes swipes at what the authors consider short-sighted administrators and politicians who, in an effort to fill chairs, lowered admissions standards while offering trendy new programs and a "supermarket" of courses. In what Margaret Cannon in the Toronto *Globe and Mail* calls a "screech of outrage," the authors prescribe a return to the elitist universities of decades past, with high admissions standards, standardized college entrance exams, and a core curriculum emphasizing language, literature, philosophy, science, math, and the arts.

In *Eldorado: Canada's National Uranium Company,* Bothwell returns to economic analysis, examining Eldorado's history between 1926 and 1960. By 1959, uranium had become one of Canada's most valuable exports. In light of uranium's strategic importance in nuclear weapons production, Eldorado occupied a prominent place on the Canadian economic landscape, particularly during the Cold War period of the 1950s. Peter Cook in the Toronto *Globe and Mail* calls *Eldorado* an "unashamedly corporate book, written at the firm's behest," but notes that it is "scrupulously researched and written with care," narrating a chapter of Canadian history that had important implications for the country's economic and foreign policies.

With *Pirouette: Pierre Trudeau and Canadian Foreign Policy,* Bothwell and coauthor Granatstein shift their focus to Canadian foreign policy during the years when Pierre Trudeau was the nation's prime minister. When Trudeau took office in 1968, he brought with him the promise of a new approach to foreign policy, one that would be elegant, hard-edged, and would allow Canada to occupy a more visible place on the world stage, especially with the

United States distracted by Vietnam. Instead, the authors write, "the fundamentals of Canadian foreign and defence policy altered scarcely at all in his time in power, but never once in his long tenure did Pierre Trudeau fail to captivate the country with the illusion of changes." The book chronicles Trudeau's "pirouette"—his dance—with four American presidents and his rocky relationship with the newly emergent European community—all conducted with a sense of flair and style. Writing in the Toronto *Globe and Mail,* reviewer John English calls *Pirouette* a "pioneering study" and "a remarkable survey" of Trudeau and of Canada's role in world affairs.

BIOGRAPHICAL/CRITICAL SOURCES:

BOOKS

Bercuson, David J., Robert Bothwell, and J. L. Granatstein, *The Great Brain Robbery: The Decline of Canada's Universities,* McClelland & Stewart, 1984.
Bothwell, Robert, Ian Drummond, and John English, *Canada, 1900-1945,* University of Toronto Press, 1987.
Bothwell, Robert, and J. L. Granatstein, *Pirouette: Pierre Trudeau and Canadian Foreign Policy,* University of Toronto Press, 1990.

PERIODICALS

Globe and Mail (Toronto), September 8, 1984; November 24, 1984; May 30, 1987; August 25, 1990.
Times Literary Supplement, July 3, 1981, p. 748.

*   *   *

BOULLE, Pierre (Francois Marie-Louis) 1912-1994

OBITUARY NOTICE—See index for *CA* sketch: Born February 20, 1912, in Avignon, France; died January 30, 1994, in France. Novelist and screenwriter. Boulle's writings vary from espionage and adventure novels to futuristic fantasies, many of which were praised by reviewers for their suspenseful plots and revealing psychological portraits. After taking an engineering degree in France, Boulle worked in Indochina on a rubber plantation, later becoming part of the French resistance in Asia during World War II. His wartime experiences, including a stint as a prisoner of war of the Vichy French forces, provided a backdrop for his war novels. The best known of these is *Le Pont de la riviere Kwai,* published in English as *The Bridge on the River Kwai,* which Boulle later adapted into an award-winning film. Another noted screen adaption was made of his futuristic 1963 story *Planet of the Apes,* which envisions a world in which apes have evolved as the

dominant intelligent species and reign over the primal humans. Boulle reminisces about his own World War II imprisonment in his 1967 autobiography *My Own River Kwai.* His other books include *William Conrad, Le Sacrilege malais, Jardin de Kanashima,* and his last work, *A Nous Deux, Satan,* which was published in 1992.

OBITUARIES AND OTHER SOURCES:

BOOKS

Twentieth-Century Science Fiction Writers, 3rd edition, St. James, 1991.

PERIODICALS

Chicago Tribune, February 1, 1994, section 3, p. 13.

*   *   *

BOURQUE, Antoine
See BRASSEAUX, Carl A(nthony)

*   *   *

BOWER, John Morton 1942-

PERSONAL: Born June 3, 1942, in Mansfield, Nottingham, England; son of Leslie (a shoe retailer) and Miriam (a shoe retailer; maiden name, Morton) Bower; married Nicola Mary Cross, August 16, 1967 (divorced, 1979); married Caroline Rosemary Boon (a veterinary surgeon), August 13, 1983; children: Sophie, Rachel, Rebecca, Tom, Jack. *Education:* Liverpool University, B.V.Sc., 1965; Royal College of Veterinary Surgeons, M.R.C.V.S., 1965. *Religion:* Church of England. *Avocational Interests:* Sailing, wine, ornithology, trout fishing, reading.

ADDRESSES: Office—Veterinary Hospital, Colwill Rd., Plymouth, Devonshire PL6 8RP, England.

CAREER: Associate veterinary surgeon in London, England, 1965-68, and Maidenhead, Berkshire, England, 1968-69; Veterinary Hospital, Plymouth, Devonshire, England, principal veterinarian, then senior partner, 1969—; writer. Consultant-advisor for Pet Plan Insurance Co., 1991—; director of Veterinary Drug Co., 1993—.

MEMBER: American Animal Hospital Association, British Veterinary Association (president, 1989-90), British Small Animal Veterinary Association (president, 1984-85), Cornish Cat Club (vice-president, 1986—), Kennel Club.

AWARDS, HONORS: Melton Award for services to small animal practice, British Small Animal Veterinary Association, 1990.

WRITINGS:

(With David Youngs) *The Health of Your Dog,* Alpine Press, 1989.

(With John Gripper and Dixon Gunn) *Veterinary Practice Management,* Blackwells/Pergammon Press, 1989.

Contributor to periodicals, including *Wild about Animals* and *Dogs Monthly.*

VIDEOS

A Kind Goodbye, Society for Companion Animals Study (SCAS), 1988.

(With Roger Mugford) *Common Behavioral Problems of Dogs,* Allan White Video Company, 1989.

Caring for Your New Puppy, Royal Veterinary College, 1990.

WORK IN PROGRESS: Teach Yourself First-Aid for Pets; The Dog Owner's Veterinary Manual.

SIDELIGHTS: John Bower told *CA:* "The purchase of a single veterinarian, small-animal practice in 1969 in Plymouth, Devonshire, was my single most important career decision. I soon discovered that the practice of progressive, sound (advanced—but not high-tech) veterinary surgery and medicine combined importantly with an ability and desire to listen, explain, and communicate with my clients led to a rapid growth in the practice. This led to my interest in veterinary practice management, involvement in veterinary politics, and writing books."

*   *   *

BRADSHAW, Michael 1935-

PERSONAL: Born July 9, 1935, in London, England; son of Ernest (a furniture salesperson) and Winifred Alice (a homemaker; maiden name, Harris) Bradshaw; married Valerie Irene McQuire (a registered nurse), 1962; children: Paul Michael, John Nicholas. *Education:* Queen Mary College, London, B.A. (with honors), 1957, M.A., 1959; University of Leicester, Ph.D., 1985. *Politics:* "Liberal conservative." *Religion:* Baptist. *Avocational Interests:* Playing the church organ and the piano.

ADDRESSES: Home—57 Frensham Ave., Glenholt, Plymouth PL6 7JN, England.

CAREER: Teacher of geography and geology at a secondary school in Godalming, England, 1959-68; College of St. Mark and St. John, Plymouth, England, teacher of geography and geology and department head, 1968-93; retired, 1993.

MEMBER: Institute of British Geographers, Geographical Association (England), National Geographic Society (United States), Association of American Geographers.

AWARDS, HONORS: International visitor grant from U.S. Department of State, 1978.

WRITINGS:

A New Geology, English Universities Press, 1968, 2nd edition, 1973.

(With E. A. Jarman) *Reading Geological Maps: Geological Map Exercises,* Hodder & Stoughton, 1969.

Earth: The Living Planet, Halstead, 1977.

(With J. Abbott and A. Gelsthorpe) *Earth's Changing Surface,* Halstead, 1978.

Earth: Past, Present, and Future, Hodder & Stoughton, 1981.

(With P. Guinness) *North America: A Human Geography,* Barnes & Noble, 1984.

Regions and Regionalism in the United States, University Press of Mississippi, 1988.

The Appalachian Regional Commission, University Press of Kentucky, 1992.

(With R. Weaver) *Physical Geography,* Mosby, 1993.

(With R. Weaver) *Essentials of Physical Geography,* W. C. Brown, in press.

WORK IN PROGRESS: World Regional Geography, publication by W. C. Brown expected in 1996.

SIDELIGHTS: Michael Bradshaw told *CA:* "My writings have two focuses. One is the natural environment (geology, physical geography); the other is the geography of the United States. The first formed an early career emphasis, and the second came later, linked to a course I taught, the establishment of a Centre for North American Studies at the College of St. Mark and St. John, and my doctoral studies on U.S. federal programs in Appalachia. I have traveled widely in the United States, and was influential in establishing a student exchange program between the college in Plymouth and Purdue University. The exchange program began in 1979 and continues.

"I see the combination of writing about both environmental topics and social/political issues as related to my view of geography as a subject and also to my personal Christian faith. Since retiring from college teaching and administration in 1993, I devote half my working time to writing and half to church administration.

"Much of my writing is now for U.S. publishers, mainly in the form of college textbooks. Although I was initially surprised that someone living and teaching in England should be asked to write for American students, modern communications and the fresh approach of an 'outsider' appear to be successful in this market."

BRADY, James B. 1939-

PERSONAL: Born August 30, 1939, in Harlingen, TX; married Diane White. *Education:* Southern Methodist University, B.A., 1961; University of Texas, J.D., 1964, Ph.D., 1970.

ADDRESSES: Home—62 Twilight Lane, East Amherst, NY 14051. *Office*—Department of Philosophy, 616 Baldy Hall, State University of New York at Buffalo, Amherst, NY 14260.

CAREER: State University of New York at Buffalo, Amherst, lecturer, 1967-70, assistant professor, 1970-73, associate professor of philosophy, 1973—, associate chair and director of undergraduate studies in department of philosophy, 1970-72, assistant provost, faculty of social sciences, 1972-73, associate provost, 1973-75, co-director of Baldy Center for Law and Social Policy, 1978-81. Oxford University, visiting senior member of Linacre College, 1975.

MEMBER: American Philosophical Association, Phi Beta Kappa, Phi Delta Phi.

AWARDS, HONORS: Received grants from Mitchell Fund and Baldy Fund, 1974 and 1979, National Science Foundation and National Endowment for the Humanities, 1978-80, and Marvin Farber Fund, 1989; Chancellor's Award for Excellence in Teaching, State University of New York, 1985.

WRITINGS:

(Editor with Newton Garver) *Justice, Law, and Violence,* Temple University Press, 1991.

Contributor of articles and reviews to journals, including *Houston Law Review, Buffalo Law Review,* and *Ethics.* Associate editor, *Humanist,* 1969-74, and *Texas Law Review.*

*   *   *

BRAND, Dionne 1953-

PERSONAL: Born January 7, 1953, in Guayguayare, Trinidad; immigrated to Canada. *Education:* University of Toronto, B.A., 1975, graduate studies at Ontario Institute for Studies in Education.

ADDRESSES: Agent—Women's Educational Press, 517 College St., Suite 233, Toronto, Ontario, Canada M6G 4A2.

CAREER: Poet, writer, and journalist. Associated with Black Education Project, Toronto, Ontario, Canada; Immigrant Women's Centre, Toronto, Caribbean women's health counselor; Agency for Rural Transformation, Grenada, information and communications officer, 1983.

AWARDS, HONORS: Publisher's Grant and Artist in the Schools Award, both from Ontario Arts Council, 1978; Canada Council Arts Grant, 1980; Ontario Arts Council grant, 1982.

WRITINGS:

'*Fore Day Morning* (poems), Khoisan Artists, 1978.
Earth Magic (poems), illustrated by Roy Crosse, Kids Can Press, 1980.
Primitive Offensive (poems), Williams-Wallace, 1982.
Winter Epigrams and Epigrams to Ernesto Cardenal in Defense of Claudia (poems), introduction by Roger McTair, Williams-Wallace, 1983.
Chronicles of the Hostile Sun (poems), Williams-Wallace, 1984.
(With Krisantha Sri Bhaggiyadatta) *Rivers Have Sources, Trees Have Roots: Speaking of Racism,* Cross Cultural Communication Centre, 1986.
Sans Souci, and Other Stories, Firebrand Books, 1989.
No Language Is Neutral (poems), Coach House Press, 1990.
(With Lois De Shield) *No Burden to Carry: Narratives of Black Working Women in Ontario, 1920s-1950s,* Women's Press, 1991.

Contributor to periodicals, including *Spear* and *Contrast.*

SIDELIGHTS: "Dionne Brand is one of the best young poets writing in Canada today," Libby Scheier asserts in her *Books in Canada* review of Brand's collection *Primitive Offensive.* A native Trinidadian who immigrated to Canada, Brand holds a bachelor's degree in English from the University of Toronto; her published works include poetry, fiction, and nonfiction. She has also worked actively for the black community in Canada through her affiliation with the Black Education Project and as a Caribbean counselor with the Immigrant Women's Centre.

Critics note that Brand's work is highly political. "To read her poetry is to read not only about her but also about her people, her identification with their struggles both in the metropole of Canada and in the hinterland of the Caribbean," comments Himani Bannerji in *Fifty Caribbean Writers.* The poetry in *No Language Is Neutral,* says Erin Moure in *Books in Canada,* "is one of waking and attentiveness, to one's own history, one's pain as a woman, as an immigrant to the place of foreign habits, to one's own sexuality." In the title poem, Moure says, Brand explores the lives of women who know "what it means to be black and women and to struggle constantly with that 'bloodstained blind of race and sex'." Moure feels that the collection contains some of "Brand's most engaging poetry."

Sans Souci, and Other Stories, a collection of short stories, "follows Brand's own cycle of growing up in Trinidad, moving to Canada as a teenager and returning to Grenada during the revolution to reconnect politically and spiritually with the Caribbean," reports Rhonda Cobham in the *Women's Review of Books.* In Cobham's opinion, Brand is a "militantly feminist and anti-imperialist writer." Cobham finds that female sexuality is a prominent theme of this collection, which contains stories of people who struggle to find a place in a world that is racist as well as sexist.

Brand's talent is not limited to poetry and fiction. *Rivers Have Sources, Trees Have Roots: Speaking of Racism,* co-authored with Krisantha Sri Bhaggiyadatta, seeks to educate readers against racism through a combination of interviews and "succinct and simply stated analysis," says *Canadian Forum* contributor Leslie Sanders. Through the testimony of the book's black, Native American, and Asian subjects, Sanders reports, the reader is led to realize that "racism is a deliberate attack on the self-image of the other." The authors also chart some of the history of the struggle against racism in Toronto, and Sanders believes that Brand and her coauthor "succeed admirably in their educative purpose." In *No Burden to Carry* Brand again uses personal recollections and interviews as the narrative support to illustrate her point. Through the accounts of fifteen black women, this book traces the role of black women in the history of Canada. Merilyn Simonds Mohr, writing in *Books in Canada,* says that reading the book "is like spending an afternoon with a roomful of charming, strong, witty women who have a lifetime of stories to share."

While Brand's work has been applauded for its thematic content, she is also recognized as an accomplished writer. Scheier says of *Primitive Offensive,* "The language is sharp and vibrant, the imagery original and evocative, the rhythmic phrasing beautifully achieved." Similarly, Cobham calls "Madame Alaird's Breasts," a short story from *Sans Souci,* "a perfect vignette of adolescent female eroticism" and declares that Brand is "*the* new Caribbean woman writer to watch." Cobham praises the whole collection, but she is especially appreciative of the technical expertise of "I Used to Like the Dallas Cowboys." The story relates the changing perception of America through the eyes of a woman facing probable death during the American invasion of Grenada in 1983. Cobham lauds it as "political art at its searing best." And while Brand has already won acclaim for both her poetry and her prose, it is Cobham's assessment that "there is more and better to come, and when Brand produces her magnum opus it's going to be out there with the big names: Toni Morrison, Toni Cade Bambara, Derek Walcott, Wilson Harris."

BIOGRAPHICAL/CRITICAL SOURCES:

BOOKS

Dance, Daryl Cumber, editor, *Fifty Caribbean Writers: A Bio-Bibliographical Critical Sourcebook,* Greenwood, 1986.

PERIODICALS

Books in Canada, December, 1983, p. 31; December, 1990, pp. 42-43; May, 1992, pp. 52-53.
Canadian Forum, January, 1988, pp. 39-40.
Women's Review of Books, July, 1990, pp. 29-31.*

* * *

BRASSEAUX, Carl A(nthony) 1951- (Antoine Bourque)

PERSONAL: Born August 19, 1951, in Opelousas, LA; son of Ferdinand, Jr. (an electrical technician) and Odile Valajean (a homemaker; maiden name, Johnson) Brasseaux; married Glenda Marie Melancon (a teacher and administrator), July 21, 1973; children: Ryan Andre, David Marc, Aimee Elizabeth. *Education:* University of Southwestern Louisiana, B.A. (cum laude), 1974, M.A., 1975; University of Paris, doctorate (summa cum laude), 1982. *Avocational Interests:* Photography, computers.

ADDRESSES: Home—111 Granada Dr., Lafayette, LA 70504-3820. *Office*—Center for Louisiana Studies, University of Southwestern Louisiana, P.O. Box 40831, Lafayette, LA 70504-0831.

CAREER: University of Southwestern Louisiana, Lafayette, assistant director of Center for Louisiana Studies, 1975—, curator of colonial records collection, 1980—, adjunct assistant professor, 1987-90, assistant professor of history, 1990—; writer. Consultant to various businesses, organizations, and institutions.

MEMBER: French Colonial Historical Association, Southern Historical Association, Gulf Coast Historical Association, Louisiana Historical Association.

AWARDS, HONORS: Chevalier, l'Ordre des Palmes Academiques, 1991.

WRITINGS:

HISTORY

(With Glenn R. Conrad and R. Warren Robison) *The Courthouses of Louisiana,* University of Southwestern Louisiana, 1977.
(Editor, translator, and annotator) *A Comparative View of French Louisiana: The Journals of Pierre Le Moyne d'Iberville and Jean-Jacques-Blaise d'Abbadie,* Uni-

versity of Southwestern Louisiana, 1979, second edition, 1980.

(Editor with Mathe Allain) *A Franco-American Overview: Louisiana,* National Assessment and Dissemination Center for Bilingual/Bicultural Education (Cambridge, MA), Volume 5, 1981, Volume 6, 1981, Volume 7: *The Postbellum Period,* 1982, Volume 8: *French Louisiana in the Twentieth Century,* 1982.

(Editor with Conrad, and annotator) Marc de Villiers du Terrage, *The Last Years of French Louisiana,* translated by Hosea Phillips, University of Southwestern Louisiana, 1982.

(Compiler with Conrad) *Gone But Not Forgotten: Records from South Louisiana Cemeteries,* Volume 1: *St. Peter's Cemetery, New Iberia, Louisiana,* Center for Louisiana Studies, 1983.

Denis-Nicolas Foucault and the New Orleans Rebellion of 1768, McGinty Publications, 1987.

The Founding of New Acadia: Beginnings of Acadian Life in Louisiana, 1765-1803, Louisiana State University Press, 1987.

(Translator with Emelio Garcia and Jacqueline K. Voorhies, annotator with Voorhies, and editor) *Quest for the Promised Land: Official Correspondence Regarding the First Acadian Migration to Louisiana, 1764-1769,* Center for Louisiana Studies, 1989.

In Search of Evangeline: Origins and Evolution of the Evangeline Myth, Blue Heron Press, 1989.

Lafayette, Where Yesterday Meets Tomorrow: An Illustrated History, Windsor Publications, 1990.

The Foreign French: French Immigration into the Mississippi Valley, 1820-1900, Center for Louisiana Studies, Volume 1: *1820-1839,* 1990, Volume 2: *1840-1848,* 1992, Volume 3: *1820-1900,* 1993.

Scattered to the Wind: Dispersal and Wanderings of the Acadians, 1755-1809, Center for Louisiana Studies, 1991.

(Editor and annotator, with Conrad) *The Road to Louisiana: The Saint-Domingue Refugees, 1792-1809,* Center for Louisiana Studies, 1992.

Acadian to Cajun: Transformation of a People, 1803-1877, University Press of Mississippi, 1992.

(With Claude Oubre and Keith P. Fontenot) *A People Apart: Creoles of Color in Louisiana's Prairie Region, 1766-1890,* University Press of Mississippi, in press.

REFERENCE WORKS

(With Conrad) *A Selected Bibliography of Scholarly Literature on Colonial Louisiana and New France,* Center for Louisiana Studies, 1982.

(With Conrad) *Louisiana History: The Journal of the Louisiana Historical Association. Index to Volumes I to XXV,* Louisiana Historical Association, 1985.

(With Michael James Foret) *A Bibliography of Acadian History, Literature, and Genealogy, 1955-1985,* Nicholls State University, 1986.

(With Conrad) *Louisiana History: The Journal of the Louisiana Historical Association. Index to Volumes XXVI to XXX,* Louisiana Historical Association, 1990.

(With Conrad) *A Bibliography of Scholarly Literature on Colonial Louisiana and New France,* Center for Louisiana Studies, 1992.

OTHER

(Under pseudonym Antoine Bourque) *Trois Saisons: Nouvelles, contes, et fables,* Centre d'Etudes louisianaises, 1988.

Work represented in anthologies, including *Acadie tropicale: Poesie de Louisiane,* Centre d'Etudes louisianaises, 1983. Managing editor of Attakapas Historical Association's Special Publications Series, 1975-77. Associate editor of and contributor to *Dictionary of Louisiana Biography,* 1982-88. Contributor to periodicals, including *Feux Follets* and *Louisiane.* Managing editor of *Attakapas Gazette,* 1975-79, and *Louisiana History,* 1993-96; consulting editor of *Louisiana Review,* 1976-82, and *Attakapas Gazette,* 1979—; associate editor of *Louisiana Francophone Review,* 1984-86. Member of editorial board of *Gulf Coast Historical Review,* 1987—.

WORK IN PROGRESS: France's Forgotten Legions: Service Records of French Military and Administrative Personnel Stationed in the Mississippi Valley, 1699-1769, five volumes; *The Steamboats of the Teche Country; Santo Domingo Refugees: A Reference List;* research on Louisiana's Cajuns from 1877 to the present, indigenous flora and fauna of the Gulf Coast, and Acadian migrations.

SIDELIGHTS: Carl A. Brasseaux told *CA:* "As a professional historian, I have always believed that general histories—those which are most widely read by the general public and which are thus most responsible for shaping public consciousness about the past—should be 'mosaics' reflecting the composition of the general public.

"Like approximately one-third of all Louisianians, I am a Cajun. During my childhood, Cajun culture was threatened with destruction by the 'melting pot' mentality. I have devoted my career to exploring the history of the various French groups that have coalesced over the last two hundred years to form the Cajun and Creole communities. It is my fervent hope that authors of future general histories of the Lower Mississippi Valley area will utilize my works in creating a new, and hopefully more representative, 'mosaic' of the past."

BRATA, Sasthi 1939-

PERSONAL: Born Sasthibrata Chakravarti, July 16, 1939, in Calcutta, India; son of Sasi Kanta (an engineer) and Hemnalini Chakravarti; married Pamela Joyce Radcliffe (divorced). *Education:* Presidency College, Calcutta, India, B.S. (with honors), 1960. *Politics:* "Left of center, traditional radical."

ADDRESSES: Home—Brata's Corner, 33 Savernake Rd., Hampstead, London NW3, England. *Agent*—Barbara Lowenstein, 50 West 57th St., New York, NY 10107.

CAREER: Full-time writer. *Statesman* (magazine), London columnist, 1977-80. Worked variously in Europe and New York as a lavatory assistant, kitchen porter, bartender, air conditioning engineer, and postal worker.

AWARDS, HONORS: Arts Council Grant (United Kingdom), 1971, 1979.

WRITINGS:

AUTOBIOGRAPHY

My God Died Young, Hutchinson, 1968.
A Search for Home, Orient, 1975.
Astride Two Worlds: Traitor to India, B.I. Publications, 1976, published in England as *Traitor to India: A Search for Home,* Elek, 1976.

NOVELS

Confessions of an Indian Woman Eater, Hutchinson, 1971, published in India as *Confessions of an Indian Lover,* Sterling, 1973.
She and He, Orient, 1973.
The Sensuous Guru: The Making of a Mystic President, Sterling, 1980.
India: Labyrinths in the Lotus Land, Morrow, 1985.

OTHER

Eleven Poems (poetry), Blue Moon, 1960.
Encounter (short stories), Orient, 1978.

SIDELIGHTS: Sasthi Brata told *CA:* "All my work is drawn from my own experiences. In the 'nonfictional' books, I have used fictional devices, and in fictional works I have used reportage techniques. Be warned, however, that not every hero in every novel is representative of all of me. In a review of the late Yukio Mishima's novels, I wrote: 'The obsessionally autobiographical writer may be an invisible man.' Although no lies are told, there may be very little empirical truth in what is presented to the reader because imagination is exercised and it is not necessarily made clear where the fiction ends and the truth begins, or vice versa."

That Brata is an autobiographical writer is apparent—though whether "obsessionally" so or not is a judgment subjective to individual readers. *My God Died Young,* written while the author was still in his twenties, narrates the essential facts of his life. He was born in Calcutta, India, to an affluent Brahmin (the upper class of India's social caste system) family who spoiled and indulged him, then sent him at age eleven to a rigid English-speaking school in Calcutta. It soon became clear that he was a gifted student; in college, where he earned honors in physics, he was also an accomplished debater. But he grew increasingly estranged from the traditional India of his parents, so after college he left home to work for an engineering firm in London, England. He later returned to India with vague plans to put down roots and enter into a traditional arranged marriage. He did neither. In *Astride Two Worlds: Traitor to India,* Brata continues his life story, enriching it with discussions of Indian politics and his experiences with racial discrimination in England. While Brata resides in England, the country of his birth is a strong presence in his writing; he is drawn by the pull of two countries and two widely disparate cultural traditions.

The critical reaction to *My God Died Young* was somewhat mixed. In *Books Abroad,* Leona Bagai praised the book for being "explicit, candid, and fairly objective." Similarly, Christopher Wordsworth, writing in the *Observer,* found the book to be a "vivid, well-written account." What bothered critics was what Wordsworth called the book's "superciliousness," or what Donald Gropman in the *Christian Science Monitor* similarly called its "pretension, pomposity, and . . . sophomoric urge to shock and impress." Concluded Robert Berkvist in the *New York Times Book Review:* "This is a young man's book, verging on the pompous at times."

Brata's novels are in many ways continuations of his autobiographies. The best-selling *Confessions of an Indian Woman Eater* features the exploits—a good many of them explicitly sexual—of Amit Ray, a man who leaves his Calcutta home and eventually lands in England, where he enjoys a successful writing career. Writing in *Books & Bookmen,* J. A. Cuddon expressed reservations about the novel's preoccupation with sexuality but enjoyed its "winningly naive and inquisitive" protagonist and praised the author for his "powers of description" and "realistic" dialogue.

Brata's subsequent novels include *She and He,* whose Arab-French hero tries to write the "Great English Novel" by filling in the blank pages of an unfinished novel written by his girlfriend. In 1980 he wrote *The Sensuous Guru,* a book about a successful New York guru who writes a pornographic autobiographical novel that wins the Pulitzer Prize. The stature he gains from his book and its subsequent awards eventually gets him elected to the presidency of the United States. In 1985 Brata returned to the subject of his homeland for *India: Labyrinths in the Lotus Land.*

BIOGRAPHICAL/CRITICAL SOURCES:

PERIODICALS

Books Abroad, spring, 1969.
Books and Bookmen, June, 1971.
Christian Science Monitor, December 12, 1968.
Observer, July, 1968.
New Statesman, April 23, 1971.
New Yorker, November 23, 1968.
New York Times Book Review, October 20, 1968.*

*   *   *

BREMMER, Ian A. 1969-

PERSONAL: Born November 12, 1969, in Baltimore, MD; son of Arthur Helmuth and Marie Jean (a homemaker) Bremmer. *Education:* Attended Sophia University, 1987, and University of Essex, 1987-88; Tulane University, B.A. (magna cum laude), 1989; Stanford University, M.A., 1991, doctoral work, 1991-94. *Politics:* "Not that simple." *Religion:* Roman Catholic.

ADDRESSES: Home—755 University Ave., No. 2, Palo Alto, CA 94301. *Office*—Department of Political Science, Stanford University, Stanford, CA 94305-2044.

CAREER: Stanford University, Stanford, CA, Hrair Hovnanian fellow, 1990-94. Foundation for Global Community, member of steering committee, 1992, 1993; consultant to National Geographic Society. Disc jockey for radio stations in Oklahoma, California, Vermont, and England.

MEMBER: Association for the Study of Nationalities (member of executive committee, 1992—), American Political Science Association, American Association for the Advancement of Slavic Studies, National Association for the Advancement of Armenian Studies, American Professional Society of the Bay Area, Berkeley-Stanford Program in Post-Soviet Studies, Armenian Benevolent Union (member of executive board of San Francisco chapter, 1990—), Pi Sigma Alpha (president, 1988-89).

AWARDS, HONORS: Fellow of MacArthur Foundation, 1992.

WRITINGS:

(Editor with Norman Naimark) *Soviet Nationalities Problems,* Stanford Center for Russian and East European Studies, Stanford University, 1990.
(Editor with Raymond Taras, and contributor) *Nation and Politics in the Soviet Successor States,* Cambridge University Press, 1993, 2nd edition, 1994.

(Editor with Raymond Taras, and contributor) *Transitions to and From Democracy: Liberalism and Nationalism Compared,* Cambridge University Press, 1994.
(With Alexander Hrushevsky) *Fraternal Illusions: A History of Russians in Ukraine,* Canadian Institute for Ukrainian Studies, in press.

Work represented in anthologies, including *Soviet Social Reality in the Mirror of Glasnost,* edited by Jim Riordan, St. Martin's, 1992. Contributor of articles and reviews to history and political science journals. Book review editor, *Stanford Journal of International Affairs,* 1991—; *Nationalities Papers,* member of editorial board, 1992—, guest editor, 1994.

SIDELIGHTS: Ian Bremmer told *CA:* "I had come up with the idea for *Nations and Politics* in the summer of 1990, shortly after I had arrived at Stanford, while attending a conference and listening to well-known Sovietologists discuss the 'nationalities explosion' under the leadership of Mikhail Gorbachev. Reasonably fresh to the field, I was surprised at how state-centric and even Moscow-centric the debate was: nations were not actors, but had reacted to mistakes in Soviet policy. The fundamental question was not how the national movements would build states, but how Gorbachev would keep the situation under control. I intended to focus, not on the Soviet nation (which, in fact, did not exist), but on the nations of the former U.S.S.R. (which did). *Nations and Politics* was to be a book on the national movements themselves and their aspirations to statehood. What determines how these movements would express themselves? How would the successor states function?

"As you might imagine, securing a publisher was rather difficult. I received rejections from every decent university press I could think of, and the complaints were largely the same. There's no 'Soviet' in the book, virtually no mention of Gorbachev, 'nationalities' is just a flash-in-the-pan issue, and so on. I was getting quite frustrated when the August coup occurred in 1991. Within two weeks, almost every publisher I had contacted (and a couple I hadn't) wanted to know what I had done with the text.

"The timing was fortunate, to say the least. What strikes me as most remarkable, however, is that the same process which created obstacles in the publication of my volume has left *Nations and Politics* as the only text presently available on the Soviet successor states.

"A final point: youth creates both surprise and resentment in a field where those who used to dominate are assiduously grappling with paradigms lost. I was twenty when my first book appeared; *Nations and Politics* first appeared in England before my twenty-third birthday. My favorite comment came during the subsequent fighting in Moscow. I was there at the time, returning from a research project in Kazakhstan and, as the events unraveled, I had become a frequent commentator for CNN cable news. Filming an interview atop their roof on Kutuzovsky Prospekt, the correspondent could contain herself no longer, and asked, 'Aren't you a little young to be a Soviet expert?' 'Yes,' I replied, 'but I'm just the right age to be a *post*-Soviet expert.' It is a very fast-moving field, and there are few honest-to-God social scientists who are trained to consider the successor states as the basis for comparative research. I have been fortunate, thus far, in working on filling that niche; hopefully my present research will continue along the same path."

*   *   *

BREWERTON, Derrick (Arthur) 1924-

PERSONAL: Born February 26, 1924, in London, England; son of Arthur Ernest Brewerton (a civil servant) and Dorothy Kathleen (Bath) Brewerton (a homemaker); married Joan Catherine Wells (a child psychiatrist), March 21, 1953; children: Catherine Mary Sims, Peter John, Sally Anne. *Education:* McGill University, B.Sc., 1945, M.D., C.M., 1947; Royal College of Physicians, M.R.C.P., 1952, F.R.C.P., 1969. *Religion:* Church of England.

ADDRESSES: Home—62 Denbigh St., London SW1V 2EX, England.

CAREER: Consultant rheumatologist in London, England, 1957-89. University of London, professor, 1982-89. Consultant physician at Royal National Orthopaedic Hospital, 1957-73, and Westminster Hospital, 1958-89.

MEMBER: Royal Society of Medicine, British Society for Rheumatology, American College of Rheumatology, Alpha Omega Alpha.

AWARDS, HONORS: Robecchi Prize, 1975; Ambuj Nath Bose Prize, Royal College of Physicians, 1977; Geigy Prize, 1977; Zeiter Prize, American Academy of Rehabilitation, 1984.

WRITINGS:

(Editor) *Immunogenetics in Rheumatic Diseases,* Saunders, 1977.
All About Arthritis: Past, Present, Future, Harvard University Press, 1992.

Contributor to scientific and medical journals.

SIDELIGHTS: Derrick Brewerton told *CA:* "Love of medicine has been my career, as a clinician, researcher, and teacher. My specialty is arthritis, and a large part of all my working days has been spent listening to the problems of people with this painful, disabling condition.

Many of the physicians who have made recent discoveries in the quest for the causes of arthritis are my friends, and I too have experienced the wonderment and exhilaration of contributing to major advances in research. These are stirring times for rheumatologists. Soon today's researchers will achieve their final goal, and new methods of prevention and treatment will transform the outlook for everyone with arthritis.

"I strongly believe that the fascination and the excitement of current progress in arthritis research should be shared by all general readers. In my book *All About Arthritis* I have made past researchers come alive on the page by reading extensively about them and by attempting to understand what they felt when they made their major discoveries. To help me describe today's remarkable new phase of research, colleagues in many countries have told me about their breakthroughs and disappointments, why they did what they did, and what they thought at the time.

"Presenting arthritis research through the eyes of the discoverers enabled me to write the book like a detective story, and as little like a textbook as possible. Although the book contains extensive information about genes, molecules, and diseases, it is mainly about people—especially those, great and small—who have contributed to medical research, as well as those who go through life as a constant companion."

*   *   *

BRINKLEY, William (Clark) 1917-1993

OBITUARY NOTICE—See index for *CA* sketch: Born September 10, 1917, in Custer, OK; died of an overdose of barbiturates, November 22, 1993, in McAllen, TX. Writer. Recognized for his novels that revolve around the sea and the Navy, Brinkley is remembered in particular for his 1956 best-selling *Don't Go Near the Water.* Set in the Pacific Theater during World War II, the comedic novel was made into a film in 1957 and grossed more than four million dollars. Brinkley began his career as a journalist for the *Daily Oklahoman* and the *Washington Post* in the early 1940s, before joining the U.S. Navy in 1942 and serving in the Pacific and Mediterranean. Following the war, he returned to the *Washington Post* for a brief time, then joined the staff of *Life,* where he worked as a staff writer and Washington correspondent. Turning to a freelance writing career in the late 1950s, Brinkley penned such novels as 1978's *Breakpoint,* 1981's *Peeper: A Comedy,* and 1988's *Last Ship.* In 1986 he received the Citation for Achievement Award from William Jewell College.

OBITUARIES AND OTHER SOURCES:

BOOKS

Who's Who in America, 47th edition, Marquis, 1992.

PERIODICALS

Chicago Tribune, November 28, 1993, section 2, p. 8.
Los Angeles Times, November 27, 1993, p. A36.
New York Times, November 25, 1993, p. D19.
Washington Post, November 25, 1993, p. C4.

*   *   *

BROAD, Robin 1954-

PERSONAL: Born January 26, 1954, in Manchester, NH; daughter of Edward Margoles and Muriel (Rooff) Broad; married John Cavanagh. *Education:* Williams College, B.A. (summa cum laude), 1977; Princeton University, M.P.A., 1980, Ph.D., 1983.

ADDRESSES: Home—1401 Newton St. N.E., Washington, DC 20017. *Office*—International Development Program, School of International Service, American University, 4400 Massachusetts Ave. N.W., Washington, DC 20016-8001.

CAREER: Xavier University, Mindanao, Philippines, professor of economic development and environmental studies and research associate, 1977-78; Chulalonghorn University, Bangkok, Thailand, economic researcher, 1979; University of the Philippines, Manila, visiting research associate, 1980-81; U.S. Treasury Department, Office of Multilateral Development Banks, Washington, DC, international economist, 1983-84, InterAmerican Development Bank desk officer, 1983-85; senior staff economist for U.S. Congressman Charles E. Schumer, Washington, DC, 1985-87; Carnegie Endowment for International Peace, resident associate, 1987-88; American University, Washington, DC, assistant professor of environment and development, 1990—. Producer of the Philippine segment of the documentary film *The Global Assemblyline,* broadcast by Public Broadcasting System, 1987. National Security Archives, member of editorial board, 1990; International Labor Rights Education and Research Fund, member of advisory council, 1988—; consultant to World Council of Churches and International Foundation for Development Alternatives.

MEMBER: Institute for Food and Development Policy (member of board of directors, 1990—), Council on Foreign Relations, Philippine Development Forum (founder, 1989; member of board of directors, 1989—), Phi Beta Kappa, World Wildlife Fund.

AWARDS, HONORS: Shared Emmy Award, news and documentary category, American Academy of Television

Arts and Sciences, 1987, for *The Global Assemblyline;* international affairs fellow of Council on Foreign Relations, 1987-88; grant from International Peace and Security Program, John D. and Catherine T. MacArthur Foundation, 1988-90; grant from Henry Luce Foundation, 1991; nominated for Lionel Gelber Prize, 1993, for *Plundering Paradise.*

WRITINGS:

Unequal Alliance: The World Bank, the International Monetary Fund, and the Philippines, University of California Press, 1988.
(With husband John Cavanagh) *The Philippine Challenge: Sustainable and Equitable Development in the 1990s* (monograph), Philippine Center for Policy Studies, 1991.
(With husband John Cavanagh) *Plundering Paradise: The Struggle for the Environment in the Philippines,* University of California Press, 1993.

Work represented in anthologies, including *Development Debacle: The World Bank in the Philippines,* edited by Walden Bello, Institute for Food and Development Policy, 1982; *Debt Reader,* Freedom From Debt Coalition (Quezon City), 1991; and *Paradigms Lost: The Post Cold War Era,* edited by Chester Hartman and Pedro Vilanova, Pluto Press (London), 1992. Contributor to professional journals and newspapers.

*   *   *

BROD, Harry 1951-

PERSONAL: Born February 1, 1951, in Berlin, Germany; son of Sam (an automobile dealer) and Lotti (a homemaker; maiden name, Schuefftan) Brod; married Maria Papacostaki (a homemaker), August 10, 1980; children: Artemis, Alexi. *Education:* New York University, B.A., 1972; University of California, San Diego, M.A., 1975, Ph.D., 1981. *Religion:* Jewish.

ADDRESSES: Home—3413 Moore St., Los Angeles, CA 90066.

CAREER: University of Southern California, Los Angeles, lecturer, 1982-84, associate professor of philosophy, 1984-87; writer. Lecturer and visiting instructor at various institutions, including Antioch College of Los Angeles, Kenyon College, and University of California, Los Angeles.

MEMBER: National Organization for Men against Sexism (national spokesperson, 1990—), Men's Studies Association (cochair, 1991—).

AWARDS, HONORS: Scholarship from New York State regents, 1968-72; Fulbright-Hays grant, 1976-77; dissertation fellowship from University of California, 1977-78; faculty research and innovation fund grant from University of Southern California, 1986-87; Fulbright grant, 1986-87; liberal arts fellowship from Harvard Law School, 1987-88.

WRITINGS:

Hegel's Philosophy of Politics: Idealism, Identity, and Modernity, Westview, 1992.

CONTRIBUTOR

Robert L. Perkins, *History and System: Hegel's Philosophy of History,* State University of New York Press, 1984.
Carol Kort and Ronnie Friedland, editors, *The Fathers' Book,* G. K. Hall, 1986.
Peter G. Stillman, editor, *Hegel's Philosophy of Spirit,* State University of New York Press, 1987.
Michael Kimmel, *Changing Men: New Directions in Research on Men and Masculinity,* Sage, 1987.
Elizabeth Wright, editor, *Feminism and Psychoanalysis: A Critical Dictionary,* Basil Blackwell, 1992.
Tamar M. Rudavsky, editor, *Gender and Judaism,* New York University Press, in press.

Contributor to periodicals, including *American Behavioral Scientist, Changing Men, Hospital and Community Psychiatry, Humanities in Society, Hypatia: A Journal of Feminist Philosophy,* and *Tikkun.*

EDITOR

The Making of Masculinities: The New Men's Studies, Allen & Unwin, 1987, second edition, Routledge, in press.
A Mensch among Men: Explorations in Jewish Masculinity, Crossing Press, 1992.
(With Michael Kaufman) *Theorizing Masculinity,* Sage, 1994.
Can(n)ons of Masculinity: The Hidden History of Masculinities in Western Political Theory, Humanities Press, in press.

Founding editor of *Men's Studies Review* (now *masculinities*), 1983-85, consulting editor, 1985-86, associate editor, 1992—. Guest editor of various periodicals, including *Journal of the National Association for Women Deans, Administrators, and Counselors,* summer, 1986; *American Behavioral Scientist,* October, 1987; and *Changing Men: Issues in Gender, Sex, and Politics,* summer/fall, 1987.

Member of editorial board of "Perspectives on Gender" series and "Critical Studies on Men and Masculinities" series, both for Chapman & Hall; "Research on Men and Masculinity" series for Sage; and "Men and Masculinity" series for University of California Press and Beacon Press. Also member of editorial board for various periodicals, in-

cluding *Bridges: A Journal for Jewish Feminists and Our Friends* and *masculinities.*

OTHER

Work represented in anthologies, including *Men, Masculinities, and Social Theory,* edited by Jeff Hearn and David Morgan, Unwin Hyman, 1990; *Pornography: Private Right or Public Menace?,* edited by Robert M. Baird and Stuart E. Rosenbaum, Prometheus, 1991; *Rethinking Masculinity: Philosophical Explorations in Light of Feminism,* edited by Larry May and Robert Strikwerda, Rowman & Littlefield, 1992; and *Moral Controversies: Race, Class, and Gender in Applied Ethics,* edited by Steven Jay Gold, Wadsworth, 1993.

SIDELIGHTS: Harry Brod is an authority in both Hegelian philosophy and men's studies. It is in the latter field that he is probably most known. The *Los Angeles Times,* for example, described him as "one of the nation's first academic specialists in men's studies" and added that he "devotes his professional energies to the study of the male experience." In the same article, Brod affirmed that "the variety of male experiences—of masculinities—has not been recorded," and he contended that "studying the past is the first step toward improvement."

BIOGRAPHICAL/CRITICAL SOURCES:

PERIODICALS

Los Angeles Times, August 12, 1987, p. E9.

*   *   *

BRODBER, Erna (May) 1940-

PERSONAL: Born April 20, 1940, in Woodside, St. Mary, Jamaica; daughter of Ernest (a farmer) and Lucy (a teacher) Brodber. *Education:* University College of the West Indies (now University of the West Indies), B.A. (honors), 1963, M.Sc., 1968, Ph.D.; attended McGill University, and University of Washington, beginning in 1967. *Religion:* Twelve Tribes of Israel (a Rastafarian sect).

CAREER: Worked as civil servant; worked as a teacher in Montego Bay, Jamaica; served as head of history at St. Augustine High School for Girls, Trinidad; Ministry of Youth and Community Development, Jamaica, children's officer, beginning in 1964; University of the West Indies, lecturer in sociology, in the 1970s; Institute of Social and Economic Research, supernumary fellow, 1972-73, staff member, 1974-83; free-lance writer and researcher. Visiting scholar at University of Michigan, Ann Arbor, 1973; visiting fellow at School of African and Asian Studies of University of Sussex, 1981. Appeared in revue titled *Eight O'Clock Jamaica Time,* 1972.

AWARDS, HONORS: Received scholarships from the University of the West Indies, and the Jamaican government, 1960; University of the West Indies postgraduate award, 1964; Ford Foundation fellowship for pre-doctoral research, 1967; National Festival award, Jamaica Festival Commission, 1975, for short story "Rosa"; Association of Commonwealth Universities staff fellowship, 1980.

WRITINGS:

Abandonment of Children in Jamaica, University of the West Indies, Institute of Social and Economic Research, 1974.

Yards in the City of Kingston, University of the West Indies, Institute of Social and Economic Research, 1975.

Jane and Louisa Will Soon Come Home (novel), New Beacon Books, 1980.

Perceptions of Caribbean Women: Towards a Documentation of Stereotypes, introduction by Merle Hodge, University of the West Indies, Institute of Social and Economic Research, 1982.

Myal (novel), New Beacon Books, 1988.

Rural-Urban Migration and the Jamaican Child, United Nations Educational, Scientific, and Cultural Organization (UNESCO), Regional Office for Education in Latin America and the Caribbean, 1986.

Author, with J. Edward Greene, of *Reggae and Cultural Identity in Jamaica,* 1981; author of *A History of the Second Generation of Freemen in Jamaica, 1907-1944;* author of short story, "Rosa," *Festival Commission,* 1975. Contributor to periodicals, including *Journal of Ethnic Studies* and *Jamaica Journal.*

SIDELIGHTS: Erna Brodber's first novel "immediately earned a place as a masterpiece within the canon of Caribbean fiction," says Rhonda Cobham in the *Women's Review of Books.* Born in Jamaica, Brodber was the child of parents actively involved in local community affairs in their hometown of Woodside. In this way, Brodber, a sociologist and researcher by vocation, was exposed to the importance of community affiliations at an early age. Brodber came to the United States on a research scholarship soon after she graduated from the University of the West Indies. It was here that she discovered the black power and women's liberation movements, two ideas that influenced her greatly. Back in Jamaica Brodber received a master's degree in sociology, also from the University of the West Indies. Since then she has published numerous nonfiction works in her field, but it was with the publication of her first novel, *Jane and Louisa Will Soon Come Home,* that Brodber established herself as a fiction writer. *Jane and Louisa Will Soon Come Home* was followed by *Myal,* her second novel, in 1988. Both books have been well received by critics and deal with issues central to Caribbean life.

Jane and Louisa Will Soon Come Home is set in a small rural community. In this book Brodber examines the importance and influence of traditional Jamaican society through the life of her protagonist, Nellie. Nellie, a woman who has lost her sense of self due to societal pressures, learns to use her community's strength to heal herself. She can do this, however, only if she learns to connect with and understand the significance of the past. Nellie's family teaches her to alienate herself from her black ancestry and community because their connection with the white community has resulted in prosperity. Therefore, Nellie learns to look down at the Creole community. At the end of the book, however, she learns that it is only when she accepts this community and becomes a part of it that she will heal completely.

Jane and Louisa Will Soon Come Home also explores the problems facing Caribbean women through the contradictory images of womanhood experienced by Nellie. The fissure in Nellie's self begins at puberty, when others view her increasing sexual maturity as a change to be ashamed of, leading Nellie to view herself and her womanhood as something negative. To solve the problem, Nellie is sent to live with her Aunt Becca, a woman who advises Nellie to avoid men and repress her sexuality completely. Set against this idea is the pressure of the sexual liberation prevalent at the university Nellie attends. These contradictions result in a breakdown of Nellie's self. Her first sexual encounter leaves her traumatized, leading her to deny her femininity altogether and therefore also her identity. This remains the case until Nellie learns to reconstruct herself as a unified being who has fused within her the many different aspects of womanhood by rejecting the traditional stereotypes she had previously accepted as models of female identity.

Myal, Brodber's second novel, also deals with issues of identity in Caribbean society. *Myal* is the story of Ella O Grady, a young Jamaican girl adopted by a Welsh woman, Maydene Brassington, who rescues Ella from her poverty. Ella's connection with Maydene results in Ella's dislocation from her own culture and religion. But as Cobham explains, she finally establishes a connection with her own milieu with the help of Maydene, Brassington's Jamaican husband, and a local shaman, "who create a spiritual safety-net to pull her out of the morass of cultural alienation and spiritual violation that claims her after her white American husband betrays her." She finally becomes a teacher at the local school, where she uses her own life experiences to render new meanings in the stories of the reading primers used by her students.

According to Cobham, Brodber's narrative refers explicitly to Claude McKay's *Banana Bottom,* where the protagonist, also rescued by an Englishwoman, must break her ties with that culture completely to find self-realization. Brodber's book, unlike McKay's, acknowledges the contribution of Maydene Brassington and other white women like her who, through marriage or birth, have created connections within traditional Jamaican society. Cobham feels that *Myal* establishes Maydene Brassington "as an amazingly credible figure" who is accepted by the other village shamans at the end of the book.

Cobham's final assessment of *Myal* classifies it as a "work of unquestioned achievement" in which Brodber deals with one of the most complex issues in Caribbean society: "the place and relevance of white West Indians and the colored middle class in a predominantly black society, in which both groups have disturbing past and present histories as oppressors." In both novels, Brodber's vision is of integration. The acceptance of common Creole society is as important to Nellie's self-realization in *Jane and Louisa Will Soon Come Home* as, conversely, Maydene Brassington, a white woman who has become part of Caribbean shamanic healing, is to Ella's reclamation. For Nellie and Ella the feeling of fragmentation dissipates only when they accept all the variances that comprise their world and become part of it.

BIOGRAPHICAL/CRITICAL SOURCES:

PERIODICALS

Women's Review of Books, July, 1990, pp. 29-31.*

*   *   *

BRODERICK, John   1927-1989

PERSONAL: Born July 30, 1927, in Athlone, Ireland; died May 28, 1989, in Bath, Avon, England; buried in Athlone; father owned a bakery business. *Education:* Attended St. Joseph's College, Ireland.

CAREER: Writer, 1961-89.

MEMBER: Irish Academy of Letters.

AWARDS, HONORS: Irish Academy of Letters award, 1975.

WRITINGS:

The Chameleons, Obolensky, 1961, published in England as *The Pilgrimage,* Weidenfeld & Nicolson, 1961.
The Fugitives, Obolensky, 1962.
Don Juaneen, Weidenfeld & Nicolson, 1963, Obolensky, 1965.
The Waking of Willie Ryan, Weidenfeld & Nicolson, 1965.

An Apology for Roses, Calder & Boyars, 1973.
The Pride of Summer, Harrap, 1976.
London Irish, Barrie & Jenkins, 1979.
Trial of Father Dillingham, Boyars, 1981.
A Prayer for Fair Weather, Boyars, 1984.
The Rose Tree, Boyars, 1985.
The Flood, Boyars, 1987.
The Irish Magdalen, Boyars, 1991.

Also the author of *Cite Pleine de Reves,* written in French and published in France in 1974. Author of the radio plays *The Enemies of Rome,* 1979, and *A Share of the Light,* 1981. Contributor to various publications, including the *Irish Times, Hibernia,* and *Figaro.*

Broderick's manuscript is housed at the Longford/Westmeath County Library.

SIDELIGHTS: Irish novelist John Broderick's career saw a rather marked shift in critical perception by the time of his death in 1989. Once called a "sour, dour, awkward satirist" by the *Dictionary of Irish Literature* for novels like *The Fugitives* and *An Apology for Roses* that were "highly critical of life in the Irish Midlands," Broderick won praise for his "genial country humor" in the last novel he saw published, *The Flood.* Broderick's early works provoked much critical emphasis on theme, perhaps because the author himself put a great deal of emphasis upon the matter. In Broderick's own words, published in *Contemporary Novelists* in 1986, his novels "deal with many themes: the difficulty of loving; the predicament of homosexuals in a hostile society; the strength of genuine religious feeling, and the weakness of its opposite; the frequency with which the strong overcome the weak; the apparent triumph, in many cases, of the unworthy. But the real theme . . . is the power of money." Yet Broderick's later works more often than not inspired discussions on form rather than theme; novels like *A Prayer for Fair Weather* often resisted categorization by reviewers.

Don Juaneen, one of Broderick's early novels earned praise from several reviewers. *New York Times Book Review* columnist Martin Levin noted that among the "Hibernian specialties" of this story of suburban angst are its "fine sense of place and a catalytic touch of poetry." According to a review by S. P. Ryan in *Best Sellers,* Broderick evidenced "the authentic Irish way with words." J. R. Frakes suggested in *Book Week* that the novel moves the reader to "care about its people . . . and recoil at the shock of recognition." One London *Times* reviewer, however found favor with an element that sets *Don Juaneen* apart: "there is something peculiar and original in this novel," the critic asserted. "Tragedy strikes, but nothing is really changed by it." That defining element would run through many of Broderick's ensuing works.

1973's *An Apology for Roses* touches on the familiar themes of lust and greed; in it, a parish priest enters into an illicit relationship and avarice pervades a small Irish town. In the opinion of a *Times Literary Supplement* reviewer, one of the novel's virtues is that it "generally reflects a strange but convincing local attitude toward religious beliefs and church rules, a shallow, taken-for-granted piety and disobedience." *The Trial of Father Dillingham* is also built around a clergyman's moral crisis, but is made of different structure. *Times Literary Supplement* reviewer M. G. McCulloch likened the novel to a detective story, but noted that unlike conventional mystery, its appeal is rooted in character rather than plot. For the critic, this detail is both a strength for the novel and the source of its ultimate weakness. Broderick "succeeds . . . in portraying a group of people whose kindly discretion in their dealings with one another is entirely credible," McCulloch professed, but the author's credibility wanes "when he confronts the philosophical problems he poses for himself." In the critic's opinion, Broderick's solutions to the human mysteries of *The Trial of Father Dillingham* are too easy.

With a later book, Broderick followed a similar structural path. "*The Rose Tree* is conceived and written, clearly, not as a mystery story but as an exploration of psychological depths," wrote Toby Fitton in the *Times Literary Supplement*. Like McCulloch, Fitton took exception to Broderick's unraveling of his mysteries, suggesting in this case that the resolution simply involves revealing information that had been withheld. For Douglas Sun in the *Los Angeles Times*, however, *The Rose Tree* grows "taut and compelling as it picks up speed and . . . previously suppressed conflicts open like raw sores."

A Prayer for Fair Weather earned praise from Tim Heald in the London *Times* who noted that Broderick "writes beautifully . . . he evokes a spooky underworld of misfits and derelicts deftly and convincingly; and he has a nice sardonic touch." Ultimately, however, the novel failed for the critic because, in Heald's mind, it returned to the conventions of its genre rather than rising above them. Crime columnist Newgate Callendar in the *New York Times Book Review*, however, pronounced *A Prayer for Fair Weather* "sensitive and serious."

Broderick's writing appealed on a completely different level in 1987's *The Flood*. Constance Decker Kennedy urged *New York Times Book Review* readers to ignore the book's thin plot (which involves land speculation) and enjoy its many and lively characters. "This is a first-rate comic novel," she asserted, "and its lush characterization and language richly recommend it." A reviewer for *Publishers Weekly* sounded a similar note: What matters in *The Flood* are its "genial country humor . . . the toler-

ance of human foible, and most of all, the parade of characters."

Broderick wrote *The Flood* as the first part of a trilogy he intended to set in Bridgeford, an Irish village, in the 1930s. He died before he could complete the revisions of the second novel in the series, *The Irish Magdalen,* which was published posthumously in 1989. A *Publishers Weekly* reviewer speculated as to the extent of the novel's weaknesses ("occasional awkward passages," an overall lack of polish, and, especially, its phonetically spelled dialect) that would have remained had the author completed his work. Nevertheless, the reviewer concluded that *The Irish Magdalen* "has the power to delight as it evokes village life with its intrigues and secrets." Another critic, however, found strengths in some of the very weaknesses the *Publishers Weekly* review described: "it's the outrageous, ripe comic dialogue, all rendered phonetically, that provides the fun," wrote Robert Carver in the London *Observer*.

BIOGRAPHICAL/CRITICAL SOURCES:

BOOKS

Contemporary Novelists, Gale, 1986.
Dictionary of Irish Literature, Greenwood Press, 1979.
Rafroidi, Patrick, and Maurice Harmon, editors, *The Irish Novel of Our Time,* Publications de l'Universite de Lille, 1976.

PERIODICALS

Best Sellers, December 1, 1965.
Book Week, January 2, 1966, p. 12.
Los Angeles Times Book Review, October 13, 1985, p. 16.
New York Times Book Review, October 31, 1965, p. 68; December 5, 1965, p. 56; September 2, 1984, p. 12; December 27, 1987, p. 18.
Observer (London), March 17, 1991, p. 58.
Publishers Weekly, August 21, 1987, p. 54; January 11, 1991, p. 89.
Spectator, September 1, 1979, p. 19.
Times (London), February 23, 1984.
Times Literary Supplement, May 31, 1963, p. 393; February 9, 1973, p. 141; July 9, 1976, p. 841; February 19, 1982, p. 198; May 10, 1985, p. 528.*

*   *   *

BROIDO, Ethel   1917-

PERSONAL: Born December 26, 1917, in New York, NY; daughter of Benjamin (a dentist) and Bertha Rubenstein; married Ephraim Broido, 1939 (divorced, 1954); children: Jonathan, Michal Broido Gurion. *Education:* Attended St. Martin's School of Art, London, 1940-41, 1944-45, Tel Aviv University, 1962-63, and New York

School of Interior Design, 1973-74. *Politics:* Liberal. *Religion:* Jewish.

ADDRESSES: Home and office—8 Bezalel St., Tel Aviv, Israel 64683.

CAREER: Am Oved Publishing Co., art director, 1950-55; U.S. Information Service, worked in publication department, 1956-57; El Al Israel Airlines, advertising manager, 1958-62; ZIM Shipping Lines, advertising manager, 1962-65; Gordon Gallery, Tel Aviv, Israel, cofounder, 1965, director, 1965-69; American-Israel Culture Foundation, New York City, director of Gallery of Israeli Art, 1969-72; Bloomingdale's, New York City, worked in interior design department, 1973-74; NBC News, Israel Office, administrator and translator in Tel Aviv and Herzlia, 1975-87; free-lance writer and translator, 1987—. Graphic designer and editor of publications for Histadruth, Israel's federation of labor.

WRITINGS:

(Translator) Moshe Gil, *A History of Palestine, 634-1099,* Cambridge University Press, 1992.

Author of film scripts for Israeli filmmakers, including Jewish Agency. Contributor of articles, translations, and reviews to periodicals.

WORK IN PROGRESS: Translating *Warsaw between the Wars,* by Israel Gutman, for Holocaust Memorial Museum, Washington, DC; translating personal memoirs of a Holocaust survivor, by A. Aviel.

*   *   *

BROOK, Elaine (Isabel) 1949-

PERSONAL: Born May 23, 1949, in London, England; daughter of Alec Oscar Turner (an experimental engineer) and Isabel Stanley (an artist); married Lhakpa Sherpa (a Himalayan guide), April 19, 1986. *Education:* Loughborough College of Education, certificate in education, 1971; Leicester University, certificate in ecology, 1974. *Religion:* Buddhist.

ADDRESSES: Home—Derbyshire, England. *Agent*—Jonathan Cape, 32 Bedford Sq., London WC1B 3EL, England.

CAREER: Primary school teacher in London, England, 1974-77; commercial artist in Calgary, Canada, 1977-80; mountain guide and freelance photojournalist in the United Kingdom and Nepal, 1980-85; freelance writer, 1985—; Himalayan Travel (a trekking agency), Buxton, England, 1987—. Also worked as a mountain guide for Fantasy Ridge Alpinism in Colorado. Sponsored trek to Mt. Everest base camp with Julie Donnelly to support

Guide Dogs for the Blind Association. Appeared in television film with Donnelly about communication between the sighted and the blind.

MEMBER: Royal Geographical Society (fellow), Tibetan Community in Britain.

WRITINGS:

The Wind Horse, Cape, 1986, Dodd, Mead, 1987.
Land of the Snow Lion, Dodd, Mead, 1987.

Contributor of articles to periodicals, including *Mountain* and *Prima.*

SIDELIGHTS: English author and adventurer Elaine Brook spent several years as a teacher and a commercial artist before leading expeditions to various mountain ranges. Her travels have taken her from Peru to Alaska, but she is best known for her climbing trips to the Himalayan mountains in Nepal and Tibet. Brook's first book, *The Wind Horse,* coauthored with Julie Donnelly, tells the story of how Brook guided Donnelly, a blind woman, up to the base camp on Mt. Everest. Her second, *Land of the Snow Lion,* recounts a previous journey on which she was the only woman in a group of male mountain climbers.

Donnelly described her first encounter with Brook for Shirley Flack in *Woman's Own:* "Elaine was going through some journals she'd kept from a trip to Nepal and said: 'Would you like to hear some?' I'm a great armchair traveler, so I was fascinated by the Himalayas. As she talked I really began to imagine myself traveling there. Those marvelous places, the people, came to life in my mind." Not long after that, Brook was helping Donnelly learn to climb at sites in the United Kingdom, so that she could accompany her to the Himalayas.

Their eventual excursion to Everest raised four thousand British pounds for an organization that trains guide dogs for the blind. The trip, however, not only produced a sense of accomplishment and money for charity, but gained Brook a husband. For it was on the climb that she and Donnelly chronicled in *The Wind Horse* that she was guided by Lhakpa Sherpa. As June Southworth put it in the *Daily Mail,* "He fell in love with her . . . when he realized she spoke fluent Nepalese and laughed at his jokes. She fell in love with him when she saw him carrying Julie on his back across slippery stepping stones through icy waters, murmuring his catchphrase: 'No problem.'" Brook further explained to Southworth that "unfortunately, it's the custom in his country for the girl to do the asking, and in ours it's traditionally down to the boy, so neither of us told the other we'd fallen in love. In the end, I just told him I was going back to England, and did he want to come?" The two were married in 1986, the same year that *The Wind Horse* was published in the United Kingdom.

Brook also told Southworth about the expedition that resulted in her second book, *Land of the Snow Lion.* It was her first excursion to the Himalayas, and she was the only woman with a group led by mountaineer Doug Scott. In the words of the *Daily Mail* reporter: "Yearning to see Tibet, she jumped at the chance, and promptly found herself in the foothills of a mountain called Shishapangma, with a bunch of male chauvinists who bickered constantly and forgot all the niceties of behaviour." Disgusted with her companions, Brook left the party, and wound up wandering in Tibet, where she met and lived with the natives. "She was investigated for spying, bitten by a rabid dog and beaten up in the Dalai Lama's Potala palace," elaborated Southworth.

Brook told *CA:* "Insight into Himalayan culture and Buddhist metaphysics means that much of my work involves a conscious shift in perspective between Western and Eastern viewpoints."

BIOGRAPHICAL/CRITICAL SOURCES:

PERIODICALS

Bristol Evening Post, March 23, 1987.
Daily Mail (London), March 17, 1987, p. 7.
Manchester Evening News, November 4, 1987.
Outside, August 1985, p. 13.
Woman's Own, January 10, 1986, pp. 51-52.

*   *   *

BROWN, Lloyd L(ouis)   1913-

PERSONAL: Born 1913, in St. Paul, MN; married in 1937; two children.

ADDRESSES: Home—156-20 Riverside Drive West, Apartment 16-I, New York, NY 10032.

CAREER: Writer. *Military service:* U.S. Air Force, 1942-45; became staff sergeant.

WRITINGS:

Iron City (novel), Masses and Mainstream, 1951.
(With Paul Robeson) *Here I Stand,* Othello Associates, 1958, reissued with preface by Brown, Beacon Press, 1988.

Also author of pamphlets, including *Young Workers in Action: Story of the South River Strike,* Youth Publishers, 1932; *The Conspiracy against Free Elections* (unsigned), Pittsburgh Civil Rights Committee, 1941; *Lift Every Voice for Paul Robeson,* Freedom Association, 1951; *Stand Up for Freedom: The Negro People vs. the Smith Act,* New Century Publishers, 1952; and *Paul Robeson Rediscovered,* American Institute for Marxist Studies, 1976. Con-

tributor of articles and reviews to *New Masses,* short stories and criticism to *Masses and Mainstream,* and nonfiction to *Freedomways.*

Iron City has been translated into German, Japanese, Chinese, Polish, and several other languages.

BIOGRAPHICAL/CRITICAL SOURCES:

PERIODICALS

Phylon, Volume 12, 1951.

*   *   *

BROWN, Peter Harry   1939-

PERSONAL: Born November 16, 1939, in Abilene, TX; son of Frances and Jervis Brown; married 1976; wife's name, Pamela A. *Education:* Attended the University of Arizona, Southern Methodist University, and the University of California, Los Angeles.

ADDRESSES: Home and office—1414 South Greenfield Ave., No. 110, Los Angeles, CA 90025. *Agent*— International Creative Management, 40 West Fifty-seventh St., New York, NY 10019.

CAREER: Writer. *Dallas Morning News, San Diego Union,* and Gannett Newspapers, investigative crime reporter, 1964-76; *Los Angeles Times* and *Washington Post,* entertainment reporter, 1977-88. *Military service:* Served in intelligence division of California Air National Guard.

AWARDS, HONORS: Heywood Broun Award for Investigative Reporting, 1971; California Associated Press Award for Enterprise Reporting, 1972; New Mexico-Colorado Award for Feature Writing, 1976; Florida Newspaper Publisher's Award for Spot News Reporting, 1978; Gannett Award for Feature Writing, 1978.

WRITINGS:

(With Zelda Cini and Bob Crane) *Hollywood: Land and Legend,* Arlington House, 1980.
The Real Oscar: Behind the Academy Awards, Crown, 1982.
(With Pamela Ann Brown) *The MGM Girls: Behind the Velvet Curtain,* St. Martin's, 1983.
Such Devoted Sisters: Those Fabulous Gabors, St. Martin's, 1985.
Kim Novak: Reluctant Goddess, St. Martin's, 1986.
(With Jim Pinkston) *Oscar Dearest: Six Decades of Scandal, Politics and Greed behind Hollywood's Academy Awards, 1927-1986,* Harper, 1987.
(With Patte B. Barham) *Marilyn: The Last Take,* Dutton, 1992.

Contributor to periodicals, including *Parade, US Magazine, TV Guide, Los Angeles Magazine, Redbook, Life, International Herald-Tribune, London Times,* and *People.*

WORK IN PROGRESS: Howard Hughes: The Untold Story, "the first personal history ever written on one of the twentieth century's most puzzling geniuses," with Pat H. Broeske.

SIDELIGHTS: Author Peter Harry Brown has written both biographies of actors and studies of the Academy Awards. Penned with Jim Pinkston, *Oscar Dearest: Six Decades of Scandal, Politics and Greed behind Hollywood's Academy Awards, 1927-1986* is an unauthorized, mostly critical history of the Academy Awards, also known as the Oscars, which are presented annually by the Academy of Motion Picture Arts and Sciences for notable film work. Reviewing *Oscar Dearest* in the *Los Angeles Times Book Review,* Hal Kanter noted: "Brown and Pinkston display no effort to question facts or anecdotes as they blithely smirk and sneer at every branch of the Academy." Kanter continued: "In fairness, Brown and Pinkston cannot be accused of boring a reader; their book is generously illustrated, and their detailed captions are often amusing." According *Village Voice* contributor Brett Harvey, *Oscar Dearest* "is most fun about details like clothes . . . and feuds."

In *Marilyn: The Last Take,* Brown and his coauthor Patte B. Barham take as their subject the American actor Marilyn Monroe, who appeared in a number of popular films before her early 1962 death, which is usually attributed to suicide. *Los Angeles Times Book Review* contributor John Rechy noted: "Where *The Last Take* is strongest is in its reporting of studio politics. With journalistic clarity, Peter Harry Brown and Patte B. Barham convincingly link the decision to fire Marilyn from her last film [the unfinished *Something's Got to Give*] with the financial disaster 20th Century-Fox faced." Stephanie Gutmann, writing in *National Review,* judged the book "a sophisticated, unsentimental account of motivations and behavior," and *Variety* contributor Alec Foege called *The Last Take* "easily one of the most exhaustive studies ever devoted to the tragic star."

Brown told *CA:* "With the excellent works of [American biographer] James Spada and Scott Berg, the art of the show business biography has entered a new phase—gone are the days when you could string together a series of salacious anecdotes and call it biography. Now, you have to tell a complete story—a three dimensional portrait. In fact, many of the best-selling biographies of the 1970s and 1980s will be rewritten by 'revisionist authors' who will take probing looks at the fact manipulation that began in the late 1970s. Readers now demand sources because the tabloidization of journalism has made books one of the few places readers can go for objective reporting."

BIOGRAPHICAL/CRITICAL SOURCES:

PERIODICALS

Los Angeles Times Book Review, February 24, 1985, p. 9; March 29, 1987, p. 3, 9; October 18, 1992, p. 8.
National Review, October 5, 1992, p. 68.
New York Times Book Review, March 29, 1987, p. 23.
Variety, September 7, 1992, p. 67.
Village Voice, March 31, 1987, p. 51.
Washington Post Book World, March 29, 1987, p. 12; August 16, 1992, p. 13.

*   *   *

BUFORD, Bill 1954-

PERSONAL: Born William Holmes Buford, October 6, 1954, in Baton Rouge, LA; son of William H. (a physicist) and Helen (Shiel) Buford; married Alicja Kobiernicka, 1991. *Education:* University of California, Berkeley, B.A., 1977; King's College, Cambridge, M.A., 1979.

ADDRESSES: Home—England. *Office*—Granta Publications Ltd., 2-3 Hanover Yard, Noel Road, Cambridge N1 8BE, England.

CAREER: Granta magazine, editor, 1979—; chair of Granta Publications.

WRITINGS:

NONFICTION

Among the Thugs: The Experience and the Seduction of Crowd Violence, Secker & Warburg, 1991, Norton, 1992.

EDITOR OF GRANTA MAGAZINE ISSUES PUBLISHED IN BOOK FORM BY VIKING

The End of the English Novel, 1981.
Best of Young British Novelists, 1983.
Dirty Realism, 1983.
Greetings from Prague, 1984.
Travel Writing, 1984.
Richard Ford—The Womanizer, 1992.
Biography, 1993.
Krauts!, 1993.
The Best of Young British Novelists II, 1993.

SIDELIGHTS: Although born in the United States, Bill Buford has lived in England since 1977. After receiving a master's degree from King's College, Cambridge, he became editor of *Granta* magazine, one of England's most prestigious literary reviews, and has since become chair of Granta Publications. Under Buford's editorship, several issues of *Granta* have been published in book form, testimony to the review's influence as a showcase for the best in contemporary literature and criticism. Representative titles include two issues featuring selections from some of England's best new novelists, including authors William Boyd, Martin Amis, Salman Rushdie, and Maggie Gee. Another issue-turned-book is *Dirty Realism,* which showcases some of the new writing talent in the U.S. by authors Jayne Anne Phillips, Raymond Carver, Tobias Wolff, Bobbie Ann Mason, and others. Taken together, these volumes serve as an anthology documenting significant trends in contemporary literature.

Buford's ability to identify these trends has depended in part on his immersion into contemporary English culture. One day in the mid-1980s, he saw firsthand a disturbing side to that culture: the wanton violence perpetrated by mobs of soccer fans. These "lads," as they call themselves (they are often dubbed in the press as "thugs" or "hooligans"), use professional soccer matches as a pretext for drunken rampages leading not just to property damage but often to death. Buford found himself fascinated by the violence. He became an insider, ingratiating himself with such leading hooligans as Steamin' Sammy, Daft Donald, and Barmie Bernie. Buford travelled with the lads to soccer venues throughout Britain and Europe. *Among the Thugs: The Experience and Seduction of Crowd Violence* records his experiences.

In the *Washington Post Book World,* Jonathan Yardley praised *Among the Thugs* for being "vivid and precise" in its descriptions of the denizens of this bizarre world and the peculiar forms of violence they inflict. (Buford confesses that he took part in some milder forms of that violence and attests to the exhilaration such mob behavior can induce.) Similarly, Richard Eder in the *Los Angeles Times Book Review* found the book "vividly, comically and horrifyingly reported" and marked by "powerful setpieces." In *Among the Thugs,* however, Buford does not just report; he tries to probe the psychology that lies behind the violence, "the moment when many, many different people cease being many, many different people and become . . . a crowd." He concludes that the rioters are not the poor and underprivileged, lodging a protest against those who have more; as he states in the book, they come, rather, from "a highly mannered suburban society stripped of culture and sophistication and living only for its affectations: a bloated code of maleness, an exaggerated, embarrassing patriotism, a violent nationalism, an array of bankrupt anti-social habits. This bored, empty, decadent generation . . . uses violence to wake itself up."

The critics extended *Among the Thugs* a cordial reception. Although Yardley found the book "imperfect," he concluded: "[Buford's] best is very good: animated, witty and so pungent you can taste the stale lager and smell the fetid

air." And in the *New York Times Book Review,* Clancy Sigal called *Among the Thugs* "an important, perhaps prophetic book . . . both exciting and sad at the core."

BIOGRAPHICAL/CRITICAL SOURCES:

BOOKS

Buford, Bill, *Among the Thugs: The Experience and the Seduction of Crowd Violence,* Norton, 1992.

PERIODICALS

Los Angeles Times Book Review, June 14, 1992, p. 3.
New York Times Book Review, June 7, 1992, p. 9.
Times (London), November 2, 1991, p. 48.
Times Literary Supplement, February 13, 1981, p. 170; April 15, 1983; August 12, 1983.
Washington Post Book World, May 31, 1992, p. 3.

*   *   *

BUFORD, William Holmes
See BUFORD, Bill

*   *   *

BULMER-THOMAS, Ivor   1905-1993

OBITUARY NOTICE—See index for *CA* sketch: Born November 30, 1905, in Cwmbran, Monmouthshire, England; died October 7, 1993. Government official and writer. Bulmer-Thomas led a varied career that included editorships and journalistic stints in the 1930s, membership in Parliament during the 1940s, membership in the House of Laity of the Church Assembly beginning in the 1950s, and authorship of numerous books, beginning with the biography *Our Lord Birkenhead: An Oxford Appreciation* in 1930. Bulmer-Thomas earned both his bachelor's and master's degrees from Oxford University and worked for the London *Times* and the London *News Chronicle* before serving in the British Army during World War II. He was elected to Parliament in 1942, rising to the position of Under-Secretary to the Ministry of Civil Aviation. By the early 1950s he had turned his attention to the church, focusing in particular on preserving religious buildings. He founded and later served as honorary director of the Friends of Friendless Churches and chaired the Ancient Monuments Society. He published more than ten books throughout his career, including *Top Sawyer: A Biography of David Davies of Llandinam* in 1938, *Warfare by Words* in 1942, *East Shefford Church* in 1978, and *Dilysia: A Threnody* in 1987.

OBITUARIES AND OTHER SOURCES:

BOOKS

Who's Who, 146th edition, St. Martin's, 1994, p. 269.

PERIODICALS

Times (London), October 8, 1993, p. 21.

* * *

BURGESS, Anthony
See WILSON, John (Anthony) Burgess

* * *

BURGESS, Robert J(ohn) 1961-

PERSONAL: Born August 4, 1961, in Metairie, LA; son of John Jacob (an executive in the paper industry) and Doris (a homemaker; maiden name, Keating) Burgess. *Education:* University of Denver, B.S.B.A. (summa cum laude), 1983; Loyola University of Chicago, M.B.A. (with honors), 1984. *Politics:* Republican. *Religion:* Roman Catholic. *Avocational Interests:* Card collecting, sports, rock music.

ADDRESSES: Home and office—Marketing Advocates, Inc., 6702 South Ivy Way, Suite B1, Englewood, CO 80112. *Agent*—Peter Miller, PMA Literary and Film Management, Inc., 220 West 19th St., Suite 501, New York, NY 10011.

CAREER: United Bank of Colorado, Denver, analyst, 1984-85; Coors Brewing, Golden, CO, senior analyst, 1985-88; U.S. West Telecommunications, Englewood, CO, in marketing, 1988-91; Marketing Advocates, Inc., Englewood, founder, 1990, president, 1991—. Adjunct faculty member, University of Denver and University of Colorado at Denver, both 1991—. South Metropolitan Denver Chamber of Commerce, small business counselor, 1992—; Denver Entrepreneurship Academy, member of board of directors, small business counselor, 1992—.

MEMBER: American Marketing Association (past president of Colorado chapter), Market Research Association.

WRITINGS:

Silver Bullets: A Soldier's Story of How Coors Bombed the Beer Wars, St. Martin's, 1993.

Author of "Quick Consult," a monthly column, *Denver Business Journal,* 1993.

WORK IN PROGRESS: Even a Fool Can See, a novel; research for a book on developing entrepreneurial enterprises in the 1990s.

BURKE, Kenneth (Duva) 1897-1993

OBITUARY NOTICE—See index for *CA* sketch: Born May 5, 1897, in Pittsburgh, PA; died of heart failure, November 19, 1993, in Andover, NJ. Literary critic, philosopher, and writer. Burke was well known in literary circles for his theories on language and literature. He was considered a prominent force in the New Criticism movement—a critical approach to literature that focuses on the text itself and excludes extrinsic information—and also was recognized for originating "dramatism," a school of thought which, in part, emphasizes the connection between language and moral action. Leading a varied career, Burke worked as music critic for *Dial* and *Nation* magazines during the 1920s and 1930s, then, beginning in the late 1930s, turned to serving in educational posts at several institutions, such as the University of Chicago, as well as Princeton, Harvard, and Wesleyan universities. During the course of his career, he recorded his insights into language and rhetoric in numerous books, including *The Philosophy of Literary Form: Studies in Symbolic Action; A Rhetoric of Motives; Language as Symbolic Action: Essays on Life, Literature, and Method; Dramatism and Development;* and *On Symbols and Society.* He translated works of the German writers Thomas Mann and Emil Ludwig and also penned poems, short stories, and critical essays. Among the numerous honors he garnered during his lifetime were the 1981 National Medal for Literature and the 1984 Elmer Holmes Bobst Award.

OBITUARIES AND OTHER SOURCES:

BOOKS

The International Who's Who, 57th edition, Europa, 1993, p. 231.

PERIODICALS

New York Times, November 21, 1993, p. 48.
Washington Post, November 23, 1993, p. E5.

* * *

BURKE, Richard E. 1953-

PERSONAL: Born February 25, 1953, in Buffalo, NY; son of Robert E. and Anne (a writer and producer) Burke. *Education:* Georgetown University, B.S., 1975, B.A., 1975.

ADDRESSES: Office—American Literary Products, Inc., Suite 143, 8721 Santa Monica Blvd., West Hollywood, CA 90069. *Agent*—John Hawkins, John Hawkins and Associates, 71 West Twenty-third St., Suite 160, New York, NY 10010.

CAREER: Administrative assistant/chief of staff for U.S. Senator Edward Kennedy, Washington, D.C., 1971-81.

American Electro Products (electronics), senior vice president for marketing and director of human resources; Congress Video Group, chair and CEO; National Entertainment Group (producer and distributor of video cassettes), president; affiliated with *The European Gourmet: Guide to Best Restaurants in Europe.* On board of trustees, Martha Graham Dance Company.

WRITINGS:

(With William Hoffer and Marilyn Hoffer) *The Senator: My Ten Years with Ted Kennedy,* St. Martin's, 1992.

WORK IN PROGRESS: Writing a second book, to be published in 1994.

SIDELIGHTS: Richard E. Burke has worked for Democratic senator and controversial public figure Edward "Ted" Kennedy for ten years, and, in 1978, rose to the position of the senator's chief of staff. Burke has written an expose of the politician's performance both in office and behind the scenes. Reviewing *The Senator: My Ten Years with Ted Kennedy* for the *Los Angeles Times Book Review,* Al Raksin noted Burke's seeming conviction that "Kennedy failed his country" because of episodes involving alcohol and young women, but also noted the lack of bitterness that Burke evinces toward his subject. Though Burke expresses disappointment in the senator's failure to uphold the ideals of his position, the work portrays the author himself as a young man attempting to play along with his employer's exploits. "Whether this book creates yet another [scandal for Ted Kennedy] will depend on your view of a senator's primary job," Raksin concluded.

Burke told *CA:* "The story was my life and how a young man can be engulfed in the 'glamour and fast life of Washington' and the tremendous influence a powerful man like Kennedy can have on others. It was also a story Americans need to know—what you see is not always what is reality."

BIOGRAPHICAL/CRITICAL SOURCES:

PERIODICALS

Los Angeles Times Book Review, October 25, 1992, p. 6.

*   *   *

BUTLER, Samuel   1835-1902

PERSONAL: Born December 4, 1835, in Nottinghamshire, England; died of pernicious anemia, June 18, 1902, in London, England; son of Thomas (a cleric and headmaster) and Fanny (Worsley) Butler. *Education:* St. John's College, Cambridge, first-class degree in classics, 1858.

CAREER: English author and painter. Worked in London as an amateur lay assistant to a cleric for a time following graduation. Owned and operated a sheep run in New Zealand, 1859-64. Director of a Canadian tanning-extract company, Montreal, 1870s. Had several paintings exhibited at the Royal Academy in London.

WRITINGS:

A First Year in Canterbury Settlement, Longmans, Green, 1863, Dutton, 1915.
The Evidence for the Resurrection of Jesus Christ, as Given by the Four Evangelists, Critically Examined (published anonymously), Williams & Norgate, 1865.
Erewhon; or, Over the Range (published anonymously), Truebner, 1872, revised edition, 1872, published under own name, 1873, revised edition, Richards, 1901, Dutton, 1907.
The Fair Haven: A Work in Defence of the Miraculous Element in Our Lord's Ministry upon Earth, Both as Against Rationalistic Impugners and Certain Orthodox Defenders, by the Late J. P. Owen, Edited by W. B. Owen, with a Memoir of the Author (published anonymously), Truebner, 1873, Kennerly, 1914.
Life and Habit: An Essay After a Completer View of Evolution, Truebner, 1878, Dutton, 1910.
Evolution, Old and New; or, The Theories of Buffon, Dr. Erasmus Darwin, and Lamarck, as Compared with That of Mr. Charles Darwin, Cassion, 1879.
Unconscious Memory: A Comparison between the Theory of Dr. Ewald Hering, Professor of Physiology at Prague, and the Philosophy of the Unconscious of Dr. Edward von Hartmann; with Translations from These Authors, Bogue, 1880, Dutton, 1910.
Alps and Sanctuaries of Piedmont and the Canton Ticino, Bogue, 1882, Dutton, 1913.
Selections from Previous Works, with Remarks on Mr. G. J. Romanes' "Mental Evolution in Animals," and a Psalm of Montreal, Truebner, 1884.
(With Henry Festing Jones) *Gavottes, Minuets, Fugues, and Other Short Pieces for the Piano,* Novello, 1885.
Luck or Cunning as the Main Means of Organic Modification? An Attempt to Throw Additional Light upon the Late Mr. Charles Darwin's Theory of Natural Selection, Fifield, 1886.
Ex Voto: An Account of the Sacro Monte or New Jerusalem at Varallo-Sesia, with Some Notice of Tabachetti's Remaining Work at the Sanctuary of Crea, Truebner, 1888, Longmans, Green, 1890.
(With Jones) *Narcissus: A Cantata in the Handelian Form,* Weekes, 1888.
A Lecture on the Humour of Homer, January 30th 1892; Reprinted with a Preface and Additional Matter from the "Eagle," Metcalfe, 1892.
On the Trapanese Origin of the "Odyssey," Metcalfe, 1893.

The Life and Letters of Dr. Samuel Butler, Headmaster of Shrewsbury School 1798-1836, and Afterwards Bishop of Lichfield, two volumes, Murray, 1896, one volume, Dutton, 1924.

The Authoress of the "Odyssey," Where and When She Wrote, Who She Was, the Use She Made of the "Iliad," and How the Poem Grew under Her Hands, Longmans, Green, 1897, Dutton, 1922.

(Translator) *The Iliad of Homer, Rendered into English Prose,* Longmans, Green, 1898, Dutton, 1921.

Shakespeare's Sonnets Reconsidered, and in Part Rearranged; With Introductory Chapters, Notes, and a Reprint of the Original 1609 Edition, Longmans, Green, 1899.

(Translator) *The Odyssey, Rendered into English Prose,* Longmans, Green, 1900, Dutton, 1920.

Erewhon Revisited Twenty Years Later, Both by the Original Discoverer of the Country and by his Son, Richards, 1901, Dutton, 1910.

The Way of All Flesh, edited by R. A. Streatfeild, Richards, 1903, Dutton, 1910.

Essays on Life, Art and Science, edited by Streatfeild, Richards, 1904.

(With Jones) *Ulysses: An Oratorio,* Weekes, 1904.

God the Known and God the Unknown, edited by Streatfeild, Fifield, 1909, Yale University Press, 1917.

The Note-Books of Samuel Butler: Selections, edited by Jones, Fifield, 1912, Kennerly, 1913.

The Collected Works of Samuel Butler (definitive edition), twenty volumes, edited by Jones and A. T. Bartholomew, Cape, 1923-26, Dutton, 1925.

Butleriana, edited by Bartholomew, Nonesuch, 1932.

Further Extracts from the Note-Books of Samuel Butler, edited by Bartholomew, Cape, 1934.

Samuel Butler's Notebooks: Selections, edited by Geoffrey Keynes and Brian Hill, Dutton, 1951.

LETTERS

Samuel Butler and E. M. A. Savage, Letters 1871-1885, edited by Keynes and Hill, Cape, 1935.

The Family Letters of Samuel Butler (1841-1886), edited by Arnold Silver, Stanford University Press, 1962.

The Correspondence of Samuel Butler with His Sister May, edited by Daniel F. Howard, University of California Press, 1962.

OTHER

Also contributor of articles, letters, and poems to periodicals, including *Eagle, Press* (New Zealand), *Universal Review, Examiner,* and *New Quarterly Review.*

Butler's works are housed in the Samuel Butler Collection at St. John's College, Cambridge, the Carol A. Wilson Collection of Butler manuscripts at the Chapin Library at Williams College, Williamston, MA, and at the British Museum.

SIDELIGHTS: Victorian novelist and essayist Samuel Butler is now recognized as one of the important literary figures of the period, but he was virtually ignored by the public and critics until after his death, and had to pay for the publication of most of his works himself. He experienced a small measure of success with his satiric fantasies *Erewhon* and *Erewhon Revisited,* but it was not until his scathing attack on the Victorian family *The Way of All Flesh* was published posthumously that Butler was lionized by author George Bernard Shaw and others. In addition to his critically acclaimed novels, Butler also penned many works on evolution—which he supported, but disagreed with pioneering evolutionist Charles Darwin on the theory of natural selection—and wrote essays on art and literature.

Butler was born on December 4, 1835, in Nottinghamshire, England. His father was a cleric, as was his grandfather, who was the bishop of Lichfield in addition to having been headmaster of Shrewsbury School. Butler's childhood was harsh and repressive, much as that of character Ernest Pontifex in *The Way of All Flesh.* Butler did, however, have the opportunity to go abroad to Italy on family vacations as a boy. Because his father wished him to be a cleric also, Butler eventually enrolled at St. John's College, Cambridge, where he obtained a degree in classics.

Butler began writing while still in college, and he had several pieces published in his college journal, the *Eagle.* His early topics included the art of writing and his travels in Europe during his vacations. But while studying for the clergy, Butler started to have many religious doubts. Nevertheless, he still tried to bend to his father's will for a time, apprenticing himself as a lay assistant to a cleric who ministered to the poor in London. Eventually, however, Butler stood up to his father. They argued for some time over another suitable career for Butler; then his father provided enough money for him to emigrate to New Zealand and buy a sheep run.

On the ship to New Zealand, Butler committed a symbolic act of defiance against his pious family—he read Edward Gibbon's *History of the Decline and Fall of the Roman Empire,* a work considered scandalous by most Victorians. Once in New Zealand, Butler did well as a sheep rancher, but he also found time to write. His most significant effort proved to be his letters about life in New Zealand, which his father had published with Butler's permission as *A First Year in Canterbury Settlement* in 1863. As Lee E. Holt explained in the *Dictionary of Literary Biography,* the volume was "designed in part as a 'how-to' manual to interest would-be emigrants," and "vividly narrates the events of the three-month voyage from England, telling the reader how to equip himself for such a trip; describes the towns of Lyttleton and Christchurch; and, with considerable attention to financial details, explains how to go about acquiring a sheep run. It gives an account of explorations that eventually led Butler to the discovery of a mountain and a pass later named for him." Butler also contributed to newspapers in New Zealand, notably several articles on evolution. The first of these, supporting and defending the theories of Charles Darwin, came to the attention of the evolutionist himself, beginning a friendship between the two men which was not to last.

When Butler had almost doubled the capital his father had given him for the sheep run, he returned to London. But rather than concentrate on his writing, Butler attempted to begin a career as an artist. He studied painting, and had several pictures exhibited at London's Royal Academy, but after thirteen years concluded that he would never become a truly great artist and gave it up. Some of his paintings, however, are still known today, such as *Family Prayers,* which he completed in 1864.

Though focusing on art, Butler did continue to write. In 1865 he published, at his own expense, a treatise attacking the historical accuracy of the Biblical accounts of Jesus' crucifixion on the basis that the descriptions of this event in the four Gospels did not match. After this, he worked on the satirical fantasy *Erewhon.* At about the same time, he became close friends with one of his fellow art students, Eliza Mary Ann Savage, who encouraged him in his writing. Savage believed that Butler had it within him to create truly great novels, and the correspondence between the two of them lasted until her death in 1885. Savage read and commented upon all of Butler's works, including *Erewhon.* In this novel, a nameless protagonist (later called Higgs in the sequel) explores a mountain pass in New Zealand only to enter upon a strange kingdom in which machines are banned, the sick are punished, and criminals are treated by "straighteners" until they are cured of their tendency toward wrongdoing. Many cherished Victorian institutions, including Christianity, are satirized along the way. *Erewhon* was first published anonymously in 1872, though in later editions Butler attached his name to the work. It was the most popular book he published in his lifetime.

Arthur Waugh, in his book *Tradition and Change: Studies in Contemporary Literature,* declared that *Erewhon* "is a comprehensive satire of Victorian England, drawing out the absurdities of the time to their logical conclusion. . . . But it was a creative satire, not a destructive. It was designed to help the age to rehabilitate itself by getting into honest relations with its own motives and purposes. It was, above all things, the satire of a man who has ideals, and who desires to instil those ideals into his fellow-men; but who, at the same time, having a natural aversion from

the preaching business, finds it more congenial to drive his meaning home through an undercurrent of humorous exaggeration." Edmund Wilson, writing in the *New Republic,* was a shade more ambiguous in his praise, but nevertheless put Butler in good company, claiming that *Erewhon* "is not a production which one can compare to 'Candide' or 'Gulliver's Travels': it is not the definite expression of a satiric point of view based on mature experience, it is simply the brilliant first book of a young man. It does not pretend either to the logic of [Jonathan] Swift or the singleness of intention of Voltaire: it is rather merely a device for uniting an assortment of satirical ideas—in some cases, reductions to absurdity of English ideas and institutions; in others, whimsically suggested improvements on them." Holt, however, minced no words in calling *Erewhon* "probably the most effective book of its kind in English literature since [Jonathan] Swift's *Gulliver's Travels.*"

Butler's next satiric project was *The Fair Haven: A Work in Defence of the Miraculous Element in Our Lord's Ministry upon Earth, Both as Against Rationalistic Impugners and Certain Orthodox Defenders, by the Late J. P. Owen, Edited by W. B. Owen, with a Memoir of the Author.* A complex novel, *The Fair Haven* included both a contrived defense of the inconsistencies of the New Testament by the fictional J. P. Owen, and an account of his crisis of faith and eventual collapse into insanity and death narrated by his brother. As is often the case with good satire, *The Fair Haven* fooled some of its readers—those who believed and supported a more traditional approach to Christianity—into thinking it was a legitimate defense of traditional faith. Butler gleefully remedied this in the preface to later editions of the work.

After *Fair Haven,* Butler turned his attention to evolution. Since his years in New Zealand, Butler had come to disagree with Darwin about the process of natural selection, believing that evolution was too important to be left to the chance that natural selection implied. Instead Butler felt that evolution was guided by unconscious memory and the desire to improve, passed down from organism to organism, including man. "For example," explained Holt, "accomplishments which we have in common with our remotest ancestors, such as digestion, are in us most unconscious and most beyond our control; whereas more recent acquisitions such as speech, the arts and sciences, and the upright position are much more within our control." Butler continued to explore this theme in works such as *Life and Habit: An Essay after a Completer View of Evolution, Evolution, Old and New; or, The Theories of Buffon, Dr. Erasmus Darwin, and Lamarck, as Compared with That of Mr. Charles Darwin,* and *Unconscious Memory: A Comparison between the Theory of Dr. Ewald Hering, Professor of Physiology at Prague, and the Philosophy of the Uncon-*

scious of Dr. Edward von Hartmann; With Translations from These Authors. Among other claims Butler made in these books was the one that Charles Darwin had been given too much credit for originality in his research on evolution, and that he had gotten many of his ideas from previous writers. In *Luck or Cunning as the Main Means of Organic Modification? An Attempt to Throw Additional Light upon the Late Mr. Charles Darwin's Theory of Natural Selection,* Butler is particularly sharp in his criticism of his fellow evolutionist.

During the 1880s and 1890s, Butler turned his hand toward the criticism of art and literature. In matters of art, Butler preferred the more primitive sculptors and painters, such as Tabachetti, as opposed to what he termed "high-falutin'" artists such as Michelangelo, and put forth his ideas on the subject in books such as *Ex Voto: An Account of the Sacro Monte or New Jerusalem at Varallo-Sesia, with Some Notice of Tabachetti's Remaining Work at the Sanctuary of Crea.* In literature, Butler came up with some interesting theories. One such was that the ancient Greek epic poem the *Odyssey* was not written by a man named Homer but rather by a woman. In *The Authoress of the "Odyssey," Where and When She Wrote, Who She Was, the Use She Made of the "Iliad," and How the Poem Grew under Her Hands,* he points to the domestic detail and dominance of female characters as evidence. Butler also translated both the *Iliad* and the *Odyssey* into more simple English than previous translators had used. Another of Butler's literary theories was that William Shakespeare's sonnets had been written to a lower-class, homosexual lover—this view was put forth in Butler's *Shakespeare's Sonnets Reconsidered, and in Part Rearranged; With Introductory Chapters, Notes, and a Reprint of the Original 1609 Edition.* During this period, Butler dabbled in music as well, composing with his friend and eventual biographer Henry Festing Jones after the manner of Handel, who had long been Butler's favorite composer.

Butler also issued *Erewhon Revisited.* In this sequel, the narrator Higgs returns to *Erewhon* to find that he has a son by a love affair he had had there, and that the Erewhonians now have a new religion, based on his seemingly miraculous escape by balloon twenty years earlier. Again, Butler's primary target is traditional Christian belief, as G. D. H. Cole explains in his biography, *Samuel Butler:* "The ascent of the Sun-Child [Higgs] into heaven and the subsequent growth of the legend of his divinity are an open and direct satire on the entire supernatural element in the Christian religion, an attempt to show, logically, how the beliefs embodied in it could have developed without any real foundation, and how vested interests could have grown up round them, committed to uphold their influence by all means. This, however well done, could not be quite such fun as the sheer irresponsibility of

the paradoxes of the earlier book." Raymond Chapman, in his *Victorian Debate: English Literature and Society, 1832-1901,* called *Erewhon Revisited* "a slighter work [than *Erewhon*] out of a weary mind." He further complained that "the new parody of Christianity is dreary."

Erewhon Revisited was the last of Butler's works to be published during his lifetime. He died of pernicious anemia in 1902. Among his papers he left instructions for the publication of *The Way of All Flesh,* a novel he had begun shortly after finishing *Erewhon.* He did not want it published until after all of his siblings had died, fearing it would hurt them, dealing as it did with their family. But his instructions were not followed, and *The Way of All Flesh* saw print in 1903. This novel, the most famous of Butler's works, chronicles three generations of the Pontifex family, and, for the childhood of Ernest Pontifex at least, closely follows the history of the Butler family. Ernest is severely repressed while growing up, and is beaten for such horrible offenses as saying "tum" instead of "come" at the age of eight. Chapman observed of it: "Not objective enough to be pure fiction, too fictional to be documentary, *The Way of All Flesh* still has a great deal to say about Victorian society. Butler attacks his age where it felt most confident—or perhaps was most stoutly defending its anxiety. He strikes at the middle-class values, the axioms of respectability. At a period when satire was a rare literary form, though self-criticism was increasing, he combines the two and batters away at the walls which are bastions for the majority but prisons for him." Wilson commented on the autobiographical nature of the work, saying that Butler "grew up in the narrowest, the most snobbish, the most bigoted and the most ungracious atmosphere which the Protestant nineteenth century produced. He rebelled against it and broke away from it, and he damned it forever in his masterpiece 'The Way of All Flesh', which is likely to survive as one of the classical accounts of how hateful life could become when the successful English middle class mixed avarice with religion." Similarly, George Bernard Shaw announced in the *Saturday Review* that Butler's father "was a genial old gaffer out of doors but at home was tyrant, judge, jury, and executioner all in one. A hydrogen bomb could not have blasted his reputation more devastatingly after his death than his dutiful son did with his novel." *The Way of All Flesh* is still popular; as late as 1962 William Maxwell proclaimed in the *New Yorker* that "if the house caught on fire, the Victorian novel I would rescue from the flames would be not 'Vanity Fair' or 'Bleak House' but Samuel Butler's 'The Way of All Flesh.' It is read, I believe, mostly by the young, bent on making out a case against their elders, but Butler was fifty when he stopped working on it, and no reader much under that age is likely to appreciate the full beauty of its horrors, which are the horrors not of the Gothic novel but of family life. Every contemporary novelist with a developed sense of irony is probably in some measure, directly or indirectly, through [George Bernard] Shaw and Arnold Bennett and E. M. Forster and D. H. Lawrence, indebted to Butler."

BIOGRAPHICAL/CRITICAL SOURCES:

BOOKS

Bekker, Willem G., *An Historical and Critical Review of Samuel Butler's Literary Works,* Nijgh & Van Ditmar's, 1925.

Cannan, Gilbert, *Samuel Butler: A Critical Study,* Folcroft Library Editions, 1915.

Chapman, Raymond, *The Victorian Debate: English Literature and Society, 1832-1901,* Basic Books, 1968.

Cole, G. D. H., *Samuel Butler,* revised edition, Longmans, Green, 1961.

Dictionary of Literary Biography, Gale, Volume 18: *Victorian Novelists After 1885,* 1983, Volume 57: *Victorian Prose Writers After 1867,* 1987.

Farrington, Benjamin, *Samuel Butler and the Odyssey,* Cape, 1929.

Fort, Joseph, *Samuel Butler, l'escrivain: Etude d'un style,* J. Biere, 1935.

Garnett, R. S., *Samuel Butler and His Family Relations,* Dutton, 1926.

Greenacre, Phyllis, *The Quest for the Father,* International Universities Press, 1963.

Harkness, Stanley, *The Career of Samuel Butler (1835-1902): A Bibliography,* Burt Franklin, 1955.

Harris, John F., *Samuel Butler, Author of "Erewhon": The Man and His Work,* Folcroft Library Editions, 1973.

Holt, Lee E., *Samuel Butler,* revised edition, Twayne, 1989.

Hoppe, A. J., *A Bibliography of the Writings of Samuel Butler,* Bookman, 1925.

Howard, Daniel F., *Victorian Fiction: A Second Guide to Research,* Modern Language Association, 1978.

Jeffers, Thomas L., *Samuel Butler Revalued,* Pennsylvania State University Press, 1981.

Joad, C. E. M., *Samuel Butler,* Parsons, 1924, Small, Maynard, 1925.

Jones, Henry Festing, and A. T. Bartholomew, *The Samuel Butler Collection at Saint John's College, Cambridge,* W. Heffer, 1921.

Jones, Joseph, *The Cradle of Erewhon,* University of Texas Press, 1959.

Meissner, Paul, *Samuel Butler, der Juengerer,* Tauchnitz, 1931.

Muggeridge, Malcolm, *Earnest Atheist: A Study of Samuel Butler,* Putnam, 1936.

Norrman, Ralf, *Samuel Butler and the Meaning of Chiasmus,* Macmillan, 1986.

Pestalozzi, Gerold, *Samuel Butler der Juengerer Versuch einer Darstellung seiner Gedankenwelt,* Universitaet Zuerich, 1914.

Raby, Peter, *The Life of Samuel Butler,* Hogarth, 1990.

Rattray, Robert F., *A Chronicle and an Introduction: Samuel Butler,* Duckworth, 1935.

Sinclair, May, *A Defence of Idealism,* Macmillan, 1917.

Stillman, Clara G., *Samuel Butler: A Mid-Victorian Modern,* Viking, 1932.

Stoff, Rudolf, *Die Philosophie des Organischen bei Samuel Butler,* Phaedon Verlag, 1929.

Twentieth-Century Literary Criticism, Gale, Volume 1, 1978, Volume 33, 1989.

Waugh, Arthur, *Tradition and Change: Studies in Contemporary Literature,* Chapman & Hall, 1919.

Willey, Basil, *Darwin and Butler—Two Versions of Evolution,* Chatto & Windus, 1960.

PERIODICALS

New Republic, May 24, 1933, pp. 35-37.

New Yorker, October 13, 1962.

Samuel Butler Newsletter, Volume 3, numbers 1 and 2, 1980; Volume 4, number 1, 1981; Volume 6, number 1, 1986.

Saturday Review, April 29, 1950, pp. 9-10.*

—*Sketch by Elizabeth Wenning*

C

CAESAR, (Isaac) Sid(ney) 1922-

PERSONAL: Born September 8, 1922, in Yonkers, NY; son of Max (a restaurant owner) and Ida (Raffel) Caesar; married Florence Levy, July 17, 1943; children: Michele, Richard, Karen. *Education:* Studied saxophone and clarinet at Juilliard School of Music. *Avocational Interests:* Collecting guns.

ADDRESSES: Agent—Tom Korman, Agency for the Performing Arts, 9000 Sunset Blvd., Ste. 1200, Los Angeles, CA 90069.

CAREER: Performer and writer. Worked variously as movie usher and doorman; saxophonist and clarinetist with the Charlie Spivak, Claude Thornhill, and Shep Fields dance bands, New York City, beginning in 1939. Performer in stage productions, including *Tars and Spars,* 1945; *Make Mine Manhattan,* 1948; *Little Me,* 1962; *Four on a Garden,* 1971; *Last of the Red Hot Lovers,* 1972; *The Prisoner of Second Avenue* and *Double Take,* both 1974; *Night of One Hundred Stars,* 1982; *Die Fledermaus* (opera), 1988; *An Evening with Sid Caesar . . . The Legendary Genius of Comedy,* 1989; *Sid Caesar and Company: Does Anybody Know What I'm Talking About?,* 1989; and *Together Again,* 1990. Actor in motion pictures, including *Tars and Spars,* 1946; *Guilt of Janet Ames,* 1947; *It's a Mad, Mad, Mad, Mad World,* 1963; *The Spirit is Willing,* 1967; *A Guide for the Married Man,* 1967; *Ten from Your Show of Shows,* 1973; *Airport '75,* 1974; *Silent Movie,* 1976; *Fire Sales,* 1977; *The Cheap Detective* and *Grease,* both 1978; *History of the World, Part One,* 1981; *Grease 2,* 1982; and *Cannonball Run II,* 1984. Performer in television shows, including *Admiral Broadway Revue,* 1949; *Sid Caesar's Your Show of Shows,* 1950-54; *Caesar's Hour,* 1954-57; *Sid Caesar Invites You,* 1958; *The Sid Caesar Show,* 1963-64; *The Hollywood Palace,* 1964-70; also in numerous television specials, films, and other programs. *Wartime service:* U.S. Coast Guard Orchestra, 1942-45.

AWARDS, HONORS: Donaldson Award, 1949, for *Make Mine Manhattan;* named best television comedian by *TV Guide,* 1950; named man of the year by *Radio Daily,* 1950; award for best television comedian from *Look,* 1951, for *Your Show of Shows;* gold medal from Catholic War Veterans of America; Emmy Award for best actor from Academy of Television Arts and Sciences, 1951, for *Your Show of Shows;* award for best television comedian from *Look,* 1956, for *Caesar's Hour;* Emmy Award for best continuing performance by a comedian in a series, 1956, for *Caesar's Hour;* received five Emmy awards in 1957; Sylvania Award, best comedy/variety show of 1958, for *Sid Caesar Invites You;* nomination for Antoinette Perry award (Tony award) for best actor, League of American Theaters and Producers, 1963, for *Little Me;* inducted into U.S. Hall of Fame, 1967, and Television Hall of Fame, 1987; Emmy Award for outstanding television special, for *The Sid Caesar, Imogene Coca, Carl Reiner, Howard Morris Special.*

WRITINGS:

(With Bill Davidson) *Where Have I Been?* (autobiography), Crown, 1982.

Also writer for *Six On, Twelve Off* (stage revue), 1942-44; and *Your Show of Shows* (television special), 1976.

SIDELIGHTS: Sid Caesar is a celebrated comedian who enjoyed particular success on television in the late 1950s. Beginning his show business career in his teens as a saxophone and clarinet player, Caesar played during World War II in the Coast Guard's orchestra, where he entertained his fellow musicians with a variety of offbeat monologues. Caesar's comedic talents earned him a role in the Coast Guard revue *Tars and Spars,* which toured America in the mid-1940s. Caesar also appeared in the revue's film version, which won him increased recognition as a comic performer. By the late 1940s Caesar was working as a comedian in nightclubs and theaters and was gaining considerable attention. He also realized success in the 1948 Broadway revue *Make Mine Manhattan.* In 1949 Caesar made his television debut on *Admiral Broadway Revue.* The medium proved an ideal forum for Caesar's versatility, and the following year he was accorded his own program, *Your Show of Shows.* This series, which showcased Caesar and fellow performer Imogene Coca in various comic sketches, quickly established him as a master comic. Mel Gussow, writing in the *New York Times* in 1982, recalled how "in the 1950s Sid Caesar was the funniest man in America." Finding Caesar "a mimic and mime with verbal and visual virtuosity," Gussow added that "he was a natural for the young medium of television, and he became the first celebrated Saturday night live performer."

Caesar enjoyed continued success with subsequent shows including *Caesar's Hour,* which aired in the mid-1950s, and *Sid Caesar Invites You,* which aired in 1958. In the 1960s, Caesar concentrated on work in film. He was among the many comedians to appear in the 1963 comedy *It's a Mad, Mad, Mad, Mad World.* He also remained active in television, where he hosted or was guest in numerous specials. In addition, Caesar served as the regular host of the long-running comedy showcase *Love American Style.*

In the following decades Caesar worked regularly on stage and in film and television. His stage work included *An Evening with Sid Caesar . . . The Legendary Genius of Comedy* and *Sid Caesar and Company: Does Anybody Know What I'm Talking About?,* two revues playing in New York City in 1989. The previous year, he appeared at the Metropolitan Opera as Frosch in *Die Fledermaus.* His film performances in the 1980s include a turn as caveman in *History of the World, Part One.* On television Caesar continued to appear in various specials, including some shows paying tribute to Caesar's heyday of the 1950s, which Gussow deemed the "halcyon years for American humor."

In his autobiography, *Where Have I Been?,* Caesar recounts his longtime struggle with substance abuse and psychological difficulties. Here Caesar depicts himself as a volatile, ever-suspicious comic who feared that his talents would actually disappear. Incapable of addressing his concerns, Caesar instead wallowed in alcohol and drugs, what Caesar termed his "twenty year blackout." Only in the late 1970s, after years of self-destructive behavior, did he finally begin to overcome these disorders. Caesar credits psychoanalysis as playing a significant role in his newfound stability.

Where Have I Been? was described by Gussow as "the harrowing story of an artist's gradual awakening to the suffering he has inflicted on the people in his life and, especially, on himself." Frank Rich, writing in the *New York Times Book Review,* acknowledged that the "self-revelations are unsparing." *New Republic* contributor Dick Cavett noted that the book "has the inspirational quality of any good recovery tale," affirming that Caesar "has survived the double-barreled ordeals of success and prolonged self-destruction."

BIOGRAPHICAL/CRITICAL SOURCES:

BOOKS

Allen, Steve, *Funny Men,* Simon & Schuster, 1956, pp. 105-18.
Caesar, Sid, and Bill Davidson, *Where Have I Been?,* Crown, 1982.
Freeman, Lucy, editor, *Celebrities on the Couch,* Price, Stern, 1970, pp. 27-39.

PERIODICALS

American Film, December, 1982, p. 72.
Los Angeles Times, May 10, 1984, p. 1.
Los Angeles Times Book Review, December 19, 1982.
New Republic, December 20, 1982, pp. 36, 38.
New York Times, October 11, 1982, p. D1.
New York Times Book Review, October 24, 1982, pp. 7, 32.*

*   *   *

CAINE, Barbara   1948-

PERSONAL: Born April 2, 1948, in Johannesburg, South Africa; daughter of Donald Charles (a doctor) and Peggy Jean (a writer; maiden name, Sussman) Caine; partner of Larry Boyd (a teacher); children: Tessa Boyd-Caine, Nicholas Boyd-Caine. *Education:* University of Sydney, B.A. (with honors), 1969; University of Sussex, M.Phil., 1975. *Politics:* "Feminist!"

ADDRESSES: Office—Department of History, University of Sydney, Sydney, New South Wales 2006, Australia.

CAREER: University of Sydney, Sydney, New South Wales, Australia, assistant professor of history and director of women's studies department, 1989—.

MEMBER: Australian Women's Studies Association (president, 1991-92).

WRITINGS:

Destined to Be Wives: The Sisters of Beatrice Webb, Oxford University Press, 1986.

(Editor with E. A. Grosz and Marie de Lepervanche) *Crossing Boundaries: Feminisms and the Critique of Knowledges,* Allen & Unwin, 1988.
Victorian Feminists, Oxford University Press, 1992.

WORK IN PROGRESS: A history of English feminism, to be published in 1996; researching "the women question in England, 1880 to 1945."

SIDELIGHTS: Feminist scholar Barbara Caine's body of work revolves around the issues of women's status in nineteenth-century England. Caine writes in the realm of collective biography, a format that brings often-forgotten women to light while tying in the currents of thought and action that united them during a specific era. Her first work, *Destined to Be Wives: The Sisters of Beatrice Webb,* published in 1986, is a biographical account of British industrialist Richard Potter's daughters. Caine's second book, 1988's *Crossing Boundaries: Feminisms and the Critique of Knowledges,* consists of a collection of essays coedited with E. A. Grosz and Marie de Lepervanche. *Victorian Feminists,* published in 1992, is a treatise on the sometimes contradictory facets of four progressive women in fin de siecle England.

Destined to Be Wives fills more than a century's worth of chronology and analysis of the lives of the nine Potter sisters. Daughters of a tyrannical father but a well-educated mother, the siblings were representative of the full spectrum of British middle-class women during the Victorian and Edwardian eras. Caine based much of her research for the book on the private papers of Beatrice Webb, who achieved renown as a social investigator and historian of local government and administration. Caine begins her study with the eldest, Lallie, who was born in 1845 and led a traditional life as the spouse of a prominent businessman. The work concludes with the youngest and most iconoclastic, Rosie, who died in 1949. In her book Caine presents the idea that the sisters, with the exception of Beatrice, were fated by social custom of the era to lead quiet and domestic existences—lives in which their talents and intelligence lay primarily unused.

Citing some differences between the sisters in *Destined to be Wives,* Caine attempts to attribute some of their dissimilarities to their chronological place within the family. The author shows that the lives and opinions of each of the sisters present a broad portrayal of the political, sexual, religious, and economic diversity within British society in the post-Industrial Revolution age. *Times Literary Supplement* critic Jose Harris described the book as "stylishly written and imaginative," deeming it an example "of the best and most unbiased kind of women's history."

Caine's 1992 work *Victorian Feminists* is another collective biography. It focuses on four rather divergent British activists of the late-nineteenth and early-twentieth centuries. The women profiled—Emily Davies, Josephine Butler, Millicent Fawcett, and Frances Power Cobbe—were all significantly linked with a particular cause or movement of the period and each played an instrumental role in its ultimate success. Davies, for instance, championed equal access to higher education for women and was the founder of Girton College of Cambridge University. Caine demonstrates how multifaceted these women were, sometimes to the point of espousing arch-conservative views on other issues. For example, Cobbe, a suffragist, contended that women have the right to lead independent lives yet also maintained that it was a daughter's obligation to look after her parents throughout their old age. In *Victorian Feminists,* Caine dispels any ideas that the first women's-liberation activists were also extreme radicals. However, some critics noted that three of the four women had already been the subject of critical works. Claire Tomalin, writing in the London *Times,* described Caine as "a fine historian," noting that *Victorian Feminists* "raises some interesting issues."

BIOGRAPHICAL/CRITICAL SOURCES:

PERIODICALS

Times (London), April 2, 1992, p. 4.
Times Literary Supplement, April 10, 1987, p. 375; June 19, 1992, p. 12.

*   *   *

CALASSO, Roberto 1941-

PERSONAL: Born May 30, 1941, in Florence, Italy; son of Francesco and Melisenda (Codignola) Calasso; married Fleur Jaeggy. *Education:* University of Rome, D.Litt., 1966.

ADDRESSES: Office—Adelphi Edizioni, Via S. Giovanni sul Muro 14, 20121 Milan, Italy.

CAREER: Adelphi Edizioni (publishing house), Milan, Italy, editorial director, 1968—.

AWARDS, HONORS: Ehrenkreuz Litteris et Artibus award, 1981.

WRITINGS:

L'Impuro Folle, 1974, translated into French by Daniele Salavene as *Le Fou impur,* Presses Universitaires de France, 1976.
La rovina di Kasch, Adelphi, 1983.
(Editor) Friedrich Wilhelm Nietzsche, *Ecce homo: Come si diventa cio che si e* (autobiography), Italian translation from the original German *Ecce Homo,* Adelphi, 1985.

Le Nozze di Cadmo e Armonia, Adelphi, 1988, translation by Tim Parks published as *The Marriage of Cadmus and Harmony,* Knopf, 1993.

Contributor of articles to professional journals.

SIDELIGHTS: Italian writer, editor, and publisher, Roberto Calasso is author of *The Marriage of Cadmus and Harmony,* described by *Los Angeles Times* contributor Richard Eder as "a portrait of Greek belief" and a "strange and alluring book about Greek myths and their power upon us." In reflecting upon figures from Greek mythology such as Zeus, Homer, Persephone, Achilles, and Ovid, Calasso assembles a wide-ranging discussion of full-length poetic drama, contradictory versions of specific story-fragments, and an abundance of epigrammatic imagery. Calasso also explains the relationship between the stories and the real-life settings in which they occur. *New Yorker* reviewer Gotham Wannabe disclosed that the work "is not fiction, history, or literary criticism, not a collection of aphorisms or rhapsodic Cliffs Notes on the classical, but a little of all these; like the deities themselves, it is constantly changing form." Eder described Calasso's writing in the *Los Angeles Times* as "gnomic and down to earth, colloquial and abstract, brilliantly focused and digressive to the point where it wanders off, gets lost and reappears in another quarter."

The Marriage of Cadmus and Harmony opens by telling the mythical tale of Europa and the Bull, repeating the story in progressively embellished versions. Calasso's discussion then drifts to several other Greek myths, eventually leading to the story of the marriage of Cadmus and Harmony. A cycle is created as the title story leads back to the story of Europa and the Bull in that Cadmus is Europa's sister, for whom he is searching when he encounters Harmony. Calasso looks upon the title work as the first in a ring of myths that would set the foundation for subsequent European literature.

A constantly recurring theme in Calasso's work is the paradoxical notion that the Greek gods must submit to the laws of nature, while they at the same time are autonomous and immortal. As *New York Times Book Review* contributor Mary Lefkowitz explained, "Mr. Calasso's gods seem more like powerful human beings than the slow but relentless enforcers of justice in whom the ancient Greeks for centuries believed." Commenting on this dynamic in Calasso's work in the *Los Angeles Times,* Eder found that "the concept is supremely liberating and supremely modest" and that "the result is a transfiguring electric spark between positive and negative poles." Claiming that the author's telling of Classic Greece is tailored after contemporary thoughts and traditions, Lefkowitz stated that "Mr. Calasso is writing for an audience that is more interested in the interaction of gods with men

and (especially) women than in rehashings of the origins of gods who in [the readership's] opinion never existed." Lefkowitz concluded in the *New York Times Book Review* that rather than being a scholarly work, *The Marriage of Cadmus and Harmony* is "a serious entertainment, meant to be enjoyed in the process, but to leave the reader with some lingering sense that what seemed remote and forgotten is in some way part of his own very different world."

BIOGRAPHICAL/CRITICAL SOURCES:

PERIODICALS

Los Angeles Times Book Review, March 11, 1993, p. E4.
New Yorker, March 12, 1993, pp. 31-35.
New York Times Book Review, March 14, 1993, p. 12.*

*   *   *

CALLEN, Michael (Lane)   1955-1993

OBITUARY NOTICE—See index for *CA* sketch: Born April 11, 1955, in Rising Sun, IN; died of AIDS, December 27, 1993, in Los Angeles, CA. Singer, composer, and writer. Callen was recognized nationwide for his more than ten-year battle with AIDS and for his dedication to supporting others who suffer from the disease. Diagnosed with AIDS in the early 1980s, Callen became a political activist on the part of others with the disease, and was a founding member of numerous coalitions, institutes, and task forces to research AIDS and offer support, including People with AIDS Coalition, Committee for Sexual Responsibility, National Association of People with AIDS, and Community Research Initiative. Callen publicized his message frequently on television talk shows, such as *Phil Donahue, 20/20,* and *Good Morning, America,* and also spoke in front of both houses of Congress as well as before the President's Commission on AIDS. His writings reflect his devotion to AIDS support as well; among his titles are 1990's *Surviving AIDS,* which details the lives of a group of long-time AIDS sufferers, and 1983's *How to Have Sex in an Epidemic: One Approach,* which he co-wrote. Throughout his lifetime Callen remained active in the music industry, singing with the New York City Gay Men's Chorus, releasing a solo album entitled *Purple Heart* in 1988, and performing with "The Flirtations," an a cappella group that has recorded two albums and that appeared in the 1993 film *Philadelphia. Legacy,* a compilation of Callen's new musical works, is scheduled to be published posthumously.

OBITUARIES AND OTHER SOURCES:

PERIODICALS

Los Angeles Times, December 29, 1993, pp. B1, B4.
New York Times, December 29, 1993, p. D19.

CAMBIE, R(ichard) C(onrad) 1931-

PERSONAL: Born November 11, 1931, in Tauranga, New Zealand; married Mary Constance Minchin (a consultant), 1956; children: Paul Carlton, Kenneth Gilbert. *Education:* University of New Zealand, B.Sc., 1954, M.Sc. (with first class honors), 1955, Ph.D., 1958; Oxford University, D.Phil., 1962; University of Auckland, D.Sc., 1964.

ADDRESSES: Home—21D Southern Cross Rd., Kohimaramara, Auckland, New Zealand.

CAREER: University of Auckland, Auckland, New Zealand, junior lecturer, 1957, lecturer, 1958-60, senior lecturer, 1961-63, associate professor, 1964-69, professor of organic chemistry, 1970—, head of department, 1984-91. Australian National University, visiting professor, 1981; Chinese University of Hong Kong, visiting professor, 1981; University of the South Pacific, visiting professor, 1982 and 1983; University of Melbourne, Wilsmore visiting professor, 1986. New Zealand National Committee for Chemistry, member, 1972-83, chair, 1979-82; UNESCO Network for Chemistry of Natural Products in Southeast Asia, New Zealand representative to coordinating board, 1975-86. Mount Wellington Borough Council, guardian of Tamaki Estuary, 1973-75. Coach of Auckland and New Zealand champion rowing crews, 1966 and 1968.

MEMBER: New Zealand Institute of Chemistry (fellow), Royal Society of New Zealand (fellow; member of council, 1979-81), Auckland Institute and Museum (life member), Chemical Society (London; fellow), Auckland University Rowing Club (life member of committee; president, 1958-71, 1973-81, and 1983—); Auckland University Rugby Football Club (vice president, 1958—).

AWARDS, HONORS: Pressed Steel fellow, Oxford University, 1961-62; ICI Medal, New Zealand Institute of Chemistry, 1964; Hector Medal, Royal Society of New Zealand, 1967; Research Medal, New Zealand Association of Scientists, 1969; Nuffield fellow, University of Sussex, 1981.

WRITINGS:

(With S. G. Brooker and R. C. Cooper) *New Zealand Medicinal Plants,* Heinemann (Auckland), 1981, third edition, Reed (Victoria, Australia), 1991.
(With Brooker and Cooper) *Economic Native Plants of New Zealand,* Botany Division, DSIR, 1988.
(With Cooper) *New Zealand's Economic Native Plants,* Reed, 1991, Oxford University Press, 1992.
Figian Medicinal Plants, Commonwealth Scientific and Industrial Research Organization (CSIRO; Victoria, Australia), 1994.

Contributor of more than three hundred articles to periodicals. *Australian Journal of Chemistry,* member of editorial board, 1987—.

*   *   *

CARISTI, Dom(inic) 1956-

PERSONAL: Born March 30, 1956, in New York, NY; son of Santo (a chef) and Concetta (a seamstress; maiden name, Arena) Caristi; married Kimberly Sipe (an artist), May 23, 1981; children: Anthony, Nicole. *Education:* University of Miami, Coral Gables, FL, B.A., 1977; Central Missouri State University, M.A., 1982; University of Iowa, Ph.D., 1990. *Religion:* Roman Catholic.

ADDRESSES: Home—300 Rockwell Ave., Ames, IA 50014. *Office*—Department of Journalism, 211 Hamilton Hall, Iowa State University, Ames, IA 50011.

CAREER: St. Mary's College, Winona, MN, assistant professor of mass communication, 1980-88, department head, 1985-88; Missouri Southern State College, Joplin, assistant professor of communications and general manager of K57DR-TV, 1988-92; Iowa State University, Ames, assistant professor of journalism and mass communications, 1992—. KWNO-Radio, part-time air personality, 1980-83; Ozarks Public Television, producer and director, 1989-92. Joplin Solid Waste Commission, member, 1989-92.

MEMBER: Broadcast Education Association (vice-chairperson of Law and Policy Division), Association for Education in Journalism and Mass Communication.

AWARDS, HONORS: Volunteer of the Year Award, Ozarks Public Television, 1992.

WRITINGS:

Expanding Free Expression in the Marketplace: Broadcasting and the Public Forum, Greenwood Press, 1992.

Contributor to scholarly journals, including *Suffolk University Law Review.*

WORK IN PROGRESS: A textbook for undergraduate mass media law classes; research on the reassigned electromagnetic spectrum.

SIDELIGHTS: Dom Caristi told *CA:* "Having spent the last fourteen years in higher education, my writing is mostly academic in nature. My first book was recognized as a scholarly contribution to a narrow area of First Amendment issues. The book contains about nine hundred references. I continue to study and write about First Amendment issues, particularly as they apply to electronic media."

CARLEBACH, Michael L(loyd) 1945-

PERSONAL: Born March 3, 1945, in New York, NY; son of William and Priscilla (Wardwell) Carlebach; married Margot Ammidown; children: Adam, Joshua. *Education:* Colgate University, A.B. (cum laude), 1967; Florida State University, M.A., 1980; Brown University, Ph.D., 1988.

ADDRESSES: Home—3634 Bayview Rd., Coconut Grove, FL 33133. *Office*—Photography Sequence, School of Communication, University of Miami, Coral Gables, FL 33124.

CAREER: Miami Herald, Miami, FL, staff photographer, 1969; *Village Post,* staff photographer, 1969-72; University of Miami, Coral Gables, FL, instructor, 1973-78, assistant professor, 1980-83, 1985-87, associate professor of photography, 1987—, coordinator of Photography Sequence, director, Program in American Studies. U.S. Environmental Protection Agency, photographer for Project Documerica, 1973; U.S. State Department, documentary photographer for Cuban-Haitian Task Force, 1980; freelance photographer, with group and solo exhibitions in the United States and abroad. Miami-Dade Community College, guest curator at Wolfson Campus, 1986, distinguished visiting professor, 1990; Louis Wolfson II Media History Center, member of advisory board, 1986-87, member of executive board, 1987-90. Coconut Grove Civic Club, member of board of directors, 1989-90.

MEMBER: National Press Photographers Association, Society of Professional Journalists, Phi Beta Kappa, Pi Sigma Alpha.

WRITINGS:

(Photographer) Arlene Brett and Eugene F. Provenzo, Jr., *The Complete Block Book,* Syracuse University Press, 1983.
The Origins of Photojournalism in America, Smithsonian Institution Press, 1992.
(With Eugene Provenzo) *Farm Security Administration Photographs of Florida,* University Press of Florida, 1993.
(Photographer) Arlene Brett, Robin Moore, and Eugene F. Provenzo, Jr., *The Complete Playground Book,* Syracuse University Press, 1993.

Work represented in anthologies, including *Hanging Out: Stereographic Prints From the Collection of Samuel Wagstaff, Jr. at the J. Paul Getty Museum,* edited by Nancy Versaci and Judith Tolnick, Bell Gallery, Brown University, 1984. Contributor of articles and photographs to periodicals, including *Journal of Decorative and Propaganda Arts, Miami, Time, Newsweek, U.S. News and World Report, Modern Photography,* and *New York Times.*

WORK IN PROGRESS: Photojournalism in America, 1880-1936, Smithsonian Institution Press, publication scheduled for 1995.

*   *   *

CARLING, Alan H(ugh) 1949-

PERSONAL: Born November 25, 1949, in Ipswich, Suffolk, England; son of David (an administrator of nursing homes) and Freda (a medical social worker; maiden name, Williams) Carling; married, 1974; wife's name, Christine Ann (separated, 1992); children: Sarah, David. *Education:* Emmanuel College, Cambridge, B.A., 1971; University of Essex, M.A., 1974, Ph.D., 1984. *Politics:* Socialist. *Religion:* None.

ADDRESSES: Home—58 Wilmer Dr., Bradford, West Yorkshire BD9 4AS, England. *Office*—Department of Interdisciplinary Human Studies, University of Bradford, Bradford, West Yorkshire BD7 1DP, England.

CAREER: University of Bradford, Bradford, England, senior lecturer, 1976—, association of university teachers, president, 1992-94.

MEMBER: British Sociological Association.

WRITINGS:

Social Division, Verso, 1991.

Contributor to periodicals, including *Science and Society* and *New Left Review.*

WORK IN PROGRESS: Research on issues of social class, gender, and ethnicity, and on rational choice theory, evolutionary models, and the growth of democracy.

SIDELIGHTS: Alan H. Carling told *CA:* "I was trained as a mathematician, but became fascinated by questions of social and political theory, having been radicalized as a member of the late sixties student generation. I found it difficult to combine my intellectual and social interests until I discovered the current known as analytical Marxism in the early 1980s, and especially the work of Gerry Cohen at Oxford, Jon Elster in Chicago, Erik Wright in Wisconsin, and John Roemer at the University of California, Davis. My book *Social Division* is an attempt to extend their methods of analysis from questions of social class into the domains of gender and ethnicity. I consider myself a socialist, and am an active trade unionist in the times left over from single parenthood."

CARSON, Barbara Harrell 1943-

PERSONAL: Born May 3, 1943, in Rockledge, FL; daughter of Burien (a civil servant) and Evelyn Winnell Farr (a homemaker) Harrell; married Robert G. Carson (a professor), June 12, 1962; children: Ashley, Bethany. *Education:* Florida State University, B.A. (summa cum laude), 1964; Johns Hopkins University, M.A., 1965, Ph.D., 1968. *Politics:* Democrat.

ADDRESSES: Home—221 Glenridge Way, Winter Park, FL, 32789. *Office*—Box 2619, Rollins College, Winter Park, FL 32789.

CAREER: Towson State College, Baltimore, MD, assistant professor of English, 1968-71; University of Massachusetts, Amherst, assistant professor of English, 1971-72; Florida Technological University, Orlando, FL, adjunct instructor, 1973-79; Valencia Community College, Orlando, adjunct instructor, 1973-79; Rollins College, Winter Park, FL, adjunct instructor, 1973-79, assistant professor, 1979-81, associate professor, 1981-88, professor of English, 1988—.

MEMBER: Phi Beta Kappa, Phi Kappa Phi.

AWARDS, HONORS: Florida State University Women's Scholarship Plaque for highest academic average among senior women; Gilman and Faculty of Philosophy Fellowships, Johns Hopkins University, 1964-68; National Endowment for the Humanities, fellowship, 1970-71; Arthur Vining Davis fellowship, Rollins College, 1982, "for outstanding contributions to the academic mission of the College"; one of eight national finalists in CASE Professor of the Year Competition; Hugh McKean Award, Rollins College, 1985; faculty research grant, Rollins College, 1990-92; *Eudora Welty: Two Pictures at Once in Her Frame* was named one of the Outstanding Academic Books of 1993 by *Choice* magazine.

WRITINGS:

Eudora Welty: Two Pictures at Once in Her Frame, Whitston (Troy, NY), 1992.

Contributor to numerous periodicals.

* * *

CARTER, John Marshall 1949-

PERSONAL: Born April 6, 1949, in Leaksville, NC; son of Howard Cecil (a truck driver) and Virginia (a mill worker; maiden name, Smith) Carter; married Suzon Grogan, August 9, 1974 (divorced April 15, 1991); married Pamela Cash Paul (a teacher), October 19, 1993; children: Alyson Annette; stepchildren: Alexander Joseph Paul, Abby Catherine Paul. *Education:* Elon College, B.A.,

1971; University of North Carolina at Greensboro, M.A., 1975; University of Illinois at Urbana-Champaign, Ph.D., 1983. *Politics:* Republican. *Religion:* Baptist. *Avocational Interests:* Songwriting, music, fishing, basketball.

ADDRESSES: Home—217 1/2 Spring St., Thomasville, NC 27360. *Office*—Thomasville Middle School, 400 Unity St., Thomasville, NC 27360.

CAREER: University of North Carolina at Greensboro, adjunct professor of education and history, 1988-90; Oglethorpe University, Atlanta, GA, assistant professor of education, 1990-93; Thomasville Middle School, Thomasville, NC, history teacher, 1993—.

MEMBER: North American Society for Sport History, Medieval Academy of America, American Historical Association, National Council for the Social Studies, National Academy of Recording Arts and Sciences, Phi Alpha Theta.

AWARDS, HONORS: St. Nicholas Prize, Center for Medieval and Renaissance Studies, University of California, Los Angeles, 1983; received grants from the National Endowment for the Humanities, 1984, and Deutscher Akademischer Austauschdienst, 1985 and 1987.

WRITINGS:

Wampus Cats and Dan River Rimes (poetry), Leaksville Press, 1978.
Studies in the History of Medieval Sport, MA-AH Publishing, 1980.
Sports and Pastimes of the Middle Ages, Brentwood Press, 1984.
The Bayeux Tapestry as a Social Document: Selected Readings, Ginn, 1985.
Confessions of a Space Cadet: The Transformation of a Teacher, Hamilton Press, 1987.
Ritual and Record: Sports Records and Quantification in Pre-Modern Societies, Greenwood Press, 1990.
Medieval Games, Greenwood Press, 1990.

Contributor to periodicals, including *Journal of Sport History, American Benedictine Review, Social Education,* and *International Journal of Sport History.*

WORK IN PROGRESS: Sports and Games of the Middle Ages: An Annotated Bibliography; biography of the knight, William Marshal; research on "the social studies teacher as hero."

SIDELIGHTS: John Marshall Carter told *CA:* "From the age of five or six I was interested in sports. I played organized sports in elementary, junior high, and senior high school, and a bit in college; I also coached at the high school level. After deciding to earn a doctorate in history, I discovered the newly emerging sub-discipline of sports history and almost immediately began to do research on sports and games in medieval society. For me, doing this research allowed me to correlate two important activities of my life.

"In addition to historical research and the writing of poetry and short prose, songwriting has been an ever-present interest of mine. From the time that I heard my first 'Yeah! Yeah! Yeah!' from the Beatles in 1964, I have continued to write (and publish some) pop songs."

*   *   *

CASSON, Mark (Christopher) 1945-

PERSONAL: Born December 17, 1945, in Grappenhall, Cheshire, England; son of Stanley Christopher (a minister of the Church of England) and Dorothy Nowell (a homemaker; maiden name, Barlow) Casson; married Janet Penelope Close (a teacher), July 26, 1975; children: Catherine Mary. *Education:* University of Bristol, B.A., 1966; graduate study at Churchill College, Cambridge, 1966-69. *Politics:* "No party affiliation." *Religion:* Church of England. *Avocational Interests:* Collecting books, steam railways.

ADDRESSES: Home—6 Wayside Green, Woodcote, Reading, Oxfordshire RG8 0OJ, England. *Office*—Department of Economics, University of Reading, Box 218, Reading RG6 2AA, England.

CAREER: University of Reading, Reading, England, lecturer, 1969-76, reader, 1976-81, professor of economics, 1981—, head of department, 1987—. Public speaker in England and the United States; consultant to World Bank, Commission of the European Communities, and International Labor Office. Oxford Diocesan Synod, member, 1991—.

MEMBER: Royal Economic Society (member of council, 1985-90).

AWARDS, HONORS: Business Book of the Year Award from *Newsweek.*

WRITINGS:

Introduction to Mathematical Economics, Nelson, 1973.
(With Peter J. Buckley) *The Future of the Multinational Enterprise,* Macmillan, 1976.
Alternatives to the Multinational Enterprise, St. Martin's, 1979.
Youth Unemployment, Macmillan, 1979.
Unemployment: A Disequilibrium Approach, Martin Robertson, 1981.
The Entrepreneur: An Economic Theory, Barnes & Noble, 1982.
Economics of Unemployment: An Historical Perspective, MIT Press, 1983.

(Editor) *The Growth of International Business,* Allen & Unwin, 1983.
Unemployment Theory before Keynes, Martin Robertson, 1983.
(With Peter J. Buckley) *The Economic Theory of the Multinational Enterprise: Selected Papers,* St. Martin's, 1985.
(Coauthor) *Multinationals and World Trade: Vertical Integration and the Division of Labour in World Industries,* Allen & Unwin, 1986.
The Firm and the Market: Studies in Multinational Enterprise and the Scope of the Firm, MIT Press, 1987.
(Editor) *Entrepreneurship,* Edward Elgar, 1990.
(Editor) *Multinational Corporations,* Edward Elgar, 1990.
Enterprise and Competitiveness: A Systems View of International Business, Clarendon Press, 1990.
The Economics of Business Culture: Game Theory, Transaction Costs, and Economic Welfare, Clarendon Press, 1991.
(Editor) *Global Research Strategy and International Competitiveness,* Basil Blackwell, 1991.
(Editor) *International Business and Global Integration,* Macmillan, 1992.
(Editor with Peter J. Buckley) *Multinational Enterprises in the World Economy: Essays in Honour of John Dunning,* Edward Elgar, 1992.
(Editor with John Creedy) *Industrial Concentration and Economic Inequality: Essays in Honour of Peter Hart,* Edward Elgar, 1993.

Contributor to journals in economics, business history, transport studies, political science, and social psychology. Member of editorial board, *Journal of International Business Studies.*

WORK IN PROGRESS: Leadership and Organization, a monograph for interdisciplinary readers; research on business networks and business culture; research on rational action modeling in social science.

SIDELIGHTS: Mark Casson told *CA:* "I have always found the most interesting things to be those that I am *not* supposed to be working on. My research interests, therefore, evolve continually. I find it difficult to finish one thing before moving on to the next. Indeed, I am never quite sure what the next thing will turn out to be.

"My boyhood ambition was to run a railway. I studied hard for this, reading in the evenings and ignoring the official school curriculum. University economics seemed a suitable preparation for a career in railway management, but as my enthusiasm for economics grew, my interest in railways waned. I went into economic research, specializing in statistical techniques to handle errors in data. The algebraic manipulations involved were very mechanical, however. Despite the professional status conferred by such technical work, I looked around for something more interesting to do.

"The department I worked in specialized in international business issues, but the specialists ignored a fundamental point which (together with a colleague, Peter Buckley) I was able to identify. The point is that many firms invest abroad in order to avoid licensing their technology to foreign firms. If licensing becomes more attractive, however, then more firms are likely to remain at home. Using this idea, we correctly predicted, contrary to opinion at the time, that large firms would not continue to expand abroad until a few of them dominated the world economy.

"Although technology is the driving force in modern international business, the origins of technological innovations are not well understood. Indeed, modern economics has, in general, little to say about the process of change. Even core issues like how markets adjust from one equilibrium to another are not fully understood. To try to understand change, I wrote *The Entrepreneur,* in which I argued that the direction of change is governed by the judgment of a relatively small number of key individuals.

"Unfortunately, the book followed conventional economics too closely, in that it is assumed that profit was the dominant motive of the entrepreneur. It ignored the role of the entrepreneur as a leader: as someone who founds a firm, structures its organization, and inspires loyalty from its employees. This neglected role of leadership became the theme of *The Economics of Business Culture.* I argued that leaders play a vital role in instilling that sense of obligation without which no institution (firm, polity, or society) can function properly. I am now developing these ideas more systematically in a work provisionally titled *Leadership and Organization.*

"I see my work on leadership as extending the traditional techniques of economic modeling, based on rational action, into areas previously colonized by sociologists and psychologists, who have instead emphasized the irrational in human behavior. I argue that, because moral behavior is emotionally rewarding, it is perfectly rational to be moral. Leaders control exactly how emotionally rewarding it is. Weak leadership reduces the emotional reward, and so encourages selfish, materialistic behavior. This in turn means that legal coercion must be substituted for moral obligation in order to make organization work. If leadership becomes so weak that personal morality simply becomes a lifestyle option—just another aspect of consumer choice—then coercion becomes the only reliable form of organization. More choice, but less freedom, is the paradoxical result.

"The answer, I suggest, is not 'stronger' leadership (in the dictatorial sense) but better leadership—leadership by example, by persuasive argument, by sacrificial commit-

ment. For various reasons, neither politicians nor the clergy seem able to provide such leadership in the West. In economic terms there is an unfulfilled demand for leaders, and it is not clear where the supply is going to come from. It would be nice to think that intellectuals could play a role, but so many of them are now professional careerists, and highly specialized ones at that, the inspirational ideas are themselves in very short supply.

"I am unclear where this line of reasoning is going to lead me next. An earlier generation of economists who tackled issues of this kind went on to study the economic theory of religion, or attempted to develop an economic theory of history. Definitive analysis of such topics is probably impossible to achieve, but simply rediscovering some of these early insights would be a useful contribution in its own right."

*   *   *

CAVE, Kathryn 1948-

PERSONAL: Born June 22, 1948, in Aldershot, Hampshire, England; daughter of Henry Wilson (a research scientist) and Eve Wilson (a teacher); married Martin Cave (a professor), July, 1972; children: Eleanor, Joseph, Alice. *Education:* Oxford University, B.A., 1969; graduate studies at Massachusetts Institute of Technology, 1969-70, and Birmingham University, 1972-73. *Avocational Interests:* Teaching tennis, coaching athletes, walking, poetry, theater, travel.

ADDRESSES: Home—11 West Common Road, Uxbridge, Middlesex UB8 IN2, England. *Office*—Frances Lincoln Ltd., Apollo Works, 5 Charlton King's Road, London N5, England. *Agent*—Gina Pollinger, 222 Old Brompton Road, London SW5 OBZ, England.

CAREER: Penguin Publishing, London, England, editor, 1970-71; Blackwell (publishers), Oxford, England, editor, 1971-72; Metier (publishers), Hayes, England, technical editor, 1987-88; Frances Lincoln Ltd., London, England, editorial director for children's nonfiction, 1990-92; writer.

AWARDS, HONORS: Many Happy Returns was named one of the best ten books of the year, Federation of Children's Book Group, 1986.

WRITINGS:

Dragonrise, Penguin, 1984.
Many Happy Returns, Transworld, 1986.
Just in Time, illustrated by Terry McKenna, Potter, 1988.
Poor Little Mary, Penguin, 1988.
Henry Hobbs, Alien, illustrated by Chris Riddell, Penguin, 1990.
Jumble, illustrated by Riddell, Blackie, 1990.

William and the Wolves, Penguin, 1991.
Out for the Count, illustrated by Riddell, Simon & Schuster, 1991.
Running Battles, Penguin, 1992.
Something Else, illustrated by Riddell, Viking/Penguin, in press.

SIDELIGHTS: "Most of my stories are concerned with the gap between our own perceptions of reality and those of other people," Cave explained. "I like the borderline where logic turns into madness." When Cave's oldest daughter, Eleanor, became involved in sports, the author "had plenty of chances to watch children, parents and coaches cross that borderline, under the influence of sheer obsession—it's always fascinating to see single-minded pursuit of any objective (sometimes it's horrifying too, of course)." Cave explores the humorous side of this theme in her book *Running Battles.* "I hope it is funny, although the issues involved are really no joke," she commented.

BIOGRAPHICAL/CRITICAL SOURCES:

PERIODICALS

Publishers Weekly, June 1, 1992, p. 61.
School Library Journal, May, 1992, p. 86.

*   *   *

CAVE, Thomas
    See STEWARD, Samuel M(orris)

*   *   *

**CAVENDISH, (Michael) William (Patrick)
1964-**

PERSONAL: Born December 9, 1964, in England. *Education:* Magdalen College, Oxford, B.A. (with first class honors), 1986, M.Sc. (with distinction), 1987; doctoral study at St. Antony's College, Oxford, 1990—.

ADDRESSES: Office—St. John's College, Oxford University, Oxford OX1 3JP, England; and c/o Dr. R. Choto, 9 Fife Ave., Harare, Zimbabwe.

CAREER: Oxford University, Oxford, England, research assistant at Institute of Economics and Statistics, 1987; Central Bank of Lesotho, research economist, 1987-89; Oxford University, research assistant at Unit for the Study of African Economies, 1990, research officer at Finance, Industry, and Trade Centre, Queen Elizabeth House, 1990; World Bank, Washington, DC, research economist, 1991; Oxford University, research supervisor at Centre for Continuing Education, 1992, lecturer in environmental economics, 1992-93, junior research fellow of St. John's

College, 1993—. University of Zimbabwe, research associate at Institute of Food, Nutrition, and Family Sciences, 1993-94.

MEMBER: American Economic Association.

AWARDS, HONORS: Fellow in Lesotho, Overseas Development Institute, 1987-89; *Adjusting Privatization: Case Studies From Developing Countries* was selected an outstanding academic book for 1992 by *Choice.*

WRITINGS:

(With C. Adam and P. S. Mistry) *Adjusting Privatization: Case Studies From Developing Countries,* James Currey, 1992.
(With Dennis Anderson) *Efficiency and Substitution in Pollution Abatement: Three Case Studies,* World Bank, 1992.

Work represented in anthologies, including *The World Economy Under Environmental Constraints,* edited by V. Bhaskar and A. Glyn, WIDER (Helsinki), 1993.

*   *   *

CECIL-FRONSMAN, Bill   1953-

PERSONAL: Born December 24, 1953, in Raleigh, NC; son of Richard P. (a publisher) and Margery Lila (a secretary; maiden name, Copping; present surname, Childers) Cecil; married Sally Francis Fronsman (a grant writer), June 6, 1976; children: Cassandra Patricia Cecil-Fronsman Rodriequez, Dorthea Margery. *Education:* Reed College, B.A., 1976; Southern Oregon State College, M.A., 1977; University of North Carolina at Chapel Hill, Ph.D., 1983. *Politics:* "Democratic socialist." *Religion:* Episcopalian.

ADDRESSES: Home—1609 Southwest Wayne Ave., Topeka, KS 66604. *Office*—Department of History, Washburn University, Topeka, KS 66621.

CAREER: Washburn University, Topeka, KS, associate professor of history, 1989—.

WRITINGS:

Common Whites: Class and Culture in Antebellum North Carolina, University Press of Kentucky, 1992.

WORK IN PROGRESS: Blood on the Prairie: The Story of "Bleeding Kansas."

*   *   *

CHANDLER, David Leon   1937(?)-1994

OBITUARY NOTICE—See index for *CA* sketch: Born c. 1937; died of complications from diabetes, January 23,

1994, in Denver, CO. Journalist and author. Chandler is remembered for heading a Pulitzer Prize-winning news team at Florida's *Panama City News-Herald* in the early 1960s. Chandler joined the *News-Herald* staff as a reporter in 1959, after serving in the Navy and merchant marine. Three years later his news team garnered a Pulitzer Prize for public service for a series of articles focusing on corruption in the local sheriff's office. Chandler later worked as a reporter and correspondent for the *New Orleans States-Item, Life,* the Norfolk, Virginia *Ledger-Star,* and *People,* as well as a free-lance writer. In 1980 he received the Virginia Press Association Investigative Reporting Award and the Scripps Howard Distinguished Journalism Citation. Chandler's historical biographies include *Henry Flagler: The Astonishing Life and Times of the Visionary Robber Baron Who Founded Florida* and, with his wife, Mary Voelz Chandler, *Binghams of Louisville: The Dark History Behind One of America's Great Fortunes.* The author's *Jefferson Conspiracies: A President's Role in the Assassination of Meriwether Lewis* is scheduled for publication in 1994.

OBITUARIES AND OTHER SOURCES:

PERIODICALS

Los Angeles Times, January 28, 1994, p. A26.

*   *   *

CHAPPELL, William (Evelyn)   1908-1994

OBITUARY NOTICE—See index for *CA* sketch: Born September 27, 1908, in Wolverhampton, England; died January 1, 1994, in Rye, East Sussex, England. Dancer, designer, theatre director, and author. Chappell is best remembered for his contributions to English ballet. He began his career in the 1920s, studying as a dancer with Marie Rambert's Notting Hill studio and appearing in such productions as *The Little Hut* and *L'Apres-Midi.* It was in his subsequent work as a costume designer, however, that he distinguished himself. Often working with minimal budgets, Chappell designed visually striking yet functional dance apparel for such 1930s productions as *Capriol Suite* and *Les Rendezvous.* He later pursued set design and the direction of such productions as *The Lyric Revue* and *Six of One.* Chappell also wrote extensively on ballet, contributing to journals and publishing the books *Studies in Ballet* and *Fonteyn: Impression of a Ballerina.*

OBITUARIES AND OTHER SOURCES:

BOOKS

Who's Who, 146th edition, St. Martin's, 1994.

PERIODICALS

Times (London), January 8, 1994, p. 17.

CHARMLEY, John   1955-

PERSONAL: Born November 9, 1955, in Birkenhead, England; son of John (a "docker") and Doris (a bartender; maiden name, Halliwell) Charmley; married (Ann) Dorothea Bartlett (a homemaker), July 23, 1977; children: Gervase and Gerard (twins). *Education:* Pembroke College, Oxford, received B.A. and M.A.; received Ph.D., c. 1979. *Politics:* Conservative. *Religion:* Church of England.

ADDRESSES: Home—209 Earlham Rd., Norwich, Norfolk, England. *Office*—University of East Anglia, Norwich, England. *Agent*—Felicity Bryan, Curtis Brown, 162-168 Regent St., London W1R 5TB, England.

CAREER: University of East Anglia, Norwich, England, lecturer, 1979-c. 1993; Westminster College, Fulton, MO, Churchill Memorial professor, c. 1993—; writer.

MEMBER: Royal Historical Society (fellow).

AWARDS, HONORS: Churchill College fellowship, 1986.

WRITINGS:

Duff Cooper: The Authorized Biography, Weidenfeld & Nicolson, 1986.
(Editor) Evelyn Shuckburgh, *Descent to Suez: Foreign Office Diaries, 1951-56,* Weidenfeld & Nicholson, 1987, Norton, 1987.
Lord Lloyd and the Decline of the British Empire (biography), St. Martin's, 1988.
(Editor with Eric Homberger) *The Troubled Face of Biography,* Macmillan, 1988, St. Martin's, 1988.
Chamberlain and the Lost Peace (biography), Hodder & Stoughton, 1989, I. R. Dee, 1989.
Churchill, The End of Glory: A Political Biography, Hodder & Stoughton, 1992, Harcourt, 1992.

SIDELIGHTS: Historian and educator John Charmley is internationally recognized for his authoritative biographies focusing on political figures in modern English history. His first work, published in 1986, is *Duff Cooper: The Authorized Biography.* Utilizing previously unpublished documentation, Charmley follows the life of Alfred Duff Cooper, the former English ambassador to France. Cooper's political, personal, and social life has fascinated the British public ever since he resigned from public office in protest over the Munich Pact of 1938 (an agreement between Great Britain, France, Italy, and Germany which ceded part of Czechoslovakia to Germany); British prime minister Winston Churchill publicly commended Cooper for his resistance to Adolph Hitler. Martin Fagg in *Times Educational Supplement* called Charmley's work "an appropriately stylish and admirably concise account" of Cooper's life. David Pryce-Jones noted in the *Times Literary Supplement* that the biography provides "intimate detail." Woodrow Wyatt in the London *Times* commented that "Cooper thought the purpose of being alive was to enjoy it. . . . [and] Charmley gives numerous examples of Cooper's wit. . . . Cooper would have been delighted with young Mr. Charmley's book."

In his next work, 1987's *Descent to Suez: Foreign Office Diaries, 1951-56,* Charmley edits the personal diaries of Sir Evelyn Shuckburgh, private secretary to Anthony Eden, the head of the British Foreign Office during the mid-1950s. In his diaries, Shuckburgh discusses his involvement in the Suez Crisis, a political predicament which erupted over control of the Suez Canal and which resulted in the invasion of Egypt by Great Britain. Included in the book are reports on the Geneva Conference on Indochina and significant details of Shuckburgh's career which contribute "new material" and provide "an important footnote to history," noted Genevieve Stuttaford in *Publishers Weekly.* According to William Roger Louis in the *Times Literary Supplement,* "the diaries throw new light on the private thoughts of British officials on two of the landmarks on the road to Suez, the Czech arms deal of September 1955 and the sacking of General Sir John Glubb by King Hussein of Jordan in April of the next year." *Descent to Suez* was published on the thirty-year anniversary of the Suez crisis.

Three more British political figures became the focus of Charmley's ongoing biographical studies—George Lloyd, the subject of *Lord Lloyd and the Decline of the British Empire,* published in 1988; Neville Chamberlain, the subject of *Chamberlain and the Lost Peace,* published in 1989; and Winston Churchill, the subject of Charmley's most controversial work, *Churchill, The End of Glory: A Political Biography,* published in 1992. Called a "revisionist" biography by many critics, *Churchill, The End of Glory* finds fault with the former prime minister for certain errors of judgment and political blunders during World War II. William E. Schmidt, in an article for the *New York Times,* noted Charmley's implication "that Churchill missed opportunities in the early years of the war that might have brought the fighting in Western Europe to an earlier end, and thereby preserved Britain's independence and its empire." The underlying thesis of the book, according to several reviewers, is that Churchill could have made a peace agreement with Adolph Hitler as early as May, 1940, and thereby avoided "mortgaging" the British empire to the United States for wartime aid, as well as opening the English home front to socialist influences.

Charmley's iconoclastic conclusions have drawn opposing arguments from critics. Admitting to the need for a "true historical record" and a more balanced biography than Churchill's own published memoirs, Robert Rhodes James wrote in the *Times Literary Supplement* that "there was a time after 1955 when it was virtually impossible to write anything sensible about Churchill, because this

would involve criticism, which was unthinkable about the Greatest Man of The Century." Much of the controversy of *Churchill, The End of Glory* centered around Charmley's perceived "missed opportunity" of a treaty with Germany. While acknowledging that the work is "impressively researched," Churchill's official biographer Martin Gilbert was quoted by William E. Schmidt in the *New York Times* as dismissing the book's central claim of a reasonable peace establishment with Hitler. Likewise, Richard Overy in the London *Observer* declared: "To suggest . . . that it would have been more in Britain's interest to place its future in German hands than run the risk of continued fighting, is so preposterous as barely to merit discussion. . . . The conditions Hitler wanted to impose on Britain in July, 1940, would have made it a virtual satellite, another Vichy. . . . Even this would have been torn up when it suited Hitler." James, in his *Times Literary Supplement* article, also rejected the idea of a treaty with Hitler, writing that "the essential truth was that Hitler was intent on a policy of brutal aggrandizement, backed by overwhelming military power, and could not be deterred by territorial concessions or treaties." However, James praised the book's "genuine discussions" and pointed to the essential question raised by Charmley's research: "was Churchill right?"

Charmley told *CA:* "I write biographies because I'm interested in people and because people ask me to write them."

BIOGRAPHICAL/CRITICAL SOURCES:

PERIODICALS

Books, January, 1993, p. 8.
Choice, March, 1991, p. 1199.
New York Times, January 9, 1993, p. A2.
New York Times Book Review, May 29, 1988, p. 15.
Observer (London), December 13, 1987, p. 22; August 20, 1989, p. 38; January 17, 1993, p. 51.
Publishers Weekly, January 23, 1987, p. 54.
Spectator, September 26, 1987, pp. 33-34; December 16, 1989, pp. 28-29.
Times Educational Supplement, November 7, 1986, p. 29.
Times Literary Supplement, May 16, 1986, p. 527; October 31, 1986, pp. 1207-1209; January 27-February 2, 1989; January 8, 1993, pp. 7-8.
Times (London), April 10, 1986.

—*Sketch by Linda Tidrick*

*　　*　　*

CHAUDHURI, Pranay 1957-

PERSONAL: Born October 31, 1957, in Medinipur (West Bengal), India; son of Pratap (a government employee) and Taranga Chaudhuri; married April 22, 1984; wife's name, Krishna; children: Plaban. *Education:* University of Calcutta, B.Sc. (with first class honors), 1977, B.Tech. (with first class honors), 1980; Jadavpur University, M.E. (with first class honors), 1983, Ph.D., 1988.

ADDRESSES: Home—P.O. Box 29605, Safat, Kuwait. *Office*—Department of Electrical and Computer Engineering, University of Kuwait, P.O. Box 5969, Safat 13060, Kuwait.

CAREER: Indian Institute of Technology, Kharagpur, lecturer in computer science and engineering, 1984-89; James Cook University of North Queensland, Townsville, Australia, lecturer in computer science, 1988-90; University of New South Wales, Sydney, Australia, senior lecturer in computer science and engineering, 1990—. University of Kuwait, associate professor, 1993—.

AWARDS, HONORS: Best Speakers Award from National Seminar on Computer and Robotics, Madras, India, 1984; M. N. Saha Memorial Award from Institution of Electronics and Telecommunication Engineers, New Delhi, India, 1987; Outstanding Young Computer Scientist grant from International Information Science Foundation, Tokyo, Japan, 1992; grants from Australian Research Council, 1992, and University of Kuwait, 1993.

WRITINGS:

Parallel Algorithms: Design and Analysis, Prentice-Hall Australia, 1992.

Contributor of about forty articles and reviews to scientific journals.

WORK IN PROGRESS: Research on parallel and distributed computing, algorithm design and analysis, and graph theory.

*   *   *

CHENETIER, Marc 1946-

PERSONAL: Born November 1, 1946, in Blois, France; son of a state employee; married Odile Genevieve Antoine (a program coordinator), August 29, 1969; children: Marion, Chloe. *Education:* University of Tours, B.A., 1967, M.A., 1968; University of Paris III-Sorbonne Nouvelle, Agregation d'Anglais, 1970, Doctorat d'Etat, 1979.

ADDRESSES: Home—39 rue de l'Amiral-Mouchez, 75013-Paris, France. *Office*— Ecole Normale Superieure, 31 Avenue Lombart, F-92266, Fontenay-aux-Roses, France.

CAREER: Scholar and translator. Centre Pedagogique Regional de Tours, teacher of English in training, 1969-70; Stanford University, Stanford, CA, lecturer in

French, 1970-72; University of Paris III-Sorbonne Nouvelle, France, assistant professor, 1972-79; University of Orleans, Orleans, France, professor, 1980-91; Ecole Normale Superieure, Fontenay-aux-Roses, France, professor of American literature, 1991—. University of East Anglia, Norwich, England, visiting professor, 1979-80; Stanford University, visiting professor, 1981; University of Virginia, Charlottesville, visiting professor, 1983-84; Princeton University, visiting professor, 1987. *Military service:* National Service, 1970-72.

MEMBER: Societe des Anglicistes de l'Enseignement Superieur, Association Francaise d'Etudes Americaines (treasurer, 1976-82), Association Europeenne d'Etudes Americaines (adjunct treasurer, 1981-83), Groupe Rene Tadlov de Recherche sur la Litterature Americaine Contemporaine (founder), Centre d'Etudes et de Recherches sur la Culture Anglo-Americaine, Orleans (founder), Laboratoire Orleans-Tours de Litterature Americaine (founder), Society for the Study of Midwestern Literature, Vachel Lindsay Association, Amis de Tor House (Association Robinson Jeffers), Association des Traducteurs Litteraires de France, Societe des Amis de Maurice-Edgar Coindreau (founding member), Jury du Prix Maurice Edgar Coindreau (founding member), Societe Tocqueville, Groupe de Recherches Americaines, Association Inter-Universites Americaines.

AWARDS, HONORS: Scholarship, American Council of Learned Societies, 1975; Fullbright Scholarship, 1983; fellow, Salzburg seminar, 1985; Chevalier des Palmes Academipues, 1987.

WRITINGS:

TRANSLATOR

(With wife, Odile Chenetier) G. W. Parkyn, *Vers un modele conceptuel d'education permanente,* Presses de l'UNESCO, 1973.
Richard Brautigan, *Un Prive a Babylone,* (title means "Dreaming of Babylon"), Christian Bourgois, 1981.
Jonathan Baumbach, *Ce soir, on joue mes reves* (title means "Reruns"), Editions Ramsay, 1983.
Richard Brautigan, *Memoires Sauves du vent* (title means "So The Wind Won't Blow It All Away"), Christian Bourgois, 1983.
William Byron, *Cervantes,* Julliard, 1984.
Elizabeth Swados, *Lea et Lazare* (title means "Lea and Lazar"), Editions de l'Acropole, 1984.
Willa Cather, *Le Mort et e Archevque* (title means "Death Comes for the Archbishop") Editions Ramsay, 1986.
Cather, *Mon ennemi mortal* (title means "My Mortal Enemy"), Editions Ramsay, 1986.
Jerome Charyn, *Le Nez de Pinocchio* (title means "Pinocchio's Nose"), Le Setuil, 1990.

Also translator of *Au cacus de cacus de ce pays,* by William Gass; *Demendiz le programme,* by Robert Cooves; *Fiskadoro,* by Denis Johnson; *Continents a la Derive,* by Russell Banks; and *Pionniers, Une Lome Purdue,* and *La Un des notres,* all by Cather.

OTHER

(With John Barson) *Textuellement,* Holt, 1974.

(Editor) *Selected Letters of Vachel Lindsay,* Burt Franklin, 1979.

By Signs Obsessed: The Aesthetics of Vachel Lindsay, University Microfilms International, 1981, published as *L'Obsession des signes: L'Esthetique de Vachel Lindsay (1879-1931),* Atelier de Reproduction des Theses, 1984.

(Editor with Rob Kroes) *Impressions of a Gilded Age: The American fin de siecle,* EAAS, 1983.

Richard Brautigan, Methuen, 1983.

Critical Angles: European Views of Contemporary American Literature, Southern Illinois University Press, 1985.

Au-Dela du soupcon, (title means "Beyond Suspicion"), Le Seuil, 1989, University of Pennsylvania Press, 1994.

Also author of *La Fiction Americaine de 1960 a 1985* (title means "American Fiction from 1960 to 1989"), Le Seuil. Contributor to anthologies, including *MidAmerica II,* edited by David Anderson, Midwestern Press, 1975; *Le Discours de la violence dans la culture Americaine* (title means "Discourse of Violence in the American Culture"), edited by Regis Durand, Presses Universitaires de Lille, 1979; *Poetic Knowledge: Circumference and Center,* edited by Roland Hagenbuchle and J. T. Swann, Bouvier Verlag Herbert Grundmann, 1980; *Traditions in Twentieth Century American Literature,* edited by Marta Sienicka, Poznan, 1982; *American Literary Scholarship 1981,* edited by J. Woodress, Duke University Press, 1983; and *American Poetry: Between Tradition and Modernism 1865-1914,* edited by Roland Hagenbuchle, Verlag Friedrich Pustet, 1984. Contributor to *Encyclopedia Universalis,* and *Encyclopedie Larousse.*

Also editor or co-editor of special issues of scholarly journals, including *Trema, Revue Francaise d'etudes Americaines, Bas de casse, Delta, Focus, Le Magazine Litteraire, Europe,* and *La Quinzaine litteraire.* Contributor to periodicals, including *La Quinzaine litteraire, Caliban, Quotidien de Paris, Revue Francaise d'etudes Americaines, Trema, Nouvelle Revue Francaise, Northwest Review, Nouvelles Litteraires, Stanford French Review, Review of Contemporary Fiction, Les Cahiers de l'Herne, Delta, Journal of American Studies, Vachel Lindsay Newsletter, American Book Review, Les Langues modernes,* and *Times Higher Education Supplement.*

SIDELIGHTS: Marc Chenetier is a distinguished French scholar of American literature whose best known work in the United States is his volume of the letters of American poet Vachel Lindsay, who lived from 1879 to 1931. Chenetier travelled to twenty-five depositories throughout the United States to garner close to two thousand letters of which two hundred comprise this volume. The letters shed light on the exuberance and dedication with which Lindsay pursued his vision of an America whose potential remained unrealized. According to Chenetier in his introduction to *Selected Letters of Vachel Lindsay,* the poet's "main idea was to unify expression so that the country could take hold of itself once more, renew its mythology, revivify it, and reorganize the national unconscious."

According to Chenetier, Lindsay's most famous works were his first published—1913's "General William Booth Enters into Heaven," and "The Congo"—which appeared in the influential magazine *Poetry* during World War I. Lindsay's inability to garner similar attention and respect for later works led to his increasing frustration with the American public, and it exacerbated the author's already fragile mental state. Included in *Selected Letters of Vachel Lindsay* is the last letter Lindsay wrote to his four-year-old son, Nicholas, asking him to "be brave." Lindsay killed himself at the age of fifty-two by drinking a cleaning solution. Chenetier writes: "These pages poignantly illustrate the despair born of incomprehension that gradually pervaded a man of trust and hope, the constant hammering of a warped image that reduces a face to a mere mask and a rich and many-colored personality to a paranoid and a repetitive entertainer."

Selected Letters of Vachel Lindsay received warm praise from American reviewers for the gaps it fills in Lindsay scholarship. Poet, novelist, and critic James Dickey remarked in the *New York Times Book Review* that "beyond a few superficial assumptions gleaned from the author-notes of anthologies, I have never, before reading these letters, known much of what sort of man Lindsay actually was, or how he lived and worked, that he had studied medicine and trained as an artist before devoting himself mainly to poetry." Novelist and Lindsay scholar Mark Harris commented in his *Chicago Tribune* review: "In the past we mainly guessed at some events. Here now a great deal is revealed to us, all the more heart-stirring for its being told by Lindsay himself from the depths of his torment." Susan Wood in the *Washington Post Book World* concluded that "These letters . . . reveal Lindsay as a much more interesting and prophetic poetic theorist than one might have imagined. . . . Scholars of 20th-century American literature will find it a valuable source."

BIOGRAPHICAL/CRITICAL SOURCES:

BOOKS

Chenetier, Marc, editor, *Selected Letters of Vachel Lindsay,* Burt Franklin, 1979.

PERIODICALS

Chicago Tribune, November 4, 1979, section 7, p. 1; November 4, 1979, section 7, pp. 1-2.
New York Times Book Review, December 23, 1979, pp. 9, 17-18.
Washington Post Book World, January 13, 1980, pp. 9, 14.

*   *   *

CHIRAS, Daniel D. 1950-

PERSONAL: Born October 26, 1950, in New York, NY; son of Stanley J. (in chemical manufacturing) and Mary F. (a homemaker) Chiras; married September 28, 1986; wife's name, Kathleen Ann (in real estate); children: Skyler, Forrest. *Education:* Kansas State University, B.A. (cum laude), 1971; University of Kansas, Ph.D., 1976. *Avocational Interests:* Hiking, cross-country skiing, kayaking, softball, tropical fish, organic gardening.

ADDRESSES: Home and office—7652 Gartner Rd., Evergreen, CO 40439.

CAREER: Free-lance writer, 1980—. Adjunct professor, University of Denver and University of Colorado. Colorado Environmental Coalition, member of board of directors, 1987-90, head of Environmental Health Committee, 1988-93, president, 1990-92; Speakers for a Sustainable Future, co-founder, 1989, member of advisory board, 1989—; Colorado's Ocean Journey, member of scientific advisory board, 1991—; Center for Environmental Solutions, member of board of directors, 1993—; Sustainable Futures Society, co-founder, 1993, president and director of sustainable development and policy analysis, 1993—.

MEMBER: North American Association for Environmental Education, Rocky Mountain Cichlid Association, Southern Colorado Aquarium Society, Phi Kappa Phi.

AWARDS, HONORS: Award from Colorado Energy Research Institute, 1980; Governor's Award for Service, Volunteers for Outdoor Colorado, 1985.

WRITINGS:

Environmental Science: Action for a Sustainable Future, Benjamin-Cummings, 1985, 4th edition, 1994.
Environmental Science: A Framework for Decision Making, Addison-Wesley, 1989.
(With Oliver S. Owen) *Natural Resource Conservation,* Macmillan, 5th edition, 1990.

Beyond the Fray: Reshaping the American Environmental Response, Johnson Books, 1990.
Human Biology: Health, Homeostasis, and the Environment, West Publishing, 1991, 2nd edition, 1994.
Lessons From Nature: Learning to Live Sustainably on the Planet, Island Press, 1992.
Biology: The Web of Life, West Publishing, 1993.
Study Skills for Science Students, West Publishing, 1994.
(Editor) *Regional Issues: Supplement to Environmental Science,* Benjamin-Cummings, 1994.

Author of "Earthbeat," a column in *Journal of the Southern Colorado Aquarium Society.* Author of the "Environment Section," for the annual *Science Year.* Contributor of articles to scientific journals and newspapers. Co-editor, *Environmental Carcinogenesis and Ecotoxicology Reviews.*

WORK IN PROGRESS: Readings in Biology, for West Publishing; *Best Environmental Books: Summaries of America's Best Environmental Books.*

SIDELIGHTS: Daniel D. Chiras told *CA:* "When people find out that I'm a writer and that I work at home, they usually comment on my discipline. To me, discipline has nothing to do with my success. I'd write if it were illegal! I enjoy it that much.

"But writing has not always been an easy road to travel. When I decided to embark on a full-time writing career, I left a postdoctoral fellowship at Harvard and moved to a leaky cabin in the mountains of Colorado. With electricity and a refrigerator as my only amenities, I drew water from a well and used an outhouse even on the coldest Colorado nights. I spent a year writing in the cabin accompanied by all the neighbors' dogs, who arrived as soon as their masters had left for work. When I wasn't writing, I was sending off stories, articles, and book proposals, and receiving one rejection after another. I could have heated the cabin with pink slips that year.

"Undaunted (well, actually, a bit distressed after a year of no success) I moved to a farmhouse near Bozeman, Montana. Although it marked a definite improvement in living conditions, with running water and an indoor privy, my success as a writer didn't improve much that year. I continued to write day in and day out, but managed to succeed in publishing only one article, despite the fact that I'd finished my third book and God knows how many short stories and articles. Desperate, I contemplated going to law school. After being accepted, though, I decided to try one more year of writing. I swore I'd dig ditches, if necessary, to support my writing addiction.

"A few months later, I landed my first book contract. And what a contract! It was a writer's dream come true. The publisher paid all my writing and living expenses for seventeen months while I wrote *Environmental Science.* Ironically, the idea for this book had been rejected by several publishing companies of note. One editor, in fact, went so far as to admonish me for working on it, now that I was no longer a full-time professor. He stated quite emphatically that authors who didn't teach really couldn't write successful texts. Today, the success of *Environmental Science* reinforces my belief that editors, valuable as they are, are not always right!"

*   *   *

CHIU, Tony

PERSONAL: Born in China; immigrated to United States; married; children: two daughters. *Avocational Interests:* Has twice traveled around the world.

CAREER: Journalist and writer.

WRITINGS:

THRILLERS

Port Arthur Chicken, Morrow, 1979, reprinted as *Onyxx,* Berkley, 1981.
Realm Seven, Bantam, 1984.
(With Robert Ballard) *Bright Shark,* Delacorte, 1992.

OTHER

Making the Best Deal: Your Home, Simon & Schuster, 1986.
Making the Best Deal: Your Health and Wealth, Simon and Schuster, 1986.
(With Ross Perot) *Ross Perot in His Own Words,* Warner, 1992.

Has written for various publications, including Time-Life Books, *People,* and *New York Times.*

SIDELIGHTS: Tony Chiu is a versatile journalist and writer who has produced fiction, nonfiction, including a volume on 1992 presidential candidate Ross Perot, and a wide range of profiles and public-interest pieces for *People.* Chiu has received a number of reviews among major periodicals for his thrillers, including *Port Arthur Chicken* and *Realm Seven.*

In *Port Arthur Chicken,* Chiu's first effort in the genre, Chinese-American journalist Ray Huang inadvertently witnesses the murder of an American geologist. Once he begins his investigation into the American's death, Huang finds himself the target of murderous conspirators plotting worldwide control. Among the more extreme villains Huang encounters are a deadly poetry aficionado and an unrelenting militarist. Richard Freedman, writing in the *New York Times Book Review,* reported that *Port Arthur Chicken* (which was reprinted in 1981 as *Onyxx*) contains

"enough paranoid plotting . . . to sustain any six espionage novels," but he added that Huang is an "engaging" protagonist and concluded that "the reality of [Chiu's] details and the high spirit of his writing charm away all disbelief."

Among Chiu's other thrillers is *Realm Seven,* the story of a woman, Andrea Mattson, who discovers that her daughter is involved in a life-threatening computer game with Nazi-like aspects. After Mattson expresses her concerns to her ex-husband, he is found dead. Likewise, she discusses matters with her lover, whereupon he, too, is mysteriously killed. Soon she is compelled to track the game, called Realm, to its center at a computer complex operated by scientists and war-games players.

With Robert Ballard, Chiu wrote *Bright Shark,* a techno-thriller in which Navy scuba divers discover portions of an Israeli ship that supposedly sank more than twenty years earlier. Soon the novel's protagonists, diver Edna Haddix and federal official Wendell Trent, run afoul of both Israeli agents and American authorities eager to suppress knowledge concerning the submerged Israeli vessel. *Chicago Tribune* reviewer Peter Gorner—who noted that Chiu's collaborator, Ballard, is a pioneer in the development of aquatic research technology—declared that *Bright Shark* manages to "convey the excitement of underwater exploration and explain how it's done."

BIOGRAPHICAL/CRITICAL SOURCES:

PERIODICALS

Chicago Tribune, April 22, 1992, section 5, p. 3.
Los Angeles Times Book Review, September 30, 1984, p. 8.
New York Times Book Review, November 18, 1979, p. 14; August 16, 1981, p. 27.*

*   *   *

CHRISTENSON, James A. 1944-

PERSONAL: Born June 8, 1944, in Paso Robles, CA; married Patricia Lyle; children: Eric, Kellie. *Education:* Gonzaga University, B.A., 1968; Washington State University, M.Ex., 1970, Ph.D., 1972.

ADDRESSES: Home—2705 Camino La Zorrella, Tucson, AZ 85718. *Office*—Cooperative Extension, Forbes 301, College of Agriculture, University of Arizona, Tucson, AZ 85721.

CAREER: North Carolina State University, Raleigh, assistant professor, 1972-75, associate professor of statistics, 1975-76, extension community development specialist, 1972-76; University of Kentucky, Lexington, associate professor, 1976, founder and director of Survey Research Center, 1979-82, professor of sociology, 1981-89, head of department, 1982-89; University of Arizona, Tucson, associate dean and director of Cooperative Extension, 1989—. International Research Group in Extension, co-founder, 1988.

MEMBER: International Rural Sociological Association, American Sociological Association, Rural Sociological Society (president, 1986-87), Community Development Society, Southern Sociological Society.

AWARDS, HONORS: Shared departmental teaching award, American Sociological Association, 1984.

WRITINGS:

(Editor with Jerry W. Robinson, Jr.) *Community Development in America,* Iowa State University Press, 1980.
(With Paul D. Warner) *The Cooperative Extension Service: A National Assessment,* Westview, 1984.
(Editor with Robinson) *Community Development in Perspective,* Iowa State University Press, 1989.
(With Cornelia B. Flora) *Rural Policies for the 1990s,* Westview, 1991.
Rural Data, People, and Policy, Westview, 1994.

Work represented in anthologies. Contributor of more than a hundred articles to periodicals. *Rural Sociology,* editor, 1982-86.

*   *   *

CHUAN-HSIANG
See SHIH, Chih-yu

*   *   *

CICCONE, Madonna Louise Veronica
See MADONNA

*   *   *

CLARK, Jerome   1946-

PERSONAL: Born November 27, 1946, in Canby, MN; son of Delmer Randolph (a railroad depot agent) and Kathleen (a homemaker; maiden name, Garvey) Clark; married Penelope French, August 20, 1976 (divorced, July, 1985); married Nancy Conrad (in desktop publishing), September 24, 1988; children: Alex French (stepson), Evan Keith, Molly Susannah. *Education:* Attended South Dakota State University, 1964-66; and Moorhead State University, 1966-69. *Politics:* Democrat. *Religion:* Agnos-

tic. *Avocational Interests:* Folk, blues, and vernacular music, history, politics, literary fiction.

ADDRESSES: Home and office—612 North Oscar Ave., Canby, MN 56220. *Agent*—L. T. Mead, 379 Burning Tree Court, Half Moon Bay, CA 94019.

CAREER: Fate, Highland Park, IL, associate editor, 1976-87, senior editor, 1987-89, then in St Paul, MN, consulting editor, 1989-93; writer, 1989—. Songwriter, with Robin and Linda Williams, 1978—; J. Allen Hynek Center for UFO Studies, vice-president, 1987—.

AWARDS, HONORS: Awards for outstanding academic reference work from *Choice, Library Journal,* and New York Public Library, 1990, for *New Age Encyclopedia;* outstanding academic reference book award from *Choice,* 1992, for *The Emergence of a Phenomenon;* Isabel Memorial Award, Fund for UFO Research, 1992.

WRITINGS:

(With Loren Coleman) *The Unidentified: Notes Toward Solving the UFO Mystery,* Warner Books, 1975.
(With Coleman) *Creatures of the Outer Edge,* Warner Books, 1978.
(With D. Scott Rogo) *Earth's Secret Inhabitants,* Tempo Books, 1979.
(With J. Gordon Melton and Aidan A. Kelly) *New Age Encyclopedia,* Gale, 1990, published as *New Age Almanac,* Visible Ink Press, 1991.
The UFO Encyclopedia, Omnigraphics, Inc., Volume I: *UFOs in the 1980s,* 1990, Volume II: *The Emergence of a Phenomenon: UFOs From the Beginning Through 1959,* 1992, Volume III: *High Strangeness: UFOs From 1960 Through 1979,* in press.
UFO Encounters: Sightings, Visitations, and Investigations, Publications International, 1992.
Encyclopedia of Strange and Unexplained Physical Phenomena, Gale, 1993, published as *Unexplained! 347 Strange Sightings, Incredible Occurrences, and Puzzling Physical Phenomena,* Visible Ink Press, 1993.

Contributor to periodicals, including *Omni.* Editor, *International UFO Reporter,* 1985—.

WORK IN PROGRESS: A guide to cryptozoological animals; books on messianic flying-saucer cults and on modern beliefs and movements, focused on alternative realities and otherworldly beings.

SIDELIGHTS: Jerome Clark told *CA:* "My interest in UFOs and other anomalies of science goes back to my childhood, when I read *The Report on Unidentified Flying Objects* written by Edward J. Ruppelt, a retired Air Force officer who, in the early 1950s, had headed Project Blue Book. One of the relative handful of non-silly books on UFOs, *Report* took a hard-headed, objective approach which eschewed the extremes of belief and disbelief. Though it was published in 1956, it remains one of the essential works in the literature. Probably if I had read one of the silly books, I would have dismissed the subject on the spot and gone on to other things.

"Nearly four decades later, the UFO question continues to interest me, not only as a yet-unanswered scientific question, but for all that it tells us about the human response to the unknown. In the face of the unknown, human beings either embrace it and fill in all the blanks with their imaginations and spiritual yearnings, or deny it just as fervently. In all likelihood, the mystery would have been solved long ago if cool heads, backed by the necessary funding and other resources, had applied themselves and approached the question with the proper intellectual detachment. Why that didn't happen is, I'm sure, a matter that will occupy philosophers, sociologists, and historians of science all through the twenty-first century. The denial of the UFO phenomenon by many elite scientists may be equated with the denial of evolution by many prominent Victorian scientists. In that sense Carl Sagan may be our Sir Richard Owen.

"Still, where UFO claims are concerned, there is much to be skeptical about, and gullibility, error, and fraud—not to mention simple loose thinking—have done much to marginalize the issue. Proponents of UFOs are as often as not their own worst enemies.

"My own approach has nothing to do with occultism, with which I am entirely out of sympathy, and I do not consider myself a paranormalist either. I am strictly an Old Age materialist/rationalist, and I define myself simply as an anomalist. Magical thinking will no more help us answer the questions raised by UFO sightings and reports of cryptozoological animals than will dogmatic refusal to investigate. Though some anomalies give every appearance of being beyond our current capacity to explain, that tells us only that there are things we don't know. It does *not* validate the supernatural or intimate a larger divine order. As we seek the answers, science and reason remain, as they have through the entire history of human inquiry, our best guides.

"Even more than anomalistics, my major passion in life is traditional music—the sort of music performed by mountain ballad singers, rural and urban blues artists, Hawaiian slack-key guitarists, Cajun and zydeco accordian pumpers, barrelhouse piano pounders, Western swing fiddlers, Appalachian banjo pickers, Tex-Mex conjuntos, bluegrass bands, and other practitioners of authentic regional styles. If I had it to do over again, I'd be a historian of American folk music.

"Related to this is my secondary occupation, songwriting. The only instrument I play is the stereo, but since the late 1970s I have written lyrics for Robin and Linda Williams (known to all listeners of Garrison Keillor's public radio programs) who have recorded our collaborative efforts on their own albums. Our songs have also been covered by Emmylou Harris, Tom T. Hall, Mary Chapin Carpenter, George Hamilton IV, and others. Harris's version of our *Rollin' and Ramblin' (The Death of Hank Williams)* was made into a music video in 1991."

*   *   *

CLARKE, Cheryl 1947-

PERSONAL: Born May 16, 1947, in Washington, DC; daughter of James and Edna Clarke. *Education:* Howard University, B.A., 1969; Rutgers University, M.A., 1974; Rutgers University, M.S.W., 1980.

ADDRESSES: Home—247 Liberty Ave., Jersey City, NJ 07307.

CAREER: Poet and free-lance writer. Member of New York Women Against Rape, 1985-88; co-chair of the board, Center for Gay and Lesbian Studies, City University of New York Graduate Center, 1990-92; member of steering committee, New Jersey Women and AIDS Network; administrator, Office of the Provost, Rutgers University, New Brunswick, NJ.

WRITINGS:

Narratives: Poems in the Tradition of Black Women, illustrated by Gaia (Gay Belknap), Women of Color Press, 1983.
Living as a Lesbian (poems), Firebrand, 1986.
Humid Pitch: Narrative Poetry, Firebrand, 1989.
Experimental Love, Firebrand, 1993.

Collections magazine, member of editorial collective, 1981-90.

SIDELIGHTS: Cheryl Clarke is a poet with a unique perspective, according to critics. As the titles of her collections make clear, her work finds its roots in her experience not only as an African American, but also as a lesbian and feminist. For Clarke, this vantage point serves not to limit, but rather to enrich her writings. Drawing upon certain long-standing traditions in black culture, particularly oral narratives, as well as jazz, blues, and gospel music, she fuses these elements with a lesbian and feminist sensibility to create poems with a voice that, in the words of *Belles Lettres* reviewer Jane Campbell, "reverberate with uncompromising toughness, piercing joy, and sensual delight."

Clarke's first collection, *Narratives: Poems in the Tradition of Black Women,* consists of fifteen poems in a style that

Calvin Hernton described in *Parnassus* as "oral narratives, liberating and testimonial, written from a lesbian-feminist perspective." The poems address a variety of themes from the viewpoint of numerous narrators; as Ruthan Robson of *New Pages* noted, the speakers of the poems in this volume are "marvelous and varied," and include mothers, older women, young black girls, wives, lesbians, and sisters. Through these voices, Clarke explores what Hernton identified as her central thematic concerns: "to expose and condemn sexual repression while providing truth, honesty, and sustenance for the liberation of black women." The narratives celebrate the possibility of community among women and also expose what Hernton called "the many daily small hells of black women," including the violence directed toward women by men, and the difficulties of being a black woman in a society dominated by white men.

Living as a Lesbian and *Humid Pitch: Narrative Poetry,* published in 1986 and 1989, respectively, continue the themes Clarke develops in her first collection, but with a marked change in poetic direction. "Clarke, the self-proclaimed narrative poet," Dorothy Allison noted in her *Voice Literary Supplement* review of *Living as a Lesbian,* breaks out "into lyrical song, jazz melodies played in counterpoint to uncompromising political judgements." Retaining her emphasis on what Hernton labeled as "women-identified" symbolism and allusions in her earlier work, Clarke reaches out to aspects of the larger African American culture, especially jazz, to form what Allison described as "something completely original"—poems with "raw and immediate power." This fusion of poetry, music, and sensuality is further elaborated throughout *Humid Pitch.* The poem "Epic of Song," for example, details an erotic relationship between three female singers and musicians. As Campbell remarked, the poem is not simply "a celebration of women's love for women; Clarke's epic explores the connections among eroticism, creativity, and work—the power available to those who fuse art and life." Yet even with her emphasis on the sensual, Clarke does not focus on it exclusively. The volume also contains poems which address the perils of being gay in a small town, the discovering of one's sexual identity, and the strength of a bond between sisters. Campbell's closing comments on *Humid Pitch* might serve as both a summary of Clarke's poetry as a whole and many of her critics' responses to it. "Informing [the book]," Campbell wrote, "are women's capacities to survive, love, and nurture; one leaves the book with new reverence for our strength, complexity, and diversity."

BIOGRAPHICAL/CRITICAL SOURCES:

PERIODICALS

Belles Lettres, fall, 1990, p.53.

New Pages, fall, 1984, p. 23.
Parnassus, spring-summer-fall-winter, 1985, p. 518-550.
Voice Literary Supplement, February, 1987, p. 21.*

*   *   *

CLARKE, Patricia 1926-

PERSONAL: Born July 30, 1926, in Melbourne, Australia; daughter of John Laurence (a teacher) and Annie Teresa (McSweeney) Ryan; married Hugh Vincent Clarke (a writer), 1961; children: John Hugh, Justin Patrick, Brigid Jane Clarke Veale. *Education:* Attended University of Melbourne, 1943-44.

ADDRESSES: Home—14 Chermside St., Deakin, Canberra, Australian Capital Territory 2600.

CAREER: Australian News and Information Bureau, journalist in Melbourne and Canberra; Australian Broadcasting Co., Canberra, journalist in Press Gallery; M. B. Newton Publications, editor and journalist; National Capital Development Commission, editor and journalist.

MEMBER: Australian Journalists Association, Australian Society of Authors, National Press Club of Australia, Canberra Historical Society (member of council, 1987—).

AWARDS, HONORS: Grants from Australia's Literature Board, 1987, 1989; Harold White fellow, National Library of Australia, 1993.

WRITINGS:

The Governesses: Letters from the Colonies, 1862-1882, Hutchinson, 1985.
A Colonial Woman: The Life and Times of Mary Braidwood Mowle, 1827-1857, Routledge, Chapman & Hall, 1986.
Pen Portraits: Women Writers and Journalists in Nineteenth Century Australia, Allen & Unwin, 1988.
Pioneer Writer: The Life of Louisa Atkinson, Novelist, Journalist, Naturalist, Allen & Unwin, 1990, Paul and Co. Publishers Consortium, 1991.
(Editor with Dale Spender) *LifeLines: Australian Women's Letters and Diaries, 1788-1840,* Paul and Co. Publishers Consortium, 1992.
Tasma: The Life of Jessie Couvreur, Allen & Unwin, 1994.

Editor, *Canberra Historical Journal,* 1987—.

WORK IN PROGRESS: A biography of Roza Praed.

*   *   *

CLAVEL, Pierre

PERSONAL: Married, wife's name Anne S. (a city planner and lawyer), March 20, 1960; children: Caroline,

Pierre A., Thomas A. *Education:* Haverford College, A.B., 1957; University of North Carolina at Chapel Hill, M.R.P., 1959; Cornell University, Ph.D., 1966.

ADDRESSES: Home—109 Cornell St., Ithaca, NY 14850. *Office*—Department of City and Regional Planning, 106 West Sibley Hall, Cornell University, Ithaca, NY 14853.

CAREER: Blair Associates, Providence, RI, city planner, 1960-62; University of Puerto Rico, Rio Piedras, assistant professor of planning, 1965-67; Cornell University, Ithaca, NY, began as assistant professor, became professor of city and regional planning, 1967—. City of Ithaca, member of Rental Housing Commission, 1990-92. *Military service:* U.S. Army, 1959, 1961-62.

MEMBER: Association of Collegiate Schools of Planning (vice-president, 1977-79), American Planning Association.

AWARDS, HONORS: Davidoff Award from Association of Collegiate Schools of Planning, 1990.

WRITINGS:

(Editor with William W. Goldsmith) *Urban and Regional Planning in an Age of Austerity,* Pergamon, 1980.
Opposition Planning in Wales and Appalachia, Temple University Press, 1983.
The Progressive City: Planning and Participation, Rutgers University Press, 1986.
(Editor with Wim Wiewel) *Harold Washington and the Neighborhoods: Progressive City Government in Chicago,* Rutgers University Press, 1991.
(With N. Krumholz) *Regenerating American Cities: Equity Planners Tell Their Stories,* Temple University Press, in press.

*   *   *

CLAYTON, Richard Henry Michael   1907-1993
(William Haggard)

OBITUARY NOTICE—See index for *CA* sketch: Born August 11, 1907, in Croydon, Surrey, England; died October 27, 1993. Civil servant and author. Under the pseudonym William Haggard, Clayton achieved success as the author of the "Colonel Charles Russell" series of suspense novels. Educated at Oxford, Clayton began his career as a magistrate with the Indian Civil Service in 1931, advancing to the position of sessions judge before joining the Mahratta Light Infantry in 1939. Seven years later he returned to England, and became controller of the Enemy Property Branch of the British Civil Service Board of Trade in 1957. Clayton published his first spy thriller—the well-received *Slow Burner*—the following year, and

continued to develop the series until 1990. Considered intelligent and refined, the works attracted a readership throughout Europe and the U.S. The central character, Colonel Charles Russell, is affiliated with a fictional branch of the British intelligence establishment known as the Security Executive, and is involved in international affairs. Clayton retired from the Board of Trade in 1969 to pursue a full-time writing career; among his "Colonel Charles Russell" novels are *The Arena, The Mischief Makers,* and *The Vendettists.* The author also published suspense novels apart from the series, such as *The Martello Tower* and *The Expatriates.*

OBITUARIES AND OTHER SOURCES:

BOOKS

Who's Who, 146th edition, St. Martin's, 1994, p. 369.

PERIODICALS

Times (London), November 5, 1993, p. 21.

*   *   *

CLOVIS, Allen M.   1953-

PERSONAL: Born March 10, 1953, in Salina, KS; children: Anna Marie. *Education:* Washburn University of Topeka, B.B.A., 1975, B.A., 1990, J.D., 1993; Troy State University, M.S., 1984; Naval Postgraduate School, M.A., 1986. *Religion:* Lutheran. *Avocational Interests:* Golf, flying, music, reading, tennis.

ADDRESSES: Office—5709 Southwest 21st St., Topeka, KS 66614.

CAREER: U.S. Air Force officer, 1975-90, with assignments in multinational management, supervision, planning, logistics, operations, training, and evaluation; served in England and Germany. Law office of R. Alan Bibler, attorney, 1993—.

MEMBER: Kansas Authors Club, Washburn University of Topeka Alumni Association, Naval Postgraduate School Alumni Association, Tau Kappa Epsilon, Air Force Association, Army Navy Country Club, Royal Air Force Club, Table for Eight Writers Group.

AWARDS, HONORS: Military: Defense Meritorious Service Medal, Air Force Meritorious Service Medal, and Air Force Commendation Medal. *Other:* J. Donald Coffin Memorial Book Award from Kansas Authors Club, 1993, for *The Potsdam Protocol.*

WRITINGS:

The Potsdam Protocol (novel), Lone Tree Publishing, 1993.

WORK IN PROGRESS: The Tripoli Protocol.

COLEMAN, Mary DeLorse 1954-

PERSONAL: Born June 5, 1954, in Forest, MS; daughter of John and Catherine Coleman; married Joe Laymon (divorced, November, 1978); children: Kiese. *Education:* Jackson State University, B.A., 1975; University of Wisconsin—Madison, M.A., 1977, Ph.D., 1989; postdoctoral study at University of Maryland at College Park, 1989-90, and Harvard University, 1992-93. *Politics:* Independent. *Religion:* Baptist.

ADDRESSES: Home—327 Swallow Dr., Branden, MS 39042. *Office*—Department of Political Science, Jackson State University, 1400 Jr. Lynch St., Jackson, MS 39217-0001.

CAREER: Jackson State University, Jackson, MS, associate professor of political science and acting chairperson of department. Consultant to Blackside, Inc.

MEMBER: American Political Science Association, National Conference of Black Political Scientists, Southern Political Science Association.

AWARDS, HONORS: Best Teacher Award from National Conference of Black Political Scientists, 1990; liberal arts fellow, Harvard Law School, 1992-93.

WRITINGS:

Legislators, Law, and Public Policy, Greenwood Press, 1993.

Work represented in anthologies, including *The New Black Politics,* edited by Michael Preston, Longman, 1984, 2nd edition, 1987; *Mississippi Politics,* edited by J. Parker, Chatman Press, 1993; and *Political Behavior,* edited by Stanes Walton, Praeger, 1993.

WORK IN PROGRESS: Shelter in the Times of Storms: Exit From Poverty in Sunflower County, Mississippi.

SIDELIGHTS: Mary DeLorse Coleman told *CA:* "When I wrote *Legislators, Law, and Public Policy* I was finishing doctoral requirements at the University of Wisconsin—Madison. It was my good fortune to have a superb dissertation adviser and committee. The standards were quite high, and yet I had the knowledge of the subject matter and the living history of having grown to young adulthood in Mississippi. My course work was completed in record time, but the writing of the dissertation, and eventual book, took many years. Between streams I began a teaching career at Jackson State University.

"Ever since I have been old enough to observe human behavior, I have taken an interest in writing and thinking. I grew up in a small town of about three-thousand people. My mother and father and my siblings were a supportive cast, as was the community—school, church, and neighborhood. I had a wealth of confidence in myself as a stu-

dent and, later, as a divorcee and mother, I transferred values I had learned as a child to my son. These values included freedom of expression, character, and poise under stress. These values were imparted to me by my parents during the era of segregation in Mississippi. I was undaunted by racism. Racism was an annoyance; it was not a predictor of my fate or a noose around my neck, as it had been for some in the generations preceding mine.

"I now see in the young faces of my students, and I hear in their voices, a less strident confidence and determination in their tasks and career goals. I feel a special duty to hang in there and give them all I can and to demand from them the very best. I also find the time to write and think about the circumstances under which some children and their families succeed, while others fail. Writing remains a central part of the way I give expression to joys, fears, and hopes. Nurturing the mind every day is a prerequisite to becoming a good writer. Examination of the self and the other is the stuff of good writing."

*   *   *

CONROY, Thomas F(rancis) 1935-

PERSONAL: Born November 16, 1935, in Pittsburgh, PA; son of Thomas R. (a business executive) and Dora Frances (a teacher; maiden name, Schultz) Conroy; married Patricia Frances Haushalter (a retailer), October 16, 1961; children: Thomas Richard, Mary Patricia, Brian Francis, Eileen Bridget Dyer, Kieran Ann Zastrow, Griffin Daniel. *Education:* Attended University of Notre Dame, 1953-56; University of Pittsburgh, A.B., 1960. *Religion:* Roman Catholic. *Avocational Interests:* Aviation history, ornithology, stamp collecting.

ADDRESSES: Home and office—10030 Sterling, Allen Park, MI 48101.

CAREER: Pittsburgh National Bank, Pittsburgh, PA, credit manager and analyst, 1960-65; Jones & Laughlin Steel Corp., Pittsburgh, analyst and forecaster, 1965-66; Armco Steel Corp., Middletown, OH, market analyst, 1966-71; Diversey-Wyandotte Corp., Wyandotte, MI, market analyst and economist, 1971-80; R. L. Polk and Co. (marketing firm), Taylor, MI, senior analyst, 1985-88; Market Pathfinders, Allen Park, MI, proprietor, 1988-93. Southeast Michigan Census Council, member, 1993. *Military service:* U.S. Air Force, 1956-59.

WRITINGS:

(Editor) *Markets of the United States for Business Planners: Historical and Current Profiles of 183 United States Urban Economies by Major Sector and Industry with Maps, Graphics, and Commentary,* two volumes, Omnigraphics, 1992, 2nd edition, 1994.

Contributor to periodicals, including *American Demographics.* Editor of *BirdScope Newsletter,* 1978-82.

WORK IN PROGRESS: The Best Places to Start a New Business/Life (tentative title).

SIDELIGHTS: Thomas F. Conroy told *CA:* "During my career as a corporate market researcher and economist, I learned the importance of local-area economic change to businesses of all sizes and to the households that depend on them. Businesses are constantly faced with the need to place sales people, stores, distributors, and factories in specific places. While there is a wealth of local statistical information available, it is often outdated, inappropriate, or difficult and expensive to access. Little has been done to integrate this information and present it in an inexpensive, easy-to-use format. My magazine article 'Billion-Dollar Babies' and the book *Markets of the United States for Business Planners,* are first attempts in this direction. I am also researching additional information to support future publications and information products. A potential product would be a book describing the fastest-growing counties in the United States, both statistically and (especially) in prose that describes the benefits and problems experienced in high-growth areas."

*   *   *

COOPER, Melrose
   See KROLL, Virginia L(ouise)

*   *   *

COOPER, R(obert) C(ecil) 1917-

PERSONAL: Born November 24, 1917, in Wellington, New Zealand; son of William George (a chief postmaster) and Alice Celia (a homemaker; maiden name, Clutten) Cooper; married Jessica S. Scott, December 16, 1938 (deceased); married Una Vivienne Cassie Dellow (a scientist), September 29, 1984; children: (first marriage) Robert Scott, Jessica Scott. *Education:* University of New Zealand, B.Com., 1942, B.A., 1951; Washington University, Ph.D., 1953. *Avocational Interests:* Gardening.

ADDRESSES: Home—1/117 Cambridge Rd., Hamilton, New Zealand.

CAREER: New Zealand Public Service, New Zealand, worked as cadet, clerk, and section head in education, audit, state advances, and rehabilitation departments, 1945-58; Auckland War Memorial Museum, Auckland, New Zealand, botanist, 1948-68, assistant director, 1968-71; assistant at a high school in Te Kao, New Zealand, 1971-75. Washington University, St. Louis, MO,

university fellow and research assistant at Missouri Botanic Garden, 1951-53; Auckland Cancer Research Unit, collected plant samples in New Zealand and the Pacific, including New Guinea, 1953-58. *Military service:* New Zealand Army, warrant officer, 1942-43.

MEMBER: Art Galleries and Museums Association of New Zealand (life member; fellow), New Zealand Farm Forestry Association, New Zealand Tree Crops Association, New Zealand Botanical Society, Society for the History of Natural History.

WRITINGS:

(With S. G. Brooker and R. C. Cambie) *New Zealand Medicinal Plants,* Heinemann (Auckland), 1981, third edition, Reed (Victoria, Australia), 1991.
(With Brooker and Cambie) *Economic Native Plants of New Zealand,* Botany Division, DSIR, 1988.
(With Cambie) *New Zealand's Economic Native Plants,* Reed, 1991, Oxford University Press, 1992.

Contributor of articles to professional journals.

SIDELIGHTS: R. C. Cooper told *CA:* "When I met my father-in-law Robert Scott for the first time, he asked me what books I had read, what plants I knew, and what languages I could speak. He was so formidable that I hastily enrolled in botany and German classes, ending some sixteen years later with a doctoral degree from Washington University, in St. Louis, Missouri.

"On my return to New Zealand in 1953, I was asked to provide samples of plants for the Auckland Cancer Research Unit to test for anti-leukemic activity. In the end, the unit synthesized an anti-leukemic drug, which is now in use. I was then asked to list New Zealand's medicinal plants, and this list was published first as a handbook of the Auckland Museum. It was later rewritten for Heinemann. In fact, the list has followed me ever since I started compiling it in 1959. My coauthor Stan Brooker, an industrial chemist, is deceased. R. C. Cambie, professor of chemistry at the University of Auckland, continues to gather information for the next edition.

"My children tell me I would not pass the university examinations they have taken, and my grandchildren face a future where computers, DNA probes, and other gadgetry dominate. I do wonder, however, whether members of the new generation at work actually know the plants they are torturing—pardon, experimenting with. To me, the 'old-fashioned' botany we learned in the 1940s and 1950s is still the only sound basis for research with plants."

CORBETT, Richard (Graham) 1955-

PERSONAL: Born January 6, 1955, in Southport, England; son of Harry Graham (a World Health Organization official) and Kathleen Zita (Bryant) Corbett; married Inge van Gaal (marriage ended); married Anne de Malsche; children: Tom, Hannah, Laura. *Education:* Attended Oxford University, 1973-76. *Politics:* Labour ("democratic socialist").

ADDRESSES: Home—18 Della Faille Laan, 2020 Antwerp, Belgium. *Office*—European Parliament, rue Belliard, 1040 Brussels, Belgium.

CAREER: International Youth Organizations, Brussels, Belgium, secretary general of European Coordination Bureau, 1977-81; European Parliament, Brussels, member of Secretariat, 1981-89, member of Socialist Group, 1989—.

MEMBER: Jeunesse Europeenne Federaliste (president, 1979-81), GMB Trade Union (president, 1990—), Fabian Society.

WRITINGS:

(With F. Jacobs and M. Shackleton) *The European Parliament,* Westview, 1990, 2nd edition, 1992.
The Treaty of Maastricht, Longman, 1993.

Contributor to periodicals.

SIDELIGHTS: Richard Corbett told *CA:* "My book *The Treaty of Maastricht* describes the Maastsricht process from initial conception, through the negotiations and the ratification procedures. In addition to the full text of the treaty, it contains many of the key documents of the negotiation phase."

*   *   *

CORRADO, Anthony 1957-

PERSONAL: Born February 4, 1957, in Fall River, MA; son of Anthony and Jeannette (a bank teller; maiden name, Drainville) Corrado. *Education:* Catholic University, B.A., 1979, M.A., 1982; Boston College, Ph.D., 1990. *Politics:* Democrat.

ADDRESSES: Office—Department of Government, Colby College, Waterville, ME 04901.

CAREER: Colby College, Waterville, ME, instructor, 1986-89, assistant professor, 1989-94, associate professor of government, 1994—. The White House, Washington, DC, personnel officer for the Office of Presidential Personnel, 1980-81; Capitol Services, Inc., Washington, DC, executive director, 1981-82; Mondale for President, deputy campaign manager, 1984; Dukakis for President, consultant, 1988; Kerrey for President, national campaign co-ordinator, 1992; Clinton for President Committee, consultant, 1992.

MEMBER: American Political Science Association, New England Political Science Association, Phi Beta Kappa.

AWARDS, HONORS: University President's Award, Catholic University, 1979; O'Neill Fellow, Boston College, 1985-86; John C. Donovan Prize, New England Political Science Association, 1991.

WRITINGS:

Creative Campaigning, Westview Press, 1992.
Paying for Presidents, Twentieth Century Fund, 1993.
(With Herbert Alexander) *Financing the 1992 Election,* M. E. Sharpe, in press.

WORK IN PROGRESS: Research on presidential campaign finance regulation and the presidential selection process, including the consequences of new rules and candidate strategies.

*   *   *

CORRICK, James A. 1945-

PERSONAL: Born September 12, 1945, in Astoria, OR; son of James (a captain in the United States Navy and a college professor) and Harriet (a food technologist; maiden name, Perry) Corrick; married Gay Miller (a naturalist and sculptor), November 26, 1982. *Education:* University of Tennessee, B.S., 1967, M.S., 1969, M.A., 1971; University of Arizona, Ph.D., 1981. *Politics:* Independent. *Religion:* "None."

ADDRESSES: Home and office—4402 East Cooper Circle, Tucson, AZ 85711-4260. *Agent*—Henry Rasof, 4800 Osage Dr., No. 24, Boulder, CO 80303.

CAREER: Writer and editor, Tucson, AZ, 1979—; University of Arizona, Tucson, tutor, 1981-82; L5 Society, Tucson, editor, 1985-87; National Space Society, Washington, DC, editor, 1987; Muscular Dystrophy Association, Tucson, science writer, 1991-92.

MEMBER: Tucson Book Publishers Association, Arizona Sonora Desert Museum, Southern Arizona Arthropod Association, Tucson Zoological Society, Arizona Historical Society.

AWARDS, HONORS: National Defense Education Act fellow, 1967 and 1968.

WRITINGS:

The Human Brain: Mind and Matter, Arco, 1983.
Recent Revolutions in Chemistry, Franklin Watts, 1986.
Recent Revolutions in Biology, Franklin Watts, 1987.
Career Preparation, Chaparral, 1988.

Double Your Pleasure: The Ace SF Double, Gryphon, 1989.

The World of Nature: Farm Animals, W. H. Smith, 1991.

Mars, Franklin Watts, 1991.

Muscular Dystrophy, Franklin Watts, 1992.

Science People, Profiling the Men and Women of Science, volume 1, WP Press, 1993.

Contributor to books, including *Earthwise: Energy,* WP Press, 1993. Has also published articles and short stories. Editor of journals, including *L5 News,* 1985-87; *Space Frontier,* 1986-87; and *Space Advocate,* 1987.

WORK IN PROGRESS: The Low Middle Ages and *The High Middle Ages,* for Lucent Books, publication expected 1994; *The DNA Scalpel: Human Genetic Engineering,* for Enslow, publication expected 1995; *The Planet Seekers; Creation Station,* a novel; and research for *The Bone Warriors.*

SIDELIGHTS: James A. Corrick commented: "My father's reading of the *Oz* books to my sister and me certainly put me on the road to becoming a writer. First, I became an omnivorous reader and avid book collector (I bought my first book, which I still have, when I was eleven). Because my father and mother had technical backgrounds, I also became interested in science, and for a time, I seriously thought I would be a scientist who wrote. However, two years of graduate studies in biochemistry made me realize that writing was much more important. The science, of course, would eventually come back into my life when I became the author of several popular science books.

"I spent a decade as a graduate student in English, reading and studying as wide a variety as I could: nothing from classical poetry to modern journalism escaped me. In the end, I found that education useful, even though the practical craft of being a writer forced me to set aside most of the more esoteric lore I had picked up.

"I believe that all good nonfiction rests squarely on good, thorough research. The writer's job then is to take that research and present it in a clear, concise, organized manner. Personally, I like facts, and so tend to pack my books with as many facts as they can comfortably hold, but never so many that they get in the reader's way."

Corrick's first book, *The Human Brain: Mind and Matter,* is a basic text covering the brain and its functions. Topics discussed include parts of the brain, chemical and electrical reactions, memory, and sleep. Illustrations and pictures complement the text. A reviewer in *Choice* noted that the book is written "in a very simple, easy-to-follow format and style," although "rather limited" in content and depth. *School Library Journal* contributor Kathryn Weisman judged *The Human Brain* to be a "succinct yet broad overview of the human brain." And Stephen Cox, writing in *Book Report,* commented in his conclusion that "Corrick's book is an excellent, concise work. The material is current, thought-provoking and readable."

BIOGRAPHICAL/CRITICAL SOURCES:

PERIODICALS

Analog, December, 1989, p. 185.
Book Report, May/June, 1984.
Choice, January, 1984.
School Library Journal, January, 1984; December, 1986, p. 114; August, 1987, p. 91; September, 1991, p. 263.
Voice of Youth Advocates, April, 1987, p. 43; August, 1987, p. 135; December, 1991, p. 333.

*   *   *

CORRIGAN, Simon 1964-

PERSONAL: Born April 30, 1964, in Barnsley, England; son of Denys (a journalist) and Rita (a schoolteacher; maiden name, Danforth) Corrigan. *Education:* Attended Chetham's School of Music, 1980-82; Trinity College, Cambridge, B.A. (with honors), 1985, M.A. (with honors), 1991. *Politics:* "Left of center." *Religion:* None. *Avocational Interests:* Piano, bridge, gay rights, psychoanalysis, nightclubs, word games.

ADDRESSES: Home—15 Loveridge Rd., London NW6 2DW, England. *Agent*—James Hale, 47 Peckham Rye, London SE15, England.

CAREER: Writer.

AWARDS, HONORS: Betty Trask Prize, Society of Authors, 1993, for *Tommy Was Here.*

WRITINGS:

Tommy Was Here (thriller), Andre Deutsch, 1993.

WORK IN PROGRESS: Sweets from Strangers, a novel; researching psychoanalytic theory.

SIDELIGHTS: Simon Corrigan is the author of *Tommy Was Here,* a thriller about a mother, Imogen, who has travelled from London to Paris in search of her missing son, a piano student. Imogen's quest takes her into the seedier areas of Paris where she meets a series of unappealing individuals, including Pierre, a male prostitute, and Paul, a music teacher who has, apparently, been the missing son's lover. The startling journey that leads Imogen toward her son is also one of self-discovery. Although Imogen grows sickened by her son's world, she finds herself succumbing to Pierre's seductive charm. "In the process of her search, she is forced to face up to aspects of her own repressed character and desires," commented *Times Liter-*

ary Supplement contributor Tim Gooderham, who found *Tommy Was Here* "accomplished." In the *Independent on Sunday* Mark Sanderson described it as a "perceptive, graceful and gripping book."

Corrigan told *CA:* "I've written as long as I can remember. I want to convey a very personal vision of the appalling cruelty of human relationships—particularly familial relationships—within the framework of a popular genre—the thriller—and to do this in the best sentences of my generation. My working habits are irregular, but so is my life. The writers who have most influenced me are Marcel Proust and Gustav Flaubert. I think Graham Greene's *Brighton Rock* is the best modern British novel. I am not much impressed with contemporary novelists, but would make exception for Muriel Spark, Ian McEwan, and Donna Tartt. My advice for aspiring novelists: practice conveying thought, which is far more difficult and more important than 'realistic dialogue,' whatever the Hemingway apologists may claim; don't try to do sex in prose; write about what seduces you; read Flaubert."

BIOGRAPHICAL/CRITICAL SOURCES:

PERIODICALS

Daily Mail (London), August 20, 1992.
Independent on Sunday, August 16, 1992.
Times Literary Supplement, August 21, 1992, p. 17.

*   *   *

COTTRET, Bernard 1951-

PERSONAL: Born April 23, 1951, in Boulogne/Seine, France; son of Bernard (a classical singer) and Genevieve (a classical singer; maiden name, Bonnaud) Cottret; married Monique Astruc (a historian), September 22, 1973; children: Yann. *Education:* Ecole Normale Superieure de Saint-Cloud, Agregation d'anglais, 1976; University of Paris X, Dr. es Lettres, 1988. *Politics:* "Humanist." *Religion:* Protestant.

ADDRESSES: Home— 1 Res. du Lac, 94470 Boissy-Saint-Leger, France. *Office—*Universite de Versailles-Saint-Quentin-en-Yvelines, 23 rue du Refuge, 78000 Versailles, France.

CAREER: Oxford University, Merton College, Oxford, England, lecturer in French, 1972-73; University of Paris IV, Sorbonne, Paris, France, assistant professor, 1981-89; University of Lille III, Lille, France, professor of British Studies, 1989-92; University of Versailles-Saint-Quentin-en-Yvelines, Versailles, France, professor, 1992—, and chairman of arts department. University of Paris, Sorbonne, member of Institut de Recherches sur les Civilisations de l'Occident Moderne; University of Charleston,

Charleston, SC, member of faculty, summer, 1994; consultant to Bibliotheque Nationale. *Military service:* French Army, 1977-78. French Army Reserve; became honorary lieutenant.

AWARDS, HONORS: Prix Monseigneur Marcel; Silver Medal from Academie Francaise, 1993, for *Cromwell.*

WRITINGS:

Terre d'exil, Aubier, 1985.
La Glorieuse Revolution, Gallimard, 1988.
Le Christ des Lumieres, Le Cerf, 1990.
The Huguenots in England, Cambridge University Press, 1991.
Cromwell, Fayard, 1992.
Bolingbroke, Klincksieck, 1992.

Contributor to periodicals, including *Reforme.*

WORK IN PROGRESS: Bolingbroke's Political Works, for Macmillan; research on American colonial history and on Ireland.

SIDELIGHTS: Bernard Cottret told *CA:* "My main concern has been with comparative history. My starting point was Huguenot immigration to England in the early modern period, but I have since moved on to intellectual and political history, with Bolingbroke and other authors. My second major field of interest is religious or, to be more explicit, the links between faith and action. This has led me to investigate Oliver Cromwell's career. My American friends now press me to study their own brand of Puritanism, and a quick visit to Salem, Massachusetts, has fully convinced me.

"Though I would not describe myself as a writer, in the literary or fictional sense of the word, I do thoroughly enjoy imparting my discoveries and emotions to the reader. If I had not been able to write, I would certainly have sung, like my parents. It was my grandmother, a painter, who told me endlessly about the good bad old days. History is inseparable from storytelling and what Jules Michelet called 'the resurrection of the past.' I have since learned a great deal from my wife and from various encounters in the academic world, and I have developed over the years a real passion for teaching."

*   *   *

COVIN, David L(eroy) 1940-

PERSONAL: Born October 3, 1940, in Chicago, IL; son of David and Lela Jane (Clements) Covin; married Judy Bentinck Smith; children: Wendy, Holly. *Education:* University of Illinois, B.A., 1962; Colorado University, M.A., 1966; Washington State University, Ph.D., 1970.

ADDRESSES: Office—Director of Pan African Studies, California State University, 6000 J St., Sacramento, CA 95819.

CAREER: California State University, Sacramento, assistant professor of government and ethnic studies, 1970-74, associate dean of general studies, 1972-74, associate professor of government and ethnic studies, 1975-79, professor of government and ethnic studies, 1979, director of Pan African Studies. Union Graduate School, adjunct professor, 1979; state of California, consultant, 1979. Women's Civic Improvement Club, executive board member, 1987—.

MEMBER: National Party of Congress (delegate), National Black Independent Political Party, Black Science Resource Center (acting chair, 1987—), Sacramento chapter of National Rainbow Coalition Organization Committee, Sacramento Area Black Caucus (chair, 1988—).

AWARDS, HONORS: Community service award, Sacramento Area Black Caucus, 1976; grant, California Council for Humanities Public Policy, 1977; Sacramento community service award, Sacramento Kwanza Commission, 1978; Man of the Year, Omega Psi Phi, 1982; community service award, All African People, 1986; Meritorious Performance Award, California State University, 1988; John C. Livingston Distinguished Faculty Lecture, California State University, 1992.

WRITINGS:

Brown Sky, Path Press, 1987.

Also contributor of short stories and articles to periodicals, including the *Journal of Black Studies.* Contributing editor to *Rumble.*

*   *   *

COWDEN, Robert H.   1934-

PERSONAL: Born November 18, 1934, in Warren, PA; son of Wallace Hapgood (a banker) and Astrid (an actress; maiden name, Sundelof) Cowden; married Jacqueline Mailloux (an opera singer), November 26, 1959; children: Christopher, Jonathan, Jennifer Cowden Bertaccini, Marc, Adrienne. *Education:* Princeton University, A.B., 1956; University of Rochester, B.Mus. (with distinction), 1959, M.Mus. (with distinction), 1960, D.M.A., 1966; Musikhochschule, Frankfurt, Germany, Diploma, 1963. *Politics:* Democrat. *Religion:* Episcopalian.

ADDRESSES: Home—18195 Via Encantada, Monte Sereno, CA 95030. *Office*—School of Music, San Jose

State University, 1 Washington Sq., San Jose, CA 95192-0001.

CAREER: University of Rochester, Rochester, NY, instructor, summers, 1961 and 1964-65; Jacksonville University, Jacksonville, FL, assistant professor of music and director of Opera Workshop, 1966-68; Wayne State University, Detroit, MI, assistant professor, 1968-72, adjunct professor of music, 1972-74, director of graduate program in lyric theater, 1968-72, director of fine and applied arts, College of Lifelong Learning, 1972-74, executive producer of television adult education activities, 1972-74, director of Hilberry Classic Theatre, 1969-70, and Lyric Theatre, 1970-71; University of Nebraska, Omaha, J. J. Isaacson Professor of Music and department head, 1974-76; San Jose State University, San Jose, CA, professor of music, 1976—, department head, 1976-82. Chautauqua Opera Company, director and coordinator of Apprentice Artist Program, 1968; California State Summer School for the Arts, member of music faculty and head of Music Division, 1987—.

Michigan Opera Theatre, director, 1969-70; Detroit Symphony Orchestra, director, 1969-72; Banff School of Fine Arts, director, 1971; University of Windsor, director, 1972; performer with Boston Arts Festival, Stadttheater Hildesheim, Metropolitan Opera National Company, and Chautauqua Opera Association. Director of numerous educational television programs for Public Broadcasting System, American Broadcasting Co., and National Broadcasting Co. Detroit Metropolitan Black Arts, founding member of board of directors, 1968-76; Opera Omaha, member of board of directors, 1975-76; Music/Arts Consortium, founding member, 1977-82; New Sounds San Jose, member of founding committee, 1977-83; Montalvo Center for the Arts, member of advisory board, 1982-87; consultant to Nebraska Arts Council and Stratford Shakespeare Festival, Stratford, Ontario.

MEMBER: National Opera Association (member of board of directors, 1977-79).

AWARDS, HONORS: Fulbright scholar in Germany, 1961-63; scholar at Bayreuth Musikfestspiel, 1962; grant from National Endowment for the Humanities, 1985.

WRITINGS:

(Translator) Giuseppe Verdi, *Un Ballo in Maschera,* Edwin F. Kalmus, 1970.
The Chautauqua Opera Association, 1929-1958: An Interpretive History, National Opera Association, 1974.
(Compiler) *Concert and Opera Singers: A Bibliography of Biographical Materials,* Greenwood Press, 1985.
(Compiler) *Concert and Opera Conductors: A Bibliography of Biographical Materials,* Greenwood Press, 1987.

(Compiler) *Instrumental Virtuosi: A Bibliography of Biographical Materials,* Greenwood Press, 1989.

(Editor in chief) *Opera Companies of the World: Selected Profiles,* Greenwood Press, 1992.

Classical Singers of the Operatic and Recital Stages, Greenwood Press, 1994.

Translator of the operas *Der Wildschuetz* by Lortzing, *Der Jasager* by Brecht and Weill, and *La Serva Padrona* by Pergolesi. Contributor of articles and reviews to music journals.

WORK IN PROGRESS: Commercial and Entertainment Singers of the World, publication by Greenwood Press expected in 1996; *Triumph of the American Singer: A Century of Encores,* a cultural history.

SIDELIGHTS: Robert H. Cowden told *CA:* "Writing, for me, has always emerged naturally from my other artistic involvements, as a performer, director, producer, and teacher. John Collier once suggested that our activities, indeed our passions and commitments, should thrust us 'a little way over the rim of the horizon.' Total involvement in any art demands plunging into the oceans of information which might cast some light on its many dimensions. Thus, my writing is always a journey of discovery, a journey undertaken for myself. My publishers then make it possible to share that particular journey with others, a rather miraculous event. At that point it becomes someone else's journey, and I am back looking at new road maps. The next journey is undertaken because I have no other choice; it is inevitable."

*   *   *

COX, Paul(us)   1940-

PERSONAL: Born April 16, 1940, in Venlo, Netherlands; immigrated to Australia, 1965; son of Wim (a documentary film producer) and Else (Kliminack) Cox; children: Ezra, Kyra, Marilis.

ADDRESSES: Office—Illumination Films, 1 Victoria Ave., Albert Park, Melbourne, Victoria 3206, Australia. *Agent*—S.T.E. Representation, 9301 Wilshire Blvd., Suite 312, Beverly Hills, CA 90210.

CAREER: Photographer, screenwriter, and director of motion pictures. Worked as teacher of photography and cinematography, 1971-82; Illumination Films (independent production company), Melbourne, Victoria, Australia, cofounder (with Tony Llewellyn-Jones), producer, and director, beginning c. 1975. Photographs exhibited at various institutions. Actor in motion pictures, including *Where the Green Ants Dream,* 1985, *Golden Braid,* 1991, and *Careful.*

AWARDS, HONORS: Recipient of numerous honors, including Silver Hugo Award, Chicago Film Festival, 1983, and award for best film, Valladolid Film Festival, 1984, both for *Man of Flowers;* Awgie Award for best original screenplay, Australian Writers Guild, 1984, and awards for best film and best director, Houston Film Festival, 1985, all for *My First Wife;* and Australian Human Rights Award for best feature film, 1991, for *A Woman's Tale.* Honoree at several special tributes and retrospectives, including at Hof International Film Festival, 1984, Ghent International Film Festival, 1986, Olympic Film Festival, Calgary, 1988, Calcutta International Film Festival, 1990, and Film Society of Lincoln Center, New York, 1992.

WRITINGS:

(With Ulli Beier) *Home of Man: The People of New Guinea,* Nelson (Australia), 1971.

(Photographer) Ulli Beier, *Mirka,* Macmillan (Australia), 1980.

Also author of *Reflections,* an autobiography.

SCREENPLAYS; AND DIRECTOR

Illuminations, Melbourne Filmmakers Coop., 1976.

(Writer with Susan Holly Jones) *Inside Looking Out,* Illumination Films, 1977.

(Writer with John Clarke) *Lonely Hearts,* Samuel Goldwyn, 1981.

(Writer with Bob Ellis) *Man of Flowers,* Spectrafilm, 1983.

Death and Destiny: A Journey into Ancient Egypt, Illumination Films, 1984.

(Adaptor with Bob Ellis) *My First Wife,* Illumination Films, 1984, International Spectrafilm, c. 1985.

(Writer with Ellis and Norman Kaye) *Cactus,* International Spectrafilm, 1986.

Vincent: The Life and Death of Vincent van Gogh (based on the letters of Vincent van Gogh), Illumination Films, 1988.

Island, Atlantis, 1989.

(Writer with Barry Dickins) *Golden Braid* (adapted from a short story by Guy de Maupassant), Illumination Films, 1990, Cabriolet Films, 1991.

(Writer with Dickins) *A Woman's Tale,* Orion Classics, 1991.

The Nun and the Bandit (based on the book by E. L. Grant Watson), Illumination Films, 1992.

Exile (documentary; based on the novel *Priest Island* by E. L. Grant Watson), Illumination Films, 1993.

Also writer and director of *The Journey,* 1972; and writer (with John Larkin) and director of *Homecoming,* Illumination Films. Writer and director of short films, including *Matuta,* 1965; *Time Past,* 1966; *Skindeep,* 1968; *Marcel,* 1969; *Symphony,* 1969; *Mirka,* 1970; *Phyllis,* 1971; *We Are All Alone My Dear,* 1975; *Ways of Seeing,* 1977; and *Rit-*

ual, 1978. Also creator of original concept for, and director of *Kostas,* Illumination Films, c. 1978.

Also writer and director of documentary films, including *Calcutta,* 1970; *All Set Backstage,* 1974; *For a Child Called Michael,* 1979; *The Kingdom of Nek Chand,* 1980; *Underdog,* 1980; and *Handle with Care,* 1985.

JUVENILE TELEPLAYS; AND DIRECTOR

The Secret Life of Trees, Australian Children's Television Foundation, 1986.
The Gift, Australian Children's Television Foundation, 1988.

Also writer and director of the episode "Paper Boy" for the television program *WonderWorks,* PBS, c. 1987.

SIDELIGHTS: Paul Cox is an Australia-based filmmaker who has realized increasing international acclaim since the early 1980s. After initially establishing himself as a photographer, Cox began his filmmaking career in 1965, the same year that he emigrated from his native Netherlands to Australia. During the late 1960s Cox worked exclusively in the short-film genre. In the early 1970s he continued to make short films, but he also began making feature-length documentaries and narrative works. In 1970 he completed his first documentary, *Calcutta,* and in 1972 he wrote and directed the narrative film *The Journey.* Throughout the remainder of the decade Cox continued to make short films, documentaries, and narrative films. In addition, he collaborated with Ulli Beier on the volume *Home of Man: The People of New Guinea,* and in 1980 he supplied the photographs for Beier's book *Mirka.*

International attention came to Cox only after the Australian cinema gained recognition as the next New Wave in the early 1980s. At this time films such as *Picnic at Hanging Rock, Breaker Morant, My Brilliant Career,* and *The Chant of Jimmie Blacksmith* found favor with American art-house audiences. Unlike these relatively commercial productions which would lead their directors to Hollywood careers, Cox's films are of a more personal nature, and thus they are often perceived as European in influence and style.

This is particularly true of *Man of Flowers,* Cox's first work to gain substantial praise in the United States. This 1983 film concerns an eccentric, aging art devotee who writes letters to his dead mother and regularly pays a young woman to disrobe before him to the strains of *Lucia di Lammermoor. Man of Flowers,* with its unlikely protagonist, is a quirky, often contemplative work, one replete with vivid seascapes, haunting flashbacks and peculiar comedic elements, including an obnoxious abstract artist who tries, with fatal consequences, to coerce the hero into patronage. *Man of Flowers* readily established Cox as an accomplished, uncompromising artist, and though the

film is not as well known as some of his later works, it is nonetheless championed by some critics as his masterpiece.

As the Australian New Wave continued to gain attention in the 1980s, Cox too won acclaim, though critics inevitably distinguished him from his more overtly commercial peers. Among Cox's other films to win acclaim at this time were *Lonely Hearts,* the story of a love that develops between two pathetic, middle-aged people, and *My First Wife,* a disturbing 1984 drama about a marital breakup. In the latter work, a classical music broadcaster learns that his wife of ten years no longer loves him. His futile efforts to alternately win back her affection and punish her bear grim consequences. *Los Angeles Times* reviewer Sheila Benson deemed *My First Wife* "a penetrating, indelibly memorable film," and she hailed Cox as "one of the most powerful and interesting [filmmakers] currently at work."

Among Cox's other films from the mid-1980s is *Cactus,* the story of a love that develops between a blind man and an already married woman whose own sight is declining. Dave Kehr wrote in the *Chicago Tribune* that *Cactus,* like the earlier *Lonely Hearts* and *Man of Flowers,* is a film "describing the condition of a painfully sensitive, romantic individual at the mercy of a world of danger and treachery." Kehr conceded that *Cactus,* with its somewhat elusive heroine, is flawed, but he added that in creating the film Cox nonetheless "remains a distinct and troubling personality."

By the late 1980s, fervor for the Australian cinema had diminished considerably, particularly since many of Australia's more distinguished artists had, by this time, commenced working in America. Cox, though, remained based in Australia, and he continued to practice his more personalized filmmaking. In 1988 he completed *Vincent: The Life and Death of Vincent van Gogh,* a typically unusual work about the life and art of the great painter. Here Cox forgoes dramatic actors and merely presents, instead, footage of both van Gogh's art and of the places where the painter lived and worked. The soundtrack is comprised of both musical selections and readings—by John Hurt—of van Gogh's letters. *Christian Science Monitor* critic David Sterritt proclaimed *Vincent* "one of the season's most unusual movies" and added that it is "often dazzling to watch and to listen to."

In 1990 Cox wrote and directed *Golden Braid,* a film—derived from a Guy de Maupassant tale—about a clockmaker who becomes infatuated with a strand of hair. *New York Times* reviewer Caryn James, while decrying the work's "artiness," acknowledged that *Golden Braid* "is so sincere that it deserves respect."

Cox followed *Golden Braid* with *A Woman's Tale,* a film about an elderly, cancerous woman who aspires to a dignified death. Cox planned the film as a vehicle for its lead actress, Sheila Florance, who died only a few days after winning an Australian award for her performance. The *Washington Post*'s Rita Kempley described *A Woman's Tale* as "an honest and keen-witted reflection on living well to the last breath," and she proclaimed Cox an "idiosyncratic director . . . [of] little miracles." *National Review*'s John Simon hailed *A Woman's Tale* as "a rare, honest, moving but not maudlin, melancholy but not depressing film," and he acknowledged the "art" of Cox's script—written with Barry Dickins—and direction.

BIOGRAPHICAL/CRITICAL SOURCES:

PERIODICALS

Chicago Tribune, April 23, 1987, p. E13.
Christian Science Monitor, March 11, 1988, p. 21; September 17, 1991, p. 11.
Los Angeles Times, May 9, 1985, p. F1; March 8, 1991, p. F13; June 30, 1992, p. F1.
National Review, May 25, 1992, pp. 45-46.
New York Times, March 16, 1988, p. C25; October 5, 1990, p. C10; April 30, 1992, p. C16; February 11, 1993, p. C23.
Washington Post, June 12, 1992, p. C7.

*   *   *

CRAIS, Clifton C(harles) 1960-

PERSONAL: Born March 4, 1960, in New Orleans, LA; son of Gustave Henry and Olga Yvonne Crais; married Pamela Scully (a professor), October 16, 1987. *Education:* University of Maryland at College Park, B.A., 1982; Johns Hopkins University, M.A., 1984, Ph.D., 1988.

ADDRESSES: Home—234 North Pearl St., Granville, OH 43023. *Office*—Department of History, Seitz House, Kenyon College, Gambier, OH 43022-9623.

CAREER: Kenyon College, Gambier, OH, visiting instructor, 1987-88, assistant professor, 1988-93, associate professor of history, 1993—, founder and chairperson of Kenyon Seminar, 1990-93. University of London, member of Institute of Commonwealth Studies, London School of Oriental and African Studies, 1985—, member of Institute of Historical Research, 1985-86; Rhodes University, South Africa, university research scholar at Institute of Social and Economic Research, 1985, 1992; University of Cape Town, South Africa, visiting assistant professor, 1988-89, visiting associate of Centre for African Studies, 1988-89, 1991-92; guest on radio programs. Conducted field work in Ciskei and Transkei, South Africa, 1992, 1993.

MEMBER: World History Association, American Historical Association, African Studies Association, Greater Lakes Collegiate Association (African studies representative, 1992—).

AWARDS, HONORS: Fulbright fellow in South Africa, 1984-85; grants from National Endowment for the Humanities and American Council of Learned Societies, both for South Africa, 1993.

WRITINGS:

White Supremacy and Black Resistance in Pre-Industrial South Africa: The Making of the Colonial Order in the Eastern Cape, 1770-1865, Cambridge University Press, 1992.
(Editor with Nigel Worden, and contributor) *Breaking the Chains: Slavery and Its Legacy in Nineteenth-Century South Africa,* Witwatersrand University Press, 1993.

Contributor of articles and reviews to periodicals, including *Journal of Social History* and *African Studies.*

WORK IN PROGRESS: "Not in a Distant Time": Subaltern Visions and the Political Imagination in South Africa, the Eastern Cape, 1856-1963, for Heinemann; *A Contested Past: Culture, Consciousness, and the Production of History in South Africa.*

SIDELIGHTS: Clifton C. Crais told *CA:* "My youth was characterized by change and instability. Born in New Orleans into a working-class family, at the age of twelve I moved in with my eldest sister's family. In the next five years we lived in Mississippi, California, Maryland, and Tunisia. I attended about fourteen different schools before I graduated from high school in 1977. I developed an interest in Africa during my undergraduate years at the University of Maryland and began research on South Africa at the Johns Hopkins University. My work has primarily centered around understanding the histories of white supremacy and black resistance, and the intellectual history of South Africa, as well as the ethics and poetics of historical production. I work very regularly, rising at 6:00 A.M. each morning and writing before classes. I don't wait for inspiration but write even when I am feeling uninspired. I have been influenced by the work of French post-structuralists like Michel Foucault and, in African history, by the work of David William Cohen."

*   *   *

CRANSTON, Maurice (William) 1920-1993

OBITUARY NOTICE—See index for *CA* sketch: Born May 8, 1920, in London, England; died of a heart attack,

November 5, 1993, in London, England. Philosopher, educator, and author. Cranston was a prominent interpreter of seventeenth- and eighteenth-century philosophy. He began his career as a lecturer in social philosophy at the University of London in 1950. Nine years later he began lecturing in political science at the London School of Economics and Political Science, where he was promoted to professor and remained until 1985. Cranston was an honorary fellow of St. Catherine's College of Oxford University in 1984 and the London School of Economics in 1991, and in 1987 was named Commandeur de l'Ordre des Palmes Academiques. He specialized in the writings of Jean-Jacques Rousseau, publishing *Jean-Jacques: The Early Life and Work of J. J. Rousseau* in 1983 and translating Rousseau's *Discourse on Inequality.* He was also the editor, with Peter Mair, of *Langage et Politique,* and received the James Tait Memorial Prize for his 1957 work, *John Locke: A Biography.*

OBITUARIES AND OTHER SOURCES:

BOOKS

Who's Who in the World, 12th edition, Marquis, 1994.

PERIODICALS

New York Times, November 12, 1993, p. A31.
Times (London), November 9, 1993, p. 21.

*   *   *

CRAVEN, Avery (Odelle)   1885(?)-1980

PERSONAL: Born August 12, 1885 (some sources say 1886), in Warren County (near Ackworth), IA; died January 21, 1980; son of Oliver and Mary E. (Pennington) Craven; married Grace Greenwood, October 2, 1914 (died, 1936); married Georgia D. Watson, September 26, 1938; children: (first marriage) one daughter. *Education:* Simpson College, A.B., 1908; Harvard University, A.M., 1914; University of Chicago, Ph.D., 1923; University of Cambridge, M.A., 1952.

CAREER: Simpson College, Indianola, IA, instructor, 1908-11; College of Emporia, Kansas, assistant professor, 1920-22; Michigan State College (now Michigan State University), East Lansing, assistant professor, 1923-24; University of Illinois, Urbana, assistant professor, 1924-26, associate professor, 1926-28; University of Chicago, Chicago, IL, associate professor, 1928-29, professor of American history, 1929-72, professor emeritus, beginning in 1972; University of Sydney, Australia, distinguished foreign professor of history, 1947-48; Cambridge University, professor of American history and institutions, 1952-53. Lecturer at American Seminar, Salzburg, 1953; visiting professor at University of Wisconsin,

1964-67; University of Maryland, 1967-68; and at University of Colorado, University of North Carolina, University of Southern California, Northwestern University, and Western Michigan University; distinguished foreign lecturer with the American Studies Committee in Japan, 1967. Member of Civil War Centennial Commission, beginning in 1958; member of Lincoln Sesquicentennial Commission, beginning in 1959.

MEMBER: American Historical Association (president, 1930), Organization of American Historians (president, 1963-64), American Agricultural Society (past president), Japanese Society of American Studies, Southern Historical Association (vice-president, beginning in 1950; president, 1952), Phi Beta Kappa.

AWARDS, HONORS: Honorary degrees from Simpson College, 1946, Tulane University, 1952, Wayne State University, 1957, University of South Carolina, 1961, Western Michigan University, 1963, and Purdue University, 1969.

WRITINGS:

Soil Exhaustion as a Factor in the Agricultural History of Virginia and Maryland, 1606-1860, University of Illinois Studies in the Social Sciences, 1926.
Edmund Ruffin, Southerner: A Study in Secession, Appleton, 1932.
The Repressible Conflict, 1830-1861, Louisiana State University Press, 1939.
Democracy in American Life: A Historical View, University of Chicago Press, 1941.
The Coming of the Civil War, Scribner, 1942, second edition, University of Chicago Press, 1966.
(With Walter Johnson) *The United States: Experiment in Democracy,* Ginn, 1947.
(With Walter Johnson and F. Roger Dunn) *A Documentary History of the American People,* Ginn, 1951.
The Growth of Southern Nationalism, 1848-1861, Louisiana State University Press, 1953.
Civil War in the Making, 1815-1860, Louisiana State University Press, 1959.
(With Walter Johnson) *American History,* Ginn, 1961.
An Historian and the Civil War, University of Chicago Press, 1964.
Reconstruction: The Ending of the Civil War, Holt, 1969.
(And illustrator) *Rachel of Old Louisiana,* Louisiana State University Press, 1975.

Also coauthor of *Sources of Culture in the Middle West;* author of *A Frontier Cycle,* Wayne State University Press, 1958; *The American Tragedy: The Civil War in Retrospect,* with Frank E. Vandiver, introduction by Bernard Mayo, Hampden-Sydney College, 1959; and *Politics and the Crisis of Eighteen-Sixty,* with William E. Baringer and Don E. Fehrenbacher, Books on Demand. Author of introduction to *Lincoln Takes Command,* by John S. Tilley. Contributor of articles to professional journals.

Simpson College in Indianola, Iowa, holds many of Craven's manuscripts and notes and much of his correspondence.

SIDELIGHTS: Noted historian and educator Avery Craven was best known for his volumes on the U.S. Civil War and life in the antebellum South. He was labeled a revisionist by most critics for his view—presented in titles such as *The Repressible Conflict, 1830-1861, The Coming of the Civil War,* and *Civil War in the Making, 1815-1860*—that the Civil War was not the inevitable conflict presented by previous historians, but rather the result of emotional propagandizing by both sides. Craven's works are seen by many as being too sympathetic to the Southern cause; many others, however, would agree with John David Smith in the *Dictionary of Literary Biography* who concluded that "Craven's works remain important. They underscore the value of moderation, the folly of war, and the hope for life in a rational universe. He raised salient questions and offered alternative, albeit often controversial, historical explanations."

Craven was born to Quaker parents in Iowa. His father, however, was born in North Carolina, and Craven himself spent a brief period there during his very early childhood. This later was used by critics who accused Craven of bias on behalf of the Old South and slavery, but the historian pointed to his Quaker background as antithetical to racism and noted that his parents had left the South in the 1880s to escape those negative aspects of Southern culture.

Craven began his career as an educator teaching geology at Simpson College in Iowa. He became interested in history only when he was asked to teach a few courses in it. His interest, however, led him to return to school at Harvard University, where he studied history under the direction of famed historians Edward Channing and Jackson Turner. When he completed his master's degree at Harvard, Craven journeyed to the University of Chicago to work on his doctorate, this time experiencing the teaching of William E. Dodd and Marcus W. Jernegan. His doctoral thesis became his first published work, *Soil Exhaustion as a Factor in the Agricultural History of Virginia and Maryland, 1606-1860.*

His work on the agricultural history of the South led to Craven's interest in Civil War topics and personalities, and his next important work was a biography of Edmund Ruffin, who was both an agricultural reformer and one of the most radical Southern leaders of the antebellum period. Ruffin fired the first shot at Fort Sumter at the war's beginning in 1861, and when the Union was victorious over the Confederacy in 1865, he took his own life in his despair. *Edmund Ruffin, Southerner: A Study in Secession*

was Craven's attempt to portray a Southern type in the life history of one man, and the book was well received. H. S. Commager, reviewing the biography in *Books,* noted that "the choice of subject is exceptionally happy, the technique masterly, the portrait finished and impressive." A critic for *Times Literary Supplement* concluded that "Craven has done more than recall the figure of Edmund Ruffin: he has, with great art, recreated the proud spirit of the South that became madness and destroyed all that it most loved."

Craven's "most popular book," according to Smith, is *The Coming of the Civil War,* first published in 1942. "Here is a deliberate, measured, lucid recital of the way one calamitous blunder after another, and not inexorable destiny, made the conflict inevitable," explained G. W. Johnston in *Books.* But Commager, writing in the *New York Times,* lamented that in *The Coming of the Civil War* Craven wrote "less objectively than we had hoped," and cautioned that "the unwary reader will need to be reminded that there were happier states than that of slavery and that no free Negro was ever known to run the other way." Allan Nevins in the *Saturday Review of Literature* called the book "a biased and partial treatment of a very complex phase of American history." Nevertheless, Nevins also conceded that *The Coming of the Civil War* "is full of fresh material, it throws much new light on public feeling [during the period of] 1830-1860 and the forces which produced it, and it compresses a vast deal of erudition into a concise and often beautifully written exposition."

In 1959 Craven issued a series of lectures he had given as *Civil War in the Making, 1815-1860.* The lectures in book form explore in greater depth the mounting tensions that led to the war, and Craven here observes that prior to 1840 the arguments between North and South were based on practical concerns, but that afterward the debate tended to center on more abstract ideals. R. F. Nichols lauded the volume in the *American Historical Review,* declaring that "American scholarship is richer for this unique exercise." R. B. Harwell in the *Chicago Tribune* praised the title as well, labeling it "a brilliant, straightforward summary of the background of America's favorite armchair war." He went on to assert that Craven's "text is studded with pungent statements that give meaning to both past and present."

Craven had a more personal work, *An Historian and the Civil War,* printed in 1964. A collection of Craven's essays written during a thirty-five year span, it illustrates the evolution of his opinions and theories about the war. "If, as these essays prove, Craven has so qualified and modified his opinions that he can no longer be properly used as a whipping boy by irate young neo-abolitionists," David Donald announced in the *Journal of American History,* "he has preserved a lofty purpose and a humane temperament which give him deserved rank among our more thoughtful and eloquent historians." A *Times Literary Supplement* reviewer gave the simple compliment that "these essays well deserve reprinting."

Despite the summarizing nature of *An Historian and the Civil War,* Craven added to his chronicling of that momentous event in U.S. history in 1969 with *Reconstruction: The Ending of the Civil War.* In it, he examines both the presidential and congressional approaches to Reconstruction and discusses the importance of the period in forming the social conditions of more modern times. He concludes that Reconstruction ended with an emphasis on individual responsibility rather than major social actions. A *Publishers Weekly* reviewer hailed Craven's "fresh perspectives," while Elmer D. Johnson in *Library Journal* recommended it for both "history collections" and "high school libraries."

Craven retired from his long-time academic post at the University of Chicago in 1972. As a professor emeritus, however, he issued one more book, *Rachel of Old Louisiana,* in 1975. He died in 1980.

BIOGRAPHICAL/CRITICAL SOURCES:

BOOKS

Dictionary of Literary Biography, Volume 17: *Twentieth-Century American Historians,* Gale, 1983, pp. 126-131.

PERIODICALS

American Historical Review, July, 1959, p. 969.
Books, April 24, 1932, p. 7; May 17, 1942, p. 5.
Chicago Tribune, March 29, 1959, p. 2.
Journal of American History, December, 1964, p. 483.
Library Journal, March 15, 1969, p. 1143.
New York Times, May 24, 1942, p. 3.
Publishers Weekly, January 27, 1969, p. 92.
Saturday Review of Literature, May 30, 1942, p. 5.
Times Literary Supplement, May 26, 1932, p. 379; October 15, 1964, p. 936.*

—*Sketch by Elizabeth Wenning*

*   *   *

CRAWLEY, Aidan Merivale 1908-1993

OBITUARY NOTICE—See index for *CA* sketch: Born April 10, 1908, in Kent, England; died November 3, 1993. Legislator, journalist, and author. Best known as the founder and first editor-in-chief of Britain's *Independent Television News,* Crawley was involved in a variety of occupations during the course of his career. He excelled in cricket at Oxford University, and was affiliated with news-

papers including the *Daily Mail* before joining the Royal Auxiliary Air Force in 1936. Crawley flew in the Balkans and Egypt in World War II, and was shot down in enemy territory. His experience as a prisoner of war led to his 1956 book, *Escape from Germany.* After the war Crawley was elected to Parliament as a member of the Labour party, becoming Parliamentary Private Secretary to Secretaries of State for the Colonies, as well as Under-Secretary of State for Air. When he was voted out of office in 1951, Crawley turned to television news, producing documentaries and serving as special correspondent for the *Sunday Times* until 1955, when he founded *Independent Television News.* Although he returned to Parliament in 1962, Crawley went on to chair *London Weekend Television* from 1967 to 1971, when he became its president. He was the author of *DeGaulle: A Biography, Dial 200-200,* and his 1988 autobiography, *Leap Before You Look.*

OBITUARIES AND OTHER SOURCES:

BOOKS

Who's Who, 144th edition, St. Martin's, 1992, p. 423.

PERIODICALS

Times (London), November 4, 1993, p. 21.

*   *   *

CREIGHTON, Linn 1917-

PERSONAL: Born June 7, 1917, in Kuling, China; son of Roy Lamont (a missions architect) and Clara (Linn) Creighton; married Lois Richardson Glover (a minister), May 25, 1946; children: Patricia Creighton Kaminski. *Education:* Harvard University, A.B., 1939; Union Theological Seminary, B.D., 1948; Princeton Theological Seminary, Th.M., 1963, Th.D., 1972. *Politics:* Democrat. *Religion:* Presbyterian.

ADDRESSES: Home and office—17 Kendal at Longwood, Kennett Square, PA 19348.

CAREER: Newton Trust Co., Newton, MA, clerk, 1940-41; South Kent School, teacher of French and Latin, 1941-42; pastor of Presbyterian church in Flemington, NJ, 1950-83; writer. *Military service:* U.S. Naval Reserve, active duty as intelligence officer, 1943-45; became lieutenant junior grade.

MEMBER: Old Guard Club (Princeton, NJ).

WRITINGS:

Bicentennial History of the Presbyterian Church in Flemington, NJ, privately printed, 1991.
Beyond This Darkness (novel), Herald Press, 1993.

SIDELIGHTS: Linn Creighton told *CA:* "As a minister of a thousand-member church, where preaching is at a premium, I always wrote each weekly sermon in full manuscript form, then took only an outline with me into the pulpit. This method required hours of work, so I felt desperate one Christmas Eve when pastoral emergencies had eaten up all my preparation time. It was not until late in the evening that I hit upon the idea of meeting the three wise men in the desert, a modern man face-to-face with ancient biblical personalities, the twentieth century in confrontation with the first. To my surprise, the sermon was a smash, which encouraged me upon retirement to use the same idea to write a novel about a modern man, in this case a skeptic, taken back in time to meet ten people who were friends or enemies of Jesus of Nazareth.

"So far as I am aware, this formula has not been used on a theme like mine. I like to think that, through dialogue and plenty of action, it makes the scripture on which it is based relevant to our own time. Certainly the novel is an easy read, with a highly fluid style developed over many years of preaching. In novel form, with the attitudes of faith and skepticism well honed, *Beyond This Darkness* presents both as clear choices, and could serve in its unique form as a vivid introduction to the New Testament."

*   *   *

CREMO, Michael (A.)   1948-
(Drutakarma Dasa)

PERSONAL: Born July 15, 1948, in Schenectady, NY; son of Salvatore F. (a military intelligence officer) and Nora L. (a homemaker; maiden name, Rossi; present surname, Nelson) Cremo; married Barbara Cantatore, 1985 (divorced, 1992). *Education:* Attended George Washington University, 1966-68. *Politics:* "The politics of spiritual transcendence." *Religion:* "Devotee of Lord Krishna." *Avocational Interests:* Reading Sanskrit and Bengali literature of the bhakti tradition, travel to sacred places, meditation, poetry, "making new spiritual friends."

ADDRESSES: Office—Bhaktivedanta Institute, P.O. Box 99584, San Diego, CA 92169.

CAREER: Initiated as a disciple of A. C. Bhaktivedanto, Swami Prabheyada, 1976; Bhaktivedanta Book Trust, San Diego, CA, writer and editor, 1980-86; Bhaktivedanta Institute, San Diego, research associate, 1984—. International Society for Krishna Consciousness (ISKCON), teacher of bhakti-yoga, 1973—, member of governing body of Philosophical Research Group, 1991—; public affairs consultant for ISKCON Communications, 1980—;

Govardhan Hill, director, 1988—. *Military service:* U.S. Navy, communications yeoman, 1969-71.

MEMBER: History of Science Society, American Archaeological Association, Ancient Astronauts Society, Louisiana Mounds Society.

WRITINGS:

(Under pseudonym Drutakarma Dasa; with Michael Grant writing as Mukunda Goswami, and Austin Gordon writing as Bhutatma Dasa) *Coming Back: The Science of Reincarnation,* Bhaktivedanta Book Trust, 1982.

(Under pseudonym Drutakarma Dasa; with Michael Grant writing as Mukunda Goswami, and Austin Gordon writing as Bhutatma Dasa) *Chant and Be Happy: The Power of Mantra Meditation,* Bhaktivedanta Book Trust, 1982.

(Under pseudonym Drutakarma Dasa; with Michael Grant writing as Mukunda Goswami, and Austin Gordon writing as Bhutatma Dasa) *The Higher Taste: A Guide to Gourmet Vegetarian Cooking and a Karma-Free Diet,* Bhaktivedanta Book Trust, 1983.

(With Richard L. Thompson) *Forbidden Archeology: The Hidden History of the Human Race,* Govardhan Hill, 1993.

Contributor to spiritual periodicals and to newspapers, under the pseudonym Drutakarma Dasa. Contributing editor, *Back to Godhead,* 1977—; editor, *As It Is* (newspaper), 1980-84; associate editor, *ISKCON World Review,* 1984—.

VIDEOTAPES

Coming Back: Reincarnation in America, ITV Productions, 1984.

Healthy, Wealthy, and Wise (accompanies *The Higher Taste*), ITV Productions, 1984.

Katha-Kali (documentary), ITV Productions, 1985.

Jagannatha Puri, ITV Productions, 1986.

(With Richard L. Thompson) *Human Evolution: A Conflict Between Fact and Theory,* Bhaktivedanta Institute/Govardhan Hill, 1987, abridged edition, 1994.

(Under pseudonym Drutakarma Dasa; with Michael Grant writing as Mukunda Goswami) *Divine Nature: Spiritual Perspective on the Environmental Crisis,* Bhaktivedanta Book Trust, 1994.

WORK IN PROGRESS: The Trees That Could Not Be: A Paleontological Enigma from the Salt Range of Pakistan, with Lori Erbs, for Bhaktivedanta Institute, completion expected in 1995; *Descent of Man: An Alternative View of Human Origins,* with Richard L. Thompson, publication by Bhaktivedanta Institute expected in 1996; *Supernatural Cell: A New Look at Vitalism,* with Danakeli Dasi, publication by Bhaktivedanta Institute expected in 1996; *Jaws of Moulin Quignon: Reopening the Case of an Archeological Mystery,* publication by Bhaktivedanta Institute expected in 1996.

SIDELIGHTS: Michael Cremo told *CA:* "The soul that I am entered its present body at the moment I was conceived in the fall of 1947. I appeared from my mother's womb on July 15, 1948. That birth was probably one of millions I have experienced since I left my real home in the spiritual world. My mother tells me that, when I was a baby, she would give me alphabet soup, and sometimes I would not eat it, but would just spell out words in the bowl. From that, I take it that I must have practiced writing in many previous existences. In this life, I recall always having wanted to be a writer.

"From the very beginning, my life has been a spiritual quest for love and truth, in the material context of late twentieth-century earth-planet existence. During the Korean war, my father re-entered the United States Air Force, and from that time my life was one of periodic change and travel. I went to high school at an American school in Germany and spent my vacations traveling all over Europe. Once, in the spring of 1965, in a youth hostel in Stockholm, I met some kids who had been to India and back, traveling overland. I decided I would someday do the same thing. I also became deeply interested in Eastern philosophy, particularly Indian esoteric teachings. I kept travel diaries, wrote poetry, and tried my hand at autobiographical short fiction.

"My career ambitions involved becoming a diplomat or intelligence officer, marrying a beautiful, cultured woman, while simultaneously becoming an author of esoteric fiction and poetry. During my last year of high school in St. Petersburg, Florida, I took a creative writing course. The next year I entered George Washington University. Over the next two years, I became immersed in the counterculture and gradually gave up my plan to enter government service. I continued my investigations into Eastern philosophy and esoteric spiritual teachings.

"In 1968 I left college and went to Europe on a voyage of self-discovery. I took a boat from Haifa to Istanbul, where the pull toward the East was so strong that I found myself heading overland to India. I got as far as Tehran, lost my nerve, and turned back. Later, from a naval weather outpost in Iceland, I left without authorization and traveled overland again, getting as far as Kabul, Afghanistan. I encountered a psychic barrier I could not surmount and returned to Iceland.

"After my general discharge from the United States Navy, and after carefully studying the *Bhagavad-gita,* a gift of some Hare Krishna people at a Grateful Dead concert, I decided that I should absorb myself in the yoga of devotion to the mysterious Lord Krishna. At first I practiced on my own, but eventually decided to join the Krishna temple in Washington, D.C. Later I moved to Los Angeles to join the staff of the International Society for Krishna Consciousness, and to write for the Bhaktivedanta Book Trust. By 1980 I was regarded as an accomplished writer. To date my books have sold more than ten million copies and have been translated into many languages.

"With Richard L. Thompson, a founding member of the Bhaktivedanta Institute, I began a series of books aimed at both scholarly and popular audiences. The first to be published was *Forbidden Archeology: The Hidden History of the Human Race.* This book shows that archaeologists and anthropologists, over the past one hundred and fifty years, have accumulated vast amounts of evidence showing that humans like ourselves have existed on this planet for tens of millions of years. We show how this evidence has been suppressed, ignored, and forgotten because it contradicts generally-held ideas about human evolution."

*   *   *

CRONIN, John F(rancis) 1908-1994

OBITUARY NOTICE—See index for *CA* sketch: Born October 4, 1908, in Glens Falls, NY; died January 2, 1994, in Baltimore, MD. Cleric and author. Cronin was a Roman Catholic priest who was considered an expert on labor and social issues. He was educated at the Sulpician Seminary (now the Theological College of Catholic University of America) in Washington, D.C., and was ordained a priest as a member of the Society of St. Sulpice in 1932. Beginning the following year, Cronin served as an instructor in economics at St. Mary's Seminary and University in Baltimore, advancing to the level of professor. While at St. Mary's he became involved in labor relations and developed an expertise in socio-economic issues. Cronin attracted national attention in 1945 when he was named assistant director of the Department of Social Action at the National Catholic Welfare Conference (now the National Conference of Catholic Bishops) in Washington, a position he held for twenty-two years. In the early 1960s Cronin worked to elicit the support of religious groups for civil rights legislation. He returned to St. Mary's Seminary as a professor of Christian ethics in 1967. A staunch supporter of the Civil Rights Movement, as well as an ardent opponent of Communism, Cronin frequently spoke about political and social issues on behalf of his church. He received a 1944 Pabst Award for an essay on postwar employment, as well as the Papal Benemerenti Medal in 1957. Cronin's writings include *Catholic Social Principles* and *Problems and Opportunities in a Democracy.*

OBITUARIES AND OTHER SOURCES:

BOOKS

American Catholic Who's Who, Volume 23: *1980-1981,* National Catholic News Service, 1979, p. 159.

PERIODICALS

New York Times, January 5, 1994, p. D21.

*   *   *

CURRIE, Lauchlin (Bernard)   1902-1993

OBITUARY NOTICE—See index for *CA* sketch: Born October 8, 1902, in West Dublin, Nova Scotia, Canada; died of a heart attack, December 23, 1993, in Bogota, Colombia. Economist, government official, educator, and author. Currie is remembered for having assisted President Franklin D. Roosevelt with the formulation of the New Deal policy in the 1930s. Currie received a doctorate in economics from Harvard University in 1931, and two years later accepted a position as professor of international economics at the Tufts University Fletcher School of Law and Diplomacy. He was named assistant director of research and statistics at the Federal Reserve Board in Washington, D.C., in 1934. He also became a citizen of the United States around that time. Appointed Roosevelt's special economic assistant in 1939, Currie composed several reports for the White House on domestic economic policy, international trade, and post-war amends. He also represented the president on missions to China and Switzerland, and remained in government until after Roosevelt's death in 1945.

Currie's career took a turn, however, three years later, when Elizabeth Bentley, a U.S. informer and former Soviet spy, accused him of having delivered information to Soviet espionage agents. The Federal Bureau of Investigation (FBI) also claimed that Currie had given information to the Soviets, possibly unknowingly. Although the charges were never proven, and Currie denied them before the House Un-American Activities Committee, his career in the United States never recovered. He moved permanently to Colombia in 1950, eventually becoming a naturalized citizen. Currie spent the next three decades serving as economic consultant to the Colombian Government and its agencies. In 1981 he began teaching at the Universidad de los Andes in Bogota, and in 1982 he became a member of the council of economic advisers to the president of Colombia. He was also an adviser to the Colombian Institute of Housing and Loans. Currie was decorated by the governments of Nationalist China, Colombia, and Venezuela. As a writer he was prolific in both English and Spanish, with publications including *The Basis of a Development Program for Colombia, Governmental Planning and Political Economy,* and *Taming the Megalopolis: A Design for Urban Growth.*

OBITUARIES AND OTHER SOURCES:

PERIODICALS

New York Times, December 30, 1993, p. B6.
Times (London), January 10, 1994, p. 17.
Washington Post, December 31, 1993, p. D4.

D

DACYCZYN, Amy 1955-

PERSONAL: Surname is pronounced "decision"; born September 21, 1955, in Ayer, MA; daughter of Nord William Davis, Jr. (a newsletter publisher) and Ann (a homemaker; maiden name, Shipton) Davis; married James D. Dacyczyn (a circulation manager and homemaker), December 11, 1982; children: Alec, Jamie, Neal, Rebecca, and twins Bradley and Laura. *Education:* Attended Vesper George School of Art. *Politics:* "Yes." *Religion:* Presbyterian.

ADDRESSES: Home—P.O. Box 222, Leeds, ME 04263. *Office*—*Tightwad Gazette,* R.R. 1, Box 3570, Leeds, ME 04263-9710.

CAREER: Publisher of *Tightwad Gazette,* a monthly newsletter, c. 1990—. Guest on talk shows; public speaker on thrift.

WRITINGS:

The Tightwad Gazette: Promoting Thrift as a Viable Alternative Lifestyle, Villard Books, 1993.

WORK IN PROGRESS: A collection of articles from years three and four of the *Tightwad Gazette* newsletter.

SIDELIGHTS: Amy Dacyczyn has turned a talent for thriftiness into fodder for an underground newsletter, *Tightwad Gazette,* and a book of the same title. Practicing what Dacyczyn calls "the Zen of advanced tightwaddery" was at first a necessity for this former Navy wife, and mother of six children. Through such money-saving measures as buying oatmeal in feedstore lots, finding uses for dryer lint, and reusing "disposable" items like vacuum-cleaner bags, plastic bags, and aluminum foil, Dacyczyn was able to save forty-three thousand dollars over a seven-year period from her husband's thirty thousand dollar a year petty officer's salary, and put it all into buying the family home. In 1990, she and husband Jim began publishing Amy's thrifty secrets in a monthly newsletter. Dacyczyn's book, *The Tightwad Gazette: Promoting Thrift as a Viable Alternative Lifestyle,* provides a selection of articles from the first two years of the newsletter's publication.

Dacyczyn "began the *Tightwad Gazette* not just to make money but to create a support group for penny pinchers afraid to admit that they, too, root around in other people's trash," explained Clare Ansberry in the *Wall Street Journal.* In her writings, Dacyczyn calls this activity "treasure hunting," and encourages readers to instill in themselves "an aversion to stupid expenditures." She includes recipes for such domestic items as dog food biscuits among her other tips for saving money, and emphasizes that refusing to throw anything away is good for the environment. While reviewers agreed that some of Dacyczyn's ideas seem a bit extreme, the author was praised for the good humor with which she dispenses advice. Denise Perry Donavin remarked in her *Booklist* review of *Tightwad Gazette* that the work is "fun to read even for a spendthrift." Reviewer Bill Katz in *Library Journal* concluded that "the recipes, ideas, and practical steps toward self-sufficiency will involve any perceptive reader."

BIOGRAPHICAL/CRITICAL SOURCES:

BOOKS

Dacyczyn, Amy, *The Tightwad Gazette: Promoting Thrift as a Viable Alternative Lifestyle,* Villard Books, 1993.

PERIODICALS

Booklist, January 1, 1993, p. 775.
Library Journal, April 15, 1992, pp. 49-50.
Wall Street Journal, November 19, 1991, section A, pp. 1, 15.

d'AMBOISE, Jacques Joseph   1934-

PERSONAL: Surname is pronounced "dom-*bwaz*"; original name, Jacques Joseph d'Amboise Ahearn; born July 28, 1934, in Dedham, MA; son of Andrew Patrick (a telegraph operator, then a nurse) and Georgette (a nurse; maiden name, d'Amboise) Ahearn; married Carolyn George (a dancer, then a photographer), January 1, 1956; children: George, Christopher, Charlotte and Catherine (twins). *Education:* Attended American School of Ballet, New York City, beginning c. 1942. *Religion:* Catholic.

ADDRESSES: Office—National Dance Institute, 244 West 71st St., New York, NY 10023.

CAREER: New York City Ballet Co., dancer, beginning c. 1949, principal dancer, 1953—; motion picture dance credits include *Seven Brides for Seven Brothers, Carousel,* and *The Best Things in Life Are Free;* appeared in Broadway production of *Shinbone Alley;* appeared in television specials, including *Sandlot Ballet.* School of American Ballet, instructor; National Dance Institute, founder and director, 1976—; State University of New York at Purchase, School of Dance, professor and dean, 1977-80.

WRITINGS:

(With wife, Carolyn George, and Hope Cooke) *Teaching the Magic of Dance,* Simon & Schuster (New York, NY), 1983.

SIDELIGHTS: Although born in Massachusetts, Jacques Joseph d'Amboise grew up on the streets of New York's Washington Heights, where he frequently ran with gangs. At the age of eight he became a student at the American School of Ballet, where he studied under the demanding, world-renowned George Balanchine, who became almost a second father to him. By the age of twelve he was dancing ballet professionally, and when Balanchine formed the New York City Ballet, he enlisted d'Amboise as a dancer. In 1953 d'Amboise—by this time a high school dropout—was designated a principal dancer, launching his career as America's leading male ballet dancer. He appeared not only in a wide range of traditional ballet roles but in films and television specials as well.

Eventually d'Amboise's career was cut short by the accumulation of minor injuries. So in the 1970s, he turned to teaching. He accepted a position as dean of the School of Dance at the State University of New York at Purchase, but he chafed at the administrative details and left after a few years. His real love was children, particularly the underprivileged children of New York City's streets, many of whom were from the same tough neighborhoods in which he had grown up. In 1976 he founded the National Dance Institute, and in the 1980s, he used that organization to raise funds enabling him (and a small staff) to teach dance to schoolchildren. Nearly every day of the week,

d'Amboise, who had danced on every important stage in the United States and Europe, could be seen in his beat-up Volkswagen headed off to a school, where he conducted dance classes for adoring children—more than one thousand total in the program, most of them boys. His goal is not to train professional dancers. Rather, it is to bring to students his own joy in dancing as a form of expression, remembering how the dance brought order and beauty to his own life when he was young.

In *Teaching the Magic of Dance,* which d'Amboise coauthored in 1983 and for which his wife, Carolyn George, provided photographs, he shares his experiences with teaching dance. Much of the book consists of anecdotes and informal discussions of what teaching dance has been like for him. In addition, in one section of the book coauthor Hope Cooke describes what goes into the production of a show. A reviewer for *Publishers Weekly* called *Teaching the Magic of Dance* "ebullient" and an "absolute must for any lover of the dance."

BIOGRAPHICAL/CRITICAL SOURCES:

PERIODICALS

New York Times April 12, 1981.
Publishers Weekly, October 7, 1983, p. 92.

*   *   *

DASA, Drutakarma
See CREMO, Michael (A.)

*   *   *

DAVIDSON, Dana H.   1949-

PERSONAL: Born August 20, 1949, in Santa Rosa, CA; daughter of Richard H. Hinze (a professor) and Nancy (a homemaker; maiden name, Wilson) Hinze; married Dan Davidson (an attorney), December 28, 1976; children: one son and one daughter. *Education:* Northwestern University, B.S., 1970; Vanderbilt University, M.A., 1972; Claremont Graduate School, Ph.D., 1977. *Avocational Interests:* Child development and welfare.

ADDRESSES: Office—Department of Human Resources, University of Hawaii—Miller Hall 110, Honolulu, HI 96822.

CAREER: University of Hawaii—Manoa, Honolulu, instructor in human development and the family, 1977—. Peking University, Peking, China, visiting scholar, 1992.

MEMBER: State Advisory Council for Gifted Children, NAEYC, AHEA, Phi U honorary society.

AWARDS, HONORS: University of Hawaii Regent's Medal for Excellence in Teaching, 1992.

WRITINGS:

(With Joseph J. Tobin and David Y. H. Wu) *Preschool in Three Cultures: Japan, China, and the United States,* Yale University Press, 1989.

(With Kiki Davis and Terry Lawhead) *Hawaii for Kids: A Family Guide to the Islands,* Bess Press, 1990.

WORK IN PROGRESS: Childhood: An Interdisciplinary Approach.

SIDELIGHTS: Dana H. Davidson, with Joseph H. Tobin and David Y. H. Wu, is the author of *Preschool In Three Cultures: Japan, China, and the United States,* an in-depth study of the effect of preschools on society and the ways that preschools reflect societal trends. Davidson's book does not seek to determine which of the three countries studied has the superior preschool system, but rather looks at how each culture perceives children's and parents' needs. Davidson finds all three cultures have experienced similar changes in the last quarter-century, primarily concerning the societal role of women (the traditional caretakers of children). As the number of women in the workplace has increased, the number of those at home has decreased, leaving fewer mothers, aunts, grandmothers, and neighbors to care for small children. This, plus a migration of people from their homes to other, often urban, parts of the country, and away from available family members and friends, has necessitated the development of group care centers.

In preparing their book, Davidson and coauthors Tobin and Wu videotaped a day's activities in Japanese, Chinese, and American preschools, later returning to each country to show educators the edited tapes. Basic cultural differences in education and beliefs about child raising were evident as the educators viewed the classroom activities. Whereas American preschools strive for a low student-teacher ratio so that each child receives individual attention, Japanese teachers work with many more students, believing the teacher should give more attention to the class as a group, rather than as individuals. Similarly, Chinese teachers stress the importance of the child as part of a collective ensemble, rather than the development of an individual personality.

Davidson also finds that, although all three cultures place great emphasis on the development of language skills, their motives for teaching them differ. The Japanese view language as an expression of group solidarity and allow students to speak when and in whatever way they wish. The Chinese, on the other hand, teach recitation to promote proper diction, but frown upon spontaneous verbal interaction between the children, as it may turn the child's attention away from his or her teacher's instruction. American preschools, unlike their Eastern counterparts, promote language skills in order to prompt self-expression and a sense of personal identity.

In matters of discipline, sharp contrasts were found among the cultures. America's "time out" method, or the removal of the misbehaving child to an isolated area, was foreign to the Chinese, whose authoritarian teaching methods squelch misbehavior before it has a chance to occur, while the Japanese children were only punished when their behavior exceeded the tolerance of the other children.

Preschool in Three Cultures has been praised by several critics, among them *New York Times Book Review* critic Penelope Leach, who writes: "The book should be required reading for professionals in early education and makes thought-provoking reading for anyone aware of his or her own cultural blinkers and interested in glimpsing the world outside them." *Los Angeles Times Book Review* critic Carole C. Kemmerer writes that *Preschool in Three Cultures* "is not a trivial exploration. It is scholarly and detailed but readily readable. . . . Its style is clear, its methodology fascinating. . . . *Preschool in Three Cultures* is a must read for those who take social issues seriously."

Davidson told *CA:* "The success of our video and text may be due to the increased awareness people find from reading our book. We ask people to examine what is important to them for our children. As with many studies such as this, the 'unfamiliar' helps us to see the 'familiar' more clearly."

BIOGRAPHICAL/CRITICAL SOURCES:

PERIODICALS

Los Angeles Times Book Review, June 18, 1989, p. 8.
New York Times Book Review, June 25, 1989, pp. 26-28.

*   *   *

DAVIS, Helen Dick   1899-1992

PERSONAL: Born October 3, 1899, in New London, WI; died February 27, 1992, in Auburn, AL; daughter of William Henry (in lumber industry, also a planter) and Susa (a homemaker; maiden name, Blackwood) Dick; married Reuben G. Davis (a writer), March 9, 1926 (died, 1966); children: Louvica, Nicholas Dick. *Education:* University of Wisconsin—Madison, B.A., 1921. *Religion:* Presbyterian. *Avocational Interests:* Church, reading, cooking breads and pastries, lecturing, letter writing.

CAREER: Writer in Philipp, MS, 1928-36, Hendersonville, NC, 1936-39, Carter, MS, 1939-59, Yazoo City, MS, 1959-73, and Auburn, AL, 1973-92. Grader and part-time teacher in English department of Yazoo City public school, 1969-73.

MEMBER: Phi Beta Kappa.

WRITINGS:

(With husband, Reuben G. Davis; published under husband's name only) *Butcher Bird* (novel), Little, Brown, 1936.

(With husband, Reuben G. Davis; published under husband's name only) *Shim* (novel), Bobbs-Merrill, 1953.

(With husband, Reuben G. Davis, and Mary Hamilton) *Trials of the Earth: The Autobiography of Mary Hamilton,* University Press of Mississippi, 1992.

Contributor of collaborative short fiction with husband, Reuben G. Davis, to such periodicals as the *Saturday Evening Post, Ladies Home Journal, Country Gentleman, Redbook,* and *Bluebook;* book reviewer for local newspapers.

WORK IN PROGRESS: The author's son, Nicholas Dick Davis, intends to publish excerpts from journals and unpublished short stories by Helen Dick Davis.

SIDELIGHTS: Speaking of his mother's and father's careers, Nicholas Dick Davis told *CA:* "Although *Trials of the Earth: The Autobiography of Mary Hamilton* involved mostly my mother, Helen, and Mary Hamilton, most of her other published works were written in close partnership with my father, Reuben G. Davis (who died in 1966). They also coauthored about a dozen short stories, two unpublished novels, and about two dozen unpublished short stories.

"Life in the Mississippi Delta among both blacks and whites constitutes the bulk of their subject matter. Several short stories and the book *Butcher Bird* have all-black characters. A particularly difficult problem which they struggled with was how to write black dialect in a form intelligible to New York publishers without stripping away its rich color and without resorting to the painful distortions of Uncle Remus. It is interesting to see their language evolve from the more literal forms of their 1926 short stories to a much smoother but equally expressive interpretation in *Butcher Bird* (1936). This process of accurately portraying the Negro culture of the South was ended by the New Deal policies of the 1930s and any writing which did not portray that culture as cruelly oppressed was rejected. Thus an art form which had been more than a decade in the making had to be abandoned—at least in the eyes of my parents and the market.

"In the 1930s they produced *Trials of the Earth, Butcher Bird,* several short stories, and a wrote a long novel which was never published. This intense level of production was never to be equalled, due in part to my father's ill health.

"Now, as I read the unpublished manuscripts and leaf through the thick pile of rejection slips, I am overwhelmed by the strength and cheerfulness with which they bore their disappointments and by the tenacity with which they continued to create until they died. The acceptance of *Trials of the Earth* five months before my mother's death was an incredible triumph."

BIOGRAPHICAL/CRITICAL SOURCES:

PERIODICALS

New York Times Book Review, December 13, 1992.

    [Sketch reviewed by son, Nicholas Dick Davis.]

*   *   *

DAVIS, Reuben G.   1889-1966

PERSONAL: Born December 22, 1889, in Charleston, MS; died May 28, 1966, in Yazoo City, MS; son of Reuben (a plantation owner) and Vicelou (a homemaker) Davis; married Helen Dick (a writer), March 9, 1926 (died, 1992); children: Louvica, Nicholas Dick. *Education:* Attended Mississippi College. *Religion:* Methodist. *Avocational Interests:* Fishing, hunting, shooting, African dialects, history, storytelling.

CAREER: Writer in Philipp, MS, 1928-36, Hendersonville, NC, 1936-39, Carter, MS, 1939-59, and Yazoo City, MS, 1959-66. Worked as a planter, timber foreman, railroad flagger, plantation manager, and surveyor for Tallahatchie Lumber Co.; served on local flood control boards and in local agricultural organizations. *Military service:* U.S. Army, 20th Engineers, 1917-19; served in France and England.

WRITINGS:

(With wife, Helen Dick Davis; published under Reuben G. Davis's name only) *Butcher Bird* (novel), Little, Brown, 1936.

(With wife, Helen Dick Davis; published under Reuben G. Davis's name only) *Shim* (novel), Bobbs-Merrill, 1953.

(With wife, Helen Dick Davis, and Mary Hamilton) *Trials of the Earth: The Autobiography of Mary Hamilton,* University Press of Mississippi, 1992.

Contributor of collaborative short fiction with wife, Helen Dick Davis to periodicals.

SIDELIGHTS: For more information on the career of Reuben G. Davis, please refer to the entry on his wife, Helen Dick Davis, in this volume.

    [Sketch reviewed by son, Nicholas Dick Davis.]

de CARVALHO, Fernando Jose Cardim 1953-

PERSONAL: Born September 4, 1953, in Sao Paulo, Brazil; son of Julio Alves de Carvalho Filho and Dinorah Cardim de Carvalho; married Fernanda Lopes (a sociologist), December 1, 1973; children: Thiago Lopes. *Education:* University of Sao Paulo, B.A., 1975; University of Campinas, M.A., 1978; Rutgers University, M.A., 1984, Ph.D., 1986.

ADDRESSES: Home—Rua General Gois Monteiro 8, Bloco A, Apt. 603, Rio de Janeiro, RJ 22290-080, Brazil. *Office*—Faculty of Economics and Business Administration, Federal University of Rio de Janeiro, Rua Pasteur 250, Rio de Janeiro, RJ 22290, Brazil.

CAREER: Brazilian Central Statistical Office, economic analyst, 1978-82; Fluminense Federal University, Niteroi, Brazil, assistant professor, 1981-85, associate professor of economics, 1985-93; Federal University of Rio de Janeiro, Rio de Janeiro, Brazil, professor of economics, 1993—. Rutgers University, instructor, 1984-86; University of Campinas, visiting professor, 1986, 1991; Federal University of Rio de Janeiro, visiting professor, 1986-92, inflation analyst at Boletim de Conjuntura, Industrial Economics Institute, 1986-89.

MEMBER: National Association of Graduate Schools of Economics (chairperson, 1992-94).

WRITINGS:

Mr. Keynes and the Post Keynesians: Principles of Macroeconomics for a Monetary Production Economy, Edward Elgar, 1992.

Work represented in anthologies, including *Economic Problems of the 1990s,* edited by P. Davidson and J. Kregel, Edward Elgar, 1991; *The Megacorp and Macrodynamics: Essays in Memory of Alfred Eichner,* edited by W. Milberg, M. E. Sharpe, 1992; and *Post Keynesian Economics,* edited by P. Wells, Kluwer Academic Publishers, 1993. Contributor to economic journals.

WORK IN PROGRESS: A study of the theory of monetary policy; a book on the workings of intense inflationary processes; research on the roots of stability and instability of capitalist economies.

SIDELIGHTS: Fernando Jose Cardim de Carvalho told *CA:* "Currently I am working on three closely related areas: a study of the theory of monetary policy, contrasting the views of the main schools of thought, the monetarists and Keynesians, and developing a post-Keynesian alternative approach. I am also interested in the workings of intense inflationary processes and the roots of stability and instability of capitalist economies. This third area of research involves more abstract problems, including some philosophical debates around the notions of order, uncertainty, and chaos, and the related problems of determinism and free will. I have already published some papers on this, but much more work will have to be done before results can be presented in a more definitive form."

*   *   *

de la BILLIERE, Peter (Edgar de la Cour) 1934-

PERSONAL: Born April 29, 1934, in Plymouth, England; son of Claude Dennis Delacour de Labilliere (a naval surgeon) and Frances Christine Wright Lawley; married Bridget Constance Muriel Goode, February 13, 1965; children: Edward, Nicola, Phillida. *Education:* Attended Staff College, 1966, and Royal College of Defence Studies 1983. *Religion:* Church of England. *Avocational Interests:* Family, down market apiculture, farming, squash, tennis, sailing.

ADDRESSES: Agent—Curtis Brown & John Farquharson, 162-168 Regent St., London W1R 5TB, England.

CAREER: British Army, career officer, 1952-1992. Joined King's Shropshire Light Infantry, 1952; joined Special Air Services Regiment, 1956, director of Special Air Services, 1978-83; served in several countries, including Japan, Korea, Sudan, Oman, and Egypt; held several posts as commanding officer, including command of British Army training team in Sudan, 1977-78, British forces in the Falkland Islands, 1984-85, and British forces in the Middle East, 1990-91; permanent peacetime commander of Joint Forces Operations Staff, 1987-90; Middle East adviser to Ministry of Defence, 1991-92; Robert Fleming Holdings, non-executive director, 1992—. Member of council of Royal United Services Institute for Defense Studies, 1975-77; chair of Joint Services Hang Gliding, 1986-89; Duke of York's Military School, 1988-90; trustee of Imperial War Museum, 1992; board member of FARM Africa.

MEMBER: Special Air Service Association (president, 1991), Army Sailing Association (commodore, 1989-91), Army Cadet Force (president, 1992—), Southampton Master Mariners Association (Stowaway member), Farmers' Club, Special Forces Club.

AWARDS, HONORS: Mentioned in despatches, 1958; Military Cross, 1959 and Bar, 1966; Companion of the Distinguished Service Order, 1976; Commander, Order of the British Empire, 1983; Knight Commander, Order of the Bath, 1988; Knight Commander, Order of the British Empire, 1991; Freeman of the City of London, 1991; Honorary Freeman of Fishmongers' Co., 1991; Chief Commander, Legion of Merit, United States Department of Defense, 1992; Deputy Lieutenant Hereford and Worcester, 1993; also received the Meritorious Cross from Canada; Order of Abdul Aziz, second class, from Saudi Arabia; Order of Bahrain, first class; Kuwait Decoration, first class; and Qatar Sash of Merit; honorary doctorate from Cranfield Institute of Technology, 1992, and University of Durham, 1993.

WRITINGS:

Storm Command: A Personal Story, HarperCollins, 1992.

Contributor to periodicals, including *Newsweek.*

WORK IN PROGRESS: Looking for Trouble (an autobiography).

SIDELIGHTS: Peter de la Billiere was declared "the most decorated man in the British Army" by *Los Angeles Times* reviewer William Tuohy. In his long and distinguished career, de la Billiere was stationed in the Middle East for a number of years, and in 1990 he was was appointed Commander of British Forces in the Middle East. In this capacity, he worked closely with the United States Army to resolve the Persian Gulf crisis following Iraq's invasion of Kuwait. De la Billiere's best-selling book, *Storm Command: A Personal Story,* is an account of that operation, including the role played by the British armed forces. Reviewing the book for the London *Observer,* Julian Thompson commended de la Billiere for writing an "excellent" and balanced narrative of the operation.

BIOGRAPHICAL/CRITICAL SOURCES:

PERIODICALS

Boston Globe, January 27, 1991, p. 16.
Economist, October 10, 1992, p. 111.
Los Angeles Times, October 6, 1990, p. A12.
Observer (London), November 8, 1992, p. 60.

*　　　*　　　*

de LOMELLINI, C. A.
　　See KELLEY, (Kathleen) Alita

*　　　*　　　*

DENNING, A. T.
　　See DENNING, Alfred Thompson

*　　　*　　　*

DENNING, Alfred
　　See DENNING, Alfred Thompson

DENNING, Alfred Thompson 1899-
(A. T. Denning, Alfred Denning, Baron Denning, Lord Denning)

PERSONAL: Born January 23, 1899, in Whitchurch, Hampshire, England; son of Charles (a draper) and Clara Denning (a school teacher); married Mary Harvey, 1932 (died, 1941); married Joan (Taylor) Stuart; children: (first marriage) one son. *Education:* Magdalen College, Oxford, bachelor's degree (with honors), 1920, jurisprudence degree (with honors), 1922. *Avocational Interests:* Legal research, country walks, croquet.

ADDRESSES: Home—The Lawn, Whitchurch, Hants RG28 7AS, England.

CAREER: Lawyer, jurist, and author. Called to the Bar, London, England, 1923; in private practice; appointed king's counsel, 1938; High Court of Justice, judge, 1944; Lord Justice of Appeal, 1948-57; Lord of Appeal in Ordinary, 1957-62; Master of the Rolls, 1962-82. Chancellor, Diocese of Southwark, 1937-44, and of London, 1942-44; Birkbeck College, president, 1952-83; British Institute of International and Comparative Law, member, 1959-86; Committee on Legal Education for Students from Africa, chair, 1962; Royal Commission on Historical Manuscripts, chair, 1962-82; Security Enquiry, head, 1963; Lincoln's Inn, treasurer, 1964; British Broadcasting Corporation (BBC-TV), Dimbleby lecturer, 1980. *Military service:* Royal Engineers, 1918-19, served in France.

MEMBER: Athenaeum Club.

AWARDS, HONORS: Eldon Scholar, Oxford, 1921; Prize Student, Inns of Court; honorary fellow of Magdalen College, Oxford, 1948, and Nuffield College, Oxford, 1982; numerous honorary degrees from universities, including London, 1960, Cambridge, 1963, Leeds, 1964, McGill, 1967, Dalhousie, 1970, Wales, 1973, Columbia, 1976, Tilburg (Netherlands), 1977, British Columbia, 1979, Sussex, 1980, and Nottingham, 1984.

WRITINGS:

Freedom under the Law (lecture), Stevens, 1949.
The Changing Law, Stevens & Sons, 1953.
The Road to Justice, Stevens & Sons, 1955.
The Discipline of Law, Butterworth, 1979.
The Profumo-Christine Keeler Affair: Lord Denning's Report Presented to the Parliament by the Prime Minister, New York Popular Library, 1963, published in England as *Lord Denning's Report,* His Majesty's Stationery Office, 1963.
The Due Process of Law, Butterworth, 1980.
The Family Story, Butterworth, 1981.
What Next in the Law, Butterworth, 1982.
The Closing Chapter, Butterworth, 1983.
Landmarks in the Law, Butterworth, 1984.

(Compiler) *Leaves from My Library: An English Anthology,* Butterworth, 1986.

Author of works under the royal titles Lord Denning and Baron Denning and under the names A. T. Denning and Alfred Denning. Author of numerous speeches and lectures delivered at universities and broadcast by the British Broadcasting Corporation (BBC-TV), including *Gems in Ermine,* Oxford University Press, 1964, and *Misuse of Power,* 1980. Coeditor with Sir Thomas Willes Chitty and Cyril Pearce Harvey of the two-volume *Smith's Leading Cases,* thirteenth edition, 1929; coeditor with Arthur Grattan-Bellew of *Bullen and Leake's Precedents of Pleadings in the Superior Courts of Common Law,* ninth edition, 1935.

Lord Denning's Report has been translated into French.

SIDELIGHTS: During a judicial career which spanned thirty-seven years Lord Alfred Denning became known for his activist stance on the bench and his authorship of numerous works about his often controversial judgments. "Praise him or deplore him, Lord Denning could never be ignored," Allan C. Hutchinson pointed out in *Books and Bookmen.* "He was a judicial gang of one; a maverick in legal garb. He has left an indelible mark on the career of the common law."

Denning grew up in a family in which duty, religion, and intelligence were emphasized. After graduating from Oxford with honors in mathematics, Denning taught for a year at a prominent public school. He realized that teaching did not appeal to him, however, and returned to Oxford where he studied law as the recipient of the prestigious Eldon Scholarship. During his fifteen years in private practice as a barrister, Denning built a successful career. By 1938 he was appointed king's counsel and began his prominent years on the bench.

Denning's writings were geared strictly to a professional legal audience until 1963, when he was appointed investigator of the Profumo affair (a sex scandal that rocked the government of Conservative British Prime Minister Harold Macmillan). Denning delved into Secretary of State John D. Profumo's affair with a party girl, Christine Keeler, who was also involved with a Russian intelligence officer attached to the Russian embassy in London. *Lord Denning's Report* supplied the facts of the case to a ready audience, selling ten thousand copies in two days. John Sparrow, writing in the *New York Review of Books,* called the volume "surely the raciest and most readable Blue Book ever published." Though Denning found no evidence that state secrets were compromised, confidence in the government plummeted. A month after its publication, Prime Minister Macmillan resigned for "health reasons."

During his summer vacation of 1978 Denning wrote *The Discipline of Law,* in which he reviews a selection of his judgments. Denning states in the book that "the principles of law laid down by the judges in the nineteenth century—however suited to the conditions of that time—are not suited to the social necessities and social opinion of the twentieth century. They should be moulded and shaped to meet the needs and opinions of today." Denning's activism on the bench has stirred controversy and made his judgments—and writings—of particular interest to colleagues. "*The Discipline of Law* consists almost wholly of an account of the more important cases in which the author has been involved, illustrated by extensive quotations from his own judgments," wrote A. W. B. Simpson in the *Times Literary Supplement.* The critic noted that "the discussion only rarely ranges outside purely legal material, and gives an impression of intense cultural isolation. The aim is to convince and convert; the intended audience is law students, and Lord Denning has an unflattering view of their powers of assimilation." However, according to reviewer Louis Blom-Cooper in the *Spectator, The Discipline of Law* "provides the layman and the specialist reader with a canter through [Denning's] most outstanding judicial utterances. If there is selectivity and an undercurrent of self-justification in the chronicles of a crusader, it is all served up in the same delightful manner that one experiences whenever one is privileged to be in his court. One may quarrel, even violently, with the content; but one can admire the spirit in which it is expounded."

Denning has also been in the public eye for his televised lectures and writings of a non-technical nature. In the *Listener* David Pannick described Denning's autobiographical work *Family Story* as "compelling, if undemanding, reading for all those fascinated by a lawyer who has exerted a greater influence on English law this century than any of his brethren. Lord Denning makes no shocking revelations. . . . What we are offered is a simple, rather moving account of one man's values and of what has inspired ('motivated' is not a word he would use) and consoled him." Hugh Massingberd, a reviewer for the *Spectator,* commented, "In this extraordinary volume, punctuated by numerous sub-headings, copious quotations from Shakespeare and others in the manner of a commonplace book, and composed in his inimitable short sentences . . . Lord Denning distills his unique brand of wisdom in telling us about his family and his own life in and out of the courts. A charmingly vivid picture emerges of provincial English life based on hard work, commonsense, and Christian behaviour."

In *Family Story* Denning explains, "I avoid long sentences like the plague because they lead to obscurity." Assessing the effectiveness of what he called Denning's "precise, unadorned literary style," Pannick commented: "Words complicate and ambiguously translate the intuitive values he holds dear. Description and comment, for him, need no qualification. This produces an effective lyrical quality to some of the passages." In the London *Times* Peta Fordham found *A Family Story* "naive yet profound," and commented that "for a Judge in high office to display a quality of innocence which has enabled him to view the whole of life with the clear eyes of a child, plus the maturity of a fine brain, is indeed a rare achievement; and this is the real personal disclosure of the book."

In the book *What Next in the Law* Denning discusses law reform using "a pastiche of extracts, judicial and literary, strung together with his stabbing and fresh prose," according to Hutchinson in *Books and Bookmen.* David Pannick in the *Times Literary Supplement* remarked that "the style in which Lord Denning presents his thoughts on law reform will be familiar to readers of his earlier books. There is a great deal of history that could come from a schoolboy essay. . . . The sentences are short, and the presentation intimate." *What Next in the Law* was recalled when Denning's comments about black jurors prompted the threat of a libel suit and it was later altered and republished. However, the negative publicity surrounding the book played a part in Denning's retirement, ending his lengthy career on the bench. In the *Times Literary Supplement* Neil MacCormick stated that "one cannot but regret the manner of ending of Lord Denning's brilliant, erratic and tempestuous career as Master of the Rolls; but one cannot doubt that the publication of the book and the reaction it rightly and predictably provoked among the black communities and particularly the jurors assailed in one section of it made imperative its author's decision to retire."

The Closing Chapter is Denning's account of his last months as Master of the Rolls and the events that led to his retirement. "The interest of the book is largely in the information it provides on the attitudes and beliefs of an important judge and on his failure to understand the problem of judicial bias," commented Pannick in the *Listener.* Christopher Staughton, writing in the London *Times,* found *The Closing Chapter* so enlightening that he stated, "A law student who has not read this book will not necessarily be failed in his examinations, but he should be."

BIOGRAPHICAL/CRITICAL SOURCES:

BOOKS

Denning, Alfred, *The Discipline of Law,* Butterworth, 1979.
Denning, *The Family Story,* Butterworth, 1981.

PERIODICALS

Books and Bookmen, August, 1982, p. 38.

British Book News, July, 1984, pp. 390-392; March, 1985, p. 153.
Listener, March 15, 1979, pp. 379-380; April 23, 1981, p. 546; August 12, 1982, p. 21; January 12, 1984, p. 24.
New Statesman, January 19, 1979, p. 78; February 24, 1984, p. 22.
New York Review of Books, February 25, 1965, p. 23.
Punch, May 27, 1981, p. 845; February 2, 1984, p. 51.
Spectator, February 17, 1979, p. 23; June 13, 1981, pp. 20-21; June 5, 1982.
Times (London), May 28, 1981; January 7, 1984.
Times Literary Supplement, October 28, 1965, p. 965; December 7, 1979; October 1, 1982; November 9, 1984, p. 1279.*

*   *   *

DENNIS, Peggy   1909-1993

OBITUARY NOTICE—See index for *CA* sketch: Born January 1, 1909, in Brooklyn, NY; died of complications resulting from several strokes, September 25, 1993, in San Francisco, CA. Political organizer, journalist, and author. Dennis devoted much of her career to the cause of the Communist Party. Beginning her involvement in internal party organizing in the mid-1920s, she served for a number of years as a courier of messages between Communist leaders in the United States and those in European countries. In 1928 she married Eugene Dennis, who later became general secretary of the American Communist Party and was imprisoned in the late 1940s for conspiring to overthrow the U.S. government. Peggy was the editor of her husband's book about the experience, *Letters from Prison.* In the early 1950s Dennis began applying her political sentiments to a career in journalism, authoring the column, "Comradely Yours, Peggy Dennis" and editing the women's page in the *Sunday Worker.* She also contributed to other publications, including *Progressive* and *Socialist Revolution,* and from 1961 to 1968 was foreign editor of *People's World.* Dennis left the Communist Party in the mid-1970s on account of leadership conflicts, and in 1977 saw publication of her *Autobiography of an American Communist: A Personal View of a Political Life, 1925-1975.* She and Eugene Dennis were the subject of a 1992 public television documentary, *Love in the Cold War,* produced by American Experience and Windfall Films.

OBITUARIES AND OTHER SOURCES:

PERIODICALS

New York Times, October 12, 1993, p. B9.

DICKE, Thomas S(cott) 1955-

PERSONAL: Born November 9, 1955, in St. Marys, OH; son of Dale E. (a small business owner) and Kathryn (a small business owner; maiden name, Springer) Dicke; married Judith Burke (a legal secretary), October 12, 1985; children: Rachel, Samuel. *Education:* Bowling Green State University, B.S.Ed., 1979; Ohio State University, M.A., 1983, Ph.D., 1988. *Politics:* "Independent Democrat." *Religion:* Roman Catholic.

ADDRESSES: Home—617 South Weller, Springfield, MO. *Office*—Department of History, Southwest Missouri State University, 901 South National Ave., Springfield, MO 65802-0089.

CAREER: High school teacher of history, geography, and political science in Hebron, IL, 1979-81; Ohio State University, Columbus, instructor, 1987-88, lecturer, 1988-89; University of Georgia, Athens, temporary assistant professor, 1989-90; Southwest Missouri State University, Springfield, assistant professor, 1990-93, associate professor of history, 1993—.

MEMBER: Organization of American Historians, Business History Conference, Economic and Business Historical Society.

WRITINGS:

Franchising in America: The Development of a Business Method, 1840-1980, University of North Carolina Press, 1992.

Contributor of articles and reviews to history and business journals.

* * *

DIOP, David Mandessi 1927-1960

PERSONAL: Born July 9, 1927, in Bordeaux, France; died in a plane crash in August, 1960, near Dakar, Senegal; father was a medical doctor. *Education:* Attended Lycee Marcelin Berthelot near Paris, France in the late 1940's.

CAREER: Teacher at Lycee Maurice Delafosse in Dakar, 1957-58; school principal in the town of Kindia, Guinea, 1958-60.

WRITINGS:

Coups de pilon: poemes, Presence Africaine (Paris), 1956.
Hammer Blows and Other Writings [by] David Mandessi Diop, translated and edited by Simon Mpondo and Frank Jones, Indiana University Press, 1973.
Hammer Blows: Poems [by] David Mandessi Diop, translated and edited by Mpondo and Jones, Heinemann, 1975.

David Diop: 1927-1960: temoignages, etudes/Societe africaine de culture (published in French and English), Presence Africaine, 1983.

Contributor to anthologies, including *Anthologie de la nouvelle poesie negre et malgache,* L. S. Senghor, Presence Africaine, 1947; *An Anthology of African and Malagasy Poetry in French,* Clive Wake, editor, Three Crowns Press, 1965; *Modern Poetry from Africa,* Moore and Beier, editors, Penguin, revised edition, 1968.

BIOGRAPHICAL/CRITICAL SOURCES:

BOOKS

David Diop: 1927-1960: temoignages, etudes/Societe africaine de culture, Presence Africaine, 1983, published in French and English.

PERIODICALS

Choice, March, 1974, p. 101; October, 1975, p. 971.*

* * *

DISTLER, Ann G.
See GOETHE, Ann

* * *

DOLBIER, Maurice (Wyman) 1912-1993

OBITUARY NOTICE—See index for *CA* sketch: Born May 5, 1912, in Skowhegan, ME; died October 20, 1993, in Providence, RI. Performer, editor, and author. Dolbier attended the Whitehouse Academy of Dramatic Arts in Boston, Massachusetts, and toured with Shakespearean theatre companies early in his career. He also worked as a radio news editor, announcer, and program director, but spent the bulk of his career as a journalist and a writer of fiction, humor, plays, and children's tales. Dolbier was named literary editor of the *Providence Journal* in 1951. Five years later he began composing the "Books and Authors" column and reviewing books for the *New York Herald Tribune,* which was later renamed the *New York World Journal Tribune.* When that paper went out of business in 1967, Dolbier returned to his prior position at the *Providence Journal. The Magic Shop, Torten's Christmas Secret,* and *Paul Bunyan* are among his writings for children, while his adult works include *All Wrong on the Night: A Comedy of Theatrical Errors* and *The Mortal Gods.* One of Dolbier's plays, *Jenny, the Bus That Nobody Loved,* has been broadcast on television.

OBITUARIES AND OTHER SOURCES:

BOOKS

Authors of Books for Young People, 3rd edition, Scarecrow, 1990, p. 190.

PERIODICALS

New York Times, October 23, 1993, p. 10.

*   *   *

DOOLEY, Roger B(urke) 1920-1993

OBITUARY NOTICE—See index for *CA* sketch: Born May 15, 1920, in Buffalo, NY; died of a heart attack, October 29, 1993, in New York, NY. Educator, film scholar, and author. Dooley's 1981 publication, *From Scarface to Scarlett: American Films in the 1930s,* is considered a valuable resource in that it covers five thousand films in fifty genres. Dooley began his career as an instructor in English at his alma mater, Canisius College, in 1946. He later taught at a number of institutions, including Queensborough Community College of the City University of New York, where he chaired the English Department in the early 1960s. Dooley became a professor at Manhattan Community College of the City University of New York in 1964, was appointed department chair in 1972, and was named professor emeritus upon his retirement in 1985. In addition to teaching, Dooley was a film reviewer for *Marriage* and the *Villager* between 1956 and 1974. He is the author of novels concerning Irish Americans in Buffalo, including *Less Than Angels* and *Gone Tomorrow.* He also published *A Study Guide to Modern British and Irish Drama* and spent ten years writing *From Scarface to Scarlett.*

OBITUARIES AND OTHER SOURCES:

BOOKS

Who's Who in Writers, Editors, and Poets, 1989-1990, December Press, 1989, p. 142.

PERIODICALS

New York Times, November 11, 1993, p. D23.

*   *   *

DOOLITTLE, James H(arold) 1896-1993
(Jimmy Doolittle)

PERSONAL: Born December 14, 1896, in Alameda, CA; died following a stroke, September 27, 1993, in Pebble Beach, CA; buried at Arlington National Cemetery, Arlington, VA; son of Frank H. (a carpenter) and Rosa C. (Shephard) Doolittle; married Josephine E. Daniels, December 24, 1917 (died, 1988); children: James H. (deceased), John P. *Education:* University of California at Berkeley, A.B., 1918; Massachusetts Institute of Technology, M.S., 1924, Sc.D., 1925. *Avocational Interests:* Shooting and fishing.

CAREER: Boxed professionally while in college; enlisted in the U.S. Army Air Corps, 1917, served as flying instructor during World War I, commissioned as first lieutenant, 1920, involved in development of military navigation, assigned to various test-facility stations during the late 1920s, resigned his commission for the first time in 1930, remained on reserve duty; Shell Oil Co., manager of the aviation department, 1930-40, vice president and director, 1946-59; returned to active duty in the U.S. Army Air Corps, 1940, supervised the transformation of automobile factories for airplane manufacture for war effort until 1942, then joined Army Air Forces in Washington, D.C., to plan the raid on Tokyo, Japan, which he subsequently led, promoted to brigadier general, then transferred to England where he organized the Twelfth Air Force and commanded its invasion of North Africa, directed intensive bombing of Germany, 1944-45, attained rank of lieutenant general by the end of World War II, in 1985 promoted to full general in the reserves by President Ronald Reagan. Served on several boards concerned with military and aviation development, including the National Advisory Committee for Aeronautics and the Air Force Science Advisory Board; set several flight records during the 1920s and 1930s, including first pilot to successfully execute an outside loop, first pilot to fly across the continental United States in less than twenty-four hours, and several land speed records.

AWARDS, HONORS: Winner of numerous awards for work in advancing aeronautics, including the Harmon Trophy and Daniel Guggenheim Medal; recipient of airplane racing awards, including the Thompson Trophy and Bendix Trophy; Congressional Medal of Honor, 1942, for bombing raid on Tokyo during World War II; honorary Knight Commander of the Order of Bath, 1945; Sylvanus Thayer Award, United States Military Academy, 1983, for distinguished military service; awarded Presidential Medal of Freedom by U.S. President George Bush, 1989.

WRITINGS:

(With Carroll V. Glines) *I Could Never Be So Lucky Again: The Memoirs of General James H. "Jimmy" Doolittle,* Bantam, 1991.

CONTRIBUTOR

(Author of introduction) Getz, C. W., editor, *The Wild Blue Yonder: Songs of the Air Force,* Redwood Press, 1981.

(Author of foreword) Toliver, Raymond F., *Fighter General: The Life of Adolf Galland,* AmPress, 1990.

(Author of foreword) Gabreski, Francis, *Gabby: A Fighter Pilot's Life,* Crown, 1991.

(Author of foreword) Boyne, Walter J., *Silver Wings: A History of the United States Air Force,* Simon & Schuster, 1993.

SIDELIGHTS: General James H. "Jimmy" Doolittle was one of the best-known American heroes of World War II. A daring aviator, planner, and commander, he led the 1942 U.S. Army Air Corps bombing raid on Tokyo, as well as other Japanese cities, that was credited with turning the tide of American wartime morale. Doolittle received the Congressional Medal of Honor for this mission, but his contributions to the U.S. war effort were much greater than this one raid. As the United States entered World War II, Doolittle helped supervise the conversion of automobile factories to manufacture airplanes that would be needed to fight the Axis powers (a wartime alliance of Germany, Italy, and Japan); even before that, his work with Shell Oil Company led to the production of a high-octane gasoline for airplanes that gave the United States an edge over Germany. After the Tokyo raid, Doolittle was sent to England to supervise air campaigns both in North Africa and Germany, and, at the close of the war, served for a time under General Douglas MacArthur. Towards the end of his life, Doolittle, with the help of author Carroll V. Glines, told the story of his long, eventful existence in *I Could Never Be So Lucky Again: The Memoirs of General James H. "Jimmy" Doolittle.*

Doolittle was born December 14, 1896, in Alameda, California. His father was a carpenter, but he dreamed of striking it rich and he took his family to Nome, Alaska, to prospect for gold when the future aviator was still a young child. They eventually returned to California, however, settling in the Los Angeles area. There, as an adolescent, Doolittle began displaying an interest in flight. An obituary writer for the *Los Angeles Times* recorded that in 1910 Doolittle "witnessed an event that changed his life forever—the great air meet at Dominguez Field. . . . Among other heroics the 13-year-old . . . gawked at were Glenn Curtiss breaking the world's speed record for aircraft, whizzing along at 55 m.p.h., and Louis Paulhan setting a world altitude record, a then dizzying 4,165 feet." Two years later, Doolittle was at work on his own glider made from wood and fabric; though he crashed it on his first flight attempt, undaunted, he repaired it and crashed it yet again.

In 1916, Doolittle matriculated at the University of California at Berkeley to study mining engineering. But in 1917, he quit to enlist in the Aviation section of the U.S. Army—the U.S. Air Force would not come into existence until 1947. Doolittle trained as a pilot and hoped to see air combat in World War I, but he so impressed his flight instructors that they made him one of their own—he trained others to fly and thus remained in the United States while men that he taught went into battle. The year of his enlistment saw another milestone in Doolittle's life as well—he married his high school sweetheart, Josephine Daniels.

After World War I, Doolittle remained in the U.S. Army Air Corps while continuing his education. He was among the first men to receive a doctorate in aeronautics from the Massachusetts Institute of Technology. During his time in the army, he helped test many new planes. He continuously sought to expand human accomplishments in flight; in 1922 he became the first man to fly non-stop across the continental United States. He piloted his plane from Florida to California in what was then a blistering twenty-one hours and nineteen minutes. He also was the first to make a flight and landing relying solely on instruments. As the London *Times* put it in their obituary of Doolittle, "this helped to revolutionize commercial aviation." Doolittle also learned how to fly seaplanes and won the prestigious Schneider Trophy race in one of them. He even spent time stunt flying and wing walking. Another of Doolittle's accomplishments in an airplane was to be the first to successfully complete an outside loop. On the road to all of these triumphs, however, the pilot crashed several times, but he was always fortunate enough to come out of these disasters virtually unscathed. He is considered by many to have made as great or greater a contribution to aviation as famed pilot Charles A. Lindbergh, whose fame is primarily based on making the first solo nonstop transatlantic flight.

Though Doolittle loved his work with the Army, Shell Oil Company offered to triple his salary, and he resigned his commission to join the oil giant in 1930, remaining in the U.S. Army Reserves and continuing to help them develop planes. While with Shell, Doolittle pushed the company to produce high-octane airplane fuels, which greatly improved the performance of American plane engines. Another part of his job was competing in air races and aviation exhibitions in the United States and Europe; while performing this duty Doolittle set what was then the land speed record of 296 m.p.h. in the Gee Bee—a plane the *Los Angeles Times* described as "fast, unstable and overpowered," and of which Doolittle was one of the few successful flyers.

In 1940, with the United States on the verge of entering World War II, Doolittle returned to active duty with the Army Air Corps. His first assignment was helping to ready factories for military production, especially that of airplanes. After the Japanese pilots bombed the U.S. military facilities at Pearl Harbor in Hawaii, however, Doolittle was assigned to the Army Air Force headquarters in

Washington, D.C., where, at the request of then-president Franklin D. Roosevelt, they were planning a retaliatory strike on the Japanese. A *Los Angeles Times* obituary writer quoted a previous interview with the pilot as Doolittle told how he won the task of leading the mission on Tokyo after he had begun training the crew that would carry it out: "I asked Gen. Arnold if I might personally lead the mission. . . . He said, 'No, I want you here on my staff.' He apparently saw the disappointment on my face because the[n] he said, 'Well, if Biff Harmon [Arnold's chief aide] has no objection, I have no objection.' So I saluted and ran as fast as I could to Harmon's office." Arnold apparently intended to call Harmon and tell him to refuse Doolittle, but the pilot told the *Los Angeles Times*: "I got to Harmon's office before the call and he said 'I have no objection if Gen. Arnold has no objection.'"

The Tokyo mission, at first felt to be impossible by many military planners, turned out to be more difficult than Doolittle had anticipated. The aircraft carrier, the *Hornet*, was spotted by Japanese ships long before the planes were scheduled to take off; so Doolittle ordered his men to leave shortly after their detection. Because of this, they did not have enough fuel to make it to their intended landing strips in unoccupied China. The planes' crew members, including Doolittle himself, were forced to bail out after dropping their bombs on Japan, and some had to find their way through enemy-occupied territory. Though most of the soldiers survived, the planes did not, and Doolittle at first feared he would be court martialed for foolishly losing so much expensive equipment. Instead he was promoted to brigadier general and given the Congressional Medal of Honor, because although the bombs did little actual damage, they did succeed in demoralizing the Japanese and raising American morale tremendously. After that mission, Doolittle spent the remainder of the war in England and Italy supervising the Twelfth, Fifteenth, and Eighth Air Forces; as commander of the last "he directed the strategic bombing of Germany until the end of the war in Europe," reported Bart Barnes in the *Washington Post*. As the London *Times* observed, "in contrast with Bomber Command's night 'area offensive,'" Doolittle's pilots made daylight raids and "stuck to precision attacks."

After World War II, Doolittle returned to work for Shell Oil, this time as vice president and director. But he remained involved with the military he loved, serving on several advisory committees. He helped develop the U.S. Air Force as a separate military division from the army, and he was a part of the National Advisory Committee for Aeronautics, which later became the National Aeronautics and Space Administration, or NASA. Doolittle retired from all these activities, however, in 1959. In 1991, with coauthor Glines, the noted aviator discussed not only

his famous raid on Tokyo but the rest of his distinguished career as well in *I Could Never Be So Lucky Again.* The book was well received; John F. Wukovits in the *Chicago Tribune* hailed it as "a dramatic account," but noted that "though Doolittle rubbed elbows with some of history's greats, they play secondary roles here. . . . The narrative resonates most when Doolittle speaks lovingly of his wife, Josephine, when he describes the bond he feels toward the men who accompanied him to Tokyo, and when he tells tales of flying and of the marvelous machines he piloted." Walter J. Boyne in the *Washington Post Book World* concurred, lauding *I Could Never Be So Lucky Again* as a "satisfying and long overdue autobiography" and observing that the book "provides new and needed insight into Jimmy Doolittle's amazingly multi-faceted talents." Two years after *I Could Never Be So Lucky Again* was published, Doolittle died following a stroke at his son's home in Pebble Beach, California. He was given a burial service with full military honors and laid to rest in Arlington National Cemetery in Arlington, Virginia.

BIOGRAPHICAL/CRITICAL SOURCES:

BOOKS

Doolittle, James H., and Carroll V. Glines, *I Could Never Be So Lucky Again: The Memoirs of General James H. "Jimmy" Doolittle,* Bantam, 1991.
Glines, *Doolittle's Tokyo Raiders,* Van Nostrand, 1964.
Reynolds, Quentin, *The Amazing Mr. Doolittle: A Biography of Lieutenant General James H. Doolittle,* Appleton-Century-Crofts, 1953.
Thomas, Lowell, and Edward Jablonski, *Doolittle: A Biography,* Doubleday, 1976.

PERIODICALS

Tribune Books (Chicago), December 1, 1991, p. 4.
Washington Post Book World, July 28, 1991, p. 8.

OBITUARIES:

PERIODICALS

Chicago Tribune, October 2, 1993, section 2, p. 19.
Los Angeles Times, September 28, 1993, p. A1.
New York Times, September 29, 1993, p. B8.
Times (London), September 29, 1993, p. 19.
Washington Post, September 29, 1993, p. D4.*

—Sketch by Elizabeth Wenning

*   *   *

DOOLITTLE, Jimmy
See DOOLITTLE, James H(arold)

DORAN, David K. 1929-

PERSONAL: Born June 23, 1929, in Chadwell Heath, England; son of Harry (a clerk) and Anne (a homemaker; maiden name, Goddard) Doran; married Maureen Massam (a business administrator), August 15, 1959; children: Susan, Nigel. *Education:* University of London, B.Sc., 1950, D.I.C., 1953. *Politics:* Conservative. *Religion:* Baptist. *Avocational Interests:* Golf, collecting stamps.

ADDRESSES: Home and office—17 Blake Hall Cres., London E11 3RH, England.

CAREER: G. Wimley, London, England, chief structural engineer, 1965-85; consulting civil and structural engineer in London, 1985—. *Military service:* British Army, Royal Engineers, 1953-55; served in Malaya.

MEMBER: Institution of Civil Engineers (fellow), Institution of Structural Engineers (fellow; member of council, 1983-89), City and Guilds Institute (fellow), Wanstead Golf Club (chairperson, c. 1988-89).

AWARDS, HONORS: Lewis Kent Award from Institution of Structural Engineers, 1993.

WRITINGS:

(Editor) *Construction Materials Reference Book,* Butterworth-Heinemann, 1992.

WORK IN PROGRESS: Construction Materials; research on alkali-silica reactions in concrete and on bridge access gantries and tracks.

SIDELIGHTS: David K. Doran told *CA:* "I have had a fascinating career in civil and structural engineering. This has taken me all over the world, giving me the enjoyment and enrichment of travel. I have reached the stage where I am trying to put something back into an industry in which it has been exciting to work. I am active on a number of technical committees, which enables me to blend my experience with that of others and distill it into reports for the benefit of fellow professionals."

*   *   *

DOUGLAS, Emily (Taft) 1899-1994

OBITUARY NOTICE—See index for *CA* sketch: Born April 19, 1899, in Chicago, IL; died January 28, 1994, in White Plains, NY. Member of Congress and author. Douglas, a Democrat from Illinois, was elected to a seat in the U.S. House of Representatives in 1944. A member of the House Foreign Affairs Committee and a unitarian, she was an advocate of international cooperation to provide relief efforts in Europe after World War II. In addition, she prompted legislation for providing library books

to rural areas in the United States and fostered civil rights. In 1947 Douglas left Congress and began writing historical literature. Her first book, *Appleseed Farm,* features the American pioneer known as Johnny Appleseed. *Margaret Sanger: Pioneer of the Future,* her most acclaimed work, details the life of the birth-control and women's rights proponent.

OBITUARIES AND OTHER SOURCES:

BOOKS

Who's Who in America, 37th edition, Marquis, 1972.

PERIODICALS

Chicago Tribune, February 1, 1994, p. 12.

*   *   *

DOYLE, Paul I(gnatius) 1959-

PERSONAL: Born February 5, 1959, in Cincinnati, OH; son of Robert J. (a consultant) and Mary (an office manager; maiden name, Heitker) Doyle; married Susan Kramer, December 28, 1984; children: Kramer Augustine, Margaret Elizabeth. *Education:* Received a B.A. degree from the University of Notre Dame, and an M.A. degree from the University of West Virginia. *Religion:* Roman Catholic.

ADDRESSES: Home—1122 Warwick Court, Holland, MI 49424. *Office*—3601 J. F. Donnelly Dr., Holland, MI 49424.

CAREER: Delta Management Group, Portland, OR, vice-president, 1987-92; Donnelly Corp., Holland, MI, operations development manager, 1992—.

WRITINGS:

(With father, Robert J. Doyle) *GainManagement: A Process for Building Teamwork, Productivity, and Profitability throughout Your Organization,* AMACOM, 1991.

Contributor to periodicals, including *Oregon Business.*

SIDELIGHTS: Paul I. Doyle told *CA:* "There are two aspects of management I feel are critical to develop in the next ten years in American business: strategic analysis and vision and first-line leadership. Everything in between is relatively simple. Strategic planning will define the future, and first-line leadership will achieve it."

*   *   *

DOYLE, Robert J. 1931-

PERSONAL: Born July 29, 1931, in Pittsburgh, PA; married Mary E. Heitker, August 20, 1955; children: Ellen

Doyle Mizener, Marie Doyle Ingman, Paul, Patrick, Barbara, Thomas, Moira. *Education:* Xavier University, B.S., 1952, M.B.A., 1959. *Religion:* Roman Catholic.

ADDRESSES: Home and office—2660 Southwest Garden View Ave., Portland, OR 97225.

CAREER: Ford Motor Co., Cincinnati, OH, personnel administrator, 1957-64; Wolverine World Wide, Rockford, MI, training director, 1964-67; Donnelly Mirrors, Inc., Holland, MI, director of human resources, 1967-74; Precision Castparts Corp., Portland, OR, director of personnel, 1974-75; Hay Associates, Seattle, WA, principal, 1975-77; Delta Management Group, Portland, OR, president, 1977—. Scanlon Plan Associates, co-founder and past president. *Military service:* U.S. Army, artillery commander with Special Forces and senior parachutist, 1952-55; served in Korea; became captain.

MEMBER: American Society for Training and Development (founding president of Grand Rapids chapter), Society for Human Resource Management, AQP.

WRITINGS:

Gainsharing and Productivity, AMACOM, 1983.
(With son Paul I. Doyle) *GainManagement: A Process for Building Teamwork, Productivity, and Profitability throughout Your Organization,* AMACOM, 1992.

SIDELIGHTS: Robert J. Doyle told *CA:* "From its earliest days in the 1930s, the Scanlon Plan has captured the imagination of those who see a need to renew the world of work. My two books represent an ongoing effort to bring this great idea to the attention of managers, workers, and union officials. If we are ever to have a truly civil society, the places where people work must be made more equitable, civil, and full of opportunities for personal achievement and growth. *GainManagement* and its predecessor *Gainsharing and Productivity* are my contributions to this effort."

*   *   *

DOYLE, Roddy   1958-

PERSONAL: Born in 1958 in Dublin, Ireland; married; wife's name, Belinda; children: two sons.

ADDRESSES: Home—Dublin, Ireland. *Agent*—Patti Kelly, Viking Books, 375 Hudson St., New York, NY 10014; Secker & Warburg, 54 Poland St., London W1V 3DF, England.

CAREER: Lecturer at universities, playwright, screenwriter, and novelist.

AWARDS, HONORS: The Van was shortlisted for Britain's Booker Prize, Book Trust (England), 1991; Booker Prize, 1993, for *Paddy Clarke Ha Ha Ha.*

WRITINGS:

NOVELS

The Commitments, Heinemann, 1988, Random House, 1989.
The Snapper, Secker & Warburg, 1990, Penguin, 1992.
The Van, Viking, 1991.
Paddy Clarke Ha Ha Ha, Secker & Warburg, 1993.

The Snapper has been translated into Japanese and Czechoslovakian.

SCREENPLAYS

(With Dick Clement and Ian La Frenais) *The Commitments* (based on the novel by Doyle), Twentieth Century-Fox, 1991.
The Snapper (based on the novel by Doyle), Miramax Films, 1993.

ADAPTATIONS: The Snapper was adapted for a British Broadcasting Corporation (BBC) production, and won the People's Choice Award for Best Film at the Toronto Film Festival.

SIDELIGHTS: Roddy Doyle's trilogy of novels about the Irish Rabbitte family, known informally as the "Barrytown trilogy," has been internationally acclaimed for wit, originality, and powerful dialogue. Each of the three books—*The Commitments, The Snapper,* and *The Van*—focuses on a single character of the large Rabbitte family who live in Barrytown, Dublin. They are "a likeable, rough, sharp-witted clan," declared Lawrence Dugan in *Chicago Tribune.* Typical working-class citizens, the Rabbittes are a vivacious and resilient household, lustily displaying an often ribald sense of humor. "These books are funny all the way down to their syntax," claimed Guy Mannes-Abbott in *New Statesman & Society,* "enabling Doyle to sustain my laughter over two or three pages."

The Commitments is, perhaps, Doyle's most well-recognized work. The successful novel was adapted in 1991 into a very popular screenplay by Doyle, Dick Clement, and Ian La Frenais, and directed by award-winning filmmaker Alan Parker. In both the novel and the film, Doyle's wit and originality are evident. The main character, Jimmy Rabbitte, inspired by the rhythm and blues music of James Brown, B. B. King, and Marvin Gaye, resolves to form an Irish soul band in Dublin. He places a musicians-wanted ad in the paper: "Have you got Soul? If yes, . . . contact J. Rabbitte." And so is born the "Commitments," with Jimmy as the manager of a group which includes Imelda, a singer, and Joey "The Lips" Fagan, a musician who claims to have "jammed with the man" James Brown. "The rehearsals, as Mr. Doyle chronicles them," wrote Kinky Friedman in *New York Times,* "are authentic, joyous, excruciating and funny as hell." Dugan, in the *Chicago Tribune,* described *The Commitments* as "a beautifully told story about the culture that absorbed the Vikings, Normans, Scots and British now trying its luck with black America." Doyle "possesses a rare gift for capturing the metaphysical lift of live music," enthused David Fricke in *Rolling Stone.* "In Doyle's hands, the band . . . take[s] on an uncommon vibrancy." The film version stars an all-Irish cast, including Robert Arkins, Andrew Strong, and singer Maria Doyle performing such 1960s hits as "Mustang Sally" and "In the Midnight Hour." A *People* critic reviewed the film and concluded, "the cathartic power of music has never been more graphically demonstrated."

Doyle's second novel, *The Snapper,* focuses on Sharon Rabbitte, Jimmy's older sister, who is young, unmarried, and pregnant. Refusing to reveal the identity of the father of her "snapper," Sharon's predicament has the Rabbitte household in a tizzy, and she becomes the target of humorous speculations by the Barrytown citizens. As a result of Sharon's pregnancy, relationships within the family undergo various transformations ranging from the compassionate (dad Jimmy Sr.) to the murderous (mom Veronica), while Sharon herself tries to understand the changes within her own body: "me uterus is pressin' into me bladder," she explains on one of her numerous trips to the "loo." A *Los Angeles Times Book Review* critic noted that "few novels depict parent-child relationships—healthy relationships, no less—better than this one, and few men could write more sensitively about pregnancy."

Like *The Commitments, The Snapper* is written in the Irish vernacular, with little descriptive intrusion, and with an enormous sense of humor. John Nicholson in the London *Times* pointed to Doyle's "astonishing talent for turning the humdrum into high comedy" in the novel. He also singled out the characters' vernacular banter for critical praise—"the dialogue of *The Snapper* crackles with wit and authenticity." This is a "very funny" novel, admitted Tania Glyde in the London *Times,* yet she further pointed out that "it is also sad . . . Sharon's life . . . would be tragic without the support of her large and singular family." *Times Literary Supplement* critic Stephen Leslie asserted that "*The Snapper* is a worthy successor to *The Commitments.*"

Shortlisted for Britain's prestigious Booker Prize, Roddy Doyle's third Rabbitte novel, *The Van,* changes the focus to Jimmy Sr., the ribald, fun-loving father of the Rabbitte family, who has been recently laid off work. Jimmy and his best friend, Bimbo, open a portable fast-food restaurant—Bimbo's Burgers—housed in a greasy van that is a health inspector's nightmare. The antics of the two friends running the business provide much of the hilarity of the book; for example, they mistakenly deep-fry a diaper,

serve it up to a customer like cod, and then flee—restaurant and all—from his wrath, hurling frozen fish at their victim from the back of the van. Jimmy and his friends are Irish laborers "whose idea of wit and repartee is putting on fake Mexican accents and 'burstin' their shite' at jokes about farting," wrote Anne-Marie Conway in *Times Literary Supplement.* "*The Van* is not just a very funny book," insisted Mannes-Abbott, "it is also faultless comic writing."

Critical response towards *The Van* was enthusiastic, with many reviewers finding a special appeal in what a *Publishers Weekly* commentator called Doyle's "brash originality and humor that are both uniquely Irish and shrewdly universal." Reviewer Tim Appelo in the *Los Angeles Times Book Review* maintained that "Roddy Doyle has perfect pitch from the get-go. He can write pages of lifelike, impeccably profane dialogue without a false note or a dull fill, economically evoking every lark and emotional plunge in the life of an entire Irish family." Ann-Marie Conway sums up her comments by saying "*The Van* could have been depressing; that it is warm and funny . . . is a tribute to an interesting new writer on the Irish scene."

Doyle's next book, *Paddy Clarke Ha Ha Ha,* was awarded the prestigious Booker Prize in 1993. The novel is written from the point of view of Paddy Clarke, a ten-year-old Irish boy, whose often humorous escapades become gradually more violent and disturbing as the story progresses. John Gallagher in the *Detroit News and Free Press* commented on Doyle's effective use of a stream of consciousness narrative, and noted a "theme of undeserved suffering. . . . *Paddy Clarke Ha Ha Ha* matures into an unforgettable portrait of troubled youth."

BIOGRAPHICAL/CRITICAL SOURCES:

BOOKS

Doyle, Roddy, *The Commitments,* Random House, 1989.
Doyle, Roddy, *The Snapper,* Penguin, 1992.

PERIODICALS

Chicago Tribune, August 9, 1992, p. 5.
Detroit News and Free Press, December 12, 1993,
Los Angeles Times Book Review, July 19, 1992, p. 6; September 20, 1992, p. 3.
New Statesman & Society, August 23, 1991, pp. 35-36.
New York Times, July 23, 1989, p. 11.
New York Times Book Review, October 8, 1993.
People, August 26, 1991, pp. 13-14.
Publishers Weekly, May 25, 1992, p. 36.
Rolling Stone, September 21, 1989, p. 27.
Times (London), August 16, 1990; October 5, 1991, p. 51.
Times Literary Supplement, December 21-27, 1990, p. 1381; August 16, 1991, p. 22; November 5, 1993, p. 14.

Washington Post Book World, August 10, 1992, p. B2.*

—Sketch by Linda Tidrick

* * *

DRAPER, James P(atrick) 1959-

PERSONAL: Born September 26, 1959, in Detroit, MI; son of James Wilson (a lawyer) and Alice Patricia (a homemaker; maiden name, Sullivan) Draper. *Education:* Attended Colgate University, 1977-78, and University of London, 1978-79; Princeton University, B.A., 1981; Oxford University, M.Phil., 1984; also attended Columbia University, 1988, and University of Denver, 1991.

ADDRESSES: Home—113 Merriweather Rd., Grosse Pointe Farms, MI 48236. *Office*—Gale Research, Inc., 835 Penobscot Building, Detroit, MI 48226-4094.

CAREER: Worked as a desk clerk in Detroit, MI, summers, 1977-81; Oxford University, New College, Oxford, England, instructor in English literature, 1982-84; Gale Research, Inc., Detroit, editor, 1985—. 1832 Committee (England), director, 1983—; consultant to pension fund management organizations and to filmmakers and producers, including Grossman Films.

MEMBER: Bibliographical Society of America, Bibliographical Society (London), Architectural Society (officer, 1981-83), Medieval Society (London), Oxford Bibliographical Society, Oxford Society of Bibliophiles, Grolier Club, Princeton Club, New College Society, Book Club of Detroit, Detroit Club, American Friends of the Vatican Library, Johnson and Chesterton Club, Phi Beta Kappa.

AWARDS, HONORS: Outstanding Reference Source Award from American Library Association, 1993, for *Black Literature Criticism.*

WRITINGS:

(Editor and contributor) *Literature Criticism from 1400-1800,* Volumes III-XIV, Gale, 1986-91.
(Editor) *Black Literature Criticism,* three volumes, Gale, 1992.
(Editor) *World Literature Criticism, 1500 to the Present,* six volumes, Gale, 1992.
(Editor) *DISCovering Authors* (CD-ROM database), Gale, 1993, Canadian edition, 1993.
(Editor) "Contemporary Literary Criticism" series, Gale, 1993—.

Contributor to books, including *Modern Arts Criticism, Shakespearean Criticism,* and *Poetry Criticism.* Contributor to journals and periodicals.

WORK IN PROGRESS: Research on fifteenth-century English laments of the Virgin Mary.

DREW, Eileen 1957-

PERSONAL: Born April 17, 1957, in Casablanca, Morocco; daughter of Walter H. Drew (a foreign service officer) and Muriel M. (McGuire) Drew; married Lance Rosedale, 1985. *Education:* Attended Ewha Women's University, Seoul, Korea, 1976; University of California, Santa Cruz, B.A., 1979; University of Arizona, Tucson, M.F.A., 1986.

ADDRESSES: Home—765 Keeler Ave., Berkeley, CA 94708. *Office*—Mount Diablo Adult Education ESL, Loma Vista Adult Center, 1266 San Carlos Ave., Concord, CA 94518.

CAREER: Institut Nsona-Mpangu, Zaire, instructor, 1979-81; Lao Family Community, Inc., Richmond, CA, instructor, 1986-88, English as a Second Language (ESL) coordinator, 1988; Mount Diablo Adult Education ESL, Loma Vista Adult Center, Concord, CA, instructor in ESL, 1989—. California Medical Association, San Francisco, secretary, 1982-83; Writers at Work, Tucson, AZ, co-president, 1985-86.

AWARDS, HONORS: Katherine Anne Porter Prize, *Nimrod,* 1985, for "Ancient Shells," published in *TriQuarterly;* Charles Angoff Award, *Literary Review,* 1987; recipient of literary award from *Black Warrior Review,* 1987-88; Drue Heinz Literature Prize finalist, 1988, Milkweed National Fiction Award, 1989, and *New York Times* notable book citation, 1990, all for *Blue Taxis: Stories about Africa.*

WRITINGS:

Blue Taxis: Stories about Africa, foreword by Rosellen Brown, Milkweed Editions, 1989.
(With Kathleen Coskran) *Kennedy: From the Center of the Earth; Stories Out of the Peace Corps,* Clover Park Press, 1991.

Contributor of fiction to periodicals, including *Antioch Review, Black Warrior Review, Literary Review, TriQuarterly,* and *Nimrod.* Co-editor, *Orangewood,* 1977; staff editor, *Quarry West,* 1978-79; staff editor, *Sonora Review,* 1984-86.

WORK IN PROGRESS: The Ivory Crocodile, a novel.

SIDELIGHTS: Eileen Drew's *Blue Taxis: Stories about Africa* is a collection of nine short stories told through the voices of young, female Americans who are missionaries, diplomats' daughters, or teachers of English in Africa. Drew, who was born into a foreign service family in Morocco and who has lived in several African countries, is intimately familiar with the continent's landscape, folklore, and life, which adds impact to her critically acclaimed stories, according to critics. "Some first story collections cascade language . . . deftly," writes *New York Times Book*

Review commentator Carol Spindel. "But they say little about anything substantive. *Blue Taxis* is different; these stories work their way around a very real dilemma: the ambivalent relationship of Americans . . . toward the 'third world.' " Spindel adds that "to know Africa we need to read African writers, but to know ourselves we can read Eileen Drew." Reviewer Penny Kaganoff in *Publishers Weekly* notes Drew's "wit and singular powers of observation," and proclaims *Blue Taxis* an "exceptional debut collection."

BIOGRAPHICAL/CRITICAL SOURCES:

PERIODICALS

New York Times Book Review, February 25, 1990, p. 21.
Publishers Weekly, September 8, 1989, p. 63.

*   *   *

DUFFY, Brian 1954-

PERSONAL: Born December 14, 1954, in New York, NY; son of William and Adeline Duffy; married Jo Walsh, December 27, 1978. *Education:* Fairfield University, B.A., 1977; Northwestern University, M.A., 1980.

ADDRESSES: Office—*U.S. News and World Report,* 2400 N St. N.W., Washington, DC 20037.

CAREER: Affiliated with *Miami Herald,* Miami, FL, 1980-86; *U.S. News and World Report,* Washington, DC, senior writer, 1986-88, assistant managing editor, 1988—.

WRITINGS:

(With Steven Emerson) *The Fall of Pan Am 103: Inside the Lockerbie Investigation,* Putnam, 1990.
Head Count (novel), Putnam, 1991.

Regular contributor to *U.S. News and World Report.*

WORK IN PROGRESS: A book about the justice department, for Simon & Schuster; a novel.

SIDELIGHTS: Investigative reporter Brian Duffy's first full-length book, *The Fall of Pan Am 103: Inside the Lockerbie Investigation,* was written with former colleague Steven Emerson. The 1990 volume is a detailed analysis of a major news story the authors covered as journalists. In December of 1988, a bomb hidden in a portable cassette player exploded on board a Pan Am flight heading from London to New York. The explosive, contained in a luggage compartment, destroyed the plane, killing 270 people, including all passengers and crew as well as some residents of Lockerbie, Scotland, where the debris landed. Terrorist activity was suspected from the onset, and a massive international investigation was begun that threatens to last into the twenty-first century.

The Fall of Pan Am 103 provides a synopsis of the world events leading to the explosion, a chronicle of the efforts involved in pinpointing the culprits, and a look at some of the key players on both sides. Duffy and Emerson review the international scenario played out after the downing of an Iranian passenger plane in July of 1988 by a missile fired from the U.S.S. Vincennes, an American ship patrolling the Persian Gulf. This action led to the retaliatory bomb on Flight 103. The book also questions the security procedures at major international airports, especially in the major international air-travel hub of Frankfurt, Germany, where the flight originated. The authors contend that it is possible to provide airtight security to prevent acts of terrorism but that such procedures would prove intolerably long and exhaustive for both passengers and airlines. *The Fall of Pan Am 103* also relates the conflict surrounding a bomb threat made prior to the flight that was not publicly disclosed and is the subject of an ethical debate as well as pending lawsuits by victims' families.

Duffy and Emerson detail the efforts involved in reconstructing the entire plane and its contents, which lay strewn over a vast stretch of the Scottish landscape. It was this effort that provided investigators with the clues necessary to piece together the origins of the explosive device. However, once it was traced to a small fringe Palestinian group centered in Germany, a deeper web of intrigue developed. Two months earlier, German counter-terrorist operatives had cracked the ring that was believed to be responsible for the bombing of Flight 103, but had bungled the initial investigation and released the suspects due to lack of sufficient evidence. Duffy and Emerson describe how German authorities attempted to cover their errors and further delayed the investigative efforts once this information came to light.

The Fall of Pan Am 103 received much critical attention upon publication. Many reviewers criticized the authors for a trite style of writing and a narrative that appeared to be pieced together too hastily, but often forgave them in light of the ongoing and unresolved nature of the subject matter. Robert H. Kupperman, writing in the *Los Angeles Times,* noted that "Emerson and Duffy successfully cover the human side of the tragedy" and concluded that the book "is worthwhile reading." *Tribune Books* critic Anthony Olcott described the volume as "a gripping marriage of thriller and forensic procedural." A *New York Times* reviewer commented that *The Fall of Pan Am 103* "pulls together most available material with impressive clarity, adding new angles, dispelling false leads and leaving little room for interest to flag."

Duffy is also the author of *Head Count,* a comic political novel published in 1991. The author draws on his background in international relations to construct a thriller involving a deteriorating African nation, a gang of bandits in charge, and the out-of-work terrorists from Eastern Europe that enter the fray.

BIOGRAPHICAL/CRITICAL SOURCES:

PERIODICALS

Globe and Mail (Toronto), April 7, 1990.
Los Angeles Times, August 7, 1990.
New York Times, June 9, 1990.
Tribune Books (Chicago), May 5, 1990, p. 5.
Washington Post Book World, May 6, 1990, p. 1.

*   *   *

DUNCAN, Dave   1933-

PERSONAL: Born June 30, 1933, in Newport-on-Tay, Scotland; immigrated to Canada, 1955; naturalized Canadian citizen, 1960; married Janet Hopwell, 1959; children: one son, two daughters. *Education:* University of St. Andrews, B.Sc., 1955.

ADDRESSES: Home—P.O. Box 1, Site 13, SS 3, Calgary, Alberta, Canada T3C 3N9. *Agent*—Richard Curtis Associates, 171 East 74th St., Suite 2, New York, NY 10021.

CAREER: Worked as geologist, 1955-76; manager of geological consulting business, 1976-86; writer.

MEMBER: Science-Fiction Writers of America, Writers Guild of Alberta.

AWARDS, HONORS: Canadian Science Fiction and Fantasy Award, Canadian Science Fiction and Fantasy Association, 1990, for *West of January.*

WRITINGS:

"THE SEVENTH SWORD" FANTASY SERIES, PUBLISHED BY BALLANTINE/DEL REY

The Reluctant Swordsman, 1988.
The Coming of Wisdom, 1988.
The Destiny of the Sword, 1988.

"A MAN OF HIS WORD" FANTASY SERIES, PUBLISHED BY BALLANTINE/DEL REY

Magic Casement, 1990.
Faery Lands Forlorn, 1991.
Perilous Seas, 1991
Emperor and Clown, 1992.

"A HANDFUL OF MEN" FANTASY SERIES, PUBLISHED BY BALLANTINE/DEL REY

The Cutting Edge, 1992.
Upland Outlaws, 1993.
The Stricken Field, 1993.
The Living God, 1994.

OTHER FANTASY PUBLISHED BY BALLANTINE/DEL REY

A Rose-Red City, 1987.
The Reaver Road, 1992.
The Hunters' Haunt, in press.
The Cursed, in press.

SCIENCE-FICTION NOVELS PUBLISHED BY BALLANTINE/ DEL REY

Shadow, 1987.
West of January, 1989.
Strings, 1990.
Hero!, 1991.

WORK IN PROGRESS: A fantasy trilogy entitled "The Great Game," including the books *Past Imperative, Present Tense,* and *Future Indefinite,* publication expected in 1996.

SIDELIGHTS: Dave Duncan is a prolific writer of fantasy and science fiction novels. Most of his works in the fantasy genre fall into one of several series, known as "The Seventh Sword," "A Man of His Word," and "A Handful of Men." Among Duncan's science fiction novels is *Shadow,* a tale of events on a distant planet colonized thousands of years ago by earthlings. The narrative involves intrigue at a royal palace, where a false prince kills the king and assumes rule of the land. Tom Easton, writing in *Analog Science Fiction/Science Fact,* affirmed that *Shadow* serves as evidence of Duncan's "admirable progression in authorial confidence, storytelling deftness, and writerly skills."

Duncan told *CA:* "Even as a child I wanted to be a writer, but not to the exclusion of wanting to earn a decent living. In the summer of 1984 I began writing a novel, more or less on the spur of the moment, thinking it would be a fun thing to try. I rapidly became hooked to the point where I began sneaking time away from my work. I wrote a huge fantasy novel, a science fiction novel, and then a rewrite of the fantasy as a trilogy. After all that I produced *A Rose-Red City.* In the spring of 1986 the oil business collapsed. For the first time in thirty years I was out of work. Two weeks after I completed my last consulting project, Del Rey publishers offered to buy *A Rose-Red City.* I followed with *Shadow* and then another rewrite of the trilogy, 'The Seventh Sword.' It was the final version that began to attract attention from readers."

BIOGRAPHICAL/CRITICAL SOURCES:

PERIODICALS

Analog Science Fiction/Science Fact, June, 1988, pp. 179-80; October, 1990, pp. 183-84; July, 1991, p. 311.
Locus, April, 1993.
Quill & Quire, August, 1992.

DURO, Paul 1953-

PERSONAL: Born February 10, 1953, in Nottingham, England; son of Griffin (a shopkeeper) and Margaret Irene (a secretary; maiden name, Heathcote) Duro. *Education:* University of Essex, B.A. (with honors), 1978, M.A., 1980, Ph.D., 1984.

ADDRESSES: Home—71 The Hermitage, Medley St., Chifley, Australian Capital Territory 2606. *Office*— Department of Art History, Australian National University, G.P.O. Box 4, Canberra, Australian Capital Territory 2601.

CAREER: Newcastle upon Tyne Polytechnic, Newcastle upon Tyne, England, associate senior lecturer, 1984-88; Australian National University, Canberra, lecturer in art history, 1989—.

MEMBER: Art Association of Australia (member of executive board, 1990-91), Association of Art Historians (England), Societe de l'Histoire de l'Art Francaise.

AWARDS, HONORS: Fellow or scholar of British Institute in Paris, 1980-81, and French government, 1983; grant from British Academy, 1986.

WRITINGS:

(With Michael Greenhalgh) *The Essential Art History,* Bloomsbury Publishing, 1993.
(Editor and author of introduction) *The Rhetoric of the Frame: Essays Toward a Theory of the Frame in Art,* Cambridge University Press, 1994.

Editor of the book *Perspectives on Academic Art,* [Canberra], 1991. Contributor of articles and reviews to art journals.

WORK IN PROGRESS: The Academy and the Limits of Painting in Seventeenth-Century France.

*   *   *

DYCK, Ian 1954-

PERSONAL: Born July 23, 1954, in Saskatoon, Saskatchewan, Canada; son of Clifford John (a farmer) and Agnes Mary (a farmer; maiden name, Bourne) Dyck. *Education:* University of Saskatchewan, B.A., 1980, M.A., 1982; University of Sussex, D.Phil., 1985.

ADDRESSES: Office—Department of History, Simon Fraser University, Burnaby, British Columbia V5A 1S6, Canada.

CAREER: University of Saskatchewan, Saskatoon, Saskatchewan, Canada, instructor, 1985-87; University of Lethbridge, Lethbridge, Alberta, Canada, assistant professor, 1987-88; Simon Fraser University, Burnaby, British Columbia, Canada, associate professor of history, 1988—.

WRITINGS:

(Editor) *Citizen of the World: Essays on Thomas Paine,* St. Martin's, 1988.
William Cobbett and Rural Popular Culture, Cambridge University Press, 1992.

WORK IN PROGRESS: The Cottage Charter: Rural Song in England, 1500—.

E

EGUDU, R. N.
See EGUDU, Romanus N(nagbo)

* * *

EGUDU, Romanus N(nagbo) 1940-
(R. N. Egudu)

PERSONAL: Born February 1, 1940, in Ebe, Nigeria. *Education:* University of Nigeria, B.A. (with honors), 1963; Michigan State University, Ph.D., 1966.

CAREER: St. Paul's School, Eke, Enugu, Nigeria, principal, 1963; University of Nigeria, Nsukka, lecturer in English and African literature, 1966-67; University of Benin, Benin City, Nigeria, head of Department of English. African representative of *Journal of the New African Literature and the Arts,* 1966-68.

MEMBER: African Literature Association, Association of African Literary Critics.

AWARDS, HONORS: Poetry Prize, Michigan State University, 1966; Certificate of Merit, International Biographical Center.

WRITINGS:

(Compiler and translator with Donatus I. Nwoga) *Poetic Heritage: Igbo Traditional Verse,* Nwankwo-Ifejika, 1971, published as *Igbo Traditional Verse,* Heinemann, 1973.
(Collector and translator) *The Calabash of Wisdom and Other Igbo Stories,* illustrated by Jennifer Lawson, NOK Publishers, 1973.
Four Modern West African Poets, NOK Publishers, 1977.
(Under name R. N. Egudu) *Modern African Poetry and the African Predicament,* Barnes & Noble, 1978.
African Poetry of the Living Dead: Igbo Masquerade Poetry, Edwin Mellen, 1992.

Also author of *The Study of Poetry,* 1977. Work represented in anthologies, including *Modern Poetry from Africa,* Penguin, 1963; *Commonwealth Poems of Today,* John Murray, 1967; and *New Voices of the Commonwealth,* Evans Brothers, 1968. Contributor to periodicals, including *Black Orpheus, Transition, Outposts,* and *Okike.* Associate editor of *Paideuma: Journal of Ezra Pound Scholarship;* editorial consultant for *Conch;* member of review staff for *Books Abroad: An International Literature Journal.*

SIDELIGHTS: Romanus N. Egudu is a Nigerian university professor whose internationally published work includes his own poetry, translations of poetry and tales from the Igbo language, and advanced-level critical works on African poetry and its context. His own poetry often concerns the theme of injustice. It was influenced, he once said, by a roster of English poets from John Donne to W. B. Yeats.

Of his critical works, *Four Modern West African Poets* presents the English-language verse of Christopher Okigbo and John Pepper Clark of Nigeria, Lenrie Peters of Gambia, and Kofi Awoonor of Ghana. The critical material was part of Egudu's doctoral thesis and emphasizes the special position from which these poets write, mainly, their deep roots in local cultures and fluency in European languages and culture. This situation allows them to communicate their personal, African experiences to a worldwide audience.

Egudu widened his scope to include twentieth-century English-language poetry from West, East, and South Africa in *Modern African Poetry and the African Predicament.* Egudu discusses individual poems and the poets' overall work as well as their political and social contexts. Reviewing this last work, a *Choice* writer commented that in dealing with these various issues, "Egudu is often brilliant."

BIOGRAPHICAL/CRITICAL SOURCES:

PERIODICALS

Choice, February, 1974, p. 1672.
World Literature Today, autumn, 1978, p. 679.*

*   *   *

EHRET, Terry 1955-

PERSONAL: Born November 12, 1955, in San Francisco, CA; daughter of Stephen Henry II (an accountant) and Adelaide (a teacher; maiden name, O'Connor) Ehret; married Donald Nicholas Moe (a teacher), April 7, 1979; children: Allison, Caitlin, Annelisa. *Education:* Stanford University, A.B. (with distinction), 1977; attended Chapman College, 1979-80; San Francisco State University, M.A. (with honors), 1984. *Politics:* Democrat. *Religion:* "Catholic by tradition."

ADDRESSES: Home—924 Sunnyslope Rd., Petaluma, CA 94952.

CAREER: Children's Health Council, Palo Alto, CA, tutor and researcher, 1975-77; high school teacher of English, psychology, and art history in Salinas, Belmont, and San Francisco, CA, 1977-90; Santa Rosa Junior College, Santa Rosa, CA, instructor in English, 1990—. California Poets in the Schools, poet and teacher, 1990—; Sonoma State University, lecturer, 1993; gives readings from her works.

MEMBER: American Federation of Teachers, American Association of University Women, National Council of Teachers of English, California Association of Teachers of English.

AWARDS, HONORS: Special Mention, Pushcart Literary Prize, 1991; National Poetry Series Award, 1992, for *Lost Body.*

WRITINGS:

(With Steve Gilmartin and Susan Herron Sibbet) *Suspensions* (poems), White Mountain Press, 1990.
Lost Body (poems), Copper Canyon Press, 1993.

Contributor of poems to *Feminist Poetics, Paragraph, Five Fingers Review, San Francisco Poetry,* and *Vivo.*

WORK IN PROGRESS: A fictional treatment of the story of the Trojan War; a series of poems exploring Spanish painter Pablo Picasso's portrayal of women.

SIDELIGHTS: Terry Ehret told *CA:* "One of the greatest obstacles and greatest sources of insight in my creative life has been motherhood. I began writing poetry in the light of the emerging feminist critical theory and spent several years struggling to reconcile my definition as a writer and as a mother, categories which I tended to view as mutually exclusive. Consequently, I have been drawn to the lives and works of women who have confronted these often conflicting roles, and especially to those who have invented ways to nurture their artistic ambitions as devotedly as they have nurtured their children: Harriet Beecher Stowe, Ursula LeGuin, Carolyn Kizer, Kathleen Fraser, Sacajawea, and many more I have yet to discover.

"In general, I'm intrigued by definitions, how they can empower and limit us, and what lies beyond their boundaries. I'm interested in the source of western culture's concepts of violence and desire, and so I am trying to explore this in a retelling of the Trojan War legend. I want to know how relationships define us, particularly those of the most intimate nature where boundaries between self and other break down. This is the motivation behind most of the poems in *Suspensions* and *Lost Body,* as well as the series I am currently working on, based on Spanish painter Pablo Picasso's portraits of women. As a writer, I'm interested in how language defines our thoughts, our lives, our experience, how certain poetic forms embody assumptions about beauty and the meaning of our experiences, how the act of composition itself can be a deeply political act.

"As part of an effort to explore what lies beyond the reach of definitions, I often work outside the boundaries of traditional form. When I do choose to adopt certain formal limitations, my intention is generally to push against the form, explore the tension the form exerts. The controlling devices I most often employ are patterns of rhythm and repetition, believing, as German poet Rainer Maria Rilke did, that sound is the root of poetry and that listening, not to the self, but to a deeper singing inside the heart, is the source of inspiration."

*   *   *

EIGHNER, Lars 1948-

PERSONAL: Born November 25, 1948, in Corpus Christi, TX; son of Lawrence Clifton (an aircraft mechanic) and Elizabeth (a teacher of the deaf; maiden name, Vail) Eighner. *Education:* Attended University of Texas, 1966-69. *Politics:* "Skeptical democrat." *Avocational Interests:* Computer bulletin boards, electronic games.

ADDRESSES: Home—Austin, TX. *Agent*—Steven Saylor, 1711 Addison St., Berkeley, CA 94703-1501.

CAREER: Austin State Hospital, Austin, TX, attendant and ward worker, c. 1980-87. Worked variously for a drug-crisis program, and as a free-lance writer.

WRITINGS:

(Contributor) *Bayou Boy and Other Stories* (short fiction), Gay Sunshine Press, 1985, Badboy Books, 1993.
Lavender Blue, Liberty Books, 1988.
Travels with Lizbeth (autobiography; includes essay "On Dumpster Diving"), St. Martin's Press, 1993.
B.M.O.C., Badboy Books, 1993.

Eighner's works have been published in *Threepenny Review,* the *Utne Reader,* and *Harper's.* His essay "On Dumpster Diving" has been included in anthologies, including *The Pushcart Prize: Best of the Small Presses,* 1992.

WORK IN PROGRESS: Writing two "erotic" novels, and considering work on a fictional detective story.

SIDELIGHTS: Travels with Lizbeth is Lars Eighner's account of surviving for three years as one of America's homeless. The work has been compared to W. H. Davies's *Autobiography of a Super-Tramp,* and Jack London's *The People of the Abyss,* both early-twentieth century travel narratives which offer a rare view of life on the streets. Eighner's book began as a series of letters to friends relating the circumstances that quickly took him from a job in a mental institution in Texas to homelessness, wandering the streets with his dog, Lizbeth, and hitchhiking to California and back in search of employment and lodging.

In an article that appeared in *Publishers Weekly,* Molly McQuade quoted Eighner's recollection that "I didn't undertake homelessness to have something to write about. . . . I didn't contemplate publication at all." Yet, for the grandson of poet Alice Ewing Vail, literary aspirations were not diminished with circumstances. Typed on equipment found in the garbage, Eighner's manuscript nevertheless found favor with Wendy Lesser, an editor at the *Threepenny Review* who first published the essays, as well as with numerous subsequent reviewers. McQuade assessed *Travels with Lizbeth* as "a portrait of the artist as a homeless man who writes for his own survival."

Critics remark that Eighner's unusual prose style carries echoes of the nineteenth-century fiction he favors. His "voice and form are . . . unconventional," noted Jonathan Raban in the *New York Times Book Review,* "by turns grandiloquent and simple, alienating and compelling." For example, in *Travels with Lizbeth* Eighner writes: "I do not mind admitting that I love my dog. But anyone who has had to sleep by the side of the road in some wild place may appreciate that an extra pair of keen ears, a good nose and sharp teeth on a loud, ferocious ally of unquestionable loyalty have a certain value that transcends mere sentiment. . . . She loves human attention and like Browning's duchess she is pleased indiscriminately whencesoever it comes." Eighner's editor at St. Martin's Press, Michael Denneny, summarized the author's style

in *Publishers Weekly* as "sharp, precise, sober and oddly classical." Disdaining a conventional form—Eighner explains that "a homeless life has no story line"—*Travels with Lizbeth* is a series of vignettes highly praised by critics for the beauty of its language, and its insightful commentary on contemporary life. Raban concluded: "In lavish, patient detail, it re-creates the grammar, point of view and domestic economy of the unhoused life, and if there's any justice in the world it should guarantee its author a roof over his head for the rest of his days."

Eighner told *CA:* "I have been studying and practicing writing since I was eleven. I was not making enough money at writing to support myself as a housed person, but I was writing well before I became homeless. There are not many good writers digging in dumpsters—but there are good carpenters, good auto workers, and good painters who have fallen on hard times. A writer needs talent, luck, and persistence. You can make do with two out of three, and the more you have of one, the less you need of the others. You can't do without training and practice."

BIOGRAPHICAL/CRITICAL SOURCES:

BOOKS

Eighner, Lars, *Travels with Lizbeth,* St. Martin's Press, 1993.

PERIODICALS

New York Times Book Review, October 10, 1993, pp. 1, 33-34.
Publishers Weekly, May 10, 1993, pp. 28-29.

*   *   *

EISENDRATH, Polly Young
See YOUNG-EISENDRATH, Polly

*   *   *

ENGLISH, O(liver) Spurgeon   1901-1993

OBITUARY NOTICE—See index for *CA* sketch: Born September 27, 1901, in Presque Isle, ME; died October 3, 1993, in Haverford, PA. Physician and author. English believed that mental and physical problems can be related, and he was a pioneer in discussing the correlation. As a physician, English worked in psychiatric hospitals and taught psychiatry at the university level. He worked in the psychopathic department at Philadelphia General Hospital from 1933 to 1947. He also held various positions, including head of the department of psychiatry, at Temple University from 1933 to 1964. After leaving Temple, English opened a private practice in psychiatry. For his contributions to his field, English received the 1968 American Academy of Psychotherapists Award. His publication, with Edward Weiss, titled *Psychosomatic Medicine: A Clinical Study of Psychophysiologic Reactions,* discusses his views on the association between mental and physical ailments. He also wrote *Personality Manifestations in Psychosomatic Illness: Visual Aid Charts to Psychotherapy,* and, with Gerald H. J. Pearson, *Common Neuroses of Children and Adults.*

OBITUARIES AND OTHER SOURCES:

BOOKS

Who's Who in America, 43rd edition, Marquis, 1984.

PERIODICALS

Washington Post, November 9, 1993, p. B5.

*   *   *

ERICKSON, Darlene (E.) Williams   1941-

PERSONAL: Born November 5, 1941, in Bay City, MI; daughter of Durward Joseph (a manager) and Laura Mae (a homemaker; maiden name, Monoghan) Williams; married Lawrence E. Erickson, Jr. (a manager), June 30, 1962; children: Lawrence E. III, Mary Ellen. *Education:* Aquinas College, B.A., 1963; Western Michigan University, M.A., 1970; Miami University, Ph.D., 1989; graduate study at Illinois State University, Ohio State University, Denison University, University of Toledo, and Ashland College. *Politics:* Independent. *Religion:* Roman Catholic.

ADDRESSES: Home—1283 Berwyn Lane N., Newark, OH 43055. *Office*—Ohio Dominican College, 1216 Sunbury Rd., Room 223 Erskine, Columbus, OH 43219.

CAREER: Newark High School, Newark, OH, teacher, 1977-84; Central Ohio Technical College, Newark, 1980-82, coordinator of gifted programs, 1984-89; Ohio State University-Newark, instructor, 1988; Ohio Dominican College, Columbus, associate professor, 1989—, chair of Freshman Year Experience, 1990-91, chair of Faculty Development Committee, 1991-92, chair of department of English, 1991—, coordinator of Council of Independent Colleges grant, 1992—. Miami University, teaching fellow, 1985-86; Ashland-Otterbein College, adjunct professor, 1987-88.

MEMBER: International Society for Contemporary Literature and Theatre (program chair, 1993), Modern Language Association, National Council of Teachers of English, National Association for Gifted Children and Adults, American Association of University Women, Midwest Modern Language Association, Gifted Coordinators of Central Ohio (president, 1988-89), Ohio Legisla-

tive Liaison Committee on the Gifted, Ohio State Committee on Written Expression, Weathervane Playhouse Board, Phi Kappa Phi, Alpha Kappa Gamma (honorary).

AWARDS, HONORS: Conley Award, Ohio Dominican College, 1991; Outstanding Teacher Award nominee, Miami University, 1987.

WRITINGS:

Illusion Is More Precise than Precision: The Poetry of Marianne Moore, University of Alabama Press, 1992.

Reviewer for *Christianity and Literature* and *Christianity Today.*

WORK IN PROGRESS: A book about poet Anne Sexton, emphasizing her works, not merely her biography. Researching writers Alice Walker and Toni Morrison.

SIDELIGHTS: Darlene Williams Erickson told *CA:* "My writing career began at age thirteen when I won my first regional essay contest and earned fifty dollars. Since that affirmation I have enjoyed the challenge of discovering my world and myself on paper and helping others to do the same. Like Chaucer's clerke, 'Gladly would I learn, and gladly teach.'

"There is no doubt that I am a product of my age and of my gender. The women's movement has helped me find my voice and my subject matter. Not that I write only about women's issues; I consider myself a *personist,* not a feminist, but the refreshing voices of women in the twentieth century and their ability to articulate new causes has given me real inspiration. When I discovered Marianne Moore's poetry, I knew I had found the dominant female voice of this century. Her mind is both challenging and captivating, her ideas fresh and healing. (One finds oneself believing in prophets all over again.) I have grown up with the 'political' voices of the women's movement; now I think it's time to celebrate the literary ones, those who will turn the twenty-first century toward a better world, aesthetically as well as practically. I especially enjoy laughter and a sound sense of humor, a love of language, a delight in puns, a fearlessness in pursuit of truth. I celebrate healing and search out the voice of the other, and find in that voice new dimensions of myself.

"Perhaps my own sense of my own 'minority' status has caused me to listen carefully for voices from the past and from the present to which most of us have not listened. I demand excellence, but continue to be surprised where and how I find it. I cherish womanhood, motherhood, teaching, creativity, professionalism, family, friends, and the continuity of the human spirit. I am pleased that I have the opportunity to test out new ideas with my students. Many semesters I find that I learn more than I have taught.

"My husband's career has taken me to live in several parts of this country. I am pleased to have seen the United States from many sides. And I often present papers in Europe; that experience has helped me observe the American experience with new insights and far less parochialism."

*   *   *

ESEOGHENE
See BARRETT, (Eseoghene) Lindsay

*   *   *

ESQUIVEL, Laura   1951(?)-

PERSONAL: Born c. 1951, in Mexico; daughter of Julio Caesar Esquivel (a telegraph operator) and Josephina Esquivel; married Alfonso Arau (a film director); children: Sandra. *Education:* Attended Escuela Normal de Maestros, Mexico. *Avocational Interests:* Cooking.

ADDRESSES: Home—Mexico City, Mexico.

CAREER: Novelist and screenwriter; writer and director for children's theater. Worked as a teacher for eight years.

AWARDS, HONORS: Ariel Award nomination for best screenplay, Mexican Academy of Motion Pictures, Arts and Sciences, for *Chido One.*

WRITINGS:

SCREENPLAYS

Like Water for Chocolate, based on her novel of the same title, Miramax, c. 1993.

Also author of *Chido One,* released in 1985, and *Little Ocean Star,* a children's feature, released in 1994.

NOVELS

Como agua para chocolate: novela de entregas mensuales con recetas, amores, y remedios caseros, Editorial Planeta Mexicana, 1989, translation by Carol Christensen and Thomas Christensen published as *Like Water for Chocolate: A Novel in Monthly Installments, with Recipes, Romances, and Home Remedies,* Doubleday, 1991.

Esquivel's novel has been translated into numerous languages.

WORK IN PROGRESS: Regina, the screenplay of a film about a female Christ, based on Antonio Belasco Pina's novel of the same name.

SIDELIGHTS: Mexican author Laura Esquivel, who gained international recognition with her first novel,

Como agua para chocolate (Like Water for Chocolate), began her literary career as a screenwriter. Working in partnership with her husband, the Mexican director Alfonso Arau, Esquivel wrote the screenplay for a 1985 Mexican release *Chido One,* which Arau directed. The film's success prompted the couple to continue their collaboration, and Arau became the director when Esquivel adapted *Like Water for Chocolate* for the screen. Both the novel and movie have been enormously popular. A number one best-seller in Mexico in 1990, the book has been translated into numerous languages, including an English version, which enjoyed a longstanding run on the *New York Times Book Review* best-seller list in 1993. The movie, according to *Publishers Weekly,* has reported record-breaking attendance, to become one of the highest-grossing foreign films of the decade. Employing in this work the brand of magic realism that Gabriel Garcia Marquez popularized, Esquivel blends culinary knowledge, sensuality, and alchemy with fables and cultural lore to capture what *Washington Post* reviewer Mary Batts Estrada calls "the secrets of love and life as revealed by the kitchen."

Like Water for Chocolate is the story of Tita, the youngest of three daughters born to Mama Elena, the tyrannical owner of the De La Garza ranch. Tita is a victim of tradition: as the youngest daughter in a Mexican family she is obliged to remain unmarried and to care for her mother. Experiencing pain and frustration as she watches Pedro, the man she loves, marry her older sister Rosaura, Tita faces the added burden of having to bake the wedding cake. But because she was born in the kitchen and knows a great deal about food and its powers, Tita is able to bake her profound sense of sorrow into the cake and make the wedding guests ill. "From this point," as James Polk remarks in the *Tribune Books,* "food, sex and magic are wondrously interwoven." For the remainder of the novel, Tita uses her special culinary talents to provoke strange reactions in Mama Elena, Rosaura, Tita's other sister, Gertrudis, and many others.

Food has played a significant role in Esquivel's life since she was a child. Remembering her early cooking experiences and the aromas of foods cooked in her grandmother's house, she told Molly O'Neill of the *New York Times* that "I watch cooking change the cook, just as it transforms the food. . . . Food can change anything." For Esquivel, cooking is a reminder of the alchemy between concrete and abstract forces. Esquivel's novel of cooking and magic has been well-received by critics. Writing in the *Los Angeles Times Book Review,* Karen Stabiner remarks that Esquivel's novel "is a wondrous, romantic tale, fueled by mystery and superstition, as well as by the recipes that introduce each chapter." James Polk, in the *Chicago Tribune,* writes that "*Like Water for Chocolate* (a Mexican colloquialism meaning, roughly, agitated or excited) is an inventive and mischievous romp—part cookbook, part novel."

BIOGRAPHICAL/CRITICAL SOURCES:

PERIODICALS

Los Angeles Times Book Review, November 1, 1992, p. 6.
New Republic, March 1, 1993, pp. 24-25.
New York Times, March 31, 1993, pp. C1, C8.
Time, April 5, 1993, pp. 62-63.
Tribune Books (Chicago), October 18, 1992, p. 8.
Washington Post, September 25, 1992, p. B2.*

*   *   *

ESTES, Clarissa Pinkola   1943-

PERSONAL: Born in 1943 in northern Indiana; married; children: three daughters. *Education:* Loretto Heights College, B.A. (with distinction), 1976; The Union Institute, Cincinnati, OH, Ph.D., 1981; Charter of Zurich, postdoctoral diploma (certified as a Jungian analyst), 1984.

ADDRESSES: Home—Colorado and Wyoming. *Agent*—Ned Leavitt Agency, 70 Wooster St., Suite 4-F, New York, NY 10012.

CAREER: Psychoanalyst in private practice, Denver, CO, 1971—. Developer and teacher of "Writing as Liberation of the Spirit" program in state and federal prisons throughout the U.S., 1971—; Women in Transition Safe House, Denver, co-coordinator, 1973-75; C. G. Jung Center for Education and Research, executive director; co-founder and co-director of Colorado Authors for Gay and Lesbian Equal Rights; founder, Guadelupe Foundation (human rights organization).

MEMBER: International Association of Analytic Psychology, Inter-Regional Society of Jungian Analysts.

AWARDS, HONORS: Rocky Mountain Woman's Institute fellowship and grant, 1990, for *Las Brujas* (a work in progress); Las Primeras award, MANA, National Latina Foundation (Washington, DC), 1993, for lifetime social activism and literature; Book of the Year Honor Award, American Booksellers Association, 1993, and Colorado Authors League Award, 1993, both for *Women Who Run with the Wolves: Myths and Stories of the Wild Woman Archetype;* Joseph Campbell Keepers of the Lore Award, Joseph Campbell Festival of Myth, Folklore, and Story, 1994.

WRITINGS:

Women Who Run with the Wolves: Myths and Stories of the Wild Woman Archetype, Ballantine, 1992.

The Gift of Story: A Wise Tale about What Is Enough, Ballantine, 1993.

Nine original audio cassette recordings, including *The Creative Fire: Myths and Stories about the Descent and Ascent of Creativity, Warming the Stone Child: Myths and Stories about the Abandoned and the Unmothered Child, The Radiant Coat: Myths and Stories of the Crossing between Life and Death, How to Love a Woman: On Intimacy and the Erotic Life of Women, In the House of the Riddle Mother: Common Archetypal Dreams of Women, The Wild Woman Archetype: Myths and Stories of the Instinctual Nature of Women, The Red Shoes: On Torment and the Recovery of Soul Life, The Boy Who Married an Eagle: Myths and Stories about Male Individuation,* and *The Gift of Story: A Wise Tale about What Is Enough,* all released by Sounds True, 1992. Contributor of poetry to numerous publications.

WORK IN PROGRESS: The Dangerous Old Woman and the Power of Age: Myths and Stories of the Wise Woman Archetype, part two of a larger manuscript of one hundred tales with psychological commentary, of which *Women Who Run with the Wolves* is the first of five volumes to be published; *Las Brujas.*

SIDELIGHTS: In the book *Women Who Run with the Wolves: Myths and Stories of the Wild Woman Archetype* author Clarissa Pinkola Estes uses folklore and fairy tales to address certain psychological issues affecting women. As a Jungian analyst, Estes has been trained in the exploration of archetypes (numinous images and ideas that arise in humans universally), and she has focused her explorations on the female psyche, an entity which has long been ignored as a subject for study. "Traditional psychology is often spare or entirely silent about deeper issues important to women, the archetypal, the intuitive, the sexual and cyclical, the ages of women, a woman's way, a woman's knowing, her creative fire," Estes writes in *Women Who Run with the Wolves.* "This is what has motivated my work on the Wild Woman archetype for the better part of two decades."

Estes was born to *mestizo* parents of Spanish and Mexican ancestry and was later adopted by Hungarian immigrants to the United States. From these diverse cultures the traditions of story as a healing act came into her life; in an interview conducted by her publisher, Estes related that she "spent many hours seated at the feet of old Hungarian and Latina women who storytell in plain voices. For them, story is a medicine which strengthens and arights the individual and community. From them I learned that story greases and hoists the pulleys, shows us the way out, down, in and around, cuts for us fine, wide doors in previously blank walls—doors that lead us to our own knowing as wildish women."

The tales and myths included in *Women Who Run with the Wolves* are drawn from stories Estes heard first-hand from family and friends who are from the Inuit, Asian, European, Mexican, African, and Greek cultures as well as others. Stories, Estes says, are "medicine"—they provide a person with a link to that self-knowledge which is buried, but which is also available if one knows how to dig for it. "It's almost like [a] psychic DNA," Estes told Elizabeth Hand in the Detroit *Metro Times*. "You recognize it when it comes to you." Similar to Swiss psychiatrist Carl Jung's use of archetypes, Estes proposes that "stories as medicine" stimulate imagination and strengthen various aspects of the psyche. Estes metaphorically compares the woman who has realized her essential nature—a woman who is "able to rely on gut feelings to make choices," in the words of a reviewer in *Publishers Weekly*—to a strong and persistent animal: the wolf. "[Wolves] are deeply intuitive, intensely concerned with their young, their mate[s], and their pack. They are experienced at adapting to constantly changing circumstances, they are fiercely stalwart and very brave. So that is where the concept of the wild woman archetype crystallized for me, in the study of wolves," Estes writes in *Women Who Run with the Wolves*.

"My work is dedicated to the idea of taking these ancient stories that have been used as instruction for thousands of years, and using them as the basis of naming the parts of the psyche that a person needs to go forth under any circumstance," Estes related in the Detroit *Metro Times*. "It doesn't matter if electricity has not been invented yet, that we're in the gaslight era, or now we're in the electronic era, and we're going to be in the virtual reality era—doesn't matter. Everything remains the same, because it's ancient."

Estes told *CA:* "There are several ways to describe the language of my work, depending on how deeply one looks. I'll try to briefly describe some of the main structural underpinnings. I come from the working class—the old fashioned word used to be 'the underclass.' Though we struggled and lost much in many ways, we were vastly rich in ethnic culture, song, dance, poetry, and story. My basic writing language stays close to home—the northwoods and orchards, brutal winters and summers, running for the root cellar ahead of tornadoes—all these are inside me. Nothing goes onto the page that does not pass through these, and more.

"I was not able to go to college until my late twenties, too late to wash away the dirt-language of home. The word-pictures of my elders (few of my elders were literate; they were immersed instead in the high oral tradition) became my true language, one that uses the personal 'we' and the personal 'you.' I use the personal voice, for in my work I am not talking about women as a topic, I am talking about the *we,* the *you* and the *I* of womanliness. I have married this, my original language, to the language of scholarship and analytical psychology. I had in mind that I might be able to thusly construct a kind of literate orchestra in my work with more than one instrument carrying the tone, some in point, others in counterpoint.

"Underneath this—which some readers perceive and write to me about—are the rhythms of enchanting poetry. Enchanting as a verb, not an adjective. As in the healing chants of *curanderisma* and *esme* that my *abuelitas* and *nagymamas* (grandmothers) taught, as in the poetics of fairy and folk tales given me by my family and friends, as in my own work as a poet, there is a hymnal quality to a long chain of words. I use these qualitative strophes or rhythms in my writing because they do the work needed; penetrating past the ego, reaching into spirit and soul.

"I see that in some ways it is still shocking for a woman to write in original voice. So much of women's psyche is unmapped as yet. We barely know what women's various writing languages will look and sound like once allowed to come upward from their bones to meet with intellect, rather than to be devised from intellect alone. In Spanish we talk about *La voz*, The Voice, the voice that creates. It has a certain beat, a strophe. That strophe is important to my work and underlies it all.

"So, these aspects, and others from my life, dictated that my larger life's work, of which *Women Who Run with the Wolves* is a portion, be as purposeful works of art as I could make them, as well as treatises on depth psychology and the old healing ideas from my own ethnic background. The latter, incidentally, which relies on many methods, one specifically being story as medicine, has been a part of Latina and *mesemondok* culture since time out of mind. Psychology—the study of the soul—is not, as you know, one hundred years old. It did not begin with, nor was it solidly conceptualized by, Freud. Psychology is thousands of years old. It began with anyone and everyone who heard a voice greater than their own, and who felt compelled to seek its source.

"When interviewers ask me to describe my background, I say 'Mother, poet, activist, writer, *cantadora*, psychoanalyst.' I think it is good to be named by the endeavors we have worked hard to master. Which incidentally includes women remaining just as they are, forever if they so choose, and women wishing to devote themselves to a single endeavor as well.

"Some interviewers have expressed their surprise at the public's taking up my work and want to know why so many seem to have found it moving. I ask these questions in return: 'What do you think has happened in our culture that we become surprised when a soulful work affects many people? What condition does this mean our culture is really in?' As best I can tell, women (and men) have responded to my work for many personal reasons, but all having to do with their concern with matters of spirit, as well as their desire to caretake all of life in and around themselves for as far as they can reach.

"We receive many letters from men, most of whom say in one form or another, 'This book is for men too,' that men have a feminine nature also, and that the work has helped them understand the more mysterious sides of their mothers, wives, daughters, friends and lovers. Also near to my heart are the many letters we receive from women in their seventies, eighties, and nineties, many of whom are artists, both known and not yet well known. The psychoanalytic community, for the most part, has had overwhelming praise for this work. Most feel such a book was long overdue and say that it has helped them immeasurably in having a structure and a language to speak about the instinctive nature of women, and more so the symbolic function of the psyche.

"In 1971, in response to thinking that so little of psychology seemed to apply to actual women and to *all kinds* of women in the real world—middle class, working class, educated, not educated, Latinas, African Americans, Japanese Americans, Italian Americans and so on, recent immigrants, lesbians, women from religious orders, widows, artists, intellectuals, women in prison, women activists and on and on—I began writing the one hundred fairy tales, myths and psychological commentary that comprise my work. In essence, it is a work that de-pathologizes the innate and instinctual nature, and that asserts that all women are born gifted. Upon beginning a scholarly inquiry, I had found that the central issue was an ages-old reviling of various innate and powerful aspects of the feminine that not only constitute the feminine inheritance, but which are absolutely essential to women's psychic life, and to the strong living of that life in the outer world. Without these aspects, women psychically die.

"I have this feeling that sometimes comes over me—I call it 'the wind of Santa Ana'—and it fills up my blouse and my skirt and causes my hair to fly back. I was filled with the wind of Santa Ana, and that is what, back then, made me stand up at my desk and say, 'By God, I'm going to write about gifted and talented women, and the creative center of the psyche.'

"I laugh now, because I seemed so young then and had no idea what a vast subject I was undertaking. When I laid down the first fifteen hundred pages of writing, which means two to three pages of research notes for every written page—well, I may have had ten thousand pages altogether. Of manuscript actually ready to go, about 2,200 pages. *Women Who Run with the Wolves* represents the first five hundred pages.

"I initially thought the lack of psychoanalytic material about real women and their real and diverse lives was a vacuum. When I looked more closely, however, I could see that perhaps the classical psychologists of old were, as I was for a time, almost overwhelmed by the enormous laceration in the psyches of women that appeared to reach out over and down throughout the centuries. This laceration ran through entire cultures, and across many cultures, not just in individuals. I began to wonder, 'What can I use as suture for this?' How does one sew the edges of such a huge abyss together? Something that has been dead for so long that the flesh around the edges of the wound has become necrotic. It is painful. What can help? It became a question accompanied by not a little despair at the paucity of modern options. In the end, the answer I came to was story, story as medicine from the old healing traditions. Not as *the* answer. But as help, assistance for mending and strengthening the modern psyche. And further, accurate structural underpinnings that were as necessary to this work as were the lyric components.

"Some booksellers have shelved my work in several sections of their stores at the same time, as well as in specific sections: Psychology, Women's Studies, Mythology, Spiritual Development, and Poetry being the most common ones. Some feel it defies category, or has begun a new one of its own. I feel it is just 'the work' and hopefully more an artwork than a book of pages alone. I have little appetite for a few who want to call my work by those tiresome old merchandising phrases, 'self-help' or 'new age,' although maybe it is of the Self (another name for the soul in analytical psychology) with a capital S. If I were pushed to it, I would call my work something like 'psychology in the truest sense of the word,' that is, the study of the soul. The maturation process of each individual is unique and cannot be codified into a 'do these ten easy steps and all will be well.' No, this work is not for everyone. And it is not easy. For those who do take it up, it is better approached as a contemplative work that is best integrated through a slow reading of the texts, a going away, thinking about it, dreaming about it all and then returning to the work once again in one's own rhythm, at one's own speed—rather than trying to finish the book at a breakneck pace.

"I think that at the center of my work is something far more difficult to articulate. I have been asked if my lifetime of social activism is compatible with my analytic work. I cannot imagine that they could ever be separate from one another. Now, and since the time I was a little child, when I look out over the world, I have felt the relentless sensation of brokenheartedness, but I have also felt an unshakable and inspired hope for humankind. Sometimes this is mixed with anger, sometimes not. These seemingly contradictory but powerful forces of the broken heart—a heart that is broken open and stays open---commingled with hope are, I believe, the enduring underpinnings for effecting ongoing and positive psychic and social change.

"My heart has broken open many times. During the forced repatriation of Mexicano field workers in the upper Midwest. The winter a toddler on our road fell through the ice and drowned because a negligent landowner failed to fence his pond. The day a faulty thresher dragged my friend's father to his death. The day my aunts were tricked into working at lightning speed after being promised a small bonus; after exhausting themselves, the line man raised their daily production quotas to inhuman heights. Seeing ulcerated veins on the legs of my friend's mother, lesions from ten babies in ten years while trying to follow religious proscriptions against birth control. Watching the men come home with their heads down the day the Studebaker factory closed with little warning. The day I saw my Magyar foster father writhe in agony while the radio broadcaster announced that the Soviets had invaded Hungary with tanks while the peasants had nothing to fight with but their fists. The day boys I grew up with who played 'guns' in snow forts, and girls, who played 'nurses' at the roadside, came back standing or laid down from Khe Sanh and the Tet. There were many breakings, not just one, but time and again. And still.

"I have found a word in German that describes this feeling: *Schmerzenreich*—it means rich in sorrow, ability to bear sorrow—this essential ability for activism . . . and poetry . . . and psychoanalytic work. There is another phrase I have found also that describes this drive I feel, it is the Hebrew 'tikkun olam,' the moral duty to help repair the world soul on a daily basis. In my work of writing and amplifying the tales and stories given me by family and friends across many different cultures, in all the ways I have described here and a few more somewhat mysterious ones as well, I am striving in the end to balance two forces. My grandmothers and aunts gave me the understanding about what it was to be *La cantadora*, and *mesemondo*, that is, a keeper of stories. Part of this tradition is to be able to carry the *cante*, a special kind of feeling in the song or story. This feeling tone must be equally divided with sorrow on one side, and joy on the other. These two together are necessary and inseparable. It is this 'necessary and inseparable' mystery that I am trying to delve, not from the outside by just simply describing these phenomena as might have occurred had I used a solely intellectual approach, but by describing them from the inside, from what I hope is the marrow, the place where life is constantly being replenished without our interference or intervention."

BIOGRAPHICAL/CRITICAL SOURCES:

BOOKS

Estes, Clarissa Pinkola, *Women Who Run with the Wolves: Myths and Stories of the Wild Woman Archetype,* Ballantine, 1992.
Notable Hispanic American Women, Gale, 1993.

PERIODICALS

Bloomsbury Review, September/October, 1993; November/December, 1993.
Los Angeles Times, August 27, 1992, pp. E1, E9.
Metro Times (Detroit), August 18-24, pp. 12-13.
Newsweek, December 21, 1992, p. 59.
People, December 21, 1992, p. 82.
Publishers Weekly, October 5, 1992, p. 29; December 14, 1992, p. 64.
Psychological Perspectives, winter, 1993.
Round Table Press Review of Contemporary Contributions to Jungian Psychology, January/February, 1994.
Washington Post Book World, August 30, 1992.

*   *   *

EYER, Diane E(lizabeth) 1944-

PERSONAL: Born March 21, 1944, in Buffalo, NY; daughter of Charles R. Eyer (an engineer) and Elizabeth M. Eyer (a librarian); married Jack W. Byer (a professor) July 6, 1991. *Education:* Bucknell University, B.A., 1966; University of Pennsylvania, Ph.D. (with distinction), 1988.

ADDRESSES: Agent—Beth Vesel, Sanford J. Greenburger Associates, 55 Fifth Ave., New York, NY 10003.

CAREER: Rutgers University, New Brunswick, NJ, instructor, 1985-89; Temple University, Philadelphia, PA, instructor, 1986-87; University of Pennsylvania, Philadelphia, lecturer, 1991—; full-time writer. University of Pennsylvania, teaching assistant, 1983-85, research assistant, 1984-87. Institute of Pennsylvania Hospital, poetry therapist, 1971-73; Philadelphia Institute for Gestalt Therapy, counselor, 1971-75; assistant therapist in private practice; producer, narrator, and editor of various documentary and educational films; editorial consultant to publications.

MEMBER: International Society for the History and Sociology of Science, Human Sciences Division, National Women's Studies Association, Cheiron Society, Historians of the Behavioral and Social Sciences, Society for Research and Child Development, Philadelphia Independent Filmmakers and Video Artists Association.

AWARDS, HONORS: New York State Regents scholarship, 1962.

WRITINGS:

Studying Literacy in Morocco: A Model (documentary film script), Middle East Center, University of Pennsylvania, 1988.

Mother-Infant Bonding: A Scientific Fiction, Yale University Press, 1992.

Motherwork/Motherguilt, Ticknor & Fields, in press.

Contributor to books, including *The Psychology of Women: Ongoing Debates,* edited by Mary Roth Walsh, Yale University Press, in press; *Birth Management: A Biosocial Perspective,* edited by M. E. Lamb and J. Lancaster, Aldine, in press. Reporter and feature writer for the *Bethlehem Globe-Times;* contributor of articles to periodicals, including the *Wall Street Journal, USA Today Weekend Magazine, Esquire,* and *Glamour.*

WORK IN PROGRESS: Child Development: The Moral Science, for Yale University Press, publication expected in 1996; researching the history of developmental psychology, child growth studies, women in abusive relationships, and the fallibility of attachment theories.

SIDELIGHTS: Diane E. Eyer told *CA:* "I'm a psychologist at heart and that means that I always think there are very interesting reasons for what people do, behind the reasons that people actually give for what they do. To uncover these complications gives me a great sense of having tracked down 'the truth' (Nancy Drew was my girlhood role model so perhaps my inner core is private investigation). In graduate school at the University of Pennsylvania, I became fascinated with the question of what psychologists thought was normal or healthy. In pursuing the question, I was struck by the frequent fads in child rearing that were based on such psychological concepts. I decided to investigate one psychological construct, postpartum maternal bonding, to see how science interacted with social forces to create this fad. That study became a book, *Mother-Infant Bonding: A Scientific Fiction.* I'm also writing a history of developmental psychology and a book for a more general audience which investigates the effects of attachment theory on contemporary families. Since I am discovering that truth is stranger than fiction, perhaps one day I will simply turn to writing fiction."

*   *   *

EZELL, Edward C(linton)   1939-1993

OBITUARY NOTICE—See index for *CA* sketch: Born November 7, 1939, in Indianapolis, IN; died of renal cell cancer, December 23, 1993, in Woodbridge, VA. Historian and author. Ezell was an authority in the history of military small arms. He taught social studies at North Carolina State University from 1966 to 1970 and history at Sangamon State University from 1970 to 1974. Also during this time period, he dealt in small arms operations as vice president of the Singapore armaments dealer Interarms Asia. After teaching, he obtained the position of historian for the National Aeronautics and Space Administration (NASA). He became curator of the National Firearms Collection and supervisor of the Division of Armed Forces History at the National Museum of American History in 1982. And beginning in 1986, Ezell founded and directed the Institute for Research on Small Arms in International Security. He wrote and contributed to numerous books about history and small arms, including *The Great Rifle Controversy: The Search for the Ultimate Infantry Rifle, From World War II to Vietnam and Beyond, Small Arms Today: The Latest Reports on the World's Small Arms and Ammunition,* and *Personal Firepower: Infantry Weapons of Vietnam.* He also edited *Small Arms of the World.*

OBITUARIES AND OTHER SOURCES:

BOOKS

Who's Who, 145th edition, St. Martin's, 1993.

PERIODICALS

Washington Post, December 25, 1993, p. C4.

F

FABRICANT, Michael B. 1948-

PERSONAL: Born August 23, 1948, in New York, NY; son of George Wenig/David Fabricant and Harriet (a bookkeeper) Fabricant; married Betsy Werner (a social services administrator), July 4, 1971; children: Nicole Werner, Matthew William. Education: University of Pittsburgh, B.A., 1970; Brandeis University, Ph.D., 1975. Politics: Social Democrat. Religion: Jewish.

ADDRESSES: Home—118 Lincoln Ave., Elizabeth, NJ 07208. Office—129 East 79th St., New York, NY 10021.

CAREER: Community Service Society, New York City, research associate, 1975-80; Hunter College, New York City, assistant professor, 1980-85, associate professor, 1985-88, professor of social work, 1988—. Member of board of directors for National Coalition for the Homeless, Union County Legal Services, Elizabeth Coalition to House the Homeless, and St. Joseph's Social Service Center; consultant to American Red Cross, Henry Street Settlement, and John Jay College of Criminal Justice of the City University of New York.

WRITINGS:

Deinstitutionalizing Delinquent Youth, Schenkman, 1980.
Juveniles in the Family Court, Lexington Books, 1983.
(With S. Burghardt) Working Under the Safety Net, Sage Publications, 1987.
(With S. Burghardt) The Welfare State Crisis and the Transformation of Social Service Work, M. E. Sharpe, 1992.

WORK IN PROGRESS: Rebuilding Community in an Era of Heightened Individualism.

FANCHER, Betsy 1928-
(Betsy Hopkins Lochridge)

PERSONAL: Born October 17, 1928, in Atlanta, GA; daughter of John L. (an attorney) and Elizabeth (Hawkins) Hopkins; married Marshall Lochridge, March 18, 1950 (marriage ended); married John K. Fancher, Jr., October 17, 1959; children: (second marriage) three stepdaughters. Education: Wesleyan College, A.B., 1949.

CAREER: Ida Williams Library, Atlanta, GA, page, then assistant librarian, 1940-43; Atlanta Constitution, Atlanta, writer, beginning 1944, became daily columnist and book editor; Macon Telegraph, Macon, GA, reporter, 1945-49; South Today, associate editor; Atlanta magazine, senior editor; writer. Activist in civil rights work; volunteer for Emaus House Chaplaincy of the Episcopal Church, Atlanta.

AWARDS, HONORS: Creative Writing Award, Wesleyan College, 1949; Georgia Writers Association's fiction award, 1956, for Blue River, and nonfiction award, 1971, for The Lost Legacy of Georgia's Golden Isles.

WRITINGS:

(Under name Betsy Hopkins Lochridge) Blue River (short stories; includes "The Town," "Foots," "Will Davis," and "Ida Sims"), Macmillan, 1956.
Voices from the South: Black Students Talk about Their Experiences in Desegregated Schools, Southern Regional Council, 1970.
The Lost Legacy of Georgia's Golden Isles, photographs by Peter Hudson, Doubleday, 1971.
Savannah: A Renaissance of the Heart, Doubleday, 1976.

Also author of an unpublished novel, The Profit and the Loss. Contributor of articles to periodicals, including Saturday Evening Post, Gentlemen's Quarterly, Saturday Review, and Holiday.

Blue River was translated into Italian and published in Braille.

SIDELIGHTS: Blue River, Betsy Fancher's 1956 award-winning short story collection, was described by a reviewer for the *New York World-Telegram* as a "near masterpiece," and yet it is the only fiction the author, a long-time journalist, has published. The volume, a series of sixteen stories about the fictional Southern town of Blue River, was written when Fancher was living in Pittsburgh, Pennsylvania—away from her Georgia home. "The characters are primarily derivations or composites of people I had known in Georgia before my first marriage," the author told a *Dictionary of Literary Biography Yearbook* (*DLBY*) interviewer. "*Blue River* began out of homesickness—it took me back to Atlanta. It was an experiment in writing."

The first story in the collection, "The Town," provides a comprehensive background of Blue River. The narrative begins with the town's settlement by a Baptist minister who, after having a vision of an angel of God, sets out with his family in a covered wagon on a mission to convert Indians to his faith. Reaching Blue River after a disastrous journey, the minister dies without having encountered a single Indian. The story continues through the town's early years of prosperity, the establishment of slavery, the Civil War, World War I, the Great Depression of the 1930s, and finally to the town's decline.

The next fourteen stories focus on relationships among Blue River's townspeople, highlighting the power structures that have evolved between blacks and whites and between men and women. The story "Foots" explores the relationship between the title character, a black gardener, and his abusive employer, an elderly woman he calls Miz Sarah. In the story, Miz Sarah, after accusing Foots of having stolen money that she has in fact mislaid, orders him to go into the pantry and remove his clothes so that she can search them. Orin Anderson summarized in *DLBY*: "Foots's relationship with his employer, 'Miz Sarah' (the Grandmother), is amiable and fond, but rigidly set in a master-and-servant mold which seems a legacy of the days of slavery, for the Grandmother blames him for her failings, and he feels that she could not exist if he were not there to shoulder both his burden and hers."

In "Will Davis," the education of a highly intelligent black boy receives special attention from the town's schoolmaster and rector. At their prodding, the boy eventually goes north, where he finds impenetrable racial barriers instead of the world of opportunities he had been led to expect. Returning to Blue River, he lashes out at his mentors, who never made the realities of racism known to him. After hitting the rector and cursing his "little prissy white God," the boy is hunted down and lynched.

Blacks are not the only citizens of Blue River who cope with oppression and injustice. Many of the characters featured in Fancher's stories are women who seek, but do not necessarily find, freedom from male dominance. The title character of "Ida Sims," scorned by the town for promiscuous behavior, leaves Blue River to live with an artist and study composition in New York. When the artist expects Ida to assume the traditional female role she hoped to leave behind, she returns to grim prospects in her unsympathetic hometown.

New York World-Telegram contributor Sterling North compared Fancher's writing to other great Southern women writers, asserting that with *Blue River* Fancher "immediately steps into the class of Katherine Ann Porter and Shirley Ann Grau as one of the most distinguished short story writers ever to come out of the Southland." Anderson, comparing her to Southern writer Eudora Welty, lauded Fancher for "capturing the essence of 'Southern-ness,'" and for "her perception of the inherent linking factors of the South: the preeminent role of women, the legacy of slavery, the casual familiarity with religion, the saturation of history, and the bond of place." Anderson also observed that "Fancher's insight into the history and lives of Blue River's black people . . . elevates the book to masterpiece or 'near masterpiece,'" as it was called in the *New York World-Telegram.*

Although her first "experiment in writing" proved successful, Fancher has not penned any more short stories. Her marriage in 1959 to her second husband—who had three daughters—nudged her into journalism and nonfiction. "*Blue River* stands alone because becoming an instant mother with my second marriage made fact more interesting to me than fiction," the author said in her *DLBY* interview. "I was deeply embroiled in life; I had no room of my own, and I had to make a living, so I embraced journalism." Journalism was not simply a practical or second choice for Fancher, who began her career as a reporter while still in high school. An activist in the civil rights movement of the 1960s and later in human rights campaigns, Fancher appreciated the power of good journalistic writing and the place of fact in the literary world. The author told *DLBY:* "I believe journalism to be an art form as precise and exacting as poetry. It is *the* art form of our fast-paced, modern lives. My own career in journalism has been rich and challenging. I was at my typewriter during the entire course of the civil rights struggle in the South. There wasn't time for fiction when fact was so exciting, even dangerous."

Along with articles and daily newspaper columns, Fancher has written several nonfiction books over the years. Her 1971 publication, *The Lost Legacy of Georgia's Golden Isles,* won the author her second Georgia Writers Association Award and fared well with critics. The book provides a cultural, historical, and geographical description of the islands off Georgia's coast, with material as diverse as the inhabitants of these islands. Fancher tracks the evolution of Jekyll Island, at one time an elegant resort area for multimillionaires such as the Rockefellers and the Morgans, and now a middle-class American vacation spot. She emphasizes the racial history of the islands, from slavery to reconstruction to the nineteenth-century black separation movement on Sapelo Island. There is a chapter about the Gullahs, a group thought to be descendants of slaves taken from the Gola tribe in Liberia, who inhabit the islands today, often in poverty and harsh conditions. George E. Snow wrote in *Best Sellers:* "In a style that is eminently readable Miss Fancher evokes the spirit of these islands with a sure sense of history and an unfailing eye for the human, the tragic, and, yes, even the dramatic. . . . But for all this, the author is neither saccharine nor evasive of what are major issues in this or any other age."

BIOGRAPHICAL/CRITICAL SOURCES:

BOOKS

Dictionary of Literary Biography Yearbook: 1983, Gale, 1984, pp. 227-233.

PERIODICALS

Best Sellers, March 15, 1971, p. 541.
Georgia Review, April, 1971.
Library Journal, February 15, 1971.
New York Herald Tribune Book Review, November 25, 1956, p. 18.
New York World-Telegram, September 26, 1956.
Saturday Review, October 20, 1956.*

—*Sketch by Sonia Benson*

*   *   *

FECIT
See BARCLAY, Robert

*   *   *

FEDOROFF, Nina (V.) 1942-

PERSONAL: Born April 9, 1942, in Cleveland, OH; daughter of Vsevolod (an engineer) and Olga (a translator; maiden name, Snegireff; present surname, Stacy) Fedoroff; married Patrick Gaganidze (divorced, 1978); married Michael Broyles (a musicologist), June 16, 1990; children: (first marriage) Natasha Gaganidze MacPherson, Kyr. *Education:* Syracuse University, B.S., 1966; Rockefeller

University, Ph.D., 1972. *Avocational Interests:* Music (flute), gardening, tennis, skiing.

ADDRESSES: Home—5214 Tilbury Way, Baltimore, MD 21212. *Office*—Department of Embryology, Carnegie Institution of Washington, 115 West University Parkway, Baltimore, MD 21210.

CAREER: Biological Abstracts, Philadelphia, PA, assistant manager of Translational Bureau, 1962-63; free-lance translator and abstracter from Russian to English, 1963-66; Syracuse Symphony Orchestra, Syracuse, NY, flutist, 1964-66; University of California, Los Angeles, acting assistant professor of biology, 1972-74; Carnegie Institution of Washington, Baltimore, MD, staff scientist, 1975—. Johns Hopkins University, professor of biology, 1979—; University of Maryland at College Park, member of scientific advisory board, Center for Agricultural Biotechnology, 1987—. National Science Foundation, member of developmental biology panel, 1979-80; Congressional Office of Technology Assessment, member of scientific advisory panel on applied genetics, 1979-80; National Institutes of Health, member of recombinant DNA advisory committee, 1980-84; National Research Council and National Academy of Sciences, member of Commission on Life Sciences, 1984-90, and biotechnology committee, 1988-90; Japanese Human Frontier Science Program, member of scientific advisory committee, 1988; U.S.-U.S.S.R. Interacademy Workshop on Plant Molecular Biology Applied to Agriculture, co-chairperson, 1989; BIO-SIS, member of board of trustees, 1991—; International Science Foundation, member of board of directors, 1992-93; *Plant Journal,* member of the scientific advisory panel, 1992—; consultant to United AgriSeeds, Dow Elanco, and U.S. Department of Agriculture.

MEMBER: International Society for Plant Molecular Biology, Genetic Society of America (member of board of directors, 1990-93), American Society for Cell Biology, American Society for Biochemistry and Molecular Biology, American Association for the Advancement of Science, National Academy of Sciences, American Academy of Arts and Sciences, Phi Beta Kappa, Sigma Xi.

AWARDS, HONORS: Damon Runyon-Walter Winchell fellow, 1974-75; fellow of National Institutes of Health, 1975-77; Howard Taylor Ricketts Award, 1990; Merit Award from National Institutes of Health; named Outstanding Contemporary Woman Scientist by New York Academy of Sciences, 1992.

WRITINGS:

(Editor with D. Botstein) *The Dynamic Genome: Barbara McClintock's Ideas in the Century of Genetics,* Cold Spring Harbor Laboratory Press, 1992.

Work represented in scientific anthologies. Contributor of numerous articles to scientific journals and newspapers, including *Sciences* and *Scientific American.* Editor of *Gene,* 1981-84, and *Perspectives in Biology and Medicine,* 1990—; member of board of reviewing editors, *Science,* 1985.

WORK IN PROGRESS: Research on the regulation mechanism of plant transposable elements and on the uses of these elements in gene isolation.

*   *   *

FELLINI, Federico   1920-1993

OBITUARY NOTICE—See index for *CA* sketch: Born January 20, 1920, in Rimini, Italy; died of cardiac arrest, October 31, 1993, in Rome, Italy. Film director and screenwriter. Winner of numerous awards for filmmaking, Fellini was known for crafting personal motion pictures that delved into the human condition, often using avant-garde or grotesque visual imagery. His work, which ran the gambit from neo-realism to surrealism, was often praised by critics for its originality and boldness. Fellini's career in the entertainment field began in his youth, first as a cartoonist and later as a member of a vaudeville troupe. He moved on to radio comedy writing before venturing into screenwriting. His filmmaking career got a boost when he met director Roberto Rossellini and began collaborating with him on various motion pictures, including the 1945 documentary *Open City.*

An accomplished and controversial director, he also wrote the scripts for each of his twenty feature films, such as *La Dolce Vita* ("The Sweet Life"), *City of Women, Fred and Ginger,* and *Intervista* ("Interview"). Such achievements earned him critical praise, including credit for reviving Italy's demoralized film industry after World War II. Several of his works—*8 1/2, La Strada* ("The Road"), *The Nights of Cabiria,* and *Amarcord* ("I Remember")—won Academy Awards as best foreign films. Fellini himself was also the recipient of a lifetime achievement Oscar in 1993. During his career, Fellini also chronicled various facets of his life and film work in books such as *Fellini on Fellini* and *La mia Rimini.*

OBITUARIES AND OTHER SOURCES:

BOOKS

Contemporary Theatre, Film, and Television, Volume 7, Gale, 1989, pp. 126-127.
Who's Who in the World, 11th edition, Marquis, 1992, p. 349.

PERIODICALS

Chicago Tribune, November 7, 1993, p. 6.

Los Angeles Times, November 1, 1993, p. 1A.
New York Times, November 1, 1993, p. 1A; November 3, 1993, p. D24; November 4, 1993, p. D22.
Times (London), November 1, 1993, p. 17.

*   *   *

FERGUSON, Kathy E.   1950-

PERSONAL: Born November 16, 1950, in Anderson, IN; daughter of Al (a farmer) and Laura Sears (a factory worker; maiden name, Rinker) Ferguson; married Gilad Ashkenazi (a mechanic), March 10, 1986; children: Oren, Ari. *Education:* Purdue University, B.A., 1972; University of Minnesota—Twin Cities, Ph.D., 1976.

ADDRESSES: Home—Honolulu, HI. *Office*—Women's Studies Program, University of Hawaii at Manoa, Honolulu, HI 96822.

CAREER: Siena College, Albany, NY, professor of political science, 1976-85; University of Hawaii at Manoa, Honolulu, professor of political science and women's studies, 1985—.

WRITINGS:

Self, Society, and Womankind, Greenwood Press, 1980.
The Feminist Case against Bureaucracy, Temple University Press, 1984.
The Man Question, University of California Press, 1993.

WORK IN PROGRESS: Kibbutz Journal: Reflections on Gender, Race, and Militarism in Israel, for Trilogy Press; research for a book on the military in Hawaii, with Phyllis Turnbull.

SIDELIGHTS: Kathy E. Ferguson told *CA:* "I write in order to explain things to myself. Writing helps me to digest life, to seize ideas and experiences and make them my own. Since having children, I've found myself relaxing into writing, approaching it more eagerly and with much less anxiety. Perhaps because I have so little time to write, I cherish that time."

*   *   *

FERLING, John E.   1940-

PERSONAL: Born January 10, 1940, in Charleston, WV; son of Ernie L. (an industrial production supervisor) and Ruth (a homemaker; maiden name, McCracken) Ferling; married Carol Millette (a homemaker), September 5, 1965. *Education:* Sam Houston State University, B.A., 1961; Baylor University, M.A., 1962; West Virginia University, Ph.D., 1971. *Religion:* Lutheran.

ADDRESSES: Home—335 Kramer St., Carrollton, GA 30117. *Office*—Department of History, West Georgia College, Carrollton, GA 30118.

CAREER: Morehead State University, Morehead, KY, assistant professor of history, 1965-68; West Chester State University, West Chester, PA, associate professor of history, 1970-71; West Georgia College, Carrollton, professor of history, 1971—.

MEMBER: Institute of Early American History and Culture, Society of Historians of the Early American Republic, Organization of American Historians.

WRITINGS:

The Loyalist Mind, Pennsylvania State University Press, 1977.
A Wilderness of Miseries, Greenwood Press, 1981.
The First of Men: A Life of George Washington, University of Tennessee Press, 1988.
John Adams: A Life, University of Tennessee Press, 1992.
Struggle for a Continent, Harlan, Davidson, 1992.
John Adams: A Bibliography, Greenwood Press, 1993.

WORK IN PROGRESS: Adams, Jefferson, and Hamilton: A Comparative Biography.

*   *   *

FERRARO, Barbara 1943-

PERSONAL: Born December 4, 1943, in Boston, MA; daughter of Charles (a comptroller) and Lillian (a homemaker; maiden name, DeGuglielmo) Ferraro. *Education:* Emanuel College, B.A., 1966; Loyola University, M.P.S., 1976; McCormick Theological Seminary, D.Min., 1981. *Politics:* Democrat. *Religion:* Roman Catholic. *Avocational Interests:* Jogging, skiing, and gardening.

ADDRESSES: Office—1109 Quarrier St., Charleston, West Virginia 25301.

CAREER: Entered the Order of the Sisters of Notre Dame de Namur (a Roman Catholic religious order for women) in 1962; took final vows, 1965, left the order, 1988; teacher, parish minister, 1966-81; codirector of Covenant House (a shelter and counseling center for the homeless), Charleston, WV, 1981—.

MEMBER: National Organization for Women (NOW), Catholics for a Free Choice, National Women's Ordination Conference, National Abortion Rights Action League.

AWARDS, HONORS: Margaret Sanger Award, Women's Health Center of West Virginia, 1986; People of Courage Award, Catholics for a Free Choice, 1986; Champion for Choice Award, Catholics for a Free Choice of New York, 1987; Susan B. Anthony Award, National Alliance for Women, 1987, 1988; Prophetic Figure Award, National Women's Ordination Conference, 1987; Religious Freedom Award, National Religious Coalition for Abortion Rights, 1987; Clara Bell Educational Award, Pittsburgh National Abortion Rights Action League, 1988; award from the National Refuse and Resist Organization, 1988; third annual Hero Award, *Mother Jones* magazine, 1989; Women of the Professions Celebrate Women Award, 1989; Citizen of the Year, West Virginia Chapter of National Association of Social Workers, 1990; Book of the Year Award, West Virginia Library Association, 1990, for *No Turning Back;* Jesse Bernard Wise Women award, Center for Women Policy Studies, 1991.

WRITINGS:

The Inside Stories: Thirteen Valiant Women Challenging the Church, edited by Annie Milhaven, Twenty-third Publications, 1987.
(With Patricia Hussey and Jane O'Reilly) *No Turning Back: Two Nuns' Battle with the Vatican over Women's Right to Choose,* Poseidon Press, 1990.

WORK IN PROGRESS: A play based on *No Turning Back.*

SIDELIGHTS: Former nuns Barbara Ferraro and Patricia Hussey collaborated on the book *No Turning Back: Two Nuns' Battle with the Vatican over Women's Right to Choose.* This book, published in 1990, was also written with the assistance of writer Jane O'Reilly. It details the struggle Ferraro and Hussey underwent in the mid-1980s when, as nuns, they spoke out in opposition to the firmly-entrenched position of the Roman Catholic Church on the issue of reproductive freedom. Their story, as told in *No Turning Back,* discusses the changing roles that female members of Catholic religious communities have undergone since the 1960s and is also a bellwether of the overall status of women within the male-dominated ecclesiastical hierarchy.

The authors describe in *No Turning Back* the reasons why they chose to join a religious community, what that life embodied, and why they decided to leave it behind. Ferraro joined the Order of the Sisters of Notre Dame de Namur in 1962, which was a time when nuns lived in strict adherence to the medieval vows of chastity, poverty, and obedience. Ferraro recounts in the book how the nuns of her era lived—their heads shaven under a full habit, forbidden to touch a child, and completely detached from the outside world. Until recently, nuns were confined within convent walls, under tight supervision, and their work in the lay community was limited to teaching school or nursing. However, in the mid-1960s changes occurred within the Catholic church dictated by the Second Vatican Council. Ferraro details how the reforms returned her and the other nuns to the world outside of the convent. They were told to remove their habits and circulate among other people. Using their religious training and conviction, they began developing new ways of bringing the church's message and charity to humanity.

Coauthor Hussey entered the religious community inspired, in part, by the Vatican's new mission. She joined the Sisters of Notre Dame de Namur in 1967, and participated in many of the innovations that the religious orders were then undertaking. Hussey did not wear the "old" habit nor a spiked band on her arm once a week as Ferraro had done, and she had the opportunity to choose how her skills could be best utilized in helping others. The younger sister was interested, like Ferraro, in the area of pastoral ministry—serving the community in ways that had previously only been open to male clergy. The authors met when they were assigned to be apartment-mates while theological students in Chicago in the late 1970s. They later became directors of the Covenant House, a day shelter for the disadvantaged in Charleston, West Virginia. The authors tell how this direct and sometimes difficult work with those who were the victims of society's ills helped shape their strong convictions on reproductive freedom. They worked with young women, some still in their teens, who had been victims of rape and incest. They also counseled women in the poverty-stricken Appalachian community who told them they could not afford to adequately care for another child. Ferraro and Hussey began to question the Church's strict opposition to abortion and birth control.

The impetus behind *No Turning Back* was a full-page advertisement in the *New York Times* in October of 1984. The ad, paid for by a group called the Catholics for a Free Choice, stated that the Catholic church's ban on abortion did not represent the "only legitimate Catholic position" in the United States. The announcement called for an open discussion on the issue of reproductive freedom and patently opposed any legislation "that curtails the legitimate exercise of freedom of religion and conscience or discriminates against poor women." Ferraro and Hussey's names appeared as signees in the ad, along with ninety-five others. Twenty-four of the names were nuns, along with four male clerics. The Vatican began a battle with all of the members of religious orders who had publicly stated their opposition to the church doctrine. As told in *No Turning Back*, it was at this point that the authors began to question their future role in an institution that disallowed women any voice in the formulation of church doctrine nor any dissent at all from its members.

No Turning Back details the four years of meetings, memorandums, and wars of will that Ferraro and Hussey experienced. The governing bodies that oversaw the different orders managed to extract retractions or recantations from all of the nuns except Ferraro and Hussey by 1986. As the authors point out, however, many of the recantations were coerced from nuns who had originally signed a neutral declaration, only to see it published in the Catholic press as a full apology of their original opinion and affirmation of the Church's position. Ferraro and Hussey continued their work at Covenant House, but were continually summoned to meetings with their superiors from the Sisters of Notre Dame and even a papal delegation. The authors detail in *No Turning Back* the isolation they felt within the religious community and the sometimes extreme tactics the ecclesiastical officials would use to try to get them to withdraw their position. The Order of the Sisters of Notre Dame originally supported their right to dissent, but later withdrew and began pressuring the two to recant. The formal process of dismissal began. However, the battle to bring them back into line with Church doctrine helped to solidify their convictions. In July of 1988, Ferraro and Hussey left the religious order that they had joined shortly after their teens and began life as lay people. *No Turning Back,* in addition to chronicling the path that brought the authors to that point, also discusses their adjustment to life outside the religious community.

Ferraro and Hussey's first book received media attention, partly due to the fact that they had already become spokespeople for one side of the divisive controversies sweeping the Catholic church. Eugene Kennedy, writing in the *New York Times Book Review,* praised *No Turning Back* for its multifaceted approach—the biographical and factual chronicle that "absorbs the reader with its central narrative," and its companion "compelling account" of their growth as both religious and lay persons. For more information on Patricia Hussey, see her sketch in this volume.

BIOGRAPHICAL/CRITICAL SOURCES:

PERIODICALS

Commonweal, December 21, 1990, pp. 759-760.
Ms., December, 1988, pp. 64-67.
New York Times, June 12, 1988, sec. 4, p. 28; July 22, 1988, p. A8.
New York Times Book Review, September 23, 1990, p.7.
Publishers Weekly, August 24, 1990.
Washington Post, October 13, 1990, sec. B., p. 7.*

* * *

FEYDY, Anne Lindbergh
See SAPIEYEVSKI, Anne Lindbergh

FIGGIE, Harry E., Jr. 1923-

PERSONAL: Born October 28, 1923, in Lakewood, OH; married; three children. *Education:* Case Institute of Technology (now Case Western Reserve University), B.S., 1947, M.S., 1951; Harvard University, M.B.A., 1949; Cleveland Marshall Law School, LL.B., 1953.

ADDRESSES: Office—Figgie International, Inc., 4420 Sherwin Rd., Willoughby, OH 44094.

CAREER: Employed by Western Automatic Screw Machine Corporation, Parker-Hannifin Corporation, and Booz, Allen, & Hamilton; A. O. Smith Corporation, vice-president for industrial products, 1962-64; Figgie International, Inc. (formerly A-T-O, Inc.), Willoughby, OH, chairman of the board and chief executive officer, 1964—. Director and chairman of Clark Reliance Corporation.

MEMBER: World Business Council.

AWARDS, HONORS: Freedoms Foundation award; Globe of Leadership award from National Association of OTC Companies.

WRITINGS:

The Cost Reduction and Profit Improvement Handbook, Van Nostrand Reinhold, 1983, revised edition published as *The Harry Figgie Guide to Cost Reduction and Profit Improvement,* with foreword by John S. R. Shad, Probus Publishing, 1988.
A Dream Comes True: The Story of Figgie International, Newcomen Society of the United States, 1985.
Cutting Costs: Executive's Guide to Increased Profits, with foreword by John S. R. Shad, AMACOM, 1990.
(With Gerald J. Swanson) *Bankruptcy 1995: The Coming Collapse of America and How to Stop It,* foreword by Warren B. Rudman, Little, Brown, 1992.

SIDELIGHTS: Harry E. Figgie, Jr., is the author of numerous works primarily aimed at an audience of his peers—executives and managers of corporate America. Figgie, who holds a law degree, worked in various capacities for manufacturing firms before founding the Ohio-based company Figgie International in 1964. The business is the holder of numerous smaller subsidiaries that are engaged in the production of various goods, from fire extinguishers to baseballs. The story of this enterprise was authored by Figgie and published under the title *A Dream Comes True: The Story of Figgie International,* a volume that appeared in 1985. This and other works on the subject of maximizing corporate profit received scant critical attention from the mainstream media, but the 1992 tome *Bankruptcy 1995: The Coming Collapse of America and How to Stop It* catapulted the executive to the pages of a major news magazine.

Bankruptcy 1995 was coauthored with Gerald J. Swanson, a professor of economics at the University of Arizona. In the volume, the authors detail the various fiscal policies that they predict will lead the United States economy down a certain path to complete financial ruin. The work discusses the dramatic increase in the national debt, a figure that reflects the government's spending patterns. In the early 1980s the United States was the world's largest creditor nation and the national debt had reached one trillion dollars. However, in little over a decade since that figure has soared to four trillion dollars, placing the United States at the forefront of the world's prevailing debtor nations. Figgie and Swanson evaluate the reasons that have led to this enormous public debt, including extravagant congressional disbursements, lack of leadership in recent presidents, and consumer spending patterns.

To provide an example of where the authors believe the country is heading, *Bankruptcy 1995* sets forth a fictionalized account of a middle-American, middle-class family whose lives are destroyed by the sudden collapse of the national economy. Overnight, both the husband and wife are unemployed and unemployable, their credit lines are rescinded, their bank has gone under, they suddenly can't afford necessities such as food, and their daughter's college closes, rendering even their children permanently useless. Figgie and Swanson construct this dramatic scenario to remind those who can afford to purchase a book just what economic collapse really entails. Their prognostication is echoed in the book's foreword, written by former Republican senator Warren Rudman, who coauthored a significant legislative deficit-reduction plan in the mid-1980s which attempted to put the brakes on government spending. The volume urges citizens to become involved in halting the catastrophe by voicing their opinions to their political leaders. The authors further postulate that a freeze on federal spending will prove beneficial, as will the creation of a committee comprised of captains of industry providing their input on the direction of the economy.

Critical analysis of *Bankruptcy 1995* faulted the author's thesis on several grounds. Stanley W. Cloud, writing on the book and its message in *Time* magazine, asserted that "Figgie overstates the problem—using some highly dubious statistics in the process—and understates the solution." Cloud also took issue with the stable of scapegoats that the book had blamed for the current economic debacle, demonstrating that "the kind of leveraged buyouts with which [Figgie] made his fortune helped push up the *private* debt that also plagues the United States these days." If the collapse that Figgie and Swanson forecast is indeed imminent, Cloud maintains, then their "lame measures are too little and too late to prevent it."

BIOGRAPHICAL/CRITICAL SOURCES:

PERIODICALS

Time, December 28, 1992, p. 29.

*   *   *

FINKE, Ronald A. 1950-

PERSONAL: Born June 10, 1950, in Columbus, OH. *Education:* University of Texas at Austin, B.S., 1972, B.A., 1974; Massachusetts Institute of Technology, Ph.D., 1979. *Avocational Interests:* Cycling, hiking, imaging.

ADDRESSES: Office—Department of Psychology, Texas A&M University, College Station, TX 77843-4235.

CAREER: University of California, Davis, assistant professor of psychology, 1981-83; State University of New York at Stony Brook, assistant professor of psychology, 1983-88; Texas A&M University, College Station, associate professor of psychology, 1988—.

MEMBER: Phi Beta Kappa, Sigma Xi.

AWARDS, HONORS: Fellow of National Science Foundation, Cornell University, 1979, and Sloan Foundation, Stanford University, 1980.

WRITINGS:

Principles of Mental Imagery, MIT Press, 1989.
Creative Imagery: Discoveries and Inventions in Visualization, Lawrence Erlbaum, 1990.
(With T. B. Ward and S. M. Smith) *Creative Cognition: Theory, Research, and Applications,* MIT Press, 1992.
(Editor with S. M. Smith and T. B. Ward) *The Creative Cognition Approach,* MIT Press, 1994.

Work represented in anthologies, including *Sensory Experience, Adaptation, and Perception,* edited by L. Spillmann and W. Wooten, Lawrence Erlbaum, 1984; *Handbook of Perception and Human Performance,* Volume II, edited by K. R. Boff, L. Kaufman, and J. P. Thomas, Wiley, 1986; and *Creativity Research Handbook,* edited by M. A. Runco and M. Stein, Hampton, in press. Contributor of numerous articles and reviews to academic journals and other magazines, including *Scientific American* and *Nature.*

WORK IN PROGRESS: Chaotic Cognition: Principles and Applications, with J. Bettle; *Creative Realism: Magical Ideas and Practical Implications; Mental Imagery and Visual Thinking; A Psychological Study of Imaginary Sciences; The New Creativity,* with T. B. Ward and S. M. Smith; *Chordic Cognition: A Synthesis of Ordered and Chaotic Thinking; The Psychology of Stupidity: Everyday Patterns of Maladaptive Cognition,* with S. M. Smith and

T. B. Ward; *Creative Explorations: Idealisms and Illusions.*

SIDELIGHTS: Ronald A. Finke told *CA:* "My dominant research interest has been the relationship between cognitive and perceptual processes. In my earlier work, I demonstrated that imagery and perception share many of the same kinds of neural mechanisms, and that imagery can influence a variety of perceptual processes, including visual recognition, discrimination, extrapolation, and the coordination of vision and movement. More recently, extensions of this work have clarified the role that imagery plays in creative thinking, and have led to the discovery of new techniques for generating creative concepts and inventions. My colleagues and I have developed a general model of creative cognition, based on these findings, in an attempt to identify the specific types of cognitive processes and structures that give rise to creative ideas and products. This work has practical implications for improving creative thinking and design, and may eventually lead to the development of more creative forms of artificial intelligence."

*   *   *

FISHER, David 1946-
(Ray Lilly)

PERSONAL: Born April 16, 1946, in New York, NY; son of Irving and Sylvia Fisher. *Education:* Syracuse University, B.A., 1968.

ADDRESSES: Agent—Joan Stewart, William Morris Agency, 1350 Avenue of the Americas, New York, NY 10019.

CAREER: Free-lance writer and ghostwriter. *Life,* New York City, staff writer-reporter, 1970-72. Comedy writer for Joan Rivers and others.

WRITINGS:

COLLABORATIONS

(With "Joey") *Joey Collects,* Ace Books, 1980.
(With Reginald Bragonier, Jr.) *What's What: A Visual Glossary of the Physical World,* Hammond, 1982.
(With Bragonier) *What's What in Sports: The Visual Glossary of the Sports World,* Hammond, 1984.
(With Ron Luciano) *The Umpire Strikes Back,* Bantam, 1984.
(With Luciano) *Strike Two,* G. K. Hall, 1984.
(With Tommy Lasorda) *The Artful Dodger,* Arbor House, 1985.
(With Luciano) *The Fall of the Roman Umpire,* Bantam, 1986.
(With Gene Klein) *First Down and a Billion: The Funny Business of Pro Football,* Morrow, 1987.

(With Luciano) *Remembrance of Swings Past,* Bantam, 1988.

(With Anthony Read) *The Deadly Embrace: Hitler, Stalin, and the Nazi-Soviet Pact, 1939-1941,* Norton, 1988.

(With Read) *Kristallnacht: Unleashing the Holocaust,* Viking, 1989.

(With George Burns) *All My Best Friends,* Putnam, 1989.

(With Sparky Lyle) *The Year I Owned the Yankees: A Baseball Fantasy,* Bantam, 1990.

(With Patty Brown) *The Book of Memories,* edited by Elizabeth Davis, Perigee, 1990.

(With John Boswell) *Fenway Park: Legendary Home of the Boston Red Sox,* Little, Brown, 1992.

(With Read) *The Fall of Berlin,* Norton, 1993.

Also coauthor of other works, including (with "Joey") *The Happy Hitman;* (with Jhan Robbins) *Tranquility without Pills,* 1972; (with Robbins) *How to Make and Break Habits,* 1973; (with "Joey") *Killer,* 1973; (with "Joey") *Hit Number Twenty-nine,* 1974; (with Jack Clouser) *The Most Wanted Man in America,* 1974; (with Cecile Mileto) *Louie's Widow,* 1975; (with Read) *Colonel Z: The Life and Times of a Master of Spies,* 1984; (with Burns) *Gracie: A Love Story,* 1988; and (with Luciano) *Baseball Lite,* 1989.

NOVELS

The War Magician, Coward-McCann, 1983.

Also author of *The Pack,* 1976; author of a novel under the pseudonym Ray Lilly.

NONFICTION

Operation Lucy: Most Secret Spy Ring of the Second World War, Coward, 1981.

Morality and the Bomb: An Ethical Assessment of Nuclear Deterrence, St. Martin's, 1985.

Across the Top of the World: To the North Pole by Sled, Balloon, Airplane, and Nuclear Icebreaker, Random House, 1992.

Also author of *The Incredible Scooter Cops,* 1974; *Rules of Thumb for Engineers and Scientists,* revised edition, 1991; and *The H. R. Factor,* 1992.

OTHER

Ghostwriter of numerous works, including a biography of Malcolm X for children.

SIDELIGHTS: David Fisher has had a long and prolific career as a free-lance writer about diverse topics: he has written or ghostwritten more than thirty books on baseball, politics, and true crime. Frequently, he has collaborated with personalities from sports, show business, or the underworld to write insider accounts of worlds that many

people are fascinated by but that few have direct access to for themselves. Reviewers have praised Fisher's work for its colorful and pithy bird's-eye views.

The Umpire Strikes Back, for example, cowritten with umpire and sports commentator Ron Luciano, was lauded by *Chicago Tribune Book World* reviewer Clarence Peterson as a "delightful account of the baseball world as it looks from behind the plate." Another baseball tale, *The Year I Owned the Yankees: A Baseball Fantasy,* was written with Sparky Lyle, a former New York Yankees relief pitcher who fantasized about spending a year as owner of the team. Writing in the *New York Times Book Review,* Michael Caruso called the book "engaging and unpredictable" with "some hilarious moments, many involving a rather Nixonian [former Yankee owner] George Steinbrenner, who is obsessed with sneaking into Yankee Stadium to get his old job back."

Although Fisher has written some works by himself, notably three novels, he has focused most of his career on collaborating with others. Fisher told *Los Angeles Times* writer Richard Sandomir that as a child, he had dreams other than ghostwriting and collaborating: he wanted to write a syndicated humor column and a Broadway play. For a time, he was a comedy writer for Joan Rivers, then a staff reporter for *Life* magazine. Soon, however, he was ghostwriting a children's biography of Malcolm X for his agent, as well as a novel that appeared under the pseudonym Ray Lilly.

Fisher's first entry into the kind of collaboration that was to make his career, however, was *The Happy Hitman,* a book he wrote with a man pseudonymously identified as "Joey." Joey worked for the Mafia and provided Fisher with an inside view of organized crime. Fisher went on to collaborate with even more famous figures, including San Diego Chargers owner Gene Klein, actor and comedian George Burns, and former umpire Luciano.

The people who have worked with Fisher praise his ability to help them tell their stories and explore the worlds they know. "He took my character, molded and polished me a little," Luciano told Sandomir. "He really created me." Lyle credits Fisher with helping him develop the fantasy of owning the Yankees for a year: "I'd never met David before and never thought about owning the Yankees," Lyle told Sandomir. "But he came to the house, we made a bunch of tapes, and he understood me. He asked what would happen here or what would happen there. We let our imagination go. Then he went to work."

Fisher himself told Sandomir that he enjoys finding the distinctive voice of each of his collaborators. But, he adds, he is always aware that the real star of the book is not him but his collaborator. In fact, if he does his job right, he won't even be noticed. "Collaborating is a job. It's how I earn my living. There's no great satisfaction to it. But there are great opportunities. I've gotten to be so many people."

BIOGRAPHICAL/CRITICAL SOURCES:

PERIODICALS

Chicago Tribune, December 4, 1989.
Chicago Tribune Book World, April 25, 1982, section 2, p. 7.
Los Angeles Times, May 11, 1990.
Los Angeles Times Book Review, May 12, 1986, p. 14.
New York Times Book Review, August 3, 1986, p. 16; April 26, 1987, p. 12; April 1, 1990, p. 11.

*   *   *

FLEETWOOD, Mick 1947-

PERSONAL: Born June 24, 1947, in Cornwall, England; married Jenny Boyd (divorced); married Sara Recor, April 24, 1988; children: (first marriage) Lucy, Amy.

ADDRESSES: Office—c/o Warner Bros. Records, 3300 Warner Blvd., Burbank, CA 91505.

CAREER: Rock musician. Drummer with John Mayall, 1967, and with Fleetwood Mac, 1967—; contributor to Fleetwood Mac recordings, including *Bare Trees,* 1975, *Fleetwood Mac,* 1976, *Rumours,* 1977, *Tusk,* 1979, *Mirage,* 1982, *Tango in the Night,* 1987, and *Behind the Mask,* 1990; released solo recording, *The Visitor.* Appeared in motion picture *The Running Man,* 1987. Opened supper club, Fleetwood's, Los Angeles, CA, 1991.

WRITINGS:

WITH STEPHEN DAVIS

Fleetwood: My Life and Adventures in Fleetwood Mac, Morrow, 1990.
My Twenty-Five Years in Fleetwood Mac (sound recording and text), discography by Frank Harding, Hyperion, 1991.

SIDELIGHTS: Mick Fleetwood, leader and partial namesake of Fleetwood Mac, one of rock music's most long-lived, successful, and tumultuous bands, set down his memories in the 1990 autobiography co-written with Stephen Davis, *Fleetwood: My Life and Adventures in Fleetwood Mac.* Reviewer Robert Waddell, writing in the *New York Times Book Review,* called the book "slapdash" and the life recorded in it "cliched," but *Chicago Tribune* reviewer Lynn Van Matre and interviewer Greg Kot found considerably more appeal in both the book and the man. Van Matre called *Fleetwood: My Life and Adventures in Fleetwood Mac* an "engaging, better-than-average rock

autobiography," while Kot wrote, "it only seems like the usual rock-star tale," admiring it instead as "a tale about persistence." Kot also praised the depictions of the recording-studio work behind *Rumours,* the second-highest-selling pop album of all time with more than 20 million copies sold.

Fleetwood proclaims in his autobiography that "I'm going to be an eighty-year-old rocker, and they'll have to take me out and shoot me to get me to stop." This sentiment derives from the fact that Fleetwood still loves his work despite the many pitfalls that have beset him and his band since their inception. The band Fleetwood Mac was actually founded by its talented lead guitarist, Peter Green, a publicity-shy man who named the group after his drummer (Fleetwood) and bassist (John McVie). After leading Fleetwood Mac to success in Britain, Green left the band suddenly in 1969, taking menial jobs as the years went by and sinking, in Kot's words, into "various stages of mental despair." Two other guitarists in the band also underwent abrupt personality shifts, one succumbing to emotional problems and one leaving the band to join a religious cult. Beset by these personnel difficulties, the band's fortunes faded for a time, but Fleetwood, accompanied by John McVie and his wife Christine, carried on.

In 1976, as the remnants of the group prepared to record a new album, they discovered, through a fluke, an aspiring Los Angeles duo, female singer-songwriter Stevie Nicks and male guitarist-singer-songwriter Lindsey Buckingham. The new members immediately transformed the group's sound, through Buckingham's prodigious flair for a "hook" in his song writing and his guitar solos, and through the new richness that the combination of Nicks and Christine McVie gave the vocals. The result, the best-selling album *Fleetwood Mac,* was a major comeback, and the follow-up a year later, *Rumours,* was an even bigger hit.

Money began pouring in, and with it, the excesses of the rock life. Group members began taking cocaine regularly, and at the same time, they were beset by rifts in their personal relationships. Buckingham and Nicks, who had been romantically involved, broke up, and Nicks and Fleetwood became secretly involved. The McVies divorced amid tremendous acrimony. In another round of changes, a decade later, Buckingham quit the group to launch a solo career despite his colleagues' pleas for him to stay. Fleetwood, the grand old man and leader of the group, hired two new guitarists, Billy Burnette and Rick Vito. A successful tour followed. Then, after the group's 1990 album, *Behind the Mask,* Nicks and Christine McVie—the former of whom had established a particularly successful solo career—announced that they would no longer tour with the band, though they would still record with it. Further changes seemed inevitable, Fleetwood told

Kot, because of the impracticality of singers' recording for a group without going on tour. But, as Fleetwood said at the end of his *Tribune* interview, the departure of certain band members will in no way signal the end for Fleetwood Mac. "This is the last hurrah for this stage of the band," Fleetwood told Kot, "but we'll carry on."

BIOGRAPHICAL/CRITICAL SOURCES:

PERIODICALS

Chicago Tribune, October 8, 1990; October 17, 1990.
Los Angeles Times, November 26, 1986, sec. VI, p. 1.
New York Times Book Review, November 18, 1990, p. 22.*

* * *

FOWLER, Karen Joy 1950-

PERSONAL: Born February 7, 1950, in Bloomington, IN; daughter of Cletus and Joy Arthur (Fossum) Burke; married Hugh Fowler, 1972; children: Ryan, Shannon. *Education:* Attended University of California, Berkeley, 1968-70, B.A., 1972; attended State University of New York, 1970-71; University of California, Davis, M.A., 1974.

ADDRESSES: Agent—Wendy Weil, Wendy Weil Agency, 747 Third Ave., New York, NY 10017.

CAREER: Novelist and short story writer. Cleveland State University, Cleveland, OH, writer in residence, 1990—.

AWARDS, HONORS: John W. Campbell Memorial Award (Hugo Award) for best new writer, World Science Fiction Society, 1987; received grant from the National Endowment for the Arts, 1988; Commonwealth Club Medal, 1991, for *Sarah Canary.*

WRITINGS:

Artificial Things (anthology), Bantam, 1986.
Peripheral Vision (anthology), Pulphouse, 1990.
Sarah Canary (novel), Holt, 1991.

Work represented in periodicals, including *Pulphouse.*

WORK IN PROGRESS: A novel set in northern Michigan just after World War II.

SIDELIGHTS: Winner of a 1987 Hugo Award for best new writer, Karen Joy Fowler is the author of two short-story collections and a novel that use fantastical characters and situations to bring to light various aspects of human nature. Her work has been well received by critics, many of whom have expressed a desire to read more of Fowler's writing, mostly classified as science fiction.

In her first anthology, *Artificial Things,* Fowler compiled thirteen short stories, many of which had appeared previ-

ously in periodicals. Applauding the stories as worthy "examples of both literary form and style," *Voice of Youth Advocates*'s Allison Rogers Hutchison especially recommended the work to writing students. The critic also praised Fowler's skillful use of fantastic plotlines and characters to show the human world in a different light. Fowler accomplishes this by presenting humans through the eyes of her alien characters. For instance, in one story, insectile aliens probe the mind of a poet, while in another, humans in the far future study replicants who re-enact historical events. Karen S. Ellis noted in *Kliatt* that although many of the stories in *Artificial Things* were abstract, the "study of human nature" was an important theme in Fowler's work.

In 1990 Fowler issued her second collection of short stories. Titled *Peripheral Vision,* the volume garnered further praise for Fowler as an emerging writer. Reviewing the work in the *Washington Post Book World,* Gregory Feeley lauded Fowler as a "writer of clarity and humor." In particular, the reviewer cited "The Faithful Companion at Forty" and "Contention" as examples of Fowler's interest in writing modern stories which, he felt, retained the element of fantasy "without shifting their centers of gravity." This sense of fantasy also pervades Fowler's novel, *Sarah Canary,* an account of the adventures of a mysterious woman called Sarah Canary and a Chinese immigrant laborer named Chin.

The book begins when Sarah—who has been variously described by critics as a mysterious wild creature and an enigmatic woman who speaks in grunts and strange sounds—is entrusted in Chin's care after she wanders into his labor camp. Chin is asked to take Sarah to an asylum, but before he can accomplish this task, he is jailed. Separated from Sarah, the imprisoned Chin vows to free her, marking the beginning of their adventures together. Accompanying them on their journey are B. J., an escapee from a mental institution, and Adelaide Dixon, a free-thinking lecturer. The narrative follows the characters through a bizarre series of events until they reach San Francisco, where Chin escapes to China and eventually becomes a government bureaucrat. Sarah, on the other hand, vanishes without a trace or explanation.

The plot of *Sarah Canary* is loosely structured and has lent itself to numerous interpretations. Barbara Quick, writing in the *New York Times Book Review,* said that the story presents a "dreamscape" through which Fowler reveals a "tableau of the Pacific Northwest in the 1870s." And *Los Angeles Times Book Review*'s Richard Eder described *Sarah Canary* as "part ghost story, part picaresque adventure," an unusual narrative style that has allowed Fowler to present an ironic and painful vision of late-nineteenth century America. Explaining that the main characters of the book are representative of the victims of that age, Eder drew parallels between events in history and the action of the story. For example, he believes the character of Chin evokes the large number of Chinese immigrants who worked on building American railroads, while the female characters reveal the plight of women at the time. Another reviewer, Michael Dorris, wrote in Chicago *Tribune Books* that *Sarah Canary* is a "full-tilt allegory, an uncompromising work of imagination that asks its readers to not merely suspend disbelief but to surrender it." Describing the landscape of the book as mythic, Dorris called Sarah "a cipher, an embodiment of each individual's deeply buried need for mystery in life." And Quick says in her final assessment that *Sarah Canary* "is an extraordinarily strong first novel" that "whets the appetite for what . . . [Fowler] will serve up next."

BIOGRAPHICAL/CRITICAL SOURCES:

BOOKS

Fowler, Karen Joy, *Sarah Canary*, Holt, 1991.

PERIODICALS

Kliatt, April, 1987, pp. 29-30.
Los Angeles Times Book Review, October 20, 1991, pp. 3, 7.
New York Times Book Review, November 10, 1991. p. 18.
Tribune Books (Chicago), December 15, 1991, section 14, pp. 1, 9.
Voice of Youth Advocates, June, 1987, pp. 89-90.
Washington Post Book World, April 29, 1990, p. 8.

*   *   *

FOWLKES, Diane L(owe)   1939-

PERSONAL: Born October 30, 1939, in Memphis, TN; daughter of Erskine Havis (an electronics technician) and Brenda (a homemaker; maiden name, Bisplinghoff) Lowe; married Edward Oliver Fowlkes III, August 12, 1962 (marriage ended, February, 1969); married Lawrence Everman Noble, Jr. (a professor), February 17, 1973. *Education:* Southwestern at Memphis (now Rhodes College), B.A., 1961; Georgia State University, M.A., 1971; Emory University, Ph.D., 1974. *Politics:* Democrat. *Religion:* "Ancient Earth Goddess." *Avocational Interests:* Reading, hiking, exercise and health, movies, horse racing.

ADDRESSES: Home—Atlanta, GA. *Office*—Department of Political Science, Georgia State University, Atlanta, GA 30303.

CAREER: Georgia State University, Atlanta, assistant professor, 1973-80, associate professor, 1980-92, professor of political science, 1992—, director of women's studies program, 1992—. Worked as a secretary, 1961-70. Diable

Stable, Ltd. (breeders and racers of thoroughbred horses), president. Women's Policy Group/Women's Policy Education Fund, vice-president, 1992—.

MEMBER: American Political Science Association, National Women's Studies Association, Women's Caucus for Political Science, Southeastern Women's Studies Association.

AWARDS, HONORS: Woodrow Wilson fellow, 1971-72; grant from Women's Educational Equity Act Program, 1979-82; senior Fulbright scholar at Open University, Milton Keynes, England, 1985-86.

WRITINGS:

How Feminist Theory Reconstructs American Government and Politics (monograph), American Political Science Association, 1983.
(Coeditor) *Feminist Visions: Toward a Transformation of the Liberal Arts Curriculum*, University of Alabama Press, 1984.
White Political Women: Paths From Privilege to Empowerment, University of Tennessee Press, 1992.

Work represented in books, including *Party Politics in the South*, edited by Robert Steed, Laurence Moreland, and Tod Baker, Praeger, 1980; *Political Women: Current Roles in State and Local Government*, edited by Janet A. Flammang, Sage Publications, 1984; and *Feminism and Epistemology: Approaches to Research in Women and Politics*, edited by Maria J. Falco, Haworth, 1987. Writer for the television series *Democratic Government and Politics*, British Broadcasting Corp., 1987. Contributor to political science, social science, and women's studies journals.

WORK IN PROGRESS: Building Bridges Through Feminist Politics of Identity.

SIDELIGHTS: Diane L. Fowlkes told *CA:* "I was politicized during the sixties by the civil rights and black power movements, and by the split with my parents as they moved 'right' and I moved 'left.' I returned to school to study political science and to gain a more formal understanding of what had been happening in my life. It was not until I began to work in women's studies that I began to gain more insight into the dynamics of 'the personal is political,' the intersection of women's movements with civil rights and black power movements, and the distance we still have to travel on uncleared trails to reach, in fact to create, an egalitarian polity. My current explorations in identity politics among feminists are attempts to learn about bridge-building across socially constructed hierarchical differences."

FOX, Samuel 1905-1993

OBITUARY NOTICE—See index for *CA* sketch: Born March 18, 1905, in Chicago, IL; died December 23, 1993, in Chicago, IL. Attorney, accountant, educator, and author. Fox began his lengthy career in law and accounting in 1928, working as an attorney in Chicago. More than ten years later, he obtained a position as a budget accountant with the U.S. Rubber Company in Indiana. In 1943 Fox started a three year stint as a regional enforcement attorney for the U.S. Office of Price Administration. Following this experience, the author began educating students at the University of Illinois at Chicago Circle, earning the Silver Circle Teacher of the Year Award in 1972. One year later, he moved to Roosevelt University where he became a professor of accountancy—a position he held until 1985. Throughout his life, Fox lectured and wrote books on law and accounting topics, including *Law of Decendents Estates, Workbook on Managerial Law,* and *Principles of International Accounting.* Fox was also a sports columnist for the *Park Ridge Herald* and a drama critic for *Des Plaines Suburban Times* from 1946 to 1966.

OBITUARIES AND OTHER SOURCES:

BOOKS

Who's Who in America, 47th edition, Marquis, 1992.

PERIODICALS

Chicago Tribune, January 11, 1994, p. 6.

*   *   *

FRAME, Ronald (William Sutherland) 1953-

PERSONAL: Born May 23, 1953, in Glasgow, Scotland; son of Alexander (an advertising agent) and Subel D. (Sutherland) Frame. *Education:* University of Glasgow, M.A., 1975; Jesus College, Oxford, B.Litt., 1979.

ADDRESSES: Office—c/o Hodder Headline, 338 Euston Rd., London NW1 3BH, England. *Agent*—Michael Shaw, Curtis Brown Ltd., 162-8 Regent St., London W1R 5TB, England.

CAREER: Writer, 1981—.

AWARDS, HONORS: Betty Trask Award for first novel, Society of Authors, 1984, for *Winter Journey;* Television Industries Award and Samuel Beckett Prize, both 1986, both for *Paris: A Television Play;* Scottish Arts Council Spring Book Award, 1987, for *A Long Weekend with Marcel Proust.*

WRITINGS:

FICTION

Winter Journey (novel), Beaufort, 1984.

Watching Mrs. Gordon and Other Stories (short stories), Bodley Head, 1985.
A Long Weekend with Marcel Proust: Seven Stories and a Novel, Bodley Head, 1986.
Sandmouth People (novel), Bodley Head, 1987, published in the United States as *Sandmouth,* Knopf, 1988.
A Woman of Judah: A Novel and Fifteen Stories, Bodley Head, 1987, Norton, 1989.
Penelope's Hat (novel), Simon & Schuster, 1989.
Bluette (novel), Hodder & Stoughton, 1990.
Underwood and After (novel), Hodder & Stoughton, 1991.
Walking My Mistress in Deauville, Hodder & Stoughton, 1992.
The Sun on the Wall, Hodder & Stoughton, 1994.

Contributor to short story anthologies, including *Seven Deadly Sins,* Severn, 1985; *Winter's Tales 3,* edited by Robin Baird-Smith, St. Martin's, 1987; *20 under 35,* edited by Peter Straus, Sceptre, 1988; *Scottish Short Stories,* HarperCollins, 1993; *Best Short Stories,* Heinemann, 1993; and *Telling Stories 2,* Hodder & Stoughton, 1993.

RADIO PLAYS

Winter Journey (adapted from novel by Frame), BBC Radio 4, 1985.
Twister, BBC Radio 4, 1986.
Rendezvous, BBC Radio 4, 1987.
Cara, BBC Radio 3, 1988.
Marina Bray, BBC Radio 3, 1989.
A Woman of Judah (adapted from novel by Frame), BBC Radio 4, 1993.

TELEVISION PLAYS

Paris: A Television Play; with Privateers, broadcast on BBC-1 Television, published by Faber, 1987.
Out of Time, Channel 4, 1987.
Ghost City, BBC Television, 1994.

WORK IN PROGRESS: A novel, tentatively titled *The Old Verities;* an adaptation of *A Long Weekend with Marcel Proust* for BBC Radio; two novellas, *The Lantern-Bearers* and *The Misses Hemington.*

SIDELIGHTS: Scottish writer Ronald Frame chronicles the dysfunctional side of postwar middle-class Britain in his works of fiction. Many characters in his novels and short stories are troubled by certain facets of their past and wrestle to keep parts of it concealed, while other characters strive to decipher the motivations behind the behavior of those around them. In his body of work, Frame relies heavily on eliciting a period mood to set the tone. Critics have often commented favorably on the author's talent in evoking the era of postwar Britain, a country ravaged by the long war years and unsettled by the resulting changes in national identity. Frame had penned numerous short stories, some of which he also adapted into radio and television plays, before writing his first novel, *Winter Journey.*

Winter Journey is an acclaimed work of fiction that won the Betty Trask Award in 1984, an honor bestowed upon an inaugural novel by a writer under the age of thirty-five. The novel's plot blends the melodrama of an unhappy family with political intrigue and is told in flashback from a child's point of view. The narrator, Annoele Tomlinson, is the offspring of a chic but duplicitous mother, Laura, and Simon, an equally-devious diplomat father. In recollections about her family, Annoele remembers little of Simon, forever overseas on assignment, but revels in the details of her mother's spoiled and tempestuous persona. She is entranced by Laura's glamorous clothes and lifestyle, yet as a mother she remains to Annoele as distant as the girl's faraway father.

The journey of the title takes place as the ten-year-old Annoele and Laura travel to Prague to visit Simon, who has been posted there. The three motor through Europe during the holiday season and the acrimonious marriage between Annoele's parents reaches a crisis point as they kick up rancorous scenes that result in evictions from various hostelries. Critics have noted how this chain of events mirrors the biblical flight of the Holy Family, and it culminates in an automobile accident resulting in the death of one parent. The ensuing investigation into Simon's career reveals a dark secret about his postwar diplomatic activities. Annoele's search into the mystery behind her parents' disastrous lives forms the basis for the novel's structure. *Winter Journey* was well-received by critics. A review of the work in the *New Yorker* asserted that Frame's novel "requires and rewards close attention." Christopher Hawtree of the *Times Literary Supplement* described the slim volume as "a decidedly individual creation, and makes one impatient for something on a larger scale."

A collection of Frame's short stories was the follow-up to his celebrated first novel. The collection, entitled *Watching Mrs. Gordon and Other Stories,* appeared in 1985. Like many of Frame's other works, the selections in *Watching Mrs. Gordon* take place in the milieu of a rigid British middle class and involve a cast of characters who have paid a dear price in order to maintain the appearance of a civilized life. Many of the stories revolve around themes of deception and hidden identities, and the true nature of the characters is often revealed by an unusual secret that looms somewhere within the structure of each plot. In the title work, an older man is locked into a marriage with a younger beauty with a concealed past. Another piece unfolds as a woman nervously anticipates a biography of her deceased husband, a noted archaeologist. The volume, entitled *Feet of Clay,* will expose his long-hidden homosexuality. *Times Literary Supplement* critic Gerald Mangan faulted the dismal ambiance of the stories, but granted

that Frame "draws some cool moments of comedy from them."

Another collection of Frame's fiction appeared the following year under the title *A Long Weekend with Marcel Proust: Seven Stories and a Novel.* The shorter works, which lead the reader to the novella at the end, are reminiscent in some ways of the nineteenth-century French writer immortalized in its title. They rely on the minutiae of surfaces and objects, and time and place, to set the tone for the drama behind the characters' seemingly placid lives. In "The Lunch Table," two affluent married women, nearing middle-age, meet regularly to fondly reminisce about their youth, refusing to discuss anything that might give away a hint of dissatisfaction about their present lives. Another work, "The Blue Jug," portrays a now-aged femme fatale, former muse of a celebrated artist, as she looks back on her life through the visual incantations of his paintings. The final piece, "Prelude and Fugue," is set in wartime London and told from multiple viewpoints of several narrators. Its protagonist is Helen Wilmot, a young girl traumatized by both her earlier childhood and the ongoing Blitzkrieg. The story is unusually structured with Helen's discourse in one column of text and those of other voices running parallel on the same page. As the aerial bombardment reaches a crescendo, Helen thinks back to her odd relationship with her father and the treatment suffered in the care of a sadistic nanny. Helen strives to maintain a sense of self, but begins to think she may have already been killed, and that those around her are also the walking dead.

In reviewing *A Long Weekend with Marcel Proust,* Valentine Cunningham of the *Observer,* although commending the prose in "The Blue Jug" as "finely tactile writing," summarized the volume's end effect as "marginalia [that] reads as over-contrived and coldly mannered." In a critique of the work for the *New Statesman,* however, Michelene Wandor asserted that "Frame is a writer who relies on care, logic and distance, creating unsettling patterns with aplomb." Mark Casserley of the *Times Literary Supplement* proclaimed that "Frame's prose is astringent, careful and clear," and lauded the effect of "Prelude and Fugue." The depiction of the heroine's distress in the novella, Casserley remarked, is "a powerful testimony to Frame's psychological depth, his awareness of interpersonal tensions, and the special dimension of the continued everyday existence within which his protagonist strives to remain."

Frame returned to the format of the full-length novel with the 1987 publication of *Sandmouth People,* which appeared in the United States under the shortened title *Sandmouth* the following year. The work takes place on St. George's Day in April, 1953, in the seaside town of Sandmouth, England. Like many of Frame's previous works, its multitudinous cast of characters lead corrupt lives, each driven by a shameful past or a duplicitous present. In their diversity they represent the nuanced class levels of postwar British society: bank clerks, aristocrats, and artists remain on equally decadent footing in the vacation resort. Through the characters and their actions *Sandmouth* provides a detailed frozen-in-time snapshot of one day of this era, depicting the nation's changing moral standards, newly-formed class structure, and stultifying reliance on ritual and custom to somehow hold it all together.

The work, although essentially devoid of a formal plot, begins and ends with an excerpt from a detective novel that sets the stage for the unsolved death of Sandmouth's resident madwoman, Tilly. The mute daughter of a wealthy family, her presence at every stage of the narrative is her downfall when she is witness to one of the many depraved escapades that take place during the course of the day. *Sandmouth* garnered mixed reviews. Stevenson Swanson, critiquing the volume for *Tribune Books,* maintained that "it is difficult to work up much concern for any of the characters," and further noted that the absence of plot "also keeps the reader at a distance." *Times Literary Supplement* critic Cunningham faulted the novel for relying too heavily on the sins of the flesh as motivation for its characters. The reviewer remarked that "for all its mass of occasional delights . . . *Sandmouth People* disappoints." London *Times* critic Stuart Evans, on the other hand, praised Frame's treacherous characters, remarking that the author "is adept at creating monsters," and complimented the final sum of its parts as "inventive throughout its considerable length."

Frame's ensuing volume was 1987's *A Woman of Judah: A Novel and Fifteen Stories.* The smaller works contained within it are typical of the author's previous short stories, their characters locked in a civilized world of skeletons and sexual deceit. In "Rendezvous," an adulterous affair continues for over two decades, shadowed by the unasked question of whether or not the woman had aborted a pregnancy years earlier. In the title work, an aged judge recalls for the narrator his sojourn in a small English town in the 1930s. The locale's most intriguing character was the doctor's wife, with whom the young lawyer became infatuated. Although the townspeople were themselves no paragons of virtue, the attractive and enigmatic woman became the focus of their righteous venom. Anthony Sattin of the *Times Literary Supplement* lauded the characters of Frame's volume as "well conceived," and stated that as an author "one of his greatest strengths is the use of significant detail to create atmosphere and character."

Penelope's Hat is the title of another full-length work of fiction by Frame. In the 1989 novel he again utilizes a story-within-a-story structure, relating the reminiscences of acclaimed writer Penelope Milne in autobiographical

form. The hat of the title is a metaphoric reference to the phases of Penelope's life, as she donned distinctive headgear to both signify her current state as well as to safeguard against her notoriety. The aging writer recalls the events in her past and the manner through which she transformed them into her fiction. She recounts the saga of her deceptive husband, who is thought to have perished in an automobile accident after six years of marriage. Penelope later discovers that she had been instead married to a man who had successfully duped her with a fictional persona. He reappears at various points in the course of her life, and the reader is left wondering which of her recollections are true and which exist only in Penelope's imagination.

In a review of *Penelope's Hat* for the *New York Times Book Review,* critic Linda Barrett Osborne asserted that Frame "writes with a quiet intelligence, grace of language and eye for manners." *Times Literary Supplement* writer Patricia Craig commended the author's descriptive powers, remarking that "all the different eras of Penelope's life are evoked with conviction." Yet Craig also questioned the scope of the novel, musing that "we can't help feeling that it might have benefited from being quite ruthlessly compressed." Rita Kashner of *Tribune Books* wrote that the novel "begins promisingly," but its "relentless unrolling of tales . . . and the rather flat, thematic characters who people them" prevent the reader from becoming engaged. Kashner suggested that perhaps the volume would have been better constructed as a series of shorter works, noting that "Frame's real strength is as a writer of short fiction."

Bluette, a 1990 novel, evoked comparisons with *Penelope's Hat* from critics. Both share an indefatigable heroine who moves through the fast-paced and gilded chapters of her life yet remains an enigma. Frame again places *Bluette*'s protagonist, Catherine Hammond, in a postwar British milieu of questionable morals and sometimes-degenerate sexuality. Catherine flits through the rarefied circles of fashion magazines, 1950s London nightlife, and the show-business enchantment of Hollywood. Her arduous journeys across continents and through the decades is driven by the search for the father of her illegitimate child. Frame again fills in the elements of his characters' lives with descriptive detail of expensive apparel and posh interiors. Hawtree of the *Times Literary Supplement* described *Bluette* as "fantasy gone mad," condemning it as "a perplexing, sad development in a writer who began with some rewarding stories." London *Times* reviewer Sally Edworthy remarked that although the reader "is left admiring the inexhaustible display of crisp phrases," the presentation of the protagonist was less than ideal. "Catherine," the critic wrote, "is kept at a remove, on display as it were, behind the glass of distancing, deflecting prose." Other reviewers found Frame's experimental approach more rewarding. Trevor Royle, in an essay about Frame's work for *Contemporary Novelists,* praised *Bluette* as "vast, sprawling, and eclectic," and a work "that marks Frame as one of the most innovative writers of his generation."

In *Underwood and After,* a novel that appeared in 1991, Frame again reconstructs a saga around the reminiscences of a bewildered narrative voice. In this work the middle-aged Ralph recollects the charmed life he led as a youth when he became a chauffeur for a wealthy and well-connected man. Ralph was mystified by the source of Mr. Chetwynd's riches and for years afterward remained intrigued by the memories of the dissipated yet glamorous characters that comprised his boss's social set. His recollections are renewed by the appearance of a daughter of one of the circle's now-deceased denizens, a young woman who has sought Ralph out to provide him with her mother's diaries. The memoirs help to reconstruct some of the strange events of the time and the motivations behind their instigators. Candace Rodd of the *Times Literary Supplement* described the work as "a bizarre blend of period melodrama and postmodernist flourish, the point of which, concealed in serpentine coils of plot and gnomic authorial speculation, remains resolutely knotted."

BIOGRAPHICAL/CRITICAL SOURCES:

BOOKS

Contemporary Novelists, St. James Press, 1991.

PERIODICALS

Books & Bookmen, July, 1985, p. 35.
Library Journal, April 1, 1986, p. 160.
New Statesman, November 21, 1986, pp. 28-29.
New York Times Book Review, October 13, 1991, p. 22.
New Yorker, July 14, 1986, p. 83.
Observer, June 9, 1985, p. 24; December 14, 1986, p. 23.
Publishers Weekly, January 17, 1986, p. 61; April 7, 1989, p. 125.
Times Literary Supplement, September 21, 1984, p. 1065; July 5, 1985, p. 747; July 26, 1985; October 17, 1986, p. 1169; May 15, 1987, p. 515; December 11, 1987, p. 1374; August 11, 1989, p. 878; July 6, 1990, p. 731; August 2, 1991, p. 18.
Times (London), September 4, 1986; April 2, 1987; July 5, 1990.
Tribune Books (Chicago), February 21, 1988, p. 7; October 20, 1991, pp. 8, 10.

—*Sketch by Carol Brennan*

FRANTZ, Joe B. 1917-1993

OBITUARY NOTICE—See index for *CA* sketch: Born January 16, 1917, in Dallas, TX; died of complications from diabetes, November 13, 1993, in Houston, TX. Historian and author. Frantz was a scholar of American West history, educating and writing about this topic throughout his life. He devoted more than thirty-five years to teaching at the University of Texas at Austin where he served in many roles, including Walter Prescott Webb Professor Emeritus of History from 1977 to 1985. He was commended for his excellence in teaching when he was chosen for the Lemuel Scarborough Award. In conjunction with his work on the University of Texas's Oral History Project on President Lyndon B. Johnson, Frantz worked as a White House history consultant from 1968 to 1969, during which time he collected information about the life and accomplishments of Johnson. Frantz received the Carr P. Collins Award for his book *Gail Borden: Dairyman to a Nation.* His other works include *The Forty-Acre Follies,* and with M. Cox, *Lure of the Land: Texas County Maps and the History of Settlement.*

OBITUARIES AND OTHER SOURCES:

BOOKS

Writers Directory: 1992-1994, St. James Press, 1991.

PERIODICALS

Chicago Tribune, November 21, 1993, p. 10.

*   *   *

FREYER, Tony (Allan) 1947-

PERSONAL: Born December 28, 1947, in Indianapolis, IN; married; children: one. *Education:* San Diego State University, A.B. (with honors), 1970; Indiana University—Bloomington, M.A., 1972, Ph.D., 1975.

ADDRESSES: Home—3850 Derby Downs Dr., Tuscaloosa, AL 35405. *Office*—School of Law, University of Alabama, Box 870382, Tuscaloosa, AL 35487-0382.

CAREER: Indiana University—Bloomington, lecturer in law, 1974-75, Bicentennial of the Constitution Lecturer, 1984; University of Arkansas at Little Rock, assistant professor, 1976-80, associate professor of history, 1980-81; University of Alabama, Tuscaloosa, associate professor, 1983-86, professor of history and law, 1986-90, university research professor, 1990—. Harvard University, Harvard-Newcomen business history fellow at Harvard Business School, 1975-76, fellow of Charles Warren Center, 1981-82; University of California, Los Angeles, visiting professor, winter/spring, 1987. University of London, London School of Economics and Political Science, senior

Fulbright scholar and visiting professor, autumn, 1986; Vanderbilt University, Martin Luther King, Jr. Lecturer, 1991; Australian National University, senior Fulbright scholar, summer, 1993.

MEMBER: American Historical Association, American Society for Legal History, Organization of American Historians, Phi Beta Kappa.

AWARDS, HONORS: Grants or fellowships from American Philosophical Society, 1978, American Bar Foundation, 1978-79, Arkansas Endowment for the Humanities, 1978 and 1980-81, National Endowment for the Humanities, 1978 and 1985, Hagley Museum and Library, 1979-80, University of Wisconsin—Madison, 1981, Earhart Foundation, 1982 and 1985, and Judicial Conference of the United States, 1991.

WRITINGS:

Forums of Order: The Federal Courts and Business in American History, JAI Press, 1979.
Harmony and Dissonance: The Swift and Erie Cases in American Federalism, New York University Press, 1981.
The Little Rock Crisis, Greenwood Press, 1984.
(Editor) *Justice Hugo L. Black and Modern America,* University of Alabama Press, 1990.
Hugo L. Black and the Dilemma of American Liberalism, Scott, Foresman, 1990.
Regulating Big Business: Antitrust in Great Britain and America, 1880-1990, Cambridge University Press, 1992.
Producers versus Capitalists: Constitutional Conflict in Antebellum America, University Press of Virginia, 1994.
(With Timothy Dixon) *Discretion and Dependence: A History of the Alabama Federal Courts,* Carlson Publishing, 1994.
(Editor) *A Frank Johnson Reader,* Carlson Publishing, 1994.

Work represented in books, including *Federalism and the Judicial Mind,* edited by Harry N. Scheiber, 1992, and *The Warren Court in Historical Perspective,* edited by Mark Tushnet, University Press of Virginia, in press. Contributor of about seventy articles and reviews to history and law journals. Member of editorial board, *Business History Review,* 1985—, and *Law and History Review,* 1993—.

*   *   *

FROHNMAYER, John 1942-

PERSONAL: Born June 1, 1942, in Medford, OR; son of Otto J. (a lawyer) and Marabel B. (a homemaker) Frohnmayer; married Leah Thorpe (a homemaker), June 10, 1967; children: Jason, J. Aaron. *Education:* Stanford University, B.A., 1964; attended Union Theological Seminary, 1964-65; University of Chicago, M.A., 1969; University of Oregon, J.D., 1972. *Politics:* Republican. *Religion:* Presbyterian. *Avocational Interests:* Singing, rowing, skiing.

ADDRESSES: Home and office—200 11th St. SE, Washington, DC 20003.

CAREER: Tonkon, Torp, Galen, Marmaduke, and Booth (law firm), Portland, OR, trial lawyer, 1972-89; National Endowment for the Arts, Washington, DC, chairperson, 1989-92; writer. *Military service:* U.S. Navy Reserve, 1966-69, attained rank of lieutenant.

AWARDS, HONORS: First Amendment Award, People for the American Way, 1992; Governor's Arts Award, Oregon, 1993.

WRITINGS:

Leaving Town Alive: Confessions of an Arts Warrior, Houghton Mifflin, 1993.

WORK IN PROGRESS: A novel, a non-fiction book, and numerous articles.

SIDELIGHTS: John Frohnmayer served as chairperson of the National Endowment for the Arts (NEA) from 1989 until 1992, during some of the agency's most turbulent times. On the right he was beset by religious conservatives such as the Reverend Donald Wildmon, leader of the American Family Association, and Senator Jesse Helms, who felt that the organization Frohnmayer headed should not give grants to artists whose art could be deemed obscene. When Frohnmayer attempted to compromise with these conservatives, allowing himself to be guided by the 1989 Helms amendment restricting art content for grants, he came under fire from artists and free speech advocates on the left. When he reversed decisions denying grants to controversial artists and exhibits, he was criticized— much like the man who appointed him, President George Bush—as wavering too often on important issues. Finally, when conservative Republican presidential candidate Patrick Buchanan threatened to make Bush's "liberal" stance on the NEA an issue in the 1992 presidential election campaign, Bush asked for Frohnmayer's resignation.

After leaving his post, Frohnmayer chronicled his difficult experiences in a book, *Leaving Town Alive: Confessions of an Arts Warrior.* Among the topics he discusses in the volume is his insertion, into the listed terms and conditions of endowment grants that recipients had to sign, the entire text of the Helms amendment banning obscene art. Critics saw this as a type of "loyalty oath"; Frohnmayer reveals that he was attempting to provoke the courts to overturn the Helms amendment as unconstitutional. The ex-chairperson also discusses his naivete and unpreparedness for what Grace Gluek described in the *New York Times Book Review* as "the totally politicized endowment . . . and the Federal agency's tormented relations with neanderthal Congressmen, the religious right, the craven Bush Administration and the arts community, which in situations like this acts out." Although several reviewers of *Leaving Town Alive* took the opportunity to criticize Frohnmayer's tenure with the NEA, many nevertheless praised his book. Gluek noted that Frohnmayer "offers some considered advice . . . and some philosophical reflection," and Jonathan Yardley of the *Washington Post Book World* hailed it as "valuable" and "enlightening."

Frohnmayer told *CA:* "Perhaps life, or education, or wisdom is a process of watching our illusions being dashed, our naivete extinguished. I came to Washington to head the National Endowment for the Arts under President Bush under the illusion that people of good faith, committed to making ours a richer society, could make a difference. What I found was that many in Washington who controlled the fate of the arts had agendas in which the arts were merely a pawn. Scratch one illusion. I felt that one could succeed in Washington on the basis of (or at least could maintain) ideals. Wrong. Extinguish what Washington insiders call 'political naivete.'

"So I thought I would write a book. I chronicle one outsider's journey through the rude and frustrating world of Washington politics. This book, honestly told, will provide a roadmap for the landmines and self-defeating hubris of our federal government. Wrong again. The book was reviewed—in Washington, New York, and Los Angeles—by essentially the same forces that keep Washington functioning the way it doesn't. The notion that the book enlightened anyone, or changed anyone's mind, is one I no longer hold—another bit of naivete extinguished. On hotly debated issues, people tend to form opinions and hold them.

"So was it 'worth it' to write the book? Damn right. The other two alternatives—to leave government to the politicians and political insiders, or not to leave an accurate account of what happened for those who come after and perhaps can do better—are not acceptable to me."

BIOGRAPHICAL/CRITICAL SOURCES:

PERIODICALS

Los Angeles Times Book Review, May 9, 1993, pp. 3, 9.
New York Times Book Review, May 2, 1993, pp. 3, 21.
Washington Post Book World, April 18, 1993, p. 3.

FUNICIELLO, Theresa 1947-

PERSONAL: Born in 1947, in Ballston Spa, NY; daughter of Anthony and Mary (Siano) Funiciello; married Tom Sanzillo (a public servant), 1984; children: Nanine. *Education:* Bard College, B.A., 1970; graduate study at Graduate Center of the City University of New York. *Avocational Interests:* Gardening, film, music.

ADDRESSES: Home—Woodstock, NY. *Office*—P.O. Box 444, Woodstock, NY 12498. *Agent*—Nancy Rose, Levine, Hall & Plotkin, 1740 Broadway, New York, NY 10019.

CAREER: Downtown Welfare Advocate Center, executive director, 1976-81; Youth Project, regional director, 1981-83; New York State Department of Social Services, special assistant to the commissioner, 1983-84; consultant to social welfare agencies and the New York State Legislature, 1984-88; writer, 1987—. Guest on television and radio programs, including *Phil Donahue, The McNeil Lehrer News Hour, Sally Jessie Raphael,* and *The Today Show.*

AWARDS, HONORS: Revson fellow at Columbia University and Center for Women in Government; John Hay Whitney fellow.

WRITINGS:

Tyranny of Kindness: Dismantling the Welfare System to End Poverty in America, Atlantic Monthly Press, 1993.

Work represented in anthologies. Contributor to magazines and newspapers, including *Dissent, Nation, Social Policy, Christianity and Crisis,* and *City Limits.* Contributing editor, *Ms.,* 1990—.

SIDELIGHTS: Theresa Funiciello told *CA:* "I write about the dirtiest word in the English language—welfare. *Tyranny of Kindness* reflects twenty years of work as a welfare mother, an organizer of welfare mothers, an establishment insider, and an inveterate researcher. I attempt to insert the voice of welfare mothers into the public debate on welfare and poverty in this country. I seek to expose how this voice has been kept out by the panoply of 'do-gooders' in charitable institutions, politics, and the media.

"My writing takes a number of directions. First, it portrays a complex portrait of welfare mothers as caregivers to the nation's poorest children. As a feminist, I emphasize the heroism and grace of women facing, and overcoming, enormous obstacles.

"Second, my work is muck-raking and investigative. Tens of billions of dollars are wasted annually through government contracts and charitable contributions 'to benefit poor people,' but most of it never gets to them. I expose some of the largest charities in the country to penetrate this money enigma and reveal the ripoffs of taxpayers and poor people alike. I take a hard look at the power relationships that sustain the poverty industry in this country: who benefits, who doesn't.

"Third, my work is change-oriented. If poor women's interests and the unpaid work they do were genuinely considered in the public debate on poverty, alternative policies, including a more generous system of income distribution, would be fashioned."

*   *   *

FURDYNA, Anna M. 1938-
(Alauda Arvensis, Aurelia Happenstance)

PERSONAL: Born August 13, 1938, in Warsaw, Poland; naturalized U.S. citizen; daughter of Konstanty (a military psychiatrist) and Maria (a pediatrician; maiden name, Baranowski) Swider; married Jacek K. Furdyna, June 25, 1960 (divorced, March, 1984); children: Zofia H., Wanda M., Julia A., Jadwiga E. *Education:* Illinois Institute of Technology, B.S. (with distinction), 1960; Northwestern University, M.S., 1963. *Politics:* "Centrist-eclectic and pacifist." *Religion:* "Neo-Christian."

ADDRESSES: Home—5439 West George, Chicago, IL 60641.

CAREER: Worked as a laboratory assistant in high-energy physics, 1959; Massachusetts Institute of Technology, Cambridge, staff physicist at National Magnet Laboratory, 1964-66; Purdue University, West Lafayette, IN, teaching assistant in physics, 1968-69; free-lance translator, 1972-78; Purdue University, research assistant at Center for Information and Numerical Analysis, 1978-79; freelance translator, 1979—.

MEMBER: World Future Society (director of local chapter, 1993-94).

WRITINGS:

(Translator) K. Slomczynski and T. Krauze, editors, *Class Structure and Social Mobility in Poland,* M. E. Sharpe, 1978.

(Translator) Iwo Birula-Bialynicki, M. Cieplak, and J. Kaminski, *Theory of Quanta,* Oxford University Press, 1992.

Translator of *Nativity Moderne,* a play by Ireneusz Iredynski, and the libretto for *Auschwitz Oratorio,* by Alina Nowak, 1974; translator of poems by K. J. Galczynski and A. Warzecha; translator of songs by Bulat Okudzhava, Agnieszka Osiecka, Olearczyk, and Wozniak. Contributor of articles, poems, and translations to periodicals. Some poems appear under the pseudonyms Alauda Arvensis and Aurelia Happenstance.

WORK IN PROGRESS: Survival Papers for Earth Civilization and Associated Poems, with Julian Hahn; *A Phenomenological Alternative to Born and Bohm Readings of Quantum Physics,* with Julian Hahn.

SIDELIGHTS: Anna M. Furdyna told *CA:* "My scientific-semantic avocation began early when, as a student of physics, I noticed to what extent a high level of verbal expression is instrumental in conveying and *engendering* physical concepts. It became a fascination to me to formulate scientific ideas as precisely and compellingly as possible. Eventually the momentum of this fascination carried me into literary prose translation and finally to the creation and re-creation of poems in English. As I get older, I realize more and more the value of translation as a social yeast of discovery and progress.

"For inspiration in scientific writing, I owe much to D. Bohm, E. Peck, P. Roman, H. Muirhead, and H. Ohanian. For intellectual stimulation and critical moral support, as well as conceptually creative collaboration, I am indebted to Julian Hahn, whose semantic prowess is a constant challenge."

G

GALLAS, John (Edward) 1950-

PERSONAL: Born January 11, 1950, in Wellington, New Zealand; son of Fredrick (a teacher) and Nancy (a teacher) Gallas. *Education:* University of Otago, B.A. (with honors), 1971; Merton College, Oxford, M.Phil., 1974. *Politics:* None. *Religion:* None. *Avocational Interests:* Cycling, swimming, tile painting, the Leicester City Football Club.

ADDRESSES: Home—40 London Rd., Coalville, Leicestershire LE6 2JA, England.

CAREER: University of Otago, Dunedin, New Zealand, assistant lecturer in English, 1975; Terry's Restaurant, York, England, assistant chef, 1976-77; University of Liverpool, Liverpool, England, archivist, 1977-78; Cizakca Lisesi, Bursa, Turkey, English teacher, 1980; Robert Smyth School, Market Harborough, England, English teacher, 1981-87; Akademi, Diyarbakir, Turkey, English teacher, 1988; Student Support Service, Leicester, England, teacher of students with special needs, 1989—.

WRITINGS:

Practical Anarchy (poems), Carcanet Press, 1989.
Flying Carpets over Filbert Street (poems), Carcanet Press, 1993.

WORK IN PROGRESS: A third collection of poems, including two long narratives.

SIDELIGHTS: John Gallas told *CA:* "I am a slow and unsteady worker surrounded by reference books, whose mild anarchism is informed by uncertainty as to the naturalness of our relationships with each other, nature, and (dis)order."

GALLO, Robert C(harles) 1937-

PERSONAL: Born March 23, 1937, in Waterbury, CT; son of Francis Anton and Louise Mary (Ciancuilli) Gallo; married Mary Jane Hayes, July 1, 1961; children: Robert Charles, Marcus. *Education:* Providence College, B.A., 1959; Jefferson Medical College, M.D., 1963. *Avocational Interests:* Swimming, reading historical novels, tennis, and theater.

ADDRESSES: Office—Laboratory of Tumor Cell Biology, National Cancer Institute, National Institutes of Health, 9000 Rockville Pike, Bethesda, MD 20892.

CAREER: University of Chicago, Chicago, IL, intern and resident in medicine, 1963-65; National Cancer Institute, Bethesda, MD, clinical associate, 1965-68, senior investigator in human tumor cell biology, 1968-69, head of section on cellular control mechanisms, 1969-72, chief of laboratory on tumor cell biology, 1972—. Served with United States Public Health Service beginning in 1965. George Washington University, adjunct professor of genetics, 1980; University of Medicine & Dentistry of New Jersey, adjunct professor of microbiology, 1985—; Johns Hopkins University, adjunct professor of biology, 1985. International Comparative Leukemia and Lymphoma Association, United States representative to world committee, 1981. Member of board of governors, Franco American AIDS Foundation and World AIDS Foundation, both 1987.

MEMBER: American Society of Biological Chemists, American Society of Clinical Investigation, American Association of Physicians, National Academy of Sciences (elected into membership, 1988; elected into Institute of Medicine, 1989).

AWARDS, HONORS: Superior Service Award, United States Public Health Service, 1975; CIBA-GEIGY awards in biomedical sciences, 1977 and 1988; Otto Herz Memorial Award for basic research on malignant processes (Israel), 1982; Albert Lasker awards, for basic biomedical research, 1982, and for clinical research, 1986; Abraham White Award in biochemistry, George Washington University, 1983; Prix Griffuel, Association for the Development of Research on Cancer (France), 1983; American Cancer Society Medal of Honor, 1983; Commissioned Corps Distinguished Service Medal, 1984; Charles S. Mott Medal, General Motors Cancer Research Foundation, 1984; Lucy Worthham Prize in cancer research, Society for Surgical Oncology, 1984; Barbara Bohen Pfeifer Award for Scientific Excellence, 1984; National American-Italian Foundation Award for Medicine and Cancer Research, 1984; Armand Hammer Cancer Research Award, 1985; Rabbi Shai Shacknai Memorial Prize and Lectureship, Hadassah Medical School, Hebrew University (Israel), 1985; special award, American Society for Infectious Disease, 1986; Birla International Award for Science (India), 1986; Gairdner Foundation International Award for Biomedical Research (Canada), 1987; Richard and Hinda Rosenthal Foundation Award, American College of Physicians, 1988; Japan Prize in preventative medicine, 1988; eleven honorary degrees.

WRITINGS:

FOR GENERAL READERS

Virus Hunting: AIDS, Cancer, and the Human Retrovirus: A Story of Scientific Discovery, Basic Books, 1991.

EDITOR; SCIENTIFIC PUBLICATIONS

(With Rolf Neth) *Modern Trends in Human Leukemia: Biological, Biochemical, and Virological Aspects,* Grune, 1974.

Recent Advances in Cancer Research: Cell Biology, Molecular Biology, and Tumor Virology, CRC Press, 1977.

(With Prem S. Sarin) *International Encyclopedia of Pharmacology and Therapeutics,* Section 103: *Inhibitors of DNA and RNA Polymerases,* Pergamon Press, 1980.

(With Vincent T. Marchesi) *Differentiation and Function of Hematopoietic Cell Surface: Proceedings of the UCLA Symposium Held at Keystone, Colorado, February 15-20, 1981,* Alan Liss, 1982.

(With Myron E. Essex and Ludwik Gross) *Human T-cell Leukemia/Lymphoma Virus: The Family of Human T-lymphotropic Retroviruses, Their Role in Malignancies and Association with AIDS,* Cold Spring Harbor Laboratory, 1984.

(With Dominique Stehelin and Oliviero E. Varnier) *International Symposium: Retroviruses and Human Pathology,* Humana, 1985.

(With Giuseppe Della Porta and Alberto Albertini) *Monoclonals and DNA Probes in Diagnostic and Preventative Medicine,* Raven Press, 1987.

(With others) *Viruses and Human Cancer: Proceedings of a UCLA Symposium Held in Park City, Utah, February 2-9, 1985,* Alan Liss, 1985.

(With Jean-Pierre Allain and Luc Montagnier) *Human Retroviruses and Diseases They Cause: Symposium Highlights, May 12-13, 1988, Abbott Park, Illinois,* Excerpta Medica-Princeton, 1988.

(With Flossie Wong-Staal) *Retrovirus Biology and Human Disease,* Dekker, 1989.

(With Gilbert Jay) *The Human Retroviruses,* Academic Press, 1991.

Member of the editorial boards of numerous scientific journals.

OTHER

Contributor of more than 950 articles to periodicals and scientific journals, including *Science, Nature, Scientific American,* and *Proceedings of the National Academy of Sciences.*

SIDELIGHTS: In 1984 Dr. Robert C. Gallo and his colleagues published a series of articles that documented their discovery of the virus that causes acquired immunodeficiency syndrome (AIDS). This accomplishment was an important first step in the battle against the fatal disease, and it was initially thought to have been the highest achievement in Gallo's career to that point. The scientist's claims soon became a source of controversy, however, when French researchers insisted that they had first documented the same virus. The debate over the discovery raised questions about Gallo's ethics and research practices and led to investigations by journalists and by the National Institutes of Health. This controversy was one of the subjects addressed in Gallo's 1991 book, *Virus Hunting: AIDS, Cancer, and the Human Retrovirus: A Story of Scientific Discovery.* In summing up the work, *New York Review of Books* contributor Michael Specter wrote that "*Virus Hunting* is Gallo's feverish attempt to defend a reputation that has fallen under legal, scientific, and political attack." The book details Gallo's version of events surrounding the discovery of the AIDS virus and also provides a firsthand account of his medical research career.

Gallo's interest in medicine began at an early age. As he relates in *Virus Hunting,* his sister was afflicted with leukemia when she was only six years old, and her death launched Gallo on his quest to help those who suffered from similar diseases. After completing his medical studies, Gallo joined the staff at the National Cancer Institute in 1965. By 1972 he was heading his own laboratory at the institute, where he concentrated on the study of leukocytes, the white blood cells that increase abnormally in leukemia victims.

In 1976 Gallo's team made a significant breakthrough with the discovery of interleukin-2, a growth factor that allowed scientists to grow T-cells—one kind of white blood cell—for the first time. The ability to reproduce these cells in the laboratory significantly aided cancer and virus research—including subsequent AIDS research—and is now used to grow so-called "killer" T-cells that are utilized in the treatment of some cancers.

After further studies, Gallo came to the conclusion that some human leukemias, like many animal leukemias, could be caused by a virus—genetic material that has the ability to invade cells and take over their reproductive processes, ultimately spreading throughout the body of the host. This theory proved difficult for Gallo to document, however. When he first announced that he had isolated a human leukemia virus, Gallo was criticized by some researchers, and his findings were soon disproved, even by Gallo himself. Despite this setback, Gallo continued his studies. In 1980 he successfully proved the presence of the first human retrovirus, named HTLV-I, and in 1982, the second, HTLV-II. HTLV-I was then found to be a cause of some forms of leukemia and neurological disease. With these discoveries Gallo was confirmed as one of the country's preeminent cancer researchers, and he would soon employ his talents to confront a new medical challenge.

Beginning in the early 1980s, large numbers of patients were diagnosed with a fatal failure of the immune system. This condition was termed acquired immunodeficiency syndrome, or AIDS, and medical researchers were soon pursuing the cause of the epidemic. Gallo quickly recognized similarities between AIDS and the form of leukemia caused by the HTLV virus; both diseases were most prevalent in Africa and the Caribbean, and both were transmitted by intimate contact between humans, including sexual intercourse and blood. Guided by these factors, Gallo's research pursued the hypothesis that a new HTLV-related retrovirus was the cause of AIDS.

Meanwhile, other scientists were exploring the disease. A French team at the Pasteur Institute headed by Luc Montagnier identified a virus—named LAV—that they found in a man with swollen lymph glands. They did not have evidence that the virus caused AIDS, but there was suspicion that it might. Continuing their own research, Gallo's team soon identified a similar virus that they named HTLV-III, and they announced their findings within a year after the French team had identified LAV. It was Gallo's team, however, that definitively established that this virus was the cause of AIDS—something the French scientists had failed to do—and it was Gallo's team that developed an accurate and sensitive blood test to detect the viral infection.

The ensuing controversy over the virus began when Gallo's team was awarded the patent to the AIDS blood test over the French team. While Gallo conceded that Montagnier's team was the first to isolate the virus, he maintained his laboratory's pioneering role in determining the cause of the disease and developing the blood test. The French, conversely, felt that their contribution had not been recognized in awarding the patent. The dispute became more heated when it was found that not only were the two viruses—LAV and one of Gallo's HTLV isolates—very similar, their genetic patterns were almost identical. This similarity led many authorities to believe that the two viruses had come from the same person. For this reason, Gallo was accused in media reports of stealing Montagnier's samples, identifying the same virus that the Frenchman had already documented, then claiming the discovery as his own. The controversy soon became an international dispute when France sued the United States over patent rights that had been awarded to Gallo rather than Montagnier.

The controversy surrounding Gallo received considerable attention, in part, because of his stature in the scientific community. "Gallo is easily one of the country's most famous scientists," wrote Malcolm Gladwell in the *Washington Post,* "frequently mentioned as a Nobel Prize contender, and a man whose research publications were cited . . . during the last decade more often than those of any other scientist in the world." While the dispute about the AIDS virus cast a shadow over Gallo's distinguished career, many journalists felt that the conflict also weakened the overall fight against the disease. Specter, in *New York Review of Books,* charged that "by insisting for so long that he and Montagnier had different viruses, regally dismissing suggestions to the contrary, Gallo may have impeded the development of a vaccine." A spokesperson for Gallo's staff responded to this charge by telling *CA,* "obviously, a vaccine has not been developed, even to this date, and there is no logic to thinking that a difference in the viruses would somehow impede our working on a vaccine with one or the other. Moreover, the early belief that there were some important differences in the two viruses mostly arose from some inaccurate results by the French group on some of the features of LAV." Though questions remain about the cause of the dispute, many have felt that the battle between the two scientists drew attention from their most important job: finding a cure for AIDS. "Coming as it did in the early stages of an epidemic that was already causing suffering throughout the world," Specter wrote, " . . . the hostility between two leading scientists seemed particularly odious."

After a long review of records from Gallo's lab, the legal dispute was settled out of court. A mutual agreement was reached recognizing the contributions of each team, thereby giving Gallo and Montagnier duel credit for the discovery of the AIDS virus. The two scientists jointly published an account of their respective groups' retroviral research in a 1987 edition of *Nature*. The account acknowledged that the AIDS virus was first isolated in France in 1983 but grown in culture properly and linked to the cause of AIDS by Gallo's team in 1984.

The *Nature* report became the basis of the joint agreement, but it was far from the first time that the two scientists had worked together. A spokesperson for Gallo relates that the American researcher had aided the French team with reagents and techniques during their discovery and had openly acknowledged the earlier French identification of LAV on many occasions. Montagnier's staff had, likewise, provided Gallo's team with blood samples from AIDS patients during their research. Experts later hypothesized that it was this practice of sharing samples that caused one sample to contaminate another, resulting in the duel identification of similar viruses. Despite the controversy that resulted from the contamination, both Gallo and Montagnier declared the value of their collaborative relationship in the *Nature* report: "Both sides wish it to be known that from the beginning there has been a spirit of scientific cooperation and a free exchange of ideas, biological materials and personnel between Dr. Gallo's and Dr. Montagnier's laboratories. This spirit has never ceased despite the legal problems and will be the basis of renewed mutual cooperation in the future." In a *Discover* article, Gallo further defended the relationship between his laboratory and Montagnier's, stating that "the competition accelerated the pace [of research] enormously—the conflict arose, in a sense, because of the pace. Without the blood test that resulted from the work done in our two laboratories, many additional lives might have been lost."

Though the legal agreement seemed to have put an end to the dispute, the controversy regarding the AIDS virus was soon rekindled. In 1989, *Chicago Tribune* reporter John Crewdson published a series of articles that again examined Gallo's research practices. The reporter detailed the exchange of samples in 1983 and the resulting contamination—though Crewdson suggested that such a contamination could have been intentional as well as accidental. Crewdson also alleged that Gallo's team engaged in several unorthodox research practices, such as mixing together samples from different patients. These practices might have been undertaken, the reporter speculated, to cover up evidence of the theft of the French virus.

Crewdson's allegations were taken seriously in at least one official circle, and a congressional committee requested the National Institutes of Health (NIH)—the government organization that funds the Gallo's research—to investigate the charges. Gladwell, writing about the investigation in the *Washington Post,* noted that it was "an inquiry with-

out precedent in the history of the NIH. . . . No other investigation has taken so long, dealt with a scientific discovery of such importance or directly implicated so distinguished a researcher."

Virus Hunting was published after Crewdson's allegations were made public, and Gallo argues in the book that his team used standard research practices and that their conduct was ethical. In reviewing *Virus Hunting, New York Times Book Review* contributor Natalie Angier agreed with Gallo's defense on this point, noting that "his description of the key experiments in 1983 and 1984 that led to the final isolation of the AIDS virus are intelligent and persuasive, particularly to a reader who has heard the other side of the story." Gallo also maintains in the book that his laboratory had identified other strains of the virus that were definitely different from the French strain. It was this fact, a spokesperson for Gallo later related, that "convinced all investigations that [Gallo] had no intention of stealing the French virus isolate."

Many critics found that Gallo's book was a direct response to Crewdson's allegations. "*Virus Hunting* might never have been written," Specter noted in *New York Review of Books,* "or at least would have been an altogether different book, had not Crewdson so directly questioned Gallo's integrity." Angier found that Gallo's attempts to refute the journalist made *Virus Hunting* a "problematic book" and added that "it is hard to see how anybody not familiar with all the charges could follow the ins and outs of Dr. Gallo's defenses." Other critics, however, have treated *Virus Hunting* as an important new document in the continuing conflict over the AIDS virus and a revealing look at the process of scientific research. J. D. Robinson, writing in the *Washington Times,* noted that "a series of fascinating themes runs through *Virus Hunting*. The complexity, subtlety and uncertainty of fundamental biological research jumps out from page after page." Warwick Coppleson's review in the *Journal of the American Medical Association* was also positive, noting that "the level of science here is quite well handled. . . . Someone with no scientific background can read this account with compelled interest." Coppleson summarized *Virus Hunting* as "a strange and interesting book that covers a range of topics and makes fascinating reading on the whole."

Since publication of *Virus Hunting*, Gallo's reputation has been exonerated. Further scientific findings were reported in 1991 that showed accidental contamination from a fast-growing strain of HIV had occurred in samples from both Gallo's lab and Montagnier's lab. It was also reported that both scientists had isolated samples independent from the original specimens that had appeared so similar. This information further supported Gallo's claim that he had isolated the virus independent of French samples. Charges made by a government agency—the Office of Research Integrity—were eventually withdrawn in 1993 after an appeals board found that the allegations against a member of Gallo's staff were without basis. The appeals board decision, as quoted in *Time,* was decisively in favor of Gallo's team. "One might anticipate," the review board wrote, "after all the sound and fury, there would be at least a residue of palpable wrongdoing. That is not the case."

After a long battle to clear his name, Gallo is now better able to concentrate on further viral research, especially in regard to AIDS. *Virus Hunting,* meanwhile, stands as a chronicle of his past research and the scientist's own account of his work on the deadly AIDS virus. Commenting on the book, Angier noted that "Dr. Gallo shows himself to be a formidable gladiator who firmly believes in the vast importance of his scientific contributions. One cannot help admiring his courage for taking his case to the public."

BIOGRAPHICAL/CRITICAL SOURCES:

BOOKS

Newsmakers 91, Cumulation, Gale, 1991.

PERIODICALS

Discover, October, 1989, pp. 31-36.
Journal of the American Medical Association, December 18, 1991, pp. 3351-52.
Nature, Volume 326-2, April, 1987, pp. 435-36.
New York Review of Books, August 15, 1991, pp. 49-52.
New York Times Book Review, March 24, 1991, p. 3.
New York Times Magazine, December 26, 1993, p. 12.
Scientific American, December, 1985, pp. 88-98; January, 1987, pp. 46-56; October, 1988, pp. 40-48
Time, May 20, 1991, p. 50; November 22, 1993, p. 61.
Washington Post, August 17, 1990, p. A8; October 6, 1990, p. A3; February 28, 1991, p. A3; April 22, 1991, p. C4.
Washington Times, April 22, 1991.

—Sketch by Jeff Hill

* * *

GARCIA, Alfredo 1952-

PERSONAL: Born January 13, 1952, in Santiago, Cuba; son of Cristobal and Rosalina Garcia; married; wife's name, Cynthia O.; children: Christina, James. *Education:* Received B.A. from Jacksonville University; received M.A. and J.D. from University of Florida. *Religion:* Roman Catholic.

ADDRESSES: Home—10484 Southwest 114th Terrace, Miami, FL 33176. *Office*—School of Law, St. Thomas University, 16400 Northwest 32nd Ave., Miami, FL 33054.

CAREER: University of Texas at San Antonio, assistant professor, 1987-89; St. Thomas University, Miami, FL, associate dean of School of Law, 1989—.

WRITINGS:

The Sixth Amendment in Modern American Jurisprudence, Greenwood Press, 1992.

* * *

GASKELL, Ivan 1955-

PERSONAL: Born February 26, 1955, in Somerset, England; son of George and Catherina (van Leeuwen) Gaskell; married Jane Whitehead, 1981; children: Leo. *Education:* Oxford University, M.A. (history), 1976; University of London, M.A. (art history), 1980; Cambridge University, Ph.D. *Politics:* Socialist. *Religion:* Church of England.

ADDRESSES: Home—Lexington, MA. *Office*—Fogg Art Museum, Harvard University, 32 Quincy St., Cambridge, MA 02138.

CAREER: University of London, London, England, assistant curator of Warburg Institute, 1980-83; Cambridge University, Cambridge, England, fellow of Wolfson College, 1983-91; Harvard University, Cambridge, MA, curator of paintings and sculpture at Fogg Art Museum, 1991—. Cambridge Darkroom Gallery, chair of board of directors, 1989-91.

MEMBER: College Art Association, Historians of Netherlandish Art.

WRITINGS:

The Thyssen-Bornemisza Collection: Seventeenth-Century Dutch and Flemish Painting, Philip Wilson, 1990.

Contributor to journals, including *Burlington, Apollo, Art History, British Journal of Aesthetics, Print Quarterly, Creative Camera,* and *Performance.*

EDITOR; "CAMBRIDGE STUDIES IN PHILOSOPHY AND THE ARTS" SERIES

(With Salim Kemal) *The Language of Art History,* Cambridge University Press, 1991.
(With Kemal) *Landscape, Natural Beauty, and the Arts,* Cambridge University Press, 1993.
(With Kemal) *Explanation and Value in the Arts,* Cambridge University Press, 1993.

WORK IN PROGRESS: Editing additional volumes for the series "Cambridge Studies in Philosophy and the

Arts," with Salim Kemal, for Cambridge University Press.

*   *   *

GAT, Azar 1959-

PERSONAL: Born June 24, 1959, in Haifa, Israel; son of Eli and Josepha (Ram) Gat; married Ruth Reich, October 13, 1983; children: Tamar. *Education:* Haifa University, B.A. (with distinction), 1978; Tel Aviv University, M.A. (with distinction), 1983; Oxford University, D.Phil., 1986.

ADDRESSES: Home—9 Ha'eshel St., Ramat Gan, Israel. *Office*—Department of Political Science, Tel Aviv University, Ramat Aviv, Tel Aviv, Israel.

CAREER: Tel Aviv University, Tel Aviv, Israel, lecturer, 1987-91, senior lecturer in political science, 1991—. *Military service:* Israel Defense Forces Reserve; present rank, major.

WRITINGS:

The Origins of Military Thought from the Enlightenment to Clausewitz, Oxford University Press, 1989.
The Development of Military Thought: The Nineteenth Century, Clarendon Press, 1992.

WORK IN PROGRESS: Fuller, Liddell Hart, and Twentieth-Century War.

BIOGRAPHICAL/CRITICAL SOURCES:

PERIODICALS

Times Literary Supplement, April 6, 1990, p. 377.

*   *   *

GAY, John H. 1928-

PERSONAL: Born December 2, 1928.

ADDRESSES: Office—Humanities Division, Box 277, Cuttington University College, Monrovia, Liberia.

CAREER: Cuttington University College, Monrovia, Liberia, chair of humanities division.

WRITINGS:

(With Michael Cole) *The New Mathematics and an Old Culture: A Study of Learning among the Kpelle of Liberia,* Holt, 1967.
(With William Welmers) *Mathematics and Logic in the Kpelle Language,* Institute of African Studies, 1971.
(With Cole and others) *The Cultural Context of Learning and Thinking,* Basic Books, 1971.
Red Dust on the Green Leaves: A Kpelle Twins Childhood, introduction by Jerome Bruner, photographs by Har-

rison Owen, University of Ibadan Press, 1971, Inter-Culture Associates, 1973.
Universals of Human Thought: Some African Evidence, Cambridge University Press, 1981.
(With David Hall and Gerhard Deborath) *Poverty in Lesotho, a Mapping Exercise,* Lesotho Food Management Unit, 1992.

BIOGRAPHICAL/CRITICAL SOURCES:

PERIODICALS

Choice, April, 1974, p. 294.*

*   *   *

GEDMIN, Jeffrey (N.) 1958-

PERSONAL: Born May 13, 1958; son of Victor Gerald (an electrical engineer) and Dorothy (a telephone representative; maiden name, Nickerson) Gedmin; married Jeana Williams (a clinical psychologist), May 22, 1993. *Education:* Attended Dolmetscher Institute, Munich, Germany, 1977; University of Salzburg, 1977-78; American University, B.A., 1980, M.A., 1982; attended Friedrich Schiller University, 1984, Paedagogische Hochschule Erfurt, 1985, and Johns Hopkins School of Advanced International Studies, 1986; Georgetown University, Ph.D., 1990. *Religion:* Roman Catholic.

ADDRESSES: Home—10161 Oakton Terrace Rd., Oakton, VA 22124. *Office*—American Enterprise Institute for Public Policy Research, 1150 17th St. N.W., Washington, DC 20036.

CAREER: High school teacher in Washington, DC, 1981-88, also head of modern foreign language department and director of foreign exchange programs for Germany, Czechoslovakia, Austria, Greece, Turkey, Egypt, the U.S.S.R., and Australia; American Enterprise Institute for Public Policy Research, Washington, DC, research fellow, Foreign Policy Program, 1988—. Georgetown University, adjunct professor, 1985—. Guest on radio and television programs.

WRITINGS:

The Hidden Hand: Gorbachev and the Collapse of East Germany, American Enterprise Institute for Public Policy Research, 1992.

Contributor of numerous articles and reviews to political science journals. Guest editor, *World Affairs,* spring, 1990.

WORK IN PROGRESS: Closing Europe's Door? German Attitudes Toward America in the 1990s, for American Enterprise Institute for Public Policy Research.

SIDELIGHTS: Jeffrey Gedmin told *CA:* "There were two major turning points in my career. In 1978 I spent an academic year in Salzburg, Austria, where I studied music. This ignited my interest in German language and literature, which led to my teaching for seven years at Gonzaga College High School, a private Jesuit boys' school in Washington, DC. Then, in the 1980s, I traveled frequently to Eastern Europe, especially East Germany. I made enormously important friendships; I also learned what freedom, and its absence, meant. Finishing my Ph.D. at Georgetown University, I wanted to pursue work in which I could focus on East-West relations, the problems of Communism, and the challenges for democracy.

"My current work focuses on American interests in Europe after the Cold War."

* * *

GEORGE, Judith W(ordsworth) 1940-

PERSONAL: Born August 26, 1940, in Yorkshire, England; daughter of Arthur (a teacher) and Esther (Wordsworth) Holt; married Peter George, 1963 (marriage ended, 1981); children: Catharine, Felicity. *Education:* Oxford University, M.A., 1963, Diploma in Education, 1964; University of Edinburgh, Ph.D., 1985. *Religion:* Christian.

ADDRESSES: Home—Edinburgh, Scotland. *Office*—Open University, 10 Drumsheugh Gardens, Edinburgh EH3 7QJ, Scotland.

CAREER: Open University, Edinburgh, Scotland, deputy Scottish director. Consultant in education in curriculum development and "technologies in distance education."

WRITINGS:

Venantius Fortunatus: A Latin Poet in Merovingian Gaul, Oxford University Press, 1992.

Work represented in anthologies, including *Translated Texts for Historians,* Liverpool University Press, in press.

* * *

GEORGE, Margaret 1943-

PERSONAL: Born January 19, 1943, in Nashville, TN; daughter of Scott George (a foreign service officer) and Dean (Crain) George; married Paul L. Kaufman (a physician), April 12, 1970; children: Alison. *Education:* Tufts University, B.A., 1964; Stanford University, M.A., 1966. *Avocational Interests:* Film and pop culture, photography, reptiles.

ADDRESSES: Agent—Jacques de Spoelberch, 9 Shagbark Rd., Wilson Pt., South Norwalk, CT 06854.

CAREER: National Institutes of Health, science writer, 1966-70; Washington University, newswriter, 1970-72; freelance novelist, 1973—.

MEMBER: Archaeological Institute of America, St. Andrew's Scottish Society, Wisconsin Screenwriters Forum (secretary), Council for Wisconsin Writers, Royal Stuart Society, Wisconsin Herpetology Society, Venomous Snake Society.

AWARDS, HONORS: Oppie Award, best biographical novel, Southwestern Booksellers Association, 1986, for *The Autobiography of Henry VIII; With Notes by His Fool, Will Somers;* first place, book-length fiction, Council for Wisconsin Writers, 1986, for *The Autobiography of Henry VIII; The Autobiography of Henry VIII* was named best novel of 1986 by the Wisconsin Library Association; Outstanding Achievement by Wisconsin Author award, Wisconsin Library Association, 1993, for *Mary Queen of Scotland and the Isles.*

WRITINGS:

The Autobiography of Henry VIII; With Notes by His Fool, Will Somers, St. Martin's, 1986.
Mary Queen of Scotland and the Isles, St. Martin's, 1992.

WORK IN PROGRESS: A biography/epic of the life of Cleopatra, for St. Martin's, publication expected in 1996.

SIDELIGHTS: Margaret George spent fifteen years doing the research for her first historical novel, *The Autobiography of Henry VIII; With Notes by His Fool, Will Somers.* As the title implies, the book purports to tell the story of the famous English king, oft-criticized for his brutality to his wives and his advisors, from his own point of view. George uses the literary device of a secret autobiography, commented upon in footnotes by Henry's court jester, and, as Philippa Toomey reported in the London *Times,* "Henry is a hero to the author and she puts forward a persuasive case for him." Rather than a greedy man desirous of both Church lands and a male heir, for instance, George explains Henry's historic break with the Catholic Church as resulting from deep spiritual doubts—Henry asks the question of whether marrying his brother's widow caused God to punish him by withholding a son from him. Barbara Tritel in the *New York Times Book Review* observed that "George contributes intriguing material to the popular mythology" of Henry VIII's wives, and further commented on the book's "delightful detail." Though Mollie Hardwick in the *Washington Post Book World* lamented "the odd incongruity" of an occasional modern term, she concluded that "the writing is smooth and stylish enough that it is hard to believe that this is a first novel" and that "the historical detail and period flavor are . . . well conveyed."

George's next novel, *Mary Queen of Scotland and the Isles,* was published in 1992. This time the author tackled the story of Mary Stuart, the tragic Queen of Scotland whose own intrigues, combined with betrayals by her advisors, religious differences, her position in line for the English throne, and the general turbulence of the times, resulted in her beheading at the hands of Henry VIII's daughter, Elizabeth I. Though Sheila Paulos in the *New York Times Book Review* complained that George was too sympathetic to her subject, she conceded that the author's "intriguing vision never wavers." Christopher Pavek lauded *Mary Queen of Scotland and the Isles* in the *Library Journal,* declaring that George "again shows exemplary research skills while improving significantly on her storytelling abilities."

George told *CA:* "I come from a Southern background, and was born in Nashville, Tennessee. My early childhood was spent at various overseas posts where my father, a career diplomat, was stationed. These included Taiwan, Israel, and Germany. From the time I was seven, I created stories and wrote books, mainly to entertain myself. Although I kept them secret when I was writing them, once they were finished I would send them to publishers. My first completed book-length one (150 pages—I always liked length!), a novel about the Old West, was sent to Grosset & Dunlap when I was twelve. Then followed several other novels, on very different subjects, at approximately five-year intervals. *The Autobiography of Henry VIII* was my first published novel—thirty years after I submitted my first efforts to a publisher.

"Growing up in the 1950s, I really liked the big-screen epics of the era, and I am sure that has influenced my work. An obituary of filmmaker David Lean described his work as 'elegant, detailed, and panoramic'—and I realized that was what I had aimed for in my work, trying to get down on paper what he got on the screen. At the same time, I think epics should be gorgeous and entertaining as well. Too many of them get weighted down with research and self-importance. If a story cannot stand on its own as a drama, then it isn't fiction, but something else.

"I credit my Southern background and the King James version of the Bible with my saga-like approach to storytelling and my love for the beauty of words. I use only published works in the public domain. For details, I am grateful to the historians Agnes Strickland, Lacey Baldwin Smith, and Michael Grout."

BIOGRAPHICAL/CRITICAL SOURCES:

PERIODICALS

Library Journal, August, 1992, p. 148.
New York Times Book Review, October 12, 1986, p. 28; November 1, 1992, p. 20.

Times (London), May 28, 1987, p. 17.
Washington Post Book World, August 17, 1986, p. 4.

*   *   *

GEWERTZ, Deborah B.   1948-

PERSONAL: Born June 12, 1948, in New York, NY; daughter of Max Goldsmith and Frederica Lascher Goldsmith; married Frederick Errington; children: Alexis. *Education:* Attended Princeton University, 1968-69; Queens College of the City University of New York, B.A., 1969; Graduate Center of the City University of New York, Ph.D., 1977.

ADDRESSES: Office—Department of Anthropology and Sociology, Amherst College, Amherst, MA 01002.

CAREER: Queens College of the City University of New York, Flushing, NY, adjunct lecturer, 1972; Graduate Center of the City University of New York, New York City, supervisor of Human Relations Area Files, 1972-73; Hunter College of the City University of New York, New York City, adjunct instructor, 1976-77; Amherst College, Amherst, MA, assistant professor, 1977-83, associate professor, 1983-88, professor of anthropology, 1988—, chairperson of Department of Anthropology and Sociology, 1985-87, Elizabeth Bruss Reader in Anthropology and Women's Studies, 1985-87. Australian National University, research fellow, Research School for Pacific Studies, 1983-84. Conducted field research among the Chambri and their neighbors of the East Sepik Province, Papua New Guinea, 1974-75, 1979, 1983-84, and 1987-88, in Rock Creek MT, summers, 1985-86, 1988-89, and 1992, and among the Karavarans and their neighbors of the Duke of York Island Group, East New Britain Province, Papua New Guinea, 1991.

MEMBER: American Anthropological Association (fellow), Association for Social Anthropology in Oceania, Association for Cultural Anthropology (fellow).

AWARDS, HONORS: Miner D. Crary fellow, 1979; National Endowment for the Humanities, fellow, 1979, grant, 1987-88; grant from Wenner-Gren Foundation for Anthropological Research, 1980-81.

WRITINGS:

Sepik River Societies: A Historical Ethnography of the Chambri and Their Neighbors, Yale University Press, 1983.

(Editor with Edward Schieffelin, and contributor) *History and Ethnography in New Guinea,* Oceania Monographs (Sydney), 1985.

(Editor and contributor) *Myths of Matriarchy Reconsidered,* Oceania Monographs (Sydney), 1988.

(With Frederick Errington) *Cultural Alternatives and a Feminist Anthropology: An Analysis of Culturally Constructed Gender Interests in Papua New Guinea,* Cambridge University Press, 1989.

(With Frederick Errington) *Twisted Histories, Altered Contexts: Representing the Chambri in a World System,* Cambridge University Press, 1991.

Work represented in anthologies, including *Dealing With Inequality,* edited by Marilyn Strathern, Cambridge University Press, 1987; *Contemporary Pacific Studies,* edited by Victoria Lockwood and others, Prentice-Hall, 1992; and *Occidentalism,* edited by James Carrier, in press. Association for Social Anthropology in Oceania, member of editorial board of monograph series, 1982-87, and editor of special publications. Contributor of articles and reviews to scholarly journals.

WORK IN PROGRESS: Articulating Change in the "Last Unknown", with Frederick Errington.

*   *   *

GIFALDI, David   1950-

PERSONAL: Born February 24, 1950, in Brockport, NY; son of Americo and Angie (maiden name, DiNicola) Gifaldi; married Marita Keys, November 25, 1989. *Education:* Duquesne University, B.A., 1972; Western Washington University, elementary and secondary teaching credentials. *Avocational Interests:* Reading, swimming, backpacking, gardening, baseball.

ADDRESSES: Home—4305 Northeast Skidmore Street, Portland, OR 97218.

CAREER: Bellingham School District, Bellingham, WA, and Vancouver School District, Vancouver, WA, substitute teacher, 1980-83; Vancouver School District, teacher, 1985—.

MEMBER: Society of Children's Book Writers and Illustrators, National Educational Association.

AWARDS, HONORS: Nomination to the Mark Twain Award Master List, Missouri Association of School Librarians, 1988-89, for *One Thing for Sure;* Best Book for Reluctant Young Adult Readers, American Library Association, 1990, and Michigan Library Association Young Adult Forum Award nominee, both for *Yours till Forever;* Junior Literary Guild selection (now Junior Library Guild), for *One Thing for Sure.*

WRITINGS:

NOVELS

One Thing for Sure, Clarion Books, 1986.
Yours till Forever, Lippincott/HarperCollins, 1989.

Gregory, Maw, and the Mean One, Clarion Books, 1992.
Toby Scudder, Ultimate Warrior, Clarion Books, 1993.

OTHER

The Boy Who Spoke Colors (an original folktale), illustrated by Carol Greger, Houghton Mifflin, 1993.

Also contributor to periodicals, including *Cricket, Teen, Highlights for Children, Alive! for Young Teens, Children's Digest* and *Jack and Jill.*

WORK IN PROGRESS: A book of poems for middle grade readers.

SIDELIGHTS: David Gifaldi grew up in a small town near Lake Ontario named Holley, New York. "Summers in Holley were filled with baseball, band concerts, carnivals, and playing Tarzan off the rope swings at various swimming holes," he commented. "Winters were for ice skating and sledding. The town had an outdoor rink, really just a scooped out pond that the firemen would fill when the cold came down from Canada. There was a little shed for changing and taking a breather after playing hockey or trying out some of the figure skating moves we kids saw on TV. The best was skating at night with the floodlights on and stars shivering in the dark overhead . . . the cold sucking your breath. I recall the sound of skate blades on ice, the cries of children and adults at play, and the warm feeling inside knowing that Christmas was just a week away." It was during his childhood that the magic of books opened up for Gifaldi. In fact, he credits his third grade teacher with introducing him to literature. She read books such as *Tom Sawyer* daily after recess, and Gifaldi said he looked forward to being carried away to visit with characters from these books.

Though Gifaldi began writing poetry and keeping a journal after college, he said he did not get serious about writing until he met Richard Peck at a summer workshop, who greatly encouraged Gifaldi to write. While completing a teacher certification program at Western Washington University, Gifaldi also took a correspondence writing course. His persistence in writing stories for children led to his first sale of a short story to *Children's Digest.* He continued to write while supporting himself as a substitute teacher.

It was while substitute teaching for a fifth grade class that Gifaldi got the idea for his first novel, *One Thing for Sure.* He described this experience to *Junior Literary Guild:* "A boy got up during sharing time, and said, 'My father's in jail.' This statement was followed by an uneasy quiet. The other students didn't know how to respond. It was as if everyone was wondering what it would be like if their own father was in prison." In the novel, twelve-year old Dylan is shocked and disillusioned when his father is arrested. Since he lives in a small town, he must deal with being labeled a thief himself and defend his father at the same time he resents him. A review in *Publishers Weekly* noted "Gifaldi has great flair for figurative language" and uses it to demonstrate Dylan's perception of the world.

Gifaldi's next novel, *Yours till Forever,* was named a 1990 American Library Association Best Book for Reluctant Young Adult Readers. Rick, a high school senior, notices his two friends were born the same day his parents were killed in a car accident. As the young couple falls in love, Rick suspects they are the reincarnation of his parents and will die the same tragic death. Through the combination of Eastern religion and American high-school life "the concept of forever takes on special meaning . . . in a competently sketched tale," noted Margaret A. Bush in *Horn Book.* Carolyn Cushman described the book as "an involving and intelligent tale of teenagers just starting out in life" in her *Locus* review. She also commented on the book's educational exploration of the topic of reincarnation.

Gifaldi's more recent books mimic the style of folktales and tall tales. *Gregory, Maw, and the Mean One* is a tall tale in which the Mean One goes back into the past to reclaim his lost heart, so he will not have to continue to be so mean. A review in *Publishers Weekly* stated Gifaldi's "clever writing bears a subtle though worthwhile message about the potential good in everyone."

Gifaldi said he enjoys both teaching and writing because the two go together. The teaching experiences and the students themselves give him numerous ideas to write about. "I like writing for young people because I enjoy looking at the world through the eyes of a ten or twelve or sixteen-year old. Things always seem fresher that way. Growing up is hard. But it's also a time of wonder and discovery. Writing keeps me on my toes, wondering and discovering."

BIOGRAPHICAL/CRITICAL SOURCES:

PERIODICALS

Horn Book, September/October, 1989, p. 627.
Junior Literary Guild, October, 1986.
Locus, July, 1989, p. 50.
Publishers Weekly, August 22, 1986, p. 99; August 3, 1992, p. 72.
School Library Journal, October, 1993, p. 124.

*   *   *

GIL, Moshe 1921-

PERSONAL: Born February 8, 1921, in Bialystok, Poland; son of Meir (in the textile industry) and Freidl (Yuszynski) Gitler; married Shoshana Herland (a registered nurse), 1950; children: Hagit Gil Halberstamm, Dinah Gil Moyal, Esther Gil Naftali. *Education:* Tel Aviv University, B.A., 1966, M.A., 1968; University of Pennsylvania, Ph.D., 1970.

ADDRESSES: Office—Carter Building, Tel Aviv University, Tel Aviv, Israel 69978.

CAREER: Imprisoned in concentration camp during World War II and released in 1944; member of Kibbutz Reshafim, Bet Shean Valley, Palestine, 1945—; Tel Aviv University, Tel Aviv, Israel, associate professor, 1974-80, professor, 1980—, dean of humanities, 1986-89. *Military service:* Served in Israel Defense Forces.

WRITINGS:

Documents of the Jewish Pious Foundations, E. J. Brill, 1976.
The Tustaris (in Hebrew), Tel Aviv University, 1981.
Palestine during the First Muslim Period (in Hebrew), Tel Aviv University, 1983.
A History of Palestine, 634-1099, translated from Hebrew by Ethel Broido, Cambridge University Press, 1992.

WORK IN PROGRESS: A history of Jews in Muslim lands during medieval times, particularly the study of medieval Judeo-Arabic manuscripts such as the *Cairo Geniza.*

*   *   *

GILLETT, Grant (Randall) 1950-

PERSONAL: Born June 2, 1950, in Auckland, New Zealand; son of Arthur Randall (a piano tuner) and Pauline Marguerite (maiden name, Richardson; later surname, Hinemoa) Gillett; married Shirley Anne Saunders, January 6, 1972; children: Rachel. *Education:* Received B.Sc., M.Sc., M.B., and Ch.B. from University of Auckland; received D.Phil. from Oxford University. *Politics:* "Moderate." *Religion:* Christian.

ADDRESSES: Home—164 Maitland St., Dunedin, New Zealand. *Office*—Bioethics Centre, University of Otago, Dunedin, New Zealand.

CAREER: Resident and lecturer in neurosurgery, Auckland, New Zealand, 1977-83; Oxford University, Oxford, England, fellow in philosophy, 1986-88; University of Otago, Dunedin, New Zealand, associate professor of medical ethics and consultant neurosurgeon, 1988—, and honorary lecturer in philosophy. Oxford University, fellow of Magdalen College; consultant to New Zealand Department of Health.

MEMBER: Royal Australasian College of Surgeons (fellow).

AWARDS, HONORS: Senior scholar, St. Cross College, Oxford.

WRITINGS:

Reasonable Care, Bristol Press, 1989.
Representation, Meaning, and Thought, Oxford University Press, 1992.
Practical Medical Ethics, Oxford University Press (New Zealand), 1992.
The Mind and Its Discontents, Oxford University Press, 1994.

WORK IN PROGRESS: Neurophilosophical Investigations.

SIDELIGHTS: Grant Gillett told *CA:* "From my teenage years I was interested in the puzzles surrounding the human mind, in the context of a scientific world view. When I entered medical school and encountered neuroscience, I developed a major interest in the brain and its function. My knowledge in this area just intensified the problems, and I pursued a master's degree in psychology. On the way through this degree, I was waylaid by philosophy. Serious study in philosophy had to be deferred until I had completed my medical training and then my specialist training in neurosurgery, which took me to Oxford. Oxford was the ideal setting in which to do a doctorate in philosophy, and that was followed by an appointment as a fellow (by examination) in philosophy at Magdalen College. This was one of the haunts of a longtime hero of mine, C. S. Lewis. Although I was not writing in the same area as he, I felt that he shared many of my concerns (he had, of course, died long before my appointment there). I had originally intended to avoid questions in the philosophy of language, but I found my primary concern with the mind, the brain, and the nature of a person did not allow me to ignore this area of philosophy and, so, stimulated by the remarks of others, in 1986 I began to write *Representation, Meaning, and Thought.* Six years and many rewrites later, the book was completed, and in the process it had spawned a rash of other bits and pieces of philosophical writing that had led me into medical ethics. I am still deeply engaged in fundamental philosophical inquiry, but I also manage to combine the two sides of my life in medical ethics teaching and writing. I also continue to practice as a neurosurgeon."

*   *   *

GLASSMAN, Bruce   1961-

PERSONAL: Born September 15, 1961, in San Francisco, CA; son of Richard (a publisher) and Sonja (a homemaker) Glassman; married Tracy Hughes (a clinical social worker), June 23, 1985. *Education:* Wesleyan University, B.A.

ADDRESSES: Office—Blackbirch Press, 1 Bradley Rd., Woodbridge, CT 06525.

CAREER: Blackbirch Press, Inc., Woodbridge, CT, editorial director, 1985—.

WRITINGS:

YOUNG ADULT FICTION

The Marathon Race Mystery, illustrated by Jackie Rogers, Troll, 1985.

NONFICTION

The Crash of '29 and the New Deal, Silver Burdett, 1986.
Everything You Need to Know about Step-Families, Rosen Publishing, 1988.
Everything You Need to Know about Growing up Male, Rosen Publishing, 1991.
New York: Gateway to the New World, Blackbirch Press, 1991.

BIOGRAPHY

J. Paul Getty: Oil Billionaire, edited by Nancy Furstinger, Silver Burdett, 1989.
Mikhail Baryshnikov, Silver Burdett, 1990.
Arthur Miller, Silver Burdett, 1990.
Wilma Mankiller: Chief of the Cherokee Nation, Blackbirch Press, 1992.

WORK IN PROGRESS: A full length romantic comedy for the theater; television screenplays for HBO.

SIDELIGHTS: Bruce Glassman concentrates his creative efforts on nonfiction for children. His nonfiction debut was a book for Silver Burdett's "Turning Points in American History" series entitled *The Crash of '29 and the New Deal,* which discusses the stock market crash and the Great Depression that followed it. According to a reviewer in *Booklist:* "Glassman does a good job of crisply explaining how these disasters occurred and the impact they had on American society, beginning with the panic on Wall Street in October, 1929."

Glassman continues to write nonfiction, particularly biographies of influential historical figures. His 1992 book *Wilma Mankiller: Chief of the Cherokee Nation* describes not only the life of Mankiller, but introduces some of the events and people important to the Cherokee at this time: Sequoyah, the Cherokee alphabet, and the Trail of Tears. "Extensive coverage is given to Mankiller's accomplishments and struggles for the Cherokee," writes Lisa Mitten in the *School Library Journal,* "but Glassman also discusses the chief's efforts to counter Cherokee and Indian stereotypes in the United States."

Glassman has also written a book about New York and several titles in Rosen Publishing's "Need to Know" series. The first, *Everything You Need to Know about Step-Families* is written in a conversational style and is designed to be appealing to even the most reluctant readers. Says Karen K. Radtke in *School Library Journal:* "Glassman is very supportive of readers and tries to explain in real terms how everyone's feelings are valid."

In *Everything You Need to Know about Growing up Male,* Glassman again uses a conversational tone to present both the facts and feelings connected to puberty. "Glassman's text for boys is a straightforward, clearly written summary," observes Stephanie Zvirin in *Booklist.* "Aimed at reluctant readers, it is easy to read and filled with teen-appealing photographs and helpful diagrams."

BIOGRAPHICAL/CRITICAL SOURCES:

PERIODICALS

Booklist, August, 1986, p. 1687; January 1, 1990, p. 908; September 15, 1990, p. 154; July, 1991, p. 2044; October 15, 1991, p. 426.
Bulletin of the Center for Children's Books, November, 1986.
School Library Journal, December, 1986, p. 116; April, 1989, p. 112; March, 1990, p. 243; August, 1991, p. 202; April, 1992, p. 132.
Voice of Youth Advocates, April, 1991, p. 56; December, 1991, p. 336.

*   *   *

GLISSON, J(ake) T. 1927-

PERSONAL: Born March 15, 1927, in Cross Creek, FL; son of J. Tom (a wholesaler and farmer) and Pearlee (a homemaker; maiden name, Josey) Glisson; married Patricia Apone (a nurse), 1950; children: Nick, Tom, Steve, Jennie, Bill. *Education:* Attended Ringling School of Art, 1951, and Associated Art School, Miami, FL, 1952. *Religion:* Roman Catholic. *Avocational Interests:* Flying, whitewater rafting, exploring.

ADDRESSES: Home and office—P.O. Box O, Evinston, FL 32633.

CAREER: Artist and writer. Chief executive officer of Motivation Systems and Jaake' Creations. Steinmetz Studio, Sarasota, FL, photographer, 1950; Newman Lynde Advertising Agency, Miami, FL, artist and illustrator, 1951; Advertising Trade Services of New York, Miami, artist and illustrator, 1952; *All Florida,* Ocala, art director, 1954; Cape Haze Marine Laboratory, Cape Haze, FL, artist, 1955; Social and Visitors Guides, Sarasota, chief executive officer and art director, 1964; Wild Wald Center,

Menden, Germany, art director and conceptual artist, 1983. U.S. Army, Chemical Corps College, illustrator, 1956; National Mobile Home Dealers and Owners Association magazine, chief executive officer and art director, 1957; Florida State Museum, art director, designer, and producer of traveling museums, 1968. Creator of sets, story boards, and special effects for the film *Where the River Flows North.* Explored the Manso River in Argentina and Chile, sponsored by National Geographic Society. Florida Council for the Humanities, member; Southern Academy of Letters, Arts and Sciences, honorary member. *Military service:* U.S. Army Air Forces, 1945-47.

MEMBER: Marjorie K. Rawlings Society (charter member of board of directors), Florida Historical Society, Marion County Historical Society.

WRITINGS:

The Creek, University Press of Florida, 1993.

WORK IN PROGRESS: Escape From Caska (tentative title); *Siggsby Scruggs,* a play.

*   *   *

GOBLE, Alan 1938-

PERSONAL: Born January 21, 1938, in Brighton, East Sussex, England; son of Reginald (a railway clerk) and Cynthia (Cope) Goble; married, wife's name, Valerie (a window dresser), September 14, 1963. *Avocational Interests:* Theater, literature, travel.

ADDRESSES: Home—7 Raphael Rd., Hove, East Sussex BN3 5QP, England.

CAREER: Civil servant. Currently assistant official receiver, Department of Trade and Industry.

WRITINGS:

(Editor) *The International Film Index: 1895-1990.* Volume 1: *Film Titles,* Volume 2: *Directors, Filmography and Indexes,* Bowker-Saur, 1991, revised edition, Centenary of Cinema, in press.

SIDELIGHTS: Alan Goble told *CA:* "I have had a life-long interest in the cinema. The first film I remember seeing, in 1945, was *De Letzte Chance,* directed by Leopold Lindtberg. It was a Swiss film, unusual in England just after the war. I live in a town that helped in the birth of the cinema. A group of people known as the Hove School made films here as early as 1895. My favorite film is *Elmer Gantry* (1960), starring Burt Lancaster."

GODWIN, Peter (Christopher) 1957-

PERSONAL: Born December 4, 1957, in Zimbabwe. *Education:* Received M.A. from Cambridge University.

ADDRESSES: Office—White City, 201 Wood Lane, London W12, England.

CAREER: Sunday Times, London, England, roving foreign correspondent, 1983-85, correspondent from Eastern Europe, 1985-86, and Africa, 1986-89, diplomatic correspondent, 1989; BBC-TV, London, foreign correspondent, 1990—.

MEMBER: Foreign Correspondents Association.

AWARDS, HONORS: Special Commendation from British Press Awards, 1984.

WRITINGS:

(With Ian Hancock) *Rhodesians Never Die: The Impact of War and Political Change on White Rhodesia, 1970-1980,* Clarendon Press, 1993.

Contributor to periodicals, including *Wall Street Journal, Sunday Times Magazine,* and *Illustrated London News.*

*   *   *

GOETHE, Ann 1945-
(Ann G. Distler, Ann Goette)

PERSONAL: Born December 12, 1945, in Baton Rouge, LA; daughter of Carl Conrad (a school administrator) and Eleanor (a journalist; maiden name, Canright) Goethe; married P. A. Distler, April, 1966 (divorced July, 1980); children: Paul, Gretchen, Tod. *Education:* Attended Bavat College, Tulane University, and Bennington College. *Politics:* "Often Democrat." *Religion:* "Pantheist."

ADDRESSES: Home—509 Rose Ave., Blacksbury, VA 24060. *Agent*—Sandra Dijkstra, 1155 Camino, Del Mar, CA 92014.

CAREER: Writer. Worked as dancer and actress. Founded Blacksburg New School, 1971.

AWARDS, HONORS: First prize in Louisiana poetry contest, 1960.

WRITINGS:

Midnight Lemonade (novel), Delacorte, 1993.

Also contributor—sometimes as Ann G. Distler or Ann Goette—to periodicals, including *Carolina Quarterly* and *Southern Review.*

WORK IN PROGRESS: A novel.

SIDELIGHTS: Ann Goethe is the author of *Midnight Lemonade,* a novel about the trials and tribulations of a young woman in the South. The novel's heroine is Katherine Roberts, who was raised in a small town and educated at a convent. After abandoning collegiate studies, Roberts is drawn into a relationship with a professor in his early thirties. Within several weeks Roberts marries the professor, but in the ensuing years the union becomes increasingly unsatisfactory. Katherine even turns to alcohol as a means of consoling herself while her husband indulges in extramarital flings. After obtaining a divorce, Katherine enters into another relationship. But that action bears significant repercussions, and Katherine endures further unhappiness. Dulcie Leimbach, writing in the *New York Times Book Review,* declared that the ending of *Midnight Lemonade* is "affecting."

BIOGRAPHICAL/CRITICAL SOURCES:

PERIODICALS

New York Times Book Review, May 23, 1993, p. 29.

*   *   *

GOETTE, Ann
See GOETHE, Ann

*   *   *

GOLANY, Gideon S. 1928-

PERSONAL: Born January 23, 1928; son of Jacob and Rajina Golany; married Esther Klein (a counselor), January, 1956; children: Ofer, Amir. *Education:* Hebrew University of Jerusalem, B.A., 1956, M.A., 1962, Ph.D., 1966; Institute of Social Studies, The Hague, Diploma in Comprehensive Planning, 1965; Technion-Israel Institute of Technology, M.Sc., 1966; also attended University of Northern Colorado, 1971-73, and Summer Seismic Institute for Architectural Faculty, 1978.

ADDRESSES: Home—292 Douglas Dr., State College, PA 16803. *Office*—Department of Architecture, 210 Engineering Unit C, Pennsylvania State University, University Park, PA 16802.

CAREER: Kibbutz Bea'ri, Negev, Israel, founder and active member, working as a builder, 1946-52; Ministry of Education and Culture, Jerusalem, Israel, general secretary of Scout Union Organization, 1956-58; Ministry of the Interior, Jerusalem, principal assistant to the general director, 1958-60, principal assistant for village planning, 1960-62, senior planner in Department of Regional and National Planning, 1962-63; Technion-Israel Institute of Technology, Haifa, Israel, lecturer in architecture and town planning, 1963-67; Cornell University, Ithaca, NY, lecturer in city and regional planning, 1967-68; Virginia Polytechnic Institute and State University, Blacksburg, associate professor of urban and regional planning, 1968-70; Pennsylvania State University, University Park, professor of urban and regional planning, 1970-87, research professor of urban design and planning, 1987-91, distinguished professor of urban design, 1991—, chairperson of Graduate Program in Architecture, 1970-77, faculty research fellow of Institute for Arts and Humanistic Studies, 1981, coordinator of China programs in Division of Environmental Design and Planning, 1984-89, director of the division's doctoral program, 1986-89. Planning Team Office (Haifa), partner, 1964-69; Golany Associates: New Town Planning, Natural Resource Economics, and Urban and Regional Planning and Design, principal, 1968—. Ben-Gurion University of the Negev, visiting professor at Institute for Desert Research, 1975-76; Technion-Israel Institute of Technology, visiting professor, 1979-80; Hebrew University of Jerusalem, visiting professor, 1980; University of Western Australia, visiting professor, 1980; Open University (Milton Keynes, England), visiting professor, 1981-82; University of Roorkee, visiting professor, 1982-83; Waseda University, visiting professor, 1990-91; University of Tokyo, visiting professor at Research Center for Advanced Science and Technology, 1991, endowed chair of Urban Development Engineering, 1992-93. Indian Institute of Human Settlements, member of advisory board, 1982—; American Biographical Institute, member of honorary educational advisory board, 1984—; Babylonian Jewry Heritage Center, member of academic committee, 1992. *Military service:* Hagana, 1946-48. Israeli Army, 1948-50, 1956, and 1967.

MEMBER: International New-Towns Association, American Planning Association, American Underground Space Association, Association for Arid Land Studies, Association of Engineers and Architects in Israel (overseas member), China Research Society of Ancient Architecture (foreign director, 1988).

AWARDS, HONORS: Grants from Government of the Netherlands, 1965, National Science Foundation, 1972-74, and Laboratory for Environmental Design and Planning, 1981 and 1986; Fulbright award for India, 1982-83; grant from National Academy of Sciences (for China), 1984; honorary professor of Institute of the History of Natural Science, 1988; Tongji University, honorary advisory professor, 1988; honorary professor of Academia Sinica (China Academy of Sciences), 1989; China Academy of Management Science, honorary professor of Research Institute of the Culture of World Cities, 1989; Xian Institute of Metallurgy and Construction Engineering, honorary professor, 1989; grant from National Endowment for the Arts, 1990-91; Fulbright award for Japan, 1990-91.

WRITINGS:

The Geography of Israel, Chachik (Tel-Aviv), 1962.

(Co-author) *New Geographical Dictionary,* two volumes, Mesada Publishers (Jerusalem), 1966.

New-Town Planning and Development: A Worldwide Bibliography, Urban Land Institute (Washington, DC), 1973.

(Co-editor and contributor) *The Contemporary New Communities Movement in the United States,* University of Illinois Press, 1974.

(Editor and contributor) *Strategy for New Community Development in the United States,* Dowden, Hutchinson & Ross, 1975.

New-Town Planning: Principles and Practice, Wiley, 1976.

(Editor and contributor) *Innovations for Future Cities,* Praeger, 1976.

International Urban Growth Policies: New-Town Contributions, Wiley, 1978.

Urban Planning for Arid Zones: American Experiences and Directions, Wiley, 1978.

(Editor and contributor) *Arid-Zone Settlement Planning: The Israeli Experience,* Pergamon, 1979.

(Editor and contributor) *Housing in Arid Lands: Design and Planning,* Architectural Press (London), 1980.

(Editor and contributor) *Desert Planning: International Lessons,* Architectural Press (London), 1982.

(Editor and contributor) *Design for Arid Regions,* Van Nostrand, 1983.

Earth-Sheltered Habitat: History, Architecture, and Urban Design, Van Nostrand, 1983.

Earth-Sheltered Dwellings in Tunisia: Ancient Lessons for Modern Design, University of Delaware Press, 1988.

Urban Underground Space Design in China: Vernacular and Modern Practice, University of Delaware Press, 1989.

Design and Thermal Performance: Below-Ground Dwellings in China, University of Delaware Press, 1990.

Chinese Earth-Sheltered Dwellings: Indigenous Lessons for Modern Urban Design, University of Hawaii Press, 1992.

Environmental Ethic for Urban Design (in Chinese), Liaoning Publishing House (Shenyang), 1993.

Design of Baghdad Indigenous Jewish House and Quarter (in Hebrew), Babylonian Jewry Heritage Center Publishing House (Or Yehuda), 1993.

Work represented in anthologies, including *Earth-Covered Buildings and Settlements,* Volume II, edited by Frank L. Moreland, Forrest Higgs, and Jason Shih, University of Texas at Arlington, 1979; *Urban Innovation Abroad: Problem Cities in Search of Solutions,* edited by Thomas L. Blair, Plenum, 1984; and *Chinese Landscape: The Village as Place,* edited by Ronald G. Knapp, University of Hawaii Press, 1992. Contributor of more than sixty articles to architecture and planning journals.

WORK IN PROGRESS: Baghdad Indigenous House Design: The Jewish Case, 1993; *Design of the Geo-Space City,* with T. Ojima; *Urban Design and Thermal Performance; Urban Design of Ancient Chinese Cities; Evolution of Urban Design in History.*

SIDELIGHTS: Gideon S. Golany told *CA:* "Throughout more than three decades of my academic career, my research, writing, and publications have focused on the subjects of design for traditional society when confronted with modern technology and modern management, new town planning and design, urban design in stressful climates, and earth-sheltered space design. My concern is for future city design, while one of my major themes has been the introduction of the lessons to be learned from ancient and vernacular design to modern and future practice.

"My approach is one of comprehensive design, in which I try to understand the forces affecting our environment (physical, social, economic, climatic, and so on) and bring them into synthesis in my writing. An interdisciplinary approach is 'one of never tiring to dig deep' into other related disciplines and of investigating research findings into teaching. My existing work is now focusing on design of the geo-space city, design principles of ancient Chinese cities, urban design and thermal performance, and the evolution of urban design in history.

"My mission is to produce a generation of comprehensive environmental urban designers and to upgrade the quality of practitioners. The last ten years of field survey and research in China and Japan have deeply enriched and stimulated my profession."

*   *   *

GOLDMAN, Ivan G. 1942-

PERSONAL: Born November 21, 1942, in Chicago, IL; son of Sidney (a grocer) and Shirley (a homemaker; maiden name, Balaban); married Connie Buys (a designer of computer games); children: three. *Education:* Southern Illinois University, B.A., 1965; University of Kansas, M.A., 1967. *Religion:* Jewish.

ADDRESSES: Agent—Michael Hamilburg, Mitchell J. Hamilburg Agency, 292 South La Cienega Blvd., Suite 312, Beverly Hills, CA 90211.

CAREER: Kansas City Star, Kansas City, MO, reporter; *Washington Post,* Washington, DC, reporter; *Los Angeles Times,* Los Angeles, CA, editor; California State University, Dominguez Hills, associate professor of communications; writer. Commentator for *Marketplace,* American Public Radio. *Military service:* Served in U.S. Army; member of Volunteers for Israel.

AWARDS, HONORS: Fulbright scholarship, 1989.

WRITINGS:

(With Mike Rothmiller) *L.A. Secret Police: Inside the L.A.P.D. Elite Spy Network,* Pocket Books, 1992.

Correspondent for *Ring.*

WORK IN PROGRESS: House Money, a novel; research for a nonfiction book on "Las Vegas and the changing face of the gambling industry."

SIDELIGHTS: Ivan G. Goldman has worked for such publications as the *Washington Post* and the *Los Angeles Times.* He collaborated with Mike Rothmiller, a former Los Angeles police detective, on *L.A. Secret Police: Inside the L.A.P.D. Elite Spy Network.* This 1992 book charges that the Los Angeles Police Department included a special division, numbering nearly sixty personnel, that compiled information—and, in effect, even spied—on individuals ranging from local politicians to residing celebrities. The division reported to Police Chief Daryl F. Gates, who is—in the wake of various controversies—now retired from active duty. *L.A. Secret Police* led to an internal investigation of the Los Angeles police department by Gates's replacement, Police Chief Willie Williams.

Goldman told *CA:* "I began my career as a reporter, and the newspaper life took me into exciting places and circumstances. Unfortunately, like so many journalists, I became burned out on reporting the world into the prism formula of the daily newspaper. So I became a professor, but eventually I did not feel comfortable training people to work in a profession I did not love. I knocked around the world a bit but eventually used my family's needs as a rationalization to once again get drawn into the world of daily journalism.

"At age forty nine I was toiling for a big-city newspaper when I was thrown out on the street as part of the downsizing craze. Through incredible luck I immediately secured a book contract, wrote *L.A. Secret Police,* and watched it hit the best-seller list. As any self-respecting author would do under the circumstances, I took my family to Europe. When I returned, I discovered that I wasn't rich after all. But it was all a wonderful experience, teaching me once again that we have to make our own lives and not allow them to be fashioned by the whims of others. It's a lesson I've had to learn over and over."

For more information on *L.A. Secret Police,* see the entry on Goldman's collaborator, Mike Rothmiller, in this volume.

GOLDMAN, Katherine (Wyse) 1951-

PERSONAL: Born November 14, 1951, in Cleveland, OH; daughter of Marc A. (an advertising executive) and Lois (an advertising executive and writer; maiden name, Wohlgemuth) Wyse; married Henry F. Goldman (a reporter), July 11, 1982; children: Max, Molly. *Education:* Attended Chatham College, 1969-71; Wheaton College, B.A., 1973. *Politics:* Independent Democrat. *Religion:* Jewish. *Avocational Interests:* Baseball, education, modern art, flowers.

ADDRESSES: Home—Wynnewood, PA. *Office*—P.O. Box 560, Pound Ridge, NY 10576. *Agent*—Jay Acton, Acton, Dyster, Leone & Jaffe, 79 Fifth Ave., New York, NY 10003.

CAREER: Cleveland Press, Cleveland, OH, intern, 1971; *Taunton Daily Gazette,* Taunton, MA, stringer, 1972-73; Random House, Inc., New York City, copywriter, 1973-74; Wyse Advertising, New York City, senior copywriter, 1974-82; *Shop,* New York City, associate editor, 1979-80; Richardson, Myers and Donofrio, Philadelphia, PA, associate creative director, 1983-86; operator of a consulting business for advertising and promotion, 1986—.

AWARDS, HONORS: Gold Award, Philadelphia Television/Radio Advertising Club, 1984 and 1985; recipient of regional Addy Awards; Gold Award, Business/Professional Advertising Association; awards from Delaware Advertising Club, Best of Baltimore, and Philadelphia Art Directors Club.

WRITINGS:

(Co-author) *Disco Beauty,* Simon & Schuster, 1980.
My Mother Worked and I Turned Out Okay, Villard, 1993.

WORK IN PROGRESS: Another book about working mothers, for Villard.

SIDELIGHTS: Katherine Goldman told *CA:* "I never really knew I was a writer. All I knew was that I wasn't terrified when I had to put pen to paper. I approached it as though I were talking to somebody. That conversational style appears in all of my writing. I started out by writing sales promotion material for the Random House schoolbook sales force. Then I went into advertising. There, I've always thought that if I can put the basics of a product into terms that I can understand, then I can explain it to anybody else.

"I try to find the common denominator in my audience, and I believe that my own thoughts and concerns are not much different from those of other people. I can always make myself believe that I need the product that I'm advertising, but then, I do choose the products I work on.

I turned down an assignment to write a direct mail piece for the National Rifle Association and another to write ads for a manufacturer of pesticides because I didn't believe in them.

"When I decided that *My Mother Worked and I Turned Out Okay* was the title of a book and not the headline of an ad, I approached it the same way I have approached all of my professional writing. I had a strong concept: working mothers are not taking anything away from their children; they're giving them tremendous benefits, and working mothers will feel a lot better when they know this. Then I set out to find the input from those who would substantiate my premise. I gathered all their words, organized them into small, understandable chunks, then put them together. I wanted the book to be like a conversation among lots of people. I believe it is in the words of the not-so-famous, rather than the political speeches, scientific treatises, and important biographies, where we find the real soul of our society.

"I've always liked to read journals and letters to find out what the world is really like. I also believe that the best way to learn is from sharing the experiences of others—the good, the bad, and everything else. For my research pool, I chose adult children of working mothers, because only adults have any kind of perspective on their childhoods. Before the grown-up decisions and commitments of career, life partners, and progeny, it is impossible to know what you thank your mother for. I was lucky enough to hear some very fresh voices, and yes, they did support my thesis.

"Besides my own mother and the natural pull of the genes, I've been influenced by many writers. I love Mark Twain, William Faulkner, Thomas Hardy, Charles Dickens, George Eliot, Gustave Flaubert, and the short stories of O. Henry and Dorothy Parker. I also enjoy many modern women writers, like Sue Grafton, Mary Gordon, and Margaret Atwood. I'm sitting here with a long list of first novels by young writers, and I want to get to it. I'm joining a reading club. I also read lots of journals, and letters between mothers and daughters, and stories of early pioneers and turn-of-the-century immigrants. It is all leading me to explore relationships and tough experiences, and to find the good that comes of it."

*   *   *

GOLDSTEIN, Michael S. 1944-

PERSONAL: Born August 1, 1944, in New York, NY; son of Abraham and Rose Goldstein. *Education:* Queen's College, B.A., 1965; Brown University, M.A., 1967, Ph.D., 1971.

ADDRESSES: *Office*—Department of Community Health Sciences, School of Public White Rhodesia, 1970-1980,

CAREER: Brown University, Providence, RI, lecturer, 1970-71; University of California, Los Angeles, assistant professor, 1971-78, head of the division of Behavioral Sciences and Health Education, 1978-80, associate professor, 1978-88, vice chair of the department of Public Health, 1988-89, chair of department of Community Health and Sciences, 1989-91, professor of public health and sociology, 1988—. Planning Department of the Jewish Federation Council of Greater Los Angeles, member of research advisory committee, 1977-89; American Civil Liberties Union of Southern California, member of board of directors, 1987-89; member of various committees, including "Healthy Kids-Healthy California" advisory committee, 1987-89, and "California Healthy Cities Project" steering committee, 1989—, both for California State Department of Education; Society for the Study of Social Problems, Division of Health, Health Policy and Health Services, cochair, 1991-1993.

MEMBER: American Sociological Association, American Public Health Association, Society for the Study of Social Problems, Hastings Institute of Society, Ethics, and the Life Sciences.

WRITINGS:

The Health Movement: Promoting Fitness in America, Twayne/Macmillan, 1992.

Contributor to periodicals, including *Sociology of Education, The New England Journal of Medicine, American Journal of Public Health, Contemporary Sociology,* and *The Journal of Applied Social Sciences.* Associate editor of *Journal of Health and Social Behavior,* 1985-87; member of editorial board of *The Yearbook of Cross-cultural Therapy Research,* 1992—.

*   *   *

GORDON, Vivian V(erdell) 1934-

PERSONAL: Born April 15, 1934, in Washington, DC; daughter of Thomas and Susie Verdell; married Ronald Clayton Gordon (divorced); children: Ronald Clayton Jr., Susan Gordon Akkad. *Education:* Virginia State University, B.S., 1955; University of Pennsylvania, M.A., 1957; University of Virginia, Ph.D., 1974.

ADDRESSES: *Office*—Department of African American Studies, State University of New York, Albany, NY 12222.

CAREER: Women's Christian Alliance Child Welfare Agency, Philadelphia, PA, social worker, 1956-57; Library of Congress Legislative Reference Service, Washington, D.C., research assistant, 1957, education and social analyst, 1957-63; U.S. House of Representatives Committee on Education and Labor, Washington, D.C., coordinator of research, 1963; Upward Bound Project, University of California, Los Angeles, assistant director, 1966-67; California State College (now California State University, Los Angeles), director of Education Participation in Community Program, 1967-69; University of Virginia, Charlottesburg, teaching assistant, 1971-73, assistant professor and department chairperson, 1973-79, associate professor of sociology, 1979-84; State University of New York at Albany, associate professor of African and Afro-American Studies, 1987—. Black scholar in residence, Gettysburg College, 1978; visiting Black scholar, Ball State University, 1981; visiting professor, Wellesley College, 1987. Coordinator of the National Council for Black Studies Student Contest, 1984-89; and consultant to Albany Annual Critical Black Issues Conference.

MEMBER: National Council for Black Studies, Association of Black Sociologists, Association of Black Women Historians.

AWARDS, HONORS: Outstanding Service Award, Parents Association of Jordan High School, 1968; Bethune-Roosevelt Award, The Society of Artemas of the University of Virginia, 1974, for outstanding contributions to race relations at the university; Martin Luther King Award, Alpha Phi Alpha, 1982, for service to students; Award for Distinguished Service to Students and Community, National Association for the Advancement of Colored People (NAACP) branch of the University of Virginia, 1983; Distinguished Service to Students Award, Council of Black Students Organizations at the University of Virginia, 1984; Outstanding Service to African Students, State University of New York African Students Association, 1985; Albany Black Arts and Culture Award, 1985; Outstanding Black Woman, State University of New York, 1989; Outstanding Service to Black Students, State University of New York, 1989; Martin Luther King Service Award, 1990.

WRITINGS:

The Self-Concept of Black Americans, University Press of America, 1977.
Lectures: Black Scholars on Black Issues, University Press of America, 1979.
Black Women, Feminism and Black Liberation: Which Way?, Third World Press, 1984.
Kemet and Other Ancient African Civilizations, Third World Press, 1991.
(With Lois Smith Owens) *Think about Prisons and the Criminal Justice System* (part of the "Think" series), Walker, 1992.

Author of educational publications for the Legislative Reference Service, Council of State Governments, and United States Government Printing Office, 1958-62. Member of the editorial board of *The Negro Education Review,* 1985-86.

SIDELIGHTS: Vivian V. Gordon has produced many studies, centering on subjects from driver's education to prisons. In *Black Women, Feminism and Black Liberation: Which Way?,* she had the opportunity to unite many of her areas of knowledge, methodologies, and concerns. "The author," wrote Beverly H. Robinson in *The Black Scholar,* "conducts a systematic analysis of those issues with which Black women and Black men have grappled since the emergence of the so-called women's liberation movement." Those issues include coalition politics and how they bear upon any alliance of black and white women within the movement, the strong identification between white women and white men, and the cause and effect relationship between the Civil Rights movement and the emergence of Women's Studies.

Ironically, that latter connection resulted in the attempted erasure, in academia, of any difference between black women's and white women's problems. Gordon's historical review reveals this to be a damaging mistake. Her contemporary research with a sample of black women, moreover, shows them connecting their own liberation with the liberation of the entire African American community—male and female, upper and lower class. Unification of that community, through education and bridge-building, is and should be the black woman's priority, she concludes.

In noting that Gordon's conclusions agree with many other black feminist writings, Robinson comments that the book is still a valuable addition to those previous views. Gordon's long career has allowed her to experience social problems which affect black Americans from a wide range of perspectives—that of a social worker, researcher and analyst, and educator. "Vivian Gordon," concludes Robinson, "has analyzed all of the possible issues that must be considered for the development of a theoretical perspective on political alternatives for Black women."

BIOGRAPHICAL/CRITICAL SOURCES:

PERIODICALS

The Black Scholar, March, 1985.*

*   *   *

GOTTLIEB, Carl

PERSONAL: Born March 18, in New York, NY; son of Sergius M. (an engineer) and Elizabeth (a medical admin-

istrative assistant) Gottlieb; married Allison Caine, 1970 (divorced, 1982). *Education:* Received B.S. from Syracuse University.

ADDRESSES: Office—c/o Writers Guild of America, West, 8955 Beverly Blvd., West Hollywood, CA 90048. *Agent*—c/o APA, 9000 Sunset Blvd., Los Angeles, CA 90069.

CAREER: Screenwriter, director, and actor. Director of films, including *The Absent-Minded Waiter* (short), 1977; and *Caveman,* 1981. Director of television programs, including *The Music Scene,* 1969-70; and *Delta House,* 1977. Actor in films, including *Maryjane,* 1968; *M*A*S*H,* 1970; *Up the Sandbox,* 1972; *Jaws,* 1975; *Cannonball,* 1976; *The Jerk,* 1979; *The Sting II,* 1983; *Johnny Dangerously,* 1984; and *Amazon Women on the Moon.* Actor in television programs, including *The Ken Berry "Wow" Show,* 1972; *The Super,* 1972; and *The TV TV Show,* 1977. Actor in The Committee (improvisational comedy troupe), San Francisco, CA, 1963-68. Instructor at University of Southern California and Sundance Institute. *Military service:* U.S. Army, 1961-63.

MEMBER: Academy of Motion Picture Arts and Sciences, Writers Guild of America, West (vice-president, 1991-95).

AWARDS, HONORS: Emmy Award for outstanding writing in a comedy, variety, or music program, Academy of Television Arts and Sciences, 1969, for *The Smothers Brothers Comedy Hour.*

WRITINGS:

SCREENPLAYS

(With Peter Benchley) *Jaws* (based on the novel by Benchley), Universal, 1975.
(With Cecil Brown) *Which Way Is Up?,* Universal, 1977.
(With Howard Sackler) *Jaws II,* Universal, 1978.
(With Steve Martin and Michael Elias) *The Jerk* (from a story by Martin and Gottlieb), Universal, 1979.
(With Rudy DeLuca) *Caveman,* United Artists, 1981.
(With Richard Matheson) *Jaws 3-D* (based on a story by Guerdon Trueblood), Universal, 1983.
(With Robert Boris and Bruce Jay Friedman) *Dr. Detroit* (based on a story by Friedman), Universal, 1983.

TELEPLAYS

The Smothers Brothers Comedy Hour (series), Columbia Broadcasting System (CBS), 1967-69.
The Summer Smothers Brothers Show (series), CBS, 1968.
The Super (series), American Broadcasting Companies (ABC), 1972.
Flip Wilson . . . Of Course (special), National Broadcasting Company, (NBC), 1974.
The Flip Wilson Special, NBC, 1974.

The Flip Wilson Comedy Special, NBC, 1975.

The New Lorenzo Music Show (pilot), ABC, 1976.

The Deadly Triangle (pilot), NBC, 1977.

(With Alvin Boretz) *Crisis in Sun Valley* (pilot), NBC, 1978.

Also writer of episodes of the series *The Odd Couple,* ABC, and *The Bob Newhart Show,* CBS.

BOOKS

The Jaws Log, Dell, 1975.

(With David Crosby) *Long Time Gone: The Autobiography of David Crosby,* Doubleday, 1988.

WORK IN PROGRESS: A feature film, *Illegals,* for Ithaca Films.

SIDELIGHTS: With Peter Benchley (the author of the novel upon which the movie was based), Carl Gottlieb collaborated on the screenplay for what would become one of the highest-grossing movies of all time—*Jaws.* Gottlieb began his eclectic career in show business as an improvisational actor in The Committee, a California comedy troupe, in the 1960s. He went on to play small roles in popular movies like *Up the Sandbox, Johnny Dangerously, Amazon Women on the Moon, The Jerk,* and *Jaws,* the latter two of which he also cowrote. Gottlieb has been a director for television and film, and his television writing includes Emmy Award-winning work for *The Smothers Brothers Comedy Hour.* He is also the author of two books of nonfiction.

It is for his screenplays, however, that Gottlieb is best known. *Jaws,* the thriller of the summer of 1975, saw a tiny New England community terrorized by a great white shark at the height of tourist season. While Benchley's novel was a best seller in its own right, some of the movie's phenomenal success was credited to the pared-down writing of its screenplay, which resulted in a more action-oriented film. A reviewer for *Time* magazine, in a cover story that described the movie as "an efficient entertainment machine," called the film script "a shrewd adaptation" of the original work. The *Time* contributor also told the story of the conflict arising from the five different versions of the screenplay, the final version of which "was rejiggered nightly out on location." The making of *Jaws* featured its own peculiar terrors. While waiting to film a scene at sea in which Gottlieb played a small part, the *Time* reviewer recalled, Gottlieb "fell overboard and was nearly decapitated by the boat's propellers." The story would be told again in Gottlieb's *Jaws Log,* a book chronicling the making of the movie. According to a commentator in *Publishers Weekly,* the account is in the form of "a gossipy, seemingly candid, occasionally testy journal" replete with details about the locals of Martha's Vineyard (where the movie was filmed) and behind-the-scenes glimpses of the cast and crew members.

Gottlieb refrained from acting in the less popular sequels *Jaws II* and *Jaws 3-D,* although he returned to coauthor the screenplay of each. The films' critical reception, like their box-office success, was less enthusiastic than that of the originals. Vincent Canby questioned the need for a sequel in his review of *Jaws II* in the *New York Times.* Kevin Thomas of the *Los Angeles Times* felt that the script of *Jaws 3-D* (cowritten by Gottlieb and Richard Matheson from a story by Guerdon Trueblood) neglected characterization in the name of action and special effects. Thomas concluded, however, that the film is "fast-moving and unpretentious." The reviewer also found it "a respectably made action thriller."

From the terror and subtle humor of the *Jaws* films, Gottlieb moved on to pen the screenplays of three relatively successful comedies. *The Jerk,* written by its star, Steve Martin, in collaboration with Michael Elias and Gottlieb, was well received by Janet Maslin in the *New York Times:* The reviewer described the 1979 movie as being "by turns funny, vulgar and backhandedly clever, never more so than when it aspires to absolute stupidity." Maslin was similarly pleased with Gottlieb's follow-up effort, *Caveman,* which Gottlieb also directed. Starring Ringo Starr, the drummer for the immensely popular rock group the Beatles, and set in the year One Billion B.C., *Caveman* appealed to Maslin as a movie that is "nicely whimsical, and elaborate in a way that no fantasy film this side of outer space has lately been. It's dopey, but it's also lots of fun." Like *The Jerk, Dr. Detroit* worked as a vehicle for the humor of its comedian/actor star—in this case, Dan Aykroyd. Some critics felt the movie's script (penned by Bruce Jay Friedman, Gottlieb, and Robert Boris from a Friedman story) was undercut by a patchwork collaboration. Nevertheless, Gene Siskel of the *Chicago Tribune* pointed out the movie's "many goofy, entertaining scenes," while Thomas in the *Los Angeles Times* called it "a boisterous, cheerfully crass piece of nonsense that serves its purpose just fine in allowing Aykroyd to show off his wares."

Gottlieb's writing took a more serious turn in 1988, when he allowed rock musician David Crosby's powerful story of drug addiction and recovery to come to the fore in *Long Time Gone: The Autobiography of David Crosby.*

Gottlieb told *CA:* "I'm currently sharing what I know with other writers, teaching at the University of Southern California and Sundance Institute, and through service at the Writers Guild and elsewhere."

BIOGRAPHICAL/CRITICAL SOURCES:

PERIODICALS

Chicago Tribune, December 14, 1979, p. 13; May 6, 1983.
Los Angeles Times, May 6, 1983; July 25, 1983.
New York Times, June 16, 1978; December 14, 1979, p. C12; April 17, 1981; May 6, 1983.
Publishers Weekly, June 30, 1975, p. 60
Time, June 23, 1975, p. 42.
Washington Post, May 9, 1983.

*   *   *

GRANGER, (Patricia) Ann   1939-
(Ann Hulme)

PERSONAL: Born July 12, 1939, in Portsmouth, England; daughter of Eugene (an officer in the Royal Navy) and Norah (a homemaker; maiden name, Davey) Granger; married John Hulme (a civil servant), 1966; children: Timothy, Christopher. *Education:* Royal Holloway College, London, B.A. (with honors), 1962. *Religion:* Anglican.

ADDRESSES: Home—34 Longfields, Bicester, Oxfordshire OX6 7QL, England. *Agent*—Al Zuckerman, Writers House, 21 West Twenty-sixth St., New York, NY 10010; and Carole Blake, Blake Friedmann, 37-41 Gower St., London WC1E 6HH, England.

CAREER: Worked as English teacher in France, 1960-61; worked in visa section of British embassies in Europe, including Zagreb, Belgrade, Prague, and Vienna, 1962-66; writer.

MEMBER: Society of Authors, Crime Writers Association, Mystery Writers of America, Writers in Oxford.

WRITINGS:

"MITCHELL AND MARKBY" SERIES; MYSTERY NOVELS

Say It with Poison, St. Martin's, 1991.
A Season for Murder, Headline, 1991, St. Martin's, 1992.
Cold in the Earth, Headline, 1992, St. Martin's, 1993.
Murder among Us, Headline, 1992, St. Martin's, 1993.
Where Old Bones Lie, Headline, 1993, St. Martin's, 1994.
A Fine Place for Death, Headline, 1994.

HISTORICAL ROMANCE NOVELS, UNDER PSEUDONYM ANN HULME

Summer Heiress, Mills & Boon, 1981.
The Gamester, Mills & Boon, 1982.
The Emperor's Dragoon, Mills & Boon, 1983.
Daughter of Spain, Mills & Boon, 1984.
A Woman of the Regiment, Mills & Boon, 1985.
The Hungarian Adventures, Mills & Boon, 1985.
The Unexpected American, Mills & Boon, 1988.

The Flying Man, Worldwide, 1988.
A Scandalous Bargain, Mills & Boon, 1988.
Captain Harland's Marriage, Mills & Boon, 1989.
False Fortune, Mills & Boon, 1989.
Whisper in the Wind, Worldwide, 1989.

Also author of *A Poor Relation,* 1979, *Interlaken Intrigue,* 1986, *The Garden of the Azure Dragon,* 1986, and *No Place for a Lady,* 1988.

Hulme's works have been translated into French, Swedish, Finnish, and German.

WORK IN PROGRESS: A five-part serial mystery, *The Smugglers' Stair,* and a new Mitchell and Markby novel, *Flowers for His Funeral,* to be published by Headline.

SIDELIGHTS: Ann Granger is perhaps best known as the author of a series of mystery novels featuring heroine Meredith Mitchell (a British Foreign Office employee), and her crime-solving partner, chief inspector Alan Markby. Several reviewers have noted Granger's compelling characters and her sensitive portrayal of human relationships. In a *Publishers Weekly* review of *Say It with Poison,* Sybil Steinberg determined that Mitchell and Markby must solve a murder which can only be done through "an understanding of the inner lives of those connected with the events," and concluded that this book will "be savored by connoisseurs of characterization." Likewise, Granger's well-drawn settings are noted for heightening the suspense of the narrative. Steinberg wrote in *Publishers Weekly* that, in Granger's *Cold in the Earth,* both the characterization as well as "the atmospheric Cotswolds setting give this tale uncommon depth."

Granger told *CA:* "It's always difficult to explain just why a writer writes. I was a bookish child. When I was young my mother would read aloud to me until her voice gave out. Later, I had an inspired English teacher who encouraged me to read a wide variety of literature. So I read Fyodor Dostoyevsky, for example, when I was in my early teens. I've retained a great love of long, nineteenth-century novels ever since. Crime writers whose works I admire include Ngaio Marsh, Agatha Christie, Nicolas Freeling, Erle Stanley Gardner, Emma Lathen, and Barbara Paul, among many others.

"My crime novels have country settings. But the settings are modern villages reflecting rural life as it is today, and not at the time of the Golden Age of writers. The characters face modern problems as well as timeless situations. I always try to include an element of humor in my writing as I believe it is integral to the human experience."

BIOGRAPHICAL/CRITICAL SOURCES:

PERIODICALS

Publishers Weekly, February 22, 1991, p. 214; January 27, 1992, p. 90; February 22, 1993, p. 84.

*   *   *

GREENBERG, Elinor Miller 1932-

PERSONAL: Born November 13, 1932, in Brooklyn, NY; daughter of Ray (a wholesale supplier) and Susan (a homemaker and salesperson; maiden name, Weiss) Miller; married Manuel Greenberg (self-employed), December 26, 1955; children: Andrea Susan, Julie Elizabeth, Michael Alan. *Education:* Mount Holyoke College, B.A., 1953; University of Wisconsin—Madison, M.A., 1954; University of Northern Colorado, Ed.D., 1981. *Politics:* Democrat. *Religion:* Jewish. *Avocational Interests:* Travel.

ADDRESSES: Home and office—EMG and Associates, 6725 South Adams Way, Littleton, CO 80122.

CAREER: Loretto Heights College, Denver, CO, director of University Without Walls, 1971-79, assistant academic dean for adult education and public service, 1981-84, assistant to the president, 1984-85; Pathways to the Future, Englewood, CO, founding executive director, 1986-91; EMG and Associates (consulting and publishing business), Littleton, CO, president and chief executive officer, 1991—. University of Maryland at College Park, research associate at Institute for Research on Adults in Higher Education, 1991. Council for Adult and Experimental Learning, regional manager and executive officer for Mountains and Plains Region, 1979-91; Project Leadership, executive director, 1986—; National Center for Strategic Planning and Resource Development, senior counsel. Interdisciplinary Telecommunications Program, member of executive board; Colorado 2000, chairperson of Goal Five Team; Colorado Telecommunications Advisory Commission, chairperson of K-12 Visioning Team; Colorado Legal and Judicial Education Board, member; Colorado Women's Economic Development Council, member; Colorado Mathematics, Science, and Technology Commission, co-chairperson, 1992—; committee member of Colorado Commission on Higher Education, Colorado Private Occupational Schools Advisory Committee, Colorado State Board for Community Colleges and Occupational Education, and U.S. Department of Education; worked with National Women's Business Council and U.S. Department of Labor; senior consultant to U.S. West Foundation and University of Colorado at Denver. International Women's Forum, member of board of directors, 1986-89, currently member of board of directors of its Leadership Foundation; Women's Forum of Colo-

rado, president, 1986; Colorado Women's Leadership Coalition, co-founder, 1988, member of executive committee, and co-chairperson of Coalition Development Committee; member of LARASA/Hispanic Agenda Higher Education Oversight Commission, Women's Equity Fund, and Hermitage Retreat.

MEMBER: B'nai B'rith (and its Anti-Defamation League).

AWARDS, HONORS: Minoru Yasui Volunteer Award; named Woman of the Decade, 1970; honorary degrees from St. Mary-of-the-Woods College and Professional School of Psychology.

WRITINGS:

(Editor with Kathleen M. O'Donnell and William H. Bergquist, and contributor) *Educating Learners of All Ages,* Jossey-Bass, 1980.

(With William H. Bergquist and Ronald A. Gould) *Designing Undergraduate Education: A Systematic Guide,* Jossey-Bass, 1981.

(Co-editor and contributor) *New Partnerships: Higher Education and the Nonprofit Sector,* Jossey-Bass, 1982.

(With Stephanie Allen, Lois J. Zachary, and others) *Enhancing Leadership,* EMG and Associates, 1989.

Weaving: The Fabric of a Woman's Life, EMG and Associates, 1991.

Journey for Justice: From Colorado to Germany, EMG and Associates, 1993.

(With William H. Bergquist and G. Alan Klaum) *In Our Fifties: Voices of Men and Women Reinventing Their Lives,* Jossey-Bass, 1993.

Columnist for *Littleton Independent, Denver Business Journal,* and *Colorado Woman News.* Contributor of more than a hundred-fifty articles to periodicals. Guest editor, *Liberal Education,* 1992.

WORK IN PROGRESS: Research on the information superhighway and on integrated community networks.

SIDELIGHTS: Elinor Miller Greenberg told *CA:* "My life work has been to weave the fabric of self, others, and community into coherent and relevant projects and programs that integrate adult development, institutional change, and societal trends and realities. In doing so, I have remained at the cutting edge in higher education, school reform, nonprofit development, and business/economic development. My career reveals periods of innovative organizational activity, alternated with periods of reflection and writing. I draw my writing from my experience and study, then communicate to larger audiences through public speaking, workshops, and service on boards and commissions. I often work in the margins, between sectors, and view my work as pace-setting and creative.

"My special concerns and commitments are to human rights, women's issues, diversity, and equal opportunity. Throughout my life, my work has been directed toward these ends. I view the coming years, and our entrance into the twenty-first century, as focused on demography, technology, and the new global economy and political climate. My current and future efforts will be devoted to ensuring that technological change, especially the information superhighway, is directed to access for diverse Americans and participation in the new global economy."

*   *   *

GREGG, Davis W(einert) 1918-1993

OBITUARY NOTICE—See index for *CA* sketch: Born March 12, 1918, in Austin, TX; died of cancer, October 27, 1993, in Bryn Mawr, PA. Insurance professional, educator, and author. Gregg is remembered for the changes he implemented to the programs offered at American College of Life Underwriters, which in 1976 modified its name to American College. In 1940 he began his career as an underwriter, later directing his insurance knowledge to educating students at Ohio State University. Following his position at Ohio State, he became a trustee at American College of Life Underwriters. From 1954 to 1982 he served as president and then was named a Distinguished Professor of Economics. At the University of Pennsylvania, Gregg founded, directed, and chaired the Boettner Institute of Financial Gerontology. He penned the work *Group Life Insurance,* and edited books such as, with Vane B. Luca, *Life and Health Insurance Handbook* and, with John D. Long, *Property and Liability Insurance Handbook.* He also edited more than thirty volumes of the "Irwin Series in Risk and Insurance."

OBITUARIES AND OTHER SOURCES:

BOOKS

Who's Who in America, 48th edition, Marquis, 1994.

PERIODICALS

New York Times, October 29, 1993, p. B10.

*   *   *

GRIMOND, Joseph 1913-1993

OBITUARY NOTICE—See index for *CA* sketch: Born July 29, 1913, in St. Andrews, Scotland; died of a stroke, October 24, 1993, on the Orkney Islands, Scotland. Political leader and author. As leader of Britain's Liberal Party, Grimond was known for his humor and idealism. Before his political career, he worked briefly as the European di-

rector of personnel for the United Nations Relief and Rehabilitation Administration. In 1950 he became a Liberal member of the British Parliament for Orkney and Shetland, a position he held for almost four decades. Beginning in 1956, Grimond was elected the head of the Liberal Party. During the years he lead the party, the Liberal leverage in elections increased, but not enough to gain substantial power. In 1967 Grimond resigned from his leadership position. After leaving Parliament, Grimond joined the House of Lords. He wrote a number of books expressing his political views, including *The Liberal Challenge, The Common Welfare,* and *A Personal Manifesto.* His other works include *Memoirs, The St. Andrews of Jo Grimond,* and *Britain: A View from Westminster.*

OBITUARIES AND OTHER SOURCES:

BOOKS

Writers Directory: 1988-1990, St. James Press, 1988.

PERIODICALS

New York Times, October 27, 1993, p. D24.
Times (London), October 26, 1993, p. 17.
Washington Post, October 27, 1993, p. D5.

*   *   *

GROSS, Martha 1931-

PERSONAL: Born September 27, 1931, in Chicago, IL; daughter of Matthias Joseph (in business) and Myrtle Eileen (an artist; maiden name, Ray) Propst; married Sol W. Gross (in business), December 21, 1961 (died, 1976); children: Jennifer Ray. *Education:* Studied acting at Chicago School of Expression and Dramatic Art as a child; attended University of Chicago, 1954-57. *Politics:* Republican. *Religion:* Roman Catholic. *Avocational Interests:* Painting, cooking, ham radio, aerial ballet, dancing, bowling.

ADDRESSES: Office—Lifestyle Section, *Sun-Sentinel,* 200 East Las Olas Blvd., Fort Lauderdale, FL 33301-2293. *Agent*—Joyce Flaherty, 816 Lynda St., St. Louis, MO 63122.

CAREER: Worked as a professional actress on television and radio in Chicago, IL, 1948-51; U.S. Navy, Waukegan, IL, computer programmer, 1957-59; Metropolitan Life Insurance Co., New York City, computer programmer, 1959-60; *Singles Directory* (magazine), Hollywood, FL, editor and publisher, 1976-79; talk show host for WRBD-Radio, Fort Lauderdale, FL, and WKAT-Radio, Miami, FL, 1979-80; *Sun-Tattler* (newspaper; now defunct), Hollywood, bi-weekly columnist, 1981-83; *Sun-Sentinel* (newspaper), Fort Lauderdale, columnist-editor, 1983---;

free-lance novelist, 1993—. Makes appearances with the local Hanneford Circus performing "The Web" (an aerial ballet) for various charities in southern Florida.

AWARDS, HONORS: Named Poet Laureate of Hollywood, Florida, 1994.

WRITINGS:

Return to Love (romance novel), Zebra, 1993.
One Kiss (romance novel), Zebra, 1993.

Contributor of novellas to romance anthologies, including *To Mother with Love* and *Merry Christmas My Love,* both Zebra, both 1993.

WORK IN PROGRESS: A romance novel, and an untitled novel for Zebra, to be published in 1994.

SIDELIGHTS: Columnist and novelist Martha Gross had a varied professional life that included being both an actress and a computer programmer before she became a writer during the mid-1970s. While penning columns for two southern Florida newspapers, first the *Sun-Tattler* and then the *Sun-Sentinel,* however, she began to seek out new experiences. As a society columnist, Gross has been involved in many charitable events, and for these events she has engaged in activities that range from driving a formula race car in an actual race to performing aerial ballet twenty-five feet above the floor for a circus. She records her experiences in her column, and, as Kevin Lane reported in *Fort Lauderdale Downtown,* "she has been catapulted off a Navy carrier deck in a small plane. . . . She has piloted the Goodyear Blimp, a Navy hydrofoil . . . and a nuclear sub 180 feet under the ocean's surface. Some people have called Martha Gross the George Plimpton of the newspaper world."

In 1993, Gross ventured into fiction with her first romance novel, *Return to Love.* Written for Zebra Books' "To Love Again" series, the narrative relates the story of two young protagonists who first meet at a high school science fair and recognize their mutual attraction, yet go their separate ways for thirty-five years until both wind up widowed and living in the same condominium complex. Gross has also published a second book, entitled *One Kiss,* and has had two romance novellas published in the Zebra anthologies *To Mother with Love* and *Merry Christmas My Love.* Two more romance novels are in the works, and Gross intends after that to write mainstream fiction.

Gross told *CA:* "How do I write? I just sit at a keyboard and start tapping. I don't get writer's block. Newspaper writers aren't allowed. I don't feel inspired today? Tough. I write anyway. (I don't want to be switched to the classified department.) If the results are crummy, at least now there's something to rewrite, to soup up. A forty-hour week? Ha! First comes the endless dressing up and the par-

ties, then the unforgiving deadlines. But I do meet such fascinating people. The rich and famous. The accomplishers. The stars.

"When I finally gave in to the urge that had been nudging me for decades, to write a novel, with my tight schedule, what then? I'll tell you what then. These days, my glasses are held together by safety pins—no time to get them fixed. No time for anything. My car gets washed once in twelve to fifteen months. My nails are always a mess. I can hardly walk through the entry hall of my apartment. I dump things there when I dash in and pick them up as I dash out. I rarely sit down for meals. I eat while I write, while I drive—rice cakes, bagels, fruit. With all those crumbs on the floor, I'm lucky I don't get mice in my car. You get the picture. Part of my problem is I simply cannot resist a chance at a good story. Life is short. If you want to do it all, you have to keep moving. People over fifty needn't dry up and quit. I have lots of mountains yet to climb. When someone mentions a new, interesting hands-on story idea, all I can say is 'Hey, gang, wait for me!' "

BIOGRAPHICAL/CRITICAL SOURCES:

PERIODICALS

Fort Lauderdale Downtown, December, 1992, p. 15.

*　　*　　*

GROSSE, W. Jack 1923-

PERSONAL: Born April 3, 1923, in Cincinnati, OH; son of Wilbur J. and Marguirette (Forbes) Grosse; married Norma Lee Kirby, December 13, 1947; children: Douglas W., Lisa Lynn. *Education:* Chase College of Commerce, B.S.C., 1952; Xavier University, M.B.A., 1954; Northern Kentucky State College (now University), J.D., 1962, LL.D., 1972; Case Western Reserve University, LL.M., 1969.

ADDRESSES: Home—3860 Vineyard Green Dr., Cincinnati, OH 45255. *Office*—Chase College of Law, Northern Kentucky University, Highland Heights, KY 41099.

CAREER: Dun & Bradstreet, credit reporter, 1946-47; Fifth-Third Bank, credit manager, 1947-54; Chase College of Commerce, Cincinnati, OH, professor and associate dean, 1954-62; Northern Kentucky University, Highland Heights, professor of law and assistant dean of Chase College of Law, 1962-64; Clarkson College of Technology, Potsdam, NY, professor, 1964-66; Northern Kentucky University, professor of law, 1966-68; Xavier University, Cincinnati, professor and assistant dean, 1968-70; Northern Kentucky University, professor of law, 1970-91, professor emeritus, 1991—, dean of Chase College of Law,

1970-78, interim dean, 1992-93, member of board of trustees, university counsel, 1979-81. Private practice of law, 1962—. Underwriters Publishing Co., author of insurance summaries, 1962-82, editor, 1962—. Ohio Valley Environmental and Natural Resources Law Institute, president; Ohio State Bar Foundation, fellow; Cincinnati Bar Foundation, member of board of trustees. Pro Seniors, Inc., member of board of trustees; Northern Kentucky Legal Aid Society, member of board of trustees; Northern Kentucky Family Service, member of advisory committee.

MEMBER: American Bar Association, American Society for Legal History, American Society for Political and Legal Philosophy, Selden Society, Ohio State Bar Association, Kentucky Bar Association, Cincinnati Bar Association.

WRITINGS:

(Coauthor) *Government Contract Law,* Ohio State Research Foundation, 1970.

School Law Handbook, Chase Center for Public Law, Northern Kentucky University, 1981.

The Protection and Management of Our Natural Resources: Wildlife and Habitat, Oceana, 1992.

Natural Resource Law: Cases and Materials, two volumes, Gateway Press, 1993.

(With C. Maxwell Dieffenbach and Stanley E. Harper) *A Centennial History of Chase College of Law,* W. H. Anderson, 1994.

Contributor to law and education journals.

*   *   *

GRUBB, Michael (J.) 1960-

PERSONAL: Born February 29, 1960, in Southall, England; son of Mortyn (a mini-cab driver and philosopher) and Anne (a solicitor; maiden name, Bath) Grubb; married Anne-Christine Davis (a lecturer in physics), July 12, 1986; children: Tara Davis. *Education:* Attended Cambridge University. *Politics:* "Pragmatic idealist."

ADDRESSES: Home—Cambridge, England. *Office*—Energy and Environmental Programme, Royal Institute of International Affairs, Chatham House, 10 St. James's Sq., London SW1Y 4LE, England.

CAREER: Royal Institute of International Affairs, London, England, head of Energy and Environmental Programme.

WRITINGS:

Energy Policies and the Greenhouse Effect, Dartmouth Publishing, Volume 1: *Policy Appraisal,* c. 1990, Volume 2: *Country Studies and Technical Options,* c. 1991.

WORK IN PROGRESS: A study of renewable energy strategies for Europe.

SIDELIGHTS: Michael Grubb told *CA:* "A childhood enthusiasm for 'creative writing,' suppressed during the requirement to study English grammar and Shakespeare in secondary school, finally began to find expression more than fifteen years later, after completion of a physics degree. Writing short pieces on subjects ranging from the causes of the Ethiopian famine and Indira Gandhi's assassination, to the subjects of nuclear weapons and energy supply, generated the confidence and skills for communication. Since then I have been aware of a passion both for understanding complex issues and for communicating such understanding.

"My research position at the Energy and Environmental Programme at Chatham House has given full range for these interests. Tackling the threat of global warming combines so many diverse interests: technical aspects of energy supply, nuclear power, and the alternatives; the struggle between the ideological simplicity of free markets and the practical limitations to intervention; the domestic politics of powerful interest groups twisting perceptions in a bid to deflect effective action away from their sector; and the international politics of nations trying to face up to—or run away from—a global constraint. Underlying all these are the basic human psychology and economic structures which drive the search for ever greater consumption.

"After one report on the negotiating issues, and two extensive volumes on energy policies and the Greenhouse Effect, I am mostly conscious of how much more remains to be said. Yet an excessive focus on one topic, however large and important, has to be tempered. My book on the Earth Summit Agreements seeks to answer for a broader audience a basic question that bothered me after witnessing, in Rio, the biggest international conference process in history: what did it achieve? Is the world really starting to grapple with the reality that the expansion of human activity is pushing at the limits of the planet and, if so, what in the realm of political reality can be done about it? I will not be surprised if writing and speaking under this broad theme occupies most of my career."

The author also discussed his work in progress with *CA:* "Renewable energy sources, like wind, solar power, and energy from plants, are emerging as serious candidates for energy supply after being eclipsed for two hundred years. My book in progress examines how Europe can seize the opportunities offered."

BIOGRAPHICAL/CRITICAL SOURCES:

PERIODICALS

Financial Times, November 23, 1990.
Safe Energy, June/July, 1992.

*   *   *

GUILLOU, Jan 1944-

PERSONAL: Born in 1944 in Sweden.

ADDRESSES: Agent—c/o Norstedt Publishers, Box 2052, S-103, 12 Stockholm, Sweden.

CAREER: Worked as a reporter at a small radical magazine in Sweden during the early-1970s; convicted of espionage in 1973; author, c. 1976—.

WRITINGS:

Journalistik 1967-1976, Oktober, 1976.
(With Marina Stagh) *Irak—det nya Arabien,* Norstedt, 1977.
(With Jan Hakan Dahlstrom) *Artister: Intervjuer och portratt,* Norstedt, 1979.
Reporter, Oktoberforl, 1979.
Justitiemord: Fallet Keith Cederholm, foreword by Henning Sjostrom, Askelin & Hagglund, 1983.
(With Goran Skytte) *Nya berattelser: Fran Geijer till Rainer,* Askelin & Hagglund, 1984.
I nationens intresse: Coq Rouge, Norstedt, 1988.
Fiendens fiende, Norstedt, 1989, translation by Thomas Keeland published as *Enemy's Enemy,* Knopf, 1992.
Vendetta: Coq Rouge VI, Norstedt, 1991.
Ingen mans land: Coq Rouge VII, Norstedt, 1992.

SIDELIGHTS: In the early-1970s, Swedish author Jan Guillou was working as a reporter for a small magazine when he and his partner discovered a secret military intelligence organization at work in Sweden. The pair reported their investigations, which, among other things, proved that this organization violated Swedish law by planting informants in left-wing associations and also went against the Swedish policy of neutrality by aiding Israel in that country's clashes with Arab nations in the Middle East. Guillou and his partner were convicted of espionage for their work and served short sentences. When he began writing novels, Guillou drew upon this experience to craft a series of espionage thrillers. His books are very popular in Sweden; the first one was notable for its similarity to the actual assassination of former Swedish Prime Minister Olof Palme. As Guillou related to *CA:* "Most of the stories in my novels are authentic, and most of the characters *do* exist in real life; some of them are my friends and some my enemies."

Guillou's first book to be published in the United States is *Fiendens fiend,* which was translated by Thomas Keeland and published as *Enemy's Enemy.* Like several of Guillou's other novels, *Enemy's Enemy* features Swedish spy Carl Hamilton—a protagonist *Publishers Weekly* described as "a Nordic James Bond with a touch of angst." The book has what is considered an unusual structure for the espionage genre and is divided into four parts that find Hamilton in an equal number of intrigue situations. In one section Hamilton's reputation is questioned as charges of complicity with Russian enemies is leveled; his heroic side is showcased in a jaunt to Lebanon; his skills as a master spy are put to use in Moscow; and he finally ends up back in Sweden, nobly completing his mission. Kenneth Mintz in the *Library Journal* liked *Enemy's Enemy,* declaring it to be "a thoughtful spy thriller that succeeds" in spite of a few flaws.

BIOGRAPHICAL/CRITICAL SOURCES:

PERIODICALS

Chicago Tribune, February 16, 1992, sec. 14, p. 4.
Library Journal, January, 1992, p. 174.
Publishers Weekly, November 29, 1991, p. 43.*

*   *   *

GUNZBERG, Lynn M. 1944-

PERSONAL: Born April 21, 1944, in Buffalo, NY; daughter of Arthur (an executive) and Aline (Dubin) Gunzberg; married Anthony Molho (a professor), December 23, 1984. *Education:* University of Wisconsin—Madison, B.A., 1966; University of California, Berkeley, M.A., 1968, Ph.D., 1982. *Avocational Interests:* Choral singing, gardening.

ADDRESSES: Home—83 Keene St., Providence, RI 02906. Office—Office of the Dean of the College, Brown University, Box 1865, Providence, RI 02912.

CAREER: Brown University, Providence, RI, assistant professor of Italian, 1982-87, associate dean of the college, 1986—, adjunct associate professor, 1993—. Member of Planned Parenthood and Providence Singers.

MEMBER: Modern Language Association of America, National Association of Women in Education, American Association of University Women.

WRITINGS:

Strangers at Home: Jews in the Italian Literary Imagination, University of California Press, 1992.

Contributor to literature journals.

WORK IN PROGRESS: Research on Italian Jewish writers and on Italian emigration.

GUTTMANN, Hadassah 1952-

PERSONAL: Born June 4, 1952, in New York, NY; daughter of Jacob (a designer of men's clothes) and Helen (a nurse; maiden name, Schnall) Guttmann; married Peter Cutrin, 1975 (divorced, 1982). *Education:* Queens College of the City University of New York, B.Mus., 1976, M.A., 1978; New York University, Ph.D. (with honors), 1991. *Politics:* Democrat. *Religion:* Jewish. *Avocational Interests:* Giving and attending musical concerts, art, history, animals, walking, theater.

ADDRESSES: Home—62-43 136th St., Flushing, NY 11367. *Office*—Department of Music, Nassau Community College of the State University of New York, Garden City, NY 11530-6793.

CAREER: Nassau Community College of the State University of New York, Garden City, adjunct associate professor of music, 1984—. Lucy Moses Music School, Abraham Goodman House, Merkin Concert Hall, teacher, director, and coordinator, 1992—; Guteri Trio, director. Pianist, performing at chamber music concerts in and around New York City and on radio and television programs.

MEMBER: Music Teachers National Association (member of board of directors, 1991-92), Music Educators National Conference, American Society for Jewish Music, College Music Society, Phi Delta Kappa, Pi Kappa Lambda.

AWARDS, HONORS: Grants from Queens Council on the Arts, 1979—.

WRITINGS:

The Music of Paul Ben-Haim: A Performance Guide, Scarecrow, 1992.

WORK IN PROGRESS: Research for a book on several contemporary composers.

H

HAGGARD, William
See CLAYTON, Richard Henry Michael

*   *   *

HAGY, James William 1936-

PERSONAL: Born January 21, 1936, in Abingdon, VA; son of Charles A. (a farmer) and Amanda (Price) Hagy. Education: King College, A.B., 1956; East Tennessee State University, M.A., 1966; University of Georgia, Ph.D., 1969. Politics: Democrat.

ADDRESSES: Office—Department of History, College of Charleston, Charleston, SC 29424.

CAREER: College of Charleston, Charleston, SC, member of history faculty, 1969—. American Academy in Rome, Dr. Russell Scott Director of School of Classical Studies, 1976; University of South Carolina, fellow of Institute for Southern Studies, 1987, 1989. Conducted archaeological work in Sardinia, 1985, 1989.

MEMBER: Phi Alpha Theta.

AWARDS, HONORS: Grants from Colonial Williamsburg, 1970, National Endowment for the Humanities, 1975, 1991, 1992, Canadian Department of External Affairs (for Royal Military College, Kingston, Ontario), 1978, Government of Saudi Arabia, 1981, and Southern Regional Educational Board, 1989; Fulbright fellow in Pakistan, 1983, and India, 1988.

WRITINGS:

Castle's Woods: Frontier Virginia Settlement, 1769-1799, Russell County Library, 1966.
Castle's Woods and Early Russell County, 1769-1799, Russell County Historical Society, 1979.

People and Professions in Charleston, S.C., 1782-1802, Clearfield, 1992.
This Happy Land: The Jews of Colonial and Antebellum Charleston, University of Alabama Press, 1993.
To Take Charleston: The Civil War on Folly Island, Pictorial Histories, 1993.

Work represented in anthologies, including Canada: A Sociological Profile, edited by W. E. Mann, Copp, Clark, 1971. Contributor of articles to history and archaeology journals and literary journals, including Antigonish Review and Queen's Quarterly.

*   *   *

HAHN, Lewis E(dwin) 1908-

PERSONAL: Born September 26, 1908, in Swenson, TX; son of Edwin D. (a manager of a lumber yard) and Ione (a homemaker; maiden name, Brewster) Hahn; married Elizabeth Herring, June 30, 1932 (died August 24, 1991); married Mary Anne King (a genealogist), September 1, 1992; children: Helen Elizabeth Hahn Cameron, Mary L. Hahn Francis, Sharon K. Hahn Crowell. Education: University of Texas at Austin, B.A. and M.A., both 1929; University of California, Ph.D., 1939. Politics: Democrat. Religion: Unitarian-Universalist.

ADDRESSES: Home—Route 2, Reed Station Rd., Box 621, Carbondale, IL 62901. Office—Department of Philosophy, Southern Illinois University at Carbondale, Carbondale, IL 62901.

CAREER: University of Missouri—Columbia, instructor, 1936-39, assistant professor, 1939-46, associate professor of philosophy, 1946-49; Washington University, St. Louis, MO, professor of philosophy, 1949-63, department head, 1949-63, associate dean of Graduate School of Arts and

Sciences, 1953-54, dean, 1954-63; Southern Illinois University at Carbondale, research professor of philosophy, 1963-77, professor emeritus, 1977—, visiting professor, 1981—. Princeton University, visiting lecturer, 1947; Baylor University, distinguished visiting professor, 1977, 1979, 1980. Illinois Philosophy Conference, president, 1969-71. UNESCO, member of U.S. National Commission, 1965-67.

MEMBER: American Association for the Advancement of Science (fellow), American Philosophical Association (member of executive board, 1950-54, 1970-73), American Association of University Professors, American Society for Aesthetics, Southwestern Philosophical Society (president, 1955), Southern Society for Philosophy and Psychology (president, 1958-59), Missouri Philosophical Association (president, 1949-50), Phi Beta Kappa.

AWARDS, HONORS: Distinguished Service Award, Southern Illinois University, 1993.

WRITINGS:

A Contextualistic Theory of Perception, University of California Press, 1942.
(Editor with Paul Arthur Schilpp) *The Philosophy of Gabriel Marcel,* Open Court, 1984.
(Editor with Schilpp) *The Philosophy of W. V. Quine,* Open Court, 1986.
(Editor with Schilpp) *The Philosophy of John Dewey,* Open Court, 1989.
(Editor with Schilpp) *The Philosophy of G. H. von Wright,* Open Court, 1989.
(Editor with Harold M. Kaplan and Ralph E. McCoy) Charles D. Tenney, *The Discovery of Discovery,* University Press of America, 1991.
(Editor) *The Philosophy of Charles Hartshorne,* Open Court, 1991.
(Editor) *The Philosophy of A. J. Ayer,* Open Court, 1992.

Contributor to books, including *Value: A Cooperative Inquiry,* Columbia University Press, 1949; and *Guide to the Works of John Dewey,* Southern Illinois University Press, 1970. Contributor to philosophy journals. Editor of the series "Library of Living Philosophers," Open Court, 1981—.

WORK IN PROGRESS: Editing nine volumes for Open Court's "Library of Living Philosophers," on the philosophy of Paul Ricoeur, Paul Weiss, H. G. Gadamer, Donald Davidson, Roderick M. Chisholm, P. F. Strawson, Thomas S. Kuhn, Juergen Habermas, and Seyyed Hossein Hasr; writing a family history.

SIDELIGHTS: Lewis E. Hahn told *CA:* "As editor of the 'Library of Living Philosophers,' I am very much interested in world dialogue in philosophy. My philosophical outlook is contextualistic, in that I think of contextualism as one of the better ways of making sense of our world and our place in it. This world view stresses change and the intimate relationship between people and their environment."

*   *   *

HAIRSTON, William (Russell, Jr.) 1928-

PERSONAL: Born April 1, 1928, in Goldsboro, NC; son of William Russell Hairston and Malissa Carter Hairston; married Enid Carey; children: Ann Marie. *Education:* Received B.A. from University of Northern Colorado; attended Columbia University and New York University.

ADDRESSES: Home—5501 Seminary Rd, No. 511-S, Falls Church, VA 22041.

CAREER: Author, playwright, actor, director, producer, and public administrator. Scriptwriter for U.S. government presentations; professional actor, 1950-57, performing in New York City, on tour, in summer stock, in television shows, including *Harlem Detective* (1953), and featured in the Metro-Goldwyn-Mayer film, *Take the High Ground* (1953); Greenwich Mews Theatre, New York City, production coordinator and coproducer, 1963; New York Shakespeare Festival (NYSF), New York City theater manager, 1963-64; director of *Jericho-Jim Crow* by Langston Hughes, produced in New York City, 1964; NYSF Mobile Theatre Unit, codirector of community relations, 1965; Arena Stage, Washington, DC, assistant to executive director, 1965-66; Democratic National Committee, correspondent and radio news editor, 1968; District of Columbia, Executive Office of the Mayor, executive manager of office of personnel, 1970-90.

MEMBER: Authors League of America, Dramatists Guild, American Society of Public Administrators, District of Columbia Police and Firefighters Retirement and Relief Board (chair, 1979-90), Boy Scouts of America (member of executive board of National Capitol Area Council).

AWARDS, HONORS: Ford Foundation Theatre Administration Grant, 1965-66; NEA Literary Study Grant, 1967; Silver Beaver Award, Boy Scouts of America (National Capitol Area), 1988; Group Theatres Multi Cultural Playwrights Festival Award, 1988, for *Ira Frederick Aldridge (The London Conflict);* Meritorious Public Service Award, District of Columbia, 1990.

WRITINGS:

Swan-Song of the 11th Dawn (three-act workshop reading), produced in New York, 1962.
Walk in the Darkness (three-act stage play; adapted from the novel by Hans Habe), produced at Greenwich Mews Theatre, New York City, 1963.

Curtain Call, Mr. Aldridge, Sir! (stage play; adapted from the radio script by Ossie Davis), produced in New York, 1966.

Black Antigone (one-act stage play; adapted from *Antigone* by Sophocles), produced at North Carolina Regional and State Drama Festival, 1966.

The World of Carlos (novel), illustrated by George Ford, Putnam, 1968.

Ira Frederick Aldridge (The London Conflict) (stage play), Four Workshop Productions, The Group Theatre, Seattle, WA, 1988.

Sex and Conflict (novel), University Editions, 1993.

Also author of scripts for the U.S. Information Agency, including *Apollo 11—Man on the Moon* (half-hour television program), *Media Hora* (half-hour television series for Latin American countries), *Festival of Heritage* (half-hour film on the "African diaspora" produced in association with the Smithsonian Institute), *Jules Verne vs. Real Flight to the Moon, Yosemite National Park* (short film), *English Training—Teaching English as a Second Language, Chicago: Portrait of a City, Masterworks of Art from Zaire,* and *Operation Money-wise ("Breadbasket")* (produced for the Social Security Administration). Also editor and publisher of the government employer's newsletter *D.C. Pipeline.*

*   *   *

HALDEMAN, H(arry) R(obbins)   1926-1993

OBITUARY NOTICE—See index for *CA* sketch: Born October 27, 1926, in Los Angeles, CA; died from an abdominal tumor, November 12, 1993, in Santa Barbara, CA. Government official, business consultant, and author. Haldeman gained notoriety for his involvement in the 1972 Watergate scandal—a scheme devised by top-ranked government officials, including President Richard M. Nixon, to cover up the Committee to Reelect the President's connection with the burglary of the Democratic National Committee's headquarters. For his role in the conspiracy, Haldeman, Nixon's chief of staff, was forced to resign from his position and was later indicted on conspiracy, perjury, and obstruction of justice charges. He spent eighteen months in prison, and when he was released, he distanced himself from politics, becoming involved instead with business and real estate ventures and working as a business consultant. With Joseph DiMona, Haldeman related his memories of the Watergate scandal in his 1978 book *The Ends of Power.*

OBITUARIES AND OTHER SOURCES:

BOOKS

Who's Who in America, 48th edition, Marquis, 1994.

PERIODICALS

Chicago Tribune, November 13, 1993, p. 19; November 14, 1993, p. 9.
Los Angeles Times, December 13, 1993, pp. A1, A18-A19.
New York Times, November 13, 1993, p. 31.
Times (London), November 15, 1993, p. 17.
Washington Post, November 13, 1993, p. A12.

*   *   *

HAMBREY, Michael (John)   1948-

PERSONAL: Born March 20, 1948, in Sedgley, Staffordshire, England; son of Frederick Charles (a minister of religion) and Alison Mary (a nurse; maiden name, Snape) Hambrey. *Education:* Victoria University of Manchester, B.Sc., 1970, Ph.D., 1974; Cambridge University, M.A., 1978. *Religion:* Anglican. *Avocational Interests:* Mountain walking, skiing, wildlife and landscape photography, choral singing (church choirs).

ADDRESSES: Home—1 Hill Cottages, Montgomery Hill, Wirral, Merseyside L48 1NG, England. *Office*—School of Biological and Earth Sciences, Liverpool John Moores University, Byrom St., Liverpool L3 3AF, England.

CAREER: Swiss Federal Institute of Technology, Zurich, postdoctoral research associate, 1974-77; Cambridge University, Cambridge, England, senior research associate, 1977-91, fellow of St. Edmund's College, 1978-91; chartered geologist, 1991; Liverpool John Moores University, Liverpool, England, professor of quaternary geology, 1991—.

MEMBER: Royal Geographical Society (fellow), Geological Society of London (fellow), Arctic Institute of North America.

AWARDS, HONORS: Polar Medal from Queen Elizabeth II, 1989.

WRITINGS:

(Editor with D. Harlan) *Earth's Pre-Pleistocene Record,* Cambridge University Press, 1981.
(With I. J. Fairchild, B. W. Glover, A. D. Stewart, and others) *Late Precambrian Geology of the Scottish Highlands and Islands,* Geologists Association, 1991.
(With Jurg C. Alean) *Glaciers,* Cambridge University Press, 1992.
Glacial Environments, University of London Press, 1994.

Contributor of nearly a hundred articles to scientific journals.

WORK IN PROGRESS: A long-term glacial history of Antarctica and its connection to global sea level and climatic changes; research on the early geological evolution of the Arctic/North Atlantic region.

SIDELIGHTS: Michael Hambrey told *CA:* "I was born in the overcrowded and once heavily polluted industrial heartland of England. My career as a geologist and glaciologist has, in contrast, taken me to some of the remotest corners of the planet, including the Canadian Arctic, Greenland, Spitsbergen, Alaska, and Antarctica. I have also undertaken field work in northern Norway, the Swiss Alps, and China.

"My interest in geology in general and glacial environments in particular came about as a result of youthful fell-walking activities in the English Lake District, Wales, and the Scottish Highlands. Opportunities for work in increasingly icy parts of the world evolved progressively from that time onward.

"Because of the international character of my research, I have worked for extended periods at institutions in Switzerland, Germany, and New Zealand. Although, for the greater part of my career, I have been based at Cambridge University, one of the world's leading centers of polar research. I was appointed to Cambridge in 1991 to head an expanding earth science department at Liverpool John Moores University.

"The discipline of scientific writing for peer-reviewed specialist journals is the primary means by which a scientist's credibility is judged, but there is little scope for conveying the beauty of the environments in which the work is undertaken, either in the written word or in the form of photographs. Writings *Glaciers* with Jurg Alean was a means of sharing some of our fascination for the subject with the general public. It also provided an outlet for the publication of some of the best photographs obtained during our researches."

*　　　*　　　*

HAMPSHIRE, Stuart (Newton)　1914-

PERSONAL: Born October 1, 1914, in Healing, Lincolnshire, England; son of George N. and Marie (West) Hampshire; married Renee Orde-Lees Ayer, 1962 (some sources say 1961; deceased, 1980); married Nancy Cartwright, 1985; children: two daughters. *Education:* Received degree from Balliol College, Oxford, 1936.

ADDRESSES: Office—5 Beaumont Rd., The Quarry, Headington, Oxford, England.

CAREER: All Souls College, Oxford University, Oxford, England, fellow and lecturer in philosophy, 1936-40, domestic bursar and research fellow, 1955-60; University College, University of London, London, England, lecturer in philosophy, 1947-50, Grote Professor of Philosophy of Mind and Logic, 1960-63; New College, Oxford University, fellow, 1950-55; Princeton University, Princeton, NJ, 1963-70, began as professor of philosophy, became chair of philosophy department; Wadham College, Oxford University, warden, 1970-84; Stanford University, Stanford, CA, professor emeritus. *Military service:* Served in British Army and Foreign Office, 1940-45, became personal assistant to Minister of State, 1945.

MEMBER: American Philosophical Association (served as president), Arts Council.

AWARDS, HONORS: Elected fellow of British Academy, 1960, and of the American Academy of Arts and Sciences, 1968; made Knight of the British Empire, 1979; Hon. D.Litt, Glasgow, 1973.

WRITINGS:

Spinoza, Penguin Books, 1951.
(Editor and author of introduction and interpretive commentary) *The Age of Reason: The 17th Century Philosophers,* Houghton, 1956.
Thought and Action, Chatto & Windus, 1959, Viking, 1960.
Feeling and Expression: An Inaugural Lecture Delivered at University College, London, 25th October, 1960, H. K. Lewis, 1961.
Freedom of the Individual, Harper & Row, 1965, expanded edition published by Princeton University Press, 1975.
Philosophy of Mind, Harper & Row, 1966.
(With Conor Cruise O'Brien and Northrop Frye) *The Morality of Scholarship,* edited by Max Black, Cornell University Press, 1967.
Modern Writers and Other Essays, Chatto & Windus, 1969, Knopf, 1970.
Freedom of Mind and Other Essays, Princeton University Press, 1971.
Morality and Pessimism (The Leslie Stephen Lecture), Cambridge University Press, 1972.
(Editor with Leszek Kolakowski) *The Socialist Idea: A Reappraisal,* Weidenfeld & Nicolson, 1974.
Knowledge and the Future (Fawley Foundation Lecture), University of Southampton, 1976.
Two Theories of Morality (Thank-Offering to British Fund Lectures), Oxford University Press, 1977.
(Editor and contributor) *Public and Private Morality* (essays), Cambridge University Press, 1978.
Morality and Conflict, Basil Blackwell, 1983.
Innocence and Experience, Harvard University Press, 1989.

Contributor to *David Hume: A Symposium,* edited by D. F. Pears, St. Martin's, 1963. Contributor to periodicals, including the *Philosophical Review.*

SIDELIGHTS: Stuart Hampshire has had a long and prolific career as an esteemed academic and author. His field of expertise lies in the area of philosophy, but Hampshire has attempted to place his specific theories into a more contemporary and broad spectrum that encompasses literature, psychology, and politics. His critical analysis of various facets of philosophical reasoning has brought him acclaim and set him apart from many of his intellectual colleagues. Hampshire began teaching at the university level after graduating from Oxford and has since continued to hold various academic posts. His first published work was an examination of the seventeenth-century Dutch philosopher Benedict de Spinoza, which appeared in 1951. Reviewers of Hampshire's body of work often cite Spinoza as an evident influence in the author's views. The subject matter of much of his writing centers around the question of what influences knowledge and the origins of free will. In *World Authors: 1950-1970,* Hampshire stated, "I believe aesthetics, ethics, and political philosophy are parts of a single inquiry, now often called the philosophy of mind." This approach, which emphasizes the less accessible facets of thinking, is separate from the standard methodology philosophers adhere to, which centers around science and logic and therefore can be proven true or false.

One of the first of Hampshire's works to receive attention in academic circles was *Thought and Action,* published in 1959. In breaking away from the customary proposition that learning is a passive action springing forth from the act of observation, Hampshire theorized that one achieves knowledge by a more active role. *Thought and Action* set forth the idea that one's intentions and conduct greatly influence the educational experience. Hampshire also postulated that two types of self-knowledge play a role in human behavior and the outcome of personal will. The first type can be viewed as an indication of resolve, and it stands in contrast to the more manipulative form of self-knowledge based in Freudian psychiatry. This issue was explored further in Hampshire's next major work, *The Freedom of the Individual.*

Published in 1965, *The Freedom of the Individual* appeared when Hampshire was chair of the department of philosophy at Princeton University. The volume examines the nature of human will and the linguistic facets that encircle the debate over thought, action, and knowledge. The author sets forth his own arguments that break with many of the tenets that support various branches of analytical philosophy that developed through the centuries, including positivism and physicalism. *The Freedom of the Individual* probes these areas by postulating and expounding on statements of determination and describing how they do not fit into a prescribed or predictable path of consequence. In reviewing the work for the *Partisan Review,* Henry David Aiken disputed some areas regarding Hampshire's line of reasoning, but described the general debate as "freshly and imaginatively argued."

Another of Hampshire's work to receive attention was 1967's *The Morality of Scholarship,* cowritten with Conor Cruise O'Brien and Northrop Frye and edited by Max Black. Hampshire's three essays contained therein present an overview of the dilemmas enveloping modern academia. His next work, *Modern Writers and Other Essays,* appeared in 1969 and marries the author's viewpoints with literary analysis. The volume is a collection of twenty-two selections of his writings that appeared previously in various periodicals. Hampshire discusses the relevance of authors such as James Joyce, Marcel Proust, and Virginia Woolf, along with the moral theories of philosophers such as Bertrand Russell. *Modern Writers*'s connecting theme, according to Hampshire's introductory essay, is the thread between distinct branches of philosophical thought and styles of literary expression, and he addresses each of the essays within this framework. In a review of the tome for the *Observer,* Karl Miller praised the clarity of Hampshire's writing in remarking that the "the beauty of this book is that it states directly and without prevarication what is important, and what is salient, about each writer." Martin Seymour-Smith, commenting on the volume for the *Spectator,* stated that Hampshire's "unobtrusive scrupulosity, combined with his lack of dogmatism, makes almost everything he has to say about literature interesting."

Freedom of Mind and Other Essays was Hampshire's next collection of previously-published works. The 1971 volume contains fourteen selections of his writings, many of them originally devised as speeches. They again address the issue of individual self-determinism and the nature of freedom in a modern society. Reviewer Peter Caws, writing on the volume for the *New Republic,* observed Hampshire's obvious debt to the philosophy of Spinoza and praised the author's well-reasoned continuation of Spinoza's ideas on the nature of human existence. Caws faulted, however, the inaccessibility of Hampshire's ideas to the general audience, which he felt, in essence, goes against the grain of both Hampshire's and Spinoza's viewpoints. The critic did praise the selections in the book that were originally written as speeches, however, remarking that "Hampshire writes with elegance . . . as examples of philosophical prose at its best and most intelligible these would be hard to match."

Another of Hampshire's numerous volumes was 1977's *Two Theories of Morality.* Originally a lecture given to the British Academy, the book explores the divergent theories of Spinoza and the ancient Greek philosopher Aristotle. The following year, *Public and Private Morality,* a collection of essays for which Hampshire served as editor, was published. Hampshire himself was the author of two of the six entries in the volume. The various essays emphasize the dilemma of finding a common principle to guide public institutions—such as bodies of government—that reflects a conscious moral objective and concern for humanity. The authors discuss the contention that public servants are often allowed far more leeway in official behavior than normally demanded of an individual citizen, and they cite such examples as the Vietnam War to support their theories. In a review of *Public and Private Morality* for the *Spectator,* Anthony Quinton observed that "Hampshire's two essays are . . . imaginative and generally thought-provoking, even if somewhat loosely bolted together considered as arguments."

In *Morality and Conflict,* published in 1983, Hampshire again addresses the plausibility of constructing a moral framework that governs all facets of human behavior. Some of the selections in this work previously appeared in preceding volumes, such as *Two Theories of Morality* and *Public and Private Morality,* but here they are thematically united around Hampshire's central thesis regarding moral decisions. He rejects the utilitarian concept of judging actions simply by their consequences, postulating that each act must instead be assessed according to the cultural conventions that regulate the individual party.

In the title chapter, the author argues that societies devise their own sets of morals, that conflicts result from the diversity of human opinion, and that reconciling divergent moral philosophies is nearly impossible. As an example, Hampshire addresses the issue of regulating sexual conduct according to a standard moral code and how each specific community will have its own definition of such. The essay also explores the theory that no solution to a moral dilemma will have a complete absence of negative repercussions. Commenting on *Morality and Conflict* for the *New York Review of Books,* Ronald Dworkin described the collection as "subtle and beautifully written." Thomas Nagel, writing in the *New York Times Book Review,* described the volume as "valuable and provocative" and praised the author's "pure, ageless style." Nagel summarized *Morality and Conflict* as "an outstanding example of serious moral reflection, historically informed and alive to the difficulties of theory and the limits of human possibility."

Innocence and Experience is another tract on the moral questions that influence societal behavior. In this 1989 work, Hampshire rejects the notion that an ideal community is based on a shared unanimity of belief. The author instead argues that dissonance within a group, when it also has a fair system of dispute resolution, leads to a more flexible and humane society. Hampshire also addresses the need for due process to govern all human relations, asserts that individuals have a right to their own sets of needs and goals, and maintains that the construction of a framework

to resolve the resulting conflicts is the best hope for harmonious human coexistence. In a review of *Innocence and Experience* for the *New York Times Book Review,* John T. Noonan, Jr. faulted Hampshire for failing to place his arguments within a necessary historical context, adding that some of his theories expose him as "hopelessly Romantic." The critic did praise several aspects of the book, however, finding them to be "contributions to the charting of the moral landscape." *Times Literary Supplement* reviewer Adam Morton criticized the author's failure to cite some of today's most enveloping moral dilemmas, such as the issue of religious fundamentalism, but praised him for having "shown how rich and varied the connections are between questions of political morality and questions of moral pluralism."

BIOGRAPHICAL/CRITICAL SOURCES:

BOOKS

World Authors: 1950-1970, H. W. Wilson, 1975.

PERIODICALS

Books, February, 1970.
Nation, February 19, 1968, pp. 246-47.
New Republic, October 23, 1971, pp. 24-27; February 10, 1979, pp. 39-40.
New York Review of Books, October 24, 1985, p. 37.
New York Times Book Review, April 8, 1984, p. 24; February 25, 1990, p. 28.
Observer, January 4, 1970.
Partisan Review, summer, 1967, pp. 474-79.
Spectator, February 7, 1970, p. 180; November 18, 1978, pp. 20-21.
Times Literary Supplement, February 26, 1970, p. 216; January 27, 1984, p. 83; February 16, 1990, p. 164.*

—*Sketch by Carol A. Brennan*

*   *   *

HANSON, Earl D(orchester) 1927-1993

OBITUARY NOTICE—See index for *CA* sketch: Born February 15, 1927, in Shahjahanpur, India; died of a heart attack, October 26, 1993, in Middletown, CT. Educator and author. Hanson was known for his commitment to teaching ethical science to students becoming scientists. He also encouraged improvements in the scientific education of nonscientists. He began his career as an instructor at Yale University, becoming an assistant professor in 1954. He accepted a position in 1960 at Wesleyan University as an associate professor. Ten years later he was presented with the Harbison Distinguished Teaching Award, and the title of Fisk Professor of Natural Science followed in 1972. His publications include *Animal Diversity* and

Understanding Evolution. He edited and contributed to *Recombinant DNA Research and the Human Prospect* and contributed to *Paramecium: A Current Survey* and *Methods in Cell Physiology.*

OBITUARIES AND OTHER SOURCES:

BOOKS

Who's Who in America, 48th edition, Marquis, 1994.

PERIODICALS

New York Times, October 28, 1993, p. D27.

*   *   *

HAPPENSTANCE, Aurelia
See FURDYNA, Anna M.

*   *   *

HARDER, Leland   1926-

PERSONAL: Born July 1, 1926, in Hillsboro, KS; son of Menno S. (a teacher) and Katherine (a beautician; maiden name, Wiens) Harder; married Bertha Fast (a teacher), August 8, 1951; children: John, Thomas. *Education:* Bethel College, North Newton, KS, B.A., 1948; Michigan State College (now University), M.A., 1950; Bethany Theological Seminary, Chicago, IL, M.Div., 1952; Northwestern University, Ph.D., 1962. *Politics:* Independent. *Religion:* Mennonite. *Avocational Interests:* Family history.

ADDRESSES: Home—P.O. Box 363, North Newton, KS 67117.

CAREER: Pastor of a Mennonite church in Chicago, IL, 1952-57; Mennonite Biblical Seminary, Elkhart, IN, professor, 1958-83; Great Plains Seminary Education Program, Newton, KS, director, 1983-86; Church Member Profile Research Project, associate director, 1988-92. *Military service:* U.S. Navy, 1944-46.

WRITINGS:

Anabaptists Four Centuries Later, Herald Press, 1975.
The Pastor-People Partnership: The Call and Recall of Pastors from a Believer's Church Perspective, Institute of Mennonite Studies, 1983.
(Editor) *Perspectives on the Nurturing of Faith,* Institute of Mennonite Studies, 1983.
(Editor) *The Sources of Swiss Anabaptism,* Herald Press, 1985.
(Editor with Leo Driedger) *Anabaptist-Mennonite Identities in Ferment,* Institute of Mennonite Studies, 1990.
Doors to Lock and Doors to Open: The Discerning People of God, Herald Press, 1993.

Publisher of *Family History,* a quarterly periodical.

WORK IN PROGRESS: A biography of Jacob A. Wiebe, the founder of the Crimean Mennonite Brethren; research on lesser-known episodes in American Mennonite history.

SIDELIGHTS: Leland Harder told *CA:* "Drawing on ideas and insights accumulated from twenty-five years of teaching at a theological seminary, my book, *Doors to Lock and Doors to Open: The Discerning People of God,* is about the Christian process of discernment. By discernment, I mean learning more and more about what it was that Jesus came to teach about the call to faith. The book explores how faith is formed and integrated, who we are and what we can believe, the creative tension between individualism and corporate accountability, the partnership between pastors and people in the church. It discusses how to think biblically about the biases against women that St. Paul tried to transmit to his New Testament churches, how Christians can be peacemakers and make political decisions. The book covers many other ethical discernments like abortion, capital punishment, and homosexuality. The process of writing this book almost led me to believe Reuel Howe's supposition that retirement really can be the commencement of 'the creative years.'"

*   *   *

HARER, John B.   1948-

PERSONAL: Born December 14, 1948, in Atlanta, GA; son of Robert J. (a manager of a soft drink plant) and Sherry (a teacher; maiden name, Peard) Harer; married Shelley M. Deutschle, January 8, 1972 (divorced, August 23, 1988); married Susan Smith Meisel (a teacher), October 14, 1988; children: Justin Marshall, Brian Scott. *Education:* Bloomsburg University, B.S., 1972; Millersville University, Certificate in Library Science, 1975; Clarion University, M.S.L.S., 1978; University of Baltimore, M.P.A., 1986; further graduate study at Texas A&M University, 1989—. *Politics:* Democrat. *Religion:* United Church of Christ. *Avocational Interests:* Tennis, bicycling, touring Civil War battlefields, travel.

ADDRESSES: Home—306 Bolton, College Station, TX 77840. *Office*—Sterling C. Evans Library, Texas A&M University, College Station, TX 77843-5000.

CAREER: American International School, Duesseldorf, Germany, librarian, 1979-80; Radford University, Radford, VA, head of circulation at McConnell Library, 1980-83; Towson State University, Towson, MD, head of circulation at Cook Library, 1983-88; Texas A&M University, College Station, head of access services at Sterling C. Evans Library, 1988—. Literacy Volunteers of America, tutor, 1993—.

MEMBER: American Library Association, Library Administration and Management Association, American Civil Liberties Union (president of local chapter, 1976-79), Beta Phi Mu, Phi Alpha Alpha.

WRITINGS:

Intellectual Freedom: A Reference Handbook, American Bibliographical Center-Clio Press, 1992.
(With Steven Harris) *Censorship of Expression in the 1980s: A Statistical Survey,* Greenwood Press, 1994.

Editor of "Information and Instruction Technologies," a column in *Library Hi-Tech News,* 1989-91.

WORK IN PROGRESS: A chapter on library circulation, to be included in a major library science textbook.

SIDELIGHTS: John B. Harer told *CA:* "It is difficult for me to be passionless about intellectual freedom, but it is doubly so when, as a librarian, I am confronted with a book censorship attempt. Words and ideas are sacrosanct, and even the most disagreeable must be critiqued or disconfirmed, never suppressed. Anything else dangerously risks the destruction of our democratic form of government and, more importantly, our individual liberties. As a librarian, I view access to books and other creative works as a basic human right. However, I recognize that there are trends in society—such as the growing influence of television violence, the proliferation of hardcore pornography, and the rise in hate-speech incidents—that disturb large segments of the population. It is this confluence of the principles of intellectual freedom with these societal discords that portends a difficult period for speech rights in the next several years. It is my hope that, through my research, these tensions can be eased in some way and that my books will contribute to a greater understanding of intellectual freedom and its exercise in this nation.

"My first book, *Intellectual Freedom: A Reference Handbook,* was designed to aid individuals in learning more about First Amendment rights. The four rights of the First Amendment are interconnecting and interdependent. Freedom of religion cannot be realized without freedom of speech, for example. The resource book contains a vast array of information, ranging from a discussion of the philosophical underpinnings of intellectual freedom, to books, films, and multimedia materials of relevance. I have tried to build as much balance as possible into the data it contains, treating individuals and materials from both political spectra as equally as possible.

"My second book, *Censorship of Expression in the 1980s: A Statistical Survey,* was written with my colleague Steven Harris. We recognized the need for more statistics on the types and level of censorship that has occurred in the past decade. This research is a comprehensive compilation of all incidents of censorship reported in four major intellec-

tual freedom periodicals: the *Newsletter on Intellectual Freedom, Censorship News,* the *Attacks on the Freedom to Learn,* and the *Student Press Law Center Report.* We have also benchmarked our results with two major censorship studies of earlier decades. The most disturbing trend we found is the strength of the attacks against the works of Judy Blume, a well-known young adult author."

*　　*　　*

HARING, Lee 1930-

PERSONAL: Born June 30, 1930, in New York; son of Forrest Chapman (a theatrical executive) and Cecilia (a musician; maiden name, Lee) Haring; married Margery Cornwell, January 19, 1963 (divorced, 1973); married Bea Vidacs, May 27, 1983 (divorced, 1990); married Susan V. (an educator), March 17, 1991; children: Bartholomew Cornwell, Timothy Paul. *Education:* Haverford College, A.B., 1951; Columbia University, A.M., 1952, Ph.D., 1961. *Religion:* Society of Friends (Quakers).

ADDRESSES: Home—60 Plaza St., No. 1M, Brooklyn, NY 11238. *Office*—Department of English, Brooklyn College of the City University of New York, New York, NY 11210.

CAREER: Guilford College, Greensboro, NC, assistant professor of English, 1953-56; Brooklyn College of the City University of New York, Brooklyn, NY, lecturer, 1957-61, instructor, 1961-67, assistant professor, 1967-73, associate professor, 1973-81, professor of English, 1981—.

MEMBER: International Society for Folk Narrative Research, American Folklore Society, New York Folklore Society, Folklore Fellows International, Modern Language Association of America.

AWARDS, HONORS: Fulbright Scholar Award, Council for International Exchange of Scholars, 1975-76 and 1989-90.

WRITINGS:

The Gypsy Laddie, Hargail Music Press, 1962.
Folk Songs for Guitar, Novello, 1964.
Malagasy Tale Index, FFC (Helsinki), 1982.
Verbal Arts in Madagascar, University of Pennsylvania Press, 1992.
Ibonia, Epic of Madagascar, Bucknell University Press, 1994.

WORK IN PROGRESS: A study of myth and folktale in the western Indian Ocean, completion expected in 1995.

HARRIGER, Katy J(ean) 1957-

PERSONAL: Born June 1, 1957, in San Antonio, TX; daughter of Russell E. (an air force officer) and Jean (a journalist and homemaker; maiden name, Kautenburg) Harriger; married Robert J. Griffiths (a college professor), June 20, 1981; children: Aaron. *Education:* Edinboro University of Pennsylvania, B.A. (magna cum laude), 1979; University of Connecticut, M.A. (with distinction), 1981, Ph.D. (with distinction), 1986.

ADDRESSES: Home—3391 Poteat Court, Winston-Salem, NC 27106. *Office*—Box 7568, Reynolda Station, Winston-Salem, NC 27109.

CAREER: University of Connecticut, Hartford Branch, instructor in political science, 1983, 1984; Wake Forest University, Winston-Salem, NC, instructor, 1985-86, assistant professor, 1986-91, associate professor of politics, 1991—, and Zachary T. Smith Professor, also resident scholar at Spice II Bicentennial Institute, 1987, 1988. Forsyth County Celebration of the Bicentennial of the Constitution, member of planning committee, 1986-89.

MEMBER: American Political Science Association, American Association of University Professors (vice president, 1992-93; president, 1993-94), North Carolina Political Science Association (member of executive council, 1989—; vice president, 1992-93; president-elect, 1993-94), Phi Kappa Phi, Omicron Delta Kappa.

AWARDS, HONORS: Ford Foundation grant, 1986; grant from National Commission on the Bicentennial of the U.S. Constitution, 1990; award from North Carolina Political Science Association, 1991.

WRITINGS:

Independent Justice: The Federal Special Prosecutor in American Politics, University Press of Kansas, 1992.

Work represented in anthologies, including *Politics and the Legal Bureaucracy,* edited by Cornell W. Clayton, University Press of Kansas, 1993. Contributor of articles and reviews to political science and history journals and newspapers.

*   *   *

HARRIS, Robert (Dennis) 1957-

PERSONAL: Born March 7, 1957, in Nottingham, England; son of Dennis Harris (a printer) and Audrey (Hardy) Harris; married Gillian Hornby (a journalist), 1988; children: one son, one daughter. *Education:* Selwyn College, Cambridge, B.A. (with honors), 1978. *Politics:* "Supporter of the British Labour Party." *Avocational In-*terests: Reading history, walking, fishing, listening to music.

ADDRESSES: Home—The Old Vicarage, Kintbury, Berkshire R915 OTR, England.

CAREER: British Broadcasting Corporation (BBC-TV), England, researcher and film director for *Tonight, Nationwide,* and *Panorama,* 1978-81, reporter for *Newsnight,* 1981-85, and for *Panorama,* 1985-87; *Observer,* London, England, political editor, 1987-89; Thames TV, England, political reporter for *This Week,* 1988-89; *Sunday Times,* London, political columnist, 1989-92.

WRITINGS:

(With Jeremy Paxman) *A Higher Form of Killing: The Secret Story of Gas and Germ Warfare,* Chatto & Windus, 1982, published in the United States as *A Higher Form of Killing: The Secret Story of Chemical and Biological Warfare,* Hill & Wang, 1982.
Gotcha!: The Media, the Government, and the Falklands Crisis, Faber & Faber, 1983.
The Making of Neil Kinnock, Faber & Faber, 1984.
Selling Hitler, Pantheon, 1986, Penguin, 1987.
Good and Faithful Servant: The Unauthorized Biography of Bernard Ingham, Faber & Faber, 1990.
Fatherland (novel), Random House, 1992.

Harris's work has been translated into several languages.

WORK IN PROGRESS: Enigma, a wartime thriller; and a biography of John Le Carre.

SIDELIGHTS: Robert Harris had written several books of nonfiction during the 1980s before the publication of his popular 1992 novel *Fatherland.* Constructed around the premise that Adolf Hitler led the Nazis to victory in World War II, with Germany defeating both Great Britain and the Soviet Union and fighting the United States to an uneasy deadlock, *Fatherland* became a bestseller, selling three million copies worldwide. Several of Harris's previous nonfiction works, such as *A Higher Form of Killing: The Secret Story of Chemical and Biological Warfare* and *Gotcha!: The Media, the Government, and the Falklands Crisis,* also deal with war and its repercussions. In *Selling Hitler* Harris details the 1983 hoax in which a counterfeiter claimed to have discovered the diaries of the dead Nazi leader.

Fatherland is set in 1964 on the eve of an important visit by the president of the United States, Joseph P. Kennedy, to the German Fuhrer, Adolf Hitler, in a Berlin which is now the site of the grandiose Great Hall (built to the specifications of Nazi architect Albert Speer, the building can accommodate 180,000 people). The Allies have lost World War II, the wartime British prime minister, Winston Churchill, is in exile in Canada, and Germany now controls all of Europe and a good part of the Soviet Union. Against this background a German police detective, Xavier March, investigates the murder of a Nazi party official and in the course of his probe unearths a terrible secret with wide-ranging implications. Pursued by the gestapo, March attempts to publicize a crime of immeasurable dimensions—the systematic murder of millions of European Jews, whom the world believes to have been nonviolently relocated to the East. "March's inquiries jeopardize the crowning achievement of Hitler's three decades in office: world peace," commented Mark Horowitz in the *Los Angeles Times Book Review*. Coming at a time when the American president is making overtures to end the cold war with Germany, "revelations of a Holocaust would make appeasement impossible," Horowitz explained.

Critic Newgate Callendar wrote in the *New York Times Book Review* that *Fatherland* is an "absorbing, expertly written novel. . . . [It] is a bleak book. But what concerns the author is the indestructibility of the human spirit, as exemplified by Xavier March." In *Time* John Skow stated that Harris's "brooding, brown-and-black setting of a victorious Nazi regime is believable and troubling, the stuff of long nights of little sleep." And in the *Los Angeles Times Book Review* Horowitz remarked that "*Fatherland* works fine as a sly and scary page-turner."

A true account of the Hitler diary hoax, *Selling Hitler* reveals the extent to which greed influenced the publishing industry to overlook the veracity of the supposedly newly-discovered diaries in favor of their marketability. "One merit of Robert Harris's thorough and mordantly funny account of the diaries scandal in *Selling Hitler* is that he lets no one off the hook," commented James M. Markham in the *New York Times Book Review*. The diaries were originally obtained by a reporter for the German magazine *Stern;* according to Jonathan Alter in *Newsweek,* "Executives at *Stern*'s parent company, Gruner and Jahr, smelled money. Not wanting to see the bubble burst, *Stern* subjected the papers to only the most cursory handwriting examination." Markham noted in the *New York Times Book Review* that Harris presents "an unsettling portrait of the press baron, Rupert Murdoch, who aggressively bought up rights to the diaries for his corporation . . . and then nonchalantly dismissed their fraudulence with an unhappily memorable one-liner: 'After all, we are in the entertainment business.' " Reviewer Paul Hallam wrote in *New Statesman* that Harris tells this "sick saga . . . with skill and wit."

BIOGRAPHICAL/CRITICAL SOURCES:

PERIODICALS

Los Angeles Times Book Review, July 5, 1992, pp. 2, 9.
New Statesman, May 1, 1987.
Newsweek, May 26, 1986, p. 70.

New York Review of Books, December 17, 1992, pp. 38-44.
New York Times Book Review, April 13, 1986, pp. 11-12; June 28, 1992, p. 28.
Observer (London), February 13, 1983.
Spectator, March 12, 1983, pp. 20-22.
Time, July 6, 1992, pp. 75-76.
Times Educational Supplement, April 3, 1983, p. 27.
Washington Post Book World, July 11, 1982, pp. 1-2.

*   *   *

HARTIG, John H.   1952-

PERSONAL: Born September 16, 1952, in Vancouver, WA; son of Theodore A. (a Lutheran minister) and Virginia B. (a teacher; maiden name, Schwenke) Hartig; married Patricia DiBattista (an attorney), March 14, 1981; children: Danielle V., Elizabeth K. *Education:* Eastern Michigan University, B.S., 1974, M.S., 1977; University of Windsor, Ph.D., 1985. *Religion:* Lutheran.

ADDRESSES: Home—2357 Ashby, Trenton, MI 48183. *Office*—Department of Chemical Engineering, Wayne State University, 5050 Anthony Wayne Dr., Detroit, MI 48202.

CAREER: University of Michigan Great Lakes Research Division, Ann Arbor, research assistant, 1976-78; Michigan Department of Natural Resources, Lansing, water quality specialist, 1978-82; International Joint Commission, Windsor, Ontario, environmental scientist, 1985-91; Wayne State University, Detroit, MI, associate professor of chemical engineering, 1992—; writer. Member of Rouge River Basin Committee, 1983-92, and board of directors of Wittenberg University, 1988-90.

MEMBER: International Association for Great Lakes Research, American Society of Limnology and Oceanography, American Water Resources Association, Water Environment Federation, North American Lake Management Society, Great Lakes Institute, Sigma Xi.

AWARDS, HONORS: Fellowship from Environmental Protection Agency, 1982; Sustainable Development Award for civic leadership from Global Tomorrow Coalition, 1993.

WRITINGS:

(Editor with M. A. Zarull) *Under Raps: Towards Grassroots Ecological Democracy in the Great Lakes Basin,* University of Michigan Press, 1992.

Contributor, with others, to books, including *Toxic Contamination in Large Lakes,* Volume 3: *Sources, Fates, and Controls of Toxic Contaminants,* edited by N. W. Schmidtke, Lewis Publications, 1988; *Global Freshwater*

Quality: A First Assessment, edited by M. Meybeck, D. Chapman, and R. Helmer, Alden Press, 1989; and *Water Resource Planning and Management: Saving a Threatened Resource—in Search of Solutions,* edited by M. Karamouz, American Society of Civil Engineers, 1992. Contributor to periodicals, including *Environmental Management, International Environmental Affairs, Journal of Great Lakes Resources, Michigan History,* and *Water Resources Bulletin.*

SIDELIGHTS: John H. Hartig is a limnologist specializing in the Great Lakes. He told *CA:* "My primary interest is in finding practical solutions to environmental problems. The focus of my work is to apply an ecosystem approach to the rehabilitation and preservation of the Great Lakes. Through use of an ecosystem approach I attempt to account for societal, economic, and environmental linkages using an inclusive, shared decision-making process. A long-term goal is to achieve sustainable development. *Under Raps* attempts to celebrate the small and large victories being experienced through the Great Lakes Remedial Action Plan (RAP) program and encourages a spirit of partnership in restoring and maintaining the integrity of the Great Lakes."

*   *   *

HARTLEY, Cathy J. 1965-

PERSONAL: Born January 31, 1965, in Skipton, North Yorkshire, England; daughter of J. R. Hartley (a teacher) and C. M.-J. (Marton) Hartley (a teacher). *Education:* Clare College, Cambridge, B.A., 1988, M.A., 1992. *Politics:* Socialist. *Religion:* Atheist. *Avocational Interests:* Cats, politics, reading.

ADDRESSES: Home—London, England. *Office*—Europa Publications Ltd., 18 Bedford Sq., London WC1B 3JN, England.

CAREER: Europa Publications Ltd., London, England, assistant editor, 1988-90, editor, 1990—.

WRITINGS:

EDITOR

European Communities: An Encyclopedia and Directory, Europa, 1991.
The International Who's Who of Women, Europa, 1992.

Also editor of *The USA and Canada, 1994,* 1993, and *The International Foundation Directory,* 1994.

HAUPTMAN, Robert 1941-

PERSONAL: Born August 14, 1941, in New York, NY; son of Irving (a professor) and Sigrid (a teacher; maiden name, Anker) Hauptman; married Terry Herman (a poet and artist), September 7, 1968. *Education:* Wagner College, B.A. (cum laude), 1964; attended University of Innsbruck, 1965; Ohio University, M.A., 1967, Ph.D., 1971; attended University of Iceland, 1971; State University of New York at Albany, M.L.S., 1977; University of Pittsburgh, Certificate of Advanced Study in Library Science, 1984. *Avocational Interests:* Hiking, skiing, climbing, history and philosophy of science, natural history, philosophy, classical music, travel.

ADDRESSES: Office—LRS, St. Cloud State University, 720 Fourth Ave. S., St. Cloud, MN 56301.

CAREER: University of Oklahoma, Norman, humanities librarian and assistant professor of library science, 1980-84; St. Cloud State University, St. Cloud, MN, reference librarian and associate professor of library science, 1984—.

MEMBER: American Alpine Club, Phi Kappa Phi.

WRITINGS:

Twenty Poems Adjuring Death, [Wilmington, VT], 1973.
The Pathological Vision: Jean Genet, Louis-Ferdinand Celine, and Tennessee Williams, Peter Lang Publishing, 1984.
Ethical Challenges in Librarianship, Oryx, 1988.
(With Carol Anderson) *Technology and Information Services,* Ablex Publishing, 1993.

Work represented in anthologies, including *Magazines for Libraries,* edited by Bill Katz, Bowker, 3rd edition, 1978, 7th edition, 1993; and *English and American Literature: Sources and Strategies for Collection Development,* edited by William McPheron, American Library Association, 1987. Contributor of numerous articles and reviews to academic and commercial periodicals, including *North Stone Review, Catholicism in Crisis, Multicultural Review, Travel and Leisure, Poets and Writers,* and *New England Journal of Medicine.* Special editor, *Library Trends,* 1992, and *Reference Librarian;* founding editor of *Journal of Information Ethics,* 1992—.

WORK IN PROGRESS: Strangers in Strange Lands: Twentieth Century Travel Literature, a monograph; *Information Ethics: A Reader,* with Richard Stichler; research on intellectual strategies, academic dishonesty, and scientific book illustration.

SIDELIGHTS: Robert Hauptman told *CA:* "I am, first and foremost, an academic scholar. My primary interest is literary criticism, but the quirks of academic life have led me away from literature into other areas, including librarianship and information ethics. The scholarly material is important, but my favorite genre is the personal essay; I have written on water, walking, climbing, and some bizarre encounters in my travels.

"My writing is influenced not only by my academic work, but also by some other pursuits. These include the design and construction of a large house in the woods of Vermont; I have been working on this, basically by myself, with hand tools, for a decade, and it is almost finished. Other interests include my love of mountains, which I manifest by climbing them: Orizaba, Shasta, Aiguille du Tour, Rainier, and others; and travel. In 1993 my wife and I circumnavigated the globe, with stops in many esoteric lands. I have lived in or visited thirty-four countries all over the world."

* * *

HAWTHORNE, Douglas B(ruce) 1948-

PERSONAL: Born August 12, 1948, in Mineola, NY; son of Frank Douglas (an air force officer) and Jean Rae (an accounting clerk; maiden name, Spencer) Parker; married Marjorie Jo Rheinscheld (a physical therapist), December 21, 1979. *Education:* Pima Community College, A.A., 1981; University of Arizona, B.A. (with high distinction), 1983, M.A., 1985. *Politics:* Republican. *Religion:* Protestant. *Avocational Interests:* Space research, collecting space memorabilia, attending the theater.

ADDRESSES: Home and office—5946 North Camino Del Conde, Tucson, AZ 85718-4312.

CAREER: Tombstone Epitaph, Tombstone, AZ, city editor and reporter, 1985; Territorial Publishers, Inc., Tucson, AZ, copy editor and reporter, 1986-87; free-lance journalist, 1987—. Arizona Department of Economic Security, new and continued claims deputy, summer, 1982. *Military service:* U.S. Naval Reserve, 1965-69.

MEMBER: National Space Society, Aerospace Ambassadors, Aviation Space Education Association, British Interplanetary Society (fellow), University of Arizona Alumni Association, Phi Theta Kappa, Phi Kappa Phi, Golden Key.

AWARDS, HONORS: Pima Community College Liberal Arts Faculty Recognition Award, 1980; Tucson (Arizona) Radio and Television Broadcasters scholarship, 1981.

WRITINGS:

Men and Women of Space, Univelt, 1992.

WORK IN PROGRESS: Revising *Men and Women of Space;* research on "the unflown Soviet/Russian cosmonauts."

SIDELIGHTS: Douglas B. Hawthorne told *CA:* "My intense interest in the exploration and development of space began with the launch of the Soviet cosmonaut Yuriy A. Gagarin in April, 1961. I was twelve years old at the time, and my interest has never waned. Over the years I have accumulated an extensive collection of space-related books and memorabilia and established contacts in both the United States and other countries. I believe that mankind's destiny is to travel among the stars and spread the seed of life to other worlds. In 1978, I narrowed my focus to the biographies and careers of the astronauts, cosmonauts, and other people selected for spaceflight training around the world. My first book, *Men and Women of Space,* was written after years of research, interviews, and telephone conversations."

* * *

HAYNES, Gary (Anthony) 1948-

PERSONAL: Born September 30, 1948, in Long Beach, CA; son of Ellsworth Wallace and Martha Louise (Ryan) Haynes; married Janis Rose Klimowicz (an archaeologist), May, 1989. *Education:* University of Maryland at College Park, B.A., 1970; Catholic University of America, M.A., 1978, Ph.D., 1981.

ADDRESSES: Office—Anthropology Department, University of Nevada, Reno, NV 89557.

CAREER: Smithsonian Institution, Washington, DC, research associate, 1981-85; George Washington University, Washington, DC, associate professor, 1982; University of Nevada, Reno, assistant professor, 1985-88, associate professor, 1988—. Catholic University of America, visiting assistant professor, 1981; Hwange Research Trust, Reno, and Bulawayo, Zimbabwe, Africa, chairperson, 1987—.

MEMBER: American Quaternary Association, Society for American Archaeology, Society of Vertebrate Paleontology, Zimbabwe Scientific Association.

AWARDS, HONORS: Grants from National Geographic Society, Louis Leakey Foundation, National Science Foundation, and United States National Research Council; Fulbright Senior Scholar Research Award; International Research and Exchanges Board Award.

WRITINGS:

Mammoths, Mastodonts, and Elephants, Cambridge University Press, 1991.

Editor of *Nevada Archaeologist,* 1987—.

WORK IN PROGRESS: A book, *The Forest with a Desert Heart;* research on the history and prehistory of Zimbabwe's national parklands and the paleoenvironments of the Kalahari Beds region of Zimbabwe.

HAYNES, John Earl 1944-

PERSONAL: Born November 22, 1944, in Plant City, FL; son of John Milner (an educator) and Sarah Elizabeth (Farmer) Haynes; married Janette Marie Murray (an educator), December, 1971; children: Joshua, Amanda, William. *Education:* Florida State University, B.A., 1966; University of Minnesota—Twin Cities, M.A., 1968, Ph.D., 1978. *Religion:* Anglican Catholic.

ADDRESSES: Home—10041 Frederick Ave., Kensington, MD 20895. *Office*—Manuscript Division, Library of Congress, Washington, DC 20540-4780.

CAREER: Library of Congress, Washington, DC, twentieth-century political historian in Manuscript Division, 1987—. *Military service:* U.S. Army

MEMBER: Historians of American Communism (president, 1992-93).

WRITINGS:

Dubious Alliance: The Making of Minnesota's DFL Party, University of Minnesota Press, 1984.
Communism and Anti-Communism in the United States: An Annotated Guide to Historical Writings, Garland Publishing, 1987.
(With Harvey Klehr) *The American Communist Movement,* Twayne, 1992.

Editor of *Historians of American Communism* (newsletter), 1982-92.

WORK IN PROGRESS: A book on anti-communism in American life; editing several volumes of documents on American communism from Soviet archives.

SIDELIGHTS: John Earl Haynes told *CA:* "I enjoy the study of history because it allows me to understand how and why human history happened the way it did. I enjoy writing about it because, once I have come to an understanding of how and why something came about, I want to tell others. I find writing about communism and anti-communism interesting because the conflict over communism was one of the defining events of the twentieth century."

*   *   *

HENDERSON, William McCranor 1943-

PERSONAL: Born August 4, 1943, in Charlotte, NC; son of William (an anthropologist) and Nancy (a playwright; maiden name, Wallace) Henderson; married Carol Douglas (a journalist), 1975; children: Olivia, Colette. *Education:* Oberlin College, B.A., 1965; attended University of Iowa, 1965-66. *Politics:* Independent. *Religion:* "Non-affiliated."

ADDRESSES: Office—CB# 3520, Greenlaw Hall, University of North Carolina at Chapel Hill, Chapel Hill, NC 27599-3520. *Agent*—Russell & Volkening, Inc., 50 West 29th St., New York, NY 10001.

CAREER: Freelance editor and sound recordist for documentary films, New York City, 1966-68; producer of the short film *Zelenka,* late 1960s; WBAI-FM, New York City, staff producer and host of free-form "Medicine Hat" program, 1969-70; musician, Boston, MA, 1970-75; freelance audio-visual writer and producer, Boston and New York City, 1977-88; screenwriter, Los Angeles, CA, 1979-81; University of North Carolina at Chapel Hill, teacher of creative writing, 1989—.

AWARDS, HONORS: CINE Golden Eagle award, 1968, for film *Zelenka.*

WRITINGS:

Stark Raving Elvis, Dutton, 1984.
I Killed Hemingway, St. Martin's, 1993.

WORK IN PROGRESS: Applestock Nation, a novel about the 1960s.

SIDELIGHTS: William McCranor Henderson has combined popular culture and satire in his two novels, *Stark Raving Elvis* and *I Killed Hemingway.* Henderson has a diversified resume that includes a stint at the prestigious University of Iowa Writer's Workshop, behind-the-scenes work on documentary films, and playing guitar and electric violin for various Boston-area rock bands. Henderson had produced radio plays and an acclaimed short film in the late 1960s and early 1970s, but *Stark Raving Elvis* was his first foray into the novel form. The work met with favorable reviews upon publication in 1984, and was followed nearly a decade later by Henderson's second novel, *I Killed Hemingway.*

Stark Raving Elvis is a parody of the gargantuan mythos surrounding Elvis Presley, the so-called "King of Rock and Roll," whose popularity has endured since his 1977 death. Henderson's novel weaves together various facets of the King's legend and legacy as the book's protagonist, Byron "Blue Suede" Bluford, makes almost the same fateful life journey as his idol. Bluford discovers he has a talent for imitating Presley in a 1958 talent contest in his hometown of Portland, Maine. He then becomes obsessed with Elvis, first a devoted fan, then a first-rate imitator. His fixation on the singer culminates in a 1976 meeting with Presley, a year before the King's death. At that fateful encounter, the bloated and catatonic Elvis presents Bluford with one of his prized revolvers as a gift.

When Presley expires the following year, Bluford is ready to step into his shoes and joins the legions of Elvis impersonators on the road to stardom in Las Vegas. Yet Bluford soon learns that his act, that of the young, lean, and rebellious Elvis of the 1950s, does not play as well in Vegas as the overweight, sequinned King of later years. He adjusts his stage persona accordingly, then flirts with the same self-destruction that claimed Presley.

In reviewing *Stark Raving Elvis* for the *New York Times Book Review,* critic Nikki Giovanni described it as "a funny, revealing novel that shows what happens to those who refuse to let youth go." *Village Voice* writer Ed Ward commented that "*Stark Raving Elvis* tells a story that's simultaneously preposterous and profoundly concerned with contemporary American culture and its myths." Ward summarized Henderson's first attempt at the novel form by asserting that the author "has a fine ear for dialogue and a way of writing that doesn't condescend to his characters or ring false."

Henderson's second novel, 1993's *I Killed Hemingway,* is another humorous and satirical look at a celebrity, author Ernest Hemingway, whose posthumous fame has extreme consequences for a number of the novel's characters. The plot is set in motion when a publishing firm receives a portion of an autobiography written by a ninety-three-year-old man in Key West, Florida, who claims to have murdered Hemingway. Eric "Pappy" Markham, the author of the memoir, alleges that he was the macho man that Hemingway idolized, imitated, and eventually plagiarized, robbing Pappy of the fame he deserved. As revenge, Markham killed Hemingway in 1961, making it appear to be a suicide, and he now wants to reveal the true story to the world.

Sensing that the memoir could be a sensational best-seller, the publishing company dispatches Elliot McGuire to investigate Pappy's claims. To this point in his life McGuire has, like Pappy Markham, been obsessed with Hemingway. As a boy, McGuire sent an angry letter to Hemingway, and the author's suicide a few days later has haunted McGuire for years. He later became a renowned Hemingway scholar, but his career faltered when he was ostracized by his intellectual peers for a drunken statement made at a literary event. Now he has become a hack biographer for wealthy customers, a job he despises. He is in the midst of developing his own biography-based self-help system, Life Forms, when a friend lands him the job of sizing up Pappy Markham's memoir. Though the assignment is a lucrative change for McGuire, he finds Markham's claims ludicrous.

Once in Key West, McGuire discovers that Pappy has no memoir, but when the old man offers him a large portion of the advance to ghost-write a manuscript, McGuire

agrees. Pappy's tales of boozing and womanizing in 1920s Paris are compelling, portraying Markham as even more Hemingway-esque than the writer himself. When the finished book becomes a best-seller, McGuire is consumed with guilt, and he resolves to clear Hemingway's name by revealing Pappy as a fraud. The resulting intrigue allows Henderson to satirize print media, television talk shows, and other elements of popular culture while paving the way for a final showdown between Pappy and McGuire.

I Killed Hemingway met with favor from reviewers for its biting look at the mythology of extinct celebrities. "His ability to shatter an icon," a *Publishers Weekly* reviewer noted, "then glue the pieces back together, unnerves his readers as surely as it does his exhausted, desperate characters." Robert Grudin of the *New York Times Book Review* was also enthusiastic. He found that Henderson's theme evoked some very real complexities of literary success and reputation and lauded the work as "complex, amusing and palpably symbolic."

Henderson told *CA:* "I was born in Charlotte, North Carolina, in 1943, and grew up in Chapel Hill. As a boy I was musical and seemed to be headed, if anywhere, in that direction. In high school I led a double life: secret reader and symphony violinist, and rock 'n' roll guitarist. During the school year my bands worked the fraternity circuit. When school was out I disappeared to play in classical summer festival orchestras, accompanying festival-hopping soloists like Isaac Stern, Beverly Sills, and Grant Johannesen.

"I didn't write anything until late in my college years, and when I did, it was poetry. Senior year at Oberlin, I won the Plum Creek Review poetry prize, and after graduation went on to the University of Iowa's Writer's Workshop. Accepted as a poet, I decided (in an act of prophecy and idiocy) to switch, if I could, into the fiction program. It was easy: I simply talked the program secretary into making the necessary changes and—presto, I was a fiction writer. I had never actually written fiction, but that seemed only a minor obstacle. It was a good time for fiction at Iowa. Kurt Vonnegut was there, along with Nelson Algren, Jose Donoso, and Vance Bourjailly. But, unprepared as I was, I spooked myself by doing so poorly that I withdrew from the program, and it was a good fifteen years before I would try fiction again.

"In the meantime I went to New York and got into the technical side of documentary filmmaking, ending up a freelance film editor and location sound recordist. My short film *Zelenka* won a CINE Golden Eagle award and was seen in festivals around the world. In 1969 I made a sideways move into radio where I managed to write and produce a number of radio plays for WBAI-FM in New York where I was a staff producer and had my own live free-form magazine show, 'Medicine Hat.' This was the 'psychedelic' era at WBAI and the on-air personalities were young, mischievous, and unpredictable. The station maintained a marvelous pop music collection, and I filled my show with curious and esoteric word-tapes and collages of album cuts. Little by little, my delight with the explosion of new music was drawing me back into rock 'n' roll. One day, on impulse, I bought not one but two guitars, a vintage Fender Stratocaster and a beat-up Gibson Les Paul. I had my mother ship me my old Fender Twin Reverb amplifier, and I walked into the station manager's office and resigned from WBAI.

"After a summer in Berkeley, California, I moved to Boston and spent the next five years making my living in various rock 'n' roll road bands, including two years with Cambridge bar legend John Lincoln Wright. Marriage and old age (I was over thirty!) ended this phase of my life. Settling down in Cambridge, I got work as a freelance audio-visual writer and producer while my wife plied her trade as a modern dancer. I specialized in soundtracks, music editing, and jingle writing. We moved back to New York for two years, then out to Los Angeles, where I took a crack at learning the screenwriting trade. After two years, I had absorbed quite a bit of screenplay technique (valuable lessons, especially in plot structure, or as they call it out there, 'story'), but my wife and I began to realize we were not cut out for endless summer, or the entertainment 'company town' character of Los Angeles. We bolted for Calais, Maine, near the Canadian border, where we took work as a gardener-handyman team for some rich summer folks with a mansion and twelve acres. Here I finally faced up to my long-buried ambition to write fiction and banged out the first draft of *Stark Raving Elvis*.

"Two years later, *Stark Raving Elvis* was published. Not long after that, I began the early work on *I Killed Hemingway*. Today I have a third novel underway and a teaching job at the University of North Carolina at Chapel Hill. My wife (same one) is now a freelance magazine journalist, and my daughters are seven and ten. When I look back it's hard to believe how long and tortuous a route I took to get where I knew I'd end up all along. But it's been a life, and not a bad one at that."

BIOGRAPHICAL/CRITICAL SOURCES:

PERIODICALS

Boston Globe, December 30, 1984.
Boston Herald, November 18, 1984.
New York Times, August 30, 1987, p. 34.
New York Times Book Review, December 9, 1984, p. 26; May 9, 1993, p. 9.
Philadelphia Inquirer, October 14, 1984.
Publishers Weekly, January 25, 1993.
San Francisco Chronicle, April 18, 1993.
Village Voice, January 29, 1985, pp. 47-48, 57.

HENRY, Stuart (Dennis) 1949-

PERSONAL: Born October 18, 1949, in London, England; immigrated to United States, 1984; son of Lionel Victor (a chef) and Dorothy (an office worker; maiden name, Knowles) Henry; married Lee Doric (an art therapist), March 5, 1988. *Education:* University of Kent at Canterbury, B.A. (honors), 1972, Ph.D., 1976. *Avocational Interests:* House renovation and repair.

ADDRESSES: Home—Manchester, MI. *Office*—Department of Sociology, Anthropology, and Criminology, Eastern Michigan University, 712 Pray Harrold, Ypsilanti, MI 48197-2207.

CAREER: University of London, Institute of Psychiatry, London, England, research sociologist at Addiction Research Unit, 1975-78; University of Middlesex, Enfield, England, research fellow at Centre for Occupational and Community Research, 1978-79; Nottingham Polytechnic, Nottingham, England, senior lecturer in social studies, 1979-83; Old Dominion University, Norfolk, VA, assistant professor of sociology and criminal justice, 1984-87; Eastern Michigan University, Ypsilanti, associate professor, 1987-92, professor of sociology and criminal justice, 1992—. Guest on radio and television programs.

MEMBER: American Society of Criminology, Academy of Criminal Justice Sciences, Law and Society Association, Industrial Relations Research Association.

AWARDS, HONORS: Grants from British Economic and Social Research Council, 1978-81, and National Science Foundation, 1990-93; Teaching Excellence Award from State of Michigan, 1990.

WRITINGS:

(With D. Robinson) *Self-Help and Health: Mutual Aid for Modern Problems,* Martin Robertson, 1977.
The Hidden Economy: The Context and Control of Borderline Crime, Martin Robertson, 1978, Loompanics Unlimited, 1988.
(Editor) *Informal Institutions: Alternative Networks in the Corporate State,* St. Martin's, 1981, published in England as *Can I Have It in Cash?,* Astragal Books, 1981.
Private Justice: Toward Integrated Theorizing in the Sociology of Law, Routledge & Kegan Paul, 1983.
(Editor) *Degrees of Deviance: Student Accounts of Their Deviant Behavior,* Avebury Press, 1989, Sheffield Publishing, 1990.
(With R. Cantor and S. Rayner) *Making Markets: An Interdisciplinary Perspective on Economic Exchange,* Greenwood Press, 1992.
(Editor with L. A. Ferman and L. E. Berndt) *Work beyond Employment in Advanced Capitalist Countries: Classic and Contemporary Perspectives on the Infor-*

mal Economy, Volume I: *Concepts, Evidence, and Measurement,* Volume II: *Revisions and Criticism,* Edwin Mellen, 1993.

(With E. H. Pfuhl) *The Deviance Process,* 3rd edition, Aldine de Gruyter, 1993.

(Editor) *Social Control: Aspects of Non-State Justice,* Dartmouth Press, 1993.

(Editor) *Inside Jobs: A Student Guide to Criminal Justice Careers,* Sheffield Publishing, 1994.

Work represented in anthologies, including *Transcarceration: Essays in the Sociology of Social Control,* edited by J. Lowman, R. Menzies, and T. Palys, Gower Press, 1987; *Rules, Decisions, and Inequality in Egalitarian Social Groups,* edited by J. Flanagan and S. Rayner, Gower Press, 1988; and *The Futures of Criminology,* edited by D. Nelken, Sage Publications, 1994. Contributor of numerous articles and reviews to periodicals, including *Annals of the American Academy of Political and Social Science, British Journal of Criminology, British Journal of Law and Society, New Society,* and *Sociological Review.* Member of editorial board, *Howard Journal of Criminal Justice,* 1983—.

WORK IN PROGRESS: Criminological Theory, with W. Einstadter, for Harcourt; *Constitutive Criminology: A Critical Deconstructionist Paradigm,* with D. Milovanovic; revising *Degrees of Deviance: Student Accounts of Their Deviant Behavior* for Sheffield Publishing; research on justice in workplace discipline and discharge; research on postmodern criminological theory.

SIDELIGHTS: Stuart Henry told *CA:* "I was brought up as the only son of working-class parents in a south London suburb. I was the first in my family to go to college and to earn a bachelor's degree. From the streets of London, sociology had an immediate attraction, and the doctoral thesis I later pursued reflected the networks of dealing and trading that formed the hidden economy of my neighborhood. Since graduating I have gone on to teach at universities, first in England and since 1984 in the United States, where I live with my American wife.

"In my research and publications I attempt to capture the diversity of human creativity *outside* of their formal roles and institutions. I have examined private and non-state systems of justice, self-help and mutual aid, as well as continuing my studies of informal economies."

*   *   *

HERLIHY, James Leo   1927-1993

OBITUARY NOTICE—See index for *CA* sketch: Born February 27, 1927, in Detroit, MI; died from an overdose of sleeping pills, October 21, 1993, in Los Angeles, CA.

Actor, educator, playwright, and author. Herlihy is best remembered for his stage plays and novels, which present vivid depictions of the downtrodden or troubled. Following a stint in the U.S. Navy during World War II, Herlihy embarked on a career in the entertainment field spanning more than forty years. He began performing on stage while a student at the Pasadena Playhouse College from 1948 to 1950. He also began writing plays, seeing his *Streetlight Sonata* produced in Pasadena in 1950. By 1958 Herlihy's work (*Blue Denim*) had found its way to the Broadway stage. Among his other popular plays was the trilogy *Stop, You're Killing Me.*

Herlihy also tried his hand successfully in other writing genres. In the 1950s he penned scripts for television; in the 1960s he crafted the critically acclaimed novels *Midnight Cowboy* and *All Fall Down,* both adapted for film within several years of publication. His last novel, *Season of the Witch,* was released in 1971. He also found time to give acting workshops at Hollywood's Milton Katselas and to teach at the City College of the City University of New York, University of Arkansas, Colorado College, University of Southern California, and other schools. He also continued to act, starring in the 1981 film *The Four Friends.*

OBITUARIES AND OTHER SOURCES:

BOOKS

Contemporary Theatre, Film, and Television, Volume 1, Gale, 1984, p. 241.
Who's Who in America, 48th edition, Marquis, 1994.

PERIODICALS

Chicago Tribune, October 24, 1993, section 2, p. 7.
Los Angeles Times, October 23, 1993, p. A26.
New York Times, October 22, 1993, p. B9.
Times (London), November 20, 1993, p. 21.

*   *   *

HINE, Darlene Clark   1947-

PERSONAL: Born February 7, 1947, in Morley, MO; daughter of Levester (a truck driver) and Lottie Mae (a homemaker; maiden name, Thompson) Clark; married William C. Hine, 1970 (marriage ended, 1974); married Johnny E. Brown, 1981 (marriage ended, 1986); children: Robbie Davine. *Education:* Roosevelt University, B.A., 1968; Kent State University, M.A., 1970, Ph.D., 1975. *Politics:* Democrat. *Religion:* Baptist.

ADDRESSES: Home—2357 Burcham Dr., East Lansing, MI 48823. *Office*—Department of History, 301 Morrill Hall, Michigan State University, East Lansing, MI 48824.

CAREER: South Carolina State College, Orangeburg, assistant professor of history and coordinator of black studies, 1972-74; Purdue University, West Lafayette, IN, assistant professor, 1974-79, associate professor, 1979-85, professor of history, 1985-87, interim director of Africana Studies and Research Center, 1978-79, vice-provost, 1981-86; Michigan State University, East Lansing, John A. Hannah Professor of History, 1987—. Arizona State University, distinguished visiting professor, 1985; University of Delaware, distinguished visiting professor of women's studies, 1989-90; lecturer at colleges and universities, including Harvard University, University of Virginia, University of Texas at Austin, Arkansas College, Williams College, University of Arizona, Howard University, Carnegie-Mellon University, Utah State University, Cornell University, University of Michigan, Washington University, and University of Galway. Indiana Committee for the Humanities, member, 1983-85; Medical College of Pennsylvania, member of advisory board for Black Women Physicians Project, 1987-89; Consortium of Social Science Associations, member of board of directors, 1987-91; consultant to Florentine Films, MacArthur Foundation, and Meharry Medical College.

MEMBER: American Historical Association, Organization of American Historians (chair of Elliott Rudwick Book Prize, 1991), Association for the Study of Afro-American Life and History (member of executive council, 1979-84; second vice president, 1986-89), Association of Black Women Historians (founding member and director of publications; vice president, 1981-82; chair of Letitia Brown Memorial Publication Prize Committee, 1986-87), Berkshire Conference of Women Historians, Southern Historical Association (member of executive council, 1990-92), Southern Association for Women Historians (vice president, 1983-84; president, 1984-85), Phi Alpha Theta.

AWARDS, HONORS: Fellow of Rockefeller Foundation, 1980; grants from Eleanor Roosevelt Institute, 1980-81, Fund for the Improvement of Post Secondary Education, 1980-82, National Endowment for the Humanities, 1982-83 and 1984-85, and Ford Foundation, 1991; essay competition award, DeGolyer Institute of American Studies, Southern Methodist University, 1982; named a Sagamore of the Wabash by the governor of Indiana, 1985; fellow, American Council of Learned Societies and National Humanities Center, both 1986-87; Otto Wirth Award, Roosevelt University Alumni Association, 1988; Women's Honors in Public Service, Minority Fellowship Programs, and Cabinet on Human Rights Award, American Nurses Association, 1988; Letitia Woods Brown Book Award, Association of Black Women Historians, 1990; Lavinia L. Dock Book Award, American Association for the History of Nursing, 1990; Outstanding Academic Book Award, *Choice*, 1990; Outstanding Book Award, Gustavus Myers Center, 1990; Special Achievement Award, Kent State University Alumni Association, 1991.

WRITINGS:

Black Victory: The Rise and Fall of the White Primary in Texas, KTO Press, 1979.

When the Truth Is Told: A History of Black Women's Culture and Community in Indiana, 1875-1950, National Council of Negro Women, 1981.

(Editor) *Black Women in the Nursing Profession: An Anthology of Historical Sources,* Garland Publishing, 1985.

(Editor) *Black Women in the Middle West Project: A Comprehensive Resource Guide, Illinois and Indiana,* Indiana Historical Bureau, 1985.

(Editor and contributor) *The State of Afro-American History: Past, Present, and Future,* Louisiana State University Press, 1986.

Black Women in White: Racial Conflict and Cooperation in the Nursing Profession, 1890-1950, Indiana University Press, 1989.

(Editor) *Black Women in the United States, 1619-1989,* sixteen volumes, Carlson Publishing, 1990.

(Editor with Clayborne Carson, David Garrow, and Vincent Harding) *Eyes on the Prize, a History of the Civil Rights Era: A Reader,* Penguin, 1991.

(Editor) *Black Women in America: An Historical Encyclopedia,* Volumes I-II, Carlson Publishing, 1993.

(Editor with D. Barry Gaspar) *Black Women and Slavery in the Americas,* Indiana University Press, 1993.

(Editor with Carson) *Milestones in African American History,* sixteen volumes, Chelsea House, 1993.

Work represented in books, including *Lady Bountiful Revisited: Women, Philanthropy, and Power,* edited by Kathleen D. McCarthy, Rutgers University Press, 1990; *The Great Migration in Historical Perspective,* Indiana University Press, 1991; and *Lure and Loathing,* edited by Gerald Early, Penguin, 1993. Editor, "Blacks in the Diaspora Series," Indiana University Press, 1984. Contributor of articles and reviews to history, black studies, and women's studies journals. Editor, *Truth: The Newsletter of the Association of Black Women Historians,* 1978-79; member of editorial board, *Journal of Negro History,* 1979-87, *Umoja: A Scholarly Journal of Black Studies,* 1980-84, *Journal for Higher Education Management* (formerly *Journal of the American Association of University Administrators*), 1984-87, and *Hampton University Journal of Ethnic Studies,* 1984-89; member of editorial advisory board, *Journal of Women's History,* 1987—, and *Nursing History Review.*

WORK IN PROGRESS: The Origins of Modern African American Society and Culture, 1931-1954 and *Madam C.*

J. Walker, completion of both expected in 1995; research on the history of black civil rights lawyers, black physicians, black theologians, and blacks in science.

SIDELIGHTS: Darlene Clark Hine told *CA:* "Ever since I learned to read, I have been fascinated by words and books. It was not until a high school civics teacher gave me a copy of American author James Baldwin's *Giovanni's Room* that I imagined that, as a black person, I too could put words and images together to make books.

"My interest in African American history began while I was an undergraduate student attending Roosevelt University in Chicago. Actually, I turned to the study of black history in search of answers regarding the genesis and intransigence of white racism. I was profoundly troubled by the civil rights movements, and the images of water hoses and police dogs turned against unarmed protestors still haunt my memories. I imagined that history perhaps held both the explanations and the solutions to the problem of white racism. This search for answers and solutions led me to pursue graduate studies at Kent State University, where I studied with American author and educator August Meier. My first book, *Black Victory: The Rise and Fall of the White Primary in Texas,* was a revision of my doctoral dissertation. It reflects my concerns with the antecedents to the modern civil rights movement.

"During the 1980s, I began to research and write on the history of black women, adding gender and class to my arsenal and analytical categories. I published *Black Women in White: Racial Conflict and Cooperation in the Nursing Profession, 1890-1950* in 1989. After editing a sixteen-volume series of articles and unpublished dissertations on black women for Carlson Publishing in 1990, I assumed that I had done enough. I was wrong. Ralph Carlson persuaded me to edit *Black Women in America: An Historical Encyclopedia.* My reluctance gave way to an urgency to produce and make accessible as much accurate information about black women as possible. The encyclopedia is intended to place a stone in the shoe of every American historian. The encyclopedia will make it difficult, if not impossible, to ignore or exclude black women and their deeds, contributions, and experiences in the American pageant."

*   *   *

HIRSCHFELD, Yizhar 1950-

PERSONAL: Born February 6, 1950, in Jerusalem, Israel; son of Eli (a merchant) and Stafrira (a homemaker) Hirschfeld; married; wife's name, Hannah (an archaeologist), January 4, 1983; children: Tammar, Daphna, Irit. *Education:* Hebrew University of Jerusalem, B.A., 1974, M.A.,

1982, Ph.D., 1987; postdoctoral study at Yale University. *Politics:* Labor.

ADDRESSES: Home—6 Haarazim St., Motza 90820, Israel. *Office*—Israel Antiquities Authority, P.O. Box 586, Jerusalem 91004, Israel.

CAREER: Israel Antiquities Authority, Jerusalem, director of excavations for the Roman Bath of Hammat Gader, 1978-82, the site of Ramat Hanadiv, 1984-93, and the site of Tiberias, 1989—. Hebrew University of Jerusalem, guest lecturer at Institute of Archaeology. *Military service:* Israel Defence Forces.

AWARDS, HONORS: Rothchild Award for Yale University.

WRITINGS:

The Survey of Israel: Herodium Map, Israel Antiquities Authority, 1985.
The Judean Desert Monasteries in the Byzantine Period, Yale University Press, 1992.
Palestinian Dwelling Houses, Franciscan Press, 1994.

WORK IN PROGRESS: A final report on the excavations of the Roman bath of Hammat Gader, with Giora Soler; reports on the excavations of Tiberias and Ramat Hanadiv.

SIDELIGHTS: Yizhar Hirschfeld told *CA:* "Field work in archaeology is creative work; new data comes out of the dust and sends us regards from ancient civilizations. Through my books I try to organize this information, explain it, and use it to paint a picture. Exposing an ancient monastery may give us a lovely and vivid picture of the daily life of the monks. A Roman bath is no less vivid. I want to tell the stories of the people who lived in the late antique period. It is a challenge for me to do it well and, above all, it is a kind of spiritual amusement."

*   *   *

HOLMES, Geoffrey (Shorter) 1928-1993

OBITUARY NOTICE—See index for *CA* sketch: Born July 17, 1928, in Sheffield, England; died November 25, 1993, in Settle, North Yorkshire, England. Historian, educator, and writer. Holmes's historical studies of late-seventeenth and early-eighteenth century Britain made important contributions to contemporary understanding of the era. Beginning his academic career as a lecturer at the University of Glasgow in Scotland, Holmes continued his teaching duties at the university while researching his first book, *British Politics in the Age of Anne,* which became a respected text after its publication in 1967. He moved to the University of Lancaster in 1969, where he remained until his retirement from full-time teaching in 1983. He authored numerous books, including *The Electorate and the National Will in the First Age of the Party, Augustan England: Professions, State and Society 1680-1730,* and *Politics, Religion and Society in England 1679-1742,* was coauthor of *Stuart England,* and also coedited *The London Diaries of William Nicholson, Bishop of Carlisle, 1702-1718.*

OBITUARIES AND OTHER SOURCES:

BOOKS

The International Who's Who, 57th edition, Europa, 1993.

PERIODICALS

Times (London), December 14, 1993, p. 19.

*   *   *

HOLST, Johan J(oergen)   1937-1994

OBITUARY NOTICE—See index for *CA* sketch: Born November 29, 1937, in Oslo, Norway; died following a stroke, January 13, 1994, in Oslo, Norway. Norwegian government official, international negotiator, and author. Long associated with Norway's Ministry of Defense, Holst published numerous volumes on security issues. In 1993 he became the Norwegian foreign minister and played an instrumental role in the negotiations between Israel and the Palestinian Liberation Organization (PLO) that led to limited Palestinian self-rule in the Gaza Strip and West Bank areas of the Middle East. Holst worked in the United States as a research assistant at Harvard University's Center for International Affairs from 1962 to 1963 and at the Hudson Institute in Croton, New York, from 1967 to 1969. In Norway he served as senior researcher at the Norwegian Defense Research Establishment from 1963 to 1967, worked for the Norwegian Institute of International Affairs beginning in 1969, and moved to the Ministry of Defense in 1976. He was a state secretary at the Ministry of Foreign Affairs from 1979 to 1981 when he returned to the Institute of International Affairs. He was named Norway's defense minister beginning in 1986, and he assumed his duties as foreign minister in 1993. His books include *Why ABM?: Policy Issues in the Missile Defense Controversy, Five Roads to Nordic Security,* and *Beyond Nuclear Deterrence: New Arms, New Aims.*

OBITUARIES AND OTHER SOURCES:

BOOKS

Who's Who in the World, 12th edition, Marquis, 1993.

PERIODICALS

Chicago Tribune, January 16, 1994, p. 6.
Los Angeles Times, January 14, 1994, p. A22.

New York Times, January 14, 1994, p. D18.
Times (London), January 14, 1994, p. 17.

*   *   *

HOODBHOY, Pervez   1950-

PERSONAL: Born July 11, 1950, in Karachi, Pakistan; son of Amirali and Malek Hoodbhoy; married Hajra Ahmad (a teacher), 1974; children: Asha Amirali, Alia Amirali. *Education:* Massachusetts Institute of Technology, Ph.D. (nuclear physics), 1978.

ADDRESSES: Office—Department of Physics, Quaid-e-Azam University, Islamabad, Pakistan.

CAREER: Quaid-e-Azam University, Islamabad, Pakistan, physicist, 1973—. Director and producer of a television series on popular science.

WRITINGS:

Islam and Science, Zed Books, 1991.
M. A. Beg Memorial Volume, World Scientific, 1991.

Writer of thirteen educational programs for Pakistan Television.

*   *   *

HOOKS, Bell
See WATKINS, Gloria

*   *   *

HOOPER, Maureen Brett   1927-

PERSONAL: Born August 5, 1927, in Chino, CA; daughter of Herbert E. (a minister) and Adelaide A. (a homemaker) Hooper. *Education:* University of California, Los Angeles, B.A., 1949; California State University, Northridge, M.A., 1960; University of Southern California, Ed.D., 1969. *Avocational Interests:* Travel, concerts and plays, reading.

ADDRESSES: Home—1635 Hilts Ave., Los Angeles, CA 90024. *Office*—c/o University of California, Los Angeles, Department of Music, 405 Hilgard Ave., Los Angeles, CA 90024-1616.

CAREER: Los Angeles Unified School District, Los Angeles, CA, music teacher, 1949-62; University of California, Los Angeles, senior lecturer of music education, 1962-91, emeritus lecturer, 1991—. Curriculum consultant and music textbook consultant; speaker and clinician for gifted and talented programs; director of the American Suzuki Institute West.

MEMBER: Society of Children's Book Writers and Illustrators, Golden Key Fraternity (honorary member), Los Angeles City Elementary Schools Music Teachers' Association, Inc. (lifetime member).

WRITINGS:

The Violin Man (middle grade novel), Boyds Mills Press, 1991.
The Christmas Drum (picture book), Boyds Mills Press, in press.

Also author of professional articles and curriculum guides.

WORK IN PROGRESS: The Orange Clarinet (picture book), *The Year the Rabbit Dance Began* (picture book), *Mrs. Periwether's Piano* (middle grade novel), and *The Almost Terrible Tuba Tragedy* (picture book).

SIDELIGHTS: Maureen Brett Hooper commented: "A few years ago I became an admirer of Suzuki string students. I admired not only their skills but the joy with which they made music. I wanted somehow to be a part of it. My cello had stood dormant in a corner of my closet for many years, so I knew teaching would not do. Then one day I surprised myself by deciding to write a book for these students. It would not be a book about the facts of music, although those books are important, but a book about the wonders of making music. From that decision came my first book. Now I spend much of my time writing other stories on this theme. And as I write, I learn more and more about this mystical power we call music."

*   *   *

HOPKINSON, Deborah 1952-

PERSONAL: Born February 4, 1952, in Lowell, MA; daughter of Russell W. (a machinist) and Gloria D. Hopkinson; married Andrew D. Thomas (a teacher); children: Rebekah, Dimitri. *Education:* University of Massachusetts— Amherst, B.A., 1973; University of Hawaii, M.A., 1978. *Avocational Interests:* Reading, hiking, swimming, history.

ADDRESSES: Home—3561-D Pinao St., Honolulu, HI 96822. *Office*—East-West Center, 1777 East-West Rd., Honolulu, HI 96848.

CAREER: Manoa Valley Theater, Honolulu, HI, marketing director, 1981-84; University of Hawaii Foundation, Honolulu, development director, 1985-89; East-West Center, Honolulu, development director, 1989—. Creative Fund Raising Associates, Honolulu, consultant,

1991—. Board member of the National Society of Fund Raising Executives, Aloha Chapter, 1985-91.

MEMBER: Society of Children's Book Writers and Illustrators, National League of American Pen Women.

AWARDS, HONORS: Merit award, Society of Children's Book Writers and Illustrators, 1991; work-in-progress grant recipient, Society of Children's Book Writers and Illustrators, 1993.

WRITINGS:

Pearl Harbor, Dillon Press/Macmillan, 1991.
Sweet Clara and the Freedom Quilt, illustrated by James Ransome, Knopf, 1993.

WORK IN PROGRESS: Stories about the settling of the West and lighthouses, and a book about the Civil War.

SIDELIGHTS: "As a girl, I always wanted to be a writer," Deborah Hopkinson commented, "But I never knew what I wanted to write. Then, when my daughter Rebekah was about three, we were reading a lot of children's books. Having a full-time career and a child, I was very busy. But I thought, 'Maybe I'll try writing for children. At least the books are short!' I have since found out that simply because a story is short, that doesn't mean that it is easy to write!"

Hopkinson's first book, *Pearl Harbor,* was published in 1991 as part of Dillon Press's "Places in American History" series. Aimed at older children, the book tells the story of the bombing of Pearl Harbor during World War II and includes photographs showing Pearl Harbor both during the war and today.

For her second book, Hopkinson decided to try her hand at fiction. *Sweet Clara and the Freedom Quilt* is about a slave girl who is separated from her mother and sent to work in the fields. She lives with an elderly woman named Aunt Rachel, who teaches her to sew. Clara becomes a seamstress, but she is always preoccupied with thoughts of her mother and freedom. Clara overhears other slaves discussing the "underground railroad," and decides to use her sewing skills to help herself and other slaves escape. In her spare time, she sews a quilt; but instead of patchwork, Clara's quilt is a map detailing an escape route. When she finally does escape the plantation, she leaves the quilt for other slaves.

Hopkinson commented: "The idea for *Sweet Clara and the Freedom Quilt* came to me while listening to a radio story about African-American quilts. I consider this story a wonderful gift, and feel very happy that I was able to tell it." The story "brings power and substance to this noteworthy picture book," writes a reviewer for *Publishers Weekly* who concludes, "This first-rate book is a triumph of the heart."

In addition to her books, Hopkinson also writes short stories, especially for *Cricket* magazine. While her main interest "is stories that also tell about history," she adds, "I also like to write about girls, because when I was a girl, there weren't many stories about the exciting things that girls can do!"

BIOGRAPHICAL/CRITICAL SOURCES:

PERIODICALS

Bulletin of the Center for Children's Books, July/August 1993, p. 346.
Publishers Weekly, February 8, 1993, p. 87; July 12, 1993, pp. 25-26.
School Library Journal, June 1993, p. 76.

*   *   *

HOPPE, Matthias   1952-

PERSONAL: Born December 5, 1952, in Schluechtern, Germany; son of Bodo (a preacher) and Gisela (a musician and homemaker) Hoppe; children: Aniela. *Education:* Attended University of Erlangen (Germany), 1971-74, and University of Munich, 1974-78. *Avocational Interests:* Playing piano, composing music, painting, photography.

ADDRESSES: Home and office—Bucheckernweg 3, D-81547, Muenchen, Germany.

CAREER: Journalist and author, 1981—. Television journalist, 1985-87; *Ambiente* magazine, editor, 1990-92. Press speaker for the German peace movement, 1983, and for *Die Gruenen,* 1984-85.

MEMBER: IG Medien (German Writers Association).

AWARDS, HONORS: Fourth prize in a writing contest, *Eltern* magazine, 1991.

WRITINGS:

(With Klaus Gerosa, Beate Kuhn, and Ursula Kopp) *Lexikon fuer Waldfreunde* (dictionary; title means "All about the Forest"), Bucher Verlag, 1982.
Muenchen April '82: Ostermaersche, SPD-Parteitag, Demonstrationen (documentary), SBV-Verlag, 1982.
Was macht Arno im Sommer oder Ein Schneemann hat Heimweh (picture book; title means "What Does Arno Do in Summer; or, A Snowman Is Homesick"), illustrated by Rolf Faenger, Coppenrath Verlag, 1989.
Das kleine Buch der grossen Wunder (aphorisms; title means "Little Book about Great Miracles"), ars edition, 1990.

Die Maus und der Elefant, Bohem Press, 1990, translation published as *Mouse and Elephant,* illustrated by Jan Lenica, Little, Brown, 1991.

Contributor to periodicals, including *Stern, Die Zeit, Abendzeitung, Frankfurter Rundschau,* and *Ambiente.* Also contributor to German television.

WORK IN PROGRESS: A sequel to *Mouse and Elephant;* other children's books; a novel, tentatively titled *Havana in Dresden;* a stage play, tentatively titled *Mosquitos under the Bridge,* about people who live under a bridge.

SIDELIGHTS: Matthias Hoppe commented: "When my daughter Aniela was five years old, she wanted me to tell her my own stories before going to bed—no more reading any book stories. So I had to find new stories for children, another one each day. One day I began to note down my ideas. With a friend of mine, a talented illustrator, I developed my first children's book in 1989: *Was macht Arno im Sommer oder Ein Schneemann hat Heimweh,* a story about a snowman. So it began.

"Writing is my hobby and business. To express what you have seen, your experiences, your thoughts, together with imagination and the will to do something for this world—that's what I want. Not only for children but also for adults, politically, psychologically, ecologically."

*   *   *

HORD, Frederick (Lee)   1941-
(Mzee Lasana Okpara)

PERSONAL: Born November 7, 1941, in Kokomo, IN; son of Noel E. and Jessie (maiden name, Tyler) Hord; divorced; children: Teresa D. Hord-Owens, F. Mark, Laurel E. *Education:* Indiana State University, B.S., 1963, M.S., 1965; Union Graduate School, Ph.D., 1987.

ADDRESSES: Office—Director of Black Studies, Knox College, Box 13, Galesburg, IL 61401.

CAREER: Wabash College, Crawfordsville, IN, professor of black studies, 1972-76; Indiana University, guest lecturer in black studies, 1976; Community Service Administration, research director, 1977-80; Frostburg State University, Frostburg, MD, assistant director of minority affairs, 1980-84; Howard University, Washington, DC, professor of Afro-American studies, 1984-87; West Virginia University, Morgantown, WV, Center for Black Culture, director, 1987-88; Knox College, Galesburg, IL, director of black studies, 1988—. Performer/lecturer with PANFRE, 1981—; regional consultant for NAMSE; consultant on black studies for Aframeric Enterprises.

MEMBER: Association for Black Culture Centers (founder).

AWARDS, HONORS: Governor's Award, 1963, for Outstanding Black Male Scholar in Indiana Colleges and Universities.

WRITINGS:

After(h)ours (poems), Third World Press, 1974.
Into Africa, the Color Black (poems), Third World Press, 1987.
Reconstructing Memory: Black Literary Criticism (essays), Third World Press, 1991.

Contributor of poems and articles to journals, including *Black Books Bulletin, Western Journal of Black Studies, Black American Literature Forum, West Virginia Law Review,* and *Obsidian II.* Consulting editor of *Nightsun.*

BIOGRAPHICAL/CRITICAL SOURCES:

PERIODICALS

Choice, April, 1992, p. 1225.
Reference and Research Book News, October, 1991, p. 34.
Small Press Book Review, November, 1991, p. 14.*

*   *   *

HOUSE, James S. 1944-

PERSONAL: Born January 27, 1944, in Philadelphia, PA; son of James, Jr., and Virginia Miller (Sturgis) House; married Wendy Fisher; children: Jeff, Erin. *Education:* Haverford College, B.A., 1965; University of Michigan, Ph.D., 1972.

ADDRESSES: Home—2309 Brockman, Ann Arbor, MI 48104. *Office*—Institute for Social Research, University of Michigan, Box 1248, Ann Arbor, MI 48106.

CAREER: Duke University, Durham, NC, began as instructor, became associate professor of sociology, 1970-78; University of Michigan, Ann Arbor, associate professor and associate research scientist, 1978-82, professor of sociology and research scientist in sociology and epidemiology, 1982—, chairperson of Department of Sociology, 1986-90, director of Survey Research Center at Institute for Social Research, 1991—, and faculty associate at Institute of Gerontology.

MEMBER: American Sociological Association, Academy of Behavioral Medicine Research (fellow), Society for Epidemiological Research, American Association for the Advancement of Science (fellow).

AWARDS, HONORS: Guggenheim fellow, 1986-87.

WRITINGS:

Work, Stress, and Social Support, Addison-Wesley, 1981.

(Editor with K. Warner Schaie and Dan Blazen, and contributor) *Aging, Health Behaviors, and Health Outcomes,* Lawrence Erlbaum, 1992.
(Editor with Karen Cook and Gary Fine, and contributor) *Sociological Perspectives on Social Psychology,* Allyn & Bacon, in press.

Contributor to sociology journals and other periodicals, including *Science.* Associate editor, *Work and Stress,* 1985-88, and *Social Psychology Quarterly,* 1988-91.

WORK IN PROGRESS: Adding Life to Years: Psychosocial Factors in the Maintenance of Health and Effective Functioning in Middle and Late Life, completion expected in 1996.

SIDELIGHTS: James S. House told *CA:* "I have been involved, for two decades, in research and writing on the relation of social stress and social support to physical and mental health. My current research focuses on the role of psychosocial factors (including social stress and social support) in the maintenance of health and effective functioning over the life course, including the reciprocal relationship between health and paid work or other productive activity. Currently I am examining variations in socioeconomic differentials in health and effective functioning over the life course, and the role of a broad range of psychosocial factors in producing those differences."

*   *   *

HOUSTON, Pam 1962(?)-

PERSONAL: Born c. 1962 in New Jersey; daughter of a businessperson and an actress; married Mike Elkington (a safari guide), c. 1992. *Education:* Received B.A. (with honors) from Denison University and Ph.D. from University of Utah. *Avocational Interests:* Skiing, white-water rafting, rock-climbing.

ADDRESSES: Home—Jensen, UT. *Agent*—Liz Darhansoff, 1220 Park Avenue, New York, NY 10128.

CAREER: Writer and hunting and rafting guide in the American West and Alaska. Has worked as a horse trainer, ski instructor, bartender, flag person on a highway crew, and instructor in literature and creative writing at Denison University; has appeared on talk shows.

WRITINGS:

Cowboys Are My Weakness: Stories, Norton, 1992.

SIDELIGHTS: Pam Houston has a dual career, writing during wintertime and working as a river guide in the American West and in Alaska during the summer. Both aspects of her career have contributed to the wide success she has achieved with the publication of her first book,

Cowboys Are My Weakness: Stories. Houston drew on her outdoor experiences to produce a sequence of twelve stories, typically narrated in the first person by a young woman who undergoes a strenuous lifestyle in order to pursue modern-day "cowboys"—defined by Houston as ruggedly attractive but emotionally inarticulate outdoorsmen. In an interview with Molly O'Neill for *New York Times,* Houston declared that a cowboy is the kind of man who "couldn't use the word 'love' in a sentence." In the title story, a picture-perfect cowboy takes the narrator home after a night of western dancing, and, while the narrator speculates about a romantic evening, the cowboy declares, "I'd like to give you a great big kiss, but I've got a mouthful of chew."

Cowboys Are My Weakness attracted considerable positive critical attention and appeared on best-seller lists, making Houston a familiar figure both in print interviews and on talk shows. In those forums, Houston described her varied life experiences, which include winning a tennis tournament at age thirteen and then quitting the sport; graduating second in her college class, then taking a transcontinental bicycle tour with a friend and ending up in Colorado; and learning the ropes of outdoor living in order to follow the men with whom she was infatuated. According to O'Neill's *New York Times* profile, Houston "hauled wild-sheep carcasses on her back across Alaskan mountains, camped in snow caves and defied a river that just a day before had killed a woman—all for the love of various men." When Houston married, it was to a former safari guide from South Africa.

More than one critic commented approvingly that Houston has staked out for women the territory previously claimed for men by writers such as American authors Ernest Hemingway and Richard Ford. Eliza Clark, reviewing *Cowboys Are My Weakness* for the Toronto *Globe and Mail,* called the stories "fresh, and often funny" and described Houston's style as "clear and spare, persuasive as a flexed muscle." Houston's characters, said Clark, "follow their cowboys into the wilderness, but what they discover is their own unique relationship to nature, risk and ego." A *New Yorker* critic stated that Houston's characters, both male and female, remain shadowy, but applauded Houston's "sturdy sense of humor" and "gift for poetic description." Judith Freeman, in the *Los Angeles Times Book Review,* called *Cowboys Are My Weakness* a "brilliant first collection," attesting that the stories "strike at the heart, and end up revealing much about the complex state of relations between men and women." Houston's "enduring theme," according to Freeman, is "the capacity of women to endure romantic disappointments," and Houston's narrative voice is "so perfectly natural, it's as if she simply found it one day, wholly formed and perfect, like an arrowhead picked up while walking through the desert."

BIOGRAPHICAL/CRITICAL SOURCES:

BOOKS

Houston, Pam, *Cowboys Are My Weakness: Stories,* Norton, 1992.

PERIODICALS

Globe and Mail (Toronto), April 25, 1992.
Los Angeles Times Book Review, February 23, 1992, pp. 3, 8.
New Yorker, February 24, 1992, pp. 101-102.
New York Times, January 12, 1992, section 7, p. 10; July 15, 1992, pp. C1, C8.*

*   *   *

HOUTS, Marshall (Wilson) 1919-1993

OBITUARY NOTICE—See index for *CA* sketch: Born June 28, 1919, in Chattanooga, TN; died November 24, 1993, in Laguna Niguel, CA. Federal law enforcement agent, lawyer, educator, and writer. Houts wrote numerous books on legal and medical procedures, and his 1967 nonfiction book *Where Death Delights: The Story of Dr. Milton Helpern and Forensic Medicine* became the basis for the popular television series *Quincy M. E.* Trained as a lawyer, Houts became an FBI agent in 1941, then turned to legal practice in 1946, eventually becoming a municipal judge in Pipestone, Minnesota, from 1947 to 1951. Houts practiced law in California beginning in 1951, and he later taught college courses at the University of California, Los Angeles in 1954, at Michigan State University from 1955 to 1957, and at Pepperdine University beginning in 1972. In 1972 he also became a clinical professor of forensic pathology at the University of California, Irvine, where he remained until his death. The author of over forty books, Houts recently published *Jesus' Two Sanhedrin Acquittals: Their Legacies of Due Process of Law, Cousin Charlie the Crow,* and *Eisenhower: Turning the World toward Peace,* which he cowrote with Harold Stassen.

OBITUARIES AND OTHER SOURCES:

BOOKS

Who's Who in America, 48th edition, Marquis, 1994.

PERIODICALS

Los Angeles Times, November 27, 1993, p. A36.
New York Times, November 30, 1993, p. B10.
Washington Post, November 29, 1993, p. B4.

HU, Xu-wei 1928-

PERSONAL: Born March 9, 1928, in Zhejiang Province, China; son of Shi-liu (an editor) and Han-xiang (Liu) Hu; married Ye-chun Huang (a teacher), August 24, 1957; children: Tian-yu, Tian-jun, Tian-xin. *Education:* People's University of China, B.A., 1953.

ADDRESSES: Home—3-307 Baofangnanli, Datun Rd., Beijing 100101, China. *Office*—Institute of Geography, Chinese Academy of Sciences, Beijing 100101, China.

CAREER: Institute of Geography, Chinese Academy of Sciences, Beijing, China, assistant professor, 1954-78, associate professor, 1978-86, professor of geography, 1986—, deputy director of academic committee and deputy director of experts committee for regional development research. International Engineering Consulting Corp., member of experts committee, 1986—; Guiding Committee for China's Cities, deputy director, 1990—.

MEMBER: Regional Science Association of China (vice-chair, 1990—), Geographical Society of China (deputy director of Professional Committee of Economic Geography, 1991—), Urban Planning Society of China (executive member, 1990—; director of Academic Committee of Regional Planning and Urban Economics, 1993—), Urban Economics Society of China (executive member, 1986—), Territorial Economics Society of China (deputy secretary general, 1982—).

AWARDS, HONORS: National Science and Technology Progress awards, third level, 1988, first level, 1992.

WRITINGS:

(With others) *East China Economic Geography,* Science Press, 1959.
(With others) *Northeast China Economic Geography,* Science Press, 1963.
(Editor) *The Distribution of Cities and Industries in Regional Study,* Science Press, 1986.
(Editor with Yue-man Yeung) *China's Coastal Cities,* University of Hawaii Press, 1990.
(Editor) *China's Coastal Zone: Social and Economic Survey,* Ocean Press, 1992.
Economic Regions: Planning and Organizing, Science Press, 1994.

Editor in chief, *Economic Geography.*

WORK IN PROGRESS: Research on the mechanics of concentration and diffusion for economy and population in China's urban agglomerated regions.

SIDELIGHTS: Xu-wei Hu told *CA:* "I was born into an intellectual family. When I was a child, I liked writing and published some essays. Since I entered the university, I have been interested in economic geography. Originally I thought that spreading knowledge of economic geography could arouse people's patriotic enthusiasm. In 1953 I came to the Institute of Geography. In the first several years, I took part in compiling *Annals of China's Geography* and was in charge of compiling *East China Economic Geography* and *Northeast China Economic Geography.* During that period, I was conscious that economic geography should go further to serve the national economy and should not describe the present condition of regional economic geography. For this reason, I had been engaged in research on regional planning and allocation of productive forces and had published some papers summarizing this research. Since the reforms, China's coastal opening zone has become the briskest zone, so I have focused on that."

*   *   *

HUFFER, Lynne 1960-

PERSONAL: Born September 22, 1960, in Rochester, NY; daughter of William (a doctor) and Elisabeth (affiliated with the Girl Scouts of America; maiden name, McConnell) Huffer; married David Myers (divorced, 1990). *Education:* Attended Wells College, 1978-79, 1980-81; Ohio University, B.A., 1984; University of Michigan, Ph.D., 1989. *Politics:* Left.

ADDRESSES: Home—409 Ellsworth Ave., New Haven, CT 06511. *Office*—French Department, Yale University, New Haven, CT 06511.

CAREER: Yale University, New Haven, CT, assistant professor of French literature and women's studies, 1989—.

WRITINGS:

Another Colette, University of Michigan Press (Ann Arbor), 1992.

WORK IN PROGRESS: Beyond the Mother, completion expected in 1996.

*   *   *

HUGHES, Glenn 1951-

PERSONAL: Born December 18, 1951, in Seattle, WA; son of Glenn Arthur (a professor) and Cleta Fay (a teacher; maiden name, Rogers) Hughes. *Education:* University of Washington, Seattle, B.A. (English literature), 1972, B.A. (history), 1976, M.A. (history), 1979; Boston College, M.A. (philosophy), 1985, Ph.D., 1989.

ADDRESSES: Home—202 West Mandalay, San Antonio, TX 78212-1503. *Office*—Department of Philosophy, St.

Mary's University, 1 Camino Santa Maria, San Antonio, TX 78228.

CAREER: St. Mary's University, San Antonio, TX, associate professor of philosophy, 1990—.

MEMBER: International Association of Philosophy and Literature, American Philosophical Association, Eric Voegelin Society, Lonergan Philosophical Society.

WRITINGS:

Mystery and Myth in the Philosophy of Eric Voegelin, University of Missouri Press, 1993.

Contributor of poems to magazines, including *Poetry Northwest, Poetry East,* and *Prairie Schooner.*

WORK IN PROGRESS: A series of articles on transcendence.

SIDELIGHTS: Glenn Hughes told *CA:* "I've worked as a taxi driver, printing press operator, housepainter, boat refinisher, hospital office coordinator, film sound recordist and sound editor, and theater director. I have one foot in academe, one foot out—a precarious and necessary balance."

*　　*　　*

HULME, Ann
See GRANGER, (Patricia) Ann

*　　*　　*

HUNT, Marsha 1946-

PERSONAL: Born in 1946, in Europe; children: Karis.

CAREER: Model, actress, singer, and writer.

WRITINGS:

Real Life (autobiography), Chatto & Windus, 1986.
Joy (novel), Dutton, 1990.
Free (novel), Dutton, 1993.

SIDELIGHTS: Both of Marsha Hunt's published novels are, in a sense, voyages of self-discovery—voyages during which, with both humorous and tragic effect, blinders are lifted from the eyes of the main characters. The main characters of the books are African Americans who have for some time failed to notice changes in the world around them, at the same time ignoring terrible truths concerning the people to whom they have been closest.

Hunt's first novel, *Joy,* gains much of its inside knowledge of the entertainment industry and those who have been swept up into its limelight from Hunt's own experiences as a singer, songwriter and actress, most famous for her starring role in the London production of *Hair.* The central character and narrator is Baby Palatine, an elderly, church-going woman, who is travelling from California to New York to assist in the funeral of Joy Bang, one of three sisters she helped raise. The three had gained brief stardom in the sixties as a girl group calling itself Bang Bang Bang. The group crashed as quickly as it had become famous, leaving the sisters free to pursue the excesses of their respective personalities. Joy was Baby's favorite, her "God-sent child;" Baby ignored Joy's corruption while she was alive and continues to do so as she recollects Joy's life during the trip eastward. It is not until the very end of the novel that Baby realizes the unpleasant truth and her own part in creating it. At that point a bloodfest ends the novel, leaving many critics agreeing with Jewelle Gomez, who wrote in *The Women's Review of Books* that "the additional deaths in the final pages seem gratuitous and completely at odds with the humorous bantering style of Baby P.'s narrative."

Teenotchy, the protagonist of *Free,* Hunt's second novel, carries a weightier repression: that of the rape and murder of his mother. As a teenager in turn of the century Germantown, Pennsylvania, he is "a slave to habit," working as a servant for the same man his mother had worked for—a man who had a role in her murder and afterward had become Teenotchy's kindly protector. Teenotchy's journey of self-discovery comes when an upper-class Englishman visits and takes him to England. He falls in love with his benefactor and also learns a great deal about himself, though the novel ends tragically.

BIOGRAPHICAL/CRITICAL SOURCES:

BOOKS

Hunt, Marsha, *Free,* Dutton, 1993.
Hunt, *Joy,* Dutton, 1990.
Hunt, *Real Life,* Chatto & Windus, 1986.

PERIODICALS

Booklist, December 1, 1990, p. 717.
Books, May, 1991, p. 16; July, 1992, p. 11.
Essence, July, 1991, p. 36.
Kirkus Reviews, November 15, 1990, p. 1559.
Lambda Book Report, May, 1991, p. 40.
Library Journal, January, 1991, p. 152.
Listener, April 12, 1990, p. 25.
New Statesman and Society, April 13, 1990, p. 36.
Publishers Weekly, December 7, 1990, p. 69.
Punch, June 8, 1990, p. 37.
Spectator, May 12, 1990, p. 38.
Times Literary Supplement, August 7, 1992, p. 18.
Women's Review of Books, June, 1991, p. 20.*

HUNTER, T. Willard 1915-

PERSONAL: Born September 22, 1915, in Emmett, ID; son of Stuart McK. (a college professor) and Louise (a homemaker; maiden name, Willard) Hunter; married Mary Louise Merrell (a college personnel administrator and homemaker); children: Thomas M., Willard M., Robert S. (deceased). *Education:* Carleton College, B.A. (summa cum laude), 1936; attended Harvard University, 1936-38; Andover Newton Theological School, M.Div., 1973, S.T.M., 1977. *Politics:* Independent. *Religion:* Congregational/United Church of Christ. *Avocational Interests:* Hiking, photography.

ADDRESSES: Home and office—525 West Sixth St., Claremont, CA 91711.

CAREER: Moral Re-Armament, Washington, DC, staff executive, 1938-56; Macalester College, St. Paul, MN, associate general secretary, 1957-59; Claremont Colleges, Claremont, CA, coordinator of development, 1959-66; Independent Colleges of Southern California, Los Angeles, executive vice-president, 1966-70; pastor of Congregational churches in New England, California, Hawaii, and Minnesota, 1970-80. School of Theology, Claremont, assistant to the president, 1976-80. *Military service:* U.S. Army, Infantry, 1944-45.

MEMBER: Phi Beta Kappa, Rotary International, Claremont University Club, Andiron Club.

AWARDS, HONORS: Guinness Book of World Records, 1984 and 1985, for marathon oration; preaching prize, Andover Newton Theological School, 1973; grand marshall, Claremont Fourth of July parade, 1987.

WRITINGS:

The Tax Climate for Philanthropy, Council for the Advancement and Support of Education, 1968.
We Mutually Pledge, privately printed, 1982.
The Spirit of Charles Lindbergh: Another Dimension, Madison Books, 1993.

Also author, with Jim Newton, of *Uncommon Friends.* Work represented in anthologies, including *Vital Speeches of the Day,* 1990 and 1993. Weekly columnist for newspapers in California and Illinois. Correspondent for *Himmat,* in the 1960s. Contributor to periodicals, including *Modern Maturity.*

WORK IN PROGRESS: The Man behind the Twelve Step Miracle: Frank Buchman and the Oxford Group, 1995.

HURT, Harry III 1951-

PERSONAL: Born November 13, 1951, in Houston, TX; son of Harry Hurt, Jr., and Margaret (Birting) Hurt; married Alison Beelew (a restaurant owner), August 7, 1993. *Education:* Graduate of Choate School (cum laude), 1969, and Harvard College (magna cum laude), 1974.

ADDRESSES: Office—P.O. Box 365, Sag Harbor, NY 11963. *Agent*—Bob Dattila, Phoenix Literary Agency, 315 South "F" St., Livingston, MT 59047.

CAREER: Texas Monthly, Austin, TX, senior editor, 1975-86; *Newsweek,* New York City, correspondent based in Los Angeles, CA, 1988-90.

WRITINGS:

Texas Rich: The Hunt Dynasty from the Early Oil Days through the Silver Crash, Norton, 1981.
For All Mankind, Atlantic Monthly Press, 1988.
Lost Tycoon: The Many Lives of Donald J. Trump, Norton, 1993.

SIDELIGHTS: Harry Hurt III is a former *Newsweek* correspondent who has distinguished himself with his coverage of a group of astronauts since their monumental lunar landings, his tracing of the Hunt dynasty in Texas from its beginning to its glory days, and his chronicling of one of America's wealthiest tycoons, Donald Trump. In his first book, *Texas Rich: The Hunt Dynasty from the Early Oil Days through the Silver Crash,* Hurt tells how a cunning and hustling man named Haroldson Lafayette Hunt, Jr., swindled two con men out of their claim to an East Texas oil field. With a promise of thirty thousand dollars and some notes assuring that he would relieve the men of their oil field if it proved a burden, Hunt claimed it from them with a small amount of money. He soon became one of the wealthiest persons in the world. Hurt reports that Hunt's economic success sprang from his interest in the East Texas field. Wishing to protect his oil interests, Hunt pushed politicians to establish the Texas Railroad Commission, an organization that insured rationing so that depletion of the oil field would be avoided.

The remainder of Hunt's life lacks the excitement and interest of his earlier days, according to Steve Lohr in the *New York Times.* Hunt spawned three families, and much of Hurt's book chronicles the internal fighting among them for a piece of the fortune. Bunker and Herbert, two of Hunt's fifteen children, became the main trustees in securing the Hunt fortune, only to lose a good deal of money themselves when the silver market crashed in 1980. Hunt himself lost seventy-one million dollars after his food business failed.

Hurt's book has been called "a painstakingly researched, restrained and well-written account" by Lohr in the *New*

York Times. And writing in *Washington Post Book World,* L. J. Davis comments that "Harry Hurt III has done a commendable job of sorting out the [Hunt's] affairs, getting a grip on the members' personal histories and walking them through the days of their lives."

Hurt followed his first book with *For All Mankind,* a look at the lives of a group of astronauts twenty years after their history-making moon landings. Drawing on books by and interviews with the astronauts, Hurt discovers what the men have done since the landings and what they think of their past achievements. Lee Dembart of the *Los Angeles Times* affirms that "Hurt manages to portray each of the astronauts as distinct individuals—no small accomplishment." Hurt examines the relationship between Neil Armstrong and Buzz Aldrin, the first and second men, respectively, to walk on the moon. Apparently, according to Hurt, Aldrin is still bothered by the fame that Armstrong has received for being first. Focusing on the psychiatric distress that the astronaut suffered since his departure from NASA (National Aeronautical Space Administration), Hurt writes that Aldrin is still seeking a worthy career goal for himself—one that will "snap him out of 'the melancholy of all things done.' " *For All Mankind* recalls the memories that the other astronauts have of their space explorations as well. As reported by Peter Gorner in the *Chicago Tribune,* Apollo 12's Alan Bean commented on his perspective of the Earth from space, saying that it appeared as though there were "nothing holding [the planet] up."

For All Mankind "homes in on the spiritual revelations that rocked some of the astronauts," writes Gorner in the *Chicago Tribune.* Dembart notes in the *Los Angeles Times* that *For All Mankind* "correctly views America's voyages to the moon as a stunning and pioneering achievement that laid the groundwork for the future exploration of space and scientific advance." And Chicago *Tribune Books* reviewer Walter J. Boyne comments that "Harry Hurt III provides a disconcerting analysis of the contemporary response to the adventure of space." The critic concludes: "*For All Mankind* is one of those books that we earthlings need to re-read every few years, just to remind ourselves of how much we can do—and how greatly we can err."

Hurt's third book is *Lost Tycoon: The Many Lives of Donald J. Trump;* it "deconstructs but does not quite skewer" Trump, as Genevieve Stuttaford writes in *Publishers Weekly.* Relying on a good number of sources, Hurt traces various events in Trump's life, such as his relationships with Marla Maples and ex-wife Ivana, his plastic surgery, and his business practices that have resulted in the loss of money and property.

BIOGRAPHICAL/CRITICAL SOURCES:

PERIODICALS

Chicago Tribune, November 2, 1988.
Los Angeles Times, November 8, 1988.
New York Times, August 20, 1981.
Publishers Weekly, April 26, 1993, p. 66.
Tribune Books (Chicago), November 27, 1988, pp. 1, 8-9.
Washington Post Book World, June 9, 1981.

—Sketch by Ken Rogers

*   *   *

HUSSEY, Patricia (Ann) 1949-

PERSONAL: Born November 7, 1949, in Milford, CT; daughter of Walter (a district manager) and June (a state employee; maiden name, Hornish) Hussey. *Education:* Southern Connecticut State College, B.S., 1972; Jesuit School of Theology, M. Div., 1979; licensed as a Certified Social Worker, 1986. *Politics:* Democrat. *Religion:* Roman Catholic. *Avocational Interests:* Jogging, skiing, reading.

ADDRESSES: Office—Covenant House, 1109 Quarrier St., Charleston, WV 25301. *Agent*—Freya Manston Associates Inc., 145 West Fifty-eighth St., New York, NY 10019.

CAREER: Entered the Order of the Sisters of Notre Dame de Namur (a Roman Catholic religious order for women) in 1967, took final vows, 1980, left the order, 1988; co-director of Covenant House (a shelter and counseling center for the homeless), Charleston, WV, 1981—. St. Teresa's School, Providence, RI, teacher, 1972-73; Long Lane School, Middletown, CT, youth service worker, 1973-76, recreation worker, 1977; United States Representative for the Sisters in Initial Formation, Rome, Italy, 1978; Stringer and Racker, Providence, RI, jewelry factory worker, 1979-81; Advent House (a shelter for the homeless and battered women), volunteer, 1979-81.

MEMBER: Catholics for a Free Choice, National Association for the Advancement of Colored People, National Organization for Women, National Abortion Rights Action League, Central American Human Rights Coalition, Coalition Against Apartheid, West Virginia Health Right, West Virginia Human Resource Association, West Virginia FREE, Community Council of Kanawha County, West Virginia, Coalition for the Homeless (Kanawha Valley), Charleston East Community Development Corporation, Conference for Agency Executives, Mayor's Task Force on Homelessness, Women and Employment, Women's Health Center Nominating Committee.

AWARDS, HONORS: Margaret Sanger Award, Women's Health Center of West Virginia, 1986; People of Courage

Award, Catholics for a Free Choice, 1986; *Esquire Register* Award for Outstanding American Men and Women Under Forty, 1986; Champion for Choice Award, Catholics for a Free Choice, 1987; Susan B. Anthony Award, National Organization of Women (NOW), 1987 and 1988; Prophetic Figure Award, NOW, 1987; Religious Freedom Award, National Religious Coalition for Abortion Rights, 1987; award, National Refuse and Resist Organization, 1988; Clara Bell Educational award, 1988; Women in the Professions Celebrate Women award, West Virginia Women's Commission, 1989; Third Annual Hero Award, *Mother Jones,* 1989; Book of the Year Award, West Virginia Library Association, 1990, for *No Turning Back: Two Nuns' Battle with the Vatican Over Women's Right to Choose;* Jesse Bernard Wise Women Award, Center for Women's Policy Studies, 1991.

WRITINGS:

(With Barbara Ferraro and Jane O'Reilly) *No Turning Back: Two Nuns' Battle with the Vatican Over Women's Right to Choose,* Poseidon Press, 1990.

SIDELIGHTS: Patricia Hussey is a former nun who left her religious community, the Roman Catholic Order of the Sisters of Notre Dame de Namur, in 1988 amid controversy. She and her colleague Barbara Ferraro were outspoken critics of the Vatican's stand on women's reproductive rights. Hussey and Ferraro, with coauthor Jane O'Reilly, chronicled their lives as nuns and their struggle with church hierarchy in 1990's *No Turning Back: Two Nuns' Battle with the Vatican Over Women's Right to Choose.* For more information on this work, see the entry on Barbara Ferraro in this volume.

Hussey told *CA:* "Women and men in our country and throughout the world have identified with our story because it is each and all of our stories. If we act with integrity in our daily lives, in our workplace, and in our faith communities, we are bound to deal with adversity and struggles. Let us hope we have support to be strong and the courage and humor to go through all of life."

BIOGRAPHICAL/CRITICAL SOURCES:

PERIODICALS

Commonweal, December 21, 1990, pp. 759-760.
Ms., December, 1988, pp. 64-67.
New York Times, June 12, 1988, section 4, p. 28; July 22, 1988, p. A8.
New York Times Book Review, September 23, 1990, p.7.
Washington Post, October 13, 1990, p. B7.

I-J

IGUS, Toyomi 1953-

PERSONAL: Born October 10, 1953, in Iowa City, IA; daughter of Will (an attorney) and Kazumi (a home-maker; maiden name, Tamori) Gibson; married Darrow Igus (an actor); children: Kazumi, Kenji. *Education:* Barnard College, B.A., 1974. *Politics:* Liberal Democrat.

ADDRESSES: Office—P.O. Box 10421, Marina Del Rey, CA 90295.

CAREER: L.A. Style, Los Angeles, CA, associate managing editor, 1986-89; University of California at Los Angeles Center for Afro-American Studies Publications, managing editor, 1990—.

MEMBER: American Black Book Writers Association, Society of Scholarly Publishing.

WRITINGS:

(With Veronica Freeman Ellis, Diane Patrick, and Valerie Wilson Wesley; and editor) *Book of Black Heroes,* Volume 2, *Great Women in the Struggle,* Just Us Books, 1992.
(Editor with Charles Roland) *Life in a Day of Black L.A.: The Way We See It,* Center for Afro-American Studies, 1992.
When I Was Little, Just Us Books, 1992.

Contributor of articles and reviews to the *American Black Bookwriters Association Journal.* Co-author of several plays and screenplays, including *Zeke: History of Blacks in the Movies. American Black Book Writers Association Journal,* executive editor, 1986-1992.

SIDELIGHTS: Toyomi Igus, a woman of Japanese and African-American descent and a graduate of Barnard College, has spent fifteen years in the West Coast publishing industry. During these years, she has written for various trade and consumer magazines, coauthored several plays and scripts, and edited periodicals such as *L.A. Style.* Since 1992 she has been the managing editor of CAAS Publications, an academic press at the Center for Afro-American Studies, which is affiliated with the University of California, Los Angeles. Igus coordinated and edited a project for CAAS entitled *Life in a Day of Black L.A.,* a collection of photographic essays produced by black Los Angeles photographers. *Life in a Day of Black L.A.* has since been reproduced as a traveling exhibition.

It was not until the birth of her daughter, Kazumi, and her son, Kenji, that Igus was motivated to write books for children. The first to be published was the product of a project that Igus coordinated, edited, and cowrote, *Book of Black Women,* Volume 2, *Great Women in the Struggle.* This work spotlights more than eighty historical and contemporary women of African descent. The writer's second book for children, 1992's *When I Was Little,* was written solely by Igus. In this picture book, a little boy visiting his grandfather imagines life without televisions, VCRs, and video games, and also learns that the need for love and sharing is one thing that will not change with time.

BIOGRAPHICAL/CRITICAL SOURCES:

PERIODICALS

Horn Book, fall, 1992, p. 331.
School Library Journal, August, 1992, p. 166.

*   *   *

INWOOD, Christiane Sourvinou
See SOURVINOU-INWOOD, Christiane

ISAACS, Arnold R. 1941-

PERSONAL: Born February 6, 1941, in New York, NY; son of Harold Robert (a writer) and Viola (a social worker; maiden name, Robinson) Isaacs; married Kathleen Taylor (a teacher), November 23, 1962; children: Jennifer Anne, Katherine Muir, Robert Turnbull. *Education:* Harvard University, B.A. (magna cum laude), 1961.

ADDRESSES: Home and office—2006 West Joppa Rd., Lutherville, MD 21093.

CAREER: Sun, Baltimore, MD, reporter, 1962-66, chief of Rio de Janeiro bureau and chief Latin America correspondent, 1966-69, correspondent in Washington D.C. bureau, 1969-72, chief of the Saigon bureau, Vietnam, 1972-73, chief of the Hong Kong bureau and chief Asia correspondent, 1973-78, Sunday features editor, 1978-81; free-lance writer, 1981—. Towson State University, Baltimore, MD, visiting scholar, 1983, lecturer, 1984-85; Johns Hopkins University, Baltimore, MD, lecturer, 1983-84, visiting professor of communications, 1983—.

MEMBER: Phi Beta Kappa.

AWARDS, HONORS: Without Honor: Defeat in Vietnam and Cambodia named as Notable Book of the Year by the *New York Times,* and American Library Association, both 1983.

WRITINGS:

Without Honor: Defeat in Vietnam and Cambodia, Johns Hopkins University Press, 1983.
(With editors of Boston Publishing Company) *Pawns of War: Cambodia and Laos,* Boston Publishing Company, 1987.

Associate editor of *Current,* 1961-62. Contributor to periodicals, including *New Republic, New York Times, Washington Post,* and *Chicago Tribune.*

SIDELIGHTS: The son of Harold Isaacs, a well-known foreign correspondent, Arnold R. Isaacs has achieved his own measure of fame with the publication in 1983 of *Without Honor: Defeat in Vietnam and Cambodia,* his lauded account of the last period of the war in Vietnam. Like his father, Isaacs forged a career in journalism in which he saw service as a foreign correspondent. The author told *CA* that during his eighteen years with the Baltimore *Sun,* he "reported from more than forty foreign countries," often in the capacity of bureau chief. It was during Isaac's heading of the Saigon bureau from 1972-73 that he became, as he described it, "responsible for coverage of the Vietnam war and the conflicts in neighboring Cambodia and Laos." The author "continued to travel frequently to Vietnam and covered the final three months of the war in 1975, leaving Saigon in the U.S. helicopter evacuation on the final day before it fell to the North Vietnamese." Many

of the events of that time would make their way into *Without Honor,* including Isaacs's account of the evacuation. "Particularly moving" is the way the *Washington Post Book World* described these passages. Douglas Pike, writing in *New York Times Book Review,* stated that *Without Honor* "offers vivid recollections of key moments in the war, set down with honesty by a man who saw and felt deeply."

In *Without Honor,* Isaacs attempts to depict the time and events in great detail, and many critics felt he succeeded. "The thud and the blood of combat and the wailing of mortally wounded nations are here," commented *Los Angeles Times* writer Paul Dean, "so are the softer sounds of negotiations, riffled documents, the sigh of broken agreements and the tinkle of glasses on conference tables." According to a review by Harry G. Summers Jr. in the *Washington Post Book World,* Isaacs's concentration "on the period between the withdrawal of U.S. combat forces in 1973 and South Vietnam's eventual collapse in 1975 . . . is particularly useful, for too many Americans still perceive the war as waged by simple peasant revolutionaries in black pajamas armed with crude and primitive weapons." Further, in focusing on the "internal conditions that led to the collapse of South Vietnam, Cambodia, and Laos rather than on the enemy action," the critic acknowledged that Isaacs's report "forces us to consider the very real problems of coalition warfare."

Without Honor found particular favor for its style and tone—one that forces the reader to experience its painful subject. Pike described the style as "impressionistic, offering chunks and fragments of the Vietnam experience, intuitively selected, it would seem, and set down in tones ranging from moodiness to bitter cynicism. It reminds one of the musings of a police reporter who has seen too much of humanity's worst side." Gene Lyons warned in *Newsweek* that "Isaacs's account of the madhouse confusion of the Thieu regime's last days will be more than many will want to read, revealing as it does a client state grown so sick of war and so corrupt that elemental human bonds could not hold." For the *Chicago Tribune*'s Jack Fuller, the prose of *Without Honor* "is often so vivid that you find yourself transported back to that nightmarish time and place."

Isaacs "has produced a sound and interesting narrative," wrote R. B. Smith of the *Times Literary Supplement,* "which succeeds in combining vivid images of the war with the statistics and analysis that are essential for historical perspective." For many critics *Without Honor* is valuable both as a history and a warning—for being what Dean described as "a raw but necessary history" of a painful past. Commenting on one of Isaacs's descriptions of Saigon sleeping beneath an uneasy, artillery-lit sky, Fuller related that: "The horizon Isaacs directs our attention to is irretrievably behind us now. When the sky flashes, it shows us a place of suffering and dishonor, a wracked landscape this book will make all the more difficult to put out of mind."

BIOGRAPHICAL/CRITICAL SOURCES:

PERIODICALS

Chicago Tribune, October 16, 1983, p. 33.
Los Angeles Times, December 18, 1983, p. 5.
Newsweek, October 3, 1983, p. 90.
New York Times Book Review, October 16, 1983, pp. 9, 38; December 16, 1984, p. 32.
Times Literary Supplement, May 25, 1984, p. 593.
Washington Post Book World, October 2, 1983, pp. 1-2, 14; February 10, 1985, p. 12.

*   *   *

ISRAEL, Lee   1939-

PERSONAL: Born December 3, 1939, in New York, NY; daughter of Jack Israel (a grocer) and Sylvia (Komarow) Israel. *Education:* Brooklyn College (now of the City University of New York), A.B., 1961. *Politics:* Socialist. *Avocational Interests:* "Literary forgery."

ADDRESSES: Home and office—98 Riverside Drive, New York, NY 10024. *Agent*—Jean Free, Jay Caron-Brooke Associates, 101 W. 55th St, New York, NY 10019.

CAREER: WRVR-FM Radio, New York, NY, producer and broadcaster; *Eros* magazine, associate editor; Virginia Kirkus Service (now *Kirkus Reviews*), New York, NY, book reviewer.

WRITINGS:

Miss Tallulah Bankhead, Putnam, 1971.
Kilgallen, Delacorte, 1979.
Estee Lauder: Beyond the Magic, Macmillan, 1985.

Contributor to numerous newspapers and magazines, including *Cosmopolitan, Esquire, McCall's, Ms., New York Times, Playbill, Saturday Review, Theater Week* and *Village Voice.*

WORK IN PROGRESS: A biography of Vanessa Redgrave.

SIDELIGHTS: Turning her investigative and narrative powers on overlooked subjects—outspoken, controversial women who worked hard to become highly successful—biographer Lee Israel has worked to expand the coverage of women's lives and accomplishments. "We are not accustomed to finding heroes in middle-aged, quirky women," wrote novelist Rita Mae Brown in a *Washington Post Book World* review of Israel's work. Sympathetic to

their difficulties, Israel credits her female subjects for their outstanding achievements, but she also delves deeper to reveal, sometimes painfully, their personal struggles and shortcomings. Because of this, Israel tends to include troubling details that her subjects omit from their own autobiographies.

Actress Tallulah Bankhead, the subject of Israel's 1971 biography, *Miss Tallulah Bankhead,* was both an outrageous original and a typically beautiful, self-centered Southern belle. Drawing on many sources for her research, including Tallulah's sister Eugenia, Israel tells the life story of this talented and tumultuous woman. She examines Bankhead's feelings about sex, drugs, and exhibitionism, as well as her relationships. The biographer omits neither the Bankhead family's convoluted prejudices, nor Tallulah's lackadaisical attitude toward her craft.

Reporter and columnist Dorothy Kilgallen is the subject of Israel's 1979 book *Kilgallen.* Using, again, many varied sources, Israel tells the story of Kilgallen's enigmatic life and equally mysterious death. The daughter of a reporter, Kilgallen followed in her father's footsteps, covering murders and other crimes. The young woman achieved international celebrity with her coverage of a highly publicized 1936 air race around the world. Israel covers Kilgallen's scandalous affair with musician Johnnie Ray, as well as her secret interview with Jack Ruby following the assassination of President John F. Kennedy. Brown, in a review of *Kilgallen* in *Washington Post Book World,* praised the work: "Without bogus psychologizing the author manages to present a complex, compelling woman and help us understand why she did what she did. *Kilgallen* deserves to be ranked with serious biography just as its subject deserves to be ranked a serious journalist." The reviewer also placed credence in Israel's theory that Kilgallen, who allegedly committed suicide, may have actually been murdered as a result of her inside knowledge of Kennedy's assassination.

Israel's 1985 biography of the cosmetics magnate, *Estee Lauder: Beyond the Magic,* was overshadowed by the nearly simultaneous release of Lauder's own autobiography, *Estee: A Success Story,* published by Random House. Marylin Bender, writing in the *New York Times Book Review,* compared the two books and found that Israel's work "comes off as a cut-rate job. It reads as though it had been rushed to the printing plant." But even harsh critics credited Israel for doing her usual far-reaching research. "Lee Israel, by checking the New York State census records and past editions of the Manhattan telephone directory and by tracking down relatives, among other sources, has done her dogged spadework," wrote G. Bruce Boyer in the *Washington Post Book World.* Revealing that the vaguely aristocratic cosmetics queen was actually born Josephine Esther Mentzer, a child of poor Jewish immigrants who grew up in Corona, Queens, New York, Israel portrays the woman's skills and achievements in building a billion-dollar, international business from Youth-Dew—a face cream concocted by her uncle. The biographer also discusses Lauder's attempts to enhance her social status and her competitive nature. Although Lauder's autobiography drew attention from Israel's book, critic Martha Duffy wrote in *Time* that it may have been Israel's initial efforts that prompted Lauder to write her own story. "It is . . . possible," the critic wrote, "that [Lauder's] own gutsy book would not have seen print without the challenge of Israel's research."

BIOGRAPHICAL/CRITICAL SOURCES:

PERIODICALS

Chicago Tribune, February 10, 1980, p. 4.
New York Times Book Review, November 17, 1985, p. 16.
Time, November 11, 1985, p. 90.
Village Voice, December 10, 1979, p. 54.
Washington Post Book World, November 18, 1979, p. 11; November 24, 1985, p. 5.

*　　*　　*

JAMES, W(illiam) Martin (III) 1952-

PERSONAL: Born February 8, 1952, in Lake Charles, LA; son of William Martin, Jr. (a chemical engineer) and Dorothy (a homemaker; maiden name, McGinty) James; married Susan Janelle Chansler (a case worker), December 6, 1974; children: Christopher William Martin, Gregory Bennett. *Education:* University of Arkansas, B.A., 1974, M.A., 1977; Catholic University of America, Ph.D., 1987. *Politics:* Independent. *Religion:* Roman Catholic.

ADDRESSES: Home—516 Teresa Dr., Benton, AR 72015. *Office*—Department of Political Science, Henderson State University, P.O. Box 7611, Arkadelphia, AR 71999.

CAREER: Foreign affairs research assistant to U.S. Senator Henry Bellmon, 1977-78; legislative and research assistant to U.S. Representative Bill Alexander, 1978-83; research director for Arkansas's auditor of state, 1983-88; Henderson State University, Arkadelphia, AR, assistant professor, 1988-91, associate professor of political science, 1991—. Accredited observer of elections in Angola, 1992; testified before the U.S. Senate Foreign Relations Committee.

MEMBER: American Political Science Association, United States Strategic Institute, Foreign Policy Research Institute, Southwestern Political Science Association, Southern Political Science Association, Arkansas Political Science Association (member of executive board), Little Rock Foreign Relations Council, Phi Alpha Theta, Pi Gamma Mu, Pi Sigma Alpha.

WRITINGS:

(With J. Peter Vanneman) *Soviet Foreign Policy in Southern Africa: Problems and Prospects,* Africa Institute of South Africa, 1983.
A Political History of the Civil War in Angola, 1974-1990, Volume I, Transaction Books, 1991.

Contributor of about twenty articles to scholarly journals and newspapers.

WORK IN PROGRESS: A Political History of the Civil War in Angola, 1974-1990, Volume II; research on the African National Congress (ANC) and Inkatha in South Africa.

SIDELIGHTS: W. Martin James told *CA:* "Southern Africa is one of the least understood regions in the world. This is particularly true in the case of Angola and the UNITA rebel movement. Having studied UNITA for more than twenty years, I am astonished at the amount of ignorance that surrounds the group. Even worse, the media often portray UNITA as the villain, despite having data to the contrary. As in life, nothing in Angola is in black and white. The reality is much more fascinating."

*　　*　　*

JANOWSKY, Oscar Isaiah 1900-1993

OBITUARY NOTICE—See index for *CA* sketch: Born January 15, 1900, in Suchawola, Poland; died of a stroke, November 4 (one source cites November 5), 1993, in Princeton, NJ. Historian, educator, and writer. Janowsky's historical texts concentrated on recent Jewish history, helping to establish him as an advocate of Jewish and minority rights. Janowsky began his long association with City College of the City University of New York in 1924, where he served as director of graduate studies in the 1950s and retired as a professor in 1966. He was an advisor on refugees to the League of Nations in 1935 and was affiliated with many Jewish rights groups, including the National Jewish Welfare Board from 1946 to 1947, the Commission for Study of Jewish Education in the United States from 1952 to 1957, and B'nai B'rith from 1961 to 1964. Janowsky also worked in conjunction with the Commission to Study the Organization of Peace. His books include *The Jews and Minority Rights, 1898-1919, People at Bay, The Jews: Their History, Culture, and Religion,* and *The Education of American Jewish Teachers.*

OBITUARIES AND OTHER SOURCES:

BOOKS

The Writers Directory: 1992-1994, St. James Press, 1991.

PERIODICALS

New York Times, November 6, 1993, p. 54.
Washington Post, November 8, 1993, p. D6.

* * *

JARVIE, Gordon (Iain) 1941-

PERSONAL: Born August 4, 1941, in Edinburgh, Scotland; son of Alexander and Daisy (Beattie) Jarvie; married Frances Kelly (a teacher), 1974; children: Sally, Andrew. *Education:* Trinity College, Dublin, B.A., 1964, M.A., 1966; University of Sussex, M.Phil., 1966. *Avocational Interests:* Hill walking, reading, exploring.

ADDRESSES: Home—81 Comiston Dr., Edinburgh EH10 5QT, Scotland. *Office*—Canongate Press, 14 Frederick St., Edinburgh EH2 2HB, Scotland.

CAREER: Purdue University, West Lafayette, IN, David Ross fellow in English, 1967-68; Oxford University Press, London, England, editor, 1969-71; Collins Publishers, Glasgow, Scotland, editor, 1971-82; Oliver & Boyd (publisher), Edinburgh, Scotland, editor, 1982-89; Canongate Press, Edinburgh, editor, 1993—.

WRITINGS:

(With wife, Frances Jarvie) *Edinburgh: A Capital Story,* Chambers, 1991.
Scottish Names, Chambers, 1992.
Punctuation Guide, Chambers, 1992.
Bloomsbury Grammar Guide, Bloomsbury Publishing, 1993.
Scottish Castles, H.M.S.O., 1994.
Scottish Saints and Holy Places, H.M.S.O., 1994.

EDITOR

The Wild Ride and Other Scottish Stories (juvenile), Kestrel, 1986.
The Genius and Other Irish Stories (juvenile), Puffin, 1988.
Scottish Short Stories (for young people), Oxford University Press, 1992.
A Friend of Humanity: Selected Short Stories of George Friel, Polygon, 1992.
Scottish Folk and Fairy Tales (juvenile), Puffin, 1992.
Irish Folk and Fairy Tales (juvenile), Puffin, 1992.
Great Golf Stories, Michael O'Mara, 1993.
The Scottish Reciter, Blackstaff Press, 1993.

WORK IN PROGRESS: Research on children's reading, folklore, and aspects of Scottish literature.

SIDELIGHTS: Gordon Jarvie told *CA:* "I have worked most of my life as an editor, so I have a professional, even a vested, interest in the written word; hence, the books on grammar and punctuation. A lot of my editorial time has been spent helping teachers devise effective reading schemes for school children; hence, probably, my tendency to dream up anthologies. As a Scot in a minority culture (by many criteria), I have always been keen for young fellow Scots to have access to their own literature."

* * *

JEDRZEJEWICZ, Waclaw 1893-1993

OBITUARY NOTICE—See index for *CA* sketch: Born January 29, 1893, in Spiczynce, Ukraine; died November 30, 1993, in Cheshire, CT. Historian, government official, and author. Jedrzejewicz produced a number of works that concentrated on the history of Poland, especially during the period between the two World Wars. His background in this area was based on first-hand experience, as he had served in various government and military posts in Poland in the 1920s and 1930s, before coming to the United States in 1941. Jedrzejewicz began his affiliation with the Pilsudski Institute of America in 1943, and was a professor at Wellesley College from 1948 to 1958 and at Ripon College from 1958 to 1963. His writings include the memoir *P. O. W. I Batalion Warzawski: Moja Sluzba 1914-15, Polish Americans in Polish Politics, Diplomat in Berlin, 1933-39: Papers and Memoirs of Josef Lipski, Ambassador of Poland,* and the two volume work *Chronicles of the Life of Josef Pilsudski.*

OBITUARIES AND OTHER SOURCES:

BOOKS

International Authors and Writers Who's Who, 9th edition, Melrose, 1982.

PERIODICALS

New York Times, December 8, 1993, p. B8.

* * *

JEFFRIES, Ian 1942-

PERSONAL: Born September 9, 1942, in Pontypool, Gwent, Wales; son of Ivor (a coal miner) and Bessie (a homemaker; maiden name, Watkins) Jeffries. *Education:* National University of Wales, B.A., 1964; University of London, Ph.D., 1974. *Politics:* Liberal Democrat. *Religion:* Atheist.

ADDRESSES: Home—32 Lon Cadog, Cwmgwyn, Sketty, Swansea SA2 0TS, Wales. *Office*—Department of Economics, National University of Wales, University College of Swansea, Singleton Park, Swansea SA2 8PP, Wales.

CAREER: National University of Wales, University College of Swansea, lecturer in economics and member of Centre of Russian and East European Studies, 1966—.

WRITINGS:

(Editor) *The Industrial Enterprise in Eastern Europe,* Praeger, 1981.

(Editor with Manfred Melzer) *The East German Economy,* Croom Helm, 1987.

A Guide to the Socialist Economies, Routledge, 1990.

(Editor) *Industrial Reform in Socialist Countries: From Restructuring to Revolution,* Edward Elgar, 1992.

Socialist Economies and the Transition to the Market, Routledge, 1993.

SIDELIGHTS: Ian Jeffries told *CA:* "I feel strongly that economics has grown worryingly apart from other subjects and has become far too abstract and specialized. My broad-ranging, 'real world' books represent my efforts to reverse these (in my opinion) unhealthy trends. Academics should also be prepared to invest in new areas. For example, I had to shift ground almost entirely when most of the communist regimes collapsed in 1989."

*   *   *

JERSILD, Arthur T(homas)   1902-1994

OBITUARY NOTICE—See index for *CA* sketch: Born November 12, 1902, in Elk Horn, Iowa; died January 17, 1994, in Beaufort, SC. Psychologist, educator, and author. Jersild authored several influential texts on child psychology and education, including *In Search of Self* and *When Teachers Face Themselves.* He began teaching at Barnard College in 1927, then moved to the University of Wisconsin—Madison in 1929. In 1930 he joined the faculty of Columbia University and remained at the university for the rest of his academic career. Other titles he produced include *Mental Set and Shift,* the long-lived text book *Child Psychology,* and *Psychology of Adolescence.*

OBITUARIES AND OTHER SOURCES:

BOOKS

Who's Who in Writers, Editors, and Poets, 1989-1990, December Press, 1989.

PERIODICALS

New York Times, January 22, 1994, p. 10.

*   *   *

JEWISON, Norman (Frederick)   1926-

PERSONAL: Born July 21, 1926, in Toronto, Ontario, Canada; son of Percy Joseph (a manager of a general store and post office) and Dorothy Irene (Weaver) Jewison; married Margaret Ann Dixon (a former model), July 11, 1953; children: Kevin Jefferie, Michael Philip, Jennifer Ann. *Education:* Attended Malvern Collegiate Institute, 1940-44; Victoria College (now University of Toronto), B.A., 1950. *Politics:* Liberal. *Religion:* Protestant. *Avocational Interests:* Skiing, yachting, tennis.

ADDRESSES: Office—Knightsbridge Films Ltd., 18 Gloucester St., 5th Floor, Toronto, Ontario M4Y 1L5, Canada. *Agent*—c/o William Morris Agency, 151 El Camino Dr., Beverly Hills, CA 90210.

CAREER: Director of films, including *The Art of Love,* 1965, *In the Heat of the Night,* 1967, and *Gaily, Gaily,* c. 1970; director and producer of films, including *The Russians Are Coming, the Russians Are Coming,* 1966, and *Fiddler on the Roof,* 1970; director and coproducer of films, including *Jesus Christ Superstar,* 1972, *And Justice for All,* 1979, *A Soldier's Story,* 1984, *Agnes of God,* 1985, and *Moonstruck,* 1987; coauthor of screenplay for *Jesus Christ Superstar,* 1973; director of television programs, including episodes of *Your Hit Parade,* 1958, and of specials, including *Tonight with Harry Belafonte,* 1959; director and producer of television programs, including *The Judy Garland Show,* 1963-64. Affiliated with Canadian Broadcasting Corporation (CBC-TV), 1952-58; Columbia Broadcasting System (CBS-TV), producer and director, 1958-61; British Broadcasting Corporation (BBC-TV), actor and writer. Institute for American Studies, Salzburg, Austria, faculty member, 1969; D'Avoriaz Film Festival, president, 1981—; Centre for Advanced Film Studies, director, 1987—. *Military service:* Royal Canadian Navy, 1945-46.

MEMBER: Directors Guild of America (electoral board member), Canadian Arts Council.

AWARDS, HONORS: Emmy award, 1960, for *The Fabulous Fifties;* Academy Award Nomination, best picture, 1967, for *The Russians Are Coming, the Russians Are Coming;* Golden Globe Award and Academy Award, both for best director, both 1968, for *In the Heat of the Night;* Academy Award nominations, best picture and best director, both 1972, for *Fiddler on the Roof;* LL.D., University of Western Ontario, 1974; director of the year, National Association of Theatre Owners, 1982; officer, Order of Canada, 1982; honored by the American Civil Liberties Union, 1984; International Moscow Film Festival winner and Academy Award nomination, best picture, both 1985, for *A Soldier's Story;* Golden Globe nomination, best film, and Academy Award nomination, best director, both 1988, for *Moonstruck.*

WRITINGS:

(With Melvyn Bragg) *Jesus Christ Superstar* (screenplay), Universal, 1973.

SIDELIGHTS: Norman Jewison once told Allan Gould, an interviewer for *Influence,* that among all the films he had made, one of the two that most satisfied him was *Jesus Christ Superstar*—"because I made a film out of a phonograph record," he explained. "And that's difficult to do. And it's an opera, and there aren't many operas made into films that have reached so many people. It has some of my best work, photographically, and in directorial vision." In addition to directing *Jesus Christ Superstar,* Jewison also cowrote, with Melvyn Bragg, the film's screenplay.

Jesus Christ Superstar, which had started out as an album and then became a Broadway play, was brought to the screen by Jewison in 1973. With book and lyrics by Tim Rice and music by Andrew Lloyd Webber, the rock opera featured seven young tourists in Israel who recreate the last days of Christ. Although the film was criticized for what some critics felt were its anti-semitic elements, *New York Times* reviewer Howard Thompson said the film had "some interesting aspects. One is the brilliant opening, the 'overture,' as a busload of players arrives to make the film, in the film within-a-film format." Yet for all the negative criticism it received, the movie *Jesus Christ Superstar* was a huge success with the public, grossing nearly twenty million dollars in box office receipts. Jewison's decision to film the movie on location in Israel was cited by critics to be among the movie's strengths, as was its unusual and lavish production.

"I believe my first obligation is to the writer and the material," Jewison told the *Chicago Tribune*'s Julia Cameron in speaking of his concerns as a producer and director. "I like writers. God, I enjoy writers! . . . Although there is a certain amount of natural improvisation that occurs when shooting a movie, if you don't have a strong script, one that's logical and definitive, then usually you get into trouble. So you see, it all starts with the writer and the writer's idea."

In addition to being an author himself, Jewison has collaborated with numerous successful writers. Paul D. Zimmerman praised Jewison in *Newsweek* for the director's handling of reporter Ben Hecht's farcical story in the film *Gaily, Gaily.* The critic wrote that "Jewison tells it with . . . bravado" and asserted that Jewison "nailed the twists of [Hecht's] plot." Jewison has twice filmed the original scripts of John Patrick Shanley, who, like Jewison, was nominated for an Academy Award for 1987's *Moonstruck.* Strong writing has been associated with numerous Jewison projects; several of his critically acclaimed films, such as *Agnes of God* and *A Soldier's Story,* are adaptations of original plays. *In the Heat of the Night,* for which Jewison received the best director Oscar in 1967, was the winner of the best screenplay award as well.

Jewison is also one of the forces behind the creation of Toronto's Canadian National Center for Film Studies, described by Charles Champlin in the *Los Angeles Times* as the director's homeland's "equivalent of the American Film Institute."

BIOGRAPHICAL/CRITICAL SOURCES:

PERIODICALS

Chicago Tribune, September 8, 1985.
Influence, interview with Allan Gould, c. 1985.
Los Angeles Times, March 24, 1988.
Newsweek, January 5, 1970.
New York Times, August 8, 1973; May 14, 1978.
Washington Post, July 13, 1985.*

*   *   *

JOHNSON, Andrew 1949-

PERSONAL: Born July 26, 1949, in Saltash, Cornwall, England; son of John Metcalfe (a teacher) and Anne (a homemaker; maiden name, Selley) Johnson; married Alison Findlay Rice (a writer), 1973; children: Sarah. *Education:* St. John's College, Cambridge, M.A., 1970; Balliol College, Oxford, D.Phil., 1973. *Politics:* "Green—liberal." *Religion:* Church of England. *Avocational Interests:* Woodwork, sailing.

ADDRESSES: Office—10 High St., Knapwell, Cambridgeshire, England.

CAREER: Schoolteacher, 1973-77; hotelier, 1978-90; publisher, 1990—.

WRITINGS:

Factory Farming, Basil Blackwell, 1991.

Contributor to periodicals. Reviews editor, *Environmental Values.*

WORK IN PROGRESS: Research on environmental ethics.

*   *   *

JOHNSON, Scott 1952-

PERSONAL: Born November 23, 1952, in Chicago, IL; son of Roy and Gladys (Hurt) Johnson; married Susan Newton, September 28, 1985; children: Ethan Lucas, Jordan Guthrie. *Education:* Indiana University, B.A. (with honors), 1974; University of Massachusetts, M.F.A., 1978. *Avocational Interests:* Backpacking, hiking, bicycling, acoustic music (guitar and mandolin).

ADDRESSES: Home—25 Wright Ave., Mahopac, NY 10541. *Office*—c/o Pleasantville High School, Romer

Ave., Pleasantville, NY 10570. *Agent*—Richard Parks Agency, 138 East 16th St., New York, NY 10003.

CAREER: Pleasantville High School, Pleasantville, NY, teacher of English and creative writing, 1978—.

MEMBER: National Conference of Teachers of English, New York State English Council, Sierra Club, Nature Conservancy.

AWARDS, HONORS: Fulbright exchange teacher, 1983; National Endowment for the Humanities independent study fellowship, 1987; *One of the Boys* was selected as one of the "Best Book for Young Adults" by the American Library Association, 1993.

WRITINGS:

One of the Boys (young adult novel), Atheneum, 1992.
Overnight Sensation (young adult novel), Atheneum, 1994.

Contributor of articles and short stories to *English Journal, TriQuarterly,* and *Ploughshares.*

SIDELIGHTS: Scott Johnson commented: "There aren't too many second chances in life, and writing for young people, for me, is a way to get back and live through some of those choices and decisions I had to make—and often didn't make too wisely. When I write I get to watch some character, some boy or girl I've come to feel close to over the course of a book, struggle with choices that he or she must now face."

In *One of the Boys,* Johnson has created a character who faces some rough choices. Eric is a "nice" kid who, out of the desire to fit in, joins up with the wrong crowd. Randy Meyer wrote in *Booklist* that "Johnson has written a tough, quickly paced story about the irony and complexity of peer pressure. . . . The pain and promise of friendship come clear in a story that demonstrates that there are no easy choices."

Johnson's ability to empathize with adolescents comes from his continuing contact with them in his position as a high school teacher. He first discovered young adult novels as a teacher; his favorites, he commented, provided him "with a direct line to my past, to those adolescent sensations that haunted and tortured all of us, and other times left us soaring with glee. That teenager from long ago is still inside, still seeing the world as unjust and overly complicated, still crying out for understanding, some guidance and maybe a little bit of attention. We need to listen to that teenager, and [young adult] books help to put us in touch."

Growing up, Johnson never really considered himself a writer. "I was destined to be a zoologist," he commented. "It only took a couple of semesters memorizing the arte-

rial circulation in reptilian hearts, or hunting the pituitary gland of fetal pigs, and before I knew it, I was trading in my developmental anatomy text at the college bookstore for used paperbacks of Dickens, Fitzgerald, and Twain.

"A short time after that I admitted to myself, cautiously, at first, nervous for the consequences—I was a writer. At least I wanted to be. Even back then I knew the best writers only made it look easy. But I wanted to take my turn. There was something in fiction that reminded me of the tales told around the fire on my old Boy Scout camping trips. Tales swapped, with everyone hoping the next one would be even better—scarier, wilder, more real than life. And as we lay there, each snap of a twig or rustle of a leaf outside our tent was surely the telltale sign of some creature we had thrilled to around the fire, drawing near, long after the last story was spoken. That's how fiction works, I think. 'Good story,' we say, when the storyteller reaches the end, but that's not the half of it. The true measure of fiction is how much it grows inside you, how much the tale still burns after the campfire is only embers."

BIOGRAPHICAL/CRITICAL SOURCES:

PERIODICALS

Booklist, April 1, 1992.

* * *

JOHNSON, U(ral) Alexis 1908-

PERSONAL: Born October 17, 1908, in Falun, KS; son of Carl Theodore and Ellen (Forsse) Johnson; married Patricia Ann Tillman, 1932 (died, 1981); children: Judith Ann Zerbe, Stephen Tillman, William Theodore K., Jennifer Ellen Johnson Bishop. *Education:* Occidental College, A.B., 1931; attended Georgetown University, 1932. *Avocational Interests:* Golf.

ADDRESSES: Office—3133 Connecticut Ave. N.W., Washington, DC 20008. *Agent*—Leona Schecter, 3748 Huntington St. N.W., Washington, DC 20015.

CAREER: U.S. Foreign Service, 1935-77; served in Asia, 1935-40 (prisoner in China, 1941-42), and South America, 1942, consul in Yokohama, Japan, 1945, deputy director of Department of State's North East Asian affairs, 1949-51, director of Department of State's North East Asian affairs, 1951, deputy assistant to secretary of state for Far Eastern affairs, 1951-53, ambassador to Czechoslovakia, 1953-58, representative to Geneva Conference, 1954, representative in talks with China, 1955-57, ambassador to Thailand, 1958-61, deputy undersecretary of state for political affairs, 1961-64 and 1965-66, deputy ambassador to Vietnam, 1964-65, ambassador to Japan, 1966-69, undersecretary of state for political affairs, 1969-73, envoy to Strategic-Arms Limitation Talks (SALT), 1973-77; George Washington University, Washington, DC, adjunct professor of international relations at Sino-Soviet Institute, 1977-83; writer. Consultant to Department of State, 1977-82, and Department of Defense, 1979-81; director of Atlantic Council, 1977—; vice president of Washington Institute of Foreign Affairs, 1979—; chair of U.S. Group on Sea Lanes of Communication, 1980—.

MEMBER: Associated Japan-America Societies of United States.

AWARDS, HONORS: Royal Cypher Medal from king of Thailand, 1962; Rockefeller Public Service Award for contribution to field of foreign affairs, 1965; Career Service Award from National Civil Service League, 1969; Distinguished Service Award from New York chapter of Association of the United States Army, 1970; President's Award for Distinguished Federal Civilian Service, 1971; Distinguished Alumni Award from Delta Sigma Rho-Tao Kappa Alpha, 1971; Distinguished Service Award from Department of Defense, 1977; Distinguished Honor Award from Department of State, 1977; President's Medal from Georgetown University, 1977; Alumni Seal Award from Occidental College, 1978; award from Association of Diplomatic and Consular Officers, 1980; Jit Trainor Award for Distinction in the Conduct of Diplomacy from Georgetown University's Institute for Study of Diplomacy of Foreign Service School, 1981; Foreign Service Cup from American Foreign Service Association, 1981; First Class Order of Rising Sun from emperor of Japan, 1982.

WRITINGS:

(Editor) *The Common Security Interests of Japan, the United States, and NATO,* Atlantic Council, 1981.
(Editor) *China Policy for the Next Decade,* Atlantic Council, 1984.
(With Jef Olivarius McAllister) *The Right Hand of Power* (memoir), Prentice-Hall, 1984.

SIDELIGHTS: U. Alexis Johnson was a longtime United States foreign service figure specializing in Asian relations. He began his service work in 1935 as a language officer in Japan, and in the remaining years of the decade he also worked in Korea and China. In 1941 he was captured and held prisoner of war in Manchuria. He obtained his freedom the following year and soon served on General Douglas MacArthur's staff at Yokohama, Japan. In the decade after World War II, Johnson continued to work in Asia, interrupted by two stints in Czechoslovakia. From 1958 to 1961 he was ambassador to Thailand, and from 1961 to 1964 he was deputy undersecretary of state for political affairs. He then served a mid-1960s stint in Vietnam, after which he was named ambassador to Japan. Johnson remained active politically into the late 1970s, re-

tiring in 1977 after representing the United States in the Strategic-Arms Limitation Talks (SALT) with the former Soviet Union.

After leaving the foreign service Johnson worked as consultant to various state departments. In addition, he remained active in foreign-affairs groups and served as adjunct professor of international affairs at Georgetown University's Sino-Soviet Institute.

Johnson has been the editor of two books, *Common Security Interests of Japan, the United States, and NATO* and *China Policy for the Next Decade,* and in 1984—in collaboration with Jef Olivarius McAllister—he completed a memoir, *The Right Hand of Power.* Robert Manning, writing in the *New York Times Book Review,* observed that Johnson's memoir constitutes "a useful handbook of many State Department operations in the 1950s, '60s, and '70s"; the reviewer added that the book provides "insights into how professional diplomats strive to do their job."

Johnson told *CA:* "I wrote *The Right Hand of Power* because I wanted to contribute my own experiences and observations to the many historical events in which I participated, and in some way contribute to stimulating interest in history, an area in which I feel Americans tend to be very deficient."

BIOGRAPHICAL/CRITICAL SOURCES:

BOOKS

Johnson, U. Alexis, and Jef Olivarius McAllister, *The Right Hand of Power,* Prentice-Hall, 1984.

PERIODICALS

New York Times Book Review, September 23, 1984, p. 30.
Washington Post, October 4, 1984, p. B10.

*   *   *

JONES, Dennis 1945-
(R. D. Jones)

PERSONAL: Born June 29, 1945, in Canada; son of Robert A. and Edna Jones; married Pamela (a librarian), August 5, 1966 (marriage ended); married Sandra, June 20, 1990. *Education:* York University, B.A., 1969, M.A., 1970.

ADDRESSES: Agent—Authors Marketing, 217 Degrassi St., Toronto, Ontario, Canada.

CAREER: London Board of Education, London, Ontario, office manager, 1971-85; writer.

WRITINGS:

(As R. D. Jones) *Fenris Option,* Tower, 1981.

Rubicon One, General Publishing, 1983, Thorndike Press, 1984.

Russian Spring, Beaufort Books, 1984.

Barbarossa Red, Little, Brown, 1985.

Winter Palace, Little, Brown, 1988.

Concerto, St. Martin's, 1989.

The Minstral Boy, Random House, 1991.

SIDELIGHTS: Dennis Jones is the author of what he described for *CA* as "political-military-espionage thrillers, usually concerning scenarios for limited or global nuclear war in the next two decades." Margaret Cannon of the Toronto *Globe and Mail* takes the description a step further, pointing out the "overtones of East-West confrontation" in Jones's novels and the "plots drawn from the front pages of the daily papers." It's a combination that is targeted for popular success. "I am a commercial writer," Jones told *CA,* "and my books are directed to the mass market."

With novels like *Winter Palace* and *Concerto,* Jones has been pleasing a critical audience as well. For Arthur Krystal in the *New York Times Book Review,* Jones's "rendering of Russia's moral and political landscape" in *Russian Spring* "tempts one to judge this thriller by standards that ordinarily apply to serious fiction." The novel relates the tale of Andrei Mikhailov, a young KGB official so disenchanted by his country's war in Afghanistan that he agrees to provide crucial information to the United States, unwittingly at the expense of his beloved uncle. Krystal termed the book "gripping," including it in the ranks of suspense novels like *Gorky Park.* For Derrick Murdoch, columnist for the Toronto *Globe and Mail,* the resemblance of *Russian Spring* to serious fiction is a weakness rather than a strength. The critic writes that the novel "takes off impressively enough," but the "Chekhovian" angst of Mikhailov—a reference to Russian author Anton Chekhov—throws off what the critic sees as an otherwise straightforward thriller. The *Times Literary Supplement* sees Mikhailov's moral quandary as implausible in an officer of the KGB, but concludes that "good military detail and action" outweigh the minor problems in *Russian Spring.*

Barbarossa Red, Jones's next effort, was described by Margaret Cannon in the *Globe and Mail* as "another solid, well-crafted political thriller." For Cannon, Jones's story of a U.S.-Soviet Union missile accord undercut by German suspicion and defection succeeds despite its large cast of characters wide-ranging settings. Daniel Akst in the *Los Angeles Times Book Review* detected a wooden quality in Jones's handling of characters and dialogue, but found that these shortcomings were offset by "clean prose, suspense and a good story."

Winter Palace marked a further critical success for Jones. Cannon in the *Globe and Mail,* for instance, found much to praise in a novel that postulates a Russian plan to expel its entire Jewish population, an undertaking that allows the hard-line Communist government to smuggle spies into the U.S. Applauding Jones for incorporating historical material in the novel, Cannon pronounced *Winter Palace* "unquestionably his best so far." Brian D. Johnson in a *Maclean's* review complained of a lack of surprises in the book but called it "a sprawling, high-action novel" with an "elaborate" plot. In an article in the *Los Angeles Times Book Review,* Karen Stabiner deemed *Winter Palace* "a heart-stopping international thriller."

The kidnapping of former Soviet premier Mikhail Gorbachev is the premise of Jones's *Concerto,* published in 1989. Like the novels that precede it, *Concerto* found favor for its tightly woven plot and topicality. Newgate Callendar of the *New York Times Book Review* called it "a good, readable novel," and a *Publishers Weekly* review noted the author's "sympathetic hero, taut pacing and keen eye for contemporary politics." Bob Allen, writing in the *Washington Post Book World,* was also enthusiastic, stressing the manner in which Jones "painstakingly constructs his numerous, finely detailed action sequences with something resembling architectural brilliance."

BIOGRAPHICAL/CRITICAL SOURCES:

PERIODICALS

Globe and Mail (Toronto), September 15, 1984; October 26, 1985; June 4, 1988.

Los Angeles Times Book Review, August 31, 1986, p. 5; April 17, 1988, p. 10.

Maclean's, June 20, 1988, p. 58.

New York Times Book Review, January 6, 1985, p. 20; March 28, 1986, p. 50; June 17, 1990, p. 19.

Publishers Weekly, April 19, 1985, p. 80; April 20, 1990, p. 57.

Times Literary Supplement, June 7, 1985, p. 644.

Washington Post Book World, May 6, 1990, p. 10.

*   *   *

JONES, Lawrence K. 1940-

PERSONAL: Born April 5, 1940, in Fargo, ND; son of Stanley A. and Irene (Galyen) Jones; married Jeanine Wehr (a media specialist), June 29, 1964; children: Mark, Juliet. *Education:* California State University, Sacramento, B.A., 1963; University of Pennsylvania, M.S.Ed., 1967; University of Missouri—Columbia, Ph.D., 1971. *Avocational Interests:* Sailing, hiking, canoeing, amateur radio.

ADDRESSES: Office—Department of Counselor Education, North Carolina State University, Box 7801, Raleigh, NC 27695.

CAREER: High school teacher in Tarsus, Turkey, 1963-66; Philadelphia Child Study Center, Philadelphia, PA, teacher, 1967; counselor at a junior high school in Greece, NY, 1967-68; Fort Roots Veterans Administration Hospital, Little Rock, AR, counseling psychology intern, 1970; Stephens College, Columbia, MO, instructor in psychology, 1970-71; North Carolina State University, Raleigh, assistant professor, 1971-76, associate professor, 1976-84, professor of counseling psychology, 1984—, acting head of department, 1976-84. Vanderbilt University, visiting associate professor with Overseas Program in England and West Berlin, 1979-80. Social Security Administration, vocational expert witness for Bureau of Hearings and Appeals, 1976—.

MEMBER: American Counseling Association, National Career Development Association, American School Counselors Association, Association for Assessment in Counseling, North Carolina Counseling Association, North Carolina School Counselors Association, North Carolina Career Development Association.

AWARDS, HONORS: The Encyclopedia of Career Change and Work Issues was listed among the American Library Association's Outstanding Reference Sources of the Year in 1993.

WRITINGS:

(Editor) *The Encyclopedia of Career Change and Work Issues,* Oryx, 1993.

Work featured in books, including *Treating the Offender: Problems and Issues,* edited by Riedel and P. A. Vales, Praeger, 1977. Contributor of about thirty articles to education and counseling journals. Member of editorial board, *Career Development Quarterly,* 1980-88.

WORK IN PROGRESS: Research on work skills, "helping individuals identify skills they possess, learn ones that are transferable and saleable, and market them to employers in situations such as school-to-work transitions and job hunts for those who have been 'laid off.'"

SIDELIGHTS: Lawrence K. Jones told *CA:* "Creating *The Encyclopedia of Career Change and Work Issues* has been my most satisfying professional experience. The encyclopedia is a vehicle for pulling together, in one source, the expertise of more than a 150 authorities. They wrote on every imaginable work issue, offering information and practical advice on topics as diverse as sexual harassment, biological work hazards, and mentoring. The process was gratifying for several reasons.

"First, the cooperation I received from these experts was inspiring. Despite their heavy schedules, they wrote these articles without monetary compensation. I believe most saw this as their way of making life easier for working women and men. I was uplifted by their commitment.

"Second, a guiding theme for my work has been 'to help others help themselves,' and the encyclopedia gave me an opportunity to do this. It was this theme that led me to go to Turkey as a teacher in the 1960s, and then on to the counseling field, eventually becoming a counselor educator. I am concerned about the many difficulties workers face today. More than 200 people die in the United States each day from occupational-related diseases or injuries; millions work full-time but are unable to earn enough money to rise above the poverty line; there is unemployment, underemployment, discrimination, and more. I hope that many will find the encyclopedia helpful.

"Finally, there has been the satisfaction of meeting a challenge. After having the book proposal rejected by ten publishers, after three years and hundreds of phone calls, letters, and computer disks, and with the outstanding contributions of the editor and staff of Oryx Press, the book has received positive reviews."

*　　*　　*

JONES, R. D.
　See JONES, Dennis

*　　*　　*

JONES, Steve   1961-

PERSONAL: Born March 7, 1961, in Chicago, IL; son of George (a civil engineer) and Sofia (a librarian; maiden name, Sekulic) Jones. *Education:* University of Illinois at Urbana-Champaign, B.S., 1983, M.S., 1984, Ph.D., 1987. *Avocational Interests:* Popular music recording, tennis.

ADDRESSES: Home—505 South Gary, No. 24, Tulsa, OK 74104. *Office*—Department of Communication, University of Tulsa, Tulsa, OK 74104.

CAREER: Skokie Public Library, Skokie, IL, assistant librarian, 1977-79; University of Illinois at Urbana-Champaign, Urbana, instructor in communications and media studies, 1986, and journalism, 1987; University of Wisconsin—Eau Claire, assistant professor of journalism, 1987-90; University of Tulsa, Tulsa, OK, visiting assistant professor, 1990-91, assistant professor of communication, 1991—, acting head of department, 1993—, director of Communication Program in England, 1992—. Invisible Hand Media (multimedia production firm), director,

1984—; record producer and recording studio engineer, 1983—; consultant to Beecham Products. Youth Services of Tulsa, volunteer, 1990—.

MEMBER: International Communication Association, International Association for the Study of Popular Music (member of executive board, 1987-93; executive secretary of U.S. organization, 1990-91), International Society for Arts, Sciences, and Technology, Performing Artists Network of North America, American Association of University Professors, Association for Education in Journalism and Mass Communication, Society for Ethnomusicology, Society for the Philosophy of Technology, Society for the Study of Symbolic Interaction, Speech Communication Association, Union for Democratic Communications, Midwest Sociological Society, Mensa, Amnesty International, Greenpeace.

AWARDS, HONORS: Poynter fellow, College Newspaper Advisers Seminar, 1989; grant from Association for Recorded Sound Collections, 1991; nominated for Excellence in Historical Recorded Sound Research Award from Association for Recorded Sound Collections, and BMI/ *Rolling Stone* Gleason Award, both 1993, for *Rock Formation.*

WRITINGS:

Rock Formation: Music, Technology, and Mass Communication, Sage Publications, 1992.
(Editor) *Cybersociety: Computer-Mediated Communication and Community,* Sage Publications, 1994.

Work represented in anthologies, including *A Sourcebook of American Literary Journalism,* edited by Thomas Connery, Greenwood Press, 1992; *Cassette Mythos,* edited by Robin James, Autonomedia, 1992; and *Rock 'n' Roll: Politics, Policies, and Institutions,* edited by Tony Bennett, Larry Grossberg, and others, Routledge & Kegan Paul, 1993. Contributor to periodicals, including *Wired, Sound Choice, Creem, Goldmine,* and *Modern Recording and Music.* Editor, *Tracking: Popular Music Studies,* 1987-92, and *Popular Music and Society,* spring, 1990; member of editorial board, *Journalism Monographs,* 1988—.

WORK IN PROGRESS: A general reader in popular music studies.

SIDELIGHTS: Steve Jones told *CA:* "My work is informed by the writing and thinking of James Carey, former dean of the College of Communication at the University of Illinois. Carey seeks to understand the intricate relationships between social relations and communication technologies, as do I. My own particular interests have led me to examine the mediation of reality, of authentic experience and its interpretation, as we devise and develop technologies of simulation like virtual reality.

"This is also why I am interested in the study of popular music. It forms a core, or center, for youth (but also, increasingly, for adults) who are coping with and coming to terms with reality. As a communication medium, popular music forms the critical common thread of our social and mediated experiences. It is part and parcel of all our mass media, but usually is overlooked by serious scholars, who relegate it to the background of visual forms (or to the dustbin)."

K

KALETSKI, Alexander 1946-

PERSONAL: Born, April 21, 1946, in Montchegorsk, Soviet Union (now Russia); immigrated to the United States, 1975; son of Seimone I. (a construction company president) and Cecilia A. (Zabina) Kaletski; married Lena Braslov (an actress), 1968 (divorced, c. 1977). *Education:* Attended Tula Military Institute (Russia), 1964-65; attended Moscow Theatre and Film Institute, 1965-69. *Politics:* Republican.

ADDRESSES: Home—334 East Seventy-third St., Number 4C, New York, NY 10021.

CAREER: Actor, musician, educator, artist, and author. Actor in films, theater, and television, Moscow, Soviet Union, 1965-69; songwriter, musician, and language instructor, United States, 1975-77; fabric designer, New York City, 1977-83; artist-illustrator, New York City, 1975-85; writer.

WRITINGS:

Metro: A Novel of the Moscow Underground, Viking, 1985.

WORK IN PROGRESS: A novel about the adventures of a Russian in America; a movie script, *In and Out,* 1993.

SIDELIGHTS: In 1985, soon after the publication of his first novel, *Metro: A Novel of the Moscow Underground,* Alexander Kaletski told *CA:* "Writing *Metro,* my goal was to tell Americans the truth about the Soviet regime, to paint a clearer picture of everyday life in Russia, and to speak for those who don't have freedom to speak for themselves." Kaletski elaborated further on the process of writing the novel, which, he said, was "ninety percent" his own life story.

Kaletski explained that writing the book was a much harder process than he originally expected, mainly because he discovered how difficult it was to meet his own artistic standards. Altogether, *Metro* took more than five years to write, in part because Kaletski first wrote it in his native Russian and then translated it into English himself. Perhaps as a result, Kaletski cites both Russian writers—Fyodor Dostoyevsky and Mikhail Bulgakov—and an American writer—Ernest Hemingway—as his major influences.

Metro is the story of Sasha K---, a young Soviet actor and singer, who, like the author, is deeply disaffected with his native land. Although the book is subtitled "A Novel of the Moscow Underground," it concerns not so much an organized political "underground" as a more anarchic subculture—the black-market, semi-criminal, drug-and-alcohol culture of hustlers and con men. Again like the author, Sasha K---- comes up with an elaborate scheme to emigrate: he pretends to be Jewish and melt in with the large number of Jews that the Soviet Union, during the mid-1970s, was allowing to leave.

Critics were generally receptive to *Metro,* which *Washington Post* reviewer Anthony Olcott called "an entertaining story of living in and leaving the Soviet Union." Reviewing *Metro* in the *Los Angeles Times,* Elaine Kendall praised Kaletski's ability to portray the grim tale with "rambunctious" comedy and a "frenetic" pace. Kendall characterized the book as "black comedy, with shafts of youthful exuberance piercing the prevailing gloom."

The *Washington Post*'s Olcott was concerned, however, that Kaletski's extremely bleak portrait of Soviet life might reflect not so much the truth as Kaletski's efforts to please anti-Soviet American readers: "the sensational nature of some of Kaletski's incidents also suggests that *Metro* might be tailored to its audience, and Kaletski is telling us what he thinks we want to hear." *Village Voice* critic William Grimes also praised the book with reservations. Grimes wrote: "there are times when the book lurches from incident to incident. Yet at its best, *Metro*'s drunken ramble through a Russia of crooks, confidence men, and fat officials harks back to the freewheeling Soviet satire of the '20s. Evidently Kaletski has noticed an absurdity or two in our own society, since a sequel is already in the writing. To his credit, the prospect of a follow-up volume feels like a promise, not a threat."

BIOGRAPHICAL/CRITICAL SOURCES:

PERIODICALS

Los Angeles Times, August 13, 1985.
New York Times Book Review, June 30, 1985, p. 20.
Times Literary Supplement, December 13, 1985.
Village Voice, August 6, 1985, p. 50.
Washington Post, May 29, 1985; July 23, 1985.

* * *

KARMILOFF-SMITH, Annette Dionne 1938-

PERSONAL: Born July 18, 1938, in London, England; daughter of Jack Smith and Doris Findlay; married Igor Karmiloff, July, 1965 (marriage dissolved, 1992); children: Yara-Natasha, Kyrena-Laure. *Education:* Universite de Lille, Certificat d'Etudes Bilingues, 1957; Holborn College of Law and Languages, Postgraduate Diploma in International Conference Interpretation, 1965; Universite de Geneve, Diplome General de Psychologie de l'Enfant, 1970, Licence en Psychologie, 1970, Diplome de Specialisation en Psychologie Genetique, 1976, Doctorat en Psychologie Genetique et Experimentale, 1977.

ADDRESSES: Home—1 Lutton Terr., Flask Walk, London NW3 1HB, England. *Office*—Medical Research Council, Cognitive Development Unit, 4 Taviton St., London WC1H 0BT, England.

CAREER: American University of Beirut, Beirut, Lebanon, associate in psychology and research consultant at UNWRA/UNESCO Institute of Education, 1970-72; research collaborator with Jean Piaget at Centre International d'Epistemologie Genetique, 1972-79, director of studies, 1979; Max Planck Institute, Nijmegen, Netherlands, research associate, 1979-82; Medical Research Council, London, England, senior scientist in Cognitive Development Unit, 1982—. University of London, honorary professor, 1988; visiting professor at Universite Libre de Bruxelles, 1985, Max-Planck Institute for Psychiatry, 1986, University of Chicago, 1987, University of Barcelona, 1988, Carnegie-Mellon University, 1991-92, and University of Madrid, 1994; Tel Aviv University, member of international advisory council of Unit for Human Development. Jean Piaget Archives, member of scientific advisory board; guest on television and radio programs in the United States and Europe; consultant to Salk Institute for Biological Studies, BBC-TV, and British Museum.

MEMBER: Williams Syndrome Association (member of medical advisory panel), British Psychological Society (member of council, 1988-91), Jean Piaget Society, Society for the Study of Behavioural Phenotypes, American Society for Philosophy and Psychology, American Cognitive Science Society.

AWARDS, HONORS: Sloan fellow in computer science, Yale University, 1978; honorary professorial fellow in cognitive science, University of Sussex, 1979-81; Sloan fellow in cognitive science, University of California, Berkeley, 1981; named to the Academia Europaea, 1992; named fellow of the British Academy, 1993.

WRITINGS:

A Functional Approach to Child Language, Cambridge University Press, 1979.
(With W. M. Levelt and A. Mills) *Child Language Research in ESF Countries,* European Science Foundation, 1981.
Beyond Modularity: A Developmental Perspective on Cognitive Science, MIT Press, 1992.
(With J. L. Elman, E. Bates, M. H. Johnson, and others) *Rethinking Innateness: Connectionism in a Developmental Framework,* MIT Press, in press.

Work represented in anthologies, including *Thinking: Readings in Cognitive Science,* edited by P. Johnson-Laird and P. Wason, Cambridge University, 1978; *The Child's Construction of Language,* edited by W. Deutsch, Academic Press (London), 1981; and *Epigenesis of the Mind: Essays in Biology and Knowledge,* edited by S. Carey and R. Gelman, Lawrence Erlbaum, 1991. Co-editor of the series "Cognitive Development," Basil Blackwell, 1985—, and "The Developing Child," Harvard University Press, 1989—. Contributor of articles and reviews to scholarly journals. Editor, *British Psychological Society Developmental Newsletter,* 1989-91; associate editor for cognitive development, *Behavioral and Brain Sciences,* 1982—; member of editorial board, *Cognitive Science,* 1980-83, *Cahiers de Psychologie Cognitive,* 1981-88, *Journal of Child Language,* 1981-90, *Cognition,* 1987-92, *Language and Cognitive Processes,* 1985—, *Mind and Language,* 1986—, *Cognitive Development,* 1990—, and *Substratum,* 1992—.

WORK IN PROGRESS: Exploring Abnormal Development: A Window on the Nature/Nurture Debate, for Basil Blackwell.

SIDELIGHTS: Annette Dionne Karmiloff-Smith told *CA:* "My main broad interest is the difference between human and non-human intelligence, or what is specifically human about human cognition. I attempt to probe this, often using microdevelopmental, rather than macrodevelopmental, methods, in human children's representational change in a number of different areas. I have focused on the child as a linguist, the child as a scientist, the child as psychologist, and the child as a notator. More recently, I have been in the process of exploring these questions in abnormal populations by comparing different behavioral phenotypes in which there is either across-the-board cognitive retardation (Down syndrome) or across-domain dissociations (proficient face processing and language skills in Williams syndrome, compared to severe problems in spatial cognition, number and problem solving). In particular, I have focused on within-domain dissociations, particularly within language, comparing Williams syndrome to subjects with hydrocephalus and associated myelomeningocele."

*   *   *

KEHDE, Ned   1940-

PERSONAL: Born April 27, 1940, in St. Louis, MO; son of Edward (a restaurateur) and Ruth (a restaurateur; maiden name, Garstang) Kehde; married Pat Micheals (a bookseller), March 28, 1980; children: Gretchen, John Cayton, Nancy Cayton, Anna. *Education:* University of Missouri—Columbia, B.A., M.A., 1967. *Religion:* Roman Catholic.

ADDRESSES: Home—1636 Learnard, Lawrence, KS 66044.

CAREER: Free-lance writer, 1967—. University of Kansas, archivist, 1970—.

WRITINGS:

The American Left, 1955-1970, Greenwood Press, 1976.
(Editor) *Dictionary of Contemporary Quotations,* John Gordon Burke, 1978.
(Editor) *Index to "The Sporting News,"* John Gordon Burke, 1992.

Outdoor columnist, *Lawrence Journal-World,* 1992-93. Contributor to *In-Fisherman.* Editor, *Access,* 1976—.

*   *   *

KELL, Joseph
See WILSON, John (Anthony) Burgess

*   *   *

KELLEY, Alec E(rvin)   1923-

PERSONAL: Born November 6, 1923, in Houston, TX; son of Alfred Allee (a farm implement dealer) and RayOla

(a homemaker; maiden name, Fielder) Kelley; married K. Alita Haley (a professor of modern languages and a translator), May 29, 1970. *Education:* Attended Edinburg Junior College (now University of Texas—Pan American), 1940-42; University of Texas at Austin, B.S., 1944; Purdue University, M.S., 1949, Ph.D., 1956. *Politics:* Democrat. *Religion:* Humanist. *Avocational Interests:* Opera, travel, recreational writing.

ADDRESSES: Home—1086 King Rd., MP-215, Malvern, PA 19355-1975.

CAREER: Manhattan Project, Chicago, IL, chemist, 1944-46; University of Arizona, Tucson, began as assistant professor, became professor of chemistry, 1952-87, professor emeritus, 1988—. Wesleyan University, Middletown, CT, professor, summers, 1967-68; Pennsylvania State University, Delaware County Campus, Media, professor, 1993. W. M. Symposia, Inc., member of board of directors, 1992—. Hospitality International (Tucson), member of board of directors, 1970-85; Humanist Community of Tucson, member of board of directors and "occasional president," 1958-92. *Military service:* U.S. Army, 1944-46; received Meritorious Unit Award.

MEMBER: American Chemical Society, American Humanist Association, U.S. Servas (area representative, 1986-92).

WRITINGS:

(Translator with wife Alita Kelley) Jose Promis, *The Identity of Hispanoamerica,* University of Arizona Press, 1991.

WORK IN PROGRESS: Translating *The Chilean Novel of the Last Hundred Years,* by Jose Promis, with wife Alita Kelley.

SIDELIGHTS: Alec E. Kelley told *CA:* "My professional career has been mostly that of a chemist and a professor of chemistry. Even during that time, I was particularly concerned with good writing, of precision and clarity, which I consider essential in scientific papers and desirable in all writing; though the style may be experimental, the desired effect should be conveyed as well as possible. I began writing *as a writer* only after my retirement from teaching, when I began collaborating with my wife on some of her writings.

"I have never set out to write a book, though I have three, unpublished, that I am currently working on. They seem just to have grown—one a set of selections of memoirs, another a group of short stories and a novel. As a night person, I usually do most of my writing during the two or three hours after midnight.

"The writers whose works have most influenced me include Jane Austen, for her clarity of vision and gentleness of presentation even when being most critical, Bertrand Russell, for the precision and straight-forwardness of his style, and Robert Barnard, for his cynical satire."

*   *   *

KELLEY, (Kathleen) Alita 1932-
(C. A. de Lomellini)

PERSONAL: Born November 19, 1932, in Bradford, Yorkshire, England; daughter of Harry (a textile mill overseer) and Jeanette (a homemaker; maiden name, Chandler) Haley; married Carlos De Luchi Lomellini, September 17, 1951 (divorced May 25, 1970); married Alec Ervin Kelley (a professor of chemistry), May 29, 1970; children: (first marriage) Gianna De Luchi Lomellini Cooper, Patricia De Luchi Lomellini Benson. *Education:* University of Arizona, B.A., 1981, M.A., 1986, Ph.D., 1992. *Religion:* Humanist.

ADDRESSES: Home—1086 King Rd., MP-215, Malvern, PA 19355-1975. *Office*—Department of Spanish and French, Pennsylvania State University, Delaware County Campus, 25 Yearsley Mill Rd., Media, PA 19063-5596.

CAREER: Teacher of English as a second language in Lima, Peru, and Cuzco, Peru, 1962-68; Wiesman and Co., Tucson, AZ, commercial translator and office manager, 1970-92; Pennsylvania State University, Delaware County Campus, Media, assistant professor of Spanish and French, 1992—. Teacher of English and French literature and civilization at schools in Lima, 1963-68; U.S. Embassy, Lima, teacher of Italian, 1967-68. Hospitality International (Tucson), member of board of directors, 1970-85; Humanist Community of Tucson, program coordinator, 1970-92.

MEMBER: International Society for Humor Studies, Modern Language Association of America, American Association of Teachers of Spanish and Portuguese, American Literary Translators Association, American Translators Association, Latin American Studies Association.

AWARDS, HONORS: Grants from Tinker Foundation, 1986-87, and National Endowment for the Humanities, 1993.

WRITINGS:

UNDER NAME C. A. DE LOMELLINI

(Translator) Jane Radcliffe, *Lima Rooftops* (poems), Solo Press, 1978.
Shared Images (poems), Rivelin Grapheme Press, 1982.
Dreams of Samarkand (poems), Rivelin Grapheme Press, 1982.
Ineffable Joys (poems), Redbeck Press, 1983.
Antimacassars (poems), Rivelin Grapheme Press, 1984.

Target Practice (poems), Redbeck Press, 1994.

UNDER NAME ALITA KELLEY

(Translator with husband Alec E. Kelley) Jose Promis, *The Identity of Hispanoamerica,* University of Arizona Press, 1991.
(Translator) Charles M. Tatum, editor, *New Chicana/Chicano Writing 2,* University of Arizona Press, 1992.
(Translator with Edith Grossman) Julio Ortega, *Goodbye, Ayacucho and Moscow Gold* (stories), Latin American Literary Review Press, 1994.

WORK IN PROGRESS: Translating *The Chilean Novel of the Last Hundred Years,* by Jose Promis, with husband Alec E. Kelley; translating the poems *Bolereando el llanto,* by Rosina Conde; research on translation theory and on contemporary Peruvian writers.

SIDELIGHTS: Alita Kelley told *CA:* "My writing career began, with translations, when I was in my thirties. Although I had written poems and stories for my own amusement from the time I was a child, I never considered trying to publish them until I started publishing translations. Then I'm afraid I thought, 'I can do as well as this.'

"I never think in terms of writing books, only in getting ideas down. Often I write out of a sense of fear, or to affirm my existence to myself. I believe this to be my usual motivation. My working habits depend on my current *modus vivendi.* Earning a steady living has been an obsession all my life. When my work permits, I write regularly, very early in the morning. I write poetry when an idea comes to me and rewrite early in the morning; I am a morning person.

"Apart from affirming my existence to myself, I can't say I have ever felt a purpose exists for my writing, or for anything else. That wouldn't fit in with my outlook on existence, which I see as purposeless. I write because I feel a compulsion, but I can't explain it and don't understand it.

"The last writer I read influences me. I admire many writers enormously, but I don't think about their writing, or they would shame me into silence. I don't try to write like anyone else, consciously at least, but my interior life is permanently dialogical.

"If I were in a financial position to live as I would like to— independent, with no obligations and with time to write—I would spend four to five hours every morning writing. But who knows? I might dissipate the rest of my life drinking, overeating, and living it up."

KEMP, Peter (Mant Macintyre) 1915-1993

OBITUARY NOTICE—See index for *CA* sketch: Born August 19, 1915, in Bombay, India; died October 30, 1993. Soldier, reporter, and author. Kemp's conservative political beliefs led him to take part in a number of wars as both a soldier and journalist. He saw his first fighting in 1936 in the Spanish Civil War, where he served with the fascist forces led by General Francisco Franco. After being wounded several times in Spain, Kemp's next campaign was with the British Army in World War II, where he undertook a number of special missions. After the war he began selling insurance for Imperial Life Assurance Company, though he took time off to cover a number of world trouble spots, including Southeast Asia, Central America, South America, Rhodesia, and Albania, for papers including the *Tablet* and *Sunday Telegraph*. He retired from insurance work in 1980. His experiences are recounted in a number of books, including *Mine Were of Trouble, No Colours or Crest, Alms for Oblivion,* and the autobiography *The Thorns of Memory*.

OBITUARIES AND OTHER SOURCES:

BOOKS

Who's Who in the World, 3rd edition, Marquis, 1976.

PERIODICALS

Times (London), November 6, 1993, p. 19.

*   *   *

KEMP, Tom 1921-1993

OBITUARY NOTICE—See index for *CA* sketch: Born February 28, 1921, in London, England; died December 22, 1993, in Gravesend, England. Economist, educator, and author. Kemp's writing examined the interplay of political and economic factors, concentrating on a variety of subjects from the nineteenth and twentieth centuries. Beginning as a research assistant at the University of Southampton in 1947, Kemp then moved to the University of Hull, becoming a lecturer in 1950 and remaining at the university, with the exception of two years spent abroad, until his 1986 retirement. His first book was *Theories of Industrialism* in 1967, and he followed with numerous influential texts, including *Industrialisation in Nineteenth Century Europe, Historical Patterns of Industrialisation, Industrialisation in the Non-Western World,* and *The Climax of Capitalism: The U.S. Economy in the Twentieth Century*.

OBITUARIES AND OTHER SOURCES:

PERIODICALS

Times (London), January 21, 1994, p. 19.

KENDRICK, Alexander 1911(?)-1991

PERSONAL: Born c. 1911 in Philadelphia, PA; died of a heart attack, May 17, 1991, in Philadelphia, PA; married Sara Kunitz (died, 1981).

CAREER: Journalist, foreign correspondent, and author. Affiliated with the *Ledger,* Philadelphia, PA; later affiliated with the *Inquirer,* Philadelphia, 1940s; Columbia Broadcasting System (CBS), began as radio and television correspondent, became bureau chief.

AWARDS, HONORS: Sigma Delta Chi Award for editorial writing, Society of Professional Journalists, 1942.

WRITINGS:

Prime Time: The Life of Edward R. Murrow, Little, Brown, 1969.
The Wound Within: America in the Vietnam Years, 1945-1974, Little, Brown, 1974.

SIDELIGHTS: After earning a reputation as a respected newspaper journalist, Alexander Kendrick became a broadcaster for the Columbia Broadcasting System (CBS) on radio and television, working under famed broadcasting pioneer Edward R. Murrow. He continued with CBS until his retirement in the mid-1970s. During his career Kendrick penned two books, one of which was a biography of his renowned colleague.

Prime Time: The Life of Edward R. Murrow, published in 1969, chronicles both Murrow's career as an adult and various experiences that Murrow went through as a child and an adolescent. Kendrick also details Murrow's confrontation with United States Senator Joseph McCarthy over the politician's endeavor to manipulate Americans into becoming paranoid over the threat of communism in the 1950s. *New York Times Book Review* contributor Eric F. Goldman lauded Kendrick's portrayal, asserting that "this biography proves worthy of its subject—a richly informed, incisive, pungent book, admiring and affectionate but not forgetting the Murrow canon that candor is a high form of devotion." Kendrick's work is regarded as one of the authoritative sources on Murrow, providing many previously unknown details of the broadcaster's encounters with the famous people upon whom he reported, such as British Prime Minister Winston Churchill and U.S. Senator Robert F. Kennedy.

Kendrick next published *The Wound Within: America in the Vietnam Years, 1945-1974,* which traces the American role in the Vietnamese War from its roots in the Cold War atmosphere that followed World War II. Kendrick also draws parallels between the events of the War itself and corresponding occurrences in American society while the War was being waged. As Herbert Mitgang noted in the *New York Times, The Wound Within* "carefully summarizes what was going on when colleges were in turmoil; in the civil rights movements; in the Federal trials against draft resisters; in various forms of antisocial behavior against 'the system.' "

BIOGRAPHICAL/CRITICAL SOURCES:

PERIODICALS

Commonweal, January 17, 1975, pp. 331-33.
New York Times, August 24, 1974, p. 23.
New York Times Book Review, September 28, 1969, pp. 1, 40.
Times Literary Supplement, May 14, 1970, p. 543.

OBITUARIES:

PERIODICALS

New York Times, May 19, 1991.*

*   *   *

KHAN, Mahmood H(asan) 1937-

PERSONAL: Born September 8, 1937, in Rampur, Uttar Pradesh, India; son of Amir Hasan (in the military) and Araishi (a homemaker; maiden name, Begum) Khan; married Aiysha Sultana (a homemaker); children: Rummana Hemani, Mansoor Hasan. *Education:* University of Sindh, B.Sc., 1957, M.A., 1960; Institute of Social Science, M.S.S., 1963; Agricultural University (Wageningen, The Netherlands), Ph.D., 1966. *Politics:* "Social" Democrat. *Religion:* Islam.

ADDRESSES: Home—2338 Oneida Dr., Coquitlam, British Columbia V3J 7A8, Canada. *Office*—Dept. of Economics, Simon Fraser University, Burnaby, British Columbia V5A 1S6, Canada.

CAREER: Simon Fraser University, Burnaby, British Columbia, Canada, assistant professor, 1966-68, associate professor, 1969-79, professor of economics, 1980—. Consultant to various organizations, including Asian Development Bank, International Monetary Fund, The World Bank, United Nations Food and Agricultural Organization, United States Agency for International Development (US-AID), and Canadian International Development Agency.

MEMBER: American Economics Association, American Agricultural Economics Association, International Association of Agricultural Economists, Canadian Asian Studies Association, Pakistan Society of Development Economists.

WRITINGS:

Economics of the Green Revolution in Pakistan, Praeger, 1975.

Underdevelopment and Agrarian Structure in Pakistan, Westview, 1981.
Rural Change in the Third World, Greenwood Press, 1992.
Third World Sustainable Agriculture in Egypt, Lynne Rienner, 1993.
Egyptian Women in Agricultural Development, Lynne Rienner, 1994.

Also author of numerous journal articles.

WORK IN PROGRESS: Research on rural poverty and development in Pakistan and Egypt.

SIDELIGHTS: Mahmood H. Khan told *CA:* "My modest writings began in 1966 as part of my academic career in economic development. My major interest was to analyze the process of agricultural development in Pakistan, including a study of technological change (the 'green' revolution) and the land system (agrarian structure). I have maintained my focus on rural poverty and rural development, but expanded the scope of my writings from Pakistan to Egypt. Almost all of my research can be called 'academic,' but I have always focused on the role of public policy. I have been influenced by the writings of several writers and scholars, including Gunnar Myrdal, Jan Tinbergen, T. W. Schultz, and J. K. Galbraith. My humble advice to young scholars and writers is to make a commitment and focus your energies on that commitment. The goal should be to help improve the human condition."

*   *   *

KIM, Byoung-lo Philo 1960-

PERSONAL: Born November 11, 1960; son of Do-bin (a pastor) and Chung-hee (Oh) Kim; married Helen Choi, June 27, 1987; children: Grace Eugene, James Dong-jin. *Education:* Sung Kyun Kwan University, B.A., 1984; Indiana State University, M.A., 1986; Rutgers University, Ph.D., 1991. *Religion:* Protestant.

ADDRESSES: Home—13-206 Gubanpo Apt., Banpobon-Dong, Sucho-Gu, Seoul 137-049, Korea. *Office*—C.P.O. Box 8232, Seoul, Korea.

CAREER: Writer. *Military service:* Korean Army; became second lieutenant.

MEMBER: Korean Sociological Association.

WRITINGS:

Two Koreas in Development: A Comparative Study of Principles and Strategies of Capitalist and Communist Third World Development, Transaction Books, 1992.
The Bibliographical Explanation of the Work of Kim Il Sung (in Korean), Research Institute for National Unification (Korea), 1993.

WORK IN PROGRESS: The Bibliographical Explanation of the Work of Kim Jung-Ih, written in Korean.

*   *   *

KINOY, Arthur 1920-

PERSONAL: Born September 29, 1920, in New York, NY; son of Albert (a schoolteacher) and Sarah Jane (a social worker; maiden name, Forstadt) Kinoy; married Susan Knopf, 1945 (divorced, 1971); married Barbara Webster (a bookkeeper and office manager), October 12, 1972; children: Peter, Joanne. *Education:* Harvard University, A.B., 1941; Columbia University, L.L.B., 1947.

ADDRESSES: Home—72 North Fullerton, Montclair, NJ 07042. *Office*—Department of Law, Rutgers University, Newark, NJ 07102.

CAREER: Donner, Kinoy & Perlin (law firm), New York City, partner, 1950-60; Kunstler, Kunstler & Kinoy (law firm), partner, 1964-67; Rutgers University, New Brunswick, NJ, professor of law, 1964—, became Distinguished Professor of Law and emeritus professor. Center for Constitutional Rights, founder and copresident. *Military service:* Served in U.S. military in World War II Italian campaign; received Battle Stars.

MEMBER: National Lawyers Guild (vice president, 1966-67), National Committee for Independent Political Action (co-chairperson).

WRITINGS:

Rights on Trial: The Odyssey of a People's Lawyer (autobiography), Harvard University Press, 1983.

Also author of numerous law review articles and published legal briefs, including *Conspiracy on Appeal,* an appellate brief on behalf of the Chicago Eight.

SIDELIGHTS: Arthur Kinoy is currently Distinguished Professor of Law Emeritus at Rutgers University, but the public is more likely to recognize his name because of his passionate involvement with "activist" legal causes since the early 1950s. Then a young lawyer in private practice, he represented many people placed before the McCarthy Committee and the Un-American Activities Committee, both established to identify and blacklist people with communist sympathies. Kinoy was also an appellate counsel for Morton Sobell in the celebrated Rosenberg "atom spies" case, in which Julius and Ethel Rosenberg were accused of giving confidential information on American nuclear technology to Soviet officials. Later he represented such organizations as the Mississippi Freedom Democratic Party, the Student Nonviolent Coordinating Committee, and the Southern Christian Leadership Confer-

ence. He was chief counsel in the successful appeal of the so-called Chicago Eight, who were arrested and convicted for violating the Federal Anti-Riot Statute at the 1968 Democratic National Convention in Chicago. More generally, he has worked tirelessly to protect the First Amendment rights of citizens, obtaining the first-ever federal injunction against the Un-American Activities Committee. On the cover of his book, *Rights on Trial: The Odyssey of a People's Lawyer,* is a photograph of him being arrested and physically removed from the committee hearing room by federal marshals.

Rights on Trial is Kinoy's account of his forty years as a "people's lawyer." It documents his efforts to challenge attempts by the government or big business to interfere with people's constitutional rights. It demonstrates his belief that the lawsuit and the test case are the people's most effective weapons against illegal government behavior. *Rights on Trial* is also a roll call of the landmark civil rights and First Amendment cases in which Kinoy has had a prominent hand, many of which have shaped the contemporary judicial climate.

BIOGRAPHICAL/CRITICAL SOURCES:

BOOKS

Kinoy, Arthur, *Rights on Trial: The Odyssey of a People's Lawyer,* Harvard University Press, 1983.

PERIODICALS

New Republic, December 26, 1983, pp. 33-34, 36.
Publishers Weekly, September 16, 1983, p. 112.

*   *   *

KIRCH, Patrick V(inton) 1950-

PERSONAL: Born July 7, 1950, in Honolulu, HI; son of Harold William and Barbara Ver (MacGarvin) Kirch; married Debra Connelly, March 3, 1979 (divorced, 1990). *Education:* University of Pennsylvania, B.A., 1971; Yale University, M.Phil., 1974, Ph.D., 1975.

ADDRESSES: Office—Department of Anthropology, University of California, Berkeley, CA 94720.

CAREER: Associated with University of Hawaii at Manoa, Honolulu, beginning 1979, affiliated associate professor of anthropology, 1982-84; University of Washington, Seattle, associate professor, 1985-87, professor of anthropology, 1987-89, director of Thomas Burke Memorial Washington State Museum, 1984-89; University of California, Berkeley, professor of anthropology, 1989—, curator of oceanic archaeology at Hearst Museum of Anthropology, 1989—, director of Archaeological Research Facility, 1992—. Bernice P. Bishop Museum, associate anthropologist, 1974-75, anthropologist, 1975-85, head of Division of Archaeology, 1983-84, research associate, 1984—; conducted archaeological and ethnographic field work in the Cook Islands, Samoa, Tonga, Papua New Guinea, the Marshall Islands, Tikopia, Anuta, the Solomon Islands, Wallis and Fortuna, the Loyalty Islands, and Hawaii. Washington State Centennial Commission, member of Lasting Legacy Committee, 1986-88.

MEMBER: American Anthropological Association (fellow), Society for American Archaeology, Association for Field Archaeology, Prehistoric Society (England; honorary member), Polynesian Society (New Zealand), New Zealand Archaeological Association, Pacific Scientific Associates, Sigma Xi.

AWARDS, HONORS: Elected member of National Academy of Sciences, 1990; elected member of American Academy of Arts and Sciences, 1992; grants from National Science Foundation, 1976-91, Hawaii Committee for the Humanities, 1981, Institute of Museum Services, 1985-88, National Endowment for the Arts, 1985, National Geographic Society, 1986 and 1989, Wenner-Gren Foundation for Anthropological Research, 1986, M. J. Murdock Charitable Trust, 1987, and National Endowment for the Humanities, 1988.

WRITINGS:

Marine Exploitation in Prehistoric Hawai'i: Archaeological Investigations at Kalahuipua'a, Hawai'i Island, Department of Anthropology, Bernice P. Bishop Museum, 1979.

(With D. E. Yen) *Tikopia: The Prehistory and Ecology of a Polynesian Outlier,* Bishop Museum Press, 1982.

(With Jeffrey T. Clark) *Archaeological Investigations of the Mudlane-Waimea-Kawaihae Road Corridor, Island of Hawai'i: An Interdisciplinary Study of an Environmental Transect,* Hawaii State Department of Transportation, 1983.

The Evolution of the Polynesian Chiefdoms, Cambridge University Press, 1984.

Feathered Gods and Fishhooks: An Introduction to Hawaiian Archaeology and Prehistory, University of Hawaii Press, 1985.

Niuatoputapu: The Prehistory of a Polynesian Chiefdom, Burke Museum, 1988.

(With Marshall Sahlins) *Anahulu: The Anthropology of History in the Kingdom of Hawaii,* Volume I: *Historical Ethnography,* Volume II: *The Archeology of History,* University of Chicago Press, 1992.

The Wet and the Dry: Irrigation and Agricultural Intensification in Polynesia, University of Chicago Press, 1994.

EDITOR

(With Marion Kelly) *Prehistory and Ecology in a Windward Hawaiian Valley: Halawa Valley, Molokai,* Department of Anthropology, Bernice P. Bishop Museum, 1975.

Island Societies: Archaeological Approaches to Evolution and Transformation, Cambridge University Press, 1986.

(With Terry L. Hunt) *Archaeology of the Lapita Cultural Complex: A Critical Review,* Burke Museum, 1988.

Prehistoric Hawaiian Occupation in the Anahulu Valley, O'ahu Island: Excavations in Three Inland Rockshelters, Archaeological Research Facility, Department of Anthropology, University of California, Berkeley, 1989.

Contributor of about a hundred articles to scientific journals.

*   *   *

KLEENE, Stephen Cole   1909-1994

OBITUARY NOTICE—See index for *CA* sketch: Born January 5, 1909, in Hartford, CT; died of pneumonia, January 25, 1994, in Madison, WI. Mathematician, educator, and author. Kleene's work with logic and recursion theory laid important groundwork for the development of computer science by helping determine the functions that can and cannot be accomplished by a computer. Long associated with the University of Wisconsin—Madison, Kleene began as an instructor at the university in 1935. He was an associate professor at Amherst College from 1941 to 1942, then returned to Madison after serving in World War II. Kleene became a full professor in 1948 and was the Cyrus C. MacDuffee Professor of Mathematics from 1964 until his retirement in 1979. His tenure also included stints as the chair of the departments of mathematics and numerical analysis and the dean of the College of Letters and Science. *Introduction to Metamathematics* was Kleene's debut publication, and his other titles included *The Foundations of Intuitionistic Mathematics,* which he cowrote with Richard Eugene Vesley, and *Logic,* which was published in 1980. Kleene was awarded the National Medal of Science in 1990.

OBITUARIES AND OTHER SOURCES:

BOOKS

Who's Who in America, 48th edition, Marquis, 1994.

PERIODICALS

Chicago Tribune, January 30, 1994, sec. 2, p. 7.
New York Times, January 27, 1994, p. D21.

KLEINFELD, Vincent A. 1907-1993

OBITUARY NOTICE—See index for *CA* sketch: Born February 10, 1907, in New York; died of heart ailments, October 9, 1993, in Palm Beach, FL. Lawyer, educator, and author. Kleinfeld began his lengthy career as an attorney with the United States Government in 1935. In 1953, he cofounded the Washington, DC, law firm Kleinfeld, Kaplan and Becker, where he specialized in food and drug law until his retirement in 1991. Kleinfeld taught for fifteen years at New York University's law school and subsequently for more than two decades at the law school of George Washington University. In addition to editing a number of volumes containing court decisions that concerned food and drug cases, Kleinfeld cowrote *Federal Food, Drug, and Cosmetic Act* and authored *Legal and Business Problems of the Cosmetic Industry* and *Federal Regulation of the Drug Industry.*

OBITUARIES AND OTHER SOURCES:

PERIODICALS

Washington Post, October 14, 1993, p. B4.

*   *   *

KLEVEN, Elisa 1958-
(Elisa Schneider)

PERSONAL: Name is pronounced "clay-ven"; born October 14, 1958, in Los Angeles, CA; daughter of Stanley (a doctor) and Lorraine Art (an artist) Schneider; married Paul Kleven, July, 1984; children: Mia. *Education:* University of California, Berkeley, B.A., 1981, teaching credentials, 1983.

ADDRESSES: Home—1028 Peralta Ave., Albany, CA 94706.

CAREER: Berkeley Hills Nursery School, Berkeley, CA, nursery school teacher, 1978-80; weaver and toy maker, 1980-84; Prospect School, El Cerrito, CA, fourth-grade and art teacher, 1984-86; writer and illustrator.

MEMBER: Society of Children's Book Writers and Illustrators, Amnesty International, World Wildlife Fund, Humane Society of the United States, Phi Beta Kappa.

AWARDS, HONORS: Parent's Choice award for illustration for *Abuela; Abuela* was also named a notable book by the American Library Association and a "Fanfare" book by *Horn Book.*

WRITINGS:

(Under name Elisa Schneider) *The Merry-Go-Round Dog,* Knopf, 1988.
Ernst, Dutton Children's Books, 1989.
The Lion and the Little Red Bird, Dutton, 1992.

(And illustrator) *The Paper Princess,* Dutton, 1994.

Ernst was translated into Japanese and Chinese.

ILLUSTRATOR

Isabel Wilner, *B Is for Bethlehem,* Dutton, 1990.
Arthur Dorros, *Abuela,* Dutton, 1991.
Tricia Brown, *The City by the Bay,* Chronicle, 1993.
Karen Lotz, *Snow Song Whistling,* Dutton, 1993.

SIDELIGHTS: Elisa Kleven commented: "A comment I hear often about my work is, 'It looks like you were having fun when you made this!' I never know exactly how to respond. I agonize a lot over my stories and my pictures: Is this a stupid idea? Is this a cluttered illustration?

"Yet once the flow and excitement of creation carries me safely beyond the internal critical voices, picture-book-making is indeed fun—so much fun I can't imagine not doing it. Creating the little make-believe world of a book—bringing characters to life, 'dressing' them, naming them, worrying over and loving them, giving them landscapes to roam in and skies to fly through—gives me the same deep joy and satisfaction that playing with beloved dolls and toys gave me in childhood.

"My advice to aspiring writers/illustrators of picture books would be to value and love your imaginations. Try not to forget that you're creating books for *children*—try to remember what you were thrilled and intrigued by, and what you loved, as a child. Don't be slick or gimmicky; while creating, try not to think about 'the market'—just the children."

BIOGRAPHICAL/CRITICAL SOURCES:

PERIODICALS

Booklist, October 15, 1991.
Children's Book Review Service, January, 1990, p. 51.
Horn Book, November/December, 1991, p. 726; May/June, 1992, p. 321.
Kirkus Reviews, May 15, 1992, p. 672.
Los Angeles Times Book Review, November 26, 1989, p. 27.
Newsweek, December 16, 1992, p. 68.
New York Times Book Review, June 21, 1992, p. 27.
Publishers Weekly, May 18, 1992, p. 68; October 4, 1993, p. 78.
School Library Journal, December, 1989, p. 84; July, 1992, p. 60.

*   *   *

KNAPP, Sara D. 1936-

PERSONAL: Born June 5, 1936, in New York, NY; daughter of Henry W. (a naval officer) and Alice (Ortgies)

Dusinberre; married Richard S. Knapp (divorced, 1968). *Education:* College of William and Mary, B.A., 1958; State University of New York at Albany, M.L.S., 1964, M.A., 1973.

ADDRESSES: Home—8 Ableman Ave., Albany, NY 12203. *Office*—University Library, State University of New York at Albany, 1400 Washington Ave., Albany, NY 12203.

CAREER: Albany Medical Center, Albany, NY, social case work aide, 1958-63; New York State Library, Albany, assistant library supervisor in Division of Library Development, 1964-67; State University of New York at Albany, assistant librarian, 1967-70, associate librarian, 1970-79, librarian, 1979—, cataloger, 1967-68, head of Periodicals Section, 1968-69, head of Serials and Bindery Department, 1969-71, reference librarian, 1971-72, head of Bibliographic Services Unit, 1972, coordinator of Computer Search Service Unit, 1972—. Bibliographic Retrieval Services, Inc., editor of the database *BRS/TERM,* 1983-89; consultant to Medical Reliance Co. and Bancroft Group. Capital District Library Council, member, 1969—, chairperson of Computer Based Reference Services Committee, Online Users Group, 1975-76. Colonie Public Library, volunteer, 1965-67; Clinton Square Neighborhood House, volunteer, 1965-67; Volunteers in Technical Assistance, volunteer for library research, 1967—; First Unitarian Church of Albany, chairperson of Channing Bookstore, 1966-68, 1970-71; Wheels to Independence, vice-president, 1974; Albany County Department of Social Services, member of advisory board of Infoline, 1979-85; member of Westlawn Neighborhood Improvement Association.

MEMBER: American Library Association (member of board of directors of Reference and Adult Services Division, 1978-79; member of executive committee of Machine Assisted Reference Section, 1979-80), Association of College and Research Libraries, American Society for Information Science, United University Professions, Eastern New York Association of College and Research Libraries, State University of New York Librarians Association.

AWARDS, HONORS: Isadore Gilbert Mudge Award from American Library Association, 1984.

WRITINGS:

BRS Training Workbook: An Introduction to Searching on the BRS System With Practice Exercises From the ERIC Database, Bibliographic Retrieval Services, 1979, revised edition, 1981.
(Compiler) *The Contemporary Thesaurus of Social Science Terms and Synonyms: A Guide for Natural Language Computer Searching,* Oryx, 1993.

Contributor of articles to library journals. Member of editorial board, *College and Research Libraries,* 1980-81.

WORK IN PROGRESS: Research on alternative methods of teaching search logic.

SIDELIGHTS: Sara D. Knapp told *CA:* "My writing has been related to my work. My biggest interest has been to make intelligible the apparently confusing details of online searching. My book reflects my interest in retrieving meaningful results from online searches. Using the right word(s) can help users to find the most relevant information."

*   *   *

KNIGHT, Julia 1957-

PERSONAL: Born in 1957, in Chorleywood, Hertfordshire, England; daughter of Peter G. K. (a civil engineer) and Marjorie (a secretary; maiden name, Merrett) Knight. *Education:* Polytechnic of North London, B.A. (with first class honors), 1987; University of Westminster, M.A. (with distinction), 1993. *Politics:* "Leftish and feminist." *Avocational Interests:* Cajun music, gardening, textiles.

ADDRESSES: Home—London, England. *Education:* School of Media Arts, University of Luton, 75 Castle St., Luton, Bedfordshire LU1 3AJ, England.

CAREER: Albany Video Distribution, London, England, co-manager, 1987-91; free-lance writer and lecturer, London, 1991-92; University of Luton, Luton, England, lecturer in media studies, 1992—. Cinenova Film and Video Distribution Company, member of management committee.

AWARDS, HONORS: Governors Award, Polytechnic of North London, 1987; Grant from British Academy, 1988.

WRITINGS:

Book Publishing, Wayland, 1988.
Women and the New German Cinema, Verso, 1992.

Work represented in anthologies, including *The Women's Companion to International Film,* edited by A. Kuhn and S. Radstone, Virago, 1990; *Screening Out Women: Lesbianism and Film,* edited by T. Wilton, Routledge, 1994; and *An Introduction to Film Studies,* edited by G. Nelmes, Routledge, in press. Contributor of articles and reviews to professional journals. British corresponding editor, *Perfect Beat.*

WORK IN PROGRESS: Editing a book on British experimental video for Arts Council of Great Britain; research on women and technology and on the new media technology.

SIDELIGHTS: Julia Knight told *CA:* "Two things have played a major role in my career: my 'discovery' of feminism in my early-twenties and my decision to do an evening class in film studies, which motivated me to return to university as a mature student. This combination of events gave me an interest in the representation of women in film, as well as the work of women directors. Since then, my interests have diversified and expanded, but remain informed by feminist politics."

*   *   *

KOLODNY, Nancy J.   1946-

PERSONAL: Born March 18, 1946, in New York, NY; daughter of Lawrence M. (a doctor) and Estelle (Srebnik) Shapiro; married Robert Charles Kolodny (a doctor, researcher, and writer), June 6, 1966; children: Linda Hillary, Lora Elizabeth, Lisa Michelle. *Education:* Barnard College, B.A., 1967; Washington University, M.A., 1969, M.S.W., 1980.

ADDRESSES: Office—Behavioral Medicine Institute, 885 Oenoke Ridge Rd., New Canaan, CT 06840.

CAREER: University City High School, University City, MO, English teacher, 1967-69; South Boston High School, South Boston, MA, English teacher, 1970-71; Clayton High School, Clayton, MO, English teacher, 1971-72; Bulimia Anorexia Self Help, St. Louis, MO, psychiatric social worker and eating disorder therapist, 1981-83; Behavioral Medicine Institute, New Canaan, CT, psychiatric social worker and eating disorder therapist, 1983—. Class correspondent, Barnard College, New York City, 1982-87; board member, Saxe Middle School, New Canaan, CT, 1985-88; board member, Fairfield County Seven Sisters Alumnae seminars, 1985-92; creator/facilitator of "Closing the Gap," a high school parent-student communication program, New Canaan High School, 1987-89. Consultant to University of Bridgeport, Home Box Office, and Allegra Films; public speaker on eating disorders, adolescence and parenting.

MEMBER: National Association of Social Workers, American Association of University Women (board member, 1987-89; member of committee on women, 1989), Kappa Delta Pi.

AWARDS, HONORS: Editor's Choice Award, *Booklist,* 1987, and Best Book Award nomination, *Voice of Youth Advocates,* 1988, both for *When Food's a Foe; Smart Choices* was named a Young Adult's Choice book by the International Reading Association, 1988.

WRITINGS:

(With Mark Schwartz) *Instructor's Manual for "Human Sexuality" by Masters, Johnson, Kolodny,* Little, Brown, 1982; revised edition, 1988.

(With Felix E. F. Larocca) *Anorexia and Bulimia Facilitator's Training Manual: A Primer, the BASH Approach,* Midwest Medical Publications, 1983.

(With Robert C. Kolodny, Thomas E. Bratter, and Cheryl Deep) *How to Survive Your Adolescent's Adolescence,* Little, Brown, 1984.

(With R. C. Kolodny and Bratter) *Smart Choices: A Guide to Surviving at Home and in School, Dating and Sex, Dealing with Crises, Applying to College, and More,* Little, Brown, 1986.

When Food's a Foe: How to Confront and Conquer Eating Disorders, Little, Brown, 1987, revised edition, 1992.

Contributor to *New Directions Quarterly Sourcebook*'s mental health series, Jossey-Bass, 1984.

SIDELIGHTS: As a psychiatric social worker and an eating disorder therapist, Nancy J. Kolodny writes about the types of problems she treats in the Behavioral Medical Institute. Kolodny's books help today's adolescents to face such challenges effectively. Patty Campbell, writing about self-help books for the *Wilson Library Bulletin,* reports: "Although self-help for adults has proliferated, such books for teenagers have been relatively scarce."

Campbell describes Kolodny's *Smart Choices* as "an encyclopedia of advice for every conceivable social problem of adolescence, [covering] not only parents, sex, school, and emotions, but drugs and alcohol, eating disorders, divorce, pregnancy, loneliness, depression, suicide, death, and how to persuade your friends not to break the law." Also included in *Smart Choices* are some other problems today's teenagers may face, including bulimia, contraception, tattoos, attending one's first funeral, and how to handle the persistence of military recruiters. Problems experienced in everyday conflicts within families and among friends are also discussed, thereby giving teenagers a chance to help understand their family dynamics as well as their relationships with friends. A *Publishers Weekly* reviewer writes: "An up to date, extensive bibliography and a tone of respect make *Smart Choices* a 'smart choice' to have on hand."

Kolodny's *When Food's a Foe: How to Confront and Conquer Eating Disorders* not only describes anorexia and bulimia but also helps to guide teenagers who are afflicted with these disorders. The information on self-image, eating disorder symptoms, how to get help and how to help others, makes the book appropriate for many adolescent readers. Kolodny uses teen-related analogies and quotes from adolescent anorexics and bulimics to appeal to her youthful audience. Kolodny also incorporates questions, suggestions, and words of encouragement to the readers. Information on how to face the problem and change the behavior which leads to eating disorders is detailed using quizzes designed to help the reader examine their self-image and self-esteem. With the number of such cases on the rise, Shirley Carmony, writing for *Voice of Youth Advocates,* calls *When Food's a Foe* "an excellent addition to a school library. It is both readable and timely."

BIOGRAPHICAL/CRITICAL SOURCES:

PERIODICALS

Bulletin of the Center for Children's Books, February, 1988, p. 119.
Children's Book Review Service, April, 1987, p. 100.
Publishers Weekly, December 26, 1986, p. 62; December 11, 1987, p. 67.
School Library Journal, January, 1987, p. 84; March, 1988, p. 221.
Voice of Youth Advocates, February, 1988, p. 296; August, 1988, p. 118.
Wilson Library Bulletin, December, 1986, pp. 50-51.

*   *   *

KOSTERS, Marvin H(oward)   1933-

PERSONAL: Born August 4, 1933, in Corsica, SD; son of Albert (a farmer) and Alice (a homemaker; maiden name, Vander Luit) Kosters; married Bonnita Eckels (a teacher), December 28, 1962; children: Mark Alan, Elise Lyna Kosters Van Noord, Barbara. *Education:* Calvin College, B.A., 1960; University of Chicago, Ph.D., 1966. *Religion:* Christian Reformed. *Avocational Interests:* Genealogy, bicycling.

ADDRESSES: Home—4033 North 27th St., Arlington, VA 22207. *Office*— American Enterprise Institute for Public Policy Research, 1150 17th St. N.W., Washington, DC 20036.

CAREER: RAND Corp., Santa Monica, CA, economist, 1965-69; President's Council of Economic Advisers, Washington, DC, senior economist, 1969-71; U.S. Cost of Living Council, Washington, DC, associate director for economic policy, 1971-74; American Enterprise Institute for Public Policy Research, Washington, DC, resident scholar, 1974; Office of the Assistant to the President for Economic Affairs, Washington, DC, staff member, 1974-75; American Enterprise Institute for Public Policy Research, director of Center for the Study of Government Regulation, 1976-86, resident scholar and director of economic policy studies, 1987—. U.S. Department of Labor, Manpower Administration, associate administrator for policy, evaluation, and research, 1971, member of Task

Force on Economic Adjustment and Worker Dislocation, 1975-76; Civil Aeronautics Board, member of advisory committee on procedural reform, 1975; Committee for Economic Development, member of research advisory board, 1989-92; consultant to U.S. Department of the Treasury and Council on Wage and Price Stability. Teacher at University of Chicago, summers, 1964-65, and University of California, Los Angeles, 1966-69. *Military service:* U.S. Army, 1953-55.

MEMBER: American Economic Association.

WRITINGS:

(With Dawson Ahalt) *Controls and Inflation: The Economic Stabilization Program in Retrospect,* American Enterprise Institute for Public Policy Research, 1975.
(Editor with Timothy B. Clark and James C. Miller III) *Reforming Regulation,* American Enterprise Institute for Public Policy Research, 1980.
(Editor and contributor) *Workers and Their Wages: Changing Patterns in the United States,* American Enterprise Institute for Public Policy Research, 1991.
(Editor and author of introduction) *Personal Savings, Consumption, and Tax Policy,* American Enterprise Institute for Public Policy Research, 1992.
(Editor) *Fiscal Politics and the Budget Enforcement Act,* American Enterprise Institute for Public Policy Research, 1992.

Work represented in anthologies, including *The Economics of Labor Relations,* edited by H. R. Northrup, Irwin, 1972; *Income Maintenance and Labor Supply: Econometric Studies,* edited by Glen G. Cain and Harold W. Watts, Markham, 1973; and *Toward a New Industrial Policy,* edited by Michael L. Watcher and Susan M. Watcher, University of Pennsylvania Press, 1981. Contributor to periodicals.

*   *   *

KOUROUMA, Ahmadou   1940-

PERSONAL: Born in 1940, on the Ivory Coast.

CAREER: Writer. Living in exile.

WRITINGS:

Les Soleils des Independences, Seuil, 1968, translation by Adrian Adams published as *The Suns of Independence,* Africana, 1981.
Monne, Outrages et Defis, Seuil, 1990, translation by Nidra Poller published as *Monnew,* Mercury House, 1993.

SIDELIGHTS: Using degraded African princes as the focal points of his two novels, Ahmadou Kourouma has written angry satires about the disasters wrought in black Africa by both colonialism and post-independence black African governments. Critics have found exceptional both this unflinching anger and its modes of expression.

Kourouma's stylistic innovations were evident in his first novel, *The Suns of Independence,* both in the French original and the subsequent English translation. "The first novel of Ahmadou Kourouma" remarked Suzanne Gasster in the *French Review,* "marked the beginning of the adaptation of French deliberately opened to African language. From the African folk narration came a headlong rhythm, syntax reversals, and exclamations from different narrative sources." In *The Suns of Independence,* much of the material for this language play is given by the fallen prince himself, Fama, who, discarded by the postcolonial dictatorship and slightly daft, makes a bare living by giving ritual orations. Prey to the seemingly arbitrary forces in power, his situation worsens until he is fatally wounded crossing a newly established territorial border.

The title of Kourouma's second novel, *Monnew,* means "shame." It describes the fate of another prince, Djigui. In his own interest he cooperates with the French conquest of the Malinke peoples at the end of the nineteenth century, resulting in much slaughter and ruination of the kingdom. Kourouma uses a series of eyewitness narrators to relate the downfall. There are frequent comments on these recitations, anonymous voices responding with proverbial words from Malinke folklore or Islam; another verbal layer is provided by the misinterpretations given to Djigui—and, possibly to the reader—by French translators and local soothsayers.

But despite the continual verbal interest of the novel, it ends in much the same contemporary mood as *The Suns of Independence,* revealing the same priorities of that novel noted by John F. Povey in the *World Literature Today:* "the disaster of modern Africa must be exposed in words that burn with the bitterness of their despair. As the author concludes, colonized or independent, Africans will keep on suffering 'until such times as God unpeels the curse stuck fast in their black backsides.' "

BIOGRAPHICAL/CRITICAL SOURCES:

BOOKS

Zell, Hans M., and others, *A New Reader's Guide to African Literature,* Holmes & Meier, 1983.

PERIODICALS

African Today, Volume 31, number 1, 1984, p.71.
Booklist, June 1, 1974, p. 1084.
French Review, October, 1991, p. 171.
Times Literary Supplement, October 18, 1985, p. 1180.
World Literature Today, winter, 1983, p. 159.*

KRAEUTER, David W. 1941-

PERSONAL: Surname rhymes with "writer"; born April 21, 1941, in Homestead, PA; son of Harold A. (a plumber) and Dorothy L. (a schoolteacher; maiden name, Honse) Kraeuter. *Education:* Geneva College, B.A., 1963; University of Pittsburgh, M.L.S., 1968. *Politics:* Independent. *Religion:* Agnostic. *Avocational Interests:* Reading, electronics, music.

ADDRESSES: Home—506 East Wheeling St., Washington, PA 15301. *Office*—Library, Washington and Jefferson College, Washington, PA 15301.

CAREER: Washington and Jefferson College, Washington, PA, assistant librarian, 1968-92, associate librarian, 1992—. *Military service:* Pennsylvania National Guard, 1963-65. U.S. Army Reserve, 1965-69.

MEMBER: Pittsburgh Antique Radio Society (secretary, 1986-90).

AWARDS, HONORS: Ace Author Certificate from Antique Wireless Association, 1992.

WRITINGS:

Radio and Television Pioneers: A Patent Bibliography, Scarecrow, 1992.
British Radio and Television Pioneers: A Patent Bibliography, Scarecrow, 1993.

Contributor to periodicals, including *Tropical Fish, Antique Radio Classified,* and *Hobbyist.* Editor, *Pittsburgh Oscillator: Journal of the Pittsburgh Antique Radio Society,* 1986—.

WORK IN PROGRESS: Editing *The KDKA Papers,* about the pioneer radio station KDKA; research on radio and television history.

SIDELIGHTS: David W. Kraeuter told *CA:* "I have always liked the idea that books can 'trap' information and make it available, more or less forever, to anyone who wants it. It took years to gather and organize the information in my bibliographies, but now it can be available to anyone in minutes."

*   *   *

KRAMER, Ted
See STEWARD, Samuel M(orris)

*   *   *

KRATZ, Martin P. J. 1955-

PERSONAL: Born October 30, 1955, in Edmonton, Alberta, Canada; son of Hans (a teacher and consultant) and

Juliana (a social worker; maiden name, Jonas) Kratz; married Margaret Burghardt, June 20, 1976 (marriage ended October 29, 1983); married Christina Harley (a property manager), February 6, 1988; children: Stephanie, Robert, Alexandra, Marcus. *Education:* University of Alberta, B.Sc. (with distinction), 1981, LL.B. (with distinction), 1984. *Religion:* Roman Catholic. *Avocational Interests:* Skiing, sailing, soccer, flying (VFR private pilot), cycling, painting in acrylics and oils, writing occasional fiction and poetry, reading, collecting art and music, teaching and attending live theater.

ADDRESSES: Home—Edmonton, Alberta, Canada. *Office*—Bennett Jones Verchere, 1000 Canadian Utilities Centre, 10035-105 St., Edmonton, Alberta, Canada T5J 3T2.

CAREER: Celanese Canada Ltd., Clover Bar, Alberta, chemical operator, 1974-76; Pitney Bowes Canada Ltd., Edmonton, Alberta, service representative, 1976-77; Texaco Exploration, Bonnie Glen, Alberta, engineering trainee, 1978; University of Stuttgart, Stuttgart, Germany, research assistant at Institute fuer Thermodynamik und Warmetechnik, 1979; Alberta Oil Sands Technology and Research Authority, Edmonton, engineer, 1980; Canadian Association of Fire Chiefs, consulting engineer, 1981; Alberta Court of Appeal and Court of Queen's Bench, Edmonton, law clerk, 1984-85; Ogilvie and Co., Edmonton, barrister and solicitor, 1985-88; Cruickshank Karvellas (law firm), Edmonton, barrister and solicitor, 1988-89, partner, 1989-91; Bennett Jones Verchere, Edmonton, lawyer, 1991—. University of Alberta, lecturer, 1986—; University of Calgary, lecturer, 1987—; speaker at universities throughout Canada. Kratz Consulting, consultant, 1983—; NeuroSpheres Ltd., acting president, 1993—. Montana Board of Professional Engineers and Surveyors, member in training, 1981-91; Alberta Science and Technology Leadership Awards Foundation, vice-president and member of board of directors, 1982—.

MEMBER: International Federation for Information Processing (chairperson of Computer Security Law Working Group), Licensing Executives Society of Canada and the United States, Canadian Bar Association, Canadian Information Processing Society (chairperson of Intellectual Property Committee, 1987—), Patent and Trademark Institute of Canada, Data Processing Management Association (national chairperson of Government Relations Task Force; member of board of directors of Edmonton chapter), Canadian Information Processing Society (founder and director of Edmonton Computer Security Special Interest Group; chairperson of Intellectual Property Standing Committee), Canadian Advanced Technology Association (counsel to Alberta Section), American Bar Association (Science and Technology Section and Patent, Copyright, and Trademark Section), U.S. Trademark Association, Society for Computers and Law (England), Alberta Society of Software Developers, Electronic Industry Association of Alberta (general counsel, 1986—), Edmonton Bar Association, Polar Ski Club (past president).

WRITINGS:

(With Philip Fites and Alan Brebner) *Control and Security of Computer Information Systems,* with instructor's guide, Computer Science Press, 1988.
(With Philip Fites and Peter Johnson) *The Computer Virus Crisis,* Van Nostrand, 1989, 2nd edition, 1991.
(With others) *Information System Security Handbook,* Van Nostrand, 1993.

Contributor of more than a hundred articles to professional journals.

WORK IN PROGRESS: Security Law; Intellectual Property Law; Industrial Espionage: A Guide, completion expected in 1995; a user's guide to copyright and industrial design; research on using the opportunities under the free trade agreement; research on annotated government procurement agreements.

SIDELIGHTS: Martin P. J. Kratz told *CA:* "The future of our economies and societies depends, in part, on the encouragement and development of advanced technology and entertainment industries. These industries are highly dependent on intellectual property rights for the protection of creative effort. They are also fields in which Canada, the United States, and other advanced nations may excel and be successful. It is important that the creators and those who use or work with creative products or services have a better understanding of the rights with which they work. Further, it is vital that the legal system continues to review the forms of protection available and implement timely and meaningful changes to protect these industries."

*   *   *

KRIEG, Joann P(eck)   1932-

PERSONAL: Born August 19, 1932, in New York, NY; daughter of Samuel Wilson (in sales) and Alice (a homemaker; maiden name, LaRose) Peck; married John W. Krieg, March 29, 1952; children: Lisa Krieg MacLeman, John Steven. *Education:* Hofstra University, B.A., 1974, M.A., 1975; Graduate Center of the City University of New York, Ph.D., 1979. *Politics:* Independent. *Avocational Interests:* Opera.

ADDRESSES: Home—4045 Massachusetts Ave., Island Park, NY 11558. *Office*—Department of English, Hofstra University, Hempstead, NY 11550.

CAREER: Hofstra University, Hempstead, NY, associate professor of English, 1978—. Walt Whitman Birthplace Association, member of board of trustees and past president.

MEMBER: Modern Language Association of America, American Studies Association, Northeast Modern Language Association, Phi Beta Kappa.

AWARDS, HONORS: Fulbright award, 1992.

WRITINGS:

Walt Whitman, Here and Now, Greenwood Press, 1985.
To Know the Place: Teaching Local History, Long Island Studies Institute, 1986.
Dwight D. Eisenhower: Soldier, President, Statesman, Greenwood Press, 1987.
Evoking a Sense of Place, Heart of the Lakes Publishing, 1988.
(With Paul Harper) *John F. Kennedy,* Greenwood Press, 1988.
Long Island and Literature (monograph), Heart of the Lakes Publishing, 1989.
Long Island Architecture, Heart of the Lakes Publishing, 1991.
Epidemics in the Modern World, Twayne, 1992.

*   *   *

KRITSICK, Stephen M(ark)   1951-1994

OBITUARY NOTICE—See index for *CA* sketch: Born November 2, 1951, in Cambridge, MA; died of lymphoma related to acquired immunodeficiency syndrome (AIDS), January 16, 1994, in Lexington, MA. Veterinarian, television commentator, and author. Kritsick was affiliated with a number of institutions during his veterinary career, including the Animal Medical Center and the Park East Animal Hospital, both located in New York City. In 1990, he became a staff veterinarian of the Humane Society of the United States, and he also served as the Society's national spokesperson. Kritsick appeared in segments dedicated to animals on the children's television show *Romper Room* for nearly a decade, on the Cable News Network feature "People and Pets" in the early 1980s, and on *Good Morning America.* Kritsick, who was preparing a book about acquired immunodeficiency syndrome (AIDS) at the time of his death, coauthored *Creature Comforts: The Adventures of a City Vet* and wrote *Dr. Kritsick's Tender Loving Cat Care.*

OBITUARIES AND OTHER SOURCES:

PERIODICALS

Chicago Tribune, January 17, 1994, section 4, p. 10.
Los Angeles Times, January 20, 1994, p. A32.

New York Times, January 18, 1994, p. B11.
Washington Post, January 18, 1994, p. D8.

*   *   *

KROLL, Virginia L(ouise)   1948-
(Melrose Cooper)

PERSONAL: Born April 28, 1948, in Buffalo, NY; daughter of Lester H. (a United States immigration inspector) and Helen (a registered nurse and model; maiden name, Szewczyk) Kroll; married David Haeick (in construction); children: Sara, Seth, Joshua, Hannah, Katya, Noah. *Education:* Attended State University of New York at Buffalo and Canisius College. *Religion:* Roman Catholic. *Avocational Interests:* Reading, crafts, friends.

ADDRESSES: Home—214 Maple Ave., Hamburg, NY 14075. *Office*—c/o Publicity Director, Four Winds Press, 866 Third Ave., New York, NY 10022.

CAREER: Fifth grade teacher in the Buffalo, NY, area, 1968-69 and 1980-81; Hamburg Memorial Youth Center, Hamburg, NY, recreation assistant, 1978-80. Medaille College, Buffalo, college instructor for Writing for Children course, 1993.

WRITINGS:

PICTURE BOOKS

Helen the Fish, illustrated by Teri Weidner, Albert Whitman and Co., 1992.
My Sister, Then and Now, illustrated by Mary Worcester, Carolrhoda Books, 1992.
Masai and I, illustrated by Nancy Carpenter, Four Winds Press/Macmillan, 1992.
Naomi Knows It's Springtime, illustrated by Jill Kastner, Boyds Mills Press, 1993.
Woodhoopoe Willie, illustrated by Katherine Roundtree, Charlesbridge Publishing, 1993.
Africa Brothers and Sisters, illustrated by Vanessa French, Four Winds Press/Macmillan, 1993.
A Carp for Kimiko, illustrated by Roundtree, Charlesbridge Publishing, 1993.
I Wanted to Know All about God, illustrated by Debra Reid Jenkins, William B. Eerdmans Publishing, 1994.
Beginnings, illustrated by Stacey Schuett, Albert Whitman and Co., 1994.
Pink Paper Swans, illustrated by Nancy Clouse, William B. Eerdmans Publishing, 1994.
Sweet Magnolia, illustrated by Laura Jakes, Charlesbridge Publishing, 1994.
The Seasons and Someone, illustrated by Tatsuro Kiuchi, Harcourt Brace Jovanovich, 1994.
Faraway Drums, illustrated by Floyd Cooper, Little, Brown, in press.

Hands Fit, Boyds Mills Press, in press.

UNDER PSEUDONYM MELROSE COOPER

I Got a Family, illustrated by Dale Gottlieb, Henry Holt, 1993.
Life Riddles (chapter book), Henry Holt, 1994.
I Got Community, illustrated by Gottlieb, Henry Holt, in press.

OTHER

When Will We Be Sisters?, Scholastic, 1993.
Jaha and Jamil Went down the Hill, illustrated by Roundtree, Charlesbridge Publishing, 1994.
Handy Hairstyles and Dandy Do's, illustrated by Kay Life, Charlesbridge Publishing, 1994.
I Saw a Whale, Seacoast Publications, 1994.
Butterfly Boy, Boyds Mills Press, in press.

Contributor to periodicals.

SIDELIGHTS: Kroll commented: "All I ever wanted to be is an author. And now that I am one, all I ever want to be is an author. In between the desire and the realized dream, I became a mother. Good thing. My six children and one grandchild give me stories every day. So do the children I visit in schools. There is a story in everyone I meet, everything I encounter, because they induce wonder.

"*Masai and I* began as a discussion with my former fifth graders about each other's heritage. *Helen the Fish* involves the experiences of three of my children and a pet goldfish. *My Sister, Then and Now* deals with the struggles of mental illness, which I have seen in two families who are close to me. *Life Riddles* includes many true incidents of my personal struggle with poverty. My brother, 'Donald the drummer,' gave me the idea for the musical percussionist in *Woodhoopoe Willie* and my sister, Nancy, a wildlife rehabilitator, for *Sweet Magnolia*. The list goes on. . . ."

Kroll might be considered an inspiration for many writers since most of her books were accepted from the "slush pile." Despite the positive response from editors, Kroll has had several negative responses which bothered her. One was a prejudice some editors had against a white author writing about other cultures. Kroll feels it's foolish to believe a white person is not capable of writing "black material." She doesn't want to write about a suburban middle-class white woman's world. So she writes whatever she has a desire to write.

Masai and I is about a young African American girl who is learning about the Masai culture in school. Each day she goes home and compares herself to an East African child she is studying. She wonders where a Masai girl would sleep, what she would do in her free time, what she would wear, eat, etc. Readers learn that while the everyday lives of Americans are different than the everyday lives of the Masai, children are still children, no matter where they live. Martha Topol in the *School Library Journal* calls *Masai and I* "an interesting, richly blended book that connects two different worlds . . . pointing out similarities and differences."

Another type of prejudice which Kroll has had to deal with is that some felt she was writing too many books too fast. She addressed this criticism by using a pseudonym. She chose one which neither reveals her sex nor hints at her race. The first time she submitted a manuscript under the new name, it was immediately accepted.

Kroll has had a lot of people tell her how wonderful it is that she has a gift that she can get paid for. Her comment is, "This is true, but talent needs work. A gift can sit there and look beautiful, but it is worth nothing at all until is it unwrapped and used properly."

BIOGRAPHICAL/CRITICAL SOURCES:

PERIODICALS

Children's Book Review Service, spring, 1992, p. 135.
Kirkus Reviews, September 1, 1992, p. 1131.
Publishers Weekly, June 29, 1992, p. 62; December 28, 1992, p. 26.
School Library Journal, June 6, 1992, p. 96; October, 1992, p. 91; November, 1992, p. 94.

*   *   *

KUH, Katharine (W.) 1904-1994

OBITUARY NOTICE—See index for *CA* sketch: Born July 15, 1904, in St. Louis, MO; died January 10, 1994, in Manhattan, NY. Curator, editor, and author. Kuh founded the first commercial avant-garde art gallery in Chicago, Illinois, the Katharine Kuh Gallery, in 1936, where the works of several of modern art's most respected painters were exhibited. During World War II, Kuh joined the Art Institute of Chicago's public relations office. Later she edited the Institute's periodical *Quarterly*, and in 1953 she became the curator of modern painting and sculpture. During the 1960s and 1970s, Kuh served as the *Saturday Review*'s art editor and advised the First National Bank of Chicago on its corporate art collection. Kuh's writings include *Art Has Many Faces, Leger, The Artist's Voice, Break-Up: The Core of Modern Art*, and *The Open Eye: In Pursuit of Art*.

OBITUARIES AND OTHER SOURCES:

BOOKS

Who's Who in American Art, 1991-1992, 19th edition, Bowker, 1990.

PERIODICALS

Chicago Tribune, January 16, 1994, p. 6.
New York Times, January 12, 1994, p. B7.

*   *   *

KUKREJA, Veena 1960-

PERSONAL: Born August 30, 1960, in Delhi, India; daughter of U. C. (an industrialist) and K. D. (a homemaker) Kukreja. *Education:* University of Delhi, degrees in political science, 1976 and 1978, M.Phil., 1982, Ph.D., 1987. *Politics:* "Considerably left of center." *Religion:* "Faith in human values."

ADDRESSES: Home—House 27, Road 5, East Punjabi Bagh, New Delhi 110 026, India. *Office*—Department of Political Science, University of Delhi, Delhi 110 007, India.

CAREER: University of Delhi, Delhi, India, lecturer at Shivaji College, 1979-80, lecturer at Janaki Devi College, 1981-89, lecturer in political science, 1989—.

MEMBER: Indian Council of World Affairs, Institute for Defence Studies and Analysis, India International Centre.

WRITINGS:

Military Intervention in Politics: A Case Study of Pakistan, NBO (New Delhi), 1985.
Civil-Military Relations in South Asia, Sage Publications, 1991.

Contributor of articles to political science journals.

WORK IN PROGRESS: A book on military politics in Bangladesh; research on South Asian politics.

SIDELIGHTS: Veena Kukreja told *CA:* "In the early 1980s, when I was writing a seminar paper titled 'The Military's Role in Pakistan,' my supervisor Professor M. P. Singh aroused my interest in the theories of civil-military relations. I found that the literature on civil-military relations in developing countries has been prodigious in recent years, but the serious scholarly interest seems to concentrate on regions outside South Asia. This region comprises an important segment of the coup-zone displaying contrasting, as well as similar, patterns of civil-military relations—for example, Pakistan and Bangladesh on the one hand, and India on the other.

"All three began with a civilian government, but two of them soon succumbed to military rule. Pakistan virtually remained under military rule for twenty-five of the forty-five years of its existence. Bangladesh, until the downfall of General Ershad, except the years 1972 to 1975 and the four months of Abdur Sattar's civilian rule, has been ruled essentially by men in uniform. However, not a single full-length comparative study of any aspect of the military role and rule in Pakistan and Bangladesh has yet been attempted.

"The existing literature consists of either purely theoretical studies or largely empirical ones. My study seeks to fill the gap by applying a much-needed theoretical framework to the study of actual patterns of civil-military relations in South Asia. One feature that makes my work unique is that it is not confined to understanding the reasons for military intervention in politics, but it systematically deals with strategies and tactics for survival and legitimization adopted by the armed forces in Pakistan and Bangladesh once they seized power. This contributes to an understanding of why some military regimes fail and others succeed."

*   *   *

KUNZ, Kathleen 1935-

PERSONAL: Born September 22, 1935, in St. Louis, MO; daughter of Edward James (a high school business manager) and Kathleen Julia (a comptometrist; maiden name, Gamache) King; married Donald Albert Kunz, Sr. (a military officer and certified public accountant), January 9, 1957; children: Donald, Kathleen Kunz Walker, Patricia Kunz Alikhani, Stephen, Lawrence, Robert. *Education:* St. Louis University, B.S., 1957; University of Oklahoma, M.A., 1981. *Politics:* "Mostly Democrat." *Religion:* "Decidedly Catholic." *Avocational Interests:* Hot air ballooning, backpacking, travel.

ADDRESSES: Home—Norman, OK. *Office*—H. H. Herbert School of Journalism, University of Oklahoma, 860 Van Vleet Oval, Norman, OK 73019. *Agent*—Spencer King Associates, 595 Main St., Suite 1602, Roosevelt Island, New York, NY 10044.

CAREER: World Literature Today, Norman, OK, secretary, 1978-79; University of Oklahoma, Norman, instructor in English, 1980-81, visiting instructor in journalism, 1981—.

MEMBER: Mystery Writers of America, Sisters in Crime, National Journalism Society, National Jesuit Honor Society, Alpha Sigma Nu, Kappa Tau Alpha.

WRITINGS:

Murder Once Removed (novel), Walker and Co., 1993.

Contributor of about fifty articles to magazines, including *Parents', Good Housekeeping, Mothers Today, Working Parents, Oklahoma Today,* and *Preschooler.*

WORK IN PROGRESS: Death in a Private Place, the second novel in the Terry Girard mystery series; research on St. Genevieve for the third mystery in the series.

SIDELIGHTS: Kathleen Kunz told *CA:* "I write because I feel guilty when I don't. I also have a strong feeling for history, not so much dates and places, but exploring in fiction what happens between the dates on a person's tombstone. How does it affect that person or character, and what does he do as a result?"

*   *   *

KUSHIGIAN, Julia A.   1950-

PERSONAL: Born July 17, 1950, in New York, NY; daughter of Jack Paul (an accountant) and Rose (an artist; maiden name, Nevart) Kushigian; married Charles Augustus Secor, Jr. (a dealer in imported automobiles), November 25, 1989. *Education:* New York University, M.A., 1975; Yale University, M.A., 1980, M.Phil., 1981, Ph.D., 1984. *Religion:* Congregationalist.

ADDRESSES: Home—15 Country Club Dr., Ledyard, CT 06339. *Office*—Connecticut College, Box 5562, New London, CT 06320.

CAREER: Connecticut College, New London, associate professor of Hispanic studies and head of department, 1985—. Literacy Volunteers of America, member of Greater New London board of directors.

MEMBER: International Institute of Iberoamerican Literature, Modern Language Association of America, Latin American Studies Association, American Association of Teachers of Spanish and Portuguese, American Association of University Women, Northeast Modern Language Association, NECLAS.

WRITINGS:

Orientalism in the Hispanic Literary Tradition: In Dialogue with Borges, Paz, and Sarduy, University of New Mexico Press, 1991.

WORK IN PROGRESS: Growing up in Spanish America: The "Bildungsroman" in Spanish American Literature.

L

La BERGE, Ann F. 1944-

PERSONAL: Born June 2, 1944, in Jacksonville, FL; daughter of William John Fowler and Leigh Rydholm Fowler; married Bernard La Berge, June 19, 1969; children: Leigh Claire, Julia Louisa. *Education:* Middlebury College, A.B., 1965; Vanderbilt University, M.A.T., 1966, M.A., 1969; University of Tennessee, Knoxville, Ph.D., 1974.

ADDRESSES: Home—2814 Mt. Vernon Ln., Blacksburg, VA 24060. *Office*—Center for the Study of Science in Society, Price House, Virginia Polytechnic Institute and State University, Blacksburg, VA 24061.

CAREER: Virginia Polytechnic Institute and State University, Blacksburg, visiting assistant professor, 1979-81, assistant director of Center for the Study of Science in Society, 1981-85, program coordinator, 1985-86, visiting assistant professor of history, 1986-88, assistant professor of Center for Programs in the Humanities, 1989—, and Center for the Study of Science in Society, 1991—.

MEMBER: International Society for the History, Philosophy, and Social Studies of Biology, American Association for the History of Medicine, History of Science Society, American Historical Association, Society for French Historical Studies, Society for the Social History of Medicine, British Society for the History of Science, Societe francaise pour l'histoire des sciences de l'homme, Western Society for French History, Southern Historical Association (European History Section).

AWARDS, HONORS: Grants from National Library of Medicine, 1975-80, American Council of Learned Societies, 1982 (for Paris) and 1985, and National Endowment for the Humanities, 1985 and 1991-93.

WRITINGS:

(Editor with Arthur Donovan) *Working Papers in Science and Technology Studies: Ethics in Engineering,* Center for the Study of Science in Society, Virginia Polytechnic Institute and State University, 1982.
(Editor with Doris Zallen) *Readings in Humanities, Science, and Technology,* Pocahontas Press, 1992.
Mission and Method: The Early Nineteenth-Century French Public Health Movement, Cambridge University Press, 1992.
(Editor with Mordechai Feingold, and contributor) *French Medical Culture in the Nineteenth Century,* Rodopi, 1993.

Contributor of articles and reviews to history journals.

WORK IN PROGRESS: Editing and writing contributions for *Reinterpreting Paris Medicine, 1790-1850,* with Caroline Hannaway; research on early French medical microscopy, 1820-1860, and medical statistics in nineteenth-century France.

*   *   *

LaDUKE, Betty 1933-

PERSONAL: Born January 13, 1933, in New York, NY; daughter of Sam (a house painter) and Helen (a factory worker; maiden name, Peskin) Bernstein; married Vincent LaDuke, 1958 (died, 1963); married Peter Westigard (a professor of entymology), July 14, 1965; children: (first marriage) Winona, (second marriage) Jason. *Education:* Attended Denver University, 1950-51, Cleveland Institute of Art, 1951-52, and Instituto Allende, 1953-54; California State University, B.A., 1959, M.A., 1963. *Avocational Interests:* Walking, traveling, sketching, research on women artists and multi-cultural issues.

ADDRESSES: Home—610 Long Way, Ashland, OR 97520. *Office*—Department of Art, Southern Oregon State College, Ashland, OR 97520.

CAREER: Southern Oregon State College, Ashland, professor of art, 1964—; artist and writer. Art works exhibited in various institutions, museums, and galleries, including Galerie Arte Moderne, Mexico City, Mexico, 1956; Crocker Art Museum, Sacramento, CA, 1972; University of Washington, Pullman, 1978; Lucien Labaudt Gallery, San Francisco, CA, 1980; Women's Caucus for Art, Houston, TX, 1983; Eastern Washington State University, Cheney, 1984; Maude Kern Art Center, Eugene, OR, 1987; In Her Image Gallery, Portland, OR, 1989; International Oasis Gallery, Savannah, GA, 1990; Schneider Art Museum, Ashland, 1992; and Maier Museum of Art, Lynchburg, VA, 1993. Works exhibited in one-person shows, including *Impressions of India, China: An Outsider's Inside View, Print Impressions: Third World Cultures, Impressions of Latin America,* and *Africa: Between Myth and Reality.*

MEMBER: International Society for Education through the Arts, National Arts Education Association, National Women's Studies Association, Women's Caucus for Art, Phi Kappa Phi.

AWARDS, HONORS: Honorable mention for painting from City Center Gallery, 1958; first prize in printmaking from California State College of Los Angeles, 1962; honorable mention for printmaking from Friends of the Museum of Art (Eugene, OR), 1967; Award for printmaking from Oregon College of Education, 1969; second prize for printmaking from Rochester Religious Art Festival, 1969; purchase prize for printmaking from Ninth Pacific Northwest Annual, 1969; first prize for painting from Oregon State Fair, 1970; purchase prize from Graphics 1971, 1971; purchase prize for painting from Coos Art Museum, 1972; grants from Carpenter Foundation, 1973, 1974, 1978, 1980, 1983, and 1984; grants from Collins Foundation, 1974 and 1976; grants from Southern Oregon State College, 1975-77, 1984, 1986, 1987, and 1992; grants from Oregon Committee for the Humanities, 1978-80 and 1982; grant from Oregon Art Commission, 1980; Faculty Award of Excellence from Southern Oregon State College, 1986; Governor's Award for the Arts from the State of Oregon, 1993.

WRITINGS:

Companeras: Women, Art, and Social Change in Latin America, City Lights, 1985.
Africa through the Eyes of Women Artists, Africa World Press, 1990.
Women Artists: Multi-cultural Visions, Red Sea Press, 1991.

WORK IN PROGRESS: An Artist's Journey from the Bronx to Timbuctu.

SIDELIGHTS: Betty LaDuke is a diverse artist who has distinguished herself in media ranging from printmaking to painting. Her work is largely inspired by her travels, as is evidenced by such one-person exhibitions as *Impressions of India, China: An Outsider's Inside View, Impressions of Latin America,* and *Africa: Between Myth and Reality.* In addition to producing art works, LaDuke has published the volumes *Companeras: Women, Art, and Social Change in Latin America* and *Africa through the Eyes of Women Artists.* For her work she has received numerous awards and honors, including the Governor's Award for the Arts from the State of Oregon in 1993.

Speaking about her art and about her exhibition entitled *Africa Between Myth and Reality,* LaDuke told *CA:* "After five intense visits I look back and realize that my African travels were also a personal spirit journey. Like a serpent shedding skin, I cast aside routine responsibilities to experience an extraordinarily different world view. Though it was only a brief period of sharing some of the intimacies of people's daily lives, customs, and traditions, I was left deeply touched in long-lasting ways. These feelings received visible expression in the paintings and prints later produced in my home studio. I refer to this series of images, created between 1986 and 1992, as *Africa: Between Myth and Reality.* They evolved in response not only to external stimuli but to inner-felt emotions."

BIOGRAPHICAL/CRITICAL SOURCES:

BOOKS

Foss, Karen, and Sonya Foss, *Women Speak: The Eloquence of Women's Lives,* Waveland Press, 1991.
Gadon, Elinor, *The Once and Future Goddess: A Symbol for Our Time,* Harper, 1989.
Orenstein, Gloria Feman, *The Reflowing of the Goddess,* Pergamon Press, 1990.
Orenstein, *Multi-Cultural Celebrations: Betty LaDuke Paintings, 1972-1992,* Pomegrante Publications, 1993.

*   *   *

LAKE, Timothy
See BATES, Tom

*   *   *

LAKOS, Amos 1946-

PERSONAL: Born July 31, 1946, in Arad, Romania. *Education:* Hebrew University of Jerusalem, B.A., 1972; University of British Columbia, M.L.S., 1977.

ADDRESSES: Office—Porter Library, University of Waterloo, Waterloo, Ontario, Canada N2L 3G1.

CAREER: University of Waterloo, Waterloo, Ontario, reference and collections development librarian, 1977—.

MEMBER: Association of Israel Studies.

WRITINGS:

International Terrorism: A Bibliography, Westview, 1986.
International Negotiations: A Bibliography, Westview, 1989.
Terrorism, 1980-1990: A Bibliography, Westview, 1991.

WORK IN PROGRESS: The Foreign Relations of Israel: A Bibliography, completion expected c. 1996.

SIDELIGHTS: Amos Lakos told *CA:* "I am a professional librarian. I am interested in providing better access to subject materials in my area, which happens to be political science and international relations. I believe that, as a librarian, I have a better understanding of what students need in a bibliography. The reviews of my bibliographies prove this. I am also interested in collection management and information management."

*   *   *

LAMONT, Michele   1957-

PERSONAL: Born December 15, 1957, in Toronto, Ontario, Canada; daughter of Jacques and Jeanine (Page) Lamont; married Frank Dobbin (a sociologist), 1987. *Education:* University of Ottawa, B.A. (general studies), 1977, B.A. (political science), 1978, M.A., 1979; Universite de Paris, D.E.A., 1979, Ph.D., 1983.

ADDRESSES: Home—7 Hart Ave., Hopewell, NJ 08525. *Office*—Department of Sociology, Princeton University, Princeton, NJ 08544-2180.

CAREER: Stanford University, Stanford, CA, postdoctoral research fellow in sociology, 1983-85; University of Texas at Austin, assistant professor of sociology, 1985-87; Princeton University, Princeton, NJ, assistant professor, 1987-92, associate professor of sociology, 1993—, fellow of Wilson College, 1987-89, faculty associate of Center for International Studies, Woodrow Wilson School of Public and International Affairs, 1990—, fellow of Rockefeller College, 1990—. Harvard University, visiting fellow, Center for European Studies, 1987; Ecole des Hautes Etudes en Sciences Sociales (Paris), visiting fellow, Group for Political and Moral Sociology, 1992; New York Public Library, scholar in residence, Schomburg Center for Research in Black Culture, 1992; New York University, visiting fellow, Institute of French Studies, 1993. Lecturer at Washington University, St. Louis, MO, Brooklyn College

of the City University of New York, Centre Culturel de Cerisy-LaSalle, Cornell University, Harvard University, and Sorbonne, University of Paris; guest on Canadian radio programs.

MEMBER: Association Internationale des Sociologues de Langue Francais, American Sociological Association (member of council of Culture Section, 1992-95), American Anthropological Association, Council for European Studies, Society for the Social Studies of Science, Society for the Study of Social Problems, Sociologists for Women in Society, Tocqueville Society.

AWARDS, HONORS: Fellow of French Ministry of Foreign Affairs, 1978-82; postdoctoral fellow, Government of Quebec, 1983-85; grants from Social Sciences and Humanities Research Council of Canada, 1984, 1985, French-American Commission of Exchange Universities, 1987, National Science Foundation and American Sociological Association, 1987, Andrew W. Mellon Foundation, 1988-89, Lilly Endowment, 1988-89, Boesky Family Fund, 1989, and Peter Lewis Fund, 1992; fellow of German Marshall Fund, 1992-93; grant from National Science Foundation, 1992-95.

WRITINGS:

(Editor with Marcel Fournier) *Cultivating Differences: Symbolic Boundaries and the Making of Inequality,* University of Chicago Press, 1992.
Money, Morals, and Manners: The Culture of the French and the American Upper-Middle Class, University of Chicago Press, 1992.

Work represented in anthologies, including *Comparative Social Research,* edited by Craig Calhoun, JAI Press, 1989; *Frontiers of Social Theory: The New Synthesis,* edited by George Ritzer, Columbia University Press, 1990; and *Between States and Markets: The Public Sphere in Advanced Industrial Societies,* edited by Robert Wuthnow, Princeton University Press, 1991. Contributor of articles and reviews to sociology journals. Co-editor of *Sociologie et Societes,* 1989. Associate editor, *Cambridge Cultural Social Studies;* member of editorial board, *Theory, Culture, and Society.*

WORK IN PROGRESS: Class, Race, and Boundaries in France and the United States; editing *Symbolic Boundaries and Principles of Legitimation in Comparative Perspective,* with Laurent Thevenot, completion expected in 1995; research on patterns of symbolic boundaries in the United States.

LAMPERT, Hope 1960-

PERSONAL: Born August 23, 1960, in Boston, MA; daughter of Nelson Robert (a surgeon) and Elisabeth (a teacher; maiden name, Ogden) Lampert. *Education:* Harvard University, A.B. (magna cum laude), 1981.

CAREER: Newsweek, New York City, business reporter, 1981-83; *Washingtonian,* Washington, DC, staff writer, 1983; free-lance writer.

WRITINGS:

NONFICTION

Till Death Do Us Part: Bendix versus Martin Marietta, Harcourt, 1983.
Behind Closed Doors: Wheeling and Dealing in the Bank World, Atheneum, 1986.
True Greed: What Really Happened in the Battle for RJR Nabisco, New American Library, 1990.

Contributor to periodicals, including *Manhattan, Inc.*

SIDELIGHTS: Hope Lampert has distinguished herself as a writer who has depicted some of the more sensational events in American business. Her first book, *Till Death Do Us Part: Bendix versus Martin Marietta,* details the drama that ensued when the Bendix Corporation's chair, William Agee, launched a miscalculated takeover of Martin Marietta, an aeronautics firm, in the early 1980s. The Marietta company, in turn, risked self-destruction in order to thwart Agee. As *New York Times* reviewer Christopher Lehmann-Haupt related, "Bendix tried to take over Martin Marietta without even the courtesy of a by-your-leave; Marietta retaliated by fusing a doomsday bomb that would blow up both companies if Bendix invaded."

Providing a backdrop to the ill-fated takeover, Lampert also examines the relationship between Agee and Mary Cunningham. Cunningham had worked at Bendix amid speculation that she and Agee were romantically involved. She left the company but reappeared a few years later as Agee's new wife and consultant in the takeover plans. Lampert relates Cunningham and Agee's appetite for power and money through the recollections of people close to the couple. Agee is portrayed as an error-prone executive who achieved his high status at Bendix through a series of happy accidents. Cunningham is less flatteringly described as a conniving and ruthless climber who often took credit for ideas that were not her own.

Upon publication in 1983, *Till Death Do Us Part* was accorded praise as a compelling and incisive depiction of corporate intrigue. Thomas W. Lippman, for instance, wrote in the *Washington Post Book World* that in the book Lampert "has done an outstanding job of reporting the inside details of this billion-dollar chess game." *Time* reviewer John S. DeMott affirmed that *Till Death Do Us Part* "is excellently reported and loaded with lively reconstructed dialogue," and Marjorie Lewellyn Marks remarked in the *Los Angeles Times Book Review* that Lampert "has superbly researched and reconstructed the context of a merger match play."

Lampert followed *Till Death Do Us Part* with *Behind Closed Doors: Wheeling and Dealing in the Banking World,* in which—as Michael M. Thomas observed in the *New York Times Book Review*—she relates "tales of high financial adventure." Included in the volume are accounts of bank sales and aggressive takeover ventures. Thomas, in his review of *Behind Closed Doors,* declared that "there is a lot of good stuff here."

In 1990 Lampert published *True Greed: What Really Happened in the Battle for RJR Nabisco.* Here she charts what Scot J. Paltrow, writing in the *Los Angeles Times Book Review,* described as "the protracted, vicious bidding war" that resulted in the leveraged buyout of RJR Nabisco by the Kohlberg, Kravis, Roberts investment firm, known as KKR. A leveraged buyout is a situation in which borrowed money and securities are used to purchase a controlling majority of a company. The buyout was precipitated by Nabisco president F. Ross Johnson's attempt, along with a group of investors, to buy up the company's stock shares and take Nabisco into private ownership. Johnson sought to do this without the services of the influential KKR firm. This slight so infuriated KKR executives that they undertook their own takeover of Nabisco. The entire affair was replete with escalating stock prices—Nabisco share prices ultimately surpassed one hundred dollars—and extraordinary business maneuverings. Johnson, for instance, even demanded—and was, on one account, accorded—authority to negate his own firing. "In retrospect," Paltrow reported, "it's clear that the RJR battle was a watershed in the history of deal madness: it was the beginning of the end." Nancy Goldstone wrote in the *Washington Post Book World* that *True Greed* provides "a crisp rendition [that] focuses on the mechanics of the deal."

BIOGRAPHICAL/CRITICAL SOURCES:

PERIODICALS

Los Angeles Times Book Review, August 28, 1983, p. 9; January 28, 1990, pp. 1, 13.
New York Review of Books, March 29, 1990, p. 3.
New York Times, July 5, 1983, p. 19.
New York Times Book Review, October 26, 1986, p. 28; January 21, 1990, p. 7.
Time, July 4, 1983, p. 44; February 19, 1990, p. 71.
Washington Post Book World, July 31, 1983, pp. 5, 14; January 14, 1990, p. 9.

LANCASTER, Roger N(elson) 1959-

PERSONAL: Born June 28, 1959, in La Grange, NC; son of Gene R. (a farmer and repair person) and Faith (a teacher and homemaker; maiden name, Lane) Lancaster. *Education:* University of North Carolina—Chapel Hill, B.A. (summa cum laude), 1982; University of California, Berkeley, M.A., 1983, Ph.D., 1987. *Politics:* Socialist. *Religion:* "I believe in humanity."

ADDRESSES: Home—New York, NY. *Office*—Department of Anthropology, Schermerhorn Hall No. 452, Columbia University, New York, NY 10027.

CAREER: Evergreen State College, Olympia, WA, faculty member, 1987-88; George Mason University, Fairfax, VA, assistant professor of anthropology, 1988-93; Columbia University, New York City, associate professor of anthropology, 1993—.

MEMBER: American Anthropological Association (fellow), American Ethnological Society, Latin American Studies Association, Democratic Socialists of America, Kroeber Anthropological Society.

AWARDS, HONORS: C. Wright Mills Award from Society for the Study of Social Problems, 1992, for *Life Is Hard.*

WRITINGS:

Thanks to God and the Revolution: Popular Religion and Class Consciousness in the New Nicaragua, Columbia University Press, 1988.
Life Is Hard: Machismo, Danger, and the Intimacy of Power in Nicaragua, University of California Press, 1992.

Contributor to periodicals, including *American Ethnologist, Christopher Street, Cultural Anthropology, Ethnology, Identities, People's Voice, Signs,* and *Social Science and Medicine Quarterly.* Book review editor of *Anthropological Quarterly,* 1992-93.

WORK IN PROGRESS: The Queer Body, a book on gay theory; editing *Sex, Politics, and Religion: Contingencies and Convergences in Late Twentieth Century Social Movements;* co-editing, with Nancy Scheper-Hughes, *Gender/Sexuality: An Interdisciplinary, Cross-Cultural Reader.*

SIDELIGHTS: Roger N. Lancaster is an esteemed anthropologist specializing in Latin American culture. He told *CA* that his first book, *Thanks to God and the Revolution: Popular Religion and Class Consciousness in the New Nicaragua,* "explores some of the enduring issues of social science theory by way of Nicaragua's experience with revolution and religion." Ilja A. Luciak, writing in the *American Political Science Review,* observed that *Thanks to God and the Revolution* "stands out as an eloquent and cogent analysis" and that it "makes a major contribution to the realignment of Marxist-Christian relations."

In Lancaster's next book, *Life Is Hard: Machismo, Danger, and the Intimacy of Power in Nicaragua,* he analyzes the effect of the Sandinistan revolution on the urban poor of Nicaragua. A *Times Literary Supplement* reviewer described *Life Is Hard* as both "a study of popular revolution" and "a modern work of ethnography," and Lancaster himself affirmed to *CA* that the book explores "the experiences that ultimately undermined the revolution." James Quesada noted in *Barricada Internacional* that *Life Is Hard* "should be taken to heart in enlarging our understanding of the daunting path revolutionary processes must inevitably tread." In 1992, *Life Is Hard* garnered the C. Wright Mills Award from the Society for the Study of Social Problems.

Lancaster told *CA:* "My writing is always at least partly autobiographical, in the sense that the problems I raise, the questions I set out to answer, emerge from my own experiences in the world. My work is also unapologetically partisan in that it begins from a contemplation of injustice, a feeling of empathy and identification with those who are unnecessarily suffering.

"Everything convinces me that we can no longer afford the dog-eat-dog reality of predatory capitalism. Even if capitalism can outrun the class and regional conflicts it creates, planet-wide environmental degradation is the logical terminus of this system. I do not pretend to hold out ready-made solutions. But the social movements of the coming century will be born in the concrete struggles of men and women around the world. Hopefully, the emerging movements will restore socialism to its original ideals: economic equality, participatory democracy, openness, and generosity."

BIOGRAPHICAL/CRITICAL SOURCES:

PERIODICALS

American Political Science Review, June, 1990, pp. 692-93.
Barricada Internacional, May, 1993.
Chronicle (San Francisco), February 28, 1993.
Journal for the Scientific Study of Religion, December, 1990, pp. 538-40.
Los Angeles Times, January 3, 1993.
Report on the Americas, February, 1993.
Times Literary Supplement (London), May 7, 1993.

*   *   *

LANDON, Margaret (Dorothea Mortenson) 1903-1993

OBITUARY NOTICE—See index for *CA* sketch: Born September 7, 1903, in Somers, WI; died of a stroke, December 4, 1993, in Alexandria, VA. Missionary and author. Landon's 1944 book, *Anna and the King of Siam*, inspired the popular Richard Rodgers and Oscar Hammerstein musical *The King and I*. In 1956 *The King and I* was filmed, starring Deborah Kerr as Welsh governess and teacher Anna Leonowens and Yul Brynner as the King of Siam, a role for which he received the Best Actor Academy Award. *Anna and the King of Siam* was sparked during Landon and her husband's missionary stay in Siam (now Thailand) in the 1920s and 1930s, during which time Landon served as a school principal. She also wrote the novel *Never Dies the Dream*.

OBITUARIES AND OTHER SOURCES:

BOOKS

American Women Writers: A Critical Reference Guide from Colonial Times to the Present, Volume 2, Ungar, 1980, pp. 496-497.

PERIODICALS

Chicago Tribune, December 6, 1993, section 1, p. 11; December 12, 1993, section 2, p. 10.
New York Times, December 6, 1993, p. D9.
Times (London), December 17, 1993, p. 23.
Washington Post, December 5, 1993, p. B5.

*   *   *

LANSBURY, Coral   1933-1991

PERSONAL: Born August 3, 1933, in Melbourne, Australia; immigrated to the United States, 1969; naturalized United States citizen, 1973; died of cancer, April 2, 1991, in Philadelphia, PA; daughter of Oscar (an actor) and May (a singer; maiden name, Morle) Lansbury; divorced; children: Malcolm Turnbull. *Education:* Attended University of Sydney; University of Auckland, M.A., 1967, Ph.D., 1969.

CAREER: University of Waikato, Waikato, New Zealand, senior lecturer in English, 1967-69; Rosemont College, Rosemont, PA, associate professor of English, 1970-73; Drew University, Madison, NJ, visiting professor of English and history, 1973-76; Rutgers University, Camden, NJ, professor, 1976-80, distinguished professor of English, 1980-91, dean of English graduate school, 1984-91; writer.

MEMBER: Modern Language Association (former president of Victorian executive committee), Northeast Modern Language Association, Victorian Studies Association (former president), Royal Australian Historical Society.

AWARDS, HONORS: Grant from American Council of Learned Societies, 1972-73; Guggenheim fellowship; National Endowment for the Humanities fellowship; Lindback Award.

WRITINGS:

Arcady in Australia, Melbourne University Press, 1971.
Elizabeth Gaskell: The Novel of Social Crisis, Elek, 1975.
The Reasonable Man: Trollope's Legal Fiction, Princeton University Press, 1981.
Elizabeth Gaskell, Twayne, 1984.
The Old Brown Dog: Women, Workers, and Vivisection in Edwardian England, University of Wisconsin Press, 1986.

Contributor to periodicals, including *Dickens Studies*, *Meanjin Quarterly*, and *Modern Language Studies*.

NOVELS

Ringarra, Harper, 1986.
Felicity, Dutton, 1987.
The Grotto, Knopf, 1989.
Sweet Alice, Dutton, 1989.

Also author of unreleased novel *Opium!*

OTHER

Also author of various screenplays and television scripts.

SIDELIGHTS: Coral Lansbury, in addition to writing the scripts for various films and television productions, has distinguished herself with both her literary criticism and her novels. Her initial publications were devoted to English literature. In 1975, for instance, she wrote *Elizabeth Gaskell: The Novel of Social Crisis*, in which she argues that Victorian novelist Gaskell is worthy of ranking among such revered English storytellers as Charles Dickens and George Eliot. And in 1981 Lansbury published *The Reasonable Man: Trollope's Legal Fiction*, where she analyzes Anthony Trollope's massive novels by relating their straightforward narrative form to Trollope's experience as a copier of legal documents. Andre Wright, in his *Times Literary Supplement* assessment of *The Reasonable Man*, deemed it "an original and welcome contribution to the understanding of Trollope," and he concluded that the book "takes its place among the works with which readers of Trollope will want to become acquainted."

In the mid-1980s Lansbury also began publishing novels. Her first tale, *Ringarra*, concerns an American Quaker who finds herself irresistibly drawn to a powerful sheep farmer in Australia. In the *New York Times Book Review*, Merle Rubin acknowledged that the novel is within the Gothic genre, and she deemed it "suspenseful, thoughtful, tightly controlled and deftly plotted." Lansbury followed *Ringarra* with *Felicity*, in which a slovenly art historian uncovers a smuggling operation and eventually lands in a Tunisian harem while trailing art treasures to Switzerland.

Chicago *Tribune Books* reviewer John Espey called *Felicity* "a splendidly funny farce," and *New York Times Book Review* critic Fay Weldon hailed the novel as "joyful" and noted, "The sheer delight, the animation and relish are infectious."

In 1989 Lansbury published *The Grotto,* which chronicles the exploits of Sicilian-born Australian Gwen Harcourt de Marineo during the first half of the twentieth century. Among Gwen's more harrowing experiences is her discovery, while pregnant, that her future spouse, a stranger whom she has nonetheless agreed to marry, has been killed. Don G. Campbell, writing in the *Los Angeles Times Book Review,* proclaimed *The Grotto* "thoroughly engrossing and entertaining." And John Mortimer wrote in the *New York Times Book Review* that Lansbury's novel features "excellent portraits" and is comprised of prose that is "constantly elegant."

Sweet Alice, Lansbury's other novel published in 1989, concerns an eccentric, middle-aged aristocrat who travels from her native England to Australia in hopes of acquiring a considerable inheritance. In his *New York Times Book Review* critique, Erich Segal described *Sweet Alice* as a "delightfully breezy novel" and "a lighthearted tale with a smile a minute."

BIOGRAPHICAL/CRITICAL SOURCES:

PERIODICALS

Los Angeles Times Book Review, March 19, 1989, p. 10.
New York Times Book Review, March 23, 1986, p. 25; November 8, 1987, p. 7; May 21, 1989, p. 15; November 12, 1989, p. 57.
Times Literary Supplement, November 14, 1975, p. 1352; March 19, 1982, p. 322.
Tribune Books (Chicago), September 27, 1987, p. 7; March 12, 1989, p. 5.*

*   *   *

LARSEN, Torben B. 1944-

PERSONAL: Born January 12, 1944, in Copenhagen, Denmark; son of Poul Frederik and Eva Larsen; partner of Nancy Fee. *Education:* University of Copenhagen, M.Sc., 1970, D.Sc., 1984.

ADDRESSES: Home—358 Coldharbour Lane, London SW9 8PL, England; and Jakobys alle 2, 1806 Frederiksberg, Denmark.

CAREER: International Planned Parenthood Federation, family planning specialist in Beirut, Lebanon, and London, England, 1970-84; Danish International Development Agency, New Delhi, India, family planning specialist, 1984-86; free-lance researcher and writer, 1986—. University of Florida, research associate; conducted entomological field studies in Nigeria, Spain, Morocco, Nigeria, Bulgaria, Jordan, Yemen, Papua New Guinea, India, Ecuador and the Galapagos Islands, Kenya, Botswana, and Ghana. *Military service:* Danish Army, Royal Danish Infantry, 1962-64; became lieutenant.

WRITINGS:

Butterflies of Lebanon, National Council for Scientific Research (Beirut), 1974.
(With K. Larsen) *The Butterflies of Oman,* Bartholomew (Edinburgh), 1980.
The Butterflies of Saudi Arabia and Its Neighbours, Stacey International (London), 1984.
The Butterflies of Egypt, Apollo Books (Svendborg), 1990.
The Butterflies of Kenya and Their Natural History, Oxford University Press, 1991.

Also author of *The Butterflies of Botswana and Their Natural History,* in press. Contributor of more than a hundred articles to scientific journals. Member of editorial advisory board, *Tropical Lepidoptera.*

WORK IN PROGRESS: Research for *Butterflies of West Africa: Origins, Natural History, Diversity, and Conservation.*

SIDELIGHTS: Torben B. Larsen told *CA:* "Since compulsory military service and teaching at the University of Copenhagen during my final student years, my career has been in development aid, especially family planning, health, and population, with an emphasis on evaluation. Since 1986 I have been working as a family planning evaluation consultant and free-lance photojournalist, in order to get the necessary time for entomological research.

"Since my childhood in India I have been deeply interested in butterflies, and most of my spare time has been devoted to entomological research throughout the world. This has resulted in several books and more than a hundred scientific articles, as well as a qualification from the University of Copenhagen as doctor of sciences, one of very few such degrees ever conferred on a non-biologist.

"My main interests are biodiversity, biogeography, ecology, and conservation of African butterflies and their use as indicator species in environmental impact assessment and for ecological monitoring. I am currently spending three months a year studying butterflies in the remaining rainforest in West Africa."

LEAN, Garth Dickinson   1912-1993
(Tenax)

OBITUARY NOTICE—See index for *CA* sketch: Born December 26, 1912, in Cardiff, Wales; died October 17, 1993, in Oxford, England. Journalist and author. While a student in Oxford, England, Lean became affiliated with the Oxford Group, later known as Moral Re-Armament (MRA), which espoused the belief that the way to bring about social change was religious experience that inspired personal change. He himself belonged to the Church of England, and in the 1940s and 1950s he worked to convert people in both England and North America. Lean contributed a political column to *Time and Tide* under the pseudonym Tenax from 1965 to 1975; his many books include religious volumes written with Arnold Henry Moore Lunn and several biographies, including *John Wesley, Anglican; God's Politician: William Wilberforce's Struggle;* and *Frank Buchman: A Life,* which is considered his finest work.

OBITUARIES AND OTHER SOURCES:

PERIODICALS

Times (London), November 2, 1993, p. 21.

*   *   *

Le DOEUFF, Michele   1948-

PERSONAL: Born April 16, 1948, in Motreff, Brittany, France; daughter of primary schoolteachers. *Education:* Attended Ecole Normale Superieure de Fontenay; Sorbonne, University of Paris, License, 1968, Agregation de philosophie, 1971, Ph.D., 1980; University of Nanterre, Habilitation, 1993. *Politics:* "Feminist." *Religion:* None.

ADDRESSES: Home—34 rue de Poitou, 75003 Paris, France; and 25 West St., Osney, Oxford OX2 0BQ, England.

CAREER: High school philosophy teacher, 1971-73; Ecole Normale Superieure de Fontenay, Fontenay, France, assistant professor, 1973-80, *maitre-assistante,* 1980-86; Centre National de la Recherche Scientifique, Paris, France, researcher, 1986-93. Speaker for French Planned Parenthood Movement.

MEMBER: O.I.R.A. (Oxford).

WRITINGS:

L'Imaginaire philosophique, Payot (Paris), 1980, translation published as *The Philosophical Imaginary,* Athlone, 1989, Stanford University Press, 1990.

(With Margaret Llasera) *Francis Bacon: La Nouvelle Atlantique,* Payot (Paris), 1983.

(Translator) *Shakespeare: Venus et Adonis,* Alidades (Paris), 1986.

L'Etude et le rouet: Des femmes, de la philosophie, etc., Editions du Seuil (Paris), 1989, translation published as *Hipparchia's Choice: An Essay Concerning Women, Philosophy, etc.,* Basil Blackwell, 1991.

Francis Bacon: Du Progres et de la promotion des savoirs, Gallimard (Paris), 1991.

Contributor of numerous articles to periodicals.

WORK IN PROGRESS: Translating Bacon's *New Atlantic,* for Flammarion; *Le Motif du bas-bleu* (tentative title; title means "The Bluestocking Motive"), a sequel to *Hipparchia's Choice.*

SIDELIGHTS: Michele Le Doeuff told *CA:* "Though not at the fore of the 1968 Parisian movement, I clearly belong to the 1968 generation. In 1971 I joined the then-budding feminist movement, and have been an activist for reproductive rights since then, with occasional work in support of battered wives or women raped by their fathers. My favorite avocational interest is to take the government to task about their policy concerning women, though I enjoy gardening as well. My one religious practice is to pick a bone with the Roman Catholic church about contraception.

"In 1986 I took a position as a researcher in philosophy at the Centre National de la Recherche Scientifique in Paris. Considered at that time as a specialist of Sir Francis Bacon, things went alright for me until I published *L'Etude et le rouet.* That book put an end to my career at the CNRS, despite the fact that I continued to publish on Bacon. The president of the Philosophy Committee wrote to me that they were reluctant to admit 'feminine works' (*'des travaux feminins'* which, if it means anything in French, could be a phrase referring to needlework)."

*   *   *

LEHMAN, Donna (Jean)   1940-

PERSONAL: Born February 14, 1940, in Berne, IN; daughter of Edison Kenneth (a farmer and carpenter) and Berniece Evangeline (a homemaker; maiden name, Liechty) Lehmann; married Michael Jon Lehman (a project engineer), October 4, 1959; children: Bruce, Pamela Lehman Migues, Carl. *Education:* International Business College, secretarial degree, 1959; attended Indiana University-Purdue University at Fort Wayne, 1973, 1984. *Politics:* Republican.

ADDRESSES: Home—Fort Wayne, IN. *Office*—c/o Herald Press, 616 Walnut Ave., Scottdale, PA 15683.

CAREER: Private secretary for a church of the First Assembly of God, Fort Wayne, IN, 1959-61; Fort Wayne

State Developmental Center, Fort Wayne, private secretary and office manager, 1961-65; Samaritan Pastoral Counseling Center, Fort Wayne, administrative assistant, 1984; free-lance writer. Fort Wayne State Developmental Center, member of Human Rights Committee, 1991—; Environmental Education Coalition, member of Northeast Indiana Speakers Bureau, 1991—; Fort Wayne Parkinsons Support Group, co-president, 1993.

MEMBER: Fort Wayne Christian Writers Group.

WRITINGS:

What on Earth Can You Do? Making Your Church a Creation Awareness Center, Herald Press, 1993.

Work represented in anthologies, including *Walking Together in Faith: A History of the Central District Conference, 1957-1900,* edited by Elaine Rich, Historical Committee of the Central District Conference, 1993; and *A History of the Maplewood Mennonite Church,* edited by David Habegger, in press. News editor for the feature "Women at Work," *Central District Reporter,* 1980-83. Contributor to periodicals, including *Women in Mission.*

SIDELIGHTS: Donna Lehman told *CA:* "I joined the Environmental Education Coalition after being diagnosed with Parkinsons Disease. Through the coalition's Speakers Bureau I have conducted workshops at churches, businesses, schools, and organizations on practical ways to improve the environment. My husband and I are now co-presidents of the Fort Wayne Parkinsons Support Group."

BIOGRAPHICAL/CRITICAL SOURCES:

PERIODICALS

The News-Sentinel (Fort Wayne), August 16, 1993, p. 1A.

* * *

LEVINE, Milton I(sra)   1902-1993

OBITUARY NOTICE—See index for *CA* sketch: Born August 15, 1902, in Syracuse, NY; died of heart failure, December 22, 1993, in New York, NY. Physician, educator, editor, and author. Levine was affiliated with the New York Hospital for more than forty years as a pediatrician and, at the same time, taught at the Cornell University Medical College, becoming professor emeritus in 1971. Levine commented daily on child care for the Columbia Broadcasting System (CBS) Radio Network from 1968 to 1979. In 1972, he founded and became editor of the periodical *Pediatric Annals.* Levine's books, many of which were written with his wife, Jean H. Seligmann, include *The Wonder of Life: How We Are Born and How We Grow Up, Helping Boys and Girls Understand Their Sex Roles,*

Your Overweight Child, and *The Parent's Encyclopedia of Infancy, Childhood, and Adolescence.*

OBITUARIES AND OTHER SOURCES:

PERIODICALS

New York Times, December 24, 1993, p. B7.

* * *

LEWIS, Naomi

PERSONAL: Born in Norfolk, England. *Education:* Attended a women's college in London, England.

ADDRESSES: Home—3 Halsey House, 13 Red Lion Square, London WC1 R4QF, England.

CAREER: Worked variously as a teacher in Switzerland and England and as an advertising copywriter; *New Statesman,* London, England, reviewer; British Broadcasting Corporation (BBC-Radio), England, broadcaster; writer, editor, and translator.

MEMBER: Royal Society of Literature (fellow).

WRITINGS:

A Visit to Mrs. Wilcox (essays), Cresset Press, 1957.
(Author of English text) *Leaves,* illustrated by Fulvio Testa, Andersen, 1980, Peter Bedrick, 1983.
Once upon a Rainbow, illustrated by Gabriele Eichenauer, Cape, 1981.
(With Tony Ross) *Hare and Badger Go to Town,* illustrations by Ross, Andersen, 1981.
Come with Us (poems), illustrations by Leo Lionni, Andersen, 1982.
(With Janice Thompson) *Marco Polo and Wellington: Search for Solomon,* Cape, 1982.
Puffin, illustrated by Deborah King, Lothrop, 1984.
Swan, illustrated by Deborah King, Lothrop, 1985.
A School Bewitched (based on Edith Nesbit's *Fortunatus Rex, or The Mystery of the Disappearing Schoolgirls*), illustrated by Errol Le Cain, Blackie, 1985.
(With James Kruess) *Johnny Longnose* (picture book with poetry), illustrated by Stasys Eidrigevicius, North-South, 1989.
The Mardi Gras Cat (poetry), Heinemann, 1993.

RETELLER

The Story of Aladdin, illustrated by Barry Wilkinson, H. Z. Walck, 1970.
The Three Golden Hairs: A Story from the Brothers Grimm, illustrated by Francoise Tresy, Hutchinson, 1983.
Wayne Anderson and Leonard Price, *A Mouse's Tale,* illustrated by Wayne Anderson, Cape, 1983, Harper, 1984.

Jutta Ash, *Jorinda and Joringel* (based on *Jorinde und Joringel* by the Brothers Grimm), Andersen Press, 1984.

Hans Christian Andersen, *The Flying Trunk and Other Stories from Hans Andersen,* Prentice-Hall, 1986.

The Stepsister, illustrated by Allison Reed, Dial Books, 1987.

Stories from the Arabian Nights, illustrated by Anton Pieck, Holt, 1987.

Cry Wolf and Other Aesop Fables, illustrated by Barry Castle, Oxford University Press, 1988.

ADAPTOR

Andersen, *The Snow Queen,* illustrated by Toma Bog-danovic, Scroll Press, 1968, new adapted version with illustrations by Le Cain, Viking, 1979, with an introduction by Lewis and illustrated by Andrea Barrett, Holt, 1988.

The Butterfly Collector, illustrated by Fulvio Testa, Prentice-Hall, 1979.

TRANSLATOR

(And author of notes and introduction) Andersen, *Hans Andersen's Fairy Tales,* illustrated by Philip Gough, Puffin, 1981.

Andersen, *The Wild Swans,* illustrated by Angela Barrett, Peter Bedrick, 1984.

Heide Helene Beisert, *My Magic Cloth: A Story for a Whole Week,* illustrated by Beisert, North-South, 1986.

Jutta Ash, *Wedding Birds* (adapted from a traditional German song), Andersen, 1986.

Andersen, *The Swineherd,* illustrated by Dorothee Duntze, North-South, 1987.

(And adaptor) *Proud Knight, Fair Lady: The Twelve Lais of Marie de France,* illustrated by Andrea Barrett, Viking, 1989.

Jacob Grimm, *The Frog Prince,* illustrated by Binette Schroeder, North-South, 1989.

Siegfried P. Rupprecht, *The Tale of the Vanishing Rainbow,* illustrated by Jozef Wilkon, North-South, 1989.

(And author of introduction) Andersen, *The Nightingale,* illustrated by Josef Palecek, North-South, 1990.

Kurt Baumann, *Three Kings,* illustrated by Ivan Gantschev, North-South, 1990.

Andersen, *Thumbelina,* North-South, 1990.

(And editor) Andersen, *The Steadfast Tin Soldier,* illustrated by P. J. Lynch, Harcourt, 1992.

(And adaptor) Kurt Baumann, *The Hungry One: A Poem,* illustrated by Stasys Eidrigevicius, North-South, 1993.

EDITOR

Christina Rossetti, *Christina Rossetti* (poems), E. Hulton, 1959.

The Best Children's Books of . . . , six annual volumes, Hamish Hamilton, 1964-69.

(And annotator and author of introduction) Emily Bronte, *A Peculiar Music: Poems for Young Readers,* Macmillan, 1971.

(And annotator) *Fantasy Books for Children,* National Book League, 1975, new edition, 1977.

Edith Nesbit, *Fairy Stories,* illustrated by Brian Robb, E. Benn, 1977.

(And author of introduction) *The Silent Playmate: A Collection of Doll Stories,* illustrated by Harold Jones, Gollancz, 1979, Macmillan, 1981, abridged edition published as *The Magic Doll: A Collection of Doll Stories,* Magnet, 1983.

A Footprint on the Air: An Anthology of Nature Verse, illustrated by Liz Graham-Yool, Hutchinson, 1983, published as *A Footprint in the Air: A Collection of Nature Verse,* Knight, 1984.

Messages: A Book of Poems, Faber & Faber, 1985.

Grimms' Fairy Tales, illustrated by Lidia Postma, Hutchinson, 1985.

Jacob Grimm, *The Twelve Dancing Princesses and Other Tales from Grimm,* illustrated by Postma, Dial Books, 1986.

William Shakespeare, *A Midsummer Night's Dream,* illustrated by Sylvie Monti, Hutchinson, 1988.

OTHER

Also author of the preface to *Twentieth-Century Children's Writers,* 3rd edition, St. James Press, 1989. Contributor to periodicals, including London *Observer, New Statesman, Listener, New York Times, Times Literary Supplement,* and *Times Educational Supplement.*

SIDELIGHTS: Naomi Lewis is a respected critic and anthologist who is also much-admired as a children's book author, poet, translator, and adaptor. Of her work as a commentator, anthologist and editor, a reviewer for *Junior Bookshelf* remarked: "What sets Naomi Lewis in a class apart from the general run of critics today is her breadth of sympathies and her ability to see the course of literature whole, so that each new book can be set into its proper slot in the grand structure." In addition, Lewis is the author of several original stories and collections of poetry, including *The Mardi Gras Cat.*

Lewis has received acclaim for the numerous books that she has edited, adapted, retold, and translated, scholarly work that she continues to perform on a regular basis. She came to prominence as a literary critic for the *New Statesman,* a eminent British periodical, and has also shared her knowledge on radio for the BBC. One of her first publications was the *Best Children's Books* series, a British annual bibliography. A review of the 1965 edition which appeared in the *Times Literary Supplement* found that Lewis "applies to children's books the standards of adult criticism that the best of them deserve."

She continues to uphold these standards in bringing the work of other writers to the attention of modern audiences; in editing, adapting, and translating these works she provides her readers not only with accessible versions, but critical essays that detail the background of each story. Reviewers have noted that Lewis's books, such as *A Peculiar Music, Proud Knight, Fair Lady,* and *Stories from the Arabian Nights,* have made these unique works available to young readers for the first time.

BIOGRAPHICAL/CRITICAL SOURCES:

PERIODICALS

Books for Keeps, November, 1990, pp. 14-15.
Bulletin of the Center for Children's Books, February, 1984.
Growing Point, January, 1980; November, 1985, p. 4538; January, 1989, pp. 5081-82.
Horn Book, February, 1982.
Junior Bookshelf, October, 1981, p. 199; August, 1982, pp. 133-34; February, 1986, pp. 35-36; June, 1989, pp. 132-33.
Kirkus Reviews, June 15, 1986, pp. 937-38; January 15, 1987, p. 136; August 1, 1987, pp. 1159-60; September 1, 1987, p. 1322.
Listener, December 30, 1971, p. 911; November 6, 1980.
Los Angeles Times Book Review, October 23, 1988.
New York Times Book Review, November 11, 1979, pp. 58, 64; July 9, 1989.
Observer (London), December 23, 1979, p. 36.
Publishers Weekly, April 10, 1972, p. 58; July 9, 1979, p. 106; August 13, 1979, p. 66; June 27, 1986, p. 86.
School Library Journal, January, 1980, p. 64; October, 1982, p. 142; May, 1987, p. 85.
Times Educational Supplement, November 20, 1981, p. 31; November 2, 1984, p. 26; June 7, 1985, p. 55; February 13, 1987, p. 48.
Times Literary Supplement, June 9, 1966, p. 519; July 2, 1970, p. 714; December 14, 1979; July 24, 1981, p. 841; November 9, 1984; November 29, 1985, p. 1361.

*   *   *

LEWIS, Robert W. 1930-

PERSONAL: Born December 15, 1930, in Elrama, PA; son of Robert W. (a railroad engineer) and Beryl (Dillon) Lewis; married Leila Jose, September 3, 1955 (marriage ended, September, 1978); children: Lisa Lewis Spicer,

Nina. *Education:* University of Pittsburgh, B.A., 1952; Columbia University, M.A., 1958; University of Illinois at Urbana-Champaign, Ph.D., 1963. *Politics:* Socialist. *Religion:* Roman Catholic. *Avocational Interests:* Canoeing, gardening.

ADDRESSES: Home—Turtle Oaks, Route 1, Box 111-D, Manvel, ND 58256-9732. *Office*—Department of English, University of North Dakota, Grand Forks, ND 58202-7209.

CAREER: University of Nebraska, Lincoln, instructor in English, 1955-58; University of Texas at Austin, assistant professor of English, 1963-69; University of North Dakota, Grand Forks, associate professor, 1969-71, professor, 1971-90, Chester Fritz Distinguished Professor of English, 1990—. Fulbright professor at University of Catania, in Italy, 1967-68, and Ain Shams University, in Egypt, 1975-76. North Dakota Humanities Council, chair, 1982-84; North Dakota Museum of Art, president of board of directors, 1990-92; Ernest Hemingway Foundation, member of board of directors. *Military service:* U.S. Army, 1952-80; became lieutenant colonel.

MEMBER: Modern Language Association of America, American Association of University Professors, Hemingway Society (president, 1987-92).

WRITINGS:

Hemingway on Love, University of Texas Press, 1965.
(Editor) *Hemingway in Italy and Other Essays,* Praeger, 1990.
A Farewell to Arms: The War of the Words, Twayne, 1992.

General editor of a series about the major books of Ernest Hemingway, for Southern Illinois University Press. Contributor to periodicals, including *Humanist.* Editor, *North Dakota Quarterly,* 1982—.

WORK IN PROGRESS: A family biography.

SIDELIGHTS: Robert W. Lewis told *CA:* "Ever since I was in elementary school, I was encouraged to write, and I liked to write. As a college senior, the first short story I sent out won a prize and was published. I was briefly deluded into thinking that writing was a snap. I became an English teacher to learn further about writing and to put bread on the table. Teaching never left much time for writing, but a day that goes by without even a little bit of writing, such as letters to friends and the keeping of a journal, is a half-lived day.

"I haven't written short stories in a number of years, but besides the critical writing that is my main occupation, I fancy myself as a poet and have had a few poems published. Editing the *North Dakota Quarterly* is like teaching: it keeps me close to writing, but is a drain on writing time. The combination of teaching, editing, and writing is, however, a fine life for me."

*   *   *

LILLY, Ray
See FISHER, David

*   *   *

LINDBERGH, Anne
See SAPIEYEVSKI, Anne Lindbergh

*   *   *

LINDISFARNE, Nancy   1944-
(Nancy Lindisfarne-Tapper, Nancy Tapper)

PERSONAL: Original name Nancy Starr Self; born October 10, 1944, in St. Louis, MO; naturalized British citizen, 1990. *Education:* Attended Grinnell College, 1964-66; Washington University, St. Louis, MO, B.A., 1966; London School of Oriental and African Studies, London, M.Phil., 1968, Ph.D., 1979.

ADDRESSES: Office—Department of Anthropology and Sociology, London School of Oriental and African Studies, University of London, Thornhaugh St., Russell Sq., London WC1H 0XG, England.

CAREER: Writer and educator.

WRITINGS:

(Under name Nancy Tapper) *Bartered Brides: Politics, Gender, and Marriage in an Afghan Tribal Society,* Cambridge University Press, 1991.
(Editor with Andrea Cornwall, and contributor) *Dislocating Masculinity: Comparative Ethnographies,* Routledge & Kegan Paul, 1993.

Work represented in anthologies, including (under name Nancy Tapper) *Central Asia: Tradition and Change,* edited by S. Akiner, Routledge & Kegan Paul, 1991; *The Future of Anthropology: Its Relevance to the Contemporary World,* edited by A. Ahmed and C. Shore, Athlone Press, 1993; and *Reassessing Anthropological Responsibility,* edited by V. Stolcke, Routledge & Kegan Paul, 1993. Contributor of more than forty articles to scholarly journals, from 1968-93 under the name Nancy Tapper, in 1991 under the name Nancy Lindisfarne-Tapper, and since 1993 under the name Nancy Lindisfarne.

LINDISFARNE-TAPPER, Nancy
See LINDISFARNE, Nancy

*   *   *

LINDSAY, Frederic   1933-

PERSONAL: Born August 12, 1933, in Glasgow, Scotland; son of Henry (a plumber) and Catherine (a teacher; maiden name, Kelly) Lindsay; married Shirley Russell (a teacher), January 5, 1957; children: Susan, Alison, Robert, Elspeth. *Education:* Glasgow University, M.A. (with first-class honors), 1960; attended Edinburgh University, 1966-67. *Politics:* Scottish National Party. *Religion:* Humanist. *Avocational Interests:* Reading, films, theatre, hill walking.

ADDRESSES: Home and office—2A Hopelands Rd., Silverburn, Penicuik EH26 9LH, Scotland. *Agent*—Curtis Brown, 162-168 Regent St., London W1R 5TB, England.

CAREER: Annan Academy, instructor in English, 1960-66; Hamilton College of Education, lecturer in English and applied linguistics, 1966-78; writer, 1979—.

MEMBER: International PEN Scottish Centre (vice-president), Society of Authors in Scotland (chair), Committee of Scottish Arts Council (member of literature committee).

AWARDS, HONORS: Scottish Arts Council literature awards for *Brond* and *A Charm Against Drowning.*

WRITINGS:

And Be the Nation Again (poems), Akros Publications, 1975.
Brond (novel), Macdonalds, 1984.
Jill Rips (novel), Deutsch, 1987.
A Charm Against Drowning (novel), Deutsch, 1988.
After the Stranger Came (novel), Deutsch, 1992.

Also author of radio plays for children, and of plays for Scottish Youth Theatre; author of several commissioned, but unproduced, film scripts. Adaptor of *Brond* into a three-part television work, 1987.

WORK IN PROGRESS: A novel, *In the Belly of the Whore,* to be published in 1995.

SIDELIGHTS: Frederic Lindsay told *CA* that he has enjoyed a "life-long involvement with Scottish culture and politics. For me the novel continues to be of all literary forms the most rewarding; financially, though, doing film scripts buys time to write books. Despite common sense and most of the evidence, I cling to the hope that there may actually be a posterity for which it's worth writing as well as one can."

Lindsay's first novel, *Brond,* drew praise from reviewers such as Gerald Mangan in the *Times Literary Supplement,* who admired the many levels of meaning in the narrative. "Lindsay's first novel opens and proceeds very much in the manner of a cryptic, fast-cutting thriller," Mangan wrote, but has an undercurrent of political allegory hidden within the suspense of the story. *Brond* is set in Glasgow and dramatizes the plight of a university student who witnesses a murder. The murderer, the student comes to realize, is Brond, a respected figure in the academic arena. The student faces danger, uncertainty, and fear as Brond sets out to destroy him as well. Mangan concluded his review by writing that "*Brond* largely transcends its local meanings, both as a Kafkaesque allegory and as a novel of initiation into adulthood." A *New Statesman* critic, Nick Kimberley, commenting on British crime novels, wrote that the Glasgow location in both *Brond* and *Jill Rips* "has much to offer in the way of tenebrous locations and shady ethics," and he noted the author's skillful use of "crime, character, language and location."

Lindsay's *Charm Against Drowning* is also set in Glasgow, and focuses on George Campbell, a teacher at a London training college. In the book, Campbell is faced with a number of problems, among them a mentally unstable wife and a heroin-addicted eighteen-year-old daughter, Chris. Hoping to rehabilitate Chris away from the influence of drug-pushers, Campbell kidnaps her and takes her to a remote ancestral island. However, with the arrival of Ramsay, a man who seems to have an evil hold on Chris, violence erupts and Campbell fears for his daughter's safety as well as for his own sanity. While some reviewers questioned Lindsay's use of violence in the story, London *Times* reviewer John Nicholson praised the work, declaring that *A Charm Against Drowning* "veers between realism and fairy-tale, [and] is a worthy successor" to Lindsay's previous books.

In his fourth novel, *After the Stranger Came,* Lindsay moves from the London underworld to academics in a Scottish university. Based on a 1930s true-life criminal hypnotist in Adolf Hitler's Germany, *After the Stranger Came* is occupied with the question of duality and with the fragility of personality. In the story, Lindsay returns to his distinctive concerns with extreme emotions and family relationships. Calling Lindsay an "established author of good psychological thrillers," London *Times* critic Stephen Hargrave deemed *After the Stranger Came* "well-paced and convincing."

BIOGRAPHICAL/CRITICAL SOURCES:

PERIODICALS

New Statesman, May 22, 1987, p. 31.
Publishers Weekly, May 12, 1989, p. 280.

Scotsman, June 20, 1992.
Scottish Literary Journal, winter, 1989.
Times (London), April 14, 1988; July 18, 1992, p. 43.
Times Literary Supplement, February 15, 1985, p. 179; May 20, 1988, p. 553.
Today, April 9, 1987.

*   *   *

LINDSAY, Loelia (Mary) 1902-1993

OBITUARY NOTICE—See index for *CA* sketch: Born February 6, 1902, in London, England; died November 1, 1993. Duchess and author. Lindsay's marriage to the second Duke of Westminster was one of the largest English social events of 1930. The marriage soured, however, and ended in divorce in 1947. Lindsay's 1961 book, *Grace and Favour: The Memoirs of Loelia, Duchess of Westminster,* examines her experiences during her marriage to the duke, a wealthy landlord. In addition to being an associate editor of *House and Garden,* Lindsay published the photograph collection *Cocktails and Laughter: The Albums of Loelia Lindsay.*

OBITUARIES AND OTHER SOURCES:

PERIODICALS

Times (London), November 4, 1993, p. 21.

*   *   *

LINDSTROM, Lamont (Carl) 1953-

PERSONAL: Born May 11, 1953, in Oakland, CA; son of Eddie Gustav (a research chemist) and Jean Ann (an investment consultant; maiden name, Hoffman) Lindstrom; married Cynthia Frazer (a librarian), June 19, 1976; children: Elsa Katiri, Carla Marie, Nora Rika. *Education:* Attended University of California, Santa Cruz, 1971-73; University of California, Berkeley, A.B., 1975, M.A., 1976, Ph.D., 1981.

ADDRESSES: Home—3752 West 111th St. S., Sapulpa, OK 74066. *Office*—Department of Anthropology, University of Tulsa, Tulsa, OK 74104.

CAREER: Australian National University, Canberra, visiting research scholar, Research School of Pacific Studies, 1977-79; Southwestern at Memphis, Memphis, TN, visiting assistant professor, 1981-82; University of Tulsa, Tulsa, OK, assistant professor, 1982-88, associate professor, 1988-92, professor of anthropology, 1992—, department chair, 1991—. East-West Center, fellow of Institute of Culture and Communication, 1987-88; National Endowment for the Humanities, seminar director, 1991 and 1993. Conducted anthropological field studies in Tanna,

Vanuatu, 1978-79 and 1982-83; in Australia, Papua New Guinea, Fiji, Vanuatu, and the Solomon Islands, 1985; in Guadalcanal, the Solomon Islands, and Tanna, 1987; Vanuatu, 1988; and Port Moresby, Papua New Guinea, 1988-89.

MEMBER: American Anthropological Association, Association for Social Anthropology in Oceania (member of board of directors, 1986-89; member of editorial board, 1988—), Royal Anthropological Institute, Pacific History Association, Pacific Arts Association, Polynesian Society, Japanese Society for Oceanic Studies, Vanuatu Natural Science Society, Phi Beta Kappa.

AWARDS, HONORS: Pacific fellow, English Speaking Union, 1978-79; Fulbright grant, 1979; fellow of National Endowment for the Humanities, 1984; grant from Wenner-Gren Foundation for Anthropological Research, 1988; Fulbright scholar in Vanuatu and Papua New Guinea, 1988; grant from National Endowment for the Humanities, 1990; Rockefeller Foundation fellow, Center for Pacific Island Studies, University of Hawaii at Manoa, 1990-91; Masayoshi Ohira Memorial Prize, 1992, for *The Pacific Theater.*

WRITINGS:

Kwamera Dictionary: Nikukua Savai Nagkiariien Nininife, Research School of Pacific Studies, Australian National University, 1986.

Drugs in Western Pacific Societies: Relations of Substance (monograph), University Press of America, 1987.

(Editor with G. M. White, and contributor) *The Pacific Theater: Island Recollections of World War II,* University Press of Hawaii, 1989.

(With G. M. White) *Island Encounters: Black and White Memories of the Pacific War,* Smithsonian Institution Press, 1990.

Knowledge and Power in a South Pacific Society, Smithsonian Institution Press, 1990.

(With V. Lebot and M. Merlin) *Kava: The Pacific Drug,* Yale University Press, 1992.

Cargo Cult: Strange Stories of Desire From Melanesia and Beyond, University of Hawaii Press, 1993.

Work represented in books, including *Disentangling: Conflict Discourse in Pacific Societies,* edited by K. Watson-Gegeo and G. White, Stanford University Press, 1990; *Rethinking Context: Language as an Interactive Phenomenon,* edited by C. Goodwin and A. Duranti, Cambridge University Press, 1992; and *Artistic Heritage in a Changing Pacific,* edited by P. Dark and R. Rose, Crawford House Press, 1993. Contributor of articles and reviews to anthropology journals.

WORK IN PROGRESS: Big Wok: Wol wo tu long vanuatu, an oral history of World War II in Vanuatu, to

be published in both English and Bislama (Vanuatu pidgin English); research on the anthropology of creativity.

SIDELIGHTS: Lamont Lindstrom told *CA:* "Humans are fascinating, although the human sciences can get tedious. I try to write anthropology so that it reads at least as interestingly and lively as the people I describe. Once in a while I succeed. Within academia, anthropology's knowledge of other cultures has often been kept out on the fringes of the curriculum. From within anthropology, my writing goes even further toward the edge: to faraway South Pacific peoples and their strange stories of cargo cult, powerful knowledge, inspirational drugs, and Pacific war memories. It is out there, on the edge, where we discover some of the most interesting news about ourselves."

*   *   *

LIPMAN, Eugene Jay   1919-1994

OBITUARY NOTICE—See index for *CA* sketch: Born October 13, 1919, in Pittsburgh, PA; died of brain cancer, January 14, 1994, in Bethesda, MD. Rabbi, educator, editor, and author. Lipman began his long affiliation as a rabbi with Temple Sinai in Washington, DC, in 1961; he became rabbi emeritus in the mid-1980s and served as the president of the Central Conference of American Rabbis from 1987 to 1989. Often involved in social and civil rights causes, Lipman was once president of the National Capital Area Chapter of the American Civil Liberties Union (ACLU). He taught religion at American University during the 1960s and theology at Catholic University of America in the late 1960s and 1970s. Lipman cowrote *Justice and Judaism: The Work of Social Action,* coedited *The American Synagogue: A Progress Report* and *A Tale of Ten Cities: The Triple Ghetto in American Religious Life,* and edited and translated *The Mishnah: Oral Teachings of Judaism.* He also wrote the 1988 book *Yamim Nora'im: Sinai Sermons.*

OBITUARIES AND OTHER SOURCES:

BOOKS

Who's Who in America, 48th edition, Marquis, 1994.

PERIODICALS

New York Times, January 15, 1994, p. 28.
Washington Post, January 15, 1994, p. B5.

*   *   *

LOCHRIDGE, Betsy Hopkins
   See FANCHER, Betsy

LONG, Frank Belknap   1903-1994
(Lyda Belknap Long)

OBITUARY NOTICE—See index for *CA* sketch: Born April 27, 1903, in New York, NY; died January 2, 1994, in Manhattan, NY. Editor and author. A prolific science fiction and fantasy writer whose early work was published in the pulp magazines *Weird Tales* and *Astounding Science Fiction,* Long was awarded the World Fantasy Convention's Life Achievement Award in 1978 and the Bram Stoker Life Achievement award in 1988. He was an associate editor for several magazines during the 1950s, including *Mike Shayne Mystery Magazine* and *Satellite Science Fiction.* Occasionally writing under the name Lyda Belknap Long, Long authored a number of novels, including *The Horror from the Hills* and *Rehearsal Night,* but was considered most successful with short stories, which have been published in collections such as *The Hounds of Tindalos; John Carstairs, Space Detective;* and *Night Fear.* His *Autobiographical Memoir* was published in 1985.

OBITUARIES AND OTHER SOURCES:

BOOKS

Twentieth-Century Science Fiction Writers, 3rd edition, St. James Press, 1991, pp. 499-501.

PERIODICALS

Chicago Tribune, January 9, 1994, p. 6.
New York Times, January 5, 1994, p. D21.

*   *   *

LONG, Lyda Belknap
See LONG, Frank Belknap

*   *   *

LORD DENNING
See DENNING, Alfred Thompson

*   *   *

LOVEJOY, Thomas E.   1941-

PERSONAL: Born August 22, 1941, in New York, NY; divorced; children: Elizabeth and Katherine (twins), Anne. *Education:* Yale University, B.S., 1962, Ph.D., 1971.

ADDRESSES: Office—Smithsonian Institution, Washington, DC 20560.

CAREER: Yale University, New Haven, CT, zoological assistant on prehistoric expedition to Nubia, 1963, zoolog-

ical assistant at Peabody Museum of Natural History, 1963, collected birds in Kenya for the museum, 1964; Smithsonian Institution, Washington, DC, research assistant on Belem Project, National Museum of Natural History, 1970; Academy of Natural Sciences of Philadelphia, Philadelphia, PA, executive assistant to the science director and assistant to the vice-president for resource and planning, 1972-73; World Wildlife Fund of the United States, program director, 1973-78, vice-president for science, 1978-85, executive vice-president, 1985-87; Smithsonian Institution, assistant secretary for environmental and external affairs, 1987—; U.S. Department of the Interior, science adviser, 1993.

Wildlife Preservation Trust International, member of board of directors, 1973—, chairperson of board, 1974-89, honorary chairperson, 1989—; Henry Foundation for Botanical Research, member of board of directors, 1975—; International Union for the Conservation of Nature and Natural Resources, member of Species Survival Commission, 1975—, member of Commission on Ecology, 1980—, chairperson of Tropical Forest Working Group, 1981-87; American Committee for International Conservation, director, 1975-78; International Council for Bird Preservation, member of Parrot Working Group, 1976—, and Tropical Forest Bird Working Group, 1981; International Crane Foundation, member of board of advisers, 1977—; Resources for the Future, member of Forestry Advisory Committee, 1979—, member of board of directors, 1989—; Charles A. Lindbergh Fund, chairperson of Conservation Committee, 1979-82; Jersey Wildlife Preservation Trust, member of council, 1981—; Rocky Mountain Biological Laboratory, member of board of trustees, 1983—; Horizon Communications, member of scientific review board, 1985—; Fundacion Peruana para la Conservacion de la Naturaleza, member of economic council, 1985-87, and scientific council, 1988—; New York Botanical Garden, member of board of governors, 1986—; Center for Plant Conservation, member of board of trustees, 1987—; United States Man and the Biosphere Program, chairperson, 1987-92; Rachel Carson Council, Inc., member of board of directors, 1987-92; Rainforest Alliance, member of board of directors, 1988—; Fundacion Maquipucuna, member of board of directors, 1988—; Peruvian Cultural Center, member of board of directors, 1989—; World Resources Institute, member of board of directors, 1989—; Earth Communications Office, chairperson of advisory board, 1989—; Parliamentarians Global Action for Disarmament, Development, and World Reform, member of Global Environment Advisory Group, 1989—; Woods Hole Research Center, member of board of directors, 1989—; National Institute for Global Environmental Change, member of national policy council, 1990—; Tropical Forest Foundation, chairperson, 1991—; Environmental Defense Fund, member of national council, 1991—; Greenwire, member of board of analysts, 1991—; Walter Orr Roberts Institute, member of steering committee, 1991—; National Environmental Education and Training Foundation, ex-officio member of board of trustees, 1991—; Rainforest Conservancy, member of advisory board of trustees, 1991—; Alley Foundation, member of board of directors, 1991—; State of Maryland, member of Historic St. Mary's City Commission, 1992—; Sustainable Biosphere Project, member of senior advisory board, 1993—; Rondon-Roosevelt Center, member of board of directors, 1993—; Institute of Ecosystem Studies, member of board of trustees, 1993—.

Executive Office of the President, member of U.S.-Brazil Panel on Science and Technology, 1986-87; member of White House Science Council, 1988-89; member of President's Council of Advisers for Science and Technology, 1990-93; National Research Council, member of Committee on Federal Acquisition of Lands for Conservation, 1990-93; United Nations Conference on Environment and Development, representative of U.S. delegation, 1992. WNET-TV, founder of the television series *Nature,* 1980, principal scientific adviser, 1980-87; *Discover,* judge of Environment Award, 1991—; *Conde Nast Traveler,* judge of annual environmental award, 1992—.

University of Pennsylvania, research associate in biology, 1971-74; University of Washington, Seattle, visiting lecturer at Center for Environmental Studies, 1981; University of California, Santa Barbara, Manley Lecturer, 1981; Woods Hole Marine Biological Laboratory, Charles A. Lindbergh Lecturer, 1981; Yale University, visiting lecturer, 1982; Claremont Colleges, David French Lecturer, 1983; Denison University, Ronneberg Lecturer, 1987; University of California, Davis, Storer Symposium Lecturer, 1990. Academy of Natural Sciences of Philadelphia, research associate in ornithology, 1971—, member of board of trustees, 1987-93; Smithsonian Institution, research associate of International Center for African, Near Eastern, and Asian Cultures, 1984-87.

Manhattan Life Corp., member of board of directors, 1976-86, chairperson of board, 1986, member of executive committee, 1979-86, chairperson of committee, 1982-87, director of Manhattan Life Insurance Co., 1974-75, 1987—.

MEMBER: International Society for Tropical Ecology, World Wildlife Fund (member of national council, 1989—), Nature Conservancy, American Association for the Advancement of Science (fellow), American Institute of Biological Sciences (president, 1991-92), American Ornithologists Union (fellow), American Society of Ichthyologists and Herpetologists, American Society of Mammalogists, American Society of Naturalists, American Society of Zoologists, Association of Field Ornithologists,

Association for Tropical Biology, Cooper Ornithological Society, Cornell Laboratory of Ornithology, Ecological Society of America, Institute of Ecology, National Academy of Sciences, National Wildflower Research Center, Society for Conservation Biology (past president), Society for the Study of Evolution, Society of Systematic Zoology, Wildlife Society, Council on Foreign Relations, Association of Systematics Collections, American Society for the Protection of Nature in Israel, Ozone Society (member of board of trustees, 1990—), Xerces Society, Royal Society for the Encouragement of Arts, Manufactures, and Commerce (fellow), British Ecological Society, British Ornithologists Union, British Ornithologists Club, Deutsche Ornithologen Gesellschaft, Fauna and Flora Preservation Society, Malayan Nature Society, Royal Australian Ornithologists Union, Royal Society for the Protection of Birds, Southern African Ornithological Society, Eastern Bird Banding Association, Northeastern Bird Banding Association, Rocky Mountain Biological Laboratory, Linnean Society of New York, New York Academy of Sciences, New York Zoological Society (scientific fellow), Zoological Society of Philadelphia, Linnean Society of London (fellow), Zoological Society of London, Century Association, Cosmos Club, Knickerbocker Club, Lawn Club (New Haven, CT).

AWARDS, HONORS: Rockefeller Foundation grant for Belem Virus Laboratory, Belem, Brazil, 1965; Ibero-American Award from Ibero-American Ornithological Congress, 1983; Certificate of Merit from Goeldi Museum Belem, 1985; commander, Order of Merit of Mato Grosso, 1987; Medal from Brazilian National Parks, 1987; commander, Order of Rio Branco, 1988; award for best social inventions from London's Institute for Social Inventions, 1988, for a proposed Debt-for-Nature Swaps program; D.Sc. from Colorado State University, 1989; Carr Medal from University of Florida, 1990; D.Sc. from Williams College, 1990; D.H.L. from Lynn University, 1991; Frances K. Hutchinson Medal from Garden Clubs of America, 1992; named to Global 500 Roll of Honor by United Nations Environment Program, 1992; Rainforest Champion Award from Rainforest Alliance, 1992; named honorary member of National Park Service of Costa Rica, 1993; grants from Man and the Biosphere Program, Andrew W. Mellon Foundation, Carnegie Foundation, Chapman Fund of the American Museum of Natural History, Conservation Foundation, U.S. Departments of Agriculture, State, and the Interior, Environmental Protection Agency, Explorers Club, U.S. Forest Service, Homeland Foundation, MacArthur Foundation, Marcia Brady Tucker Foundation, National Geographic Society, National Institute of Health, National Park Service, National Science Foundation, Packard Foundation, Pew Memorial Trusts, Sequoia Foundation, W. Alton Jones Foundation, and Weyerhaeuser Family Foundation.

WRITINGS:

(With J. H. Rappole, E. S. Morton, and J. Ruos) *Nearctic Avian Migrants in the Neotropics,* U.S. Government Printing Office, 1983.

(Editor with G. T. Prance, and contributor) *Key Environments: Amazonia,* Pergamon, 1985.

(Editor with A. W. Diamond) *Conservation of Tropical Forest Birds,* International Council for Bird Preservation, 1985.

(Editor with R. L. Peters, and contributor) *Global Warming and Biological Diversity,* Yale University Press, 1992.

Work represented in numerous books, including *Tropical Rainforests: Diversity and Conservation,* edited by F. Almeda and C. M. Pringle, California Academy of Sciences, 1988; *Four Neotropical Forests,* edited by A. H. Gentry, Yale University Press, 1990; and *The Earth as Transformed by Human Action,* edited by B. L. Turner II, W. C. Clark, R. W. Kates, and others, Cambridge University Press, 1990. Contributor of numerous articles and reviews to scientific journals, popular magazines, and newspapers, including *National Parks, Environmental Journal, Atlantic Naturalist, Earth Summit Preview, American Scientist,* and *Time.* Member of editorial board, *Zoo Biology,* 1982—.

WORK IN PROGRESS: Three books, including one on biotechnology and biological diversity.

SIDELIGHTS: Thomas E. Lovejoy told *CA:* "I am a tropical biologist and conservation biologist who has worked in the Amazon of Brazil since 1965. My doctoral thesis introduced the technique of banding to Brazil and identified patterns of community structure in the first major long-term study of birds in the Amazon. As the program director of the World Wildlife Fund of the United States, I was responsible for its scientific, western hemisphere, and tropical forest orientation. I have tried to bring the tropical forest problem to the fore as a public issue, and I am one of the main protagonists in the science and conservation of biological diversity.

"I also conceived of the Minimum Critical Size of Ecosystems project, a joint research project of the Smithsonian Institution and Brazil's National Institute for Amazon Research. This project, considered a centerpiece of the newly-emerging discipline of conservation biology, is essentially a giant experiment designed to define the minimum size for national parks and biological reserves, as well as management strategies for small areas.

"In the field of international conservation, I originated the concept of debt-for-nature swaps. Several such swaps of international debt for conservation projects have been initiated (including ones in Bolivia, Costa Rica, Ecuador, the Philippines, Madagascar, and Zambia), and others are being developed."

*   *   *

LUCAS, Eileen 1956-

PERSONAL: Born July 23, 1956, in Chicago, IL; daughter of Robert (a commercial artist) and Patricia (a homemaker; maiden name, Costello) O'Donnell; married Joseph Lucas (a shipping, receiving, and assembly manager), April 4, 1981; children: Travis, Brendan. *Education:* Attended School of Irish Studies (Dublin, Ireland), 1976; Western Illinois University, B.A. (with honors), 1977.

ADDRESSES: Home—167 Fontana Avenue, P.O. Box 89, Fontana, WI 53125.

CAREER: Writer of juvenile nonfiction books.

MEMBER: Society of Children's Book Writers and Illustrators, Council for Wisconsin Writers.

WRITINGS:

Vincent Van Gogh, F. Watts, 1991.
Peace on the Playground, F. Watts, 1991.
Acid Rain, Children's Press, 1991.
Water: A Resource in Crisis, Children's Press, 1991.
Jane Goodall, Millbrook Press, 1992.
The Cherokees, Millbrook Press, 1993.
The Mind at Work, Millbrook Press, 1993.
The Ojibwas, Millbrook Press, 1994.
American Conservationists, Naturalists and Environmentalists, Facts on File, 1994.
The Everglades, Steck Vaughn, 1994.

SIDELIGHTS: "I feel I am very lucky to have been able to make a career out of two of the things I really enjoy doing—reading and writing," Eileen Lucas commented. "I enjoy communicating about things I read and think about through the written word. I think that these are valuable skills for anyone, regardless of the career they choose.

"Being a mother is a very important part of who I am and it just feels right for me to write for and about kids," she noted. Lucas wrote *Vincent Van Gogh* in order to share with children the story of the artist's life—how he struggled to create beauty and how he remained true to himself despite many personal problems. She wrote *Peace on the Playground* so that children would know that there are other alternatives to problem solving besides using violence.

Lucas writes about subjects that concern her deeply, and tries to share her information with children at all different age levels. "As I read and I write I am learning all the time," acknowledged Lucas. "I learn about the subjects I am working on, and I learn about writing. I think learning is very exciting, and so I am always excited about what I do."

BIOGRAPHICAL/CRITICAL SOURCES:

PERIODICALS

Booklist, May 1, 1991, p. 1710; January 1, 1992, p. 827; March 1, 1992, p. 1269; May 1, 1992, p. 1596; May 15, 1992, pp. 1679-80.
Kirkus Review, October 1, 1991, p. 1289.
School Library Journal, July, 1991, p. 83; December, 1991, p. 112.

*   *   *

LUCAS, John A.   1927-

PERSONAL: Born December 25, 1927, in Boston, MA; son of Apostal (a candy maker) and Antigone (a homemaker; maiden name, Zhitomy) Lucas; married Joyce Vaughan (a librarian), July 31, 1955; children: Mark Langley. *Education:* Boston University, B.S., 1950; University of Southern California, M.A., 1952; Pennsylvania State University, M.A., 1954; University of Maryland at College Park, Ph.D., 1961. *Politics:* Republican. *Religion:* Christian Scientist. *Avocational Interests:* Jogging.

ADDRESSES: Home—618 South Fraser St., State College, PA 16801.

CAREER: Track and field coach at high schools, preparatory schools, and universities, 1949-72; Pennsylvania State University, University Park, senior research and teaching professor of sport history, 1961-93. International Olympic Committee, member of various sub-committees and official Olympic lecturer. *Military service:* U.S. Army, 1945-47; served in Japan and Korea.

WRITINGS:

(With Ronald Smith) *Saga of American Sports,* Lea & Febiger, 1977.
The Modern Olympic Games, A. S. Barnes, 1980.
Future of the Olympic Games, Human Kinetics, 1992.

Contributor of more than two hundred articles to journals in the United States and abroad.

WORK IN PROGRESS: A History of the United States Olympic Committee (USOC), 1896-1994.

SIDELIGHTS: John A. Lucas told *CA:* "I was born in Boston to very, very poor, immigrant parents who had come to America from Albania before World War I. They had four sons, all of them nurtured in a loving and disciplined household and stimulated by a powerful work

ethic. Although our parents were unlettered, they never knew the formal definition of that phrase. All of us graduated from Boston's best academic high schools, but only I went to college; the other three had to go to work during the late 1930s. I was a student-athlete of better-than-average abilities through the 1940s and 1950s, almost making the United States Olympic team in 1952. I coached high school, preparatory school, and university track teams before turning wholly in the direction of teaching and research."

*   *   *

LUKE, Mary
See LUKE, Mary M(unger)

*   *   *

LUKE, Mary M(unger)   1919-1993
(Mary Luke)

OBITUARY NOTICE—See index for *CA* sketch: Born March 24, 1919, in Pittsfield, MA; died after a brief illness, November 24, 1993, in New Haven, CT. Historian and writer. Luke was perhaps best noted for her biographies of Tudor royalty, including 1967's *Catherine, the Queen,* which looks at Catherine of Aragon's ill-fated marriage to King Henry VIII of England, *A Crown for Elizabeth,* published in 1970, which followed Queen Elizabeth I's long reign, and *The Nine Days Queen: A Portrait of Lady Jane Grey,* a 1986 publication focusing on Grey's brief hold on the throne of England. Luke was also the author of *The Ivy Crown: A Biographical Novel of Queen Katherine Paar,* and she sometimes wrote under a shorter form of her name. Before writing books, she had worked in the advertising industry and, during World War II, for a documentary film company and RKO Pictures.

OBITUARIES AND OTHER SOURCES:

PERIODICALS

New York Times, November 25, 1993, p. D19.

*   *   *

LYONS, Louis   1937-

PERSONAL: Born November 25, 1937, in London, England; son of Israel (a chemist) and Ann (Rashbass) Lyons; married Batya Meller, November 17, 1963 (died, 1991); children: Dalia, Simona. *Education:* Cambridge University, B.A. (with first class honors), 1958; Oxford University, D.Phil., 1962. *Religion:* Jewish.

ADDRESSES: Home—Jesus College, Oxford University, Oxford OX1 3BW, England. *Office*—Nuclear Physics

Laboratory, Oxford University, Keble Rd., Oxford, England.

CAREER: Oxford University, Oxford, England, tutor and fellow of Jesus College, 1969—, university lecturer in nuclear physics, 1970—, vice-principal of Jesus College, 1992—. Royal Society visiting professor, 1987-89.

WRITINGS:

Statistics for Nuclear and Particle Physicists, Cambridge University Press, 1986.

A Practical Guide to Data Analysis for Physical Science Students, Cambridge University Press, 1991.

Contributor to scientific journals.

WORK IN PROGRESS: A mathematics book for first-year science students, two volumes, for Cambridge University Press; experimental studies of elementary particles, using the LEP storage rings at CERN in Geneva.

M

MACCOBY, Hyam 1924-

PERSONAL: Born March 20, 1924, in Sunderland, England; son of Ephraim Meyer (a teacher) and Fanny (a homemaker; maiden name, Rabinowitz) Maccoby; married Cynthia Davies (a teacher), June 14, 1950; children: David, Deborah, Melanie. *Education:* Balliol College, Oxford University, B.A., 1951, M.A., 1952. *Religion:* Jewish.

ADDRESSES: Home—Surrey, England. *Office*—Leo Baeck College, 80 East End Rd., London N3 2SY, England. *Agent*—A. P. Watt, 26 Bedford Row, London WC1, England.

CAREER: Worked as a teacher in various schools, 1952-75; Leo Baeck College, London, England, lecturer and librarian, 1975—. Imperial College, London University, London, lecturer, 1976-78. *Military service:* Royal Signals, 1943-46; signalman; received Long Service and Good Conduct Medals.

MEMBER: British Association for Jewish Studies, European Association for Jewish Studies, Society for Jewish Study.

AWARDS, HONORS: Balliol College, Oxford University, schoolmaster fellowship, 1973-74; *Jewish Quarterly/ Wingate Literary Prize* for nonfiction, 1993, for *Judas Iscariot and the Myth of Jewish Evil;* emeritus fellowship and honorary doctorate, both from Leo Baeck College, both 1994.

WRITINGS:

Revolution in Judaea: Jesus and the Jewish Resistance, Orbach and Chambers, 1973, Taplinger, 1980.
(With Wolf Mankowitz) *The Day God Laughed: Sayings, Fables, and Entertainments of the Jewish Sages,* Robson, 1978.

(Editor) *Judaism on Trial: Jewish-Christian Disputations in the Middle Ages,* Associated University Presses, 1982.
The Sacred Executioner: Human Sacrifice and the Legacy of Guilt, Thames & Hudson, 1982.
The Disputation (teleplay), Channel Four (England), 1986.
The Mythmaker: Paul and the Invention of Christianity, Harper, 1986.
(Editor) *Early Rabbinic Writings* (anthology), Cambridge University Press, 1988.
Judaism in the First Century, Sheldon Press, 1989.
Paul and Hellenism, SCM, 1991.
Judas Iscariot and the Myth of Jewish Evil, Peter Halban, 1992.

Contributor to numerous magazines and journals, including *Encounter, Listener, Times Literary Supplement, Commentary, New Testament Studies,* and *New Society.* Associate editor of *The Jewish Quarterly* and assistant editor of *European Judaism.*

SIDELIGHTS: Hyam Maccoby, a lecturer and librarian at London's Leo Baeck College, is chiefly interested in the history of Jewish-Christian relations, especially the origin, development, and cure for anti-Semitism. He examines these issues from theological, historical, psychological, and anthropological angles, with the distinct advantage of being able to study the Bible, the Talmud, and related historical documents in their original languages.

His first book, *Revolution in Judaea,* is a study of the life of Jesus from the standpoint of a Talmudic scholar. Maccoby concludes that Jesus was a Pharisee, that he was identical to his fellow Roman prisoner Barbabbas, that his enemies were the Romans, not the Jews, and that the Gospels depoliticized him and whitewashed the Romans, putting the blame for Jesus's death on the Jews. The book caused great controversy, giving rise to extended correspondence in the *Times Literary Supplement.* Some reviewers were not kind: Julian N. Hartt in the *New York Times Book Review* called the book a "resounding failure," and a *Times Literary Supplement* reviewer concluded, "Without the support of historical, cultural and religious expertise, Mr. Maccoby's imagination tends to run out of control." *Revolution in Judaea* did garner some critical support, however. *Times Literary Supplement* contributor A. J. Ayers recommended the book, stating that "it convincingly represents Jesus as a leader of the Jewish resistance." Writing in the *Spectator,* Alan Brien opined that *Revolution in Judaea* "casts a light on the events" of history and religion. Brien also stated that Maccoby's writing displays convincing arguments and information "which no author writing on the subject has . . . been able to match."

Maccoby's next two books are collections. *The Day God Laughed* is an anthology from the Talmud, showing its humor, love of life, and humanism. In *Judaism on Trial,* the author examines the "Disputations" between the Jews and Christians in the Middle Ages, translating and editing the most important documents in those debates and explaining their historical and theological background. In *The Sacred Executioner,* Maccoby returns to authorship to explore the anthropological and psychological background of anti-Semitism. He argues that it stems from ancient rites of human sacrifice, where the sacrificer was cursed and driven from the community, which then washed its hands of guilt for the sacrifice, even though the sacrifice was regarded as necessary for the community's salvation. Contending that the Christian myth is mainly responsible for anti-Semitism by casting the Jews in the role of Christ killers, a variation of the ancient "Sacred Executions" motif, the book again aroused controversy. J. Duncan M. Derrett in the *Times Literary Supplement* dismissed *The Sacred Executioner* as a "pastiche" in which "the august discipline of history is prostituted." In the *New York Times Book Review,* however, Norman K. Gottwald concluded that the book "can challenge us to a fundamental rethinking of the inhumanity at the heart of our inherited religions." And John Gross wrote in the *Observer* that *The Sacred Executioner* "is a rich, closely packed book, with many fascinating insights."

With *The Mythmaker,* Maccoby turned his attention to the origins of Christianity. His thesis is that Paul, not Christ, was the real founder of Christianity, and that Paul distorted the career of Jesus—in Maccoby's view, a Jewish, anti-Roman revolutionary—into a "salvation-cult" modeled on Gnostic mystery-religions that were deeply anti-Semitic. *The Mythmaker* was yet another lightning rod for criticism; in the *New York Times Book Review,* J. Louis Martyn questioned the entire foundation of evi-

dence on which the book rested, and J. L. Houlden in the *Times Literary Supplement* faulted it for "obscurities" and "highly selective" use of evidence.

Two of Maccoby's more recent books are essentially continuations of his earlier work. *Paul and Hellenism* is a study of central Pauline doctrines, again arguing that their roots lie not in Judaism but in the mythology of Gnosticism, which Paul uses to initiate the anti-Semitism later developed in the form of deicide in the Gospels. *Judas Iscariot and the Myth of Jewish Evil* applies the central thesis of *The Sacred Executioner* to the story of Judas, concluding that Judas was an "invention," an "arch-traitor" created in the Gospels to encapsulate "Jewish treachery"; hence, a source of anti-Semitism. Reviewers continued to show reluctance to accept Maccoby's views. In the *Times Literary Supplement,* John M. G. Barclay takes the author to task for "oversimplifications" and an unjustified "animosity towards Paul" in *Paul and Hellenism*; and while a *Times* reviewer found Maccoby's thesis in *Judas Iscariot* "attractive," the critic professed "astonishment" at some of the author's conclusions and finds "serious difficulties" with some of the inconsistencies those conclusions create.

Writing about his work, Maccoby told *CA:* "I consider it is my life work to combat anti-Semitism by revealing its origins in religious paranoia and thus help towards the development of a healthier form of religion, in which the Jewish-Christian conflict will be resolved."

BIOGRAPHICAL/CRITICAL SOURCES:

PERIODICALS

Expository Times, October, 1991.
Jewish Journal of Sociology, December, 1983.
Journal of Jewish Studies, summer, 1993.
Listener, August 10, 1978.
New York Times Book Review, January 18, 1981, pp. 10-11; December 18, 1983, p. 7; July 20, 1986, p. 8.
Observer, November 14, 1982.
Spectator, December 20, 1986, p. 58.
Sunday Telegraph, December 28, 1986.
Sunday Times, December 5, 1982; March 8, 1992.
Times (London), February 13, 1992, Life & Times section, p. 5.
Times Literary Supplement, March 8, 1974; May 3, 1974, p. 481; April 1, 1983, p. 330; March 28, 1986, p. 336; May 8, 1992, p. 26.

*   *   *

MACINTYRE, Ben   1963-

PERSONAL: Born in 1963.

CAREER: Journalist and author. Worked as foreign affairs reporter for England's *Sunday Correspondent* and New York bureau chief of London *Times.*

WRITINGS:

Forgotten Fatherland: The Search for Elisabeth Nietzsche, Farrar, Straus, 1992.

Contributor to periodicals, including the *New York Times Book Review.*

SIDELIGHTS: Journalist Ben Macintyre's first book, *Forgotten Fatherland: The Search for Elisabeth Nietzsche,* details the life of German philosopher Friedrich Nietzsche's sister Elisabeth and the ways in which she affected the life and writings of her brother. As Macintyre explains in the book, Elisabeth not only destroyed Nietzsche's relationship with Lou Andreas Salome, a woman he proposed marriage to, but she herself married a rabid anti-Semite, Bernhard Forster. The Forsters traveled to Paraguay in 1886 to form an idealistic, "pure" Aryan community, but when it failed and Forster committed suicide, Elisabeth returned to Germany to take care of her brother, who by that time was seriously mentally ill.

Macintyre notes in *Forgotten Fatherland* that though Friedrich Nietzsche had already published several works of philosophy, he was not yet famous. Under Elisabeth's care—and with her revising his works so that they appeared to embrace fascism and anti-Semitism when originally they did not—Nietzsche's prestige began to increase. After his death, but still within the lifetime and influence of Elisabeth, his philosophy was adopted and used by Adolf Hitler and the Nazi regime. Indeed, when Elisabeth died at the age of eighty-nine in 1935, Hitler gave her a state funeral and wept over her casket. As Macintyre told Jon Elsen in the *New York Times Book Review,* Elisabeth "did a brilliant job of making [Nietzsche] famous and at the same time making him infamous. She overlaid him with her own views—but she did it in a very stylish way."

In addition to relating these events in *Forgotten Fatherland,* Macintyre also tells of his own journey to the remains of the Paraguayan colony that Elisabeth and her husband founded. There, Simon Collier reported in the *New York Times Book Review,* "a handful of descendants of the original families still survived, still scraped a modest living from the poor soil, still spoke German with a thick Saxon accent and still preserved a residual notion of Aryan supremacy." They also displayed the effects of severe inbreeding. George Steiner, reviewing *Forgotten Fatherland* in the *New Yorker,* praised Macintyre for linking these two aspects of Elisabeth Nietzsche's story together, calling it "a sparkling idea" that "yields vivid travel writing and information of a ghostly but fascinating sort."

BIOGRAPHICAL/CRITICAL SOURCES:

PERIODICALS

Los Angeles Times, September 24, 1992, p. E2.
New Republic, November 9, 1992, p. 50.
New Yorker, October 19, 1992, pp. 122-26.
New York Times Book Review, October 4, 1992, p. 9.
Times (London), April 9, 1992, p. 4.
Washington Post Book World, September 27, 1992, p. 5.*

*   *   *

MACK, Beverly (B.) 1952-

PERSONAL: Born February 27, 1952, in Hartford, CT. *Education:* University of Connecticut, B.A., 1973; University of Wisconsin—Madison, M.A., 1978, Ph.D., 1981.

ADDRESSES: Office—Department of African and African-American Studies, 104 Lippincott Hall, University of Kansas, Lawrence, KS 66045-2107.

CAREER: Conducted field work in Kano, Nigeria, 1979-80; Bayero University, Kano, tutor in African drama and English composition, 1980, lecturer in African oral and written literature and African-American literature, 1982-83; Georgetown University, Washington, DC, adjunct assistant professor of African history, 1984-85; Yale University, New Haven, CT, assistant professor of Hausa language and African literature, 1986-87; George Mason University, Fairfax, VA, adjunct assistant professor, 1987-88, visiting assistant professor of English, 1988-93; University of Kansas, Lawrence, assistant professor of African and African-American studies, 1993—. Nigeria-U.S. Business Council, program assistant, 1984; South East Consortium for International Development, project assistant at Center for Women in Development, 1984-86; American Medical Students Association, language instructor, 1989; consultant to U.S. Agency for International Development, Center for Applied Linguistics, and the film series *National Geographic Explorer.*

AWARDS, HONORS: Fulbright grants for Nigeria, 1979-80, 1989; Woodrow Wilson grant, 1980-81; grants from National Endowment for the Humanities, 1985, 1992, and Ford Foundation (for Nigeria), 1987.

WRITINGS:

(Editor and annotator) Hauwa Gwaram and Hajiya 'Yar Shehu, *'Alk'alami a Hannun Mata'* (title means "A Pen in the Hands of Women"), Northern Nigerian Publishing, 1983.
(Editor with Catherine M. Coles, and contributor) *Hausa Women in the Twentieth Century,* University of Wisconsin Press, 1991.

Work represented in anthologies, including *The Human Commodity: Perspectives on the Trans-Saharan Slave Trade,* Frank Cass, 1992; *African Encounters With Domesticity,* edited by Karen Tranberg Hansen, Rutgers University Press, 1992; and *Queens, Queen Mothers, Priestesses, and Power: Case Studies in African Gender,* edited by Flora Kaplan, Southern Illinois University Press, 1993. Contributor of articles and reviews to magazines and newspapers.

WORK IN PROGRESS: Nana Asma'u's Collected Works in Translation, with Jean Boyd; *The Popular Song: Hausa Women's Poetic Voice.*

*   *   *

MADONNA 1958-

PERSONAL: Born Madonna Louise Veronica Ciccone, August 16, 1958, in Bay City, MI; daughter of Silvio (an engineer) and Madonna Ciccone; married Sean Penn (an actor), August 16, 1985 (divorced, 1989). *Education:* Attended University of Michigan, 1976-78.

ADDRESSES: Office—c/o Sire Records, 75 Rockefeller Plaza, New York, NY 10019. *Agent*—Creative Artists Agency, 9830 Wilshire Blvd., Beverly Hills, CA 90212.

CAREER: Singer, actress, dancer, and musician. Worked as an artist's model in New York City, c. late 1970s; Alvin Ailey Dance Theater, New York City, dancer, c. late-1970s; backup singer and drummer for the band Breakfast Club, 1980; backup singer and dancer for disco singer Patrick Hernandez in Paris, France, 1980-81; singer in New York-based bands the Millionaires, Modern Dance, and Emmy, 1981-83; solo performer 1983—; songwriter and recording artist on solo albums, including *Madonna,* 1983, *Like a Virgin,* 1984, *True Blue,* 1986, *Like a Prayer,* 1989, *I'm Breathless,* 1990, and *Erotica,* 1992; actress in feature films, including *Vision Quest,* 1985, *Desperately Seeking Susan,* 1985, *Dick Tracy,* 1989, and *Truth or Dare,* 1991; also served as executive producer of *Truth or Dare.* Appeared on Broadway in the role of Karen in *Speed-the-Plow,* 1988.

AWARDS, HONORS: Grammy Award nomination for best female pop performance, National Academy of Recording Arts and Sciences, 1986, for "Crazy for You," from the soundtrack to the movie *Vision Quest.*

WRITINGS:

Sex, photographed by Steven Meisel and edited by Glenn O'Brien, Warner Books, 1992.

Also writer or co-writer of numerous songs.

SIDELIGHTS: World-renowned pop star Madonna has established herself as one of the most pervasive, influen-

tial, and written-about performers of the 1980s and 1990s. The singer, songwriter, and actor has released numerous best-selling albums, appeared in feature films, and is reported to be one of the wealthiest women in contemporary show business. She is the head of her own production company that firmly retains control over everything released under her name, and she boasts a sixty million dollar contractual agreement with the media conglomerate Time/Warner, Inc. Her many public incarnations include new-wave temptress, Marilyn Monroe clone, dancing Barbie in a bullet bra, and androgynous diva. Legions of fans both young and old across the world contribute to her success and have catapulted her to the status of one of the era's most assailed and coveted women.

Many aspects of Madonna's personal life have been thoroughly chronicled in the media, including a failed marriage to actor Sean Penn, a romance with actor Warren Beatty, and friendships with other women such as comedian Sandra Bernhard. Even minor circumstances of her upbringing in suburban Detroit, Michigan, have been subject to speculation. Raised in a large Italian-Catholic family, she suffered the loss of her mother to cancer when she was two, and her father eventually remarried their housekeeper. Madonna studied dance at the University of Michigan, but left after two years and moved to New York City. After dancing professionally for a time, she began singing in dance-music bands in the early 1980s. At this time the disco era was fading out and giving rise to a fresh hybrid somewhere between the slick synthesized sound of disco and an edgier new-wave sensibility. The fledgling performer not only caught on to this new trend, but soon appeared at the forefront of it. Her first album, entitled *Madonna,* was released in 1983. The work, like her later albums, contained material she had written herself and sold millions of copies. During the next few years Madonna reached international pop-diva stardom as her albums went platinum, world tours sold out, and legions of young female fans copied her look. She has appeared in numerous films and in 1991 served as executive producer of *Truth or Dare,* a documentary movie that chronicles one of Madonna's concert tours.

Late 1992 saw the multimedia appearance of a variety of consumer goods from Madonna, hyped for months prior and timed for release as the Christmas season loomed. The package included her new album *Erotica,* along with a racy extended video, but the showpiece of the ensemble was a coffee-table-type book of photographs and text entitled *Sex.* The visuals were shot by fashion photographer Steven Meisel and interspersed with Madonna's commentary as edited by journalist Glenn O'Brien. *Sex's* heavy price tag of fifty dollars and its secretive Mylar-wrapped packaging attracted media attention upon its release, as did the book's controversial contents.

Sex depicts the star engaged in various acts of a sexual nature, most of which might be considered aberrant behavior by middle America. None of the photographs depict actual sexual acts, but rather meaning-laden images related to various forms of sexuality. The photos, which often feature other celebrities such as actor Isabella Rossellini and rap singer Vanilla Ice, continue the eroticism that Madonna has been known for candidly exploring in her videos—mild sadomasochistic acts, bisexuality, and multiple partners. Text written by Madonna is woven into the photographic tenor of the work, taking the form of observations on power and sexual games played between partners, impassioned letters to anonymous lovers, and the musings of an alter ego, a dominatrix by the name of Dita.

Sex received an extraordinary amount of media attention upon publication, as representatives from all segments of society voiced their opinions of the book. Critical reaction was mixed. Caryn James of the *New York Times Book Review* criticized the "chintzy look" of the tinted photographs, adding that "only a few bold images are characteristic of . . . Meisel's best work." James faulted the volume as "less the display of an erotic imagination than a cliched catalogue of what the middle class—her target audience, after all—is supposed to consider shocking." JoAnn Wypijewski, on the other hand, took a more approving stance regarding the book. Writing in the *Nation,* Wypijewski termed some of the images in the book "irresistibly exhilarating," and mused that those who try to pigeonhole both Madonna and the various facets of human sexuality manifested in the book are wrong in their attitudes. Wypijewski addressed critics of *Sex* in hypothesizing that "what disturbs is the suggestion that [sexual preferences] might not stay neatly in their boxes, that sexuality might be something that is not always fixed and whose expression might ring with contradictions."

BIOGRAPHICAL/CRITICAL SOURCES:

BOOKS

Contemporary Musicians, Volume 4, Gale, 1991.

PERIODICALS

Nation, December 14, 1992, pp. 744-748.
New York Times Book Review, October 25, 1992, p. 7.
Rolling Stone, December 10, 1992.*

*   *   *

MAGNER, Lois N.   1943-

PERSONAL: Born June 8, 1943, in Brooklyn, NY; daughter of Max (an accountant) and Ethel (a teacher; maiden name, Schachner) Magner; married Ki-Han Kim (a biochemist), September 14, 1972; children: Oliver J. *Educa-*

tion: Brooklyn College of the City University of New York, B.S., 1963; University of Wisconsin—Madison, Ph.D., 1968. *Politics:* Democrat. *Religion:* Jewish. *Avocational Interests:* Reading, gardening.

ADDRESSES: Home—3804 Capilano Dr. W., West Lafayette, IN 47906. *Office*—Department of History, University Hall, Purdue University, West Lafayette, IN 47906-1358.

CAREER: Purdue University, West Lafayette, IN, postdoctoral research associate in biochemistry, 1968-72, assistant professor, 1973-78, associate professor, 1978-93, professor of history, 1993—, assistant dean of School of Humanities, Social Science, and Education, 1979-80, director of Women's Resource Office, 1985-87.

MEMBER: International Association for the Study of Traditional Asian Medicine, American Historical Association, American Association for the History of Medicine, History of Science Society, Association for Asian Studies, Sigma Xi.

AWARDS, HONORS: Fellow of National Institutes of Health, 1968-70 and 1973; grants from Indiana Committee for the Humanities, 1979, and National Library of Medicine, 1984-86.

WRITINGS:

A History of the Life Sciences, Dekker, 1979, 2nd edition, 1993.
A History of Medicine, Dekker, 1992.

Work represented in books, including *Critical Essays on Charlotte Perkins Gilman,* edited by Joanne Karpinski, G. K. Hall, 1992; *The History and Geography of Human Disease,* edited by Kenneth F. Kiple, Cambridge University Press, 1992; and *Leaders of the World,* edited by Deborah Klezzmer, Gale, 1994. Contributor of articles and reviews to scientific and history journals.

WORK IN PROGRESS: A History of Korean Medicine: Comparative Aspects of the History of Medicine in Korea, China, and Japan, based in part on the author's translation of Kim Tu-jong's *History of Korean Medicine,* completion expected in 1995; *The Feminist Response to Darwinism,* "an analysis of the writings of Charlotte Perkins Gilman, Antoinette Brown Blackwell, Elizabeth Cady Stanton, Eliza Burt Gamble, and the response to the work of Charles Darwin, Herbert Spencer, and other founders of modern evolutionary theory—part of a larger study of the question of the use and abuse of scientific theories"; a history of food and nutrition in Korea, to be included in a book.

MALTESE, John Anthony 1960-

PERSONAL: Born August 19, 1960, in Point Pleasant, NJ; son of John (a professor of music) and Eva May (Campbell) Maltese. *Education:* Duke University, B.A. (magna cum laude), 1982; Johns Hopkins University, M.A., 1986, Ph.D., 1988. *Religion:* Presbyterian. *Avocational Interests:* Promoting the arts; collecting historic autographs, historic recordings, and films of classical musicians.

ADDRESSES: Home—136 Jolly Lane, Athens, GA 30606. *Office*—Department of Political Science, Baldwin Hall, University of Georgia, Athens, GA 30602.

CAREER: Duke University, Durham, NC, instructor in political science, 1982; Johns Hopkins University, Baltimore, MD, instructor in political science, 1987; University of Georgia, Athens, assistant professor of political science, 1989—. Guest on radio and television programs.

MEMBER: American Political Science Association, American Judicature Society, Southern Political Science Association.

AWARDS, HONORS: Herbert Hoover presidential research grant, Herbert Hoover Library, 1990-91; Frank Luther Mott-Kappa Tau Alpha National Research Award, 1992, for *Spin Control.*

WRITINGS:

(Editor and contributor) *The Accompanist: An Autobiography of Andre Benoist,* Paganiniana Publications, 1978.
Spin Control: The White House Office of Communications and the Management of Presidential News, University of North Carolina Press, 1992, revised edition, 1994.
(With Charles C. Euchner) *Selecting the President,* Congressional Quarterly Press, 1992.

Work represented in anthologies, including *The Congressional Quarterly Guide to the Presidency,* Congressional Quarterly Press, 1989; *The Oxford Companion to the Supreme Court,* Oxford University Press, 1992; and *The Encyclopedia of the American Presidency,* Simon & Schuster, 1993. Contributor of articles and reviews to political science and music journals.

WORK IN PROGRESS: The Selling of Supreme Court Nominees: Politics and the Senate Confirmation Process, for Johns Hopkins University Press; *The Constitutional Presidency,* with Michael Nelson, Macmillan.

SIDELIGHTS: John Anthony Maltese told *CA:* "One of my hobbies is the preservation of historic recordings and films of classical musicians in performance. My father and I have amassed one of the largest private collections in the world of published and unpublished violin recordings dating back to the 1890s. Rare performances from our collection have been used for historic reissues by record companies throughout the world."

*   *   *

MANN, Jack 1917(?)-
(Jackie Mann)

PERSONAL: Born c. 1917, in England; married; wife's name, Sunnie (an equestrian instructor; died November 30, 1992).

ADDRESSES: Home—High Cyprus Bldg., Nicosia, Cyprus.

CAREER: Middle East Airlines, Lebanon, pilot. Owner of Pickwick Bar, Beirut, Lebanon, until 1989. *Military service:* Royal Air Force (England) fighter pilot in World War II.

WRITINGS:

UNDER NAME JACKIE MANN

(With wife, Sunnie Mann, and Tess Stimson) *Yours Till the End: Two Survivors of the Hostage Crisis—Their Amazing Story* (autobiography), Heinemann, 1992.

SIDELIGHTS: In 1989, Jackie Mann was living with his wife, Sunnie, in Beirut, Lebanon, a city that he remembered as elegant and sophisticated, a resort and commercial center where a former Royal Air Force fighter pilot and Middle East Airlines pilot could enjoy a comfortable retirement running a British pub for his fellow expatriates. As Beirut degenerated into chaos and civil war in the 1980s, the British Embassy repeatedly, and without success, urged the Manns to leave. The couple, however, was convinced that none of the religious factions that fought for control of the city would have any interest in a husband and wife in their mid-seventies. But on May 12, 1989, they learned that they were wrong. Jackie was coming out of a bank in West Beirut when he was seized by a band of gunmen. At first he thought he was being robbed, but it soon became apparent that he was one more in a long series of Western hostages used as political pawns by Islamic extremists. His abductors demanded the release of "comrades" being held in London for the 1987 slaying of a Palestinian cartoonist, Ali Naji al-Adhami, although Scotland Yard insisted that no one was being held for that crime. Mann was finally released on September 24, 1991, apparently in response to Israel's release of Shiite Muslim prisoners and the return of the bodies of several Lebanese guerrillas.

Yours Till the End: Two Survivors of the Hostage Crisis—Their Amazing Story is Mann's account of his twenty-eight-month ordeal. Written with Sunnie, who stayed in Lebanon after the kidnapping and who describes in the book her efforts to win her husband's release, *Yours Till the End* is a story of survival. Jackie details his isolation as he was held blindfolded and in chains in a series of hideouts, sleeping on dirty mattresses, and enduring beatings and sexual advances at the hands of inept captors who wanted only to be rid of him. Despite his age and the torture he endured, Mann returned to a hero's welcome in relatively good condition.

Yours Till the End met with a mixed reception. Although a *Publishers Weekly* reviewer praised the book for recreating the drama of the ordeal in "homely detail," other reviewers were more critical. Writing in the *Los Angeles Times*, Carolyn See was troubled by the Manns' "ignorance" of the extent of the trouble in the Middle East, and what she perceived as their couldn't-care-less attitude about the historical events unfolding around them. Richard Owen, in the London *Times*, lamented that the book neglected in-depth "reflections on the spirit of man in confinement," but nevertheless recommended that people "should at least read Jackie's side of the story and consider how they would cope with being chained up in a series of small rooms on dirty mattresses for two and a half years."

BIOGRAPHICAL/CRITICAL SOURCES:

PERIODICALS

Los Angeles Times, February 1, 1993, p. E6.
Publishers Weekly, November 9, 1992, p. 68.
Times (London), April 25, 1992.
Times Literary Supplement, June 29-July 5, 1990, p. 687.*

*   *   *

MANN, Jackie
See MANN, Jack

*   *   *

MANN, Paul (James) 1947-

PERSONAL: Born January 16, 1947, in Northumberland, England; son of James William (a police officer) and Patience Hales (a nurse at a residential psychiatric facility; maiden name, Jones) Mann; married Nancy Gwenith (a teacher), August 18, 1979; children: Jessica, Alexandra, Sarah. *Education:* Attended high school in Northumberland. *Politics:* "Progressively incorrect." *Religion:* None. *Avocational Interests:* Scuba diving, kayaking, canoeing, desert trekking, cross-country skiing, wilderness hiking.

ADDRESSES: Office—P.O. Box 171, Cape Neddick, ME 03402. *Agent*—Arnold Goodman, Goodman Associates, 500 West End Ave., New York, NY 10024.

CAREER: Free-lance journalist, 1963-87; novelist, 1987—.

MEMBER: American Authors Guild, Australian Society of Authors.

WRITINGS:

The Libyan Contract, Pinnacle Books, 1988.
The Beirut Contract, Pan Macmillan, 1989.
The Traitor's Contract, Knightsbridge, 1990.
The Britannia Contract, Carroll & Graf, 1993.
Season of the Monsoon, Fawcett Columbine, 1993.

Contributor to magazines and newspapers.

WORK IN PROGRESS: The Ganja Coast; a sequel to *Season of the Monsoon;* another volume in the "Sansi" series.

SIDELIGHTS: Paul Mann told *CA:* "I grew up in the northeast of England, with a father who was a working class Tory and a police officer, and a mother who was a manic-depressive alcoholic and a nurse in a lunatic asylum. An acute sense of the absurd was therefore inevitable. I was a highly itinerant newspaper and magazine journalist from 1963 to 1987. I wrote my first novel, a thriller, by the self-imposed deadline of age forty (and wrote it in six weeks to make the date) because I thought writing thrillers was easy. It is. *The Britannia Contract* is probably my best, and probably my last.

"*Season of the Monsoon* marks a determined attempt to move into upmarket genre fiction and seems to have been successful; I have contracted to write three more novels like it. The challenge will be to maintain quality and avoid stereotyping. My life of itinerancy has left me virtually stateless, which can be an asset because it spares me any excess of nationalism, though it also undermines any sense of regional perspective. I have lived in Britain, the United States, Australia, and Canada, and intend returning to the United States permanently in 1994, where the robust publishing industry seems happy to impose an identity on me."

*   *   *

MANN, Sunnie 1914(?)-1992

PERSONAL: Born c. 1914, in England; died of lung cancer, November 30, 1992, in Nicosia, Cyprus; married Jackie Mann (a retired airplane pilot).

CAREER: Equestrian instructor in Beirut, Lebanon, until 1989.

WRITINGS:

Holding On (autobiography), Bloomsbury, 1990.
(With husband, Jackie Mann, and Tess Stimson) *Yours Till the End: Two Survivors of the Hostage Crisis—*

Their Amazing Story (autobiography), Heinemann, 1992.

Also author of numerous articles.

SIDELIGHTS: In May, 1989, Sunnie Mann was living with her husband, Jack Mann, in West Beirut, Lebanon. "Jackie" had been a World War II Spitfire pilot and later a trainer pilot for a commercial Lebanese airline. When Jackie retired, the couple decided to remain in Lebanon, where they had lived since 1946. They failed to recognize, however, that the sophisticated port city that they called home was rapidly disintegrating into civil war as Christian and fundamentalist Muslim factions fought for control of Lebanon. The couple, British by birth, ignored repeated efforts by the British Embassy to persuade them to leave. The kidnappings of Westerners during the 1980s were highly publicized, but the Manns were convinced that no one would be interested in them because, at seventy-five, they felt they were too old. Jackie ran a pub and Sunnie taught at an equestrian center, and both seemed to remain oblivious to the political chaos surrounding them.

On May 12, 1989, Jackie was seized in broad daylight by Muslim extremists, beginning a two-and-a-half-year captivity. Sunnie remained in Lebanon, trying, alongside other hostages' wives, to win her husband's release by keeping pressure on the news media. She tells the story of her efforts in two accounts. The first, *Holding On,* was written while Jackie was still a captive; later, after his release, the couple published *Yours Till the End: Two Survivors of the Hostage Crisis—Their Amazing Story,* which records (with the help of ghost writer Tess Stimson) their separate experiences during the ordeal. Once her husband was imprisoned, Sunnie relates how she coped alone with the recurrent bombings of the city and the resultant lack of food, water, and electricity, and her frustration over the fruitless attempts to persuade the British Embassy to help find her husband. She recounts her dismay over the abduction of her adored pet poodle, the brutal killing of the horses at her equestrian center, and conflicting reports about whether her husband was dead or alive. David P. Snider in *Library Journal* averred that *Holding On* "poignantly captures the spirit of all those left behind in hostage situations."

Critical reaction to the books was mixed. Carolyn See in the *Los Angeles Times* faulted *Yours Till the End* for reflecting the Manns' indifferent, "studied imperviousness" to the sweep of historical events that was going on around them. However, Richard Owen in the London *Times,* while lamenting that the book lacked an analysis of events surrounding the kidnapping, nonetheless commended the narrative for its "overall effect . . . one of a gentle chat, sitting with them on their veranda in Nicosia, with occasional explanatory passages in between, in women's maga-

zine style." Roger Owen in the *Times Literary Supplement* praised *Holding On* for its "forthright and colourful" style. And a reviewer for *Publishers Weekly* concluded that the "homely detail" of *Yours Till the End* is effective in conveying the writers' "mutual devotion and staunchness of spirit."

BIOGRAPHICAL/CRITICAL SOURCES:

PERIODICALS

Library Journal, March 15, 1991, p. 102.
Los Angeles Times, February 1, 1993, p. E6.
Publishers Weekly, November 9, 1992, p. 68.
Times (London), April 25, 1992.
Times Literary Supplement, June 29-July 5, 1990, p. 687.

OBITUARIES:

PERIODICALS

Los Angeles Times, December 3, 1992, p. A42.*

*   *   *

MANTON, Kenneth G.   1947-

PERSONAL: Born August 11, 1947, in Toronto, Ontario, Canada. *Education:* Princeton University, B.A. (cum laude), 1969; Duke University, M.A., 1971, Ph.D., 1974.

ADDRESSES: Office—Center for Demographic Studies, Duke University, 2117 Campus Dr., Box 90408, Durham, NC 27708-0408.

CAREER: Duke University, Durham, NC, postdoctoral fellow of Center for Demographic Studies, 1974-77, research associate, 1977-82, assistant director of the center, 1977-78, acting director, 1978-79, assistant director, 1979—, lecturer at the university, 1978-79, adjunct assistant professor, 1978-82, associate research professor and adjunct associate professor, 1982-85, research professor of demographic studies, 1985—, assistant medical research professor at Medical Center, 1978-82, 1986—, senior fellow of Center for the Study of Aging and Human Development, 1980—, head of World Health Organization Collaborating Center for Research and Training in the Methods of Assessing Risk and Forecasting Health Status Trends as Related to Multiple Disease Outcomes, 1986-94. Consultant to National Academy of Sciences, International Institute for Applied Systems Analysis, and Systems Science, Inc.

MEMBER: International Epidemiological Association, International Union for the Scientific Study of Population, American Statistical Association, Population Association of America, Human Biology Council, Southern Demographic Association.

AWARDS, HONORS: Fellow of Sandoz Foundation, 1982-83; Mindel C. Sheps Award in Mathematical Demography and Demographic Methodology from Population Association of America, 1990; Allied-Signal Inc. Achievement Award in Aging from Johns Hopkins Center on Aging, 1991; grants from National Institute on Aging, Health Care Financing Administration, U.S. Environmental Protection Agency, National Institutes of Health, National Institute of Mental Health, National Institute of Child Health and Human Development, U.S. Congressional Office of Technology Assessment, U.S. Centers for Disease Control, Library of Congress Congressional Research Service, World Health Organization, Elfride Draeger Foundation, National Cancer Institute, Social Security Administration, National Institute of Justice, LaJolla Management Corp., United Nations Children's Fund, U.S. Senate Special Committee on Aging, Commonwealth Fund, National Center for Health Statistics, U.S. General Accounting Office, Veterans Administration, Sloan Foundation, Travelers Foundation, Hospital Corp. of America, Health Insurance Corp. of America, World Bank, Marriott Corp., National Science Foundation, Urban Institute, U.S. Department of Agriculture, SOLON Consulting Group, American Association of Retired Persons, U.S. Bureau of the Census, Commonwealth of Pennsylvania, Mathematical Policy Research, Inc., and Parke-Davis Pharmaceutical Research.

WRITINGS:

(With Eric Stallard) *Recent Trends in Mortality Analysis,* Academic Press (Orlando, FL), 1984.

(With Wilson B. Riggan and others) *U.S. Cancer Mortality Rates and Trends, 1950-1979,* Volume IV: *Maps* and *Cartographic Presentation,* U.S. Government Printing Office, 1987.

(With Stallard) *Chronic Disease Risk Modelling: Measurement and Evaluation of the Risks of Chronic Disease Processes,* Charles Griffin, 1988.

(Editor with Richard Suzman and David Willis, and contributor) *The Oldest-Old,* Oxford University Press, 1992.

(Editor with Burton H. Singer and Richard Suzman, and contributor) *Forecasting the Health of Elderly Populations,* Springer-Verlag, 1993.

(With Max A. Woodbury and H. Dennis Tolley) *Statistical Applications Using Fuzzy Sets,* Wiley, 1993.

(With Eric Stallard) *Asbestos-Related Diseases and Exposures,* Springer-Verlag, in press.

Work represented in anthologies, including *Models of Noncommunicable Diseases: Health Status and Health Service Requirements,* edited by W. Morgenstern, E. Cigan, R. Prokhorskas, and others, Springer-Verlag, 1992; *The Epidemiological Transition: Policy and Planning Implications for Developing Countries,* edited by J. N. Gribble and S. H. Preston, National Academy Press, 1993; and *Studies of the Economics of Aging,* edited by D. Wise, University of Chicago Press, 1994. Contributor of over three hundred articles and reviews to professional journals. Associate editor, *Journal of the American Statistical Association,* 1985-89; member of editorial board, *Journal of Gerontology: Social Sciences.*

WORK IN PROGRESS: Research on demography, metropolitan structure and suburbanization, biomathematical models of human mortality and morbidity, and multivariate statistical methodology; research on urban sociology, methodology, statistics, human ecology, and population epidemiology.

SIDELIGHTS: Kenneth G. Manton told *CA:* "My current research interests include forecasting the morbidity, disability, and mortality among the nation's elderly, reimbursement and maintenance of quality of care for both acute and long-term care services consumed by the elderly, mathematical modeling of physiological aging processes of human mortality at advanced ages, and differentials in those processes by gender and race, as well as cross-nationally."

*   *   *

MARBACH, Ethel
See POCHOCKI, Ethel Frances

*   *   *

MARCINKO, Richard   1940-

PERSONAL: Born November 21, 1940, in Lansford, PA; son of George L. (a coal miner) and Emilie T. (Pavlik) Marcinko; married Kathy Black, 1962 (marriage ended, 1985); married Nancy Alexander, September 4, 1993; children: (first marriage) Kathy, Richie; (stepdaughters from second marriage) Brandy, Tiffany.

ADDRESSES: Home—Alexandria, VA. *Office*—c/o Witherspoon Associates, Inc., 157 West 57th St., Suite 700, New York, NY 10019.

CAREER: U.S. Navy, 1958-89; became commander; served in Sea, Air, Land unit (SEALS) in Vietnam, 1966-68; naval attache in Cambodia, 1973; president of Special Operational Security (SOS) Temps, Inc.; conductor of motivational and team-building seminars for corporations through Richard Marcinko, Inc.

WRITINGS:

(With John Weisman) *Rogue Warrior* (autobiography), Pocket Books, 1992.

WORK IN PROGRESS: Rogue Warrior II; Red Cell, publication expected in 1994; *Rogue Warrior III;* contracted to write *Rogue Warrior IV* and *Rogue Warrior V.*

SIDELIGHTS: Richard Marcinko is coauthor of *Rogue Warrior,* an account of his often harrowing experiences during his thirty-year career in the U.S. Navy. *Rogue Warrior,* written with John Weisman, provides a particularly grueling depiction of life in the Navy's Sea, Air, and Land unit (SEALS), in which Marcinko served as a commander. In the mid-1960s he fought in Vietnam, and in the 1970s and 1980s he served in SEALS counter-terrorist operations. "I'm good at war," Marcinko confided to *People* in 1992. "My philosophy is, kill them before they kill us." In the same *People* profile he complained about the managerial function of many career officers and declared, "Even in Vietnam, the system kept me from hunting and killing as many of the enemy as I would have liked." David Murray, assessing *Rogue Warrior* in the *New York Times Book Review,* proclaimed Marcinko's story "fascinating," and Robert Lipsyte, writing in the *Los Angeles Times Book Review,* acknowledged the book's "sheer readability." Lipsyte observed that *Rogue Warrior* possesses "a manic energy."

Marcinko told *CA:* "Since the demise of the Soviet Union there are now at least five hundred Dick Marcinkos out there who used to work for the KGB, GRV, and SPETS-NAZ; who own no property; who didn't write a bestseller; who don't have a retirement fund; who have to make a living doing what they do best. Some maniac is going to buy their talents and use them for personal gain. There is no world order. Today's world is like a box of rubber bands. Today the 'tail is wagging the dog' instead of 'the dog wagging the tail.' I'll always have fresh experiences to write about. I get the data from my experience as president of Special Operational Security (SOS) Temps, Inc., contracted worldwide. Through Richard Marcinko, Inc., I conduct motivational and team building seminars for Fortune 500 companies. Once again I *take on* the bureaucracy. Some things never change! Namely me."

BIOGRAPHICAL/CRITICAL SOURCES:

PERIODICALS

Los Angeles Times Book Review, April 5, 1992, p. 2.
New York Times Book Review, April 19, 1992, p. 12.
People, May 4, 1992, pp. 155-56.
Playboy, April, 1992, p. 26.

MARKER, Sherry 1941-
(Alice Whitman)

PERSONAL: Born August 10, 1941, in Evanston, IL; daughter of Tom Marker and Mary McSherry (a writer); children: Jessica Alice Nenner, Sarah Whitman Nenner. *Education:* Attended Smith College, 1959-61; Radcliffe College, B.A. (cum laude), 1964; attended American School of Classical Studies, 1964-65, and University College, London, 1965-66; University of California, Berkeley, M.A., 1970. *Politics:* Democrat. *Religion:* Catholic.

ADDRESSES: Home and office—25 Tyler Ct., Northampton, MA 01060.

CAREER: Freelance writer. Smith College, Northampton, MA, lecturer, 1992—.

MEMBER: Melanoma Foundation, American Cancer Society.

AWARDS, HONORS: Sword of Hope, Massachusetts American Cancer Society, 1987, for the best first-person newspaper piece on cancer published in 1987; Support of Education Medal, Council for Advancement and Support of Education, 1988, for an article published in an alumni magazine.

WRITINGS:

BOOKS FOR YOUNG ADULTS

London, Black Birch, 1990.
Cooperation, Black Birch, 1991.

TRAVEL BOOKS

The Meteora, Efstathiadis, 1984.
The Peloponnese, Efstathiadis, 1984.
Athens, Attica, and the Islands of the Argo-Saronic Gulf, Efstathiadis, 1985.
Macedonia, Thessaly, and Epirus, Efstathiadis, 1987.
Athens, Efstathiadis, 1988.
Philip of Macedon and the Royal Sites of Macedonia, Efstathiadis, 1989.
Athens and Attica, Kedros, 1990.
The Peloponnese, Kedros, 1990.

BIOGRAPHIES AND AMERICAN HISTORY

Illustrated History of the United States, Bison-Crown, 1988.
Norman Rockwell, Bison-Crown, 1989.
Edward Hopper, Bison-Crown, 1990.

Contributor to *Great Generals of the American Civil War and Their Battles,* 1986, *World Almanac of the American West,* 1986, *Treasures of Ancient Greece,* 1987, *Facts on File Scientific Yearbook,* 1987, *Chronology of Twentieth Century History,* 1992, and *Cambridge Dictionary of*

American Biography, 1993. Also contributor to Penguin/ Berlitz traveler's guides.

OTHER

Contributor, sometimes under the pseudonym Alice Whitman, of articles and reviews to periodicals, including *New York Times, Hampshire Life, San Juan Star, Travel and Leisure, Horizon, Museum Insights, Smith College Alumnae Quarterly,* and *Journal of the American Academy of Religion.*

WORK IN PROGRESS: Research on United States history.

SIDELIGHTS: Sherry Marker has written several travel guides and many historical books. Although the majority of her work is designed for adult audiences, Marker has written two books for young adults. The first, *London,* describes the city of London, its history, and its people. *Cooperation,* published in 1992, is a discussion of the need for people to help one another in varying situations.

Marker commented on her emergence as a writer: "A few years ago, my dear octogenarian friend Vivian Anagnostaki, remarked that 'getting older is very interesting. Everything starts to pull together.' Even in my 50's, I can see that she's right. When I first began to study Ancient Greek as an undergraduate, how could I have known that long after I'd stopped seriously reading Ancient Greek, I'd be passably fluent in modern Greek? In 1976, I bought a small house in the Peloponnese where I have yet to miss a summer. While avoiding working on my Ph.D. thesis in Ancient History, I wrote an article on buying the house which was published in the *New York Times.* One thing led to another and I began to do articles on Greece, England, and New England for the *New York Times* travel section. At the same time, I cranked out a series of guides to Greece for two Greek publishers. These were not 'serious' guides, but rather the sort of thing weary travellers buy in airports and skim in their hotel rooms. Happily, since 1990, I have been writing for two guides that are serious: the Berlitz guides to Greece and Turkey.

"What lies ahead? More of all of the above, I hope. Something I hope doesn't lie ahead: any repetition or resumption of the two bouts of cancer I've had since 1980. That experience has made me a firm believer in the philosophy which Horace expressed as 'Carpe Diem' and the Shakers' Mother Anne stated as 'Do all your work, as though you had a thousand years to live, and as you would if you knew you must die tomorrow.' "

MARKEY, Kevin 1965-

PERSONAL: Born May 5, 1965, in Kittery, ME; son of Martin James (a clinical psychologist) and Sarah Marie (McTaggart) Markey. *Education:* Georgetown University, A.B., 1988. *Religion:* None. *Avocational Interests:* Sailing, pinball, jazz music.

ADDRESSES: Home and office—2321 Ontario Rd. N.W., Washington, DC 20009.

CAREER: New England Monthly, associate editor, 1988-90; free-lance writer, 1990—. *Family Fun,* associate editor, 1992.

MEMBER: Authors Guild, Mungo Park Full Brass Band and Whisky Society (member of board of trustees).

WRITINGS:

(Coauthor) *More How Do They Do That?,* Morrow, 1993.

Contributor to *The Ultimate Baseball Book,* edited by Daniel Okrent and Harris Lewine, Houghton, 1992; and *Our Times: The Illustrated Encyclopedia of the 20th Century,* edited by Lorraine Glennon, Turner Publishing, in press.

WORK IN PROGRESS: The Blue Fifth, a novel.

*   *   *

MARTIN, Claire 1933-

PERSONAL: Born December 6, 1933, in San Francisco, CA; daughter of Clair Devere (a geologist) and Mary (a homemaker; maiden name, McGowan) Jones; married Chet Martin (a radio news correspondent), February 12, 1955; children: Claire, Craig, Stephen, David, Philip, Eileen Gottlieb, Richard. *Education:* Received B.A. from Mount St. Mary's College and M.L.S. from Immaculate Heart College. *Avocational Interests:* Tennis, skiing, scuba diving, reading, knitting.

ADDRESSES: Home—96 Benthaven Ct., Boulder, CO 80303. *Agent*—Pesha Rubinstein, 37 Overlook Terrace, Apt. 10, New York, NY 10033.

CAREER: Los Angeles Public Library, Los Angeles, CA, children's librarian, 1971-75; children's librarian in Rahway, NJ, and Fanwood, NJ, 1976-83; County College of Morris, Randolph, NJ, reference librarian, 1986-88.

MEMBER: Society of Children's Book Writers and Illustrators, Author's Guild.

AWARDS, HONORS: Honor book, Society of Illustrators, 1991, for *The Race of the Golden Apples,* illustrated by Leo and Diane Dillon; Gold Medal, Society of Illustrators, 1992, for *Boots and the Glass Mountain,* illustrated by Gennady Spirin; Martin was commended by City of Los Angeles as a contributor of outstanding children's programs.

WRITINGS:

I Can Be a Weather Forecaster, Children's Press, 1987.

My Best Book: A Year-Round Journal of Personal Bests, Black Birch, 1989.

The Race of the Golden Apples, illustrated by Leo and Diane Dillon, Dial, 1991.

Boots and the Glass Mountain, illustrated by Gennady Spirin, Dial, 1992.

Contributor to *Wonders and Winners,* Scott, Foresman, 1985.

ADAPTATIONS: The Race of the Golden Apples was featured on *Mrs. Bush's Story Time,* ABC Radio Network.

WORK IN PROGRESS: "Other retellings and original picture books."

SIDELIGHTS: Claire Martin commented: "I was raised in the city of San Francisco, in the shadow of St. Anne's Church and School, but my family moved for a few years to the 'mother lode' country of California, where my father owned and worked a gold mine (this was during World War II). We lived on a farm in a town called Rescue. Those childhood years gave me a taste for the freedom of country living. They also instilled in me a love of animals. What they did not provide was much schooling. When we returned to San Francisco and I went back to the parochial school, I was totally out of step with the rest of the class.

"During that period of isolation, I drowned myself in books. I remember reading *Lorna Doone,* one of my father's favorites. My reading also included *The Idylls of the King* and other versions of the Arthurian Cycle. My all-time favorite book still remains *The Once and Future King.* I loved noble narrative poems like 'Horatius at the Bridge,' and devoured the poems of Gerard Manley Hopkins.

"The seed for my writing was planted when, as a children's librarian, the book *Sir Gawain and the Loathly Damsel* by Joanna Throughton crossed my desk. What a wonderful way to introduce children to a rather obscure medieval tale, I thought. And then I thought, maybe I can do that! It wasn't until many years later, after my seven children were adults, that I tried to retell tales that I had loved. My only regret is that I did not start sooner."

A reviewer for *Publishers Weekly* called Martin's first picture book, *The Race of the Golden Apples,* "a stylish, lucid retelling of the myth of Atalanta," a girl who was raised from a baby by the goddess Diana after she was abandoned by her father, who only wanted sons. As a young woman, Atalanta reluctantly returns to the kingdom of her father and agrees to marry in order to give him an heir, but insists she will only accept a man who can outrun her. The young man in love with her, Hippomenes, is aided by Venus in his quest to win her hand. Ann Welton wrote in the *School Library Journal:* "Martin's retelling is clear and romantic, maintaining suspense until the finish line."

In *Boots and the Glass Mountain,* Martin retells a Norwegian fairy tale depicting a young farmboy who tames the wild horses owned by the fearful trolls who descend from the mountain every Midsummer's Night. In this reverse Cinderella-tale, the boy, Boots, rides the horses in a competition for the princess's hand in marriage and is transformed into a prince. A *Publishers Weekly* reviewer described Martin's narration in *Boots and the Glass Mountain* as "tinged with romance, mystery and drama," making it "well suited to read-aloud enjoyments."

Martin commented: "There are so many stories and tales that exist in formats that are daunting to children. Perhaps, if they are introduced to them in beautifully illustrated books, then they'll hunger for more."

BIOGRAPHICAL/CRITICAL SOURCES:

PERIODICALS

American Bookseller, March, 1992, p. 19.

Booklist, November 15, 1987, p. 570; September, 1991; August, 1992, p. 2015.

Bulletin of the Center for Children's Books, November, 1991, p. 69.

Children's Book Review Service, September, 1991.

Horn Book, July/August, 1992, pp. 457-58.

Kirkus Reviews, July 15, 1991.

Publishers Weekly, June 28, 1991; July 13, 1992, p. 54.

School Library Journal, October, 1991, p. 111; July, 1992, p. 70.

* * *

MARTIN, George E. 1932-

PERSONAL: Born July 3, 1932, in Batavia, NY; son of William George and Annabelle (Simons) Martin; married Margaret M. Stewart (a professor of biology), December 19, 1969. *Education:* New York State College for Teachers, A.B., 1954, M.A., 1955; University of Michigan, Ph.D., 1964.

ADDRESSES: Home—R.D.1, Box 274, Voorheesville, NY 12186-9755. *Office*—Department of Mathematics and Statistics, State University of New York at Albany, Albany, NY 12222.

CAREER: University of Rhode Island, Kingston, assistant professor of mathematics, 1964-66; State University of New York at Albany, began as assistant professor, became professor of mathematics, 1966—. *Military service:* U.S. Army, 1955-57.

MEMBER: American Mathematical Society, Mathematical Association of America, National Council of Teachers of Mathematics, Society for Industrial and Applied Mathematics, Association of Mathematics Teachers of New York State.

WRITINGS:

Foundations of Geometry and the Non-Euclidean Plane, Springer-Verlag, 1975.
Transformation Geometry: An Introduction to Symmetry, Springer-Verlag, 1982.
Polyominoes: A Guide to Puzzles and Problems in Tiling, Mathematical Association of America, 1991.

WORK IN PROGRESS: Geometric Constructions; research on polymorphic tilings of the plane.

SIDELIGHTS: George E. Martin told *CA:* "I am a geometer who writes exceedingly slowly about topics in mathematics that I find interesting. It can be said that none of my three books in print deals with a fashionable area of mathematics. Each has been inspired by my research or teaching. I am fortunate, however, that these books have been very favorably reviewed. In this, I thank fate as much as my own ability; it is my impression that much in publishing does depend on luck. I hope to continue writing books on mathematics; only in my wildest dreams could I turn to fiction."

*   *   *

MARTIN(-BERG), Laurey K(ramer) 1950-

PERSONAL: Born March 23, 1950, in Chicago, IL; daughter of Frederick Richard (a retailer) and Marilyn Jean (a homemaker; maiden name, Chidsey; present surname, Benson) Kramer; married William James Berg (a professor), February 1, 1986; children: Jennifer Anne Spurlock, Jessica Lyn, Stirling Brooke Martin, Hunter Kirk Martin. *Education:* Stanford University, B.A. (with honors), 1971; University of Wisconsin—Madison, M.A., 1975, Ph.D., 1982.

ADDRESSES: Home—5201 Pepin Place, Madison, WI 53705. *Office*—Department of French and Italian, 618 Van Hise Hall, University of Wisconsin—Madison, 1220 Linden Dr., Madison, WI 53706.

CAREER: University of Wisconsin—Madison, lecturer, 1982-83, visiting assistant professor, 1983-86, lecturer, 1986-92, senior lecturer in French, 1992—. Amnesty International, translator, 1988—.

MEMBER: American Association of Teachers of French, American Association of University Supervisors, Coordinators, and Directors of Foreign Language Programs, American Conference on the Teaching of Foreign Languages, Central States Conferences Advisory Council, Wisconsin Association of Foreign Language Teachers, Phi Beta Kappa.

WRITINGS:

(With husband William J. Berg) *Images,* Holt, 1990.
(With Berg) *Emile Zola Revisited,* Twayne, 1992.

Work represented in anthologies, including *Approaches to Teaching "Madame Bovary",* edited by L. M. Porter and E. F. Gray, Modern Language Association of America, 1993; and *The French Novel from LaFayette to Desvignes,* edited by Patrick Brady, New Paradigm Press, 1993. Contributor of articles and reviews to academic journals.

WORK IN PROGRESS: Paroles, a textbook, with Sally Sieloff Magnan, Yvonne Ozzello, and husband William J. Berg, publication expected in 1995; *Gustave Flaubert Revisited,* with Berg, Twayne, 1996; *The Poetry of Modern Activity: Physical, Social, and Systemic Movement in Zola's "Au Bonheur des Dames".*

*   *   *

MARTIN, Robert M.   1942-

PERSONAL: Born April 2, 1942, in Philadelphia, PA; son of George J. (a teacher of business studies) and Ethel (a teacher) Martin; married; wife's name, Frances (a university administrator), July, 1970; children: Erica, Joanna. *Education:* Columbia University, B.A., 1963; University of Michigan, Ph.D., 1971. *Religion:* "Druid Non-Euclidian."

ADDRESSES: Home—1543 Edward St., Halifax, Nova Scotia, Canada B3H 3H8. *Office*—Department of Philosophy, Dalhousie University, Halifax, Nova Scotia, Canada B3H 3S5.

CAREER: Dalhousie University, Halifax, Nova Scotia, assistant professor, 1968-75, associate professor, 1975-88, professor of philosophy, 1988—.

WRITINGS:

The Meaning of Language, MIT Press, 1987.
The Philosopher's Dictionary, Broadview Press, 1991.
There Are Two Errors in the the Title of This Book, Broadview Press, 1992.

SIDELIGHTS: Robert M. Martin told *CA: "There Are Two Errors in the the Title of This Book* is a collection of entertaining philosophical puzzles. They make some of the deepest and most interesting problems in philosophy comprehensible to people with no training in academic philosophy."

*   *   *

MARTIN, Russell 1952-

PERSONAL: Born July 25, 1952, in Durango, CO; son of Claude Vincent (an insurance agent) and Jean (a tailor and homemaker; maiden name, Rutherford) Martin; married Karen Holmgren (an artist), 1977; children: none. *Education:* Colorado College, B.A., 1974.

ADDRESSES: Home—15201 County Rd. 25, Dolores, CO 81323. *Agent*—Barney M. Karpfinger, Karpfinger Agency, 357 West 20th St., New York, NY 10011.

CAREER: Telluride Times, Telluride, CO, reporter, 1975-78, managing editor, 1978-79. Full-time writer, 1979—. Colorado College, visiting assistant professor of English, 1985, 1987, 1989, 1992; Colorado Rocky Mountain School, visiting scholar, 1992. Teacher at workshops, including Steamboat Writers' Conference, 1985, Southern Utah University Creative Writing Conference, 1992, and Desert Writers' Workshop, 1993.

AWARDS, HONORS: Ford Foundation Venture Grant, 1973, for the short story collection *Piecing;* Thomas Watson Foundation fellowship, 1974-75, for independent international work in creative writing; *Entering Space: An Astronaut's Odyssey* chosen as the official book of the United States pavilion at Expo '86, Vancouver, British Columbia, Canada; Caroline Bancroft History Prize, 1990, for *A Story That Stands Like a Dam: Glen Canyon and the Struggle for the Soul of the West.*

WRITINGS:

NONFICTION

Cowboy: The Enduring Myth of the Wild West, Stewart, Tabori & Chang, 1983.
(With Joseph P. Allen) *Entering Space: An Astronaut's Odyssey,* Stewart, Tabori & Chang, 1984.
The Color Orange: A Super Bowl Season with the Denver Broncos, Henry Holt, 1987.
Matters Gray and White: A Neurologist, His Patients, and the Mysteries of the Brain, Henry Holt, 1987.
A Story That Stands Like a Dam: Glen Canyon and the Struggle for the Soul of the West, Henry Holt, 1990.
Out of Silence: A Journey Into Language, Henry Holt, 1994.

Contributor of articles to periodicals, including *Time, Science Digest,* and *New York Times Magazine.*

FICTION

Beautiful Islands, Simon & Schuster, 1988.

Also the author of the short story collection *Piecing.*

EDITOR, AND AUTHOR OF INTRODUCTION

(With Marc Barasch) *Writers of the Purple Sage: An Anthology of Recent Western Writing,* Viking/Penguin, 1984.
New Writers of the Purple Sage: An Anthology of Contemporary Western Writers, Penguin, 1992.

WORK IN PROGRESS: The Shapes of Creeks and Rivers, a novel.

SIDELIGHTS: "When I ride horses these days, I always strap spurs to my boots, not because our plug horses require them, but because the feel and the *sound* of the jangle of spurs when I walk is simply stirring as hell and strangely satisfying," Russell Martin reflects in *Cowboy: The Enduring Myth of the Wild West.* "Sometimes, I even go out in a cowboy hat and wear it as proof that I belong somewhere, that I'm rooted in a region." Martin, born and raised in western Colorado, writes with a sense of rootedness to the land and a knowledge of life in the West which is revealed to readers in *Cowboy* and in the two volumes of western writing that he has edited. He has also written a novel and a number of nonfiction works on such diverse topics as space travel, the human brain, and a major dam project.

As a child Martin took part in America's hero worship of the cowboy, a myth that has endured for well over a century. In *Cowboy,* Martin discusses the truth behind the legendary symbol of the American West. He focuses on William F. "Buffalo Bill" Cody, a former frontier scout who founded the popular Wild West Show, a production which traveled internationally and contributed significantly to the romantic notion of the cowboy as a larger than life hero. Nicholas Lemann in the *New York Times Book Review* called *Cowboy* "intelligent" and "well-researched" with "great honesty" about the realities of cowboy life, then and now.

Martin's interest in the American West also extends to his role as editor. In *Writers of the Purple Sage: An Anthology of Recent Western Writing* (and its later companion volume, *More Writers of the Purple Sage: An Anthology of Contemporary Western Writers*), he compiled short stories, excerpts from novels, essays, and poems by new and established writers whose works capture some essential element of the western landscape. Dennis Drabelle, a reviewer for the *Washington Post Book World,* called *Writers of the Purple Sage* "a model anthology. The selections reach a consistently high level and are self-contained." Martin's own short story—"Cliff Dwellers"—is "immodestly" included in the volume, according to Drabelle, "but it so good that one can only approve."

Although Martin is steeped in knowledge of the West, he has written works which have explored various other subjects. To produce his 1987 book *Matters Gray and White: A Neurologist, His Patients, and the Mysteries of the Brain,* he spent nearly a year observing the work of a childhood friend who practices neurology in Colorado, pseudonymously referred to in the volume as Dr. John Ferrier. *Matters Gray and White* records the drama that unfolds when patients learn that they have such incapacitating brain disorders as Alzheimer's disease. The reader is taken into the operating room to observe firsthand—and in detail—the removal of a brain tumor. Martin describes Dr. Ferrier's activities "with uncommon sensitivity and understanding," according to Donovan Fitzpatrick in the *New York Times Book Review.* "There is not much euphoria, but a good deal of tension in Ferrier's daily life. Basically he acts as a detective, often under great pressure, looking for what went wrong in the brains of people who come to him with bizarre complaints," informed Maya Pines in the *Washington Post Book World.* She went on to call *Matters Gray and White* "an honest and moving book," one that "leaves us full of awe."

In *A Story That Stands Like a Dam: Glen Canyon and the Struggle for the Soul of the West,* Martin discusses a controversial construction project which will have a lasting affect on the Western landscape. In the 1950s and early 1960s, Glen Canyon on the Lower Colorado River became a battleground between the forces of development—represented by the builder of the Glen Canyon Dam—and environmental organizations which sought to prevent its construction. Although the dam is considered a major engineering feat, in the view of environmentalists it is responsible for having wiped out an irreplaceable natural wonder. Martin explains that after Glen Canyon, people involved with the environmental movement became a viable political force, moving swiftly and decisively to block projects that in their view threatened to destroy natural areas. Although the dam was built, the opposition it aroused eventually forced the federal Bureau of Reclamation to concede in 1987 that it would probably build no more dams. In the *Los Angeles Times Book Review,* Charles Bowden praised Martin's book, calling it "well written, well researched, well paced" and "an excellent introduction for the general reader to the civil war that has disturbed the West in general and the Southwest in particular for thirty years."

Martin switched to writing fiction with *Beautiful Islands,* his first novel. It tells the story of Jack Healy, family man and astronaut, whose life is disrupted by his schizophrenic brother and faithless wife, as well as his own efforts to carry on a romance with a childhood friend. The real-life

Challenger space shuttle disaster also figures into the story. *Beautiful Islands,* which explores the nuances and complexities of personal and family relationships as its protagonist reexamines his role in the space program, met with a respectful critical reception. Polly Morrice in the *New York Times Book Review* praised its "shapely structure and nicely realized settings," while Toby Olson in the *Los Angeles Times Book Review* found the book "extremely gentle."

BIOGRAPHICAL/CRITICAL SOURCES:

BOOKS

Martin, Russell, *Cowboy: The Enduring Myth of the Wild West,* Stewart, Tabori & Chang, 1983.

PERIODICALS

Bloomsbury Review, July/August, 1990, pp. 6-8.
Chicago Tribune, December 18, 1989.
Los Angeles Times Book Review, May 22, 1988, p. 5; September 11, 1988, p. 14; November 12, 1989, p. 2.
New York Times Book Review, December 11, 1983, p. 15; April 26, 1987, p. 25; May 8, 1988, p. 20.
Publishers Weekly, November 21, 1986, p. 44.
Tribune Books (Chicago), August 4, 1991, p. 8.
Washington Post Book World, December 14, 1984; November 21, 1986, p. 44; February 1, 1987, p. 9; November 12, 1989, p. 17.

*   *   *

MARX, Anthony W. 1959-

PERSONAL: Born February 28, 1959, in New York, NY; son of Peter and Marion Marx; married Karen Barkey (a professor), September 7, 1992. *Education:* Attended Wesleyan University, Middletown, CT, 1977-79; Yale University, B.A., 1981; Princeton University, M.P.A., 1986, M.A., 1987, Ph.D., 1990.

ADDRESSES: Home—New York City. *Office*—Department of Political Science, Columbia University, 420 West 118th St., Room 701, New York, NY 10027.

CAREER: University of Pennsylvania, Philadelphia, administrative aide to the president, 1981-84; SACHED Trust, Johannesburg, South Africa, consultant, 1984, 1986; CASE, Johannesburg, visiting fellow, 1988, 1990; Columbia University, New York City, assistant professor of political science, 1990—. Fund for Education in South Africa, member of board of trustees, 1990—; consultant to United Nations Development Program.

MEMBER: American Political Science Association, African Studies Association, Council on Foreign Relations.

AWARDS, HONORS: Fellow of U.S. Institute of Peace and Social Science Research Council, 1992-93; Guggenheim fellow, 1993-94.

WRITINGS:

Lessons of Struggle: South African Internal Opposition, 1960-1990, Oxford University Press, 1992.

Contributor to periodicals and scholarly journals.

WORK IN PROGRESS: A Comparison of State-Making and Racial Mobilization in South Africa, the United States, and Brazil, completion expected in 1995.

*   *   *

MASALHA, Nur 1957-

PERSONAL: Born January 4, 1957, in Galilee, Israel; naturalized British citizen, 1987; son of Fadel and Fatima Masalha; married; wife's name, Stephanie. *Education:* Hebrew University, B.A., 1979, M.A., 1983; School of Oriental and African Studies, London, Ph.D., 1988.

ADDRESSES: Home—105 Belgrave Rd., Wanstead, London E11 3QR, England. *Office*—Centre for Middle Eastern and Islamic Studies, University of Durham, South End House, South Rd., Durham City DH1 3TG, England.

CAREER: Hebrew University, Jerusalem, teaching and research assistant, 1979-82; Neve Shalom School for Peace, Neve Shalom, Israel, director, 1982-83; University of London, part-time lecturer, 1985-86; Institute for Palestine Studies, Washington, DC, Constantine Zurayk research fellow, 1989-92; University of Bristol, Bristol, England, part-time lecturer in development, administration and planning with special reference to the Middle East, 1991; Centre for Middle Eastern and Islamic Studies, University of Durham, honorary fellow, 1993—.

MEMBER: Institute of Historical Research—University of London; Galilee Center for Social Research (fellow).

AWARDS, HONORS: Scholarships from the Social Science Faculty of Hebrew University, 1979-82, the Jerusalem Fund, 1983-85, Central Research Fund of the University of London, 1984-85, and the Palestine Studies Trust, 1993.

WRITINGS:

Tard al-Filastiniyyun: Mafhum al-"transfer" fi al-fikr wa-al-takhtit al-Suhyuniyyan, 1882-1948, [Beirut], 1992, published in the United States as *Expulsion of the Palestinians: The Concept of "Transfer" in Zionist Political Thought, 1882-1948,* Institute for Palestine Studies, 1992.

(Editor) *The Palestinians in Israel,* Galilee Centre for Social Research, 1993.

"Transfer" in the Post-1948 Period: Israel and the Palestinians, Institute for Palestine Studies, in press.

Contributor to scholarly journals, including *Middle Eastern Studies, Journal of Palestine Studies, Scandinavian Journal of Development Alternatives, Middle East International, Race and Class,* and *The Palestine Yearbook of International Law;* translator and editor of academic articles and papers.

WORK IN PROGRESS: Researching the subject of the Iraqi Army and the Assyrian crisis of 1933.

SIDELIGHTS: Nur Masalha is an Israeli-Palestinian historian whose 1992 book, *Expulsion of the Palestinians: The Concept of "Transfer" in Zionist Political Thought, 1882-1948,* shed new light on one aspect of the conflict that has consumed Arab-Israeli relations for generations. Masalha's volume appeared on bookshelves at a time when world attention was focused on Israel's expulsion of the four hundred refugee Palestinians who spent the early winter months of 1993 camped on a hillside in southern Lebanon. Both Arab and Western leaders condemned Israel's action as a violation of international humanitarian agreements. Masalha's book received favorable critical attention in reviews for questioning both past and present Israeli attitudes toward the Palestinian people.

Expulsion of the Palestinians examines the roots of the strife whose origins date back to the late nineteenth century. As the book points out, Palestine had been occupied for centuries by a large population of indigenous Arabs, although the land itself was originally part of the Ottoman Empire, and later became a territory under British control. The Zionist movement, dating back to the turn of the century, called for a homeland for the world's widely-dispersed Jewish population, a place of refuge from centuries of persecution and genocide. According to the author, Zionist leaders judged the area of Palestine to be this homeland based on scriptural references. *Expulsion of the Palestinians* chronicles the tensions between the indigenous community and the Jewish settlers who began to occupy Palestinian areas. A Royal Commission of Inquiry, commonly called the Peel Commission, was sent from London to investigate the situation and make recommendations. The resultant report, submitted in 1937, recommended that Palestine be divided with sections of the populations "transferred" from one territory to another, to effect a homogenous population in each area—a solution which was rejected by both sides.

Masalha used recently declassified documents from Israeli archives to show that Zionist leaders wrestled for decades with the question of how to deal with the indigenous population. The sources show that both conservative and liberal Israeli leaders privately felt that the only possible way to secure a true Israeli state was the eviction of numerous Palestinians. The conflict worsened after World War II when hundreds of thousands of European Jews flocked to Palestine upon learning of the genocide that had taken place during the Holocaust. The official creation of the state of Israel came in 1948, after Britain had given up control of the area. A full-scale war between the Arab and Israeli forces erupted, with Israel emerging victorious. *Expulsion of the Palestinians* debunks the commonly-held view that at the time all remaining Palestinians fled their homeland on their own, spurred on by public radio broadcasts. However, the book affirms that Jewish forces expelled Palestinians across the borders, then razed the villages to the ground to dispel any possible hopes of returning. Soon, new Israeli settlements sprang up in the rubble, effectively erasing any reminders of the former inhabitants. It was believed that Jewish military leaders acted independently in their treatment of the Palestinians when they took these actions, but the most telling sources from Masalha's research depict a concrete vision shared by the founders of the state of Israel. A revealing example comes from the journal of Yosef Weitz, who headed the Population Transfer Committee, an official Zionist agency whose task was to induce Palestinians to leave the area. Examining Weitz's previously private documents, Masalha revealed Weitz's 1940 statement that "among ourselves it must be clear that there is no room for both peoples in this country. . . . The only way is to transfer the Arabs from here to neighbouring countries. Not a single village or a single tribe must be left."

Expulsion of the Palestinians elicited praise from critics. Most reviewers cited Masalha's exhaustive use of Israeli archival materials to force a rethinking of commonly-held views on the Arab-Israeli conflict. Ian Gilmour in the *Guardian Weekly* asserted that many of the Israeli justifications for their military actions during this period "will not survive Masalha's quietly devastating research." *Times Literary Supplement* critic Lawrence Tal described *Expulsion of the Palestinians* as a work that "helps to contextualize the debate with an articulate, well-researched analysis." Michael Adams, writing on the volume for the *Middle East International,* noted that "Masalha is careful to maintain a scholarly detachment," and summarized the work as "an important and scrupulous piece of revisionist history. It is also a text which should be studied by those who are still trying . . . to put an end to the tragedy of which Palestine and the Palestinians have been the victims for half a century."

Masalha told *CA:* "My main interest is the modern history and politics of the Middle East. As a Palestinian born and brought up in Israel, and a political scientist trained at the Hebrew University of Jerusalem and the University of

London, I endeavored in my book *Expulsion of the Palestinians* to explore an important part of Palestine/Israel history with a new, innovative approach, away from old myths and dogmas. Perhaps my academic experience at the Hebrew University from 1976 to 1982 was the most important single motivation for writing this major work. During this period, I was employed as a research and teaching assistant in the political science department. There was not a single time at which the crucial subject of 'transfer in Zionist political thought' was ever discussed. The main reason for this academic self-censorship was, of course, the fact that my Israeli lecturers believed that any discussion of Zionist 'transfer' plans and activities would not be in the 'national interest.' Unfortunately, in Israel, like many parts of the world, academic institutions are there largely to serve the 'national interest.' Israel's national consensus has deliberately and systematically excluded the Arab citizens of Israel. Numerically they constitute eighteen percent of the total population, and have over sixteen thousand university graduates—but only fifteen Arabs out of a total of six thousand academics are employed by Israeli universities. There are, of course, revisionist historians and dissident academics in Israel, but the vast majority of Israeli historians of the Middle East are linked to the Israeli establishment. Against my background of academic experience at the Hebrew University, I have endeavored to develop my own independent and critical approach to the history of the Palestinian-Israeli conflict. As a Middle Easterner teaching Middle East studies in the West, I attempt to challenge common Western myths, prejudices, and misconceptions, with the same critical and independent approach I employ in my scholarship."

BIOGRAPHICAL/CRITICAL SOURCES:

BOOKS

Masalha, Nur, *Expulsion of the Palestinians: The Concept of "Transfer" in Zionist Political Thought, 1882-1948,* Institute for Palestine Studies, 1992.

PERIODICALS

Financial Times, December 2, 1992.
Guardian Weekly, January 24, 1993.
Middle East International, January 22, 1993, pp. 18-19.
Times Literary Supplement, June 4, 1993, pp. 5-6.

*   *   *

MATUSOW, Barbara   1938-

PERSONAL: Born November 15, 1938, in Philadelphia, PA; daughter of Joseph (an attorney) and Clara (a homemaker; maiden name, Baehr) Matusow; married John H.

Nelson (a journalist), December 7, 1974. *Education:* Pennsylvania State University, B.A. (with honors), 1960.

ADDRESSES: Home and office—4528 Van Ness St. N.W., Washington, DC 20016. *Agent*—Arnold Goodman, 500 West End Ave., New York, NY 10024.

CAREER: United Nations, New York, NY, guide, radio writer, 1963-68; WRC-National Broadcasting Co. (NBC), Washington, DC, NBC News trainee, 1968-69; Columbia Broadcasting System, CBS News, New York City, radio news writer, producer, reporter, television assignment editor, 1969-72; WNBC-TV, New York City, news editor, writer, field producer, 1972-73; WRC-TV, Washington, DC, assignment editor, producer, 1973-76; WJLA-TV, Washington, DC, assistant news director, operations, 1976-77, producer, 1977-78; free-lance magazine writer and television producer, 1978—. Also taught French for junior high school and English for the Berlitz organization in Paris, France.

MEMBER: Phi Beta Kappa.

WRITINGS:

The Evening Stars: The Making of the Network News Anchor, Houghton, 1983.

Associate editor of *Washington Review,* 1977—. Contributor to numerous magazines and newspapers, including *Washington Post, Washington Journalism Review, Masthead, Los Angeles Times,* and *Philadelphia Inquirer.*

SIDELIGHTS: Barbara Matusow is an author whose extensive career in broadcast journalism heightened her interest in the history of that particular medium. In her book *The Evening Stars: The Making of the Network News Anchor,* she examines how it evolved from basic news reading to a cult of personality in which news anchors are stars and rank among the most respected authority figures in society. When television viewers a generation ago tuned in to the first network evening news broadcasts by the American Broadcasting Company (ABC), the face they saw was that of John Daly. Daly was already known to the public not as a journalist but as the moderator of the TV game show *What's My Line?* In time, however, the network news anchor became a more credible figure: for millions of viewers Walter Cronkite was a trusted figure, and Chet Huntley and David Brinkley became icons representing journalism's role in protecting citizens from the misinformation of those in power. In the 1970s and 1980s, the major news anchors—Dan Rather, Barbara Walters, Tom Brokaw, Peter Jennings, and others—evolved into media stars, able to negotiate multi-million-dollar contracts and exert an enormous amount of control over the form and content of the news they presented. Walters was even able to negotiate the services of a regular hairdresser

and first-class accommodations whenever her assignments took her on the road.

In *The Evening Stars,* Matusow documents the rise to power of this television elite. On one level the book is a collection of anecdotes that reveal the pettiness, ambition, and egotism of which the network stars can sometimes be guilty—although in the *New York Times Book Review,* Carol Verderese concluded that the author depicts those stars as largely "principled, dedicated and responsible professionals." On another level, the book is an examination of the role of journalism and journalists in shaping American society and in influencing the way Americans view important public issues. On this level it invites readers to ask with the author: "What of the anchor who turns out to be lacking in personal integrity? What is to stop him if, in the quest for higher ratings or personal aggrandizement, he sensationalizes the news or ignores dull but vital stories for fear of driving viewers away? The sobering reality is that very little *can* be done. . . ."

The Evening Stars met with a mixed critical reception. In the *Los Angeles Times Book Review,* Bill Stout excoriates the book for "bias" and partiality, for "faulty" premises and "leaky" theories, and for showing "little understanding of how television works." In contrast, Roger Piantadosi in the *Washington Post Book World* found that the book's subjects are "carefully profiled and put into much-needed perspective" and that the portraits are "ultimately fair." Verderese concluded her review by stating: "Barbara Matusow's retrospective . . . is well researched and abundant with detailed anecdotes revealing the complex personalities behind the television images."

BIOGRAPHICAL/CRITICAL SOURCES:

PERIODICALS

Los Angeles Times Book Review, August 14, 1983, p. 3.
New York Times, June 20, 1983.
New York Times Book Review, November 27, 1983, pp. 16-17.
Washington Post Book World, August 2, 1983.

*   *   *

McANDREWS, John
 See STEWARD, Samuel M(orris)

*   *   *

McCAFFREY, James M.   1946-

PERSONAL: Born May 10, 1946, in Springfield, IL; son of Edward J. (an attorney) and Margaret (a secretary;

maiden name, Oberriter) McCaffrey; married Ellen Sandel (a bookkeeper), May 28, 1971; children: Michael K. *Education:* Attended University of Illinois at Urbana-Champaign, 1964-66; Springfield Junior College, A.A., 1968; University of Missouri—Rolla, B.S., 1970; University of Houston, M.E., M.A., Ph.D., 1990. *Avocational Interests:* Participating in re-enactments of historic events: Civil War battles, fur trade rendezvous, and battles of the Texas revolution.

ADDRESSES: Office—Department of History, University of Houston—Downtown, 1 Main St., Houston, TX 77002.

CAREER: Structural engineer, 1970-86; University of Houston—Downtown, Houston, TX, professor of history, 1989—.

MEMBER: Organization of American Historians, Company of Military Historians, Society for Military History, Crossroads of Texas Living History Association.

AWARDS, HONORS: Fellow of U.S. Military Academy, 1991.

WRITINGS:

This Band of Heroes: Granbury's Texas Brigade, C.S.A., Eakin Publications, 1985.
Army of Manifest Destiny: The American Soldier in the Mexican War, 1846-1848, New York University Press, 1992.

WORK IN PROGRESS: Writing the memoirs of Brigadier General John F. Kinney, U.S. Marine Corps (retired), who was a fighter pilot in World War II, a prisoner of war of the Japanese who escaped after more than three years in prison, and who later served in Korea.

*   *   *

McCULLOUGH, David Willis   1937-

PERSONAL: Born October 2, 1937, in Canonsburg, PA; son of Willis L. and Dorothy (Davies) McCullough; married Frances Monson (an editor), November 20, 1965; children: Benjamin, Katherine. *Education:* University of Rochester, B.A., 1959; attended Stanford University, 1959-60.

ADDRESSES: Home—117 Villard Ave., Hastings-on-Hudson, NY 10706.

CAREER: Book-of-the-Month Club, member of the editorial department, 1964—, member of editorial board, 1980—.

MEMBER: PEN, Mystery Writers of America, Association for Gravestone Studies, Century Association.

AWARDS, HONORS: Books-Across-the-Sea Ambassador of Honor Award, English-Speaking Union, 1984, for *Brooklyn . . . And How It Got That Way;* Washington Irving Book Selection, Westchester Library Association, 1993, for *Think on Death.*

WRITINGS:

People, Books and Book People, Crown, 1981.
Brooklyn . . . And How It Got That Way, photographs by Jim Kalett, Dial, 1983.
(Editor) *Great Detectives: A Century of the Best Mysteries from England and America,* Pantheon, 1984.
(Editor) *American Childhoods: An Anthology,* Little, Brown, 1987.
(Editor) *City Sleuths and Tough Guys,* Houghton, 1989.
Think on Death: A Hudson Valley Mystery, Viking, 1991.
Point No-Point: A Ziza Todd Mystery (sequel to *Think on Death*), Viking, 1992.

Contributor of introductions to *The Manchurian Candidate* by Richard Condon, Book-of-the-Month Club, 1988, and *The Old Eagle-Nester: The Lost Legends of the Catskills* by Doris W. Brooks, Black Dome Press, 1992.

SIDELIGHTS: Longtime editor for the Book-of-the-Month Club, David Willis McCullough has compiled anthologies, written a mystery series, and depicted the history of Brooklyn. *People, Books and Book People* is a collection of short interviews with ninety authors whose books were marketed through the Book-of-the-Month Club. The interviews originally appeared in the *Book-of-the-Month Club News*'s "Eye on Books" column. "This is not a book to inspire adulation—either of interviewees or interviewer," maintained Marilyn Murray Willison in the *Los Angeles Times Book Review.* "What the reader does feel, however, is a quiet sense of admiration for the creative process. Reading McCullough's book is like taking a stroll with someone who has accomplished what you'd like to be able to do. The big and small legends of the literary world appear delightfully approachable."

Brooklyn . . . And How It Got That Way is a highly photo-illustrated look at the history of the New York borough. "McCullough has captured a lot of it [the Brooklyn story] in his sparklingly written, soundly researched account," praised Frances A. Koestler, a Manhattan-based reviewer for the *Washington Post.* "As with most local histories, it's the raisins and not the bran that make this book worth reading," remarked *Voice Literary Supplement* critic Bill McKibben. McCullough's topics include seventeenth-century Brooklyn and its founder Henry Hudson, the beginnings of the Brooklyn Dodgers baseball team, local celebrities, the development of Coney Island, the construction of the Brooklyn Bridge, and the ghettoization of the borough.

McCullough compiled an anthology of crime stories, *City Sleuths and Tough Guys,* which begins with selections from nineteenth-century writers and provides representative samples from later masters. He further embraced the detective genre with a pair of his own mysteries—*Think on Death* and *Point No-Point*—which are set in New York and feature the young Presbyterian minister Ziza Todd. The plot of *Think on Death* revolves around the revelation of a family secret of a nineteenth-century Utopian community and a long lost heir to a fortune. In her review of *Think on Death,* Marilyn Stasio commented in the *New York Times Book Review* that "cool, clear and mighty refreshing to encounter in a first novel, David Willis McCullough's fluid prose might have tumbled down the slopes of the Catskill Mountains." In *Point No-Point,* Ziza Todd returns to solve the mystery of a high school student's death on the Hudson River waterfront.

BIOGRAPHICAL/CRITICAL SOURCES:

PERIODICALS

Los Angeles Times Book Review, April 26, 1981; August 21, 1983.
New York Times, August 15, 1981.
New York Times Book Review, January 20, 1991; April 5, 1992.
Voice Literary Supplement, May, 1983.
Washington Post Book World, May 23, 1983.

* * *

McGLOTHLEN, Ronald L(ee) 1947-

PERSONAL: Born March 20, 1947, in Galesburg, IL; son of Lamont C. (an insurance executive) and Betty C. (a homemaker) McGlothlen; married Elvera Tegnelia (a teacher), August 23, 1975; children: Carrie Ann. *Education:* Attended Aurora College, 1965-67, Bradley University, 1967-69 and 1970-71, Colgate Rochester Divinity School, 1969-70, and Northern Illinois University, 1975-76 and 1984-92. *Religion:* Christian.

ADDRESSES: Home—76 Sheridan Street, Elgin, IL 60123.

CAREER: Northern Illinois University, DeKalb, part-time assistant professor. Department associate at Northwestern University.

AWARDS, HONORS: Louis Knott Koontz Award, Pacific Coast Branch of American Historical Association, 1990.

WRITINGS:

Controlling the Waves: Dean Acheson and U.S. Foreign Policy in Asia, Norton, 1993.

Contributor of articles to *Pacific Historical Review* and *Military History.*

WORK IN PROGRESS: An article on the origins of the Marshall Plan.

SIDELIGHTS: Ronald L. McGlothlen told *CA:* "My first book, *Controlling the Waves: Dean Acheson and U.S. Foreign Policy in Asia,* is written on three levels. At its most basic level, it is the story of how a group of men, led by Dean Acheson, reconstructed and reconfigured the economy of the Pacific Rim following World War II. Their policies and paradigms led directly to the Korean War, the Vietnam War, the United States commitment on Taiwan, the cold war with China, the rise of modern Japan, and the phenomenal expansion of America's Asian trade. On the second level, this book is a candid snapshot which exposes the bare-knuckle realities behind the making of United States foreign policy. On the third level, *Controlling the Waves* is a carefully drawn portrait of irony (inspired by Danish philosopher Soren Kierkegaard's *The Concept of Irony*). Dean Acheson, the book's principal protagonist, is a man struggling with the limits of his own understanding while striving to orchestrate a degree of political and economic control in Asia (hence the title) which is ultimately beyond his country's reach. More than anything else, it is this concept of irony applied to the pursuit of power which gives the book its cutting edge, and I hope to develop other thought provoking themes in my future works."

* * *

McGUCKIAN, Medbh 1950-

PERSONAL: First name pronounced "Maeve"; born August 12, 1950, in Belfast, Northern Ireland; daughter of Hugh Albert (a schoolteacher) and Margaret (Fergus) McCaughan; married John McGuckian (a teacher), 1977; children: three sons and one daughter. *Education:* Queen's University, Belfast, B.A., 1972, M.A., 1974. *Religion:* Roman Catholic.

ADDRESSES: Home—Belfast, Ireland. *Agent*—Oxford University Press, Walton St., Oxford OX2 6DP, England.

CAREER: Dominican Convent, Fortwilliam Park, Belfast, Northern Ireland, teacher, 1974; St. Patrick's College, Knock, Belfast, instructor, 1975—; Queen's University, Belfast, writer-in-residence, c. 1985-88.

AWARDS, HONORS: National Poetry Competition prize, 1979, for "The Flitting"; Eric Gregory award, 1980; Rooney prize, 1982; Ireland Arts Council award, 1982; Alice Hunt Bartlett award, 1983, for *The Flower Master;* Cheltenham Literature Festival Poetry Competition prize, 1989.

WRITINGS:

VERSE

Single Ladies: Sixteen Poems (chapbook), Interim Press, 1980.

Portrait of Joanna (chapbook), Ulsterman, 1980.

(With Damian Gorman and Douglas Marshall) *Trio Poetry,* Blackstaff Press, 1981.

The Flower Master, Oxford University Press, 1982.

The Greenhouse, Steane, c. 1983.

Venus and the Rain, Oxford University Press, 1984.

(Editor) *The Big Striped Golfing Umbrella: Poems by Young People from Northern Ireland,* illustrated by Anne Carlisle, Arts Council of Northern Ireland, 1985.

On Ballycastle Beach, Oxford University Press, 1988.

(With Nuala Archer) *Two Women, Two Shores,* New Poets, 1989.

Marconi's Cottage, Gallery, 1991.

Also author of poem, "The Flitting." Contributor to periodicals; editor of *Fortnight.*

SIDELIGHTS: Irish poet Medbh McGuckian has won acclaim for her imaginative verse, her lyricism, and her themes on the feminine psyche. McGuckian's work has been compared to verse by such poets as Marianne Moore and Elizabeth Bishop, and she has been called an "Irish Emily Dickinson" by Anne Stevenson in *Times Literary Supplement.* Using lyrical language—rich in sound and emotion—to express the thoughts and feelings of the speaker, McGuckian juxtaposes the concrete experiences of domestic life with evocative, dreamlike imagery. The resultant poetry is sometimes described as esoteric, often erotic, and highly symbolic. Calvin Bedient, writing in *Parnassus,* enthused that McGuckian "is Ireland's first great female poet—indeed, arguably its most original. No doubt she's too difficult and Romantic to please everyone, at least right off. But of twentieth-century poets writing in English, she strikes me as one of the most original and compelling—and as easily the most *white-hot* Irish poet since [William Butler] Yeats."

McGuckian was born to a Catholic family in Belfast, Northern Ireland, the third of six children. She attended school at a Dominican convent from 1961 to 1968, and then enrolled at Queen's University to study English. At Queen's, McGuckian was influenced by Seamus Heaney, a teacher who, although only in his early thirties, was already widely recognized as a gifted poet. In addition, McGuckian's classmates included promising young poets Paul Muldoon and Frank Ormsby. After graduation McGuckian began issuing her work in various local newspapers and magazines, and landed a job teaching English in Fortwilliam Park. The next year, 1975, she accepted a position as English teacher at St. Patrick's College in Knock,

and two years later married a geography teacher, John McGuckian. In 1979, McGuckian won the National Poetry Competition award for her poem "The Flitting," and the next year published her first chapbooks, *Single Ladies: Sixteen Poems,* and *Portrait of Joanna.*

"I believe wholly in the beauty and power of language, the music of words, the intensity of images to shadow-paint the inner life of the soul," McGuckian was quoted as saying in *Contemporary Poets.* Typically, McGuckian's images are drawn from either the home—furniture, children, rooms—or from nature—flowers, trees, roots, rain—which the poet uses to create a metaphor symbolizing the feminine subconsciousness. In other words, the persona's contemplations on the concrete often express intimate feelings of a woman's spirit. With 1982's award-winning *Flower Master,* McGuckian's reputation as a poet of originality was firmly established. "Her poems are haunted by the mysterious loves of the plants . . . and their means of survival," wrote Hugh Haughton in *Times Literary Supplement.* "She's a poet of vegetable processes, drawn to enigmatically mute, exotic blossoming." McGuckian's verse is, therefore, often described as "mysterious," and, in the words of Neil Corcoran in *Dictionary of Literary Biography (DLB),* often "uninterpretably rich and strange."

In her 1984 publication, *Venus and the Rain,* McGuckian uses metaphors which have a disconcerting power to fuse experience to form "new realities," according to Michael O'Neill in *Times Literary Supplement.* The speaker, Venus, "is transposed from classical mythology into a post-Newtonian universe," wrote Jon Cook in *New Statesman;* a scientific universe which is juxtaposed on the mythological when Venus becomes nostalgic for the past. Cook concluded that "the poem moves out of a mythic frame into a scientific one, only to recombine the two in a way that can recall the capacity of [John] Donne or [William] Empson to make poetry out of scientific theory." In the verse, Venus and the Moon are female, while Mars, the Sun, and the Rain are male; hence, sexuality is approached obliquely through symbolism "without falling prey to the conventions of pornography," as Cook pointed out in his *New Statesman* essay.

Other reviewers have noted McGuckian's use of language—the syntax, the rhythms and cadences, and the tensions and stresses of her vocabulary. Neil Corcoran in *DLB* wrote that "a characteristic strategy is to develop and elaborate an initial image, in a beautifully lucid, flowing syntax, to a point where intense physicality is weighted with a moral and emotional (in some poems, almost a 'metaphysical') burden of suggestion and implication." McGuckian often relies upon the associations readers bring to a word or phrase to lend significance or meaning to the poem—yet some critics complain that the "soft focus" is too indistinct to interpret. O'Neill concluded in

Times Literary Supplement that "*Venus and the Rain* is a gifted collection, yet it leaves the reader hoping that at some stage in this talented poet's career language will serve less as a screen and more as a torch."

But what Alan Jenkins in the London *Observer* called a "reckless disregard for sense" has been seen by others as, in the words of Calvin Bedient in *Parnassus,* "purely imaginative" poems, crafted "glamorously as well as cryptically." In a review of *On Ballycastle Beach* Bedient insisted that McGuckian "treat[s] language not as a public pie but as the four and twenty blackbirds to be freed from it." The danger, as Clair Wills pointed out in her *Times Literary Supplement* essay, is that "widespread recognition of the beauty and power of [McGuckian's] poetry has been matched by a similarly widespread uncertainty with regard to its meaning," and this ambivalence can result in an impatient reader's "denunciation . . . of the poems as nothing more than a metaphorical game." Likewise, Richard Tillinghast in *New York Times Book Review* commented on a frustrating disorientation in reading the poet's 1991 *Marconi's Cottage:* "McGuckian's poems are less cryptic than mysterious, because 'cryptic' implies that a key is available," he observed. However, "after several readings one starts to feel at home." Tillinghast concluded that, though not recommended for beginners, "these poems are not to be missed."

BIOGRAPHICAL/CRITICAL SOURCES:

BOOKS

Contemporary Literary Criticism, Volume 48, Gale, 1988, pp. 274-79.
Contemporary Poets, 4th edition, St. James Press, 1985.
Dictionary of Literary Biography, Volume 40: *Poets of Great Britain and Ireland since 1960,* Gale, 1985.

PERIODICALS

New Statesman, August 31, 1984, p. 26.
New Statesman and Society, August 26, 1988, p. 38; August 28, 1992, p. 36.
New York Times Book Review, August 30, 1992, p. 12.
Observer (London), July 10, 1988, p. 42.
Parnassus, Volume 16, number 1, 1990, pp. 195-217.
Times (London), January 24, 1985.
Times Literary Supplement, August 21, 1981, p. 952; August 13, 1982; p. 876; October 29, 1982, p. 1200; November 30, 1984, p. 1393; August 19-25, 1988, p. 915; July 10, 1992, p. 23.*

—Sketch by Linda Tidrick

McGUIRE, William 1917-

PERSONAL: Born November 8, 1917, in St. Augustine, FL; son of William Joseph McGuire (an accountant) and Edna Laurie (Musgrave) McGuire; married Anne Georgia Collins (an editor), November 13, 1947 (marriage ended); married Paula Van Doren (an editor and writer), May 28, 1965; children: (first marriage) John, Edward; (second marriage) Mary. *Education:* University of Florida, Gainesville, A.B., 1938, M.A., 1939; graduate study at Johns Hopkins University, 1939-41. *Politics:* Independent left. *Religion:* No affiliation.

ADDRESSES: Home and office—219 Washington Rd., Princeton, NJ 08540.

CAREER: St. Augustine Record, St. Augustine, FL, reporter, summers of 1934 and 1935; *Baltimore Sun,* Baltimore, MD, reporter, 1941; *New Yorker,* New York City, reporter, 1943-46; United Nations Secretariat, editor and reporter, 1946-49; Bollingen Foundation, New York City, special editor of "Bollingen Series," 1949-56, managing editor, 1956-67; Princeton University Press, Princeton, NJ, associate editor of "Bollingen Series," 1967-82; various writing and editing projects on independent basis, 1983—. Former trustee of Vladimir Nabokov Literary Trust; former board member of Frances G. Wickes Foundation, Archives for Research in Archetypal Symbolism, and C. G. Jung Institute (New York City); board member of C. G. Jung Foundation (San Francisco, CA).

MEMBER: PEN, St. Augustine Historical Society, Marjorie Kinnan Rawlings Society.

WRITINGS:

(Editor with others) *Collected Works of C. G. Jung,* numerous volumes, Bollingen Foundation/Pantheon Books, 1953-67, Princeton University Press, 1967-83.
(Editor) *The Freud/Jung Letters: The Correspondence between Sigmund Freud and C. G. Jung,* translated by R. F. C. Hull and Ralph Manheim, Princeton University Press, 1974.
(Editor) *C. G. Jung Speaking: Interviews and Encounters,* translated by R. F. C. Hull and others, Princeton University Press, 1977.
Bollingen: An Adventure in Collecting the Past, Princeton University Press, 1982, second edition, 1989.
(With John C. Burnham) *Jelliffe: American Psychoanalyst and Physician,* University of Chicago Press, 1983.
(Editor) C. G. Jung, *Dream Analysis: Notes of the Seminar Given in 1928-1930,* Princeton University Press, 1984.
Poetry's Catbird Seat: The Consultantship in Poetry in the English Language at the Library of Congress, 1937-1987, Library of Congress, 1988.

(Editor) C. G. Jung, *Analytical Psychology: Notes of the Seminar Given in 1925,* Princeton University Press, 1989.

(Coauthor) *American Social Leaders,* ABC-Clio, 1993.

Also author of *Second C. G. Jung Memorial Lecture,* [London], 1984. Author of foreword to *A Secret Symmetry: Sabina Spielrein between Jung and Freud,* by Aldo Carotenuto, Pantheon Books, 1982, and introductions to *The Undiscovered Self: With "Symbols and the Interpretation of Dreams,"* by C. G. Jung, Princeton University Press, 1990, and *Psychology of the Unconscious,* by C. G. Jung, Princeton University Press, 1991.

SIDELIGHTS: For three decades William McGuire wielded an editorial hand over the "Bollingen Series," the creation of Paul and Mary Mellon. The Mellons, wealthy Americans who during the 1930s had become interested in the psychology of C. G. Jung, started a publishing program to bring Jung's writings and other original works on comparative religion, myth, and literature to the English-speaking public. To realize their program, in 1942 they created the Bollingen Foundation, named after a village on the Lake of Zurich, Switzerland, where Jung had a retreat. The foundation also supported scholars with fellowships and grants, funded the Bollingen Prize in Poetry, and published the A. W. Mellon Lectures on the Fine Arts, given at the National Gallery of Art. Throughout his tenure as an editor of the Bollingen Series, McGuire collaborated in preparing Jung's collected works for publication. McGuire told *CA:* "Forty years of work with the *Baltimore Sun,* the United Nations, the *New Yorker,* and the Bollingen Series exposed me to an entertaining and catholic range of subjects. Central in the Bollingen program was the *Collected Works of C. G. Jung,* of which I was house editor throughout. That, together with several years of involvement in Freudian psychoanalysis, made an appropriate background for editing *The Freud/Jung Letters* and other works in that vein. The Library of Congress project grew out of interests generated in the Bollingen work."

McGuire recounted the foundation's history in his *Bollingen: An Adventure in Collecting the Past,* in which he combined his memories of the people associated with the foundation and authors with whom he worked with factual information from foundation records to tell the inside story of a unique supporter of American intellectual life. "The moment was clearly ripe for McGuire's chronicle," declared S. Schoenbaum in the *Washington Post Book World.* "*The Adventure* is hardly given to irreverence . . . but it is candid; mistakes are not glossed over." Calling the work "delightful," Thomas Bender, in the *New York Times Book Review* conversely remarked that McGuire "tempers his sympathetic attachment with a winning sense of irony, even irreverence." "The main handicap for the ordinary reader is, I expect, the plenitude of names,

titles, and financial details, which can make the going something of a slog at times," Schoenbaum conceded. "Still the narrative remains shapely, and McGuire writes with lucid economy; he is no doubt an excellent editor."

BIOGRAPHICAL/CRITICAL SOURCES:

PERIODICALS

New York Times Book Review, November 14, 1982, p. 24.
Times Literary Supplement, December 17, 1982, p. 1387.
Voice Literary Supplement, October, 1982, pp. 1, 12-15.
Washington Post Book World, November 14, 1982, p. 4.

*   *   *

McKENNA, Colleen O'Shaughnessy 1948-

PERSONAL: Born May 31, 1948, in Springfield, IL; daughter of Joseph F. (a civil engineer) and Ruth Short (an office manager) O'Shaughnessy; married J. Frank McKenna III (an attorney), March 25, 1972; children: Collette, Jeff, Laura, Steve. *Education:* Slippery Rock University, B.S., 1970; post-graduate studies at Carnegie Mellon University and Pitt University. *Religion:* Roman Catholic.

ADDRESSES: Home—101 Fox Ridge Farms, Pittsburgh, PA 15215.

CAREER: Third and fourth grade teacher in Bethel Park, PA, 1970-1973; writer. Member of St. Lucy's Auxillary.

MEMBER: Society of Children's Book Writers and Illustrators.

AWARDS, HONORS: Award of Excellence, Slippery Rock University, 1992.

WRITINGS:

"MURPHY" SERIES

Too Many Murphys, Scholastic, 1988.
Fourth Grade Is a Jinx, Scholastic, 1989.
Fifth Grade: Here Comes Trouble, Scholastic, 1989.
Eenie, Meanie, Murphy, No, Scholastic, 1990.
Murphy's Island, Scholastic, 1991.
The Truth about Sixth Grade, Scholastic, 1991.
Mother Murphy, Scholastic, 1992.
Camp Murphy, Scholastic, 1993.

JUVENILE

Merry Christmas, Miss McConnell!, Scholastic, 1990.
Good Grief, Third Grade, Scholastic, 1993.
Roger Friday: Live from the Fifth Grade, Scholastic, in press.

"COUSINS" SERIES

Not Quite Sisters, Scholastic, 1993.
Stuck in the Middle, Scholastic, 1993.

YOUNG ADULT

The Brightest Light, Scholastic, 1993.

WORK IN PROGRESS: Scout's Honor; also sequels to *The Brightest Light, Murphy's Island,* and *Eenie, Meanie, Murphy, No.*

SIDELIGHTS: To many young readers the name Colleen O'Shaughnessy McKenna means a fun read. The kids in her stories think and talk like kids and are people other children can identify with. Reviewers have called her books warm, funny, and insightful, and have noted the way her "Murphy" books capture the chaos, struggles and joys of a loving, boisterous family. Since *Too Many Murphys* was first published in 1988, McKenna's books have become popular with children between the ages of eight and twelve.

McKenna began serious attempts at writing while in the eighth grade. Because she loved the character of Little Joe from the television series *Bonanza,* she began to write her own scripts for the show. "I wanted him to notice me. The best way to do that was to make myself the main character," she recalls. In all, McKenna wrote twenty-seven scripts, mailing the best three to *Bonanza.* "It was a good experience because I learned about the opening, middle, and end of a story."

After graduating from Slippery Rock University with a degree in elementary/special education, McKenna taught third and fourth grades in Bethel Park, Pennsylvania. While there, she began writing plays for her classes. Noting that her students enjoyed working on the plays, McKenna did not hesitate to use them to gain control of her classroom. "I guess we can't have rehearsal today because someone is throwing spitballs," she would say. The kids disciplined each other in order to rehearse.

In 1972 she married J. Frank McKenna III, and when they started their family she stopped teaching. Within six years their family had grown to include children Collette, Jeff, Laura, and Steve. It was a time for absorbing facts and learning experiences about life in a growing family and the individuals that are part of it. When her husband, an attorney, announced that he would be away from home for about fourteen weeks trying a case, he encouraged McKenna to find something to do that she would really love. "You'll go crazy being alone with four children for more than three months," he told her. She began to think, "If I could do *anything,* what would it be?" The one thing she really missed was writing, so she signed up for a course in children's literature.

One important piece of advice McKenna gained from the class was "write about what you know." She realized that being a full-time mother, it would be natural to write about her own children. "One day, my oldest daughter,

Collette, came up to me and said, 'None of my friends want to come to our crazy house. No offense, Mom, but you have too many babies. Sometimes I just wish I could be an only child.' " McKenna thought that sounded like a good story idea and she began work on her first book, *Too Many Murphys.* The story became the first in a series of books depicting the often disastrously humorous antics of the Murphy family, based on the experiences of McKenna's own children and their friends.

Too Many Murphys focuses on Collette, a third-grader who is the oldest child in her family. She feels the weight of being the one who is always responsible, setting a good example for the other three children: Jeff, Laura, and Stevie. Collette describes herself as a "midget mother" and often wishes she had more time with her parents all to herself. In a review in *School Library Journal,* Carolyn Jenks states that "the outstanding quality" of *Too Many Murphys* is realism. "The characters and the things that happen to them will be familiar to many young readers."

In the "Murphy" books Collette deals with all the pains and joys of growing up. *Fourth Grade Is a Jinx, Fifth Grade: Here Comes Trouble,* and *The Truth about Sixth Grade* all focus on learning how to relate to parents, teachers, and classmates in school. Nancy P. Reeder, reviewing *The Truth about Sixth Grade* for *School Library Journal,* comments that "all of the characters may be found in any sixth grade classroom," where "students live in the moment . . . and every event is a crisis." Making friends in new situations such as camp and a new school are explored in *Eenie, Meanie, Murphy, No* and *Murphy's Island.* Collette also learns to adjust to big changes, such as her mother's pregnancy, in *Mother Murphy.* Of her own writing, McKenna says: "In my 'Murphy' books I deliberately stretch out the awfulness and I make Collette wade through it all, not just to get the laugh, but to force her to react. It is her reactions that draw readers to her, giving them a chance to identify with her because she really is a lot like them."

Another of McKenna's books for middle-grade readers is *Merry Christmas, Miss McConnell!,* in which fifth-grader Meg Stafford and her family discover that Christmas need not be filled with expensive decorations, dinners and presents to be celebrated. McKenna balances the serious story of a family with financial difficulties with the humorous antics of Meg's friend, Raymond. Assessing *Merry Christmas, Miss McConnell!* in *School Library Journal,* Susan Hepler declares that "McKenna has a good ear and eye for sketching fifth graders in a Catholic school."

McKenna has also penned a young adult novel, *The Brightest Light.* The book follows the trials of Kitty Lee, a sixteen year old who grows as she confronts a number of new and confusing issues, including her best friend's mysterious romance and elopement with an older man. She also experiences new feelings for her old friend Cody, who asks her out on a date, and for the man whose children she babysits while his wife battles alcoholism. Although Carol A. Edwards in *School Library Journal* finds *The Brightest Light* a fairly predictable teenage romance novel, she also lauds McKenna's refusal to happily resolve all difficult issues: "To give McKenna credit, anything that couldn't be fixed in the last ten pages is realistically left hanging." A reviewer for *Bulletin of the Center for Children's Books* praises the "subtle strength" of McKenna's heroine and suggests that *The Brightest Light* is "steadily told, entirely contemporary, and deeply romantic."

Colleen McKenna enjoys making presentations about herself and her writing to young readers. She wants her love of reading and writing to help inspire children to succeed in these fields. "The first thing you have to do is entertain them," she says. "I start by acting out scenes from *Bonanza* to show them what I was like in the eighth grade. Basically I show them I'm an ordinary person who chose writing as a career." She also explains to these groups how a story is written, using *The Three Little Pigs* to illustrate what makes a story work. She talks to the children about the importance of being a reader and gives them writing tips. "I want to represent a persistent kid who loved books so much I decided to write some of my own."

BIOGRAPHICAL/CRITICAL SOURCES:

PERIODICALS

Booklist, September 15, 1992, p. 138.
Bulletin of the Center for Children's Books, October, 1988, p. 47; February, 1989, p. 152; October, 1989, p. 39; October, 1990, pp. 38, 183-84; February, 1992, p. 163.
Kirkus Reviews, September 1, 1988, p. 1325; February 1, 1989, p. 211; January 1, 1992, p. 54.
Publishers Weekly, August 26, 1988, p. 90; April 27, 1992, p. 272.
School Library Journal, December, 1988, p. 109; March, 1989, p. 178; September, 1989, p. 254; March, 1990, p. 219; October, 1990, p. 38; December, 1990, p. 105; April, 1991, p. 121; February, 1992, p. 87; December, 1992, p. 133.
Wilson Library Bulletin, January, 1991, p. 6.

—*Sketch by Mary Lois Sanders*

* * *

McKNIGHT, Stephen A. 1944-

PERSONAL: Born July 27, 1944, in Mount Airy, NC; son of Sam A. (a wholesale distributor) and Macy M. (a hosiery mill worker) McKnight; married Rebecca Semones (a teacher), June 5, 1965; children: Stephen A., Jr. *Education:* University of North Carolina at Chapel Hill, B.A., 1966; Crozier Theological Seminary, M.Div., 1969; Emory University, Ph.D., 1972.

ADDRESSES: Home—2311 Southwest 43rd Pl., Gainesville, FL 32608. *Office*—Department of History, 4131 Turlington, University of Florida, Gainesville, FL 32611.

CAREER: Emory University, Atlanta, GA, instructor in humanities, 1970-72; University of Florida, Gainesville, assistant professor of humanities and philosophy, 1972-77, associate professor of humanities and affiliate associate professor of philosophy, 1977-80, associate professor, 1980-91, professor of European intellectual and cultural history, 1991—, chairperson, Department of Humanities, 1977-80, associate professor in Florence, Italy, 1979, special adviser to the vice-president for research, 1983-86. University of North Carolina at Asheville, Carol Belk Distinguished Professor of Humanities, 1993; St. Peter's College, Will and Ariel Durant Professor of Humanities, 1994-95. U.S. Information Agency, director of Office of Academic Programs, Educational and Cultural Affairs, 1981-83; Federal Interagency Committee on Education, member and co-chairperson of subcommittee on international education, 1981-83; consultant in East Asia, Africa, Europe, Latin America, and the Middle East.

MEMBER: International Seminar for Philosophy and Political Theory (charter chairperson, 1978-80), History of Science Society, Renaissance Society of America.

AWARDS, HONORS: Grants from National Endowment for the Humanities, 1976-80, 1990, Earhart Foundation, 1980, 1987, 1989, 1991-92, Rockefeller Foundation, 1980, and Wilbur Foundation, 1989, 1993.

WRITINGS:

(Editor and contributor) *Eric Voegelin's Search for Order in History: Expanded Edition,* University Press of America, 1987.
Sacralizing the Secular: The Renaissance Origins of Modernity, Louisiana State University Press, 1989.
The Modern Age and the Recovery of Ancient Wisdom: Historical Consciousness, 1400-1650, University of Missouri Press, 1991.
(Editor and contributor) *Science, Pseudo-Science, and Utopianism in Early Modern Thought,* University of Missouri Press, 1992.

Contributor to history, political science, sociology, and religious studies journals.

WORK IN PROGRESS: Francis Bacon and Ancient Wisdom; Knowledge and Order: The Intellectual Foundations of Utopianism; "Ancient and Modern Gnosticism and Hermeticism," an essay to be included in *Ancient and*

Modern Gnosticism, edited by Robert Segal; research on Eric Voegelin's concept of Gnosticism in the light of recent research.

SIDELIGHTS: Stephen A. McKnight told *CA:* "My research and writing are devoted to European intellectual history, especially the Renaissance and the Scientific Revolution. My interest is in new research showing that the revival of the *prisca theologia,* or ancient wisdom tradition of pseudo-science (magic and alchemy) and esoteric religion (Hermeticism and the Cabala) strongly influenced the Renaissance and the Scientific Revolution. Two themes of particular interest are the modern equation of knowledge with power and the modern notion of utopian perfection. Both are strongly influenced by the *prisca theologia.*"

*   *   *

McLEAN, J. W. 1922-

PERSONAL: Born April 2, 1922, in Okmulgee, OK; son of Lawrence W. (a banker) and Margaret (a homemaker; maiden name, McGill) McLean; married Eleanor Jane Johnson, May 8, 1943; children: Margo McLean Beasley, Lawrence W., Scott J. *Education:* University of Oklahoma, B.S. (with honors), 1943. *Politics:* Republican. *Religion:* Presbyterian.

ADDRESSES: Home and office—7150 North Country Club Dr., Oklahoma City, OK 73116; and P.O. Box 25848, Oklahoma City, OK 73125. *Agent*—John T. Willig, 61 Chaffey Circle, Norwood, NJ 07648.

CAREER: Merrill, Lynch, Fenner & Bean, Tulsa, OK, account executive, 1946-48; First National Bank of Tulsa, began as trainee, became vice-president and commercial loan officer, 1949-58; Texas National Bank, Houston, began as senior vice-president, became president and chief executive officer, 1958-64; Bank of America, San Francisco, CA, senior vice-president and director of marketing, 1964-67; Liberty National Bank and Trust Co., Oklahoma City, OK, president, chairperson, and chief executive officer, 1967-87, retired, 1987; writer, lecturer, and consultant, 1987—. Federal Reserve System, director for six years and president of Federal Advisory Council, 1979. Allied Bank International, past chairperson of board of directors; Banks of Mid-America, past chairperson and chief executive officer; Reading & Bates Corp., founding director; Devon Energy Corp., member of board of directors. University of Oklahoma, adjunct professor; Center for Creative Leadership, senior adviser; conducts seminars on leadership and team building for corporate clients, large municipalities, and institutions of higher learning. Leadership in Oklahoma City, past president and chair-

person of executive committee; Oklahoma City Chamber of Commerce, past executive vice-president; Houston Chamber of Commerce, life member. Rice University, honorary life member of board of governors, 1961—. *Military service:* U.S. Army, field artillery, 1943-46; served in European theater, participating in four major European battles; received battlefield promotion to captain; received Bronze Star.

MEMBER: American Bankers Association (chairperson, credit policy division and marketing division), U.S. Golf Association (past member of executive committee), Allied Arts Association (co-founder and past chairperson of executive committee), Oklahoma Heritage Association (past president and chairperson), River Oaks Country Club (past president), Oklahoma City Golf and Country Club (past president), Oak Tree Golf Club (chairperson).

AWARDS, HONORS: Distinguished Service Citation, University of Oklahoma, 1975; Oklahoma City University, Doctorate in Commercial Science, 1980, Distinguished Service Award, 1985; Amicus Medicinae Award, College of Medicine Alumni Association, University of Oklahoma, 1985; inducted into Oklahoma Hall of Fame; named Regional Banker of the Year by *Finance;* George Washington Honor Medal from Freedoms Foundation.

WRITINGS:

Say Yes or Say Why: Fundamental Principles of Sound Bank Credit, American Bankers Association, 1964.
Cross-Selling Banking Services to Business, Bank of America, 1965.
So You Want to Be the Boss?: A CEO's Lessons in Leadership, Prentice-Hall, 1990.
(With William Weitzel) *Leadership: Magic, Myth, or Method?* AMACOM, 1991.
Conquering Quandaries, Mid-America Communications, 1992.
There Ain't No Straight Putts, Mid-America Communications, 1992.

Work represented in anthologies, including *Loan Officers Handbook.* Columnist for *Journal Record,* Oklahoma City. Contributor of more than twenty articles to banking publications.

WORK IN PROGRESS: . . . *Mere Grains of Sand* (tentative title), a book-length version of a published column. "It will involve a comprehensive focus upon the lives of leaders of this century from a wide range of professions. The object will be to delineate some key leadership skills, principles and philosophies which were common to their magnificent lives."

SIDELIGHTS: J. W. McLean told *CA:* "Of all the rewarding events of my life—including various business achievements like two major regional bank consolidations and a variety of awards and citations—a letter from one of my leadership seminar victims ranks near the top. At the end, it read: ' . . .and, Mr. McLean, pages five, six, and seven of your invaluable handout on self-knowledge very likely have saved my marriage.' "

*   *   *

McLEAN, Teresa 1951-

PERSONAL: Born April 5, 1951, in London, England; daughter of Patrick (an attorney) and Mary (a homemaker; maiden name, Geldart) McLean; married Martin Brett (a university teacher), August 18, 1984; children: Peter. *Education:* Notre Dame Convent in Lingfield, Surrey; attended Lady Margaret Hall, Oxford University, 1969-1972; Trinity College, Cambridge, Ph.D., 1979. *Religion:* Roman Catholic. *Avocational Interests:* Cricket, cooking, reading, writing.

ADDRESSES: Home—Cambridge, England.

CAREER: Cheltenham Ladies College, Cheltenham, Gloucestershire, England, history teacher, 1973-76; Oxford High School, Oxford, England, 1981-84; writer and freelance broadcaster, 1979-81. Cricket correspondent for the *Financial Times,* 1980—.

WRITINGS:

Medieval English Gardens, Viking, 1980.
The English at Play in the Middle Ages, Kensal Press, 1983.
Metal Jam: The Story of a Diabetic (autobiography), St. Martin's, 1985.
The Men in White Coats, Stanley Paul, 1987.

Also author of documentaries for British radio.

SIDELIGHTS: British author Teresa McLean has penned books on diverse subjects, including medieval gardening, diabetes, and cricket umpires. Her first such effort, *Medieval English Gardens,* was widely and favorably reviewed. As Susan Dooley explained in the *Washington Post Book World,* "what Teresa McLean has done" in this book "is to reconstruct an earlier period through plans for monasteries and castles, chronicles, paintings, poems and account books with their lists of seeds bought and produce sold, of sums paid out for garden labor and buildings." She traces the English garden from its beginnings in monastical cloisters to its development on the wealthy estates of the nobility. She observes that the medieval gardener had in general a more practical view of plants and their usefulness than his modern counterpart. But "you needn't be a medievalist or a gardener to enjoy this delightful book," according to Frances Taliaferro in the *New York Times Book Review,* because it "is full of medieval trivia to de-

light the general reader." McLean "is to be congratulated on having found so much information in primary sources," noted *Times Literary Supplement* critic John Buxton, who went on to add that "her book is very thorough" and "well arranged." Anthony Huxley in the *Spectator* praised *Medieval English Gardens* as well, asserting that "it is the detail in this book, with its ample quotations from contemporary documents and poetry, which makes it so engrossing."

In 1985's *Metal Jam,* McLean turns to her own life for material, telling of her struggle against diabetes, a disease in which the body is unable to produce the insulin necessary to break down sugars. Diabetics must rely on insulin injections to assimilate sugar into their bloodstream. McLean's form is particularly difficult to deal with because insulin causes the victim to respond unpredictably, often descending into hypoglycemia, a condition in which the sugar in the bloodstream drops to a perilous level. The story of how McLean overcame these disabling bouts with hypoglycemia to live an activity-filled life was lauded as "vivid and moving" in *Booklist.*

One of the activities that McLean pursues is acting as an occasional umpire for cricket games. Cricket is an enormously popular sport in England, on a par with baseball or football in the United States. McLean recounts the history of cricket umpires in her 1987 book, *The Men in White Coats,* named for the distinctively dapper white uniforms the umpires wear. She covers the early days of corruption in the sport and discusses the changes brought about by modern-day media coverage. "Fascinating reading," stated Nigel Andrew in the *Listener,* who went on to declare that McLean "writes with real dash."

McLean told *CA:* "I write because I love it, on subjects I like. Except for *Metal Jam,* which is about diabetes and which I wrote to pay the rent."

BIOGRAPHICAL/CRITICAL SOURCES:

BOOKS

McLean, Teresa, *Metal Jam: The Story of a Diabetic,* St. Martin's, 1985.

PERIODICALS

Booklist, January 1, 1986, p. 680.
Listener, December 3, 1987, p. 34.
New York Times Book Review, March 29, 1981, p. 16.
Times Literary Supplement, April 10, 1981, p. 418.
Washington Post Book World, May 17, 1981, p. 4.

McLEOD, Grover S(tephen) 1929-

PERSONAL: Born June 15, 1929, in Birmingham, AL; son of Grover C. and Lucille M. (a homemaker) McLeod; married, wife's name Esme (divorced); children: Susan McLeod McCullough, Joy McLeod Dorn, Peggy McLeod Honneycutt, Malcolm. *Education:* Attended Birmingham Southern College, University of Western Australia, and University of Alabama. *Politics:* None.

ADDRESSES: Home—Deerwood Lake, Shelby County, AL. *Office*—Law Offices of Grover S. McLeod, 1204 17th St. S., Birmingham, AL 35205-4798.

CAREER: Civil trial lawyer in private practice in Birmingham, AL.

WRITINGS:

Subsailor, Manchester Press (Birmingham), 1964.
Sketches from the Bar, Manchester Press, 1966.
Teodoro, Manchester Press, 1969.
About Women, Manchester Press, 1974.
Submarine Stories, Manchester Press, 1977.
Civil Actions at Law in Alabama, Manchester Press, 1980, 2nd edition, 1987.
Trial Practice and Procedure in Alabama, Manchester Press, 1983, 2nd edition, 1991.
Equitable Remedies and Extraordinary Writs in Alabama, Manchester Press, 1983.
Subduty, Southern University Press, 1986.
The Ghost of Chimera, Southern University Press, 1988.
The Sultan's Gold, Southern University Press, 1988.
The Trials of FAT, Southern University Press, 1989.
Worker's Compensation in Alabama for On-the-Job Injuries, Manchester Press, 1990.
The Legal Circus, Manchester Press, 1992.

WORK IN PROGRESS: Drake, Captain of the South Seas; Equitable Remedies and Extraordinary Writs in Alabama, 2nd edition.

SIDELIGHTS: Grover S. McLeod told *CA:* "I like books. I like to read them, and I like to write them. I am also curious about the world around me, and I pursue knowledge in order to learn. I enjoy traveling. The world is my garden."

*　　*　　*

McNARIE, Alan Decker 1954-

PERSONAL: Born August 22, 1954, in Hamilton, MO; son of Leonard J. (a farmer) and Mary Ann (a homemaker) McNarie; married Susan Decker (an attorney), September 22, 1986. *Education:* Northwest Missouri State University, B.S.Ed., 1976; University of Missouri—

Columbia, M.A., 1978, Ph.D., 1988. *Politics:* "Independent with Green leanings." *Religion:* "Methodist with Buddhist leanings."

ADDRESSES: Home—P.O. Box 10247, Hilo, HI 96721. *Office*—Hilo Law Center, 77 Mohouli St., Hilo, HI 96720.

CAREER: Midwest Friends of the Earth, copy editor of *Midwest Earth Advocate,* 1977-78 and 1982-83; U.S. Peace Corps, Washington, DC, volunteer assistant regional supervisor for Thailand, 1979-81; University of Hawaii at Hilo, assistant professor, 1988-93; Law Office of Susan Decker McNarie, paralegal, 1993-94. Big Island Poetry Festival, co-coordinator, 1993; Volcano Art Center, member, 1993—; member of Hawaii Literary Arts Council and East Hawaii Cultural Council.

MEMBER: Associated Writing Programs, Academy of American Poets, Hawaii Poets Guild, Sierra Club (member of executive committee of Moku Loa Group, 1991-93).

AWARDS, HONORS: Editors Book Award from Pushcart Press, 1992, for *Yeshua.*

WRITINGS:

Yeshua: The Gospel of St. Thomas, Pushcart, 1993.

Executive editor, *Art Centering,* 1993—.

WORK IN PROGRESS: Sword, a fantasy novel; *Across Two Wounded Mountains,* a travel and ecology book; two books of poetry, *Haunts* and *Immigrants; The Skinthold War,* a fantasy novel; research for a novel about Saipan in World War II and a novel about Sherman's march to the sea; research on old Hawaiian law cases, for possible dramatic monologues.

SIDELIGHTS: Alan Decker McNarie told *CA:* "A young man leaves his home in a small town, moves to the city, gets an education at some expense to his family, and then can't go home again. That, in one sentence, is my biography. Unfortunately, it's also the biography of a huge number of other authors—and the plot of a huge number of novels. The Literary Wanderer has become a stock character for modern American authors, from Thomas Wolfe to Tom Wolfe. That's the trouble with the old writing workshop admonition to 'write what you know': too many of us know the same life.

"I think it's the duty of writers to seek out the whole of human experience, not just the narrow circle of literary workshops. That's one reason I decided to play a two-thousand-year-old Jew in my first novel. Teoma the doubter first lodged himself in my head when I was doing some research on Gerard Manley Hopkins. I came across a translation of an ancient apocryphal book, *The Acts of St. Thomas,* which traced Thomas's journey from Palestine to southern India. It was neither great theology nor great history, but it *was* one wonderful story, full of irony, spectacle, and surprisingly human characters.

"With the apocryphal book as a starting point, I set out to broaden my experience enough to think something like Teoma. Part of that task consisted of library research, looking not just for scholarly facts, but for sensory data and first-century biases and attitudes and superstitions. I joined the Peace Corps, then traded my ticket home for an Air India fare that took me through India and Europe, and hitched a ferry to Israel to work on archaeological digs. I pored over maps for a sense of terrain and trade routes, and strolled through Third World marketplaces, looking for ancient sights and sounds and odors. Then I had to pare out a huge amount of myself that was not available to my character. How do you describe time, for instance, in an age when sundials are a rarity?

"The result was a character who looked at many of the same basic dilemmas as I did, through a very different set of lenses. But Teoma is still a wanderer, and wanderers, by their very nature, tend never to learn more about a place than can be picked up in a short sojourn. That's why my wife and I chose to stay on the big Island of Hawaii after the teaching job that brought us here evaporated. I now work as a paralegal with family violence cases, gaining still another very different perspective of human experience. We live in the rainforest, on an active volcano, and awake to the sounds of birds that live nowhere else in the world, and preserve a small patch of their ecosystem as intact as we can. Someday I'll have learned enough to write about them. Meanwhile, life is interesting."

*   *   *

MEIER, Richard (Alan) 1934-

PERSONAL: Born October 12, 1934, in Newark, NJ; son of Jerome and Carolyn (Kaltenbacher) Meier; married Katherine Gormley, 1978; children: Joseph Max, Ana Moss. *Education:* Cornell University, B.Arch., 1957. *Avocational Interests:* Furniture and tableware design.

ADDRESSES: Office—475 Tenth Ave., New York, NY 10018.

CAREER: Richard Meier and Associates, New York City, principal architect, 1963-80; Richard Meier and Partners, New York City, principal architect, 1980—. Architect with various firms, 1957-63; Cooper Union, professor of architecture, 1962-73. Cornell University College of Art, Architecture and Planning, member of advisory council, beginning in 1971; American Academy in Rome, resident architect, 1973-74; Yale University, William Henry Bishop visiting professor of architecture, 1975-77; Harvard University, visiting professor of architecture,

1977. Has participated in numerous gallery and museum exhibitions.

MEMBER: National Academy of Design, American Institute of Architects, International Academy of Architecture, American Academy and Institute of Arts and Letters, Century Club of New York.

AWARDS, HONORS: First Honor, American Institute of Architects, 1965-81; American Institute of Architects fellow, 1976; Medal of Honor, American Institute of Architects (New York), 1980; Pritzker Architecture Prize, 1984; Officier dans l'Ordre des Arts et Lettres nomination, 1984; Royal Gold Medal for Architecture, Royal Institute of British Architects, 1988.

WRITINGS:

(With Charles Gwathmey, John Hejduk, and others) *Five Architects,* Wittenborn, 1972.
Richard Meier, Architect, 1964-1976, introduction by Kenneth Frampton, afterword by Hejduk, Oxford University Press, 1976.
Shards, illustrated by Frank Stella, Petersburg Press, 1983.
Richard Meier, Architect 1964/1984, introduction by Joseph Rykwert, Rizzoli, 1985.
Architektur-Zeichnungen 1971-1984, translated as *Richard Meier: Architectural Drawings 1971-1984,* edited by Rudolf Kicken and Suzanne E. Pastor, Rudolf Kicken Galerie (Cologne, Germany), 1985.
(With Werner Blaser) *Bauten fur die Kunst,* translated by D. Q. Stephenson as *Buildings for Art,* Birkhauser (Basel, Switzerland, and Boston), 1990.
Richard Meier, Architect, 1985/1991, with essays by Frampton and Rykwert, Rizzoli, 1991.
(With Blaser) *Weishaupt Forum, Richard Meier* (trilingual edition; includes "On the New Weishaupt Forum—What Good Architecture Can Be"), Birkhauser, 1993.

Contributor to *Architecture, Shaping the Future: A Symposium and Exhibition with Ricardo Legorreta, Fumihiko Maki, Richard Meier, Richard Rogers,* introduction by Allan Temko, edited by Suzy Ticho, University of California, San Diego, 1990. Meier's works have appeared in German, French, and Italian editions.

SIDELIGHTS: Internationally renowned architect Richard Meier has been on the vanguard of modern architecture for decades. His work is prominent in major cities throughout the United States, and in 1984 he was the winner of the Pritzker Architecture Prize, the most coveted award in his profession. After earning his bachelor's degree in architecture from Cornell University in 1957, Meier spent his early professional years with several architectural firms. In 1963 he attended an exhibition at the

Museum of Modern Art, where he discovered the work of the French master architect Le Corbusier. It was a turning point artistically for Meier, and he soon founded his own firm, which has since grown steadily in size and reputation. Meier is perhaps best known for his white modern houses on Long Island, New York, as well as his work on the Museum of Decorative Arts in Frankfurt, Germany, the High Museum of Art in Atlanta, The Atheneum in New Harmony, Indiana, and the Getty Center in Los Angeles.

Richard Meier, Architect 1964/1984 is a collection of Meier's drawings along with the architect's own descriptions of his projects. Sam Hall Kaplan of the *Los Angeles Times Book Review* praised the work as "thorough and well detailed, illustrated and designed . . . sure to engage those who pursue and appreciate interior and exterior design." Writing in the *New York Times Book Review,* William H. Jordy commented, "Massimo Vignelli's design for 'Richard Meier Architect, 1964/1984' so complements the architect's own elegant buildings as to make the work seem already canonized."

BIOGRAPHICAL/CRITICAL SOURCES:

PERIODICALS

Los Angeles Times Book Review, April 7, 1985.
New York Times Book Review, December 5, 1976; March 17, 1985, pp. 13-14.

*   *   *

MELLANBY, Kenneth   1908-1993

OBITUARY NOTICE—See index for *CA* sketch: Born March 26, 1908, in Barrhead, Scotland; died December 23, 1993. Scientific researcher, educator, editor, and author. Mellanby raised controversy for his willingness to use human subjects in scientific research. As director of the Sorby Research Institute beginning in 1941, he used some of World War II's conscientious objectors to investigate the contagion of the human parasitic disease scabies. His findings, which revolutionized medical treatment of an infection that, at that time, affected two million people, were published in 1944's *Scabies,* a clinical textbook. In 1947 Mellanby was appointed principal at a newly instituted university in Ibadan, Nigeria, a post he was to retain for the next seven years. He was named Commander of the Order of the British Empire at the end of that period. In 1961 Mellanby became director of the Monks Wood Experimental Station, where he established the largest ecological laboratory in England. Mellanby was author of several books on ecology, including *Pesticides and Pollution, Waste and Pollution,* and his 1992 publication, *The DDT Story.* He also wrote a children's book, *Talpa, the*

Story of a Mole, edited *Air Pollution, Acid Rain and the Environment,* and was the founding editor of a journal, *Environmental Pollution.*

OBITUARIES AND OTHER SOURCES:

BOOKS

Who's Who, 146th edition, St. Martin's, 1994, p. 1300.

PERIODICALS

Times (London), December 24, 1993, p. 17.

*   *   *

MERQUIOR, J(ose) G(uilherme)   1941-

PERSONAL: Born April 22, 1941, in Rio de Janeiro, Brazil; son of Danilo (a lawyer) and Maria (Alves) Merquior; married Hilda Vieira de Castro, October 11, 1963; children: Julia, Pedro. *Education:* State University, Rio de Janiero, Graduate, Law and Philosophy, 1963; University of Paris, Doctor of Letters, 1972; London School of Economics, Ph.D., 1978.

ADDRESSES: Sierra Leona 270, Lomas 11010, Mexico, DF.

CAREER: Brazilian Embassy, second secretary in Paris, France, 1966-70, first secretary in Bonn, Germany, 1971-73, first secretary in London, England, 1975-79, counsellor in Montevideo, Uruguay, 1980-81, minister-counsellor in London, 1983-86, ambassador to Mexico, 1987-89, delegate to UNESCO, 1989—. King's College, London, visiting professor, 1976-78; special aide to head of civilian cabinet at the presidency of Brazil, 1981-82; University of Brasilia, professor, 1982; Brazilian charge d'affaires, London, 1985.

MEMBER: Brazilian Academy of Letters, Reform Club (London).

AWARDS, HONORS: Chevalier de l'Ordre du Merite, France, 1971; Verdienstkreuz (first class), West Germany, 1973; Member of the Victorian Order, United Kingdom, 1976; Brazilian Academy, 1979; National Book Institute, 1980; PEN, 1981; named commander of Rio Branco Order, 1982.

WRITINGS:

Formalismo e Tradicao Moderna (nonfiction), [Rio de Janeiro], 1974.
L'Esthetique de Levi-Strauss (nonfiction), [Paris], 1977.
De Anchieta a Euclides (history of Brazilian literature), [Rio de Janeiro], 1977.
The Veil and the Mask (essays), [London], 1980.
Rousseau and Weber: Two Studies in the Theory of Legitimacy (nonfiction), Routledge, 1980.

As Ideias e as Formas (nonfiction), [Rio de Janeiro], 1981.

A Natureza do Processo (nonfiction), [Rio de Janeiro], 1982.

O Argumento Liberal (nonfiction), [Rio de Janeiro], 1983.

Foucault (nonfiction), Collins Fontana, 1985, University of California Press, 1987.

Western Marxism (nonfiction), Paladin, 1985.

From Prague to Paris: A Critique of Structuralist and Post-Structuralist Thought (nonfiction), Verso, 1986.

Critica, 1964-1989 (essays), Editora Nova Fronteira, 1990.

Liberalism, Old and New (nonfiction), Twayne, 1991.

Contributor to periodicals, including *Times Literary Supplement, Europe, Government and Opposition, Journal do Brasil and Folha de Sao Paulo,* and *O Globo.*

SIDELIGHTS: For more than two decades, J. G. Merquior has written extensively on the history of ideas. Taken together, his books form a road map of intellectual history since the eighteenth-century Enlightenment. His pervading theme is an abiding belief in and commitment to the ideological traditions of liberalism and Enlightenment thought.

Merquior's first book available to English-speaking readers was *Rousseau and Weber: Two Studies in the Theory of Legitimacy.* In the volume, Merquior compares the work of eighteenth-century French philosopher and author Jean-Jacques Rousseau, with emphasis on his 1762 book *The Social Contract,* to the ideologies of German sociologist Max Weber. *Times Literary Supplement* reviewer J. A. Hall called the book "an elegant and valuable" history of the sources of legitimate political power.

Two of Merquior's books are devoted to modern structuralist and post-structuralist thought. *Foucault,* part of a series designed to offer short critiques of modern masters' major texts, examines the work of French philosopher-historian Michel Foucault. Merquior voices opposition to Foucault's views; as Bart Testa wrote in the Toronto *Globe and Mail,* Merquior exposes his subject as a "trendy, modern anarchist." While *Times Literary Supplement*'s Colin Gordon criticized the volume for being too chatty, Testa called the book "artful, concise and suggestive," but harsh in its dismissal of Foucault's system of thought.

From Prague to Paris: A Critique of Structuralist and Post-Structuralist Thought, issued in 1986, "attempts to show what structuralism, its avatars and its successors, look like on a larger intellectual map," according to Ann Jefferson in the *Times Literary Supplement.* Merquior begins by examining the Prague School, led by Roman Jakobson, lamenting its emphasis on formalist, linguistic approaches to the study of literature and culture. He then turns to the aesthetic theories of Claude Levi-Strauss, objecting to the

French writer's "revulsion against modernity." He concludes by arguing that the post-structuralists—Derrida, Lacan, and Foucault—have created what Jefferson termed "an artificially produced cultural crisis" by divorcing modern thought from its historical and cultural contexts.

With the volume *Western Marxism,* Merquior moved to a different corner of the intellectual map. His purpose in the book is to examine the political and social views of nineteenth-century German political philosopher Karl Marx's adherents in the West (in contrast to the "classical Marxists" associated more with the former Eastern bloc). His principal theme is to show that Western Marxism has emphasized what John Gray in the *Times Literary Supplement* termed "a humanist doctrine of liberation," combined with "an elitist distaste for . . . modern culture." Concluded Gray: *Western Marxism* is a "brilliant little book . . . bursting with delightful asides," an "undeceived intellectual history of Western Marxism in which all of its central paradoxes and absurdities are faithfully chronicled."

BIOGRAPHICAL/CRITICAL SOURCES:

BOOKS

Dictionnaire des Philosophes, edited by Denis Huisman, Universitaires de France, 1984.

Merquior, J. G., *From Prague to Paris: A Critique of Structuralist and Post-Structuralist Thought,* Verso, 1986.

PERIODICALS

Globe and Mail (Toronto), August 16, 1986.

Times Literary Supplement, March 20, 1981, p. 320; June 6, 1986, p. 626; September 5, 1986, p. 965; November 21, 1986, p. 1306.*

*   *   *

METCALF, Alida C. 1954-

PERSONAL: Born April 5, 1954; daughter of John T. (a naval engineer) and Helen (a homemaker; maiden name, Waterman) Metcalf; married Daniel C. Rigney (a professor), December 26, 1986; children: Matthew, Benjamin. *Education:* Smith College, B.A. (cum laude), 1976; University of Texas at Austin, M.A., 1978, Ph.D., 1983.

ADDRESSES: Office—Department of History, Trinity University, 715 Stadium Dr., San Antonio, TX 78212-7200.

CAREER: Trinity University, San Antonio, TX, associate professor of Latin American history, 1986—.

WRITINGS:

Family and Frontier in Colonial Brazil, University of California Press, 1992.

WORK IN PROGRESS: The Latin American Cultural Tradition, completion expected in 1995; *Holiness and Error: The Santidade Cult of Sixteenth-Century Brazil,* 1997.

SIDELIGHTS: Alida C. Metcalf told *CA:* "I became interested in Latin America when my father, an officer in the United States Navy, was posted to Lima, Peru. In Peru I attended a bilingual British school. I became fascinated with the culture of Peru: its history, its peoples, its incredible geography. My interest in Brazil began in college, where I was a student of Emilia Viotti da Costa, then in exile from the University of Sao Paulo. I found the comparisons between Brazil and the United States most compelling, and such issues now underlie my scholarly work."

*   *   *

MILLER, E(ugene) Ethelbert 1950-

PERSONAL: Born November 20, 1950, in New York, NY; married Denise L. King, 1982; children: Jasmine-Simone, Nyere-Gibran. *Education:* Howard University, B.A., 1972.

ADDRESSES: Office—Department of Afro-American Studies, P.O. Box 441, Howard University, Washington, DC 20059.

CAREER: African-American Resource Center, Howard University, Washington, DC, director, 1974—; Ascension Poetry Reading Series, Washington, DC, founder and organizer, 1974—. University of Nevada—Las Vegas, visiting professor of English, 1993.

MEMBER: PEN American Center, Associated Writing Programs, Institute for Policy Studies, National Writers Union, PEN/Faulkner Foundation, Cultural Alliance of Greater Washington, and D.C. Community Humanities Council.

AWARDS, HONORS: Achievement Award, Institute for Arts and Humanities, Howard University, 1978; "E. Ethelbert Miller Day" proclaimed by Mayor of Washington, DC, September 28, 1979; Washington, DC, Mayor's Art Award, 1982; Washington, DC, Arts Commission fellowship, 1989; Columbia Merit Award, 1993.

WRITINGS:

POETRY

Andromeda, [Chiva], 1974.

The Land of Smiles and the Land of No Smiles, privately printed, 1974.

The Migrant Worker, Washington Writers Publishing House, 1978.

Season of Hunger/Cry of Rain: Poems 1975-1980, Lotus Press, 1982.

Where Are the Love Poems for Dictators?, Open Hand, 1986.

First Light: New and Selected Poems, Black Classic Press, 1993.

EDITOR

(With Ahmos Zu-Bolton) *Synergy: An Anthology of Washington, D.C. Black Poetry,* Energy Blacksouth Press, 1975.

Women Surviving Massacres and Men, Anemone Press, 1977.

In Search of Color Everywhere, Stewart Tabori and Chang, 1993.

OTHER

Also author, with Amma Khalil, of *Interface,* 1972. Author of introduction to *Fast Talk, Full Volume,* Gut Punch Press, 1993. Contributor to periodicals, including *Essence, Greenfield Review, Washingtonian, Caliban, Obsidian, Black American Literature Forum, Praxis, Black Scholar, Yardbird Reader,* and *Unrealist.*

SIDELIGHTS: A self-proclaimed "literary activist" and described by others as an "aesthetic entrepreneur," prolific poet, editor, and organizer, E. Ethelbert Miller is descended from a line of proselytizers of new writing that includes Ezra Pound, Langston Hughes, Lawrence Ferlinghetti, and Ishmael Reed. Particularly noteworthy is Miller's dedication to the mission of bringing poetry into the lives of as many people as possible. In an article in the *Washington Review,* he commented, "I tried from the beginning to make my work accessible to both language and Ideas. In some ways I modeled myself after Langston Hughes—he was the writer who best embodied and articulated the hopes and dreams of our people." As a poet interested in moving society toward the goals of looking "beyond race and color" and seeking ways to "eliminate the divisions of class," Miller has confronted the fact that there are two literary cultures in operation: "There are two traditions operating within African American culture," he remarked, "one oral, the other literary. At times they intersect and influence each other. Some writers borrow readily from the oral tradition and attempt to 'stretch' their text into being more responsive to sound, music, and mobility. How you sound is still important within the African American community." Miller's poetry—with influences from "Paul Simon, Donovan, and other 1960s American folk-rock artists" combined with "some of the concerns and techniques which predominate in the poetry of the 1960s black arts movement"—blends and balances oral techniques with the modernist experiments of William Carlos Williams' poetic minimalism and American idiom and Ishmael Reed's conversational narrative idiom and pervasive irony.

Miller's career as a poet began at Howard University, where he enrolled as a history major in 1968, intending to eventually study law. Influenced by the Black Arts Movement, however, Miller went against the wishes of his family, changed his major to Afro American Studies, and began to develop his style of poetry. A decisive influence on Miller at the beginning of his career as a poet was his partnership with fellow poet Ahmos Zu-Bolton II, with whom he founded *Hoo-Doo Magazine,* a poetry journal, and edited *Synergy: An Anthology of Washington, D.C. Black Poetry.* Miller's first volume of poems, *Andromeda,* is described by Theodore R. Hudson in *Contemporary Poets* as "that of a young poet predictably concerned with values, introspection, and love." *Dictionary of Literary Biography* contributor Priscilla R. Ramsey observed that *Andromeda* already showed characteristics which were to become fixtures in Miller's poetry, including the absence of punctuation, the exploration of feelings, the narrator's grasp of "the ironic significance of his condition," and the premium the poet places on his emotional life. Themes explored in *Andromeda* include "the quest toward religious self-definition, love, and isolation," Ramsey commented. "From *Andromeda* through Miller's later work, we can watch his development of an ironic, self-aware, psychological distancing that is centered on his increasing social and political experience." Miller's next volume of verse appeared the same year. *The Land of Smiles and the Land of No Smiles,* a single long poem, "chronicles Africa's colonial history and the western exploitation of human beings as it separated African people from a cultural identity and sense of place," according to Ramsey. "The poem identifies the failure of both Africa and the West to create a new black civilization."

In *The Migrant Worker* Miller brought together a collection of poems that directly confronts conditions in Washington, D.C. Miller speaks of his own experiences in the 1960s and 1970s, and includes what *Small Press Review* calls "irreverent satires of the human condition." Ramsey sees Miller's chief distinction in *The Migrant Worker* as being "lowering the barriers between street people and intellectuals." This feature is most clearly manifested in the poems featuring Bo Willie, Miller's streetwise alter ego. In the title poem he speaks as himself, betraying the weariness that comes from living in a time of struggle: "i want to yell / join hands demonstrate / free my brothers around the world / free the world around my brothers / but the thrill is gone." Miller's next collection, *Season of Hunger/ Cry of Rain: Poems 1975-1980,* is introduced by June Jordan, a poet known for her political activism. Miller's poems in the volume are characterized by a deepening un-

derstanding of complex social and human issues. The direction toward political concerns culminated in Miller's experiments with writing poems openly concerned with Latin American politics. In an essay in the *Washington Review,* he stated that he began to recognize his own roots when he recalled that his father was born in Panama and spoke only Spanish when he reached the United States. Miller commented: "The opportunity to recite my poetry to people from Central America was a challenge. I responded by writing a series of poems in the voices of people living in the region." These poems make up much of Miller's 1986 volume, *Where Are the Love Poems for Dictators?* Miller was also "attracted to how women held up during the [Nicaraguan] war and revolution," and his interest in women had a large influence on the poems in *Where Are the Love Poems for Dictators?* Hudson commented that "sensitive to feminist concerns and attitudes, [Miller] is adept at using a female persona."

Miller's style has clarified and simplified over the years. Hudson sees Miller's poetry in terms of lines that are characteristically conversational, "sometimes idiomatic, pithy, as if they are quiet spurts of thought fragments or little whispers," adding that "Miller has a noticeable talent for the conceit . . . [and] is especially good at revelatory, pointed closure that can reverberate for the reader."

Miller brought work from his previous volumes together in 1993's *First Light: Selected and New Poems.* This volume is divided into eight sections, thematically grouping the poems so that while it is possible to read poems related by subject, it is impossible to identify the order in which they were written and published or to tell the previously published poems from the new ones. Miller's concerns are demonstrated by the way the poems are distributed in the volume, with the longest sections bringing together political poems on Latin America ("El Salvador") and often quizzical and ironic poems about love affairs ("Chinatown"). One evocative section, according to some critics, is "A Death in the Family," which groups together poems on the deaths of W. E. B. DuBois, Malcolm X, James Baldwin, C. L. R. James, and others.

Miller's reputation as a poet and advocate of a politics of inclusion is increasingly bringing him a wider exposure. While serving as vice-president of the PEN/Faulkner Foundation, he came to the attention of Richard Wiley of the University of Nevada at Las Vegas and was invited to the campus for a semester as a visiting professor. Increasingly, Miller is being recognized as an important poet; he was deemed by poet Gwendolyn Brooks to be "one of the most significant and influential poets of our time." Miller's reputation as a poet is based equally on the accessibility and honesty of his poetry and his political statements. Miller sees no separation between the roles of art and conscience; he writes in the introduction to *Fast Talk, Full*

Volume that "there is now a need for all of us to become more involved. . . . With so many changes occurring in Africa, and throughout the world, it is critical that we keep writing and dreaming."

BIOGRAPHICAL/CRITICAL SOURCES:

BOOKS

Contemporary Poets, fifth edition, St. James Press, 1991, pp. 655-656.
Dictionary of Literary Biography, Volume 41: *Afro-American Poets since 1955,* Gale, 1985, pp. 233-240.
Fast Talk, Full Volume, Gut Punch Press, 1993.

PERIODICALS

Las Vegas Accent, May 17, 1993.
New York Times, June 5, 1988.
Small Press Review, April, 1988.
Washington Post, March 11, 1987.
Washington Review, February/March, 1991.*

*   *   *

MILLER, Ian
   See MILNE, John

*   *   *

MILLER, Louise (Rolfe)   1940-

PERSONAL: Born May 9, 1940, in Chicago, IL; daughter of George Rolfe (in insurance sales) and Catherine (a teacher; maiden name, Walsh) Miller. *Education:* Attended University of Vienna, 1959-60; St. Xavier College, B.A., 1961; University of Kansas, M.A., 1965. *Politics:* Independent.

ADDRESSES: Home—626 West Waveland 1E, Chicago, IL 60613. *Office*—Catherine College, 2 North LaSalle St., Chicago, IL 60602.

CAREER: Researcher and publicist for various firms in Los Angeles, CA, 1975-77; Rand McNally, Skokie, IL, editorial director, 1977-81; freelance writer, Chicago, IL, 1981-82; Jenner & Block (law firm), Chicago, proofreader, recruiter, and trainer, 1982-85; Catherine College, Chicago, instructor in English and office skills, 1985—. Instructor in German at University of Kansas, University of Missouri, University of Illinois, Harold Washington College, and Rosary College. Writing consultant for individuals and nonprofit organizations. Member of Citizens Action Program; member of Women Employed.

MEMBER: American Society for Training and Development, National Business Education Association, Chicago Women in Publishing.

WRITINGS:

Careers for Animal Lovers and Other Zoological Types, NTC Publishing, 1991.
Careers for Nature Lovers and Other Outdoor Types, NTC Publishing, 1992.

Wildlife columnist, *Sentinel* newspaper, Woodstock, IL, 1981.

WORK IN PROGRESS: A book on cats; a German book with tapes; a follow-up book on animal lovers for younger people (10-14); a career book for night owls; short stories.

SIDELIGHTS: Louise Miller commented: "I was born and reared in Chicago, Illinois, but have lived in Kansas, Missouri, California, Germany, and Austria. As a young girl, I was fascinated with geography, travel, and language. I grew up during World War II and was especially interested in Germany, probably because I have a German heritage and Germany was so much in the news at that time (and not for good reasons). Only five years after the end of the war (1950), I knew I was going to spend some time in Europe, maybe even as a glamorous foreign correspondent for a major newspaper!

"Although that was not to be my fate, I did study in Vienna, Austria, and Bonn, Germany, in my late teens and early twenties. I went on to become a German instructor at several universities and colleges. But in the process of learning the spelling, grammar, and beautiful new sounds of this wondrous language, I was not neglecting my English—not with my grandmother (a stickler for spelling) and the sisters in the Catholic schools that I attended. I was also quite intrigued by the flexibility, rich vocabulary, and literary tradition of English and loved to compare words and sounds of both languages.

"In the late 1960s, when many foreign languages were being dropped from college and university programs, I decided to try my hand at commercial writing and editing for publishing houses in Chicago. I started out as a copy editor and writer for a brand-new, from-scratch encyclopedia on aviation and aerospace. During the 1970s, I worked full time and freelanced articles and brochures in the fields of real estate, economics, and anything else that would give me some experience. For several years, I was research director for *Compton's Encyclopedia.* During that time, I was sent to Hollywood to set up a research facility for a new TV quiz show called *Gambit.* I was also a senior editor for the *Mobil Travel Guide,* which entailed conducting research, travel writing, and supervising. I have also worked as a legal proofreader and am currently teaching English and German and conducting writing workshops. So when the publisher approached me about actually writing a book of my own, I felt I was ready.

"The important thing for me now is to write every day, to keep some quiet time to think, and always be alert to a new story idea, research project, human experience, or special interest. Then I just hope the muse will be with me when I'm near my new computer!"

*   *   *

MILLER, Tice L.   1938-

PERSONAL: Born August 11, 1938, in Lexington, NE; son of Tice M. (a farmer) and Thyra V. (a farmer and homemaker; maiden name, Lewis) Miller; married Carren J. Hammerstrom (in television operations), September 6, 1963; children: Dane T., Graeme H. *Education:* Nebraska State Teachers College at Kearney (now Kearney State College), B.A., 1960; University of Nebraska—Lincoln, M.A., 1961; University of Illinois at Urbana-Champaign, Ph.D., 1968. *Politics:* Democrat. *Religion:* Unitarian-Universalist.

ADDRESSES: Home—4630 Bingham Ct., Lincoln, NE 68516. *Office*—Department of Theatre Arts and Dance, 215 Temple, University of Nebraska—Lincoln, Lincoln, NE 68588.

CAREER: Kansas City Junior College, Kansas City, MO, instructor, 1961-62; University of West Florida, Pensacola, assistant professor, 1968-72; University of Nebraska—Lincoln, associate professor, 1972-80, professor of theater arts and dance, 1980—, department head, 1989—, fellow of Center for Great Plains Study, 1979—, executive director of Nebraska Repertory Theatre Summer Equity Company, 1988—. National Educational Theatre Convention, chairperson, 1986. *Military service:* U.S. Naval Reserve, 1962-71, active duty as supply officer, 1962-65; became lieutenant commander.

MEMBER: Association for Theatre in Higher Education (vice-president for research and publication, 1987-89), American Theatre Association (member of Midwest regional council, 1982-85), National Association of Schools of Theatre (member of Commission on Accreditation, 1994), Mid-America Theatre Conference, Nebraska Theatre Association (president, 1975).

AWARDS, HONORS: Fellow, College of Fellows of the American Theatre, John F. Kennedy Center for the Performing Arts, 1992.

WRITINGS:

Bohemians and Critics: Nineteenth Century Theatre Criticism, Scarecrow, 1981.
(Associate editor and contributor) *Shakespeare Around the Globe: Notable Postwar International Revivals,* Greenwood Press, 1986.

(Editor with Don Wilmeth) *The Cambridge Guide to American Theatre,* Cambridge University Press, 1993.
(Editor with Ron Engle) *The American Stage,* Cambridge University Press, 1993.

Work represented in books, including *The Cambridge Guide to World Theatre,* Cambridge University Press, 1988; and *When They Weren't Doing Shakespeare,* University of Georgia Press, 1989. Contributor to theater and communication journals. Member of editorial board, *Pirandellian Studies,* 1985, *Theatre Studies,* 1987—, and *Theatre History Studies,* 1981—.

WORK IN PROGRESS: The American Theatre and Public Life, 1840-1870, completion expected in 1996.

SIDELIGHTS: Tice L. Miller told *CA:* "I am interested in placing American theater in the context of American culture, to show how influence works both ways. Theater has not only reflected the culture, but in turn has influenced the culture. I am especially interested in the role theater has played in American public life, and how this has changed over the years. A native Nebraskan, I have encouraged my students to study the nineteenth-century midwestern opera houses and understand the role they played in the cultural life of the community. We must also broaden our definition of theater to include films and television."

*   *   *

MILLER, Warren   1921-1966
(Amanda Vail)

PERSONAL: Born August 31, 1921, in Stowe, PA; died of lung cancer, April 20, 1966, in New York, NY; son of Carl Miller and Rose Singer; married; children: Scott, Eve. *Education:* University of Iowa, B.A. and M.A., 1948.

CAREER: Writer. University of Iowa, Iowa City, instructor of literature, during 1950s; also worked in public relations and sales in New York City. *Military service:* Served during World War II.

AWARDS, HONORS: National Institute of Arts and Letters grant, 1961.

WRITINGS:

NOVELS

The Sleep of Reason, Secker & Warburg, 1956, Little, Brown, 1960.
The Way We Live Now, Little, Brown, 1958.
The Cool World, Little, Brown, 1959.
Flush Times, Little, Brown, 1962.
Looking for the General, McGraw-Hill, 1964.
The Siege of Harlem, McGraw-Hill, 1965.

ROMANTIC NOVELS; UNDER PSEUDONYM AMANDA VAIL

Love Me Little, McGraw-Hill, 1957.
The Bright Young Things, Little, Brown, 1958.

CHILDREN'S BOOKS

King Carlo of Capri, illustrations by Edward Sorel, Harcourt, 1958.
Pablo Paints a Picture, illustrations by Edward Sorel, Little, Brown, 1959.
The Goings-On at Little Wishful, illustrations by Edward Sorel, Little, Brown, 1959.

OTHER

Ninety Miles from Home: The Face of Cuba Today (nonfiction), Little, Brown, 1961, published in England as *The Lost Plantation: The Face of Cuba Today,* Secker & Warburg, 1961.

Literary editor for *Nation,* 1965-66; contributor to *New Yorker, Saturday Evening Post,* and *Esquire.*

BIOGRAPHICAL/CRITICAL SOURCES:

PERIODICALS

New York Times, February 13, 1972, p. 5.

OBITUARIES:

PERIODICALS

Antiquarian Bookman, May 2, 1966.
Newsweek, May 9, 1966.
New York Herald Tribune, April 21, 1966.
New York Times, April 21, 1966, p. 39.
Publishers Weekly, May 2, 1966, p. 36.*

*   *   *

MILLETT, John D(avid)   1912-1993

OBITUARY NOTICE—See index for *CA* sketch: Born March 14, 1912, in Indianapolis, IN; died November 14, 1993, in Oxford, OH. Educator and author. After receiving his doctorate from Columbia University in 1938, Millett began his career with the Social Science Research Council in New York City, later transferring to the National Resources Planning Board in Washington, D.C., for one year. During World War II Millett joined the United States Army; he achieved the rank of colonel and won the Legion of Merit award. In 1945 Millett accepted a position as associate professor at Columbia University, where he remained until 1953, advancing to director of the Center of Administrative Studies. He then served as president of Miami University in Oxford, Ohio, for nine years, and in 1964 he became the first chancellor of the state's Board of Regents, a post he held for eight years. In 1972

Millett became vice-president of the Academy for Educational Development in Washington, D.C. He was the author of numerous books on management, government planning, and educational finance. Among his publications are *The Process and Organization of Government Planning; The Liberating Arts: Essays in General Education; What Is a College For?; Decision Making and Administration in Higher Education; Management, Governance, and Leadership: A Guide for College and University Administrators;* and *Conflict in Higher Education.*

OBITUARIES AND OTHER SOURCES:

BOOKS

Who's Who in America, 45th edition, Marquis, 1988, p. 2162.

PERIODICALS

Chicago Tribune, November 21, 1993, p. 10.

*   *   *

MILNE, John   1952-
(Ian Miller)

PERSONAL: Born September 20, 1952, in Bermondsey, England; son of Alexander (a docker) and Sheila (a seamstress; maiden name, Levett) Milne; married Sarah Letitia Beresford Verity (a painter), 1983; children: Alexander, Hugh. *Education:* Attended Chelsea School of Art (London), 1976-77; Ravensbourne College of Art and Design (Chislehurst, England), B.A., 1980. *Politics:* Socialist/Labour. *Religion:* "None; educated as Roman Catholic."

ADDRESSES: Home—La Poultiere, Roz-sur-Covesnon 35610, France. *Agent*—c/o Lemon Unna and Durbridge Ltd., Pottery Lane, London W11 England.

CAREER: Police officer, 1969-73; manual worker, 1973-76; full-time writer, 1980—. Has also worked variously as a delivery driver and factory worker.

AWARDS, HONORS: Creative writing fellowship from the Council of Art—Britain, 1983-85; John Llewellyn Rhys Memorial Prize from the National Book League, 1985, for *Out of the Blue;* Writer's Guild Award for best drama serial, 1992, for *Taggart.*

WRITINGS:

CRIME NOVELS

Tyro, Hamish Hamilton, 1982.
London Fields, Hamish Hamilton, 1983.
Out of the Blue, Hamish Hamilton, 1985.

JAMES JENNER CRIME SERIES

Dead Birds, Hamish Hamilton, 1986, Viking, 1987.

Shadow Play, Heinemann, 1987, published in the United States as *The Moody Man,* Viking, 1988.
Daddy's Girl, St. Martin's, 1988.

UNDER PSEUDONYM IAN MILLER

Wet Wickets and Dusty Balls: The Diary of a Cricketing Year (novel), Hamish Hamilton, 1986.

Also writes scripts for television series, including *Taggart, The Bill, Bererac, Perfect Scoundrels, East Enders, Boon, Lovejoy, Sam Saturday, Crime Story,* and *Pie in the Sky.* Contributor of book reviews and features for *Time Out* magazine.

WORK IN PROGRESS: Alive and Kicking, a new James Jenner novel.

SIDELIGHTS: John Milne told *CA* that after completing art school, he "became a writer by accident" because he "couldn't afford any paint." Regarding personal insights, he stated that "I don't have anything to say that can't be found in my novels." Milne introduced himself to readers with the publication of his first novel, *Tyro,* in 1982. In ensuing years he defined himself as a well-respected writer of detective/mystery fiction, including his popular series of novels featuring private investigator James Jenner. Richard Brown described Milne in *Twentieth Century Crime and Mystery Writers* as "a skilled performer in what has recently become known as the new sub-genre of the 'London Novel' that has attained a near cult status in some circles."

Milne's first three crime novels serve as stylistic precursors to his later work in the Jenner series. The first, *Tyro,* moves from the violence of Belfast, Ireland, to the placidity of England's Lake District, to London, and back to Ireland. It tells the story of Joe Jackman, a British army private who tries to reconcile the dehumanizing elements of his job with the supposed virtues of army life, but he encounters disillusionment at every turn, particularly when a West Indian soldier is killed and later when he meets the bohemian friends of a love interest. Milne's next book, *London Fields,* is rooted in the London underworld; it tells the story of Elf Hicks, a small-time Cockney thief and scam artist who is led to betray his best friend by a manipulative woman and an opportunistic police officer. At the center of Milne's award-winning *Out of the Blue* is the elusive artist Paul Brown, a duplicitous painter who leads several would-be biographers on a chase from London, to Munich, to his studio in Bavaria, with murders popping up around him.

Reviewers generally regarded these early novels as an auspicious start to Milne's writing career. In the *Times Literary Supplement,* John Melmoth found *Tyro* "skillfully-rendered" and praised it for its "linguistic virtuosity." For Randy Hogan in the *New York Times Book Review,* the narrative passages of *London Fields* were "unusually graceful," and he found the book as a whole "incisive and convincing." Writing about *Out of the Blue* in the *New Statesman,* Grace Ingoldby enthused: "This is a very rich, well written story where nothing is skimped, full of insight, information and humour."

With *Dead Birds* Milne introduced readers to James Jenner, a retired cop who has lost a leg in a terrorist bombing. Wry, sardonic, resilient, intimidated by his ex-wife, Jenner hates the French and is more at home in seedy London East End locales than in some of the more elegant venues where his services as a private eye are requisitioned. In *Dead Birds,* he is hired by a shady boxing manager to look after the man's wife. The woman turns up dead the next day. In *Shadow Play* (published in the United States as *The Moody Man*), Jenner finds a corpse in a friend's London apartment. The search for his missing friend and the identity of the dead person takes Jenner to Paris and back, all the while contending with his ex-wife, uncooperative police, and a web of frame-ups and bluffs. In *Daddy's Girl,* Jenner is hired by a touring American author to find his missing daughter. Again it's off to Paris, where Jenner encounters the daughter's boyfriend, the son of a mafioso, and where he's drawn into the tangled machinations of a drug-smuggling operation.

The abiding appeal of the James Jenner mysteries is summed up in *Publishers Weekly*'s appraisal of *Daddy's Girl.* The review credited the book with having the requisite components for a well-made adventure/mystery, including beautiful women, illegal goods, "murder, mobsters and a fast-paced plot." Milne's audience of readers has grown with each successive book. Critics agree that Milne's appealing central character, his intriguing plots, and his ability to bring places to life will no doubt ensure a loyal and growing following. Brown stated in *Twentieth-Century Crime and Mystery Writers* that "John Milne has made his mark as one of the most interesting . . . English crime writers around."

BIOGRAPHICAL/CRITICAL SOURCES:

BOOKS

Twentieth-Century Crime and Mystery Writers, 3rd edition, St. Martin's, 1991, pp. 771-72.

PERIODICALS

New Statesman, April 5, 1985, p. 32.
New York Times Book Review, August 5, 1984, p. 18; June 4, 1989, p. 24.
Publishers Weekly, April 28, 1989, p. 63.
Times (London), March 28, 1985; September 25, 1986.
Times Literary Supplement, December 17, 1982, p. 1398; June 17, 1983, p. 622; January 9, 1987, p. 42.

MISURELLA, Fred 1940-

PERSONAL: Born February 28, 1940, in Newark, NJ; son of Adam R. (a tailor) and Madeline B. (a homemaker) Misurella; married Kim McKay (a professor of English), June 3, 1989. *Education:* Montclair State College, B.A., 1962; University of Iowa, M.A., 1963, Ph.D., 1975.

ADDRESSES: Home—Stroudsburg, PA. *Office*—Department of English, East Stroudsburg University, East Stroudsburg, PA 18301.

CAREER: University of Iowa, Iowa City, instructor in English, 1972-74; University of Paris, Paris, France, Fulbright lecturer, 1975-76, lecturer in American civilization and literature, 1975-77; City University of New York, New York City, adjunct professor of English, 1978; East Stroudsburg University, East Stroudsburg, PA, professor of English, 1978—. *Village Voice,* copy editor, 1978.

MEMBER: Modern Language Association of America.

AWARDS, HONORS: Award from *Kansas Quarterly* and Kansas Art Commission, 1992.

WRITINGS:

Understanding Milan Kundera: Public Events, Private Affairs, University of South Carolina Press, 1993.

Contributor of articles, poems, and reviews to periodicals, including *Partisan Review, Salmagundi, Tel Quel, Focus/Midwest, Small Pond,* and *University of Windsor Review.* Assistant editor, *Philological Quarterly,* 1974; articles editor, *Paris Metro,* 1976-77.

WORK IN PROGRESS: A Man of His Time, a collection of short fiction; *Short Time,* a novel; research on the life and philosophy of Vincent van Gogh.

SIDELIGHTS: Fred Misurella told *CA:* "I am interested in the novel and all its possible forms. Milan Kundera is the greatest practitioner of the contemporary novel, in my opinion, and I wrote my study of his work in order to increase my understanding of his art. I have also learned from his novels how to construct my own fiction and how to be a better writer of stories and novels."

*   *   *

MITCHELL, Henry (Clay, II) 1923-1993

OBITUARY NOTICE—See index for *CA* sketch: Born November 24, 1923, in Washington, DC; died of cancer, November 12, 1993, in Washington, DC. Journalist and author. In a journalism career spanning more than forty years, Mitchell got his start as a copywriter at the Washington, D.C. *Evening Star* in 1949. Moving to Memphis, Tennessee, to become a reporter for the *Commercial Appeal* in 1951, he then advanced to editor at the *Delta Review.* He began work at the *Washington Post* in 1970, retiring in 1991. He was the author of two weekly columns, "Earthman" and "Any Day." Specializing in gardening, Mitchell's articles were popular among readers for "common sense, good humor, modesty and a certain durable skepticism," according to J. Y. Smith in a *Washington Post* obituary. Other works by Mitchell include *The Essential Earthman: Henry Mitchell on Gardening,* published in 1981. In 1992 Mitchell saw publication of a second collection of his "Earthman" columns, called *One Man's Garden.*

OBITUARIES AND OTHER SOURCES:

BOOKS

Who's Who in America, 48th edition, Marquis, 1994, p. 2413.

PERIODICALS

Washington Post, November 13, 1993, p. B6 and G1.

*   *   *

MITCHELL, John 1930-

PERSONAL: Born July 16, 1930, in Los Angeles, CA; son of Homer Irving (an attorney) and Katharine (a homemaker; maiden name, Reid) Mitchell; married Margo Copeland (a ceramist), December 17, 1949; children: Ruth Mitchell de Aguilar, John Cook, Mary, Joel Beach. *Education:* Stanford University, B.A., 1952; Claremont Graduate School, M.A., 1956. *Politics:* Democrat. *Religion:* Episcopalian. *Avocational Interests:* Surfing, jogging, tennis.

ADDRESSES: Home—P.O. Box R, Kaneohe, HI 96744.

CAREER: Teacher in Pauloff Harbor, AK, 1950-51, and Kenai, AK, 1952-53; University of Hawaii, Honolulu, HI, instructor, 1954-56 and 1962-63; owner and operator of a commercial fishing business in Alaskan waters, 1953—.

AWARDS, HONORS: Pushcart Prize, 1984, for *Alaska Stories.*

WRITINGS:

Alaska Stories (fiction), Plover Press, 1984.
Exile in Alaska (stories), Plover Press, 1987.
(Translator from Spanish with daughter Ruth Mitchell de Aguilar) Jose Ruben Romero, *Notes of a Villager* (novel), Plover Press, 1988.
(Translator from Spanish with daughter Ruth Mitchell de Aguilar) Paco Ignacio Taibo II, *Calling All Heroes* (novel), Plover Press, 1990.
(Translator from Spanish with daughter Ruth Mitchell de Aguilar) Matias Montes Huidobro, *Qwert and the Wedding Gown* (novel), Plover Press, 1992.

(Translator from Spanish with daughter Ruth Mitchell de Aguilar) Silvia Molina, *Gray Skies Tomorrow* (novel), Plover Press, 1993.

WORK IN PROGRESS: The Pied Pipers, a novel about the creative writing industry.

SIDELIGHTS: John Mitchell told *CA:* "I began teaching at the age of twenty, when the minimum requirement in Alaska was a high school education. Like my study of English literature, which led to a master's degree in 1954, the work held interest for me primarily as a forum for my literary theories, which I inflicted even on gradeschool children. After 1962, I turned to commercial fishing, which had the dual benefits of money and material, of which teaching offered little. When success still proved elusive, I began translating because it forced a word-by-word attention to language and structure, which mere criticism never achieves. I was fifty-four when by this winding path I won my first national prize."

*   *   *

MITGUTSCH, Ali   1935-

PERSONAL: Born August 21, 1935; son of Ludwig and Paula Mitgutsch; married Karin Ramm, February 4, 1960; children: Oliver, Florian, Katrin. *Religion:* Catholic.

ADDRESSES: Home—Tuerkenstrasse 54, 8000 Muenchen 40, Germany. *Office*—Schraudolphstrasse 26, 8000 Muenchen 40, Germany.

CAREER: Publishing art designer. Children's book author and illustrator.

AWARDS, HONORS: Received a significant German children's book prize for *Rundherum in meiner Stadt* (title means *All around My Town*).

WRITINGS:

"START TO FINISH" SERIES; SELF-ILLUSTRATED

From Beet to Sugar (originally published as *Von der Ruebe zum Zucker*), Carolrhoda, 1981.
From Blossom to Honey (originally published as *Von der Blute zum Honig*), Carolrhoda, 1981.
From Cacao Bean to Chocolate (originally published as *Vom Kakao zur Schokolade*), Carolrhoda, 1981.
From Cement to Bridge (originally published as *Vom Zement zur Brucke*), Carolrhoda, 1981.
From Clay to Bricks (originally published as *Vom Lehn zum Ziegel*), Carolrhoda, 1981.
From Cotton to Pants (originally published as *Von der Baumwolle zur Hose*), Carolrhoda, 1981.
From Cow to Shoe (originally published as *Von der Kuh zum Schuh*), Carolrhoda, 1981.

From Fruit to Jam (originally published as *Vom Obst zur Marmelade*), Carolrhoda, 1981.
From Grain to Bread (originally published as *Vom Korn zum Brot*), Carolrhoda, 1981.
From Grass to Butter (originally published as *Vom Gras zur Butter*), Carolrhoda, 1981.
From Milk to Ice Cream (originally published as *Von der Milch zum Speiseeis*), Carolrhoda, 1981.
From Oil to Gasoline (originally published as *Vom Erdol zum Benzin*), Carolrhoda, 1981.
From Ore to Spoon (originally published as *Vom Erz zum Loffel*), Carolrhoda, 1981.
From Sand to Glass (originally published as *Vom Sand zum Glas*), Carolrhoda, 1981.
From Seed to Pear (originally published as *Vom Kern zur Birne*), Carolrhoda, 1981.
From Sheep to Scarf (originally published as *Vom Schaf zum Schal*), Carolrhoda, 1981.
From Tree to Table (originally published as *Vom Baum zum Tisch*), Carolrhoda, 1981.
From Gold to Money (originally published as *Vom Gold zum Geld*), Carolrhoda, 1985.
From Graphite to Pencil (originally published as *Vom Graphit zum Bleistift*), Carolrhoda, 1985.
From Sea to Salt (originally published as *Vom Meer zum Salz*), Carolrhoda, 1985.
From Swamp to Coal (originally published as *Vom Urwald zur Kohle*), Carolrhoda, 1985.
From Lemon to Lemonade (originally published as *Von der Zitrone zur Limonade*), Carolrhoda, 1986.
From Rubber Tree to Tire (originally published as *Vom Kautschuksaft zum Reifen*), Carolrhoda, 1986.
From Wood to Paper (originally published as *Vom Holz zum Papier*), Carolrhoda, 1986.
From Idea to Toy (originally published as *Vom Bar zum Teddy*), Carolrhoda, 1988.
From Picture to Picture Book (originally published as *Vom Maler zum Bilderbuch*), Carolrhoda, 1988.

IN ENGLISH TRANSLATION; SELF-ILLUSTRATED

World on Wheels, translated and adapted by Alice Popper, Golden Press, 1975, published in England as *All about Wheels,* Dent.
The Busy Book, Golden Press, 1976.
A Knight's Book (originally published as *Ali Mitgutsch Ritterbuch*), translation by Elizabeth D. Crawford, Clarion Books, 1991.

OTHER

(With Irmgard Haller) *Die Hexe und die sieben Fexe,* Ravensburger, 1970.

Also author of *All around My Town,* Western Publishing (originally published as *Rundherum in meiner Stadt,* Ravensburger), and *Nico Finds a Treasure,* Blackie. Author of untranslated published works, including *Unsere grosse Stadt, Bei uns im Dorf, Komm' mit ans Wasser, Wir spielen Abenteuer, In den Bergen, Rund um's Rad, Rund um's Schiff, Pirateninsel,* and *Von der Skizze zum Buch.*

SIDELIGHTS: Ali Mitgutsch is best known as an illustrator whose colorful, engaging paintings often carry a humorous element in science-oriented books for young children. His first book translated into English, *World on Wheels,* uses bright, busy illustrations to present the evolution of the wheel and its many uses. This work was followed by an extensive science-oriented series of books for young children called "Start to Finish" books, published in the United States by Carolrhoda. Including such works as *From Beet to Sugar, From Grass to Butter, From Tree to Table,* and *From Picture to Picture Book,* the series breaks down both natural and technological processes into simple terms and processes for the young reader or preschooler curious about the origin of common objects. While some reviewers have observed that the series oversimplifies some processes, many find the series effective in explaining complex topics to young children.

Another work by Mitgutsch to appear in English, *A Knight's Book,* tells the story of a young squire who learns to joust from a poor but valiant knight and then stays on at his castle to help prepare for an impending attack. The book has been praised for its informative text and colorful, detailed illustrations of medieval life. A contributor to *Kirkus Reviews* comments that the story's "greatest strength is its informational value." Another work translated for English-speaking readers, *Nico Finds a Treasure,* presents the story of a shy boy who proves his worth to the relatives he is visiting by finding a fantastic treasure. Again, Mitgutsch's colorful illustrations were singled out for critical praise.

BIOGRAPHICAL/CRITICAL SOURCES:

PERIODICALS

Booklist, October 15, 1981, pp. 300-301.
Junior Bookshelf, December, 1976, pp. 316-17; February, 1986, p. 27.
Kirkus Reviews, August 15, 1991, p. 1092.
School Library Journal, January, 1982, p. 63; October, 1991, p. 125.

*   *   *

MOEN, Matthew C. 1958-

PERSONAL: Born June 19, 1958, in Sioux Falls, SD; son of Kenneth (in business) and Verona (an educator) Moen; married; wife's name, Donna (a nurse). *Education:* Augu-

stana College, B.A., 1980; University of Oklahoma, M.A., 1983, Ph.D., 1986.

ADDRESSES: Office—5754 North Stevens, University of Maine at Orono, Orono, ME 04469.

CAREER: University of Maine at Orono, assistant professor, 1986-91, associate professor, 1992—.

WRITINGS:

The Christian Right and Congress, University of Alabama Press, 1989.
The Transformation of the Christian Right, University of Alabama Press, 1992.
(Editor with Lowell Gustafson) *The Religious Challenge to the State,* Temple University Press, 1992.

WORK IN PROGRESS: Research on the history of the National Endowment for the Arts.

SIDELIGHTS: Matthew C. Moen told *CA:* "The principal focus of my writing is the intersection of the so-called 'new Christian Right' and American political institutions. I strive to approach the subject with objectivity, explaining the rise of the Christian Right, its political impact, and its permutations over time in a fair and balanced manner."

*   *   *

MONTGOMERY, M(aurice) R(ichard) 1938-

PERSONAL: Born February 24, 1938, in Glasgow, MT; son of M. R. (an engineer) and Mary E. (a homemaker; maiden name, Poulson) Montgomery; married Florence Yoshiko Watanabe (an artist), February 16, 1963. *Education:* Stanford University, A.B., 1960; University of Oregon, M.A., 1963; Harvard University, M.Ed., 1965. *Politics:* Liberal. *Religion:* "Shaky."

ADDRESSES: Home—Lincoln, MA. *Office*—*Boston Globe,* Boston, MA 02107.

CAREER: Worked as a carpenter in California, 1955-1960; *Boston Globe* (newspaper), Boston, MA, feature writer, 1973—. *Military service:* U.S. Army and U.S. Army Reserves, discharged 1964, became staff sergeant.

AWARDS, HONORS: Nieman Fellow, Harvard University, 1983-84.

WRITINGS:

In Search of L. L. Bean, illustrated by Mary F. Rhinelander, Little, Brown, 1984.
(With Gerald L. Foster) *A Field Guide to Airplanes of North America,* illustrated by Foster, Houghton Mifflin, 1984, second edition, 1992.
Saying Goodbye: A Memoir for Two Fathers, Knopf, 1989.

The Way of the Trout: An Essay on Anglers, Wild Fish, and Running Water, illustrated by Katherine Brown-Wing, Knopf, 1991.

WORK IN PROGRESS: An untitled travel book on the Rocky Mountains and the Great Basin, for Simon & Schuster.

SIDELIGHTS: Author M. R. Montgomery has been a columnist with the *Boston Globe* for approximately two decades. In the 1980s he began writing books, and in 1984 two of his titles, *A Field Guide to Airplanes of North America* and *In Search of L. L. Bean,* were printed. The latter, which both chronicled the life of the titled company's founder—an amateur outdoorsman who hated to get his feet wet—and followed the company's rise to one of the nation's top mail-order firms, attracted more attention from critics. "From the moment you pick up M. R. Montgomery's *In Search of L. L. Bean,* you know you've got hold of something a bit unusual," hailed Christopher Lehmann-Haupt of the *New York Times.* The same critic described the book as "an edifying tale of America's development as a consuming society." David Traxel in his article for the *New York Times Book Review* concluded that Montgomery "has done a good job of tracing this Maine success story."

Montgomery chose a more personal subject for his next achievement, 1989's *Saying Goodbye: A Memoir of Two Fathers.* In this book he concentrates more on the life and death of his own father, an engineer who was reticent even within the ranks of his own family, and he pays tribute to his father-in-law, a Japanese-American physician who suffered through the discrimination faced by those of his ancestry in the United States during World War II. Cyra McFadden, reviewing *Saying Goodbye* in the *New York Times Book Review,* praised the work for its "plain telling of a tale, without affectation or flourishes but with tenderness." McFadden also observed, "In this restrained but deeply moving book, a model of good prose, fine particles breathe life." *Los Angeles Times Book Review*'s Pauline Mayer judged that "Montgomery's canvas is vast and varied, his hand sensitive and sure."

In the 1991 book *The Way of the Trout: An Essay on Anglers, Wild Fish, and Running Water,* the author explores not only practical aspects of fishing, but philosophical ones as well. As Le Anne Schreiber reported in the *New York Times Book Review,* Montgomery's "more passionate preoccupations are with the geology, biology and fluid dynamics of streams, with the behavior of trout and with the special beauty of trout country." A *Los Angeles Times Book Review* critic lauded *The Way of the Trout,* calling it "an exemplary fishing book."

BIOGRAPHICAL/CRITICAL SOURCES:

PERIODICALS

Los Angeles Times Book Review, June 18, 1989, p. 1; May 19, 1991, p. 6.
New York Times, November 16, 1984.
New York Times Book Review, December 30, 1984; June 4, 1989, p. 7; June 9, 1991, p. 13.
Washington Post Book World, January 13, 1985, p. 11.

*   *   *

MORGAN, Dan 1937-

PERSONAL: Born August 20, 1937, in New York, NY; married Elaine Shannon (a journalist). *Education:* Harvard University, B.A., 1958.

ADDRESSES: Office—Washington Post, 1150 15th St. NW, Washington, DC 20071. *Agent*—International Creative Management, 40 West 57th St., New York, NY 10019.

CAREER: Washington Post, reporter and editor, 1963—, correspondent in Bonn, Germany, and Belgrade, Yugoslavia (now Serbia), 1967-73. *Military service:* U.S. Army.

AWARDS, HONORS: Merchants of Grain was named a notable book by the American Library Association, 1979, and nominated for American Book Award, 1981; Gerald Loeb award, John E. Anderson Graduate School of Management at University of California, Los Angeles, 1984; Champion Media Award, Amos Tuck School of Business Administration at Dartmouth College, 1984; Hancock Award, John Hancock Mutual Life Insurance Company, 1984.

WRITINGS:

Merchants of Grain, Viking, 1979.
(Editor and author of introduction) Patrick Welsh, *Tales Out of School: A Teacher's Candid Account from the Front Lines of the American High School Today,* Viking, 1986.
Rising in the West: The True Story of an "Okie" Family from the Great Depression through the Reagan Years, Knopf, 1992; reissued under the title *Rising in the West: The True Story of an "Okie" Family in Search of the American Dream,* Vintage Books, 1993.

Contributor to periodicals.

SIDELIGHTS: For more than two decades Dan Morgan has been an investigative reporter for the *Washington Post.* After returning to the United States from stints as a European correspondent based in Belgrade in the former Yugoslavia, and Bonn, Germany, Morgan has covered agricultural and natural resource topics, both nationally and internationally. He has written several nonfiction books as well, including the nationwide best-seller *Merchants of Grain.*

In *Merchants of Grain* Morgan delves into the operations of the five family-owned businesses that control the international grain market (Cargill, Continental, Andre, Louis Dreyfus, and Bunge). Maintaining that grain is "the only resource in the world that is even more central to modern civilization than oil," Morgan chronicles the convoluted history of the grain trade, beginning in the nineteenth century. He also considers the weighty influence of grain marketers on domestic politics and foreign policy; among the topics he covers are the United States government's use of food as a weapon, its 1972 grain sales to Russia, Secretary of State Henry Kissinger's attempt in 1975 to coerce oil concessions from the Russians using grain as an incentive, and the Department of Agriculture's creation of an agricultural dependency in Iran.

Because privately owned companies do not have to publish annual reports there is often much secrecy surrounding them. Morgan used the few public documents which were available and interviews with former employees to write what James Risser of the *Washington Post Book World* found "an extensively researched and highly readable book" and what Marilyn Bender of the *New York Times Book Review* termed "a sprawling, sometimes untidy book with a nonetheless engrossing plot." Robert Engler commented in the *Nation* that Morgan "mixes hard data and anecdote in readable proportions." Writing in the *New Republic,* Robert Sherrill stated that Morgan "does a fine job of portraying the movement of food in the world, and its effect on whole nations. . . . There's as much high adventure as low morals in this commerce."

Interested in the Depression-era migration of midwesterners to California since he first read John Steinbeck's *The Grapes of Wrath* as a teenager, Morgan chose the subject as the theme of his next book. *Rising in the West: The True Story of an "Okie" Family from the Great Depression through the Reagan Years* is the story of four generations of the Tatham family who left Oklahoma in 1934 to make a new life in the San Joaquin Valley of California. Unlike the Okies immortalized in Steinbeck's novel who remain migrant workers, the book's central character, Oca Tatham, becomes an entrepreneur and rises to a position of wealth and influence in conservative politics. "The first third of *Rising in the West*—what could be called 'The Making of Oca Tatham'—could hardly be better," stated Greg Mitchell in the *New York Times Book Review.* "Mr. Morgan writes vividly about Oklahoma, Depression-era California and the Pentecostal Church."

Mitchell, however, suggested that the author was too subjective in his acceptance of the Tatham's claims. The critic wrote, "Every few pages a serious affliction is miraculously healed by prayer; and shortly after Ruby dies, God personally sends a message directing Oca to claim a new spouse. . . . Occasionally [Morgan] . . . serves as spin doctor, assuring us, for example, that 'the Tathams were not extremists.'" In the *Los Angeles Times Book Review* Jane Smiley, like Mitchell, raised objections to Morgan's relationship with the Tathams wherein he allowed members of the family to read and comment on the book prior to its publication. "This reader could not help feeling uncomfortable with such cooperation between observer and subject," Smiley wrote. "Clearly Morgan was moved by his close attention to the family, but this affection seems to sentimentalize his portrait, and to underplay forces and tensions in the family that may not be so agreeable or admirable."

On the other hand, *Chicago Tribune* contributor Donald Katz found *Rising in the West* a "very good book," and stated that "the result is at once a richly informative panorama of one part of American history from the 1930s to the present and a strangely depressing reminder that our most inspiring romances are, in the end, only that."

BIOGRAPHICAL/CRITICAL SOURCES:

BOOKS

Morgan, Dan, *Merchants of Grain,* Viking, 1979.

PERIODICALS

Chicago Tribune, September 27, 1992, p. 1.
Library Journal, March 1, 1980, p. 599.
Los Angeles Times Book Review, October 11, 1992, p. 2.
Nation, January 19, 1980, pp. 55-58.
New Republic, August 18, 1979, p. 27; August 30, 1980, p. 39.
New Yorker, July 23, 1979, p. 96.
New York Times, March 6, 1981, p. C15.
New York Times Book Review, May 27, 1979, p. 4; July 6, 1980, p. 19; October 11, 1992, p. 25.
Newsweek, July 9, 1979, p. 73.
Washington Post Book World, June 10, 1979, p. 1; December 2, 1979, p. 18.*

*   *   *

MORINIS, Alan 1949-

PERSONAL: Born December 8, 1949, in Toronto, Ontario, Canada; son of David (in business) and Bess (a homemaker; maiden name, Lapides) Morinis; married Beverly Spring (a physician), August 8, 1973; children: Julia Beth, Leora Evelyn. *Education:* York University,

B.A. (with honors), 1972; Oxford University, M.Litt., 1974, D.Phil., 1980.

ADDRESSES: Home—4537 Marguerite St., Vancouver, British Columbia V6J 4G7, Canada. Office—Ark Films, Inc., 305-1107 Homer St., Vancouver, British Columbia V6B 2Y1, Canada.

CAREER: Meta Communications, Vancouver, British Columbia, president, 1985-88; Ark Films, Inc., Vancouver, president, 1989—. Seva Foundation, member of board of directors.

MEMBER: CFTPA, ACCT.

AWARDS, HONORS: Rhodes scholar at Magdalen College, Oxford, 1972.

WRITINGS:

Pilgrimage in the Hindu Tradition, Oxford University Press, 1984.
Pilgrimage in Latin America, Greenwood Press, 1991.
Sacred Journeys: The Anthropology of Pilgrimage, Greenwood Press, 1992.

*   *   *

MORRIS, William   1913-1994

OBITUARY NOTICE—See index for CA sketch: Born April 13, 1913, in Boston, MA; died of congestive heart failure, January 2, 1994, in Columbus, OH. Lexicographer, educator, editor, and author. Morris was editor in chief of the best-selling American Heritage Dictionary of the English Language, first published in 1969 and subsequently revised several times. A Harvard University graduate, Morris taught English and Latin for a brief time before entering publishing, first at G. & C. Merriam and later at Grosset & Dunlap. During his fifteen years at Grosset & Dunlap he advanced from managing editor to editor in chief. He also began publishing a column about language, "William Morris on Words," which eventually grew into a syndicated column written with his wife, Mary Elizabeth Davis, "Words, Wit, and Wisdom." In 1960 Morris transferred to Grolier, Incorporated, where he served as executive editor and editor in chief of encyclopedias. Four years later, he joined the staff of American Heritage Publishing to begin work on the now-famous American Heritage Dictionary. Among Morris's other works are It's Easy to Increase Your Vocabulary and Your Heritage of Words, both for young people, and, with his wife, Harper Dictionary of Contemporary Usage and Morris Dictionary of Word and Phrase Origins.

OBITUARIES AND OTHER SOURCES:

BOOKS

Who's Who in America, 48th edition, Marquis, 1994, p. 2451.

PERIODICALS

Chicago Tribune, January 9, 1994, p. 6.
New York Times, January 4, 1994, p. D20.
Washington Post, January 6, 1994, p. B7.

*   *   *

MOSS, Miriam   1955-

PERSONAL: Born September 2, 1955, in Aldershot, England; daughter of John Kennedy (a lecturer) and Myra (a teacher; maiden name, Hunt) Moss; married Stephen White-Thomson (a publisher), July 28, 1984; children: Imogen, Morwenna, Finn. Education: Oxford University, B.Ed., 1977. Religion: Church of England.

ADDRESSES: Home and office—37 Hampstead Rd., Brighton, East Sussex, England.

CAREER: King's School, Canterbury, Kent, England, teacher, 1977-82; Imani School, Thika, Kenya, teacher, 1982-83; Windlesham House School, Findon, Sussex, England, teacher, 1983-85; writer. Creative writing teacher, 1993. Volunteer teacher of adult literacy.

MEMBER: Society of Authors (London), Amnesty International.

AWARDS, HONORS: Street Fashion and Fashion Design were listed by the American Library Association as recommended books for reluctant adult readers, 1992.

WRITINGS:

In the Pond, Macdonald, 1988.
The Fashion Industry, Wayland, 1989.
Women and Business, Wayland, 1989.
Castles, Andromeda, 1993.

"HOW THEY LIVED" SERIES

A Slave in Ancient Greece, Wayland, 1986.
A Norman Baron, Wayland, 1987.
A Schoolchild in World War II, Wayland, 1988.

"LIVING HISTORY" SERIES

The Victorians, Wayland, 1986.
The American West, Wayland, 1986.
Great Explorers, Wayland, 1986.
The Crusades, Wayland, 1986.
Ancient China, Wayland, 1987.

"TOPICS" SERIES

Language and Writing, Wayland, 1987.
Fairs and Circuses, Wayland, 1987.
Zoos, Wayland, 1987.

"COSTUMES AND CLOTHES" SERIES

Uniforms, Wayland, 1988.
Working Clothes, Wayland, 1988.
Clothes in Hot Weather, Wayland, 1988.
Clothes in Cold Weather, Wayland, 1988.
Fashionable Clothes, Wayland, 1988.
Children's Clothes, Wayland, 1988.
Traditional Costumes, Wayland, 1988.

"MY SCHOOL" SERIES

The Schools' Librarian, Wayland, 1988.
Easter, Wayland, 1988.
The School Nurse, Wayland, 1988.

"FASHION WORLD" SERIES

Fashion Model, Wayland, 1990.
Fashion Photographer, Wayland, 1990.
Fashion Designer, Wayland, 1990.
Street Fashion, Wayland, 1990.

"THREADS" SERIES

Eggs, A & C Black, 1990.
Fruit, A & C Black, 1990.

"STAY HEALTHY" SERIES

Keep Fit, Wayland, 1992.
Eat Well, Wayland, 1992.
Be Positive, Wayland, 1992.

WORK IN PROGRESS: Stories for young children; the "Weather Watch!" series of four books on the seasons, for Wayland, 1994.

SIDELIGHTS: When Miriam Moss became pregnant with her first child, she left teaching after eight years and began looking for work which she could combine with motherhood. By chance, an editor friend asked her to write a children's information book on a subject she had taught. "Three children and more than forty books later, it has proved to be a wonderful rhythm of life which suits me," Moss commented. "I work every morning and feel full of energy and excitement at the prospect of the afternoons with my children. They have proved to be a source of inspiration for my stories too. I listen to the remarkable way in which young children use language, combining unusual words to create powerful images, and I am inspired." The author is now also running creative writing workshops in schools.

BIOGRAPHICAL/CRITICAL SOURCES:

PERIODICALS

Appraisal, summer, 1988, p. 63.
Booklist, April 15, 1988, pp. 1431-32; May 15, 1991, pp. 1790-91.
Books for Your Children, autumn, 1988, p. 30; spring, 1989, p. 16.
Bulletin of the Center for Children's Books, May, 1988.
Kirkus Reviews, May 1, 1991, p. 607.
School Library Journal, July, 1991, p. 84.

*   *   *

MULLANE, (R.) Mike   1945-

PERSONAL: Born September 10, 1945, in Wichita Falls, TX; son of Hugh J. and Marjorie (Pettigrew) Mullane; married Donna Sei (a professional speaker), June 14, 1967; children: Patrick, Amy, Laura. *Education:* U.S. Military Academy, West Point, B.S., 1967; Air Force Institute of Technology, M.S., 1975; graduated from Air Force Flight Test Engineer School, Edwards Air Force Base, CA.

ADDRESSES: Home and office—1301 Las Lomas Rd. N.E., Albuquerque, NM 87106.

CAREER: U.S. Air Force, career officer, 1968-90, retiring as colonel; served in Vietnam as a weapons system operator aboard a Phantom aircraft; astronaut for National Aeronautics and Space Administration (NASA), 1978-90. Producer of the videotape *The Ten Thousand Night Dream;* USA Network, host of the series *Inside Space;* professional speaker, 1990—.

AWARDS, HONORS: Distinguished Flying Cross, Legion of Merit, NASA Space Flight Medal, inducted into International Space Hall of Fame.

WRITINGS:

Red Sky: A Novel of Love, Space, and War, Northwest Publishing, 1993.

*   *   *

MULLEN, Patrick B.   1941-

PERSONAL: Born August 22, 1941, in Beaumont, TX; son of Borden Calvin Mullen and Lorraine Terry Mullen; married Roseanne Rini, March 17, 1972. *Education:* Lamar State College, B.A., 1964; North Texas State University, M.A., 1965; University of Texas, Ph.D., 1968.

ADDRESSES: Office—Center for Folklore Studies, Ohio State University, Columbus, OH 43210.

CAREER: State University of New York College at Buffalo, assistant professor of English and folklore, 1968-69; Ohio State University, Columbus, assistant professor, 1969-72, associate professor, 1972-81, professor of folklore, 1981—, and director of Center for Folklore Studies. University of Wisconsin—Milwaukee, visiting instructor, summers, 1969-70; Institute on Folklore and Traditions of Mexican-American, Black, and Appalachian People, instructor, summer, 1978; University of Rome, Fulbright lecturer, 1983; Utah State University, visiting professor, 1990. Cuyahoga Valley National Recreation Area, member of staff, National Folk Festival, 1983.

MEMBER: International Society for Folk Narrative Research, American Folklore Society (editor of publications, 1988-93; chairperson of Publications Committee, 1990-91), Texas Folklore Society, Ohio Folklore Society (past president).

AWARDS, HONORS: National Foundation for the Arts and Humanities grant, 1967-68; John Lyman Award in American Maritime History, from North American Society for Oceanic History, 1990, for Lake Erie Fishermen.

WRITINGS:

I Heard the Old Fishermen Say: Folklore of the Texas Gulf Coast, University of Texas Press, 1978.
(With Timothy C. Lloyd) Lake Erie Fishermen: Work, Identity, and Tradition, University of Illinois Press, 1990.
Listening to Old Voices: Folklore, Life Stories, and the Elderly, University of Illinois Press, 1992.

Work represented in anthologies, including "And Other Neighborly Names": Social Process and Cultural Image in Texas Folklore, edited by Richard Bauman and Roger D. Abrahams, University of Texas Press, 1981; Popular Beliefs and Superstitions: A Compendium of American Folklore, edited by Wayland D. Hand, Anna Casetta, and Sondra B. Thiederman, G. K. Hall, 1981; and Critical Essays on E. E. Cummings, edited by Guy Rotella, G. K. Hall, 1984. Member of editorial advisory board, Encyclopaedia of American Popular Beliefs and Superstitions. Contributor of numerous articles and reviews to scholarly journals. Member of editorial board, Contemporary Legend.

WORK IN PROGRESS: Race Relations in Folklore Fieldwork.

*   *   *

MURPHY, Claire Rudolf 1951-

PERSONAL: Born March 9, 1951, in Spokane, WA; daughter of Kermit (a lawyer) and Frances Claire (a librarian; maiden name, Collins) Rudolf; married Robert Patrick Murphy (a teacher and principal), June 9, 1979; children: Conor Liam, Megan Frances. Education: Santa Clara University, B.A., 1973; University of California—Berkeley, secondary teaching credentials, 1974; University of Alaska—Fairbanks, M.F.A. in creative writing, 1987. Politics: Democrat. Religion: Catholic. Avocational Interests: Family outdoor activities, "such as biking, swimming, hiking, and cross-country skiing," running, and tennis; music (piano and voice) and community theater.

ADDRESSES: Home—221 Well St., Fairbanks, AK 99701. Agent—Liza Voges, c/o Kirchoff/Wohlberg, 866 United Nations Plaza, New York, NY 10017.

CAREER: St. Mary's Mission High School, St. Mary's, AK, teacher of English and drama, 1974-77; Fairbanks Borough School District, Fairbanks, AK, secondary school teacher of English and drama, 1977-83; Fairbanks Correctional Center, Fairbanks, writing instructor, 1984-89; University of Alaska—Fairbanks, instructor in composition, 1990-91; free-lance writer, 1991—. Alaska State Writing Consortium teacher consultant, 1984—. Member, Fairbanks Light Opera, Immaculate Conception Church, Running Club North, and Nordale School Parent-Teacher Association.

MEMBER: Alaska Society of Children's Book Writers (cochair and presenter at 1992 convention), Fairbanks Drama Association.

WRITINGS:

Friendship across Arctic Waters: Alaskan Cub Scouts Meet Their Soviet Neighbors, photographs by Charles Mason, Lodestar/Penguin, 1991.
To the Summit (young adult novel), Lodestar/Penguin, 1992.
The Prince and the Salmon People, illustrated by Dwayne Pasco, Rizzoli Children's Library, 1993.
We Are Alaska, photographs by Charles Mason, Alaska Northwest Books, 1994.
Gold Star Sister, Lodestar, 1994.

WORK IN PROGRESS: A series of sports biographies; another Alaskan native legend; a young adult novel about Alaska in World War II.

SIDELIGHTS: Claire Rudolf Murphy commented, "My first book, Friendship across Arctic Waters: Alaskan Cub Scouts Meet Their Soviet Neighbors, came about in a very unusual way. While I was working on my MFA degree I thought I wanted to write for young adults, but I wasn't quite sure. So my thesis ended up being a collection of short stories, half for young adults and half for adult readers. Afterwards I got sidetracked for a while writing newspaper and magazine articles. At one point I was trying to sell my short story 'To the Summit' to the Boy Scout magazine *Boys' Life* because I thought they would print an adventure story. I contacted the local director of the Boy Scouts in town here to talk about what kinds of articles and stories *Boys' Life* accepted. He said, 'You know, you really should write a story about the Nome Cub Scouts, this great group of boys that do all sorts of community service projects. Besides, they need some articles about Alaska.' So I wrote a query letter to *Boys' Life* about it and they said, 'Yes, write the article.' So I interviewed several Scouts, leaders and parents in Nome about their pack and wrote an article. In the article I mentioned that their dream was to take a field trip to Provideniya, Soviet Far East.

"As it turned out *Boys' Life* didn't publish my article or short story, but the local Fairbanks newspaper did and it got reprinted around the state. So news about the Cub Scouts and their dream got around. The Nome Cub Scouts used my article to help convince American government officials to let them visit Provideniya in the summer of 1989. The trip was the opportunity of a lifetime. Here I had grown up thinking of the Russians as enemies. In fact, in school during the Fifties we used to have air raid drills and many people in my neighborhood built bomb shelters to protect their families from the terrible Russians. They were our enemies. They didn't believe in God and they wanted to control the earth. Now I had the chance to get to know them for myself. During the visit I found them to be the friendliest, most articulate and most generous people in the world (next to the Irish, of course!) Many of them spoke English because English is taught in the schools from the first grade on. They all wanted to know about life in America, our government, what Russian books I had read and movies I had seen. The scouts and the young pioneers were like long-lost buddies. They knew the same games, told the same jokes and just had fun together.

"Ever since I first saw Denali (the Athabaskan Indian name for Mount McKinley, meaning 'high one,' a term commonly used by Alaskans) in 1974 it has reached out for me, as it has to many Alaskans. It is the mighty symbol of our state, a magnificent statement about the beauty of our world. Fairbanks is only 120 miles from Denali National Park and on a clear day I can see Denali, jutting out, white and mighty. It is one of the wonders of the modern world, so I felt it deserved a novel about climbing it. I wrote *To the Summit* because I believe it speaks to the idea of how much a physical challenge such as climbing Denali can help strengthen a person's inner self. People, teens particularly, can often feel powerless today, and having confidence in one's abilities can help overcome that. Though I am athletic and have been a serious competitor at different times in my life, I have to admit that I do not at this time have the drive or discipline to climb Denali's

mighty peak. However, I have great admiration for those who attempt it and feel that researching and writing this book, I have climbed Denali in spirit. And, interviewing as many climbers and guides as I did, I feel the story is as accurate as it could be without my actually climbing it.

"My third book, *The Prince and the Salmon People,* is very special to me. The salmon is my favorite wild animal, and I am concerned with how endangered they have become today. At the University of Alaska—Fairbanks library, I came upon a set of Tsimshian legends, and included in one volume was the story of the Prince and the Salmon People. After that I found other Tsimshian and Tlingit versions of the same story. I began my own retelling of the story, using the original story along with what I was learning about the Tsimshian culture. I contacted a traditional Tsimshian artist, Jack Hudson, who lives in Metlakatla, the only Tsimshian community in Alaska. He read my story and gave me important feedback. He also validated my desire to retell this story. He said he was glad I was trying to get this Tsimshian legend out to more children. As always, I wanted to make sure it was accurate because there are so many things written about Alaska, especially the native peoples, that are not accurate.

"I really wanted a Tsimshian artist to illustrate the story. After some checking around, Dwayne Pasco, from Poulsbo, Washington was recommended as an outstanding Northwest Coast Indian artist. Though Dwayne is not Indian himself, he has spent the last forty years studying and practicing the Northwest Coast Indian art form. I hope that children around the world will enjoy and learn more about the Tsimshian people from our book, also. The Tsimshian learned how to respect and take care of the salmon, so that they would return to them every spring. My hope is that we today can take better care of the salmon so that they will continue to return to us every year, instead of dying out. The book is dedicated to my brother Matt because in 1988 he and I fought the mighty king salmon one July day and it was then that I first said aloud that I wanted to write a book about the salmon.

"I care so much about our incredible state and hopefully this book conveys that love and warmth for younger readers everywhere. We have many natural resources up here, as well as a diversity of cultural groups and wild animals, and our job as Alaskans now is to protect all we have for future generations."

*   *   *

MURPHY, Cullen 1952-

PERSONAL: Born September 1, 1952, in New Rochelle, NY; son of John Cullen (an artist) and Joan (a homemaker; maiden name, Byrne) Murphy; married Anna Marie Torres (an editor), April 7, 1979; children: John C., Anna, Timothy. *Education:* Amherst College, B.A., 1974. *Religion:* Roman Catholic.

ADDRESSES: Office—Atlantic Monthly, 745 Boylston, Boston, MA 02116.

CAREER: Wilson Quarterly, Washington, DC, editor, 1977-84; *Atlantic Monthly,* Boston, MA, managing editor, 1984—.

WRITINGS:

(With William Rathje) *Rubbish!: The Archaeology of Garbage,* Harper, 1992.

SIDELIGHTS: For additional information on the work of Cullen Murphy, please refer to collaborator William Rathje's sketch in this volume of *CA.*

*   *   *

MUSACCHIO, George   1938-

PERSONAL: Surname is pronounced Mu-*sock*-yo; born November 1, 1938, in Louisville, KY; son of Saverio George and Josie (Blair) Musacchio; married Betty Wright (an elementary schoolteacher), August 18, 1962; children: Marcus, Laura. *Education:* California Baptist College, B.A., 1962; University of California, Riverside, M.A., 1965, Ph.D., 1971. *Religion:* Baptist. *Avocational Interests:* Travel, hiking, tennis, reading.

ADDRESSES: Home—Belton, TX. *Office*—College of Arts and Sciences, Box 8438, University of Mary Hardin-Baylor, Belton, TX 76513-2599.

CAREER: California Baptist College, Riverside, instructor, 1964-66, assistant professor, 1966-68, associate professor, 1968-71, professor of English and head of department, 1971-89; University of Mary Hardin-Baylor, Belton, TX, Frank W. Mayborn Professor of Arts and Sciences and dean of College of Arts and Sciences, 1990—. Visiting professor at Baylor University, 1985, Golden Gate Baptist Theological Seminary, 1987, and Calvin College, 1988.

MEMBER: Modern Language Association of America, Milton Society of America, Conference on Christianity and Literature, Southern California C. S. Lewis Society.

WRITINGS:

(Textual editor) C. S. Lewis, *The Weight of Glory,* Unicorn Press, 1977.
Milton's Adam and Eve: Fallible Perfection, Peter Lang Publishing, 1991.

Work represented in anthologies, including *Christian Education: Pilgrimage and Performance,* California Baptist College Press, 1985. Contributor of articles and reviews to academic journals. *Lamp-Post,* editor, 1977-80, contributing editor, 1991—.

WORK IN PROGRESS: C. S. Lewis, Man and Writer: Essays and Reviews.

*   *   *

MUSGRAVE, Gerald L.   1942-

PERSONAL: Born in 1942. *Education:* Received B.A. from California State University; received M.S. and Ph.D. from Michigan State University.

ADDRESSES: Office—Economics America, Inc., 612 Church Street, Ann Arbor, MI 48104.

CAREER: Various teaching positions, including professor of economics at U.S. Naval Postgraduate School, Monterey, CA, research professor at Stanford University, Stanford, CA, professor at University of Michigan, Ann Arbor; President of Economics America, Inc., Ann Arbor. Member of Recombinant DNA Advisory Committee, National Institutes of Health.

MEMBER: National Association of Business Economists (fellow; chairperson of Health Economics Roundtable).

AWARDS, HONORS: Antony Fisher International Memorial Award, 1993, for *Patient Power: Solving America's Health Care Crisis.*

WRITINGS:

(Editor) *The Galbraith Viewpoint in Perspective: Critical Commentary on "The Age of Uncertainty" Television Series,* Hoover Institution Press, 1977.
(With James Bernard Ramsey) *APL-STAT: A Do-It-Yourself Guide to Computational Statistics Using APL,* Lifetime Learning Publications, 1981.
(With John C. Goodman) *Patient Power: Solving America's Health Care Crisis,* Cato Institute, 1992, paperback version published as *Patient Power: The Free-Enterprise Alternative to Clinton's Health Plan,* Cato Institute, 1993.

Contributor of more than seventy articles to periodicals.

SIDELIGHTS: Gerald L. Musgrave told *CA:* "There is a patient power network of organizations working to make medical savings accounts available to every citizen."

MWANGI, Meja   1948-

PERSONAL: Born December, 1948, in Nyeri, Kenya; son of a domestic worker. *Education:* Attended Kenyatta College; attended the University of Iowa, 1975.

CAREER: Writer. Assistant director of the film *Out of Africa,* 1985; member of the film production team that adapted James Fox's *White Mischief,* 1988.

AWARDS, HONORS: Jomo Kenyatta Prize, 1974, for *Kill Me Quick;* Commonwealth Writers Prize nomination, 1990, for *Striving for the Wind.*

WRITINGS:

FICTION

Kill Me Quick, Heinemann Educational, 1973.
Carcase for Hounds, Heinemann Educational, 1974.
Taste of Death, East African Publishing House (Kenya, Nairobi), 1975.
Going down River Road, Heinemann Educational, 1976.
The Bushtrackers (adapted from a screenplay by Gary Strieker), Longman Drumbeat (Nairobi), 1979.
The Cockroach Dance, Longman Kenya (Nairobi), 1979.
Bread of Sorrow, Longman Kenya, 1987.
The Return of Shaka, Longman Kenya, 1989.
Weapon of Hunger, Longman Kenya, 1989.
Striving for the Wind, Heinemann Kenya, 1990; Heinemann, 1992.

SIDELIGHTS: Kenyan Meja Mwangi describes the current African social and political situation in his writings, which employ the suspense, violence, and pacing that typify the modern thriller genre. The son of a maid who worked for white families in the British town of Nyeri, Kenya, Mwangi grew up during the Mau Mau massacres and Kenya's tumultuous independence movement. While violence raged on the outskirts of town, Mwangi spent his childhood absorbing much of the white settlers' culture from both his mother's contact with the settlers in their homes and from his reading of European children's books, which were gifts from his mother's employers.

Mwangi has remained in Kenya and bases his work upon the sufferings of his people, drawing upon his experiences with the Anglo-African society and his childhood memories of the Mau Mau uprising, and combining them with a sense of place in order to dramatize his characters' lives and their struggle for survival in contemporary Africa. Several members of Mwangi's family were sent to detention camps because they had been active in the revolution. According to Simon Gikandi, writing in the *Dictionary of Literary Biography,* Mwangi recalled being held captive in a detention camp with his mother for a short time. Mwangi was so affected by what he had witnessed and the stories he had heard of the Mau Mau uprising that he

wrote about it in his first book, *Taste of Death,* when he was seventeen years old (it was not published for several years). In this novel, the young hero, Kariuki, is swept along by the passion and excitement of the Mau Mau insurrection and Kenya's fight for independence even though he does not understand the basis of the conflict and is not ready to sacrifice his own life for the rebellion. Mwangi glorifies the conflict in the novel, telling of the freedom fighters' futile attempt to avoid death at the hands of colonial forces.

Mwangi's realistic novel *Kill Me Quick* takes place after Kenya established its independence. The protagonists, two boys who are life-long friends, try to improve their lives by attending school. They move to Nairobi in order to find work, but they discover that their classroom education is worthless in the city. They become stranded in the urban jungle, without hope for improving their situation or the ability to return to their rural homes. Desperate for money, the boys turn to crime and are apprehended, and only after they are incarcerated does the quality of their lives improve. Gikandi explained that *Kill Me Quick* is considered significant "because of Mwangi's . . . journalistic style; he renders scenes with the hard and sharp ear of a reporter on the beat." A *Choice* contributor called the novel "an incisive look at the way crime is created by poverty rather than by innate evil."

In *Carcase for Hounds,* Mwangi again deals with the themes of pessimism, futility, and hopelessness. A Mau Mau soldier and his mortally wounded revolutionary commander are trapped and surrounded by hostile British forces in a forest, a situation that Mwangi uses as a metaphor for the hopelessness both the revolutionaries and the British colonial forces feel in this stand-off. "Mwangi has usurped the language of the American thriller, of Raymond Chandler, Mickey Spillane, and Chester Himes," Gikandi wrote. "His characters speak in an American idiom that is incongruous with their situation, and the authorial descriptions also seems more appropriate for the 'jungles' of Harlem or the Bronx than for those of Kenya."

In *Going down River Road,* which is considered to be his greatest achievement, Mwangi returns to the horrors of the urban jungle. According to *World Literature Today* contributor Charles R. Larson, Mwangi paints a culture "composed . . . of young bar girls, urban thugs or youths." In 1979's *The Cockroach Dance,* Mwangi attempts to realize a balance between entertaining the reader and criticizing society. His main character, a water meter reader, is driven to despair and violence by the hopelessness and injustice he witnesses every day on his job. Mwangi's novelization of Gary Strieker's screenplay *The Bushtrackers* was also published in 1979. *Black Scholar* contributor Roland S. Jefferson called it "the first indigenous novel/film to come out of Africa with an eye toward appealing to the U.S./westernized culture." The main character reacts to every situation with anger and rage. Jefferson wrote that the novel "highlights a character who views the political and justice system around him as virtually impotent and unable to extract retribution."

In 1987's *Bread of Sorrow,* Mwangi uses the thriller genre to address the problems of apartheid and racial oppression, while his 1989 Americana-packed novel *The Return of Shaka* focuses on an African prince touring the United States on a Greyhound bus, chased across the continent by hired killers. In *Weapon of Hunger,* the worst of Africa's horrors—famine, drought, civil war, the atrocities of revolution—are played against an American pop star's efforts to save the starving. Mwangi returns to African concerns with *Striving for the Wind,* a novel of contemporary rural despair and loneliness. Mwangi's depiction of the depleted Kenyan landscape and the exhausted humans who till it earned the volume a nomination for the Commonwealth Writers Prize.

BIOGRAPHICAL/CRITICAL SOURCES:

BOOKS

Dictionary of Literary Biography, Volume 125: *Twentieth-Century Caribbean and Black African Writers: Second Series,* Gale, 1993.

Zell, Hans M., and others, *A New Reader's Guide to African Literature,* Holmes and Meier, 1983.

PERIODICALS

Black Scholar, November/December, 1984, pp. 61-63.

Choice, March, 1976, p. 78; June, 1976, p. 528.

World Literature Today, autumn, 1977, p. 565.*

—*Sketch by Mel Wathen*

* * *

MYERS, John H(olmes) 1915-1993

OBITUARY NOTICE—See index for *CA* sketch: Born January 17, 1915, in Chicago, IL; died October 22, 1993, in Bloomington, IN. Accountant, educator, and writer. An expert on accounting procedures—especially in the petroleum industry—Myers worked as a certified public accountant for one year before beginning some forty-five years as an educator. In 1939 he accepted a teaching position at the University of Buffalo in New York and rose to associate professor. In 1945 Myers transferred to Northwestern University where he remained until 1968. At that time he began teaching at Indiana University, retiring as professor emeritus in 1984. Myers also authored *Statistical Presentation, Auditing Cases,* and *Business Research: Text and Cases.*

OBITUARIES AND OTHER SOURCES:

BOOKS

Who's Who in Finance and Industry, 24th edition, Marquis, 1985.

PERIODICALS

Chicago Tribune, October 26, 1993, p. 10.

N-O

NABHAN, Gary Paul 1952-

PERSONAL: Born March 17, 1952, in Gary, IN; son of Theodore B. and Wanda Mary (Goodwin) Nabhan; married Caroline C. Wilson, September 1, 1993; children: Laura, Dustin. *Education:* Received Ph.D. *Religion:* Lutheran.

ADDRESSES: Home—H.C.R. Box 626, 15872 West Aubrey Ave., Tucson, AZ 85736.

CAREER: Ethnobiologist, plant ecologist, and author. University of Arizona, Office of Arid Land Studies, research associate; affiliated with Arizona Sonora Desert Museum. Has lived and worked with Native American tribes, including the Papago Indians; cofounder of Native Seeds/Search (a nonprofit organization).

AWARDS, HONORS: Burroughs Medal, John Burroughs Association, 1987, for *Gathering the Desert.*

WRITINGS:

The Desert Smells Like Rain: A Naturalist in Papago Indian Country, North Point Press, 1982.
Gathering the Desert, illustrations by Paul Mirocha, University of Arizona Press, 1985.
Saguaro: A View of Saguaro National Monument and the Tucson Basin, photographs by George H. H. Huey, Southwest Parks and Monuments Association, 1986.
(Editor with Jane Cole) *Arizona Highways Presents Desert Wildflowers,* Arizona Highways, 1988.
Enduring Seeds: Native American Agriculture and Wild Plant Conservation, North Point Press, 1989.
(Editor) *Counting Sheep: Twenty Ways of Seeing Desert Bighorn,* University of Arizona Press, 1993.
Songbirds, Truffles, and Wolves: An American Naturalist in Italy, Pantheon Books, 1993.

Contributor to periodicals, including *Christian Science Monitor, Sierra, Wilderness,* and *Horticulture.*

SIDELIGHTS: Ethnobiologist Gary Paul Nabhan has devoted his career to advocating the preservation of desert plants and the lifestyles of native desert people—the Native American tribes of the southwestern United States. In addition to founding a seed bank to ensure the survival of as many desert plants as possible, Nabhan has penned several works concerning these plants and their relationships to the tribal people who have harvested or cultivated them.

Nabhan used the time he spent living and working among the Papago to inform the writing of his first book, *The Desert Smells Like Rain: A Naturalist in Papago Indian Country.* Matthew Schudel, reviewing the book in the *Washington Post,* described it as "part natural history, part anthropology, part folklore, part political analysis," and observed that Nabhan "is at his best describing the fragile ecology of the desert." John Peterson, writing in *Village Voice,* lauded Nabhan's ability, "in a series of spare and sometimes tantalizing selections, to convey a real sense of the people and their environment."

"To illustrate the interaction of the human desert culture with desert plant ecology," wrote *Natural History* contributor Hugh H. Iltis of Nabhan's next book, *Gathering the Desert,* "Gary Nabhan has chosen an even dozen of the more than 425 edible wild species found in the Sonoran Desert." These species include *chiltepines,* a hot pepper; *Washingtonia* fan palms; *Agave,* a species of which is used to make tequila; and *Larrea tridentata,* a creosote bush that the southwestern tribes use for many medicinal purposes. Iltis went on to assert that *Gathering the Desert* "is a splendid way to learn to love—and save—the deserts." David Mabberley, critiquing the book in the *Times Literary Supplement,* noted that "Nabhan attempts to give the reader a feeling for desert country: his prose is an amalgam of botany and agronomy, of whimsical characters of his own invention, of much doomwatch, mysticism, and folklore." The book was awarded the Burroughs Medal in 1987.

Nabhan concentrates on the specific agricultural practices of the southwestern tribes in his 1989 work *Enduring Seeds: Native American Agriculture and Wild Plant Conservation.* Peter H. Raven, writing in *Natural History,* hailed the book as "lovely, impressionistic and romantic," though he felt that "sometimes . . . Nabhan goes too far in championing the salutary effect of native agriculture on biological diversity." But Raven concluded that "by bringing us closer to the earth and its processes, Nabhan reminds us of our origins, helping us to understand that we might collectively lead better and richer lives if we are willing to preserve and consider some of the many options available."

BIOGRAPHICAL/CRITICAL SOURCES:

PERIODICALS

Natural History, March, 1986, pp. 74-76, 78-79; June, 1989, pp. 70-71.
Times Literary Supplement, May 9, 1986, p. 515.
Village Voice, October 19, 1982, p. 47.
Washington Post, May 14, 1982.

*   *   *

NAVARRE, Yves (Henri Michel)   1940-1994

OBITUARY NOTICE—See index for *CA* sketch: Born September 24, 1940, in Condom, Gascony, France; died of an overdose of barbiturates, January 24, 1994, in Paris, France. Playwright and author. Honored in 1992 by the French Academy for his numerous novels and plays, Navarre also won the Goncourt prize in 1980 for his novel *Le Jardin d'acclimatation* ("The Zoological Garden"), published in the United States as *Cronus' Children.* Known for his forthright treatment of homosexuality, the human psyche, and gender restrictions in society, Navarre often utilized symbolism and stream-of-consciousness techniques to underscore his themes. Among many others, Navarre wrote *Lady Black, The Little Rogue in Our Flesh, Romans un roman, Hotel Styx, Biographie,* and *Friends Gone with the Wind.* Among Navarre's plays are *Histoire d'amour, LaGuerre des piscines, Lucienne de Carpentras,* and *Les Dernieres clientes.* Navarre also authored several children's books.

OBITUARIES AND OTHER SOURCES:

BOOKS

Who's Who in the World, 11th edition, Marquis, 1993, p. 824.

PERIODICALS

Los Angeles Times, January 26, 1994, p. A24.
Washington Post, January 26, 1994, p. B5.

*   *   *

NEAR, Holly   1949-

PERSONAL: Born June 6, 1949, in Ukiah, CA; daughter of Russell E. (a rancher) and Anne H. (a rancher and writer; maiden name, Holmes) Near. *Education:* Attended University of California, Los Angeles, 1967.

ADDRESSES: Office and agent—Jo-Lynne Worley, P.O. Box 10408, Oakland, CA 94610.

CAREER: Folk and women's musician, record company executive, actress, and writer. Singer-songwriter and recording artist, c. 1972—; founding owner and operator of Redwood Records, beginning 1972. Has toured with Ronnie Gilbert, 1983, and with Gilbert, Pete Seeger, and Arlo Guthrie, 1985; contributor of vocals to soundtrack for *Woody Guthrie: Hard Travelin'* and anthologies *Bullets and Guitars* and *Reaganomics Blues.* Traveled with Jane Fonda and Tom Hayden on the Indochina Peace Campaign, 1972. Cofounder of Redwood Cultural Work (a nonprofit progressive multicultural organization), 1988. Lectures in the art of performance and progressive songwriting. Actress in motion pictures, including *Slaughterhouse Five, Minnie and Moskowitz,* and *Dogfight;* actress in television programs, including *All in the Family* and *L.A. Law;* actress in stage productions, including a Broadway production of *Hair* and an Off-Broadway production of *Fire in the Rain.* Appeared in the documentary *Wasn't That a Time,* the film *Women of Summer,* and the television special *Holly Near Live at the Tonder Festival.* Involved in numerous benefits and activist causes.

AWARDS, HONORS: Album of the year, National Association of Independent Record Distributors, 1979, for *Imagine My Surprise;* Woman of the Year, *Ms.* magazine, 1984; Pioneer in Woman's Music Award, *Ms.* magazine, 1987; numerous awards for civil and human rights work.

WRITINGS:

(Composer) *Still Life,* American Place Theatre, 1981.
(With Derk Richardson) *Fire in the Rain . . . Singer in the Storm* (autobiography), Morrow, 1990.
The Great Peace March, illustrations by Lisa Desimini, Holt, 1993.

(With sister, Timothy Near) *Fire in the Rain . . . Singer in the Storm* (play; adapted from Near's autobiography of the same title), first produced at San Jose Repertory Theatre, 1991, produced Off-Broadway at the Union Square Theatre, 1993.

Composer for plays *Volpone,* produced at Mark Taper Forum, Los Angeles, and *The Near Sisters Review,* produced at Royce Hall, University of California. Also composer for the television specials *A Woman Like Eve, Back from Nicaragua,* and *Women of Steel.*

RECORDINGS

Albums include *Hang in There,* with Jeff Langley, Redwood, 1972; *A Live Album,* 1975; *You Can Know All I Am,* 1976; *Imagine My Surprise,* Redwood, 1979; *Fire in the Rain,* 1981; *Speed of Light,* 1982; *Journeys,* 1983; *Lifeline,* with Ronnie Gilbert, Redwood, 1983; *Watch Out!,* 1984; *Sing to Me the Dream,* with Inti-Illimani, Redwood, 1984; *HARP,* with Gilbert, Arlo Guthrie, and Pete Seeger, Redwood, 1985; *Singing with You,* with Gilbert, Redwood, 1986; *Don't Hold Back,* 1987; *Singer in the Storm,* with Mercedes Sosa, Chameleon, c. 1990; *Holly Near: Musical Highlights* (includes selections from stage production *Fire in the Rain . . . Singer in the Storm*), c. 1993; an audio autobiography; and several compilations.

WORK IN PROGRESS: A novel; a progressive songbook for young people; ongoing songwriting work.

SIDELIGHTS: Holly Near is a renowned contemporary singer-songwriter who has won particular attention over the past two decades for her staunch social advocacy on issues such as racism, world peace, environmental concerns, and gay and lesbian rights. Although Near is probably best known as an activist musician, she actually began her performing career by working as an actress in a broad range of productions, including the film *Slaughterhouse Five* and the television series *Room 222.* She recorded her first album, *Hang in There,* in 1972, and in the ensuing years she has completed fifteen recordings selling nearly two million copies. Her albums—described by *Nation* reviewer Leslie Berman as "spirited and sassy"—are rich and varied, and they are rendered, according to Berman, in styles ranging from "naive folkie to savvy chanteuse."

In 1990 Near, with Derk Richardson, published an autobiography, *Fire in the Rain . . . Singer in the Storm,* in which she candidly relates her musical and socio-political concerns. Margot Mifflin, writing in the *New York Times Book Review,* declared that Near's autobiographical volume "documents a rare case in which an artist who was determined to fight the power actually succeeded." Near is also the author of *The Great Peace March,* a book based on a song that Near wrote for the 1986 Great March for Nuclear Disarmament. Illustrated by Lisa Desimini, the

work centers on the notion that the attainment of peace, though a struggle, is a worthy goal, and one that must begin in the heart of each individual.

Near told *CA:* "Whether I am writing, teaching, or performing, I try to achieve these goals: to inspire, educate, entertain, heal, empower, challenge, and—in doing so—to improve myself as an artist and as a human being."

BIOGRAPHICAL/CRITICAL SOURCES:

BOOKS

Contemporary Musicians, Volume 1, Gale, 1989, pp. 161-62.
Contemporary Theatre, Film, and Television, Volume 6, 1989, Gale, pp. 300-01.

PERIODICALS

Nation, October 22, 1990, pp. 463-64.
New York Times Book Review, August 5, 1990, p. 10.

*   *   *

NEWMAN, Daisy 1904-1994

OBITUARY NOTICE—See index for *CA* sketch: Born May 9, 1904, in Southport, Lancashire, England; died of heart failure, January 25, 1994, in Lexington, MA. Writer. An active member of the Quaker community in Cambridge, Massachusetts, Newman often wrote about Quaker life and history, including her history of American Quakers, *A Procession of Friends.* Her list of novels contains a number of titles for young adults, such as 1945's *Now That April's There,* 1968's *Mount Joy,* and 1975's *I Take Thee Serenity.* Other works by Newman include the novel *Indian Summer of the Heart,* published in 1982, and her 1987 autobiography, *A Golden String.*

OBITUARIES AND OTHER SOURCES:

BOOKS

The Writers Directory: 1992-1994, St. James Press, 1991.

PERIODICALS

New York Times, January 30, 1994, p. 38.

*   *   *

NEWMAN, Walter (Brown) 1916(?)-1993

OBITUARY NOTICE—See index for *CA* sketch: Born c. 1916 (some sources list 1920); died of lung cancer, October 14, 1993, in Sherman Oaks, CA. Screenwriter. Nominated for three Academy Awards—for *Ace in the Hole, Cat Ballou,* and *Blood Brothers*—Newman was also the author of *Harrow Alley,* an unproduced screenplay that has nevertheless become a cult classic with film students and within the industry itself. Newman graduated from New York University and went on to study law at Harvard University. He began his career in radio, writing dramas such as *The Halls of Ivy,* and the pilot episode for the *Gunsmoke* series. Newman also issued scripts for the screen, including *The Man With the Golden Arm, The True Story of Jesse James,* and *The Champ.*

OBITUARIES AND OTHER SOURCES:

PERIODICALS

Chicago Tribune, October 17, 1993, p. 7.
Los Angeles Times, October 16, 1993, p. A24.
New York Times, October 16, 1993, p. 11.

*   *   *

NGEMA, Mbongeni 1955-

PERSONAL: Born in 1955, in a township outside Durban, South Africa.

CAREER: Worked as a laborer; musician and actor, 1976-78; performed with Gibson Kente's theater company, South Africa, 1979-c. 1981; Committed Artists theater company, South Africa, founder, playwright and director, 1982—.

AWARDS, HONORS: Tony Award nomination—best director, League of American Theatres and Producers, 1987, for *Asinamali!*

WRITINGS:

PLAYS

(With Percy Mtwa) *Woza Albert!* (produced in South Africa, 1981, produced in United States, 1984), Methuen, 1983, reprinted, Heinemann, 1988.
Asinamali!, produced in Lamontville, South Africa, 1983, produced in Harlem, New York City, September, 1986.
(With Hugh Masekela) *Sarafina!* (musical), produced in Johannesburg, South Africa, then in New York City, June, 1987.

Also author and director of a play produced in Durban, South Africa, c. 1978.

OTHER

(With William Nicholson) *Sarafina!* (feature film based on the musical), Buena Vista, 1992.

SIDELIGHTS: Despite the variety of Mbongeni Ngema's theatrical productions—ranging from a satirical fantasy, to a dramatic ensemble piece combining elements of agit-prop and street theater, to an exuberant musical—his works are united by their frenetic energy, their humor in the face of oppression, their defiance of apartheid, and their celebration of life and of black South African culture. While his plays are relentlessly political in protesting apartheid—the South African system of racial segregation and discrimination against non-whites—Ngema is also committed to the production of quality theater. "I wanted technique as well as the truth," he told *Africa Report* interviewers Margaret A. Novicki and Ameen Akhalwaya in discussing his play *Asinamali!* "What was the key for me was a play that we could do for people in [the black tent cities near Durban, South Africa] but that could also be performed on a Broadway stage. . . . They should go and see it because it's good theatre. At the same time, it should be about the spirit of our people."

Born and raised in the black townships around Durban, South Africa, Ngema worked as a laborer and a guitarist before becoming involved in local theatrical productions as a musician and actor. During a tour of the western United States in 1982, he was inspired by the work of the Mexican-American company El Teatro Campesino, which was producing theater for and by farm workers. On his return to South Africa, he brought together a number of artists, actors, writers, and musicians in the Durban area to form Committed Artists, a theater company intended to serve the cultural needs of the black townships and tent cities. He also began collaborating with Percy Mtwa, a fellow South African actor and playwright, on a satirical play in which Christ's Second Coming takes place in South Africa, the Afrikaaner government attempts to exploit the Messiah for political gain, and Christ is ultimately banished to a high-risk black penitentiary on Robben Island. First produced in South Africa in 1981 and presented in the United States in 1984, *Woza Albert!* won international acclaim.

Ngema's next production, *Asinamali!,* presented a view of black life in South Africa through the eyes of five black prisoners, who re-enact the events that led to their arrests. The five men, noted Frank Rich in the *New York Times,* had "been variously victimized by racist laws, unemployment, forced separation from their families, violent police tactics and a seeming infinity of daily humiliations." The actors themselves were people from the townships who had taken part in Ngema's drama workshops, and the play was based on actual events surrounding the concurrent protests against rent increases in Lamontville, a black township near Durban. The play's title, *Asinamali!,*—meaning, "We have no money!"—was the slogan of the Lamontville protesters, whose leader, Msizi Dube, was murdered at the instigation of the South African authorities. Four days after the play opened, police raided a performance and arrested several of the actors, one of whom received an eight-year sentence.

In 1986, in collaboration with Duma Ndlovu, a black South African emigre writer, Ngema brought *Asinamali!* to the United States, where it premiered in Harlem. Rich described the play as a "stunningly performed tapestry of satire, tragedy and reportage from the land of apartheid. . . . Ngema's staging eschews realism for a tightly choreographed melding of indigenous ritual, storytelling and musical theater." Despite its tragic themes and serious political message, reported Humm in *Variety,* "*Asinamali!* is a joyous expression of human individuality and the life force that oppression can't extinguish. . . . Ngema . . . has a sly fondness for low comedy which lightens what is essentially somber material." Reviewing the play in *Maclean's,* Mark Abley quoted a Zulu saying cited in the play itself: "We laugh even though there is death."

The 1987 musical *Sarafina!* was inspired by the 1976 student uprisings in Soweto protesting the government's attempt to impose classroom instruction in Afrikaans, the language of the ruling white South African minority. Hundreds of black schoolchildren were killed by South African police and soldiers during the uprising. In the play, a group of students is putting together a show to celebrate the imagined release of Nelson Mandela, a black anti-apartheid leader who had been imprisoned by the South African authorities since 1962. (Mandela's actual release would not occur until 1990.) One of the students—the title character, Sarafina—is briefly detained by the authorities, interrogated and tortured. Produced in collaboration with South African emigre jazz trumpeter Hugh Masekela, the play makes use of the black South African pop music known as "Mbaqanga," which taps into the indigenous African musical tradition as well as black American jazz and gospel, white missionary hymns, Motown rhythm-and-blues and contemporary rock. "I decided the show had to celebrate the spirit of the students and the power of Mbaqanga, which I call the music of liberation," Ngema told *New York Times* contributor Robert Palmer. The director held auditions throughout the country to choose a cast of 24 young people, most of them in their teens, whom he then trained for the production.

The show opened in Johannesburg, South Africa early in 1987 and in New York City later that year. In *Sarafina!,* Clive Barnes wrote in the *New York Post,* "you will encounter perhaps the most joyous music to be heard in New York City. . . . Ngema's achievement simply in forging this troupe into a cutting-edge theater force is almost incredible." The production suffered somewhat from a "rudimentary book" and a tendency toward "cliche," wrote John Simon in *New York.* Nonetheless, he added, it also possessed "the strength, spirit, and savvy with which to overcome [its flaws]." "Spontaneously performed and precisely choreographed, the musical numbers provide a running commentary on the children's experiences—the acts of protest, troops and police in the classroom, imprisonment and torture, and the funerals of the victims," reported John Beaufort in the *Christian Science Monitor.* "The score of *Sarafina!*—whether driven by timeless drums or jazzy horns or electric guitar—evokes the cacophony of life in a black society both oppressed and defiant, at once sentenced to hard labor and ignited by dreams of social justice," wrote Rich in the *New York Times.* Concluded Barnes, "*Sarafina!* lives—and celebrates man, while dramatizing man's injustice."

A movie version of *Sarafina!,* directed by Darrell James Roodt and starring Whoopi Goldberg and Leleti Khumalo, was released by Buena Vista in 1992. *Voices of Sarafina!,* a film documentary by Nigel Noble about the American production of the musical, appeared in 1988.

BIOGRAPHICAL/CRITICAL SOURCES:

BOOKS

Contemporary Literary Criticism, Volume 57, Gale, 1990, pp. 339-347.

PERIODICALS

Africa Report, July/August, 1987, pp. 36-39.
Christian Science Monitor, October 28, 1987.
Maclean's, November 10, 1996, p. 79.
New Statesman, January 15, 1993.
Newsweek, September 22, 1986, p. 85.
New York, September 29, 1986, pp. 98, 100; November 9, 1987, pp. 124, 128.
New York Post, October 26, 1987.
New York Times, September 12, 1986, p. C3; October 25, 1987, pp. H5, H15; October 26, 1987, p. C15.
Variety, September 17, 1986, p. 112.*

*   *   *

NICHOLSON, Jack 1937-

PERSONAL: Born April 22 (some sources say April 28), 1937, in Neptune, NJ; son of June Nicholson; married Sandra Knight, 1961 (divorced, 1966); children: (first marriage) Jennifer; Lorraine Broussard, Raymond Broussard. *Education:* Studied acting with Jeff Corey, 1957, and several other drama teachers.

ADDRESSES: Office—c/o Sandy Bresler, Bresler, Kelly, and Kipperman, 15760 Ventura Blvd., Suite 1730, Encino, CA 94136.

CAREER: Began career in cartoon department of Metro-Goldwyn-Mayer Studios, 1957. Member of Players Ring

Theatre troupe, 1957-58. Actor in films, including *Easy Rider,* 1969, *Chinatown,* 1974, *One Flew Over the Cuckoo's Nest,* 1975, and *Terms of Endearment,* 1983; director of films, including *Goin' South,* 1978, and *The Two Jakes,* 1991; producer of films, including *Ride the Whirlwind,* 1966, and *Head,* 1968; screenwriter. Actor for television, including episodes of *Dr. Kildare* and *The Andy Griffith Show.*

AWARDS, HONORS: Academy Award nomination, best supporting actor, Academy of Motion Picture Arts and Sciences, 1969, for *Easy Rider;* Academy Award nomination, best actor, 1970, for *Five Easy Pieces;* Academy Award nomination, best actor, and Cannes Film Festival prize, both 1973, both for *The Last Detail;* Academy Award nomination, Golden Globe Award, Hollywood Foreign Press Association, and New York Film Critics Award, all for best actor, all 1975, all for *One Flew Over the Cuckoo's Nest;* Academy Award nomination, best supporting actor, 1981, for *Reds;* Academy Award, best supporting actor, 1983, and Golden Globe Award, best supporting actor, 1984, both for *Terms of Endearment;* Academy Award nomination, and Golden Globe Award, both for best actor, both 1985, both for *Prizzi's Honor;* Academy Award nomination, best actor, 1987, for *Ironwood;* Grammy Award (with Bobby McFerrin), National Academy of Recording Arts and Sciences, best children's recording, 1987, for *The Elephant's Child;* has also received awards from National Society of Film Critics and British Film Society.

WRITINGS:

SCREENPLAYS

Ride the Whirlwind, Twentieth Century-Fox, 1966.
Flight to Fury, Feature Films, 1966.
The Trip, American International, 1967.
(With Bob Rafelson) *Head,* Columbia, 1968.
(With Jeremy Larner) *Drive, He Said,* (adapted from novel by Larner), Columbia, 1970.

Also author of *Thunder Island,* 1963. Contributed foreword to *Winnin' Times: The Magical Journey of the Los Angeles Lakers,* by Scott Ostler and Steve Springer, Macmillan, 1986.

SIDELIGHTS: Jack Nicholson has achieved tremendous popularity and success as a screen actor in roles as varied as those of Jake Gittes in *Chinatown,* Eugene O'Neill in *Reds,* and the Joker in *Batman.* "In a business where money masquerades as art and box-office receipts constitute culture, Nicholson dominates the industry on his own terms. Not only is he one of the richest actors in Hollywood, he is also, arguably, its most revered artist," commented Nancy Collins in *Vanity Fair.* Although Nicholson's greatest fame can be attributed to his movie perfor-

mances—several of which have won Academy Awards—he also wrote screenplays early in his career. According to Tim Cahill in *Rolling Stone, Ride the Whirlwind* (a 1966 western scripted by Nicholson) is now a cult classic.

Stardom did not come quickly for Nicholson, however. He started out in Hollywood during the mid-1950s as a mail carrier in the cartoon department at Metro-Goldwyn-Mayer, attending acting classes with other future celebrities such as producer Roger Corman and actress Sally Kellerman. His first movie role, in 1958, was for an independent feature produced by Corman (who would become commonly known as the "King of the Quickies"). After appearing in other low-budget films (or B-movies) as well as various television shows throughout the 1960s, Nicholson finally received critical notice in 1969 for his role as George Hanson in *Easy Rider.* By 1975—the year for which he won an Academy Award for his portrayal of Randall Patrick McMurphy in *One Flew Over the Cuckoo's Nest*—Nicholson had established himself as a major Hollywood star, having also acted in critically-acclaimed features like *The Last Detail* (1973) and *Chinatown* (1974); Ty Burr in *Entertainment Weekly* stated that these films rate among those which "contain [Nicholson's] most incisive, compelling, and lasting performances."

While Nicholson was appearing in B-movies throughout the 1960s, he was also engaged in other aspects of filmmaking; besides producing and directing, he started writing his own scripts. Quoted in *Rolling Stone,* Nicholson commented that "filmmaking is a collaborative art, and collaboration is what I've studied. I learned that a good actor can always be interesting, but fine acting involves the whole piece. And if you write or direct or produce as well as act, you understand that. Orson Welles once told me that the ideal figure for the theater is a writer who acts. Shakespeare, Moliere, Charlie Chaplin were all actors who wrote." Two films released in 1966 were made from screenplays by Nicholson, *Flight to Fury* and *Ride the Whirlwind* (which he also produced). "Both of these films are brooding, mystical, psychological Westerns which have enjoyed considerable success in Europe but never got off the ground in the United States," Bill Davidson remarked in the *New York Times.*

Nicholson's next script was *The Trip,* which was produced and directed by Corman and released in 1967. Bosley Crowther, writing in the *New York Times,* described the premise of *The Trip* as "how one feels and what one sees in the mind's eye when high on psychedelic drugs." The plot revolves around the character Paul, played by Peter Fonda, who seeks an escape from everyday pressures through experimentation with LSD. Various hallucinatory special effects were employed by the filmmakers to simulate Paul's drug-induced state as he maneuvers from one dreamlike encounter to the next. "*The Trip* . . . has its unusual and experimental aspects and is a quite remarkable venture for so totally an exploitation-minded firm as American International, under whose aegis Corman flourishes," stated Hollis Alpert in the *Saturday Review.*

Head, which Nicholson co-wrote and produced with director Bob Rafelson, stars the pop musical group The Monkees (a band created for the television series of the same name by Rafelson and producer Bert Schneider to capitalize on the success of the popular British rock group the Beatles). Released in 1968, *Head* does not have a distinct storyline, but instead follows members of The Monkees through various humorous situations. Although *New York Times* critic Renata Adler declared that the film was "dreadfully written," she did point out that "there are some funny moments—an old joke about a regiment of Italian soldiers surrendering to a single man, a policeman posing girlishly before a mirror, a scene in which [The Monkees] are cast as dandruff in the hair of a giant Victor Mature."

Despite the lukewarm reception *Head* received from critics, Nicholson's work on the project did not go completely unappreciated. Bill Davidson wrote in the *New York Times* that "Schneider and Rafelson were sufficiently impressed with Nicholson's over-all capabilities as a film maker . . . that they asked him to join their company, B.B.S. Productions, to write and produce *Drive, He Said,* from a novel by Jeremy Larner. Most important of all to Nicholson, he was also going to direct the picture." *Drive, He Said* concerns a star college basketball player named Hector Bloom who—according to Vincent Canby in the *New York Times*—"begins to feel, in [Hector's] word, disconnected. The old game doesn't quite mean what it once did." Hector (played by actor William Tepper) is distracted by events happening off the basketball court; he develops an interest in radical politics and becomes romantically attached to the wife of a professor (portrayed by Karen Black). The Vietnam War is currently being fought in Southeast Asia and, on campus, Hector is affected by the conflict when his best friend is drafted and, subsequently, driven mad by attempts to avoid conscription. Released in 1971, *Drive, He Said* "comes close to being the sort of movie about the anxieties and dilemmas of the sixties that no one ever made in the sixties," Canby commented in the *New York Times.*

Nicholson's work on *Drive, He Said* was disrupted several times by acting jobs that paid well and, more importantly, boosted his reputation at the box-office. When Rip Torn dropped out of the film *Easy Rider,* Nicholson—who had been summoned to the production location in New Orleans to oversee the budget and to soothe fraying tempers—hurriedly substituted for the role of alcoholic George Han-

son, a southern lawyer who joins the characters portrayed by Dennis Hopper and Peter Fonda on their motorcycle journey across the United States. "I felt very strongly that the movie was gonna be a very big success," Nicholson was quoted as saying in *Entertainment Weekly.* In the same publication, James Kaplan noted, "When the lights came up after *Easy Rider's* screening at the 1969 Cannes Film Festival, the audience was cheering wildly—for *him.* With one role, the B-movie exile had become an international movie star. Overnight, after eleven years." On the basis of his performance in *Easy Rider,* Nicholson received his first Academy Award nomination, for best supporting actor. Another film role he accepted during this period, that of Robert Eroica Dupea in *Five Easy Pieces,* resulted in a second Academy Award nomination, this time for best actor.

There have been no more Nicholson scripts produced as films since the early 1970s and he has directed only two other movies, *Goin' South* (1978) and *The Two Jakes* (1991). He has concentrated instead on acting over the last two decades and his talent in that arena is widely praised. Director Milos Forman, quoted in the *New York Times,* emphasized Nicholson's genius for acting over his other abilities: "I saw just one flash of Nicholson's directing brilliance in *Drive, He Said*—the scene where Karen Black is attacked by a man while birds fly free through the house. On the other hand, I see his extraordinary *acting* brilliance in every film he does, even the bad ones."

Good writing not only serves the filmmaking process, according to Nicholson, it also influences people's lives. In an interview with Cahill in *Rolling Stone* Nicholson revealed that he had always been an avid reader. "Writers provided role models. They got people thinking," Nicholson explained. In the same publication Cahill summed up the young Nicholson in literary terms: "He had an affinity for black culture, he identified with the characters at the track and pool hall. He was deadly serious about his art. What you had, in fact, was a classic Beat. It was as if, say, Jack Kerouac had taken up acting instead of writing."

BIOGRAPHICAL/CRITICAL SOURCES:

PERIODICALS

American Film, January/February, 1984.
Entertainment Weekly, January 8, 1993, pp. 15-21.
New York Times, August 24, 1967; November 7, 1968; June 14, 1971; October 12, 1975; October 6, 1978.
Rolling Stone, April 6, 1981, pp. 13-17.
Saturday Review, September 2, 1967, p. 39.
Time, August 12, 1974, pp. 44-50.
Vanity Fair, April, 1992, pp. 162-166, 222-230.*

—Sketch by Scot Peacock

NIDITCH, Susan 1950-

PERSONAL: Born July 10, 1950, in Boston, MA; son of Jacob and Betty Niditch; married Robert Doran (a professor), June 30, 1974; children: Rebecca, Elizabeth. *Education:* Radcliffe College, A.B. (cum laude), 1972; Harvard University, Ph.D., 1977. *Politics:* Democrat. *Religion:* Jewish.

ADDRESSES: Office—Religion Department, Amherst College, Amherst, MA 01002.

CAREER: University of Cincinnati, Cincinnati, OH, assistant professor of religion, 1977-78; Amherst College, Amherst, MA, assistant professor, 1978-84, associate professor, 1984-90, Elizabeth Bruss Readership, 1987-90, professor of religion, 1990—, Samuel Green Professor of Religion, 1992—, chair of department, 1986-87 and 1991-93.

MEMBER: American Academy of Religion (president of New England region, 1983-84), Society of Biblical Literature (president of New England region, 1993-94), American Folklore Society, Phi Beta Kappa.

AWARDS, HONORS: National Endowment for the Humanities fellowships, 1985-86 and 1990-91.

WRITINGS:

The Symbolic Vision in Biblical Tradition, Scholars Press (Chico, CA), 1980.
Chaos to Cosmos: Studies in Biblical Patterns of Creation, Scholars Press, 1984.
Underdogs and Tricksters: A Prelude to Biblical Folklore, Harper (New York), 1987.
(Editor) *Text and Tradition: The Hebrew Bible and Folklore,* Semeia Studies, 1990.
War in the Hebrew Bible: A Study in the Ethics of Violence, Oxford University Press (New York), 1993.
Folklore and the Hebrew Bible, Fortress/Augsburg, 1993.
Oral Worlds and Written Words: The Hebrew Bible in Context, Westminster, in press.

Journal of Biblical Literature, member of editorial board, 1984-89; *Hermeneia,* member and executive secretary of editorial board; *Harper Collins Study Bible,* associate editor.

WORK IN PROGRESS: The Religious Traditions of Ancient Israel, a study of ancient Israelite religion, Oxford University Press, 1996.

SIDELIGHTS: Susan Niditch told *CA:* "Whereas my older brother was sent for violin lessons, I attended Hebrew School beginning at the age of eight until I graduated high school. It may have had something to do with our living down the street from the local synagogue, or maybe my parents just knew I would love to learn Hebrew, but the study of the classical traditions of Judaism has always been a part of my life. In college, I thought I would do something else, but through the study of early and oral literatures with my mentor, Albert Bates Lord, I slipped back into the study of the Hebrew Bible, shoring up my literary work with philological and historical tools of the modern biblicist in a doctoral program in near eastern languages and civilizations.

"Throughout my career I have sought to understand the people behind the Hebrew Bible, their cultures and worldviews, and the literary forms in which ancient Israelite authors expressed their vital concerns. I seek to understand the many and varied voices that lie behind the tradition.

"Much of my research has been triggered by my students' questions. How, for example, is the life-affirming and just God of the Hebrew Bible imagined by Israelites to demand in a war context that entire enemy populations be killed—men, women, children, and infants? How have we as westerners been shaped by ideologies preserved in the Bible? These are some of the issues explored in my *War in the Hebrew Bible.* I also continue to weave together my interests in folklore and Hebrew Bible, exploring the ways in which the study of early and oral literatures enriches our understanding of the literary traditions of ancient Israel."

*　　*　　*

NORDICUS
See SNYDER, Louis L(eo)

*　　*　　*

NORTON, Bryan G(eorge) 1944-

PERSONAL: Born July 19, 1944, in Marshall, MI; son of Kenneth Lucien (a farmer) and Liba (a homemaker; maiden name, Miller) Norton; married Pauline Elizabeth Hosack, 1966 (divorced, 1976). *Education:* University of Michigan, B.A. (with honors), 1966, Ph.D., 1970. *Politics:* Liberal Democrat.

ADDRESSES: Home—321 Drexel Ave., Decatur, GA 30030. *Office*—School of Public Policy, Georgia Institute of Technology, Atlanta, GA 30332.

CAREER: University of South Florida, New College, Sarasota, 1970-86, began as assistant professor, became professor; Georgia Institute of Technology, Atlanta, professor of public policy, 1987—. University of Maryland at College Park, research associate at Institute for Philosophy and Public Policy, 1981-83. Two Hundred Atlanta, associated scientist, 1989—; consultant to government agencies and businesses, including U.S. Environmental Protection Agency.

MEMBER: International Society for Ecological Economics, International Society for Environmental Ethics, American Philosophical Association, Society for Conservation Biology (member of board of governors, 1988-92), Florida Philosophical Association (president, 1980-81).

AWARDS, HONORS: Gilbert White fellow, Resources for the Future, 1986.

WRITINGS:

Linguistic Frameworks and Ontology, Mouton, 1977.
(Editor) *The Preservation of Species,* Princeton University Press, 1986.
Why Preserve Natural Diversity?, Princeton University Press, 1987.
Toward Unity among Environmentalists, Oxford University Press, 1991.
Ecosystem Health: New Goals for Environmental Management, Island Press, 1992.

WORK IN PROGRESS: Editing *Ethics on the Ark,* with Michael Hutchins, Terry L. Maple, and Elizabeth Stevens; a book on theory of environmental management.

SIDELIGHTS: Bryan G. Norton told *CA:* "I grew up on a farm in southern Michigan and developed a love for both nature and ideas. I studied government and philosophy at the University of Michigan in the 1960s, absorbing a sense of social activism. These forces all came together when, in 1981, I was invited by the University of Maryland to study the policy behind the Endangered Species Act of 1973. Since then, I have concentrated on values, policy, and science associated with the protection of biological resources."

*   *   *

NORTON, Philip   1951-

PERSONAL: Born March 5, 1951, in Louth, England; son of George Earnest and Ena D. (Ingham) Norton. *Education:* University of Sheffield, England, B.A. (with first class honors), 1972; University of Pennsylvania, M.A., 1975; University of Sheffield, Ph.D., 1976. *Politics:* British Conservative Party. *Religion:* Methodist.

ADDRESSES: Office—Department of Politics, University of Hull, Hull HU6 7RX, England.

CAREER: University of Hull, Hull, England, lecturer, 1977-82, senior lecturer in politics, 1982-84, reader in politics, 1984-86, professor of government, 1986—, director of Centre for Legislative Studies, 1992—. Wroxton College, Farleigh Dickinson University, Rutherford, NJ, lecturer in political science, 1977.

MEMBER: International Political Science Association (member of research committee of legislative specialists), Politics Association, United Kingdom (president, 1993—), British Politics Group, U.S.A. (president, 1988-90), British Study of Parliament Group, American Political Science Association.

AWARDS, HONORS: Thouron Scholar, University of Pennsylvania, 1974-75; Nalgo Prize in Politics, University of Sheffield, 1977.

WRITINGS:

Dissension in the House of Commons, 1945-74, Macmillan, 1975.
Conservative Dissidents, Temple Smith, 1978.
Dissension in the House of Commons, 1974-79, Oxford University Press, 1980.
The Commons in Perspective, M. Robertson, 1981; reissued by Basil Blackwell, 1985.
(With Arthur Aughey) *Conservatives and Conservatism,* Temple Smith, 1981.
The Constitution in Flux, M. Robertson, 1982; reissued by Basil Blackwell, 1984.
The British Polity, Longman, 1984.
Parliament in the 1980s, Basil Blackwell, 1985.
(With Bill Jones and others) *Politics U.K.,* Philip Allan, 1991.
(With David M. Wood) *Back from Westminster: British Members of Parliament and Their Constituents,* University Press of Kentucky, 1993.
Does Parliament Matter?, Harvester Wheatsheaf, 1993.

EDITOR

Law and Order and British Politics, Ashgate, 1984.
(With Jack Hayward) *The Political Science of British Politics,* Harvester Wheatsheaf, 1986.
(And contributor) *Parliaments in Western Europe,* F. Cass, 1990.
Legislatures, Oxford University Press, 1990.
New Directions in British Politics?; Essays on the Evolving Constitution, Aldershot, 1991.
(With Mark Franklin) *Parliamentary Questions,* Clarendon, 1993.

Associate editor, *Political Studies,* 1987-93; editor, *Journal of Legislative Studies,* 1995—.

WORK IN PROGRESS: Parliament Since 1945; The Prime Minister in Britain.

SIDELIGHTS: As a professor of government at Hull University in England and a member of the British Conservative Party, Philip Norton writes from an authoritative position on British politics, particularly the conservative variety. Among his numerous publications are textbooks on the workings of the British Parliament, studies of conservatism, and essays on such topics as parliamentary reform and the evolution of the British constitution.

Norton compiled incidences of rebellion among elected British Conservatives in the trio *Dissension in the House of Commons, 1945-74, Conservative Dissidents,* and *Dissension in the House of Commons, 1974-79,* published over a five-year period. The first book was described by C. M. Woodhouse in the *Times Literary Supplement* (*TLS*) as "a dependable and unbiased compendium" and "a useful and unpretentious contribution." Likewise, *TLS* critic Janet Morgan called *Conservative Dissidents* "cautious and exact" and "a quantifying methodologist's dream." While Ferdinand Mount of the *TLS* faulted Norton as "a somewhat stodgy writer, prone to quote from his own earlier works," he purported, "his collation of statistical evidence and verbal recollection is fascinating and, on the whole, reliable."

In *The Commons in Perspective,* geared to an undergraduate audience, Norton explains the makeup and history of the British House of Commons. Likewise, with their primer *Conservatives and Conservatism,* Norton and coauthor Arthur Aughey define the nature of conservatism in the United Kingdom and describe its practical implications. Writing for the *Times Literary Supplement,* J. R. Vincent noted that the authors "come across as good-tempered and fair men. . . . The exposition is graceful and free from social science English." "There is pretty well everything in it which you could need to know about the Conservative Party," quipped William Waldegraves of the London *Times,* "and quite a lot you do not need to know."

Norton has served as editor of several essay collections, including *Law and Order and British Politics,* based on a 1982-83 seminar at the University of Hull. The authors of this collection delve into questions of law and order in the contexts of history, labor relations, and political parties. *Parliaments in Western Europe* brings together papers on the impacts of national parliaments in France, Italy, Germany, Ireland, Sweden, the Netherlands, and the United Kingdom—the last of which was written by Norton. Norton wrote the opening and closing of the collection *New Directions in British Politics?,* which he also edited. The volume centers on the subject of parliamentary reform in the United Kingdom.

BIOGRAPHICAL/CRITICAL SOURCES:

PERIODICALS

Times (London), September 24, 1981.

Times Literary Supplement, March 12, 1976; October 13, 1978; July 10, 1981; October 2, 1981; March 29, 1985; December 6, 1991; March 13, 1992.

*   *   *

NORTON, Robert L. 1939-

PERSONAL: Born May 5, 1939, in Boston, MA; son of Harry J. (in business) and Kathryn (Warren) Norton; married Nancy Auclair, February 27, 1960; children: Robert L., Jr., Mary Kay, Thomas J. *Education:* Northeastern University, A.S. (cum laude), 1962, B.S. (summa cum laude), 1967; Tufts University, M.S., 1970.

ADDRESSES: Home—46 Leland Rd., Norfolk, MA. *Office*—Department of Mechanical Engineering, Worcester Polytechnic Institute, 100 Institute Rd., Worcester, MA 01609.

CAREER: Polaroid Corp., Cambridge, MA, product design engineer, 1959-66; Jet Spray Cooler, Inc., Waltham, MA, project engineer, 1966-69; Tufts University, Boston, MA, instructor in surgery department, 1970-82; Worcester Polytechnic Institute, Worcester, MA, professor of mechanical engineering, 1981—. Norton Associates Engineering, president, 1971—; Polaroid Corp., senior engineer, 1979-81. Northeast Medical Center Hospitals, biomedical engineer with Tufts Surgical Research Department, 1969-71; Boston City Hospital, research associate with Tufts Surgical Service, 1971-74; Franklin Institute, lecturer in biomedical engineering, 1973-76; Tufts University, Medford, MA, assistant professor, 1974-79. Holder of more than a dozen patents, including those for a self-developing camera, a photographic shutter mechanism, a photographic film magazine, a variety of beverage dispensers, various cardiac assist apparatus, and a syringe holder.

MEMBER: American Society of Mechanical Engineers, American Society of Engineering Education (president of CoED Division, 1988-90), Sigma Xi, Pi Tau Sigma.

AWARDS, HONORS: American Society for Engineering Education, John A. Curtis Outstanding Paper Award, 1984; Merle Miller Award, best journal article, 1986, 1992; Proctor & Gamble Best Paper Award from Applied Mechanisms Conference, 1985; grants from National Science Foundation, AMP, Inc., Cadkey Corp., and Hewlett Packard Corp.

WRITINGS:

Design of Machinery, McGraw, 1992.
Machine Design: An Integrated Approach, Prentice-Hall, in press.

Work represented in anthologies, including *Modern Kinematics,* edited by A. Erdman, Wiley, 1993. Contributor to scientific journals.

* * *

NOWAK, Jan 1913-

PERSONAL: Original name, Zdzislaw Jezioranski; legally changed, 1943; born May 15, 1913, in Warsaw, Poland; immigrated to the United States, 1977; naturalized U.S. citizen, 1972; son of Waclaw Adam (in business) and Elisabeth (Piotrowski) Jezioranski; married Jadwiga Zaleski (a homemaker), September 7, 1944. *Education:* University of Poznan, M.S., 1936. *Religion:* Catholic.

ADDRESSES: Home—3815 Forest Grove Dr., Annadale, VA 22003. *Agent*—International Creative Management, 8899 Beverly Blvd., Los Angeles, CA 90048.

CAREER: BBC-Radio, London, England, editor of European service, 1947-51; Radio Free Europe, Munich, West Germany, director of Polish service, 1951-76; writer. Consultant to U.S. National Security Council, 1979-92; national director of Polish-American Congress, 1979—. *Military service:* Polish Army and Polish Resistance, 1939-45; became major in artillery corps; received Virtuti Militari, Cross of Valour, and King's Medal for Courage.

AWARDS, HONORS: Honorary doctorate from University of Poznan, 1990.

WRITINGS:

Polska droga ku wolnosci 1952-1973 (radio talks; title means "Polish Road towards Freedom"), Gryf Publications, 1974.
Polska pozostala soba (political essays; title means "Poland Faithful to Itself"), Polonis Book Fund, 1980.
Courier from Warsaw (memoir), foreword by Zbigniew Brzezinski, Wayne State University Press, 1982.
Wojna w eterze: Wspomnienia (title means "War on the Airwaves"), Odnowa, Volume 1, 1985, Volume 2, 1988.
Polska z oddali: Wspomnienia (title means "Poland from Afar"), Znak, 1992.
W poszukiwaniu nadziei, Czytelnik, 1993.

Contributor to periodicals, including *New Leader, Problems of Communism, Washington Journalism Review,* and *Washington Post.*

WORK IN PROGRESS: The English version of *War on the Airways,* which covers the BBC and Radio Free Europe years, 1948 to 1976.

SIDELIGHTS: Jan Nowak, formerly associated with BBC-Radio and Radio Free Europe, is best known in the United States as the author of *Courier from Warsaw,* an autobiographical account of his harrowing experiences as a member of the Polish Resistance during World War II. Nowak describes several dangerous missions, as well as "the horrors of the Holocaust, the Warsaw uprising and the massacre at Katyn (where Polish officers were killed by Russian troops, hoping to disguise the murders as a Nazi crime)," informed Chris Kucharski in the *Detroit Free Press.* "The author also touches on the disputed issue of how much Western leaders knew about the wartime killings of millions of East European Jews in German-occupied lands," Theodore Shabad commented in the *New York Times.*

As a courier traveling surreptitiously from Nazi-occupied Poland to London, Nowak also met leaders of the Allied war effort, such as Winston Churchill. The information Nowak delivered to the Allies, however, was met with much disbelief. According to Hugh Seton-Watson in the *Times Literary Supplement,* "Neither the London Poles nor the British could believe what he had to tell them about the destruction of Polish Jews." Seton-Watson goes on to describe a similar disbelief on the part of Poles who were told that their country would be handed over to the Soviet Union after the war: "The resistance leaders in Poland could not believe what he had to tell them about the extent to which the Allies accepted Soviet demands. In this book Nowak presents these various bewilderments most convincingly."

Jan Kott noted in the *New York Times Book Review* that "fast-paced action, unpredictable and sudden reversals, accuracy of technical detail, flawless description of places and interiors make *Courier from Warsaw* as fascinating and thrilling to read as the best of John Le Carre's novels." And in the *New York Times,* Shabad described the book as "an important historical document" which "may shed additional light on little-known episodes of the World War II period."

Nowak told *CA:* "The basic message of my writing is that in our nuclear age we are so fascinated by technological progress and modern weaponry that we tend to underestimate the human factor. In the history of human conflicts the power of ideas ultimately prevailed over military might. The experience of my mature life, first in the Resistance Movement of World War II and later as a broadcaster to a country under a totalitarian system, leads me to these conclusions, which I try to share in my autobiographical books such as *Courier from Warsaw.*"

BIOGRAPHICAL/CRITICAL SOURCES:

PERIODICALS

Detroit Free Press, September 26, 1982, p. D7.
Jewish News, October 15, 1982.

Monthly Detroit, November, 1982, pp. 47-48.
New York Times, November 22, 1982.
New York Times Book Review, October 31, 1982, pp. 3, 24-25.
Times Literary Supplement, December 10, 1982, p. 1375.
Wall Street Journal, October 15, 1982.
Washington Times, August 27, 1982.

*   *   *

NWAPA, Flora   1931-

PERSONAL: Full name, Florence Nwanzuruahu Nkiru Nwapa; born January 18, 1931, in Oguta, East Central State, Nigeria; married Gogo Nwakuche (an industrialist), 1967; children: Amede, Uzoma, Ejine. *Education:* University College, Ibadan, Nigeria, B.A., 1957; University of Edinburgh, diploma in education, 1958.

ADDRESSES: Office—Tana Press Ltd., 2A Menkiti Lane, Ogui Enugu, Nigeria. *Agent*—David Bolt Associates, 12 Heath Dr., Send, Surrey GU23 7EP, England.

CAREER: Ministry of Education, Calabar, Nigeria, education officer in inspectorate division, 1958; Queen's School, Enugu, Nigeria, education officer and teacher of English and geography, 1959-61; University of Lagos, Lagos, Nigeria, administrative officer, beginning in 1962, lecturer in creative writing and geography at International Press Institute, 1962-65, assistant registrar, until 1967; East Central State of Nigeria, member of executive council and minister of health and social welfare, 1970-71, minister of lands, survey, and urban development, 1971-74, minister of establishments, beginning in 1974; Tana Press Ltd., Ogui Enugu, Nigeria, founder, chairperson, and managing director, 1977—. Flora Nwapa Books Ltd., founder and managing director, 1977—. Alvan Ikoku College of Education, visiting lecturer, 1976-77; University of Maiduguri, visiting professor, 1989-90; East Carolina University, visiting professor, 1993; lecturer at colleges and universities, including New York University, Trinity College (Hartford, CT), Episcopal Divinity School (Cambridge, MA), University of Minnesota—Twin Cities, Sarah Lawrence College, Kalamazoo College, University of Michigan, University of Oregon, and University of Colorado, Denver. University of Ilorin, member of governing council, 1986. Commission on Review of Higher Education in Nigeria, member, 1990.

MEMBER: International PEN, African Literature Association, Association of Nigerian Authors (vice president, 1981; president for Borno State, 1989), Children's Literature Association of Nigeria, African Studies Association (U.S.).

AWARDS, HONORS: Recipient of numerous grants; Certificate of Merit, Nigeria Association of University Women, 1980; named Officer of the Order of the Niger, Federal Government of Nigeria, 1982; fellow at University of Iowa, 1984; Merit Awards for literary achievement from University of Ife, 1985, and Solidra Circle, Lagos, Nigeria, and Octagon Club, Owerri, Nigeria, both 1987.

WRITINGS:

NOVELS

Efuru, Heinemann Educational, 1966.
Idu, Heinemann Educational, 1971.
Never Again, Tana Press, 1975, Africa World Press, 1991.
One Is Enough, Tana Press, 1982, Africa World Press, 1991.
Women Are Different, Tana Press, 1986, Africa World Press, 1991.

FOR CHILDREN

Emeka, Driver's Guard, illustrated by Roslyn Isaacs, University of London Press, 1972.
My Animal Colouring Book, Flora Nwapa Books, 1977.
My Tana Colouring Book, Flora Nwapa Books, 1978.
Mammywater, illustrated by Obiora Udechukwu, Tana Press, 1979.
Journey to Space, illustrated by Chinwe Orieke, Tana Press, 1980.
The Miracle Kittens, illustrated by Emeka Onwudinjo, Tana Press, 1980.
The Adventures of Deke, Flora Nwapa Books, 1982.

OTHER

Cassava Song and Rice Song (poems), Tana Press, 1986.
This Is Lagos and Other Stories, Tana Press, 1971, Africa World Press, 1991.
Wives at War and Other Stories, Tana Press, 1986, Africa World Press, 1991.

WORK IN PROGRESS: Two novels, *The Umbilical Cord* and *The Lake Goddess;* three plays, *The First Lady, Two Women in Conversation,* and *The Sycophants; The New Game and Other Stories; The Silent Passengers and Other Stories; Miri and Other Stories;* and *The Debt and Other Stories.*

SIDELIGHTS: As a teacher, former government official, businesswoman and writer, Flora Nwapa expresses an avid interest in the traditions and momentous changes taking place in Nigeria. Such interests are a focus of her writing, whether she is educating children about the myths and spiritual beliefs of the Igbo in *Mammywater* and *Cassava Song and Rice Song* or depicting the impact of change on the women characters in her novels and short stories. All of Nwapa's works are grounded in Igbo life and culture. Her characters are drawn, like many in the African literary tradition, from the outside in, so that the orality, or the richness of African dialogue emerges. For her talent in dramatizing the special nature of Igbo women's talk, she is praised by such critics as Lloyd Brown in *Women Writers of Black Africa* and Gay Wilentz in *Binding Cultures, Black Women Writers in Africa and the Diaspora.*

Nwapa's adult fiction comprises a transformational whole, as her women characters begin by operating within the accepted traditions of Igbo society, but move outside its codes when their social, economic and spiritual needs grow beyond the Igbo ideal of how a woman should behave. Hence, as the women protagonists in *Efuru* and *Idu* maintain individual will, they "demonstrate the ability of women to transform both motherhood and childlessness into positive, self-defined and powerful experiences," notes Jane Bryce-Okunla in *Motherlands.* Greater movement outside these traditions is depicted in *Wives at War.* This new direction is signaled first by the title, which—when related to some of the stories—means not only women's participation in the Nigerian Civil War between Igbos and opposing tribal groups (also called the Biafran War), but also women's direct confrontation with men for political rights; their private bonding against paternalism and the male who cannot think realistically; and their determination to avoid being regarded solely as sexual objects.

Nwapa later wrote the novels *One Is Enough* and *Women Are Different.* In *One Is Enough,* Amaku, the protagonist, relinquishes the pre-determined role of wife against the wishes of her mother, the father of her children, and her community. In short, Amaku's transformation is typical of a number of Nwapa's previous women characters because she begins by endorsing her community's belittlement of her childless status but ends by questioning any standards which she feels may demean her self-image. *Women Are Different* follows the development of three women who begin as schoolmates, each looking to the future for husbands and family. Like Amaku, they find that, as adults, their dreams of a stable family life are unfulfilled and they must work hard to achieve financial independence, without their errant husbands' help.

Transformation and transition of women characters lie at the center of Nwapa's themes. The struggle of women as wives and mothers is interwoven with their change and emergence. In *Efuru* and *Idu* the theme of the relationship between women and their communities is essential to understanding Nwapa's portraits of the traditional wife whose status is achieved through childbirth; of the woman who achieves rank and power in seeing to it that traditions are maintained, no matter how restrictive; and of the aggressive woman who is the protector of other women as she openly and brazenly challenge the men for fair treatment. In *One Is Enough* and *Women Are Different* Nwapa celebrates the strength, imagination, and energy of women

who become economically and spiritually independent in Nigeria's fast-paced urban centers. One underlying theme in both *This Is Lagos and Other Stories* and *Women Are Different* is the loss of some traditions brought about by westernization and changes in economics and political structure. In *Kunapipi* Kirsten Holst Petersen also observes that in *This Is Lagos, Never Again,* and *Wives at War* the shift in environments causes women to lose "the secure moral universe of the village" and instead be confronted by "problems of individual survival in a city jungle with no guidelines except those provided by success, modern life and wealth, exemplified by cars, drink, wigs, etc."

Nwapa's themes clearly have a feminine slant. The power of feminine bonding is a theme she presents in *Women Are Different, Wives at War and Other Stories,* and *One Is Enough.* Nwapa does not dehumanize or reject her male characters, but as upholders of paternalistic values, they are sometimes blind or indifferent to women's needs; they impede women's progress and exploit them economically or sexually. Commenting on Nwapa's feminism in *Efuru,* critic Adewale Maja-Pearce concludes in *World Literature Written in English* that Nwapa's feminism "isn't of the strident kind. Far from hating men, she doesn't even dislike them. The women in the novel [*Efuru*] possess some extra quality that the men lack: her women are 'good' in a way that her men never are." Underscoring this theme of feminine power Brenda Berrian in the *College Language Association Journal (CLAJ)* says that "Nwapa insists that although the African woman may be vulnerable to men, she does not play a subordinate role."

While women are still at the center of these texts, *This Is Lagos, Never Again,* and *Wives at War* depict the Biafran War in terms of how it affects soldiers, women, families, villages, and towns in Biafra. Biafra, so called by the Igbos of Nigeria's Eastern Region, seceded from Nigeria on May 30, 1967, as a result of massacres of thousands of Igbos by two other tribal groups, the Yorubas and Hausas, who believed the rumor that Igbos were attempting to control all of Nigeria. In *This Is Lagos,* the story "My Soldier Brother" is one of the few told from a male perspective. An adoring youth joins his Igbo militia unit to avenge his brother's death. The irony in the story captures Nwapa's sense of tragedy in all of her war stories: those Igbos most enthusiastic about an Igbo victory seem to lose sight of the fact that they were not only losing the war but also suffering the loss of entire generations of Igbos. It is this irony of fanatic patriotism amid tremendous loss and suffering that Nwapa's heroine, Kate, observes in *Never Again.* "In Nwapa's novel, the refrain 'never again' becomes the expressed resolve that such suffering, the dehumanization, and the fragmentation would no longer be tolerated," explains Maxine Sample in *Modern Fiction Studies.* In "Wives at War" and "A Certain Death" Nwapa depicts the vital role of women in the war. They organized kitchens for starving soldiers, and they were the main force behind the Biafran Red Cross. In the case of the woman character in "A Certain Death," they saved the lives of the remaining men in their families by paying substitutes to go to war. Nwapa notes in *Never Again* and *One Is Enough* that women participated in the "attack trade." Using their acquired skills in market trade, these women bargained with the enemy, the Nigerians, for items of which the starving Biafrans were in dire need.

Often referred to as Africa's first woman novelist to publish in English, Flora Nwapa is highly credited for being a literary voice of the African woman during a period when African literature was dominated by men. She enriches the English language with Igbo folk idioms spoken largely by and about women. In her early novels Nwapa offers a view of women's lives in precolonial times; through Nwapa the African woman is no longer silent. As Elleke Boehmer observes in *Motherlands*, Nwapa gives voice to texts which challenge the conventional literary image of women created by the African male writer and which depict the evolution of female characters who define their own lives, whether or not they are mothers or wives.

Nwapa told *CA:* "I have been writing for nearly thirty years. My interest has been on both the rural and the urban woman in her quest for survival in a fast-changing world dominated by men.

"My fascination with the goddess of the lake, or the water spirit, shows up in most of my writings, especially in the children's book *Mammywater*. In research for a paper on priestesses and power among the Riverine Igbo, I came across interesting aspects of the call of power of a priestess of the Lake Goddess. The novel *The Lake Goddess* is based on my findings.

"I am interested in the ancestral worship of my people, and how it has affected their Christian beliefs. This interest was rekindled by the ceremonies I had to perform, as the first daughter, when my Christian father died.

"I would like to teach African literature, as well as work on the myth of the Lake Goddess and the Christian religion in a community whose ancestors mean so much to them."

BIOGRAPHICAL/CRITICAL SOURCES:

BOOKS

Brown, Lloyd, *Women Writers of Black Africa*, Greenwood, 1981.
Dictionary of Literary Biography, Volume 125: *Twentieth-Century Caribbean and Black African Writers, Second Series*, Gale, 1993.

James, Adeola, editor, *In Their Own Voices, African Women Writers Talk*, Heinemann, 1990.
Nasta, Susheila, editor, *Motherlands: Black Women's Writing from Africa, the Caribbean and South Asia*, Rutgers, 1992.
Wilentz, Gay, *Binding Cultures, Black Women Writers in Africa and the Diaspora*, Indiana, 1992.

PERIODICALS

Africa Woman, July/August, 1977.
African Literature Today, number 7, 1975.
College Language Association Journal, Volume 25, number 3, 1982.
Kunapipi, Volume 7, numbers 2-3, 1985.
Modern Fiction Studies, autumn, 1991.
Nigeria Magazine, June, 1966.
Presence Africaine, Volume 82, 1972.
World Literature Written in English, spring, 1985.

*   *   *

NYLANDER, Jane C. 1938-

PERSONAL: Born January 27, 1938, in Cleveland, OH; daughter of James Merritt (a paperboard manufacturer) and Jeannette (a homemaker; maiden name, Crosby) Cayford; married Daniel Harris Giffen, November 30, 1964 (divorced, June, 1970); married Richard Conrad Nylander (a museum curator), July 8, 1972; children: (first marriage) Sarah Louise, Thomas Harris; (second marriage) Timothy Frost. *Education:* Brown University, A.B. (with distinction), 1959; University of Delaware, M.A., 1961.

ADDRESSES: Home—17 Franklin St., Portsmouth, NH 03801. *Office*—Society for the Preservation of New England Antiquities, 141 Cambridge St., Boston, MA 02114.

CAREER: Historical Society of York County, York, PA, curator, 1961-62; New Hampshire Historical Society, Concord, curator, 1962-69; Old Sturbridge Village, Sturbridge, MA, curator of ceramics and textiles, 1969-84, senior curator, 1985-86; Strawbery Banke, Inc., Portsmouth, NH, director, 1986-92; Society for the Preservation of New England Antiquities, Boston, MA, director, 1992—. New England College, instructor, 1963-64; Monadnock Community College, instructor, 1964-68; Boston University, adjunct associate professor, 1978-85, adjunct professor, 1993—; University of New Hampshire, adjunct assistant professor, 1987-92. Worcester Historical Museum, trustee, 1978-84; Historic Deerfield, Inc., trustee, 1981—, head of Museum Committee, 1992—; Jones Museum, trustee, 1986-88; Portsmouth Athenaeum, trustee, 1987-90; Decorative Arts Trust, member of board of governors, 1991—; Wentworth-Coolidge Commission, member, 1991—; Historic Massachusetts, Inc., member of board of directors, 1992-93; Bentley College, member of board of advisers of New England Heritage Center, 1993—. Committee to Preserve Historic Flags Belonging to the State of New Hampshire, member, 1991-92; lecturer on New England social history and domestic life; consultant to local and national museums.

MEMBER: American Antiquarian Society, American Association of Museums, American Association for State and Local History, National Trust for Historic Preservation, Costume Society of America (member of board of directors, 1977-83; member of regional board of directors, 1984-85), National Society of the Colonial Dames of America, Garden Conservancy, Wentworth Gardner and Tobias Lear House Association, Warner House Association, Trustees of Reservations, Costume Society (England), New England Historic Genealogical Society, Colonial Society of Massachusetts (member of council, 1993—), New Hampshire Historical Society, Japan-America Society of New Hampshire (member of board of directors, 1988-92), Friends of Historic Deerfield, Boston Museum of Fine Arts, Society of Winterthur Graduates.

AWARDS, HONORS: Charles F. Montgomery Award, Decorative Arts Society, 1985, for her contribution to the book *The Great River.*

WRITINGS:

Fabrics for Historic Buildings, Preservation Press, 1977, 4th edition, 1990.
(Contributor) *The Great River,* Wadsworth Atheneum, 1985.
Our Own Snug Fireside: Image and Reality in the New England Home, 1750-1860, Knopf, 1993.

Also contributor to *Upholstery in America and Europe,* Norton, 1987; and *An American Sampler: Folk Art From the Shelburne Museum,* National Gallery of Art, 1987. Contributor of articles and reviews to history, museum, and antique journals, including *Connoisseur, Early American Life, Historic Preservation, Historical New Hampshire, Antiques,* and *Old Time New England.*

WORK IN PROGRESS: Editing the journal of Ruth Henshaw Bascom, 1794-1846; collecting and exhibiting decorative arts from nineteenth-century New England.

*   *   *

O'BRIEN, David M(ichael)   1951-

PERSONAL: Born August 30, 1951, in Rock Springs, WY; son of Ralph (an educator) and Lucile (a homemaker; maiden name, Resel) O'Brien; married Claudine Mendelovitz (a teacher), June 27, 1954; children: Benja-

min Michael, Sara Ashley, Talia Michele. *Education:* University of California, Santa Barbara, B.A., 1973, M.A., 1974, Ph. D., 1977. *Avocational Interests:* Painting, travel, and surfing.

ADDRESSES: Home—Route 12, Box 64A, Charlottesville, VA 22901. *Office*—University of Virginia, Charlottesville, VA 22901.

CAREER: University of Virginia, Charlottesville, associate professor, 1979—. Office of Administrative Assistant to the Chief Justice, Supreme Court of the United States, judicial fellow, 1981-82, research associate, 1983-84; Russell Sage Foundation, visiting fellow, 1981-82.

MEMBER: American Political Science Association, American Society for Public Administrators, Supreme Court Historical Society.

AWARDS, HONORS: Justice Thomas C. Clark Judicial Fellow Award, 1983; American Bar Association Certificate of Merit, 1985, for *Views from the Bench;* Silver Gavel Award, American Bar Association, 1987, for *Storm Center;* Fulbright fellow at Nuffield College, Oxford, 1987-88; Fulbright researcher in Japan, 1993-94.

WRITINGS:

Privacy, Law and Public Policy, Praeger, 1979.
The Public's Right to Know: The Supreme Court and the First Amendment, Praeger, 1981.
Views from the Bench: The Judiciary and Constitutional Politics, Chatham, 1985.
Storm Center: The Supreme Court in American Politics, Norton, 1986, 3rd edition, 1993.
What Process Is Due? Courts and Science Policy Disputes, RSF/Basic Books, 1987.
Constitutional Law and Politics, Norton, 1991, 2nd edition, 1994.
(With Barbara Hinkson Craig) *Abortion and American Politics,* Chatham House, 1993.
(With Stephen Wayne) *The Politics of American Government,* St. Martin's, 1994.

Co-editor of book series on "Constitutionalism and Democracy" for University Press of Virginia. Also contributor of articles to periodicals. Served on editorial board of *Public Administration Review,* 1983-87.

WORK IN PROGRESS: Crucible for Civil Liberties; a book on freedom of religion and censorship in Japan.

SIDELIGHTS: David M. O'Brien's research into American law, public policy, and the judiciary resulted in his 1986 book on the United States Supreme Court, *Storm Center: The Supreme Court in American Politics.* In the book, "O'Brien starts with a lucid explanation of the basic mechanics of the court, then carefully shows how it has changed in style and substance over two hundred years," noted Lee Dembart in the *Los Angeles Times.* A political scientist at the University of Virginia, O'Brien views the Supreme Court "as subject to . . . political weather as Congress and the executive branch," according to Walter Goodman in the *New York Times.*

In his study of the United States Supreme Court—which is composed of nine justices appointed for life by the president, with the advice and consent of the Senate—O'Brien emphasizes the judicial body's " 'political' role," according to Fred Graham in the *Washington Post Book World.* "[*Storm Center*] is about the intensely human nature of the institution, and it adds a great deal to the store of knowledge about the personal factors (a few of them political) that have simmered behind the scenes over the years." Although O'Brien discusses some of the personal conflicts between justices—including instances of anti-Semitism—he asserts that these factors never influenced important decisions. "The Justices are constrained by the forms of courtesy built into the Court's procedures (they all shake hands before a conference), by the delicacy of its political position and by other institutional and prudential considerations; unexpected alliances are formed on touchy issues," informed Walter Goodman in the *New York Times.* O'Brien also relates the processes that contribute to the court's everyday functioning, including "how much [justices] rely on law clerks, how they schedule their time, decide what cases to take, negotiate, politic, quarrel and, finally, reach their decisions," Dembart wrote in the *Los Angeles Times.*

Critics praised *Storm Center* for its clarity and detail. Goodman in the *New York Times* found it an "illuminating analysis," while Jack Fuller stated in the *Chicago Tribune,* "As a primer on the Supreme Court, *Storm Center* does its work quite well. It enriches understanding through simple, direct exposition and vivid example." In the *Washington Post Book World,* Graham suggested that "O'Brien is at his best when he is delving into White House documents, investigative records and obscure files to turn up eyebrow-raising gems of dubious judicial behavior." Dembart remarked in the *Los Angeles Times,* "The Supreme Court is a remarkable institution, and O'Brien's book does it great justice."

BIOGRAPHICAL/CRITICAL SOURCES:

PERIODICALS

Chicago Tribune, July 1, 1986.
Los Angeles Times, July 8, 1986.
New York Times, June 20, 1986.
New York Times Book Review, July 27, 1986, p. 14.
Washington Post Book World, June 15, 1986, p. 6.

O'CONNOR, Pat 1950-

PERSONAL: Born December 12, 1950, in Cork, Ireland; daughter of Denis (a creamery manager and office manager) and Shelia (a teacher and homemaker; maiden name, Kelleher) O'Connor. *Education:* Earned B.Soc.Sc. (with first class honors), 1970; National University of Ireland, University College, Dublin, M.Soc.Sc. (with first class honors), 1979; University of London, Ph.D., 1987.

ADDRESSES: Office—College of Humanities, University of Limerick, Limerick, Ireland.

CAREER: Economic and Social Research Institute, Dublin, Ireland, research assistant, 1970-73; University of London, Bedford College, London, England, research officer in Social Research Unit, 1973-79; National Institute for Social Work, London, project director in health and social security, 1979-82; Waterford Regional Technical College, Waterford, Ireland, course director, 1982-92; University of Limerick, Limerick, Ireland, lecturer in sociology and director of master's of arts program in women's studies, 1992—. E.C. Research Network on Employment and Family Life, member; Paul Partnership, member of research and evaluation committee; St. Stephen's Green Trust, adviser.

MEMBER: Sociological Association of Ireland (member of executive council, 1988-91), National Council for Education.

WRITINGS:

(With Sinclair, Vicery, and Crosbie) *Bridging Two Worlds: Social Work with the Elderly,* Gower, 1988.
Friendships Between Women: A Critical Review, Guilford, 1992.

Contributor to sociology, women's studies, and education journals.

WORK IN PROGRESS: A book on women in contemporary Irish society; an evaluation of a family rights project on families with children in care; research on resource allocation within Irish households; a study of the gender dimensions of rural community tourism.

SIDELIGHTS: Pat O'Connor told *CA:* "My mother was prevented by the Marriage Bar from entering paid employment as a second level teacher, following her graduation from college as a mature student in Ireland of the 1930s. My father, a graduate in agricultural dairy science, worked first as an assistant creamery manager in rural Cork and then as an officer manager in urban Dublin. I lived in a working-class area in Dublin from age eight to age twenty-three. I was reared with one sister in a quite authoritarian family, dominated by political and religious debate, underpinned by a love of literature, nature, a pervasive sense of God, and a critical attitude to authority.

In many ways, these influences have shaped my professional career and my personal life.

"I went to college at age sixteen, and was the only person from my class at secondary school to do so. Because of a strong social conscience, I studied social science and graduated at the age of nineteen; I have worked full-time since then. I spent the first ten years in research, and, since then, I have been teaching. I spent ten years in England, an experience which increased my tolerance immeasurably, and accentuated my love for, and yet also my alienation from, Ireland.

"I had always wanted to write, and I began publishing very steadily as I came up to my fortieth birthday. My return to Ireland, my parents' deaths, the completion of my doctorate, and the building of a house all made it somehow logical that I would begin to write more. I have been steadily interested in the lives of women. In my journal articles I have been preoccupied with mother/daughter relationships at every age and stage of life—with relationships between sisters and friends and, to a certain extent, with power and sex in marriage. These concerns have moved outwards into the area of social policy, and into a concern with male dominance in the para-professions and resource distribution within households."

*   *   *

OCULI, Okello 1942-

PERSONAL: Born in 1942 in Dokolo County, Lang'o, Uganda. *Education:* Attended Soroti College, St. Peter's College, Tororo, and St. Mary's College, Kisubi; received B.A. from Makerere University, Kampala, Uganda.

CAREER: Poet, novelist, editor, and journalist. Reporter and columnist for *People* (Uganda); news editor for *Makererean.*

WRITINGS:

Prostitute (fiction), Modern African Library, 1968.
Orphan (fiction), East African Publishing House, 1968.
Malak: An African Political Poem, illustrated by V. Murray Ngoima, East African Publishing House, 1976.
Kookolem, Kenya Literature Bureau, 1978.
(Editor) *Health Problems in Rural and Urban Africa: A Nigerian Political Economy Health Science, Ahmadu Bello University, Department of Political Science Project, 1981,* Ahmadu Bello University, Department of Political Science (Zaria, Nigeria), 1981.
Food and Revolution in Africa, Vanguard, 1986.
(Editor) *Nigerian Alternatives,* Ahmadu Bello University, Department of Political Science (Zaria), 1987.
Political Economy of Malnutrition, Ahmadu Bello University Press, 1987.

Also author and/or editor of other government and academic papers on health, nutrition, and economic conditions in Nigeria, beginning c. 1978.*

*   *   *

O'DAY, Alan (Earl)

PERSONAL: Born in Detroit, MI; divorced; children: Andrew Sean Dominic. *Education:* University of Michigan, A.B., 1962; Roosevelt University, M.A. (with honors), 1965; King's College, London, Ph.D., 1971; Northwestern University, M.A., 1986.

ADDRESSES: Home—6 York Pl., Oxford OX4 1YL, England.

CAREER: J. E. Watkins Co., Maywood, IL, worked in industry, 1962-65, part-time employee, 1965-67; University of Maryland, Overseas Program, lecturer in history, 1969-70; University of Newcastle upon Tyne, Newcastle upon Tyne, England, junior research officer, 1970-71; University of Salford, Salford, England, research assistant, 1971-72; University of East Anglia, Norwich, England, temporary lecturer in economic and social history, 1972-74; University of Giessen, Giessen, Germany, lecturer in American studies, 1974-76; University of North London, London, England, lecturer, 1976-77, senior lecturer in history, 1977-93. University of Maryland, Overseas Program, lecturer, 1975-76; University of Maryland at College Park, lecturer, summer, 1976; Johns Hopkins School of Advanced International Studies, lecturer, 1979; Oxford University, visiting research fellow of St. John's College, summer, 1985, visiting fellow of Wolfson College, 1986, senior associate of St. Antony's College, 1988-89; University of Durham, visiting fellow of St. Aidan's College, 1989; University of Edinburgh, visiting research fellow, Institute for Advanced Study in the Humanities, 1989; Concordia University, Montreal, Quebec, visiting professor, 1991-92, adjunct professor, 1992-94.

MEMBER: Royal Historical Society (fellow).

AWARDS, HONORS: Grants from Isobel Thornley Bequest, 1976, 1986, British Academy, 1978, 1985, 1987, European Science Foundation, 1984-87, Marc Fitch Fund, 1985, and Twenty-Seven Foundation, 1985-90; National Endowment for the Humanities, fellowship, 1980-81, grant, 1986.

WRITINGS:

The English Face of Irish Nationalism: Parnellite Involvement in British Politics, 1880-86, MacLean-Hunter Press, 1977, 2nd edition, Gregg Revivals (Surrey), 1993.
(Editor, and contributor) *The Edwardian Age: Conflict and Stability, 1900-1914,* Archon, 1979.

(Editor with Yonah Alexander, and co-author of introduction) *Terrorism in Ireland,* St. Martin's, 1984.

Parnell and the First Home Rule Episode, Gill & Macmillan (Dublin), 1986.

(Editor with Yonah Alexander, and contributor) *Ireland's Terrorist Dilemma,* Nijhoff, 1986.

(Editor and author of introduction) *Reactions to Irish Nationalism, 1865-1914,* Hambledon Press, 1987.

(Editor with T. R. Gourvish, and contributor) *Later Victorian Britain,* St. Martin's, 1988, corrected printing, 1990.

(Editor with Yonah Alexander, and co-author of introduction) *Ireland's Terrorist Trauma,* St. Martin's, 1989.

(Editor and author of introduction) *A Survey of the Irish in England, 1872,* Hambledon Press, 1990.

(Editor with T. R. Gourvish, and contributor) *Britain Since 1945,* Macmillan, 1991.

(Editor with D. George Boyce, and contributor) *Parnell in Perspective,* Routledge & Kegan Paul, 1991.

(Editor with Yonah Alexander, and co-author of introduction) *The Irish Terrorism Experience,* Dartmouth Publishing, 1991.

(Editor with Andreas Kappeler and Firket Adanir, and contributor) *Comparative Studies on Governments and Non-Dominant Ethnic Groups in Europe, 1850-1940,* Volume VI: *The Formation of National Elites,* New York University Press, 1992.

(Editor with John Stevenson and co-author of introduction) *Irish Historical Documents Since 1800,* Barnes & Noble, 1992.

(Editor and author of introduction) *Dimensions of Irish Terrorism,* G. K. Hall, 1993.

(Editor with Michael Hurst, and contributor) *The Speeches of Charles Stewart Parnell,* two volumes, Hambledon Press, 1994.

(Editor with Michael Bromley, and contributor) *Bibliography of Charles Stewart Parnell,* Greenwood Press, 1994.

(Editor and contributor) *Government and Institutions in the Post-1832 United Kingdom,* Edwin Mellen Press, 1994.

(Editor and contributor) *Terrorism's Laboratory: The Case of Northern Ireland,* Dartmouth Publishing, 1994.

Work represented in anthologies, including *Terrorism: Theory and Practice,* edited by Yonah Alexander, David Carlton, and Paul Wilkinson, Westview, 1979; *The Irish in the Victorian City,* edited by Roger Swift and Sheridan Gilley, Croom Helm, 1985; *The Irish in Britain, 1815-1939,* edited by Roger Swift and Sheridan Gilley, Barnes & Noble, 1989; *Recent Historians of Great Britain: Essays on the Post-1945 Generation,* edited by Walter L. Arnstein, Iowa State University Press, 1990; *Racial Violence in Britain, 1840-1950,* edited by Panikos Panayi, St. Martin's, 1993; *Roots of Rural Ethnic Mobilisation,* edited by David Howell, et. al., New York University Press, 1993; and *Governments, Ethnic Groups, and Political Representation,* edited by Geoffrey Alderman, John Leslie, and Klaus E. Pollmann, New York University Press, 1993. Contributor of numerous articles and reviews to periodicals.

*   *   *

O'KANE, James M. 1941-

PERSONAL: Born June 12, 1941, in Brooklyn, NY; son of Bernard O'Kane and Matilda Mullin; married Margaret Mary Gray in 1966. *Education:* St. Francis College, A.B. (magna cum laude), 1962; Columbia University, M.S., 1964; New York University, Ph.D. (with honors), 1968.

ADDRESSES: Office—Department of Sociology, Drew University, Madison, NJ 07940-4038.

CAREER: St. Francis College, Brooklyn, NY, instructor in sociology, 1964-67; Drew University, Madison, NJ, instructor, 1967-68, assistant professor, 1968-72, associate professor, 1972-78, professor of sociology, 1978—, chair of department, 1970-78, 1980-86, 1989-90, member of advisory council, Center for Public and Corporate Affairs, 1982-83. New York University, member of summer faculty, 1969-70, teacher at Resident Center, San Juan, PR, 1969; University of Navarra, visiting research professor, 1973. Volunteer worker in community development programs in Peruvian and Mexican villages, 1962-63; Social Science Research Associates, founder, 1974, research director, 1974—; consultant to U.S. Department of Housing and Urban Development, Media Methods, Inc., and New Jersey Department of Water Resources. Focus House, member of board of directors, 1970, 1971; Madison Community Pool Corp., member of board of trustees, 1978-89, vice-president of board, 1981, president, 1982; Discovery Club (boys' club), founder, 1979, director, 1979-85; Roman Catholic Archdiocese of New York, member of Panel of Distinguished Educators, Catholic Social Policy Coalition, 1987.

MEMBER: International Association for the Study of Organized Crime, Academy of Criminal Justice Sciences, Population Reference Bureau, American Sociological Association, Eastern Sociological Society, Omicron Chi Epsilon, Alpha Kappa Delta, Drew University Faculty Club (president, 1978), Irish Society of Drew University (co-founder, 1991).

WRITINGS:

Pamplona: A Sociological Analysis of Migration and Urban Adaptation Patterns, University Press of America, 1981.
The Crooked Ladder: Gangsters, Ethnicity, and the American Dream, Transaction Books, 1992.

Work represented in anthologies, including *Equality of Educational Opportunity: A Handbook for Research,* edited by Edmund W. Gordon and LaMar P. Miller, AMS Press, 1974; *Continuities and Discontinuities: Essays in Psychohistory,* edited by Shirley Sugerman, Drew University Publications, 1978; and *Needed Reforms in the Social Sciences,* edited by Patrick F. Fagan and Charles E. Thomann, American Society of Local Officials, 1988. Contributor of articles and reviews to journals in the social sciences and to newspapers.

*   *   *

O'KANE, Rosemary H(eather) T(eresa) 1947-

PERSONAL: Born November 18, 1947, in Enfield, Middlesex, England; daughter of William Charles and Eileen Margaret Henrietta (a telephonist and receptionist; maiden name, Lovelock) O'Kane; married Leslie Rosenthal (a lecturer in economics), March 25, 1976; children: Harriet Elizabeth Selima. *Education:* University of Essex, B.A., 1970, M.A. (with distinction), 1971; University of Lancaster, Ph.D., 1978. *Politics:* Labour. *Religion:* "Atheist/Humanist."

ADDRESSES: Home—Radway House, 259 Crewe Rd., Alsager, Cheshire, England. *Office*—Department of Politics, University of Keele, Keele, Staffordshire ST5 5BG, England.

CAREER: University of Keele, Keele, England, lecturer in political sociology, 1973—.

MEMBER: International Political Science Association, Political Studies Association.

AWARDS, HONORS: Outstanding Book Award, *Choice,* 1993, for *The Revolutionary Reign of Terror.*

WRITINGS:

The Likelihood of Coups, Gower, 1987.
The Revolutionary Reign of Terror, Edward Elgar, 1991.

Contributor to political science journals.

WORK IN PROGRESS: Terror, Force, and States; research on terror states, revolutions, and coups d'etat.

SIDELIGHTS: Rosemary H. T. O'Kane told *CA:* "Against the dominant tide in the United Kingdom, my research is directed away from Europe and toward the darker side of politics, to the study of coups d'etat, military regimes, revolutions, and terror states. My aim in writing is to develop general explanations with predictive boundaries between political sociology and comparative politics. I am firmly committed to the view that the study of 'illegitimate' government is not only important in its own right, but that it contributes to an understanding of the role played by coercion in 'legitimate' government.

"Though I am committed to the study of these dangerous, dramatic, and sometimes dreadful forms of politics, however, I admit that I never go to violent films or read frightening novels."

*   *   *

OKPARA, Mzee Lasana
See HORD, Frederick (Lee)

*   *   *

OLITZKY, Kerry M. 1954-

PERSONAL: Born December 22, 1954, in Pittsburgh, PA; son of Abraham Nathan (an engineering technician) and Frances (an inventory controller; maiden name, Reznick) Olitzky; married Sheryl Mandy Rosenblatt (a market researcher), August 28, 1977; children: Avi Samuel, Jesse Michael. *Education:* Attended American College in Jerusalem, 1971-72; University of South Florida, B.A., 1974, M.A., 1975; Hebrew Union College-Jewish Institute of Religion, Cincinnati, OH, rabbinic ordination, 1981, D.H.L., 1985. *Politics:* Democrat.

ADDRESSES: Home—Dayton, NJ. *Office*—School of Education, Hebrew Union College-Jewish Institute of Religion, Brookdale Center, 1 West Fourth St., New York, NY 10012.

CAREER: Ordained rabbi, 1981. Assistant rabbi and director of religious education for congregation Beth Israel in West Hartford, CT, 1981-84; Hebrew Union College-Jewish Institute of Religion, New York City, director of graduate studies program at School of Education, 1984—. Mature Adult Day Care Center, St. Petersburg, FL, program manager, 1976; American Jewish Archives, assistant archivist, 1978-81; B'nai B'rith Youth Organization, assistant regional director, 1978-81; Union of American Hebrew Congregations, facilitator for National Liheyot Task Force, and member of Gerontology Committee, executive committee of Joint Commission on Jewish Education, and Day School Curriculum Advisory Committee; member of National Interfaith Coalition on Aging and United Jewish

Appeal/Federation's Task Force on the Jewish Aged; Open University of Israel, member of education board. ABC-Radio, producer and moderator of *Message of Israel;* executive producer of *Torah Tapes: Contemporary Insights into the Weekly Torah Reading.* Conference on Alternatives in Jewish Education, member of steering committee, 1981; Hartford Jewish Federation, member of Older Adults Committee and Education Committee, 1981; Rabbinical Fellowship of Greater Hartford, member, 1981; Hartford Jewish Center, member of board of directors, 1981; Greater Hartford Jewish Educators Council, member, 1981-84; Center for Jewish Life, honorary member of board of directors.

MEMBER: Jewish National Fund (member of Young Associates, 1979-81), Central Conference of American Rabbis, Coalition for the Advancement of Jewish Education, Association of Reform Zionists in America, National Association of Temple Educators, Gerontology Society of America, Association for Supervision and Curriculum Development, American Society of Aging (member of Forum on Religion and Aging), Association for Jewish Studies.

AWARDS, HONORS: Grant from American Jewish Archives, 1990.

WRITINGS:

EDUCATION AND REFERENCE BOOKS

Aging and Judaism (textbook), Alternatives in Religious Education, 1980.
Critical Issues Facing American Jewish Youth: A Resource Book for Educators, Experimental Edition, Union of American Hebrew Congregations, 1982.
Come Dance with Me: Life in the Jewish Shtetl, Experimental Edition, Union of American Hebrew Congregations, 1983.
I Am a Reform Jew (student workbook), Behrman, 1986.
Explaining Reform Judaism (teacher's guide), Behrman, 1986.
My Jewish Community (student workbook), Alternatives in Religious Education, 1986.
A Jewish Mourner's Handbook, Ktav, 1991.
(With Ronald H. Isaacs) *A Glossary of Jewish Life,* J. Aronson, 1992.
When Your Jewish Child Asks Why: Answers for Tough Questions, Ktav, 1993.
Reform Judaism in America: A Biographical Dictionary and Source Book, 1824-1980, Greenwood Press, 1993.
The "How to" Book of Jewish Living, Ktav, 1993.

Work represented in anthologies, including *The Jewish Principal's Handbook,* 1983; and *Visions of Excellence: The Reform Jewish Day School,* Union of American Hebrew Congregations, 1990.

SELF-HELP BOOKS

Twelve Jewish Steps to Recovery: A Personal Guide to Turning from Alcoholism and Other Addictions, Jewish Lights Publishing, 1991.
Renewed Each Day: Daily Twelve Step Recovery Meditations Based on the Bible, two volumes, Jewish Lights Publishing, 1992.
Recovery from Codependence: A Jewish Twelve Steps Guide to Healing Your Soul, Jewish Lights Publishing, 1993.
One Hundred Blessings Every Day, Jewish Lights Publishing, 1993.

OTHER

To Grow Old in Israel: A Survey of Recent Trends and Developments, Human Sciences, 1988.
In Celebration: An American Jewish Perspective on the Bicentennial of the U.S. Constitution, University Press of America, 1988.
An Interfaith Ministry to the Aged: A Survey of Models, Human Sciences, 1988.
The Synagogue Confronts the Jewish Family of the Twenty-first Century, Union of American Hebrew Congregations and Hebrew Union College-Jewish Institute of Religion, 1988.
(Editor) *The Safe Deposit Box: And Other Stories about Grandparents, Old Lovers, and Crazy Old Men,* Markus Wiener, 1989.
Leaving Mother Russia: Chapters in the Russian Jewish Experience, American Jewish Archives, 1990.
The Discovery Haggadah, Ktav, 1992.
Hebrew, Heroes, and Holidays: The Great Jewish Fun Book, Union of American Hebrew Congregations, 1992.
Pirke Avot: A New Translation and Commentary, Union of American Hebrew Congregations, 1993.
Documents of Jewish Life, J. Aronson, 1993.

Contributor of articles, poems, and reviews to professional journals and popular magazines, including *Cobblestone* and *South Florida Review.* Editor, *Journal of Aging and Judaism;* executive editor, *Shofar;* past executive editor, *COMPASS;* member of editorial board, *Journal of Ministry in Addiction and Recovery;* coeditor of *T'shuva: Bringing the News of Jewish Recovery.*

WORK IN PROGRESS: The American Synagogue: A Historical Dictionary, for Greenwood Press; *Tales of Jewish Life,* J. Aronson; *The Big Book of Teshuvah,* J. Aronson; *Sparks beneath the Surface: A Psycho-Spiritual Commentary on the Bible,* J. Aronson; "The Jewish Welfare Board," to be included in *Encyclopedia of World War I,* Garland Publishing; "A Jewish Theology of Aging," to be included in *Handbook on Religion and Aging.* Reform Judaism editor for the *Oxford Dictionary of Judaism.*

SIDELIGHTS: Kerry M. Olitzky is a rabbi, educator, and author of a wide variety of books with Jewish themes. While much of his writing deals with issues of Jewish education or history, his reference manuals provide a broader scope of information for children, parents, or general readers. Olitzky has also published four "twelve-step" books intended to guide Jewish readers through a spiritual healing process.

Unlike his nonfiction publications, Olitzky's 1989 work, *The Safe Deposit Box: And Other Stories about Grandparents, Old Lovers, and Crazy Old Men* is a collection of tales, memoirs, and anecdotes concerning old age by Jewish writers. Issues such as Black-Jewish relations and attitudes toward the elderly are explored in some of the pieces. In addition to the title selection by Isaac Bashevis Singer, the book includes Grace Paley's "Dreamer in a Dead Language," Hugh Nissenson's "The Crazy Old Man," and short works by Dan Jacobson, Bruno Lessing, Anzia Yezierska, and Edna Ferber.

In 1992 Olitzky published *A Glossary of Jewish Life* with Ronald H. Isaacs. The book provides definitions of terms commonly used in Judaism, as well as biographical portraits of historical and contemporary figures. Divided into eight segments by subject matter, with headings including "Religious Practice" and "World Jewish History," *A Glossary of Jewish Life* also includes cross-references and a general index.

Olitzky told *CA:* "I work in several areas. My work in education generally serves a particular need. Often, I use a book to translate into reality (especially in a Jewish context) a theoretical construct from secular education. I also write in order to bring individuals closer to their Jewish roots and, in the process, closer to God. I aim to help them make their lives holy and sacred. My work in history is based on interest in particular areas, often of an esoteric nature."

BIOGRAPHICAL/CRITICAL SOURCES:

PERIODICALS

Publishers Weekly, October 13, 1989, p. 44.

*   *   *

OLSON, Everett C.   1910-1993

OBITUARY NOTICE—See index for *CA* sketch: Born November 6, 1910, in Waupaca, WI; died November 26, 1993, in Brentwood, CA. Paleontologist, educator, and author. Known for his research on the origin and evolution of invertebrate animals, Olson did pioneering work to help trace fossil records of the Paleozoic Era. In addition to scientific study, Olson spent many years teaching pale-

ontology at the college level. Olson began his teaching career as an instructor at the University of Chicago in 1935. When he left the university in 1958, Olson was associate dean of the Division of Physical Sciences. He then taught at the University of California, Los Angeles, where he became chair of the department of zoology. Olson wrote several books, including *Concepts of Evolution* and *The Other Side of the Medal.* He was also editor of the periodical *Evolution* from 1952 to 1958 and the *Journal of Geology* in the 1960s. A recipient of the Distinguished Scientist Award from the Center for the Study of Evolution and the Origin of Life, Olson was also awarded the Paleontological Medal by the Paleontological Society.

OBITUARIES AND OTHER SOURCES:

BOOKS

Who's Who in America, 48th edition, Marquis, 1994.

PERIODICALS

Chicago Tribune, December 1, 1993, section 1, p. 11.

*   *   *

OMOTOSO, Kole   1943-

PERSONAL: Born April 21, 1943, in Akure, Nigeria; married; children: three. *Education:* Attended King's College, Lagos; University of Ibadan, B.A., 1968; University of Edinburgh, Ph.D., 1972.

CAREER: Ibadan University, Ibadan, Oye, Nigeria, lecturer, 1972-76; University of Ife, Ife, Nigeria, professor, beginning c. 1976.

MEMBER: Association of Nigerian Authors (founder; national secretary, 1981-84; president, 1986-87).

WRITINGS:

Notes, Q & A on Peter Edwards' West African Narrative, Onibonoje, 1968.
Pitched against the Gods (stage play), first produced at Deen Playhouse, Ikare, Nigeria, 1969.
The Edifice, Heinemann, 1971.
The Combat, Heinemann, 1972.
Miracles and Other Stories, Onibonoje, 1973, revised, 1978.
Fella's Choice, Ethiope, 1974.
Sacrifice, Onibonoje, 1974, revised, 1978.
The Curse, New Horn, 1976.
The Scales, Onibonoje, 1976.
(Coeditor) *The Indigenous for National Development,* Onibonoje, 1976.
Shadows in the Horizon, Omotoso/Sketch, 1977.
Kole Omotoso of Nigeria (recording), Voice of America, 1978.

To Borrow a Wandering Leaf, Olaiya Fagbamigbe, 1979.

The Form of the African Novel, Olaiya Fagbamigbe, 1979, revised edition, McQuick, 1986.

Memories of Our Recent Boom, Longman, 1982.

The Theatrical into Theatre: A Study of the Drama and Theatre of the English-Speaking Caribbean, New Beacon, 1982.

A Feast in the Time of Plague, Dramatic Arts/Unife, 1983.

The Girl Sunshine, Dramatic Arts/Unife, 1983.

The Last Competition (stage play), first produced at National Theatre, Lagos, 1983.

All This Must Be Seen, Progress, 1986.

Just before Dawn, Spectrum, 1988.

Contributor to periodicals and newspapers, including Lagos *Sunday Times, Top Life,* Lagos *Sunday Concord Okike,* and *Index on Censorship.*

SIDELIGHTS: Kole Omotoso is a prominent Nigerian writer who writes both to offer answers to Nigeria's problems as well as to entertain. Omotoso's belief that the artist must help lead the way to a better life for the common people is reflected in his writing. "Art for art's sake is intellectual crap," Omotoso told J. B. Alston in *Yoruba Drama in English.* "Whereas if you are committed to communicating with everyone who reads your works, that's a very basic and responsible kind of commitment."

Omotoso, the nephew of Yoruba author Olaiya Fagbamigbe, began writing in primary school. His first influences were family folktales, and his first audience his schoolmates. By the time he was in secondary school, Omotoso began to be published, but in English, rather than his native Yoruba. Later, when he went to Great Britain to study Arabic, the racism he experienced there provided the inspiration for his first novel. With the publication of *The Edifice,* Omotoso's career blossomed.

He wrote essays, plays, short stories, and novels. Among them was *Miracles and Other Stories,* a collection that focused on the plight of poor children in Nigeria. During his career, the author's work has become increasingly politicized. The content of his novels reflects Omotoso's concern with the future of his homeland. He was strongly influenced by the shaky political climate of Nigeria, a country where military rule predominates. Omotoso struggled against the limitations of that situation.

In 1977, the author released his play *Shadows in the Horizon* privately after publishers deemed it too controversial. The piece was successful; ultimately, it was translated into Russian. Like other authors, including the well-known playwright Wole Soyinka, whom Omotoso calls his major influence, African themes are important in his work. F. Odun Balogun points out in the *Dictionary of Literary Biography* that in *Fella's Choice* and another mystery-adventure work, the 1976 book *The Scales,* Omotoso

makes communalism the basis for heroism, rather than Western individualism.

Omotoso's fiction reflects a preoccupation with the future of the common folk of one's country. In *Yoruba Drama in English* Omotoso is quoted as saying that "the conscious artist can contribute towards building a new mode of life. Anything he does—the way he presents his characters, the way he lives his own life—is likely to influence what other people are going to do."

BIOGRAPHICAL/CRITICAL SOURCES:

BOOKS

Agetua, John, *Interviews with Six Nigerian Writers,* Bendel Newspapers Corporation, 1974, pp. 9-16.

Alston, J. B., *Yoruba Drama in English,* Edwin Mellen, 1989, pp. 107-115.

Dictionary of Literary Biography: Volume 125, *Twentieth Century Caribbean and Black-African Writers, Second Series,* Gale, 1993.

Nazareth, Peter, *The Third World Writer,* Kenya Literature Bureau, 1978, pp. 71-86.

Nichols, Lee, *Conversations with African Writers,* Voice of America, 1981, pp. 218-229.

PERIODICALS

African Book Publishing Record, Number 2, 1976, pp. 12-14.

Commonwealth Essays and Studies, autumn, 1984, pp. 36-50.

Cultural Events in Africa, Number 103, 1973, pp. 2-12.

Daily Times (Lagos), March 12, 1974, p. 12.

Guardian (Lagos), June 9, 1986, p. 10.

Journal of Commonwealth Literature, Volume 25, number 1, 1990, pp. 98-108.

Notre Librairie, Volume 98, July-September, 1989, pp. 68-70.

Theatre Research International, autumn, 1982, pp. 235-244.

World Literature Written in English, April, 1977, pp. 39-53.*

*   *   *

ORKENY, Antal 1954-

PERSONAL: Born January 6, 1954, in Budapest, Hungary. *Education:* Eotvos Lorand University, M.A., 1986, Ph.D., 1993. *Politics:* Liberal. *Religion:* Agnostic. *Avocational Interests:* Travel, "making friendships."

ADDRESSES: Home—Keleti Karoly utca 44, Budapest 1024, Hungary. *Office*—Institute of Sociology, Eotvos Lorand University, P.O. Box 394, Budapest 1446, Hungary.

CAREER: Eotvos Lorand University, Budapest, Hungary, assistant professor, 1978-86, associate professor of sociology, 1987—. Columbia University, assistant professor, 1984; Economic University of Budapest, lecturer in Education Abroad Program sponsored by University of California and University of Wisconsin, 1988-89, 1990-91, director of program, 1992—; American University, lecturer in Budapest Program, 1991—; University of Michigan, research fellow at Institute for Social Research, 1992, 1993.

MEMBER: Hungarian Sociological Association.

WRITINGS:

(With Gyorgy Csepeli) *Az Alkony: A mai magyar ertelmiseg ideologiai-politikai optikaja az 1980-as evek vegen,* Eotvos Lorand University, 1990, translation published as *Ideology and Political Beliefs in Hungary: The Twilight of State Socialism,* St. Martin's, 1992.

Kaderek (title means "The Newcomers"), Eotvos Lorand University, 1991.

WORK IN PROGRESS: Everyday Perception of Social Justice in a Comparative Perspective, "based on an empirical attitude survey carried out in 1991 in fourteen different countries from eastern and western Europe, and the United States and Japan."

*   *   *

OSLIN, George P(oer) 1899-

PERSONAL: Born August 5, 1899, in West Point, GA; son of Reuben Jefferson (a dentist) and Mary (a homemaker; maiden name, Poer) Oslin; married Susannah Meigs; children: Louise Oslin Darlington (deceased), Catherine Oslin McManus, Jeanne Oslin Fernald. *Education:* Attended Trinity College (now Duke University); Mercer University, B.A., 1920; graduate study at Columbia University.

ADDRESSES: Home and office—838 Lake Shore Dr., Delray Beach, FL 33444.

CAREER: Macon Telegraph, Macon, GA, reporter, 1920-22; *Newark Ledger,* Newark, NJ, editor and reporter, 1922-23; *Newark Evening News,* Newark, reporter, 1923-29; Western Union, corporate public relations director, 1929-64, created the first singing telegram, 1933; retired, 1964. Guest on national television programs.

MEMBER: Public Relations Society of America (founder; president, in the 1940s), Sons of the American Revolution (president in New Jersey, 1940-50, and in New York, 1950s).

WRITINGS:

The Telegraph Industry, Bellman Publishing, 1941.
Talking Wires: The Way of Life in the Telegraph Industry, Row, Peterson, 1942.
The Story of Telecommunications, Mercer University Press, 1993.

Work represented in anthologies, including *The Development of American Industries,* edited by John G. Glover and Rudolph L. Lagai. Contributor to magazines.

SIDELIGHTS: George P. Oslin told *CA:* "From the day in 1929 when I became the first corporate public relations director for Western Union, I realized the need to preserve the unique history of the communications industry for future generations. I began collecting items from sources around the country and, indeed, the world. Having covered such major stories as the kidnapping of aviator Charles Lindbergh's son in 1932 and the subsequent trial and the *Hindenburg* zeppelin disaster of 1937, I had a journalistic background that prepared me for writing history as it was being made.

"Over a fifty-year period, I interviewed scientist-inventor Thomas Edison, William Henry Jackson (a Civil War soldier), and William Campbell (at the time, the last surviving Pony Express rider), and collected company documents, periodicals and books, a hundred thousand letters and diaries of industry pioneers, and hundreds of historic photographs to assemble *The Story of Telecommunications,* the first comprehensive history of the industry.

"My exhaustive research dispels such myths as Alexander Graham Bell's and Samuel Morse's inventions of the first telephone and telegraph instruments, and the Pony Express's delivery of the U.S. mail. A high school student who based her presentation on this work won the New York City History Contest in 1993. In preserving this segment of our history, I have attempted to document the fascinating account of humankind's quest for ever-improving communication with each other and with the world in which we live."

*   *   *

OUGHTON, Jerrie 1937-

PERSONAL: Born April 13, 1937, in Atlanta, GA; daughter of Edwin (a college president) and Mary Frances (an educational director and author; maiden name, Johnson) Preston; married William Paul Oughton (a business owner), November 28, 1963; children: Cher, Lisa, Shannon, Sean, Preston. *Education:* Received B.A. from Meredith College. *Religion:* Southern Baptist.

ADDRESSES: Office—c/o Publicity Director, Houghton Mifflin Co., 222 Berkely St., Boston, MA 02116-3764.

CAREER: Teacher, Raleigh, NC, 1963-64; substitute teacher and teaching assistant, Washington, NC, 1974-85; secretary with Fayette County Public Schools, 1989—.

WRITINGS:

How the Stars Fell into the Sky: A Navajo Legend, illustrated by Lisa Dessami, Houghton, 1992.

Contributor to periodicals, including *Catholic Digest* and denominational magazines.

WORK IN PROGRESS: Another Navajo legend, about the Navajo God Spider Woman and how she taught the People to weave.

SIDELIGHTS: Jerrie Oughton's career began when she was eight years old and a magazine asked her to write a review of a book for them. In high school in Raleigh, NC, she studied under the creative writing teacher, Mrs. Phyllis Peacock, who also taught the well-known Southern writer, Reynolds Price, who, in turn, taught Anne Tyler, author of such novels as *Breathing Lessons* and *The Accidental Tourist.*

For twenty years, Oughton wrote articles and short stories and received encouraging letters from some of the most prominent (and caring) editors in children's publishing. But she had written no book. Then, as Oughton commented, "There came a point which I really believe is a milestone most writers have to pass. I knew that I would be writing whether or not I ever had a book published. It is part of my make-up and if I tried to turn it off it would be as futile as stemming a flood.

"It was at this point that I sent Houghton Mifflin Co. two manuscripts. One I discussed in the cover letter. A 'P.S.' stated that I was also enclosing a manuscript for a Navajo legend called *How the Stars Fell into the Sky.* This is the book they bought. My editor linked me up with Lisa Dessami who is an extraordinary artist. When the first copy of the book came to me, I felt that I had written the words to a song and Lisa had written the music. I was astounded.

"Sometimes people ask me how I got interested in Native American lore. I admire the Navajo greatly and feel any honor and recognition that can be channeled their way is certainly richly deserved. So much of their literary heritage is oral history from their Medicine Men and others who told the stories. I was just fortunate enough to find mention of two oral legends and to be able to pass them on through my mind and soul."

P-Q

P. Q.
See QUENNELL, Peter (Courtney)

* * *

PADDISON, Sara 1953-

PERSONAL: Born February 23, 1953, in Madison, WI; daughter of Harold Arthur (a general in the U.S. Marines), and Mildred (in elementary education; maiden name, Gehrig) Hatch; children: Christian Paddison. *Education:* East Carolina University, B.F.A., 1976.

ADDRESSES: Office—Institute of HeartMath, P.O. Box 1463, Boulder Creek, CA 95006. Agent—Planetary Publications, P.O. Box 66, Boulder Creek, CA 95006.

CAREER: Institute of HeartMath, Boulder Creek, CA, vice-president, 1970-93.

WRITINGS:

Just Love the People, Planetary Publications, 1991.
The Hidden Power of the Heart: Achieving Balance and Fulfillment in a Stressful World, Planetary Publications, 1992.

SIDELIGHTS: Sara Paddison told *CA:* "As a child I was lonely, withdrawn, frightened of my own shadow. I was confused, as so many young people are today. But I was a survivor in life, always knowing there was an answer somewhere. I grew up on military bases, always moving from one base to another with my family. My life seemed like one readjustment after another. When I attended college, I found peace and family in art school. I loved art, but the people were even more important to me. I graduated from East Carolina University with a Bachelor's of Fine Arts degree and also took many courses in psychology. I came to realize that life is about loving and caring for people. That became my ambition.

"Sixteen years ago I began to simply 'listen to and follow my heart.' Little did I know that following my heart would not only vanquish my fears and insecurities but awaken a new intelligence that can perceive the holographic nature of reality, experience new depths of love, peer into DNA blueprints, and more. Today I am vice-president of the Institute of HeartMath, a nonprofit educational and research organization founded by Doc Lew Childre. We have developed a proven system of energy-efficiency and self-empowerment called HeartMath. Much of what I share in my second book, *The Hidden Power of the Heart: Achieving Balance and Fulfillment in a Stressful World,* I discovered while in the process of proving the HeartMath system side-by-side with my friends at the Institute.

"I am currently very interested and involved in leading edge science. Developing heart intelligence has given me a deeper understanding of the relationship between love and the heart/mind/brain connection. The Research Division of the Institute is engaged in several exciting areas of research which correlate mental and emotional attitudes, the heart's electrical system, and the immune system. The primary focus of this research is to understand the relationship between these systems, so people can reduce stress, boost energy levels, and enhance immune responses.

"I appreciate Doc Lew Childre for providing a step-by-step, nuts and bolts method of energy-efficiency that shows how the heart empowerment of each individual—mentally, emotionally and physically—accelerates human evolution. Uncovering this hidden power is a personal process of understanding how it works and understanding yourself."

PAKER, Saliha

PERSONAL: Born in Ankara, Turkey; daughter of a diplomat; children: Kerim (son). *Education:* University of Istanbul, B.A. (with honors), 1964, Ph.D., 1977; Bogazici University, postdoctoral degree in English, 1982.

ADDRESSES: Home—London, England, and Istanbul, Turkey.

CAREER: University of Istanbul, Istanbul, Turkey, assistant lecturer in Greek, 1967-75; Bogazici University, Istanbul, began as lecturer, became associate professor of English and classical studies, 1979-83; University of London, London School of Oriental and African Studies, London, England, part-time teacher of modern Turkish language and literature, 1983-85; University of Warwick, Coventry, England, visiting research fellow at European Humanities Research Centre, 1986-87; University of Birmingham, Birmingham, England, associate member of Centre for Byzantine, Ottoman, and Modern Greek Studies, 1988-92, honorary research fellow, 1992-95.

MEMBER: International Comparative Literature Association, Society of Authors, Institute of Linguists (fellow).

WRITINGS:

(Translator with Ruth Christie) Mehmet Ali Birand, *Shirts of Steel: An Anatomy of the Turkish Armed Forces,* I. B. Tauris, 1991.
(Translator with Christie, and author of introduction) Latife Tekin, *Berji Kristin: Tales From the Garbage Hills* (novel), Marion Boyars, 1993.

Work represented in anthologies, including *Modern Literature in the Middle East,* edited by Robin Ostle, Routledge, 1991; and *Textual Liberation: European Feminist Writers in the Twentieth Century,* edited by Helena Forsas-Scott, Routledge, 1991. Contributor of articles and translations to periodicals.

WORK IN PROGRESS: A book on the critical reception of Turkish women writers, to be published in Turkey; translating modern Turkish fiction and poetry.

SIDELIGHTS: Saliha Paker told *CA:* "When I was eight, I could speak and write in four languages: Turkish, French, Arabic, and English. Later Greek replaced Arabic. Looking back, I can now say that growing up in more than one language and culture meant living in translation, being in conscious contact with the 'other' in myself as well as with 'others' in different physical and mental environments. It involved a constant exploration of differences and similarities through language. As a result, the variety of literary and cultural perceptions and modes of expression reflected in different literatures has always held a challenge for me: the challenge to make them as meaningful in another language. This is what I have been trying

to do for some time, not only through translations, but in other forms of writing or rewriting. I no longer believe in the distinction between so-called 'major' and 'marginal' literatures, because each replenishes and revives the other in time, largely thanks to fresh translations and the responses they produce in creative minds."

*   *   *

PANAYI, Panikos   1962-

PERSONAL: Born October 18, 1962, in London, England; son of Nestoras (a pastry cook) and Chrystalla (a dressmaker; maiden name, Louca) Panayi. *Education:* Polytechnic of North London, B.A., 1985; University of Sheffield, Ph.D., 1988. *Politics:* "Radical." *Religion:* Greek Orthodox.

ADDRESSES: Home—Leicester, England. *Office*—School of Arts, De Montfort University, Leicester LE1 9BH, England.

CAREER: University of Keele, Keele, England, temporary lecturer in history, 1989-90; De Montfort University, Leicester, England, lecturer in history, 1990—. University of Osnabrueck, Alexander von Humboldt fellow, 1991-92.

WRITINGS:

The Enemy in Our Midst: Germans in Britain during the First World War, Berg, 1991.
(Editor) *Racial Violence in Britain, 1840-1950,* Leicester University Press, 1993.
(Editor) *Minorities in Wartime,* Berg, 1993.
Immigration, Ethnicity, and Racism in Britain, 1815-1945, Manchester University Press, 1994.

WORK IN PROGRESS: Research on Germans in England since the Middle Ages; research on race in postwar Germany and Europe.

SIDELIGHTS: Panikos Panayi told *CA:* "My main area of research is immigration, ethnicity, and racism in Europe since 1800, an area in which I also teach. I began as a specialist on the Germans in Britain, and this still forms my core research interest, but I have subsequently moved to broader areas, such as immigration into Britain generally, minorities in wartime, and race in postwar Germany and Europe. Perhaps the major reason for my interest lies in my own ethnicity, as I am the son of Greek Cypriot immigrants who moved to Britain in the late 1950s. However, my motivation for writing is far more complex, revolving around psychological factors."

PANKHURST, Helen 1964-

PERSONAL: Born May 8, 1964, in Addis Ababa, Ethiopia; daughter of Richard Pankhurst (a historian) and Rita Pankhurst (a librarian); married David Loakes (a research chemist), September 14, 1991. *Education:* Attended Vassar College, 1985-86; University of Sussex, B.A., 1987; University of Edinburgh, Ph.D., 1990.

ADDRESSES: Home—59 Queens Rd., Royston, Hertfordshire, England.

CAREER: Agency for Cooperation and Research in Development (ACORD), assistant regional program officer for the Horn of Africa, 1993—. MYRADA, volunteer with a Tibetan resettlement program in Karnataka, India, 1982-83; KPMG Peat Marwick, auditor, 1991-93; consultant to Canadian International Development Agency, SOS Sahel, and U.S. Agency for International Development.

WRITINGS:

Gender, Development, and Identity: An Ethiopian Study, Zed Books, 1992.

Work represented in books, including *Ethiopia: Rural Development Options,* edited by Fantu Cheru Pausewang, S. Bruuene, and Eshetu Chole, Zed Books, 1990, and *Ethiopia: Problems of Sustainable Development,* University of Trondheim College of Arts and Science, 1990.

*   *   *

PARK, Keith K. H. 1964-

PERSONAL: Born February 11, 1964, in Seoul, South Korea; son of B. W. (an international trader) and Insook (a real estate developer) Park. *Education:* Columbia University, B.A., 1986, M.A., 1988.

ADDRESSES: Home—255 South Grand Ave., Suite 1703, Los Angeles, CA 90012. *Office*—Global Strategies Group, 700 South Flower St., Suite 1100, Los Angeles, CA 90017.

CAREER: Global Strategies Group, Los Angeles, CA, partner, 1989—.

WRITINGS:

Global Equity Markets, Probus Publishing, 1991.
Global Bond Markets, Probus Publishing, 1991.
(With Steven Schoenfeld) *Pacific Rim Futures and Options Markets: A Comprehensive, Country-by-Country Reference to the World's Fastest Growing Financial Markets,* Probus Publishing, 1992.
(Editor with Antoine W. Van Agtmael) *The World's Emerging Stock Markets: Structure, Development,*

Regulations, and Opportunities, Probus Publishing, 1992.

WORK IN PROGRESS: Equity Derivatives in Quantitative Global Equity Investment; research on the world's equity derivative stock markets.

SIDELIGHTS: Keith K. H. Park told *CA:* "I find a great satisfaction in sharing my research work with professionals in the global investment community through my publications."

*   *   *

PARMELEE, David Freeland 1924-

PERSONAL: Born June 20, 1924, in Oshkosh, WI; son of Gale Freeland and Helen (MacNaughton) Parmelee; married Jean Marie Peterson, December 4, 1943; children: Helen Gale Parmelee Bruzzone. *Education:* Lawrence College (now Lawrence University of Wisconsin), B.A., 1950; University of Michigan, M.S., 1952; University of Oklahoma, Ph.D., 1957. *Politics:* Independent. *Religion:* Lutheran. *Avocational Interests:* Travel, photography, art, fishing, gardening.

ADDRESSES: Home—7433 Painted Shadows Way, Las Vegas, NV 89129. *Office*—Marjorie Barrick Museum of Natural History, 4505 Maryland Parkway, University of Nevada, Las Vegas, NV 89154-4012.

CAREER: Kansas State Teachers College (now Emporia State University), Emporia, began as assistant professor, became professor of biology, 1957-70; University of Minnesota—Twin Cities, Minneapolis, professor of biological sciences, 1970-92, chairperson of Field Biology Program, 1970-86, curator of birds at Bell Museum, 1986-92, and director of Lake Itasca and Cedar Creek biological field stations; University of Nevada, Las Vegas, research curator of ornithology, 1992—. National Science Foundation, member of polar programs, 1972-86; Scientific Committee on Antarctic Research, member, 1976-80; public lecturer. *Military service:* U.S. Marine Corps Reserve, active duty, 1943-46; served in Pacific theater.

MEMBER: Organization of Biological Field Stations (president, 1984-85), Association of Field Ornithologists (life member), Explorers Club (fellow), Coopers Club (life member), Wilson Ornithological Society (life member).

AWARDS, HONORS: Award from Kansas Wildlife Federation and Sears-Roebuck Foundation, 1966; the Antarctic site Parmelee Massif was named in the author's honor, 1977; Antarctic Service Medal, 1977; Native Son Award from Rotary International, 1982.

WRITINGS:

Bird Island in Antarctic Waters, University of Minnesota Press, 1980.

Antarctic Birds: Ecological and Behavioral Approaches, University of Minnesota Press, 1992.

Contributor of articles and illustrations to scientific journals, including *National Museum of Canada Bulletin.*

WORK IN PROGRESS: The Birds of Lake Mead National Recreation Area, completion expected in 1998; research on Arctic and Antarctic birds and on the birds of southern Nevada.

SIDELIGHTS: David Freeland Parmelee told *CA:* "Much of my research has focused on Arctic and Antarctic birds, and I am the author and artist-illustrator of numerous scientific papers and books on the ecology and behavior of birds at high latitudes. Since 1985, my wife Jean and I have worked as a team for travel companies, annually cruising to both polar regions. Our cruise in July, 1993, took us all the way to the geographic North Pole aboard the nuclear-powered Russian icebreaker *Yamal.*"

*   *   *

PARNELL, Peter 1953-

PERSONAL: Born August 21, 1953, in New York, NY; son of Sol (a textile executive) and Pearl (a dental office worker; maiden name, Bogen) Parnell. *Education:* Dartmouth College, B.A. (magna cum laude), 1974.

ADDRESSES: Home—74 Irving Place, Apt. R9, New York, NY 10003. *Agent*— Arlene Donovan, International Creative Management, 156 West Fifty-seventh St., New York, NY 10036.

CAREER: Playwright. Denver Center Theatre Company, Denver, CO, playwright-in-residence, 1983-84. Playwrights Horizons, New York City, artistic board member.

MEMBER: Dramatists Guild, Writers Guild East.

AWARDS, HONORS: Reynolds Travelling Fellowship in Playwriting, 1975-76; National Endowment of the Arts Grant, 1983-84.

WRITINGS:

PLAYS

Scooter Thomas Makes It to the Top of the World (one act; produced in Los Angeles, c. 1978), Dramatists Play Service, 1983.

Sorrows of Stephen (produced by New York Shakespeare Festival, New York City, 1979-80), Samuel French, 1982.

The Rise and Rise of Daniel Rocket (produced by Playwrights Horizons, New York City, 1982), Dramatists Play Service, 1984.

Romance Language, produced by Playwrights Horizons, New York City, 1984.

Hyde in Hollywood, produced by Playwrights Horizons, American Place Theater, New York City, 1989.

OTHER

Coauthor of movie for television, *Listen to Your Heart,* Columbia Broadcasting System, 1983.

SIDELIGHTS: Peter Parnell began writing while attending college at Dartmouth, where three of his plays won campus competitions. His early career was helped along by Israel Horowitz, founder of the Playwrights' Lab in New York, who took an interest in Parnell while the latter was still at school. Upon Parnell's return from England, where he traveled on a fellowship from Dartmouth, he came to the attention of the famous theater producer Joseph Papp, who offered suggestions on the revision of what was to be the budding playwright's first full-length work, *Sorrows of Stephen.*

Parnell's first staged work was a brief, one-act production, *Scooter Thomas Makes It to the Top of the World.* In the play, a young man packs for the funeral of his friend, Scooter, and, as he reminisces about their childhood adventures, Scooter appears and they re-live often humorous events. It is a comic, yet sorrowful story of boyhood friendships, loss, and nostalgia. In an interview with Eleanor Blau, published in the *New York Times,* Parnell described the structure of the piece as "a mixture of stand-up comedy routines and a play."

Parnell's next two plays exhibit the qualities of comic light-heartedness mixed with authentic sorrow that marked his first play. *Sorrows of Stephen* tells the story of a young man obsessed by romantic love, fueled by a shelf of nineteenth-century romantic novels, including the one from which Parnell takes his title, Wolfgang von Goethe's *The Sorrows of Young Werther.* Parnell explained the premise of this light comedy to Blau in the *New York Times:* "I found it rather funny to think of a character who valued his emotions above everything else and pursued an impossible ideal—in these times, a bit of an anachronism." Accordingly, the main character, Stephen Hurt, is, in the words of Mel Gussow, theater critic for the *New York Times,* "in love with love. He longs to be smitten and finds grand passion in everyday life." Stephen's problem with women is summarized by the main character himself who declares: "I love them. They leave me." In imitation of Goethe's callow hero, Stephen halfheartedly considers suicide after the departure of his latest lover, but, in the end, he blithely decides he will just find someone new with whom to be in love. Gussow concluded that *Sorrows of*

Stephen "is a real romantic comedy, sophisticated and sentimental, with an ageless attitude toward the power of positive love."

Like Parnell's earlier works, *The Rise and Rise of Daniel Rocket* is a comedy in which the main character's need to believe in illusions propels the action of the play. Daniel is a twelve-year-old boy whose position as an outsider in his class is mitigated by his friendship with another boy named Richard, his love for a girl named Alice, and his (secret) ability to fly, which he uses to escape the pains of childhood. Gussow, in his *New York Times* review, compared *Daniel Rocket* to other "dream-of-glory" plays—such as *Superman* and *Peter Pan*—and declared emphatically that "it is proof that old stories can always be retold." In the second act, Daniel returns to his childhood home twenty years later, both a hero and yet still the insecure little boy who ran away. While some critics were uncomfortable with the simplistic theme of this play, Parnell was also praised for the accuracy of his portrayal of the quick and violent emotions of children. "Even as *Daniel Rocket* becomes increasingly fanciful," wrote Gussow in the *New York Times,* "it remains unpretentious, and it is grounded in truth about the mutual hurtfulness of children and the need for illusion in their young lives."

Romance Language, Parnell's next play to be produced in New York, shares with his earlier works a love of nineteenth-century romantic literature, as well as a taste for fantasy. But where the earlier plays focus on the dreams and illusions of youth, this play explores the more adult themes of sexuality, responsibility, and freedom. Featuring historical characters—Walt Whitman, Emily Dickinson, Henry David Thoreau, Ralph Waldo Emerson, and Louisa May Alcott—*Romance Language* enacts the conflicts between the egalitarian ideals expressed by these writers and the perception of freedom in the twentieth century. Parnell is quoted by Leslie Bennetts in the *New York Times* as explaining that "Whitman's idea of democracy included the sexual—that expressing oneself, and being free sexually, goes hand in hand with being free in every other way. . . . In a way, the play is Whitman's dream." In the sixteen scenes which compose this play, Parnell plays out this conflict on the field of the sexual life of his characters, imagining, among other things, an actress seducing the reclusive poet Emily Dickinson, and Louisa May Alcott falling in love with General George Custer, whose nephew suffers from an obsession with a transvestite. "All the characters in the play are trying to make connections with each other," Parnell explained to Bennetts, "and something always seems to be in the way. . . . Whether they're gay or straight, they're all not connecting. But they want to, and they try."

Romance Language was generally well-received by critics. Frank Rich, writing in the *New York Times,* expressed ad-

miration for the breadth of Parnell's vision. "At evening's end," Rich observed, "the entire company at last reaches the same destination, where everyone babbles at once in a language as varied as the land they inhabit. It's the sound of Whitman's America singing, of course. And, while Mr. Parnell doesn't always keep the song going, he does leave us with an inspiring sense of how beautiful both its cacophonies and harmonies were meant to be."

In *Hyde in Hollywood,* Parnell takes on another American dream gone sour in a dramatization of what the author perceives as the hypocritical morality of Hollywood in the late 1930s. Taking the structure of a film within a play, *Hyde in Hollywood* revolves around the career of Julian Hyde, a secret homosexual, who, together with screenwriter Jake Singer, a secret communist, rebel by making a *Citizen Kane*-like film which exposes the powerful elite of the film industry. According to reviewer Frank Rich in the *New York Times,* the play symbolizes "the tyranny of all-American conformity, whether in definitions of patriotism or masculinity or race."

Like *Romance Language, Hyde in Hollywood* was praised as much for its ideas as for the playwright's execution of them. Rich noted that the underlying theme of *Hyde in Hollywood* is "the belief that a braver 30's Hollywood might have helped produce a more courageous nation than the one that was tardy in mobilizing against Hitler in one generation and against Joseph McCarthy in the next." Rich concluded that "there have been few new plays this year with as much to say as *Hyde in Hollywood* or with potentially as intriguing a way to say it. Mr. Parnell owes it to himself and his subject to keep working until his dreams are as powerful as those he wants to demolish."

BIOGRAPHICAL/CRITICAL SOURCES:

BOOKS

Parnell, Peter, *Sorrows of Stephen,* Samuel French, 1982.

PERIODICALS

New York Times, October 24, 1979, p. C21; December 12, 1979, p. C23; December 28, 1979, p. C3; January 6, 1980, p. D5; December 17, 1982; November 15, 1984; November 21, 1984; November 30, 1989.*

*   *   *

PARRISH, T(homas) Michael 1953-

PERSONAL: Born January 5, 1953, in Ada, OK; son of Thomas Zaner (a university administrator) and Frances Emmaline (a schoolteacher; maiden name, Thomas) Parrish; married Julia Elizabeth Swenson (a homemaker),

May 24, 1975; children: Theodore Stohl. *Education:* Baylor University, B.A., 1974, M.A., 1976; University of Texas at Austin, M.L.S., 1978, Ph.D., 1991. *Politics:* "Liberal-moderate Democrat." *Religion:* Southern Baptist ("moderate wing").

ADDRESSES: Home—6322 Bon Terra Dr., Austin, TX 78731-3843. *Office*—Lyndon Baines Johnson Library and Museum, 2313 Red River, Austin, TX 78704.

CAREER: Jenkins Rare Book and Publishing Co., Austin, TX, manager, 1976-91; T. Michael Parrish, Rare Americana, proprietor, 1992-93; Lyndon Baines Johnson Library and Museum, Austin, archivist and historian, 1994—. Louisiana State University, member of founders' circle and national board of directors of United States Civil War Center.

MEMBER: Organization of American Historians, Society of Civil War Historians, Association for the Bibliography of History (life member), Southern Historical Association, Society of Southwest Archivists, Texas State Historical Association (honorary life member), Texas African American Heritage Organization, Civil War Round Table of Austin (co-founder and president).

AWARDS, HONORS: Jefferson Davis Award from Museum of the Confederacy, 1992, for *Richard Taylor, Soldier Prince of Dixie.*

WRITINGS:

(With Robert M. Willingham, Jr.) *Confederate Imprints: A Bibliography of Southern Publications from Secession to Surrender,* Jenkins Publishing, 1987.
(Editor and author of introduction and notes) David French Boyd, *Reminiscences of the War in Virginia,* Jenkins Publishing, 1989.
(Editor and author of introduction) Douglas John Cater, *As It Was: Reminiscences of a Soldier of the Third Texas Cavalry and the Nineteenth Louisiana Infantry, C.S.A.,* State House Press, 1990.
Richard Taylor, Soldier Prince of Dixie (History Book Club selection), University of North Carolina Press, 1992.
(Editor with Norman D. Brown, and author of introduction) Joseph Palmer Blessington, *The Campaigns of Walker's Texas Division,* State House Press, 1993.
(Editor and author of introduction) Alfred Roman, *The Military Operations of General Beauregard in the War Between the States,* Da Capo Press, 1994.
Civil War Texana: A Bibliography and Research Guide, Book Club of Texas, in press.

Work represented in anthologies, including *The American Civil War: A Handbook of Research and Literature,* edited by Steven E. Woodworth, Greenwood Press, in press.

WORK IN PROGRESS: P. G. T. Beauregard: Power and Splendor in the Southern Confederacy, publication by Random House expected in 1996; consulting editor for the fifteen-volume work *The Papers of Robert E. Lee,* University of North Carolina Press.

*   *   *

PATRON, Susan 1948-

PERSONAL: Born March 18, 1948, in San Gabriel, CA; daughter of George Thomas (a business owner) and Rubye (a homemaker; maiden name, Brewer) Hall; married Rene Albert Patron (a rare book restorer), July 27, 1969. *Education:* Pitzer College, B.A., 1969; Immaculate Heart College, School of Library Science, M.L.S., 1972.

ADDRESSES: Office—Los Angeles Public Library, Children's Services, 630 West 5th St., Los Angeles, CA 90071.

CAREER: Los Angeles Public Library, children's librarian, 1972-79, senior children's librarian, 1979—. Served on Caldecott Committee of the American Library Association; taught courses in children's literature. Member of the board of advisors, KCET public television's *Storytime.*

MEMBER: Society of Children's Book Writers and Illustrators, Author's Guild, American Library Association, California Library Association.

WRITINGS:

Burgoo Stew, illustrated by Mike Shenon, Orchard Books, 1991.
Five Bad Boys, Billy Que, and the Dustdobbin, illustrated by Shenon, Orchard Books, 1992.
Bobbin Dustdobbin, illustrated by Shenon, Orchard Books, 1993.
Maybe Yes, Maybe No, Maybe Maybe, illustrated by Dorothy Donahue, Orchard Books, 1993.
Dark Cloud Strong Breeze, illustrated by Peter Catalanotto, Orchard Books, 1994.

Contributor to *Expectations,* an anthology for blind children published in Braille, 1992. Children's book reviewer, *School Library Journal* and *Five Owls.* Member of the board of advisors, *L.A. Parent* magazine.

WORK IN PROGRESS: A sequel to *Maybe Yes, Maybe No, Maybe Maybe.*

SIDELIGHTS: Susan Patron grew up in Los Angeles, California, the middle of three sisters, and, as she commented, "a reader, dreamer, eavesdropper, washer of cars, shiner of shoes, mower of lawns, director of elaborate neighborhood plays, and teller of stories" who knew by the time she was eight that she wanted to be a writer. "Confiding this ambition to my father," said Patron, "I received both encouragement (go ahead: if you want to be a writer, write) and excellent advice (learn how to type). He also told me I wouldn't have to go far to find story ideas; all I had to do was keep my ears open. He was right. I began eavesdropping and hearing stories everywhere."

Patron spent her junior year of college in independent study at Trinity College, in Dublin, Ireland, listening to the "gowned professors as well as the cab drivers, the children, and the pub orators—the best extemporaneous talkers in the world." Back in the states, Patron was offered a job as children's librarian at the Los Angeles Public Library, where she voraciously read children's literature, learned how to tell stories to preschoolers and elementary school children, and created a project in which older adults were recruited and taught storytelling techniques.

Beginning in 1989, Patron wrote a series of stories about Billy Que, some bad boys who are friends of his, and two "dustdobbins" (Hob and Bobbin) who live in the dust under Billy Que's bed. "I hear in my mind the voices of my Mississippi grandparents, Baby R. Della and Homer, as these stories spin out. They are meant to be told or read aloud like stories from the folk tradition. I only recently met the illustrator of these books, Mike Shenon, who draws and paints with the same wit, verve, and inventiveness as the great Irish storytellers. And by an extraordinary coincidence, his Billy Que resembles—in the kindness of his face—my husband.

"The text of *Dark Cloud Strong Breeze,* a rhythmic, circular tale for very young children, moves back and forth between the fanciful and the mundane, the wish-world and the everyday one. I had long admired the way that the artist Peter Catalanotto paints both qualities into his beautiful illustrations, so I asked my editor, Richard Jackson—a man of great vision—whether he thought Mr. Catalanotto might be interested in working on my story. To my great happiness, he was.

"I hope that by sharing vividly remembered feelings from childhood in my stories, I will be giving readers or listeners a way of recognizing and articulating their own."

BIOGRAPHICAL/CRITICAL SOURCES:

PERIODICALS

Booklist, September 15, 1991, p. 153; November 1, 1992; March 15, 1993.
Horn Book, September, 1991, p. 606; January/February, 1992; July/August, 1993.
Kirkus Reviews, July 15, 1991, p. 939; September 1, 1992, p. 1133; March 3, 1993.
Publishers Weekly, August 23, 1991, p. 61; August 31, 1992, p. 77; April 5, 1993.
School Library Journal, October, 1991, pp. 111-112; December, 1992; March, 1993; October, 1993, p. 107.

PATRY, Jean-Luc (P.) 1947-

PERSONAL: Born May 31, 1947, in Geneva, Switzerland; son of Jean (a mathematician and physicist) and Julie (a nurse; maiden name, Fueter) Patry; married Elsbeth Gehringer (a psychotherapist), July 27, 1973; children: Philippe, Carole, Eric. *Education:* Swiss Federal Institute of Technology, received diploma, 1972, D.Sc., 1976; University of Fribourg, Habilitation, 1991.

ADDRESSES: Office—Institut fuer Erziehungswissenschaften, Akademiestrasse 26, A-5020 Salzburg, Austria.

CAREER: University of Fribourg, Fribourg, Switzerland, assistant, 1975-81; Stanford University, Stanford, CA, visiting scholar, 1982-83; Lehigh University, Bethlehem, PA, visiting scholar, 1983; University of Fribourg, *maitre-assistant,* 1985-93; University of Salzburg, visiting scholar, 1984, visiting professor, 1990, professor, 1993—.

MEMBER: Swiss Educational Research Association (member of council, 1977-81, 1985—; secretary general, 1985; vice-president, 1986-90; president of the section Basic Problems in Educational Research, 1987—), Swiss Psychological Association, American Psychological Association, American Educational Research Association, Evaluation Network, Association of Psychologists and Psychotherapists in Fribourg, Empirical Educational Research Group in Germany.

WRITINGS:

IN ENGLISH

(Editor with F. Oser and A. Dick) *Effective and Responsible Teaching: The New Synthesis,* Jossey-Bass, 1992.

Contributor to professional journals.

IN GERMAN

(With R. Hirsig and H. Fischer) *Koordination von Unterrichtsthemen,* Haupt (Bern), 1977.
Feldforschung: Methoden und Probleme der Sozialwissenschaften unter natuerlichen Bedingungen, Huber (Bern), 1982.
(With M. Perrez, F. Buechel, and others) *Psychologische Beratung und Intervention: Hilfe zue Selbsthilfe in Familie und Schule,* Huber, 1985.
(With G.-A. Eckerle) *Theorie und Praxis des Theorie-Praxis-Bezugs in der empirischen Paedagogik,* Nomos (Baden-Baden), 1987.
Transsituationale Konsistenz des Verhaltens und Handelns in der Erziehung, Peter Lang (Bern), 1991.
(With E. Weber and M. Spychiger) *Musik macht Schule: Biographie und Ergebnisse eines Schulversuchs,* Die Blaue Eule (Essen), 1993.

Contributor to professional journals. Editor of the bulletin of the Swiss Educational Research Association, 1977-80; editor, *Education and Practice,* 1985—.

WORK IN PROGRESS: Research on situation specificity of action and its implications on questions such as generalizability, the relationship between theory and practice, and social behavioral goals in education and therapy; research on practitioners' ethos and responsibility, specifically the ways that teachers and other professionals make decisions in ethical dilemma situations, and how they should make such decisions.

*   *   *

PAUL, Ann Whitford 1941-

PERSONAL: Born February, 1, 1941, in Evanston, IL; daughter of George (a business executive) and Genevieve (a homemaker and poet; maiden name, Smith) Whitford; married Ronald S. Paul (a surgeon), July 21, 1968; children: Henya, Jonathon, Alan, Sarah. *Education:* University of Wisconsin—Madison, B.A., 1963; Columbia University School of Social Work, M.S.W., 1965. *Avocational Interests:* Quilting, knitting, cooking, reading, and walking.

ADDRESSES: Home and office—2531 North Catalina St., Los Angeles, CA 90027. *Agent*—Ginger Knowlton, Curtis Brown Ltd., Ten Astor Pl., New York, NY 10003.

CAREER: Writer; worked as a social worker in medical hospitals and adoption agencies, 1965-1970.

MEMBER: Society of Children's Book Writers and Illustrators, Southern California Council on Literature for Children and Young People.

AWARDS, HONORS: New York Times Notable Children's Book citation, and Notable Social Studies Book citation, both 1991, for *Eight Hands Round: A Patchwork Alphabet;* Outstanding Science Trade Book citation, and Junior Library Guild Selection, both 1992, for *Shadows Are About.*

WRITINGS:

Owl at Night, Putnam, 1985.
Eight Hands Round: A Patchwork Alphabet, HarperCollins, 1991.
Shadows Are About, Scholastic, 1992.

Also author of *The Seasons Sewn,* Harcourt-Brown Deer Press; and *In My Yard,* Scholastic.

WORK IN PROGRESS: A book about life during the Colonial period; compiling a collection of poetry.

SIDELIGHTS: Ann Whitford Paul grew up in the midwest, the oldest of five children. Although she loved books, and would often stay up late into the night to read, she did not think about writing books until the birth of her third child. She was thirty-five and her inspiration came from her children. "Except for that time after supper when teeth were brushed and baths were done, it was rarely quiet in our crowded house," Paul commented. It was then that she would sit with each child in a rocker or in bed under the covers, and together they would read. This was the impetus. Paul decided to write books that parents, grandparents, aunts and uncles, could share with the children special to them.

Between her decision to be a writer and actually becoming one there were many years of study. Paul cites three teachers as being particularly helpful: Sue Alexander, Sonia Levitin, and Myra Cohn Livingston. These three were true mentors, being both supportive and critical of her work, helping her to grow in her craft. The work began to pay off—in 1985 Putnam published her first book, *Owl at Night.* It is the simple story about two children and their family who settle down to sleep just as an owl begins his activities in the night. Susan Hepler, in her review for *School Library Journal,* called this story "a cozy catalog of nighttime activity that would make a good addition to the bedtime story collection." A *Publishers Weekly* reviewer found Paul's writing to contain "a gentle touch and a lyrical voice."

In 1991 HarperCollins published Paul's second book, *Eight Hands Round: A Patchwork Alphabet,* which was distinguished by being chosen one of the outstanding social studies books of the year. Aimed at children between the ages of 8 and 12, this work combines the alphabet-book idea with twenty-six patchwork quilt patterns, from A for Anvil to Z for Zigzag, and then presents the historical background of the past customs and events which inspired each design. Through it all "a fine history lesson emerges," states Denise Wilms in her review for *Booklist.* "A novel way to introduce patchwork's economic, social, and artistic role while relating it to history," writes a *Kirkus Reviews* critic.

Paul's next book, *Shadows Are About,* was published by Scholastic in 1992, and is also written for younger children. The rhyming text is gently flowing as it follows the shadow explorations of a brother and sister. It has a "simple, lyrical text," writes Stephanie Loer of the *Boston Globe.* Deborah Abbott, in her *Booklist* review, says that "shadows, which are about light and movement and new perspectives, take on a life of their own in this beautifully crafted picture book."

"Now that my oldest child has graduated from college," Paul commented, "I finally have an office." Paul says that in her work the first draft is always "painful," but the fun part is the revision. "I liken these to making a puzzle and trying to get all the pieces (or words) to fit in their right places." Paul encourages other aspiring writers to follow the well-known advice to "Write about what you know." She adds: "Trying to jump on the bandwagon or write to the demands of the market does not make good books. Stories that tug at a reader's emotions have to come out of the writer's strong emotions. Don't worry if your life isn't a roller coaster of grand adventure. I've never rescued a drowning person, or climbed the Himalaya Mountains, or driven a race car, but I still find plenty of material in my own quiet world that I want to share with others. In fact, I'll probably need ten lifetimes to get everything I want to say down on paper."

BIOGRAPHICAL/CRITICAL SOURCES:

PERIODICALS

Booklist, June 1, 1991, p. 1876; July, 1992, p. 1944.
Boston Globe, May 31, 1992.
Bulletin of the Center for Children's Books, July, 1991, p. 270.
Kirkus Reviews, February 1, 1991, p. 183.
New York Times Book Review, May 19, 1991, p. 29.
Publishers Weekly, October 18, 1985, p. 64.
School Library Journal, December, 1985, p. 80; July, 1991, p. 70; April, 1992, p. 98.

*   *   *

PAYNE, Darwin 1937-

PERSONAL: Born May 15, 1937, in Phalba, TX; the son of Burnice Wylie (an auditor) and Sally (a homemaker; maiden name, Jones) Payne; married Patsy N. Patterson, September 8, 1962 (divorced 1978); married Phyllis Schmitz (a newspaper editor), June 25, 1983; children: (first marriage) Mark, Scott; (second marriage) Sarah, Hannah. *Education:* University of Texas at Austin, B.J., 1959; Southern Methodist University, M.A., 1967; University of Texas at Austin, Ph.D., 1973.

ADDRESSES: Home—9021 Gunnison Dr., Dallas, TX 75231. *Office*—Center for Communication Arts, Southern Methodist University, Dallas, TX 75275.

CAREER: Reporter for *Fort Worth Press, Dallas Times Herald,* and KERA-TV in Dallas, TX, 1960-72; Southern Methodist University, professor, 1967-68 and 1972-80, acting chair of Division of Journalism, 1973-74, chair, 1980—; *The Suburban Tribune* (a suburban weekly), editor and publisher, 1985-89. *Military service:* Texas State National Guard, 49th Armored Division, 1959-63. Saw six months active duty with U.S. Army, 1959-60; recalled to active duty in 1961.

MEMBER: American Journalism Historians Association, Association for Education in Journalism, Texas State His-

torical Association, Press Club of Dallas, Sigma Delta Chi, Kappa Tau Alpha.

AWARDS, HONORS: Texas Literary Award for best non-fiction book of the year from Southwestern Booksellers Association, 1985, for *Owen Wister: Chronicler of the West, Gentleman of the East;* Friends of the Dallas Public Library Award for book making best contribution to knowledge by a Texan or about Texas from Texas Institute of Letters, 1985, for *Owen Wister: Chronicler of the West, Gentleman of the East.*

WRITINGS:

The Man of Only Yesterday: Frederick Lewis Allen, Harper, 1975.
(Editor) *Dissenting Opinion: Carl Brannin's Letters to the Editor, 1933-1976,* American Civil Liberties Foundation of Texas, 1977.
Initiative in Energy: Dresser Industries, 1880-1978, Simon & Schuster, 1979.
Dallas: An Illustrated History, Windsor Publications, 1982.
Owen Wister: Chronicler of the West, Gentleman of the East, Southern Methodist University Press, 1985.
(Editor) *Sketches of a Growing Town: Episodes and People of Dallas from Early Days to Recent Times,* Southern Methodist University Press, 1991.

Contributor to periodicals, including *Southwestern Historical Quarterly, Southwest Review, Southwestern Historical Quarterly, Dallas, The New Republic, Texas Woman,* and *Boys' Life.*

WORK IN PROGRESS: A history of Dallas in the twentieth century, with publication expected in 1994.

SIDELIGHTS: With university degrees in journalism and American history, it is not surprising that Darwin Payne has focused his literary efforts on American historical and literary figures, among them Frederick Lewis Allen, long-time editor of *Harper's,* and Owen Wister, author of the romantic western *The Virginian. The Man of Only Yesterday: Frederick Lewis Allen* chronicles Allen's life, from his school-boy days at Groton Academy to his education at Harvard University and also through the editor's years at *Harper's.* "The biographer rekindles the excitement of Allen's editing," wrote *Harper's* contributor Edward Weeks, who was Allen's former rival at *The Atlantic.* On the other hand, Alfred Kazin, writing in the *Saturday Review,* called the work "banal" and faults Payne for an omission; "his biographer has not examined [Allen's] relationship to the magazine audience," Kazin wrote, "but it is just this that makes Allen's handling of *Harper's* interesting."

In his award-winning biography *Owen Wister: Chronicler of the West, Gentleman of the East,* Payne discusses the life and times of the man who created the romantic image of the American cowboy. Although he was an educated and well-to-do Easterner, Owen Wister was attracted to his idealized image of life in the West. He popularized this image of the masculine as embodied in the cowboy in his best-selling novel *The Virginian,* which later spawned movies and television series. "Payne has captured the conflict between the myth and the reality in his detailed and comprehensive history," commented Stan Steiner, Western historian and reviewer for the *Los Angeles Times Book Review.* "At times, the details tend to overwhelm the story, as often happens in biographies, and the writing is sometimes flat and uninspired," Steiner wrote, "but this book is an important contribution to Western history and an understanding of the masculine image of the cowboy."

BIOGRAPHICAL/CRITICAL SOURCES:

PERIODICALS

Harper's, June, 1975.
Los Angeles Times Book Review, March 2, 1986.
National Review, August 23, 1985.
Saturday Review, May 3, 1975.

*   *   *

PEABODY, Richard (Myers, Jr.) 1951-

PERSONAL: Born March 14, 1951, in Washington, DC; son of Richard M. (a pet shop owner and salesperson) and Rachael (a Capitol Hill aide and National Institutes of Health administrator; maiden name, Hudson) Peabody. *Education:* Attended Ohio University, 1969-71; University of Maryland, B.A., 1973; American University, M.A., 1975. *Avocational Interests:* Guitar, movies, football, first editions, New Mexico.

ADDRESSES: Agent—Anne Edelstein Literary Agency, 310 Riverside Dr., Suite 1811, New York, NY 10025.

CAREER: Poet, writer, and editor. Worked variously as a laborer for the National Park Service and North American Van Lines, as a law firm messenger, with the C.O.S.M.E.P. book van project, and in several used and rare book shops, 1971-92; co-founder and editor of *Gargoyle* magazine, 1976-90; founder of Paycock Press, 1979; St. John's College, Annapolis, MD, fiction workshops instructor, 1985-87; The Writer's Center, Bethesda, MD, fiction workshops instructor, 1987—; Georgetown University, Washington, DC, creative writing instructor, 1993—; University of Maryland, College Park, creative writing instructor, 1993—; University of Virginia, Falls Church, fiction workshops instructor, 1993—. Co-host of weekly radio show for WPFW-FM, Washington, DC, 1978-79. Grants panelist for Montgomery County Arts

Council, 1980, Washington, DC, Commission on the Arts and Humanities, 1985-89, and Wisconsin State Arts Council, 1990. Member of Poetry Committee of the Greater Washington Metropolitan Area, 1983-89; member of board of Washington Project for the Arts, 1987-89.

MEMBER: The Writer's Center (member of board, 1979).

AWARDS, HONORS: Larry Neal Writers' Award, D.C. Commission on the Arts and Humanities, 1987, Coordinating Council of Literary Magazines Editor's Award, 1988, District of Columbia Arts Center Award, 1990, all for *Gargoyle;* Virginia Center for the Creative Arts fellow, 1990.

WRITINGS:

I'm in Love with the Morton Salt Girl (poems), Paycock Press (Washington, DC), 1979.
Monaural (fiction), Kawabata Press, 1980.
(Editor) *D.C. Magazines: A Literary Retrospective,* Paycock Press (Washington, DC), 1982.
(Editor) *Mavericks: Nine Independent Publishers,* Paycock Press (Washington, DC), 1983.
Echt & Ersatz/I'm in Love with the Morton Salt Girl (poems; includes revised and expanded version of *I'm in Love with the Morton Salt Girl*), Paycock Press (Washington, DC), 1985.
Sad Fashions (poems), Gut Punch Press, 1990.
(Editor with Lucinda Ebersole) *Mondo Barbie,* St. Martin's (New York, NY), 1993.
(Editor with Lucinda Ebersole) *Mondo Elvis,* St. Martin's (New York, NY), 1994.
(Editor with Lucinda Ebersole) *Coming to Terms: A Literary History of Abortion,* The New Press (New York, NY), 1994.

Also contributor of stories, poems, and reviews to magazines and newspapers, including *Baltimore Sun, Columbus Dispatch, Washington Post, Poetry East, Poet Lore, Taos Review,* and *Kuchibashi.*

WORK IN PROGRESS: Buoyancy and Other Myths, a poetry collection; *Kissing Games,* a novel; an untitled novel; *Literary Washington: An Illustrated History,* a literary nonfiction book; anthologies of poetry and fiction from *Gargoyle* magazine.

SIDELIGHTS: In 1976, poet, writer, and editor Richard Peabody, with two friends, founded *Gargoyle* literary magazine as a means of publishing their own work. "Once the word was out though," Peabody told Kevin Ring in *Beat Scene,* "good work started to pour in and we were rightly embarrassed by our early attempts. We quickly found there was a vibrant lit world out there filled with writers just like us." Driven by a desire to print all that he felt must be published, Peabody edited *Gargoyle* for fourteen years, despite little or no outside financial backing, and while working a myriad of odd jobs to enable him to get the magazine out. In what Ring judged as "probably one of the finest literary magazines to ever see the light of day in America," Peabody printed literary efforts by such writers as Elizabeth Tallent, Todd Grimson, Maya Sonenberg, and Rita Dove. He sometimes rejected the works of writers who went on to successful careers—as well as the manuscripts of thousands of other authors—but he claims that he returned all rejections with a hand-written note. "I tried to treat writers the way I wanted to be treated when I sent out my own work," Peabody told *CA.*

Peabody has admitted that despite the headaches brought by some writers, the task of reading every manuscript he received, and the lack of financial rewards reaped from publishing *Gargoyle,* he appreciated his position: At times he would receive what he considered to be a significant work, and he felt that by accepting such submissions for publication, he might be affording the writers some much-needed encouragement. Peabody vowed to quit publishing *Gargoyle* when it was no longer enjoyable, and in 1990, after a series of personal losses, he discontinued its publication. Asked by reviewer Ring how he felt, Peabody replied, "Relieved. The magazine became an all consuming ball and chain. After fourteen years of struggling and saving and reading other people's work, it's nice to be free to read books again or write or even take a drive in the country."

As the creator of his own poems and fiction, Peabody has been praised for his humorous, sardonic, and often self-deprecating observations of his everyday surroundings and relationships. He has fantasized about an erotic encounter with the famous young girl on the Morton salt container, expressed "Everyman's" reaction to a bad haircut in a poem appropriately titled "Another Stupid Haircut," and celebrated the chimichanga in his verses. In a *Best Sellers* review of Peabody's dual book of poems, *Echt & Ersatz/I'm in Love with the Morton Salt Girl,* Mark M. McCaffery observed, "Peabody celebrates everyday life with a deft hand and a wry smile." And commenting on *Sad Fashions,* another collection of Peabody's poems, *Athens News* writer David Bruce asserted, "You've got to like a writer who dedicates his new book of poems in this manner: 'For everyone who botched their first kiss, flunked their driver's test, missed the prom or bungled the score that would have won the game.' "

In 1993 Peabody, along with Lucinda Ebersole, co-edited *Mondo Barbie,* an anthology of fiction and poems penned by such writers as Alice McDermott, Philip Levine, and Sandra Cisneros. The volume, according to Robert Plunket in the *New York Times Book Review,* "allows some 30 writers to mull over what Barbie means, to peel away all the phony plastic and get to the real plastic underneath." In the volume, several pieces explore the cultural icon's

character—labeling Barbie as a conformist, a victim, or a spirited individual, among other terms. Other literary works feature Barbie as a doll; in several of these selections, young girls fuss over wardrobes, compare individual collections, or arrange Barbie's love life. Plunket called the work "a clever new book," while a reviewer for *Publishers Weekly* found that "Barbie's steady upholding of the American ideal of femininity through three decades of feminist upheaval provides rich material."

Peabody told *CA:* "My mother always said that she weaned me from the bottle with books. We lived above my father's pet shop until I was five and she had to keep me quiet and distracted. I was the sort of kid that fought hard to get out of the children's section at the library. I was reading the *Iliad* and *Odyssey* in third grade. I got in trouble in fifth grade because one of my teachers had a book of Norse legends that I wanted to read. He thought I was excited about the Rockwell Kent illustrations. Can you imagine? I relived the Civil War Centennial and read thrillers and science fiction until I stumbled onto Aldous Huxley quite by accident. *Brave New World* changed everything. I majored in English and studied D. H. Lawrence at the University of Maryland. Discovered F. Scott Fitzgerald and Ernest Hemingway at American University. Went overboard on the expatriates for awhile. My master's thesis was on E. M. Forster and *Howard's End.* I hitchhiked the United States in 1976. Discovered Henry Miller and Jack Kerouac who together ripped the top of my head off. These days it's Paul Bowles and Jeanette Winterson.

"I started writing seriously in 1973. I was really shy. I didn't even know there were literary magazines when I was in school. And I didn't hang around other writers. I came to poetry from trying my hand (badly) at song lyrics. The first poem I ever sent out was published in *New South Writing.* I started *Gargoyle* with two friends and we published the first issue in August, 1976. The magazine plugged me into the nerve net of small press 'zines. They opened me up to a world of possibilities. But after fourteen years and thirty-seven issues, it was time to move on. I read a lot of manuscripts, made a lot of friends, and learned a whole lot.

"My poetry has been more popular than my fiction, but I have always considered myself a fiction writer above all else. I have made numerous attempts at the novel, none of which have proved satisfying. Perhaps the success of *Mondo Barbie* will free up enough time to allow me to refocus. I believe that writing is both a blessing and a curse—intensifying life on the one hand and then allowing the visionary precious little time to experience anything. This constant trade-off is the friction that keeps my motor running.

"I believe that I am a vehicle for language, vision, god. Writing is a sacrament, a form of prayer, a floating conversation. And something I normally do from midnight until five in the morning. Always have. The object? To change somebody's life. Perhaps even your own."

BIOGRAPHICAL/CRITICAL SOURCES:

BOOKS

Magill, Frank N., *Critical Survey of Short Fiction,* Salem, 1981.
Peters, Robert, *The Great American Poetry Bake-Off* (2nd series), Scarecrow Press, 1982.

PERIODICALS

Athens News (Ohio), October 1, 1990.
Beat Scene, Volume 12, 1990.
Best Sellers, January, 1986.
Bethesda Almanac (Maryland), January 29, 1992, pp. 19-24.
New York Times Book Review, April 18, 1993, p. 7; January 9, 1994, p. 18.
Publishers Weekly, February 1, 1993; December 13, 1993.
Small Press Review, October, 1991.
Washington Post, March 16, 1987, pp. E1-E2; March 26, 1990, p. B7; April 26, 1993, pp. D1-D2; January 7, 1994, p. B2.
Washington Post Book World, September 2, 1990, p. 12.

*   *   *

PEALE, Norman Vincent 1898-1993

OBITUARY NOTICE—See index for *CA* sketch: Born May 31, 1898, in Bowersville, OH; died after a stroke, December 24, 1993, in Pawling, NY. Minister, lecturer, and author. Beginning in the 1930s, Peale cultivated an enormous following with his pioneering amalgam of religion and popular psychology which stressed simple prayer and positive thinking to overcome the troubles of life, achieve a spiritual happiness, and reap material wealth. He preached his message to thousands of appreciative followers, including such notables as Presidents Eisenhower and Nixon and numerous prominent business leaders. His advice and teachings were captured in a number of successful books which feature short, memorable maxims and steps to success. Most notable is his *The Power of Positive Thinking,* which arrived on the bestseller lists in the mid-1950s and stayed there for over three years. Presaging the spate of self-help books that would become widely popular in the 1970s and 1980s, Peale was initially criticized by some theologians, who considered his message to be overly simplistic and misleading. The continued high sales of the title, however, made it one of the most widely purchased

religious books in history. The success of *The Power of Positive Thinking* propelled Peale and his wife, Ruth, into other ventures designed to promote his ideas, including a television program and a periodical, *Guideposts.* Peale retired from his ministry at the Marble Collegiate Church in 1984 after having served for fifty-two years at the institution, which is part of the Reformed Church in America denomination. He continued to write in his retirement, crowning his list of over forty books with titles such as *The Power of Positive Living, This Incredible Century,* and *Bible Power for Daily Living.* He also penned a number of works about the life of Jesus for children, such as *The Coming of the King, He Was a Child,* and *The Story of Jesus.* Peale was the recipient of numerous awards and honorary degrees during his lifetime, including the Presidential Medal of Freedom, awarded by President Ronald Reagan in 1984.

OBITUARIES AND OTHER SOURCES:

BOOKS

Who's Who in America, 48th edition, Marquis, 1994.

PERIODICALS

Los Angeles Times, December 26, 1993, p. A1.
New York Times, December 26, 1993, p. 40; December 30, 1993, p. B6.
Times (London), December 27, 1993, p. 15.
Washington Post, December 26, 1993, p. B5.

*   *   *

PEARS, Tim 1956-

PERSONAL: Born November 15, 1956, in Tonbridge Wells, Kent, England; son of W. S. Pears (an Anglican priest) and Jill (Charles-Edwards) Scurfield. *Education:* Graduated from National Film and Television School, London, 1993. *Politics:* "As liberal as possible in a cruel world." *Religion:* "Still searching."

ADDRESSES: Home—116A Walton St., Oxford OX2 6AJ, England. *Agent*—Juliet Burton, Laurence Pollinger Ltd., 18 Maddox St., Mayfair, London W1R 0EU, England.

CAREER: Writer. Worked as a construction laborer, nurse in a mental hospital, bodyguard, house painter, security guard, farm worker, and manager of an art gallery.

MEMBER: Ebony International.

AWARDS, HONORS: Ruth Hadden Memorial Award, 1993, for *In the Place of Fallen Leaves.*

WRITINGS:

In the Place of Fallen Leaves (novel), Hamish Hamilton, 1993.

WORK IN PROGRESS: A second novel.

SIDELIGHTS: Tim Pears is the author of *In the Place of Fallen Leaves,* which he described to *CA* as a novel "about home and leaving home, about being at home and being in exile," and, more specifically, as the story of "an adolescent coming to understand her world and her place in it." The novel's heroine is thirteen-year-old Alison, who lives in a farming community with her family, including an eccentric grandmother and a somewhat deranged father. During the particularly hot summer of 1984, Alison befriends Jonathan, son of an impoverished aristocrat living nearby. While troubles develop among striking miners and similarly dissatisfied teachers, Alison and Jonathan prosper in the rural countryside, where they share experiences, thoughts, and feelings.

In the Place of Fallen Leaves also abounds with memorable secondary characters. Alison's father, for instance, is an endearing amnesiac whose mind has rotted from alcohol, and Alison's grandmother is a similarly loveable sort who holds some rather peculiar beliefs about time and magnetic fields. Also significant is Pam, Alison's sister, who forsakes the countryside for academic pursuits. Pam, as Giles Foden reported in the *Independent,* "presents a kind of sexual example for Alison or, maybe, a warning."

Upon its publication in 1993, *In the Place of Fallen Leaves* won widespread acclaim in England, where it was hailed as a significant literary debut. London *Times* reviewer Penny Perrick deemed the novel "astounding," and A. S. Byatt affirmed in the London *Telegraph* that Pears's story "is entirely satisfying." Byatt added that the work is "comic, and wry, and elegiac, and shrewd and thoughtful all at once." Giles Foden declared in the London *Independent* that *In the Place of Fallen Leaves* is "technically sophisticated" and "an unusually well-made novel." Still another enthusiast, Carla McKay, hailed Pears's novel, in her London *Daily Mail* assessment, as "a mesmeric, richly detailed evocation of rural existence." And Martyn Bedford wrote in the *Oxford Times* that with *In the Place of Fallen Leaves* Pears has produced "a moving and beautifully written book." Pears's novel, Bedford concluded, "is an utterly convincing portrayal of the life and times of the Devon countryside, deeply evocative and rich with sensuous imagery—sad and funny . . . but never mawkish."

Pears told *CA:* "I left school at sixteen knowing only that I wanted to be a poet. For ten years I did all kinds of jobs and wrote a lot of awful poetry. Then one day I transposed a poem into a short story and set it in the tiny Devon village in which I'd grown up. It was a moment of liberation:

Writing was no longer simply an intellectual process; it became physical, the world of my adolescence vividly recalled—I could smell the lanes after the rain, hear a mother calling her children in for tea, touch the sharp blades of grass we blew notes from through our fingers.

"I wrote no more poems but many stories and set them all in this small village. I found that there was nothing that interested me which couldn't be adapted to fit into this world. The stories developed eventually into *In the Place of Fallen Leaves.*

"I think human beings are preoccupied by the same things they've always been preoccupied with: Where do we come from, why are we here, where are we going? How should we live our lives? What are our hopes, responsibilities, dreams? How can we love and be loved? The things that spring us from sleep at night in a state of misery or joy. I just want to create characters I love and explore their lives."

BIOGRAPHICAL/CRITICAL SOURCES:

PERIODICALS

Daily Mail (London), April 22, 1993.
Independent (London), April 4, 1993.
Observer (London), March 21, 1993.
Oxford Times, April 23, 1993.
Telegraph (London), March 27, 1993.
Times (London), March 28, 1993.

*   *   *

PECK, David R.   1938-

PERSONAL: Born February 3, 1938, in Glen Ridge, NJ; son of Russell Lacy (a manufacturer's representative) and Dorothy Katherine (Bosworth) Peck; married Holloway Wilson (died, 1978); children: Sarah Holloway. *Education:* Colgate University, B.A., 1960; Temple University, Ph.D., 1968.

ADDRESSES: Home—635 Lombardy Lane, Laguna Beach, CA 92651.

CAREER: California State University, Long Beach, professor of English, 1967—. University of Ljubljana, Fulbright lecturer, 1984-85; University of Leeds, visiting professor, 1990-91. *Military service:* U.S. Army, 1960-62.

WRITINGS:

(With Chris Bullock) *Guide to Marxist Literary Criticism,* Indiana University Press, 1980.
(With B. Brinkman, E. Hoffman, and J. Blum) *A Guide to the Whole Writing Process,* Houghton, 1984.
Novels of Initiation: A Guidebook for Teaching Literature to Adolescents, Teachers College Press, 1989.

American Ethnic Literatures, Salem Press, 1992. (Editor with John Maitino) *Teaching American Ethnic Literatures,* University of New Mexico Press, 1994.

*   *   *

PEGRAM, Thomas R. 1955-

PERSONAL: Born November 29, 1955, in Hammond, IN; son of Raymond S. and Dorothy K. Pegram; married Patricia Mae Ingram, August 16, 1986; children: Tavish Ross Ingram Pegram, Rafferty Glenn Ingram Pegram. *Education:* University of Santa Clara, B.A. (summa cum laude), 1978; Brandeis University, Ph.D., 1988.

ADDRESSES: Office—Department of History, Loyola College, 4501 North Charles St., Baltimore, MD 21210-2699.

CAREER: Suffolk University, Boston, MA, lecturer in history, 1986-88; Ohio State University, Columbus, instructor in history, 1988-90; Loyola College, Baltimore, MD, assistant professor of history, 1990—. Simmons College, special instructor, 1987-88.

MEMBER: American Historical Association, Organization of American Historians, Maryland Historical Society, Phi Beta Kappa.

AWARDS, HONORS: Award of Superior Achievement in Scholarly Publication from Illinois State Historical Society, 1993, for *Partisans and Progressives.*

WRITINGS:

Partisans and Progressives: Private Interest and Public Policy in Illinois, 1870-1922, University of Illinois Press, 1992.

Contributor of articles and reviews to history journals and encyclopedias.

WORK IN PROGRESS: Alcohol in American Politics, an interpretive overview, publication by Ivan Dee expected in 1996; *Divisive Spirits: Politics and Alcohol Reform in the Mid-Atlantic, 1890-1933,* a monograph.

*   *   *

PEMBERTON, Gayle Renee 1948-

PERSONAL: Born June 29, 1948, in St. Paul, MN; daughter of Lounneer (executive with Urban League) and Muriel E. (homemaker and board of education worker; maiden name, Wigington) Pemberton. *Education:* University of Michigan, B.A., 1969; Harvard University, M.A., 1971,

Ph.D., 1981. *Avocational Interests:* Family biography, secondary and advanced education for minority students.

ADDRESSES: Office—Princeton University, 112 Dickinson Hall, Princeton, NJ 08544-1017.

CAREER: Biographer, teacher, academic administrator, and anti-racism activist. Has held academic posts at Smith College, Columbia University, Middlebury College, Northwestern University, Reed College, and Bowdoin College; currently associate director of Afro-American Studies at Princeton University, Princeton, NJ.

AWARDS, HONORS: Ford Foundation doctoral fellowship; W.E.B. DuBois doctoral fellowship; John Simon Guggenheim Memorial Foundation fellowship.

WRITINGS:

On Teaching the Minority Student: Problems and Strategies, Bowdoin College, 1988.
The Hottest Water in Chicago: On Family, Race, Time, and American Culture, Faber & Faber, 1992, reprinted as *The Hottest Water in Chicago: Notes of a Native Daughter,* Anchor Books, 1993.
Contributor, *Race-ing Justice/En-gendering Power: Essays on Anita Hill, Clarence Thomas and the Construction of Social Reality,* edited by Toni Morrison, Pantheon, 1992.
Contributor, *American Visions* (travel book), Holt, 1994.

Also contributor to periodicals, including *Women's Review of Books, Publishers Weekly, Chicago Tribune, Los Angeles Times, Mirabella,* and *Chicago Sun-Times.*

WORK IN PROGRESS: A book on black women and American cinema, and a book of short stories.

SIDELIGHTS: When Gayle Pemberton first published *The Hottest Water in Chicago: On Family, Race, Time, and American Culture* in 1992, she barely anticipated the events which would mark that year as well as the consciousness of most of America. In that year, however, the riots that followed the trial of four Los Angeles, California, police officers accused of beating motorist Rodney King violently reflected the pent-up frustration of many African Americans regarding their status in a white-dominated society. Pemberton's study portrays a struggling and celebratory American black middle-class and its relation to white academic, social, and political structures. In her comparison, Pemberton details the inequalities inherent in the current social system. Associate Director of Afro American Studies at Princeton University, and seasoned thoroughly with academic posts at Bowdoin, Columbia, Middlebury, Northwestern, and Smith, Pemberton provides a detailed dialogue between images of black inner city life and her memories as a black woman at predominately white universities.

New York Times Book Review contributor Nancy Mairs emphasizes Pemberton's return to a " 'double consciousness,' voiced by W. E. B. Du Bois, wherein black identity is shaped not purely by the self but only in relation to white demands or dreams of blackness." On one hand, Pemberton's subject matter and critical position suggest an indelible African American identity: black, female, midwestern, socially conscious, and politically active, much like her parents and their parents before them. Intermingled with memories of Paul Laurence Dunbar, Langston Hughes, Du Bois, Richard Wright, and Ralph Ellison, however, are the more mundane traces of her Midwest upbringing: Saturday morning cartoons, *Porgy and Bess*, the University of Michigan, 1950s game shows, and a formidable Episcopalian presence in family and community. The hottest waters of childhood identity, however, are often also the most clear: Pemberton rejoins these memories with a critique of how American normalcy can stifle a realistic understanding of an African American self or a black culture. "There are the white images that reinforce what I am not," writes Pemberton in *The Hottest Water*, "and the black ones that are supposed to define blackness, and that are in some ways naturalistic, always symbolic of the whole, designed to elicit pity, fear, or cheap sentiment. They are always there to diffuse and displace the potential meanings of black life."

Pemberton clarifies the anger and weariness of the black middle class from which she emerges in her book: "surviving in black skin saps the energies; not only does it keep real political and social power in the hands of the whites, but it makes the self no more than a sociological fact, dancing, marionette-style, to a degrading tune." An earlier 1988 monograph issue by Pemberton, *On Teaching the Minority Student; Problems and Strategies*, addresses both the burdens placed on minorities and possibilities for intercultural exchange within the American educational system. This earlier publication, more practical rather than biographical in nature than *The Hottest Waters*, nonetheless precipitated Pemberton's anger on determining the nature of black people by a name given to them from outside their communities: "Minority is a word for statisticians, not a self-identifier for their victims."

Language provides one of the greatest barriers to real change, Pemberton's work contends, coming between family members, intervening in productive academic conversations about race and cultural identity, or healing the wounds on each side of the color line over the latter half of the twentieth century. The couching of the meanings, illusions, and rules of an exclusive white civilization challenges the African American critic of the 1980s and early 1990s and obscures even the most recent past, so Pemberton argues. Reacting against the American impulse to "put it behind us," Pemberton relates in *The Hottest Wa-*

ters memories of racial conflict with an immediate need to find a language which tells both where African Americans come from and what needs to be done for the future: "It is important to know the path, the process, through which the present is made. Inducing cultural amnesia runs the risk of reproducing the medical scenario of 'the operation was a success but the patient died.' "

BIOGRAPHICAL/CRITICAL SOURCES:

BOOKS

Pemberton, Gayle, *The Hottest Water in Chicago: On Family, Race, Time, and American Culture*, Faber & Faber, 1992.
Pemberton, Gayle, *On Teaching the Minority Student: Problems and Strategies*, Bowdoin College, 1988.

PERIODICALS

New York Times Book Review, August 2, 1992, p.17.
Washington Post Book World, May 10, 1992, p. 8.*

*   *   *

PERRY, Steve 1947-

PERSONAL: Born August 31, 1947, in Baton Rouge, LA; married Dianne Waller (a political expert and newspaper publisher); children: Dal, Stephani.

ADDRESSES: Agent—Jean V. Naggar Literary Agency, Inc., 216 East 75th St., New York, NY 10021.

CAREER: Writer. Taught writing classes in the Portland and Washington County public school systems; has taught adult writing classes at the University of Washington in Seattle; briefly held a position as a staff writer for Ruby-Spears Productions, Hollywood, CA; worked variously as a swimming instructor and lifeguard, toy assembler, hotel gift shop clerk, aluminum salesperson, kung fu instructor, private detective, Licensed Practical Nurse, and Certified Physician's Assistant.

WRITINGS:

The Tularemia Gambit (mystery), Fawcett, 1981.
Civil War Secret Agent (young adult), Bantam, 1984.
(With Michael Reaves) *Sword of the Samurai* (young adult), Bantam, 1984.
Conan the Fearless (fantasy), Tor, 1986.
Conan the Defiant (fantasy), Tor, 1987.
(With Reaves) *The Omega Cage*, Ace, 1988.
Conan the Indomitable (fantasy), Tor, 1989.
Conan the Free Lance (fantasy), Tor, 1990.
Conan the Formidable (fantasy), Tor, 1990.

SCIENCE FICTION

(With Reaves) *Hellstar*, Berkley, 1984.

The Man Who Never Missed, Ace, 1985.
Matadora, Ace, 1986.
The Machiavelli Interface, Ace, 1986.
(With Reaves) *Dome,* Berkley, 1987.
The 97th Step, Ace, 1989.
The Albino Knife, Ace, 1991.
Black Steel, Ace, 1992.
Brother Death, Ace, 1992.

Also the author of *Curlwave,* Bluejay.

"ALIENS" SERIES

Earth Hive, Dark Horse/Bantam, 1992.
Nightmare Asylum, Dark Horse/Bantam, 1993.
(With Stephani Perry) *The Female War,* Dark Horse/
    Bantam, 1993.

"STELLAR RANGERS" SERIES

Peacemaker, B. Fawcett, 1993.
Guns and Honor, B. Fawcett, 1993.

OTHER

Has written numerous television scripts for animated action programs, including *Centurions, The Real Ghostbusters, Chuck Norris/Karate Commandos, The Spiral Zone, U.S. Starcom,* and *Batman.* Contributor to short fiction anthologies; contributor of short fiction works to magazines, including *Asimov's* and *Pulphouse Monthly.*

WORK IN PROGRESS: Eidetic, a mystery-suspense novel; *Spin,* science fiction for Ace; *The Forever Hormone,* science fiction for Ace.

SIDELIGHTS: Beginning in the late 1970s with contributions to numerous magazines and short fiction anthologies, Steve Perry has developed a style of fast-paced action scenes filled with expert knowledge about weapons and combat. He is best known for his science fiction/martial arts action series fiction for both young adults and adults, as well as for his "Conan" heroic fantasy novels.

Perry's "Conan" adventures, based on the Robert E. Howard fantasy character, are popular with young adult readers. These include *Conan the Formidable, Conan the Indomitable, Conan the Free Lance, Conan the Defiant,* and *Conan the Fearless. Conan the Defiant* tells a tale of a young Conan fighting an army of undead warriors. Barbara Evans, reviewing *Conan the Fearless* in *Voice of Youth Advocates,* states that "YA fans should enjoy this book. . . . It is a fast paced story with characters being good or evil."

Perry's "Matador" series targets more mature readers. This science fiction adventure series includes *The Man Who Never Missed, Matadora, The Machiavelli Interface, The 97th Step, The Albino Knife, Black Steel,* and *Brother Death.* Roland Green, in his *Booklist* review of *Black*

Steel, states that "each Matador novel now stands pretty much independently, which is a tribute to Perry's emphasis on fast action and well-choreographed battle scenes." Another reviewer, Bonnie Kunzel, in *Voice of Youth Advocates,* states, "There's blood and gore galore in this . . . entry in the Matador series."

Perry has also written for younger readers as part of the "Time Machine Series" with his *Civil War Secret Agent,* published in 1984. The premise of the series is to take the reader back in time, "armed with a data bank to give information on the age you are visiting," observes Drew Stevenson in *School Library Journal.* In this book readers are taken back in time to 1849 and asked to help Harriet Tubman and the Underground Railroad.

BIOGRAPHICAL/CRITICAL SOURCES:

PERIODICALS

Booklist, December, 1989, p. 726; July, 1991, p. 2034; January 15, 1992, p. 916.
Magazine of Fantasy and Science Fiction, July, 1987, p. 23.
School Library Journal, April, 1985, p. 103.
Science Fiction Chronicle, July, 1986, p. 38; May, 1988, p. 44; December, 1989, p. 39.
Voice of Youth Advocates, February, 1986, pp. 396, 399; June, 1986, p. 90; June, 1992, p. 113.

*   *   *

PETERS, Robert Henry 1946-

PERSONAL: Born August 2, 1946, in Toronto, Ontario, Canada; son of Joseph Harry Andrew (a dentist) and Ruth (Gregory) Peters; married Antonia Cattaneo (a biologist), February 23, 1974; children: Julian Marco, Elisa Laura. *Education:* University of Toronto, B.Sc., 1968, Ph.D., 1972. *Politics:* Social Democrat. *Religion:* None.

ADDRESSES: Home—32 Winchester, Westmount, Quebec, Canada H3Z 1J1. *Office*—Department of Biology, McGill University, 1205 Dr. Penfield Ave., Montreal, Quebec, Canada H3A 1B1.

CAREER: Instituto Italiano di Idrobiologia, postdoctoral fellow, 1972; Limnoligiscnes Institut, Vienna, Austria, postdoctoral fellow, 1973; Zoologisches Institut, Munich, Germany, postdoctoral fellow, 1974; McGill University, Montreal, Quebec, assistant professor, 1974-79, associate professor, 1979-86, professor of biology, 1986—. Instituto Italiano di Idrobiologia, visiting scientist, 1979 and 1986; consultant to Celgar Paper.

MEMBER: International Society for Theoretical and Applied Limnology, Canadian Society of Zoologists, Canadian Society of Limnology (president, 1993-96), Freshwater Biological Association, Eastern Canada-North American Lake Management Society (member of board of directors, 1990-93), American Society for Limnology and Oceanography, American Society of Naturalists.

AWARDS, HONORS: Ecology Institute Prize, 1991; Rigler Award from SCL, 1993.

WRITINGS:

Ecological Implications of Body Size, Cambridge University Press, 1983.
(With R. de Bernardi) *Daphnia,* Consiglio Nazionale delle Ricerche (Italy), 1987.
A Critique for Ecology, Cambridge University Press, 1991.
(With F. H. Rigler) *Science and Limnology,* Ecology Institute (Oldendorf, Germany), 1994.

Contributor of more than a hundred articles to scientific journals.

WORK IN PROGRESS: Predictive Limnology, with Lars Haakanson, completion expected in 1995; *Peters Predictive Ecology,* 1996; *Ecotoxicology: Flux and Impact of Organic Contaminants in Lakes; Eutrophy: The Control and Effect of Nutrient Addition to Lakes; Allometry: Respiration and Material Flows in the Plankton; Forestry: Impact of Clear Cuts on Lakes.*

SIDELIGHTS: Robert Henry Peters told *CA:* "I was born a naturalist, showing a deep fascination with the living world ever since childhood. This interest was directed to fresh water by summers on Mud Turtle Lake, near Coboconk, Ontario, with my grandparents; by my father's continuing interest in the out-of-doors; and by my winter residence in Toronto's Beach District, where Lake Ontario has a powerful presence.

"At university, I was confused by ecology (and many other subjects). It seemed an intellectual pursuit that said very little about the world around us. Then I found summer employment with F. H. Rigler, who would have the most profound effect on my thoughts of all my teachers. Rigler introduced me to both the philosophy of science and limnology (freshwater ecology), and they became the dominant forces of my intellectual life. Rigler, drawing on Karl Popper, made it clear that informative sciences made predictions about nature, admitted that ecology did not fit the Popperian model, and introduced Kuhn's ideas of scientific revolution as a necessity when the science of ecology failed to confront the issues of the day. The opportunity to meet the leading English-speaking ecologists, as part of the Fisheries Research Board Seminars, further convinced me of the poverty of ecology.

"On graduation, I elected to leave the English-speaking world to find alternative approaches. No doubt this rejection of dominant schools in ecology was promoted by the spirit of revolution of the sixties and a mistrust of American dominance reflecting the Vietnam war and longstanding Canadian sensitivities. In Europe, I made lasting trans-Atlantic friendships, found and married Antonia Cattaneo (another freshwater ecologist), and wrote an attack, 'Tautology in Ecology and Evolution,' which became widely cited and noted, much more than my firsthand research with phosphorus in lakes.

"Since then I have sought to collate existing general predictive models in ecology, to develop an effective alternative science. My most widely used work to date is an example of what such a science might prove to be. My second major work, *A Critique for Ecology,* focused again on what is wrong with ecology because, following Kuhn, a new paradigm is successful only when the failures of the existing paradigms are recognized. These critical writings are a device to weaken the establishment in ecology so that empirical, predictive, applied models will be able to take their place. This strategy is outlined in greater depth in *Science and Limnology,* an elaboration of the unpublished materials left by F. H. Rigler on his death in 1982.

"Future work will look to the process of development of predictive models, in a work spearheaded by the great Swedish limnologist Lars Haakanson. In the near future, I hope to begin work on a summary volume of great generality that will provide an empirical predictive overview of ecological science. In the meantime, a stream of publications in primary scientific journals allows me to pursue original research in eutrophication, organic contamination, pollution, productivity, and allometry to demonstrate that scientists can be generalists, to merit support from the granting agencies, and to train future scientists."

*   *   *

PHILLIPS, Kenneth J. H.   1946-

PERSONAL: Born May 16, 1946, in Isleworth, Middlesex, England; son of Kenneth V. (an accountant) and Mabel V. (Harding) Phillips. *Education:* University of London, B.Sc., 1967, Ph.D., 1972. *Politics:* "Left of center." *Religion:* Church of England. *Avocational Interests:* Running, reading, listening to music.

ADDRESSES: Home—16 Cholsey Rd., Thatcham, Berkshire RG13 4GH, England. *Office*—Division of Astrophysics, Rutherford Appleton Laboratory, Chilton, Didcot, Oxfordshire OX11 0QX, England.

CAREER: National Aeronautics and Space Administration, Goddard Space Flight Center, Greenbelt, MD, National Research Council postdoctoral fellow, 1972-75; University of Hawaii at Manoa, Honolulu, National Science Foundation postdoctoral fellow, 1975-76; Rutherford Appleton Laboratory, Didcot, England, research scientist, 1977—. Queen's University, Belfast, honorary lecturer; public speaker; broadcaster on British radio and television networks.

MEMBER: International Astronomical Union, Royal Astronomical Society.

WRITINGS:

Guide to the Sun, Cambridge University Press, 1992.

Work represented in anthologies, including *The Many Faces of the Sun,* Springer-Verlag, 1994. Contributor of more than a hundred-thirty articles to scientific journals and popular magazines.

WORK IN PROGRESS: Research on data from the Solar Maximum Mission and Japan's Yohkoh space satellite.

SIDELIGHTS: Kenneth J. H. Phillips told *CA:* "I was educated in physics and astronomy at the University of London, and I have made solar and stellar physics my specialties. My particular interests are flares on the sun and on solar-type stars, and the X-ray and ultraviolet emission from them. Using data from a number of spacecraft, including the Solar Maximum Mission of the National Aeronautics and Space Administration and the Japanese Yohkoh satellite, I have studied how such emission gives information on the physical conditions in the very hot gases (plasmas) produced when flares occur. A lot of this work has involved comparison with theoretical spectra, calculated from atomic physics codes, so I have interacted a good deal with theorists working in this area in British, American, and Japanese universities and other institutions.

"I have published extensively on flares and their radiations, and some other subjects. Drawing on my background of solar and stellar astronomy, I wrote *Guide to the Sun,* a comprehensive summary of present knowledge about our nearest star. The book includes sections on the history of solar astronomy; the solar interior, including energy source and helioseismology; the solar atmosphere, including photosphere, chromosphere, and corona; the solar wind and interplanetary space; the sun as a star; solar energy; and observation of the sun with telescopes and satellites. *Guide to the Sun* has been adopted as a course book at several British and U.S. universities. I am enthusiastic about popularizing astronomy, and have also contributed to several other educational projects."

*   *   *

PIERRE, Jose 1927-

PERSONAL: Born November 24, 1927, in Benesse-Maremne, Landes, France; son of Etienne (a tram employee) and Louise (a homemaker); married September 5, 1953; wife's name, Nicole. *Education:* Attended Ecole Normale Superieure de l'Enseignement Technique, 1951-55; Sorbonne, University of Paris, Ph.D., 1979. *Politics:* "Anarchist." *Religion:* "Sometimes animist, sometimes atheist." *Avocational Interests:* "Women, women, women, and little birds and fishes (frogs and snakes too)."

ADDRESSES: Home—2 rue Cournot, 75015 Paris, France.

CAREER: Professor of French literature, 1955-68; Centre National de la Recherche Scientifique, Paris, France, researcher, 1968-93. *Military service:* French Air Force, 1953-55.

WRITINGS:

Dictionnaire de poche du Surrealisme, Hazan (Paris), 1973, translation published by Barron's, 1974.
Dictionnaire de poche du Pop Art, Hazan (Paris), 1975, translation published by Barron's, 1977.
(Editor) *Investigating Sex: Surrealist Discussions, 1928-1932,* Routledge, Chapman & Hall, 1992.

UNTRANSLATED WRITINGS; IN FRENCH, EXCEPT WHERE NOTED

Le Cubisme, Rencontre (Lausanne), 1966.
La Futurisme et le Dadaisme, Rencontre (Lausanne), 1966.
Le Surrealisme, Rencontre (Lausanne), 1967.
Le "Ca" ira (stories), Editions surrealistes (Paris), 1967.
D'autres chats a fouetter (stories), Losfeld (Paris), 1968.
Theo Gerber, Lutz (Zurich), 1969.
Theatre: Le Vaisseau amiral ou les Portugais; Bonjour Mon OEil; Hara-Kiri (plays), Denoel (Paris), 1969.
(In German) *Konrad Klapheck,* DuMont Schauberg (Cologne), 1970.
Domaine de Paalen, Galanis (Paris), 1970.
Levare la lepre et la sete (poems), Galleria Arte Borgogna (Milan), 1970.
Gustave Moreau, Hazan (Paris), 1971.
Le Testament d'Horus (poems), Le Terrain vague (Paris), 1971.
L'Abecedaire, Losfeld (Paris), 1971.
Cardenas, La Connaissance (Brussels), 1972.
Les Automobiles (poem), Visat (Paris), 1972.
Gabriella Simossi, Tram (Athens), 1973.
Dova, Le Musee de poche (Paris), 1974.
Ceramiques de Miro et Artigas, Maeght (Paris), 1974.
Pleni Luna (poems), A. H. Grafik (Stockholm), 1974.
Qu'est-ce que Therese? C'est les marronniers en fleurs (novel), Le Soleil noir (Paris), 1974.
Position politique de la peinture surrealiste, Le Musee de poche (Paris), 1975.
Max Walter Svanberg ou le Regne feminin, Le Musee de poche (Paris), 1975.

(With Ragnar von Holten) *D'Orgeix,* Le Musee de poche (Paris), 1975.

Le Symbolisme, Hazan (Paris), 1976.

Le Surrealisme, Hazan (Paris), 1977.

Eva, Viviane et la fee Morgane (novel), Galilee (Paris), 1980.

La Haine des plages (novel), Galilee (Paris), 1980.

La Charite commence par un baiser (novel), Galilee (Paris), 1980.

Wolfgang Paalen, Filipacchi (Paris), 1980.

Tracts surrealistes et declarations collectives, Losfeld (Paris), Volume I: *1922-1939,* 1980, Volume II: *1940-1969,* 1982.

Gauguin aux Marquises (novel), Flammarion (Paris), 1982.

Surrealisme et Anarchie, Plasma (Paris), 1982.

L'Univers surrealiste, Somogy (Paris), 1983.

Magritte, Somogy (Paris), 1984.

Introduction a la peinture, Somogy (Paris), 1985.

L'Aventure surrealiste autour d'Andre Breton, Artcurial/ Filipacchi (Paris), 1986.

Marie Laurencin, Somogy (Paris), 1988.

La Fontaine close (novel), I'Instant (Paris), 1988.

Guy Johnson, Filipacchi (Paris), 1989.

Le Belvedere Mandiargues, Adam Biro/Artcurial (Paris), 1990.

L'Univers symboliste: Decadence, Symbolisme et Art Nouveau, Somogy (Paris), 1991.

Arthur Cravan le Prophete, Le Temps qu'il fait (Cognac), 1992.

Magdeleine Leclerc, Le dernier amour du marquis de Sade (play; produced in Paris, 1993), Le Lucernaire (Paris), 1993.

Poet, playwright, art critic, and art historian. Work represented in anthologies, including *Archives du surrealisme,* Gallimard (Paris), 1990. Contributor of stories, essays, and poems to periodicals.

WORK IN PROGRESS: Le Surrealisme et les Esthetiques de la Subversion, a collection of the author's recent articles on surrealism; a play in honor of Heinrich von Kleist; a novel celebrating pornographic films; another play, *L'Ennemi de Dieu ou le Meurte du Pere.*

SIDELIGHTS: Jose Pierre told *CA:* "I have always been a writer. I began my first novel at the age of seven. It is unfinished, of course. I was thirty-nine when I asked myself, 'Where are your complete works, boy?' Since then, I write, I write, and I write, even with my eyes closed.

"The major event in my life was my encounter with surrealism. I met Andre Breton in October, 1952, and from then until the death of the poet in September, 1966, I was in his nourishing shadow like a young cow in the grass.

"At the beginning, I was a bit dazzled by modern art and modern artists. My first writings were to celebrate these wondermen, or wonderwomen, who make modern art. Today, except for six or seven painters and sculptors who are my friends, I prefer dead artists! What is the message of the contemporary artist? 'Me, me, and me!'

"I wrote my first play in 1967, though it was not staged until 1981. The world of theater is really wonderful, and I continue to write plays. The one I prefer, which was staged in Paris early in 1993, was about the last love of the Marquis de Sade, Magdeleine Leclerc. It was perhaps my favorite work. But the actors—all they had to say was 'me, me, and me!'

"I published my first novel in 1974. Here there were no problems with artists or actors, only with editors. Now it is my turn to say 'me, me, and me!' All my novels are very erotic ones. Why not? With all those girls, it is less tiring to make love on paper!"

*   *   *

PIERSON, G(eorge) W(ilson) 1904-1993

OBITUARY NOTICE—See index for *CA* sketch: Born October 22, 1904, in New York, NY; died October 12, 1993, in Hamden, CT. Educator and author. Pierson's long affiliation with Yale University began in 1926, with his appointment as an instructor in English. A few years later, Pierson became an instructor in the department of history, and in 1936 he was promoted to the position of assistant professor of history. Pierson remained at Yale until 1973 when he became Larned Professor of History Emeritus. During his extensive teaching career, Pierson also held numerous administrative posts in the university, including director of the Division of the Humanities from 1964 to 1970. Pierson's interest and expertise on Alexis de Tocqueville, a nineteenth-century political scientist, led him to write his first book, *Tocqueville and Beaumont in America.* Pierson was also an active member of the American Historical Association from 1963 onwards, and he served as historian of Yale University. His books on the history of Yale include *Yale: A Short History, The Founding of Yale: The Legend of Forty Folios,* and *A Yale Book of Numbers: Historical Statistics of the College and University.*

OBITUARIES AND OTHER SOURCES:

BOOKS

Who's Who in America, 48th edition, Marquis, 1994.

PERIODICALS

Chicago Tribune, October 17, 1993, section 2, p. 6.

PINCKNEY, Darryl 1953-

PERSONAL: Born in 1953 in Indianapolis, IN. *Education:* Attended Columbia University and Princeton University.

ADDRESSES: Home—New York, NY. *Office*—c/o Penguin Books, 375 Hudson St., New York, NY 10014-3657.

CAREER: Columbia University, New York City, teacher, 1992—; critic; essayist; novelist.

AWARDS, HONORS: Hodder Fellow at Princeton University; received grants from Ingram Merrill Foundation and Guggenheim Foundation; Whiting Writers' Award, Mrs. Giles Whiting Foundation, 1986; Art Seidenbaum Award for first fiction, *Los Angeles Times,* 1992, for *High Cotton.*

WRITINGS:

High Cotton, Farrar, Straus, 1992.

Contributor to periodicals, including *New York Review of Books, Vanity Fair, Vogue, Granta,* and *New York Times.*

WORK IN PROGRESS: A critical book on African American literature.

SIDELIGHTS: The relationship between the narrator of Darryl Pinckney's picaresque novel, *High Cotton,* and its author has caused reviewers to speculate that the narrative is more of a memoir than a work of fiction. *Newsday's* Jonathan Mandell described the work as "a semi-autobiographical novel of growing up as a member of what W. E. B. DuBois called the 'talented tenth'—the African-American elite, the black middle class." Writing in *New York Review of Books,* Michael Wood lauded Pinckney's book as "delicately, intelligently tracing pieces of an uninvented life. The art is in the selection of the traces and in the angle of vision." In the course of the novel, the narrator moves from the sheltered world of his extended family into the white world, and eventually into the realm of large historical movements—the civil rights struggle and the politics of black cultural nationalism. Because of the deft handling of the complexities of the narrator's skeptical voice, a diverse historical and cultural span, and racial ambiguity, Pinckney's first novel has been widely praised, and received the 1992 *Los Angeles Times's* Art Seidenbaum Award for first fiction. In the *New York Review of Books,* Wood commented on the author's style, pointing out that "it can't let go, but it learns to relax, and at its best Pinckney's prose—funny, observant, lyrical, self-deprecating—is as good as any now being written in English."

Pinckney is a member of the fourth generation in his family to be college educated. He told Mandell that "Black life is no longer synonymous with underprivileged." Pinck-

ney's perspective was commented on in the *Washington Post Book World* by American scholar and essayist Henry Louis Gates, Jr., who wrote: "Pinckney's relation to black America's literary past is distinguished by an intense, and self-conscious, ambivalence—and he has turned that ambivalence into an advantage both intellectual and literary." Though Pinckney's *High Cotton* is heavily grounded in sociology, Gail Lumet Buckley pointed out in the *Los Angeles Times Book Review* that the novel also possesses a religious aspect, for it "questions the meaning of human suffering." Edmund White in the *New York Times Book Review* asserted that Pinckney explores dimensions of the American race problem with "excruciating honesty and the total freedom from restraint that [German poet and playwright Johann] Schiller said we find nowhere else but in authentic works of art."

BIOGRAPHICAL/CRITICAL SOURCES:

BOOKS

Contemporary Literary Criticism, Volume 76, Gale, 1993, pp. 98-113.

PERIODICALS

Los Angeles Times Book Review, November 8, 1992.
Newsday, March 8, 1992.
New York Review of Books, March 26, 1992.
New York Times, April 4, 1992.
New York Times Book Review, February 2, 1992.
Times (London), August 13, 1992.
Times Literary Supplement, August 14, 1992.
Washington Post Book World, February 23, 1992.*

*   *   *

PINEAU, Roger 1916-1993

OBITUARY NOTICE—See index for *CA* sketch: Born November 17, 1916, in Chicago, IL; died of cardiovascular illness, November 22, 1993, in Bethesda, MD. Naval historian, editor, and author. Pineau was a naval historian who is remembered for his research and writings on the pacific campaigns of the United States Navy. Pineau's career began in 1947, when, as an editorial assistant in the department of naval history, he aided in the preparation of a fifteen-volume history of the U.S. Navy. In 1957 Pineau transferred to the U.S. Department of State, working first as chief of Far East current intelligence and later as social science officer in Washington, D.C. Pineau then joined the Smithsonian Institution and was appointed managing editor of the Smithsonian Institution Press in 1966. Pineau remained with the Smithsonian until 1972, when he returned to work with the U.S. Navy as director of the Navy Memorial Museum. During his long career,

Pineau wrote several books, including *Picture History of the Pacific War*, in addition to editing books like *The Japan Expedition, 1852-1854: The Personal Journal of Commodore Matthew C. Perry*. Pineau also contributed his writing to other works, including *And I Was There, Pearl Harbor and Midway—Breaking the Secrets*.

OBITUARIES AND OTHER SOURCES:

BOOKS

International Authors and Writers Who's Who, 9th edition, Melrose, 1982.

PERIODICALS

New York Times, November 30, 1993, p. B11.
Washington Post, November 23, 1993, p. E5.

*   *   *

POCHOCKI, Ethel (Frances) 1925-
(Ethel Marbach)

PERSONAL: Name pronounced "po-chock-i"; born September 17, 1925, in Bayonne, NJ; daughter of Czeslaw Romuald (a lawyer) and Ethel (a homemaker; maiden name, Szloboda) Pochocki; married Francis Marbach, October 5, 1946 (divorced, 1970); children: Therese, Julia, Carol, Martin, Peter, Charles, Lucy, Rosemary. *Education:* Attended Katherine Gibbs Secretarial School, 1942-44. *Politics:* Democrat/Independent. *Religion:* Roman Catholic.

ADDRESSES: Home and office—RR 1, Box 110, Brooks, ME 04921.

CAREER: Writer.

AWARDS, HONORS: Lupine Award, Maine Library Association, 1992, for *Rosebud and Red Flannel*.

WRITINGS:

UNDER NAME ETHEL MARBACH

Do It Yourself Guide to Holy Housewifery, Abbey Press, 1965.
The Holy Housewifery Cookbook, Abbey Press, 1968.
My Mother and Leopold Stokowski (fiction), Alba House, 1970.

JUVENILES

Grandma Bagley Leads the Way, Augsburg/Fortress, 1989.
Grandma Bagley to the Rescue, Augsburg/Fortress, 1989.
The Attic Mice, Holt, 1990.
The Fox Who Found Christmas, Ave Maria Press, 1990.
Rosebud and Red Flannel, Holt, 1991.
The Mushroom Man, Simon & Schuster, 1993.

Wildflower Tea, Simon & Schuster, 1993.
The Gypsies' Tale, Simon & Schuster, 1994.
Saints and Heroes for Today, St. Anthony Messenger Press, 1994.

Contributor to periodicals, including *Cricket* and *Pockets*, and to anthologies, including *Cabbages and Kings*, 1991. Also author of television scripts for program, *Saints Alive*.

JUVENILES; UNDER NAME ETHEL MARBACH

Emily's Rainbow, Green Tiger Press, 1980.
The Cabbage Moth and the Shamrock, Green Tiger Press, 1981.
Soup Pot! and Christmas Tree for All Seasons, Green Tiger Press, 1981.
Once upon a Time Saints, Volume 1, St. Anthony Messenger Press, 1981.
Once upon a Time Saints, Volume 2, St. Anthony Messenger Press, 1982.
Saints in Waiting, St. Anthony Messenger Press, 1983.
Saints for the Journey, St. Anthony Messenger Press, c. 1984.
Saints for the Harvest, St. Anthony Messenger Press, c. 1985.
The White Rabbit, St. Anthony Messenger Press, 1985.
Dandelions, Fireflies and Rhubarb Pie, Upper Room Press, 1985.
Saints for the Seasons, St. Anthony Messenger Press, 1986.

Saints in Waiting, Saints for the Journey, Saints for the Harvest, and *Saints for the Seasons* were reprinted in one volume, St. Anthony Messenger Press, 1990.

WORK IN PROGRESS: A sequel to *The Attic Mice;* a book about the adventures of Mrs. Persimmon, a red squirrel.

SIDELIGHTS: Ethel Pochocki commented: "I was born in Bayonne, New Jersey, to a first-generation Hungarian mother and a Polish-born father. He had been caught teaching the catechism, a crime in Russian-occupied Poland at the turn of the century, and sentenced to exile in Siberia at the age of 19. He escaped and somehow made his way to the U.S. After studying for the priesthood in Michigan, he became a lawyer. He met my mother, a young widow, while visiting in New Jersey, and married her. I am the one and only remembrance of that union.

"I realize, after doing a variety of writing, that fairy tales and anthropomorphic stories are my first love. Yes, talking animals—*and* bugs, flowers, birds et al. At times I feel like a remnant of Victoriana, living in a time warp of nannies and nurseries, and finding it just my cup of tea. I think if I were living 100 years ago, I would have it made! I often wonder if the stories of Andersen and Grahame and Milne were submitted today, would they be accepted? Would they be considered too harsh or demanding of their young readers? They did not compromise with reality. They did not condescend. They used big words. They made no fuss over death. And their teddy bears and badgers and brave tin soldiers *talked!* I am at home and comfortable with them.

"Now the children have grown and flown, and I live with a menage of 7 cats (the number is always in a state of flux). I can write at any time I choose now. Winter is best, when I'm held willing captive by howling snowstorms, with nothing to lure or distract from the typewriter. Ideas come from anywhere and everywhere. Items in the daily paper are a great source—mystery flowers 'planted' by a hurricane, French gypsies gathering mistletoe for English Christmas festivities, turkeys being guests of a Thanksgiving dinner instead of the main course, a *Dear Abby* column on the friendship of two birds, one blind, the other crippled. A *Nova* program on bower birds. A glance out the kitchen window to see a pair of frozen long johns dancing in the wind, or a red squirrel trying to carry off a piece of cake thrown out for the birds. My own experiences: the guilt felt over vacuuming up spiders and flies (alive), frustration over a proliferation of zucchinis, a ladybug settling into a bowl of forced hyacinths, the collection of oddities on a fireplace mantel. I have an infinity of worlds to write about without ever leaving home."

*   *   *

PONSONBY, Frederick Edward Neuflize 1913-1993
(Tenth Earl of Bessborough)

OBITUARY NOTICE—See index for *CA* sketch: Born March 29, 1913, in London, England; died December 5, 1993. Public servant and author. Known for his work as a member of parliament in England, Ponsonby also served on several important assignments to other countries. Succeeding his father to the title of Earl of Bessborough in 1956, Ponsonby embarked on a long and varied political career. Following a short stint with the army, during which time he served in France and North Africa, Ponsonby returned to England where he was appointed the parliamentary secretary at the Ministry of Science in 1963. And although his interest and initiative in advancing technological cooperation between England and other countries led him to work at the Department of Technology in 1970, Ponsonby lost the position when the department was dissolved months after his appointment as minister of state. Subsequently, he was designated joint deputy leader of the English conservative representatives to the European Parliament. In 1972, a year after Ponsonby had joined the emerging assembly, he became the first British vice president of the European Parliament. Despite the de-

mands of his political career, Ponsonby was also actively involved in the theater. An active participant in the formation of the English Stage Company, Ponsonby also helped to establish the Chichester Festival Theatre. In addition to his administrative contributions to the stage, Ponsonby also authored several plays, including *Nebuchadnezzar, The Four Men,* and *Triptych.* Ponsonby's memoirs, titled *Return to the Forest,* were published in 1962, and he wrote *Enchanted Forest* in 1984.

OBITUARIES AND OTHER SOURCES:

BOOKS

Who's Who, 146th edition, St. Martin's, 1994.

PERIODICALS

Times (London), December 7, 1993, p. 21.

*   *   *

PORTER, Sue 1951-

PERSONAL: Born October 18, 1951, in London, England; daughter of Derek Leslie (a mathematician) and Elizabeth Marjorie (a secretary) Keeble; married Roger Derrick Porter (an architect); children: David, Megan. *Education:* Leicester Polytechnic College, Honors Degree in art and design.

ADDRESSES: Agent—Eunice McMullen, 38 Clewer Hill Rd., Windsor, Berkshire SL4 4BW, England.

CAREER: Writer and illustrator. Worked variously as a book designer, a laboratory research assistant, and a nurse.

MEMBER: Society of Authors (England).

AWARDS, HONORS: Runner-up for the Mother Goose Award (England), the Children's Book Award from the Arts Council of Great Britain, the Owl Award (Japan), and the Prix Verselle (France).

WRITINGS:

(Self-illustrated) *Baa, Baa, Black Sheep,* Harper, 1982.
One Potato, Macmillan, 1989.
Action Packed: 30 Ideas for Drama, Heinemann, 1990.
Play It Again: Suggestions for Drama, Heinemann, 1990.
(Self-illustrated) *Little Wolf and the Giant,* Simon & Schuster, 1990.

Also author and illustrator of *Chloe's Eggs,* Simon & Schuster.

ILLUSTRATOR

Mathew Price, *Do You See What I See?,* Harper, 1986.
Michaela Morgan, *Edward Gets a Pet,* Dutton, 1987.
Morgan, *Visitors for Edward,* Dutton, 1987.

Morgan, *Edward Hurts His Knee,* Dutton, 1988.
Morgan, *Edward Loses His Teddy Bear,* Dutton, 1988.
Rose Impey, *Letter to Father Christmas,* Delacorte, 1989.
Rex Harley, *Mary's Tiger,* Harcourt, 1990.
Impey, *Joe's Cafe,* Orchard Books, 1990.
Jana Novotny Hunter, *Ghost Games,* Doubleday, 1992.

Illustrator of Morgan's *Monster is Coming* and Impey's *Little Smasher, First Class,* and *The Baddies.*

SIDELIGHTS: Sue Porter commented that she has "designed, illustrated and sometimes written" thirty-seven books for children. Among those children's books written and illustrated by Porter, the nursery rhyme press-out book *Baa, Baa, Black Sheep* and *Little Wolf and the Giant* stand out. Porter described her working philosophy: "I would like to think that my books all share one thing in common—a gentle humour. There should always be a feeling of warmth to draw the young reader close." This warmth has succeeded in charming readers and garnering Porter the title of runner-up for several prestigious prizes around the world.

Porter recalled her career path: "A wonderfully eccentric teacher, Mr. Lamb, surprised me with the idea that I was good in art. In his class, I became runner-up in a National Art Competition." After attending comprehensive school and working as a research assistant in a laboratory, Porter studied art at Leicester Polytechnic College. "Apart from a brief period nursing," she explained, "I have worked as a designer, illustrator, and writer ever since."

Porter intends to continue creating children's books at her studio in Uppingham, England. She cautions readers who look forward to experiencing this future work: "I don't think it is always easy to pick out a book as being 'mine.' Although nowadays I often use watercolours, I love to use all kinds of media and methods, and I like to tailor the artwork to the age of the child and to the story itself."

*   *   *

POTTER, Harry (D.)   1954-

PERSONAL: Born August 19, 1954, in Glasgow, Scotland; son of Wallace Archibold and Eileen (Drummond) Potter. *Education:* Emmanuel College, Cambridge, M.A., 1978, M.Phil., 1981; Thames Valley University, LL.B., 1992. *Politics:* Socialist. *Religion:* Anglican.

ADDRESSES: *Home*—London, England. *Agent*—c/o SCM Press Ltd., 26-30 Tottenham Rd., London N1 4BZ, England.

CAREER: Called to the Bar at Gray's Inn; curate in London, England, 1981-84; Cambridge University, Cambridge, England, fellow of Selwyn College, 1984-87; Her

Majesty's Prison Service, chaplain, 1987-92; barrister at law, 1992—.

WRITINGS:

Hanging in Judgment: Religion and the Death Penalty in England from the Bloody Code to Abolition, Continuum, 1993.
Hanging and Heresy, University of Kent at Canterbury, 1993.

SIDELIGHTS: Harry Potter told *CA:* "I have degrees in history, theology, and law and a wide-ranging interest in the British criminal justice system. Working in two maximum security prisons (Wormwood Scrubs and Aylesbury) I encountered many men and boys sentenced to life imprisonment. Under the old dispensation some of them would have been hanged. I read the accounts of former prison chaplains who worked with the condemned and of the all-pervading shadow it cast over their lives and ministry. I began to research the interaction of religion and the peculiarly religious penalty of death, to discover not only a plethora of material but also that virtually nothing had been written about capital punishment since abolition, and nothing at all on the role of religion and the churches. My book *Hanging in Judgment* provides the most recent and comprehensive history of the subject ever written.

"My interest extends to the current situation in the United States. *Hanging and Heresy* traces the parallel course of abolition on both sides of the Atlantic and examines why our paths have, in recent years, diverged so markedly."

*   *   *

PRATCHETT, Terry   1948-

PERSONAL: Born April 28, 1948, in Beaconsfield, England; son of David (an engineer) and Eileen (a secretary; maiden name, Kearns) Pratchett; married; wife's name, Lyn; children: Rhianna. *Politics:* None. *Religion:* None.

ADDRESSES: *Agent*—Colin Smythe, Ltd., P.O. Box 6, Gerrards Cross, Buckinghamshire SL9 8XA, England.

CAREER: Journalist in Buckinghamshire, Bristol, and Bath, England, 1965-80; press officer, Central Electricity Board, Western Region, 1980-87; novelist.

AWARDS, HONORS: British Science Fiction Awards, 1989, for "Discworld" series, and 1990, for *Good Omens.*

WRITINGS:

"DISCWORLD" NOVEL SERIES

The Colour of Magic, St. Martin's, 1983.
The Light Fantastic, St. Martin's, 1986.
Equal Rites, Gollancz, 1986, New American Library, 1987.

Mort, New American Library, 1987.

Sourcery, Gollancz, 1988, New American Library, 1989.

Wyrd Sisters, Gollancz, 1988.

Pyramids, Penguin, 1989.

Eric, Gollancz, 1989.

Guards! Guards! Gollancz, 1989, Roc, 1991.

Moving Pictures, Gollancz, 1990.

Reaper Man, Gollancz, 1991.

Witches Abroad, Gollancz, 1991, New American Library, 1993.

Small Gods, Gollancz, 1992, HarperCollins, 1994.

Lords and Ladies, Gollancz, 1993.

Men at Arms, Gollancz, 1993.

"BROMELIAD" TRILOGY; JUVENILE FANTASY

Truckers, Doubleday, 1989, Delacorte, 1990.

Diggers, Delacorte, 1990.

Wings, Doubleday, 1990, Delacorte, 1991.

OTHER

The Carpet People (juvenile fantasy), Smythe, 1971, revised edition published by Doubleday, 1992.

The Dark Side of the Sun (science fiction), St. Martin's, 1976.

Strata (science fiction), St. Martin's, 1981.

The Unadulterated Cat, illustrated by Gray Jolliffe, Gollancz, 1989.

(With Neil Gaiman) *Good Omens: The Nice and Accurate Predictions of Agnes Nutter, Witch,* Workman, 1990.

Only You Can Save Mankind (for young adults), Doubleday, 1992.

Johnny and the Dead (juvenile), Doubleday, 1993.

WORK IN PROGRESS: A "Discworld" novel.

SIDELIGHTS: British author Terry Pratchett has penned numerous science fiction and fantasy novels, and is known primarily for his "Discworld" series and his "Bromeliad" trilogy for children. Critic David V. Barrett of *New Statesman & Society* stated that the novels of Discworld "are works of marvelous composition and rattling good stories." Discworld—as well as most of Pratchett's other works—also offers humorous parodies of other famous science fiction and fantasy writers, such as J. R. R. Tolkien or Larry Niven, and spoofs such modern trends as New Age philosophy and universal concerns like death. Nevertheless, "in among the slapstick and clever wordplay are serious concepts," as Barrett pointed out. In "genres assailed by shoddiness, mediocrity, and . . . the endless series," asserted *Locus* reviewer Faren Miller, "Pratchett is never shoddy, and under the laughter there's a far from mediocre mind at work."

Pratchett published his first work of fantasy, *The Carpet People,* in 1971. Aimed at young readers, the book describes a whole world set in a carpet, populated by crea-

tures called deftmenes, mouls, and wights. The novel's protagonist, Snibril the Munrung, travels with his brother Glurk through the many Carpet regions—which are set off by different colors—to do battle against the evil concept of Fray. A *Times Literary Supplement* reviewer recommended *The Carpet People* and further noted that "the Tolkienian echoes may draw in some older readers."

The Dark Side of the Sun and *Strata,* both science fiction novels by Pratchett, appear to spoof aspects of Larry Niven's *Ringworld* (a huge, flat world that completely circles a star), according to Don D'Ammassa in *Twentieth-Century Science Fiction Writers.* *The Dark Side of the Sun,* in D'Ammassa's words, features "manipulation of the laws of chance"—a subject which is also prominent in *Ringworld; Strata* discusses the construction of artificial planets and "resembles [*Ringworld*] in many superficial ways." Edward Dickey, reviewing *The Dark Side of the Sun* in *Best Sellers,* observed that "it should have strong appeal for science fiction fans" and called the novel "entertaining fiction lightened by occasional touches of whimsy." Allan Jenoff, critiquing *Strata* in *Science Fiction and Fantasy Book Review,* found it "amusing and readable."

Pratchett used the concept of a flat world again when he embarked upon his first Discworld novel, *The Colour of Magic.* This time, however, he took an approach more suitable to the fantasy genre than to science fiction. As Philippa Toomey reported in the London *Times:* "A great turtle swims through space. On its back are four giant elephants, on whose shoulders the disc of the world rests. We know this only because the extremely inquisitive inhabitants of the small kingdom of Krull lowered some early astrozoologists over the edge to have a quick look." The protagonist of *The Colour of Magic* is a hapless wizard named Rincewind; he teams up with a tourist from a remote portion of the disc. The result, according to W. D. Stevens in *Science Fiction and Fantasy Review,* is "one of the funniest, and cleverest, [Sword and Sorcery] satires to be written."

Rincewind returns in Pratchett's second Discworld novel, *The Light Fantastic.* This time he must try to prevent Discworld from colliding with a red star that has recently appeared in its sky. The next book in the series, *Equal Rites,* puts the emphasis on the character of Granny Weatherwax, whom Tom Hutchinson in the London *Times* hailed as "one of my favorite fantasy heroines." Granny Weatherwax is back in *Wyrd Sisters,* this time accompanied by two fellow witches—one, Magrat Garlick, likes to indulge in "New Age fripperies," according to Miller in *Locus.* In *Wyrd Sisters,* Granny and her companions form a trio of witches (reminiscent of those in William Shakespeare's play *Macbeth*) to foil the plot of the evil Lord Felmet and his wife, who have usurped the rightful king; this volume led Miller to express his amazement at Pratchett for creating "an open-ended series that just keeps getting better."

In 1989, Pratchett published the first of his Bromeliad fantasy series for children. *Truckers* introduces young readers to the nomes, four-inch high people from another planet who have crashed on earth and who have made a new world for themselves under the floorboards of a department store. Some of the nomes, however, have lived on the outside; the fun begins when one of these, Masklin, meets with the nomes of the store. When they learn that the store is going out of business and will be torn down, together they must cooperate to find a new home and to escape their old one in a human-sized truck. "A wild and hilarious chase sequence follows, with the baffled police doubting their sanity," observed a *Horn Book* reviewer. Elizabeth Ward in the *Washington Post Book World* summed up *Truckers* as "a delightful surprise" and a "benevolent little satire."

Diggers takes Masklin and his fellow nomes to their new home in an abandoned quarry. But problems ensue when humans attempt to reactivate the quarry. "In the book's funniest scene," according to Patrick Jones in *Voice of Youth Advocates,* "a group of nomes 'attacks' one of the humans, ties him to his desk chair, and stuffs a note in his hand proclaiming: 'leave us alone.' " "Satire and allegory abound," a *Horn Book* reviewer concluded of *Diggers,* but the critic also noted that the nomes' "trials and emotions are both moving and amusing." In *Wings* Masklin and his friends attempt to return to their home planet by placing the Thing—the "magic" box which in *Truckers* had warned them of the store's demise—aboard a communications satellite so that it can summon their old mother ship, which has been waiting for them throughout their earthly exile. Margaret A. Chang lauded this last book of the series in the *School Library Journal* as a "cheerful, unpretentious tale."

While Pratchett was working on the Bromeliad series, he continued to create new Discworld novels. *Pyramids,* which appeared in 1989, spoofs ancient Egypt, transparently labeled "Ankh-Morpork" by Pratchett. In *Pyramids,* loyal Discworld fans meet Teppic, a teenager who is studying to become an assassin until a relative's death leaves him Pharaoh. Other later, well-received Discworld books include *Witches Abroad,* which again features Granny Weatherwax and her witch companions. This time their mission is to stop the inevitable happy ending of a fairy tale because of the deeper disaster it will cause. In the London *Times* Hutchinson remarked on the more serious tone Pratchett employs in *Witches Abroad:* "While his jokes are still the best thing since [P. G.] Wodehouse, his intent has a very serious undertow. Addicts should especially note his concern with the fairy story itself." Miller in *Locus* warned readers of the book to "keep an eye out

for the delicious Tolkien parody," and Barrett in *New Statesman & Society* applauded the author's "cheerfully ransacking the fairy tales we all grew up with as the witches pursue their goal." Another later Discworld novel is *Small Gods,* which Miller described as "a book about tortoises, eagles, belief systems, conspiracies, religious bigotry, man's need for gods, and gods' even greater need for man."

Pratchett has continued to produce works outside of his two famed series, however. With Neil Gaiman, previously known for his authorship of graphic novels, Pratchett created *Good Omens: The Nice and Accurate Predictions of Agnes Nutter, Witch.* The story, which met with mixed reviews when it was published in 1990, spoofs the *Bible*'s book of "Revelation" and concerns the efforts of both an angel and a demon to prevent the end of the world because they have grown fond of mankind and life on Earth. Their tactics include such strategy as deliberately misplacing the Antichrist, who resides in an English suburb. Joe Queenan, critiquing the book in the *New York Times Book Review,* complained of "schoolboy wisecracks about Good, Evil, the Meaning of Life and people who drink Perrier." But Howard Waldrop in the *Washington Post* praised *Good Omens:* "When the book is talking about the big questions, its a wow. It leaves room in both the plot and the readers' reactions for the characters to move around in and do unexpected but very human things." In 1992 Pratchett penned a young adult novel, *Only You Can Save Mankind,* which, with its computer-game playing protagonist, spoofs, among other things, the 1991 Persian Gulf War.

Pratchett told *CA:* "I've been a journalist of some sort all my working life, and I suppose I tend to think of the books as a kind of journalism—although writing them is as much fun as anyone can have by themselves sitting down with all their clothes on.

"I can't speak for the United States—three thousand miles is a great barrier to casual feedback—but what does gratify me in the United Kingdom is that the 'Discworld' books, which are not intended for children, have a big following among kids who, in the words of one librarian, 'don't normally read.'

"I got my education from books. The official schooling system merely prevented me from reading as many books as I would have liked. So from personal experience I know that getting children to read is *important.* Civilization depends on it."

BIOGRAPHICAL/CRITICAL SOURCES:

BOOKS

Twentieth-Century Science Fiction Writers, St. James, 1991.

PERIODICALS

Best Sellers, November, 1976, pp. 249-50.
Fantasy Review, November, 1986, pp. 31-32.
Horn Book, March/April, 1990, p. 202; May/June, 1991, p. 332.
Locus, January 1989, p. 17; October, 1991, pp. 15, 17; June, 1992, p. 17; September, 1992, p. 66; February, 1993, p. 58.
New Statesman, August 29, 1986, p. 26; January 29, 1988, p. 30.
New Statesman & Society, January 3, 1992, p. 33.
New York Times Book Review, October 7, 1990, p. 27.
School Library Journal, September, 1991, pp. 258-59.
Science Fiction and Fantasy Book Review, April, 1982, p. 20.
Science Fiction and Fantasy Review, March, 1984, p. 35.
Times (London), February 12, 1987; August 9, 1990; November 21, 1991, p. 16.
Times Literary Supplement, April 28, 1972, p. 475.
Voice of Youth Advocates, February, 1991, p. 366.
Washington Post, December 20, 1990.
Washington Post Book World, February 11, 1990, p. 6.

—*Sketch by Elizabeth Wenning*

*   *   *

PRICE, Vincent (Leonard)   1911-1993

OBITUARY NOTICE—See index for *CA* sketch: Born May 27, 1911, in St. Louis, MO; died of lung cancer, October 25, 1993, in Los Angeles, CA. Actor, lecturer, and author. Best remembered as the master of horror and suspense for his work in classic films such as *Theatre of Blood, The Fly,* and *Masque of the Red Death,* Price devoted nearly sixty years to entertaining the young and old alike. He first began his acting career on stage, performing in dramas like *Victoria Regina.* He made a similar entree into motion pictures, starring in *The House of Seven Gables* and *The Song of Bernadette.* He began his foray into villainous roles as a member of Orson Welles' Mercury Theater and with films like *The House of Wax.* During his acting career, Price starred in more than one hundred motion pictures, most recently in *Whales of August* and *Edward Scissorhands.* He also found time to appear in some two thousand television productions, including *Night Gallery, Batman,* and *Mystery.* He continued his work on the stage, notably with the one-person-play *Diversions and Delights,* and even performed in a music video, Michael Jackson's *Thriller.*

An avid fine art historian and collector, Price served on the board of various art organizations, including the Archives of American Artists and Center for Arts of Indian Affairs. He was a member of Fine Arts committee to the White House, and he was a frequent lecturer on primitive and modern art, as well as on Dutch painter Vincent Van Gogh. Price authored several books on the subject of art, including *The Vincent Price Treasury of American Art* and, with his second wife, Mary, *The Michelangelo Bible.* He also wrote his memoirs in *I Like What I Know* and *Vincent Price: His Movies, His Plays, His Life.* The author of *The Book of Joe: About a Dog and His Man* as well as several cookbooks, he also edited an anthology of stories by American writer Edgar Allan Poe. In 1992 he was awarded the Los Angeles Film Critics Award for life achievement.

OBITUARIES AND OTHER SOURCES:

BOOKS

Contemporary Theatre, Film, and Television, Volume 4, Gale, 1987, pp. 374-376.
Who's Who in America, 48th edition, Marquis, 1994, p. 2773.

PERIODICALS

Chicago Tribune, October 26, 1993, p. 11.
Los Angeles Times, October 26, 1993, p. A3.
New York Times, October 27, 1993, p. D23.
Times (London), October 27, 1993, p. 19.
Washington Post, October 27, 1993, p. D4.

*   *   *

PRIMACK, Alice Lefler   1939-

PERSONAL: Born February 14, 1939, in Kent, OH; daughter of Glenn Q. (a professor of physics) and Mary (a homemaker; maiden name, Staley) Lefler; married Robert B. Primack (a professor of education); children: Eric, Mary-Anne, Glenn. *Education:* Eastern Illinois University, B.S., 1961; University of Wisconsin—Madison, M.L.S., 1962. *Politics:* Democrat. *Religion:* Unitarian-Universalist. *Avocational Interests:* Activities with and for children, camping, crafts.

ADDRESSES: Home—3657 Northwest 40th Pl., Gainesville, FL 32605. *Office*—Marston Science Library, University of Florida, Gainesville, FL 32611-7011.

CAREER: Ohio State University, Columbus, library intern, 1962-63, reference librarian, 1963-66; University of Florida, Gainesville, began as assistant librarian, became university librarian, 1972—.

MEMBER: Special Libraries Association, Unitarian-Universalist Fellowship (vice-president, 1981—), Alachua County 4-H (club leader and member of Advisory Council, 1990—).

WRITINGS:

How to Find Out in Pharmacy, Pergamon, 1969.
Finding Answers in Science and Technology, Van Nostrand, 1984.
Journal Literature of the Physical Sciences, Scarecrow, 1992.

Contributor to *Library Trends.*

SIDELIGHTS: Alice Lefler Primack told *CA:* "In today's information age, the ability to find, evaluate, and use information for a particular need is a survival skill. The power of information can make the difference between success or failure on the job and in one's personal life. Use of appropriate information enhances the quality of life.

"As a librarian, I am very interested in how people find information and how they choose and use the information appropriate for their particular need. I have developed a basic library research plan based on communication patterns of scientists and engineers, and on my experience of working with students who are doing library research. An important part of library research is evaluation of the sources based on the author's qualifications, critical thinking about the content, and awareness of bias both in the writer and in oneself.

"I believe that information skills do not come naturally, but must be taught. Use of a library research plan helps to prevent unnecessary effort. I have tried to teach the library research plan through my writing and in classes at the University of Florida. People who understand the patterns of information, types of information available, and how to access and use information are thereby information-literate and prepared for lifelong learning."

*   *   *

PRINCE CHARMING
See THOMAS, Rosanne Daryl

*   *   *

PROMIS, Jose 1940-

PERSONAL: Born September 23, 1940, in Santiago, Chile; son of Jose and Rosa Promis; married in 1971; wife's name, Patricia A. (a librarian); children: Jose Francisco, Esteban Patricio. *Education:* University of Chile, B.Letters, 1959, teacher's certification (with highest distinction), 1963; Instituto de Cultura Hispanica, Madrid, Spain, Diploma de Estudios Hispanicos Contemporaneos, 1964; University of Madrid, Ph.D. (with distinction), 1965. *Religion:* Roman Catholic.

ADDRESSES: Home—615 North Bedford, Tucson, AZ 85710. *Office*—Department of Spanish and Portuguese, University of Arizona, Tucson, AZ 85721.

CAREER: High school Spanish teacher in Santiago, Chile, 1962-67; University of Chile, Valparaiso, professor of Chilean literature, 1968-75; University of Arizona, Tucson, visiting professor, 1976-77, professor of Spanish-American literature and literary criticism, 1976—, acting department head, 1983-84, academic adviser for Guadalajara Summer School, 1986-87. University of Chile, Santiago, assistant professor, 1966-70; Catholic University of Valparaiso, professor, 1967-75, member of organizing committee, Institute of Languages and Literature, 1969, director of institute, 1969-71, head of Department of Literature, 1971-72; Catholic University of Chile, professor, 1973-76; Texas Christian University, Green Honor Professor, 1987; University of Playa Ancha, visiting faculty consultant, 1991—. Producer and host of cultural and literary programs on Chilean television, 1967-75.

WRITINGS:

La identidad de Hispanoamerica: Ensayo sobre literature colonial, Editorial de la Universidad de Guadalajara, 1987, revised translation published as *The Identity of Hispanoamerica,* University of Arizona Press, 1991.

Contributing editor, *Handbook of Latin American Studies,* 1987—; member of editorial board, *Journal of Hispanic Philology.*

IN SPANISH

Manual de Castellano, Editorial Universitaria (Santiago, Chile), seventh grade edition, 1968, eighth grade edition, 1968, high school edition, Volume 1, 1969, Volume 2, 1971, Volume 3, 1972, Volume 4, 1973.
Lectura y Lenguaje, Editorial Universitaria (Santiago), seventh grade edition, 1970, eighth grade edition, 1970.
La conciencia de la realidad en la literature espanola (Siglos XII-XVI), Ediciones Universitarias de Valparaiso, 1972.
Poesia romantica chilena, Editorial Nascimento (Santiago), 1975.
(Editor and contributor) *Ernesto Cardenal, poeta de la liberacion latinoamericana,* Fernando Garcia Cambeiro (Buenos Aires, Argentina), 1975.
Testimonios y documentos de la literatura chilena, Editorial Nascimento (Santiago), 1977.
La novela chilena actual, Fernando Garcia Cambeiro (Buenos Aires), 1977.
(With Jorge Roman-Lagunas) *La prosa hispanoamericana: Evolucion y Antologia,* University Press of America (Boston, MA), 1988.

La novela chilena del ultimo siglo, Editorial La Noria (Santiago), 1993.

Work represented in anthologies. Literary critic, *La Union* (Valparaiso, Chile), 1967-73. Contributor to scholarly journals. *SIGNOS: Journal of Languages and Literatures,* founder and director, 1967, member of editorial board, 1967-70; *Nueva Revista del Pacifico,* member of editorial board, 1992.

*   *   *

PULVER, Robin   1945-

PERSONAL: Born August 14, 1945, in Geneva, NY; daughter of Willard B. (a biochemist) and Alice (Alden) Robinson; married Donald Pulver (a physician), June 12, 1971; children: Nina, David. *Education:* William Smith College, B.A., 1967; attended Syracuse University. *Politics:* Democrat. *Religion:* Protestant. *Avocational Interests:* Hiking, swimming, bird-watching, reading, journal-keeping.

ADDRESSES: Home—19 Cricket Hill Dr., Pittsford, NY 14534.

CAREER: Has worked in public relations; writer.

MEMBER: Society of Children's Book Writers and Illustrators, National Coalition Against Censorship, Authors Guild, Association for Retarded Citizens, World Wildlife Fund, Sierra Club.

AWARDS, HONORS: "Pick of the Lists," American Booksellers Association, 1990, for *Mrs. Toggle's Zipper; The Holiday Handwriting School* was named a Children's Choice book, International Reading Association and the Children's Book Council, 1992.

WRITINGS:

Mrs. Toggle's Zipper, illustrated by R. W. Alley, Four Winds, 1990.
The Holiday Handwriting School, illustrated by G. Brian Karas, Four Winds, 1991.
Mrs. Toggle and the Dinosaur, illustrated by Alley, Four Winds, 1991.
Nobody's Mother Is in Second Grade, illustrated by Karas, Dial, 1992.
Mrs. Toggle's Beautiful Blue Shoe, Four Winds, in press.
Homer and the House Next Door, Four Winds, in press.

Contributor of articles and stories to periodicals, including *Highlights for Children, Jack and Jill, Pockets, Cricket,* and *Ranger Rick.*

SIDELIGHTS: Robin Pulver commented: "I have always enjoyed writing and reading. As a child, I was shy about

speaking and relied on writing to express what I knew and felt. I think I unwittingly served an apprenticeship in writing for children when I studied journalism in graduate school, then short story writing. Both forms require economy of language and respect for every word.

"My appreciation of children's books deepened when my own children were born. I remember carrying my newborn infant daughter into a children's bookstore in 1978 and being swept off my feet by the beautiful language and extraordinary art. Reading to my two children from their earliest days gave me a profound appreciation of the impact of literature on children and families. Sharing books with my bright, language-loving daughter has been a joy. Reading to my son, who is handicapped but also bright and language-loving in his own way, has been a salvation. It has brought us precious moments of calm and touchstones for moments of recognition and laughter.

"It came as a happy surprise when I found that I could write and sometimes publish stories for children. My first publications were in magazines, then I wrote a story called *Mrs. Toggle's Zipper,* which became my first picture book. My goal is to write well enough to move people and offer them a good story to share. I would like to give back to children's literature the kind of gifts I have received from it."

*   *   *

PUTNEY, Martha S.   1916-

PERSONAL: Born November 9, 1916, in Norristown, PA; daughter of Oliver B. (a laborer) and Ida (a homemaker; maiden name, Baily) Settle; married William M. Putney (a federal government clerk), 1948 (deceased); children: William M., Jr. *Education:* Howard University, B.A., 1939, M.A., 1940, postdoctoral study, 1970-71; University of Pennsylvania, Ph.D., 1955. *Politics:* "A bit left of center on most issues." *Religion:* Protestant. *Avocational Interests:* Reading, professional sports.

ADDRESSES: Home—Washington, DC.

CAREER: Bowie State College, Bowie, MD, professor of history and chair of Department of History and Geography, 1955-74; Howard University, Washington, DC, part-time lecturer, 1971-74, senior lecturer, 1974-83. *Military service:* U.S. Army, Women's Army Corps, 1943-46; became first lieutenant.

MEMBER: Association for the Study of Afro-American Life and History, Afro-American Historical and Genealogical Society, National Association for the Advancement of Colored People, Association of Howard University Retirees.

AWARDS, HONORS: Danforth Foundation fellow in black studies, 1970-71; Outstanding Book Award from Gustavus Myers Center for the Study of Human Rights in the United States, 1992, for *When the Nation Was in Need.*

WRITINGS:

Black Sailors: Afro-American Merchant Seamen and Whalemen Prior to the Civil War, Greenwood Press, 1987.
When the Nation Was in Need: Blacks in the Women's Army Corps During World War II, Scarecrow, 1992.

Contributor of articles to periodicals, including *Maryland Historical Magazine, Journal of Negro History,* and *Journal of the Afro-American Historical and Genealogical Society.* Member of editorial board, *Journal of the Afro-American Historical and Genealogical Society,* 1983-92.

WORK IN PROGRESS: A book on blacks in the army; research on the social history of Norristown, Pennsylvania, during the Great Depression.

SIDELIGHTS: Martha S. Putney told *CA:* "I joined the Women's Army Auxiliary/Women's Army Corps, with an appointment for the duration of the war emergency, because I saw no career future in the federal civil service as a statistical clerk. I had applied for a position in the public school system of Washington, DC, after passing the qualifying examination. I wasn't too hopeful that I would be taken on since, according to widely held views, this system took care of its own. I was an outsider, a Pennsylvanian. My hometown offered nothing; only non-blacks were allowed to teach or work in the public schools. The corps, which was then less than a year old, promised an opportunity to become a commissioned officer. Though I had master's degree in history, I refused to go any further South for a job, so the promise of a commission was the best option available.

"Except for three or four incidents, and in view of the existing army policy and social climate of the 1940s, my service after basic training was both satisfying and rewarding. I felt I had helped hundreds of young women to adjust to army life, and helped others to be satisfied with nothing less than a job well done. I had good assignments at the basic training center at Fort Des Moines, Iowa, and as a commanding officer of a hospital company at Gardiner General Hospital in Chicago, Illinois. Along the way, I had observed some things, heard about still other things, and received letters from some of my fellow officers and former basic trainees, telling of their experiences, both the good and the bad. I left the corps with the intention of someday writing a history of the blacks in the corps during World War II.

"I wanted to get on with a career in teaching. I returned to the federal civil service for two years to replenish my wardrobe, get a place to call my own, and do something more for my parents before it was too late. Then I took advantage of the GI Bill to pursue a terminal degree at the University of Pennsylvania, a school I had wanted to attend as an undergraduate, but had neither the resources nor encouragement from my high school administrators who, like the army, had a very low estimation of the ability of blacks to do certain things. Once it was certain that I would be granted a degree, I had no trouble getting a job. My first major research project was examining the records at the National Archives on black merchant seamen whalers. I soon discovered that the project would require years of patient research, so I put that on hold and went on to other topics. I wanted to publish, not perish.

"Once *Black Sailors* was published, I felt it was time to turn to the story of blacks in the corps. I wanted to look at the corps objectively from a historian's point of view. The one important difficulty was the paucity of documents on blacks that were made available to researchers at the National Archives, but correspondence and interviews of those who served helped to fill in some details. This is a story of black women who served during a period of national emergency. They were among the pioneers in the corps; they made a contribution to the war effort; and they deserve to have their story told, and not just be a footnote in history."

*   *   *

QUAYE, Cofie 1947(?)-

PERSONAL: Some sources spell given name Kofi; born c. 1947 near Apan, Ghana. *Education:* Attended school to ninth grade; self-educated thereafter.

ADDRESSES: Office— c/o Macmillan Education, Macmillan Publishers Ltd., 4 Little Essex St., London WC2R 3LF, England.

CAREER: Fiction writer; clerk in Registrar General's Office in Accra, Ghana.

WRITINGS:

FICTION

Sammy Slams the Gang, Moxon Paperbacks, 1970.
Murder in Kumasi, Moxon Paperbacks, 1970.
The Takoradi Kidjackers, Moxon Paperbacks, c. 1971.
Foli Fights the Forgers, Macmillan Education, 1991.

Contributor of stories to periodicals, including *When and Where.**

QUAYE, Kofi
See QUAYE, Cofie

*   *   *

QUENNELL, Peter (Courtney)   1905-1993
(P. Q.)

OBITUARY NOTICE—See index for *CA* sketch: Born March 9, 1905, in Bickley, Kent, England; died October 27, 1993, in London, England. Biographer, essayist, poet, and author. Regarded with appreciation for his writing ability, Quennell was hailed by the London *Times* as "the last genuine example of the English man of letters." Born in an aristocratic English family, Quennell was famed for his social skills, and his acquaintances included such varied figures as actress Greta Garbo and author Graham Greene. Although Quennell attempted to pursue a conventional career, first as a teacher and later working for the Ministry of Information, it was as a writer that he made his living. Quennell published more than seventy books throughout his lifetime, and his writing portfolio included translations, biographies, critical essays, and poetry. Some of Quennell's best known literary works were his volumes on the English poet Lord Byron and included such titles as *Byron: The Years of Fame* and *Byronic Thoughts: Maxims, Reflections, and Portraits from the Prose and Verse of Lord Byron*. Additionally, Quennell studied seventeenth-century English literature and published numerous books on the subject, including *Samuel Johnson: His Friends and Enemies*, and although he was widely respected as a scholar, Quennell also gained fame for his personal life, which he recounted in books such as *The Marble Foot, The Wanton Chase: An Autobiography from 1939*, and *The Pursuit of Happiness*.

OBITUARIES AND OTHER SOURCES:

BOOKS

Who's Who in the World, 12th edition, Marquis, 1993.

PERIODICALS

Chicago Tribune, November 3, 1993, p. 3.
New York Times, October 31, 1993, p. 48.
Times (London), October 29, 1993, p. 23.

*   *   *

QUINTERO, Ruben   1949-

PERSONAL: Born May 5, 1949, in Montebello, CA; son of Ruben Gonzalez and Elena (Navarro) Quintero; married Evelia Hernandez, 1973; children: Ruben, Jr., Michael, Christopher, Mark. *Education:* California State University, Los Angeles, B.A. (philosophy), 1978, B.A. (English), 1980; Harvard University, A.M., 1983, Ph.D., 1988.

ADDRESSES: Office—Department of English, California State University, 5151 State University Dr., Los Angeles, CA 90032.

CAREER: California State University, Los Angeles, associate professor of English, 1988—. *Military service:* U.S. Army, 1969-71.

WRITINGS:

Literate Culture: Pope's Rhetorical Art, University of Delaware Press, 1992.

WORK IN PROGRESS: A novel, *Chance Images;* research on eighteenth-century British satire.

R

RA, Carol F.   1939-

PERSONAL: Surname is pronounced "rah"; born October 29, 1939, in Newport, IN; daughter of Samuel Wilson (a mechanic) and Elsie Maxine (a township trustee; maiden name, Kinderman) Hawn; married J. O. Ra, June 30, 1962 (divorced, 1980); children: Stephanie, Alison. *Education:* Attended Hollins College; Indiana State University, B.S., 1961; University of Illinois, M.Ed., 1968. *Politics:* Democrat. *Religion:* Methodist.

ADDRESSES: Home—P.O. Box 718, Cayuga, IN 47928-0718. *Agent*—Harriet Wasserman, 137 East 36th St., New York, NY 10016.

CAREER: Richmond City Schools, Richmond, IN, elementary school teacher, 1961-62; Vigo County Schools, Terre Haute, IN, elementary school teacher, 1962-64; Champaign Unit 4 Schools, Champaign, IN, teacher of gifted children, 1964-68; St. James Episcopal, Roanoke, VA, preschool director, 1973-74; Hollins College, Roanoke, lecturer in early childhood education and children's literature, 1974-87; *Herald News,* Cayuga, IN, editor and columnist, 1990—.

MEMBER: Delta Theta Tau, Kappa Delta Pi.

AWARDS, HONORS: Awarded Mellon Research grant to study children's folk rhymes while teaching at Hollins College.

WRITINGS:

Trot, Trot to Boston: Play Rhymes for Baby, illustrated by Catherine Stock, Lothrop, 1987.
(With William Jay Smith) *Behind the King's Kitchen: A Roster of Rhyming Riddles,* illustrated by Jacques Hnizdovsky, Boyds Mills Press, 1992.
(With Smith) *The Sun Is Up,* Boyds Mills Press, 1993.

Contributor of adult poetry to periodicals, including *Artemis, Passages North, Roanoke Review, Wind,* and *Blue Unicorn.* Contributor to *Anthology of Magazine Verse,* 1986-88 edition.

WORK IN PROGRESS: A collection of poems for children; a collection of nonsense verse; a collection of rhyming riddles.

SIDELIGHTS: Carol F. Ra was born at home in rural Indiana on the eve of World War II, and grew up during hard times. "Our family's socializing centered around visiting, and being visited by, relatives," Ra commented. "Sunday afternoons were the favored times for getting together with aunts, uncles and cousins. The games we played were full of rhymes and rhythms. We wrote rhymes in each other's autograph albums. We chanted taunts and teases. We wrote rhyming graffiti in our textbooks (this was accepted as all children had to buy their books). In elementary school I received a book of folk rhymes and riddles for my birthday. I read and re-read it until I had memorized the collection.

"While teaching at Hollins College, Virginia, I joined the Virginia Folklore Society," Ra said. "I was especially interested in folk rhymes. At the same time, I compiled a collection of folk rhymes from my childhood. I shared the collection with my sister, who helped me remember others. While teaching at Hollins, I received a Mellon research grant to study children's folk rhymes. I studied sources at the Library of Congress, the University of Virginia, the University of North Carolina, the University of Illinois, and in the rare books room at Hollins College. Subsequently I collected play rhymes that parents could do with their toddlers—for example, face-touching, toe-counting, and knee-riding rhymes. *Trot, Trot to Boston* is the result."

Living and teaching at Hollins College, with its emphasis on literature and writing, strongly influenced Ra's writing development. She commented: "At Hollins I attended Valery Nash's poetry workshops, and readings by W.H. Auden, Eudora Welty, James Dickey, Lee Smith, R.H.W. Dillard, Jeanne Larsen, and Richard Adams, among others. Many of these writers were Hollins faculty, products of the Hollins graduate program, or writers-in-residence there. The 1992 Nobel Prize winner in poetry, Derek Wolcott, was writer-in-residence at Hollins and a guest at my home on more than one occasion. The rich conversations with these writers over dinner, and the reading of their books expanded my knowledge and appreciation of literature. I love to read. My large library of literature, including a special collection of folklore, gathers very little dust."

*　　*　　*

RASKIN, A(braham) H(enry)　1911-1993

OBITUARY NOTICE—See index for *CA* sketch: Born April 26, 1911, in Edmonton, Alberta, Canada; died of cancer, December 22, 1993, in New York, NY. Journalist and author. In a journalism career that spanned over four decades, Raskin came to be known for his incisive and accurate commentary on numerous economic issues. Beginning his career as a local college correspondent for the *New York Times* in the early 1930s, Raskin went on to become assistant editor of the newspaper's editorial page in 1964. During his long career, Raskin covered such major economic and political events as the Great Depression of the 1930s and the Second World War. Except for a brief period during World War II, when he served as the chief of industrial services in the Pentagon, Raskin stayed with the *New York Times* until his retirement in 1977. In 1961 he became a member of the editorial board of the newspaper, and when Raskin finally ended his affiliation with the *New York Times,* he was writing his own column. Raskin came to be known as an authority on labor and industrial relations, and for his articles revealing racketeering activities prevalent in labor unions he was awarded the George Polk Memorial Award in 1953. In addition to writing for the *New York Times,* Raskin also coauthored books, including *David Dubinsky: A Life With Labor.*

OBITUARIES AND OTHER SOURCES:

BOOKS

International Authors and Writers Who's Who, 12th edition, International Biographical Centre, 1991.

PERIODICALS

Chicago Tribune, December 24, 1993, p. 9.
New York Times, December 23, 1993, p. B6.

RATHJE, William (Laurens)　1945-

PERSONAL: Born July 1, 1945, in South Bend, IN; son of Karl Laurens (a property manager) and Jane (a teacher; maiden name, Heald) Rathje; married Michele Brady (a flight attendant), May 4, 1970. *Education:* University of Arizona, B.A., 1967; Harvard University, Ph.D., 1971.

ADDRESSES: Office—Department of Anthropology, University of Arizona, Tucson, AZ 85721.

CAREER: University of Arizona, Tucson, assistant professor of anthropology, 1971-76, associate professor, 1976-80, professor, 1980—. The Garbage Project (a study of human behavior based on that which humans discard), Tucson, founder, 1972, director, 1973—.

MEMBER: Society for American Archaeology, Society for California Archaeology, Phi Beta Kappa, Phi Kappa Phi, Phi Eta Sigma, Sigma Xi.

AWARDS, HONORS: Fellow of American Anthropological Association.

WRITINGS:

(Under name William L. Rathje; with Michael B. Schiffer) *Archaeology,* Harcourt, 1982.
(With Cullen Murphy) *Rubbish!: The Archaeology of Garbage,* Harper, 1992.

Contributor of articles on "garbology" and Maya archaeology to professional journals. Contributor of essays to *Early Man Magazine, Atlantic Monthly, Garbage,* and *American Waste Digest.*

SIDELIGHTS: "Garbology"—the study of contemporary garbage—is a relatively new scientific discipline pioneered by archaeologist William Rathje, founder of the Garbage Project at the University of Arizona (an endeavor which investigates the behavior of a given people by excavating and examining their rubbish). Rathje, along with *Atlantic Monthly* managing editor Cullen Murphy, is also the coauthor of *Rubbish!: The Archaeology of Garbage,* an account of Rathje's garbological findings. Besides providing insight into the domestic lives of human beings—reconstructed from the analysis of refuse—the book discusses garbage from an ecological viewpoint, exposing popular misconceptions about the nature of recyclables, the contents of landfills, and rates of biodegradation.

During the twenty years the Garbage Project has been in existence, its discoveries have included—in the words of William Grimes in the *New York Times*—"forty-year-old hot dogs, perfectly preserved . . . and [a] head of lettuce still in pristine condition after twenty-five years." Preceding his description of the project's working procedures, Grimes commented that "the research material may be disgusting, but the analytical methods are refined. Mr.

Rathje's team excavates layer by layer, their trowel a spinning bucket auger suspended from a derrick. Working back through time, they sort the contents into 150 coded categories."

Rathje and Murphy present a number of examples in *Rubbish!* of how people's daily behavior can fall into patterns. By applying archaeological methods in the study of trash from certain neighborhoods, the Garbage Project "observed that much candy gets thrown away after Valentine's Day but very little after Halloween. It found that, following health warnings about the consumption of animal fat, people began trimming a higher percentage of fat from their steaks—and simultaneously increased their consumption of less obvious fat in foods like bologna," according to Ed Zuckerman in the *Los Angeles Times Book Review*. Researchers also found that many adults overstate the quantity of vegetables in their diet while understating the amount of junk food they eat.

The authors also point out that, despite the best efforts of environmentally-conscious recyclers, much reusable garbage goes unexploited because there is no substantial market for its product. For instance, because the scrap metal business is lucrative, most automobiles are recycled; but, as Kathleen Courrier commented in the *Washington Post Book World*, "glass recycling is a politically tricky proposition, paper recycling an economic roller-coaster ride, and rubber tires 'every landfill manager's nightmare.' " And on the subject of landfills, Rathje and Murphy note that while current sites are straining to contain the nation's mountains of trash, there are numerous locations on which to create new safe landfills that could service the United States well into the future.

Several critics praised *Rubbish!* for being both instructive and enjoyable. Zuckerman, in the *Los Angeles Times Book Review,* stated that the book "put[s] important garbage issues in perspective; it demolishes myths that hamper our ability to act sensibly; as a nice bonus, it entertains as it goes about its business." In addition, Courrier remarked in the *Washington Post Book World* that "the sensible advice pitched in *Rubbish!* should serve for a decade or so before future garbage gurus dump or recycle it. But more likely to impress readers are Rathje and Murphy's delightfully fresh take on human foibles and the garbage heap of history."

BIOGRAPHICAL/CRITICAL SOURCES:

PERIODICALS

Los Angeles Times Book Review, June 28, 1992, p. 1.
New York Times, August 13, 1992, p. B1.
Washington Post Book World, July 12, 1992, p. 7.

RATZ de TAGYOS, Paul 1958-

PERSONAL: Born January 30, 1958, in New Rochelle, NY; son of Paul (a fine artist) and Helen Ratz de Tagyos. *Education:* Attended Parsons School of Design. *Politics:* "Cynical." *Religion:* None. *Avocational Interests:* Landscape painting, microtonal music, walking, bicycling, Indian food ("eating, not cooking").

ADDRESSES: Home and office—30 Eastchester Rd., Apt. 6-A, New Rochelle, NY 10801.

CAREER: Commercial artist.

AWARDS, HONORS: Certificate of Merit, Society of Illustrators; Certificate of Design Excellence, *Print* magazine.

WRITINGS:

(Self-illustrated) *A Coney Tale,* Clarion, 1992.

WORK IN PROGRESS: Showdown in Lonesome Pellet (another coney story).

SIDELIGHTS: Paul Ratz de Tagyos has received favorable attention for his first book, *A Coney Tale.* In this work, a writer for *Kirkus Reviews* notes, the author-illustrator "creates an appealing coney (rabbit) society in 17th-century Flanders, with unique enterprises like a 'pad repair shop' and an 'ear care center' and respectable coney burghers eating salad in timbered houses." After it is discovered that a huge tree is actually an enormous carrot, the rabbits find a way to unearth it. They feast on it for months and transform the hole it created into a public fountain. "Skewed perspectives create an amiably offbeat effect in the clean, crisp artwork," proclaims a reviewer for *Publishers Weekly.*

Ratz de Tagyos commented that the "characters and their traits" in *A Coney Tale* are the "result of a longtime involvement I have with someone named Constance; I called her Coney. And it was, in fact, Coney who told me what a coney is. It's a bunny-rabbit, or dupe." *A Coney Tale* "is a direct adaptation from a bedtime story," he continues. "The prototype text [of the story] was verbose and endless (that's where editors come in, and I'm lucky with mine). I came to this project more as an illustrator with a story rather than an author with pictures. I feel much more comfortable with being the illustrator, it comes naturally."

BIOGRAPHICAL/CRITICAL SOURCES:

PERIODICALS

Kirkus Reviews, March 1, 1992.
Publishers Weekly, March 30, 1992.

RAY, Dixy Lee 1914-1994

OBITUARY NOTICE—See index for *CA* sketch: Original name, Margaret Ray; born September 3, 1914, in Tacoma, WA; died from a severe bronchial condition, January 2, 1994, in Fox Island, WA. Marine biologist, educator, public official, and author. A marine biologist by profession, Ray gained fame as a vocal supporter of nuclear development. A former professor of zoology at the University of Washington, Ray's public career began in 1973 when she became the first woman to be appointed as chair of the Atomic Energy Commission. After the Commission was dissolved, Ray turned her attention to the political arena and in 1976, she was elected the first woman governor of Washington. A strikingly unconventional woman, Ray gained significant media attention because of her strong advocacy nuclear development and openly voiced impatience with environmentalist movements. She expressed her opinions on the subject in two books, *Trashing the Planet: How Science Can Help Us Deal with Acid Rain, Depletion of the Ozone, and Nuclear Waste (among Other Things)* and *Environmental Overkill.*

OBITUARIES AND OTHER SOURCES:

BOOKS

The International Who's Who, 57th edition, Europa, 1993.

PERIODICALS

Chicago Tribune, January 4, 1994, p. 11.
New York Times, January 3, 1994, p. A24.

*   *   *

REDGRAVE, Michael (Scudamore) 1908-1985

PERSONAL: Born March 20, 1908, in Bristol, Gloucestershire, England; died of Parkinson's disease, March 21, 1985, in Denham, Buckinghamshire, England; son of George Ellsworthy (an actor under the name Roy Redgrave) and Margaret (an actress; maiden name, Scudamore) Redgrave; married Rachel Kempson (an actress), 1935; children: Vanessa, Corin, Lynn. *Education:* Attended Clifton College; Magdalene College, Cambridge, M.A., c. 1932. *Avocational Interests:* Reading, music.

CAREER: Actor, producer and director of stage productions, and writer. Worked as teacher at Cranleigh School in early 1930s. Actor with Liverpool Repertory Theatre, 1934-36, Old Vic company, 1936-37, John Gielgud's company, 1937-38, Michel St. Denis's company, 1938-39, Old Vic company, 1949-50, and Shakespeare Memorial Theatre Company, 1951, 1953, and 1958; headed own theatrical company. Actor in stage productions, including *A Month in the Country,* 1943; *Macbeth,* 1947; *Hamlet,*

1950; *The Tempest,* 1951; *King Lear,* 1953; *The Merchant of Venice,* 1953; *Tiger at the Gates,* 1955; *A Touch of the Sun,* 1958; *The Aspern Papers,* 1959-60; *Uncle Vanya,* 1962; *The Master Builder,* 1963; *The Hollow Crown,* 1973; *Shakespeare's People,* 1975, and *Close of Play,* 1979. Actor in motion pictures, including *The Lady Vanishes,* 1938; *Dead of Night,* 1945; *Mourning Becomes Electra,* 1947; *The Browning Version,* 1950; *The Importance of Being Earnest,* 1952; *1984,* 1955; *The Innocents,* 1961; *The Loneliness of the Long Distance Runner,* 1963; *Oh! What a Lovely War!,* 1969; and *The Go-Between,* 1971. Actor in television productions, including *Great War* and *Lost Peace.* Director of stage productions, including *Werther,* 1966; and *La Boheme,* 1967. Speaker for recordings, including *Sir Michael Redgrave Reads "The Harmfulness of Tobacco," "A Transgression," "The First Class Passenger" by Anton Chekhov.* Governor of the British Film Institute for three years; president of the English Speaking Board. *Military service:* Royal Navy, 1941-42.

MEMBER: Garrick Club.

AWARDS, HONORS: Academy Award nomination for best actor, Academy of Motion Picture Arts and Sciences, 1947, for *Mourning Becomes Electra;* award for best actor in a full-length film, Cannes International Film Festival, and awards from Finnish Film Journalists and Film Club of Buenos Aires, all 1951, for *The Browning Version;* named Commander of the Order of the British Empire, 1952; named Commander of the Order of Danneborg, 1955; New York Critics Award, 1955, for *Tiger at the Gates;* Actor-of-the-Year Award, Variety Club, and award from London *Evening Standard,* 1958, for *A Touch of the Sun,* and 1963, for *Uncle Vanya;* knighted, 1959; Grammy Award nomination for documentary or spoken word recording, National Academy of Recording Arts and Sciences, 1962, for *Sir Michael Redgrave Reads "The Harmfulness of Tobacco," "A Transgression," "The First Class Passenger" by Anton Chekhov;* D.Litt., University of Bristol, 1966; awards from various film festivals.

WRITINGS:

The Seventh Man (one-act play; adapted from Q's story; produced in 1935), Samuel French, 1936.
The Actor's Ways and Means, Theatre Arts Books, 1953.
Mask or Face: Reflections in an Actor's Mirror, Theatre Arts Books, 1955.
The Mountebank's Tale (novel), Harper, 1959.
The Aspern Papers: A Comedy of Letters (play; adapted from Henry James's story "The Aspern Papers"), Samuel French, 1959.
Circus Boy (play; produced in 1935), Samuel French, 1963.
In My Mind's I: An Actor's Autobiography, Viking, 1983.

SIDELIGHTS: Michael Redgrave ranked among England's most respected actors. The child of performers, Redgrave entered the theatre in the mid-1930s after working as a teacher at Cranleigh School, where his stage productions had readily won him substantial recognition. He spent two years at the Liverpool Repertory Theatre before legendary director Tyrone Guthrie called him to England's prestigious Old Vic company, where he gained supporting roles in various Shakespeare productions, including *Hamlet.* In 1938 Redgrave made his film debut in *The Lady Vanishes,* directed by Alfred Hitchcock, and throughout the next several decades he worked regularly in both theatre and film in England and the United States. His children—daughters Vanessa and Lynn and son Corin—also pursued successful acting careers, although Corin eventually took up politics.

With his significant height and striking, leading-man features, Redgrave readily won a widespread following, particularly in England. But his considerable expertise—derived from both intense practice and regular study of Konstantin Stanislavsky's classic actor's guide, *An Actor Prepares*—brought him to his generation's highest echelon of British acting, where he ranked with such luminaries as Laurence Olivier, John Gielgud, Ralph Richardson, and Peggy Ashcroft. Like these performers, Redgrave mostly distinguished himself on the stage, in the classic repertoire ranging from the works of Shakespeare to Anton Chekhov and from Oscar Wilde to Eugene O'Neill.

Redgrave had already been acting for more than fifteen years before he assayed his first *Hamlet* in 1950. During the next few years he added to his Shakespeare roles with the leads in *The Merchant of Venice, King Lear,* and *The Tempest.* On film, Redgrave won distinction with works such as *Dead of Night,* in which he played a schizophrenic ventriloquist undone by his dummy, and *1984,* where he appeared as a blithely treacherous drone. He appeared in numerous motion pictures derived from stage and literary works. Among the more successful films are *The Importance of Being Earnest,* a rendering of Oscar Wilde's comedy, and *The Innocents,* director Jack Clayton's adaptation of Henry James's horrific story "The Turn of the Screw."

It is probably for his Chekhov performances that Redgrave was, ultimately, best known. In 1962 he delivered what is often considered his finest stage work when he assayed the lead in Chekhov's *Uncle Vanya.* Here Redgrave compromised his imposing physical stature by stooping and lurching about, the better to convey the defeated nature of the work's bitter protagonist. The next year, Redgrave appeared in a film version of *Uncle Vanya,* which was directed by Laurence Olivier.

Redgrave worked regularly throughout the 1960s and 1970s in both theatrical and film productions. But he eventually contracted Parkinson's disease, which impaired his memory, speech, and mobility. He made his last stage appearance in a 1979 production of Simon Gray's *Close of Play,* where he played an incapacitated stroke victim.

After withdrawing from the acting profession, Redgrave concentrated on his writing. He had executed various literary endeavors throughout his career as an actor. In 1936, for instance, he published a play, *The Seventh Man,* and in 1953 he completed *The Actor's Ways and Means,* a volume providing insights into the acting craft. In 1955 he added a similar volume, *Mask or Face: Reflections in an Actor's Mirror,* and in 1959 he even published a novel, *The Mountebank's Tale,* which details an Englishman's worldwide search for a once-acclaimed actor. The publication of two more plays, *The Aspern Papers: A Comedy of Letters* (adapted from a Henry James story), and *Circus Boy,* followed.

But it was Redgrave's *In My Mind's I: An Actor's Autobiography,* which finally appeared in 1983, that was probably his best-known publication. In this book Redgrave recounted his experiences with other acclaimed actors, including Olivier and Gielgud, and offered numerous insights into theatre life. Hilary Spurling, writing in the *Times Literary Supplement,* declared that Redgrave's autobiography provides "a powerful sense of the theatre's importance . . . as a means of exploring reality while simultaneously holding it at bay." London *Times* reviewer Sheridan Morley favorably compared Redgrave's memoir to those of Olivier and Gielgud and proclaimed it "the best written [and] most turbulent of them all."

BIOGRAPHICAL/CRITICAL SOURCES:

BOOKS

Cole, Toby, and H. K. Chinoy, editors, *Actors on Acting,* Crown, 1949, pp. 385-90.
Findlater, Bruce, *Michael Redgrave, Actor,* introduction by Harold Clurman, Theatre Arts Books, 1956.
Grebanier, Bernard, *Then Came Each Actor,* McKay, 1975, pp. 504-08.
Redgrave, Michael, *In My Mind's I: An Actor's Autobiography,* Viking, 1983.
Ross, Lillian, and Helen Ross, *Player,* Simon & Schuster, 1962, pp. 334-43.

PERIODICALS

Chicago Tribune, March 28, 1985.
New York Times Book Review, May 29, 1960, p. 18; March 11, 1984, p. 19.
Spectator, November 13, 1953, p. 546.
Times (London), October 20, 1983.

Times Literary Supplement, October 21, 1983, p. 1149.
Washington Post Book World, November 20, 1983, pp. 14, 17.

OBITUARIES:

PERIODICALS

Detroit Free Press, March 22, 1985.
Los Angeles Times, March 22, 1985, pp. 3, 25.
Newsweek, April 1, 1985.
New York Times, March 22, 1985.
Time, April 1, 1985.
Times (London), March 22, 1985.
Washington Post, March 22, 1985.*

*   *   *

REDHEAD, Brian   1929-1994

OBITUARY NOTICE—See index for *CA* sketch: Born December 28, 1929, in Newcastle upon Tyne, England; died of kidney failure, January 23, 1994, in Macclesfield, England. Reporter, radio broadcaster, and author. The anchor of *Today,* an English radio program, for nearly two decades, Redhead was one of the most renowned broadcast personalities in England. Before attaining fame as a radio announcer, Redhead worked as a journalist with the *Guardian* from 1965 to 1975. Yet, even during his journalistic career, Redhead was actively involved in broadcasting, first as the presenter of a weekly television show and later as anchor of a Radio Four talk show. In 1976 Redhead made a successful transition to a full-time broadcasting career when he became anchorperson of *Today,* a popular morning show on British Broadcasting Corporation (BBC) radio. Redhead was known for his relaxed yet penetrating analysis of contemporary politics, and he went on to present other programs for BBC radio, including election coverage. A confirmed Anglican, Redhead wrote several documentaries on the history of Christianity, including *The Christian Centuries* and *Protesters for Paradise.* Redhead was also president of the Council for National Parks for many years, and his interest in this field led him to write many books such as *Love of the Lakes* and *The National Parks of England and Wales.*

OBITUARIES AND OTHER SOURCES:

BOOKS

Who's Who, 145th edition, St. Martin's, 1993.

PERIODICALS

Los Angeles Times, January 26, 1994, p. A24.
New York Times, January 25, 1994, p. B8.
Times (London), January 24, 1994, p. 19.

REEVES, Faye Couch   1953-

PERSONAL: Born June 17, 1953, in Seattle, WA; daughter of Joseph Douglas (in the military) and Helen (a homemaker; maiden name, Dunn) Couch; married Ronald G. Reeves (a systems analyst), November 24, 1979; children: Stephanie, Caitlin. *Education:* Moorhead State University, B.A. and B.S., both 1975. *Religion:* Presbyterian.

ADDRESSES: Home and office—8101 Sprenger N.E., Albuquerque, NM 87109. *Agent*—Andrea Brown Literary Agent, 1081 Alameda, Suite 71, Belmont, CA 94002.

CAREER: KBHB Radio, Sturgis, SD, copywriter, 1975-77; Burroughs Corporation, Albuquerque, NM, account manager, 1977-79; Children's Day Out, Albuquerque, teacher, 1980-88; free-lance writer, 1988—. Member of Parent-Teacher Association and Art in the School.

MEMBER: International Reading Association.

WRITINGS:

My Witness, United Methodist Reporter, 1989.
Howie Merton and the Magic Dust, illustrated by Jon Buller, Random House, 1991.
What Really Happened to Annabelle Dupree, Toll Associates, in press.

SIDELIGHTS: Faye Couch Reeves commented: "My favorite authors—Elizabeth Enright, Beverly Cleary, Eleanor Estes—have one thing in common: they make me laugh. They also make me cry, think, and feel, but they *always* make me laugh. Humor is the saving grace of everyday life, and I feel it is the most important aspect of what I write.

"*Howie and the Magic Dust* is the first book that I have ever written. One of the main characters owns a dead cat—this came from an episode in my own childhood. The funny, real things from childhood make the best stories, especially when something important was learned along the way.

"After my first book was published, I experienced the thrill of meeting my reading public—the children! They read my book and complete the communication circle. They tell *me* what my book was about. Their imaginations make my book bigger and better. I love to go into their classrooms and hear what they want to write about and what they like to read. They help me remember what it was like to be a child. What was scary? What was funny? I, in turn, encourage them to be *writers*—even if they have no desire to be *authors.*"

REICH, Howard 1954-

PERSONAL: Born April 19, 1954, in Chicago, IL; son of Robert and Sonia Reich; married Pam Becker (a journalist), June 29, 1986. *Education:* Northwestern University, B.Mus., 1977.

ADDRESSES: Office—Chicago Tribune, 435 North Michigan Ave., Chicago, IL 60611.

CAREER: Chicago Tribune, Chicago, IL, arts critic and jazz music critic, 1983—.

AWARDS, HONORS: Fellow of Music Critics Association, 1976; awarded key to the city of Fort Worth, Texas, 1993; Beck Award from *Chicago Tribune.*

WRITINGS:

Van Cliburn, Thomas Nelson, 1993.

Contributor to magazines, including *Down Beat,* and newspapers.

SIDELIGHTS: Howard Reich told *CA:* "I have been writing about the performing arts since 1976. As the *Tribune*'s arts critic and jazz critic since 1983, I have been fortunate to interview—and write extended pieces on—leading figures in American performing arts. These include Frank Sinatra, Dizzy Gillespie, Ella Fitzgerald, Gene Kelly, Martha Graham, Red Skelton, Van Cliburn, and Andres Segovia."

*   *   *

REISS, Kathryn 1957-

PERSONAL: Surname is pronounced "reese"; born December 4, 1957, in Cambridge, MA; daughter of Edmund Alan Reiss and Dorothy Ann (Kauffman) Molnar; married Thomas Strychacz (a professor), October 2, 1981; children: Nicholas, Daniel. *Education:* Duke University, B.A., 1980; attended Rheinische-Friedrich-Wilhelms-Universitat-Bonn, 1980-81; University of Michigan, M.F.A., 1988. *Avocational Interests:* Traveling, reading, collecting old series books.

ADDRESSES: Home—3 Faculty Village, Mills College, Oakland, CA 94613. *Agent*—Marilyn E. Marlow, Curtis Brown, Ltd., 10 Astor Pl., New York, NY 10003.

CAREER: Princeton Language Group, Princeton, NJ, instructor, 1981-82; Stuart Country Day School, Princeton, director of foreign exchange, 1981-82; Princeton Young Women's Christian Association (YWCA), instructor, 1981-82 and 1984; Europa at Princeton (bookshop), manager, 1982-83; Princeton Public Library, assistant to children's librarian, 1982-83; Trenton State College, Ewing, NJ, instructor, 1984-86; University of Michigan, Ann Arbor, instructor, 1986-88; Mills College, Oakland, CA, lecturer in English, 1989—. Princeton Arts Council, writer-in-residence, 1986.

MEMBER: Society of Children's Book Writers and Illustrators, Mystery Writers of America.

AWARDS, HONORS: American Field Service scholar, 1975; Fulbright-Hayes scholar, 1980-81; New Jersey State Council on the Arts grant, 1983-84; Cowden Memorial Prize for fiction, University of Michigan, 1987; Best Books for Young Adults citation, American Library Association, 1993, for *Time Windows.*

WRITINGS:

Time Windows (novel), Harcourt, 1991.
The Glass House People (novel), Harcourt, 1992.
Dreadful Sorry (novel), Harcourt, 1993.
Pale Phoenix (sequel to *Time Windows*), Harcourt, 1994.

Contributor of short stories to periodicals, including *The Archive.* Associate editor, *The Archive,* 1979-80.

WORK IN PROGRESS: Research on earthquakes, triplets and multiple births, and life in working-class areas of nineteenth-century England.

SIDELIGHTS: Kathryn Reiss commented: "There are certain stories that simply beg to be told. I feel a kind of urgency to write when I have a good plot in mind. But if I tell the tale verbally, much of the urgency disappears. It has become important for me to keep my plot to myself until I get it down at least in a rough form. If I share a story before it's written, the writing becomes a sort of rerun. Some of the energy is lost.

"After graduating from Duke University in 1980, I went to Bonn, Germany, to study at the university there. At one point I was up to my ears in [the German poet Johann Wolfgang] Goethe's works, analyzing them, writing about them, preparing to give an oral report in class (a scary thought!)—and I decided to take a day off from work just to read something light, preferably in English—despite my promise to myself to avoid the English language as much as I possibly could. I had read all of my English novels already, and it was pouring rain outside, so a trip to the bookstore didn't seem so good. I thought to myself: 'This is your chance. You've been saying for years that you want to write a book, right? So, why not start now?' I got a pad of paper and my pen, and sat down and started writing a story. When the rain stopped, I was still engaged in my new story, and I went out to sit on my little balcony (I rented a room in a big, drafty house) and kept on writing far into the night. I continued to write in my free time until I had an entire first draft of a novel. I revised it over several years (taking breaks to get married, to go to graduate school, and to have two children) and so produced my first novel, *Time Windows.*

"I am currently a lecturer at Mills College, where I teach writing. I have a special interest in our various notions of time—memory, perception, history, time travel (as a child I was always looking for ways to travel in time; perhaps my writing is my own version of a time machine!). I have a special interest in writing for middle grade and young adult audiences, and write the sort of books now that I liked when I was the age of my readers—especially favoring books about magic or mystery. I have many other story ideas waiting on the back burner."

*　　*　　*

REITZ, Miriam   1935-

PERSONAL: Born December 25, 1935, in Regina, Saskatchewan, Canada, to U.S. citizens; daughter of William A. (a Lutheran minister) and Adele E. (a homemaker; maiden name, Huth) Reitz; married Klaus Baer (a professor of Egyptology), July 20, 1985 (died May 14, 1987). *Education:* Valparaiso University, B.A. (with honors), 1958; University of Chicago, M.A., 1962, Ph.D., 1982; Family Institute of Chicago, Certificate in Family Psychotherapy, 1971. *Politics:* "Very independent." *Religion:* Lutheran. *Avocational Interests:* Ancient Egypt, reading, bicycling, hiking in Rocky Mountain National Park, opera.

ADDRESSES: Office—North Pier, Suite 320, 401 East Illinois St., Chicago, IL 60611.

CAREER: Elementary schoolteacher in Houston, TX, 1955-58; Lutheran Home and Service for the Aged, Arlington Heights, IL, social worker, 1958-60; Cook County Department of Public Aid, Chicago, IL, social field worker, 1960-62; Lutheran Child and Family Services, River Forest, IL, staff social worker, 1962-66; Community Family Service and Mental Health Center, LaGrange, IL, social worker, 1966-68, chief social worker, 1968-72; Northwestern Memorial Hospital and Medical School, Family Institute of Chicago, Center for Family Studies, Chicago, associate director of professional education, 1972-73, director of professional education, 1973-76, part-time staff member, 1976-82, coordinator of consultation and community services, 1982-88; private clinical practice of social work specializing in family and personal relationships, 1989—. Northwestern University, member of faculty of psychiatry and behavioral sciences, 1975-91; Institute for Clinical Social Work, faculty member, 1990—. Michael Reese Hospital (now Humana), social field worker, 1960-62. Rocky Ridge Music Center Foundation, vice-president, 1989—.

MEMBER: National Association of Social Workers, American Family Therapy Association, American Association for Marriage and Family Therapy (approved supervisor), Illinois Society for Clinical Social Work, Alumni Association of the Family Institute of Chicago.

WRITINGS:

(With Kenneth W. Watson) *Adoption and the Family System: Strategies for Treatment,* Guilford, 1992.

Contributor to periodicals, including *Family Process.*

WORK IN PROGRESS: Marriage in the Postmodern Era: A Study of the First Ten Years, completion expected in 1996.

SIDELIGHTS: Miriam Reitz told *CA:* "Although I have dabbled in writing since I was eight years old, my first book came out nearly fifty years later, in 1992. People who do not have children may need to create books. Unlike becoming parents, however, writing a book seems to require enough life (and in my case, clinical practice experience) to have something to contribute.

"My co-author Kenneth W. Watson and I discovered a tremendous gap in otherwise burgeoning literature about members of the adoption triad; no coherent assessment and treatment framework existed which could inform counselors who are confronted with triad members needing help. Between us, we have more than sixty years practice experience, so we had something to say. Furthermore, we believe we share a facility for translating complex theory into easily read and applied practice wisdom. The warm response to our book, especially from clinicians who are also adoption triad members, has been gratifying.

"My current work is an individual matter. The project began with the interviews of newlywed couples that formed the basis for my doctoral dissertation, completed in 1982. Since then, I have met with the couples again at years five and ten. This rich material is the basis for my book in progress. My long-range plan is to write another book on the second decade of these marriages.

"My projections also include a book on the development of psychotherapists as artists (as opposed to mechanics), as well as a novel about the interaction between a therapist's inner life and the therapist role. Meanwhile, I continue to dabble in various media: verbal presentations, professional and informal articles, verse for personal comfort or amusement, and most recently, editing clips from movies to make a videotape for teaching purposes."

*　　*　　*

RENZI, Thomas C.   1948-

PERSONAL: Born May 18, 1948, in Philadelphia, PA; son of John D. and Lillian R. (a keypuncher) Renzi; married Deborah K., November 28, 1986; children: Matthew T. *Education:* State University of New York at Buffalo, B.F.A., 1971, Ph.D., 1989. *Religion:* Roman Catholic.

ADDRESSES: Home—Snyder, NY. *Office*—Department of English, Erie Community College, Buffalo, NY 14221.

CAREER: Professional musician and music teacher, 1971-81; State University of New York College at Buffalo, lecturer in English, 1982-87 and 1989—; Erie Community College, Buffalo, instructor in English, 1990—. Canisius College, instructor, 1984-86; D'Youville College, instructor, 1985; Daemen College, instructor, 1993. Consortium of the Niagara Frontier, instructor at Collins Correctional Facility, 1985; Niagara Frontier Radio Reading Service, volunteer reader; conducts film seminars for libraries and schools. Recording artist with Caesar's Children; teacher of drums and percussion.

MEMBER: Modern Language Association of America, National Writers Club, United University Professionals, Musicians Union.

WRITINGS:

H. G. Wells: Six Scientific Romances Adapted for Film, Scarecrow, 1992.

Author of the unpublished novel *Strip Tease* and an unpublished collection of children's fairy tales titled *The Grandfather Tales.* Contributor to periodicals, including *Lost Creek Publications* and *Cricket.*

WORK IN PROGRESS: Film adaptations of Jules Verne's *Extraordinary Journeys.*

*   *   *

REYNOLDS, Joe
  See STEWARD, Samuel M(orris)

*   *   *

RICCI, David M. 1940-

PERSONAL: Born October 21, 1940, in New York, NY; son of Thomas and Clara Ricci; married, wife's name, Iry (a psychologist), 1962; children: Ronit, Anat, Tali. *Education:* Johns Hopkins University, B.A., 1962; Harvard University, Ph.D., 1969.

ADDRESSES: Home—Mevo Dakar 1, French Hill, Jerusalem, Israel 97855. *Office*—Department of Political Science, Hebrew University of Jerusalem, Mount Scopus Campus, Jerusalem, Israel 91505.

CAREER: Pennsylvania State University, University Park, assistant professor of political science, 1966-70; He-

brew University of Jerusalem, Jerusalem, Israel, lecturer, 1971-73, senior lecturer, 1974-84, associate professor of political science and American studies, 1984—, head of American studies department, 1979-81. University of Pennsylvania, visiting professor, 1976-77; American University, visiting professor, 1984; University of Tulsa, visiting professor, 1987. Woodrow Wilson International Center for Scholars, fellow, 1981-82; Institution for Advanced Study, Princeton, NJ, fellow, 1990-91; Brookings Institution, guest scholar, 1991.

AWARDS, HONORS: Fellow of Mellon Foundation, 1990-91.

WRITINGS:

(Editor with Edward Keynes) *Political Power, Community, and Democracy,* Rand McNally, 1970.
Community Power and Democratic Theory: The Logic of Political Analysis, Random House, 1971.
The Tragedy of Political Science: Politics, Scholarship, and Democracy, Yale University Press, 1984.
The Transformation of American Politics: The New Washington and the Rise of Think Tanks, Yale University Press, 1993.

Work represented in anthologies, including *Political Science Between the Past and the Future,* edited by Anckar and Berndtson, Finnish Political Science Association, 1988; and *Studies in American Civilization,* edited by Budick, Goren, and Slonim, Magnes, 1987. Contributor to political science journals.

WORK IN PROGRESS: A book-length study of citizenship in America, "comparing what Americans have endorsed as a vision of good citizenship with what research has discovered most citizens actually do."

*   *   *

RICHARDSON, Carl 1950-

PERSONAL: Born June 20, 1950, in Chicago, IL; son of an attorney and certified public accountant and Evelyn (Smolin) Richardson. *Education:* Received B.A., M.F.A., M.Phil., and Ph.D. from Columbia University. *Politics:* "Cautiously, even pessimistically, liberal." *Religion:* "Unaffiliated Christian." *Avocational Interests:* Music.

ADDRESSES: Home—55 Park Terrace E., No. B60, New York, NY 10034.

CAREER: Writer.

MEMBER: Society for Cinema Studies.

WRITINGS:

Autopsy: An Element of Realism in Film Noir, Scarecrow, 1992.

WORK IN PROGRESS: Two novels.

SIDELIGHTS: Carl Richardson told *CA:* "My one published title is the exception, rather than the rule, in my writing career. Since it appeared, I have written a number of novels, all of which have been rejected—rejected by somebody whose opinion I, more or less, have to defer to, owing to the high cost of reader fees and a lack of aggressiveness on my part. Writing, however, is meaningful labor and, when done seriously and sincerely, more than compensates for any career disappointments."

*   *   *

RICHTER, Daniel K(arl)   1954-

PERSONAL: Born October 15, 1954, in Erie, PA; son of Robert C. M. (a pastor) and Violet (a teacher; maiden name, Fennell) Richter; married Sharon L. Mead (a translator and writer), May 10, 1980; children: Thomas, Mary. *Education:* Thomas More College, B.A. (summa cum laude), 1976; Columbia University, M.A., 1977, M.Phil., 1979, Ph.D., 1984. *Politics:* Democrat. *Religion:* Lutheran. *Avocational Interests:* Woodworking, choral music.

ADDRESSES: Home—Carlisle, PA. *Office*—Department of History, Dickinson College, Carlisle, PA 17013-2896.

CAREER: Seton Hall University, East Orange, NJ, adjunct instructor in history, 1979; Columbia University, New York City, instructor in history, summer, 1981; Pace University, New York City, adjunct instructor in social sciences, 1981-82; Millersville State College, Millersville, PA, instructor in history, 1982-83; College of William and Mary, Williamsburg, VA, assistant professor of history, 1983-85; Dickinson College, Carlisle, PA, assistant professor, 1985-91, associate professor of history and member of American studies department, 1991—. University of East Anglia, Fulbright exchange lecturer, 1992-93.

MEMBER: American Historical Association, American Society for Ethnohistory, American Studies Association, Organization of American Historians, Associates of the Institute of Early American History and Culture, Historical Society of Pennsylvania.

AWARDS, HONORS: Harold L. Peterson Award for best article in American military history, Eastern National Parks and Monument Association, and prize for best article, Daughters of Colonial Wars, both 1983, for "War and Culture: The Iroquois Experience"; National Endowment for the Humanities, fellowship for Institute of Early American History and Culture, 1983-85, grant, 1991; Columbian Quincentennial fellow, Newbery Library, 1988 and 1990; Milton Klein Prize, Pennsylvania Historical

Association, 1991, for the article "A Framework for Pennsylvania Indian History"; fellow, Philadelphia Center for Early American Studies, 1991; Ray Allen Billington Prize and Frederick Jackson Turner Award, both from Organization of American Historians, 1993, for *The Ordeal of the Longhouse.*

WRITINGS:

(Editor with James H. Merrell, and contributor) *Beyond the Covenant Chain: The Iroquois and Their Neighbors in Indian North America, 1600-1800,* Syracuse University Press, 1987.
The Ordeal of the Longhouse: The Peoples of the Iroquois League in the Era of European Colonization, University of North Carolina Press, 1992.

Work featured in books, including *The American Indian, Past and Present,* 3rd edition, edited by Roger F. Nichols, Knopf, 1986; and *A Guide to the History of Pennsylvania,* edited by Francis J. Bremer and Dennis Downey, Greenwood Press, 1993. Contributor of articles and reviews to history journals. Also author of award-winning articles "War and Culture: The Iroquois Experience" and "A Framework for Pennsylvania Indian History." Associate editor, *Ethnohistory,* 1986-92; member of editorial board, *Pennsylvania History,* 1986-90.

WORK IN PROGRESS: After Independence: Pennsylvanians and Natives in the Post-Revolutionary Era, a book of essays.

*   *   *

RIDLEY, Ronald T(homas)   1940-

PERSONAL: Born December 27, 1940, in Burwood, New South Wales, Australia; son of Stanley Raphael (a toolmaker) and Dorothy Annie (a homemaker; maiden name, Jones) Ridley; married Therese Dominguez (a poet and translator), March 1, 1965. *Education:* University of Sydney, B.A. (with honors), 1962, M.A., 1966; University of Melbourne, Litt.D., 1992. *Politics:* "Left of center." *Religion:* "Rationalism."

ADDRESSES: Home—14 Mahoney St., Fitzroy, Victoria 3065, Australia. *Office*—Department of History, University of Melbourne, Parkville, Victoria 3052, Australia.

CAREER: University of Melbourne, Parkville, Australia, lecturer, 1965-73, senior lecturer, 1974-87, reader in history, 1988—.

MEMBER: International Association of Egyptologists, Society of Antiquaries of London (fellow).

WRITINGS:

The Unification of Egypt, Refulgence Press, 1973.

(Translator from Greek, and author of commentary) *Zosimus: New History,* Australian Association for Byzantine Studies, 1982.

Gibbons' Complement: Louis de Beaufort, Istituto Veneto, 1986.

A History of Rome, Bretschneider, 1987.

The Historical Observations of Jacob Perizonius, Accademia dei Lincei, 1991.

The Eagle and the Spade: The Archaeology of Rome during the Napoleonic Era, Cambridge University Press, 1992.

WORK IN PROGRESS: The Monuments of Melbourne, for Melbourne University Press; a biography of Carlo Fea, Papal Antiquarian; *The Life and Times of Bernardino Drovetti;* research on the conventions of Roman politics, completion expected c. 2003.

SIDELIGHTS: Ronald T. Ridley told *CA:* "My education, I am proud to say, has been entirely in state schools and universities of the highest standard. I also have not been guilty of what is known in Australia as 'cultural cringe,' the belief that our own culture is second-rate. I have not gone overseas, especially to Oxford or Cambridge, to obtain a 'real' degree.

"I was reared in a working class family and have never forgotten my father's stories at the dinner table of conditions for workers and the appalling treatment of ordinary people trying to earn a modest living.

"My passion for history goes back as long as I can remember. At about the age of ten, I was ensconced in the public library, copying out the lists of Egyptian kings in their dynasties. I studied Latin and Greek at school, and that led to history. The first great work I ever read was J. B. Bury's work on Greece. At university I majored in classics, but it was the historical side which engrossed my attention. I came under the spell of two of the greatest teachers ever in this country: Geoffrey Evans and Edwin Judge. After three years of tutoring and working on a master's degree, chance offered me a temporary lectureship at Melbourne and that became permanent when black fate caused the sudden death of the ancient historian John O'Brien. I have been at Melbourne ever since.

"Somewhere along the line, I realized that history itself is only part of the story; there is also the history of history. For about twenty years I have been considering major historical works from the Renaissance to the present, trying to understand why historians write as they do. Along the way, I have brought attention to two very great, but neglected, historians, the seventeenth-century Dutch Perizonius and the eighteenth-century French de Beaufort.

"It was a small step from there to the history of archaeology. The first time I left Australia was during a study leave in 1971. I spent most of it in Rome (which is still inexhaustibly fascinating to me), but there was also a visit to Egypt. These two cultures have led me to years of work in archives, especially in Rome and Paris, where I have reconstructed the whole story of the archaeology of Rome under Napoleon and the biography of a leading nineteenth-century diplomat named Bernardino Drovetti. I am conscious of a major advantage I have in dealing with controversial topics that cross national boundaries: I am a 'cosmopolitan' and thus free of the national prejudices that dominate most of the people who write about them.

"I believe there is not a more basic or fascinating subject than history. It has no boundaries. I approve most heartily of encouraging everyone to write it. On the other hand, history is the most demanding of professions, and its mastery is something for which a lifetime will not suffice. No profession has greater responsibilities, for at the stroke of a pen one can create heroes or villains. This power requires the greatest discretion."

* * *

RIEDER, Marge

PERSONAL: Born March 11, in Cuba, NY; daughter of Conly and Evelyn Morgan; married Alvin Rieder (a marine pilot), September 17, 1949 (divorced); children: Conly, Evie. *Education:* Santa Ana College, M.A., 1978; and Newport University, Ph.D., 1979. *Politics:* Democrat. *Religion:* Protestant.

ADDRESSES: Home and office—300 North Ellis, No. 26A, Lake Elsinore, CA 92530.

CAREER: A. Stein and Co. (clothing manufacturer), Los Angeles, CA, stylist, 1948-50; real estate salesperson in Orange County, CA, 1970-74; *Times-Bulletin,* Elsinore, CA, editor and reporter, 1974-75; Lakeview Hospital, public relations director, 1975-76; hypnotherapist. Member of American Board of Hypnotherapy; registered with Hypnotists Examining Council. *Military service:* U.S. Army Air Forces, 1944.

MEMBER: American Guild of Hypnotherapists.

WRITINGS:

Mission to Millboro, Blue Dolphin Publishing, 1993.

Author of the unpublished book *Truth Revealed.*

WORK IN PROGRESS: Return to Millboro; research on "spirit releasement therapy" and its effectiveness in the treatment of drug addiction.

SIDELIGHTS: Marge Rieder told *CA:* "I first wrote professionally when I was employed by A. Stein and Company. I was a stylist, which involved public relations work and promotion. Part of my job was to entertain fashion editors from large newspapers, present each one with a new garment, and hope they would write about it. On one occasion, after presenting an editor with a garment in her size, she said, 'It looks good. Write the column and I will run it.' So I did, and she did, mistakes and all. From that day on, I was a writer.

"I became interested in past-life regression while living in Japan in 1965. From the marine post library, I obtained a copy of *The Search for Bridey Murphy* by Morey Bernstein. The book enthralled me, and I vowed someday to investigate past-life regressions. I am doing this now.

"Since 1986, I have been obsessed with writing *Mission to Millboro* and its sequel, which is even more fascinating than the first volume. Hopefully it will soon be finished and published. Then I hope to devote myself to experimenting in spirit releasement therapy. If successful, I plan to compile my research into a book."

*   *   *

RIJKENS, Rein 1913-

PERSONAL: Born February 13, 1913, in Amsterdam, Netherlands; son of Rein (a doctor) and Bertha Julia (Culp) Rijkens; married Claire Schrijver, 1936; children: Rein, Paul, Maarten.

ADDRESSES: Home—452, Ruychrocklaan, The Hague 2597 EJ, Netherlands.

CAREER: Unilever, Rotterdam, Netherlands, manager in marketing and advertising divisions, 1946-78; consultant and writer. Worked in insurance business, beginning in 1936.

MEMBER: International Advertising Association (honorary life member), European Association of Advertising Agencies (president, 1975-78).

AWARDS, HONORS: Honorary diploma, Communication, Advertising, and Marketing Education Foundation, 1982.

WRITINGS:

(With Gordon Miracle) *European Regulation of Advertising,* Elsevier (Amsterdam, Netherlands), 1986.
European Advertising Strategies, Cassell (London), 1992.

European Advertising Strategies has been published in Japanese.

Also author of *The Saga of the Directive on Misleading Advertising,* with Gordon Miracle and Alastair Tempest, International Journal of Advertising, 1988.

SIDELIGHTS: Rein Rijkens told *CA:* "I started my career in 1936 in the insurance business in Holland, and in 1946 I joined Unilever in Rotterdam, where I held managerial functions in marketing and advertising until my retirement in 1978. I then started a marketing and advertising consultancy based upon my presidency of the European Association of Advertising Agencies between 1975 and 1978. The consultancy prompted me to write, with Gordon Miracle, *European Regulation of Advertising,* which was followed by *European Advertising Strategies.* No more books are planned."

*   *   *

RILEY, Joan 1958-

PERSONAL: Born May 26, 1958, in Hopewell, St. Mary, Jamaica; children: Lethna, Bayhano. *Education:* University of Sussex, B.A. (honors), 1979; University of London, M.A. and M.Sc., 1984. *Politics:* "Left of center."

ADDRESSES: Home—London, England. *Agent*—Anthony Harwood, Curtis Brown, 162-164 Regent St., London W1R 5TB, England.

CAREER: Drug Advice and Research Office, London, England, researcher, 1983-85; CALC, London, action researcher, 1985-87; free-lance drug adviser and consultant, 1989; social welfare worker in London.

MEMBER: Society of Authors.

WRITINGS:

The Unbecoming, Women's Press, 1985.
Waiting in the Twilight, Women's Press, 1987.
Romance, Women's Press, 1988.
A Kindness to the Children, Women's Press, 1992.

WORK IN PROGRESS: An anthology, *Leave to Stay: Migration in Fiction and Poetry from the Four Corners of the Earth;* a novel, *Beachwater.*

SIDELIGHTS: Joan Riley told *CA:* "I was born in rural Jamaica, the youngest of eight children. From an early age, I found escape from the harsh reality of that childhood on the shelves of the local library. One read what was available and, for me, this ranged from Shakespeare to Greek mythology, Thomas Hobbes to Aristotle, Thomas Hardy, and Caribbean writers. At the age of seven I decided I would be a great poet, but after having one poem published at the age of nine, I 'retired' to concentrate on the common entrance exam. It was never my intention after that to become a writer, though my love for books remained.

"I studied international relations at university and, later, applied social studies, politics, and government at graduate school. As an undergraduate, I had a zeal to change the world, but after eighteen months I felt more inclined to make tangible change happen on a small scale. I became involved in social welfare as a community service volunteer, and along with vacation work stumbled across the unanswerable questions that were to fuel my writing.

"Jamaica has a projection for the outside world necessary for its image as a 'safe' tourist destination which hid the reality of misery and seething anger of a great deal of the population. I now found this 'underbelly' of society was not unique but universal. I have worked with drug users, torture victims, and social outcasts in many guises, and my personal philosophy is one of individual and collective responsibility for social situations. I am endlessly fascinated by the multiplicity of human presentations which form the human condition. My curiosity and my work provide endless areas to explore and convert into my literature."

* * *

RITCHIE, Harry 1958-

PERSONAL: Born January 7, 1958, in Kirkcaldy, Scotland; son of William and Janet (Murrie) Ritchie. *Education:* University of Edinburgh, M.A., 1979; Lincoln College, Oxford, D.Phil., 1985. *Politics:* "Scottish nationalist."

ADDRESSES: Office—Sunday Times, 1 Pennington St., London E1 9XW, England. *Agent*—Rachel Calder, Tessa Sayle Agency, 11 Jubilee Pl., London SW3 3TE, England.

CAREER: Sunday Times, London, England, deputy literary editor, 1988-92, literary editor, 1993—.

WRITINGS:

Success Stories, Faber, 1988.
Here We Go: A Summer on the Costa del Sol, Hamish Hamilton, 1993.

* * *

ROBERTS, Elfed Vaughan 1946-

PERSONAL: Born April 5, 1946, in Rhosllanerchvugog; son of John William (a coal miner) and Dorothy (Williams) Roberts; married, wife's name Dawn (a teacher), November 9, 1968; children: Gwilym, Emily, Mair. *Education:* Attended University of Wales, University College of Wales, Aberystwyth. *Politics:* "Floating." *Religion:* Church in Wales.

ADDRESSES: Home—5A Alberose, 134 Porfulham Rd., Hong Kong. *Office*—Department of Politics and Public Administration, University of Hong Kong, Hong Kong.

CAREER: University of Wolverhampton, Wolverhampton, England, senior lecturer, 1969-78; University of Hong Kong, affiliated with politics and public administration department, 1978—. Hong Kong "A" Levels Government and Politics Committee, chairperson; Hong Kong Welsh Male Voice Choir, chairperson; consultant to Royal Hong Kong Police Force.

MEMBER: Royal Asiatic Society, British International Studies Association, St. David's Society of Hong Kong (president).

WRITINGS:

(With S. Davies) *Political Dictionary for Hong Kong,* Macmillan, 1990.
(With R. D. Hill and N. Owen) *Fishing in Troubled Waters,* Centre of Asian Studies, 1991.
Social Sciences, Open Learning Institute (Hong Kong), 1991.
(With P. Bradshaw and Sum Ngai Ling) *A Historical Dictionary of Hong Kong and Macao,* Scarecrow, 1992.

Contributor to local periodicals.

WORK IN PROGRESS: Provincialism in Guangong Province; research on Hong Kong and the future.

SIDELIGHTS: Elfed Vaughan Roberts told *CA:* "My reason for writing depends, primarily, on what I am writing about. I write academic tracts for a number of reasons, not least because I am obliged to as a function of my profession. This impulse is, of course, hardly original in the intensely competitive academic environment. Whether it advances my career is a matter of superb indifference. I must admit to a sneaking gratification from seeing my name on the cover of a book and like to pleasure myself with the thought that someone, somewhere, might find what I write of some use. I do not, however, indulge in the fantasy of my setting the world alight with my modest contributions.

"Far more important to me is writing for the pure fun of seeing a blank page and letting a stream of consciousness flow across virgin space, a failing (or strength) most Welsh people share as aspirant, but usually pale, reflections of Dylan Thomas. This is why my broadcasts on local radio in such programs as *Letter From Hong Kong* give me real pleasure. It is also why I enjoy writing for the local press in Hong Kong on topics of my own choice. Here, in the problematical transition stage from British to Chinese administration, self-censorship is a major threat to the freedom of expression. The freedom to write for a wider, less rarefied audience, to dispense with accepted form, to allow for a degree of humor, and to present arguments, not necessarily backed up with turgid, evidential overkill, is what I would choose as my ideal medium of communication.

Perhaps I should try to produce the, as yet unwritten, Great Hong Kong Novel . . . "

* * *

ROBESON, Paul, Jr. 1927-

PERSONAL: Born November 2, 1927, in Brooklyn, NY; son of Paul Leroy (an actor and singer) and Eslanda Cardozo (an anthropologist; maiden name, Goode) Robeson; married Marilyn Paula Greenberg (a human resources manager), June 19, 1949; children: David Paul, Susan. *Education:* Cornell University, B.S.E.E., 1949. *Politics:* Democrat. *Religion:* Protestant. *Avocational Interests:* Sports, travel.

ADDRESSES: Home and office—350 Clermont Ave., Brooklyn, NY 11238. *Agent*—Lawrence Jordan, 250 West 57th St., Suite 1527, New York, NY 10107.

CAREER: School of Industrial Technology, New York City, teacher of electronics and power engineering, 1949-53; Plenum Press, New York City, translator, 1953-57; International Physical Index, New York City, editor, 1957-72, publisher, 1973-81; Allerton Press, New York City, translator and consultant, 1982-91. WNET-TV, host of the program *Paul Robeson: Man of Conscience,* 1986; WBAI-FM Radio, host of a weekly program *The USSR in Change,* 1986-87. American Program Bureau, lecturer, 1979-89; Program Corp. of America, lecturer, 1990-92. Manhattanville Tenants Association, president, 1962-64. *Military service:* U.S. Army Air Forces, 1946-47.

MEMBER: American Physical Society, New York Academy of Sciences, Tau Beta Pi, Eta Kappa Nu.

WRITINGS:

Paul Robeson, Jr. Speaks to America, Rutgers University Press, 1993.

Columnist for *New York Amsterdam News,* 1985-87. Contributor to periodicals, including *Jewish Currents* and *Science and Society.* Editor, *Monthly Digest of Russian Scientific Literature,* 1957-70.

WORK IN PROGRESS: The Undiscovered Paul Robeson; The Inside Paul Robeson Story; Russia in Change: The Gorbachev Revolution.

SIDELIGHTS: Paul Robeson, Jr. told *CA:* "During the 1930s, I traveled extensively with my parents, while my father pursued his career abroad as a singer and actor. I lived in England, Austria, Switzerland, and the Soviet Union, and learned to speak German and Russian fluently. In 1936 I accompanied my mother, a student of anthropology, on a three-month trip to Africa, where we

traveled and stayed in South Africa, Kenya, Uganda, and the Congo. At the age of twelve, I returned to the United States, where I completed my education.

"From 1949 until his retirement in 1965, I worked closely with my father as his personal representative and political adviser. Because he was frequently refused access to recording studios and concert halls during the 1950s, I produced, recorded, and edited many of the recordings currently in the Paul Robeson Collection. A number of them appear on compact discs and tape cassettes which have been released on major labels. After my father's retirement in 1965, I handled his personal affairs until his death in 1976.

"In May of 1980, my wife and I spent four weeks in China at the invitation of the Chinese Government. In addition to meetings with China's Vice-President Madame Soong Ching Ling and other important figures in China's major cities, our hosts arranged a special week-long visit to the Uygur Autonomous Region of Xinjiang in northwest China as part of our study of China's national minorities.

"In 1982 we were invited by the Indian Government to lecture and travel in India. During visits to six cities, a private visit with Prime Minister Indira Gandhi and meetings with other government leaders were arranged, and I lectured on the topic 'Paul Robeson: The Artist and the Universality of the African-American Cultural Tradition.' In 1989 I was invited to participate in the Earth Citizen Conference held in New Delhi in memory of Indira Gandhi.

"Since my early residence and schooling in Western Europe and the Soviet Union, I have made subsequent visits to conduct research and to lecture, thus maintaining an ongoing familiarity with the cultures and sociopolitical systems of both Eastern and Western Europe. In 1982 I joined Daniel Singer, author of *The Road to Gdansk,* as a featured speaker on a national tour in support of Poland's Solidarity Movement. In a 1983 lecture at Cornell University, I pointed to the strong possibility of fundamental political reform in the Soviet Union and, with Gorbachev's accession to power as the paramount Soviet leader in 1985, I advanced the view that his reform program was designed to achieve a gradual political revolution.

"My main concern these days is the political, economic, and cultural crisis sweeping across the United States. In the aftermath of the Cold War's end and the disappearance of major external 'enemies,' the failure of liberal democracy and its melting pot is apparent.

"The rising challenge of social democracy with its mosaic culture is already transforming American politics. Moreover, the issues of culture and economic fairness are relentlessly overtaking the issues of race and taxes.

"Abroad, it is now clear that what has occurred is the demise of Stalinism and most of Leninism, rather than the demise of Marxism. In fact, Marx and Engels are rising from the ashes in the form of a rejection of liberal 'free-market' economics and a search for populist social democracy with a mixed economy. In this global environment, America's dream of being 'the world's only superpower' is an idle one.

"America's domestic threat does not stem primarily from fundamentalist terrorism, immigration, crime, racial and ethnic divisions, or 'big government,' though all of these problems desperately need attention and practical remedies. The true threat to the long-term survival of our society is class warfare between a middle class that has benefited from twelve years of 'trickle-down Reaganomics' and the working class and poor, who have suffered as a result of United States economic priorities. This fault line lies at the annual family income of about forty-to-fifty-thousand dollars, and is the harbinger of a civil war rather than a race war.

"So it is time for the melting-pot culture, with its racial stereotypes, its exclusively middle-class value system, and its fanatical insistence on radical individualism, to yield up the stage of history to the more equitable and just mosaic culture of the future. The mosaic culture is already a part of the American tradition. President Lincoln and his Gettysburg Address placed the Union and community responsibility above President Jefferson's constitution that enshrined radical individualism, accepted slavery, and fathered the Confederacy."

*   *   *

ROBINSON, Blake   1932-

PERSONAL: Born February 29, 1932, in Worcester, MA.

ADDRESSES: Home—649 C St. S.E., Apt. 107, Washington, DC 20003.

CAREER: Translator.

WRITINGS:

(Translator) *Remember Me, God of Love: The Poetry and Prose of Sandro Penna,* Carcanet Press, 1993.

WORK IN PROGRESS: Translating Joe Bousquet's *La Tisane de sarments; Distichs,* a book of poems.

ROBINSON, Linda   1960-

PERSONAL: Born January 15, 1960, in Pittsburgh, PA; daughter of William (a corporate executive in the semiconductor industry) and L. Kathry (a homemaker; maiden name, Gregory) Robinson. *Education:* Swarthmore College, B.A. (with high honors), 1982.

ADDRESSES: Home—Miami Beach, FL. *Office*—2801 Ponce de Leon Blvd., Suite 555, Coral Gables, FL 33134.

CAREER: Wilson Quarterly, Washington, DC, assistant editor, 1982-83; *Foreign Affairs,* New York City, began as member of editorial staff, became senior editor, 1983-89; *U.S. News & World Report,* Miami, FL, Latin America correspondent, 1989—.

MEMBER: International Institute of Strategic Studies.

WRITINGS:

Intervention or Neglect: The United States and Central America Beyond the 1980s, Council on Foreign Relations Press, 1991.

Work represented in anthologies. Contributor of articles and reviews to periodicals.

*   *   *

RODGER, Richard   1947-

PERSONAL: Born in 1947 in Norfolk, England; married; children: two. *Education:* University of Edinburgh, M.A., 1969, Ph.D., 1975.

ADDRESSES: Office—Department of Economic and Social History, University of Leicester, Leicester LE1 7RH, England.

CAREER: University of Liverpool, Liverpool, England, lecturer in economic history, 1971-79; University of Leicester, Leicester, England, lecturer, 1979-88, senior lecturer in economic and social history, 1988—. University of Kansas, associate professor, 1982-83, 1987, visiting research fellow (Center for the Humanities), 1986-87; Trinity College (Hartford, CT), visiting professor, 1990.

WRITINGS:

(With D. H. Aldcroft) *A Bibliography of European Economic and Social History,* Manchester University Press, 1984, 2nd edition, 1993.
Housing in Urban Britain, 1780-1914: Class, Capitalism, and Construction, Macmillan, 1989.
(Editor) *Scottish Housing in the Twentieth Century,* Leicester University Press, 1989.
(With Linda McKenna) *The Economic History Review Index, Second Series, Volumes XXIV-XLII, 1971-1989,* Basil Blackwell, 1991.

(Editor) *European Urban History: Prospect and Retrospect,* Leicester University Press, 1993.

(Editor with R. J. Morris) *The Victorian City: A Reader in British Urban History, 1820-1914,* Longman, 1993.

(Editor with D. Reeder, D. N. Nash, and P. Jones) *Leicester in the Twentieth Century,* Alan Sutton, 1993.

Research in Urban History, Scolar, 1993.

Author of eight computing guides in the series "A Student's Guide to . . . ," including *Word 4, Cricket Graph, Excel, Filemaker Pro,* and *WordPerfect for the IBM and Macintosh.* Editor of *Urban History Yearbook,* 1987-91. Editor of *Urban History,* 1991—.

*   *   *

ROE, JoAnn

PERSONAL: Born in Crookston, MN; daughter of Casper (a farmer) and Andrea (a teacher; maiden name, Quill) Roe; married Ernest C. Burkhart (a manufacturer), December 15, 1950; children: Shelley Ann Burkhart Hanaoka, Scott Charles, Donovan Lee, Denise Jan Burkhart Swerland. *Education:* Attended University of Minnesota—Twin Cities, University of Southern California, and University of California, Los Angeles; earned A.A. degree. *Politics:* "Usually Republican." *Religion:* Presbyterian.

ADDRESSES: Home and office—5041 Meridian Rd., Bellingham, WA 98226.

CAREER: John Freiburg Advertising Agency, copywriter, 1945-46; *Guest Informant,* Los Angeles, CA, advertising writer, 1946-47; JoAnn Roe Advertising Agency, Los Angeles, owner, 1948-52; free-lance public relations and magazine writer, 1952-64; Skyhaven, Inc., Bellingham, WA, public relations manager, 1964-66; Northwestern Technology, Inc., secretary, treasurer, and member of board of directors, 1967-70; IGM Communications, Bellingham, secretary, treasurer, and member of board of directors, 1974-80, public relations manager, 1980-84; free-lance writer, 1984—. Assistance League of Bellingham, member of board of directors, intermittently, 1977—; Women of Rotary, past president.

MEMBER: Western Writers of America, National Federation of Press Women, Society of Children's Book Writers, Pacific Northwest Historians Guild, Washington Press Association (member of state board of directors).

AWARDS, HONORS: Named Woman of Achievement by Washington Press Association, 1984; local Mayor's Arts Award, 1988; Bellingham Tourism Award, 1988; President's Award from Japan-America Society; Washington Governor's Award; awards from Photographic Historical Society of New York and Pacific Northwest Booksellers.

WRITINGS:

The North Cascadians, Montevista Press, 1980.

The Real Old West, Douglas & McIntyre, 1981.

Frank Matsura, Frontier Photographer, Madrona Publishers, 1981.

F. S. Matsura, Heibonsha Publishers (Tokyo), 1983.

Sayonara Frank (television movie), broadcast by TV Asahi (Tokyo), 1984.

The Columbia River: A Historical Travel Guide, Fulcrum Publishing, 1992.

Ghost Towns and Mining Camps, Sunfire Publishers (Langley, British Columbia), 1994.

Stevens Pass, Mountaineers Books, in press.

Contributor of numerous articles and photographic illustrations to magazines.

CHILDREN'S BOOKS

Castaway Cat, Montevista Press, 1984.

Fisherman Cat, Montevista Press, 1988.

Alaska Cat, Montevista Press, 1990.

Samurai Cat, Montevista Press, 1993.

WORK IN PROGRESS: Research on Ranald MacDonald, the first teacher of English in Japan; research on the history of the Great Northern Railway and the history of Blakely Island.

SIDELIGHTS: JoAnn Roe told *CA:* "I am a professional writer, educated as such and able to write about many subjects with diverse slants. My main love is writing magazine articles, because of the extreme range of topics that one can explore. I enjoy the interviews with individuals and companies immensely, and the feeling of learning a little bit about many things. I think that visitors to an area enjoy their trips more by knowing the area's history. Outdoor subjects with a historical slant are particularly favorite topics. My adult books range through the history of places, but stress the human interest stories of the people who lived the history. My children's books seek to teach the reader about real life situations, which are carefully researched, but I also believe a children's book should have a strong plot and believable characters.

"Writing for publication requires considerable discipline to follow a trail thoroughly, yet not be distracted into subtopics that consume undue time for research. I believe most people like to read history that is not too pedantic, about people who could have been one's next door neighbors or peers."

ROOSA, Robert V(incent) 1918-1993

OBITUARY NOTICE—See index for *CA* sketch: Born June 21, 1918, in Marquette, MI; died of prostate cancer, December 23, 1993, in Port Chester, NY. Banker and author. Widely acknowledged as a financial expert, Roosa was one of the youngest people to become Undersecretary of the Treasury for monetary affairs. Prior to this appointment, Roosa had distinguished himself by attaining the rank of vice president at the Federal Reserve Bank, where he worked from 1946 to 1960. Continuing his involvement with financial affairs after his stint with the treasury, Roosa became a partner in the private banking firm of Brown Brothers Harriman & Company. He remained there until his retirement in 1991. Roosa also held numerous posts as director and trustee of organizations like the National Bureau of Economic Research and the United Nations Association. Roosa's expertise in finance also led him to write several books on the subject, including *Monetary Reform for the World Economy* and *The Dollar and World Liquidity.*

OBITUARIES AND OTHER SOURCES:

BOOKS

Who's Who in America, 47th edition, Marquis, 1992.

PERIODICALS

New York Times, December 25, 1993, p. 37.
Washington Post, December 25, 1993, p. C4.

*   *   *

ROSENBERG, Blanca 1913-

PERSONAL: Born December 26, 1913, in Gorlice, Poland; immigrated to the United States, 1949; daughter of Eli (in business) and Eleonore (Nebenzahl) Ehrenreich; married Wolf Rosenkranz (a physician; divorced, 1945); married Samuel Theodore Rosenberg (a physician; died, 1987); children: (second marriage) Alexander and Mark (twins). *Education:* Columbia University, M.S., 1955. *Politics:* Democrat. *Religion:* Jewish.

ADDRESSES: Home and office—800 West End Ave., No. 4D, New York, NY 10025.

CAREER: Veterans Administration, New York City, clinical social worker, 1955-63; Colulmbia University, New York City, professor of social work, 1963-84; private practice of individual and family counseling, 1963—.

WRITINGS:

To Tell at Last: Survival Under False Identity, 1941-45, University of Illinois Press, 1993.

Contributor to social work journals.

SIDELIGHTS: Blanca Rosenberg told *CA:* "I am a Holocaust survivor who immigrated to the United States in 1949, with my husband and twin sons, aged two-and-a-half. My book is the account of my personal memories of the Holocaust years, written originally in my native language, and translated (by me) more than forty years later. It is a book of pain and faith, love and sacrifice, loyalty and friendship and, above all, it served as a personal opportunity to mourn my losses and begin a healing process. My recent motivation to publish the book was engendered by my wish to share my life and our heritage with my children and grandchildren, an overwhelming desire to give meaning to the personal sacrifices of my family and especially my heroic brother Romek, and to bear witness so that our horrors will never be forgotten. I hope that my book and those of other Holocaust writers will stand as a bulwark against the incredible attempts of the revisionists to rewrite history by denying the existence of the Holocaust."

*   *   *

ROSS, Alan O(tto) 1921-1993

OBITUARY NOTICE—See index for *CA* sketch: Born December 7, 1921, in Frankfurt am Main, Germany; died of a brain tumor, December 21, 1993, in East Setauket, NY. Psychologist, educator, and author. Ross, who specialized in clinical psychology for children, served from 1959 to 1967 as chief psychologist at the Pittsburgh Child Guidance Center in Pennsylvania. Among the works he published during this period are *The Practice of Clinical Child Psychology* (a standard textbook), *The Exceptional Child in the Family,* and *The Professional Preparation of Clinical Psychologists.* Named professor of psychology at the State University of New York at Stony Brook in 1967, Ross oversaw the department's clinical training program until his retirement in 1991. The author of numerous professional articles, Ross also wrote *Psychological Disorders of Children* and *Psychological Aspects of Learning Disabilities and Reading Disorders.*

OBITUARIES AND OTHER SOURCES:

BOOKS

Who's Who in America, 48th edition, Marquis, 1994.

PERIODICALS

New York Times, December 24, 1993, p. B7.

*   *   *

ROTHMILLER, Mike 1950-

PERSONAL: Born October 12, 1950, in Lynwood, CA; son of John and Elizabeth Rothmiller; married May 10,

1975; wife's name, Nancy Marie (a bank executive). *Education:* Los Angeles Junior College, A.A., 1971; University of Redlands, B.A., 1978. *Avocational Interests:* Piloting, scuba diving, big-game fishing.

ADDRESSES: Agent—Michael Hamilburg, Mitchell J. Hamilburg Agency, Suite 312, 292 South La Cienega Blvd., Beverly Hills, CA 90211.

CAREER: Los Angeles Police Department, Los Angeles, CA, intelligence detective, 1972-83; television producer and reporter, 1984—; writer. *Military service:* U.S. National Guard.

WRITINGS:

(With Ivan G. Goldman) *L.A. Secret Police: Inside the L.A.P.D. Elite Spy Network,* Pocket Books, 1992.

WORK IN PROGRESS: A novel on police corruption; a high-tech thriller.

SIDELIGHTS: Mike Rothmiller is both a television producer-reporter and a writer. Before assuming these positions, he worked for eleven years as a detective in the Los Angeles Police Department, where he served in its special division on organized-crime intelligence. His division, however, actually conducted research and surveillance on a broad range of local celebrities, including baseball manager Tommy Lasorda and film actor Robert Redford. With former newspaper reporter Ivan G. Goldman, Rothmiller wrote *L.A. Secret Police: Inside the L.A.P.D. Elite Spy Network,* which serves as an expose of the intelligence division's more questionable operations. As a result of the book, Chief Willie Williams, who replaced the controversial Daryl F. Gates, initiated an internal police investigation of the unit.

For more information on Rothmiller's collaborator, see the sketch on Ivan G. Goldman in this volume.

BIOGRAPHICAL/CRITICAL SOURCES:

PERIODICALS

Boston Globe, July 11, 1992.

*   *   *

ROTNER, Shelley 1951-

PERSONAL: Born January 1, 1951, in New York, NY; daughter of William and Babette (an author and guidance counsellor) Rotner; married Stephen Calcagnino (an arts administrator), January 31, 1981; children: Emily. *Education:* Attended Syracuse University Extension Program, 1972; Syracuse University, B.A., 1972; post graduate work at Columbia University 1977; Bank Street College of Education, M.A., 1979.

ADDRESSES: Home and office—35 Columbus Ave., Northampton, MA 01060.

CAREER: Free-lance photographer, 1975—. Aggasiz Community School District, Cambridge, MA, photography instructor, 1975; Learning Guild, Boston, MA, photography instructor, 1975-76; Lincoln Community School System, Cambridge, MA, photography instructor, 1975-76; International Center of Photography, New York City, assistant photography instructor, 1977; Bank Street School for Children, New York City, photography instructor, 1977-78; United Nations Photo Library, New York City, photo researcher, 1977-78; International Center of Photography, New York City, curatorial assistant, 1977-78; United Nations and UNICEF, New York City, photographer, 1979—; The American Museum of Natural History, New York City, photography instructor, 1979. Exhibitor at galleries and museums in Holyoke, MA, Springfield, MA, Boston, New York, Seattle, and Portland, ME, including the American Museum of Natural History, and the International Center of Photography.

AWARDS, HONORS: Grand Prize, *Natural History* magazine photo competition, 1979; Third Prize, World Photographic Society, 1983, for color photographs of children; Northampton, MA, Arts Lottery, funds to take portraits of the women of the Lathrop Home for their centennial celebration, 1984; Northampton, MA, Arts Lottery, funds to exhibit community portraits, 1985; Grand Emmy Award in advertising for images used in Polaroid advertisements, The Polaroid Corporation, 1986; Finalist, *Parade*/Kodak, 1988, for a work to be published in *Parade* magazine, a book, and part of a traveling exhibit; First Prize, Zone Gallery, Springfield, MA, for color portraits.

WRITINGS:

Changes, Macmillan, 1991.
Nature Spy, Macmillan, 1992.
Action Alphabet, Picture Book Studio, 1993.
City Streets, Orchard Press, 1993.
Faces, Macmillan, 1993.

SIDELIGHTS: Shelley Rotner worked as a teacher, a photographer, and a curatorial assistant before she became involved in the creation of children's books. She commented: "After several years as an educator both in the classroom and in museum settings and after the birth of my daughter, I started to think about ideas for children's books. My daughter always loved to look at books and as she grew I started to think and write about the subjects that interested her."

ROUNDS, David 1942-

PERSONAL: Born December 26, 1942; married Susan Ashley (a college administrator), June 24, 1967; children: Nathaniel. *Education:* Harvard University, B.A., 1964; Dominican College of San Rafael, M.A., 1990. *Religion:* Buddhist.

ADDRESSES: Home—1380 Sanford Ranch Rd., Ukiah, CA 95482. *Agent*—Spieler Agency, 154 West 57th St., New York, NY 10019.

CAREER: Teacher and writer, 1964—.

WRITINGS:

Cannonball River Tales (children's stories), Sierra Club Books, 1992.
Perfecting a Piece of the World: Arthur Imperatore and the Blue-Collar Aristocrats of A-P-A, Addison-Wesley, 1993.

WORK IN PROGRESS: A series of books about people working, including a book about a trucking company, focused on craft; a book that describes a string quartet in its work of making music; and a book on spiritual practice by individuals from the major religious traditions.

*   *   *

ROWLEY, Charles K(ershaw) 1939-

PERSONAL: Born June 21, 1939, in Southampton, England; son of Frank (a company director) and Ellen (a homemaker; maiden name, Beal) Rowley; married first wife, Betty (divorced, June 17, 1971); married second wife, Marjorie Isobel (a homemaker), July 17, 1972; children: Amanda Rowley Owens, Bryan Alexander, Sarah, Peter Eliot. *Education:* University of Nottingham, B.A. (with first-class honors), 1960, Ph.D., 1964; graduate study at London School of Economics and Political Science, 1964-65.

ADDRESSES: Home—5188 Dungannon Rd., Fairfax, VA 22030. *Office*—Locke Institute, 4084 University Dr., Fairfax, VA 22030; and Center for the Study of Public Choice, George Mason University, Fairfax, VA 22030.

CAREER: University of Nottingham, Nottingham, England, lecturer in industrial economics, 1962-65; University of Kent at Canterbury, Canterbury, England, lecturer, 1965-69, senior lecturer in economics, 1969-70; University of York, Heslington, England, reader in economic and social statistics, 1970-72; University of Newcastle upon Tyne, Newcastle upon Tyne, England, David Dale Professor of Economics and head of department, 1972-83, director of Centre for Research in Public and Industrial Economics, 1974-83, dean of Faculty of Social Sciences,

1978-81 and 1983; George Mason University, Fairfax, VA, professor of economics, 1984—, dean of Graduate School and director of university research, 1986-88, director of graduate studies in economics, 1991-93, editorial and program director at Center for the Study of Public Choice, 1984-86, associate editorial director at Center, 1986-87, research associate at Center, 1984-86, senior research associate at Center, 1987—. Columbia University, research associate, 1967; University of York, Social Science Research Council senior research fellow, 1968-69; Virginia Polytechnic Institute and State University, research associate at Public Choice Center, 1974 and 1979; Emory University, visiting fellow at Legal Institute for Economists, 1982; Oxford University, Wolfson College, visiting research fellow at Centre for Socio-Legal Studies, 1984-86; Locke Institute, general director, 1989—. Center for the Study of Market Processes, member of academic advisory board, 1985—; David Hume Institute (Edinburgh), member of advisory council, 1985—; Institute of Economic Affairs, member of international advisory council, 1993—. Radioactive Waste Management Advisory Committee, member, 1968-84; consultant to Royal Swedish Academy of Sciences, London's Stock Exchange Council, and Royal Institute of British Architects.

MEMBER: European Public Choice Society (president, 1980-83; honorary life president, 1983—), Public Choice Society, American Economic Association, Mont Pelerin Society, Royal Economic Society, Southern Economic Association.

AWARDS, HONORS: Grants from Houblon-Norman and Bank of England, 1967, Shell Environmental Committee, 1970, Social Science Research Council, 1972 and 1974-84, British Department of the Environment, 1974-78 and 1979, European Community, 1977, British Office of Fair Trading, 1981 and 1983, British Port Authorities, 1981-83, John M. Olin, Inc., 1985 and 1986, Smith Richardson, Inc., 1985, Liberty Fund, Inc., 1985, 1991, and 1993, Bradley Foundation, 1987-88, 1989-90, 1991-92, and 1993-94, and Legal Services Corp., 1987; Claude Lambe fellow, 1988-89.

WRITINGS:

The British Monopolies Commission, Allen & Unwin, 1966.
Steel and Public Policy, McGraw, 1971.
(Editor and contributor) *Readings in Industrial Economics,* Volume I: *Theoretical Foundations,* Volume II: *Private Enterprise and State Intervention,* Macmillan, 1972.
Antitrust and Economic Efficiency, Macmillan, 1973.
(With Alan T. Peacock) *Welfare Economics: A Liberal Restatement,* Martin Robertson, 1975.

(With G. K. Yarrow) *The Evolution of Concentration in the United Kingdom Cement Industry,* Commission of the European Communities, 1978.

(With B. Beavis and M. Walker) *A Study of Effluent Discharges in the River Tees,* H.M.S.O., 1979.

Frihet, Rattvisa, Effektivitet, Timbro (Sweden), 1979.

(With C. Mulley, M. Walker, and J. Whittaker) *The Use of Roll-On/Roll-Off Vessels for Moving Freight via Coastal Waters within the United Kingdom,* Tees and Hartlepool Port Authority, 1982.

(With C. Mulley and J. Whittaker) *The Use of Roll-On/Roll-Off Vessels for Moving Freight Between the Ports of Tees and Harwich,* Tees and Hartlepool Port Authority, 1983.

(With C. Mulley and J. Whittaker) *The Use of Roll-On/Roll-Off Vessels for Moving Freight Between the Ports of Tees and London,* Tees and Hartlepool Port Authority, 1983.

(With A. I. Ogus) *Prepayments and Insolvency,* British Office of Fair Trading, 1984.

(Editor with J. M. Buchanan and Robert D. Tollison, and contributor) *Deficits,* Basil Blackwell, 1987.

(Editor and contributor) *Democracy and Public Choice: Essays in Honor of Gordon Tullock,* Basil Blackwell, 1987.

(Editor with Robert D. Tollison and Gordon Tullock, and contributor) *The Political Economy of Rent Seeking,* Kluwer Academic, 1988.

The Right to Justice: The Political Economy of Legal Services in the United States, Edward Elgar, 1992.

(Editor and author of introduction) *Public Choice Theory, Volume I: Homo Economicus in the Political Marketplace, Volume II: The Characteristics of Political Equilibrium, Volume III: The Separation of Powers and Constitutional Political Economy,* Edward Elgar, 1993.

(Editor and author of introduction) *Social Choice Theory, Volume I: The Aggregation of Preferences, Volume II: Utilitarian and Contractarian Goals, Volume III: Social Justice and Classical Liberal Goals,* Edward Elgar, 1993.

(Editor and contributor) *Property Rights and the Limits of Democracy,* Edward Elgar, 1993.

Liberty and the State, Edward Elgar, 1993.

(Editor with Friedrich Schneider and Robert D. Tollison) *The Next Twenty Years of Public Choice,* Kluwer Academic, 1993.

Free Trade on the Cross: The Political Economy of Trade Protection in the United States, George Mason University Press, 1993.

(With Richard Wagner) *Great Classical Liberal Economists,* Edward Elgar, 1994.

Work represented in anthologies, including *National Constitutions and International Economic Law,* edited by M.

Hilfe and E. U. Petersman, Kluwer Academic, 1993; *The Revolution in Development Economics,* edited by J. Dorn and A. A. Walters, George Mason University Press, 1993; and *The Edward Elgar Companion to Austrian Economics,* edited by P. Boettke, Edward Elgar, 1993. Contributor of numerous articles and reviews to economic journals. *Journal of Industrial Economics,* associate editor, 1977-83; *International Review of Law and Economics,* editor, 1980-87; *Public Choice,* book review editor, 1985-86, co-editor, 1990—. *Applied Economics,* member of editorial advisory board, 1968-83; *Review of Austrian Economics,* member of editorial board, 1988—.

WORK IN PROGRESS: Research on public choice, law and economics, and classical liberal political economics.

SIDELIGHTS: Charles K. Rowley told *CA:* "I am a professional economist who has become disenchanted with mainstream economics. Too many of my colleagues view individuals as pawns to be moved about on chess boards of their own construction. Devoid of any real insights into human motivation, they use mathematics as a crutch and a shield against outside evaluations of their work. Ignorant of the actual behavior of the political marketplace, they offer advice on policy that has not even a remote chance of implementation. Indoctrinated in the notion that economic efficiency is the ultimate goal, they tread roughshod over individual freedoms in the policy prescriptions that they endorse. Ignorant of the history of their discipline, they overlook insights provided by the great classical economists. Narrowed by their desire to publish in specialist journals, they expend all their effort and ingenuity in analyzing problems of unbelievable insignificance.

"My own research and writings are dedicated to countering this lemming-like journey into extinction. My book *Welfare Economics* challenges economic efficiency head-on and reworks welfare economics from the perspective of maintaining economic freedom. The book *Liberty and the State* takes this approach further, arguing the case for the balkanization of the United States into several countries, allowing individuals who love liberty to migrate from areas that manifestly do not. My book *Great Classical Liberal Economists* (coauthored with Richard Wagner) reviews the lives and writings of the forty all-time great scholars who forged the intellectual case for economic freedom, often at great personal cost, in countries dedicated to mercantilist and socialist principles. The Locke Institute, which I direct, is dedicated to the promulgation of classical liberal principles through a program of publications and conferences."

RUOFF, A. LaVonne Brown 1930-

PERSONAL: Born April 10, 1930, in Charleston, IL; daughter of Oscar (a farmer and factory worker) and Laura Alice Witters (a teacher and homemaker) Brown; married Milford A. Prasher, August 19, 1950 (divorced, 1964); married Gene W. Ruoff (a professor of English), June 10, 1967; children: Stephen C., Sharon L. *Education:* Attended University of Illinois, Chicago, 1948-50; Northwestern University, B.S., 1953, M.A., 1954, Ph.D., 1966.

ADDRESSES: Home—300 Forest Ave., Oak Park, IL 60302. *Office*—Department of English (m/c 162), University of Illinois at Chicago, 601 South Morgan St., Chicago, IL 60607-7120.

CAREER: University of Illinois, Chicago, instructor in English, 1956-57; Roosevelt University, Chicago, instructor, 1961-62, assistant professor of English, 1962-66; University of Illinois, assistant professor, 1966-69, associate professor, 1969-81, professor of English, 1981—. National Endowment for the Humanities, director of Summer Seminar for College Teachers on American Indian Literature, 1979, 1983, and 1989; American Literature Committee for the Council for International Exchange of Scholars, member, 1987-90, chair, 1990.

MEMBER: Association for Study of American Indian Literature (president, 1980), Modern Language Association (chair of Discussion Group on American Indian Literature, 1978, 1991), Society for Study of Multiethnic Literature in the United States.

AWARDS, HONORS: Fellowship, Dartmouth College, 1979, in the Native American studies program; grant, National Endowment for the Humanities Research Division, 1981; award for distinguished contributions to ethnic studies, Society for Study of Multiethnic Literature in the United States, 1986; fellowship, National Endowment for the Humanities, 1992-93.

WRITINGS:

(Editor) E. Pauline Johnson, *The Moccasin Maker* (young adult), University of Arizona, 1987.

American Indian Literatures, Modern Language Association, 1990.

Literatures of the American Indian (young adult), Chelsea House, 1990.

(Editor with Jerry W. Ward, Jr.) *Redefining American Literary History,* Modern Language Association, 1990.

Contributor to books, including *Old Indian Days,* by Charles Eastman, University of Nebraska Press, 1991. Editor of "American Indian Lives" series, University of Nebraska Press, 1985—. Consultant on Norton and Heath anthologies of American literature; member of advisory board for "Native American Bibliography" series, Scarecrow Press. Contributor to periodicals.

WORK IN PROGRESS: Oxford Book of Native American Literature, completion expected in 1995; an edition of S. Alice Callahan's *Wynema,* which "may be the first novel written by an Indian woman," for University of Nebraska Press; researching a history of literature written by American Indians from 1772 to the present.

SIDELIGHTS: A. LaVonne Brown Ruoff commented: "The impetus to my research on American Indians is the fact that I was formerly married to an Indian, and one of my two adopted children is an Indian."

*   *   *

RYCZEK, William J. 1953-

PERSONAL: Born September 15, 1953, in Middletown, CT; son of Frank L. (in manufacturing) and Katherine M. (a homemaker) Ryczek; married October 4, 1980; wife's name, Susan M. (a writer); children: Michael W., Anne Marie. *Education:* University of Connecticut, B.S., 1976; Pennsylvania State University, M.B.A., 1977; attended University of Bridgeport, 1978-79. *Politics:* Libertarian. *Religion:* None.

ADDRESSES: Home—56 Algonquin Dr., Wallingford, CT 06492.

CAREER: Barclays American Business Credit, Inc., East Hartford, CT, vice president, 1979-87; Liberty Bank, Middletown, CT, senior vice president, 1988—. University of Hartford, adjunct professor of finance.

AWARDS, HONORS: Macmillan-SABR Award, 1993.

WRITINGS:

Blackguards and Red Stockings, McFarland and Co., 1992.

WORK IN PROGRESS: When Johnny Came Marching Home; Summit at Moscow.

S

SACHS, Wolfgang 1946-

PERSONAL: Born November 25, 1946, in Munich, Germany; married Melamia Cavelli (an architect), June, 1953. *Education:* University of Tuebingen, M.A., 1971, Dipl. Theol., 1972, Ph.D., 1975.

ADDRESSES: Office—Wuppertal Institute for Climate, Energy, and the Environment, Doeppersberg 19, D-42103 Wuppertal, Germany.

CAREER: Technical University of Berlin, Berlin, Germany, assistant professor, 1975-83; Society for International Development, Rome, Italy, editor, 1984-87; Pennsylvania State University, University Park, visiting associate professor of science, technology, and society, 1987-90; Institute for Cultural Studies, Essen, Germany, fellow, 1990-93; Wuppertal Institute for Climate, Energy, and the Environment, Wuppertal, Germany, project director, 1993—.

WRITINGS:

For Love of the Automobile: Looking Back Into the History of Our Desires, translated from original 1984 German manuscript, University of California Press, 1992.
(Editor) *The Development Dictionary: A Guide to Knowledge as Power,* Zed Books, 1992.
(Editor) *Global Ecology: A New Arena of Political Conflict,* Zed Books, 1993.

Editor, *Development,* 1984-87.

WORK IN PROGRESS: Satellite View: Studies in Global Consciousness.

SADEH, Pinhas 1929-1994

OBITUARY NOTICE—See index for *CA* sketch: Born June 17, 1929, in Lwow, Poland; died of cancer, January 29, 1994, in Jerusalem, Israel. Novelist and poet. Sadeh, who immigrated in 1934 from Poland to Palestine, wrote poetry which reflected his belief in Zionism, a patriotic/religious movement which—at that time—advocated the creation of a Jewish homeland in what is now the country of Israel. An early collection of Sadeh's poems were published in 1951 as *Masah Dumah,* which means "The Burden of Dumah." By the 1960s Sadeh's writings assumed a more personal, introspective tone. Among his later books are the novels *Al Matzavo Shal Ha'adam* ("Notes on Man's Condition") and *Mot Avimelech* ("Death of Abimelech, King of Shechem") and an anthology of poetry, *Ahava* ("Love").

OBITUARIES AND OTHER SOURCES:

BOOKS

International Authors and Writers Who's Who, 11th edition, International Biographical Centre, 1989.

PERIODICALS

Chicago Tribune, January 31, 1994, p. 11.
New York Times, January 30, 1994, p. 38.

*   *   *

SALISBURY, Graham 1944-

PERSONAL: Born April 11, 1944, in Philadelphia, PA; son of Henry Forester Graham (an officer in the U.S. Navy) and Barbara Twigg-Smith; married second wife, Robyn Kay Cowan, October 26, 1988; children: Sandi Weston, Miles, Ashley, Melanie, Alex, Keenan, Zachary.

Education: California State University at Northridge, B.A. (magna cum laude), 1974; Vermont College of Norwich University, M.F.A., 1990. *Politics:* "Middle of the road."

ADDRESSES: Office—319 Southwest Washington No. 320, Portland, OR 97204. *Agent*—Emilie Jacobson, Curtis Brown Ltd., 10 Astor Pl., New York, NY 10003.

CAREER: Writer. Worked variously as a deckhand, glass-bottom boat skipper, singer-songwriter, graphic artist, and teacher; manager of historic office buildings in downtown Portland, OR.

MEMBER: Society of Children's Book Writers and Illustrators, Women's National Book Association, American Library Association, Hawaiian Mission Children's Society.

AWARDS, HONORS: Parents Choice Award, Bank Street College Child Study Children's Book Award, Judy Lopez Memorial Award for Children's Literature, Women's National Book Association, and citations as one of the best books for young adults, American Library Association, and best books of the year, *School Library Journal,* all 1992, for *Blue Skin of the Sea;* PEN/Norma Klein Award, 1992; John Unterecker Award for Fiction, Chaminade University and Hawaii Literary Arts Council.

WRITINGS:

Blue Skin of the Sea (novel), Delacorte, 1992.

Contributor to periodicals, including *Bamboo Ridge, Chaminade Literary Review, Hawaii Pacific Review, Journal of Youth Services in Libraries, Manoa: A Journal of Pacific and International Writing,* and *Northwest.*

WORK IN PROGRESS: Another novel, completion expected in 1994.

SIDELIGHTS: Graham Salisbury commented: "Embarrassing as it is to admit, especially to fellow writers, I didn't read until I was a little past thirty. Sure, I escaped with Edgar Rice Burroughs and Louis L'Amour a couple of times, and I read the required *Iliad* and *Odyssey* in high school, but I didn't read of my own choice until my first son was born. Then I read Alex Haley's *Roots,* which changed my life forever. I don't have a clue as to *why* I picked this book up, but I did, and I loved it so much that I wanted to read another, and another . . . and another. I surprised myself and quite suddenly became a voracious reader.

"Because reading eventually grew into something as large as life itself, I started feeling an urge to do some writing of my own. Maybe that's how we all come to this art—a desire to create those fantastic worlds and passionate feelings we got when reading something wonderful. I started

writing memory pieces. Eventually I found myself stretching my stories, bending the truth, twisting the realities, and surprising myself by the ease with which I could lie. Simply by stumbling in and writing lies, I discovered that writing *fiction* was what I enjoyed most.

" 'Write what you know' is good advice, but 'write what you *feel*' is better. I was raised in the Hawaiian Islands, a setting I know and a setting I love . . . . I was also raised—for the most part—without a father, and I have some big holes in my life because of it. I'm reminded of these holes constantly, nearly every day of my life. It's no surprise that I write a lot about relationships, especially family relationships, I guess because they're so important to me. If a writer can discover what is important to him or her, then that writer will have discovered the things he or she has to write about. That's why I say, write what you *feel.*

"There are so many things to learn about writing—about thought, about feelings and passions, about storytelling, about craft, about commitment, and about one's own personality and habits. But in my mind, one element is most important. Without it a writer will struggle endlessly. That element is discipline. Someone once said that a published writer is an amateur who didn't give up. There's so much truth in that. Discipline, to me, means consistent—almost habitual—writerly thinking, writing, rewriting, revising, and submitting.

"The important thing for me to understand as a writer for young readers is that though the world has changed, the basic needs of young people haven't. There are many, many kids out there with holes in their lives that they desperately want to fill. I can write about those holes. I can do this because I am human and have suffered and soared myself. Strange as it sounds to say, I—as a writer—consider myself lucky, indeed, to have all the holes I have in my own life. Because when I write, I remember, I understand, I empathize, and I feel a need to explore those holes and maybe even fill a couple of them—for myself and for any reader with a similar need who happens to stumble onto my work."

Blue Skin of the Sea is Salisbury's tale, told in a series of related stories, of a young boy growing up in Hawaii. Reviewing the book in *Five Owls,* Gary D. Schmidt called it "entertaining, moving, and poignant," and he praised the author's "ability to depict island life" and "the pressures and tensions and loves and fears of it." He felt that Salisbury "creates a compelling story of growth and change." A *Publishers Weekly* writer remarked upon the "extraordinary mood" of the work, in which Salisbury distills "the most powerful and universal experiences of adolescence."

BIOGRAPHICAL/CRITICAL SOURCES:

PERIODICALS

Five Owls, May/June, 1992.
Publishers Weekly, June 15, 1992, p. 104; July 13, 1992, p. 22.

* * *

SANDERS, Arthur 1955-

PERSONAL: Born November 15, 1955; son of Saul (a physician) and Elinor (a librarian and office manager; maiden name, Feltman) Sanders; married Deborah Pappenheimer (a painter), June 27, 1982; children: Benjamin Pappenheimer. *Education:* Franklin and Marshall College, A.B., 1978; Harvard University, Ph.D., 1982. *Politics:* Democrat. *Religion:* Jewish.

ADDRESSES: Home—3802 Forest Ave., Des Moines, IA 50311. *Office*—Department of Political Science, Drake University, Des Moines, IA 50311.

CAREER: Hamilton College, Clinton, NY, assistant professor of political science, 1982-90; Drake University, Des Moines, IA, associate professor of American politics, 1990—. WOI-TV, election analyst, 1990, 1992.

MEMBER: American Political Science Association, American Association of Public Opinion Researchers.

WRITINGS:

Making Sense of Politics, Iowa State University Press, 1990.
Victory: How a Progressive Democratic Party Can Win and Govern, M. E. Sharpe, 1992.

Contributor to political science journals.

WORK IN PROGRESS: Research on the politics of entertainment television.

SIDELIGHTS: Arthur Sanders told *CA:* "My interest is in how 'ordinary citizens' relate to the political world. My research and writings are an attempt to understand, and make understandable, those connections and thus help, in some small way, to improve the quality of democracy in our nation. I find politics and the political system fascinating, and I believe strongly in democracy, and in people taking control of their own political and social system. To do so effectively, we need to understand how that system works, how it shapes us, and how we can best organize our collective voices to shape it."

SANT CASSIA, Paul 1954-

PERSONAL: Born October 24, 1954, in Malta; son of Mario Philip (a physician) and Melina (Boffa) Sant Cassia; married Sabine-Birgitte Frank (a political scientist), July 17, 1993. *Education:* Royal University of Malta, B.A. (with first class honors), 1976; Christ's College, Cambridge, Ph.D., 1981. *Politics:* Liberal. *Religion:* "I'm working on it."

ADDRESSES: Home—Malta, Cyprus, and Cambridge and Durham, England. *Office*—Department of Anthropology, University of Durham, 43 Old Elvet, Durham, England.

CAREER: Cambridge University, Cambridge, England, research fellow at Christ's College, 1981-85, lecturer and museum curator, 1985-90; University of Durham, Durham, England, lecturer in anthropology, 1991—. Australian Institute of Multicultural Affairs, research fellow, 1982-83; University of Malta, visiting professor, 1992-94.

MEMBER: Royal Anthropological Society (fellow), Association of Anthropologists of the Commonwealth.

WRITINGS:

(With Constantina Bada) *The Making of the Modern Greek Family,* Cambridge University Press, 1991.

* * *

SANTORO, Carlo Maria 1935-

PERSONAL: Born August 14, 1935, in Ancona, Italy; son of Leone Ferdinando (an official) and Gemma Bianca (a university professor; maiden name, Zilli) Santoro. *Education:* Received LL.D. from University of Rome. *Religion:* Roman Catholic.

ADDRESSES: Home—Via C. Correnti 11, Milan 20123, Italy. *Office*—Istituto per gli Studi di Politica Internazionale, University of Milan, Via Clerici 5, Milan 20121, Italy.

CAREER: Italian Diplomatic Service, official in Rome, 1962, Geneva, Switzerland, 1964, and Brussels, Belgium, 1965-66; University of Venice, Venice, Italy, professor, 1972-79; University of Bologna, Bologna, Italy, professor, 1979-90; University of Milan, Milan, Italy, professor of international relations, 1990—, co-director of Istituto per gli Studi di Politica Internazionale, 1987—; Bocconi University, Italy, professor, 1991—. International Institute for Strategic Studies, London, England, fellow, 1980; University of Turin, Turin, Italy, visiting professor, 1980-81; Harvard University, Cambridge, MA, fellow at Center for International Studies, 1981-82, associate, 1987—; Brown University, Providence, RI, visiting professor, 1987-88;

Johns Hopkins School of Advanced International Studies, Washington, DC, visiting professor, 1990-91; consultant to Italian Ministry of Defense and Foreign Affairs.

MEMBER: International Studies Association (member of governing council), World Assembly of International Studies.

WRITINGS:

La Perla e l'ostrica, Angeli, 1987, translation published as *Diffidence and Ambition,* Westview, 1992.

Also coauthor with Stefano Draghi of *The Italian Diplomats,* 1986. Member of editorial board, *European Security.*

IN ITALIAN

Gli stati uniti e l'ordine mondiale, Editori Riunitti, 1978.
Lo Stile dell'Aquila (essays), Angeli, 1984.
(With Luigi Caligaris) *Obiettivo Difeso,* Il Mulino, 1986.
L'Italia e il Mediterraneo, Angeli, 1988.
Il Sistema di guerra, Angeli, 1988.
La politica estera di una media potenza, Il Mulino, 1991.
(Editor) *Il Mosaico Mediterraneo* (essays), Il Mulino, 1991.
(Editor) *L'Elmo di Scipio* (essays), Il Mulino, 1992.
(Editor) *Prospettive della cooperazione allo sviluppo negli anni '90,* Il Mulino, 1993.

Contributor to periodicals. Member of editorial board, *Relazioni Internazionali* and *Teoria Politica.*

SIDELIGHTS: Carlo Maria Santoro told *CA:* "I am interested in foreign and security studies, theories of the international system, and American and Italian foreign policy decision-making. More recently I have been researching subjects like nationalism, geopolitics, and ethnicity. I have written a large number of books and articles. *Diffidence and Ambition* is a discussion of the intellectual sources of American foreign policy at the beginning of World War II. Other titles include a collection of essays on American foreign and defense issues; an analysis of the Italian defense model; a book on the Italian foreign policy decision-making process; an empirical study of the Italian diplomats; and a book on the relationship between polarity and war. In 1991 I published a book on the structure of the Italian foreign policy system since the unification of Italy in 1861."

*   *   *

SAPIEYEVSKI, Anne Lindbergh   1940-1993
(Anne Lindbergh Feydy, Anne Lindbergh)

OBITUARY NOTICE—See index for *CA* sketch: Born October 2, 1940, in New York, NY; died of cancer, De-

cember 10, 1993, in Thetford Center, VT. Teacher and writer. Daughter of famed aviator Charles Lindbergh and noted poet and essayist Anne Morrow Lindbergh, Sapieyevski wrote fourteen books, some of which appear under the names Anne Lindbergh or Anne Lindbergh Feydy. A number of her novels are for children. Her most popular juvenile works, *The People in Pineapple Place* and *The Prisoner of Pineapple Place,* are realistic fantasies set in the surrounding areas of Washington, D.C., where she taught school and lived with her second husband, the composer and conductor Jerzy Sapieyevski. In 1987 she continued her teaching when she moved to Vermont, where she met and married writer and professor Noel Perrin. Among Sapieyevski's nonjuvenile writings are *The Unicorn and Other Poems* and *War within and Without: Diaries & Letters, 1939 to 1944.* Her later books include *Three Lives to Live* and *Travel Far, Pay No Fare.*

OBITUARIES AND OTHER SOURCES:

PERIODICALS

Chicago Tribune, December 12, 1993, section 4, p. 8.
New York Times, December 12, 1993, p. 60.
Washington Post, December 13, 1993, p. D6.

*   *   *

SAUTET, Claude   1924-

PERSONAL: Born February 23, 1924, in Montrouge, France; son of Jean (in business) and Marguerite (Parent) Sautet; married Graziella Escogido, 1953; children: Yves. *Education:* Attended College Saint-Euverte, 1935-38; Lycee de Coutances, 1939-40; Ecole Nationale Superieure des Arts Decoratifs, 1941; attended Institut des Hautes Etudes Cinematographiques (IDHEC), 1946-48. *Avocational Interests:* Music, painting, sculpture.

ADDRESSES: Agent—c/o Artmedia, 10 Avenue George V, 75008 Paris, France.

CAREER: Screenwriter and director. Served as technician and assistant filmmaker; *Combat,* music critic, late 1940s. Director of motion pictures beginning 1951, including *Un Coeur en hiver,* October Films, 1992.

AWARDS, HONORS: Prix Delluc, 1969, for *Les Choses de la vie;* Grand prix du cinema francais, 1972, for *Cesar et Rosalie;* Prix Jean Cocteau, 1973, for *Vincent, Francois, Paul . . . et les autres;* Academy Award nomination for best foreign-language film, 1978, for *Une Histoire simple;* Prix Georges de Beauregard for best director, 1987, and Grand prix, Florence film festival, 1987, both for *Quelques jours avec moi;* Lion d'argent, Venice film festival, Prix de la critique internationale, Venice film festival, Lionceau d'or for best film, Venice film festival, and Ciak d'or for best screenplay, Venice film festival, all 1992, all for *Un Coeur en hiver;* Grand prix de l'Academie nationale du cinema, Prix melies, best French film, Cesar Award for best director, David Di Donatello, best foreign language film, all 1993, all for *Un Coeur en hiver;* award of best foreign language film, London Film Critics Circle, 1994, for *Un Coeur en hiver.*

WRITINGS:

SCREENPLAYS

(And director) *Classe tous risques* (adapted from Jose Giovanni's novel), released in the United States as *The Big Risk,* United Artists, 1960.

(With Georges Franju, Jean Redon, Pierre Boileau, and Thomas Narcejac; and director) *Les Yeux sans visage* (title means "Eyes Without a Face"; adapted from a novel by Redon), Lux, 1962, released in the United States as *The Horror Chamber of Dr. Faustus,* Lopert, 1962.

(With Jose Giovanni and Jacques Deray; also director) *Symphonie pour un massacre* (adapted from *Les Mystifies* by Alain Reynaud-Fourton), Seven Arts-Goldstone, 1963, released in the United States as *Symphony for a Massacre,* Seven Arts-Goldstone, 1965.

(With Pascal Jardin; and director) *Monsieur* (adapted from Claude Gevel's play), Sanero, 1964.

(With Marcel Ophuls and Daniel Boulanger) *Peau de banane* (title means "Banana Peel"), Pathe, 1965.

(With Alain Cavalier, Jean-Paul Rappeneau, and Daniel Boulanger) *La Vie de chateau* (title means "A Matter of Resistance"), Royal Films, 1966.

(With Paul Guimard and Jean-Loup Dabadie; and director) *Les Choses de la vie* (adapted from a novel by Guimard), Lira Fida Sonocam, 1969, released in the United States as *The Things of Life,* Columbia, 1970.

(With Jean Cau, Jacques Deray and Jean-Claude Carriere) *Borsalino* (adapted from *The Bandits of Marseilles* by Eugene Saccomano), Paramount, 1970.

(And director) *Max et les ferrailleurs* (title means "Max and the Scrap Merchants"), CFDC, 1971.

(With Dabadie; and director) *Cesar et Rosalie,* Paramount/Orion, 1972, released in the United States as *Cesar and Rosalie,* Cinema 5, 1972.

(And director) *Vincent, Francois, Paul . . . et les autres* (adapted from *La Grande Marrade* by Claude Neron), Joseph Green Pictures, 1973, released in the United States as *Vincent, Francois, Paul . . . and the Others.*

(And director) *Mado,* Joseph Green Pictures, 1976.

(And director) *Une Histoire simple,* Quartet, 1978, released in the United States as *A Simple Story,* Quartet, 1978.

(And director) *Un mauvais fils* (title means "A Bad Son"; adapted from a story by Daniel Biasin), Sara Films/ Antenne 2, 1980.

(With Dabadie; and director), *Garcon!* (title means "Waiter!"), Sara Films/Renn Productions, 1983.

(With Jacques Fieschi and Jerome Tonnerre; and director) *Quelques jours avec moi* (adapted from a novel by Jean-Francois Josselin), Sara Films/Cinea Films, 1987, released in the United States as *A Few Days with Me,* Galaxy International, 1988.

Also author of screenplay and director of *Nous n'irons plus au bois,* 1950, and *L'Arme a gauche* (title means "Guns for the Dictator"), 1965, and *Nelly et Mr. Arnaud,* 1991. Also screenwriter for *Le Diable par la queue,* 1969.

OTHER

Contributor to periodicals, including *Avant-Scene du Cinema, Ecran, Combat,* and *Positif.*

SIDELIGHTS: Award-winning filmmaker Claude Sautet has garnered international acclaim for such works as *Les Choses de la vie* ("The Things of Life"), which he co-wrote and directed, as well as for his direction of screenplays by other writers, including *Un Coeur en hiver* ("A Heart in Winter"). Sautet entered filmmaking as a screenwriter in the early 1960s, and throughout much of that decade collaborated with other authors on a wide range of films, such as Georges Franju's *Horror Chamber of Dr. Faustus* (also known as "Eyes without a Face"), and Jean-Paul Ranneneau's World War II romance *A Matter of Resistance.* For his innovative film direction, Sautet has been called "a master craftsman" by Jack Kroll in *Newsweek,* and—in recognition for his recurring focus on everyday relationships in his writings—"a poet of friendship" by Michael Wilmington in the *Los Angeles Times.*

In the 1960s Sautet served as writer-director of *Classe tous risques* ("The Big Risk")—a film noted for its originality—and the thriller *L'Arme a gauche* ("Guns for the Dictator"), but it was in 1970, with the completion of *Les Choses de la vie* ("The Things of Life"), that he scored his first major filmmaking success. *Les Choses de la vie* concerns a love affair between Pierre, a married, middle-aged building contractor, and Helene, a much younger, single woman. Helene presses Pierre to abandon his past, but he refuses to sever all ties to his estranged wife and son. Fate, instead, intervenes when Pierre is involved in a fatal car crash. Unique to the story is Sautet's film technique where slices of the car crash scene are played at the beginning of the film and—using reference and flashback—made central to the story. *Les Choses de la vie* was accorded France's prestigious Prix Delluc for its strong characterization and imaginative cinematic craftsmanship.

With *Cesar et Rosalie* Sautet returned to exploring aspects of the love triangle. In this film an aggressive business tycoon, played by Yves Montand, vies with David, a cartoonist, for the affections of Rosalie, a winsome, introspective woman played by Romy Schneider. Eventually, the two men grow weary of their rivalry, cease their competition for Rosalie, and form their own bond of friendship. *Cesar et Rosalie* won substantial acclaim, particularly in France, where Sautet acquired loyal enthusiasts for his graphic portrayal of friendship and realistic depiction of middle-class life.

"Sautet films are distinguished by a graceful, rhythmic pacing and a recurrent theme of friendship," declared Kevin Thomas in the *Los Angeles Times*. Sautet's next film, the widely successful *Vincent, Francois, Paul . . . et les autres* ("Vincent, Francois, Paul . . . and the Others"), features three middle-aged friends, each of whom is in the throes of an emotional crisis. Sautet won praise for the film's lyrical dialogue and the sympathetic portrayal of evolving relationships between the characters. Likewise, Sautet's 1978 work, *Une Histoire simple* ("A Simple Story"), focuses on friendships. Marie, a successful designer played by Romy Schneider (who won a Cesar for her performance), finds comfort in friends and family after a failed love affair. The film was widely received as one of Sautet's greatest achievements, and was nominated for an Oscar in 1978 for best foreign-language film.

In the late 1980s Sautet's *Quelques Jours avec moi* ("A Few Days with Me") appeared as a romantic comedy about a love affair between a wealthy young man and an impoverished maid. Michael Wilmington, writing in the *Los Angeles Times,* contended that the film has "an almost irresistible narrative drive. . . . with amusingly eccentric characters and unexpected twists." Sautet explained to interviewer Kevin Thomas in the *Los Angeles Times* that the characters in *Quelques Jours avec moi* were taken from people in Sautet's own childhood: "I grew up in the outskirts of Paris in an extended family with an immense number of children. . . . I also discovered the secret loneliness of people, of being lonely in a crowd. One of the classic subjects is solitude. . . . Comedy starts when the individual starts to break out of this. I always try to create an imbalance, an edge to friendship. . . . My real subject is always uncertainty."

Sautet won a Cesar award in 1992 for his direction of *Un Coeur en Hiver* ("A Heart in Winter"), written by Yves Ullmann, Jacques Fieschi and Jerome Tonnerre. Richard Corliss in *Time* described the film as "a story of a woman's passion, told with a man's disconcerting reticence." In the story, a beautiful and talented violinist, Camille (played by Emmanuelle Beart), falls in love with an aloof violin technician, Stephane (played by Daniel Auteuil). Janet Maslin, in her *New York Times* review, noted that "Sautet

makes this story powerfully vivid . . . The film's settings, invitingly evoked, are used as landmarks in the lives of the principals." Maslin concluded that *Un Coeur en Hiver* is "a coolly elegant romance."

BIOGRAPHICAL/CRITICAL SOURCES:

PERIODICALS

Library Journal, February 1, 1990, p. 124; October 15, 1990, p. 114.
Los Angeles Times, June 25, 1989, pp. C22-23; June 28, 1993.
Newsweek, June 21, 1993, p. 65.
New York Times, April 14, 1989, p. C8; June 4, 1993, p. C3.
Time, June 21, 1993, pp. 67-68.

*   *   *

SAVAGE, Deborah 1955-

PERSONAL: Born December 15, 1955, in Northampton, MA. *Education:* University of Massachusetts, B.A., 1987.

ADDRESSES: Home—147 Woodside Ave., Amherst, MA 01002.

CAREER: Alderkill Camp, Rhinebeck, NY, teacher of arts program, 1975; University of Massachusetts, Amherst, teaching assistant for creative writing course, 1977; Wildwood Elementary School, Amherst, teacher of creative writing, 1978; The Hotchkiss School, Lakeville, CT, teacher of art, 1987; The Forman School, Litchfield, CT, teacher of English and art, 1988-91; writer, 1991—. Taught classes and workshops in wood-cut printmaking to young people and adults at various schools in Massachusetts and New Zealand, 1980-1985; guest author and workshop presenter in schools in New Zealand, Pennsylvania, New York, Massachusetts, Washington and Connecticut, 1985-91; served as guest author and workshop presenter for the Brookline Area Schools in Massachusetts, 1987-1988. Has also given presentations at the Northwest Corner Coalition for Nuclear Disarmament, the Massachusetts Association for Educational Media, the Boston Public Library Creative Writing Workshop, the International Federation of Teachers of English conference, and the American Association of University Women Book and Author luncheon. Savage has also exhibited wood-cut prints and watercolors at museums, including the Berkshire Museum, Pittsfield, MA, the Pratt Museum of Natural History, Amherst, MA, the Cape Cod Museum of Natural History, Brewster, MA, the Auckland Institute and Museum, Auckland, NZ, and the White Memorial Conservation Area Museum, Litchfield, CT.

AWARDS, HONORS: Award of Merit, American Museum Association, 1984, for Cape Cod Museum of Natural History poster; Notable Children's Book citation, American Library Association, remarkable book of literature award, *Parents Choice Magazine,* and *School Library Journal* best books citation, all 1986, all for *A Rumour of Otters.*

WRITINGS:

YOUNG ADULT NOVELS

A Rumour of Otters, Houghton, 1986.
Flight of the Albatross, Houghton, 1988.
A Stranger Calls Me Home, Houghton, 1992.
To Race a Dream, Houghton, 1993.

OTHER

Contributor of poetry to periodicals, including *Dark Horse, Spectrum,* and *Cross Currents.* Also contributor of illustrations to periodicals, including *Planning Quarterly* and *Cross Currents. Flight of the Albatross* has appeared in French and German translations.

ADAPTATIONS: Flight of the Albatross has been optioned by film companies in Germany and New Zealand.

WORK IN PROGRESS: Along a Path of Stars, a novel; *Approaching Sacred Places,* a collection of short stories.

SIDELIGHTS: Deborah Savage commented: "When I was a young girl I wrote story after story that I never finished; then, I thought it was because I grew bored with them—now I think it was because I was too young to know that stories never did end at all. I lived way out in the country surrounded by woods and hills and mountains, and I read a great deal. . . . I read so many stories at the same time they all became entwined within me like a great winding loop going forever through me. I loved to draw and paint, and often I would write stories about the things I liked to draw, just so I could draw them over and over as illustrations. My writing has remained visual like that; I write the story and illustrate it with word-pictures.

"Most of the people who came to my home when I was young were adults, and except for school, I knew very few children. Adults were bristling with stories, it seemed to me, and if they did not tell them to me I made them up. I think that is how I learned to traverse the divide between my experience of living and my writing, until now there is almost no division. Characters come from an infinite store of barely-known people who may no longer be in my life, but have left in their going a wake of richly-scented stories . . . I have only to lift my head and sniff the air, and there I find them.

"I write stories and books about young people . . . people just leaving childhood and coming into adulthood. The transformation is so intense it colors the world in a manner that never happens when they are older. I write books

about people who each are discovering the entire universe for the very first time, identifying it, naming it, finding their place in it where they will live for the rest of their life. Everything they have learned about love they must now test out for themselves, for the first time. They have gained a voice and they discover they have something to say. They discover how alone they are. These are the people I write about in my stories. It would be a mistake to say I write *for* young adults, because I do not have any specific audience in mind when I write (at least, not an audience defined by terms of age or sex or nationality)."

*   *   *

SCHECTER, Darrow   1961-

PERSONAL: Born July 10, 1961. *Education:* Attended London School of Economics and Political Science, 1981-82; Hamilton College, B.A. (cum laude), 1983; Nuffield College, Oxford, M.Phil., 1985, D.Phil., 1990.

ADDRESSES: Home—Flat 1, St. Anne's Well House, Farm Rd., Hove BN3 1FX, England. *Office*—School of European Studies, University of Sussex, Falmer, Brighton BN1 9QN, England.

CAREER: Oxford University, Oxford, England, tutor at Brasenose College, 1986-87, and St. Anne's College, 1988-89; Ecole Nationale des Sciences Politiques, Paris, France, lecturer in English and American studies, 1989-90; University of Sussex, Falmer, England, lecturer in European studies, 1990—.

MEMBER: Association for the Study of Modern Italy, Italian Cultural Institute (London), Amnesty International, Campaign for Nuclear Disarmament.

AWARDS, HONORS: Scholar, British School at Rome, 1987-88; fellow of British Academy, 1990-93.

WRITINGS:

Gramsci and the Theory of Industrial Democracy, Avebury, 1991.
(With Richard Bellamy) *Gramsci and the Italian State,* Manchester University Press, 1993.
Radical Theories: Paths Beyond Marxism and Social Democracy, Manchester University Press, 1994.

Contributor of articles and translations to periodicals.

SIDELIGHTS: Darrow Schecter told *CA:* "There can be few greater pleasures than that of communicating one's most profound convictions to other interested people. As a writer, my *categorical imperatives* are to use every means possible (researching, talking to allies and opponents, traveling, drinking with friends) in order to deepen my insights about politics and contemporary western culture, and to have the courage necessary to defend the books that result from both the attacks of critics and my own self-pity! Thus, the very tricky combination of passion and irony are the indispensable tools of my survival as an individual and a writer."

*   *   *

SCHIFF, James A(ndrew) 1958-

PERSONAL: Born December 6, 1958, in Cincinnati, OH; son of Robert Cleveland (an insurance executive) and Adele Carol (a homemaker; maiden name, Roehr) Schiff; married Elizabeth Ann York (a lawyer), June 24, 1989; children: James Walker. *Education:* Duke University, B.A., 1981; New York University, M.A., 1985, Ph.D., 1990. *Avocational Interests:* Golf, film.

ADDRESSES: Home—2345 East Hill Ave., Cincinnati, OH 45208.

CAREER: University of Cincinnati, Cincinnati, OH, assistant professor of English, 1989—. Director of Mercantile Library, 1991—, First National Bank of Northern Kentucky, 1992—, WCET-TV, 1993—, and Cincinnati Preservation Association, 1993—.

MEMBER: Modern Languages Association (MLA), South Atlantic Modern Languages Association (SAMLA).

WRITINGS:

Updike's Version: Rewriting "The Scarlet Letter", University of Missouri Press, 1992.

Contributor to periodicals, including *South Atlantic Review, Southern Review,* and *Studies in American Fiction.*

WORK IN PROGRESS: A novel; a "comprehensive critical study covering John Updike's entire oeuvre."

SIDELIGHTS: James A. Schiff, who teaches English at the University of Cincinnati, is the author of *Updike's Version: Rewriting "The Scarlet Letter",* an analysis of American author John Updike's three novels—*A Month of Sundays, Roger's Version,* and *S.*—derived, in various measures, from nineteenth-century American author Nathaniel Hawthorne's *The Scarlet Letter.* Schiff casts Updike's trilogy as both postmodern parody and incisive social commentary. Donna B. Massey, writing in *Critique,* deemed *Updike's Version* "clear, well-researched, and informative," and concluded that the volume "establishes [Schiff] as an important critical voice on Updike." Carl S. Horner, writing in *American Literature,* called the book "a study of considerable critical importance," and *Christianity and Literature* contributor Margaret Hallissy wrote: "Schiff has done an admirable piece of work in ex-

plicating an important literary and theological influence on one of the twentieth century's major writers."

Schiff told *CA:* "I first became interested in a career in literature while at Duke University, where I studied with [American] novelist Reynolds Price. A brilliant writer, Price proved also to be a rare and generous teacher, and in class I learned that literature does indeed *matter* and that a career in literature is possible.

"I continue to read and write about contemporary American literature, and the writers, besides John Updike, who interest me most include Price, Toni Morrison, and Don DeLillo."

BIOGRAPHICAL/CRITICAL SOURCES:

PERIODICALS

American Literature, December, 1993, pp. 815-16. *Christianity and Literature,* summer, 1992, pp. 508-10. *Critique,* summer, 1993, pp. 269-70.

*   *   *

SCHMID, Wolfram George 1930-

PERSONAL: Born August 5, 1930, in Munich, Germany; son of Wolfram (a model maker) and Maria (a homemaker; maiden name, Zirngibl) Schmid; married Hildegarde Einhauser (a homemaker), August 1, 1953; children: Michael, Henry, Hildegarde, Wilhelmina, Siegfried.

ADDRESSES: Home—4417 Goodfellows Court, Tucker, GA 30084-2701.

CAREER: Practiced architecture and landscape architecture, 1952-64, and forest products engineering and silviculture, 1964-92. North American Plant Protection Council, member; creator of the garden Hosta Hill, 1969.

MEMBER: American Hosta Society (member of national board of directors, 1984—; historian, 1989—), American Horticultural Society, Hardy Plant Society, Royal Horticultural Society, British Hosta and Hemerocallis Society, Netherlands Hosta Society, Gesellschaft der Stauden, Georgia Perennial Plant Association, Georgia Hosta Society (founder, 1984; president, 1984-86 and 1994-96; editor, 1984-88 and 1992-93).

WRITINGS:

The Genus Hosta—Giboshi Zoku, edited by Gilbert S. Daniels, Timber Press, 1991.

Contributor to botany magazines.

SCHNEIDER, Elisa
  See KLEVEN, Elisa

* * *

SCHOUVALOFF, Alexander 1934-

PERSONAL: Born May 4, 1934, in London, England; son of Paul (an art director for films, under the name Paul Sheriff) and Anna (a teacher; maiden name, Raevsky) Schouvaloff; married Gillian Baker (divorced); married Daria de Marindol, November 18, 1971; children: (first marriage) Alexander. *Education:* Jesus College, Oxford, M.A., 1956. *Religion:* Russian Orthodox.

ADDRESSES: Home—10 Avondale Park Gardens, London W11 4PR, England. *Agent*—Artellus, 30 Dorset House, London N.W.1, England.

CAREER: H. M. Tennent (theatrical production management company), London, England, manager, 1959-64; Central Office of Information, London, information officer, 1964; Edinburgh Festival, Edinburgh, Scotland, assistant director, 1965-67; North West Arts Association, Manchester, England, founding director, 1967-74; Victoria and Albert Museum, London, founding curator of Theatre Museum, 1974-89; London Archives of the Dance, trustee, 1976—; Theatre Design Trust, chair, 1993—. *Military service:* British Army, 1957-59; became second lieutenant.

MEMBER: International Society of Libraries and Museums of the Performing Arts (secretary general, 1980-90), Society for Theatre Research (member of executive committee, 1975-89), Garrick Club.

WRITINGS:

(Editor) *Place for the Arts,* Seel House Press, 1970.
The Summer of the Bullshine Boys (novel), Quartet Books, 1979.
(With Victor Borovsky) *Stravinsky on Stage,* Stainer & Bell, 1982.
The Thyssen-Bornemisza Catalogue of Theatre and Ballet Designs, Sotheby Publications, 1987.
The Theatre Museum, Scala, 1987.
Theatre on Paper, Sotheby Publications, 1990.
Leon Bakst: The Theatre Art, Sotheby Publications, 1991.

Author of two plays broadcast by BBC-Radio.

WORK IN PROGRESS: Imperial Domes, on Russian Orthodox churches built outside Russia before the revolution, for Philip Wilson.

SIDELIGHTS: Alexander Schouvaloff told *CA:* "I began by writing several plays, none of which was professionally produced. One, however, was produced experimentally as a training exercise at a school for television directors. It made people laugh, so I thought I could write dialogue. I still want to write plays, but for the last twenty-five years I have been busy as an arts administrator and confined my writing to subjects connected with my work. I did publish one novel and hope that it will not be the only one. The trouble is that I am lazy when it comes to writing.

"I hope that the books I have written about the theater, particularly my last book on the theater art of Leon Bakst, will provide some new insight, add to the available information, and correct some previous faults and misconceptions. I enjoy research and go to original sources whenever possible. I was taught by a distinguished historian of the circus never to rely on the veracity of facts in earlier publications; but that implies that others should not rely on me either.

"I am sure I have absorbed influences from French and Russian writers, especially Stephane Mallarme, Andre Gide, Paul Valery, Albert Camus, Nikolay Gogol, and Anton Chekhov. I admire many American writers, particularly Alfred Hayes. Does T. S. Eliot count as American? And Raymond Chandler? Of English writers I regard Graham Greene as a great master. Winston Churchill gave me, when I was still a schoolboy, the only important tip: he told me to keep it simple and write short sentences. It is a precept to which it is often difficult to adhere."

* * *

SCHROEDER, Barbet 1941-

PERSONAL: Born April 26, 1941, in Teheran, Iran; Swiss citizen. *Education:* Attended the Sorbonne, University of Paris.

ADDRESSES: Agent—Creative Artists Agency, 9830 Wilshire Blvd., Beverly Hills, CA 90212.

CAREER: Director of motion pictures, including *The Charles Bukowski Tapes* (a collection of 50 four-minute clips), 1985; *Barfly,* 1987; *Reversal of Fortune,* 1990; and *Single White Female,* 1992. Producer of films, including *Ma Nuit chez Maud,* 1970, and *L'Amour, l'apres-midi,* 1972; coproducer of such films as *Chinese Roulette,* 1977, and *The American Friend,* 1977. Actor in films, including *La Boulangere de Monleau,* 1963; *Les Carabiniers,* 1968; *Celine and Julie Go Boating,* 1974; and *Roberte,* 1979. Founded Les Films du Losange, 1963.

AWARDS, HONORS: Academy Award nomination, best director, Academy of Motion Picture Arts and Sciences, and Golden Globe, best director, Hollywood Foreign Press Association, both 1990, both for *Reversal of Fortune.*

WRITINGS:

SCREENPLAYS; AND DIRECTOR

(Screenplay with Paul Gegauff) *More,* Cinema V, 1969.

La Vallee, 1972, released in the United States as *The Valley (Obscured by Clouds),* Lagoon Associates, 1972.

Idi Amin Dada (documentary), Prestige, 1974.

(Screenplay with Paul Voujargol) *Maitresse,* Gaumont, 1976.

Koko, le gorille qui parle (documentary), 1977, released in the United States as *Koko, the Talking Gorilla,* New Yorker, 1978.

(Screenplay with Pascal Bonitzer and Steve Baes) *Tricheurs* (title means "The Cheaters"), Films Galatee/Roissy Films, 1983.

OTHER

Contributor to periodicals, including *Cahiers du Cinema* and *L'Air du Paris.*

SIDELIGHTS: Barbet Schroeder is a distinguished filmmaker whose eclectic canon is comprised of both arthouse films and commercial fare. In the late 1950s, when directors such as Jean-Luc Godard and Francois Truffaut were drawing attention with their freewheeling, seemingly improvised works, Schroeder—like Godard and Truffaut—was writing criticism for the French film periodical *Cahiers du Cinema.* In the 1960s, Schroeder, who had founded his own production company at the age of twenty-two and had directed his first film at the age of twenty-seven, was already an important figure in the French New Wave movement.

In 1963, Schroeder founded Les Films du Losange, which primarily showcased the films of Eric Rohmer, a filmmaker whose early works include *La Carriere de Suzanne* and *La Collectioneuse.* The company also funded *Paris vu par,* a film produced by Schroeder which featured short works by various New Wave artists, including Rohmer. In the 1970s the company made its greatest gains in importance by presenting several films by such masters as Eric Rohmer and Jacques Rivette, including the latter's *Celine and Julie Go Boating,* a film which included Schroeder as a producer and a member of the cast.

In 1969 Schroeder completed *More,* his first work as writer-director. The English-language film features Stephan, a German student who completes his studies and decides to travel rather than pursue a career. He goes to Paris and befriends Charlie, a thief and gambler who, in turn, introduces him to Estelle, a modern femme fatale. Stephan soon becomes obsessed with the free-spirited, drug-using American woman, and when she leaves he commits a robbery to gain the funds necessary to track her. His search takes him to the estate of a drug-running ex-Nazi, where he discovers that Estelle is romantically involved with an-other woman. To please Estelle, Stephan begins using heroin. His inevitable addiction bears grim consequences. With its straightforward technique and graphic realism, *More* served as ample indication of Schroeder's filmmaking prowess. In the years since its release, however, the film has fallen into obscurity and has become known primarily for its musical score, which was provided by the psychedelic rock band Pink Floyd. It was released worldwide on video in 1990 by Warner Bros.

In 1972 Schroeder completed his second film, *The Valley (Obscured by Clouds),* which furthered his reputation as an uncompromising artist. In *The Valley,* a bourgeois woman adventures into the jungle and becomes increasingly involved in native culture. As she indulges her newfound interest in native customs, so too does she begin exerting her independence, and she eventually commences an affair with a decidedly iconoclastic adventurer.

Idi Amin Dada, Schroeder's next film, is a documentary that—like *More* and *The Valley* before it—revels in the unusual and disturbing. Here the subject is Ugandan dictator Idi Amin, notorious for his cruel measures and irrational actions. Amin is the deranged leader who reportedly fed prisoners to carnivorous animals and sought to establish a navy for his land-locked nation. *Idi Amin Dada* captures this fearful ruler in all his intimidating lunacy and thus functions—in effect—as a truly frightening comedy.

Schroeder followed *Idi Amin Dada* with *Maitresse,* a drama exploring sado-masochism. Here a young man blunders into the private workrooms of a professional dominatrix and covertly watches her work. The hero eventually finds true love with the dominatrix (their own sexual relationship is essentially conventional) and lures her from her bizarre—yet, presumably, lucrative—business.

With *Maitresse* Schroeder gained a fair measure of media attention, though such coverage inevitably focused on the film's subject matter instead of its actual artistry. To those reviewers focusing on Schroeder's actual achievement as a filmmaker, *Maitresse* leant further credibility to his reputation as a realist intrigued by the unlikely and unusual.

In 1978 Schroeder returned to the documentary genre with *Koko, the Talking Gorilla,* which details a gorilla's remarkable skill in communicating with humans. Schroeder next wrote and directed *Tricheurs,* the only one of his films which was not released theatrically in the United States. The work features a typically realistic examination of high-stakes gamblers. As often happens in Schroeder's films, the quirky protagonists, a man and a woman, find love with each other even as they indulge in potentially self-destructive enterprises. Curiously, though

Tricheurs has been accorded only scant attention in the United States; it too is available on videotape.

After completing *Tricheurs,* Schroeder became increasingly involved with Charles Bukowski, an American writer known for his coarse, ribald fiction. In the early 1980s Schroeder directed *The Charles Bukowski Tapes,* which is comprised of footage wherein Bukowski speaks on an endless range of subjects. This footage was divided into fifty sequences that were, in turn, broadcast independently on French television. "Some of the material is very outrageous," Schroeder told the *New York Times* in 1989. "But it was accepted as a bedtime story every night—a closing segment . . . just before the channel went to sleep." *The Charles Bukowski Tapes* is available in the United States on videotape by Lagoon Associates.

During the mid-1980s Schroeder futilely sought funding for a film he hoped to direct from an original screenplay by Bukowski. He finally found backing from Canon films, a company responsible for the distribution of films ranging from exploitation fare to European art films. The result of Schroeder's considerable efforts was *Barfly,* which was readily acclaimed for its raucous insights into the artistic temperament. The film's hero is Henry, a hard-drinking denizen of squalid East Hollywood. When not brawling with a surly bartender or insulting the occasional fans, Henry finds time to romance a fellow alcoholic, Wanda, who is beautiful but deranged. Henry and Wanda make a surprisingly appealing couple, and though they are essentially self-destructive, they nonetheless obtain—however briefly—a measure of dignity and happiness together.

Schroeder is probably best known for *Reversal of Fortune,* for which Jeremy Irons received an Academy Award for best actor. This 1991 production—which Schroeder directed from a script by Nicholas Kazan—concerns the controversial legal case involving Claus von Bulow and famed law professor Alan Dershowitz. In this unlikely satire, Irons plays von Bulow, who is accused of abetting the demise of his wife, the incredibly rich Sunny von Bulow. Faced with likely imprisonment if found guilty, von Bulow enlists the aid of Dershowitz, a supremely enterprising attorney who is initially doubtful of von Bulow's innocence. Despite this reservation, Dershowitz accepts von Bulow's case. But he never entirely abandons a general suspicion of von Bulow's conduct, and von Bulow, in turn, endeavors to charm Dershowitz while simultaneously maintaining some semblance of authority. Among the many enthusiasts of *Reversal of Fortune* was *New York*'s David Denby, who hailed the film as "brilliantly elegant, subtle, and funny."

Single White Female, Schroeder's next work, is a thriller in which Allie, a self-employed Manhattan computer maven, discovers that her new roommate is determined to assume her identity. When Allie rebels, the deranged roommate embarks on a homicidal mission. This film, which Schroeder fashioned from Don Roos's script—was deemed predictable, but Schroeder's handling of the material was considered accomplished.

Although by the late 1970s Schroeder was recognized most readily as a filmmaker, he also continued as a producer. Among the films his company Les Films du Losange coproduced were Rainer Werner Fassbinder's *Chinese Roulette* and Wim Wenders's *The American Friend.*

BIOGRAPHICAL/CRITICAL SOURCES:

PERIODICALS

Interview, August, 1992, pp. 96-97.
Newsweek, November 5, 1990, p. 80.
New York, October 29, 1990, pp. 89-90; August 31, 1992, p. 48.
New Yorker, November 2, 1987, pp. 137-40; November 19, 1990, pp. 129-30.
New York Times, January 22, 1989, p. B18.
People, November 2, 1987, p. 14.
Time, August 17, 1992, p. 63.

*   *   *

SCHWARTZMAN, Simon   1939-

PERSONAL: Born July 3, 1939, in Belo Horizonte, Brazil; son of Zolmia and Chava R. Schwartzman; married Inez Maria Farah; children: Michel, Luisa, Isabel, Felipe. *Education:* Federal University of Minas Gerais, Bacharel em Administracao Publica, 1961, Bacharel em Sociologia e Politica, 1961; Latin American School of Social Sciences, Diploma de Estudios de Pos-Graduacion, 1963; University of California, Berkeley, Ph.D., 1973.

ADDRESSES: Home—Rua Antonio Vieira 17, Apt. 1201, 22010 Leme, Rio de Janeiro, Brazil. *Office*—Nucleo de Pesquisas sobre Ensino Superior, Universidade de Sao Paulo, Rua do Anfiteatro 181, Colmeia 9, Cidade Universitaria, 05508-900 Sao Paulo, Brazil.

CAREER: Universidade Federal de Minas Gerais, Minas Gerais, Brazil, assistant professor of political science, 1964; International Peace Research Institute, Oslo, Norway, research fellow, 1965; Fundacion Bariloche, Buenos Aires, Argentina, research fellow, 1966; Instituto Universitario de Pesquisas do Rio de Janeiro, Rio de Janeiro, Brazil, professor of sociology and political science, 1969-87; Universidade de Sao Paulo, Sao Paulo, Brazil, professor of political science, 1989—, scientific director, Nucleo de Pesquisas sobre Educacao Superior, 1989—, director, Centro de Pesquisa e Gestao Tecnologica, Escola de Administracao de Empresas de Sao Paulo da Fundacao Getulio Vargas, 1989—, fellow of Instituto de Estudos Avancados, 1988-89. Woodrow Wilson International Center for Scholars, fellow, 1978; Columbia University, Edward LaRoque Tinker Visiting Professor, 1986; University of California, Berkeley, visiting professor and visiting associate at Center for Studies in Higher Education and Institute of International Studies, all 1987. Financiadora de Estudos e Projetos, researcher and program officer, 1975-78; Centro de Pesquisa e Documentacao em Historia Contemporanea do Brasil, researcher, 1979-89; Ecole des Hautes Etudes en Sciences Sociales (Paris), director of studies at Centre d'Etudes des Mouvements Sociaux, 1983; Swedish Collegium for Advanced Study in the Social Sciences, fellow, 1987-88; National Research Council of Brazil, researcher, 1988.

MEMBER: International Sociological Association (vice-president of Research Committee on the Sociology of Science and Technology), International Political Science Association, Latin American Studies Association, Brazilian Sociological Association (president, 1989-91).

AWARDS, HONORS: Grants from Ford Foundation, World Bank, Swedish Council for Planning and Coordination of Research, and Carnegie Commission on Higher Education.

WRITINGS:

A Space for Science: The Development of the Scientific Community in Brazil, Pennsylvania State University Press, 1991.

Work represented in anthologies, including *Mathematical Approaches to Politics,* edited by H. Alker, K. Deutsch, and A. H. Stoetzel, Elsevier Scientific, 1973; *Brazil's Economic and Political Future,* edited by Julian Chacel, Pamela S. Falk, and David V. Fleischer, Westview, 1986; and *Social Sciences and Modern States,* edited by Peter Wagner, Bjorn Wittrock, and others, Cambridge University Press, 1991. Contributor to professional journals. Member of editorial board, *Higher Education,* 1992-95, and *Metropolitan Universities.*

IN PORTUGUESE OR SPANISH

Sao Paulo e o Estado Nacional, Difel, 1975.
Formacao da Comunidade Cientifica no Brasil, Vinep, 1975.
(Editor) *Metodos Avanzados de Investigacion Social,* Ed. Nueva Vision (Buenos Aires), 1977.
Ciencia, Universidade e Ideologia: A Politica do Conhecimento, Zahar, 1980.
O Pensamento Nacionalista e os 'Cadernos de Nosso Tempo, Editora da Universidade de Brasilia, 1981.

Bases do Autoritarismo Brasileiro, Editora Campus e Editora da Universidade de Brasilia, 1982, 3rd edition, 1988.
Universidades e Instituicoes Cientificas no Rio de Janeiro, Conselho Nacional de Desenvolvimento Cientifico e Tecnologico, 1982.
(Editor) *Estado Novo: Um Auto-Retrato,* Editora da Universidade de Brasilia, 1983.
(With Helena Maria Bousquet Bomeny and Vera Maria Pereira Costa) *Tempos de Capanema,* Editora Paz, 1984.
(Editor with Claudio de Moura Castro) *A Pesquisa Universitaria em Questao,* Icone Editora, 1986.
(Editor with Eunice R. Durham) *O Impacto da Avaliacao na Universidade,* Editora de Universidade de Sao Paulo, 1992.

Work represented in anthologies. Contributor to scholarly journals. Member of editorial board, *Dados: Revista de Ciencias Sociais, Estudos Historicos, Revista Colombiana de Sociologia,* and *Nova Economia.*

*   *   *

SCOTT, Dennis (Courtney) 1939-1991

PERSONAL: Born December 16, 1939, in Kingston, Jamaica; died February 21, 1991, after a prolonged illness; married Joy Scott. *Education:* Attended Jamaica College; received B.A. from University of the West Indies.

ADDRESSES: Office—School of Drama, 1 Arthur Wint Dr., Kingston 5, Jamaica.

CAREER: Poet, playwright, actor, dancer, and theatrical director. Taught English and Spanish at Presentation College, Trinidad, then taught at Kingston College and Jamaica College. Became director of Jamaica School of Drama and Dean of the Four Schools of Cultural Training Centre, Kingston, Jamaica. Performed with National Dance Theater Company of Jamaica. Visiting professor, Yale University, 1983.

AWARDS, HONORS: Shubert Playwrighting Award, 1970; Commonwealth fellowship, 1972; International Poetry Forum Award, 1973, for *Uncle Time;* Commonwealth Poetry Prize, 1974; Silver Musgrave Medal, 1974; Prime Minister's Award, 1983, for contribution to art and education; Jamaican Festival Commission bronze and silver medals, for poetry; has received best director awards.

WRITINGS:

POETRY

Journeys and Ceremonies, privately published, 1969.
Uncle Time, University of Pittsburgh Press, 1973.
Dreadwalk: Poems, 1970-78, New Beacon, 1982.

Strategies, Sandberry Press, 1989.

Also contributor to *Seven Jamaican Poets: An Anthology of Recent Poetry,* edited by Mervyn Morris, Bolivar, 1971, and *Poems from "On the Offbeat"; read at the Barn Theatre, October-November, 1966, [by] Mervyn Morris, Basil McFarlane [and] Dennis Scott,* 1966.

PLAYS

Terminus, University of the West Indies Extra-Mural Department, 1966.

Echo in the Bone (produced in Kingston, Jamaica, at Creative Arts Centre, 1974), published in *Plays for Today,* edited by Errol Hill, Longmans, 1985.

The Fantasy of Sir Gawain and the Green Knight (adaptation of medieval poem; first produced in Washington, DC, at Kennedy Center, 1977), O'Neill Press, 1979.

Dog, produced in Kingston at Creative Arts Centre, 1978.

Also author of *The Crime of Anabel Campbell,* published in *Caribbean Plays for Playing,* edited by Keith Noel, Heinemann, 1985.

SIDELIGHTS: Dennis Scott is a poet and playwright whose works display an unusual and effective use of language. In *Contemporary Poets,* Edward Kamau Brathwaite commented: "You can dip into most of Dennis C. Scott's poems and come up with glories." Proficient in both his native Jamaican idiom and standard English, Scott exemplifies the split nature of the Jamaican people, descendants of slaves, free yet still dominated by the English culture. His poetry includes personal lyrics concerning relationships, political pieces in which the persona speaks as a representative of his people, and poems which express in surreal and magical imagery the human condition.

In *Uncle Time,* Scott's first major collection to appear in the United States, the author displays his ability to incorporate his dual identity as representative black Jamaican man, and as middle-class, educated, performance artist in poems that utilize both the Jamaican idiom and standard English diction and syntax. A reviewer in *Choice* remarked: "The book is of uneven quality, but all the individual poems bear the stamp of originality, interest, and excitement."

Scott's poetry relies heavily on surrealistic imagery to convey the fear and pain of existence in his beautiful but tragic homeland. The persona utilized most often in his first two major collections, *Uncle Time* and *Dreadwalk,* is heraldic, a voice speaking for a whole people. Critics note the magical quality of much of the language in poems in which the poet appears as conjurer or mythological figure. Scott's vision is often apocalyptic, with mortal danger lurking alongside the magic, as in "Infection": "But the cop was frightened, / never having seen a man make a knife / out

of moonlight and laughter. / So he shot him." In Scott's later works, which are concerned with the recovery and acceptance of the history of his people, the menace of the earlier work is less present, and reviewers note that the voice of the poems is more at peace, sympathetic rather than frightened.

The Fantasy of Sir Gawain and the Green Knight, Scott's adaptation of the famous medieval poem concerning one of the knights of King Arthur's Round Table, was commissioned for performance at the Children's Arts Festival in 1977 by a troupe composed of both hearing and deaf actors. Reviewers commended the charm of Scott's rendering of the medieval legend as a fairy tale and noted its appropriateness for a wide range of players. A critic in *Horn Book* concluded: "The terse dialogue is a skillful simplification of the rich complexity of the original story."

Scott has also written a play, *Echo in the Bone,* which presents a wake on a Jamaican plantation as the catalyst for working through the emotional legacy of slavery.

BIOGRAPHICAL/CRITICAL SOURCES:

BOOKS

Contemporary Poets, St. James, 1991.
Dictionary of Literary Biography, Volume 125, *Twentieth-Century Caribbean and Black African Writers, Second Series,* Gale, 1993.

PERIODICALS

Callaloo, summer, 1990, p. 570.
Choice, May, 1974, p. 440; March, 1980, p. 85.
Horn Book, June, 1980, pp. 314-15.*

*   *   *

SCOTT, Kenneth   1900-1993

OBITUARY NOTICE—See index for *CA* sketch: Born May 4, 1900, in Waterbury, CT; died of pneumonia, December 11, 1993, in Maryland. Genealogist, professor, and author. An academic who published over fifty books and hundreds of articles during his long career, Scott served as a professor at institutions including Western Reserve University (now Case Western Reserve University), Upsala College, Wagner College in Staten Island, New York, and Queens College of the City University of New York. He was also a past president of the New York Genealogical and Biographical Society. Many of Scott's writings are the result of his interest in genealogy, such as *Genealogical Data from the Pennsylvania Chronicle, 1767-1774, New York Marriage Bonds, 1753-1783,* and *British Aliens in the United States during the War of 1812.* He also displayed his interest in America's history of counterfeiting in a number of books, including *Counterfeiting in Colonial America.* In addition, Scott wrote of ancient Rome. His last work, *Naturalizations in the Marine Court, New York City, 1834-1840,* was published in 1991.

OBITUARIES AND OTHER SOURCES:

BOOKS

Who's Who in Genealogy and Heraldry, Volume 1, Gale, 1981, pp. 181-82.

PERIODICALS

New York Times, December 15, 1993, p. B12.

* * *

SCOTT, Leonard B. III 1948-

PERSONAL: Born January 2, 1948, in Bremerhaven, Germany; son of Leonard B. (a military officer) and Eileen (Niles) Scott; married Jammye Clark; children: three. *Education:* Central State University of Oklahoma, M.E., 1978; graduated from U.S. Army War College, 1988. *Politics:* Conservative Republican. *Religion:* Protestant.

ADDRESSES: Home—1808 Canary Dr., Edmond, OK 73034.

CAREER: U.S. Army, became colonel, served in Vietnam War; writer.

AWARDS, HONORS: Numerous military distinctions, including Silver Star Medal, Air Medal for Valor, Purple Heart, and Bronze Star.

WRITINGS:

MILITARY NOVELS

Charlie Mike, Ballantine, 1985.
The Last Run, Ballantine, 1987.
The Hill, Ballantine, 1989.
The Expendables, Ballantine, 1991.
Iron Men, Ballantine, 1993.

WORK IN PROGRESS: Forged in Honor, a military novel.

SIDELIGHTS: Leonard B. Scott III is a distinguished army colonel who has published several military novels. Among his writings, many of which are set during the Vietnam War, are *The Hill,* in which two Oklahoma stepbrothers serve as paratroopers in the Vietnam conflict's pivotal Hill 874 encounter; and *The Expendables,* about the troops of an air cavalry unit fighting against the North Vietnamese Army. Scott is also the author of *Iron Men,* the story of three distinguished German soldiers who seek revenge against a Nazi officer who ordered the execution

of their unit—on grounds of betrayal to the German cause—at the close of World War II.

Scott told *CA:* "I write to educate as well as tell a story. I want the reader to care for and be with my main characters—if the reader doesn't laugh or cry and feel the same emotions of my characters then I have failed.

"I'm one of those guys who battled with college English and lost. People who know me are still in shock that I'm published. But I could always spin a good yarn and bore 'em to tears with 'war stories.' I had books in my head and knew I could write despite what my teachers had told me. The dam broke while I was stationed at the Pentagon. I got involved in the Vietnam memorial ceremony and saw many of my old comrades from the war. Seeing them and reliving the old days squelched my fears of attempting to write—I *had* to tell our story of the war and how it really was.

"Writing is a lonely business, so it's good to hear from readers and get their feedback. Because I've had no schooling, I'm uncomfortable giving technical advice. What I do know is this: You can't talk and think about it—you have to sit down and do it. The only other advice I give is, don't try and write the perfect first sentence or paragraph—it's not possible. Drive on and finish your story, then go back and do your rewrites. And never, ever give up. Keep at it. Persistence is the key."

* * *

SEAMAN, P. David 1932-

PERSONAL: Born January 31, 1932, in Connellsville, PA; married Mary Miller (a homemaker), January 27, 1953; children: Nancy Dawn Seaman Agan, Mark David, Donald Paul. *Education:* Asbury College, A.B., 1957; University of Kentucky, M.A., 1958; Indiana University—Bloomington, Ph.D., 1965. *Religion:* Methodist.

ADDRESSES: Home—4221 East White Aster St., Phoenix, AZ 85044. *Office*—Department of Anthropology, Northern Arizona University, Box 15200, Flagstaff, AZ 86011.

CAREER: Asbury College, Wilmore, KY, instructor, 1957-65, professor of languages and head of division of languages, 1965-67; Northern Arizona University, Flagstaff, associate professor, 1967-70, professor of linguistics, 1970—, staff member of NDEA English as a Second Language Institute, 1968, founder and director of National Science Foundation Summer Linguistics Institute, 1968-73. Toronto Institute of Linguistics, visiting instructor, summer, 1961; Allegheny College, visiting instructor, summer, 1961; Drew University, visiting instructor, summer, 1962; State University of New York College at Oswego, visiting professor, summer, 1965; Marylhurst College, visiting professor, summer, 1966; University of Athens, senior Fulbright lecturer, 1969-70. Greek Ministry of Education, American representative on English language textbook committee, 1969-70; U.S. Educational Foundation in Greece, head of English Language Program in Greece, 1969-70; Athens College, director of Linguistic Institute for Greek Teachers of English, summer, 1970; linguistic consultant to Panhellenic Association of Foreign Language Schools and Pyrsos Foreign Language Schools. Loglan Language Institute, member of national board of scientific advisers, 1990—. Arizona Academy of Science, head of Anthropology section, 1968-69; lecturer on Native Americans and sociolinguistics; consultant to Zuni Tribal Council and Bureau of Indian Affairs. Flagstaff Chamber of Commerce, member of committee on university relations, 1968-69; Coconino Estates Swimming Pool Association, member of board of directors, 1971-73; Flagstaff Medical Center, member of cost containment committee, 1980-81. University Heights Corp., director, 1972-86; Flagstaff Medical Center, member of finance committee, 1980—. *Military service:* U.S. Army, 1953-54; served in Korea; received Commendation Medal.

AWARDS, HONORS: Fellow at East-West Center, Honolulu, HI, 1992.

WRITINGS:

Modern Greek and American English in Contact, Mouton, 1972.
(Editor with Steve Weber) *Havasupai Habitat: A. F. Whiting's Ethnography of a Traditional Indian Culture,* University of Arizona Press, 1985.
Hopi Dictionary: Hopi-English, English-Hopi, Grammatical Appendix, Northern Arizona University, 1985, revised edition, 1993.
(Editor) *Born a Chief: The Nineteenth Century Hopi Boyhood of Edmund Nequatewa,* University of Arizona Press, 1993.
The A. F. Whiting Collection: User Guide and Index, Northern Arizona University, 1993.

Contributor of articles and reviews to humanities, anthropology, and linguistics journals.

WORK IN PROGRESS: Linguistic research on Native American cultures, especially the tribes of Arizona.

BIOGRAPHICAL/CRITICAL SOURCES:

PERIODICALS

American Anthropologist, December, 1986.
National Geographic, March, 1990.

SEDYCH, Andrei
See ZWIBAK, Jacques

*   *   *

SELF, Will 1961-

PERSONAL: Born in 1961, in London, England; son of Peter Self (a college professor) and Elaine (Rosenbloom) Self (a publisher); married Kate Chancellor, June 13, 1990; children: Alexis, Madeleine. *Education:* Attended Oxford University, 1979-92, received M.A. (with honors). *Politics:* None. *Religion:* None.

ADDRESSES: Agent—Ed Victor, 162 Wardour St., London W1V 3AT, England.

CAREER: Worked as a clerk and a laborer. Full-time writer.

AWARDS, HONORS: Shortlisted for John Llewellyn Rhys Prize, 1991; Geoffrey Faber Memorial Prize, 1992; voted one of twenty best young British writers in *Granta,* 1993.

WRITINGS:

The Quantity Theory of Insanity (short stories), Bloomsbury, 1991.
Cock and Bull (two novellas), Atlantic Monthly Press, 1992.
My Idea of Fun: A Cautionary Tale (novel), Atlantic Monthly Press, 1994.

Contributor of cartoons to periodicals, including *New Statesman* and *City Limits,* and of articles and reviews to periodicals, including *Esquire, Harpers,* and *Independent.*

WORK IN PROGRESS: Junk Male, a book of essays on drug addiction; and *Between the Conceits,* a book of short stories.

SIDELIGHTS: The works of Will Self can be distinguished by their black humor and uncompromising themes. Self is the author of short stories, which are collected in *The Quantity Theory of Insanity,* as well as longer works of fiction like the two novellas which comprise *Cock and Bull.* In 1994 Self issued his first full-length novel, *My Idea of Fun: A Cautionary Tale.* His themes include such dark subjects as madness and sexual confusion, although Nick Hornby in the *Times Literary Supplement* pointed out that "greyness intrigues him even more; it is its fascination with the institutional and the mundane that gives his work a paradoxical drama." In *Vanity Fair,* Zoe Heller observed that "the tone of *Quantity Theory*—both energetic and strangely lugubrious—was often profoundly discomfiting. And it was not difficult to guess that Self's thematic preoccupations—madness, altered states, the sinister authority of the psychiatric establishment—refracted a painful biography.''

Self reveals an intimate knowledge of drug culture in his fiction, having used various substances like marijuana, amphetamines, and cocaine while he was a teenager. Eventually, he became addicted to heroin; Self described himself in *Vanity Fair* as a "hard-core junkie" for almost eight years before he finally received treatment to end his habit. Heller noted in *Vanity Fair* that "the very texture of his prose bears the influence of his familiarity with drugs. . . . He has a gloriously vast vocabulary and a fetish for polysyllabic words. . . . It is most noticeable that where his vocabulary becomes most clotted, where his sentences require the most frequent application to the dictionary, he is often attempting to pin down the nuance of a precise psychic or physical experience—drug derived perceptions for which no quotidian phrases are available."

Madness is a topic which repeatedly appears within the stories of *The Quantity Theory of Insanity.* In "Ward 9" an art therapist suffers a nervous breakdown and enters a mental asylum. The title story is based upon the proposition "that sanity is a finite quantity in any given social group," according to Hornby in the *Times Literary Supplement.* Hornby pointed out that Self's stories are "full of dreary but threatening institutions," and added, "Though you wouldn't want to live in the Self universe . . . in the end, you are grateful that he has gone through the agonies necessary for its creation."

The pair of novellas in *Cock and Bull* both concern the inexplicable metamorphosis which transforms the respective main characters into the opposite sex. In *Bull,* a one-time rugby player named John Bull awakens one morning to discover that he has a vagina located behind his knee. "John Bull's behavior grows more and more feminine as he starts coping with premenstrual tension, water weight gain and hormonal ups and downs," Michiko Kakutani elaborated in the *New York Times.* Seeking help from his physician, Bull visits Dr. Alan Margoulies, but the doctor becomes obsessed with Bull's condition and attempts to seduce him. "Margoulies's infatuation with Bull—or, rather, his new plaything—is a witty satire on the kind of man who is obsessed with women's sex organs and ignores the rest of them," commented Rhoda Koenig in *New York.* The reviewer also informed that "the doctor gets his comeuppance, and Bull, who also acquires feminine qualities of vulnerability, finds satisfaction in a unique homosexual relationship."

Like Bull, the protagonist of *Cock* also undergoes a sexual transformation; this time, Carol, a homemaker, grows a penis and develops increasingly masculine traits. She begins to dominate her alcoholic husband and eventually—according to Julie Wheelwright in the *New Statesman*—

"enacts a rape as revenge for her husband's sexual ineptitude." Kakutani pointed out in the *New York Times* the perceived "blatant sexism" of the novella, writing, "In *Cock,* we learn that the woman who stands up for herself relinquishes her femininity and literally turns into a man, in Carol's case a particularly foul-minded man filled with homicidal rage." However, Wheelright in the *New Statesman* believed that the altered sexual physiology of Bull and Carol "appear as satirical metaphors of liberation." Self explained in *Vanity Fair* that he wrote *Cock and Bull* to voice his "anger at the way gender-based sexuality is so predetermined, the way we fit into our sex roles as surely as if we had cut them off the back of a cereal packet and pasted them onto ourselves."

BIOGRAPHICAL/CRITICAL SOURCES:

PERIODICALS

Granta 43, spring, 1993, p. 259.
New Statesman, October 30, 1992, p. 35.
New York, May 17, 1993, p. 87.
New York Times, May 31, 1993.
Times Literary Supplement, December 20, 1991, p. 25; October 9, 1992, p. 22.
Vanity Fair, June, 1993, pp. 125-127, 148-151.

*   *   *

SHAPIRO, Fred(eric) C(harles)   1931-1993

OBITUARY NOTICE—See index for *CA* sketch: Born February 3, 1931, in Washington, DC; died of pancreatic cancer October 22, 1993, in Manhattan, NY. Journalist and author. A reporter for newspapers including the *Philadelphia Daily News, Baltimore News-Post,* and *New York Herald Tribune,* Shapiro won acclaim for his coverage of the 1989 Tiananmen Square demonstration in Beijing, China. Shapiro's account of the Chinese Communist Party's brutal quelling of the peaceful anti-government protest was published in the *New Yorker,* a periodical on which he once worked as a staff writer. Shapiro had moved to China in 1987 to serve as an editor for the official New China News Agency, a post he resumed after the Tiananmen Square demonstration. His writings on the event earned him an Overseas Press Club prize. He was also awarded the 1969 Robert F. Kennedy journalism prize for his writings on George Whitmore, who was falsely accused of murder. Shapiro also coauthored the book *Race Riots, New York 1964.*

OBITUARIES AND OTHER SOURCES:

PERIODICALS

New York Times, October 23, 1993, p. 10.
Washington Post, October 27, 1993, p. D5.

SHASHA, Dennis (E.) 1955-

PERSONAL: Born August 15, 1955, in White Plains, NY; son of Alfred (in business) and Hanina (a painter; maiden name, Zilkha) Shasha; married, wife's name, Karen (an artist), June 5, 1983; children: Cloe, Tyler. *Education:* Yale University, B.S., 1977; Syracuse University, M.S., 1980; Harvard University, Ph.D., 1984. *Politics:* Liberal. *Religion:* Jewish.

ADDRESSES: Office—Courant Institute of Mathematical Sciences, New York University, 251 Mercer St., New York, NY 10012.

CAREER: New York University, New York City, assistant professor, 1984-90, associate professor of computer science, 1990—. Worked for Bell Laboratories and Unix System Laboratories, American Telephone and Telegraph, 1987—, and Marble Associates, Inc., 1993—; technical consultant to Ellis Island Restoration Commission.

WRITINGS:

The Puzzling Adventures of Dr. Ecco, W. H. Freeman, 1988.
Codes, Puzzles, and Conspiracy, W. H. Freeman, 1992.
Database Training: A Principled Approach, Prentice-Hall, 1992.

WORK IN PROGRESS: Profiles of fourteen great computer scientists.

SIDELIGHTS: Dennis Shasha describes his books *The Puzzling Adventures of Dr. Ecco* and *Codes, Puzzles, and Conspiracy* as "adventures of a mathematical detective, whose problems are often algorithmic or combinatoric in nature."

The author added: "I'm not really a writer. Mostly I like to invent puzzles, tell stories, and explain things so even I could understand them. My motivation when researching books is to learn new ideas and how they came about. My goal for the finished book is to convey both the problem that a clever idea addresses and the kernel of the solution. My hope is that readers will enjoy what they read and be inspired to new discoveries."

*   *   *

SHAW, Martin 1947-

PERSONAL: Born June 30, 1947, in Driffield, East Yorkshire, England; son of Sir Roy (a former secretary general of the Arts Council of Great Britain) and Lady Gwenyth Shaw; married Joanna Close, July 21, 1989. *Education:* London School of Economics and Political Science, B.A. (with first class honors), 1968; University of Hull, Ph.D., 1993.

ADDRESSES: Office—Department of Sociology and Anthropology, University of Hull, Hull HU6 7RX, England.

CAREER: University of Durham, Durham, England, lecturer in sociology, 1970-72; University of Hull, Hull, England, senior lecturer and reader in sociology, 1972—.

WRITINGS:

Marxism and Social Science, Pluto, 1975.
(Editor) *War, State, and Society,* St. Martin's, 1984.
(Editor) *Marxist Sociology Revisited,* Macmillan, 1985.
(Editor) *The Sociology of War and Peace,* Macmillan, 1987.
Dialectics of War, Pluto, 1988.
Post-Military Society: Militarism, Demilitarization, and War at the End of the Twentieth Century, Temple University Press, 1992.

*   *   *

SHAW, Patrick W. 1938-

PERSONAL: Born July 30, 1938, in Denison, TX; son of Henry W. (a manual laborer) and Sadie (a homemaker; maiden name, Snell) Shaw; married Patricia Foss (an office manager), June 17, 1967; children: Allison P., Erin P. *Education:* Austin College, B.A., 1962; North Texas State University, M.A., 1965; Louisiana State University, Ph.D., 1972. *Politics:* Democrat. *Religion:* Protestant. *Avocational Interests:* Hiking, photography, restoring old cars, Native American history.

ADDRESSES: Home—6128 Lynnhaven Dr., Lubbock, TX 79413. *Office*—Department of English, Texas Tech University, Lubbock, TX 79409.

CAREER: University of Missouri—Rolla, instructor in English, 1966-67; Louisiana State University, instructor in English, 1968-72; Texas Tech University, Lubbock, professor of English, 1972—. Worked variously as an assistant manager of a cinema, an advertising artist for a newspaper, and a public relations writer for an insurance company.

MEMBER: American Association of University Professors, South Central Modern Language Association, Rocky Mountain Modern Language Association, Central Council of Teachers of English, Phi Kappa Phi.

AWARDS, HONORS: Grant from National Endowment for the Humanities, 1989.

WRITINGS:

Literature: A College Anthology, with instructor's manual, Houghton, 1977.
Willa Cather and the Art of Conflict: Re-Visioning Her Creative Imagination, Whitston, 1992.

Work represented in books, including *Major Literary Characters: Antonia,* edited by Harold Bloom, Chelsea House, 1991; and *A New Study Guide to Steinbeck's Major Works,* edited by Tetsumaro Hayashi, Scarecrow, 1993. Contributor of about forty articles and stories to periodicals, including *South Central Review, Southern Studies, American Notes and Queries, Studies in Contemporary Satire, Mark Twain Journal,* and *American Imago.*

WORK IN PROGRESS: Two novels, *Slope* and *The Big Shaggy;* a critical study of the American novels and criticism of the 1950s; a book on Willa Cather.

SIDELIGHTS: Patrick W. Shaw told *CA:* "With the exception of several short stories published some years ago, my writing has been academic. For the past two or three years, however, at least half of my writing time has been devoted to fiction. I have finished two novels, both of which are contemporary western mysteries set in the canyon lands off the eastern edge of the Llano Estacado in West Texas.

"Aside from a desire to escape the negative elements of academia, I am not sure what motivates my writing, critical or creative. Most contemporary trends and 'isms' of literary scholarship are bloodless and offer practically no insights into the creative process. Thus, I do not consider myself a scholar or researcher, since I have no patience with or talent for the pedantry associated with those titles. I do enjoy the challenge of literary analysis and of creating fictional characters and situations.

"My interest in Willa Cather grew somewhat ironically out of my fascination with Ernest Hemingway. I wanted to find an American author, contemporary with Hemingway, who was as much unlike him as possible—a kind of polar juxtaposition, I suppose. The more I read by and about Cather, however, the more she asserted herself as an independent, extremely subtle writer who was artistically subservient to no other writer. The range of her fiction and the complexity of her private life were intriguing and offered fresh opportunities for creative analysis.

"Prior to drifting into the academic life, I worked as an assistant manager of a second-run picture show, an advertising artist for a newspaper, and a public relations writer for an insurance company. Today I consider myself primarily a teacher, and I restrict my writing to those topics which I find intrinsically worthwhile and enjoyable."

*　　*　　*

SHAW, William 1959-

PERSONAL: Born May 17, 1959, in Newton Abbot, England; son of Warren (a writer) and Francesca (a bookseller; maiden name, Lumby) Shaw. *Education:* University of Sussex, B.A. (with honors), 1983.

ADDRESSES: Home and office—94 Hassett Rd., London E9 5SH, England. *Agent*—Peters, Fraser & Dunlop, The Chambers, Chelsea Harbour, Lots Rd., London SW10 0XF, England.

CAREER: Free-lance journalist, 1983—.

WRITINGS:

(With Richard Lowe) *Travellers,* Fourth Estate, 1993.
Happy Clappy: Spying in Guru-Land (tentative title), Fourth Estate, 1994.

Contributor to the magazine *Details.*

SIDELIGHTS: William Shaw told *CA:* "I've been a magazine journalist in the United Kingdom and the United States for ten years. Last winter a colleague and I spent two months applying what I'd learned interviewing celebrities to more ordinary mortals—Britain's new age travelers—who've abandoned their homes to live permanently on the road in an attempt to escape modern life.

"Now I'm writing a book about another group of escapists: people who join religious cults. Cult leaders usually take all the blame for what's done in their names, but for me that isn't a sufficient explanation of Waco or Jonestown. By the time I've finished the book, I'll have been an 'undercover' member of at least six British cults. I hope to learn something about what's in it for the ordinary members, and how they cooperate with the charismatic leaders to construct an alternative world."

*　　*　　*

SHEEHAN, George (Augustine) 1918-1993

OBITUARY NOTICE—See index for *CA* sketch: Born November 5, 1918, in Brooklyn, NY; died of prostate cancer, November 1, 1993, in Ocean Grove, NJ. Cardiologist, public speaker, and author. Sheehan developed a passion for recreational running at the age of forty-four; by the age of fifty he had set a world age-group record for the mile. His running interest resulted in the authorship of numerous books that incorporated his background as a cardiologist. Included in his writings are *Dr. Sheehan on Running, Running and Being: The Total Experience, Dr. Sheehan's Medical Advice for Runners,* and *This Running Life.* Sheehan quit his medical practice in 1984 to devote more time to running and to his expanding career as a public speaker—lecturing on the benefits and spiritual aspects of running. Among his other books are *Encyclopedia of Athletic Medicine* and *How to Feel Great Twenty-Four Hours a Day.* Sheehan was also a weekly columnist for the

Red Bank Register and *Physician* magazine and served as the medical editor for *Runner's World.*

OBITUARIES AND OTHER SOURCES:

BOOKS

Biography Index, 17th edition, H. W. Wilson, 1992.

PERIODICALS

New York Times, November 2, 1993, p. B9.
Times (London), November 13, 1993, p.19.

*   *   *

SHELDON, Joseph K(enneth)   1943-

PERSONAL: Born November 11, 1943, in Ogden, UT; son of Donald David (a jeweler and watchmaker) and Ina May (a clerk in the family jewelry store; maiden name, Kramp) Sheldon; married Donna Sherrie Zielaskowski (a homemaker), August, 1965; children: Jodi Gwyn Sheldon Elliott-Jones, Bret Eugene. *Education:* Received B.S. from College of Idaho and Ph.D. from University of Illinois at Urbana-Champaign. *Politics:* Independent. *Religion:* Protestant. *Avocational Interests:* Fishing, hiking, travel.

ADDRESSES: Home—202 Chestnut Grove Rd., Dillsburg, PA 17019. *Office*—Department of Natural Sciences, Messiah College, Grantham, PA 19027.

CAREER: Eastern College, St. Davids, PA, professor of biology, 1971-92; Messiah College, Grantham, PA, professor of biology, 1992—.

MEMBER: American Institute of Biological Sciences, American Entomological Society (president, 1991—), Ecological Society of America, American Scientific Affiliation (fellow), Society for Conservation Biology, Society for Ecological Restoration and Management.

AWARDS, HONORS: Award and Bronze Medal from Carnegie Hero Fund Commission, 1993.

WRITINGS:

The Rediscovery of Creation: A Bibliographical Study of the Church's Response to the Environmental Crisis, Scarecrow, 1992.
(With F. Van Dyke, D. Mahan, and R. Brand) *Redeeming Creation: A Biblical Basis of Environmental Ethics,* Abbott Martyn, 1993.

Contributor to scientific journals and religious magazines, including *Environmental Entomology, Journal of Heredity, Evolution, World Christian, Transformation: An International Dialogue on Evangelical Social Ethics,* and *Perspectives on Science and Christian Faith.*

SHELTON, Beth Anne   1957-

PERSONAL: Born June 27, 1957, in San Antonio, TX; daughter of Carroll D. and Beth (Springstube) Shelton; married Ben Agger; children: Sarah. *Education:* Southern Methodist University, B.S. (with honors), 1977; University of Texas at Austin, M.A., 1980, Ph.D., 1984.

ADDRESSES: Office—Department of Sociology, Park Hall, State University of New York at Buffalo, Buffalo, NY 14260-0001.

CAREER: Oberlin College, Oberlin, OH, assistant professor of sociology, 1984-86; State University of New York at Buffalo, assistant professor, 1986-90, associate professor of sociology and director of graduate studies, 1990—. University of Michigan, visiting scholar, 1985, 1986.

MEMBER: American Sociological Association, Sociologists for Women in Society, Southern Sociological Society.

AWARDS, HONORS: Fellow of Lilly Endowment, 1987-88.

WRITINGS:

(With Nestor Rodriguez, Joe Feagin, and others) *Houston: Growth and Decline in a Sunbelt Boomtown,* Temple University Press, 1989.
Women, Men, and Time: Gender Differences in Paid Work, Housework, and Leisure, Greenwood Press, 1992.

Work represented in anthologies, including *Research in Community Sociology,* Volume II, JAI Press, 1989; *Feminism on Theory/Sociology on Gender,* edited by Paula England, Aldine, 1992; and *Men, Work, and Family,* edited by Jane Hood, Sage Publications, 1993. Contributor of articles and reviews to sociology journals. Associate editor, *Journal of Family Issues,* 1990—.

WORK IN PROGRESS: A study of the construction of gender, race, and ethnicity in everyday family life.

*   *   *

SHERMAN, Charlotte Watson   1958-

PERSONAL: Born October 14, 1958, in Seattle, WA; daughter of Charles E. Watson and Dorothy Ray (a homemaker; maiden name, Yarbrough) Glass; married David Joseph Sherman (a diagnostic ultrasound applications specialist), June 14, 1980; children: Aisha and Zahida. *Education:* Seattle University, B.A., 1980.

ADDRESSES: Agent—Beth Vesel, Sanford Greenberger Associates, 55 Fifth Ave., New York, NY 10003.

CAREER: Fiction writer. Garvey School, instructional assistant, 1987-88; East Cherry Young Women's Christian Association (YWCA), emergency housing cooordinator, 1989; Child Welfare Services, social worker, 1989-91; Group Health Cooperative, mental health specialist, 1991-92; Young Men's Christian Association (YMCA)/ Seattle Education Center, writing workshop instructor, 1992-93.

AWARDS, HONORS: King County Arts Commission Publication Award, 1990; Seattle African-American Women's Achievement Award, 1992; Great Lakes College Association Award, 1992, for *Killing Color.*

WRITINGS:

Killing Color (short stories), Calyx Books, 1992.
One Dark Body (novel), HarperCollins, 1993.

Also contributor to *Fiction and Poetry Anthology of Writings by African-American Women,* HarperCollins, 1993. Contributor to periodicals, including *Calyx, Obsidian,* and *Obsidian II.*

WORK IN PROGRESS: Novel scheduled for publication by HarperCollins, 1994; research on women writers, creativity, and mood disorders.

SIDELIGHTS: Charlotte Watson Sherman told *CA:* "I am obsessed with exploring the terrain of psychological wounds, particularly the emotional scars of African-Americans. I never knew either of my grandfathers, though both were reputedly ministers. The paternal grandfather was a Baptist preacher; the maternal grandfather was suspected to have been Elijah Muhammed of the Nation of Islam (my mother believes she is one of his many 'outside' children). As a result, elements of the sacred seem to permeate my writing. A close relative's mental illness and my accompanying fears and fascination with those who 'live on the edge' are also motivating forces in my work."

*   *   *

SHERWIN-WHITE, A(drian) N(icholas) 1911-1993

OBITUARY NOTICE—See index for *CA* sketch: Born August 10, 1911, in Brentford and Chiswick, England; died November 1, 1993. Educator and author. Sherwin-White, who was educated at Oxford University, served as an instructor at that institution for more than thirty years. A scholar of Roman history, he put forth the notion that the Roman Empire benefited by granting equal rights to its conquered peoples. Although the Romans believed other nations to be culturally inferior, they offered citizenship to those willing to adopt Roman culture. Sherwin-White developed his historical theories in the books *The Roman Citizenship*—which won the Conington Prize and

is considered a definitive text on the subject—and *Racial Prejudice in Imperial Rome.* He also produced the first general study on the Roman scholar Pliny in the book *Historical Commentary on the Letters of Pliny the Younger,* published in 1966. Among Sherwin-White's other works are *Roman Society and Roman Law in the New Testament* and *Roman Foreign Policy in the East, 168 B.C. to A.D. 1.*

OBITUARIES AND OTHER SOURCES:

BOOKS

Who's Who, 145th edition, St. Martin's, 1993.

PERIODICALS

Times (London), November 15, 1993, p. 17.

*   *   *

SHIH, Chih-yu 1958-(Chuan-hsiang)

PERSONAL: Born August 8, 1958, in Taipei, Taiwan; son of Huai-tang and Lillian (Soong) Shih; married Eva I-hwa Ho (in finance), June 26, 1983; children: Alison, Albert. *Education:* National Taiwan University, B.A., 1980; Harvard University, M.P.P., 1984; University of Denver, Ph.D., 1988. *Avocational Interests:* Coaching basketball.

ADDRESSES: Home—Taipei, Taiwan. *Office*—Department of Political Science, College of Law, National Taiwan University, 21 Hsu Chow Rd., Taipei, Taiwan.

CAREER: Winona State University, Winona, MN, assistant professor of political science, 1987-88; Ramapo College of New Jersey, Mahwah, assistant professor of East Asian studies, 1988-90; National Taiwan University, Taipei, Taiwan, associate professor of mainland Chinese affairs, 1990—. Vanguard Foundation Research Center, coordinator, 1990-92. *Military service:* Taiwanese Army, 1982-84.

MEMBER: International Society of Political Psychology, American Political Science Association (coordinator of Conference Group on Taiwan Studies, 1990-92), Chinese Political Science Association.

AWARDS, HONORS: Stanley Hornback fellow in the United States, 1985; fellow of China Times Culture Foundation, 1986; National Science Council Award, Republic of China, 1990-93.

WRITINGS:

The Spirit of Chinese Foreign Policy: A Psychocultural View, Macmillan, 1990.
(With M. Cottam) *Contending Dramas: A Cognitive Approach to International Organizations,* Praeger, 1992.

China's Just World: The Morality of Chinese Foreign Policy, Lynne Rienner, 1993.
(With J. Adelman) *Symbolic War: The Chinese Use of Force, 1840-1980,* Institute of International Relations, 1993.
Independence, Interdependence, and Chinese Neorealism, Asia Pacific Center, University of Toronto, 1993.

Editor, *Issues and Studies.*

IN CHINESE; UNDER NAME CHUAN-HSIANG

The Deep Structure of China-Taiwan Relations, Yung-Jan, 1991.
(With N. Li) *Managing China-Taiwan Relations,* Wu Nan, 1991.
The Principles of Chinese Political Economy, Wu Nan, 1992.
The Anatomy of Chinese Legal Principles, San Min, 1993.
The Chinese Consciousness in Contemporary Taiwan, Cheng-Chong, 1993.
(With Y. Chou, F. Hu, and C. Sheng) *Chinese Constitutionalism and National Identity,* San Min, 1993.
State and Society in Contemporary China, Wu Nan, 1994.
(With Li) *Practicing China-Taiwan Relations,* Cheng-Chong, 1994.

Editor of *Pedagogy and Research in China Studies, a Newsletter.* Columnist, sometimes under name Chuan Hsiang, for popular journals and newspapers in Taiwan.

WORK IN PROGRESS: The Deep Structures of Chinese Political Economy, in English; *The Theory and Practice of Chinese Foreign Policy,* in Chinese; *A Feminist Critique of Taiwanese Politics,* in Chinese, completion expected in 1995.

SIDELIGHTS: Chih-yu Shih told *CA:* "I am interested in the psychological reading of all contemporary political affairs, especially those in China and Taiwan, in reconciling Oriental and Occidental epistemology to the political phenomenon, and in postmodern, as well as feminist, reconstructions of the notion of state sovereignty. I have produced books and articles primarily in defiance of the mainstream social science interpretation of (or refusal to interpret) perspectives taken by those 'objects' under study."

*   *   *

SHIMADA, Masahiko 1961-

PERSONAL: Born March 13, 1961, in Tokyo, Japan; son of Masao and Yoko (a homemaker; maiden name, Okubo) Shimada; married Hitomi Furuse (a homemaker), May 17, 1986. *Education:* Bachelor's degree from Tokyo University of Foreign Studies.

ADDRESSES: Home—Tamami 1-25-1, Asaoku Kawasaki-shi, 7215 Japan.

CAREER: Writer.

MEMBER: Japan Writers Association.

AWARDS, HONORS: Noma Literary Award for New Writers; Kyoka Izumi Literary Award.

WRITINGS:

Divertiment for Gentle Left, Fukutake Shoten, 1983.
When Heaven Comes Crumbling Down, Fukutake Shoten, 1985.
Unidentified Shadowing Object, Bungeishunju, 1987.
Higan Sensei, Fukutake Shoten, 1992.
Dream Messenger, Kodansha, 1993.

*   *   *

SHIRER, William L(awrence) 1904-1993

OBITUARY NOTICE—See index for *CA* sketch: Born February 23, 1904, in Chicago, IL; died December 28, 1993, in Boston, MA. Journalist, radio commentator, and author. Among a select group of journalists, Shirer is credited with transposing news events into the stuff of history. He started his career in journalism in 1925 as a European correspondent for the *Chicago Tribune.* In the early 1930s he spent time with Indian leader Mohandas K. Gandhi and later published a book, *Gandhi: A Memoir,* about the famed pacifist. His experiences reporting on the rise of Nazi Germany and its leader Adolph Hitler resulted in the book *Berlin Diary: The Journal of a Foreign Correspondent, 1934-1941.* Shirer, who had been covering the early years of World War II from Berlin, fled Germany in 1940 when he was accused of spying and in danger of being arrested. During his time in Germany, he also broadcast reports on the war for CBS, sometimes resorting to American slang to confuse Nazi censors. Along with broadcasting contemporaries Edward R. Murrow and Eric Sevareid, he helped to define a new, hard-boiled style of radio news that, in addition to relaying events with unprecedented verisimilitude, created the news media's first celebrities. In the 1950s Shirer was blacklisted as a suspected communist sympathizer, and he resorted to lecturing at colleges to support his family. He credited this period, however, with providing the time to complete the highly-praised history *The Rise and Fall of the Third Reich,* which won the National Book Award in 1961. Shirer also wrote the novels *Stranger Come Home* and *The Consul's Wife,* and a three-volume set of memoirs, *Twentieth Century Journey.* His last work was a book on the Russian author Leo Tolstoy, which was published by Simon & Schuster in the spring of 1994.

OBITUARIES AND OTHER SOURCES:

BOOKS

Who's Who in America, 48th edition, Marquis, 1994.

PERIODICALS

Chicago Tribune, January 2, 1994, p. 6.
Los Angeles Times, December 29, 1993, p. A3.
New York Times, December 30, 1993, p. B7; January 17, 1994, p. A15.
Times (London), December 30, 1993, p. 17.
Washington Post, December 30, 1993, p. B6.

*   *   *

SHOMER, Enid

PERSONAL: Born on February 2, in Washington, DC; daughter of Philip (a house painter) and Minnie (a homemaker; maiden name, Magazine) Steine; children: Nirah, Oren William. *Education:* Wellesley College, B.A.; University of Miami, M.A.

ADDRESSES: Home—4781 N.W. Eighth Ave., Gainesville, FL 32605. *Agent*—Roberta Pryor, 24 W. Fifty-fifth St., New York, NY 10019.

CAREER: University of Miami, Miami, FL, lecturer in English, 1974-80; Antioch Writer's Workshop, Yellow Springs, OH, writer-in-residence, 1988-91; Thurber House and Ohio State University, Columbus, OH, writer-in-residence, 1994. Juror, literary review panels in states of Ohio and Florida, 1988-91. Has given poetry readings on radio programs, including Voice of America in 1988, WTJU-FM in Charlottesville, VA in 1988 and 1992, and National Public Radio in 1993.

MEMBER: P.E.N., Poetry Society of America, Poets and Writers, Authors Guild, Associated Writing Programs.

AWARDS, HONORS: Eve of St. Agnes Prize, *Negative Capability,* 1985; artist fellowship, state of Florida, 1985-86 and 1991-92; Washington Prize in Poetry, 1986, for "Women Bathing at Bergen-Belsen;" *Cincinnati Poetry Review* prize, 1986, for best poem series; Jubilee Press prize, 1986, for *Florida Postcards;* Word Works Washington prize, 1987, for *Stalking the Florida Panther; Apalachee Quarterly* long poem prize, 1989, for "Datelines: Jacqueline Cochran at War's End;" National Endowment for the Arts poetry fellowship, 1989; Celia B. Wagner Award, Poetry Society of America, 1990; artist fellowship, state of Florida, 1991-92; Randall Jarrell Poetry Prize, 1992, for "My Friend Who Sings Before Breakfast;" Wildwood Poetry Prize, 1992, for "Learning CPR;" H.E. Francis Short Fiction Prize, and Fiction Award, *Iowa Woman,* both 1992, both for "On the Boil;" Iowa Short

Fiction Award, University of Iowa Press, 1992, for *Imaginary Men;* Eunice Tietjens Memorial Prize, *Poetry,* 1992.

WRITINGS:

POETRY

The Startle Effect (chapbook), American Studies Press, 1983.
Florida Postcards, Jubilee Press, 1987.
Stalking the Florida Panther, Word Works, 1988.
This Close to the Earth, University of Arkansas Press, 1992.

Poetry represented in more than two dozen anthologies, including *Bubbeh Heisehs by Shayney Maidelehs: Poetry by Jewish Granddaughters about Our Grandmothers,* Her-Books, 1989; *Ghosts of the Holocaust: An Anthology of Poetry by the Second Generation,* Wayne State University Press, 1989; *Poems from the Earth: On Nature and the Environment,* Mesilla, 1990; *WPFW 89.3 FM Poetry Anthology,* 1992; and *Poetry: A Harpercollins Pocket Anthology,* 1993. Contributor of poems to periodicals, including *Atlantic Monthly, ARETE: Forum for Thought, California Quarterly, Massachusetts Review, Midstream, New Criterion, Paris Review, Ploughshares, Poetry, Tikkun, Women's Review of Books, Writers Digest,* and *Women's Review of Books.*

OTHER

Imaginary Men (short stories; includes "On the Boil"), University of Iowa Press, 1993.

Prose represented in anthologies, including *New Visions: Fiction by Florida Writers,* Arbiter, 1989; *The Time of Our Lives: Women Write on Sex After Forty,* Crossing Press, 1993; and *An Anthology of Jewish Mother/Daughter Writings,* Beacon Press, in press.

Contributor of short stories and articles to periodicals, including *Florida Review, Midstream, New Directions in Prose and Poetry 55,* the *New Yorker, Fiction Quarterly, Florida Magazine, Helicon Nine, Negative Capability, New Yorker, Paris Review,* and *Women's Review of Books.*

WORK IN PROGRESS: A story, "Breaking Up is Hard to Do;" a new book of poems; a new collection of fiction; poem biography.

SIDELIGHTS: Enid Shomer is an award-winning poet and short story writer. She has published several volumes of verse, including *Florida Postcards, Stalking the Florida Panther,* and *This Close to the Earth,* and she has contributed poems to such publications as *Atlantic Monthly* and stories to periodicals, including the *New Yorker.* Shomer is also the author of *Imaginary Men,* which Diane Postlethwaite, a critic in the *New York Times Book Review,* described as a "fine first collection of stories." Among the tales in this volume are "Street Signs," in which the first-person narrator recounts an irate brother's move to the suburbs; the cycle "On the Land," about various individuals in rural Florida; and "On the Boil," in which an aerial surveyor becomes increasingly restricted by domestic demands. Postlethwaite affirmed in the *New York Times Book Review* that each tale in *Imaginary Men* "is a distinct pleasure."

BIOGRAPHICAL/CRITICAL SOURCES:

PERIODICALS

New Yorker, August 17, 1992, p. 28.
New York Times Book Review, April 4, 1993, p. 14.
Publishers Weekly, February 15, 1993, p. 212.

*   *   *

SILVERBURG, Sanford R.   1940-

PERSONAL: Born December 14, 1940, in Schenectady, NY; son of Harry A. (a toolmaker) and Frances (a homemaker; maiden name, Kornfeld) Silverburg; married Leanore Schwerin (a teacher of the trainable mentally handicapped); children: David, Danial. *Education:* Attended Mexico City College, 1959; Siena College, A.B., 1962; attended George Washington University and University of Maryland at College Park, both 1965; American University, M.A., 1968, Ph.D., 1973.

ADDRESSES: Home—209 Cedarwood Dr., Salisbury, NC 28147-7526. *Office*—Department of Political Science, Catawba College, Salisbury, NC 28144-2488.

CAREER: American Institute of Research, Center for Research in Social Systems, Cultural Information Analysis Center, Washington, DC, research associate, 1967-69; Catawba College, Salisbury, NC, assistant professor, 1970-75, associate professor, 1975-79, professor of political science, 1979—, head of department, 1975—. Rowan Technical Institute, instructor, 1973; University of North Carolina at Charlotte, lecturer, 1974-75; Livingstone College, visiting assistant professor, 1974; Wingate College, instructor, summers, 1976-77; Columbia Pacific University, faculty mentor, 1988—. *Military service:* U.S. Army, intelligence coordinator, 1962-65.

MEMBER: International Studies Association, Middle East Studies Association of North America, American Political Science Association, Middle East Institute, Southeast Regional Islamic and Middle East Studies Seminar, North Carolina Political Science Association (member of executive council, 1971-73, 1979-82; vice president, 1988-89; president, 1990-91).

AWARDS, HONORS: Scholar-diplomat, U.S. Department of State, 1975; National Endowment for the Human-

ities, fellow, 1975, grant for London School of Advanced Legal Studies, London, 1986; Wye faculty fellow, Aspen Institute, 1988; University of Michigan, visiting faculty scholar at Center for Near Eastern and North African Studies, 1989; grant from Center for Theoretical Studies, University of Miami, Coral Gables, FL, 1990; fellow, University of California, Los Angeles, 1990; grants for U.S. Army War College, 1991, Hoover Institution on War, Revolution, and Peace, 1992, and Air University, 1993.

WRITINGS:

(With Bernard Reich) *U.S. Foreign Policy and the Middle East/North Africa: A Bibliography of Twentieth-Century Research,* Garland Publishing, 1990.
Middle East Bibliography, Scarecrow, 1992.
(With Bernard Reich) *U.S. Relations with the Middle East and North Africa: A Bibliography,* Scarecrow, 1993.
(With Bernard Reich) *Asian States' Relations with the Middle East: A Bibliography,* Scarecrow, 1993.

Creator of the computer software program *Grade-Alyzer,* Imperial International Learning Corp., 1985. Contributor of articles and reviews to political science and international studies journals.

*   *   *

SIMMONS, Gloria Mitchell   1932-1993

OBITUARY NOTICE—See index for *CA* sketch: Born March 7, 1932, in Atlanta, GA; died of cancer, December 21, 1993, in Chicago, IL. Librarian and author. Simmons worked in the library sciences field for more than thirty years and was also the coauthor, with Helene Hutchinson, of the book *Black Culture: Reading and Writing Black.* Educated at Bennett College in North Carolina and at Atlanta University, where she was a Carnegie fellow, Simmons worked at Chicago's Harold Washington College as a teacher and reference librarian beginning in 1967. She was awarded the 1993-94 Distinguished Professor Award at Harold Washington, and, at the time of her death, was on sabbatical to write another book. Simmons also played an active role as a member of the Episcopal Church, serving on several committees.

OBITUARIES AND OTHER SOURCES:

BOOKS

Living Black American Authors, R. R. Bowker, 1973, p. 145.

PERIODICALS

Chicago Tribune, December 25, 1993, p. 11.

SINCLAIR, John L(eslie)   1902-1993

OBITUARY NOTICE—See index for *CA* sketch: Born December 6, 1902, in New York, NY; died December 17, 1993, in Albuquerque, NM. Cowboy, museum curator, and author. A Western novelist who actually lived the rugged life about which he wrote, Sinclair worked as a cowboy in New Mexico for fourteen years. He began writing in 1936, publishing his first, and best known, novel, *In Time of Harvest,* in 1943; the book was reissued in 1993. Among Sinclair's other novels are *Death in the Claimshack* and *Cousin Drewey and the Holy Twister.* He also penned several nonfiction books, including *New Mexico: The Shining Land* and *Cowboy Riding Country.* Sinclair's 1977 magazine article, "Where the Cowboys Hunkered Down," won a Western Heritage Wrangler Award from the National Cowboy Hall of Fame, as well as a Golden Spur Award from the Western Writers of America. Sinclair also served as curator for the Lincoln County Museum and was associated with the Coronado State Monument.

OBITUARIES AND OTHER SOURCES:

BOOKS

Who Was Who among North American Authors 1921-1939, Volume 2, Gale, 1976, p. 1310.

PERIODICALS

Los Angeles Times, December 20, 1993, p. A42.
Washington Post, December 21, 1993, p. C9.

*   *   *

SIROIS, Allen L.   1950-

PERSONAL: Born March 14, 1950, in Bridgeport, CT; son of Louis A. (an industrial engineer) and Mildred (a homemaker; maiden name, Hoffman) Sirois; married Linda Katherine Jackson, June, 1977 (divorced); married Paula Robin Warsh (a medical editor), October 19, 1991; children: Daniel, Kira. *Education:* Attended University of Bridgeport, 1968-70. *Religion:* Pagan. *Avocational Interests:* Writing, reading, music, cooking, playing drums.

ADDRESSES: Home—Hopewell Junction, NY. *Agent*—William Morris Agency, 1350 Avenue of the Americas, New York, NY 10019.

CAREER: Compu-Teach, Inc., New Haven, CT, art director, 1983-85; Prodigy Services, White Plains, NY, senior graphic artist, 1985—.

MEMBER: Science Fiction and Fantasy Writers of America (SFFWA), Author's Guild, Society of Children's Book Writers and Illustrators.

WRITINGS:

Dinosaur Dress Up, illustrated by Janet Sweet, William Morrow/Tambourine Books, 1992.

Also author of short stories; contributor of illustrations to magazines and journals.

SIDELIGHTS: In spite of the problems facing today's world and its people, Allen L. Sirois believes that writing fiction—story telling—is essential. Dreams are "awakened and energized" through story telling, and this, Sirois believes, must happen at an early age. He commented: "Writing needs no other justification than that fiction has the potential to illuminate at least one young mind, somewhere, and to help that mind develop the will and courage necessary to take the first tentative steps down the road to self-realization. What could be more honorable than to have helped someone to learn to think?"

*   *   *

SMITH, Charlie   1947-

PERSONAL: Born June 27, 1947, in Moultrie, GA; son of C. O. (a manufacturer and farmer) and Jeanette (a homemaker; maiden name, Early) Smith; married Kathleen Huber, September 16, 1974 (divorced June 21, 1977); married Gretchen Mattox (a poet and teacher), December 16, 1987. *Education:* Duke University, B.A. (philosophy), 1971, B.A. (English), 1971; University of Iowa, M.F.A., 1983.

ADDRESSES: Home—New York, NY. *Agent*—Marian Young, 29 Grace Court, Brooklyn Heights, NY 11201.

CAREER: Peace Corps volunteer, 1968-70; freelance writer, 1981—.

MEMBER: PEN, Academy of American Poets, Poetry Society of America (member of board of directors, 1989—).

AWARDS, HONORS: Aga Khan Prize, Paris Review, 1983, for the novella *Crystal River;* National Poetry Series Award, 1987, and Great Lakes New Poets Award, 1988, both for *Red Roads.*

WRITINGS:

NOVELS

Canaan, Simon & Schuster, 1985.
Shine Hawk, Simon & Schuster, 1988.
The Lives of the Dead, Simon & Schuster, 1990.
Chimney Rock, Henry Holt, 1993.

POETRY

Red Roads, Dutton, 1987.
Indistinguishable from the Darkness, Norton, 1990.

The Palms, Norton, 1993.
Before and After, Norton, in press.

OTHER

Crystal River (novellas), Simon & Schuster, 1991.

Contributor to literary journals and periodicals, including *Paris Review* and *New Yorker.*

WORK IN PROGRESS: The novel *Cheap Ticket to Heaven,* for Holt.

SIDELIGHTS: The writings of Charlie Smith, which include several novels and collections of poetry, have been noted by critics for their lyrical intensity and mesmerizing characters. Son of an established Georgian clan, Smith spent a few debauched years in New York City after earning degrees from Duke University. He attended the prestigious writing program at the University of Iowa and was a contributor to literary journals prior to writing his first novel, 1984's *Canaan.* Smith's works are set in deteriorated Southern landscapes populated by dissipated characters and eccentric families. *Publishers Weekly* contributor Wendy Smith described Smith's body of work as "notable for the author's—and his characters'—fearless willingness to plunge into extreme situations and primal emotions." Smith himself stated in the same article that his characters are "people who do exactly what they want to do; they see the gloriousness of being alive and the horror of it at the same time, and they drive through those things because they want to have more life."

Canaan is the tale of a Southern heiress who refuses to follow any rules save those of her own. Scion of a wealthy Southern family, Elizabeth Bonnet Burdette marries one of her own kind, J. C. Burdette, in Hawaii during World War II. Willful and tempestuous, she remains behind after the war with their small son and has numerous love affairs. The novel begins with her return to the eccentric Burdette clan's ancestral home, a large estate bestowed with the symbolic name of Canaan. Elizabeth's clashes with her conventional husband—along with her rabid and indiscriminate sexual conquests—set the stage for the novel's theme, one of confrontation between old and new traditions. Her outrageous behavior encompasses seducing her son, sleeping with her best friend, attempting to drown her sister-in-law, and setting fire to the family mansion. The skirmishes force the characters to face both the limitations placed on them by their background and those which they have set upon themselves.

Canaan received widespread attention for a first novel. Most critics praised Smith's talent for evoking the novel's turbulent action in superb prose, but criticized the heroine's overblown characterization. *Washington Post Book World* reviewer Bruce VanWyngarden commented on this shortcoming, stating that Elizabeth "works better as met-

aphor than character," but he praised Smith's capacity to create other characters that "jangle with originality." *New York Times Book Review* critic Carol Verderese noted that "Smith's prose, which can be lyrical and buoyant, becomes overwrought and hyperbolic as Elizabeth takes command." Writing in the *Los Angeles Times Book Review,* Dick Rorabeck lauded Smith's inaugural effort, describing it as "a remarkable first novel of elusive but elemental force."

Smith followed *Canaan* with the 1987 collection of poetry *Red Roads,* which deals with his Southern heritage and family relationships. A second novel, *Shine Hawk,* was published in 1988. Smith again sets his characters within a Southern landscape teeming with melodrama. Its narrator, Billy Crew, has escaped his rural Georgia past to achieve minor recognition as a painter in New York City. He returns to his swampy homeland to encounter Hazel, an old lover whose memory continues to haunt him, now married to Crew's former best friend, Frank Jackson. Crew enters the scene as the distraught Frank is traumatized by his brother Jake's death, for which he believes he may be responsible. The trio begin a journey to remove Jake's body from a trailer park, loading it onto a pick-up truck in order to bury it at the family's homestead; their travels with the rotting corpse, as told by Crew in flashback, form the crux of the narrative. Crew's voice also serves as a medium for the author's descriptive style, as Crew reflects upon his life in New York, failed marriage, longing for Hazel, and his friends' sordid family saga.

Shine Hawk received a mixed, but overall positive, critical reception. In the *New York Review of Books,* Robert Towers faulted what he perceived as the work's overabundance of gory Gothic-novel imagery, and suggested that the story might have been better served by revealing some background on the motivations that drove the book's characters. However, Towers praised Smith's gift of descriptive writing, such as "the cadenced sentences that celebrate the landscape," further commending the novelist's description of the Southern locales as "physical images [that] are brilliantly precise and evocative." In an appraisal of the novel for the *New York Times Book Review,* Lorrie Moore described it as a contemporary Southern literary example of "appalling brilliance," and found that "the characters [have] lives that both repel and impress." She concluded by stating "one feels everywhere in the novel a life and imagination laid down fully and at risk, as if it were the major literary effort—as perhaps it is—of someone terribly gifted and cursed."

In his 1990 novel *The Lives of the Dead,* Smith develops a creative male protagonist nearing middle age who is embarking on a journey. The dissipated South and its past and present riches also play a role in the plot structure. The hero of this work, cult filmmaker Buddy Drake, travels to the Gulf Coast of Florida to scout locations for his latest film venture, while simultaneously attempting to wheedle money to finance it from his wealthy ex-wife. Drake is accompanied on his travels by the trio of characters of the unmade movie in his head: the disturbing serial killer by the name of D'Nel Boyd, the bewitching Molly, and the passive dolphin-trainer Banty. The focus of *The Lives of the Dead* is the interplay between reality and fiction in the increasingly troubled mind of Drake, as the lines between the film's serial killings and Drake's past and future actions begin to blur. Smith again weaves the tale with lush and descriptive prose. *Los Angeles Times Book Review* critic Richard Eder described it as a "garish, gory and chokingly overwrought novel . . . an airless world of helpless evil." Writing in *Washington Post Book World,* reviewer James Hynes praised Smith's Faulknerian use of verbiage to set the stage for the novel's mood, calling it "a harrowing, passionate, powerfully written and unflinchingly honest book."

Smith's command of language, as praised by critics, would seem to translate effectively into the medium of poetry. A second volume of verse, *Indistinguishable from the Darkness,* appeared in 1990, but received less attention than his startling novels. A collection of three novellas, *Crystal River,* was originally written long before his success as an author and not published in full until 1991. The trio of pieces in *Crystal River* have certain similarities, while differing in actual length. Each story revolves around two close men that are either brothers or bonded by a quasi-homosexual brotherly love. They all embark upon a search for answers to questions about their past that deeply trouble them. Their journeys involve large bodies of water, and they meet with a fearsome and fearless woman who plays by her own set of rules. The element of time, playing a decisive role in the drama of the characters' lives and also in their quest for answers, is a strong element of the three stories. In the title novella, two Southern "good old boys," who are romantically involved with one another, take a canoe trip that leads them to a naked woman who forces them into sexual acts at gunpoint. In "Storyville," failed lawyer Harry Bates, long overshadowed by his successful twin brother and bewildered by his father's disappearance years before, links up with the very unstable Laura Dell. The two run off to New Orleans, where they aim in part to steal a baby to replace the one Laura has miscarried, a loss which drove her husband to commit suicide. *Crystal River* was well-received by critics, who again praised Smith's lyrical fluidity. Madison Smartt Bell, reviewing the work for *Washington Post Book World,* lauded Smith's writing for "his amazingly powerful, convincing, and beautiful prose style," and noted that this "masterful prose . . . renders the natural world and the human response to it with equal conviction, and makes the characters believable even when their behavior seems

improbable and absurd." Writing in the *New York Times Book Review,* Jill McCorkle favorably remarked on the continuity behind the three novellas, and observed that "Smith's elegant and lyrical prose is constant as well, his sentences lifting the reader to great heights and then descending to the lowest of lows."

Smith's next work was a third collection of poetry, *The Palms,* which appeared in 1993. This work again draws on the author's own background and matters of trust, betrayal, and gore, with all these elements structured in the form of lengthy and entangling sentences. Smith set his fifth novel, 1993's *Chimney Rock,* in Hollywood, California. Protagonist Will Blake shares many similarities with other lead characters in Smith's previous novels. He is at a crossroads in his life, does not have a full grasp on reality, and is enmeshed in a long and turbulent family history. As in prior works, the narrative of *Chimney Rock* is woven around a particularly melodramatic family and ends with another mansion going up in flames—this one during the frenzied 1992 Los Angeles riot. Smith stated in a *Publishers Weekly* interview that he considered *Chimney Rock* as the final part of "a kind of spiritual trilogy," one that began with *Shine Hawk* and continued with *The Lives of the Dead.* Smith mused that "they are books about people headed out energetically into the world, surrendering and charming their way into the heart of things."

BIOGRAPHICAL/CRITICAL SOURCES:

PERIODICALS

Library Journal, April 1, 1987, p. 152; February 1, 1993, p. 86.

Los Angeles Times, September 6, 1990, p. 5.

Los Angeles Times Book Review, February 17, 1985, p. 4.

New York Review of Books, February 16, 1989, pp. 18-19.

New York Times, January 19, 1985, p. 13.

New York Times Book Review, April 21, 1985, p. 24; October 2, 1988, pp. 1, 42; December 15, 1991, pp. 11-12.

Publishers Weekly, July 22, 1988, p. 41; February 1, 1993, p. 78; February 15, 1993, p. 188; May 3, 1993, pp. 279-280.

Tribune Books (Chicago), September 16, 1990, pp. 3, 6; September 22, 1991, p. 7.

Washington Post Book World, April 6, 1985; October 16, 1988, pp. 3-4; September 30, 1990, p. 6; September 8, 1991, p. 9.

*   *   *

SMITH, Christine 1945-

PERSONAL: Born February 24, 1945, in New York, NY; daughter of Richard (a building manager) and Henrietta (an elementary schoolteacher; maiden name, Coufal)

Smith; married Douglas Hunnikin (divorced, 1975). *Education:* Vassar College, B.A. (magna cum laude), 1966; New York University, M.A., 1968, Ph.D., 1975. *Religion:* Episcopalian.

ADDRESSES: Home—Via de' Federighi 7, 50123 Florence, Italy.

CAREER: Finch College, instructor in Florence, 1969-71, assistant professor, 1974-75; Rosary College, Villa Schifanoia, Florence, Italy, faculty member, 1975-81; Georgetown University, Charles Augustus Strong Center, Fiesole, Italy, adjunct assistant professor, 1981-88; Institute for Advanced Study, Princeton, NJ, member, 1988-89; American Academy in Rome, Rome, Italy, visiting scholar, 1989 and 1991; Harvard University, Center for Renaissance Studies, Villa i Tatti, Rome, Italy, visiting scholar, 1989-90; Syracuse University, Syracuse, NY, lecturer at Program in Florence, 1990-93, head of art history department, 1993—. Fashion Institute of Technology, instructor, 1969; New York University, lecturer, 1969, lecturer, 1975; Nasson College, lecturer for semester in Florence, 1975-80; State University of New York College at Buffalo, lecturer for semester in Florence, 1976-80; California State University, lecturer for semester in Florence, 1976-81; University of California, Berkeley, guest lecturer; State University of New York College at New Paltz, lecturer, 1978-80, adjunct professor, 1980; Hiram College, lecturer for semester in Florence, 1979; State University of New York, lecturer for Urbino program, 1979; Smithsonian Institution, lecturer, 1985; lecturer at University of California, Santa Barbara, Rutgers University, Sarah Lawrence College, Princeton University, Duke University, and Vanderbilt University.

AWARDS, HONORS: Grants from National Endowment for the Humanities, 1984, 1987, and 1991-93; National Gallery of Art, visiting senior fellow, Center for Advanced Study in the Visual Arts, 1985; Founders Award from Society of Architectural Historians, 1985, for the article "East or West in Eleventh Century Pisan Culture: The Dome of the Cathedral and Its Western Counterparts"; summer fellow, Dumbarton Oaks, 1985 and 1991; Guggenheim fellow, 1989-90; fellow of Getty Trust, 1990-91; grant from American Council of Learned Societies, 1991.

WRITINGS:

Ravenna, Scala (Florence), 1977.
The Baptistery of Pisa, Garland Publishing, 1978.
St. Bartholomew's Church in the City of New York, Oxford University Press, 1988.
Architecture in the Culture of Early Humanism: Ethics, Aesthetics, and Eloquence, 1400-1460, Oxford University Press, 1992.

Contributor of articles and reviews to art and architecture journals.

WORK IN PROGRESS: Architectural Descriptions in Western Europe and Byzantium: From Late Antiquity to the Renaissance, with Joseph O'Connor; *Giannozzo Manetti's "Life of Nicholas V": Translation of and Commentary on the Building Descriptions,* with Joseph O'Connor.

BIOGRAPHICAL/CRITICAL SOURCES:

PERIODICALS

American Historical Review, October, 1993, p. 1280.
Journal of the Society of Architectural Historians, June, 1980; March, 1991.

*   *   *

SMITH, Clark Ashton   1893-1961

PERSONAL: Born January 13, 1893, in Long Valley, CA; died August 14, 1961, in Pacific Grove, CA; son of Timeus and Mary Frances (Gaylord) Smith; married Carolyn Jones Dorman, 1954.

CAREER: Writer of fiction and essays; poet; journalist; painter and sculptor; also performed odd jobs and manual labor.

WRITINGS:

SHORT STORIES

The Double Shadow and Other Fantasies, privately printed, 1933.
Out of Space and Time, Arkham House, 1942.
Lost Worlds, Arkham House, 1944.
Genius Loci, and Other Tales, Arkham House, 1948.
The Abominations of Yondo, Arkham House, 1960.
Tales of Science and Sorcery, Arkham House, 1964.
Other Dimensions, Arkham House, 1970.
Zothique, introduction by Lin Carter, Ballantine, 1970.
Xiccarph, introduction by Carter, Ballantine, 1972.
The Last Incantation, introduction by Donald Sidney-Fryer, Pocket Books, 1982.
A Rendezvous in Averoigne: Best Fantastic Tales of Clark Ashton Smith, introduction by Ray Bradbury, illustrated by Jeffrey K. Potter, Arkham House, 1988.

Contributor of short stories to magazines, including *The Black Cat, The Overland Monthly, Weird Tales, Amazing Stories, Magic Carpet, Fantastic Universe, Stirring Science Stories, Wonder Stories,* and *Fantasy and Science Fiction.*

POETRY

The Star-Treader and Other Poems, A. M. Robertson, 1912.
Odes and Sonnets, Book Club of California, 1918.

Ebony and Crystal: Poems in Verse and Prose, privately printed, 1922.

Sandalwood, privately printed, 1925.

Nero and Other Poems, Futile Press, 1937.

The Dark Chateau, and Other Poems, Arkham House, 1951.

Spells and Philtres, Arkham House, 1958.

The Hill of Dionysus, a Selection, [Pacific Grove, CA], 1962.

Poems in Prose, illustrated by Frank Utpatel, Arkham House, 1964.

Selected Poems, introduction by Benjamin DeCasseres, Arkham House, 1971.

OTHER

Planets and Dimensions: Collected Essays of Clark Ashton Smith, edited and with an introduction by Charles K. Wolfe, Mirage Press, 1973.

The Black Book of Clark Ashton Smith (Smith's notebook and biographical essays), illustrated by Andrew Smith, Arkham House, 1979.

Strange Shadows: The Uncollected Fiction and Essays of Clark Ashton Smith, edited by Steve Behrends, Donald Sidney-Fryer, and Rah Hoffman, introduction by Robert Bloch, Greenwood Press, 1989.

The Devil's Notebook: Collected Epigrams and Pensees of Clark Ashton Smith, compiled by Sidney-Fryer, edited with an introduction by Don Herron, Starmount House, 1990.

Also translator of *Flowers of Evil* by Charles Baudelaire, illustrated by Jacob Epstein, published by Limited Editions Club of New York. Contributor of column to, and part-time night editor of, the *Auburn Journal.* Poetry, prose, and artwork published in chapbooks, including *Grotesques and Fantastiques* (previously unpublished drawings and poems), Gerry de la Ree, 1973, and *Klarkash-ton and Monstro Ligriv* (previously unpublished poems and art by Smith and Virgil Finlay), Gerry de la Ree, 1974.

SIDELIGHTS: Clark Ashton Smith is recognized by many critics of fantasy and science fiction as one of the foremost authors in the genre known as "weird fiction." H. P. Lovecraft, an acclaimed horror writer himself, defined a "true weird tale" in his essay "Supernatural Horror in Literature" as "something more than secret murder, bloody bones, or a sheeted form clanking chains according to rule. A certain atmosphere of breathless and unexplainable dread of outer, unknown forces must be present." Locating his stories in such mythical lands as Zothique (a futuristic realm where magic has replaced science), Smith distinguished his prose from the formulaic pulp stories of the day by fashioning fantastic plots and bizarre imagery out of poetic, and sometimes archaic, language. Writing

in a tradition which traces its roots back to the works of Edgar Allan Poe and other nineteenth-century writers of the macabre, Smith and fellow contributors Lovecraft and Robert E. Howard (creator of Conan the Barbarian) defined the "golden age" of the pulp magazine *Weird Tales* during the 1930s. Although the works of Lovecraft and Howard are still widely appreciated by readers of horror and fantasy literature—tales by both authors have been adapted into films—Smith's stories, despite their critical acclaim, are known only to a smaller and more specialized audience. "Of these three gifted men (who were all good friends and correspondents although I do not believe they ever actually met), it is Clark Ashton Smith alone who has yet to achieve the wide recognition his artistry so richly deserves," observed Lin Carter in his introduction to Smith's paperback anthology *Zothique.*

Although Smith is remembered for his "weird" stories, he perceived himself as primarily a poet. L. Sprague de Camp remarked in *Literary Swordsmen and Sorcerers* that Smith's "poems, once compared to those of [nineteenth-century English poets Lord] Byron, [John] Keats and [Algernon Charles] Swinburne, are known today to few outside of some science-fiction and fantasy fans. Few of those who nowadays make a stir in the poetic world have even heard of Clark Ashton Smith." Nonetheless, Smith's earliest poems, published in *The Star-Treader and Other Poems,* met with some critical success. In the introduction to Smith's *Selected Poems,* Benjamin DeCasseres praised the poem "The Hashish-Eater" as "a glut of beauty that leaves me breathless in one continuous reading." He also described Smith as "brother-prince to Poe, [French poet Charles] Baudelaire, [nineteenth-century English poet Percy Bysshe] Shelley, [and nineteenth-century French poet Arthur] Rimbaud."

Born in Long Valley, California, in 1893, Smith never ranged far from the place of his birth. Although his formal education ended at grammar school, he continued to read and write stories and poems with the intention of devoting his life to literature, specifically poetry. "While his withdrawal from the normal schoolboy milieu may or may not have made him a better poet, it also, probably, contributed to his later frustrating difficulties in making a living," de Camp pointed out in *Literary Swordsmen and Sorcerers.* During his writing career, Smith was sometimes forced to cut wood and pick fruit to make ends meet. In a quote published in *Literary Swordsmen and Sorcerers,* Smith described his struggle with poverty: "If I work for a living, I will have to give up my art. I've not the energy for both. And I hardly know what I could do—I'm 'unskilled labor' at anything except drawing and poetry. . . . Nine hours of work on week days leaves me too tired for any mental effort." Smith also suffered from ill health during this period, but he would improve physically by the late 1920s, finding the energy from 1929 to 1936 to complete more than one hundred short stories.

Smith had his first short stories published in the general fiction magazine *The Black Cat* in 1910; they were, according to de Camp in *Literary Swordsmen and Sorcerers,* "undistinguished tales of oriental adventure." By 1912, however, Smith's poetry met with some success and he was encouraged to contact George Sterling, one of his favorite poets and the leader of an artists' colony in Carmel, California. Sterling, a protege of author and journalist Ambrose Bierce, wrote poems reminiscent of French "Decadent" literature, a pessimistic movement that acknowledged the inevitability of moral decline and exulted unrepentingly in it. According to Brian Stableford in *The Second Dedalus Book of Decadence: The Black Feast,* Sterling's verse (the poem "A Wine of Wizardry," for example) "placed morbid meditations on destiny within a peculiar cosmic perspective." A friendship developed between Smith and Sterling—with the older poet serving as a mentor—that continued until Sterling's suicide in 1926. After Sterling introduced Smith to the writings of prominent Decadent author Charles Baudelaire, the champion and translator of Poe into French during the mid-nineteenth century, Smith, in turn, later learned French and translated Baudelaire's poems into English. Sterling also served as the subject for one of Smith's numerous essays, many of which dealt with authors Smith deemed influential.

During Smith's most fertile period of creativity, from about 1930 to 1936, he had switched over to writing fiction and was completing at least one story a month. De Camp suggests in *Literary Swordsmen and Sorcerers* that this burst of productivity is related to the fact that Smith (who was also looking after his aging parents) was making more money by writing—"even at the low rates and late payments of *Weird Tales*"—than through jobs requiring manual labor. "He regarded himself mainly as a poet who wrote prose only to pay his decrepid parent's bills," de Camp stated.

Smith's stories are clearly identifiable by his unique writing style; in the introduction to *Zothique,* Carter noted, "The short stories of Clark Ashton Smith are very much his own, and nothing quite like them has been written in America, at least since Poe." Various critics have observed the influence on Smith's fiction of Sterling, Bierce, and French author Gustave Flaubert (notably the novels *Salammbo* and *Tentation de Saint Antoine*). English author William Beckford's gothic novel *Vathek* as well as the fantasies of Irish writer Lord Dunsany and supernatural stories by Lovecraft have also been cited as important references in the formation of Smith's prose. Gahan Wilson commented in the *Magazine of Fantasy and Science Fiction* that Smith's stories "were beautifully constructed, full of lovely images and absolutely sumptuous English."

Smith's penchant for choosing obscure and archaic words, de Camp suggested in *Literary Swordsmen and Sorcerers,* stemmed from the author's self-educational technique; he would "read an unabridged dictionary through, word for word, studying not only the definitions of the words but also their derivations from ancient languages. Having an extraordinary eidetic memory, he seems to have retained most or all of it."

The author's enchantment with language—as well as his instinct for horror—is apparent in "The Garden of Adompha," a tale of Zothique. As the story begins, Adompha (the decadent ruler of an island kingdom), has instructed the wizard Dwerulas to create a secret garden in which the king might "search for novel pleasures and violent or rare sensations." Smith's prose describes the garden in the following passage: "There were many . . . weird plants, diverse as the seven hells, and having no common characteristics other than the scions which Dwerulas has grafted upon them here and there through his unnatural and necromantic art. . . . These scions were the various parts and members of human beings. Consummately, and with never failing success, the magician had joined them to the half-vegetable, half-animate stocks, on which they lived and grew thereafter, drawing an ichor-like sap. . . . On palmy boles, beneath feathery-tufted foliage, the heads of eunuchs hung in bunches."

The settings of most of Smith's stories can be divided into several different worlds. In addition to the continent of Zothique, he created the locales of Hyperborea (an arctic land of ancient Earth), Poseidonis (Atlantis), Averoigne (medieval France), and Xiccarph (a region on the planet Mars). Many of Smith's fictional heroes find themselves transported from one world to another via space travel, enchantment, or a portal to another dimension. In the story "City of the Singing Flame," the narrator discovers an invisible gateway in the rugged California countryside that leads to an alien realm. Joining other creatures of all description who are drawn to a strange monolithic city by a flame that radiates mesmerizing music, the narrator witnesses—several times—the voluntary sacrifice of certain pilgrims. "The narrator . . . ends the tale by saying that he will return to the City and immolate himself in the Flame, that he might merge with the unearthly beauty and music that he had sampled and lost," Steve Behrends informed in *Studies in Weird Fiction.* Two prominent, award-winning science fiction authors have both credited "City of the Singing Flame" as a major source of inspiration. In the introduction to Smith's *A Rendezvous in Averoigne: Best Fantastic Tales of Clark Ashton Smith,* Ray Bradbury recalled that "City" and "Master of the Asteroid" were the two tales that "more than any others I can remember had everything to do with my decision, while in the seventh grade, to become a writer." And in a letter published in *Emperor of Dreams: A Clark Ashton Smith Bibliography,* Harlan Ellison related that "City of the Singing Flame" specifically influenced his career when he discovered an anthology containing the story in his high school library. (Ellison was so impressed, he admitted in the letter that he stole the volume, writing, "I own it to this day.") Ellison further commented, "I owe the greatest of debts to Clark Ashton Smith, for he truly opened up the universe for me."

The theme of loss has appeared frequently in Smith's fiction. Behrends explained, "Smith created scores of situations in which individuals lose the things closest to their hearts, and live on only to regret their loss and to contrast their fallen state with the glory they once knew. He gave his characters the capacity to realize the extent of their loss, and to express the pain they felt." The story "The Last Incantation," according to Behrends, "contains some of Smith's finest descriptions of the emotions of loss." The plot concerns the elderly wizard Malgyris who uses magic to bring a lover, long dead, back to life. "But, once she is back, he learns with disappointment how different from his memories of her she now seems. He is disillusioned to learn that what he cannot call back is his own youth with all its idealism," stated Douglas Robillard in *Supernatural Fiction Writers.*

Among Smith's Martian stories is "The Vaults of Yoh-Vombis," about an archaeological expedition that discovers an ancient tomb in the planet's unexplored wastelands. As the archaeologists venture into the ruins of Yoh-Vombis, unaccompanied by their reluctant Martian guides, they encounter a mummified being in an inner vault whose head is covered with a mysterious black cowl; the cowl, in fact, is a brain-feeding leech-like creature. By suddenly attaching itself to the head of an expedition member, the creature controls its host and frees others of its kind. Although the story is ostensibly science fiction, Carter, writing in the introduction to Smith's paperback anthology *Xiccarph,* perceives it as a superior hybrid of genres: "Read the tale and savor the prose style: this rich, bejeweled, exotic kind of writing is the sort we most often think of as being natural to the heroic fantasy tale of magic kingdoms and fabulous eras of the mysterious past. Finally, read the story straight through and notice the actual plot. As you will find, it is precisely the sort of thing we call weird or horror fiction." Donald Sidney-Fryer stated in the introduction to Smith's paperback anthology *The Last Incantation* that "The Vaults of Yoh-Vombis" is "one of the most purely horrific stories that Smith ever created" and has "obvious parallels with such Lovecraftian masterpieces as 'The Color Out of Space' and 'The Shadow Out of Time,' as well as with such a recent 'Lovecraftian' film as *Alien.*"

Smith abruptly ceased to write fiction after the deaths of his parents (his mother died in September of 1935, his father in December of 1937). Although he would write the occasional story, "the tales actually completed after 1937 could be counted on the fingers of two hands," de Camp remarked in *Literary Swordsmen and Sorcerers.* Having also shown a flair for the visual arts throughout his life, Smith turned more to rendering his fantastic visions in paintings and sculptures. Eleanor Fait reported in a December, 1941, article in the *Sacramento Union* that Smith started sculpting out of native rock in 1935. "Visiting his uncle who owned a copper mine . . . he picked up a piece of talc, took it home, and casually carved it into a figure one day. Pleased by the result, since then, he has done more than two hundred pieces."

Smith married Carolyn Jones Dorman in 1954 and was working as a gardener to help make ends meet when he suffered a stroke in 1961 and died several months later. His unique contributions to the field of imaginative fiction were summed up by H. P. Lovecraft, who wrote to Smith in 1923 (in a letter quoted in *Howard Phillips Lovecraft: Dreamer on the Nightside*), "No author but yourself seems to have glimpsed fully those tenebrous wastes, immeasurable gulfs, grey topless pinnacles, crumbling corpses of forgotten cities, slimy, stagnant, cypress-bordered rivers, and alien, indefinable, antiquity-ridden gardens of strange decay with which my own dreams have been crowded since earliest childhood."

BIOGRAPHICAL/CRITICAL SOURCES:

BOOKS

Bleiler, E. F., editor, *Supernatural Fiction Writers,* Scribner, 1985.

de Camp, L. Sprague, *Literary Swordsmen and Sorcerers,* Arkham House, 1976.

Long, Frank Belknap, *Howard Phillips Lovecraft: Dreamer on the Nightside,* Arkham House, 1975.

Lovecraft, H. P., *Dagon and Other Macabre Tales,* Arkham House, 1965.

Sidney-Fryer, Donald, *Emperor of Dreams: A Clark Ashton Smith Bibliography,* Donald M. Grant, 1978.

Smith, Clark Ashton, *The Last Incantation,* Pocket Books, 1982.

Smith, Clark Ashton, *A Rendezvous in Averoigne: Best Fantastic Tales of Clark Ashton Smith,* Arkham House, 1988.

Smith, Clark Ashton, *Selected Poems,* Arkham House, 1971.

Smith, Clark Ashton, *Xiccarph,* Ballantine, 1972.

Smith, Clark Ashton, *Zothique,* Ballantine, 1970.

Stableford, Brian, editor, *The Second Dedalus Book of Decadence: The Black Feast,* Dedalus, 1992.

PERIODICALS

Magazine of Fantasy and Science Fiction, July, 1971, pp. 73-76.
Sacramento Union, December 21, 1941.
Studies in Weird Fiction, August 1, 1986, pp. 3-12.*

—*Sketch by Scot Peacock*

*   *   *

SMITH, David Alexander 1953-

PERSONAL: Born October 6, 1953; son of Leroy Roscoe (a drafter) and Barbara Titsworth (Thomas) Smith; married Nancy K. Hiers (in small business), in 1982. *Education:* Harvard University, A.B. (cum laude), 1975. *Avocational Interests:* Racquetball.

ADDRESSES: Home—112 Avon Hill St., Cambridge, MA 02140. *Office*—Recapitalization Advisors, 160 State St., 5th Floor, Boston, MA 02109. *Agent*—Valerie Smith, 1746 Route 44-55, RD Box 160, Modena, NY 12548.

CAREER: Boston Financial, Boston, MA, senior vice president, 1975-89; Recapitalization Advisors, Boston, founder and president, 1989—. Consultant on innovative transactions in affordable housing, principally recapitalizations, workouts, refinancings, and equity takeouts.

MEMBER: Science Fiction Writers of America, Cambridge Science Fiction Workshop, 1983—.

AWARDS, HONORS: Robert H. Armstrong Prize from American Institute of Real Estate Appraisers, 1983, for *Subsidized Housing as a Tax Shelter.*

WRITINGS:

Subsidized Housing as a Tax Shelter, Robert Stanger, 1982.

Work represented in anthologies. Author of "Syndication Topics," a column in *Real Estate Review.* Contributor of articles to real estate journals. Past contributing editor, *Real Estate Review.*

NOVELS

Marathon, Ace Books, 1982.
Rendezvous, Ace Books, 1988.
Homecoming, Ace Books, 1990.
In the Cube: A Novel of Future Boston, Tor Books, 1993.
(Editor) *Future Boston,* Tor Books, 1994.

WORK IN PROGRESS: A novel, *The Mandrake Project,* completion expected in 1995.

SMITH, Deborah 1955-

PERSONAL: Born September 27, 1955, in Atlanta, GA; daughter of Jack Edward Brown Sr. (an electrical engineer) and Dora (Power) Brown (a secretary); married Hank Smith (an electrical engineer), August 11, 1979. *Education:* University of Georgia, B.A., 1979. *Politics:* Democrat.

ADDRESSES: Home—Dahlonega, GA. *Agent*—Andrea Cirillo, Jane Rotrosen Agency, 318 East 15th St., New York, NY 10022.

CAREER: Neighbor Newspapers, Marietta, GA, reporter and editor, 1980-83; American Health Consultants, Atlanta, GA, medical writer, 1983-86; author, 1986—.

MEMBER: Romance Writers of America, Authors Guild, Georgia Romance Writers (president, 1986-87), Novelists, Inc.

AWARDS, HONORS: Lifetime Achievement Award, *Romantic Times,* 1988; Series Romantic Suspense Award, *Romantic Times,* 1991, for *Silver Fox and the Red-Hot Dove;* Maggie Award for Best Single-Title Contemporary Novel, Georgia Romance Writers, 1992, for *Miracle.*

WRITINGS:

Jed's Sweet Revenge, Bantam, 1988.
Hold on Tight, Bantam, 1988.
Caught by Surprise, Bantam, 1988.
Hot Touch, Doubleday, 1989.
The Cherokee Trilogy, Bantam, 1989.
Legends, Bantam, 1990.
Silver Fox and the Red-Hot Dove, Doubleday, 1990.
Sara's Surprise, Bantam, 1990.
Honey and Smoke, Bantam, 1990.
Stranger in Camelot, Bantam, 1991.
Heart of the Dragon, Bantam, 1991.
Follow the Sun, Bantam, 1991.
The Beloved Woman, Bantam, 1991.
Miracle, Bantam, 1991.
Blue Willow, Bantam, 1993.
Silk and Stone, Bantam, 1994.

WORK IN PROGRESS: Three contemporary novels.

SIDELIGHTS: Deborah Smith told *CA:* "I am the author of numerous 'category' romances for several publishers as well as three larger novels, both contemporary and historical. While my career has moved steadily toward general fiction (or, as some call it, 'mainstream fiction') I consider the romance genre a solid influence on my past, present, and future as a writer. Romances are often misunderstood and ignorantly dismissed as pulp fiction. This disregards the depth, scope, and quality of the genre, which focusses on relationships, family dynamics, social issues, and just about any other subject matter found in contemporary fiction of all kinds. I'm very proud to follow in a tradition that dates back to Jane Austen and the Bronte sisters, and which has as its oldest ancestor the classic mythology of all literature forms. I favor idealism and grand adventure in my stories, with a flavor of the contemporary South. A native Georgian from a long and colorful heritage, I enjoy using that heritage for inspiration."

* * *

SMITH, Lane 1959-

PERSONAL: Born August 25, 1959, in Tulsa, OK; son of Lewis (an accountant) and Mildred (Enlow) Smith. *Education:* California Art Center College of Design, B.F.A., 1983.

ADDRESSES: Home—New York, NY. *Agent*—Edite Kroll, 12 Grayhurst Park, Portland, ME 04102.

CAREER: Freelance illustrator, 1983—. Contributor of illustrations to periodicals, including *Rolling Stone, Time, Ms., Newsweek, New York Times, Atlantic,* and *Esquire.* Works have been exhibited at Master Eagle Gallery, New York City; Brockton Children's Museum, Brockton, MA; Joseloff Gallery, Hartford, CT; and in the AIGA touring show.

AWARDS, HONORS: New York Times Ten Best Illustrated Books of the Year citation, *School Library Journal* Best Book of the Year citation, *Horn Book* Honor List, American Library Association (ALA) Booklist/Editor's Choice List, and Silver Buckeye Award, all 1987, for *Halloween ABC;* Silver Medal, Society of Illustrators, *New York Times* Best Books of the Year citation, ALA Notable Children's Book citation, Maryland Black-Eyed Susan Picture Book Award, and *Parenting*'s Reading Magic Award, all 1989, for *The True Story of the Three Little Pigs;* Golden Apple Award, Bratislava International Biennial of Illustrations, 1990, Silver Medal, Society of Illustrators, 1991, and first place, New York Book Show, all for *The Big Pets; Parent's Choice* Award for Illustration, *New York Times* Best Books of the Year citation, ALA Notable Children's Book citation, all 1991, for *Glasses— Who Needs 'Em?;* Caldecott Honor Book, *New York Times* Best Illustrated Books of the Year citation, *School Library Journal* Best Books of the Year citation, *Booklist* Children's Editors' "Top of the List" citation, and ALA Notable Children's Book citation, all 1992, for *The Stinky Cheese Man.*

WRITINGS:

SELF-ILLUSTRATED

Flying Jake, Macmillan, 1989.
The Big Pets, Viking, 1990.
Glasses—Who Needs 'Em?, Viking, 1991.

The Happy Hocky Family, Viking, 1993.

ILLUSTRATOR

Eve Merriam, *Halloween ABC,* Macmillan, 1987.
Jon Scieszka, *The True Story of the Three Little Pigs,* Viking, 1989.
Jon Scieszka, *The Stinky Cheese Man and Other Fairly Stupid Tales,* Viking, 1992.

ILLUSTRATOR; "TIME WARP TRIO" SERIES; WRITTEN BY JON SCIESZKA

Knights of the Kitchen Table, Viking, 1991.
The Not-So-Jolly Roger, Viking, 1991.
The Good, the Bad, and the Goofy, Viking, 1992.
Your Mother Was a Neanderthal, Viking, 1993.

WORK IN PROGRESS: Illustrating *The Time Warp Trio Meet the XYZ Guys,* written by Jon Scieszka, the fifth installment in the "Time Warp Trio" series, for Viking.

SIDELIGHTS: Lane Smith's award-winning style of illustration captures a brand of irreverent humor that appeals to both school-aged children and adults. In both his self-illustrated works and his collaborations with author Jon Scieszka, Smith's work has been variously termed "goofy," "unconventional," and "dark," based on his exaggerated characters, unusual palette of colors, and visual jokes. The artist dismisses the idea that children cannot appreciate the parody and complex illustrations that fill his work, and also defends his use of "gross, elementary-school humor," saying in a *Horn Book* essay that "kids love it." Not only kids, but parents, teachers, and reviewers have come to love his illustrations; such success is evidenced in Smith's numerous awards, including a Caldecott Honor. Signe Wilkinson described Smith's appeal in her *New York Times Book Review* appraisal of his self-illustrated book, *Flying Jake:* "Smith's style offers a minor-key look at the world that is a welcome relief from the vast oversupply of C major art and morality found in many books for young children." Wilkinson further defended Smith's work in a review of *The Stinky Cheese Man and Other Fairly Stupid Tales* in *New York Times Book Review:* "While not conventionally beautiful, [Smith's illustrations] do what all good art must—create an alternate and believable universe."

Smith describes his childhood as a happy, stable one. He was born in Oklahoma, but he spent most of his childhood in the foothills of Corona, California, with his parents and his brother Shane. "Shane and Lane. My mom thought this was funny," Smith recalled. "Yeah, a real hoot. However, *her* brothers were named Dub, Cubby, Leo, and Billy-Joe! My dad's brothers were Tom and Jerry (this is the truth)!"

As a child, Smith developed a sense of both the fantastic and the absurd. During the summers, his family would travel back to Oklahoma. "Our family would take the old Route 66 highway," he recalled. "I think that's where my bizarre sense of design comes from. Once you've seen a 100-foot cement buffalo on top of a doughnut stand in the middle of nowhere, you're never the same."

Although such summers were memorable, Smith's favorite season as a child was autumn. He commented: "I *lived* for Halloween and I loved the old Universal Monster movies. Shane and I would watch them, then read each other horror stories with titles like 'Tales to Tremble By.' The foothills were full of dry bushes and desert trees, and in the fall we'd get a lot of creepy-looking tumbleweeds blowing through our backyard at night. I used to lay awake in bed at night and imagine what wild adventures might be happening in the hills."

Smith attended college at the California Art Center College of Design. To help pay for his tuition, he took a job as a janitor at Disneyland. "Only they didn't call it a janitor," he stated, "we were called 'custodial hosts.' One of my duties was to clean out the attractions at night. It was great to be left in the Haunted Mansion all alone. Another duty was to clean up after someone if they got sick on the Revolving Teacup ride. Like I said, it was great to be left in the Haunted Mansion all alone."

When he wasn't cleaning up the Haunted Mansion or the Revolving Teacup, Smith studied illustration, developing an interest in Pop Art and European illustration. "My instructors said, 'When you get out of school, you're never going to find work in America,' " he recalled in an essay in *Horn Book.* "I was getting worried, but then the punk/new-wave movement came, and my work seemed to fit acceptably into that category."

A year after he graduated, Smith moved to New York City. He became a successful freelance illustrator, and his work began to appear in magazines such as *Ms., Time,* and *Rolling Stone.* Shortly after he arrived in New York, Smith also made his first venture into children's books. In college, he had concentrated on drawing, and he decided to try to paint for a change. This new medium of oil painting was one that Smith would use successfully in all his children's books, even though reviewers have frequently misidentified his illustrations as watercolors or drawings. One of his first projects was a series of paintings depicting the letters of the alphabet, each inspired by his favorite holiday, Halloween. He eventually produced thirty paintings and submitted them to Macmillan.

The company was impressed with his work, and hired children's author Eve Merriam to write poems to accompany the illustrations. In *Horn Book,* Smith discussed his collaboration with Merriam: "I changed some of the artwork to fit some new poems she had written. I had *V* for 'Vampire,' and she came up with 'Viper,' which I liked a lot, because I could use the *V* for the viper's open mouth." The resulting book, *Halloween ABC,* was published in 1987. Reviewers enjoyed Smith's unique style of illustration. A *Horn Book* contributor declared that "Smith's illustrations are suitably mystical and surreal. They . . . look as though they could have come from a witch's book of evil spells." And a *Publishers Weekly* reviewer noted that Smith's "wickedly eerie paintings" perfectly complemented Merriam's text.

In the mid-1980s, Smith met writer and teacher Jon Scieszka (pronounced "sheska"), with whom he has collaborated on several irreverent, satirical children's books. Their first work, 1989's *The True Story of the Three Little Pigs,* tells the traditional fairy tale from the wolf's point of view. In the Scieszka-Smith version of the story, Alexander T. Wolf, now imprisoned at the Pig Pen, tries to present himself as a victim of misunderstanding and media hype. He explains that he visited the pigs to borrow a cup of sugar. Unfortunately, he had a very bad cold, and the first two pigs' houses were very poorly built. Hence, whenever he sneezed, he blew their houses down. He also justified eating the pigs after he killed them, explaining that it would be foolish to let the meat go bad. In *Horn Book,* Smith described how his illustrations worked with Scieszka's story: "I think Jon thought of the wolf as a con artist trying to talk his way out of a situation. But I really believed the wolf, so I portrayed him with glasses and a little bow tie and tried to make him a sympathetic victim of circumstance."

Some reviewers, such as John Peters in *School Library Journal,* noted that the dark colors—and humor—of the book would make it a success with older children and adults. Peters particularly praised Smith's illustrations for the way the wolf's "juicy sneezes tear like thunderbolts through a dim, grainy world." Noting the "fetching and glib" tone of *The True Story of the Three Little Pigs,* a *Publishers Weekly* contributor commented that Smith's pictures "eschew realism," adding a modern flair to the tale. "Smith adds brilliant contemporary illustrations," declared Donnarae MacCann and Olga Richard in their *Wilson Library Journal* assessment. "Using minimal but subtly changing browns and ochers, he combines great variety of creative modes: fanciful, realist, surreal, cartoonish."

School-children and classroom teachers were especially receptive to *The True Story of the Three Little Pigs;* the book sold more than 600,000 copies. In a *Publishers Weekly* interview with Amanda Smith, the illustrator related how he was "stupefied when [the book] took off. We would go out on signings, and every other person there was a teacher, and they would talk about how they used the book for point-of-view writing. All of a sudden we were these young educators."

On their trips to schools, Scieszka and Smith began reading other fairy-tale satires that Scieszka had written prior to *The True Story of the Three Little Pigs*. The positive reception they received from students encouraged them to create a collection of such pieces in *The Stinky Cheese Man and Other Fairly Stupid Tales*. Scieszka discussed the origins of the duo's second book in an interview with Stephanie Zvirin in *Booklist*: "*The Stinky Cheese Man* was really a collaboration. I don't think there's any way to pick apart who did what. When Lane and I went out to visit schools . . . I started reading the stories as fairy tales that *didn't* work. Lane would illustrate them as I spoke. Kids would really crack up."

A headline in *The New York Times Book Review* summed up *The Stinky Cheese Man:* "No Princes, No White Horses, No Happy Endings." One of the first stories in the book is about Chicken Licken, who runs around warning others that the sky is falling. Sure enough, animals are crushed when not the sky, but the book's table of contents unexpectedly falls on them. Elsewhere other traditional tales are turned on their heads: the ugly duckling grows up to become an ugly duck, the frog prince turns out to be just a frog, and the story "The Princess and the Pea" is retitled "The Princess and the Bowling Ball." Smith's pictures carry characters in and out of each other's stories and even into such unexpected places as the endpapers and copyright notice, causing a *Publishers Weekly* reviewer to note that "the collaborators' hijinks are evident in every aspect of the book."

The Stinky Cheese Man was a hit with many reviewers and readers, receiving a prestigious Caldecott Honor for Smith's illustrations and appearing on several notable book lists. Wilkinson wrote: "Kids, who rejoice in anything stinky, will no doubt enjoy the blithe, mean-spirited anarchy of these wildly spinning stories." "Text and art work together for maximum comic impact," noted a *Publishers Weekly* critic. Claudia Logan in *Washington Post Book World* lauded Smith's work in both *The True Story of the Three Little Pigs* and *The Stinky Cheese Man:* "Observant readers will discover visual punnery in his small details, and he tries to make his pictures resemble 'small collections of things in a museum.' His characteristically dark [illustrations] are striking and distinctive." Logan also declared that *The Stinky Cheese Man* "is perhaps the best expression to date of the collaborative process between [Smith and Scieszka] and demonstrates how offbeat their humor can be."

Scieszka and Smith have also cocreated the "Time Warp Trio" series, which is about three boys who, with the aid of a magical book, travel back in time and have assorted misadventures. The series includes the titles *Knights of the Kitchen Table, The Not-So-Jolly Roger, The Good, the Bad, and the Goofy,* and *Your Mother Was a Neanderthal.*

Aimed at middle-grade readers, the books are designed to provide exciting and humorous stories for children who are looking for more than picture books, but are not yet ready for longer chapter books. The author and illustrator hoped that by basing their tales on traditional narratives or historical events, they would encourage kids to do further reading.

In *Knights of the Kitchen Table,* for example, the characters Joe, Sam, and Fred are transported back to the medieval world of King Arthur's England. While there, the boys use their "magical" power to read and their quick-thinking to save the kingdom of Camelot by defeating an evil knight, a giant, and a dragon. The boys take a second time-journey in *The Not-So-Jolly Roger,* where they encounter the legendary pirate, Blackbeard. While *New York Times Book Review* contributor Elizabeth-Ann Sachs appreciated the "Time-Warp Trio" series, she felt that the first story was the strongest, stating that the sequel was "not nearly as much fun" as *Knights of the Kitchen Table.* Sachs also praised Smith's illustrations for the books, declaring the pictures to be "wonderfully menacing and appropriately silly." Trev Jones in *School Library Journal* enjoyed the first two books in the series, calling them "a true melding of word and pictures, and jolly good fun." Joe, Sam, and Fred travel to the wild west of the 19th-century United States in 1992's *The Good, the Bad, and the Goofy,* where they initially find themselves on a rather unexciting cattle drive. Soon, however, they must use their wits to survive various dangers, including cattle stampedes, an Indian attack, a cavalry charge, and a flash flood. Observing that the continuing "Time Warp Trio" series was sure to please readers, Gale W. Sherman in *School Library Journal* found that "Smith's typically zany pencil and charcoal drawings heighten the drama and enhance the wacky mood."

Smith has also illustrated three of his own books: *Flying Jake, The Big Pets,* and *Glasses—Who Needs 'Em?* The first two books involve children's relationships with animals. In the wordless picture book *Flying Jake,* published in 1989, a boy tries to catch his pet bird after it escapes from its cage. He suddenly begins to fly, and before long, he finds himself frolicking among the birds. Some reviewers found the action of *Flying Jake* to be confusing, especially for younger readers. A *Publishers Weekly* contributor acknowledged that it takes some effort to follow the narrative, but felt that "the effort is amply repaid" in Smith's "jaunty, fanciful and energetic" pictures. Wilkinson expressed overall disappointment in the logic of the book, but admitted that Smith "has created a rich picture poem that gives readers of any age a certain feeling about flight among the birds."

The Big Pets depicts a nighttime fantasy world in which children and gigantic animals happily coexist. It begins with a little girl and her oversized cat playing in the Milk Pool, and goes on to present other enormous animals in such places as the Bone Gardens and the Hamster Holes. *Entertainment Weekly*'s Ken Tucker gave *The Big Pets* a glowing review: "*Pets* suggests that we all share the same sort of dreams and can delight in the spookiness and serenity of the night." A reviewer for *Publishers Weekly* wrote: "This fantastic story is enhanced with dark, jewel-like paintings that exhibit an almost phosphorescent glow."

As the title indicates, *Glasses—Who Needs 'Em?* is about a boy's reluctance to wear glasses—a theme Smith is very familiar with. He told *Publishers Weekly,* "I was fitted for glasses in the fifth grade, but I never really wore them—too geeky. My instructors thought I was pretty studious because I was in the front row all the time, but I was the only fifth grader with premature crow's feet—I couldn't see the board." In *Glasses,* the young patient's feeling that glasses are only for "dorks" disappears once his optometrist enlightens him about the multitude of remarkable spectacle-wearers in the world. Both the story and art for Smith's self-illustrated book were given praise by reviewers. "Smith demonstrates 20/20 vision for the sarcastic, zany humor that children adore," stated a *Publishers Weekly* contributor. Wendy Wasserstein, reviewing the book in *New York Times Book Review,* declared *Glasses* to be "one of those perfect children's books . . . a breezy read toward an enlightened end and all the way there incredibly beautiful to look at."

In 1993 Smith published a fourth self-illustrated work, *The Happy Hocky Family,* which parodies the "Dick and Jane" stories familiar to beginning readers of the 1950s. "While poking fun at the genre, *The Happy Hocky Family* is actually an excellent choice for early readers," Steven Engelfried declared in *School Library Journal.* Smith commented that "*The Happy Hocky Family* is my favorite book to date. I am a big fan of 'hand separated' color books from the 1940s and 1950s. I did this book in that style. Each of the colors was done on a separate plate by hand (as opposed to doing a color painting and then having it separated mechanically). I tried to emulate the look of those older books even more by printing the text and illustrations on recycled brown, aged-looking paper. The design was by Molly Leach, who has won acclaim for her innovative designs on *The Stinky Cheese Man, The Big Pets,* and *Glasses, Who Needs 'Em?,* among others."

Smith continues to divide his time between children's books and magazine work. "I don't consider myself a children's book illustrator, just an all-around illustrator," he stated in *Horn Book.* He added that his success in children's books has had effect on his career. "I used to get all these assignments on murder and rape and the economy," he explained, "and now I get assigned topics such as childhood toys and children's phobias." When asked by Zvirin in *Booklist* whether he would continue to create works that use humor to turn traditional stories and ideas upside-down, Smith replied: "There are so many serious books out there and lots of people who do them really well. But there aren't many people who do really goofy work. It's so refreshing to see kids who really respond to funny stuff, and if that gets them to read . . ."

The knowledge that he is getting kids to read is only one of the rewards that Smith receives by creating books for young readers. "I just love the print medium," Smith admitted in his *Horn Book* essay. "I always thought it would be kind of depressing to work for months on a painting and then just have it hang in somebody's house. I've sold some of the paintings from the books through children's art galleries, but I've decided not to do much of that, because I miss them too much. But I have a wonderful existence—I've been able to create the children's books that come naturally to me."

BIOGRAPHICAL/CRITICAL SOURCES:

PERIODICALS

Booklist, September 1, 1992, p. 57.
Bulletin of the Center for Children's Books, October, 1993, p. 58.
Entertainment Weekly, April 26, 1991, p. 71.
Horn Book, November/December, 1987, pp. 753-54; January/February, 1990, p. 58; January-February, 1993, pp. 64-70.
Kirkus Reviews, March 1, 1988, p. 369; August 1, 1991, pp. 1015-16.
New York Times Book Review, June 12, 1988; November 12, 1989, p. 27; October 6, 1991, p. 23; November 10, 1991, p. 54; November 8, 1992, pp. 29, 59.
Publishers Weekly, July 24, 1987, p. 186; February 12, 1988, p. 83; July 28, 1989, p. 218; December 21, 1990, p. 55; May 17, 1991, p. 64; July 26, 1991, pp. 220-21; August 9, 1991, p. 56; May 11, 1992, p. 72; September 28, 1992, pp. 79-80.
School Library Journal, June/July, 1988, p. 94; October, 1989, p. 108; June, 1991, p. 91; August, 1991, p. 169; October, 1991, p. 105; July, 1992, p. 64; August, 1993; October, 1993, p. 130.
Washington Post Book World, December 6, 1992, p. 21.
Wilson Library Journal, June, 1992, p. 118.

*   *   *

SMOTHERS, Ethel Footman 1944-

PERSONAL: Born April 5, 1944, in Camilla, GA; daughter of Ira Lee (a fruitpicker) and Ethel (a maid; maiden name, Jackson) Footman; married Ernest Lee Smothers (a shipping clerk), July 15, 1964; children: Delsey, Darla,

Dana, Dion. *Education:* Grand Rapids Community College, A.A., 1981. *Politics:* Democrat. *Religion:* Seventh Day Adventist.

ADDRESSES: Home—Grand Rapids, MI.

CAREER: Amway Corp., Ada, MI, telephone order clerk, 1980-85, service specialist, 1985-92; author and speaker, 1992—.

MEMBER: Society of Children's Book Writers and Illustrators, Friends of the Library.

WRITINGS:

Down in the Piney Woods, Knopf, 1992.

WORK IN PROGRESS: Moriah's Pond, a sequel to *Down in the Piney Woods;* a children's historical fiction novel set in 1865.

SIDELIGHTS: Set in the rural South during the 1950s, *Down in the Piney Woods* is the story of Annie Rye, a ten-year-old sharecropper's daughter. During the course of the novel, Annie must confront not only the racism of a neighboring white sharecropper, but her own feelings of resentment and hostility when her three older half-sisters move in with her family. Critics praised Footman's work; a reviewer for *Publishers Weekly* stated, "This zesty first novel is chock-a-block with fresh, authentic language," and Hazel Rochman, writing in *Booklist,* added, "The pleasure is in the rhythm of the narrative voice, in the sense of place, and in the characters."

Ethel Footman Smothers commented: "*Down in the Piney Woods* is drawn from childhood memories and imagination. And when I decided to tell my story, I felt that Piney Woods rhythm in my head, with the black English and short, choppy sentences. That's the language of my childhood, and of my people. That uniqueness—that real flavor of our ancestry—must be preserved, or our children—all children—will be deprived of a rare richness that never can be recaptured. You see, it's not just black history. It's American history."

BIOGRAPHICAL/CRITICAL SOURCES:

PERIODICALS

Booklist, December 15, 1991.
Publishers Weekly, November 29, 1991; July 13, 1992.
School Library Journal, December 16, 1991.

*   *   *

SNYDER, Louis L(eo)   **1907-1993**
     (Nordicus)

OBITUARY NOTICE—See index for *CA* sketch: Born July 4, 1907, in Annapolis, MD; died of cholangitis (an in-

fection of the bile ducts), November 25, 1993, in Princeton, NJ. Historian, teacher, and author. Snyder, who was a professor of history at the City College of the City University of New York, was considered an authority on German dictator Adolf Hitler and his Nazi regime. Snyder wrote, coauthored, or edited over sixty books, many of which established his expertise on that portion of German history. In 1932 he published *Hitlerism: The Iron Fist in Germany* under the pseudonym of Nordicus. The volume correctly predicted German dictator Adolph Hitler's assumption of power as well as the persecution of Jewish populations. Snyder also wrote *From Bismarck to Hitler: The Background of Modern Germany, Encyclopedia of the Third Reich, Hitler's Elite: Nineteen Biographical Sketches of Nazis Who Shaped the Third Reich,* and *Hitler's German Enemies: Portraits of Heroes Who Fought the Nazis.*

OBITUARIES AND OTHER SOURCES:

BOOKS

Who's Who in the World, 11th edition, Marquis, 1992.

PERIODICALS

New York Times, December 7, 1993, p. B13.

*   *   *

SOLMSSEN, Arthur R(obert) G(eorge)   **1928-**

PERSONAL: Born September 29, 1928, in New York, NY; son of Kurt A. (a business executive) and Marguerite (Wasschauer-Thevoz) Solmssen; married Marsha Moffat York (a social worker), August 7, 1952; children: Peter York, Kurt A., Arthur R. G. *Education:* Harvard College, A.B., 1950; University of Pennsylvania, LL.B., 1953.

ADDRESSES: Office—Saul, Ewing, Remick and Saul, Thirty-eighth floor, Center Sq. W., Philadelphia, PA 19102.

CAREER: Saul, Ewing, Remick and Saul, Philadelphia, PA, lawyer, 1953—. *Military service:* U.S. Army, 1946-47, became corporal; U.S. Air Force Reserves, c. 1950, became second lieutenant.

WRITINGS:

Rittenhouse Square, Little, Brown, 1968.
Alexander's Feast, Little, Brown, 1971.
The Comfort Letter, Little, Brown, 1975.
A Princess in Berlin, Little, Brown, 1980.
Takeover Time, Little, Brown, 1986.

SIDELIGHTS: A lawyer since 1953, Solmssen is familiar with both law and main-line Philadelphia high society; this expertise provides a realistic backdrop for his novels featuring suspenseful courtroom battles and romantic entanglements. Solmssen's first novel, 1968's *Rittenhouse Square,* is the story of Ben Butler, a member of a prestigious Philadelphia law firm on loan to the Public Defender's office. After successfully defending a housekeeper who was accused of stealing her employer's jewelry, Butler considers remaining in the Public Defender's office, until he is assigned to defend his law-firm partner (and best friend) in a counterfeit bond issue. While many critics found the plot promising, Joseph A. Flaherty, reviewing *Rittenhouse Square* for *Best Sellers,* remarked that Solmssen deflates the excitement of the courtroom scenes by overemphasizing the character's social life. "The Public Defender's Office in a city like Philadelphia must offer material for any number of convincing novels, and even staid patrician law offices must house, as Louis Auchinloss and Hamilton Gibbs have shown, more convincing characters."

Critical reception of *Alexander's Feast,* Solmssen's next novel, was mixed. The narrative concerns a young lawyer who attempts to save the business of his firm's most important client from a hostile takeover bid. Martin Levin in the *New York Times Book Review* noted that, while Solmssen's eye for setting and dialogue is exemplary, his use of an extensive flashback concerning the main character's 1948 love affair with an Austrian countess seems to diminish the plot's tension. Levin concluded that "the effect is to reduce to anti-climax the original burden of the novel, causing this reader . . . frustration, because the original values were so damn good."

Levin found Solmssen's next publication, *The Comfort Letter,* a successful legal thriller. Like the author's earlier novels, *The Comfort Letter* is set in Philadelphia and concerns the inner workings of a corporate empire on the brink of disaster due to mismanagement and corruption. As the protagonist, lawyer Ordway Smith, becomes aware of the extent of his client's illegal activities, he discovers dimensions within himself that alter his perceptions of the law and of his life. Levin especially praised the suspenseful ending, commenting "I'm not sure that this is how things really happen, but it makes for an exciting closing."

In Solmssen's 1980 novel, *A Princess in Berlin,* the author leaves behind the courtroom atmosphere of his earlier works and delves into the history of 1920 Germany. Peter Ellis, the novel's main character, is a young man from Pennsylvania who dropped out of Harvard to drive an ambulance during World War I. After the war, Ellis joins up with Christoph, a German pilot whose life he once saved, and goes to live in Berlin where the strength of the dollar over the heavily inflated mark allows the young American to prosper. Amid Germany's financial troubles and political chaos, Ellis falls in love with Lili, a beautiful Jewish heiress. Marilyn Murray Willison in the *Los Angeles Times* noted Solmssen's "slow, haunting, measured prose.

Action doesn't tumble around, it slowly and deliberately unfolds, small revelation by small revelation. . . . Amid the background of impending Nazi horrors . . . Solmssen's quiet renderings of the brutalities arising out of economic and political desperation gives these dire events a more tragic quality."

Several critics enthusiastically praised Solmssen's portrayal of the period which directly preceded the rise of fascism in Germany. In *Washington Post Book World,* Wolf Von Eckardt wrote: "More than heart tugs, suspense, believable heroes and—much more rare in this genre—a believable villain, *A Princess in Berlin* gives us as sharply focused an insight into how and why Germany perpetrated the Holocaust as any I have seen. That makes it more than a good novel. It makes it an accomplishment, *eine Leistung.*" Moreover, some reviewers lauded Solmssen's vivid portrayal of the impact of Germany's runaway inflation on the daily lives of the people. "There are enchanting passages in this novel," wrote Todd Walton in the *New York Times Book Review,* "and the details of the mind-boggling inflation of that time in Germany are fascinating." Christopher Lehmann-Haupt in a *New York Times* review of *A Princess in Berlin* asserted, "we all know that Germany in the early 1920s experienced one of the worst inflations in history, but it takes Mr. Solmssen's fiction to show the cruel and ironic effects it worked on the German people." Von Eckardt compared the author's depiction of Berlin to "literary photo-realism" and concluded that "few history books explain in such fascinating detail the ins and outs of important events."

Solmssen told *CA:* "*Rittenhouse Square, Alexander's Feast, The Comfort Letter,* and *Takeover Time* are all about people in and around the Philadelphia law firm of Conyers and Dean. *A Princess in Berlin* takes place in Berlin during the years 1922 and 1923, and has been translated into every Western European language, plus Turkish."

BIOGRAPHICAL/CRITICAL SOURCES:

PERIODICALS

Best Sellers, June 15, 1968, p. 132.
Los Angeles Times, October 27, 1980, p. 6.
New York Times, November 3, 1980.
New York Times Book Review, November 21, 1971, p. 80; June 15, 1975, p. 26; December 14, 1980, p. 10.
Washington Post Book World, November 9, 1980, p. 4.

*   *   *

SOMERVILLE, John (P. M.) 1905-1994

OBITUARY NOTICE—See index for *CA* sketch: Born March 13, 1905, in New York, NY; died January 8, 1994, in San Diego, CA. Peace activist, philosopher, educator, and author. The founder of many groups advocating peace, Somerville coined and promoted the use of the word "omnicide" as a caution against the threat of nuclear war. A teacher of philosophy from 1928 to 1935 and also from 1937 to 1967, Somerville spent close to the last three decades of his academic career at Hunter College of the City University of New York. In 1974, he wrote *The Crisis: True Story about How the World Almost Ended,* a play concerning the ethics of the Cuban Missile Crisis, a 1962 event in which President John F. Kennedy confronted the U.S.S.R. upon discovering Soviet missile sites in Cuba. Somerville was also a contributor to international research projects for UNESCO and the author of numerous books on peace and philosophical issues, including *The Philosophy of Peace, The Philosophy of Marxism,* and *The Peace Revolution.* Somerville was the recipient of the Bertrand Russell Peace Award and the Gandhi Peace Prize.

OBITUARIES AND OTHER SOURCES:

BOOKS

Directory of American Scholars, 8th edition, Volume 3, Bowker, 1982.

PERIODICALS

Los Angeles Times, January 20, 1994, p. A32.

* * *

SORKIN, Adam J. 1943-

PERSONAL: Born August 9, 1943, in New York, NY; son of Samson Zelig (an attorney) and Anna (a teacher and retail sales clerk; maiden name, Carch) Sorkin; married Nancy Rosen (a college teacher), June 28, 1964; children: Rachel, Erica. *Education:* Cornell University, A.B. (with distinction), 1964, M.A., 1965; University of North Carolina at Chapel Hill, Ph.D., 1972. *Politics:* "Independent-minded left of center." *Religion:* "An often disappointed belief in the capacity for goodness of my fellow human beings."

ADDRESSES: Home—54 Princeton Rd., Havertown, PA 19083-3622. *Office*—Department of English, Pennsylvania State University, Delaware County Campus, Media, PA 19063-1350.

CAREER: University of Illinois at Chicago Circle, Chicago, instructor in English, 1965-66; University of North Carolina at Chapel Hill, instructor in English, 1970-71; Stockton State College, Pomona, NJ, instructor in literature, 1971-73; Drexel University, Philadelphia, PA, adjunct instructor in literature and language, 1973; Bluefield State College, Bluefield, WV, assistant professor of En-

glish, 1974-78; Pennsylvania State University, Delaware County Campus, Media, assistant professor, 1978-85, associate professor of English, 1985—. Community College of Philadelphia, adjunct instructor, 1973; University of Bucharest, Fulbright lecturer, 1980-81; gives readings in Romania, Pennsylvania, Virginia, and Washington, DC.

MEMBER: American Culture Association (member of governing board, 1989-95; area chair for literature and politics, 1985—), Modern Language Association of America, Society for Romanian Studies, Pennsylvania College English Association, Phi Beta Kappa, Phi Kappa Phi, Phi Eta Sigma, Pi Delta Epsilon.

AWARDS, HONORS: Grant from National Endowment for the Humanities, 1975; fellow at University of California, Irvine, 1976; Lilly fellow, 1979; Carl Bode Award from American Culture Association, 1987; Fulbright scholar in Bucharest, Romania, 1989; fellow in Romania, International Research and Exchanges Board, 1990-91; grant for Romania, Moldova, and Belgium, from Midwest Universities Consortium for International Activities, 1993.

WRITINGS:

(Editor and contributor) *Politics and the Muse: Studies in the Politics of Recent American Literature,* Bowling Green University, 1989.
(Translator from Romanian with Irina Grigorescu Pana, and contributor) *Selected Poems of Anghel Dumbraveanu in Romanian and English: Love and Winter,* Edwin Mellen, 1992.
(Translator from Romanian with Liliana Ursu) *Fires on Water/Focuri pe apa: Seven Poets From Sibiu/7 poeti din Sibio,* European Center for the Promotion of Poetry (Leuven, Belgium), 1992.
(Editor and author of introduction and chronology) *Conversations with Joseph Heller,* University Press of Mississippi, 1993.
(Editor with Kurt W. Preptow, and translator) *An Anthology of Romanian Women Poets,* Columbia University Press, 1994.

Translator of unpublished work *The Sky Behind the Forest: Selected Poems,* by Liliana Ursu. Work represented in anthologies, including *Columbia Pictures: Portrait of a Studio,* edited by Bernard F. Dick, University Press of Kentucky, 1992; *Contemporary East European Poetry: An Anthology,* revised edition by Emery George, Oxford University Press, 1993; and *Shifting Borders: East European Poetries of the Eighties,* edited by Walter Cummins, Fairleigh Dickinson University Press, 1993. Contributor of more than one hundred articles, translations, and reviews to scholarly and literary journals, including *Romanian Civilization, Pennsylvania English, Literary Review, Poet Lore, American Literature,* and *Exquisite Corpse.* Past editor in chief, *Dialogue;* past fiction editor, *Carolina Quarterly;* advisory editor, *Journal of American Culture,* 1991—.

WORK IN PROGRESS: Translations of Romanian poetry by Marin Sorescu and Daniela Crasnalu; translations of contemporary Flemish poetry.

SIDELIGHTS: Adam J. Sorkin told *CA:* "As a student, I envisioned myself becoming a poet, but looking back, I suspect my critical facility outstripped my emotional growth and my competence and commitment as a writer. Perhaps I restricted the scope of my imagination too greatly, but I earned a Ph.D. in English out of love of literature and respect for what it means to be a scholar and teacher, and also out of respect and love for language—its purity, its beauty, its essential life that is more than the life of any individual. Neither as a committed Vietnam war protester in the 1960s and early 1970s, nor during the personal crisis of unemployment in the early 1970s, could I conceive of working in any other field. Such work, I knew then and still believe, is not mere work.

"Over the last decade, however, I have increasingly subordinated the interests of the literary and cultural critic to those of my earlier self through the collaborative translation of the wonderfully strong, moving, vital, and varied poetry of Romania, which I discovered when I taught in Bucharest over a dozen years ago. At first, during the period of the dictatorship which ended in 1989, I felt I was engaged in an important activity by the presentation of the often oblique and symbolic, but usually implicitly dissident, expression of Romania's poets.

"In the past few years, through contact with the European Association for the Promotion of Poetry, I have also begun to work on Flemish poets, and I now realize the translation of poetry has changed me, enriched me, connected me more fully with what it means to be human and, by tying me to poetry, charged me with a responsibility for an art that I believe is not ornamental, but fundamental to what is most human in humanity, most social in societies, most sustaining in culture. When a translation is falling into place as a poem, I experience that sense of being the instrument, not just of the poet's voice compelling me from the original language, but also of an other, higher or more eternal voice to which such concepts as the Muses have traditionally given utterance—to a tongue even more truly original. The challenge of crafting an effective English version of a foreign poet's work offers me both emotional and intellectual gratification that fulfills a need, and continued work on poetry has become not just a joy, but a necessity."

SOURVINOU-INWOOD, Christiane 1945-

PERSONAL: Born January 1, 1945, in Volos, Greece. *Education:* University of Athens, B.A., 1966; Oxford University, M.A., D.Phil., 1974.

ADDRESSES: Office—Oxford, England. *Office*—University College, Oxford University, Oxford OX1 4BH, England.

CAREER: Oxford University, Oxford, England, senior research fellow.

WRITINGS:

Theseus as Son and Stepson: A Tentative Illustration of the Greek Mythological Mentality, Institute of Classical Studies, 1979.
"Reading" Greek Culture: Texts and Images, Rituals and Myths, Oxford University Press, 1991.

Also author of *Studies in Girls' Transitions: Aspects of the Arkteia and Age Representation in Attic Iconography,* 1988; and *"Reading" Greek Death: To the End of the Classical Period.* Contributor to professional journals.

WORK IN PROGRESS: Women, Religion, and Tragedy: Readings in Drama and the Polis Discourse; Reading Dumb Images: A Study in Minoan Iconography and Religion; Mutant in the Shadow: Religion in the Greek "Dark Ages"; Greek Religion: A Sourcebook.

*   *   *

SPARKS, Donald L. 1953-

PERSONAL: Born May 23, 1953, in South Carolina; son of R. Wesley, Jr. and Ethel Lee (Hill) Sparks; married Katherine Saenger (a doctor of veterinary medicine); children: Sarah, Laker (son). *Education:* George Washington University, B.A., 1976; London School of Oriental and African Studies, London, M.A., 1977, Ph.D., 1985; also attended Howard University, Georgetown University, and University of California, Los Angeles.

ADDRESSES: Home—P.O. Box 711, Sullivan's Island, SC 29482. *Office*—Department of Business Administration, The Citadel, Charleston, SC 29409.

CAREER: Staff assistant to U.S. Senator Ernest F. Hollings, Washington, DC, 1974-76; Mansell Publishers Ltd., London, England, research assistant, 1976-77; U.S. Department of State, Office of Economic Analysis, Washington, DC, regional economist for Africa, 1977-83; South Carolina Sea Grant Consortium, Charleston, senior economist and special assistant for international affairs, 1982-83, 1984-85; College of Charleston, Charleston, SC, director of policy studies at Institute for Public Affairs and Policy Studies, 1985-86; The Citadel, Charleston, assistant professor, 1986-91, associate professor of international economics, 1991—. U.S. Air Force Special Operations School, adjunct professor, 1991—; United Nations University, associate of American Council; interviewed on *Voice of America.* School of Oriental and African Studies Foundation, vice-chairperson and member of board of directors; consultant to United Nations, International Union for the Conservation of Nature and Natural Resources, and Frost & Sullivan Political Risk Forecasts, Inc.

MEMBER: European Economic Association, American Economic Association, African Studies Association, National Council on International Visitors (area coordinator), African Studies Association (England), Royal Commonwealth Society, Royal African Society, Charleston Foreign Affairs Forum (member of board of directors).

WRITINGS:

(Author of revision, with James Willis and Martin Primack) *Macroeconomics: Principles and Applications,* CAT Publishing, 2nd edition, 1989, 3rd edition, 1993.
(With December Green) *Namibia: The Nation After Independence,* Westview, 1992.
Economic and Geo-Political Bibliography of the Western Indian Ocean Island States, Centre for Indian Ocean Regional Studies, Carlton University of Technology, 1993.

Work represented in anthologies, including *Africa and the Sea,* edited by J. C. Stone, Aberdeen University Press, 1985; and *Africa South of the Sahara 1993,* Europa, 1993. Contributor of articles and reviews to periodicals, including *African Studies Review* and *Journal of Southern African Studies.* Member of editorial advisory board, *Global Risk Assessments.*

*   *   *

SPARROW, Phil
  See STEWARD, Samuel M(orris)

*   *   *

SPARROW, Philip
  See STEWARD, Samuel M(orris)

*   *   *

SPIEGELMAN, Katia   1959-

PERSONAL: Born December 23, 1959, in Dreux, France; daughter of Joel (a composer and conductor) and Gail (a

teacher; maiden name, Voelker; present surname, Barrnett Beggs) Spiegelman; married Oliver Lief (a film editor), October 9, 1993. *Education:* Simon's Rock of Bard College, A.A., 1977; Sarah Lawrence College, B.A., 1980; City College of the City University of New York, M.A., 1986.

ADDRESSES: Home and office—Brooklyn, NY.

CAREER: Assistant to author Erica Jong, 1987-89; teacher at the Eugene Lang College of the New School for Social Research, New York City, 1992—.

WRITINGS:

Soul Catcher, Marion Boyars, 1990.
Peculiar Politics: A Novel of Sexual Frustration, Marion Boyars, 1993.

*   *   *

STAMES, Ward
  See STEWARD, Samuel M(orris)

*   *   *

STANLEY, Peter W(illiam)   1940-

PERSONAL: Born February 17, 1940, in Bronxville, NY; son of Arnold A. (a business executive) and Mildred Jeannette (a homemaker; maiden name, Pattison) Stanley; married Joan Olivia Hersey, September 14, 1963 (divorced, 1978); married Mary-Jane Cullen Cosgrove, September 2, 1978; children: Laura Margaret Alexandra. *Education:* Harvard University, B.A. (magna cum laude), 1962, M.A., 1964, Ph.D., 1970; attended Jesus College, Cambridge, 1962-63.

ADDRESSES: Home—345 North College Ave., Claremont, CA 91711-4408. *Office*—President's Office, Pomona College, Claremont, CA 91711-6301.

CAREER: University of Illinois, Chicago, assistant professor of history, 1970-72; Harvard University, Cambridge, MA, assistant professor, 1972-78, lecturer in history, 1978-79; Carleton College, Northfield, MN, dean, 1979-84; Ford Foundation, program officer in charge of education and culture, 1984-87, director of education and culture program, 1987-91; Pomona College, Claremont, CA, president, 1991—. Foreign Service Institute, Arlington, VA, lecturer, 1977-89. Johns Hopkins University, Center for Research on Effective Schooling for Disadvantaged Students, member of national advisory board, 1989—; College Board, trustee, 1991—; National Foreign Language Center, member of national advisory council, 1992—; National Association of Latino Elected and Appointed Officials Educational Fund, member of board, 1992—.

MEMBER: American Association of University Professors, American Historical Association, Association for Asian Studies, Phi Beta Kappa.

AWARDS, HONORS: Frank Knox Memorial fellowship, Harvard University, 1962-63; Charles Warren fellowship, Harvard University, 1975-76.

WRITINGS:

A Nation in the Making: The Philippines and the United States, 1899-1921, Harvard University Press, 1974.
(With James C. Tomson, Jr., and John Curtis Perry) *Sentimental Imperialists: The American Experience in East Asia,* Harper, 1981.
(Editor and author of introduction) *Reappraising an Empire: New Perspectives on Philippine-American History,* Harvard University Press, 1984.

Contributor to books, including *Dictionary of American Biography.* Contributor of articles to periodicals, including *New Republic* and *Nation.*

SIDELIGHTS: Educator and author Peter W. Stanley's first published work was his Ph.D. thesis, *A Nation in the Making: The Philippines and the United States, 1899-1921.* His next book, *Sentimental Imperialists: The American Experience in East Asia* (a collaboration with James C. Tomson, Jr., and John Curtis Perry), details American involvement and foreign policy in such Asian countries as Japan, China, Korea, the Philippines, and Vietnam from 1784 to the 1970s. It traces the effect of the spirit of Christian missionary zeal and also the capitalistic impulse in American dealings with Far Eastern nations, and it draws the conclusion that it was bigoted naivete that has led the United States to enter five Asian wars since 1898. As John Leonard put it in the *New York Times,* "This book tells us with a flat lack of emphasis [that] we were—and still are—racists. Skin is more important than money." Elizabeth Peer in *Newsweek* found the book's overall theme to be America's "willful, muddle-headed insistence on evaluating ancient and complex civilizations according to our own norms."

Reviewers of *Sentimental Imperialists* have been generally positive. Leonard lauded the work as "straightforward and so cogent as to cause pain" and concluded that it "tells us more than we wanted to know about our East Asian delirium and shatters the charm." Peer called *Sentimental Imperialists* "an original, tough-minded study" which "deserves a thoughtful audience."

BIOGRAPHICAL/CRITICAL SOURCES:

PERIODICALS

Newsweek, September 14, 1981, p. 89.
New York Times, August 27, 1981.
New York Times Book Review, September 13, 1981, p. 13.
Washington Post Book World, August 23, 1981, pp. 3-4.*

*   *   *

STARR, Larry 1946-

PERSONAL: Born April 17, 1946, in Brooklyn, NY; son of Isidore (a teacher) and Esther Kay (Rubin) Starr; married Leslie Karen Stone (a teacher), December 22, 1968; children: Daniel, Sonya, Gregory. *Education:* Queens College of the City University of New York, B.A., 1967; University of California, Berkeley, Ph.D., 1973.

ADDRESSES: Home—7757 29th Ave. N.E., Seattle, WA 98115. *Office*—School of Music, University of Washington, Seattle, WA 98195.

CAREER: University of Washington, Seattle, faculty member, 1977—, currently professor of music.

MEMBER: American Musicological Society, College Music Society, Sonneck Society.

AWARDS, HONORS: Woodrow Wilson fellow, 1967-68.

WRITINGS:

A Union of Diversities: Style in the Music of Charles Ives, Schirmer Books, 1992.

Contributor to music journals.

WORK IN PROGRESS: A book on style in Gershwin's music.

SIDELIGHTS: Larry Starr told *CA:* "It is essential today for scholars in the humanities to address the broadest possible audience in their work, and this is what I strive to do. The wide potential audience for twentieth-century music has, by and large, been deserted by music scholars, and I want to address this situation."

*   *   *

STERN, James (Andrew) 1904-1993

OBITUARY NOTICE—See index for *CA* sketch: Born December 26, 1904, in County Meath, Ireland; died November 22, 1993, in Tisbury, England. Author and translator. Stern was known for his 1947 work *The Hidden Damage,* which dealt with the effects of World War II on the people of Western Europe; it also included some of the author's childhood memoirs. Also a writer of many widely anthologized short stories chronicling his world travels, Stern published collections of his stories in such volumes as *The Man Who Was Loved* and *The Stories of James Stern.* Stern, with his wife and others, also translated works by German authors, including Bertolt Brecht, Franz Kafka, and Sigmund Freud.

OBITUARIES AND OTHER SOURCES:

BOOKS

The Writer's Directory, 10th edition, St. James Press, 1991.

PERIODICALS

Chicago Tribune, November 28, 1993, section 2, p. 8.
Los Angeles Times, November 26, 1993, p. A44.
New York Times, November 24, 1993, p. D19.
Times (London), November 27, 1993, p. 19.
Washington Post, November 26, 1993, p. C6.

*   *   *

STERN, Malcolm H(enry)   1915-1994

OBITUARY NOTICE—See index for *CA* sketch: Born January 29, 1915, in Philadelphia, PA; died of a heart attack, January 5, 1994, in New York, NY. Rabbi, historian, and author. A Jewish congregation leader in Norfolk, Virginia, for almost twenty years beginning in 1947, Stern left for New York City in 1964, where he became the director of rabbinic placement for the Central Conference of American Rabbis, a position he held until 1980. He also served as the chair of the music committee for the conference from 1949 to 1983 and was responsible for admissions for the organization from 1981 to 1991. In addition, Stern was a genealogist for the American Jewish Archives, where he established himself as one of the foremost Jewish genealogists in the United States. Stern was best known for his work *American Families of Jewish Descent,* which traced the histories of more than 25,000 families who immigrated to the United States from the mid-1600s to the mid-1800s. The latest edition, published in 1991 as *First American Jewish Families,* contains over 50,000 names. Stern's research informed many American Catholics and Protestants of their Jewish heritage and also provided an integral source for the best-selling novel *The Grandees* by Stephen Birmingham.

OBITUARIES AND OTHER SOURCES:

BOOKS

Who's Who in Religion, 4th edition, Marquis, 1992.

PERIODICALS

Los Angeles Times, January 10, 1994, p. A16.

New York Times, January 7, 1994, p. A20.

*   *   *

STERN, Paul C(linton)   1944-

PERSONAL: Born December 23, 1944, in New York, NY; son of Sydney Clinton and Anne Lillian (Schechtman) Stern; married Susan Elizabeth Parkison, July 13, 1968; children: Sarah Rachel. *Education:* Amherst College, B.A., 1964; Clark University, M.A., 1969, Ph.D., 1975.

ADDRESSES: Home—8817 Ritchie Spur Rd., Ritchie, MD 20743. *Office*—Commission on Behavioral and Social Sciences and Education, National Academy of Sciences, 2101 Constitution Ave. N.W., Room HA 184, Washington, DC 20148.

CAREER: Clark University, Worcester, MA, member of Psychological Services Center, 1965-68, 1969-70; Boston Veterans Administration Hospital, Boston, MA, clinical psychology trainee, 1967-69; Elmira College, Elmira, NY, instructor, 1971-75, assistant professor of psychology, 1975-78, staff member of Counseling Center, 1976-78, director of the center, 1978; Yale University, New Haven, CT, postdoctoral fellow at Institution for Social and Policy Studies, 1978-79, research associate, 1979-80; National Academy of Sciences, Commission on Behavioral and Social Sciences and Education, Washington, DC, senior staff officer, 1980-89, principal staff officer, 1989—. National Alliance of Businessmen, awareness trainer in jobs program, 1972-77; George Mason University, research professor of sociology, 1993—. International Social Science Council, member of Working Group on Perception and Assessment of Global Environmental Change, 1991—; consultant to Elmira Correctional Facility, Consumer Energy Council of America, and U.S. Department of Energy.

MEMBER: American Association for the Advancement of Science, American Psychological Association (fellow), Society for the Psychological Study of Social Issues, Society for the Advancement of Socio-Economics, Society for Human Ecology, Society for Personality and Social Psychology, Psi Chi.

AWARDS, HONORS: National Science Foundation, fellowship, 1978-79, grant, 1993-94; Distinguished Contribution Citation from American Psychological Foundation media awards program, 1979, for the article "Motivating the Troops for the Energy War"; *Energy Use: The Human Dimension* was cited by *Choice* as one of the outstanding books of 1984.

WRITINGS:

Evaluating Social Science Research, Oxford University Press, 1979.

(With J. S. Black and J. T. Elworth) *Home Energy Conservation: Issues and Programs for the 1980s,* Consumers Union Foundation, 1981.

(Editor with E. Aronson) *Energy Use: The Human Dimension,* W. H. Freeman, 1984.

(Editor) *Improving Energy Demand Analysis,* National Academy Press, 1984.

(Editor) *Energy Efficiency in Buildings: Behavioral Issues,* National Academy Press, 1985.

(Editor with R. Axelrod, R. Jervis, and R. Radner, and contributor) *Perspectives on Deterrence,* Oxford University Press, 1989.

(Editor) *Behavior, Society, and Nuclear War,* Oxford University Press, Volume I (with P. E. Tetlock, J. L. Husbands, and others), 1989, Volume II (with Tetlock, Husbands, and others), 1991, Volume III: *Behavior, Society, and International Conflict,* 1993.

(Editor with O. R. Young and D. Druckman) *Global Environmental Change: Understanding the Human Dimensions,* National Academy Press, 1992.

Work represented in anthologies, including *Families and the Energy Transition,* edited by J. Byrne, D. A. Schulz, and M. B. Sussman, Haworth, 1985; and *Handbook of Environmental Psychology,* Volume II, edited by D. Stokols and I. Altman, Wiley, 1987. Author of columns for *Population and Environmental Psychology Newsletter,* 1978-88. Contributor of more than fifty articles and reviews to periodicals, including *American Psychologist, Bulletin of the Atomic Scientists, Challenge: Magazine of Economic Affairs,* and *Psychology Today.* Associate editor, *Evaluation Review,* 1986-89; coeditor, *Journal of Socio-Economics,* 1991—; member of editorial board, *Journal of Human Ecology,* 1992—.

WORK IN PROGRESS: Environmental Problems and Human Behavior, with Gerald Gardner, for Allyn & Bacon; revising *Evaluating Social Science Research* with Linda Kalof, Oxford University Press; editing *Perspectives on Nationalism and War* with John Comaroff, Gordon & Breach; research on the formation of attitudes about global environmental change; research on individual preferences, contingent valuation, and the legitimation of social choice.

SIDELIGHTS: Paul C. Stern told *CA:* "I was one of many people who became concerned in the early 1970s that humanity was rapidly changing the earth's environment and that the potential damage was one of the world's great problems. I wanted to do something about it but hesitated because it seemed that to do it full-time would mean getting a whole new career. My training as a psychologist seemed irrelevant to the problems of the natural environment.

"On further reflection, it occurred to me that if human behavior was the cause of environmental problems, a psychologist might be able to understand that behavior and find ways to change it. That realization turned me from college teaching to research and writing, where I became one of a relatively small community that systematically studies the way people and human institutions interact with the natural environment—practitioners of what I have come to call the second environmental science. This term contrasts the scientific study of human-environmental interactions with the study of environmental systems themselves (the first environmental science).

"My work on environmental problems in recent years has been divided between helping to strengthen the community of researchers on human-environment interactions and building needed knowledge in that field. At the National Academy of Sciences, I have directed studies that synthesize knowledge about these interactions and direct the attention of the government and others to the need to build the knowledge further. I have conducted research on energy-saving behavior in homes in order to learn why people who could save money by insulating their houses or investing in energy-efficient automobiles and appliances often do not do so (there are several good reasons), and recently I have been examining the ways people's basic human concerns affect their beliefs about the environment and their willingness to support environmental protection policies. I have also spent considerable time on other projects, including a study of what social science can contribute to preventing and resolving international conflict and a continuing project to improve communication between experts and other citizens about technological decisions.

"Presently, my colleague Gerald Gardner and I are writing a college textbook for a new field. Called *Environmental Problems and Human Behavior,* the book develops a framework, and synthesizes existing knowledge, on such questions as these: Do the roots of environmental degradation lie in a system of values and attitudes that gives the environment second-class status compared to human desires? Is the natural environment too complex for humans to understand and manage? How are the behaviors that harm the environment controlled by the situations people find themselves in? How can we intervene to change those behaviors? I hope this book will help a new generation to think systematically about these problems so it can handle them more skillfully than the present generation has."

*   *   *

STEUERLE, C. Eugene 1946-

PERSONAL: Born December 22, 1946, in Louisville, KY; son of Eugene S. (a lawyer) and R. Henrietta (a home-

maker; maiden name, Cerf) Steuerle; married Norma
Lang (a psychologist), October 3, 1970; children: Kristin
R., Lynne M. *Education:* University of Dayton, B.A.,
1968; University of Wisconsin—Madison, M.A., 1972,
M.S., 1973, Ph.D., 1975. *Avocational Interests:* Reading,
swimming.

ADDRESSES: Home—904 Beverly Dr., Alexandria, VA
22302. *Office*—Urban Institute, 2100 M St. N.W., Washington, DC 20037.

CAREER: Brookings Institution, Washington, DC, federal exchange fellow, 1983-84; Project for Fundamental
Tax Reform, Washington, DC, economic staff coordinator, 1984-86; American Enterprise Institute for Public
Policy Research, Washington, DC, director of finance and
taxation, 1986-87; U.S. Treasury, Washington, DC, deputy assistant secretary, 1987-89; Urban Institute, Washington, DC, senior fellow, 1989—. American Tax Policy
Institute, member of board of trustees; National Economists Club Educational Foundation, president; consultant
to International Monetary Fund and Internal Revenue
Service. Romans Tucker Foundation, member. *Military
service:* Earned Bronze Star.

AWARDS, HONORS: U.S. Treasury, Outstanding Performance Awards, 1979 and 1980, Exceptional Service
Award, 1989.

WRITINGS:

*Taxes, Loans, and Inflation: How the Nation's Wealth Be-
    comes Misallocated,* Brookings Institution, 1985.
Who Should Pay for Collecting Taxes?, American Enter-
    prise Institute for Public Policy Research, 1986.
The Tax Decade, Urban Institute Press, 1992.
Retooling Social Security for the Twenty-First Century,
    Urban Institute Press, 1993.

Weekly columnist. Author of magazine articles.

WORK IN PROGRESS: The New World Fiscal Order; research on the integration of tax and transfer programs.

SIDELIGHTS: C. Eugene Steuerle told *CA:* "In somewhat unusual fashion, I did not grow up seeking to be a
writer; I was required to be a writer to be able to convey
my ideas best on policy issues with which I was involved.
I probably learned to write best while working as a young
adult at the Treasury Department, where I attempted to
put together memoranda that were understandable by
those with backgrounds different than my own. Currently,
I write a weekly column that demands similar attentiveness to my readers. To the extent that I have been able to
acquire any skills along the way, I try to carry them over
to books, articles, testimonies, and other writings. Although I am not afraid to venture forth with my own conclusions, I almost always attempt to present material in

sufficient quality and quantity that readers feel free to
form their own informed conclusions."

*   *   *

STEVENS, Dick   1928-

PERSONAL: Born Richard Stevens, April 20, 1928; son
of Julius A. (a building contractor) and Hilda (Maes) Stevens; married Rebecca Harris (an artist); children: Julia,
Jessica. *Education:* Received B.A. and M.A. from University of Notre Dame; doctoral study at University of Chicago. *Religion:* None.

ADDRESSES: Home—17150 Cherokee Dr., South Bend,
IN 46635.

CAREER: University of Notre Dame, Notre Dame, IN,
professor of photography.

MEMBER: Society for Photographic Education.

WRITINGS:

(With Thomas Musial) *Reading and Writing about and
    Discussing the Great Books,* Houghton, 1970.
Making Kallitypes, Focal Press, 1993.

WORK IN PROGRESS: A history of the kallitype photographic process.

*   *   *

STEVENSON, Louise L.   1948-

PERSONAL: Born June 11, 1948, in New York; daughter
of Charles P. (a manufacturer) and Mary L. (a homemaker) Stevenson; married Philip Zimmerman (a curator), 1980; children: Lila, Katherine. *Education:* Received
B.A. from Barnard College, M.A. from New York University, and Ph.D. from Boston University.

ADDRESSES: Home—13 Edinburgh Court, Newark, DE
19711. *Office*—Department of History, Franklin and
Marshall College, P.O. Box 3003, Lancaster, PA 17604.

CAREER: University of New Hampshire, Durham, visiting lecturer in history, 1981-82; Franklin and Marshall
College, Lancaster, PA, assistant professor, 1982-89, associate professor of history and American studies, 1989—,
chair of department of history, 1991—. Community and
public service lecturer.

MEMBER: American Studies Association, American
Historical Association, Organization of American Historians, American Society of Church History, History of
Education Society, American Antiquarian Society, Berkshire Conference of Women Historians, Intellectual His-

tory Group, Mid-Atlantic Women's Studies Association, Duquesne History Forum.

AWARDS, HONORS: H. F. DuPont scholar, Winterthur Museum and Gardens, 1988; grants from Spencer Foundation, 1989, 1994; Bradley R. Dewey Award for scholarship and teaching, 1992; Andrew W. Mellon fellow, Library Company of Philadelphia, 1994.

WRITINGS:

Scholarly Means to Evangelical Ends: The New Haven Scholars and the Transformation of Higher Learning in America, 1830-1890, Johns Hopkins University Press, 1986.
Miss Porter's School: A History in Documents, two volumes, Garland Publishing, 1987.
The Victorian Homefront: American Thought and Culture, 1860-1880, Twayne, 1991.
(Editor) *Women's History: Selected Reading Lists and Course Outlines from American Colleges and Universities,* 3rd edition, Markus Wiener, 1992.

Work represented in anthologies, including *The University and the City from Medieval Origins to the Present,* edited by Thomas Bender, Oxford University Press, 1988; and *The Oxford Companion to Women's Writing in the United States,* Oxford University Press, 1993. Contributor of articles and reviews to periodicals. Member of editorial board, *Newsletter of the Intellectual History Group,* 1985-91.

WORK IN PROGRESS: A history of women's intellectual life in the United States.

*   *   *

STEWARD, Samuel M(orris)   1909-1993
   (Phil Andros, Donald Bishop, Thomas Cave,
   Ted Kramer, John McAndrews, Joe Reynolds,
   Phil Sparrow, Philip Sparrow, Ward Stames,
   Philip Young)

OBITUARY NOTICE—See index for *CA* sketch: Born July 23, 1909, in Woodsfield, OH; died of chronic pulmonary disease, December 31, 1993, in Berkeley, CA. Educator, tattoo artist, and author. After teaching English at Loyola and DePaul universities from the mid-1930s to the mid-1950s, Steward left the academic world to make a living as a tattoo artist under the name Phil Sparrow. He worked at this in Chicago, Illinois, and Oakland, California, until 1970. Although he had published a book of short stories and a novel in the 1930s, he didn't return to writing until 1977, when he produced *Dear Sammy: Letters from Gertrude Stein and Alice B. Toklas.* Steward was a friend of both of the well-known writers. Much of his later writing career was spent publishing gay erotica under the

pseudonym Phil Andros, including *$tud* and *San Francisco Hustler,* later published as *The Boys in Blue.* Steward also contributed several hundred stories to European magazines under various pseudonyms.

OBITUARIES AND OTHER SOURCES:

PERIODICALS

New York Times, January 20, 1994, p. B8.

*   *   *

STIBBE, Mark W. G.   1960-

PERSONAL: Born September 16, 1960, in London, England; son of Philip (a head teacher) and Joy Mary (a homemaker) Stibbe; married Alison Heather Teale (a homemaker and writer), July 30, 1983; children: Philip Giles, Hannah Joy, Johnathan Mark. *Education:* Cambridge University, degree in English, 1982; Nottingham University, Ph.D., 1986. *Religion:* Christian.

ADDRESSES: Office—St. Mark's Vicarage, 19 Graven Close, Grenoside, Sheffield S30 3OT, England.

CAREER: Clerk in holy orders of the Church of England, 1986—, currently vicar of St. Mark's Church, Grenoside, England. Sheffield University, honorary lecturer in biblical studies, 1989-93.

WRITINGS:

John as Storyteller: Narrative Criticism and the Fourth Gospel, Cambridge University Press, 1992.
John: A New Commentary, Sheffield Academic Press, 1993.
The Gospel of John as Literature, E. J. Brill, 1993.
John's Gospel, Routledge, 1993.
A Kingdom of Priests, Darton, Longman & Todd, 1993.

Contributor to academic journals and Christian magazines.

WORK IN PROGRESS: Research on gospel and culture, on word and spirit, and on Celtic Christianity.

*   *   *

STOCKDALE, James B(ond)   1923-
   (Jim Stockdale)

PERSONAL: Born December 23, 1923, in Abingdon, IL; son of Vernon Beard (a manufacturer) and Mabel Edith (a teacher; maiden name, Bond) Stockdale; married Sybil Elizabeth Bailey (a teacher), June 28, 1947; children: James Bond, Sidney Bailey, Stanford Baker, Taylor Burr. *Education:* U.S. Naval Academy, B.S., 1946; Stanford

University, M.A., 1962. *Politics:* Independent. *Religion:* Episcopalian.

ADDRESSES: Home—547 A Ave., Coronado, CA 92118-1917. *Office*—Hoover Institution on War, Revolution, and Peace, Stanford University, Stanford, CA 94305.

CAREER: United States Navy, ensign, 1946, retired as vice-admiral, 1979, served as naval aviator, test pilot school instructor, squadron commander of supersonic fighter planes, and air wing commander; senior naval service prisoner of war in Hanoi, Vietnam, 1965-73; Naval War College, Newport, RI, president, 1976-79; The Citadel, Charleston, SC, president, 1979-80; Hoover Institute on War, Revolution, and Peace, Stanford University, Stanford, CA, senior research fellow, 1981—; independent vice-presidential candidate as running mate to H. Ross Perot, 1992. Member of academic advisement board, U.S. Naval Academy, 1981—.

MEMBER: Ends of the Earth Society, Explorers Club, Mensa, Association of Naval Aviation, Sons of the American Revolution, Congressional Medal of Honor Society, Society of Cincinnati, Boston Tavern Club, Washington Metropolitan Club, Bohemian Club.

AWARDS, HONORS: Two Distinguished Flying Crosses; three Distinguished Service Medals; four Silver Stars; awarded the Congressional Medal of Honor; prize from the Freedoms Foundation at Valley Forge for *A Vietnam Experience,* 1985; honorary fellow of Society of Experimental Test Pilots; several honorary degrees from various colleges and universities, including the University of South Carolina, University of Massachusetts, Salve Regina College, Norwich University, The Citadel, and Brown University.

WRITINGS:

(With Mark O. Hatfield, Leon Jaworski, Joe H. Fry, and Andrew R. Cecil) *The Ethics of Citizenship,* University of Texas Press, 1981.
(With wife, Sybil Stockdale; under name Jim Stockdale) *In Love and War,* Harper, 1984, revised edition, 1990.
A Vietnam Experience: Ten Years of Reflection, Stanford University, 1985.

Contributor to books, including *To Serve With Honor* by Richard Gabriel, Greenwood Press, 1982, and *Reports From the Firing Line: Organizational Reality.* Contributor of articles to periodicals, including *Los Angeles Times, American Educator, National Review, San Jose Mercury, Wall Street Journal, Argus, United States Air Force Academy Journal of Professional Military Ethics, Naval War College Review, The Professional Journal of the American Federation of Teachers, Palo Altan, Washington Quarterly,* and *Asia-Pacific Defense Forum.*

ADAPTATIONS: In Love and War was adapted as a film for television and broadcast on NBC in 1987.

WORK IN PROGRESS: A book on the Stoic philosophers.

SIDELIGHTS: In 1992, Vice-Admiral James B. Stockdale became the running mate for independent United States presidential candidate H. Ross Perot. He gained the attention of millions of U.S. television viewers in October of that year as he debated Republican and Democratic vice-presidential candidates Dan Quayle and Al Gore. This was not Stockdale's first time in the public eye, however. In 1973, he returned home after eight years as a prisoner of war (P.O.W.) in Vietnam and was lauded for his heroism during that time; he received many military awards and also garnered the Congressional Medal of Honor. He told of his harrowing experiences in Vietnam in two books, *In Love and War,* written with his wife, Sybil, and *A Vietnam Experience: Ten Years of Reflection.* Stockdale has also worked as a college president and research scholar, and has been associated with the Hoover Institute on War, Revolution, and Peace at Stanford University for many years.

Stockdale began his career in the U.S. Navy in 1946. He rose through the ranks steadily, serving as both a pilot and a trainer of other pilots. When he was in his forties, he was the commander of a squadron of U.S. fighter planes involved in the Vietnam War. In 1965 he was shot down while flying over enemy territory. In addition to suffering a broken leg caused by his landing, Stockdale was attacked by North Vietnamese civilians who beat him severely before he was taken into the custody of the enemy North Vietnamese Army. They took him to a Hanoi prisoner of war camp, where he was often held in leg shackles. As a result of this, his broken leg never healed properly, leaving him with a permanent limp.

As a prisoner of war, Stockdale suffered torturous questioning at the hands of the enemy. He never revealed what he felt to be his most dangerous information—that the Tonkin Gulf incident, which had led to the United States becoming a combatant in the Vietnamese conflict, was based on a mistake. In 1964, U.S. ships off the coast of Vietnam believed they were under attack from North Vietnamese PT boats. Stockdale, as quoted by Mary Peterson Kauffold in the *Chicago Tribune,* discovered this was a mistaken assumption. "I had the best seat in the house to watch that event [from the air, flying over the destroyers], and our destroyers were just shooting at phantom targets—there were no [Vietnamese] PT boats there. Not a conspiracy, but a hysterical mix-up." Claiming the attack as proof of North Vietnamese aggression, the U.S. Congress soon empowered President Lyndon B. Johnson to deploy American troops in Vietnam. Stockdale's observations of the incident did not stop this process. "I reported [that there were no Vietnamese boats in the Gulf]," he told Kauffold, "and Washington received it promptly, but we went to war anyway."

Throughout his eight years of captivity, Stockdale was able to keep his captors from learning that he had witnessed the Tonkin Gulf incident. He felt that the North Vietnamese could have used this information for propaganda purposes and severely damaged the U.S. war effort. In addition to protecting the Tonkin Gulf information, Stockdale helped organize his fellow American prisoners into a useful arm of the war effort. Through the use of secret codes, he taught them to communicate with each other without their captors knowing. This not only helped preserve morale among them and aided them in resisting torture, but it also helped Stockdale get information out of Hanoi and back to the U.S. military.

Stockdale was freed and returned to the United States when U.S. involvement in the war ended in 1973. He continued his military career and served as president of the Naval War College in Newport, Rhode Island, before retiring from the military in 1979. In 1979 he also became president of another military school, the Citadel in Charleston, South Carolina, but he left after only a year. Stockdale wanted to end the severe hazing rituals practiced by the students at the college, liberalize the curriculum, and alter admission standards. When these plans met with resistance from the school's alumni and board of directors, he resigned.

Since leaving the Citadel, Stockdale has been a research scholar and educator with Stanford University's Hoover Institute on War, Revolution, and Peace, a conservative think tank. There he has explored the writings of classical philosophers and their applications to today's military, although this approach often conflicts with current military procedures. Kauffold explained that Stockdale, when asked to make suggestions about a week-long ethics program for Navy officers, proposed the use of stories from classical philosophy. These tales would then be applied to military behavior in combat. Stockdale's approach was turned down, however, and instead, reported Kauffold, "the Harvard Business Review is now the curriculum bible." This turn of events has left Stockdale disappointed with some aspects of current military education. "To reduce the virtues of a warrior to the capability of making up a military budget," Stockdale told Kauffold, "is distasteful to me because it gets [the student] out of the mindset that his job is to command men in battle."

Stockdale published his first book in 1981, a collaboration with several others entitled *The Ethics of Citizenship*. He then turned his writing efforts in a more personal direction, recounting his Vietnam experiences in a collabora-

tion with his wife, Sybil. *In Love and War* featured alternating chapters by the Stockdales. Sybil discussed her experiences as a wife of a prisoner of war who eventually became an outspoken lobbyist on behalf of the U.S. prisoners, forming an influential organization that pressured the U.S. government to take more action on the prisoners' behalf. James's chapters, meanwhile, relate his experience as a P.O.W., and his efforts to organize and support his fellow inmates. Though a *Kirkus Reviews* critic complained that *In Love and War* was "overlong," several other reviewers were much more favorable in their assessment of the Stockdales' volume. Carolyn See in the *Los Angeles Times* declared that "this is a book everyone should read," and noted that the Stockdales' story "is at once astonishing, saddening, enraging and quite literally mind-boggling. This volume, while it is invaluable as a document of the war itself, is also an extraordinary testament of (good) people who live to make war." Similarly, Duncan Spencer observed in the *Washington Post Book World* that Mr. Stockdale "has narrative gifts and an infectious bloodthirstiness," and concluded that *In Love and War* "deserve[s] to be on the bookshelf of every serious student of the late, lamented war." The book was made into a television film in 1987.

While Mrs. Stockdale was trying to obtain the release of her husband and other American prisoners of war in Vietnam, she enlisted the efforts of businessman H. Ross Perot. Thus began the long association between the Stockdales and Perot, which culminated in the independent presidential candidate naming Stockdale as his running mate in 1992. Though Perot and Stockdale did not win the election, they gained almost unprecedented support for third-party candidates. In the campaign's much-publicized vice-presidential debate, Stockdale's remarks, quoted by David E. Rosenbaum in the *New York Times*, included lines such as "Who am I?" and "Why am I here?" Though many reporters felt these remarks were indicative of a man out of his league among the professional politicians Quayle and Gore, others appreciated the retired naval officer's short statements that cut straight to the heart of issues. Rosenbaum, for instance, asserted that "there was some charm in this 68-year-old who uttered simplicities amid the bombast." In recalling his P.O.W. experience during the debate, Stockdale recounted his accomplishments and summed up his dissatisfaction with American politicians. "The best thing I had going for me," he said of his long confinement, "was I had no contact with Washington all those years."

BIOGRAPHICAL/CRITICAL SOURCES:

PERIODICALS

Chicago Tribune, October 30, 1984; April 27, 1990; October 8, 1992, section 1, p. 13.

Kirkus Reviews, September 1, 1984, p. 858.
Los Angeles Times, November 12, 1984.
New York Times, October 2, 1992, p. A19; October 14, 1992, p. A18.
Washington Post Book World, September 23, 1984, p. 5.

—*Sketch by Elizabeth Wenning*

*   *   *

STOCKDALE, Jim
See STOCKDALE, James B(ond)

*   *   *

STONE, Peter B(ennet) 1933-

PERSONAL: Born July 6, 1933, in Chadderton, Lancashire, England; son of Walter (a retail manager) and Violet (Bennet) Stone; married Jennifer Jane Wedderspoon (a journalist), July 28, 1964; children: Chamouni, Seiriol. *Education:* Received B.A. and M.A. from Balliol College, Oxford. *Politics:* "In favor of underdogs." *Religion:* Agnostic. *Avocational Interests:* Mountaineering, sailing, industrial archaeology (steam locomotives and ships).

ADDRESSES: Office—Les Corneillettes, Crozet 01170, France. *Agent*—A. P. Watt Ltd., 20 John St., London WC1N 2DR, England.

CAREER: British Broadcasting Corp. (BBC-TV), London, England, producer, 1958-64; journalist, 1964-70; United Nations Conference on the Environment, Stockholm, Sweden, senior information adviser, 1971-72; United Nations Development Forum, Geneva, Switzerland, editor in chief, 1972-83; Brundtland Commission, director of information, 1983-86. United Nations Development Business, founder; Mountain Agenda, co-founder, 1991, editor in chief, and environment consultant. *Military service:* Royal Navy, seaman officer. Royal Navy Reserve; became lieutenant.

MEMBER: Geological Society (fellow), Royal Geographical Society (fellow), Alpine Club (fellow).

WRITINGS:

Japan Surges Ahead, Praeger, 1967.
(With C. M. B. Horsfield) *The Great Ocean Business,* Hodder & Stoughton, 1971.
Did We Save the Earth at Stockholm?, Earth Island, 1973.
(Editor) *The State of the World's Mountains: A Global Report,* Zed Books, 1992.

Science correspondent for *Statist* and *British Industry Week,* 1964-70.

WORK IN PROGRESS: World Mountain Audit 1997.

SIDELIGHTS: Peter B. Stone told *CA:* "I was interested by the natural wild world from as early as I can remember, in reaction perhaps to having been born in industrial Lancashire. I have always loved climbing mountains, as well as the sea, but science came first. At Oxford, I took an expedition to the mountains of southwest Angola when that war-torn country was relatively happy. I saw erosion and rural poverty and realized that the care of the planet was likely to be two parts science to six parts communication (in the public interest) and only one part politics.

"After service in the Royal Navy, where I had the rare privilege to be trained up to the exalted rank of acting temporary probationary sub-lieutenant, I went into communications and learned the basics with the British Broadcasting Corporation. After attempts in the sixties to go it alone with conservation and development journalism, I found myself with Maurice Strong and the Stockholm Environment Conference of 1972. The rest of my career was involved with carrying United Nations environment and development information to the deaf. I saw how economic recession wiped out the environment movement twice, and how only disasters rescued it.

"There's a concept called, in astrophysics, background radiation. It is everywhere and comes from all directions. That's what environmental communication will have to be until it seeps into everything. The disasters (like Chernobyl) will help, but they have to be bad without being *too* bad. Unfortunately Mother Nature does not go in for fine-tuning to suit humanity. It will be a matter of chance. Encouragement comes from the sight of young people pressing the case in non-governmental organizations, like Greenpeace and Friends of the Earth. Writers can help enormously, but there should not be sacred texts; they do too much mischief. On the other hand, text, chapter, and verse underpin a myriad of acts to care and sustain the only earth we have."

*   *   *

STONER, K. Lynn 1946-

PERSONAL: Born August 24, 1946, in Oak Ridge, TN; daughter of Henry Herb (a chemical engineer) and Frances Evelyn (a microbiologist; maiden name, Pouns) Stoner; married Luis Eugenio Hartly Campbell (a lawyer), July 22, 1991. *Education:* Vanderbilt University, B.S., 1968; Indiana University—Bloomington, M.A., 1975, Ph.D., 1983. *Religion:* Protestant. *Avocational Interests:* Tennis, swimming, music.

ADDRESSES: Home—1617 South River Dr., Tempe, AZ 85281. *Office*—Department of History, Arizona State University, Tempe, AZ 85287-2501.

CAREER: Arizona State University, Tempe, assistant professor, 1985-91, associate professor of history, 1991—, director of Latin American Studies Center, 1993. Arizona Humanities Council, member.

MEMBER: American Historical Association, Latin American Studies Association, Council of Latin American Historians.

WRITINGS:

Latinas of the Americas, Garland Publishing, 1989.
From the House to the Streets: The Cuban Woman's Movement for Legal Reform, 1898-1940, Duke University Press, 1992.

WORK IN PROGRESS: Women Prisoners in Cuba, 1920-1940, completion expected in 1996.

SIDELIGHTS: K. Lynn Stoner told *CA:* "Two themes excited my imagination while I was a graduate student: women's history and revolution. The two coalesced in Cuban history throughout this century, as revolution has been a constant state of affairs and women have been important figures. My work has focused on the pre-revolutionary period (which is a misnomer), 1900-1940. Research has taken me to Cuba, where I have many friends and now family. As Cuba faces a new era, I am even more drawn to the island's drama, this time as an observer. History has taught me that I cannot tell Cubans what their choices should be. My compassion, however, drives me to befriend and enable where I can. It is difficult to separate intellectual and personal life when passion is allowed a vital role in each."

*   *   *

STOUFFER, Allen P.   1937-

PERSONAL: Born July 16, 1937, in Stouffville, Ontario, Canada; married; wife's name, Sarah J.; children: Scott, Kirk. *Education:* Bethel College (Missionary Church), B.A. (cum laude), 1959; attended Laval Universite, 1961, and Indiana University at South Bend, 1965; Claremont Graduate School, M.A., 1961, Ph.D., 1971. *Religion:* United Church of Canada.

ADDRESSES: Home—6 Tigo Park, Antigonish, Nova Scotia, Canada B2G 1M9. *Office*—Department of History, St. Francis Xavier University, Antigonish, Nova Scotia, Canada B2G 1C0.

CAREER: Bethel College (Missionary Church), Mishawaka, IN, instructor, 1962-64, assistant professor, 1965-70, associate professor of social sciences, 1971; St. Francis Xavier University, Antigonish, Nova Scotia, assistant professor, 1971-76, associate professor, 1977-92,

professor of history, 1992—, head of department, 1974-75, 1976-77, member of St. Francis Xavier Renaissance Singers in the 1970s. University of Moncton, summer school teacher, 1975. Antigonish Area Refugee Assistance Association for the Boat People, chair, 1979-81. Halifax Chamber Choir, member, 1980-86; Halifax Camerata Singers, member, 1987—.

MEMBER: Canadian Historical Association, Organization of American Historians, Atlantic Association of Historians.

AWARDS, HONORS: Grants from Social Sciences and Humanities Research Council of Canada, 1987-88, 1988-89, and 1989-90.

WRITINGS:

The Light of Nature and the Law of God: Antislavery in Ontario, 1833-1877, Louisiana State University Press, 1992.

Contributor of articles and reviews to history and American studies journals.

*   *   *

STOWE, Leland   1899-1994

OBITUARY NOTICE—See index for *CA* sketch: Born November 10, 1899, in Southbury, CT; died January 16, 1994, in Ann Arbor, MI. Journalist and author. Stowe's noteworthy career as a journalist was highlighted by his Pulitzer Prize-winning stories on the Paris Reparations Conference in 1929 for the *New York Herald Tribune* and his coverage of early World War II in Europe for the *Chicago Daily News.* His later articles on the war focused on events in Asia for both newspapers and radio. Among Stowe's major stories of this period was his discovery that the Chinese government was stockpiling U.S. lend-lease weapons for use against Communist insurgents rather than implementing them against their Japanese war enemy. In the late 1940s and early 1950s, he served as foreign editor of *Reporter* magazine and as the news director of Radio Free Europe. From 1956 to 1969 he taught journalism at the University of Michigan. During and after his academic career, Stowe served as a roving editor and writer for *Reader's Digest.* He published a number of books, including *Nazi Means War, Target: You, Crusoe of Lonesome Lake,* and the 1982 work, *The Last Great Frontiersman: The Remarkable Adventures of Tom Lamb.*

OBITUARIES AND OTHER SOURCES:

BOOKS

Who's Who in America, 48th edition, Marquis, 1994.

PERIODICALS

Chicago Tribune, January 17, 1994, section 4, p. 9; January 23, 1994, section 2, p. 6.
New York Times, January 18, 1993, p. B10.
Washington Post, January 18, 1993, p. D8.

*   *   *

STRACKBEIN, O(scar) R(obert) 1900-1993

OBITUARY NOTICE—See index for *CA* sketch: Born January 23, 1900, in Doss, TX; died of acute respiratory failure, November 10, 1993, in McLean, VA. Economist, lobbyist, and author. For much of his early career, Strackbein worked for the U.S. government, serving from 1924 to 1930 as an assistant trade commissioner for the Department of Commerce in Cuba and Venezuela, then later working for the Tariff Commission and the Department of Labor. After spending most of the 1940s in private industry, Strackbein founded the National Labor Management Council on Foreign Trade Policy, later to be known as the Nation-Wide Committee on Import-Export Policy. As chair, and later president, of this body, he lobbied for trade legislation for industry and agriculture. During his career he also testified before Congress on free-trade issues. A contributor to journals and newspapers, Strackbein also published books, including *American Enterprise and Foreign Trade* and *Permissiveness.*

OBITUARIES AND OTHER SOURCES:

PERIODICALS

Washington Post, November 11, 1993, p. D8.

*   *   *

SUFRIN, Mark 1925-

PERSONAL: Born July 21, 1925, in Brooklyn, NY; son of Arthur (a business executive) and Ann (a homemaker; maiden name, Putter) Sufrin. *Education:* New School for Social Research, B.A., 1950; Columbia University, M.A., 1951; attended University of California, Berkeley. *Politics:* Democrat. *Religion:* Jewish. *Avocational Interests:* Sports, photography, hiking, reading, sketching, music (classical and jazz of the 1920s-1950s).

ADDRESSES: Home and office—300 West 12th St., New York, NY 10014.

CAREER: Free-lance writer. *Military service:* U.S. Army, 1942-46, served in the Pacific Theater; became first lieutenant.

MEMBER: Society of Military Writers.

AWARDS, HONORS: Teaching fellow, Columbia University, 1950-51; British Academy of Film and Television Arts Best Short Film Award, Venice Film Festival Grand Prize—documentary, Edinburgh Film Festival Grand Prize—documentary, and Academy Award nomination, best documentary, all 1956, all for *On the Bowery.*

WRITINGS:

NONFICTION

To the Top of the World: Sir Edmund Hillary and the Conquest of Everest, Platt & Munk, 1966.
The Brave Men: Twelve Portraits of Courage, illustrated by Richard Smith, Platt & Munk, 1967.
Surfing: How to Improve Your Technique (part of "Concise Guide" series), F. Watts, 1973.

BIOGRAPHIES

Focus on America: Profiles of Nine Photographers, Scribner, 1987.
Payton, Scribner, 1988.
George Bush: The Story of the Forty-first President of the United States, Delacorte, 1989.
George Catlin: Painter of the Indian West, Atheneum, 1991.
Stephen Crane, Atheneum, 1992.
Palmyra, Knightsbridge, 1992.
F. Scott Fitzgerald, Atheneum, 1993.
Walt Whitman, Atheneum, 1994.

SCREENPLAYS

(And codirector) *On the Bowery,* Film Representations, 1956.

Also author of *Jerash.* Author and director of documentaries, *Acre* and *Home Front.*

OTHER

Raid at Matupai, Tower, 1981.
The Nightriders, Dell, 1982.
Operation Hoax (science fiction; part of "Golden Heroic Champions" series), illustrated by Dan Spiegle, Golden Book, 1985.
Defenders of the Earth: The Sun Stealers (science fiction; part of "Golden Super Adventure" series), illustrated by Fred Carrillo, Golden Book, 1986.

Also author of *A Time of Heroes.* Contributor to periodicals, including the *New York Times, Chicago Tribune,* and *New Republic.* Contributor to anthologies.

WORK IN PROGRESS: A novel about middle-class life between World Wars I and II; a nonfiction work on the development of New York City between 1890 and 1930, with emphasis on its artists, writers, architects, and photographers; a novel about the U.S. Marine who predicted the bombing of Pearl Harbor in 1921.

SIDELIGHTS: Mark Sufrin commented: "My consuming interest is social history and middle-class life between the two World Wars. 'The past,' said British author L. P. Hartley, 'is a foreign country. They do things differently there.' In my next novel I hope to illuminate the period—its crimps and pleasures, the charm and banality of its popular culture. The middle class of those years aspired and conformed with innocence, docility, and quiet courage—and barely understood how precarious its position was. My obsession is with the time author John Cheever said was 'a long lost world when the city of New York was still filled with river light, when you heard Benny Goodman quartets from a radio in a corner stationery store, and when almost everybody wore a hat.' "

* * *

SUZUKI, Yoshio 1931-

PERSONAL: Born October 12, 1931, in Tokyo, Japan; son of Ichihei (an entrepreneur) and Misako Suzuki; married Yukiko Akiyama, January 11, 1959; children: Yumiko, Kenta, Morio, Yuzo. *Education:* University of Tokyo, bachelor's degree, 1955, D.Econ., 1976.

ADDRESSES: Home—5-8, Kamitakaido 2 chome, Suginami-ku, Tokyo, Japan 168. *Office*—Nomura Research Institute, Ltd., 1-10-1 Nihonbashi, Chuo-ku, Tokyo 103, Japan.

CAREER: Bank of Japan, Tokyo, 1955-89, manager of Matsumoto branch, 1977-79, deputy director of Institute for Monetary and Economic Studies (IMES), 1979-84, director of IMES, 1984-88, executive director of Bank of Japan, 1988-89; Nomura Research Institute, Ltd., Tokyo, vice chairman of board of counselors, 1989-91; chairman of board of counselors, 1991—. Visiting lecturer, University of Tokyo, 1972-73, and University of Shinshu, 1978-79. Member of government-affiliated bodies, including tax commission, 1984-87, 1990-91, and 1992—, price stabilization policy council, 1990—, and advisory group for economic restructuring, 1993—; director and vice president of Mont Perelin Society, 1986-92.

MEMBER: Japan Association of Economics and Econometrics, Association of Money and Banking, Forum for Policy Innovation.

AWARDS, HONORS: Nikkei Cultural Prize for Economic Literature, 1967, for *Effects of Monetary Policy;* Economist's Prize, Mainichi Newspaper Company, 1974, for Japanese-language edition of *Money and Banking in Contemporary Japan;* public finance fellowship, Institute of Fiscal and Monetary Policy, Ministry of Finance, 1987.

WRITINGS:

AVAILABLE IN ENGLISH

Gendai nihon kin-yuron, Toyokeizai Shinposha, 1974, translation by John G. Greenwood published as *Money and Banking in Contemporary Japan,* Yale University Press, 1980.

Nihon kin'yu keizairon (title means "Monetary Economics in Contemporary Japan"), Toyokeizai Shinposha, 1983, translation by Robert Alan Feldman published as *Money, Finance, and Macroeconomic Performance in Japan,* Yale University Press, 1986.

(Editor) *Monetary Policy in Our Times,* MIT Press, 1985.

(Editor with Hiroshi Yomo) *Financial Innovation and Monetary Policy: Asia and the West* (proceedings of the second international conference sponsored by the Institute for Monetary and Economic Studies of the Bank of Japan), University of Tokyo Press, 1986.

(Editor) *Waga kuni no kin'yu seido,* Institute for Monetary and Economic Studies, Bank of Japan, 1986, translation published as *The Japanese Financial System,* Oxford University Press, 1987.

(Editor with Mitsuaki Okabe) *Toward a World of Economic Stability: Optimal Monetary Framework and Policy* (proceedings of the third international conference sponsored by the Institute for Monetary and Economic Studies of the Bank of Japan), University of Tokyo Press, 1988.

Japan's Economic Performance and International Role, University of Tokyo Press, 1989.

(Editor with Okabe and Junichi Miyake) *The Evolution of the International Monetary System: How Can Efficiency and Stability Be Attained?* (proceedings of the fourth international conference sponsored by the Institute for Monetary and Economic Studies of the Bank of Japan), University of Tokyo Press, 1990.

OTHER

Money and Price in Japan (in Japanese; title translated), Toyokeizai Shinposha, 1964.

Kin'yu-seisaku no kouka (title means "Effects of Monetary Policy"), Toyokeizai Shinposha, 1966.

(Editor) *Debt Management and Monetary Policy* (in Japanese; title translated), Nihonkeizai Shinbunsha, 1968.

Inflation and Currency Crisis (in Japanese; title translated), Japan Institute of International Affairs, 1971.

Monetary Theory (in Japanese; title translated), Nihonkeizai Shinbunsha, 1980.

Japanese Economy at the Crossroads (in Japanese; title translated), Toyokeizai Shinposha, 1981.

Nihon keizai to kin'yu (title means "Japan's Economy and Finance in a Changing World"), Toyokeizai Shinposha, 1981.

Kin'yu jiyuka to kin'yu seisaku (title means "Financial Deregulation and Monetary Policy"), Toyokeizai Shinposha, 1985.

(Editor) *Finance and Banking in Japan* (in Japanese; title translated), Toyokeizai Shinposha, 1986.

Monetary Policy by Bank of Japan and Its Effectiveness (in Chinese; title translated), Zhongguo Jinrong Chubanshe, 1986.

Japan's Economy and Finance in the World Framework (in Japanese; title translated), Toyokeizai Shinposha, 1987.

Financial Policy of the Transition Period: A Japanese Response to the Challenge (in Korean; title translated), Hankuk Kyungjae Shinmoonsh, 1987.

The Japanese Economy: The Sun Is Still High (in Japanese; title translated), Toyokeizai Shinposha, 1990.

How Long Japan's Economic Prosperity Will Continue (in Japanese; title translated), NTT Press, 1991.

(Editor) *Financial Words Dictionary* (in Japanese; title translated), Toyokeizai Shinposha, 1991.

(Coauthor) *Japan and the World in Post-Gulf Crisis* (in Japanese; title translated), Toyokeizai Shinposha, 1991.

(Coauthor) *Where Is Japan Going?* (in Japanese; title translated), Toyokeizai Shinposha, 1991.

Revival of the Japanese Economy (in Japanese; title translated), Toyokeizai Shinposha, 1992.

Monetary Policy in Japan (in Japanese; title translated), Iwanami Shoten, 1993.

Chief editor of *Monetary and Economic Studies,* Bank of Japan.

*　　*　　*

SWANSON, June 1931-

PERSONAL: Born June 22, 1931, in St. Louis, MO; daughter of George Joseph (an engineer) and Helen (an artist and homemaker; maiden name Bange) Charlier; married Stanley Swanson, June 4, 1954; children: Sandra, Laura, John, Steven. *Education:* University of Texas, B.A., 1952; Florida Atlantic University, M.A., 1986. *Avocational Interests:* Antiques, hiking, primitive rug hooking, gardening.

ADDRESSES: Home—15 Lisa Dr., Nashua, NH 03062.

CAREER: Elementary school teacher, 1952-1954; freelance writer, 1954—.

AWARDS, HONORS: Notable Children's Trade Book in the field of social studies, National Council for Social Studies and Children's Book Council, 1983, for *The Spice of America.*

WRITINGS:

NONFICTION

The Spice of America, illustrated by Priscilla Kiedrowski, Carolrhoda, 1983.

I Pledge Allegiance, illustrated by Rick Hanson, Carolrhoda, 1990.

David Bushnell and His Turtle, illustrated by Mike Eagle, Atheneum, 1991.

OTHER

That's for Shore (riddles), Lerner, 1991.

Also author of over 200 articles, short stories, and poems in more than 30 different magazines, for children and adults.

WORK IN PROGRESS: Two more riddle books to be published by Lerner.

SIDELIGHTS: Since the publication of her first book, *The Spice of America,* June Swanson has explored little-known aspects of American history. In *The Spice of America,* Swanson writes about such overlooked figures as Dolley Madison and Andrew Johnson, and discusses the origins of such commonplace items as blue jeans and doughnuts.

Swanson's second book, *I Pledge Allegiance,* was published on the 100th anniversary of the writing of the pledge and provides some historical background on its origin. Janie Schomberg wrote in the *School Library Journal* that programs involved with new immigrants, students with English as a second language, and social studies "will be enriched by this book; it will also be helpful in public library programs."

Swanson's *David Bushnell and His Turtle* is about the man who tried to invent the submarine in the late eighteenth century. Bushnell was a graduate of Yale University who proved that explosives could be set off underwater. His submarine (which resembled two turtle shells joined together; hence the title) was intended to attach mines to British ships. While his invention was unsuccessful, he paved the way for such inventors as Robert Fulton, who created the first successful steamboat. "A most informative sketch of the first working underwater craft and its inventor," asserted a contributor *School Library Journal.* A *Kirkus Reviews* contributor noted that the author's explanation of Bushnell's problem solving "make a fascinating story that illuminates both the technology and the society of his day."

BIOGRAPHICAL/CRITICAL SOURCES:

PERIODICALS

Kirkus Reviews, August 15, 1991.

School Library Journal, July, 1990; December, 1991.

*   *   *

SWITZER, Barry 1937-

PERSONAL: Born October 5, 1937, in Crossett, AK; son of Frank Mays (a bootlegger) and Mary Louise (Wood) Switzer; married, 1963, wife's name, Kay (divorced, 1983); children: Greg, Kathy, Doug. *Education:* Attended University of Arkansas.

ADDRESSES: Office—6 Northeast 63rd St., Suite 250, Oklahoma City, OK 73105.

CAREER: University of Arkansas, Fayetteville, AK, assistant football coach, 1960-65; University of Oklahoma, Norman, assistant football coach, 1966-72, head coach, 1973-89; insurance agent, Norman, 1976—. Affiliated with Barry Switzer Marketing (food-brokerage firm). *Military service:* Served with U. S. Army.

WRITINGS:

(With Bud Shrake) *Bootlegger's Boy,* Morrow, 1990.

SIDELIGHTS: Barry Switzer, former University of Oklahoma football coach, published his autobiography to offer his perspective of his notorious career. Entitled *Bootlegger's Boy* and coauthored by Bud Shrake, the book appeared in 1990, a year after Switzer resigned as head coach of the University of Oklahoma football team amidst scandal. Under his leadership, the Sooners (the name of the college's football team) had won three national football championships, and Switzer's record as a coach in his division remains one of the highest in college football history. Marring the team's success, however, was the frequent probationary status imposed on them by the National Collegiate Athletic Association (NCAA), college football's governing body. The Sooners were continually charged with various rules infractions, including violations in recruiting practices. In 1989 the University of Oklahoma regents demanded Switzer's resignation after scandal wracked the team and threatened to discredit college football—in the space of a month, one player shot and wounded another, two others raped a woman on campus, and the star quarterback sold cocaine to a federal narcotics agent.

The title of the autobiography, *Bootlegger's Boy,* refers to Switzer's background in rural Arkansas as the son of two alcoholics—a bootlegger father and a mother who was a former beauty queen. Switzer and his younger brother grew up near the poorer section of Crossett, Arkansas, in a house without electricity, a phone, or gas heat. The family was shunned by the majority of townsfolk, primarily for the debaucheries of the parental Switzers. These ex-

cesses culminated, while Switzer was a star athlete in high school, with his father being sentenced to prison. He also recounts the suicide of his mother when he was in college, an act Switzer blamed for many years on himself, and the later slaying of his father by a distraught female companion.

After attending the University of Arkansas on a football scholarship, Switzer joined his alma mater's coaching staff in 1960 and remained there for five seasons. He signed on with the controversial University of Oklahoma Sooners in 1965. The team had a troubled past, having already attracted the censure of the NCAA for various violations of practice. Adding to the pressures of being a Sooners coach were the fevered demands of the college's faculty and its thousands of football fans, who expected nothing less than victory from their team. Switzer served as assistant coach for six seasons before taking on the job of head coach in 1973. The Sooners then went on to win two consecutive national championships, but during the ensuing years, the team continually found itself in violation of NCAA rules. The outspoken Switzer's off-the-sidelines antics also attracted considerable attention over the years, as he drank with players and press and publicly disparaged rival coaches.

Switzer himself was seen by the sports establishment as a rebel and one who let his players "run wild." He refused to play the stern father figure that many fans and sportswriters envisioned as necessary for the primarily African American college athletes. Despite these condemnations, Switzer made great strides with his players. In addition to chalking up an outstanding winning record, he was also commended for breaking the color barrier of the star position of quarterback, a station that was traditionally held by white players. If this feat raised the eyebrows of observers, it nevertheless earned him the respect and praise of his players. In his book, the coach discusses aspects of racism in regard to college athletics and defends his other actions throughout his career. Switzer condemns the hypocritical, double-edged sword of college football, which demands lip-service to its rules, yet turns a blind eye when a winning team is bringing in advertising revenues and alumni dollars.

Bootlegger's Boy, published a year after Switzer's resignation, received attention for the former coach's unusual personal story. Switzer's clarification of his controversial football career and recounting of victorious moments comprises the bulk of the book, yet critics praised Switzer's real triumph over the adversity of his early years. Reviewing the work for *Sports Illustrated,* Rick Telander commented on the former coach's defense of his conduct in assessing that his "excuses lack balance," and "paranoia tinkles through this book like wind chimes." Telander praised the coach's early life anecdotes, however, as "page turners, macabre tales that could have come out of an earlier century." *Chicago Tribune* writer Paul Galloway also lauded this section as "riveting." *New York Times Book Review* critic Felicia E. Halpert faulted Switzer and Shrake for emphasizing the blow-by-blow details of the coach's career at the expense of a more thorough account of a broader personal story, but she commended the work's "lively, personal prose."

BIOGRAPHICAL/CRITICAL SOURCES:

PERIODICALS

Chicago Tribune, January 1, 1991, p. 10.
New York Times Book Review, October 7, 1990, p. 21.
Sports Illustrated, September 24, 1990, p. 7.*

T

TAGGARD, Mindy Nancarrow 1951-

PERSONAL: Born June 19, 1951, in Texarkana, TX; daughter of Warren George (a petroleum engineer) and Hilda (a homemaker; maiden name, Harkness) Nancarrow; married Jose Antonio Cano Miret (a lawyer and novelist), March 14, 1990. *Education:* University of New Mexico, B.A., 1972; University of Texas, M.A., 1976; University of Kansas, Ph.D., 1985.

ADDRESSES: Home—1204 Queen City Ave., Tuscaloosa, AL 35401. *Office*—Department of Art, University of Alabama, Tuscaloosa, AL.

CAREER: Oklahoma State University, Stillwater, assistant professor of art history, 1985-88; University of Alabama, Tuscaloosa, assistant professor of art history, 1988—.

MEMBER: American Society for Hispanic Art Historical Studies, Southeast College Art Conference, College Art Association.

AWARDS, HONORS: Fulbright grant for Spain, 1982-83.

WRITINGS:

Murillo's Allegories of Salvation and Triumph: "The Parable of the Prodigal Son" and "The Life of Jacob", University of Missouri Press, 1992.

WORK IN PROGRESS: Antonio del Castillo y Saavedra, pintor: Su vida y su obra.

*   *   *

TAPPER, Nancy
See LINDISFARNE, Nancy

TARKINGTON, (Newton) Booth 1869-1946
(N. Booth Tarkington)

PERSONAL: Born July 29, 1869, in Indianapolis, IN; died after a short illness, May 19, 1946, in Indianapolis, IN; son of John Stevenson Tarkington (a lawyer) and Elizabeth (Booth) Tarkington; married Laurel Louisa Fletcher, June 18, 1902 (divorced, 1911); married Susanah Robinson, November 6, 1912; children: (first marriage) Laurel (deceased). *Education:* Attended business college and art school, 1889, Purdue University, 1890, and Princeton University, 1891-93. *Politics:* Republican.

ADDRESSES: Home—Indianapolis, IN; Kennebunkport, ME.

CAREER: Novelist, essayist, and playwright. Elected to the Indiana House of Representatives, 1902-03.

MEMBER: American Academy of Arts and Letters, Ivy Club, Players Club, University Club (Indianapolis), Century Club (New York), Nassau Club (Princeton), Triangle Club (president, 1892-93).

AWARDS, HONORS: Pulitzer prizes for novel, Columbia University, 1919, for *The Magnificent Ambersons,* and 1922, for *Alice Adams*; Gold Medal, National Institute of Arts and Letters, 1933; Roosevelt Distinguished Service Medal, 1942; Howells Medal, American Academy of Arts and Letters, 1945; received honorary degrees from various institutions, including an M.A. from Princeton University, 1899, Litt.D. from Princeton University, 1918, De Pauw University, 1923, and Columbia University, 1924, and L.H.D. from Purdue University, 1939.

WRITINGS:

FICTION

The Gentleman from Indiana, Doubleday & McClure, 1899.

Monsieur Beaucaire (first serialized in *McClure's,* 1899), illustrated by C. D. Williams, McClure, Phillips, 1900, illustrated by T. M. Cleland, Limited Editions Club, 1961.

The Two Vanrevels, illustrated by Henry Hutt, McClure, Phillips, 1902.

Cherry, Harper & Brothers, 1903.

In the Arena: Stories of Political Life, illustrated by A. I. Keller, Power O'Malley, and J. J. Gould, McClure, Phillips, 1905.

The Conquest of Canaan: A Novel, illustrated by Lucius W. Hitchcock, Harper & Brothers, 1905.

The Beautiful Lady, McClure, Phillips, 1905.

His Own People, illustrated by Lawrence Mazzanovich and F. R. Gruger, Doubleday, Page, 1907.

The Guest of Quesnay, illustrated by W. J. Duncan, McClure, 1908.

Beasley's Christmas Party, illustrated by Ruth Sypherd Clements, Harper & Brothers, 1909.

The Spring Concert, Ridgeway, 1910.

The Flirt, illustrated by Clarence F. Underwood, Doubleday, Page, 1913.

The Turmoil: A Novel, illustrated by C. E. Chambers, Harper & Brothers, 1915.

"Harlequin and Columbine," and Other Stories, Doubleday, Page, 1918.

"Monsieur Beaucaire," "The Beautiful Lady," "His Own People," and Other Stories, Doubleday, Page, 1918.

The Magnificent Ambersons, illustrated by Arthur William Brown, Doubleday, Page, 1918, illustrated by Roy Andersen, Franklin Library, 1977.

Ramsey Milholland, illustrated by Gordon Grant, Doubleday, Page, 1919.

Alice Adams, illustrated by Brown, Doubleday, Page, 1921, illustrated by Jim Campbell, Franklin Library, 1979.

Gentle Julia, illustrated by C. Allan Gilbert and Worth Brehm, Doubleday, Page, 1922.

The Midlander, Doubleday, Page, 1923, published as *National Avenue* in *Growth.*

"The Fascinating Stranger," and Other Stories, Doubleday, Page, 1923.

Women, Doubleday, Page, 1925.

Looking Forward, and Others, Doubleday, Page, 1926.

Growth (contains *The Turmoil, The Magnificent Ambersons,* and *National Avenue*), Doubleday, Page, 1927.

The Plutocrat: A Novel, Doubleday, Page, 1927.

Claire Ambler, Doubleday, Doran, 1928.

Young Mrs. Greeley, Doubleday, Doran, 1929.

Mirthful Haven, Doubleday, Doran, 1930.

Mary's Neck, Doubleday, Doran, 1932.

Wanton Mally, illustrated by Joseph Simont, Doubleday, Doran, 1932.

Presenting Lily Mars, Doubleday, Doran, 1933.

Little Orvie, illustrated by Brehm, Doubleday, Doran, 1934.

"Mr. White," "The Red Barn," "Hell," and "Bridewater" (novelettes), Doubleday, Doran, 1935.

The Lorenzo Bunch, Doubleday, Doran, 1936.

Rumbin Galleries, illustrated by Ritchie Cooper, Doubleday, Doran, 1937.

The Fighting Littles, Doubleday, Doran, 1941.

The Heritage of Hatcher Ide (published serially as *The Man of the Family*), Doubleday, Doran, 1941.

Kate Fennigate, Doubleday, Doran, 1943.

Image of Josephine, Doubleday, Doran, 1945.

The Show Piece (unfinished novel), introduction by wife, Susanah Tarkington, Doubleday, 1947.

Three Selected Short Novels (contains *Walterson, Uncertain Molly Collicut,* and *Rennie Peddigoe*), Doubleday, 1947.

Also author of story "Old Fathers and Young Sons."

FOR CHILDREN AND YOUNG ADULTS

Penrod, illustrated by Gordon Grant, Doubleday, Page, 1914.

Penrod and Sam, illustrated by Worth Brehm, Doubleday, Page, 1916.

Seventeen: A Tale of Youth and Summer Time and the Baxter Family, Especially William, Harper & Brothers, 1916, illustrated by Arthur William Brown, Grosset & Dunlap, 1918, illustrated by Edwin Tunis, Harper & Brothers, 1932.

Penrod Jashber, illustrated by Grant, Doubleday, Doran, 1929.

Penrod: His Complete Story (contains *Penrod, Penrod and Sam,* and *Penrod Jashber*), illustrated by Grant, Doubleday, Doran, 1931.

PLAYS

(With Evelyn Greenleaf Sutherland) *Monsieur Beaucaire* (adapted from Tarkington's novel of the same title), produced as *Beaucaire* in New York City, 1901.

The Gentleman from Indiana, produced in Indianapolis, IN, 1905.

(With Harry Leon Wilson) *The Guardian,* privately printed, 1907, published as *The Man from Home* (produced in Chicago, IL, 1907, produced in New York City, 1908), Harper & Brothers, 1908, revised edition published as *The Man from Home: A Play in Four Acts,* S. French, 1934.

(With Wilson) *Cameo Kirby,* produced in New York City, c. 1907.

Springtime, produced in New York City, c. 1908.

(With Wilson) *Your Humble Servant* (produced in New York City, c. 1909), Rosenfield, 1908.

(With Wilson) *Foreign Exchange,* produced in New York City, 1909.

(With Wilson) *If I Had Money,* produced in New York City, 1909, produced as *Getting a Polish,* New York City, 1910.

Beauty and the Jacobin: An Interlude of the French Revolution (produced in New York City, 1912), illustrated by C. D. Williams, Harper & Brothers, 1912.

Mister Antonio: A Play in Four Acts (produced in New York City, 1916), S. French, 1935.

(With Julian Street) *The Ohio Lady* (four-act; produced in New York City, 1916), Ebert Press, 1916, published as *The Country Cousin: A Comedy in Four Acts* (produced in New York City, 1917), S. French, 1921.

Clarence: A Comedy in Four Acts (four-act; produced in New York City, 1919), S. French, 1921.

(With Wilson) *Up from Nowhere,* produced in New York City, 1919.

(With Wilson) *The Gibson Upright* (produced in Indianapolis, IN, 1919), Doubleday, Page, 1919.

Poldekin, produced in New York City, 1920.

The Intimate Strangers (three-act; produced in New York City, 1921), S. French, c. 1922.

The Wren: A Comedy in Three Acts (produced in New York City, 1921), S. French, 1922.

The Ghost Story: A One-Act Play for Persons of No Great Age (produced in 1922), Stewart Kidd, 1922.

Rose Briar, produced in New York City, 1922.

The Magnolia, produced in New York City, 1923.

(With Wilson) *Tweedles: A Comedy* (produced in New York City, 1923, produced as *Bristol Glass* in Cleveland, OH, 1923), S. French, 1924.

The Trysting Place: A Farce in One Act (produced, 1923), Stewart Kidd, 1923.

Bimbo, the Pirate: A Comedy (produced in 1926), Appleton, 1926.

The Travelers (produced in 1927), Appleton, 1927.

Station YYYY (produced in 1927), Appleton, 1927.

(Under name N. Booth Tarkington; with Wilson) *How's Your Health? A Comedy in Three Acts* (produced in New York City, 1929), S. French, 1930.

Colonel Satan, produced in New York City, 1931.

The Help Each Other Club (produced in 1933), Appleton-Century, 1934.

Lady Hamilton and Her Nelson (produced in 1945), House of Books, 1945.

Also author of *The Man on Horseback,* produced c. 1911; seventy-five episodes of *Maud and Cousin Bill* (radio plays), 1932-33; and *Aromatic Aaron Burr,* 1938.

COLLECTIONS AND SELECTIONS

The Works of Booth Tarkington, fourteen volumes, Doubleday, Page, 1918-19.

Strack Selections from Booth Tarkington's Stories, arranged by Lilian Holmes Strack, Walter H. Baker, 1926.

The Gentleman from Indianapolis: A Treasury of Booth Tarkington, edited by John Beecroft, illustrated by John Alan Maxwell, Doubleday, 1957.

On Plays, Playwrights, and Playgoers: Selections from the Letters of Booth Tarkington to George C. Tyler and John Peter Toohey, 1918-1925, edited by Alan S. Downer, Princeton University Library, 1959.

Stories, illustrated by Peter Cox, Franklin Library, 1984.

OTHER

(Illustrator) James Whitcomb Riley, *The Boss Girl,* Bowen-Merrill, 1886.

(With Kenneth Lewis Roberts and Hugh MacNair Kahler) *The Collector's Whatnot: A Compendium, Manual, and Syllabus of Information and Advice on All Subjects Appertaining to the Collection of Antiques, Both Ancient and Not So Ancient, Compiled by Cornelius Obenchain Van Loot, Milton Kilgallen, and Murgatroyd Elphinstone,* Houghton, 1923.

Looking Forward, and Others (essays), Doubleday, Page, 1926.

(Illustrator) Kenneth Roberts, *Antiquamania,* Doubleday, Doran, 1928.

The World Does Move (semiautobiographical), Doubleday, Doran, 1928.

Some Old Portraits: A Book about Art and Human Beings, Doubleday, Doran, 1939.

Christmas This Year, Earle J. Bernheimer, 1945.

Your Amiable Uncle: Letters to His Nephews, self-illustrated, Bobbs-Merrill, 1949.

Also author of the following screenplays: *Edgar and the Teacher's Pet,* 1920; *Edgar's Hamlet,* 1920; *Edgar, The Explorer,* 1921; *Get Rich Quick Edgar,* 1921; (with Tom Geraghty) *Pied Piper Malone,* 1924; (with Geraghty) *The Man Who Found Himself,* 1925. Contributor to *Commemorative Tributes to Gillette and Howard and Others,* The Academy, 1940; *Commemorative Tributes of the Academy, 1905-41,* The Academy, 1942; and *There Were Giants in the Land,* Rinehart, 1942. Work represented in *The Collected Stories of the World's Greatest Writers,* Franklin Library, 1984.

Some of Tarkington's works were translated into French and Polish.

ADAPTATIONS:

MOVIES

Cameo Kirby, Lasky Feature Play, 1914, Fox Film Corporation, 1923 and 1929.

Cherry, Vitagraph, 1914.

The Two Vanrevels, Thomas A. Edison, 1914.

Sophia's Imaginary Visitors (adaptation of *Beasley's Christmas Party*), Thomas A. Edison, 1914.

The Man from Home, Lasky Feature Play, 1914, Famous Players-Lasky Corporation, 1922.

The Gentleman from Indiana, J. C. Ivers, 1915.

The Turmoil, Columbia Pictures, 1916, Universal Pictures, 1924.

The Flirt, Bluebird Photoplays, 1916, Universal Pictures, 1922.

Seventeen, Famous Players Film Co., 1916, Paramount Pictures, 1940.

The Country Cousin, Selznick Pictures, 1919.

The Adventures and Emotions of Edgar Pomeroy (series of twelve films), Goldwyn Pictures, 1920-21.

The Conquest of Canaan, Famous Players-Lasky Corporation, 1921.

Penrod, Marshall Neilan Productions, 1922.

Boy of Mine, Associated First National Pictures, 1923.

Penrod and Sam, Associated First National Pictures, 1923, First National Pictures, 1931, Warner Brothers, 1937.

Gentle Julia, Fox Film Corporation, 1923, Twentieth Century-Fox, 1936.

Monsieur Beaucaire, Paramount Pictures, 1924 and 1946.

The Fighting Coward (adaptation of *The Magnolia*), Paramount Pictures, 1924.

Pampered Youth (adaptation of *The Magnificent Ambersons*), Vitagraph, 1925.

River of Romance (adaptation of *The Magnolia*), Paramount Famous Lasky Corporation, 1929.

Geraldine, Pathe Exchange, 1929.

Mister Antonio, Tiffany-Stahl Productions, 1929.

Monte Carlo (adaptation of *Monsieur Beaucaire*), Paramount Publix, 1930.

Father's Son (adaptation of story "Old Fathers and Young Sons"), Warner Brothers/First National Pictures, 1931, Warner Brothers, 1941.

Bad Sister, Universal Pictures, 1931.

Business and Pleasure (adaptation of *The Plutocrat*), Fox Film, 1931.

Alice Adams, RKO Radio Pictures, 1935.

Mississippi (adaptation of *The Magnolia*), Paramount Pictures, 1935.

Clarence, Paramount Pictures, 1937.

Penrod's Double Trouble, Warner Brothers, 1938.

Penrod and His Twin Brother, Warner Brothers, 1938.

Little Orvie, RKO Radio Pictures, 1940.

The Magnificent Ambersons, RKO Radio Pictures, 1942.

Presenting Lily Mars, Metro-Goldwyn-Mayer, 1943.

On Moonlight Bay (based on the "Penrod" stories), Warner Brothers, 1951.

By the Light of the Silvery Moon (adaptation of *Penrod*), Warner Brothers, 1953.

PLAYS

Ethel Hale Freeman, *Monsieur Beaucaire,* W. H. Baker, 1916.

Hugh S. Stange, Stannard Mears, and Stuart Walker, *Booth Tarkington's Seventeen,* S. French, 1924.

SIDELIGHTS: Winner of two of the first four Pulitzer prizes for literature, Booth Tarkington was best known for his narratives describing middle-class life in the American Midwest of the early twentieth century. He was a prolific writer as well. In a writing career that spanned more than five decades, Tarkington produced 171 stories, 9 novellas, 21 novels, and 19 plays, besides a number of movie scenarios, illustrations, and radio dramas. Many of his works were also adapted for film through the early part of the twentieth century. Although Tarkington was an extremely popular writer, his work did not receive overwhelming critical attention. Said James Woodress in a 1991 *Dictionary of Literary Biography* essay: "Although he had more talent than most of his contemporaries, his work never quite achieved major significance, and he had to be content with a large rather than a discriminating audience." However, Tarkington is still remembered for many of his writings, including chronicles of youth such as the "Penrod" series and *Seventeen* as well as his Pulitzer prize-winning novels *The Magnificent Ambersons* and *Alice Adams.*

Tarkington evinced an early interest in his craft. He recollected dictating a story to his sister when he was only six years old in his 1941 essay, "As I Seem to Me," published in the *Saturday Evening Post.* By age sixteen, related Tarkington, he had written a fourteen-act melodrama about Jesse James after reading William Shakespeare's work. And while enrolled in Princeton University he became the editor of three university publications. Yet he said of himself in "As I Seem to Me": "I wasn't ambitious. That is, I had no ambition to be anything or to be known as anything. I didn't yearn to be a novelist or a playwright or a distinguished illustrator. . . . I had no conscious wish to write a novel; I didn't deliberately, so to say, begin one or feel anything like the interest in writing that I did in drawing, and yet I began to write a novel." During this time Tarkington had returned to Indiana from Princeton, and he spent the next few years trying to get his work published. He said in "As I Seem to Me," "I strained and fought with writing . . . and all the while, though I knew that I worked at drawing because I liked to draw, I hadn't the least idea why I worked twice as hard at writing." During these years, when he unsuccessfully tried to get his work published, Tarkington felt as though his friends and acquaintances perceived him as a loafer. He said in his essay: "As I review those years it seems to me that my family were heroic about me; their embarrassment must have been severe."

In 1895 Tarkington left for New York City to seek fame and fortune with, as related in his semiautobiographical book *The World Does Move,* a trunk full of "the manuscripts of two plays, of an unfinished novel, and of a now-forgotten number of short stories." It was here that he stumbled upon his first publishing venture after years of struggle, when one of his novels was accepted for publication in a magazine. He said in *The World Does Move:* "Five years of printed rejection slips had not prepared one to receive even an encouraging handmade letter of rejection from an editor, much less a letter of acceptance. Such a letter must be read several times to make certain that the reader's eye is not deceived, and then at intervals to be sure that his memory has not been tricky. But no; all these readings have confirmed the accuracy of the first, it became clear that the thin young man, however embarrassing he might be in his new capacity, was definitely no longer a loafer."

The publisher had, however, asked Tarkington to make changes in the manuscript, which he began immediately. In 1896 he returned to Indiana and continued working on what later became his first novel, *The Gentleman from Indiana.* The book was published in 1899, and Tarkington became an instant success in New York. In his essay, Tarkington explained that this book resulted from a decision to respond to the myth prevalent on the East Coast that Indiana was a "backwoods state." He said: "Sensitive and even resentful, I tried to make my novel answer all this nonsense. . . . A thing the novel tried to say was that in the matter of human character the people of such an out-of-the-way midland village were as estimable as any others anywhere. . . . This, in my sensitive young fervor, was my emotional tribute to the land of my birth." Although the book was a resounding commercial success, Tarkington was viewed differently by critics. An opinion expressed in the *Independent* in 1900 faulted the book for its lack of authenticity while admitting that it was "brim full of a certain boyish enthusiasm which is delightful."

For James Branch Cabell, writing in *Beyond Life: Dizain des demiurges,* Tarkington was a highly accomplished writer who had fallen short of realizing his potential. In Cabell's opinion, the commercial success of *The Gentleman from Indiana,* matched by the similar triumph of *Monsieur Beaucaire,* "was one of the most dire calamities that ever befell American literature," and it resulted in Tarkington's concessions "to the necessity of being 'pleasant.'" *The Gentleman from Indiana* was perceived as a romance by most critics, and Tarkington was criticized for what reviewers called an optimistic and unrealistic portrayal of characters. Later, he was to receive similar criticism for another best-seller, *The Magnificent Ambersons,* for which he also won his first Pulitzer.

Tarkington followed *The Gentleman from Indiana* with *Monsieur Beaucaire,* which was serialized in *McClure's* in 1899 and published separately in 1900. The volume was written as a costume romance, which was a popular style at the time. The book was successful and was later adapted for the stage and as a feature film. Set in Bath, England, in the eighteenth century, the work describes the adventures of the Duke of Orleans as he masquerades as a barber amongst English nobility living at that popular resort. The plot revolves around the exposure of the duplicity and pretentiousness of some members of the nobility. Addressing the book in a 1937 *Indianapolis Star* article, Damon Runyon wrote that "*Monsieur Beaucaire* is ever green. It is a little literary cameo, and we read it over at least once a year."

Tarkington had moved back to New York during this time, and in 1902 he married Laurel Louisa Fletcher. It was also in this year that he was elected to a seat in the Indiana House of Representatives, a post he was forced to give up due to an illness in 1903. But, Woodress explained in the *Dictionary of Literary Biography,* Tarkington gained knowledge about politics, and this in turn affected his writing. *In the Arena,* which he issued in 1905, is a collection of short stories that were influenced by his experiences as a politician. Woodress reported that *In the Arena* even drew the attention of President Theodore Roosevelt, who consequently invited Tarkington to the White House. It was also in 1905 that Tarkington collaborated, for the first time, with Harry Leon Wilson, writing the play *The Man from Home,* which was produced in 1907. In these years Tarkington continued to write articles for literary magazines in New York as well as collaborate with Wilson on a number of plays.

Following the publication of *In the Arena,* Tarkington traveled through Europe with his wife and family for some ten years. During this time he wrote *The Beautiful Lady* and *His Own People,* periodically returning to the United States to manage productions of his plays. However, his writing was interrupted for a few years due to drinking problems and his divorce from Louisa. It was not until 1912 that he decided to pick up his writing career again. Tarkington said of this change, as quoted in Woodress's *Booth Tarkington: Gentleman from Indiana:* "Now I'm in condition as I was ten years ago, but with a very piquant realization of wasted time. . . . I want to make up for that time and have the energy to do it."

In 1914, Tarkington began issuing the "Penrod" stories, which became instant successes. The stories describe the adventures of Penrod Schofield, a young boy growing up in late-nineteenth-century America. Penrod belongs to a middle-class family, and the character's childhood antics were popular with many readers from the time the tales first began appearing in *Everybody's Magazine.* The "Penrod" stories have been compared to Mark Twain's *Tom Sawyer* by many critics and recall many of Tarkington's own memories of a childhood spent in Indiana. Woodress called the works "everyday incidents in which style and arrangement of detail are everything" in the *Dictionary of Literary Biography*. The success of the first stories prompted Tarkington to write many more, and he eventually collected them into three books: *Penrod, Penrod and Sam,* and *Penrod Jashber*. In 1931 he collectively published all the books as *Penrod: His Complete Story*. The "Penrod" books sold a half-million copies while Tarkington was still alive. In *Booth Tarkington: Gentleman in Indiana,* Woodress cites Tarkington, who felt that "Penrod" was successful "because it has kept to *true* boy and avoided book-and-stage boy." And in a letter Tarkington wrote to a friend included in the same book, the author also said: "My prices astonish me . . . I'm rather sorry for the magazines that pay 'em." Assessing the *Penrod* tales in *Dictionary of Literary Biography*, Woodress said that "Tarkington was in full mastery of his craft when he wrote these stories. His style is supple, articulate, and witty, and the tales entertain children and delight adults."

While writing the "Penrod" stories, Tarkington also began work on *Seventeen: A Tale of Youth and Summer Time and the Baxter Family, Especially William,* another collection of stories about a young protagonist. He had worked on a similar theme in an earlier work, "Mary Smith," a short story dealing with young love, for which he had received favorable attention. *Seventeen* also proved very popular with Tarkington's readers. The stories deal with incidents in the life of Willie Baxter, a young man from the American Midwest, who is in love with a woman called Lola Pratt. Woodress said that although the stories seem dated today, *Seventeen* was a major success in Tarkington's own time, selling nearly eight hundred thousand copies as well as being adapted for a play, a musical comedy, and a feature film. This collection also provided Tarkington with a major character for another book, *Gentle Julia*. The character of Florence Atwater, the protagonist of *Gentle Julia,* was inspired by the tomboyish character of Jane, Willie Baxter's sister in *Seventeen*. Woodress, in *Dictionary of Literary Biography,* said of *Gentle Julia:* "Tarkington understood girls as well as boys and, in depicting the activities of Florence, her cousin Herbert, and his buddy Henry, handles successfully the emotional and mental lag between the sexes at the age of thirteen."

By the 1920s Tarkington was living in the suburbs of Indianapolis, Indiana, and spending the summers in Kennebunkport, Maine. His observations of the life of suburban women in Indianapolis resulted in *Women,* stories of "daytime society made up of wives, teas, domestic servants, luncheons, children, literary clubs, and Amazon warfare of a highly sophisticated type," summarized Woo-

dress in the *Dictionary of Literary Biography*. And his experiences in Kennebunkport, his summer home, directly impacted *Mirthful Haven,* published in 1930. Kennebunkport was a resort town, and in Woodress's opinion "it was inevitable that a novelist of manners would sooner or later make use of the clash in values and life-styles of the natives and the summer folk." Kennebunkport was also the inspiration for Tarkington's 1932 publication *Mary's Neck.*

According to Adam J. Sorkin, discussing Tarkington's work in a 1981 *Dictionary of Literary Biography* essay, although Tarkington was a popular and prolific writer throughout his literary career, the author "wrote his best works at the time of and just after World War I." It was in these years that Tarkington received two Pulitzer Prizes, one in 1919, for *The Magnificent Ambersons,* and the other in 1922, for *Alice Adams.* Although *The Magnificent Ambersons* was a very popular book with Tarkington's readers, reviewers criticized the author for romanticizing the story, thus reducing its elements of realism. *The Magnificent Ambersons* traces the fall and reclamation of the old and wealthy Amberson family through George Amberson Minafer, the spoiled heir. The Amberson family made its fortune because of the hard work of George's grandfather, Major Amberson. However, his daughter, who marries into an equally rich family, does not instill similar values in her son, George, who grows up to be a selfish, uncaring individual. Critics agreed that Tarkington successfully built up the list of George's follies, leading the reader to anticipate his fall from arrogant self-assurance. However, the direction of the story changes dramatically when in the end George, instead of receiving just punishment for his deeds, marries the wealthy daughter of his mother's rejected suitor and thus begins the reclamation of his family. George further enhances his return to material and moral success when he takes a job in a factory. Tarkington received criticism for this ending even though he was praised for his accurate description of middle-class life of the time.

Tarkington went on to write *The Midlander,* continuing the story of the economic and historical development of America. He later combined *The Magnificent Ambersons, The Midlander,* and *The Turmoil* to form the *Growth* trilogy, which, in Sorkin's words, "deals with the growing up of a nation," a subject of "potentially monumental proportions." *The Turmoil,* published in 1915, formed the second book of the trilogy. It drew favorable attention from critics at the time. According to Sorkin, in this book Tarkington explored the "raw ugliness and savagery" that characterized the growth of the nation. Although the book was written before *The Magnificent Ambersons,* it deals with a later period in history. In *The Turmoil* Tarkington dealt with the nouveau-riche Sheridan family, who, in Sorkin's words, "typify the new makers of material wealth and vulgar worshippers of Bigness." The book relates the story of James Sheridan, an affluent man, and his son Bibbs, who wants no part of his father's vast empire. W. D. Howells, discussing the book in *Harper's,* expressed appreciation for the universality of the story of *The Turmoil.* Howells said that even though the book was particularly rooted in the American way of life, "the action of *The Turmoil* is possible everywhere that the human passions and volitions have play." William Lyon Phelps praised Tarkington in *The Advance of the English Novel* and expressed a hope that he would not surrender to the demands of the popular reading public, a criticism the author had faced in the past for the conclusion of *The Magnificent Ambersons.* However, Tarkington did receive similar censure for the ending of *The Turmoil.* Some critics found Bibbs Sheridan's sudden change from sensitive poet to successful capitalist at the end of the book contrived and unrealistic. Nevertheless Phelps called *The Turmoil* "the most ambitious and on the whole the best" novel Tarkington had written till that time, and he felt the book was proof that the author was "growing in spiritual grace."

Tarkington's other Pulitzer Prize-winning novel, *Alice Adams,* fared better with critics than *The Magnificent Ambersons.* In fact, some regarded *Alice Adams* as his best work. Sorkin lauded the book as "Tarkington's most admirable achievement, a neatly structured, deftly paced, validly observed social novel and ironic novel of manners that . . . illustrates its creator's many attributes." Carl Van Doren said in the *Nation* that in *Alice Adams* Tarkington had "produced a genuinely significant book." The work was originally conceived as the third part of the *Growth* trilogy but was not included because of its narrower focus on a single generation. Sorkin said *Alice Adams* is less idealistic than Tarkington's other work in its characterization of Alice Adams as a young American girl brought up by her socially aspiring mother to realize and achieve social and material prospects beyond her class. Alice is exhorted by her mother to marry Arthur Russell, an eligible, rich young man. The book follows Alice's attempts at snaring Russell, who eventually marries his wealthy cousin, Mildred Palmer, while Alice resigns herself to working as a typist and stenographer. Sorkin felt that in this volume "Tarkington achieves an accurate appraisal and sympathetic portrait of middle-class home life." *Alice Adams* received more favorable attention from critics that other novels Tarkington had written. In *Some Contemporary Americans: The Personal Equation in Literature* Percy H. Boynton expressed his appreciation of Tarkington's literary achievement: "In *Alice Adams* there are no eleventh-hour reprieves. Perhaps [Tarkington] has turned a corner."

Besides writing fiction, Tarkington also authored numer-

ous plays. However, he was far less successful as a playwright than he was as a novelist. Critics like Barrett H. Clark in *A Study of Modern Drama* said that Tarkington was "an enormously successful novelist" who "never took playwriting seriously." But in an evaluation of Tarkington's plays in the *Princeton University Library Chronicle,* Albert Van Nostrand proposed that the subjects Tarkington explored in his plays were remarkably similar to the ones in his books. For example, said Van Nostrand, in many plays, including *Poldekin,* Tarkington presented his "thesis . . . about the ideology of capitalism," a subject the author also explored in his "economic novels." Produced in 1920, *Poldekin* relates the story of a revolutionary group of Russians who are sent on a mission to convert America into a communist state. The protagonist, Poldekin, is hesitant to believe the philosophy of his country unquestioningly, however, and he leaves the group to discover America for himself. Van Nostrand described the characters as symbolic representations of opposing points of view. Tarkington's other plays included *Clarence,* which Barrett Clark also found noteworthy. The critic felt that in this play the author realized the promise he had displayed in his novels.

Although Tarkington continued to write many more plays and books in the years following the publication of *Poldekin* and *Alice Adams,* his eyesight had begun to fail him. Woodress quoted Tarkington in his biography of the author as saying, "I'm more afraid of using up my eyes and right hand than the supplies of the mystic workman under the outer layers." In 1930 Tarkington went completely blind. Following several operations, his sight was restored the next year. Thereafter, Tarkington continued to write children's stories until he died of an illness in 1946. Even though his work did not achieve overwhelmingly favorable critical attention, Tarkington was a very popular writer in his time and a very wealthy man. Sorkin reported that more than five million copies of Tarkington's works were sold in the first half of the twentieth century. In recent years, Tarkington has been most remembered for the "Penrod" series, *Seventeen,* and his Pulitzer Prize-winning novels. In Woodress's *Dictionary of Literary Biography* evaluation, although speculating that a revival of interest in Tarkington's work is unlikely, he felt that in his "Penrod" series Tarkington "captured the essence of unchanging childhood in unforgettable scenes and memorable characters. A few of his novels, such as the *Growth* trilogy (1927) and especially *Alice Adams* (1921), also will serve to keep his memory alive; they are works of lasting value in their authentic recreation of a time in America's past and in their statements of social significance."

BIOGRAPHICAL/CRITICAL SOURCES:

BOOKS

Boynton, Percy H., *Some Contemporary Americans: The Personal Equation in Literature,* University of Chicago Press, 1924, pp. 108-25.

Cabell, James Branch, *Beyond Life: Dizain des demiurges,* R. M. McBride, 1919, pp. 277-322.

Clark, Barrett H., *A Study of the Modern Drama: A Handbook for the Study and Appreciation of Typical Plays, European, English, and American, of the Last Three-Quarters of a Century,* Appleton, 1938, pp. 359-410.

Dictionary of Literary Biography, Gale, Volume 9: *American Novelists, 1910-1945,* 1981; Volume 102: *American Short-Story Writers, 1910-1945, Second Series,* 1991.

Fennimore, Keith J., *Booth Tarkington,* Twayne, 1974.

Mayberry, Susanah, *My Amiable Uncle: Recollections about Booth Tarkington,* Purdue University Press, 1983.

Phelps, William Lyon, *The Advance of the English Novel,* Dodd, Mead, 1916, pp. 267-301.

Tarkington, Booth, *The World Does Move,* Doubleday, Doran, 1928.

Twentieth-Century Children's Writers, 3rd edition, St. James Press, 1989, pp. 947-49.

Twentieth-Century Literary Criticism, Volume 9, Gale, 1983, pp. 451-75.

Woodress, James Leslie, *Booth Tarkington: Gentleman From Indiana,* Lippincott, 1955.

PERIODICALS

Bookman, December, 1921, pp. 394-95; March, 1927, pp. 12-21.

Harper's, May, 1915, pp. 958-61.

Independent, January 4, 1900, pp. 67-68.

Indianapolis Star, August 7, 1937.

Nation, February 9, 1921.

Princeton University Library Chronicle, autumn, 1955, pp. 13-39.

Saturday Evening Post, August 23, 1941, pp. 27, 80-88.

OBITUARIES:

PERIODICALS

Art Digest, June, 1946.

Newsweek, May 27, 1946.

New Yorker, June 1, 1946.

New York Times, May 20, 1946.

Publishers Weekly, June 1, 1946.

Time, May 27, 1946.

Saturday Review of Literature, June 1, 1946.

Wilson Library Bulletin, September, 1946.*

TARKINGTON, N. Booth
See TARKINGTON, (Newton) Booth

*   *   *

TARR, Herbert 1929-1993

OBITUARY NOTICE—See index for *CA* sketch: Born Herbert Targovik, September 10, 1929, in Brooklyn, NY; died of liver cancer, November 18, 1993, in Roslyn Heights, NY. Rabbi and author. After leaving his congregation in 1963 to pursue a full-time writing career, Tarr became a best-selling author with his novel *The Conversion of Chaplain Cohen,* about a minister in the U.S. Air Force dealing with the difficulties and inanities of the military. His works are known for combining philosophy with humor. Tarr also received favorable feedback for his novel *Heaven Help Us!,* which was adapted into a Broadway play. His other books include *So Help Me God,* published in 1979, and *A Woman of Spirit,* released in 1989.

OBITUARIES AND OTHER SOURCES:

PERIODICALS

Chicago Tribune, November 21, 1993, p. 10.
Washington Post, November 20, 1993, p. C5.

*   *   *

TAULBERT, Clifton L(emoure) 1945-

PERSONAL: Born February 19, 1945, in Glen Allan, MS; son of a preacher and Mary Morgan Taulbert; married December 22, 1973; wife's name, Barbara Ann; children: Marshall Danzy, Anne Kathryn.

ADDRESSES: Office—Freemount Corporation, 616 South Boston, Suite 302, Tulsa, OK 74119.

CAREER: University Village Inc., Tulsa, OK, administrator, beginning in 1972; Bank of Oklahoma, Tulsa, vice president of marketing; Freemount Corporation, Tulsa, president. Board member, Tulsa United Way, Thomas Gilcrease Museum, Tulsa Goodwill Industry, and the Business Industrial Development Corp.; executive board member, Tulsa Metropolitan Chamber of Commerce. National Volunteer, National Arthritis Foundation, 1985. *Military service:* U.S. Air Force, 1964-68; became sergeant.

AWARDS, HONORS: National Management Association (Oklahoma chapter), Manager of the Year, 1989.

WRITINGS:

Once upon a Time When We Were Colored (memoir), Council Oak, 1989.

The Last Train North (illustrated autobiography), Council Oak, 1992.

SIDELIGHTS: Clifton L. Taulbert emphasizes the bonds of family and community in *Once upon a Time When We Were Colored,* his memoir of growing up in a small Mississippi town during the waning days of segregation. "I did not choose to focus on the grand scheme of conflict between the races. I wanted to tell about the lives of everyday people," Taulbert told Joseph A. Cincotti in the *New York Times Book Review.* Taulbert portrays those close to him—his mother, grandparents, an extended family of aunts and uncles—as people who were "wryly cognizant of segregation but . . . decided to enjoy life anyway," wrote Rosemary L. Bray, critic for the *New York Times Book Review.* Recalling his education at the "colored" school fifty miles away and his labor as a field hand during the summers, Taulbert nonetheless presents his childhood in what Bray described as "loving memories." A critic for the *Kirkus Reviews,* pointing out Taulbert's mention of the harsh realities of the era that faced blacks (such as accepting voting as "white folks' business"), called *Once upon a Time When We Were Colored* "a heartfelt testament to a beleaguered people."

A second autobiography, *The Last Train North,* tells of Taulbert's departure from the Mississippi Delta after his graduation with honors from high school and continues through his service in the air force during the 1960s. A notable section of the book depicts the author's first meeting with his preacher father in St. Louis—"the man left the bewildered youth with relatives . . . and informed him that they 'probably' would not have a relationship," summed up a critic in *Kirkus Reviews.* In *Publishers Weekly* Genevieve Stuttaford praised *The Last Train North,* declaring that "a sense of optimism infuses this winning illustrated memoir."

BIOGRAPHICAL/CRITICAL SOURCES:

PERIODICALS

Kirkus Reviews, May 1, 1989, p. 682; May 15, 1992, p. 662.
New York Times Book Review, February 18, 1990, p. 9.
Publishers Weekly, May 25, 1992, p. 44.

*   *   *

TAVRIS, Carol (Anne) 1944-

PERSONAL: Born September 17, 1944, in Los Angeles, CA; daughter of Samuel (an insurance agent) and Dorothy (an insurance agent; maiden name, Marcus) Tavris; married Ronan O'Casey (an actor). *Education:* Brandeis University, A.B. (summa cum laude), 1966; University of Michigan, Ph.D., 1971.

ADDRESSES: Office—Human Relations Center, New School for Social Research, New York, NY 10011. *Agent*—Robert Lescher, 155 East 71st St., New York, NY 10021.

CAREER: Psychology Today (magazine), Del Mar, CA, articles editor, 1968-69, associate editor, 1969-72, senior editor, 1971-72, assistant managing editor, 1972-76; *Human Nature,* senior editor, 1978-79; *American Health,* New York City, consulting editor, beginning in 1982. On faculty of New School for Social Research, New York City, 1983—.

MEMBER: National Organization for Women, American Civil Liberties Union, Association of Women in Psychology, Phi Beta Kappa.

AWARDS, HONORS: Award from Women in Communications for *The Female Experience;* Rackham prize fellow, University of Michigan, 1971; various award lectureships.

WRITINGS:

(Editor) *The Female Experience,* CRM, Inc., 1973.
(With Carol Wade) *The Longest War: Sex Differences in Perspective,* Harcourt, 1977.
(With Susan Sadd) *The Redbook Report on Female Sexuality,* Delacorte, 1977.
Anger: The Misunderstood Emotion, Simon & Schuster, 1983.
(Editor) *EveryWoman's Emotional Well-Being,* illustrations by Sandra Forrest, Doubleday, 1986.
(With Wade) *Psychology,* Harper & Row, 1987.
The Mismeasure of Woman: Why Women Are Not the Better Sex, the Inferior Sex, or the Opposite Sex, and How Using Men as the Yardstick for Normalcy Has Given Women the Short End of the Stick, Simon & Schuster, 1992.

Contributor of column, "Mind Health," to *Vogue;* contributor of articles to periodicals, including *Harper's, Mademoiselle, Geo, Gentleman's Quarterly, Redbook,* and *Psychology Today.*

SIDELIGHTS: Carol Tavris has served as both editor and writer on topics relating to psychology for many periodicals, including *Psychology Today* and *American Health.* She is also the author of the best-selling self-help book *Anger: The Misunderstood Emotion,* as well as *The Mismeasure of Woman,* a study of society's misconceptions about female roles. In her work, Tavris often takes on widely accepted beliefs about psychology and tests the evidence against them—analyzing her subjects with "an objective grain of salt," as she and coauthor Susan Sadd wrote in *The Redbook Report on Human Sexuality.*

Tavris has published a wide range of works within her field. In 1973 she edited *The Female Experience,* which garnered an award from the group Women in Communications. Another of her books, coauthored with Sadd, began with a magazine questionnaire on female sexuality for *Redbook* and became 1977's *Redbook Report on Female Sexuality.* The authors concluded that women were generally happier with their sex lives than most previous studies had reported. Barbara G. Harrison in *Washington Post Book World* noted, however, that even with a good representative sampling of women in society the authors' conclusions have to be considered with "a healthy skepticism" and "a tentative optimism." Nevertheless, Harrison concluded that the data was analyzed "scrupulously" and recommended the book "if only as an antidote to the voices howling in the wilderness of sexual unhappiness."

In her popular 1983 book, *Anger,* Tavris suggests that psychologists who have advocated expressing anger as an aide to both mental and physical health may be wrong. Tavris contends that "anger is depression turned outward," noted Anatole Broyard in *New York Times.* In many instances, being polite and holding one's temper may better serve all concerned. "It used to be called common courtesy," Tavris wrote in *Anger.* The book offers practical advice on ways to express anger with civility, noted June Schwarzmann in the *Los Angeles Times Book Review.* "Appropriately channeled, [anger] can alter behavior, fuel social movements and right unjustices. Improperly used, it severs relationships and shreds the social fabric."

Reviewer Elsa First took issue with *Anger* in the *New York Times Book Review,* saying that "Tavris's one-dimensional behaviorism would deprive us of the possibility of continuing to study how oppression in all its forms is bad for mental health." However, most reviewers were much more positive. Anatole Broyard, for instance, critiquing the volume in the *New York Times,* asserted that "Tavris has several intelligent and witty suggestions to make," and pointed out the author's insistence that " 'ventilating' our anger does not always diminish it. Instead, it often intensifies the original feeling." June Schwarzmann in the *Los Angeles Times Book Review* also had praise for Tavris's work, labeling it "witty, provocative, and impressively documented," and declaring that her "lucid, coolly reasoned arguments in praise of civility offer hope for controlling the emotion that poisons relationships."

In *The Mismeasure of Woman,* Tavris's 1992 effort, she takes on another recent trend in psychological thought—the belief that men and women are innately very different from one another. In Tavris's opinion, where differences exist, they are the result of the social roles assigned to each sex. Tavris points out, according to Susan Jacoby in the *New York Times Book Review,* that "feminist battles for equality . . . have always elicited a reactionary barrage of

attempts to establish the immutability of certain gender differences," but that recently "the concept that women are different and therefore inferior has been replaced, in many instances, by the idealized notion that women are different but *superior* beings." Tavris, however, asserts that women and men are much more alike than different. To the claim that men are more violent and that male-dominated society is responsible for the many wars experienced throughout history, "she points to the patriotic fervor of women in wartime, the one million Soviet women in active combat in the Second World War, the liberation all women experience during all wars, and the fact that someone had to sew all those costumes for the Ku Klux Klan," commented Marian Botsford Fraser in the Toronto *Globe and Mail.* On the topic of a famous brain hemisphere study that advanced the theory that women have more communication between hemispheres than men because the fibers connecting them are bulkier than those of men, Tavris observed that the study only examined fourteen brains, and did not take into account the social roles of the subjects. Fraser predicted that many groups will find fault with this book—feminists, mainstream traditionalist psychiatrists, and some men. Diana Morgan in the *Washington Post Book World* quoted Tavris's conclusion that "instead of regarding cultural and reproductive differences as problems to be eliminated, we would aim to eliminate *the unequal consequences that follow from them*" in a policy of "equality as acceptance." Morgan lauded Tavris for doing "a good job of summarizing the research and recasting the issues from a woman's point of view."

BIOGRAPHICAL/CRITICAL SOURCES:

BOOKS

Tavris, Carol, *Anger: The Misunderstood Emotion,* Simon & Schuster, 1983.
Tavris, Carol, and Susan Sadd, *The Redbook Report on Female Sexuality,* Delacorte, 1977.

PERIODICALS

Globe and Mail (Toronto), April 11, 1992, p. C8.
Los Angeles Times Book Review, February 13, 1983, p. 3.
New York Times, February 19, 1983.
New York Times Book Review, January 30, 1983, pp. 7, 24; May 29, 1992, pp. 9-10.
Washington Post Book World, December 18, 1977, p. E5; April 5, 1992, p. 6.*

—*Sketch by Elizabeth Wenning*

* * *

TAYLOR, M(artin) J. 1952-

PERSONAL: Born February 18, 1952, in Leicester, England; son of John Maurice (an accountant) and Sheila

Mary Barbara (a secretary) Taylor; married Sharon Lynn Marlow (a teacher), December 1, 1973; children: Rebecca, Deborah, Andrew, James. *Education:* Pembroke College, Oxford, B.A. (with first class honors), 1973; King's College, London, Ph.D., 1976. *Religion:* Roman Catholic.

ADDRESSES: Home—Stockport, England. *Office*—Department of Mathematics, University of Manchester Institute of Science and Technology, P.O. Box 88, Manchester M60 1QD, England.

CAREER: University of London, King's College, London, England, research assistant, 1976-77; Oxford University, Oxford, England, junior lecturer, 1977-78; University of London, Queen Mary College, London, England, lecturer, 1978-81; Cambridge University, Cambridge, England, fellow of Trinity College, 1981-85, assistant lecturer, 1984-85; University of Manchester Institute of Science and Technology, Manchester, England, professor of pure mathematics, 1986—, head of department, 1989-91. French National Center of Scientific Research (CNRS), *chercheur associe,* 1979-80; University of Illinois at Urbana-Champaign, National Science Foundation researcher, 1981; University of Bordeaux, associate professor, 1984, visiting professor, 1992; University of Besancon, associate professor, 1988; University of Geneva, visiting professor, 1989; lecturer at institutions of higher learning throughout Europe.

MEMBER: London Mathematical Society (member of council, 1991—).

AWARDS, HONORS: Junior L. M. S. Whitehead Prize, 1982; shared Adams Prize, 1983; Leverhulme senior fellow, 1991-92.

WRITINGS:

Classgroups of Group Rings, Cambridge University Press, 1984.
(With P. Cossau-Nagues) *Elliptic Functions and Rings of Integers,* Birkhauser, 1986.
(With A. Froehlich) *Algebraic Number Theory,* Cambridge University Press, 1991.
(With J. Coolers) *L Functions in Arithmetic,* Cambridge University Press, 1991.
(With K. Roggenkamp) *Group Rings and Class Groups,* Birkhauser, 1992.

* * *

TAYLOR, Ronald J.   1932-

PERSONAL: Born October 16, 1932, in Victor, ID; son of George G. (a farmer) and Elva A. (a farmer; maiden name, Drake) Taylor; married Gloria M. Wood (a secretary), April 26, 1955; children: Ryan J., Rhonda L. Taylor

Ripplinger. *Education:* Idaho State College (now University), B.S., 1954; University of Wyoming, M.S., 1960; Washington State University, Ph.D., 1964. *Avocational Interests:* Photography, outdoor activities.

ADDRESSES: Home—4241 Northwest Rd., Bellingham, WA 98226. *Office*—Department of Biology, Western Washington University, Bellingham, WA 98225.

CAREER: Western Washington University, Bellingham, began as assistant professor, became professor of biology, 1964—, department head, 1984-89, 1990-91, and curator of university herbarium. North Cascades Institute, member, 1986-90; Washington State Natural Heritage Advisory Council, member, 1989-92; Washington State Rare Plant Consortium, member; activist for the preservation of the Lake Louise Ecological Site; environmental consultant. *Military service:* U.S. Air Force, pilot, 1954-59.

MEMBER: American Association for the Advancement of Science, American Society of Plant Taxonomy, Botanical Society of America, Northwest Scientific Association (member of board of trustees, 1989-92), Washington Native Plant Society (member of board of directors; chairperson of research advisory committee), Sigma Xi, Torrey Botanical Club.

AWARDS, HONORS: Grant from U.S. Forest Service, 1989.

WRITINGS:

(With R. W. Valum) *Sagebrush Country: Wildflowers Number Two,* Touchstone Press, 1974.
(With G. W. Douglas) *Mountain Wildflowers of the Northwest,* Binford & Mort, 1975.
Rocky Mountain Wildflowers, Mountaineers-Books, 1978.
(Editor with Alan E. Leviton) *Mosses of North America,* American Association for the Advancement of Science, 1980.
Northwest Weeds: The Ugly and Beautiful Villains of Fields, Gardens and Roadsides, Mountain Press, 1990.
Sagebrush Country: A Wildflower Sanctuary, Mountain Press, 1992.

Author of laboratory manuals, workbooks, and visual aid programs. Work represented in anthologies, including *Flora of North America,* Volumes I-II, Smithsonian Institution Press, 1993. Contributor of nearly fifty articles to scientific journals.

WORK IN PROGRESS: Field guides; research on the biosystematics of North American *Picea* species; research on *Centaurea.*

TEED, Peter (Litterland) 1924-

PERSONAL: Born January 10, 1924, in Herne Bay, Kent, England; son of Thomas Westcott (a banker) and Jane (a nurse; maiden name, Sutton) Teed; married Shirley Brenda Quantick (a painter), June 8, 1955; children: Sara, David, Julian, Robert. *Education:* Corpus Christi College, Cambridge, M.A., 1950; attended New College, Oxford, 1973. *Politics:* Liberal Democrat. *Religion:* Anglican. *Avocational Interests:* Archaeology of the neolithic period, music (especially opera), walking, gardening.

ADDRESSES: Home—3 Harts Cottages, Almondsbury, Avon BS12 4JD, England.

CAREER: Goole Grammar School, headmaster, 1964-85; also taught in Australia and throughout the United Kingdom. United Kingdom Schools Council, member, 1976-82, vice-chair of history committee; Associated Examining Board, chair of history committee. *Military service:* British Army, Royal Engineers; became captain.

MEMBER: Royal Institute of International Affairs.

WRITINGS:

Britain, 1906-51: A Welfare State, Hutchinson, 1963.
The Later Nineteenth Century: Portraits and Documents, 1868-1919, Hutchinson, 1969.
Le Grande-Bretagne de 1848 a nos jouve, Wathan, 1971.
The Twentieth Century: Portraits and Documents, 1906-1960, Hutchinson, 1972.
The Move to Europe, 1880-1972, Hutchinson, 1976.
A Dictionary of Twentieth-Century History, 1914-90, Oxford University Press, 1992.

Contributor of articles and reviews to periodicals.

WORK IN PROGRESS: A Dictionary of History, 1763-1914; revising *A Dictionary of Twentieth-Century History.*

SIDELIGHTS: Peter Teed told *CA:* "My interest in archaeology is longstanding, and I have acted as an assistant site director at the Deya Centre for Archaeological Studies on Mallorca for the past five seasons."

*   *   *

TEMPLE, Cliff 1947-1994

OBITUARY NOTICE—See index for *CA* sketch: Born January 29, 1947, in London, England; died January 8, 1994, in England. Athletic coach and journalist. A sports writer for the London *Sunday Times* for twenty-five years, Temple also coached marathon runners and wrote biographies of distance runners David Moorcroft and Brendan Foster in addition to books on fitness and coaching. He was also active in promoting club athletics and had raised funds to build a track dedicated to one of his students who died in a plane crash. Temple's books include *Jogging for Fitness and Pleasure, Marathon Made Easier,* and *The A-Z of Running.*

OBITUARIES AND OTHER SOURCES:

PERIODICALS

Times (London), January 11, 1994, p. 17.

*   *   *

TENAX
See LEAN, Garth Dickinson

*   *   *

THACKER, Jonathan W(illiam) 1967-

PERSONAL: Born September 20, 1967, in Cambridge, England; son of Michael John (a lecturer) and Sarah Ann (a teacher; maiden name, Wakefield) Thacker; married Claire Lucie Chaplain (a publisher), July 26, 1991; children: Daniel Joseph. *Education:* King's College, London, graduated (with first class honors), 1990; doctoral study at Emmanuel College, Cambridge, 1991-94.

ADDRESSES: Home—9 St. Barnabas Rd., Cambridge CB1 2BU, England.

WRITINGS:

(Translator with M. J. Thacker, and co-author of introduction and notes) *Exemplary Novels,* Volume III, Aris & Phillips, 1992.
(Translator with L. Boswell) Tirso de Molina, *Two Plays,* Absolute Classics, 1992.

WORK IN PROGRESS: Research on role-play in Spanish seventeenth-century drama.

*   *   *

THOMAS, Danny 1912(?)-1991

PERSONAL: Original name, Muzyad Yakhoob; parents "Americanized" name to Amos Jacobs; professional name chosen in 1940; born January 6, 1912 (some sources say 1914), in Deerfield, MI; died of a heart attack, February 6, 1991, in Los Angeles, CA; son of Charles and Margaret Christen (Simon) Jacobs; married Rose Marie Cassaniti, January 15, 1936; children: Margaret Julia (Marlo), Theresa Cecelia (Terre), Charles Anthony (Tony). *Education:* Attended Christian Brothers College, Memphis, TN. *Religion:* Roman Catholic.

CAREER: Entertainer, comedian, actor, and producer. Worked in radio and as master of ceremonies in various nightclubs in Detroit, MI, and Toledo, OH, 1932-40; 5100 Club, Chicago, IL, master of ceremonies and entertainer, 1940-43; CBS-Radio, host of *The Danny Thomas Show,* 1944-49; appeared in numerous nightclub engagements during the 1940s, including the Oriental Theatre, Chicago, 1943, and La Martinique, New York City, the Roxy Theatre, New York City, Ciro's, Hollywood, CA, the London Palladium, London, England, and Chez Paree, Chicago, 1945-46; overseas entertainer in the Eastern Theatre of Operations and Pacific Area of Operations during World War II. St. Jude Children's Research Hospital, Memphis, TN, founder, 1962.

Actor in motion pictures, including *The Unfinished Dance,* 1947, *The Big City,* 1948, *Call Me Mister,* 1951, *I'll See You in My Dreams,* 1951, and *The Jazz Singer,* 1953. Actor in television series, including *Make Room for Daddy* (later known as *The Danny Thomas Show*), 1953-64, *The Danny Thomas Hour,* 1967-68, *Make Room for Granddaddy,* 1970-71, *The Practice,* 1976-77, *I'm a Big Girl Now,* 1980-81, *One Big Family,* 1986-87, and the made-for-television movie *Side By Side,* 1988.

Producer with Sheldon Leonard of television productions, including *The Dick Van Dyke Show,* 1961-66, *The Andy Griffith Show,* and *Gomer Pyle, U.S.M.C.;* producer with Aaron Spelling of television productions, including *The Guns of Will Sonnett,* 1967-69, and *The Mod Squad,* 1968-73.

AWARDS, HONORS: Emmy Award, best actor starring in a regular series, Academy of Television Arts and Sciences, 1954, for *Make Room for Daddy;* named Man of the Year by the National Conference of Christians and Jews, 1957; Louella Parsons Award, Hollywood Women's Press Club, 1970; Layman's Award, American Medical Association; Better World Award, Ladies Auxiliary of the Veterans of Foreign Wars, 1972; Michelangelo Award, Boys Town of Italy, 1973; award from the Governor of Ohio, 1975; entertainment award, White House Correspondents, 1975; Humanitarian Award, Lions Club International, 1975; Nobel Peace Prize nomination, 1980-81; Father Flanagan-Boys Town Award, 1981; Murray-Green-Meany Award for Community Service, American Federation of Labor and Congress of Industrial Organizations (AFL-CIO), 1981; Hubert H. Humphrey Award, Touchdown Club, 1981; Humanitarian Award, Variety Clubs International, c. 1983; American Education Award, 1984; Congressional Medal of Honor, 1985; awarded the Sword of Loyola, Loyola University, Chicago, IL, 1985; inducted into the Academy of Television Arts and Sciences Hall of Fame, 1991. Horatio Alger Award, Horatio Alger Association of Distinguished Americans; decorated Knight of Malta; Knight Commander with Star; inducted into Knights of Holy Sepulchre by Pope Paul VI; L.H.D., Belmont Abbey, International College, Springfield, MA,

1970; L.H.D., Medical College of Toledo, 1989; LL.D., Loyola University; L.H.D., Loyola-Marymount University.

WRITINGS:

(With Bill Davidson) *Make Room for Danny* (autobiography), Putnam, 1991.

SIDELIGHTS: One of ten children born to Lebanese immigrants, Danny Thomas was born Muzyad Yakhoob. He became Amos Jacobs as a young child when his parents "Americanized" the family members' names. He grew up in various locations between southern Michigan and northern Ohio; to "condense a lot of years into one sentence," the comedian quipped in his autobiography, *Make Room for Danny,* "I was born on a horse farm in Deerfield, Michigan, over Mrs. Feldman's bakery in Toledo, Ohio." A high school dropout, Thomas found his first job in show business when he was hired to sell candy and soda in a Toledo burlesque theater. He memorized the routines of some of the comics and became fascinated with show business. He later performed with success some of these borrowed routines on a radio amateur hour. Various radio jobs and, later, nightclub emcee jobs followed until he achieved his big break at the 5100 Club in Chicago, Illinois. Initially embarrassed that he had begun to succeed in radio, only to regress to doing clubs, Thomas quickly chose a pseudonym so no one back home in Toledo would know he was again playing saloons. He chose his youngest brother's name, Danny, and his oldest brother's, Thomas, for the marquee.

Danny Thomas was a hit at the 5100 Club, with the audiences displaying an encouraging response to the young comic's stories and folksy songs. He moved his family to Chicago and signed a two-year contract to perform at the club. Danny Thomas was never to be embarrassed by a lack of success again.

Never a one-liner comedian, Thomas was a master storyteller, inspired by his Old Country relatives and friends, who perfected the art of storytelling as a form of entertainment. He learned to embellish real-life scenarios he observed, thus never running out of fresh material. When Thomas died in 1991, his son-in-law, talk-show host Phil Donahue, as quoted in the *New York Times,* said, "He would hold an audience for an unprecedented length of time in the imagery of the story he was telling, and suddenly would come the punch line, and the ceiling would crack with laughter. He wove an illusion on the stage with no props, all by himself." Larry Gelbart, writing in the *New York Times,* echoed Donahue's praise: Thomas "just got his laughs the hard way," Gelbart related. "He sought to involve his audiences in the lives of those who populated his stories. He complained for them, he ranted and raved for them—an ombudsman in search of belly laughs.

And to enhance the timeless, tribal tradition of the story-teller, Thomas echoed the rage of the Old Testament. Lebanese though he was, there was a good deal of the closet rabbi about him."

From the 5100 Club Thomas went on to host his own program on CBS-Radio from 1944 to 1949. He also broke into films during that time, appearing in his first role in *The Unfinished Dance* in 1947. But he became a household name with his television series *Make Room for Daddy*, a prime-time favorite that ran from 1953 to 1964 and has been broadcast in reruns ever since. (As Thomas explained in *Make Room for Danny*, his wife, Rose Marie, suggested the name for the series: Since Thomas was on the road so much, the family had to make room for him each time he returned home.) Later Thomas became a producer of several successful television series.

In 1991 Thomas penned *Make Room for Danny* with Bill Davidson; in the volume Thomas chronicles his life from his birth, which was attended by a veterinarian, through his early failures, to his place among the top comedians of his time. Woven among the many stories that became famous in his routines are his fond memories of fellow performers, including George Burns, Jack Benny, Lucille Ball, and Milton Berle. But at the center of his life's story is his family: his wife of more than fifty years, Rosie, and his talented children, actresses Marlo and Terre and producer Tony. Also an ever-present force in his life account is his religious faith. The work generally fared well among critics, with a *Publishers Weekly* reviewer emphasizing that the book reveals "the full flavor of Thomas's much-admired personality."

Thomas credited his good fortune in life to an incident that occurred when he was struggling to support his young family back in Detroit. Upon learning that St. Jude was the patron saint of hopeless cases, Thomas prayed to the saint, asking for direction. In return for the saint's help, Thomas vowed to build a shrine for St. Jude. Thomas's big break at the 5100 Club came soon after that prayer, and he dedicated St. Jude's Children's Research Hospital, in Memphis, Tennessee—the promised shrine—in 1962. A leading research center in the fight against childhood diseases, the hospital was, as Thomas frequently expressed, his greatest accomplishment and contribution during his lifetime. As he once asserted, as quoted in the *New York Times:* "That's my epitaph. It's right on the cornerstone: Danny Thomas, founder."

BIOGRAPHICAL/CRITICAL SOURCES:

BOOKS

Thomas, Danny, and Bill Davidson, *Make Room for Danny,* Putnam, 1991.

PERIODICALS

Chicago Tribune, October 16, 1986, p. 11.
Library Journal, November 15, 1990, p. 74.
Los Angeles Times, September 1, 1986, p. 1; April 7, 1987, p. 1.
New York Times, January 10, 1991, p. C22; February 17, 1991, p. H29.
New York Times Book Review, March 24, 1991, p. 24.
People, February 25, 1991, p. 42; April 1, 1991, p. 23.
Publishers Weekly, November 9, 1990, p. 49.

OBITUARIES:

PERIODICALS

Boston Globe, February 7, 1991, pp. 55, 65.
Chicago Tribune, February 7, 1991, p. 9.
Los Angeles Times, February 7, 1991, p. 1; February 9, 1991, p. 1.
New York Times, February 7, 1991, p. D25.
Washington Post, February 7, 1991, p. 1.*

*　　*　　*

THOMAS, David　1959-

PERSONAL: Born January 17, 1959, in Maidstone, Kent, England; son of David C. (a diplomat) and Susan (a politician; maiden name, Arrow) Thomas; married Clare Jeremy (a homemaker), June 28, 1986; children: Holly, Lucy. *Education:* Attended King's College, Cambridge, earned degrees in philosophy and history of art.

ADDRESSES: Home—Sussex, England. *Agent*—Patrick Walsh, 49 Queen Victoria St., London EC4, England.

CAREER: The Magazine, London, England, editor, 1984-85; *Today,* London, section editor, 1985-86; *You,* London, deputy editor, 1986-89; *Punch,* London, editor, 1989-92. D. T. Productions Ltd., managing director.

AWARDS, HONORS: Named Young Journalist of the Year, 1983, and Magazine Columnist of the Year, 1990.

WRITINGS:

Bilko: The Fort Baxter Story, Vermilion, 1985.
Fame and Fortune, Fontana, 1988.
Sex and Shopping, Fontana, 1988.
Great Sporting Moments, Fontana, 1989.
Not Guilty: The Case in Defense of Men, Morrow, 1993.

Contributor to British newspapers.

Thomas's work has been translated into Spanish and German.

WORK IN PROGRESS: A novel; script writing.

SIDELIGHTS: David Thomas told *CA:* "I began my career because I didn't want a regular job. I starved until I began to get regular work as a journalist. What do I hope to achieve? I want to pay the mortgage, feed my family, and entertain or inform myself and, with any luck, my readers. I wrote *Not Guilty* because I wanted to figure out why men are the way they are, and how they came to be accepted as the evil/perverse/dysfunctional half of the human race."

*   *   *

THOMAS, Julian (Stewart) 1959-

PERSONAL: Born July 6, 1959, in Epsom, Surrey, England; son of Harry John Sidney (a schoolteacher) and Kathleen Mary (a librarian; maiden name, Southwell) Thomas; married Susan Jane Pitt (a historian), January 2, 1988. *Education:* University of Bradford, B.Tech. (with honors), 1981; University of Sheffield, M.A., 1982, D.Phil., 1986. *Politics:* Labour. *Religion:* Atheist.

ADDRESSES: Home—2 Glan yr afon, Llanwnen, Lampeter, Dyfed SA48 7ED, Wales. *Office*—Department of Archaeology, University of Southampton, Southampton SO9 5NH, England.

CAREER: University of Wales, St. David's University College, Lampeter, lecturer in archaeology, 1987-93; University of Southampton, Southampton, England, lecturer in archaeology, 1994—. Speaker at institutions of higher learning, including Cambridge University, and Universities of Durham, Sheffield, Nottingham, Reading, Leiden, and Amsterdam. Board of Celtic Studies, member of Archaeology and Art Committee, 1993; conducted archaeological field work throughout England and Wales.

MEMBER: World Archaeological Congress, Royal Anthropological Institute (fellow; trustee of Emslie Horniman Anthropological Scholarship Fund, 1991), Prehistoric Society, Theoretical Archaeology Group (member of national committee, 1989), Dyfed Archaeological Trust, Dorset Archaeological and Natural History Society, Wiltshire Archaeological Society.

AWARDS, HONORS: Baguley Prize from Prehistoric Society, 1989.

WRITINGS:

(Editor with F. Baker, and contributor) *Writing the Past in the Present,* St. David's University College, University of Wales, 1990.
Rethinking the Neolithic, Cambridge University Press, 1991.

Work represented in anthologies, including *From the Baltic to the Black Sea,* edited by D. Austin and L. Alcock, Unwin Hyman, 1990; *Vessels for the Ancestors,* edited by A. Sheridan and N. Sharples, Edinburgh University Press, 1992; and *Interpretive Archaeology,* edited by C. Tilley, Routledge & Kegan Paul, 1993. Contributor of more than thirty articles and reviews to archaeology journals. Member of editorial board, *Man.*

WORK IN PROGRESS: Time, Culture, and Identity; revising *Writing the Past in the Present;* editing a book on the neolithic house in Britain and Europe; archaeological field work in Anglesey and Scotland.

SIDELIGHTS: Julian Thomas told *CA:* "My work is largely concerned with the attempt to study prehistoric societies in ways that challenge the assumptions which arise from contemporary experience. Consequently, I have explored social anthropology, sociology, phenomenology, and the philosophy of science as means of finding new perspectives on the neolithic communities of Britain and Europe. My book *Time, Culture, and Identity* attempts to extend this project by reflecting on the human experience of temporality and the construction of personal and group identities.

"Since 1990, I have been a joint director of a major landscape project on Anglesey. This project is concerned with elucidating the landscape context of a series of chambered tombs on the southern part of the island, through an extensive program of shovel-testing. The project has resulted in the discovery and partial excavation of a causewayed enclosure at Bryn Celli Wen. Work in Anglesey has been funded by the National Museum of Wales, the Board of Celtic Studies, the MacDonald Foundation, and the Society of Antiquaries of London.

"All of these interests have led me into a number of interdisciplinary collaborations, most recently with the theatrical performer Mike Pearson, with whom I am writing on the experience of place and the traces of past human activity."

*   *   *

THOMAS, Lewis 1913-1993

OBITUARY NOTICE—See index for *CA* sketch: Born November 25, 1913, in Flushing, NY; died of Waldenstrom's disease, December 3, 1993, in Manhattan, NY. Physician, educator, administrator, and author. Highly accomplished in the medical field, Thomas was also noted for his philosophical, non-scientific writings about medicine, the human race, and nature. He taught at Johns Hopkins University, Tulane University, and other institutions before becoming a professor of pathology at New York University, a post he held from 1954 to 1969. Thomas then taught at Yale University and served as the dean of its School of Medicine before becoming an employee at the world-renowned Memorial Sloan-Kettering Cancer Center, where he was its president and chief executive officer from 1973 to 1980 and its chancellor from 1980 to 1983. Following that position, he dedicated himself to research at Cornell University. In 1989, Thomas received the Albert Lasker Public Service Award for his writings which "converted countless non-scientists into appreciative spectators and supporters of biomedical research," according to the jury of that prize. He was awarded the National Book Award in Arts and Letters in 1974 for *The Lives of a Cell: Notes of a Biology Watcher* and received the American Book Award for Science for *The Medusa and the Snail* in 1981. His other works include *Et Cetera, Et Cetera* and *The Fragile Species,* the latter of which was published the year before his death.

OBITUARIES AND OTHER SOURCES:

BOOKS

Who's Who in America, 48th edition, Marquis, 1994.

PERIODICALS

Chicago Tribune, December 4, 1993, section 2, p. 19; December 5, 1993, section 2, p. 11.
Los Angeles Times, December 4, 1993, p. A22.
New York Times, December 4, 1993, p. 28.
Washington Post, December 4, 1993, p. D6.

*   *   *

THOMAS, Rosanne Daryl 1956-
(Prince Charming)

PERSONAL: Born February 25, 1956, in New Jersey; children: August Siena Cohn. *Education:* Columbia University, M.F.A., c. 1984. *Religion:* "The golden rule." *Avocational Interests:* Art, politics, travel.

ADDRESSES: Agent—Emma Sweeney Agency, 280 Riverside Dr., No. 12E, New York, NY 10025.

CAREER: Writer.

MEMBER: Authors Guild, Specialty Coffee Association of America.

AWARDS, HONORS: Angel Carver was named notable book of 1993 by the *New York Times.*

WRITINGS:

(Under pseudonym Prince Charming) *Complications* (novel), Dutton, 1988.
The Angel Carver (novel), Random, 1993.
(And illustrator) *Coffee: The Bean of My Existence* (humor), Hearst, 1994.

WORK IN PROGRESS: Lifesaver, a novel.

SIDELIGHTS: Rosanne Daryl Thomas is perhaps best known for her 1993 work, *The Angel Carver,* a modern-day fable described by Laura Shapiro in *Newsweek* as "a strange and beautiful novel," written "with the gentle precision of a master." The story follows three average New Yorkers whose lives are made extraordinary by their interaction: Jack Standini, a shoe repairer who secretly sculpts beautiful, life-sized angels in the back room of his apartment; Lucille Bixby, an innocent and forlorn young woman of nineteen who longs to resemble the legendary actress Marilyn Monroe; and Buddy Lomax, an "image banker" who plots the undoing of both Lucille and Jack with the help of a sophisticated computer named Hell. Jack happens across Lucille and, although they do not engage in physical love, becomes her consort. When Buddy encounters Lucille and learns of her desire to be Monroe, he uses the graphic capabilities of Hell to electronically alter the girl's image into that of Monroe's. Seeking to both control the young woman and make money, Buddy begins to transform Lucille into Monroe through a series of plastic surgeries. Buddy also eliminates Jack from interfering with his plans. Using Hell, Buddy creates doctored photographs of Jack and Angela, the wife who abandoned the closet sculptor forty years prior, depicting a life that Jack yearned for but never lived. A critic for *Publishers Weekly* admired the book's depiction of "age-old themes" and "timeless evils," which are woven together with "the latest advances in computer graphic technology," into a "very modern fairy tale." *The Angel Carver,* wrote Susan M. Barbieri in the *Orlando Sentinel,* "is an allegory for our age—a tale of evil and greed attempting to destroy the good, the artistically pure." "Rosanne Daryl Thomas writes as an artist might paint," concluded Louise Gregg in her book review for the *Times Record News.*

Upon publication in 1993, *The Angel Carver* won wide acclaim as a compelling, accomplished novel. Joanna Scott, writing in the *New York Times Book Review,* called *The Angel Carver* "a tender novel, vividly written, with a relentless momentum," and Susan Fromberg Schaeffer wrote in the *Chicago Tribune* that Thomas's narrative "is a beautiful and delicate book about the terrible losses life inflicts and the equally wonderful rewards it can bring those strong enough to accept it for what it is." Christopher Lehmann-Haupt, meanwhile, affirmed in his *New York Times* assessment that *The Angel Carver* "sweeps the reader up like a mischievous tornado," and Stephen Stark reported in the *Washington Post* that Thomas's novel "has the flash of real intelligence. . . . There's a lot of fate in this novel, and a real-life guardian angel."

Prior to publishing *The Angel Carver,* Thomas wrote—under the pseudonym Prince Charming—the novel *Complications.* The story follows three career women who live in an apartment complex on Manhattan's Upper East

Side. They are all searching for the perfect mate—a 1990s prince who is, according to Wendy Wasserstein in her *New York Times Book Review* assessment, "the true alternative to video dating and . . . the perfect love match." Wasserstein noted, however, that there is a "new angle" to the novel, because it is "narrated and apparently written by Prince Charming himself." As many critics opined, the unusual perspective often lends an ironic atmosphere to events in the novel.

Thomas is also the author of *Coffee: The Bean of My Existence,* a self-illustrated volume that she described to *CA* as "the humorous tale of an addict—a coffee addict, of course."

BIOGRAPHICAL/CRITICAL SOURCES:

PERIODICALS

Chicago Tribune, July 4, 1993.
Kirkus Reviews, March 15, 1993.
Library Journal, April 15, 1993.
Newsweek, July 5, 1993, p. 54.
New York Times, June 28, 1993.
New York Times Book Review, March 20, 1988, p. 13; July 11, 1993.
Orlando Sentinel, August 8, 1993.
Publishers Weekly, March 22, 1993.
St. Louis Post-Dispatch, August 1, 1993.
Times Record News (Wichita Falls, TX), June 19 and 20, 1993, p. 111.
Washington Post, August 1, 1993.

*   *   *

THOMAS, Sue
    See THOMAS, Susan-Jane

*   *   *

THOMAS, Susan-Jane   1951-
    (Sue Thomas)

PERSONAL: Born July 16, 1951, in Leicester, England; daughter of Wim Leo (an insurance underwriter) and Dora (Van der Willik) de Vos; married Tyrone Thomas, 1974 (divorced, 1984); children: Amber, Erin. *Education:* Trent Polytechnic, B.A. (with honors), 1988. *Politics:* "Left, but cynical." *Religion:* "Spiritual, but cynical."

ADDRESSES: Home—11 Roecliffe, West Bridgford, Nottingham NG2 7FY, England. *Office*—Department of English and Media Studies, Nottingham Trent University, Clifton Lane, Nottingham NG11 8NS, England. *Agent*—Anne Dubuisson, Ellen Levine Agency, 15 East Twenty-

sixth St., Suite 1801, New York, NY 10010; Clarissa Rushdie, A. P. Watt Ltd., 20 John St., London WC1N 2DL, England.

CAREER: Nottingham Trent University, Nottingham, England, lecturer in writing, 1990—. Writer in residence at Manvers Pierrepont School, 1992, and Greenwood Dale School, 1993; lecturer; participant in various workshops and writing projects. Has worked variously as a bookseller, an accounts clerk, and a bartender.

AWARDS, HONORS: Grants from Nottinghamshire New Artworks, 1989, and East Midlands Arts, 1989 and 1991; short-listed for Heinemann Fiction Award, 1990, and Arthur C. Clarke Award, 1993, and listed as "highly commended" for James Tiptree Jr. Memorial Prize, 1993, all for *Correspondence.*

WRITINGS:

UNDER NAME SUE THOMAS

Women at War (four-part radio program), BBC-Radio, 1990.
Correspondence (novel), Women's Press, 1992, Overlook Press, 1993.
Water (novel), Overlook Press, 1994.
(Editor) *Wild Women,* Overlook Press, 1994.

Also author of *Nottingham History.* Contributor to *Where No Man Has Gone Before,* edited by Lucie Armitt, Routledge, 1990, and *Bust Up!,* Women's Press, 1992. Contributor to *Without Walls* (television program), 1992. Contributor to periodicals, including *Ariel, Arts Bulletin, Guardian,* and *Microsyster.* Fiction editor of *Mosaic;* books editor of *City Life.*

WORK IN PROGRESS: Picture This . . . , a novel.

SIDELIGHTS: Susan-Jane Thomas, under the name Sue Thomas, has published novels, contributed various works to a broad range of publications, and completed multi-episode shows for both radio and television. She is perhaps best known for her first novel, *Correspondence. Boston Phoenix* contributor John P. Mello, Jr., described the book as "a complex novel about a woman who chooses to escape the unbearable pain of her being by turning herself into a cyborg, a human being whose blood and tissue have been replaced with circuit boards, hydraulics, and dermatoid." Mello noted that this work—comprised of multiple perspectives and unorthodox narrative techniques—"takes cyberpunk into the realm of adults" and deemed the novel "remarkable." Richard Foss reported in the *Los Angeles Reader* that *Correspondence* constituted "a rarity, a complex and artfully written first novel," and Lance Olsen, writing in the *Review of Contemporary Fiction,* called the book "highly original, highly complex, and highly cerebral."

Thomas told *CA:* "The subjects of my writing have been varied: cybernetics, the natural world, drowning, medicine, and the psychology of nurture. What my writings have in common is that, as ideas, they provide springboards for my imagination. I am only now beginning to realize that the rather metaphysical way in which I have always interpreted the world is one which other people can really relate to, and since I have begun to write fiction I have felt less alone. It is a constant joy to me to discover that the interpretations I had always been told were 'weird' are actually perceived by my readers as enlightening and enjoyable. To communicate at last, after forty years of creative autism, is both an inconceivable relief and a delight!"

BIOGRAPHICAL/CRITICAL SOURCES:

PERIODICALS

Boston Phoenix, May, 1993, p. 12.
Entertainment Weekly, April 23, 1993.
Los Angeles Reader, March 12, 1993.
Review of Contemporary Fiction, summer, 1993.

*   *   *

THOMPSON, Judith (Clare Francesca) 1954-

PERSONAL: Born September 20, 1954, in Montreal, Quebec, Canada; daughter of William Robert and Mary Therese (Forde) Thompson; married Gregor Campbell, October 28, 1983; children: Ariane Francesca Forde. *Education:* Queen's University, B.A., 1976; graduated from National Theatre School, Montreal, 1979.

ADDRESSES: Home—396 Brunswick Ave., Toronto, Ontario, Canada M5R 2Z4. *Office*—16 Yarmouth Rd., Toronto, Ontario, Canada MOG 1W6. *Agent*—c/o Great North, 245 Adelaide St., Toronto, Ontario, Canada.

CAREER: Playwright. Actor, 1979-80, toured with Theatre of All Possibilities (TAP), 1979; affiliated with MTC, 1980.

MEMBER: Playwrights Canada, Association of Canadian Television and Radio Artists.

AWARDS, HONORS: Governor General's Awards for Drama, Canada Council, 1984, for *White Biting Dog,* and 1989, for *The Other Side of the Dark.*

WRITINGS:

PLAYS

The Crackwalker (two-act; produced at Theatre Passe Muraille, Toronto, Canada, 1980), Playwrights Canada, 1981.
White Biting Dog (two-act; produced at Tarragon Theatre, Toronto, 1984), Playwrights Canada, 1984.

The Other Side of the Dark: Four Plays (contains *The Crackwalker, Pink, Tornado,* and *I Am Yours*), Coach House, 1989.

Also author of the play *Lion in the Streets,* published by Coach House; radio plays for CBC-Radio, including *Quickening, A Kissing Way,* and *A Big White Light;* and teleplays for the Canadian Broadcasting Corporation (CBC-TV). Screenwriter for CBC and the National Film Board.

SIDELIGHTS: The plays of Judith Thompson, a Canadian who has twice won the Governor General's Award for Drama, have been praised by critics for both their imaginative language and their compelling characters. In *Books in Canada,* Richard Paul Knowles noted that "Thompson's work is characterized by an astonishingly accurate and musical sensitivity to language, particularly the local peculiarities of precisely observed Canadian speech patterns." He also recognized the playwright's "ability to create characters that are both immediately believable and possessed of hugely complex psychological depths."

Thompson's first play, *The Crackwalker,* concerns the bleak lives of two down-and-out couples living in Kingston, Ontario. The drama "climaxes in the strangling by its haunted father of a baby whose retarded mother is both incapable of mothering and yet persistently and not ironically associated with iconography of the madonna and child," Knowles informed in *Books in Canada.* Richard Plant, also a reviewer for *Books in Canada,* considered *The Crackwalker* "a raw, powerful revelation of life" and Thompson to be "amazingly compassionate."

In *Canadian Literature* Jill Tomasson Goodwin commented that "Thompson peoples her stage with characters whose social, economic, mental, or physical condition underscores their status as outsiders." The Race family in *White Biting Dog* (described by Mark Czarnecki in *Maclean's* as "a lunatic Toronto household") are similar to the men and women of *The Crackwalker* in this respect. The Races are not only cut off from any semblance of normal family life, they are also cut off from one another. While the father is dying of cancer, the mother is having an affair. "All bonds are broken—the mother has left the father for a punk rocker, the son hates the mother for having left his father, and he has left his own wife in order to save the father," Carole Corbeil commented in the Toronto *Globe and Mail.* Paul Walsh, writing in *Canadian Theatre Review,* remarked that "*White Biting Dog* is an improvisational piling up of incidents and images that, deep down, reminds one of a nineteenth-century melodrama." Knowles stated in the *Fiddlehead* that, after the success of *The Crackwalker, White Biting Dog* reinforces Thompson's position as "a unique voice in Canadian drama, and a leader in the country's new generation of playwrights."

BIOGRAPHICAL/CRITICAL SOURCES:

PERIODICALS

Books in Canada, April, 1982, p. 10; April, 1985, pp. 22-23; March, 1990, pp. 40-41; November, 1992, p. 34.
Canadian Literature, summer, 1991, pp. 178-80.
Fiddlehead, spring, 1985, pp. 84-87.
Globe and Mail (Toronto), February 23, 1984, p. E4.
Maclean's, January 30, 1984, p. 51.
New York Times, April 8, 1987.
Quill and Quire, September, 1992, p. 68.

*   *   *

THORMAEHLEN, Marianne 1949-

PERSONAL: Name pronounced "Tor-*may*-len," and sometimes spelled Thormahlen; born May 25, 1949, in Stockholm, Sweden; daughter of Curt Erik Fritiof (a sports teacher) and Ella Louise (a natural science teacher; maiden name, Kockum) Wahlberg; married Axel Thormaehlen (a writer), May 29, 1970; children: Aasa Thormaehlen Erenius, Imke (daughter). *Education:* University of Lund, M.A., 1969, Ph.D., 1979. *Politics:* "Incorrect." *Religion:* "Indefinite."

ADDRESSES: Home—Holmby 3, S-24032 Flyinge, Sweden.

CAREER: University of Lund, Lund, Sweden, reader, 1979-86, acting professor, 1986-87, 1988-89, and senior lecturer in English literature, 1986—. Swedish Board of Trade, authorized translator and interpreter. Esloev Social Welfare Committee, past member of local council; Esloev Immigrant Council, past member of local council.

MEMBER: Modern Humanities Research Association, Dorothy L. Sayers Society, Bronte Society, Richard III Society, T. S. Eliot Society, New Society of Letters (member of board of directors).

WRITINGS:

The Waste Land: A Fragmentary Wholeness, Lund University Press, 1978.
Eliot's Animals, Lund University Press, 1984.
Rochester: The Poems in Context, Cambridge University Press, 1993.
(Editor) *T. S. Eliot at the Turn of the Century,* Lund University Press, 1994.

Translator of books into Swedish, including Harold Kushner's *When Bad Things Happen to Good People* and *Wil-*

helm, by husband, Axel Thormaehlen. Contributor to scholarly journals.

WORK IN PROGRESS: The Brontes in Their Time (tentative title); a book on self-surrender in the work of T. S. Eliot.

SIDELIGHTS: Marianne Thormaehlen told *CA:* "My research has been called neocritical, feminist, historicist, and cultural-studies-oriented, but I don't see myself as belonging to any one school of English literary criticism. In English literature, as everywhere else, fashions come and go, and so do we who teach and do research on it. The only things that endure are the literary texts themselves; all I hope to achieve, as a scholar and teacher, is bringing these texts closer to people. Monitoring theoretical developments in the discipline can lead to insights that enhance the critic's skills to some extent; but a healthy blend of perspicacity and common sense, combined with good, traditional scholarly training and a genuine devotion to literature, is far more important in the long run.

"T. S. Eliot, the Earl of Rochester, the Brontes—it seems an odd scholarly profile, and its sole rationale is love of magnificent texts joined to a feeling that those texts have somehow failed to win full recognition for the marvels inherent in them. I've wanted to strip away as much as I could of the pseudo-scholarly cant that clings to Eliot's poetry, trying to open new channels of perception by reading the lines themselves first, rather than starting by reading between them. And they are the most glorious lines! Rochester's poems came across to me as the product of a first-class poetical talent teamed with a fine intellect, both harnessed by a master craftsman who took time and trouble over his writing. The implicit charge of gifted dilettantism imparted to his verse by the conventional rakish-earl image seemed both misguided and unjust. Finally, the Brontes—and I regard Anne as her sisters' equal, chiefly by virtue of the singularly powerful *The Tenant of Wildfell Hall*—were hard-headed, working women and tough-minded intellectuals who undertook an enormous amount of self-education and put it to use in their writing. These serious and conscious artists are too often treated as though they were incapable of making art out of anything but their own myth. Compelling as the Bronte myth is, they deserve better.

"For a foreigner working in the field of English literature, obtaining recognition from Anglo-American colleagues is uphill work. Not being born to the language has both advantages and drawbacks. You don't assume to know everything, so when you encounter an unfamiliar word or phrase, you look it up, accumulating philological knowledge that would have benefited a 'native' colleague as well. On the other hand, the pleasures of articulacy in a foreign language carry dangers; you need to be aware that the virtues of plainness and conciseness are the same in any language. It calls for a self-critical eye, or a knowledgeable and ruthless copyeditor, but they are thin on the ground these days.

"Literary critics, however puny our individual stature in the general scheme of things, have an awesome collective function: to ensure that the most precious stuff created by human minds is passed on to future generations. It is a deeply satisfying and worthwhile job, with creative aspects; but we are the servants and must never forget it. The literary texts are our masters, and we must defer to them at all times. Those among us who would set up criticism as an art on a par with 'real' literature have, in my view, forgotten the *raison d'etre* of our discipline."

*   *   *

THORMAHLEN, Marianne
See THORMAEHLEN, Marianne

*   *   *

THORNE, Barrie 1942-

PERSONAL: Born May 22, 1942, in Logan, UT; daughter of David Wynne (a university professor) and Alison (a university instructor and community activist; maiden name, Cornish) Thorne; married George Peter Lyman (a university librarian), November 17, 1970; children: Andrew, Abigail. *Education:* Stanford University, B.A., 1964; Brandeis University, M.A., 1967, Ph.D., 1971.

ADDRESSES: Home—South Pasadena, CA. *Office*—Department of Sociology, University of Southern California, Los Angeles, CA 90089-2539.

CAREER: Michigan State University, East Lansing, began as assistant professor, became professor of sociology, 1971-86; University of Southern California, Los Angeles, Streisand Professor of Sociology, 1987—.

MEMBER: American Sociological Association (chair, Section on Sex and Gender, 1983-84; vice-president, 1993-94), Society for the Study of Social Problems (member of board of directors, 1987-90), National Women's Studies Association, National Organization for Women, Phi Beta Kappa, Phi Kappa Phi.

AWARDS, HONORS: Woodrow Wilson fellow, 1964; Raubenheimer Award for Outstanding Teaching, Research, and Public Service, 1992.

WRITINGS:

(With Everett C. Hughes, Agostino DeBaggis, Arnold Gurin, and David Williams) *Education for the Profes-*

sions of Medicine, Law, Theology, and Social Welfare, McGraw, 1973.
(Editor with Nancy Henley) *Language and Sex: Difference and Dominance,* Newbury House, 1975.
(Editor with Henley) *She Said/He Said: An Annotated Bibliography of Sex Difference in Language, Speech, and Nonverbal Communication* (originally published in *Language and Sex*), Know, 1975.
(Editor with Marilyn Yalom) *Rethinking the Family: Some Feminist Questions,* Longman, 1982, revised edition, Northeastern University Press, 1992.
(Editor with Cheris Kramarae and Henley) *Language, Gender, and Society,* Newbury House, 1983.
Gender Play: Girls and Boys in School, Rutgers University Press, 1993.

Member of editorial boards, *Social Problems,* 1975-93, *Signs,* 1982—, *Theory and Society,* 1990—, and *Qualitative Sociology,* 1992—.

WORK IN PROGRESS: Compiling an anthology of essays on gender, biography, emotions, and the development of the last two decades of feminist sociology, with Barbara Laslett; a comparative ethnographic study of the sites, circumstances, and activities of urban children in Los Angeles, as they vary by social class, race and ethnicity, and gender.

*   *   *

THUERY, Jacques (H. A.) 1951-

PERSONAL: Born November 27, 1951, in Rodez, Aveyron, France; son of Jean-Pierre and Marguerite H. (Roubellat) Thuery; married Beatriz L. Lopez (a physiotherapist), August 25, 1983; children: Anne, Philippe. *Education:* Institut National Polytechnique de Toulouse, Electronics Engineering Degree, 1974. *Avocational Interests:* Travel, linguistics, space exploration, history, genealogy, paleography, old books, hiking, collecting stamps.

ADDRESSES: Home—3866 Corina Ct., Palo Alto, CA 94303-4508. *Office*—Alcatel-Espace, c/o Space Systems/ Loral, 3825 Fabian Way, Palo Alto, CA 94303.

CAREER: Pontificia Universidad Catolica Madre y Maestra, Santiago de los Caballeros, Dominican Republic, professor of electromagnetic theory, microwaves, and antennas, 1974-76; Industries Micro-Ondes Internationales, Epone, France, research and development manager, 1977-80; Thomson C.S.F., Space Division, Meudon-la-Foret, France, engineer in Satellite Department, 1981-85; Alcatel-Espace, Toulouse, France, project engineer, 1983-88, assigned to Aerospatiale, Cannes, France, 1983-88, and Space Systems/Loral, Palo Alto, CA,

1989—. Former communication system analyst for Ford Aerospace.

MEMBER: Institute of Electrical and Electronic Engineers, Conseil National des Ingenieurs et Scientifiques de France, Societe des Electriciens et Electroniciens, Societe des Lettres, Sciences et Arts de l'Aveyron.

WRITINGS:

Les Micro-ondes et leurs effets sur la matiere, Lavoisier/CDIUPA, 1983, revised and expanded second edition, 1989, translation published as *Microwaves: Industrial, Scientific, and Medical Applications,* Artech House, 1992.

Contributor to scientific journals in the field of satellite technology, particularly electromagnetic compatibility.

SIDELIGHTS: Jacques Thuery told *CA:* "When I began working on *Les Micro-ondes et leurs effets sur la matiere* in 1979, it was at the request of my former corporate manager, in view of a modest booklet sponsored by CDIUPA, a French public organization. The growing size and scope of my work gave grounds for a book that was finally published by Lavoisier and CDIUPA in 1983. A second, entirely new edition followed shortly after we arrived in California. This new edition cost me hundreds of evenings and weekends, and I missed a lot of our daughter Anne's first year. It was, however, greatly improved and fully updated.

"An English translation seemed like a good idea. After some researching, I was happy enough to attract the attention of Artech House, in the field of electromagnetism. Except for a number of mistranslations, their British and American staffs put out a very nice book that was reviewed favorably by *Microwaves & RF* and *Microwave Journal.*

"My initial purpose was to cover the whole field of thermal applications of microwaves, referred to as ISM (Industrial, Scientific and Medical). Such a synthetic approach is increasingly difficult because of the rapid spreading of these techniques into very different and specialized fields. Research on the medical applications of microwaves, for instance, and particularly on the treatment of tumors, has made incredible advances in the last few years.

"Though this is certainly not the trend of our time, I find it very enjoyable to try to master a complete field and expose it didactically. I have had a couple more mammoth jobs in store for years, one on transfer orbits, and another, in co-operation with a friend, on satellite electromagnetic modeling. The income you can expect from such things, though, is much less than what you would earn picking up apples in the San Joaquin Valley. In addition, my wife,

who supported me with abnegation on *Microwaves,* has run out of patience and would most probably ask for a divorce if I reiterated. The only exception I hope I can negotiate will be for my monumental family genealogies."

*   *   *

THURSTON, H. D.
    See THURSTON, H. David

*   *   *

THURSTON, H. David   1927-
    (H. D. Thurston)

PERSONAL: Born March 24, 1927, in Sioux Falls, SD; son of H. E. Thurston (a biology teacher) and Lelia W. Thurston (a homemaker); married Betty M. Hillers (a nurse and homemaker), 1951; children: Jeffrey L., Joseph W., David M. *Education:* University of Minnesota, B.S., 1950, M.S., 1953, Ph.D., 1958. *Politics:* Independent. *Religion:* Lutheran.

ADDRESSES: Office—Department of Plant Pathology, Cornell University, Ithaca, NY 14853.

CAREER: Rockefeller Foundation, assistant plant pathologist at Ministry of Agriculture, Bogota, Colombia, 1954-56, plant pathologist, beginning in 1958, director of plant pathology program at Instituto Colombiano Agropecuario (ICA), ending in 1966, director of department of plant sciences at ICA, 1965-67; Cornell University, Ithaca, NY, professor of plant pathology and international agriculture, 1967—. Chair of board of directors of Consortium for International Crop Protection; member of panel of experts on integrated pest control for Food and Agriculture Organization. *Military service:* U.S. Air Force, 1945-46.

MEMBER: International Society for Plant Pathology (member of council), American Phytopathological Society (fellow; chair of International Cooperation Committee), Sigma Xi.

WRITINGS:

UNDER NAME H. D. THURSTON EXCEPT AS NOTED

Tropical Plant Diseases, American Phytopathological Society, 1984.
Enfermedades de Cultivos en el Tropico, translated by J. J. Galindo L., Centro Agronomico Tropical de Investigacion y Ensenanza, 1989.
(Under name H. David Thurston) *Sustainable Practices for Plant Disease Management in Traditional Farming Systems,* Westview, 1991.
(Editor with M. Smith, G. Abawi, and S. Kearl) *Los Sistemas de Siembra con Cobertura: Tapado,* Centro Agro-

nomico Tropical de Investigacion y Ensenanza and CIIFAD, 1993.

Editorial board member of *Annual Review of Phytopathology*.

WORK IN PROGRESS: Slash/Mulch Systems: Neglected Tropical Agroecosystems; research on indigenous practices for managing plant diseases, tropical plant diseases, and tropical root and tuber diseases.

SIDELIGHTS: H. David Thurston has researched and taught agricultural methodology for many years. As a result of his academic and professional interest in the field of agriculture, Thurston has published books on the subject, including *Sustainable Practices for Plant Disease Management in Traditional Farming Systems*. This book contains a summary of literature available on traditional farming approaches and also deals with important issues of interest to agricultural practitioners in many countries. Reviewing *Sustainable Practices* in the *Journal of Natural Resources and Life Sciences Education,* Charles A. Francis commended Thurston's effort in stressing the relevance of traditional farming practices, especially in the area of pest control. Francis called the book "a thorough, scholarly, and practical guide to the literature on traditional methods for diverse management." A *Choice* reviewer called *Sustainable Practices* a "very readable" work and a "classic" that can be read by, and is of relevance to, all audiences.

Thurston told *CA:* "If anyone had told me I would enjoy writing when I took freshman English at the University of Minnesota in 1945, I would have considered them certifiably insane. Today, I enjoy writing and find it both satisfying and enjoyable.

"In 1954 I was hired by the Rockefeller Foundation to work in their agricultural program in Columbia with the Colombian Ministry of Agriculture. There, I experienced a severe case of culture shock, and my initial reaction was that everything Colombian farmers were doing relative to growing crops was wrong. Due to my lack of education and experience with traditional farmers and agriculture in Colombia, my judgement on technology recommendations and appropriate areas of research were poor during my first years there. During the eleven years I worked in Colombia, however, I gained increasing respect and appreciation for the knowledge of small farmers and the basic soundness of their farming systems.

"When I began teaching at Cornell University I realized that almost all the courses and knowledge available to students there, and most other universities in the United States, concern modern agriculture. This is so even though more than half of the world's farmers are considered traditional farmers. U.S. universities train thousands of students who will return to countries where most of the agriculture is still traditional. Thus, I decided to investigate the soundness of traditional practices and began to work on *Sustainable Practices*. I also organized a course at Cornell on traditional agriculture in the tropics.

"Humans have 10,000 years of experience with traditional agriculture. Today, there are many concerns about 'modern agriculture' because it is highly energy-intensive, the genetic base is narrow, and goals of increasingly high yields and efficiency lead to monoculture and overproduction, and sometimes to serious erosion, pollution, and excessive pesticide residues. With *Sustainable Practices* I hoped to examine how traditional agriculture can contribute to an improved, sustainable 'modern agriculture' and increase our knowledge of and respect for traditional agriculture and farmers. These people often have effective, time-tested practices for growing crops and managing pests and pathogens. Also, traditional agricultural practices must be understood and conserved before they are lost with the rapid advance of modern agriculture in developing countries. Those of us from developed countries can learn much from traditional farmers and elucidate principles and practices useful in the future management of agriculture."

BIOGRAPHICAL/CRITICAL SOURCES:

PERIODICALS

Choice, October, 1993.
Journal of Natural Resources and Life Sciences Education, spring, 1992.
Mycotoxam, January-March, 1993.
Phytopathology News, April, 1992.

*   *   *

TIETENBERG, T(homas) H(arry) 1942-

PERSONAL: Born October 21, 1942, in Plattsburgh, NY; son of Harry Hall (a bank president) and Florence (a homemaker; maiden name, Moxley) Tietenberg; married Gretchen Sprague (a homemaker), October 28, 1967; children: Heidi Leigh, Eric Justin. *Education:* U.S. Air Force Academy, B.S., 1964; University of the East, Philippines, M.A., 1965; University of Wisconsin—Madison, M.S., 1970, Ph.D., 1971. *Politics:* Independent. *Religion:* Methodist.

ADDRESSES: Home—R.F.D. 3, Box 272, Augusta, ME 04330. *Office*—Department of Economics, Colby College, Waterville, ME 04901.

CAREER: Williams College, Williamstown, MA, assistant professor of economics, 1971-77; Colby College, Waterville, ME, associate professor, 1977-84, professor of economics, 1984—, C. A. Johnson Distinguished Teaching Professor, 1990-93, Mitchell Family Professor, 1993—, head of department, 1986-88, 1993-95. Federal Energy Administration, director of Macroeconomic Impact Division, 1974-75; U.S. Environmental Protection Agency, Science Advisory Board, member of Environmental Economics Advisory Committee and Clean Air Compliance Committee; conducts workshops and seminars for World Bank, Coolidge Center, U.S. Agency for International Development, and Air and Waste Management Association. *Military service:* U.S. Air Force, 1964-68; became captain; received Air Force Commendation Medal.

MEMBER: International Society for Ecological Economics, International Institute for Environment and Development (associate fellow), Association of Environmental and Resource Economists (president, 1987-88), American Economics Association, American Association for the Advancement of Science.

AWARDS, HONORS: Fulbright scholar in the Philippines, 1964-65; economic policy fellow, Brookings Institute, 1974-75; Special Achievement Award from Federal Energy Administration, 1975; Danforth associate, 1981-87; Gilbert T. White fellow, Resources for the Future, Inc., 1983-84; named Maine Professor of the Year by Council for Advancement and Support of Education, 1990; senior research fellow, Woods Hole Oceanographic Institution, 1990-91; research grants from World Bank, National Science Foundation, Organization for Economic Cooperation and Development, United Nations Conference on Trade and Development, International Institute for Applied Systems Analysis, the Swedish Government, California Energy Commission, Resources for the Future, National Institute of Mental Health, U.S. Department of Energy, German Marshall Fund, Maine State Office of Energy Resources, Maine State Department of Environmental Protection, Maine Office of the Public Advocate, Great Northern Paper Co., Central Maine Power Co., and Maine Development Foundation.

WRITINGS:

(With J. Kain and others) *The Automobile and the Regulation of Its Impact on the Environment,* University of Oklahoma Press, 1975.

Energy Planning and Policy: The Political Economy of Project Independence, Lexington Books, 1976.

Environmental and Natural Resource Economics, Scott, Foresman, 1984, 3rd edition, HarperCollins, 1992.

Emissions Trading: An Exercise in Reforming Pollution Policy, Resources for the Future, 1985.

(Editor and contributor) *Innovation in Environmental Policy: Economic and Legal Aspects of Recent Develop-*

ments in Liability and Enforcement, Edward Elgar, 1992.

Environmental Economics and Policy, HarperCollins, 1993.

Economics and Environmental Policy, Edward Elgar, 1993.

Work represented in anthologies, including *The Economics of the Environment,* edited by Wallace E. Oates, Edward Elgar, 1992; *Toward a Sustainable Maine: The Politics, Economics, and Ethics of Sustainability,* edited by Richard Barringer, Edmund S. Muskie Institute of Public Affairs, University of Southern Maine, 1993; and *The Earthscan Reader in Environmental Economics,* edited by Anil Markandya and Julie Richardson, Earthscan, 1993. Contributor of articles and reviews to scientific journals and newspapers. Member of editorial board, *Land Economics,* 1981—, *Northeastern Environmental Science,* 1982-86, *Journal of Environmental Economics and Management,* 1992—, and *Resource and Energy Economics,* 1993—.

*   *   *

TIMBRELL, Charles   1942-

PERSONAL: Born May 5, 1942, in New Jersey. *Education:* Oberlin Conservatory of Music, B.Mus.; University of Michigan, M.Mus.; further graduate study at Accademia di Santa Cecilia.

ADDRESSES: Home—1824 Wyoming Ave. N.W., Washington, DC 20009.

CAREER: Howard University, Washington, DC, associate professor of piano, 1977—. American University, instructor, 1975—; lecturer at Ecole Normale de Musique, Paris, and Universite de Paris, Orsay. District of Columbia Commission for the Arts and Humanities, panelist.

MEMBER: American Musicological Society, Washington Music Teachers Association (member of board of directors), Friday Morning Music Club.

WRITINGS:

French Pianism: An Historical Perspective, Including Interviews with Contemporary Performers, Pro/Am Music Resources, 1992.

Contributor to music journals.

WORK IN PROGRESS: A biography of French pianist Isidor Philipp; a biography of German/American pianist and composer Walter Morse Rummel.

SIDELIGHTS: Charles Timbrell told *CA:* "I am active equally as a pianist, writer, and educator. I have concertized throughout the United States and on four European tours and have recorded often for radio. My specialty is French music, about which I have published extensively. I have also interviewed numerous French pianists for various publications. As an educator, I have applied various French technical and pedagogical points of view in my teaching."

BIOGRAPHICAL/CRITICAL SOURCES:

PERIODICALS

Journal of the American Liszt Society, January-June, 1993, p. 59.

*   *   *

TIMMS, Edward   1937-

PERSONAL: Born June 3, 1937, in Windlesham, England; son of John William Timms (a parson) and Joan Timms; married Saime Goksu, April 16, 1966; children: Yusuf, Defne, Sebastian. *Education:* Attended Christ's Hospital, Horsham, England, 1946-56; Gonville and Caius College, Cambridge, M.A., 1961, Ph.D., 1967.

ADDRESSES: Office—Gonville and Caius College, Cambridge CB2 ITA, England.

CAREER: University of Sussex, Brighton, England, lecturer in European Studies, 1963-65; University of Cambridge, England, lecturer in German and fellow of Gonville and Caius College, 1965—.

WRITINGS:

(Editor, with David Kelley) *Unreal City: Urban Experience in Modern European Literature and Art* (essays), St. Martin's, 1985.

Karl Kraus, Apocalyptic Satirist: Culture and Catastrophe in Habsburg Vienna (nonfiction), Yale University Press, 1986.

Karl Kraus in neuer Sicht (title means "Karl Kraus in a New Perspective;" nonfiction), University of London, 1986.

(Editor, with Peter Collier) *Visions and Blueprints: Avant-Garde Culture and Radical Politics in Early Twentieth-Century Europe* (essays), St. Martin's, 1988.

(Editor, with Naomi Segal) *Freud in Exile: Psychoanalysis and its Vicissitudes* (essays), Yale University Press, 1988.

(Editor, with Ritchie Robertson) *Vienna 1900: From Altenberg to Wittgenstein* (essays), Edinburgh University Press, 1990.

(Editor, with Ritchie Robertson) *The Austrian Enlightenment and Its Aftermath* (essays), Edinburgh University Press, 1991.

Contributor to periodicals, including *Times Literary Supplement* and *London Review of Books.*

SIDELIGHTS: Edward Timms told *CA:* " 'Culture and Catastrophe,' the subtitle of my study of the Austrian satirist Karl Kraus, constitutes the central preoccupation of my literary-critical writings. How was it possible for a culture as advanced as that of early twentieth-century Europe to produce such a series of political disasters, from World War I, the rise of fascism, and the self-destructive effects of Communism, through to World War II and its aftermath? It is this paradox that I have tried to resolve in a series of books and articles, taking as my main reference points Sigmund Freud's depth psychology, Karl Kraus's critique of propaganda, Julien Benda's concept of the 'treason of the intellectuals,' and Bertolt Brecht's political radicalism."

Timms began his search to resolve the paradoxes of twentieth-century European culture with *Unreal City: Urban Experience in Modern European Literature and Art,* which he edited with David Kelley. The book is a collection of scholarly essays that examine "the challenge of the city" as it is reflected in such writers and artists as Rainer Maria Rilke, Paul Cezanne, Federico Garcia Lorca, Ezra Pound, and James Joyce. In the *Times Literary Supplement,* John Melmoth summarized Timms's view of turn-of-the-century urban experience as "one of disorientation and dismay, the fear of impending collapse."

Timms's quest continued with his major work, *Karl Kraus, Apocalyptic Satirist: Culture and Catastrophe in Habsburg Vienna.* The volume details the turbulent political and artistic milieu in Vienna during the waning years of the Austro-Hungarian Empire. In the book, Timms sheds light on Austro-Hungary's fiercest critic Karl Kraus. Between 1899 and 1936, Kraus published *Die Fackel (The Torch),* a monthly journal in which he single-mindedly satirized the idiosyncracies of early twentieth-century Viennese culture, particularly as they emerged from the popular press. Timms tells how Kraus also wrote *The Last Days of Mankind,* a sprawling documentary play that tried to expose the folly of World War I in its own words. Kraus's work has been unavailable to the English-speaking reader, largely because of the difficulties of translating his acerbic, aphoristic German prose. But Timms's book, according to J. P. Stern in *The Listener,* "abounds in sensitive translations of Kraus's notoriously difficult texts." *Karl Kraus,* the critic added, "is unquestionably the most detailed and thoughtful book about him in any language. Edward Timms's account skilfully interweaves his life, times and work."

Among Timms's other writings is *Freud in Exile: Psychoanalysis and its Vicissitudes,* a collection of essays that Timms edited with Naomi Segal. According to the *New*

York Times Book Review's Leston Havens, the volume explores Austrian psychologist Sigmund "Freud's battle for the modern mind." Timms and his contributors argue that the decisive event that gave victory to Freud's views was the publication of an official, standardized English-language version of the psychologist's texts under the guidance of Englishman Ernest Jones. The result was to give a scientific legitimacy—a textbook force—to Freud's difficult, sometimes ironic, often inconsistent writing. Havens called *Freud in Exile* "penetrating" and "wide-ranging," noting that the book offers fresh insights into the way Freudian psychoanalysis has come to permeate diverse areas of modern thought.

With *Visions and Blueprints: Avant-Garde Culture and Radical Politics in Early Twentieth-Century Europe*, Timms and co-editor Peter Collier gather eighteen essays that explore the intersections between art and politics in Europe between 1900 and 1939. As a group, the essays remind readers of the important role that art and literature played during this period in supporting new political views and attacking old ones. In the *New York Times Book Review*, Lennard J. Davis deemed the book "fascinating and informative" and praised the "powerful coherence" of the contributors' "emphasis on the commitment of modernist artists and thinkers to reshape their nations and the world."

BIOGRAPHICAL/CRITICAL SOURCES:

PERIODICALS

Listener, October 23, 1986, pp. 28-29.
Los Angeles Times Book Review, March 29, 1987, p. 7.
New York Review of Books, November 6, 1986, pp. 46-49.
New York Times Book Review, July 3, 1988, p. 17; October 2, 1988, p. 33.
Times, April 22, 1989.
Times Literary Supplement, August 1, 1986, p. 845.*

*   *   *

TIRION, Wil 1943-

PERSONAL: Born February 19, 1943; son of Richard (a watchmaker) and Anna (a homemaker; maiden name, van der Veer) Tirion; married Cokkie van Blitterswijk (a doctor's assistant), December 23, 1975; children: Martin, Naara. *Education:* High school graduate. *Religion:* Jehovah's Witness.

ADDRESSES: Home and office—Wisselspoor 221, 2908 AD, Capelle aan de IJssel, Netherlands.

CAREER: Worked as a clerk in the publicity department of a large firm in Rotterdam, Netherlands, 1959-66; graphic artist and designer for a printer in Rotterdam,

1966-68, and a lithographer in Rotterdam, 1968-83; freelance sky cartographer, 1983—.

MEMBER: Nederlanse Vereniging voor Weer-en Sterrenkunde.

AWARDS, HONORS: Dr. J. van der Bilt-prijs from Nederlanse Vereniging voor Weer-en Sterrenkunde, 1987.

WRITINGS:

Sky Atlas 2000.0, Desk, Field, and Deluxe Editions, Sky Publishing, 1981.
B.A.A. Star Charts 1950.0, British Astronomical Association, 1981, Enslow Publishers, 1983.
(With Ian Ridpath) *The Collins Guide to Stars and Planets*, Collins, 1984, 2nd edition, 1993, published as *The Universe Guide to Stars and Planets*, Universe Books, 1985.
B.A.A. Chart of the Heavens, British Astronomical Association, 1985, Sky Publishing, 1989.
(With Ridpath) *Gem Guide: The Night Sky*, Collins, 1985.
(With Barry Rappaport and George Lovi) *Uranometria 2000.0*, Willmann-Bell, Volume I: *The Northern Hemisphere to Minus Six Degrees*, 1987, Volume II: *The Southern Hemisphere to Plus Six Degrees*, 1988.
(With Ridpath) *The Monthly Sky Guide*, Cambridge University Press, 1987, 3rd edition, 1993.
Bright Star Atlas 2000.0, Willmann-Bell, 1989.
(With Lovi) *Men, Monsters, and the Modern Universe*, Willmann-Bell, 1989.
Cambridge Star Atlas 2000.0, Cambridge University Press, 1991.
(With Craig Crossen) *Binocular Astronomy*, Willmann-Bell, 1992.
(With David Ellyard) *The Southern Sky Guide*, Cambridge University Press, 1993.

Contributor of sky maps to books. Contributor of star maps to astronomy journals.

SIDELIGHTS: Wil Tirion told *CA:* "Almost all my life I have been interested in the stars, especially maps of the heavens. After working for eleven years as a graphic artist at a lithographic firm, I started making my first star atlas in 1977 during my free hours. It showed stars down to a magnitude of 6.5 (the whole sky on five large maps) and was published in the *Encyclopedia of Astronomy* in 1979 and, later, as a separate set of maps in *B.A.A. Star Charts 1950.0*.

"After that, still as a hobby, I started working on a larger atlas, showing stars down to a magnitude of 8.0. Its publication as *Sky Atlas 2000.0* resulted in requests from several publishers for star maps for different purposes. In 1983 I decided to quit my job as a graphic artist and began working as a full-time uranographer, or sky cartographer."

TORME, Mel(vin Howard) 1925-
(Wesley Butler Wyatt)

PERSONAL: Born September 13, 1925, in Chicago, IL; son of William (a merchant) and Sarah (Sopkin) Torme; married Candy Toxton (an actress), 1949 (divorced, 1955); married Arlene Miles (a model), 1956 (divorced, 1966); married Janette Scott (an actress), 1966 (divorced, 1977); married Ali Severson (a lawyer), 1984; children: five. *Avocational Interests:* Piloting, movie posters, World War I aircraft.

ADDRESSES: Home—Los Angeles, CA. *Agent*—Sterling Lord Literistic Inc., One Madison Ave., New York, NY 10010.

CAREER: Singer, songwriter, and actor. Performer in various music ensembles, including Mel Torme and the Mel-Tones, the Duke Ellington Band, and the Buddy Rich Band. Recordings include *Mel Torme and Friends;* (with Buddy Rich) *Together Again—For the First Time; Live at the Maisonette; An Evening with George Shearing,* 1982; *Top Drawer,* 1983; *Night at the Concorde Pavilion,* 1991; and *Nothing without You,* 1992. Actor in motion pictures, including *Higher and Higher,* 1943; *Let's Go Steady,* 1945; *Girl's Town,* 1959; *A Man Called Adam,* 1966; and *The Land of No Return,* 1981. Writer and musical adviser for *Judy Garland Show,* 1963-64; host of television series *It Was a Very Good Year,* 1971; actor in television shows, including *Love American Style* and *Night Court. Military service:* U.S. Army during World War II.

AWARDS, HONORS: Emmy Award nomination, best supporting actor, Academy of Television Arts and Sciences, 1957, for *The Comedian;* Grammy awards, best male jazz vocalist, 1982, for *An Evening with George Shearing,* and 1983, for *Top Drawer.*

WRITINGS:

The Other Side of the Rainbow: With Judy Garland on the Dawn Patrol, Morrow, 1970, reprinted as *The Other Side of the Rainbow: Behind the Scenes on the Judy Garland Television Series,* Oxford University Press, 1991.
Wynner (novel; adapted from a script Torme originally contributed to the television series *Run for Your Life*), Stein & Day, 1978.
It Wasn't All Velvet (autobiography), Viking, 1988.
Traps, the Drum Wonder: The Life of Buddy Rich, Oxford University Press, 1991.

Also author, under pseudonym Wesley Butler Wyatt, of the western *Dollarhide,* 1955. Contributor of scripts for television shows, including *The Virginian* and *Run for Your Life.* Writer of songs, including *Lament to Love, Stranger in Town, County Fair, Born to Be Blue,* and (with Robert Wells) *The Christmas Song (Chestnuts Roasting on an Open Fire).* Lyricist for songs, including *The Real Thing.* Also composer of the orchestral work *California Suite.*

WORK IN PROGRESS: My Singing Teachers.

SIDELIGHTS: Mel Torme is a respected jazz singer who has also proved himself as an actor and a writer. Even as a child growing up in Chicago, Illinois, he showed remarkable singing and acting talents. He sang professionally at age four, and he began acting in radio plays at age six. In his mid-teens he scored a success when his composition *Lament for Love* was recorded by Harry James's band. A few years later Torme relocated to California and found work as a singer. One of his performances was heard by a Hollywood executive who promptly hired Torme for *Higher and Higher,* a 1943 film that also featured fellow singer Frank Sinatra.

Following an army stint during World War II, Torme toured both American coasts. His soft, slightly husky voice inspired radio broadcaster Fred Robbins to call him "the velvet fog." Torme, however, disdained this reference, and he soon attempted to move beyond his original smooth stylings to a more ambitious musical repertoire.

In the 1950s Torme increasingly devoted himself to jazz music, which he performed with such imminent musicians as Gerry Mulligan, Buddy Rich, and Art Pepper. In addition, he pursued work as a dramatic actor. In 1957 he distinguished himself as a supporting player in a *CBS Playhouse 90* production, *The Comedian,* and was nominated for an Emmy Award. And in 1955, under the pseudonym Wesley Butler Wyatt, he even published a western, *Dollarhide.* Torme eventually adapted this work as a script for the mid-1960s television series *The Virginian.*

The 1960s proved a particularly trying decade for Torme. In late 1963 he began one season as a writer and adviser for *The Judy Garland Show.* By this time, the popular Garland's show business career was declining, due in part to her abuse of alcohol and drugs. Torme later wrote about his experiences on the Garland show in *The Other Side of the Rainbow,* an unflinching, depiction of Garland's behavior and Torme's own personal turmoil at the time. In *The Other Side of the Rainbow,* as Andrew Sarris noted in the *New York Times Book Review,* Torme provides "a knowledgeable and lucid tribute" to Garland. Sarris added, "By confronting Judy Garland in her most monstrous moments, and still being moved enough . . . to let bygones be bygones, Torme affirms the size of [Garland's] talent." And Gene Lees, writing years later in the *New York Times Book Review,* deemed *The Other Side of the Rainbow* "one of the best accounts of show business ever written from the inside."

Towards the end of the 1960s and continuing into the 1970s, Torme experienced a prolonged professional—and personal—crisis. He was disdainful of much of his recorded work from this period, particularly his releases for Atlantic Records, and he was disheartened by the lack of popularity realized by the jazz and pop standards in which he specialized. "I began to feel disoriented, as though I was on another planet," he confided to Clarke Taylor in the *Chicago Tribune.* "After all, I'd been tutored by the models like Jerome Kern, Ella [Fitzgerald], Bing [Crosby], and Frank [Sinatra], and suddenly the big hits were three- to four-chord songs."

In the mid-1970s Torme began to overcome doubts about himself and his music. Some of the change was technical—he began singing more from his diaphragm instead of his throat—and some, he concedes, was psychological. Also important, though, was the increased public awareness and appreciation for Torme and his music. By the mid-1970s, as Torme observed to Taylor in the *Chicago Tribune,* "young people seemed to at least pay court to the older music."

Torme soon received further recognition as an accomplished musician. Beginning in the mid-1970s, he performed with both symphony orchestras and jazz ensembles, and he has played in both concert halls and intimate nightclubs. His recording career has also been fruitful in recent decades, resulting in a series of prized recordings—from *Together Again—For the First Time,* which he made with jazz drummer Buddy Rich, to *Top Drawer,* which earned him a Grammy Award in 1983. But even as he enjoyed continued acclaim and success, Torme humbly disclosed to *Newsweek*'s Charles Michener, "I'm still learning how to sing."

While remaining active as a singer, Torme has also managed to maintain a literary career. In 1978 he published the novel *Wynner,* which Mary Vespa described in *People Weekly* as the story of "a big-band singer and the people in his raunchy life." Ten years later Torme completed *It Wasn't All Velvet,* an account of his own life and art that reviewers have found characteristically candid, yet inevitably upbeat. Stephen Holden, for instance, wrote in the *New York Times* of Torme's "tone of cheerful equanimity" in the book. Jonathan Yardley's *Washington Post Book World* assessment, however, voiced displeasure with Torme's extensive discussions of his marriages, "about which," Yardley noted, "he writes at rather more length than all but the most inquisitive will find agreeable." Yardley acknowledged, however, that "as a musician . . . [Torme's] a valuable natural resource," while Holden's review of the book noted that "the self-portrait that emerges is of a tough, hard-working perfectionist who is driven to prove himself in many areas."

Torme is also author of *Traps, the Drum Wonder: The Life of Buddy Rich,* a biography of the well-known jazz musician who was described by Terry Teachout in a *Washington Post Book World* critique as "the greatest drummer in the world." In *Traps,* Torme charts Rich's career from vaudeville days—Rich began performing as a toddler—to his longlasting stature as the master of jazz percussion. Teachout deemed the volume "candid and compelling," while Tom Piazza, writing in the *New York Times Book Review,* concluded that "one comes away from this very touching book with a palpable sense of Buddy Rich's complexity and with admiration for Mel Torme's accomplishment."

For Torme, success, particularly as a musician, is the result of dedication and determination. "I spent most of the fifties getting over the Velvet Fog image," he told *New Yorker* profiler Whitney Balliett in the early 1980s. "I wanted to be a jazz-oriented singer. . . . It took some running to do it." He added, "I'm singing better than I ever have, and everyone seems to agree."

BIOGRAPHICAL/CRITICAL SOURCES:

BOOKS

Simon, George T., *Best of the Music Makers,* Doubleday, 1979, pp. 574-75.
Torme, Mel, *It Wasn't All Velvet,* Viking, 1988.

PERIODICALS

Chicago Tribune, October 9, 1988.
Los Angeles Times, September 11, 1988.
Newsweek, March 22, 1982, pp. 73-74.
New Yorker, March 16, 1981, pp. 49-58.
New York Times, September 13, 1988, p. 13.
New York Times Book Review, October 11, 1970, p. 6; October 30, 1988, p. 13; January 28, 1990, p. 34; September 22, 1991, p. 46.
People Weekly, August 28, 1978; April 1, 1991.
Times Literary Supplement, June 18, 1971, p. 712.
Tribune Books (Chicago), October 9, 1988, p. 7; October 11, 1992, p. 8.
Washington Post Book World, October 9, 1988, p. 3; September 15, 1991, p. 10.

*   *   *

TORNATORE, Giuseppe 1956-

PERSONAL: Born May 27, 1956, in Bagheria, Italy.

ADDRESSES: Home—7 Via Santamaura, Rome, Italy.

CAREER: Screenwriter and director of motion pictures, including *Il Camorrista,* 1986, and *Cinema Paradiso,*

1990. Contributing director to film *Especially on Sunday,* 1993.

AWARDS, HONORS: Prize for best documentary, Salerno Film Festival, 1982, for *Ethnic Minorities in Sicily;* Special Jury Prize, Cannes International Film Festival, 1989, and award for best original screenplay, British Academy of Film and Television Arts, and Academy Award for best foreign-language film, Academy of Motion Pictures Arts and Sciences, both 1990, all for *Cinema Paradiso.*

WRITINGS:

Opera prima: Museo civico d'arte contemporanea di Gibellina, Sellerio, 1990.

SCREENPLAYS

(With Massimo De Rita) *Il Camorrista* (title means "The Professor"; adapted from Giuseppe Marrazzo's novel), Intra Film, 1986.

Nuovo Cinema Paradiso, Ariane/Cristaldifilm/TFI/ FAI/Forum, c. 1990, foreword by Vincenzo Consolo, Sellerio, 1990, abridged version released in the United States as *Cinema Paradiso,* Miramax, 1990.

(With Tonino Guerra) *Stanno tutti bene,* Erre, 1990, released in the United States as *Everybody's Fine,* Miramax, 1991.

WORK IN PROGRESS: Writing and directing a sentimental action film.

SIDELIGHTS: Giuseppe Tornatore is among Italy's more acclaimed filmmakers. Beginning his career as a wedding photographer, Tornatore first gained distinction in Italy while making documentaries for television. In 1982 he was honored with the prize for best documentary at the Salerno Film Festival for his work on *Ethnic Minorities in Sicily.* Four years later Tornatore made his debut as a feature-film director/screenwriter with *Il Camorrista* ("The Professor"), which actor Ben Gazzara described to the *Los Angeles Times* as "one of the best gangster pictures ever made." Although Tornatore himself accords considerable praise to the film, which deals with Sicilian mobsters, *Il Camorrista* remains relatively unknown in the United States.

The same cannot be said for Tornatore's next work, which is most familiar—in its abridged, English-subtitled version—as *Cinema Paradiso.* Judith Michaelson, in her *Los Angeles Times* profile of Tornatore, praised his second feature film as "one of the best-known—and loved—Italian films." However, *Cinema Paradiso,* which chronicles a youth's various experiences at a provincial cinema in post-World War II Italy, was not an immediately successful film. Indeed, Tornatore related to the *Los Angeles Times* that upon release it was signified a "catastrophe" in his na-

tive Italy. But at the 1989 Cannes Film Festival *Cinema Paradiso* captured the Special Jury Prize, and in 1990 it won an Academy Award for best foreign-language film as well as a British Academy of Film and Television Arts award for best original screenplay. *New York Times* reviewer Clyde Haberman, who described *Cinema Paradiso* as "an unabashedly sentimental work," noted that when Tornatore's film was released again in Italy it "performed respectably."

Tornatore followed *Cinema Paradiso* with *Everybody's Fine,* in which an old man leaves his native Sicily to visit his various offspring, all of whom seem too busy to visit him. Tornatore told Michaelson, in the aforementioned *Los Angeles Times* profile, that *Everybody's Fine* is about "the impossibility people have today to communicate in their private lives." Michaelson added, however, that the film also serves as "a rather dark travelogue on life in Italy today."

Besides writing and directing his own motion pictures, Tornatore was also one of three contributing directors to *Especially on Sunday,* an Italian film comprised of three love stories written by Tonino Guerra, with whom Tornatore had collaborated on the script for *Everybody's Fine.*

BIOGRAPHICAL/CRITICAL SOURCES:

PERIODICALS

Commonweal, April 6, 1990, pp. 222-23.
Los Angeles Times, June 6, 1991, pp. F1, 8-9; June 7, 1991, p. F16.
New Republic, February 19, 1990, p. 27; July 8, 1991, p. 26.
Newsweek, March 12, 1990, p. 87.
New York, February 5, 1990, p. 58.
New York Times, January 28, 1990; June 7, 1991, p. C21.
Rolling Stone, February 22, 1990, p. 39.
Time, February 5, 1990, p. 73.*

*   *   *

TOWNSEND, J(ames) Benjamin   1918-1993

OBITUARY NOTICE—See index for *CA* sketch: Born February 17, 1918, in Stillwater, NY; died of cancer, December 13, 1993, in Buffalo, NY. Educator and author. An English instructor who was also known as an art scholar, Townsend taught at Yale University and the University of North Carolina at Greensboro before accepting a post at the State University of New York at Buffalo in 1957. He served as an assistant professor, then professor of English literature, until his retirement in 1983. An art critic for journals, Townsend served as the assistant director of the National Portrait Gallery of the Smithsonian Institution in 1967 and 1968. He also wrote and edited books on American art, such as *Harvey Breverman: Paintings and Drawings, 1965-1976; Presidential Portraits;* and *Arts in America: A Bibliography.*

OBITUARIES AND OTHER SOURCES:

BOOKS

Who's Who in America, 44th edition, Marquis, 1986.

PERIODICALS

New York Times, December 18, 1993, p. 24.

*   *   *

TROMBOLD, Charles D(ickson) 1942-

PERSONAL: Born May 20, 1942, in Chicago, IL; son of Charles Dickson (a soup company executive) and Dorothy Edith (Yetter) Trombold. *Education:* University of Arizona, B.A., 1967; Southern Illinois University, Ph.D., 1978. *Religion:* Presbyterian. *Avocational Interests:* Playing the Scottish highland bagpipe, sculpture.

ADDRESSES: Home—4401 McPherson Ave., St. Louis, MO 63108. *Office*—Department of Anthropology, Washington University, St. Louis, MO 63130.

CAREER: Centro Regional de Zacatecas, Mexico, associate archaeologist, 1978-80; Central Midwest Educational Research Laboratories, St. Louis, MO, senior consultant, 1980-82; Washington University, St. Louis, research associate in anthropology, 1982—. Ball State University, visiting assistant professor, 1983; Harris Stowe State College, lecturer, 1984. Conducted field work throughout Mexico.

MEMBER: American Anthropological Association, American Association for the Advancement of Science, Society for American Archaeology.

AWARDS, HONORS: Grants from National Science Foundation, 1974, 1985-87, 1987-88, and Wenner-Gren Foundation for Anthropological Research, 1987-88.

WRITINGS:

(Editor and contributor) *Ancient Road Networks and Settlement Hierarchies in the New World,* Cambridge University Press, 1991.

Work represented in anthologies, including *Archaeological Frontiers: Papers on New World High Cultures in Honor of J. Charles Kelley,* edited by Robert Pickering, Southern Illinois University Press, 1976; *The Archaeology of West and Northwest Mesoamerica,* edited by Michael S. Foster and Phil Weigand, Westview, 1985; and *Contributions to the Archaeology and Ethnohistory of Greater Me-*

soamerica, edited by William J. Folan, Southern Illinois University Press, 1985. Contributor of articles and reviews to anthropology and archaeology journals.

WORK IN PROGRESS: Research on the culture, history, and demographic collapse of the Classic Period on the northern Mesoamerican frontier, c. 200-1300; research on core-periphery relationships in expanding early civilizations.

SIDELIGHTS: Charles D. Trombold told *CA:* "I find that there is an underlying relationship between my research and playing the Scottish highland bagpipe, specifically the type of music called *piobaireachd* (pronounced *pee*-brack) that usually dates to the seventeenth and eighteenth centuries. At first glance, there would seem to be little association between the two. This arcane classical music, however, is composed of subtle, non-Western themes and frequently obscure patterns that must be recognized and expressed (often before a judge at international competitions). The same is true in any aspect of scientific investigation."

*   *   *

TROY, Judy 1951-

PERSONAL: Born August 16, 1951, in Chicago, IL; daughter of Jack Troy (a physician) and Sylvia Troy (a conservationist; maiden name, Troy); married Miller Solomon (a professor), August 30, 1993. *Education:* University of Illinois at Chicago, B.A., 1976; Indiana University, M.A., 1981. *Religion:* Jewish.

ADDRESSES: Office—Department of English, Auburn University, 9030 Haley Center, Auburn, AL 36849. *Agent*—Georges Borchardt, Inc., 136 East 57th St., New York, NY 10022.

CAREER: Auburn University, Auburn, AL, assistant professor, 1991—. *Crazyhorse* (literary periodical), fiction editor, 1991—.

WRITINGS:

Mourning Doves, Scribner, 1993.

WORK IN PROGRESS: A novel.

SIDELIGHTS: Judy Troy is the author of *Mourning Doves,* a short story collection that focuses on contemporary characters from the American heartland. Her individual tales often feature protagonists struggling to overcome barriers to relationships that have been caused by death or divorce. According to Christopher Tilghman in the *New York Times Book Review,* Troy "writes with a tremendous and wounded heart, and in *Mourning Doves* she speaks with a voice that can't be ignored."

Troy told *CA:* "I grew up in northwest Indiana, close to Lake Michigan and near Chicago, though my stories generally take place farther west or south; I write best about places I've seen once, briefly, so that they still seem mysterious and interesting to me. I can write one or two stories about a place I have just moved to, but the longer I live there the more I have to move on, fictionally speaking.

"I write about love, mainly, though seldom love between spouses or even between lovers; my characters don't tend to stay married to one person and they don't have much luck with relationships. I think it's interesting to write about how people get by when what they have is very different from what I have. My characters all love someone or something, which in the end gives their lives humor and pathos, making their lives simultaneously better and more painful. Compassion might be more what I write about than love.

"I daydreamed a lot when I was growing up; I also read a lot. I always thought that people with less money and luck were probably happier than I was. That's probably why I write about those people now—to see what they have in their lives that I don't (or didn't, anyway). So of course I still don't know, since my characters are who I want them to be. As one reviewer implied, they might be better off being who they actually are. So in the future I'm going to try for that."

BIOGRAPHICAL/CRITICAL SOURCES:

PERIODICALS

New York Times Book Review, June 27, 1993.
Publishers Weekly, April 12, 1993, p. 46.

*   *   *

TRZEBINSKI, Errol 1936-

PERSONAL: Surname is pronounced "trebinski"; born June 24, 1936, in Brockworth, Gloucester, England; immigrated to Kenya, c. 1952; daughter of Fred Butterworth Jones (in aviation engineering development) and Kathleen Mary (Walters) Butterworth Jones; married c. 1954 (divorced); married Zbigniew Trzebinski (an architect), May 8, 1959; children: (second marriage) Bruce, Antoni, Gabriela. *Education:* Attended school until age fifteen at Wimborne Convent in Dorset, England. *Religion:* Church of England. *Avocational Interests:* Environmental issues, including the Kenya ivory ban; cinema; theater; reading; ballet; painting.

ADDRESSES: Home—P.O. Box 84045, Mombasa, Kenya. *Agent*—Vivienne Schuster (literary) and Sebastian Born (film and television), Curtis Brown, 162-168 Regent St., London W1R 5TB, England; also Emilie Jacobson, Curtis Brown, 10 Astor Pl., New York, NY 10003.

CAREER: Homemaker and mother; has worked as an advertising executive for the *Nation* group of newspapers in Nairobi, Kenya; wrote a weekly cooking column for *Nation* for four years; writer of histories and biographies, 1977—.

MEMBER: Groucho Club, London.

WRITINGS:

Silence Will Speak: A Study of the Life of Denys Finch Hatton and His Relationship with Karen Blixen, Heinemann, 1977, University of Chicago Press, 1978.
The Kenya Pioneers, Heinemann, 1985, Norton, 1986.
World without Walls: Beryl Markham (documentary film), Public Broadcasting Service (PBS), 1986.
From an Immigrant's Notebook: Isak Dinesen/Karen Blixen Centenary (documentary film), British Broadcasting Corp. (BBC), 1986.
Hemingway (documentary film), BBC, 1986.
The Lives of Beryl Markham, Norton, 1993.

Also author of essay, "A Plea for the African Elephant"; author of several cookbooks.

ADAPTATIONS: Trzebinski's *Silence Will Speak* was used as a source for the film *Out of Africa,* Universal, 1986.

WORK IN PROGRESS: Work on documentary *A Ghost Story* about Raoul Schumacher and Beryl Markham; consultant for the feature film *West with the Night,* based on Markham's autobiography; a novel set in Lamu, Kenya.

SIDELIGHTS: Errol Trzebinski's 1977 book, *Silence Will Speak: A Study of the Life of Denys Finch Hatton and His Relationship with Karen Blixen,* cast new light on the association between English aristocrat Finch Hatton and the famed author of *Out of Africa,* Baroness Blixen (also known by her pen name, Isak Dinesen). Before Trzebinski's biography, Blixen's own writings were the only gauge of the intensity of the friendship between Blixen and Finch Hatton; moreover, Finch Hatton's presence in Blixen's writings was somewhat mysterious. In Trzebinski's research through old letters and interviews of surviving friends, she focuses on Finch Hatton's life, his work as a safari leader, his "affair" with Blixen, and his preoccupation with flying in his "Gypsy Moth" airplane. Doris Grumbach in *New York Times Book Review* remarked that "Finch Hatton was a golden boy, handsome, Oxford-educated, the second son of an aristocrat, with a fine war record," who journeyed to Africa for the first time in 1910. He stayed with Blixen on and off for a few years, but, in 1931, ended the affair just before his death in a plane crash at the age of forty-four. Nicholas Mosley in the *Times Literary Supplement* observed that "Trzebinski . . . has written a well-researched, sane, illuminating biography," though he noted that it seems "to diminish Karen Blixen's portrait of Finch Hatton." *Silence Will Speak* was used as a source for the successful 1986 film version of *Out of Africa.*

Trzebinski's next book, *The Kenya Pioneers,* "is a solid history of the settler experience" from 1896 to 1920, according to Robert Baldock in the *Times Literary Supplement.* Trzebinski highlights the lives of ordinary people from Great Britain and Europe who immigrated to Kenya during the early part of the twentieth century. Though she acknowledges that these settlers often mistreated the East African tribes they encountered, she applauds the pioneering spirit of such families as the Blocks, who came from Lithuania and eventually built a hotel empire worth millions. Baldock concluded that *The Kenya Pioneers* "is very well researched and carefully presented."

When Denys Finch Hatton left Karen Blixen, he did it for Beryl Markham, the subject of Trzebinski's 1993 book. In *The Lives of Beryl Markham,* the biographer—who was personally acquainted with Markham—recounts many tales of this extraordinary woman, who was a horse trainer, a pioneer airplane pilot, and above all, a femme fatale. As Trzebinski relates, Markham had a wild childhood, in which she was free to associate with the Kipsigi tribe and learned to throw spears at game animals. Markham grew up to have many famous lovers, including members of the British royal family. As John Spurling opined in his *Times Literary Supplement* review, Trzebinski collected a vast amount of material, and though roughly assembled, Markham's "picaresque story—a mixture of farce, melodrama, abysmal selfishness, hard work (with the horses), determination and occasionally even heroism, fading at last into a melancholy vodka-spiked old age—certainly deserves to be re-examined."

Trzebinski told *CA:* "It never occurred to me that I might become a writer, despite a passion from the age of five for letter-writing. My parents' divorce when I was fifteen dictated an end to schooling. I joined the university of life instead. I intended to become a nurse, because I am fascinated by people and what motivates them, but I was then too young to train. At the height of the Mau Mau Emergency I flew to Nairobi, Kenya, to rejoin my mother for the interim; there I looked after two small children and next became a probationary nurse at the Princess Elizabeth Hospital for Women, awaiting qualification for entry to the Middlesex Hospital. Instead, I married my first husband, divorcing him as soon as the legal span of three years before this could be dissolved, had ended. My second husband, and our three children, remained in Kenya, which has since been our home.

"To help make ends meet, I took a series of jobs. I became advertising manager to a trade magazine publisher and eventually became assistant group advertisement manager for the *Nation* group of newspapers in Nairobi. I was responsible for eighteen publications. Meanwhile, the editor of the Sunday *Nation* so enjoyed meals at our home in Karen that he insisted I try my hand at producing a weekly cookery column. Having steadfastly refused for eighteen months on the grounds that I was unqualified on every count, I acquiesced and thus wrote and illustrated with line drawings my own column for four years.

"When my architect husband moved to Mombasa to supervise his firm's design for Kunduchi Beach Hotel in Dar es Salaam, we moved our family to the coast. The disruption was not considered permanent, but we have now lived in Mombasa for twenty-six years. I had always helped to supplement our family income and was used to working; so once my children were all at school, I needed to do something that would fulfill me. Having heard that the Australian publisher, Rigby, was looking for an author for a French cookery book in their 'Instant' series, I submitted a manuscript of recipes drawn from my past columns. This resulted in a contract by return post. When the little book was published, such was its success that a director flew to Mombassa from Sydney to sign me up for eight more titles. The experience gave me discipline to write every day to meet publishing deadlines, regardless of domestic trivia. But cookery writers suffer as a result of their subject, often leading dismal social lives; I became bored with the terror one appeared to strike in others when one was invited out to dinner. . . .

"In 1973 I delivered my last manuscript to Rigby, rejecting their contract for two more books. I decided to attempt a biography of Denys Finch Hatton, Karen Blixen's lover. Five years earlier I had come across his inscribed silver hip-flask in an auction room in Nairobi. On my behalf, a working colleague put in a successful bid, but kept it for himself. Had I received it, the matter might have rested, but like the grit in the shell of the oyster, I was irritated by this act, then curious. Why? I re-read *Out of Africa,* but unlike the first time round, it now seemed obvious that what lay unwritten between the printed lines held the key to Blixen's enigmatic relationship with this man.

"Like most readers of *Out of Africa* then, I longed to know more about Denys's unexplained presence in the classic. I began my quest. I was told repeatedly that there was so little known about Finch Hatton that to fill the pages of a book would be impossible—this was, perhaps, the greatest spur and challenge to continue. Two publishers, Heinemann and Hamish Hamilton, learned of my project through Nairobi's best bookshop. Letters addressed to me from both landed on my desk in the same post.

"My response to each was the same. As I had never written a book, I did not know if there would be one. Heinemann had faith in the project. Roland Gant, literary director, signed me up two years later on the strength of the letters I had written to him, the chronology I had prepared, and a collection of the photographs. A modest advance was forthcoming. In 1977, *Silence Will Speak* was published, revealing for the first time the love story between Finch Hatton and Blixen. After Robert Hirsch's review of the biography appeared in the *Los Angeles Times,* no less than eight film option enquiries followed, and within three months, the rights to the film were acquired by an unknown producer, Anna Cataldi. She sold to Columbia who then sold to Universal; *Out of Africa* excelled at the Oscars in 1986.

"Meanwhile, I had written *The Kenya Pioneers,* and my latest and third book, *The Lives of Beryl Markham* which tells another side of Finch Hatton's life—the missing part of the eternal triangle. This biography was optioned for film before I began writing it and will be one of three sources in the feature film *West with the Night,* for which I am a consultant."

BIOGRAPHICAL/CRITICAL SOURCES:

PERIODICALS

New York Review of Books, July 17, 1986, pp. 21-27.
New York Times Book Review, June 11, 1978, p. 18.
Publishers Weekly, February 21, 1986, p. 159.
Times Literary Supplement, January 13, 1978, p. 24; January 31, 1986, p. 107; April 9, 1993, p. 32.

*   *   *

TUCKER, Karen

PERSONAL: Born in Oklahoma; daughter of Kellen and Alma Slagle; married Wallace H. Tucker (an astrophysicist), 1957; children: Kerry Tucker Renshaw, Stuart.

ADDRESSES: Home—P.O. Box 266, Bonsall, CA 92003.

CAREER: Free-lance writer.

MEMBER: Author's Guild.

WRITINGS:

(With husband, Wallace H. Tucker) *The Cosmic Inquirers: Modern Telescopes and Their Makers,* Harvard University Press, 1986.
(With Tucker) *The Dark Matter: Contemporary Science's Quest for the Mass Hidden in Our Universe,* Morrow, 1988.

SIDELIGHTS: Karen Tucker, a writer, and her husband, Wallace Tucker, an astrophysicist, have merged their re-

spective specialties to produce scientific books suitable for general readers. Together they published *The Cosmic Inquirers: Modern Telescopes and Their Makers,* in 1986, and *The Dark Matter: Contemporary Science's Quest for the Mass Hidden in Our Universe,* in 1988. In *Cosmic Inquirers,* the Tuckers focus on modern astronomy and the people involved in projects on the development of specialized telescopes in five observatories—one on land, three in space, and one waiting for a launch into orbit. "The volume names and offers photographs of most of the inquirers we meet, old and young American astronomers, men responsible in one or another degree for the coming into being of the instruments" described in the book, declared Philip Morison in *Scientific American.* Besides personal interviews with the scientists, the Tuckers analyze and describe the telescopes and their capabilities, from the optical telescope on Mount Palomar, which is sensitive enough to detect a ten-watt light bulb on the moon, to the HEAC-3 gamma-ray experiment. Thomas E. Margrave wrote in *Library Journal* that the Tuckers' descriptions provide "fascinating insight" into each project, "and the 'people' stories give added appeal" to the volume.

Returning to astronomy for their next book, *The Dark Matter,* the Tuckers explore what many astrophysicists consider to be one of the most baffling mysteries of modern science—dark matter in the cosmos. As the authors point out, scientists measure the stars' orbital velocities on the outer extremes of a galaxy and, combined with the strength of the gravitational field, calculate an estimate of the total mass of that galaxy. The problem is, according to astrophysics, scientists are consistently measuring significantly more gravitational pull than expected. There seems to be an unknown mass—designated "dark matter" because it cannot be seen—that is responsible for the surplus gravitational force. In *The Dark Matter,* the Tuckers outline explanations of various scientific theories to explain dark matter, including dead dwarf stars and black holes, and show how each one has yet to solve the puzzle. "Estimates vary, but it seems that somewhere between 50% and 90% of the mass of the universe has somehow escaped detection up till now," wrote Lee Dembart in *Los Angeles Times.* The Tuckers note in the book that "the solution promises to revolutionize astronomy."

Critical response towards the Tuckers' work was favorable, with reviewers such as Bob Fleiss in *School Library Journal* praising the authors' simplification of a difficult concept so that high school-age students can come to a "basic understanding" of the subject. Dembart commented that the book is "particularly compelling" because it is not only a "comprehensive account of the problem" but also "the story of how science works" through observation, theory, and experiment. Timothy Ferris in *New York Times Book Review* concluded that "the scientific reporting is sound, and the ongoing enigma of the dark matter, with its haunting implication that we have scarcely begun to comprehend how the cosmos is put together, comes shining (or darkling) through."

BIOGRAPHICAL/CRITICAL SOURCES:

BOOKS

Tucker, Karen, and Wallace H. Tucker, The Dark Matter: Contemporary Science's Quest for the Mass Hidden in Our Universe, Morrow, 1988.

PERIODICALS

Library Journal, April 1, 1986, p. 156.
Los Angeles Times, October 18, 1988, p. 8.
New York Times Book Review, June 26, 1988, p. 25.
School Library Journal, October, 1988, pp. 177-78.
Scientific American, October, 1986, pp. 38, 43.

*   *   *

TULLOCH, Richard (George) 1949-

PERSONAL: Born September 1, 1949, in Melbourne, Australia; son of Ian Mitchell (a doctor) and Cecily Muriel (a social worker; maiden name, Dean) Tulloch; married Agnes Blaauw (a drug and alcohol counselor), October, 1977; children: Telma, Bram. Education: Melbourne University, 1968-73, received B.A., B.L., and diploma of education.

ADDRESSES: Home—172 Cavendish, Stanmore, New South Wales 2048, Australia. Agent—Cameron's Management, 163 Brougham St., Woolloomooloo, New South Wales 2011, Australia.

CAREER: Free-lance actor and musician in Melbourne and Europe, 1975-78; National Theatre, Perth, Australia, associate director, 1979-80; Toe Truck Theatre, Sydney, Australia, artistic director, 1981-83; free-lance actor, theater director, and writer, 1984—.

MEMBER: International Theatre Institute (member of Australian committee, 1990-92), Australian Writers Guild (member of the management committee, 1990-92), Actors Equity (Australia).

AWARDS, HONORS: Australian Writers Guild awards for Hating Alison Ashley: The Play and Talking to Grandma While the World Goes By, both 1988.

WRITINGS:

PLAYS

Year 9 Are Animals, Heinemann, 1983.
If We Only Had a Cat, Currency Press, 1985.
Face to Face, Cambridge University Press, 1987.
Hating Alison Ashley: The Play, Penguin Books, 1988.

Space Demons: The Play, Omnibus Books, 1990.
The Cocky of Bungaree, illustrated by Peter Tierney, Currency Press, 1991.
Could Do Better, Currency Press, 1992.

CHILDREN'S BOOKS

Stories from Our House, illustrated by Julie Vivas, Cambridge University Press, 1987.
Stories from Our Street, illustrated by Vivas, Cambridge University Press, 1989.
Rain for Christmas, illustrated by Wayne Harris, Cambridge University Press, 1989.
The Strongest Man in Gundiwallanup, illustrated by Sue O'Loughlin, Cambridge University Press, 1990.
The Brown Felt Hat, illustrated by Craig Smith, Omnibus Books, 1990.
Danny in the Toybox, illustrated by Armin Greder, Ashton Scholastic, 1990, Tambourine, 1991.
Being Bad for the Babysitter, illustrated by Coral Tulloch, Omnibus Books, 1991, Scholastic, 1992.
Barry the Burglar's Last Job, illustrated by Tulloch, Omnibus Books, 1992.
Our New Old House, illustrated by O'Loughlin, Macmillan, 1992.

OTHER

Letter to Santa (screenplay), Nine Network, 1986.
The Miraculous Mellops (television series) Ten Network, 1991.
Bananas in Pyjamas (television series), Australian Broadcasting Co., 1991—.

Also author of Talking to Grandma While the World Goes By.

WORK IN PROGRESS: Two children's books, My Rotten Little Brother and Augustus and Dorothy; a play adaptation of Oscar Wilde's The Happy Prince; and continuing work on the Bananas in Pyjamas television series.

SIDELIGHTS: Richard Tulloch commented: "I became a writer by accident. During my unemployed time I wrote some short stories for very young children and submitted them to a radio program called Kindergarten. Most of my stories were rejected but enough were accepted to give me some encouragement. My son, Bram, was then about a year old. I tried in these early stories to see things from his point of view. Things which an adult may take little interest in—a line of ants on the kitchen floor, the garbage a dog has pulled from a bin in the street, a broken mug—could be fascinating for a little boy, and gave me ideas for stories.

"Another lucky break got me into writing children's books. My daughter told me that one of her friends at school had a mother who was an artist. That mum turned out to be Julie Vivas, who was already one of Australia's most successful illustrators. I was flattered when Julie asked to see the stories I'd written for *Kindergarten* and even more flattered when she said she'd like to illustrate them for what became my first children's book—*Stories from Our House.* I've now had nine children's books published and book work takes up nearly half my time.

"I'm a very quick writer. Sometimes this is because I have to be. The television series that I now write for need a lot of material very fast. There are deadlines which have to be met. And I've often found myself getting up early to write scenes for a play which have to be rehearsed that morning. But I'm also quick because I'm afraid that if I slow down and look back I'll lose confidence in what I've just written. Stories which seemed really exciting when I wrote them can look terrible the next morning. So if I've got my teeth into something, I write it fast, edit it carefully but quickly, and get it off to a publisher before I have time to change my mind."

BIOGRAPHICAL/CRITICAL SOURCES:

PERIODICALS

Horn Book, January, 1990, p. 238; July, 1990, pp. 42, 56; spring, 1992, p. 50.
Publishers Weekly, July 24, 1987, p. 186.
Quill & Quire, spring, 1989, p. 25.
School Library Journal, February, 1988, p. 66; February, 1992, p. 78.
Times Educational Supplement, May 13, 1988, p. B8; October 6, 1989, p. 32.

U-V

UNKLESBAY, A. G. 1914-

PERSONAL: Born February 11, 1914, in Byesville, OH; son of Howard Ray (a laborer) and Madaline (a homemaker; maiden name, Archer) Unklesbay; married Wanda Strauch, September 14, 1940 (deceased); children: Kenneth, Marjorie, Carolyn Unklesbay Lambert, Allen. *Education:* Marietta College, A.B., 1938; University of Iowa, M.A., 1940, Ph.D., 1942. *Politics:* Republican. *Religion:* Methodist. *Avocational Interests:* Travel, photography.

ADDRESSES: Home—Broadway Village Dr., Columbia, MO 65201.

CAREER: U.S. Geological Survey, geologist in Alaska and Florida, 1942-45; Colgate University, Hamilton, NY, instructor in geology, 1945-46; University of Missouri—Columbia, assistant professor of geology and department head, 1947-66, vice-president for administration, 1966-79; writer.

MEMBER: Geological Society of America, American Association of Petroleum Geologists, National Association of Geology Teachers, American Institute of Professional Geologists, Association of Missouri Geologists.

AWARDS, HONORS: D.Sc. from Marietta College, 1977.

WRITINGS:

The Geology of Boone County, Missouri Geological Survey, 1952.
Common Fossils of Missouri, University of Missouri—Columbia, 1955.
Pennsylvanian Cephalopods of Oklahoma, Oklahoma Geological Survey, 1962.
(With Jerry D. Vineyard) *Missouri Geology: Three Billion Years of Volcanoes, Seas, Sediments, and Erosion,* University of Missouri Press, 1992.

Contributor to professional journals.

WORK IN PROGRESS: A history of the geology department at the University of Missouri—Columbia.

SIDELIGHTS: A. G. Unklesbay told *CA:* "I have written to help the general public, as well as fellow geologists, understand and appreciate the science of geology, and to make people aware of the long and fascinating history of our continent. I also want people to appreciate the limits to our resources and understand how to use them more wisely."

*   *   *

VADIM, Roger 1928-

PERSONAL: Original name Roger Vadim Plemiannikov; born January 26, 1928, in Paris, France; son of Igor (a vice-consul) and Marie-Antoinette (a photographer; maiden name, Ardilouze) Plemiannikov; married Brigitte Bardot (an actress), 1952 (divorced, 1957); married Annette Stroyberg (an actress), (divorced, 1961); married Jane Fonda (an actress), 1965 (divorced, 1970); married Catherine Schneider, 1975 (marriage ended); married Marie-Christine Barrault (an actress); children: Christian, Vania, Nathalie, Vanessa. *Education:* Attended Charles Dullin's drama school, c. 1944. *Avocational Interests:* Automobile racing, water skiing, boating, painting.

ADDRESSES: Home—5 Rue Turbigo, Paris 75001, France. *Office*—c/o 24-29 Beverly Ave., Santa Monica, CA 90405. *Agent*—Addis-Wechsler & Associates, 955 South Camillo Dr., Third Floor, Los Angeles, CA 90211.

CAREER: Actor in various stage productions, 1944-47; assistant to film director Marc Allegret, 1947-55; journalist with *Paris Match,* 1953-55; director of motion pictures, 1956—; writer. Actor in motion pictures, including *The Testament of Orpheus,* 1959; *Sweet and Sour,* 1963; *Edie* in *Ciao!, Manhattan,* 1972; and *Into the Night,* 1985. Director of motion pictures, including *Please Not Now,* 1961; *Pretty Maids All in a Row,* 1971; *Night Games,* 1981; *Surprise Party,* 1983; and *And God Created Woman,* 1988. Director of television productions, including "Beauty and the Beast" for *Faerie Tale Theatre.*

WRITINGS:

Memoires du diable, Stock, 1975, translation by Peter Beglan published as *Memoirs of the Devil,* Harcourt, 1977.
D'Une etoile l'autre, [France], 1986, translation by Melinda Camber Porter published as *Bardot Deneuve Fonda: My Life with the Three Most Beautiful Women in the World* (autobiography), Weidenfeld & Nicolson, 1986.

NOVELS

L'Ange affame, R. Laffont, 1982, translation by William Attwood published as *The Hungry Angel,* Atheneum, 1983.

SCREENPLAYS; AND DIRECTOR

(With Raoul J. Levy) *Et Dieu crea la femme,* Iena-U.C.I.L.-Cocinor, 1956, released in the United States as *And God Created Woman,* Kingsley International, 1957 (also released as *And Woman Was. . .Created*).
(With Peter Viertel and Jacques Remy) *Les Bijoutiers du clair de lune* (adapted from Albert Vidalie's novel *The Moonlight Jewelers*), [France], 1958, released in the United States as *The Night Heaven Fell,* Kingsley International, (also released as *Heaven Fell that Night*), 1958.
(With Roger Vailland and Claude Brule) *Les Liaisons dangereuses* (adapted from Choderlos de Laclos's novel), Marceau-Cocinor-Laetitia, 1959, released in the United States as *Dangerous Liaisons 1960,* Astor, 1961 (also released as *Dangerous Love Affairs*).
(With Brule and Claude Martin) *Et Mourir de plaisir* (adapted from Sheridan Le Fanu's novel *Carmilla*), E.G.E.-Documento, 1960, released in the United States as *Blood and Roses,* Paramount, 1961.
(Coauthor) *La Bride sur le cou,* [France], 1961, released in the United States as *Please Not Now!,* Twentieth-Century Fox, 1963.
(Contributor with Felicien Marceau) *Les Sept Peches capitaux* (includes Vadim's "Pride"), Gibe-Franco London-Titanus, 1962, released in the United States as *Seven Capital Sins,* Joseph E. Levine, 1962.
(With Claude Choublier) *Le Repos du guerrier* (adapted from Christiane Rochefort's book), Francos-Incei, 1963, released in the United States as *Love on a Pillow,* Royal, 1964 (also released as *Warrior's Rest*).

(With Roger Vailland and Claude Choublier) *Le Vice et la vertu* (adapted from the Marquis de Sade's works *Justine* and *La Nouvelle Justine*), Gaumont-Trianon-Ultra, 1963, released in the United States as *Vice and Virtue,* Metro-Goldwyn-Mayer, 1965.
(With Claude Choublier) *Chateau en suede* (adapted from Francoise Sagan's play), Les Films Corona-Spectacles Lubroso-Euro International, 1963, released in the United States as *Nutty, Naughty Chateau,* Lopert, 1964.
(With Jean Anouilh) *La Ronde* (adapted from Arthur Schnitzler's play), [France], 1964, released in the United States as *Circle of Love,* Walter Reade, 1965.
(With Jean Cau and Bernard Frechtman) *La Curee* (adapted from Emile Zola's novel), Marceau-Cocinor, 1967, released in the United States as *The Game Is Over,* Royal, 1966.
(Contributor with Pascal Cousin and Clement Biddle Wood) *Histoires extraordinaire* (includes Vadim's "Metzengerstein" [adapted from Edgar Allan Poe's story]), Les Films Marceau-Cocinor-P.E.A., 1968, released in the United States as *Spirits of the Dead,* American International Pictures, 1969.
(With Terry Southern, Brian Degas, Claude Brule, Jean-Claude Forest, Clement Biddle Wood, Tudor Gates, and Bittorio Bonicelli) *Barbarella* (adapted from Forest's book), Paramount, 1968 (also released as *Barbarella, Queen of the Galaxy*).
(Coauthor) *Don Juan 1973; ou, Don Juan etait une femme,* [France], 1973, released in the United States as *Ms. Don Juan,* 1973 (also released as *If Don Juan Were a Woman*).

Also coauthor and director of *Sait-on jamais?,* 1957, released in the United States as *No Sun in Venice,* (also released as *When the Devil Drives*); *La Jeune Fille assassinee,* 1974, released in the United States as *Charlotte; Une Femme fidele* (title means "A Faithful Woman"), 1976.

OTHER SCREENPLAYS

(With Hugh Mills) *Blackmailed* (adapted from Elizabeth Myers's novel *Mrs. Christopher*), Greater Film Distributors, 1950.
(With Marc Allegret) *En Effeuillant la Marguerite,* E.G.E.-Hoche, 1957, released in the United States as *Please! Mr. Balzac,* Distributors Corporation of America, 1957 (also released as *While Plucking the Daisy* and as *Mademoiselle Striptease*).
(Contributor with Marc Allegret) *Les Parisiennes* (includes Allegret and Vadim's "The Tale of Sophie"), Francos-Incei, 1962, released in the United States as *Tales of Paris,* Times Film Corp., 1962 (also released as *Of Beds and Broads*).

Also author of *Futures vedettes.*

SIDELIGHTS: Roger Vadim is a filmmaker who is at least as well known for his personal exploits—notably his romances with various actresses—as he is for his actual screen work. Vadim was born in Paris in 1928, and his life was forever changed when, at age nine, he witnessed his father's death from cardiac arrest. "I aged more in that instant," Vadim later wrote in *Memoirs of the Devil,* "than I have ever aged since."

After the father's death, Vadim's family was reduced to poverty. Vadim, his mother, and his younger sister roamed France and subsided on handouts and meager earnings. During World War II, when Germany occupied France, Vadim lived in the Alps, where his mother managed a hostel that also served as a safe refuge for Jews and others hunted by the Germans. Vadim himself guided many of the fugitives to relative safety by conducting them through the mountains into neutral Switzerland. In 1944, Nazi leaders assumed quarters near the Alpine hostel. Consequently Vadim's mother moved her family, and they eventually returned to Paris as the French forces were proclaiming the city's liberation from German rule.

Soon after returning to Paris, Vadim entered the drama school conducted by Charles Dullin at the Theatre Sarah Bernhardt. Through the theatre Vadim befriended Marc Allegret, a film director at Francoeur Studios. Allegret, in turn, introduced Vadim to prominent intellectuals, including writers Jean Genet and Andre Gide. In 1949, through Allegret's introduction, Vadim met Brigitte Bardot, who would become the first famous love of his life. Though the attractive Bardot had already been featured in a fashion magazine, she was only sixteen when she met Vadim and thus was still under the considerable influence of her parents, who were devout Catholics. Despite parental disapproval, Vadim and Bardot persisted in their romance, and in 1952, after Vadim complied with demands from Bardot's parents that he convert to Catholicism and gain steady employment, the couple wed.

By the early 1950s Vadim had turned to screenwriting. His ambition, however, was to direct. Moreover, he desired to cast his wife, Bardot, in the lead of his films. Bardot, by this time, had already appeared in various features directed by Allegret. Vadim, though, hoped to launch Bardot as a major sex symbol. His wife's physical attractiveness and sexuality, Vadim envisioned, would be the means by which the pair might gain greater popularity.

In 1955 Vadim found financial backing for his directorial debut. The result of his initial efforts was *And God Created Woman,* a daringly provocative drama featuring Bardot as a sexually reckless young woman who romps with both her husband and his brother. While the work contained no true frontal nudity, it did include some sequences in which Bardot appeared in various stages of undress. As

such, *And God Created Woman,* while tame by today's standards, sparked considerable controversy, with some reviewers condemning it as pornography. Such publicity, in turn, lured the curious public, and soon enough *And God Created Woman* proved a substantial box-office success. Bardot, moreover, was well on her way to becoming an international celebrity, a role with which she would grow increasingly uncomfortable in the ensuing decades.

Vadim, meanwhile, was a success with his first filmmaking endeavor. Indeed, *And God Created Woman* came to represent, at least to some observers, a significant change in European film. This change, largely attributed to the French New Wave that included Francois Truffaut and Jean-Luc Godard, involved increased realism, and spontaneity, as well as less reliance on glamour and studio artifice. *And God Created Woman,* with its vivid storyline and unflinching handling of sexual themes, seemed—at least to some viewers—emblematic of the New Wave in cinema.

In 1957 Vadim finished a second work, *No Sun in Venice* (also known as *When the Devil Drives*). But this film failed to match the popularity, or even the notoriety, of *And God Created Women,* although, like the earlier work, it too included some provocative sex scenes. In 1958 Vadim teamed again with Bardot for *The Night Heaven Fell,* a thriller in which Bardot's character falls in love with a young man plotting to kill her uncle. This film, decried as dull and slow, did little to enhance the stature of either Bardot or Vadim. For Bardot, it proved merely another in a long succession of films—from *Love Is My Profession* to *Ms. Don Juan* fifteen years later—that simply exploited her sexual appeal. And for Vadim, it served as further indication that he was probably most successful, as a director, when exploiting the sexual appeal of his leading actress, whomever that might be. Strangely enough, though the cinematic aims of Bardot and Vadim seemed compatible, they made only a few more films together. Moreover, by the time that *The Night Heaven Fell* was released, the couple were divorced.

Vadim followed *The Night Heaven Fell* with *Dangerous Liaisons 1960,* a modernized working of Choderlos de Laclos's classic epistolary novel of 1782. With *Dangerous Liaisons 1960* Vadim again risked the censor's wrath, for the film included risque footage of actress Annette Stroyberg, who had become his second wife. Despite this potentially scandalous footage, *Dangerous Liaisons 1960* failed to match the attention and success realized by the earlier *And God Created Woman.* But when *Dangerous Liaisons 1960* was re-released in 1987 to capitalize on the success of director Stephen Frear's adaptation of de Laclos's novel, the film scored a fair measure of respect. Kevin Thomas, for instance, wrote in the *Los Angeles Times* that

Vadim's film "has stood the test of time," and added that it manages to "dazzle, stun and amuse."

Vadim teamed again with Stroyberg with *Blood and Roses,* which features Stroyberg as a somewhat vapid vampire. This film gained more attention for its cinematography—by Claude Renoir—than for Stroyberg's performance. In 1961, shortly after *Blood and Roses* was released, Stroyberg and Vadim divorced.

Among Vadim's other films from the early 1960s are *Please Not Now!,* which features Bardot as a model who falls in love with a fashion photographer, and *Love on a Pillow,* which casts Bardot as a resourceful woman who uses her sexuality to distract a young man from suicide. As with *When the Devil Drives,* these Bardot-Vadim collaborations failed to match the public interest accorded *And God Created Woman.*

Following his divorce from Stroyberg, Vadim was increasingly seen in the company of Catherine Deneuve, an actress—like Bardot and Stroyberg—known for her beauty. Vadim cast Deneuve in only one film, *Vice and Virtue,* which he adapted from the Marquis de Sade's *Justine* writings. The film, which Vadim set in a Nazi bordello in Paris, won little acclaim, though it confirmed his pictorial flair, particularly with regard to set designs. Deneuve and Vadim were engaged to be married, but the union never happened. Instead, Vadim met actress Jane Fonda, and in 1965 he married her. Vadim cast Fonda in a range of films, but only one, *Barbarella,* won box-office success. This 1968 film, which cast Fonda as a scantily-clad space maiden, was decried by many critics as mere camp, but it found considerable favor with paying audiences throughout the world. Today it remains popular as a cult classic.

Unfortunately for Fonda and Vadim, other earlier ventures were found less appealing. *La Ronde,* Arthur Schnitzler's play about a succession of romances, had already been filmed masterfully by Max Ophuls, and Vadim's 1964 version showed few fresh insights. Equally unsuccessful was *The Game Is Over,* in which Fonda portrays a young woman who enters into sexual relations with her stepson. In *Barbarella,* Fonda and Vadim eventually found success, but with that film Fonda finally came to resent Vadim's fashioning of her as a sex symbol. The couple worked together only once more, in the "Metzgenstern" episode of *Spirits of the Dead,* before they divorced.

Prior to their divorce, Fonda and Vadim had moved from Paris to Los Angeles. But after they parted company Vadim worked with less regularity. In 1971 he directed *Pretty Maids All in a Row,* a comedy featuring Rock Hudson as a homicidal high-school counselor regretfully compelled to dispatch an assortment of seductive students. Vadim next reunited with Bardot for *Ms. Don Juan* (also known as *If Don Juan Were a Woman*), which featured Bardot as the promiscuous adventurer. This film, despite what critics deemed as an unpromising storyline, won some recognition as an entertaining, light-hearted romp. But by the time of its release Bardot had become particularly unhappy with her life as a sex symbol, and she withdrew from acting and concentrated instead on animal-rights advocacy.

Vadim continued working, but his career was slowing. In 1981 he directed *Night Games,* about a rape victim incapable of resuming sexual relations with her husband. She overcomes her fears and inhibitions only after engaging in a series of couplings with a night-time visitor disguised as a bird. And in 1988 Vadim directed a remake of *And God Created Woman,* but this feature, as Vadim conceded, shared little with the earlier work bearing the same title. In the 1988 version, a rock singer leaves prison and determines to develop her career despite an unwanted marriage, one entered into only to facilitate her release from jail.

As Vadim's film career waned, his literary career developed. In 1975 he issued an autobiographical volume translated as *Memoirs of the Devil.* Here Vadim tactfully recalls his sexual exploits. Likewise, in the volume translated as *Bardot Deneuve Fonda,* Vadim recounts life with the beautiful actresses whose names provide the book's title. Despite his association with these actresses in their younger days, Vadim is careful to refute charges that he served as a manipulative mentor. "I'm no Svengali or Doolittle-like professor," he contended to *Film Comment.* "I'm a gardener who waters but does not cut."

Vadim is also author of a semi-autobiographical novel, *The Hungry Angel,* about a sixteen-year-old's sexual awakening in Paris shortly after the Allies liberated the city from the Germans in 1944. The protagonist, Julien, is in love with twenty-year-old Sophie, an aspiring playwright. During their first night together, the couple fall victim to a German bombing, and Sophie is paralyzed. Julien then enters into various sexual entanglements and becomes a theatre director, but he also remains close to Sophie. Misadventure ensues, but by novel's end both Sophie and Julien seem about to realize continued success with their respective theatre careers.

Although Vadim has flourished as both a filmmaker and writer, he seems aware that he is perhaps better known to many for his liaisons with beautiful actresses. But he disagrees when critics charge that he exploited his lovers or exhibited them to his own greater glory. He told *Film Comment:* "I can take valid criticism from a critic. I'm certainly not beyond reproach. But I've also been treated unfairly at times and I wonder if it doesn't come from unconscious jealousy. If these critics would direct, they would probably sin in a way quite the opposite of what they accuse me of—out of jealousy they would hide their women from us."

BIOGRAPHICAL/CRITICAL SOURCES:

BOOKS

Vadim, Roger, *Memoirs of the Devil,* Harcourt, 1977.
Vadim, Roger, *The Hungry Angel,* Atheneum, 1983.
Vadim, Roger, *Bardot Deneuve Fonda,* Weidenfeld & Nicolson, 1986.

PERIODICALS

Chicago Tribune, November 3, 1989.
Film Comment, April, 1988.
Los Angeles Times, September 16, 1989.
New York, April 7, 1986, pp. 62-63.
New York Times, June 5, 1987, p. C10; March 4, 1988, p. C22.
New York Times Book Review, October 16, 1977, p. 24; December 11, 1983, p. 16; April 20, 1986, p. 22.
People Weekly, May 5, 1986.
Time, April 28, 1986, p. 73; January 7, 1991, p. 4.*

*   *   *

VAIL, Amanda
See MILLER, Warren

*   *   *

van ALPHEN, Ernst   1958-

PERSONAL: Full name, Ernestus Johannes van Alphen; born December 4, 1958, in Schiedam, Netherlands. *Education:* Attended Harvard University, 1985-86, and Sorbonne, University of Paris, 1987; University of Utrecht, Ph.D. (cum laude), 1988.

ADDRESSES: Home—Stadionweg 44, 1077 SM Amsterdam, Netherlands. *Office*—Faculty of Letters, National University of Leiden, Van Wijkplaats 2, Postbus 9515, 2300 RA Leiden, Netherlands.

CAREER: University of Utrecht, Utrecht, Netherlands, instructor in modern Dutch literature, 1989-91; University of Nijmegen, Nijmegen, Netherlands, assistant professor of comparative literature and financial manager of Department of General Arts, 1990-92; National University of Leiden, Leiden, Netherlands, instructor, 1992, assistant professor of comparative literature, 1992—. University of Hawaii at Manoa, visiting professor at International Institute for Semiotic and Structural Studies, 1991; lecturer at colleges and universities, including University of London,

University of Rochester, University of Leicester, and Tel Aviv University.

AWARDS, HONORS: Fellow of National Endowment for the Humanities, University of Rochester, 1989; fellow of Dutch National Foundation for Scientific and Scholarly Research, Free University of Amsterdam's Interdisciplinary Program of Word and Image Studies, 1989-90.

WRITINGS:

Francis Bacon and the Loss of Self, Reaktion Books (London), 1992, Harvard University Press, 1993.

Work represented in anthologies, including *Death and Representation,* edited by Elisabeth Bronfen and Sarah Webster Goodwin, Johns Hopkins University Press, 1993; *The Point of Theory,* edited by Mieke Bal and Inge Boer, Amsterdam University Press, 1993; and *Perspectives on Vision,* edited by Theresa Brennan, Routledge & Kegan Paul, 1993. Contributor of articles and reviews to scholarly journals.

IN DUTCH

(Editor) Philippe Hamon, *Er staat meer dan er staat: Tekst, kennis en leesbaarheid,* Van Gorcum (Assen), 1985.
Bang voor Schennis? Inleiding in de Ideologiekritiek (title means "Afraid of Violation? Introduction to the Critique of Ideology"), HES Publishers (Utrecht), 1987.
Bij Wijze can Lezen: Verleiding en Verzet van Willem Brakmans Lezer (title means "As a Manner of Reading: The Seduction and Resistance of Willem Brakman's Reader"), Coutinho (Muiderberg), 1988.
(Editor with Irene de Jong) *Door het oog van de tekst: Essays voor Mieke Bal over visie,* Coutinho (Muiderberg), 1988.
(Editor of Dutch translation) Umberto Eco, *Lector in Fabula,* Bert Bakker (Amsterdam), 1989.
(Editor with Maaike Meijer) *De canon onder vuur: Nederlandse literatuur tegendraads gelezen,* Van Gennep (Amsterdam), 1991.
(Editor of Dutch translation) Umberto Eco, *The Limits of Interpretation,* Berk Bakker (Amsterdam), 1992.
De toekomst der herinnering: Essays over Moderne Nederlandse Literatuur (title means "The Future of Memory: Essays on Modern Dutch Literature"), Van Gennep (Amsterdam), 1993.

Work represented in anthologies. Contributor of articles and reviews to scholarly journals. Member of editorial board, *Diepzee: Tijdschrift voor het literatuuronderwijs,* 1983-85.

WORK IN PROGRESS: A book on trauma, memory, and representation.

van HEERDEN, Etienne 1954-

PERSONAL: Born December 3, 1954, in Johannesburg, South Africa; son of Gert Jacobus Olivier (a merino stud breeder and farmer) and Doreen Catherine (a math teacher; maiden name, Myburgh) van Heerden. *Education:* University of Stellenbosch, B.A. (law), 1978, B.A. (honors; cum laude), 1981, LL.B., 1982; University of Witwatersrand, M.A. (cum laude), 1987; attended International Writers' Program, University of Iowa, 1990. *Politics:* "Democrat (a rare breed in Africa)." *Religion:* "Doubt and God." *Avocational Interests:* Travel, journalism.

ADDRESSES: Home—Grahamstown, South Africa. *Office*—Department of Afrikaans and Dutch, University of Rhodes, P.O. Box 94, Grahamstown 6140, South Africa. *Agent*—Carole Blake, Blake Friedmann Literary, Film, and TV Agency, 37-41 Gower St., London WC 1E 6HH, England.

CAREER: University of Zululand, Natal, South Africa, lecturer in Afrikaans literature, 1985-87; Rhodes University, Grahamstown, South Africa, currently associate professor; has guest lectured at universities in the United States and Europe. Became Attorney of the Supreme Court of South Africa, 1984. Has worked variously as a dog handler, a deputy sheriff, a lecturer in legal practice at Peninsula Technikon, an attorney, and a copywriter and director of client services for an advertising agency.

MEMBER: Maatschappij der Nederlandse Letterkunde.

AWARDS, HONORS: Perskor Prize, Perskor Publishers, for *Matoli;* Eugene Marias Prize, South African Academy of Science and Arts, for *My Kubaan;* W. A. Hofmeyr Prize, Tafelberg Publishers, CNA Literary Award, Central News Agency Limited, ATKV Prize, and Hertzog Prize for Literature, all for *Toorberg;* CNA Literary Award, Central News Agency Limited, and ATKV Prize, both for *Liegfabriek;* honorary fellow in writing, University of Iowa; Rapport Prize for Fiction, and Honorary Listing, Noma Award for Publishing in Africa, both for *Casspirs en campari's: 'n historiese entertainment;* J & B and Financial Mail Rare Achievers Award.

WRITINGS:

Matoli (children's novel), Perskor (Johannesburg), 1978.
Obiter dictum (poems), Perskor, 1981.
My Kubaan (stories; title means "My Cuban"), Tafelberg (Cape Town), 1983.
Om te awol (novel; title means "To Go AWOL"), Tafelberg, 1984.
Toorberg (novel; title means "Mountain of Enchantment"), Tafelberg, 1986, translation by Malcolm Hacksley published as *Ancestral Voices,* Viking, 1992.

Die laaste kreef (poems; title means "The Last Cancer/Crab"), Tafelberg, 1987.
Liegfabriek (stories; title means "The Factory of Lies"), Tafelberg, 1988.
Casspirs en campari's: 'n historiese entertainment (novel), Tafelberg, 1991, translation by Catherine Knox published as *Casspirs and Camparis,* Viking, 1993.
Mad Dog and Other Stories (contains selections from *My Kubaan* and *Liegfabriek*), translated by Knox, David Philip Publishers (Cape Town), 1992.
Die stoetmeester (novel; title means "The Master of the Procession"), Tafelberg, 1993.

Works represented in anthologies, including *A Land Apart,* edited by Andre Brink and J. M. Coetzee, Faber and Faber, 1986; *Ons geduld heeft zijn grenzen,* Meulenhoff (Amsterdam), 1987; and *Time Out of Time: Contemporary Southern African Writing,* Penguin, 1990.

Van Heerden's works have been translated into Dutch, Hebrew, and French. *Toorberg* has been published in thirteen languages.

SIDELIGHTS: Toorberg is the first of South African novelist, poet, and short story writer Etienne van Heerden's novels to be translated into English. Published as *Ancestral Voices,* the multi-generational story focuses on the Moolmans, a clan that has lived and farmed on an extensive homestead, Toorberg, in the eastern Cape of South Africa for more than a century. The novel begins with the death of the last male Moolman heir, Noah (Trickle) de Pisani. The narrative shifts forward and backward in time between the investigations of the magistrate inquiring into Noah's death and a throng of ghosts—five generations of Moolman ancestors—each of whom tells his or her individual story and explains the forces that have held the clan together and doomed it to decay. Van Heerden prefaces his tale with an extensive family tree that traces both the ancestry of the Moolmans and that of their "half-breed" cousins, the blue-eyed Riets, whom the Moolmans call *Skaamfamilie* (family of shame) because they are both the descendants of an English missionary and, as van Heerden told *CA,* "they are descendants of slaves and the indigenous San ('Bushmen') hunters and Khoi ('Hottentot' tribes). They are regarded by the Moolman clan as the family of shame, therefore, because their skins are browner than those of the Afrikaner family of the farm." The theme of the novel, noted Phoebe-Lou Adams in the *Atlantic,* "is the death of a Boer Dynasty and, by implication, of white racial dominance in South Africa." Adams pointed out that, after the death of Noah, the Moolmans will fade; the *Skaamfamilie,* however, will endure.

Ancestral Voices was widely praised. A *Publishers Weekly* reviewer called the novel "spellbinding" and hailed van Heerden as "an important voice in South African fiction."

In a *New York Times Book Review* assessment, Lynn Freed concluded that the novel "provides a useful text for a study of the heritage and disposition of the Afrikaner. First published in Afrikaans in the dark days of apartheid (1986), . . . it seems to brood on history: what went before, what things have come to now." And Barend J. Toerien, writing in *World Literature Today,* declared that "as a picture of the disintegration of the white farming community in South Africa, [this] solidly structured novel makes a strong impression."

BIOGRAPHICAL/CRITICAL SOURCES:

PERIODICALS

Atlantic, August 1992, pp. 100-101.
Boston Globe, August 4, 1992, p. 28.
New York Times Book Review, August 16, 1992, p. 9.
Publishers Weekly, May 19, 1992, p. 56.
World Literature Today, summer, 1987, p. 484; summer, 1989, pp. 527-28; winter, 1989, p. 156; summer, 1992, p. 572.

*   *   *

VAUGHAN, Ronald G(eorge) 1952-

PERSONAL: Born May 13, 1952, in Toronto, Ontario, Canada; son of George Alexander (in business) and Kathleen Mary (a homemaker; maiden name, Ryan) Vaughan. *Politics:* Libertarian. *Avocational Interests:* Motorcycling, target shooting, travel.

ADDRESSES: Home and office—29 Everingham Court, Willowdale, Ontario, Canada M2M 2J6.

CAREER: Professional drummer, 1964—, drumming instructor, 1967—, and band leader, 1975-79. Self-defense instructor, 1977—; personal security consultant, 1980—.

MEMBER: National Rifle Association.

WRITINGS:

The Drumset Owner's Manual: A Heavily Illustrated Guide to Selecting, Setting Up, and Maintaining All Components of the Acoustic Drumset, McFarland and Co., 1993.

Contributor to periodicals, including *Modern Drummer* and *National Loss Prevention.*

WORK IN PROGRESS: Stay Alive (tentative title), a book of easily learned, emergency self-defense techniques; *The Paradiddle Papers* (tentative title), a novel "based on my experiences as a musician in traveling bar bands."

SIDELIGHTS: Ronald G. Vaughan told *CA:* "My book *The Drumset Owner's Manual* was written to fill a gap in percussion education literature. Ever since I began teaching at age fifteen, I have found many excellent instructional books that explained how to play the instrument. But I could never find a comprehensive manual for my students that explained the proper selection, set-up, tuning, and maintenance of the various components that comprise the acoustic drumset. After more than twenty years of waiting for someone else to do it, I finally put together all the information I'd collected over the years and wrote it myself. The book is also intended as a reference for school music teachers. Most of these individuals are not drummers, and they need a source of technical information to help them choose, tune, and maintain the drumsets used in their school music programs.

"Similarly, the book I am working on now, *Stay Alive,* was inspired by a perceived need for information. Most people have little or no knowledge of self-defense. Many of them would like to know how to survive and escape from an attack, but they can't or won't put a lot of time and effort into developing the skills. Traditional martial arts require much time, dedication, and physical conditioning before they can be used effectively in an emergency. The majority of self-defense books teach practical adaptations of sport martial arts techniques, still requiring too much time and effort for most people.

"After many years of experience as an instructor and consultant, I've distilled unconventional martial arts training into a selection of dirty tricks that can be used effectively by anyone in average physical condition. They are easy to learn and require little practice to retain. Because it is difficult to learn physical skills from photographs and instructions in a book, I keep everything as simple as possible. This book will allow most people to master basic, emergency self-defense techniques in a matter of a few hours."

Vaughan added, "For twenty years I traveled intermittently with bands, performing in bars. Road life with a band is the pared down, concentrated essence of what a working musician's life is really like. It is a snake pit of conflicting egos and the personal and professional joys and frustrations that are called paying your dues. Because the members of a band travel, eat, rehearse, perform, and room together, the pressure doesn't let up. Life is lived as though orchestrated by the Three Stooges or the Marx Brothers. Nothing that I've read has depicted road life convincingly, especially its humor. I want to do this while exploring the motivations of the people who choose this lifestyle. I've based *The Paradiddle Papers,* my work in progress, on years of notes from my road days. This is my first attempt at a novel, and I am enjoying the challenge."

VAVRA, Terry G. 1941-

PERSONAL: Born March 22, 1941, in Los Angeles, CA; son of Marvin J. (an electronics engineer) and Gwen (in real estate; maiden name, Filipy) Vavra; married Linda Dallas (a marketing consultant), December 20, 1970; children: Stacy Dallas, Kerry Lynn, Tammy Gwyn. *Education:* University of California, Los Angeles, B.S., 1964, M.S., 1967; University of Illinois at Urbana-Champaign, Ph.D., 1973. *Politics:* Republican. *Religion:* Methodist.

ADDRESSES: Home—4 Michele Court, Allendale, NJ 07401. *Office*—Marketing Metrics, 305 Route 17, Paramus, NJ 07652; and Department of Marketing, Pace University—White Plains, 1 Martine Ave., White Plains, NY 10606.

CAREER: National Broadcasting Co., New York City, director of news audience research, 1972-78; Kenyon and Eckhardt, New York City, head of research group, 1979-80; Batten, Barton, Durstine and Osborn, New York City, director of research, 1980-82; Marketing Metrics, Paramus, NJ, president, 1983—; Pace University—White Plains, White Plains, NY, associate professor of marketing, 1983—.

MEMBER: American Marketing Association, Association for Consumer Research, American Society for Quality Control, Society of Consumer Affairs Professionals, American Association of Public Opinion Research.

WRITINGS:

Aftermarketing: How to Keep Customers for Life Through Relationship Marketing, Irwin, 1992.

WORK IN PROGRESS: Research on "the importance to businesses of retaining their current customers, and how best to do this."

SIDELIGHTS: Terry G. Vavra told *CA:* "One-half-million customer affiliations are lost every day! While American businesses continue to spend heavily to attract new customers, more than eighteen million customer affiliations are broken each year because of disregard for the current customer. Meanwhile, American businesses spend an aggregate one hundred and forty billion dollars each year attempting to attract new customers.

"In my book *Aftermarketing: How to Keep Customers for Life Through Relationship Marketing,* I describe this problem and offer six proven tactics to minimize customer defection: identify and track current customers, using a customer information file; blueprint customer contact points to enhance the quality of customer interactions in these important 'moments of truth'; measure customer satisfaction to help constantly improve product and service quality; respond to customers' complaints and acknowledge their compliments; establish formal customer communication programs, including proprietary magazines or newsletters, special customer events, and affinity merchandise; and remarket to lost customers instead of considering them 'lost causes.'

"The spirit of aftermarketing is to create an organization that has as its goal converting occasional customers to customers who are so satisfied and pleased with the organization that they openly advocate it to other potential customers."

*   *   *

VERTREACE, Martha M. 1945-

PERSONAL: Born November 24, 1945, in Washington, DC; daughter of Walter Charles Vertreace (a supply officer) and Modena (Kendrick) Vertreace (a supervisor). *Education:* District of Columbia Teachers College (now University of the District of Columbia), B.S., 1967; Roosevelt University, M.A., 1971, M.Ph., 1972; Mundelein College, M.S., 1981. *Politics:* Democratic socialist. *Religion:* Roman Catholic. *Avocational Interests:* Knitting, photography, water colors.

ADDRESSES: Home—1157 East 56th St., Chicago, IL 60637-1531. *Office*—Kennedy-King College, 6800 South Wentworth Ave., Chicago, IL 60621. *Agent*—James Plath, 1108 North Clinton, Bloomington, IL 61701.

CAREER: Kennedy-King College, Chicago, IL, associate professor of English and poet in residence, 1977—. Member of board of trustees of Illinois Writers Review; member of advisory board of *City Magazine;* served as judge for Illinois Arts Council grants and Wisconsin Arts Board grants; served as Ariel judge for Triton College. Minister of Care, Saint Thomas the Apostle Church.

MEMBER: National Council of Teachers of English, Midwest Modern Language Association of America, Society of Midland Authors, Illinois Association for Teachers of English.

AWARDS, HONORS: Three literary awards from Illinois Arts Council; Excellence in Professional Writing Award from Illinois Association for Teachers of English; Hawthornden International Writers' Retreat fellow, 1992; Writers Center poetry fellow, 1993; Significant Illinois Poet Award from Gwendolyn Brooks, 1993; National Endowment for the Arts creative writing fellowship, 1993.

WRITINGS:

Second House from the Corner (poems), Kennedy-King College, 1986.
Kelly in the Mirror (juvenile), illustrated by Sandra Speidel, Albert Whitman, 1993.
Oracle Bones (poems), White Eagle Coffee Store, 1994.

Also author of *Under a Cat's-Eye Moon,* Clockwatch Review Press. Work represented in several anthologies, including *Benchmark: Anthology of Contemporary Illinois Poets,* Stormline Press, 1988; *American Women Writing Fiction,* University Press of Kentucky, 1989; *Mother Puzzles: Daughters and Mothers in Contemporary American Literature,* Greenwood Press, 1989; *The Anna Book,* Greenwood Press, 1993; and *Canadian Women Writing Fiction,* University Press of Mississippi, in press. *Oyez Review,* poetry editor; *Community Magazine,* book review editor; *Class Act,* editor; *Rhino,* co-editor; *Seams Magazine,* member of editorial board. Contributor to literary magazines.

SIDELIGHTS: Martha M. Vertreace commented: "I consider myself a poet—writing poetry primarily for the adult audience. My entry into writing children's books was quite by accident. The editor had read some of my poems and decided that I wrote with strong images. She invited me to try to write a picture book.

"When I write, my primary goal is to enjoy the experience. Perhaps, therefore, my work can bring joy to someone else. I write whenever I get the chance. I enjoy working in various forms; consequently, although most of my writing is poetry, I have published short stories, reviews, and critical essays. If I spoke of influences on my work, I would think of various poets—Richard Wilbur, Rita Dove, Amy Clampitt, Derek Walcott, Mona Van Duyn, Seamus Heaney—and many others. For me, writing is fun, although it is not necessarily easy. I began writing after the sudden death of my father when I was sixteen. It was a way to ease the tension and to focus on something else. I try not to judge my writing by asking whether or not the piece gets published; rather, my concern is that it expresses whatever I am after."

BIOGRAPHICAL/CRITICAL SOURCES:

PERIODICALS

Booklist, April 1, 1993.
Chicago Tribune, May 9, 1993, p. 6.
Publishers Weekly, March 29, 1993, p. 56.

*   *   *

VINEYARD, Jerry D.   1935-

PERSONAL: Born March 26, 1935, in Dixon, MO; son of Henry (a farmer) and Florence (a homemaker; maiden name, Giesler) Vineyard; married Helen Anderson (a homemaker), November 24, 1960; children: Monica Lynne Vineyard Randolph, Vanessa Anne Vineyard Hammons. *Education:* University of Missouri—Columbia, B.S., 1958, M.S., 1963. *Politics:* Independent.

Religion: Baptist. *Avocational Interests:* Photography, woodworking, travel.

ADDRESSES: Home—1524 Lola Lane, St. James, MO 65559-9700. *Office*—Missouri Department of Natural Resources, P.O. Box 250, Rolla, MO 65401-0250.

CAREER: Metropolitan College of Kansas City, Kansas City, MO, instructor, 1960-63; Missouri Department of Natural Resources, Rolla, information services director to deputy state geologist, 1963—.

MEMBER: National Speleological Society (honorary member), Geological Society of America (fellow), American Institute of Professional Geologists.

WRITINGS:

Springs of Missouri, Missouri Department of Natural Resources, 1974.
Geologic Wonders and Curiosities of Missouri, Missouri Department of Natural Resources, 1992.
(With A. G. Unklesbay) *Missouri Geology: Three Billion Years of Volcanoes, Seas, Sediments, and Erosion,* University of Missouri Press, 1992.

*   *   *

VITZTHUM, Hilda   1902-1993

PERSONAL: Born December 28, 1902, in Frankenmarkt, Austria; died July 6, 1993; daughter of Hubert (a court official) and Aloisia (a homemaker; maiden name, Lenzenweger) Vitzthum; married Georgi Sherbatov (an engineer and Communist Party official), 1932; children: Irina, Ruslan-Georg.

CAREER: Maid and worker in Linz, Austria, 1917-27; medical X-ray nurse in Linz, 1927-29; Communist party functionary and lecturer in Vienna, Austria, 1930-31, and Novokuznetsk, Commonwealth of Independent States, 1931-37; medical nurse at several labor camps in the C.I.S., 1938-48; worked as an interpreter in Vienna, 1949-62; writer, 1965-80.

WRITINGS:

Mit der Wurzel Ausrotten, Verlag Ernst Voegel (Munich), 1984, translation by Paul Schach published as *Torn Out by the Roots: The Recollections of a Former Communist,* University of Nebraska Press, 1993.*

[Date of death provided by Georg Vitzthum]

*   *   *

VOGEL, Virgil (Howard) J(oseph)   1918-1994

OBITUARY NOTICE—See index for *CA* sketch: Born February 25, 1918, in Keota, IA; died January 10, 1994, in Northbrook, IL. Educator and author. An authority on American Indian culture, especially nomenclature and medicinal practices, Vogel penned several books on American Indian history, including *This Country Was Ours.* He was interested in the American Indian names of cities, counties, and geographical features, writing books on the origins of place names in Illinois and Iowa. After teaching at public schools in Chicago for fifteen years, Vogel obtained a position in the history department of Harry S Truman College (part of the City Colleges of Chicago), remaining there until his retirement in 1980. In 1970 Vogel was among the group of Chicagoans who helped to rejuvenate the Charles H. Kerr Company, a publishing house known for printing radical books. As its new president, Vogel helped the company rerelease many of its books on Illinois labor history, including William H. Carwardine's *The Pullman Strike,* for which Vogel wrote a new introduction. Vogel's other publications include *American Indian Medicine,* as well as the pamphlets *The Indian in American History* and *Wisconsin's Name.*

OBITUARIES AND OTHER SOURCES:

PERIODICALS

Chicago Tribune, January 12, 1994, p. 11; January 16, 1994, p. 6.

W

WALDROP, M(orris) Mitchell   1947-

PERSONAL: Born August 22, 1947, in Augusta, GA; son of Morris Mitchell Waldrop, Sr. (an engineer), and Philo Waldrop (a homemaker; maiden name, Rabun); married Amy E. Friedlander (a historian), July 16, 1983. *Education:* University of North Carolina at Chapel Hill, B.S., 1969; University of Wisconsin—Madison, Ph.D. (physics), 1975, M.A. (science journalism), 1977.

ADDRESSES: Home and office—2430 39th St. N.W., Washington, DC, 20007. *Agent*—Peter Matson, Sterling Lord Literistic, One Madison Ave., New York, NY 10010.

CAREER: Chemical and Engineering News, Washington, DC, writer, 1977-78, West Coast bureau head in Palo Alto, CA, 1978-80; *Science,* Washington, DC, senior writer, 1980-91; free-lance writer, Washington, DC, 1991—. Judge for science awards, 1986—. Panel member of the Isaac Asimov seminars, 1984-91; member of the advisory panel of the National Air and Space Museum's Public Programs, 1990—.

MEMBER: Northern California Association of Science Writers (co-founder), District of Columbia Science Writers Association (member of board of directors, 1993—).

AWARDS, HONORS: Fellowship from International Business Machines (IBM), 1972.

WRITINGS:

Man-Made Minds: The Promise of Artificial Intelligence, Walker & Co., 1987.
Complexity: The Emerging Science at the Edge of Order and Chaos, Simon & Schuster, 1992.

Contributor of articles to periodicals, including *Science, Air and Space, Discover, Science 86, Connoisseur,* and *Mosaic,* 1979—; contributor to *Time-Life Books,* 1986-90.

WORK IN PROGRESS: The Technology of Enchantment, a popular book on software.

*   *   *

WALLACE, Edward C.   1946-

PERSONAL: Born December 30, 1946, in Bronxville, NY; son of Thomas A. Wallace, Jr., and Ida (Jackson) Wallace; married June 9, 1979; wife's name, Kathleen; children: Justin, Seth. *Education:* Miami University, Oxford, OH, B.S., 1969; Rutgers University, M.S.T., 1974; University of Texas at Austin, Ph.D., 1980.

ADDRESSES: Office—Department of Mathematics, State University of New York College at Geneseo, Geneseo, NY 14454.

CAREER: High school teacher of mathematics, computer mathematics, and physics in Whippany, NJ, 1969-81; Pan American University (now University of Texas, Pan American), Edinburg, TX, assistant professor of mathematics and computer science, 1981-85, department head, 1984-85; Lycoming College, Williamsport, PA, assistant professor of mathematics, 1985-88; State University of New York College at Geneseo, associate professor of mathematics, 1988—.

MEMBER: National Council of Teachers of Mathematics, Mathematical Association of America, American Mathematical Society, School Science and Mathematics Association, Association of Mathematics Teachers of New York State (member of executive board, 1990—), Rio Grande Valley Council of Teachers of Mathematics (president, 1983-84; editor, 1984-85), Pi Mu Epsilon.

WRITINGS:

(With J. C. Huber) *Student Activities Manual for Modern Mathematics: An Elementary Approach, Part II,* Brooks/Cole, 1985.
Roads to Geometry (includes instructor's manual), Prentice-Hall, 1992.

Contributor of numerous articles to mathematics and education journals. Associate editor, *New York State Mathematics Teachers Journal,* 1991—.

* * *

WALLACH, Erica Glaser   1922-1993

OBITUARY NOTICE—See index for *CA* sketch: Born February 19, 1922, in Schlawe, Germany; immigrated to the United States, 1957; died of cancer, December 22, 1993, in Warrenton, VA. Author and educator. Wallach became famous after the 1967 publication of her memoirs, *Light at Midnight,* which detailed her escapes from Nazi Germany and Cold War Russia. Born and raised in Germany until 1935, she and her family fled to Spain in 1935 to escape Hitler's rule; when fascist leader Francisco Franco took power in 1939 they fled again, this time to France. Wallach and her family were briefly held in a French internment camp before being rescued by League of Nations committee member Noel Field. Wallach lived with the Field family for several years, moving with them to Switzerland; there she began to work for the United States Office of Strategic Services (the government branch that would eventually become the Central Intelligence Agency) under Allen Dulles. In 1949 Noel Field and his wife disappeared in Czechoslovakia, arrested on charges of espionage. Anxious to help her friends, Wallach went to Berlin on a tip and was immediately arrested as a spy. After five years of imprisonment in Germany and then Russia, she was granted amnesty by Nikita Khrushchev and released. In 1957 Wallach joined her family in Warrenton, Virginia, where she went on to teach French and Latin at a local elementary school. Her memoirs became the basis for a television documentary and a stage play.

OBITUARIES AND OTHER SOURCES:

BOOKS

Writers Directory: 1992-1994, St. James Press, 1991.

PERIODICALS

Chicago Tribune, January 16, 1994, p. 7.
Los Angeles Times, January 20, 1994, p. A32.
Washington Post, December 24, 1993, p. B5.

WALLER, P(hilip) J(ohn)   1946-

PERSONAL: Born January 31, 1946, in Rochdale, Lancashire, England; son of Eric (a sales manager) and Marjorie (Atkinson) Waller; married Jane Christine O'Rafferty, August 14, 1971; children: Matthew James, Amy Alexandra, Joseph Lawrence. *Education:* Wadham College, Oxford, B.A., 1967.

ADDRESSES: Office—Merton College, Oxford OX 4AU, England.

CAREER: Magdalen College, Oxford, England, fellow by examination, 1968-71; Merton College, Oxford, England, fellow and tutor in modern history, 1971—; writer. Visiting professor at University of South Carolina, Columbia, 1979, and Colorado College, Colorado Springs, 1985.

WRITINGS:

Democracy and Sectarianism: A Social and Political History of Liverpool, 1868-1939, Liverpool University Press, 1981.
Town, City, and Nation: England, 1850-1914, Oxford University Press, 1983.
(Editor) *Politics and Social Change in Modern Britain: Essays Presented to A. F. Thompson,* Harvester Press, 1987.

SIDELIGHTS: P. J. Waller is a historian with particular expertise in Victorian England. His first major work is *Democracy and Sectarianism: A Social and Political History of Liverpool, 1868-1939,* a volume—according to *Times Literary Supplement* reviewer Asa Briggs—which "successfully relates Liverpool politics—often raw politics—to Liverpool society." Here Waller examines the city's long-held ties to Belfast, Ireland, and analyzes, as Briggs puts it, "religious friction and sectarian strife in Liverpool." *Spectator* reviewer Kenneth Morgan proclaimed that *Democracy and Sectarianism* "deserves the closest attention from historians of Britain as a whole, no less than those specifically concerned with Liverpool. His book is a magnificent achievement of sustained scholarship."

Among Waller's other publications is *Town, City, and Nation: England, 1850-1914,* where he delineates life in British towns during the Victorian era. In this volume Waller refutes the notion that Victorian England was essentially rural, observing that fully eighty percent of the country's population resided in cities by 1911. In addition, he explores the nature of local governments during the aforementioned period, and he emphasizes the manner in which urban England flourished in terms of welfare and cultural enrichment. Roderick Floud wrote in the *Times Literary Supplement* that *Town, City, and Nation* serves as "an admirable survey of our current knowledge of English towns in the Victorian age."

BIOGRAPHICAL/CRITICAL SOURCES:

PERIODICALS

Spectator, June 6, 1981, pp. 21-22.
Times Literary Supplement, August 21, 1981; December 16, 1983, p. 1410; December 11, 1987, p. 1371.*

*   *   *

WANSELL, (Stephen) Geoffrey 1945-

PERSONAL: Born July 9, 1945, in Scotland; son of Leslie J. (a civil servant) and Georgina (a civil servant; maiden name, Cunningham) Wansell; married Jan Vine (a teacher), May 29, 1976; children: Daniel, Molly. *Education:* London School of Economics and Political Science, London, B.S., 1966.

ADDRESSES: Home—23 Cromwell Grove, London W6 7RQ, England. *Agent*—Leslie Gardner, 38 Wigmore St., London W1H 9DF, England.

CAREER: Times Educational Supplement, London, England, reporter, 1967-70; *Times,* London, reporter, columnist, and feature writer, 1970-75; *Independent Radio News,* London, controller, 1973-75; *Observer,* London, columnist, 1977-79; *Now!,* London, columnist, 1979-81; *Telegraph Sunday Magazine,* London, columnist, 1981-85; writer.

MEMBER: Society of Authors (Great Britain), Writers Guild of America.

WRITINGS:

(With Marcel Berlins) *Caught in the Act: Children, Society, and the Law,* Penguin, 1974.
Sir James Goldsmith: The Man and the Myth, Fontana, 1982.
Cary Grant: Haunted Idol, Collins, 1983, published as *Haunted Idol: The Story of the Real Cary Grant,* Morrow, 1984.
Tycoon: The Life of James Goldsmith, Grafton, 1987.

SIDELIGHTS: Geoffrey Wansell is a British writer who has received attention for his various biographies. *Sir James Goldsmith: The Man and the Myth,* which Wansell published in 1982, concerns the exploits of a celebrated British business tycoon. Geoffrey Wheatcroft, writing in *Spectator,* deemed the biography "useful as a plain narrative of [Goldsmith's] public and . . . private lives." Wheatcroft added: "The two perennially interesting topics are money and sex. Sir James is a fruitful subject on both scores." In 1987 Wansell produced *Tycoon: The Life of James Goldsmith,* his second biography of the controversial business iconoclast. *Spectator* reviewer Brian Masters affirmed that Wansell "brings perception and honesty to

his treatment of his subject," and Richard Davenport-Hines, writing in the *Times Literary Supplement,* proclaimed the biography "fascinating."

Wansell is also author of *Haunted Idol: The Story of the Real Cary Grant* (published in England as *Cary Grant: Haunted Idol*). The work is a biography of the acclaimed film actor who distinguished himself as a debonair, sometimes beleaguered character in comedies, suspense dramas, and romances from the 1930s to the early 1960s. Gina Mallet, writing in the *New York Times Book Review,* described *Haunted Idol* as "an attempt to break up Cary Grant's impenetrably suave surface."

Wansell told *CA:* "Biography is my principal interest. I find the motivation and organization of people's lives more than enough to occupy me constantly, just as I find the desire in some to become rich and famous utterly fascinating."

BIOGRAPHICAL/CRITICAL SOURCES:

PERIODICALS

London Review of Books, December 2, 1982, p. 5.
New York Times Book Review, April 8, 1984, pp. 11-12; October 25, 1987, p. 18.
Spectator, May 22, 1982, p. 24; May 23, 1987, pp. 47-48.
Times (London), May 21, 1987, p. 17.
Times Educational Supplement, September 10, 1982, p. 32.
Times Literary Supplement, December 25, 1987, p. 1421.
West Coast Review of Books, July, 1984, p. 15.

*   *   *

WASSERSTEIN, Bernard (Mano Julius) 1948-

PERSONAL: Born January 22, 1948, in London, England; immigrated to the United States, 1980; son of Abraham Wasserstein (a professor of classics) and Margaret (Ecker) Wasserstein; married Janet Barbara Sherrard (an administrator), November 29, 1981; children: Charlotte Sophia. *Education:* Oxford University, B.A., 1969, M.A., 1972, D. Phil., 1974. *Politics:* "Moderate left." *Religion:* Jewish.

ADDRESSES: Office—Brandeis University, Department of History, Waltham, MA 02254. *Agent*—Harold Ober Associates, 40 East 49th St., New York, NY 10017.

CAREER: Nuffield College, Oxford University, Oxford, England, research fellow, 1973-75; Sheffield University, Sheffield, England, lecturer in modern history, 1976-80; Brandeis University, Waltham, MA, associate professor, 1980-82, professor of history, 1982—, director of the Tauber Institute, 1980-83, chair of history department,

1986-90, dean of Graduate School of Arts and Sciences, 1990-92. Visiting lecturer at Hebrew University of Jerusalem, Israel, 1979-80.

AWARDS, HONORS: Fellow of the Royal Historical Society, 1979; Golden Dagger Award, 1988, for *The Secret Lives of Trebitsch Lincoln;* fellowship from the National Endowment for the Humanities, 1994; fellow of the Royal Asiatic Society, 1994.

WRITINGS:

The British in Palestine: The Mandatory Government and Arab-Jewish Conflict, Royal Historical Society, 1978, second edition, Blackwell, 1991.
Britain and the Jews of Europe, 1939-1945, Oxford University Press, 1979.
(Editor with Frances Malino) *The Jews in Modern France,* University Press of New England, 1985.
The Secret Lives of Trebitsch Lincoln, Yale University Press, 1988.
Herbert Samuel: A Political Life, Oxford University Press, 1992.

WORK IN PROGRESS: Civilization and Barbarism in Europe since 1914.

SIDELIGHTS: Historian and university teacher Bernard Wasserstein has devoted himself to the study of modern history, particularly that of the Jews in Great Britain and other parts of Europe. His books on this subject have been well received, and include *Britain and the Jews of Europe, 1939-1945,* and two biographies, *The Secret Lives of Trebitsch Lincoln* and *Herbert Samuel: A Political Life.* Wasserstein himself is a native of Great Britain who taught for some years at Sheffield University before coming to the United States to serve as a professor of history at Brandeis University in Massachusetts.

"The picture which Dr. Wasserstein gives" in *Britain and the Jews of Europe,* according to Elie Kedourie in the *New York Review of Books,* "is . . . an ugly one." Wasserstein reveals the contents of archives on English policy toward the Jewish victims of the Nazi Holocaust. He tells how the English refused food aid to be carried through the economic blockade of Europe to concentration camp victims while okaying it for occupied Greece, how they constricted Jewish immigration to Palestine to placate their Arab allies, and how they stalled on plans presented by Jewish aid societies to bomb the railroad routes to concentration camps. Telford Taylor in the *New York Times Book Review* lauded *Britain and the Jews of Europe* as a "melancholy, moving and generally excellent book," and noted that "Wasserstein has not written a neutral analysis of British policies, which he attacks in a powerful concluding summary. But his book is all the more forceful for its restraint, and the author deals directly, honestly and . . .

effectively with the political arguments in defense of the British record."

In 1988's *The Secret Lives of Trebitsch Lincoln,* Wasserstein chronicles the activities of the man born Ignacz Trebitsch in Hungary who immigrated to England as a young man. Under one of his many aliases, Trebitsch Lincoln, he actually became a member of the British Parliament, but it was only one of his many scams and plots. As Wesley K. Wark reported in the Toronto *Globe and Mail,* "Trebitsch Lincoln had all the makings of a great villain. He was a man without scruples, totally amoral, uprooted from society, hungry for power and conceited beyond measure. If this were not enough, he was also clever, a superb linguist and a dab hand at the minor arts of forgery, disguise and escape. Not loveable, but certainly charismatic." In addition to being a Member of Parliament, Lincoln served stints as both a Christian missionary and a Buddhist monk, despite being born Jewish. He claimed also to be a spy, and a refusal by the British government to trade his espionage services for his freedom from forgery charges awakened in him his longtime desire to bring about the overthrow of the British Empire. To this end, perhaps, Lincoln also involved himself in early fascist movements in Germany, despite the fact that many of his co-conspirators were anti-semitic. But "in all the biggest things he tried," noted Wark, Lincoln was "a spectacular failure." John Gross in the *New York Times* declared that *The Secret Lives of Trebitsch Lincoln* "is a fascinating story, and Mr. Wasserstein makes the most of it, tracking down his quarry with wit and verve." Similarly, Douglas Porch in the *Washington Post Book World* observed that "Bernard Wasserstein has produced a very readable, impressively researched biography." Speaking in terms of previous biographies of Lincoln, *New York Review of Books* contributor H. R. Trevor-Roper asserted that "Wasserstein has gone much further, and deeper, been more critical, more reflective. This is surely the final work on a truly extraordinary career."

Wasserstein's 1992 biography, *Herbert Samuel: A Political Life,* takes as its subject a longtime British liberal politician. In the words of Roy Jenkins in the *Observer,* "Samuel was an able and diligent man of high public spirit who lived for a very long time, occupied a wide variety of public positions between 1905 and 1955, although not the ones he most coveted, and was a slight disappointment in most of them." Samuel was also Jewish, but that did not prevent him from favoring the agreement that former British Prime Minister Neville Chamberlain made in Munich, Germany, with Nazi leader Adolf Hitler. Jenkins went on to praise Wasserstein as "extremely accurate"; Peter Clarke in the *Times Literary Supplement* labeled *Herbert Samuel: A Political Life* "an exemplary account."

BIOGRAPHICAL/CRITICAL SOURCES:

PERIODICALS

Globe and Mail (Toronto), June 4, 1988.
New York Review of Books, November 22, 1979, pp. 6, 8, 10; June 2, 1988, p. 3.
New York Times, July 27, 1979; May 17, 1988.
New York Times Book Review, October 7, 1979, pp. 7, 27; June 26, 1988, p. 14.
Observer, January 19, 1992, p. 53.
Times Literary Supplement, April 22, 1988, p.439; March 6, 1992, p. 4.
Washington Post Book World, July 10, 1988, p. 7.

—Sketch by Elizabeth Wenning

* * *

WATKINS, Gloria 1955(?)-
(Bell Hooks)

PERSONAL: Born c. 1955. *Education:* Attended Stanford University.

ADDRESSES: Office—Department of Afro-American Studies, Yale University, New Haven, CT 06520.

CAREER: Social critic, educator, and writer. Yale University, New Haven, CT, assistant professor of Afro-American studies and English, beginning in the middle-1980s.

WRITINGS:

UNDER NAME BELL HOOKS

Ain't I a Woman: Black Women and Feminism, South End Press, 1981.
Feminist Theory: From Margin to Center, South End Press, 1984.
Talking Back: Thinking Feminist, Thinking Black, Between-the-Lines, 1988.
Yearning: Race, Gender, and Cultural Politics, Between-the-Lines, 1990.
(With Cornell West) *Breaking Bread: Insurgent Black Intellectual Life,* South End Press, 1991.
A Woman's Mourning Song, Writers and Readers, 1992.
Black Looks: Race and Representation, South End Press, 1992.
Sisters of the Yam: Black Women and Self Recovery, South End Press, 1993.

Also contributor to *Double Stitch: Black Women Write about Mothers and Daughters,* 1992.

SIDELIGHTS: Gloria Watkins takes an analytical yet impassioned look at how certain factors—black womanhood, feminism, the civil rights movement, critical theo-ry—cooperate and clash in the world at large and within herself. "At her best she exhibits a command of various voices that range from subtle overlays of the personal and historical to a refreshing public forthrightness that stings," writes P. Gabrielle Foreman in the *Women's Review of Books.* "Inevitably, a reader will cheer through one essay and scowl through another."

Born Gloria Watkins, the author writes under the name of Bell Hooks, the name of her great-grandmother, in order, according to Paula Giddings in *Ms.,* to "honor the unlettered wisdom of her foremothers." Indeed, it is the unheard voice of black women in general which drives her overall work.

Black women finding their voices within mainstream feminism is the focus of Watkins's first three works: *Ain't I a Woman: Black Women and Feminism, Feminist Theory: From Margin to Center,* and *Talking Back: Thinking Feminist, Thinking Black. Ain't I a Woman* is her formative work in this regard. She develops her black feminism through an examination of the special oppression under which African American women suffered and still suffer, from slavery until the time of her writing. She finds, in the web of racism, sexism, and classism that make up that oppression, that black and white women are sometimes allies and sometimes at odds. Generally, competitiveness and the white woman's vested interest in classism often drives the wedge of racism between her and her black sisters.

This thesis is further systematized in *Feminist Theory,* in which she clearly states the basic ills of the three "isms": racism, classism, and sexism have at their root the notion of domination, which is the basis of the hierarchical—or "authoritarian/bureaucratic" organization—of (at least American) society. This kind of organization is opposed to a consensual/collectivist model which would eradicate the existing forces of control, manipulation, and domination, and thus redefine power throughout society. Being at the bottom of the power structure as it now stands, black women are naturally in the vanguard of liberation from the existing structure, by their very efforts at individual self-determination. They are not, however, recognized as such by mainstream feminist organizations, who see the world with the same hierarchical eyes as do white males, wanting merely to be in their positions. Real feminism, says Watkins, should attack the whole hierarchical system.

In Watkins's third book, *Talking Back,* this paradigm is allowed to play itself out in twenty-three essays on different aspects of the black/feminist connection: from "writing autobiography, teaching women's literature, black homophobia, intimate violence, racist feminists, black porn, and politics at Yale," notes Beverly Miller in *Library Journal.*

Watkins's first three works have sometimes been seen as taking on too many voices to deal with their complex, inflammatory issues. A reviewer for *Publishers Weekly*, for example, notes that "although the author makes perceptive and provocative observations, they are diminished by redundancy and weakened by her doctrinaire Marxist rhetoric." In her review of *Feminist Theory*, Giddings wonders why black women and other women from the margins, since they *are* the vanguard, need to lobby at all to be included in other segments of the feminist movement, appearing to assign "proprietary rights to the same 'privileged' women she criticizes for their narrow perspective." And Patricia Bell-Scott, in the *Women's Review of Books*, admits to reacting defensively to some arguments that run against the feminist grain, and again points to the Marxist flavor as possibly irritating. "However," Bell-Scott continues, "we must keep in mind the author's goal, to enrich feminist discourse and 'to share in the work of making a liberatory ideology,' as we struggle with the uncomfortable issues she raises."

Though all of Watkins's work contains self-examination, her fourth book, *Yearning: Race, Gender, and Cultural Politics,* seems to reassess all her efforts, as well as her various voices. In it she continues to broaden her cultural criticism, using more and more of the theoretical tools available to (and expected from) a cutting-edge, post-modern academic. Critics like P. Gabrielle Foreman find that central to this effort is an essay, "Homeplace: A Site of Resistance," in which Watkins once more returns home to find her "location" of strength, a sense of community in the households set up by black women. This "location" helps her to solidify her base point of view, even as she sets out to examine more of her overall culture, and a black woman's part in it, from more varied and theoretical perspectives. This might be the reason that critics, among them Foreman, see her often contradicting herself and taking on the white feminists' point of view. For Foreman, though, it is her " 'intervention' into the politics of post-modern theory and practice that makes *Yearning* so timely and valuable." She tries, for example, to untangle the theories of "Otherness"—the position of outsiders within a culture—that have been primarily produced by insiders or white scholars. This includes their theorizing on "essentialism"—in this case the reality of racial groupings, and the politics of identity based on those groupings. This is a complicated question for Watkins, since blacks can be affected by both sides of this dilemma.

The reassessment of Watkins's "locations" as an African American intellectual continues in *Breaking Bread: Insurgent Black Intellectual Life*, a dialogue with social critic Cornel West. Their discussion ranges over the various crises of the black community, and how marketing to blacks, and depictions of blacks in the media, have contributed to those problems. This theme, which has threaded its way through her earlier work, is enlarged upon in *Black Looks: Race and Representation*. In its twelve chapters, she explores the implicit meaning of black images in phenomena such as advertising, Madonna's music videos, and the Hill-Thomas hearings. Her most serious indictment of the media is that it has further threatened the position of the black woman by selling black males a macho self-image. Widely greeted with approval for its ground breaking breadth and theoretical rigor, this last collection of essays caused a *Library Journal* critic to remark, "Hooks continues to produce some of the most challenging, insightful, and provocative writing on race and gender in the United States today."

BIOGRAPHICAL/CRITICAL SOURCES:

PERIODICALS

Black Enterprise, June, 1992, p. 23.
Black Scholar, January, 1983, pp. 38, 46.
Bookwatch, July 1989, p. 4; September, 1992, p. 10.
Choice, April, 1982, p. 1141; July, 1985, p. 1703.
Essence, July, 1989, p. 20.
Library Journal, December, 1981, p. 178; March 15, 1985, p. 68; December, 1988, p. 126; July, 1992, p. 109.
Ms., July, 1983, p. 24; October, 1985 p. 25.
Multicultural Review, April, 1992.
New Directions for Women, January, 1992, p. 22.
New Statesman & Society, October 22, 1982, p. 31; November 30, 1990, p. 39.
Phylon, March, 1983, p.85.
Political Science Quarterly, spring, 1983, p. 84.
Progressive, March, 1991, p. 42.
Publishers Weekly, November 18, 1988, p.72; November 22, 1991, p.49; June 15, 1992, p. 95.
Queen's Quarterly, summer, 1990, p. 318.
Sight and Sound, June, 1991, p. 36.
Village Voice Literary Supplement, June, 1982, p. 10.
West Coast Review of Books, April, 1982, p. 51.
Women's Review of Books, February, 1985, p. 3; September, 1991, p. 12.

*   *   *

WATKINSON, John   1950-

PERSONAL: Born March 29, 1950, in Hull, England; son of George R. (an electrician) and Agnes L. (Smith) Watkinson; married Annette Marie Friend, 1974 (divorced, 1988); partner of Christine Mary Lewis; children: (first marriage) Howard, Matthew. *Education:* Southampton University, B.Sc. (with honors), 1971, M.Sc., 1972. *Politics:* "No affiliations." *Religion:* None. *Avocational Interests:* Music, clocks, flying.

ADDRESSES: Home—2 Hillside, Burghfield Common, Reading RG7 3BQ, England.

CAREER: Digital Equipment Corp., lecturer, 1976-82; Sony Broadcast, Basingstoke, England, lecturer, 1982-84; Ampex Great Britain, training manager, 1984-88; Run Length Limited, director, 1988—.

MEMBER: Audio Engineering Society (fellow), British Computer Society.

AWARDS, HONORS: Outstanding Academic Book Award from *Choice,* for *The Art of Digital Audio.*

WRITINGS:

The Art of Digital Audio, Focal Press, 1988, second edition, 1993.
The Art of Digital, Focal Press, 1990, second edition, 1994.
The D-2 Digital Video Recorder, Focal Press, 1990.
Coding for Digital Recording, Focal Press, 1990.
R-Dat Digital Audio Tape, Focal Press, 1991.
The D-3 Digital Video Recorder, Focal Press, 1992.
The Digital Video Tape Recorder, Focal Press, 1994.
Introduction to Digital Audio, Focal Press, 1994.

Contributor to periodicals.

WORK IN PROGRESS: The Art of Data Recording; Non-Linear Film and Video Editing; research on video and audio data reduction and on digital audio broadcasting.

SIDELIGHTS: John Watkinson told *CA:* "I am a writer, lecturer, consultant, and designer who works in the field of audio, video, and computation. Much of my teenage life was marked by illness, and this gave me plenty of time to read and tinker. It also left me with a degree of determination and a sense of humor which rocks audiences who are expecting a deep technical lecture. The humor has a purpose: people remember what I say.

"I began writing while still an undergraduate. The articles included series on subjects such as disk drives, video recorders, and compact discs. I met Denis Mee and Eric Daniel at a recording conference. They were planning a definitive, multi-author book on magnetic recording, and invited me to write a chapter on digital audio. Like a number of contributors, I wrote too much, and they couldn't print it all. It wasn't very hard to add some more material and turn it into a book.

"One of the factors that drove me to writing was a dissatisfaction with the quality of technical books. Too many writers assume a specific existing level of knowledge on the part of the reader. If that is not you, too bad. Too many academic books seem to exist in order to glorify the author, rather than to illuminate the reader; these books tend to make the subject seem harder than it really is. I

determined that my books would never insult readers in that way.

"I have long felt that, however complex the subject, it should be possible to take a reader from zero to any depth of treatment simply by starting with the real principles and building on them in reasonably sized steps. Technical explanations tell a story, and the correct sequence of presentation is just as important as the material itself."

*   *   *

WATSON, Amy Zakrzewski   1965-

PERSONAL: Born August 4, 1965; daughter of Edward (a self-employed painter) and Justine (Bingham) Zakrzewski; married Neill Pat Watson III (a psychologist), December 1, 1990; children: Adam Zachary; (stepchildren) Anna Ruth Cory-Watson, Damon Thayer Cory-Watson. *Education:* Bloomsburg University, B.A., 1987; College of William and Mary, M.A., 1992. *Religion:* Catholic. *Avocational Interests:* Percussion, swimming, tennis.

ADDRESSES: Home and office—117 Chestnut Dr., Williamsburg, VA 23185.

CAREER: Learning and Evaluation Center, Bloomsburg, PA, writer and editor, 1987-1990; Colonial Williamsburg Foundation, Williamsburg, VA, associate editor, 1989-1992; Child Development Resource Center, Lightfoot, VA, editor, 1989—.

MEMBER: Sigma Tau Delta, Phi Kappa Pi.

WRITINGS:

The Folk Art Counting Book, Colonial Williamsburg Foundation, 1992.
Colonial Williamsburg from A to Z, Colonial Williamsburg Foundation, 1993.
Counting With the Cooper, Colonial Williamsburg Foundation, 1993.
Colonial Animals, Colonial Williamsburg Foundation, 1993.
Colonial Colors, Colonial Williamsburg Foundation, 1993.

SIDELIGHTS: "I have always had an interest in children's literature," Amy Zakrzewski Watson commented. "How do you get and hold a child's attention? How do you instruct while you entertain? What appeals to the child at different ages?" In 1992, Watson became the parent of a baby boy, Adam. "As a new mother," she explained, "my interest [in children's literature] has intensified as I try out new books on my four-month-old and see which he responds to. As a young writer, I am realizing that this is an important part of writing—researching the audience.

"Who the audience is and how they respond won't change the content, but it should dictate the delivery. It's like the mother playing airplane as she feeds the child. The food gets to the tummy almost without the child realizing it."

*   *   *

WATSON, Thomas J(ohn), Jr. 1914-1993

OBITUARY NOTICE—See index for *CA* sketch: Born January 8, 1914, in Dayton, OH; died of complications following a stroke, December 31, 1993, in Greenwich, CT. Business executive, statesman, and author. Once called "the greatest capitalist who ever lived" by *Fortune* magazine, Watson was the man credited with building his father's company, International Business Machines (IBM), into a multi-billion-dollar corporation. He was an admittedly spoiled child who spent most of his early years at private schools and then at Brown University "fooling around." However, because of his exemplary military actions in World War II, he received the U.S. Air Medal and was honored by many countries. Following his military stint, Watson joined his father's company. Taking the reins in 1952 following his father's retirement, he encouraged the company to concentrate on the emerging field of electronic computers. Under his command, IBM grew from a $700 million-per-year company to a $7.5 billion juggernaut known on Wall Street as "Big Blue." For his business leadership, Watson received the 1976 National Business Hall of Fame Award. And he was presented with honorary degrees from various universities, including Columbia, Yale, and Harvard. After his retirement from IBM in 1971, Watson was picked by President Jimmy Carter to serve as U.S. Ambassador to Moscow from 1979 to 1981. His memoirs, *Father, Son, & Co.: My Life at IBM and Beyond,* were published in 1990. Watson was also the coauthor of *A Business and Its Beliefs: The Ideas That Helped Build IBM.*

OBITUARIES AND OTHER SOURCES:

BOOKS

Who's Who in America, 48th edition, Marquis, 1994.

PERIODICALS

Chicago Tribune, January 2, 1994, p. 6.
Los Angeles Times, January 1, 1994, p. A22.
New York Times, January 1, 1994, p. 1, 9.
Times (London), January 3, 1994, p. 15.
Washington Post, January 1, 1994, p. D8.

WAUZZINSKI, Robert A. 1950-

PERSONAL: Born April 18, 1950; married; wife's name, Christy; children: Sharon Rose, Aric Robert. *Education:* Clarion State University, B.S., 1972; attended Gordon-Conwell Theological Seminary, 1974-76; Pittsburgh Theological Seminary, M.Div. (cum laude), 1978, and doctoral study; University of Pittsburgh, Ph.D., 1985.

ADDRESSES: Office—POLIS Research Center, 301 Cavanaugh Hall, Indiana University-Purdue University at Indianapolis, 425 University Blvd., Indianapolis, IN 46202-5140.

CAREER: Chatham College, Pittsburgh, PA, lecturer in philosophy and religion, 1978-80; Geneva College, Beaver Falls, PA, lecturer in religion and technology, 1985-86; Whitworth College, Spokane, WA, Edward B. Lindaman Associate Professor of Communication, Technology, and Change, 1986-92; Indiana University-Purdue University at Indianapolis, research associate and coordinator of a project on the history of religion in Indianapolis, 1992—. Trinity Episcopal School for Ministry, lecturer, 1984; Gordon-Conwell Theological Seminary, adjunct professor, 1985-86; Baylor University, Chavanne visiting scholar, 1987; Institute for Christian Studies (Toronto), adjunct professor, 1988—; Thomas F. Staley Foundation, national lecturer; lecturer at Hope College, Hong Kong Baptist College, Carnegie-Mellon University, Washington and Jefferson College, Indiana University of Pennsylvania, Allegheny College, King's College (Edmonton, Alberta), and Calvin College. Coalition for Christian Outreach, staff member, 1972-76, education adviser for staff training and development, 1972-74, scholar in residence, 1985-86; Pennsylvania Council of Churches, chaplain, summers, 1974-75; Friends of Probation, member, 1974-76; Greater Spokane Coalition against Poverty, member of board of directors, 1987-92. Guest on television and radio programs.

MEMBER: International Institute for Transfer Technology, Society for the History of Technology, American Academy of Religion.

WRITINGS:

Between God and Gold: Protestant Evangelicalism and the Industrial Revolution in America, 1820-1914, Fairleigh Dickinson University Press, 1993.

Work represented in anthologies, including *Biblical Principles and Economics,* Volume I, Navpress, 1988. Contributor of articles and reviews to periodicals, including *Third Way.*

WEAVER, Will(iam Weller) 1950-

PERSONAL: Born January 19, 1950, in Park Rapids, MN; son of Harold Howard (a farmer) and Arlys A. (Swenson) Weaver; married Rosalie Mary Nonnemacher (a teacher), March 2, 1975; children: Caitlin Rose, Owen Harte. *Education:* Attended Saint Cloud State University, 1968-69; University of Minnesota, B.A., 1972; Stanford University, M.A., 1979. *Politics:* Progressive. *Avocational Interests:* Mountain hiking, hunting and fishing, studying short story form, and rock n' roll.

ADDRESSES: Home—Bemidji, MN. *Office*—Bemidji State University, Bemidji, MN 56601. *Agent*—Lazear Agency, 430 First Ave. N., Minneapolis, MN 55401.

CAREER: Farmer, Park Rapids, MN, 1977-81; Bemidji State University, Bemidji, MN, part-time writing instructor, 1979-81, associate professor, 1981-90, professor of English, 1990—.

MEMBER: The Loft Literary Center (Minneapolis).

AWARDS, HONORS: Minnesota State Arts Board Fellowship for Fiction, 1979, 1983; "Grandfather, Heart of the Fields" was named one of "Top Ten Stories of 1984" by PEN and the Library of Congress; "Dispersal" was named one of "Top Ten Stories of 1985" by PEN and the Library of Congress; Bush Foundation fiction fellow, 1987-88; Friends of American Writers Award, 1989; Minnesota Book Award for Fiction, 1989.

WRITINGS:

Red Earth, White Earth (novel), Simon & Schuster, 1986.
A Gravestone Made of Wheat (stories; includes title story, "Going Home," "Gabriel's Feathers," "Cowman," "From the Landing," "The Bread-Truck Driver," "Dispersal," "You Are What You Drive," "Blood Pressure," and "Grandfather, Heart of the Fields"), Simon & Schuster, 1989.
Striking Out (young adult novel), HarperCollins, 1993.

Contributor to periodicals, including *Loonfeather, Prairie Schooner, Hartford Courant, San Francisco Chronicle, Kansas City Star, Chicago Tribune, Minneapolis Tribune, Newsday, Northern Literary Quarterly, Milkweed Chronicle, Library Journal, Chapel Hill Advocate,* and *Minnesota Monthly.*

ADAPTATIONS: Red Earth, White Earth was adapted as a television film, airing on the Columbia Broadcasting System (CBS-TV) in 1989.

WORK IN PROGRESS: Blaze of Glory and Other Stories; a novel for young adults titled *Farm Team.*

SIDELIGHTS: Will Weaver's first novel, *Red Earth, White Earth,* was published in 1986. He had previously garnered awards for his short stories, but *Red Earth,*

White Earth, the story of a Minnesota man who returns to the family farm in a time of crisis after having made a successful high-tech career in California, received acclaim from reviewers across the United States. Frank Levering, for instance, commenting on the book in the *Los Angeles Times Book Review* hailed Weaver as "a writer of uncommon natural talent, a backwoods pitcher with a 98 m.p.h. fastball." And Bruce Cook in Chicago *Tribune Books* declared that Weaver "is so certain with his farmers, his Indians and local types that they seem not so much created as drawn from life."

Guy Pehrsson, the protagonist of *Red Earth, White Earth,* grows up on a farm near an Indian reservation in Minnesota called White Earth. His best friend as a boy is a native American of the Chippewa tribe, Tom Little Wolf. But after an early effort at farming fails, Pehrsson leaves for California, eventually founding an extremely successful business in Silicon Valley. He returns home, however, after receiving a troubling letter from his grandfather. Back in Minnesota, Guy discovers that his father is an alcoholic, his grandfather is dying, his mother has run off with a young Native American half her age, and that the denizens of the reservation are attempting to take over his family farm and others in the area because the residents around White Earth occupy land originally made part of the reservation. The community erupts in what Alida Becker in *Washington Post Book World* termed "fistfights and shootings and arguments," and she further noted that "these maneuverings lead, of course, to the tragedy that's always been waiting in the wings." Tom Miller in the *New York Times Book Review* concluded that he "learned more about rural Minnesota after reading 'Red Earth, White Earth' than from a dozen Saturday nights with [the radio show about that state,] 'A Prairie Home Companion.' "

Weaver collected several of his short stories in 1989's *A Gravestone Made of Wheat.* The title tale concerns a farmer who wants to bury his wife on their farm and defies the law to do so; James Kaufmann in the *Los Angeles Times Book Review* lauded it as the "best" in the collection. Another story in the well-received volume is "Cowman," about a man whose marriage is failing but who finds satisfaction in giving up his factory job to return to his family farm. "The Bread-Truck Driver" is the story of an Elvis Presley-like truck driver who performs sexual services for the women along his bread route; Andy Solomon in the *New York Times Book Review* labeled the tale "a rock-and-roll lark with a haunting finish." Also noteworthy is "Dispersal," about the auction of a farm after its owner has declared bankruptcy. Meredith Sue Willis in the *Washington Post Book World* praised *A Gravestone Made of Wheat,* asserting that "in the best of [the stories], all literary pretentiousness is dropped and a wonderful weirdness rolls." Kaufmann summed up: "Weaver writes in a style as plain and sturdy as Middle Border farm architecture, his attention to the messages inherent in his stories is too steady to court ambiguity."

Weaver told *CA:* "My new book is called *Striking Out.* It is a novel for young adults. Set in the Midwest during the summer of Billy Bagg's thirteenth year, the story finds Billy and his parents trying to get beyond the death of his older brother, Robert, who died in a farming accident five years earlier. Working on the farm with his embittered father leaves Billy isolated from life in town. Through the local baseball coach's discovery of Billy's farm-strengthened arm, the family is finally able to bring their focus into the present.

"My recent turn towards fiction for young adults comes mainly from having two young adults in my family. Rather than distance myself from children in order to concentrate upon 'adult' fiction, I have found it much more logical and pleasant to listen to my children's stories—and create my own stories for them. When they are (too soon) older, I will doubtless return to the larger novel and to story collections for the mature reader. The lesson for me in this is that a writer must continually keep a weather eye toward the shifting winds of subject and metaphor and story; it is far easier to write with the breeze than to continually tack against it."

BIOGRAPHICAL/CRITICAL SOURCES:

PERIODICALS

Los Angeles Times Book Review, October 19, 1986, p. 9; March 12, 1989, pp. 1, 13.
New York Times Book Review, November 9, 1986, p. 33; March 12, 1989, p. 22.
Tribune Books (Chicago), December 21, 1986, p. 6.
Washington Post Book World, November 2, 1986, p. 8; March 26, 1989, p. 11.

*   *   *

WECKMANN, Luis 1923-

PERSONAL: Born April 7, 1923, in Ciudad Lerdo, Durango, Mexico; son of Jose Bernardo and Ana Teresa (Munoz) Weckmann; married Ibone de Belausteguigoitia, 1971 (divorced, 1981). *Education:* National University of Mexico, M.A., 1944, Ph.D. (history), 1949, Licentiate in Law, 1950; University of Paris, Ph.D. (international law), 1951; graduate study at University of California, Berkeley, and University of Munich.

ADDRESSES: Home—Villa del Cardo, Calzada del Cardo 4, San Miguel Allende 37700, Mexico. *Agent*—Florence Belsky, 427 East 77th St., New York, NY 10028.

CAREER: National University of Mexico, Mexico City, began as lecturer, became professor of history, 1944-64. University of the Americas, began as lecturer, became associate professor, 1948-64, named professor emeritus, 1991, served as dean of humanities; El Colegio de Mexico, professor, 1960-79, director of graduate seminars in history, 1979-80. Mexican Foreign Service, foreign service officer, 1952-89, ambassador to Israel, 1967-69, Austria, 1969-73, West Germany, 1973-76, Iran, 1976-79, the United Nations, 1979-82, Italy, 1982-86, and to the European Community and Belgium, 1986-88, consul general in Rio de Janeiro, Brazil, 1988-89, named eminent ambassador, 1989. United Nations, assistant secretary general for special political affairs, serving in missions to Iraq, Iran, and Cyprus, 1974-75.

MEMBER: International Law Association, Mexican Academy of History, Medieval Academy of America (corresponding member), Spanish Academy of History (corresponding member), Accademia del Mediterraneo (Rome; corresponding member), Societe Belge de Philologie et Histoire (corresponding member).

WRITINGS:

La Sociedad Feudal, Jus, 1944.
Las Bulas Alejandrinas de 1493. . . , introduction by Ernest H. Kantorowicz, Institute for Advanced Study (Princeton, NJ), National University of Mexico, 1949, second edition published as *Constantine the Great and Christopher Columbus,* Fondo de Cultura Economica, 1992.
El Pensamiento Politico Medieval, National University of Mexico, 1950, second edition, Fondo de Cultura Economica, 1992.
Las Relaciones Rranco-Mexicanas, 1823-1885, three volumes, Mexican Foreign Office, 1961-72.
Panorama de la Cultura Medieval, National University of Mexico, 1962.
La herencia medieval de Mexico, El Colegio de Mexico, 1984, translation published as *The Medieval Heritage of Mexico,* Fordham University Press, 1993, second edition, Fondo de Cultura Economica (Mexico City), 1994.
Carlota de Belgica: Correspondence, 1861-1868, Porrua (Mexico City), 1989.
The Medieval Heritage of Brazil, Fondo de Cultura Economica, 1993.
Diarios Politicos de un Embajador Mexicano, 1967-1988, Mexican Foreign Office, Fondo de Cultura Economica, in press.

WEIR, Bob 1947-

PERSONAL: Born October 16, 1947, in San Francisco, CA; son of Frederick U. (an electrical engineer) and Eleanor (a giftware importer; maiden name, Cramer) Weir.

ADDRESSES: Office—c/o Hyperion, 114 Fifth Ave., New York, NY 10011. *Agent*—Sarah Lazin, 126 Fifth Ave., Suite 300, New York, NY 10010.

CAREER: Rhythm guitarist and singer for The Grateful Dead, 1965—.

MEMBER: Seva Foundation, Creating Your Future, Rainforest Action Network.

AWARDS, HONORS: Notable Children's Trade Book in Social Studies citation, Children's Book Council, 1991, for *Panther Dream: A Story of the African Rainforest;* multiple gold and platinum record albums; honorariums.

WRITINGS:

(With sister, Wendy Weir, and soundtrack producer, performer, and narrator of audio cassette tape) *Panther Dream: A Story of the African Rainforest,* illustrated by W. Weir, Hyperion, 1991.

WORK IN PROGRESS: Children's book and tape about life under the ocean on the Great Barrier Reef, Australia, 1994.

SIDELIGHTS: Bob Weir commented: "A children's book can influence a child toward looking at life and natural order with respect and admiration by making it fun, as well as intriguing. If this happens enough, the world could be a better place in years to come. And maybe their innocent vision can bring adults a greater respect for our planet."

*   *   *

WEIR, Wendy 1949-

PERSONAL: Born October 2, 1949, in San Francisco, CA; daughter of Frederick U. (an electrical engineer) and Eleanor (a giftware importer; maiden name, Cramer) Weir. *Education:* University of California, Berkeley, B.A., 1970.

ADDRESSES: Office—c/o Hyperion, 114 Fifth Ave., New York, NY 10011. *Agent*—Sarah Lazin, 126 Fifth Ave., Suite 300, New York, NY 10010.

CAREER: Senior bank executive positions in savings and loans and banks, 1973-1985; financial consultant in the banking and insurance industries, 1985—. Director of The Mountain School, 1991—, and Coral Forest (non-profit coral reef conservation organization).

MEMBER: Rainforest Action Network.

AWARDS, HONORS: Notable Children's Trade Book in Social Studies citation, Children's Book Council, 1991, for *Panther Dream: A Story of the African Rainforest.*

WRITINGS:

(With brother, Bob Weir, and illustrator) *Panther Dream: A Story of the African Rainforest,* Hyperion, 1991.

WORK IN PROGRESS: Children's book and tape about life under the ocean on the Great Barrier Reef, Australia, 1994.

SIDELIGHTS: Wendy Weir commented: "I have always wanted to do something with my artistic talents, but was so heavily involved in making a living in the financial industry that I never took the time. Then, in my late thirties, I decided to do something that was totally *me.* I enjoy working with children, and decided to combine this interest with my art through the illustration of children's books."

Weir cowrote *Panther Dream* with her older brother, Bob Weir, the singer and rhythm guitarist for the rock band The Grateful Dead. Like his sister, Bob Weir is also involved in rainforest preservation and other environmental causes. In September, 1988, the Dead played a rainforest benefit concert at Madison Square Garden in New York City. Weir then approached her brother about the possibility of collaborating on a children's book.

"I talked to my brother . . . and asked if he wanted to continue educating people about the environment by producing a children's book and tape about the rainforest," she said. "We would write it together; I would illustrate it, and he would do the music and narration. He thought it was a great idea, and we started work on it immediately."

Weir explained that eighteen percent of the world's tropical rainforests are located in Africa. "We did extensive research on the animals . . . and the interrelationship of the Bantu farmers and the Mbuti pygmies who reside in this region. . . . The book and tape were designed not only to entertain, but to educate, and they were created in a manner that would appeal to the imagination of both normal and learning disabled children. This latter aspect is extremely important to us since Bob is severely dyslexic, and he wanted to teach children about the beauty and diversity of life in a way that would reach them on many levels."

*   *   *

WEISSER, Michael R. 1944-

PERSONAL: Born August 19, 1944, in Washington, DC; married September 3, 1966; wife's name, Susan; children:

Cybele, Amanda, William. *Education:* City College of New York, B.A., 1967; received M.A.; Northwestern University Ph.D., 1972.

ADDRESSES: Agent—Raphael Sagalyn, 1520 New Hampshire Ave., N.W., Washington, D.C. 20036.

CAREER: City College of New York, New York City, assistant professor of history, 1971-75; University of Southern Carolina, Columbia, associate professor of history, beginning in 1976; New York University, New York City, director of development; writer. Visiting assistant professor at University of California, Berkeley, 1975-76.

MEMBER: Society of Spanish and Portuguese History Studies.

WRITINGS:

The Peasants of the Montes, University of Chicago Press, 1977.
Crime and Criminality in Europe, Harvester, 1978.
A Brotherhood of Memory: Jewish Landsmanshaftn in the New World, Basic Books, 1985.

SIDELIGHTS: Michael R. Weisser is a historian who has taught at such institutions as City College of New York and the University of Southern Carolina. Among his writings is *The Peasants of the Montes,* a history of the rural people who inhabited a desolate region in south central Spain—lying between Toledo and Ciudad Real—in the sixteenth and seventeenth centuries. Using surviving historical archives of the period, Weisser interpreted the characteristic lifestyle and town-country relationships between the agrarian area of the Montes de Toledo and the surrounding life in urban Castile. Weisser "documents with chilling figures the sharp inequalities of wealth in his villages, and shows us how a small group of families dominated village life," wrote reviewer J. H. Elliott in *Times Literary Supplement.* Although Elliott found some information to be "fragmentary," he deemed *The Peasants of the Montes* "fluently written" and added that it is "fresh and interesting."

Weisser is also author of *A Brotherhood of Memory: Jewish Landsmanshaftn in the New World,* an account of Jewish efforts to maintain their cultural heritage after relocation to the United States in the nineteenth and twentieth centuries. Some settlers who joined these societies found the *shtetl,* or village mentality, to be restrictive; however, those who remained worked toward helping victims of European pogroms and the Holocaust. Irving Abrahamson asserted in *Chicago Tribune Book World* that "Weisser is a perceptive teller of their tale."

BIOGRAPHICAL/CRITICAL SOURCES:

PERIODICALS

Chicago Tribune Book World, September 29, 1985, p. 40.
Times Literary Supplement, August 5, 1977, p. 956; August 8, 1986, p. 858.

*   *   *

WEITZEL, William (Frederick)   1936-

PERSONAL: Born August 4, 1936, in Baltimore, MD; son of William Frederick (a mechanical engineer) and Margaret Anna (a homemaker; maiden name, Roeder) Weitzel; married Pauline Elizabeth Nesmith (a homemaker), August 9, 1957; children: William Frederick, Reta Louise. *Education:* Wheaton College, Wheaton, IL, B.A., 1961; University of Illinois at Urbana-Champaign, M.A., 1963; Wayne State University, Ph.D., 1966. *Religion:* Methodist. *Avocational Interests:* Golf, tennis, reading.

ADDRESSES: Home—3910 Ridgeline Dr., Norman, OK 73072. *Office*—College of Business Administration, 206 Adams Hall, University of Oklahoma, Norman, OK 73019.

CAREER: University of Minnesota—Twin Cities, Minneapolis, assistant professor of business administration, 1966-71; Target Stores, Minneapolis, vice-president of human resources, 1971-73; University of Minnesota—Twin Cities, associate professor of business administration, 1973-78; University of Oklahoma, Norman, professor of business administration, 1978-80; KPMG Peat Marwick, Chicago, IL, senior manager and elected principal, 1981-83; University of Oklahoma, Norman, OK, professor of business administration, 1983—. William Weitzel, Inc., owner, president, and management consultant and trainer, 1966—; Harold's Stores, Inc., member of board of directors and of audit, comprehensive, and planning committee, 1989—. *Military service:* U.S. Navy, petty officer, 1954-57.

MEMBER: Academy of Management, American Psychological Association, Beta Gamma Sigma, Chi Gamma Iota, Phi Kappa Phi.

WRITINGS:

(With J. W. McLean) *Leadership: Magic, Myth, or Method?,* AMACOM, 1992.

Contributor of more than fifty articles to business and administration journals.

WORK IN PROGRESS: Profile of a Leader, with J. W. McLean; research on leadership in the contemporary managerial role, on higher educational performance and redesign of the educational process, and on corporate turnarounds, comparing those in Western Europe with those in the United States.

SIDELIGHTS: William Weitzel told *CA:* "I began my writing career as an assistant professor at the University of Minnesota. After fifty-five papers for fellow academics, I decided to find a better way to communicate my ideas so a larger audience might find them of interest. That is when I tried writing a book for those who care less about assiduous documentation and more about understanding how research may be applied to practical and important issues. This led to my book *Leadership: Magic, Myth, or Method?* Now that the book has gone through several printings, my co-author J. W. McLean and I are preparing another book about the value and traits of leaders.

"We researched the lives of a number of acknowledged leaders in different vocations. Next we plan to look at what a large number of business managers think leadership is today. Some of my recent research shows that leadership behavior has changed in the last five years. From this research, we will present our understanding of the cardinal values and traits which successful leaders possess. In addition, we will document the uniqueness which also characterizes the actions of successful leaders. Our message is that 'one can do it his or her way, if one incorporates the fundamental values and traits with a unique presentation of the self as a leader of others.'

"I enjoy and have been influenced by writers who can, with conviction, present their ideas clearly, and yet seem accepting of different viewpoints from their own. Perhaps this is why I enjoy interpretive writing more than the academic presentation of research findings.

"While the leadership book is only written in American English, I have found that native-speaking Germans, Swiss, Dutch, Swedish, and Czech managers, for whom English is a second language, also seem to enjoy the book. Some of their questions, however, have made me much more careful about the use of typically American illustrations and figures of speech. Hopefully, my co-author and I will address this aspect of writing with greater care in our next book."

*   *   *

WEKESSER, Carol A. 1963-

PERSONAL: Born April 10, 1963, in Omaha, NE; daughter of Owen Vincent (an insurance analyst) and Hazel Leona (a bookkeeper; maiden name, Kirchenwitz) Winchell; married Michael Lee Wekesser (an architect), December 28, 1985; children: Grant Michael. *Education:*

University of Nebraska-Lincoln, B.A., 1985. *Politics:* Democrat. *Religion:* Lutheran.

ADDRESSES: Home—4861 Glenwood, #7, Mission, KS 66202.

CAREER: Curriculum Concepts, San Diego, CA, book editor, 1988-1990; Greenhaven Press, San Diego, senior editor, 1990-93; free-lance writer and editor, 1993—.

WRITINGS:

EDITOR; PUBLISHED BY GREENHAVEN PRESS

America's Children, 1991.
The Death Penalty, 1991.
America's Defense, 1991.
Africa, 1991.
(With others) *Sexual Harassment*, 1992.
(With others) *Europe*, 1992.
American Foreign Policy, 1993.
(With others) *The Breakup of the Soviet Union*, 1993.
Alcoholism, 1993.

WORK IN PROGRESS: The Supreme Court, Lucent Press.

*   *   *

WEST, Dorothy 1907-

PERSONAL: Born June 2, 1907, in Boston, MA; daughter of Isaac Christopher and Rachel West. *Education:* Privately tutored, attended public schools and Girl's Latin School; studied journalism, philosophy at Columbia University; attended Boston University.

CAREER: Novelist, editor, short story writer. Founded *Challenge* magazine; worked as relief investigator in Harlem during 1930s; worked on Federal Writers Project.

WRITINGS:

The Living Is Easy (novel), Houghton Mifflin, 1948.

Contributor of short stories to anthologies, including *The Best Short Stories by Negro Writers: An Anthology from 1899 to the Present*, edited by Langston Hughes, Little, Brown, 1967; *Harlem: Voices from the South of Black America*, New American Library, 1970. Contributor to *Saturday Evening Quill, Opportunity, Messenger*, and *Black World*.

SIDELIGHTS: Dorothy West's creations include a well-received novel and dozens of short stories. The literary magazine she founded during the 1930s, *Challenge* (and later *New Challenge*), brought into focus the great talent of the Harlem Renaissance by publishing the work of her friends and colleagues: Langston Hughes, Countee Cullen, Richard Wright, Arna Bontemps, Zora Neale Hurston, Wallace Thurman, and Claude McKay.

West was an only child, the daughter of an ex-slave who became a successful Boston businessman. Early tutoring at home nurtured her literary talent, and her first short story, "Promise and Fulfillment," was published by the *Boston Post* when she was still a youngster. The newspaper had contests for the best stories each week, and she became a regular winner. West submitted a piece to *Opportunity*'s competition and won, with her poet cousin Helene Johnson, second place and a trip to the awards banquet in New York City. West's story, "The Typewriter," was published in 1926, and it was viewed as an auspicious beginning for a young author.

Critics have compared West's narrative style to that of Russian author Fyodor Dostoyevsky, the author of, among other noted works, *Crime and Punishment* and *The Brothers Karamazov*. Like Dostoyevsky, West probes deeply into the minds of her characters, who face "moral, psychological and social confinement," wrote SallyAnn H. Ferguson in the *Dictionary of Literary Biography* (*DLB*). West also shares a belief in the innocent nature of children, much as the Russian novelist's work reflects.

West lived in New York City and stayed at the YWCA until a fellowship made her residence more secure. It was in New York that she was embraced by a circle of literary intellectuals, including H. L. Mencken, who were beginning to recognize the wealth of talent among black writers. West gained an agent but remained relatively obscure, referring to herself, as quoted in *DLB*, as "the best-known unknown writer of the time." For a time, she dappled in theater, performing a bit part in *Porgy and Bess*. It was writing, however, that remained her central focus. Toward the late 1920s, West's friendships with other leading black writers developed, including one with novelist and editor Wallace Thurman, whom West described in *DLB* as "the most symbolic figure of the Literary Renaissance in Harlem." A group of literary standouts, including West, Langston Hughes, and twenty other blacks, sailed to Russia in 1932 to film *Black and White*, a story of the oppression of American blacks. The project was dropped following accusations of association with Communism.

Despite the movie's demise, West remained in Russia with Hughes. Opinions vary on whether the two were romantically involved. West would propose to Hughes in a 1933 letter, but they were never to marry. West stayed in Russia nearly a year under a film contract before learning of her father's death, upon which time she returned to the United States. Once back in America, West felt guilty for not having written more (at age twenty-five), so she put together the first issue of *Challenge* with forty dollars. The periodical was published quarterly for only a few years, but it

contained the best of black literature at the time—the works of Hughes, Bontemps, McKay, Hurston, and her cousin Helene Johnson. In an effort to maintain a high calibre of writing, however, many of the submissions from young and unknown writers were not included. In this respect, West was accused of creating too tame a voice for the black writer, of not taking a chance on the new and innovative literature that was being created in the black community.

When the periodical failed in 1937, a more ambitious version, edited by Richard Wright, was launched. *New Challenge*, however, faced the same financial dilemmas as the original journal had, and it soon folded. West gained work as a welfare investigator, which inspired "Mammy," a story published in *Opportunity* in 1940. She then participated in the Federal Writers' Project until it ended in the mid-1940s, writing numerous short stories which, for the most part, went unpublished.

West's 1948 novel, *The Living Is Easy*, is a semi-autobiographical account depicting, as Ferguson described it in *DLB*, "the economic and psychological prisons upwardly-mobile blacks create for themselves by pursuing false values." The story's central figure is Cleo Judson, a neurotic beauty who marries an older, financially secure man. She then invites her three sisters and their husbands to live with them, leading to the demise of all their marriages. Some critics speculate that the novel is loosely based on the experiences of West's mother, who came from a family of twenty-two children.

Reviewing *The Living Is Easy*, Seymour Krim wrote in the *New York Times* that "the important thing about the book is its abundant and special woman's energy and beat." *Commonweal*'s Florence Codman praised West's Cleo Judson as "the predatory female on the loose, a wholly plausible, tantalizing creature." Reviewing the reissued novel in *Ms.*, Susan McHenry compared West's social commentary to that of Theodore Dreiser and Sinclair Lewis and called the author "a brisk storyteller with an eye for ironic detail." In a 1987 review of the book in the *Times Literary Supplement*, Holly Eley commented that "West's sensitive investigation of issues such as miscegenation, racial heritage and colour consciousness . . . is extremely relevant today." West has lived in semi-retirement in Massachusetts, lecturing occasionally and continuing to write short stories. Critics and afficionados hope to read more of her creations, many of which remain unpublished to this day.

BIOGRAPHICAL/CRITICAL SOURCES:

BOOKS

Dictionary of Literary Biography, Volume 76: *Afro-American Writers, 1940-1955*, Gale, 1988, pp. 187-95.

Harlem Renaissance and Beyond, G. K. Hall, 1990, pp. 343-46.

PERIODICALS

Commonweal, June 25, 1948.
Ms., March 1982, pp. 37-38.
New York Times, May 16, 1948, p. 5.
Times Literary Supplement, April 17, 1987, p. 410.*

*   *   *

WETTIG, Gerhard 1934-

PERSONAL: Born February 17, 1934, in Gelnhausen, Germany; son of Hermann (a clerk) and Kaethe (a teacher; maiden name, Leiske) Wettig; married Heide Wallowy (a family therapist), April 12, 1962; children: Andreas, Friedmunt, Tobias, Hannes. *Education:* Attended universities of Tuebingen, Freiburg, and Leeds; received Ph.D. from University of Goettingen. *Religion:* Protestant.

ADDRESSES: Home—Ringstrasse 51, D-5000 Cologne 71, Germany. *Office*—Federal Institute for East European and International Studies, Lindenbornstrasse 22, D-5000 Cologne 30, Germany.

CAREER: Historical-Political Commission of the Evangelical Research Corporation, Heidelberg, Germany, research associate, 1961-62; German Society for Foreign Affairs, Bonn, Germany, research staff member, 1962-66; Federal Institute for East European and International Studies, Cologne, Germany, senior research staff member, 1966-88, director of international relations and international security research, 1989—.

MEMBER: Deutsches Strategic-Forum, Deutsche Gesellschaft fuer Osteuropakunde, Wilson Center European Alumni Association.

AWARDS, HONORS: Prize of the German Association for the Promotion of International Conflict Research, 1989.

WRITINGS:

Entmilitarisierung und Wiederbewaffnung in Deutschland 1943-55: Internationale Auseinandersetzungen um die Rolle der Deutschen in Europa, Oldenburg (Munich), 1967.
Die Rolle der russischen Armee im revolutionaeren Machtkampf 1917: Forschungen zur osteuropaeischen Geschichte, Band 12 (West Berlin), 1967.
Politik im Rampenlicht: Aktionweisen moderner Aussenpolitik, Fischer Buecherei (Frankfurt), 1967.
Europaeische Sicherheit: Das europaeische Staatensystem in der sowjetischen Aussenpolitik 1966-72, Bertelsmann Universitaetsverlag (Duesseldorf), 1972.

Deutschlandpolitischen Interessen der Sowjetunion und der Deutsche Demokratische Republik, Bundesinstitut fuer Ostwissenschaftliche und Internationale Studien (Cologne-Ehrenfeld), 1972-73, translation by Edwina Moreton and Hannes Adomeit published as *Community and Conflict in the Socialist Camp: The Soviet Union, the German Democratic Republic, and the German Problem, 1965-72,* St. Martin's, 1975.
Der Kampf um die freie Nachricht, Edition Interfrom (Zuerich), 1975.
Frieden und Sicherheit in Europa: Problem der KSZE und der MBFR, Seewald Verlag (Stuttgart), 1975.
Broadcasting and Detente: Eastern Policies and Their Implication for East-West Relations, St. Martin's, 1977.
Die Sowjetunion, die Deutsche Demokratische Republik und die Deutschland-Frage 1965-76, Verlag Bonn Aktuell (Stuttgart), 1977.
Konflikt und Kooperation zwischen Ost und West: Entspannung in Theorie und Praxis: Ausses- und sicherheitspolitische Analyse, Osang Verlag (Bonn), 1981.
(Editor and contributor) *Die sowjetischen Sicherheitsvorstellungen und die Moeglichkeiten eines Ost-West-Einvernehmens, Osteuropa und der internationale Kommunismus 12,* Nomos Verlag (Baden-Baden), 1981.
Das Vier-Maechte-Abkommen in der Bewaehrungsprobe: Berlin im Spannungsfeld zwischen Ost und West, Berlin Verlag, 1982.
Umstrittene Sicherheit: Friedenswahrung und Ruestungsbegrenzung in Europa, Berlin Verlag (West Berlin), 1982.
(With Phillip A. Petersen and John G. Hines) *Sicherheit ueber Alles!: Krieg und Frieden in sowjetischer Sicht,* Markus (Cologne), 1986.
Alternativen der Sicherheit: Konzepte und Modelle, Schriftenreihe Innere Fuehrung, Bundesministerium der Verteidigung (Bonn), 1986.
(With Manfred Goertemaker) *USA—UdSSR: Dokumente zur Sicherheitspolitik,* Niedersachsisches Landeszentrale fuer Politische Bildung (Hannover), 1986.
Gorbatschow auf Lenin-Kurs? Dokumente zur neuen sowjetischen Politik, Rheinau-Verlag (Cologne), 1988.
Soviet Foreign Policy under Gorbachev: New Political Thinking and Its Impact, Institute for European Defence and Stategic Studies (London), 1988, State Mutual Book and Periodical Service Ltd., 1990.
High Road, Low Road: Diplomacy and Public Action in Soviet Foreign Policy (A Special Study from the Kennan Institute for Advanced Russian Studies, Woodrow Wilson International Center for Scholars, Washington, DC), Brassey's, 1989.

(Editor) *Die sowjetsche Militaermacht und die Stabilitaet in Europa, Osteuropa und der internationale Kommunismus 19,* Nomos Verlag, 1990.

Changes in Soviet Policy towards the West, Westview Press, 1991.

Nation und Konflikt in Osteuropa nach dem Zusammenbruch des Kommunismus, Bundesinstituts fuer Ostwissenschaftliche und Internationale Studien, 1992.

Russland und Deutschland in einem neuen System der europaischen Sicherheit, Bundesinstituts fuer Ostwissenschaftliche und Internationale Studien, 1992.

Work represented in numerous series on international relations, including *Berichte des Bundesinstitut fuer Ostwissenschaftliche und Internationale Studien,* 1966—. Acting editor of both German and English-language editions of *Aussenpolitik,* 1990—.

WORK IN PROGRESS: Studies on the interrelationship between domestic politics and foreign policies in Russia, the relations between successor states of the former Soviet Union, and the Soviet contribution to German unification. Researching selective problems of both East German-Soviet relations and the German problem, 1947-1990.

SIDELIGHTS: Gerhard Wettig told *CA:* "Being both a modern historian and a political scientist by training, I have devoted my research effort to these two fields of interest, primarily to the extent that the problem of German partition and unity and equally foreign policy and international security developments in Eastern Europe (including the former Soviet Union and its successor states) after 1945 are concerned. Analysis extended beyond the classical realms of interstate relations: unconventional dimensions of the countries' performance vis-a-vis the outside world such as policies on border-transgressing media activities (e.g., foreign journalists and international broadcasting) or the mixed covert-public type of 'societal' action abroad characteristic of communist regimes (which culminated in the 1979-83 struggle against the North Atlantic Treaty Organization's policies in what now appears as a desperate last effort to gain the upper hand) have been included as well. Also, focus has been directed on the foreign policy implications of domestic politics, attitudes toward human rights, control structures of a given country, ideological mindframes, and the like.

"I see a particularly important task in analyzing the new evidence on the implications of the communist system on managing the external affairs of the former East Germany and the former Soviet Union and to bring home this impact on future generations so as to immunize them against utopias of a communist and similar variety. Historical errors must not be repeated. At the same time, I feel it is both fascinating and relevant to study the effects of communist deformation and communist structures in the countries of the former Soviet orbit, notably in the eastern part of my German homeland where democracy will have to cope with this heritage for a long time to come. It is on this basis that my research work may tend to focus more on recent history, i.e., 1947-88 relations with the former Soviet and East German states, than on current East European affairs in the longer run."

*   *   *

WHEELOCK, David C. 1960-

PERSONAL: Born July 12, 1960, in Ames, IA; son of Thomas D. (a professor) and Edra (a homemaker; maiden name, Smith) Wheelock. *Education:* Iowa State University, B.S., 1982; University of Illinois at Urbana-Champaign, M.S., 1984, Ph.D., 1987.

ADDRESSES: Home—St. Louis, MO. *Office*—Federal Reserve Bank of St. Louis, P.O. Box 442, St. Louis, MO 63166.

CAREER: University of Texas at Austin, Austin, assistant professor, 1987-93; Federal Reserve Bank of St. Louis, St. Louis, MO, visiting scholar, 1991-93, senior economist, 1993—.

MEMBER: American Economic Association, Cliometrics Society, Economic History Association.

AWARDS, HONORS: Allan Nevins Prize, Economic History Association, 1988.

WRITINGS:

The Strategy and Consistency of Federal Reserve Monetary Policy, 1924-1933, Cambridge University Press, 1991.

WORK IN PROGRESS: Research on United States monetary and financial history.

*   *   *

WHITE, David Manning 1917-1993

OBITUARY NOTICE—See index for *CA* sketch: Born June 28, 1917, in Milwaukee, WI; died of complications following heart surgery, December 17, 1993, in Richmond, VA. Educator, publisher, and author. White helped coin the term "mass culture," paving the way for universities worldwide to develop curricula on popular arts and culture. A professor of journalism at Boston College, beginning in 1949, and of mass communication at Virginia Commonwealth University, beginning in 1975, White authored or edited numerous volumes on television, film, radio, cartoons and other examples of pop culture. He also served as an occasional correspondent to NBC-TV news and to National Public Radio (NPR), and as the editor-in-chief of *Television Quarterly*. White had been the general editor of the Beacon Press contemporary communication series since 1966, and after his retirement from academia in 1982, he became the president of the Marlborough House Publishing Company. He wrote *Pop Cult in America*, coauthored *Journalism in the Mass Media* and *The Celluloid Weapon: Social Comment in the American Film*, and coedited *Mass Culture: The Popular Arts in America* and *The Funnies: An American Idiom*.

OBITUARIES AND OTHER SOURCES:

BOOKS

Who's Who in America, 46th edition, Marquis, 1990.

PERIODICALS

Washington Post, December 21, 1993, p. C9.

*   *   *

WHITE, Geoffrey M.   1949-

PERSONAL: Born November 11, 1949, in Bridgeport, CT; son of Stephen Theodore (an engineer) and Marjorie Elizabeth (a homemaker) White; married Nancy Ann Montgomery (a teacher and artist), June 17, 1978; children: Michael. *Education:* Princeton University, B.A., 1971; University of California, San Diego, M.A., 1973, Ph.D., 1978. *Religion:* Agnostic.

ADDRESSES: Home—3009 Loomis St., Honolulu, HI 96822. *Office*—Program for Cultural Studies, East-West Center, Honolulu, HI 96848.

CAREER: East-West Center, Honolulu, HI, research associate, 1978-92, senior fellow and director of Program for Cultural Studies, 1992—. University of Hawaii at Manoa, affiliate graduate faculty, 1980—; University of California, San Diego, visiting lecturer, 1985-86.

MEMBER: American Anthropological Association, Association for Social Anthropology in Oceania (member of board of directors, 1984-86), American Ethnological Society, Society for Psychological Anthropology (member of board of directors, 1988-90), Society for Cultural Anthropology.

AWARDS, HONORS: Stirling Prize in Psychological Anthropology, American Anthropological Association, 1977; Masayoshi Ohira Memorial Prize, 1992, for *The Pacific Theater: Island Representations of World War II*; grants from Wenner-Gren Foundation for Anthropological Research, Social Science Research Council, National Science Foundation, National Endowment for the Humanities, and Hawaii Committee for the Humanities.

WRITINGS:

(Editor with A. J. Marsella) *Cultural Conceptions of Mental Health and Therapy*, D. Reidel, 1982.
(Editor with J. Kirkpatrick, and contributor) *Person, Self, and Experience: Exploring Pacific Ethno-Psychologies*, University of California Press, 1985.
(With F. Kokhonigita and H. Pulomana) *Cheke Holo Dictionary*, Australian National University, 1988.
(Editor with D. Gegeo, D. Akin, and K. Watson-Gegeo) *The Big Death: Solomon Islanders Remember World War II*, Institute of Pacific Studies, University of the South Pacific, 1988.
(Editor with Lamont Lindstrom, and contributor) *The Pacific Theater: Island Representations of World War II*, University of Hawaii Press, 1989.
(With Lindstrom) *Island Encounters: Black and White Memories of the Pacific War*, Smithsonian Institution Press, 1990.
(Editor with Watson-Gegeo, and contributor) *Disentangling: Conflict Discourse in Pacific Societies*, Stanford University Press, 1990.
Identity Through History: Living Stories in a Solomon Islands Society, Cambridge University Press, 1991.
(Editor with T. Schwartz and C. Lutz, and contributor) *New Directions in Psychological Anthropology*, Cambridge University Press, 1992.

Work represented in books, including *The Handbook of Emotion*, edited by M. Lewis and J. Haviland, Guilford, 1993; *Artistic Heritage of a Changing Pacific*, edited by P. Dark and R. Rose, Crawford House Press, 1993; and *Emotion and Culture*, edited by S. Kitayama and H. Markus, American Psychological Association, 1994. Contributor of articles and reviews to anthropology journals. Co-editor of *'O'O: Journal of Solomon Islands Studies*, number 4, 1988, and *Anthropological Forum*, Volume VI, number 4, 1993. Member of editorial board, *Contemporary Pacific*, 1987—, and *Ethos: Journal of the Society for Psychological Anthropology*, 1990—.

WORK IN PROGRESS: The life history of the bishop and paramount chief of the island of Santa Isabel, Solomon Islands; research on memories of the Pacific War, with a book expected to result.

SIDELIGHTS: Geoffrey M. White told *CA:* "Like many cultural anthropologists writing today, my work is motivated by an interest in problems of representation across cultural and geographic spaces marked by signs of difference. In addition to the small pleasures of field work and the process of learning and discovery that comes with the work of anthropology, the field is made more exciting than ever by shifting boundaries and methods of cultural study. Working in an institution devoted to interdisciplinary and international modes of work has offered a useful vantage point from which to resist the crust that often builds up around the received orthodoxies of established disciplines. At the moment, my research and writing is wrestling with the transition from research in small-scale Pacific Islands communities to research in mass-mediated American society. This promises an unending line of new problems and adjustments to ethnographic method."

* * *

WHITE, George Abbott 1943-

PERSONAL: Born August 28, 1943, in Chester, PA. *Education:* University of Michigan, A.B. (with honors), 1966; graduate study at Brandeis University, 1966-70, and Harvard University, 1972-74. *Politics:* Socialist. *Religion:* Episcopalian.

ADDRESSES: Agent—IMG—Julian Bach Literary Agency, 22 East 71st St., New York, NY 10021.

CAREER: Clinical psychologist, Boston, MA, 1971—; writer. Harvard University, instructor, 1969, keeper of Matthiessen Room.

MEMBER: Signet Society, Norwich Terrier Club.

AWARDS, HONORS: Woodrow Wilson fellowship, 1966; Danforth graduate fellowship, 1966-70.

WRITINGS:

(Editor with Charles Newman) *Literature in Revolution,* Holt, 1972.
(Editor) *Simone Weil: Interpretations of a Life,* University of Massachusetts Press, 1981.
(With John D. Stoeckle) *Plain Pictures of Plain Doctoring,* Massachusetts Institute of Technology Press, 1985.

Contributor to periodicals, including *Catholic Worker, Commonweal, Cross Currents, Harvard Medical Bulletin, Massachusetts Review, Quarterly Review, Sewanee Review, Southern Exposure,* and *Studies in Visual Communication.* Editor of the four-volume "Generation New Poets" series, University of Michigan Press, 1964-66, and *Simone Weil: Live Like Her?,* 1976. Guest editor of *TriQuarterly,* 1972; associate editor of *Cross Currents.*

WORK IN PROGRESS: Solo in the Void: F. O. Matthiessen and the Search for Self in America; editing *The FBI as Literary Historian.*

SIDELIGHTS: George Abbott White is a clinical psychologist who has also edited various essay collections relating to literature, politics, and philosophy. Among his best-known books is *Literature in Revolution,* which he edited with Charles Newman. Reviewer Robert Gorham Davis described this volume in the *New York Times Book*

Review as an "honest, contradictory, provocative collection of essays." Among the critics contributing to *Literature in Revolution* are Harry Levin, Noam Chomsky, Leo Marx, and Conor Cruise O'Brien; novelists also contribute essays to the anthology, notably Carlos Fuentes and Marge Piercy. J. D. O'Hara commented in the *Washington Post Book World* that readers "are offered some good scholarly essays," including "an excellent essay by Aileen Ward on [William] Blake."

White also served as editor of *Simone Weil: Interpretations of a Life,* a collection of writings by the controversial philosopher who—according to Jean Bethke Elshtain in the *Nation*—was "a trenchant critic of Marxism, a mystic who experienced Christ's presence, an intellectual who turned her icy disdain upon intellectuals and academics who live apart from the masses and yet believe themselves ordained to prescribe for them." Elshtain concluded that *Simone Weil* offers readers "a good opportunity for reflecting" on "so stringent a moral conscience."

In collaboration with John Stoeckle, a professor of medicine at Harvard University, White authored *Plain Pictures of Plain Doctoring.* The book presents eighty photographs of doctors and patients chosen from thousands commissioned by the Farm Security Administration during the Depression; White and Stoeckle provide commentary on the photos, which range from "scenes that appear to have been stolen from Norman Rockwell" to certain "haunting images," according to John G. Deaton in the *New York Times Book Review.*

BIOGRAPHICAL/CRITICAL SOURCES:

PERIODICALS

Nation, January 1, 1973, pp. 23-24; May 29, 1982, pp. 661-62.
New York Times Book Review, January 14, 1973, p. 21; October 13, 1985, p. 24.
Washington Post Book World, December 3, 1972, p. 25.

* * *

WHITE, Tim D. 1950-

PERSONAL: Born August 24, 1950, in Los Angeles, CA; son of Robert Julian and Georgia (Johnson) White. *Education:* University of California, Riverside, B.A., 1972; Received B.S., M.A., and Ph.D. from University of Michigan. *Politics:* "Darwinism." *Religion:* "Darwinism."

ADDRESSES: Office—Department of Anthropology, University of California, Berkeley, Berkeley, CA 94720-0001.

CAREER: University of California, Berkeley, professor of anthropology, 1977—.

MEMBER: American Association for the Advancement of Science, Society of Vertebrate Paleontology.

WRITINGS:

Human Osteology, Academic Press, 1991.
Prehistoric Cannibalism at Mancos SMTUMR-2346, Princeton University Press, 1992.

WORK IN PROGRESS: Paleoanthropological research on human origins in Africa.

* * *

WHITELAW, Nancy 1933-

PERSONAL: Born August 29, 1933, in New Bedford, MA; daughter of Joseph Eaton (a furniture store manager) and Mildred (a furniture store manager; maiden name, Pehrson) Eaton; married David Whitelaw (a farmer), 1955; children: Katherine Whitelaw-Barrett, Patricia Whitelaw-Hurley. *Education:* Tufts University, B.A., 1954; University of Buffalo, M.Ed., 1968. *Avocational Interests:* Grass-roots politics, volunteering in local mayor's office.

ADDRESSES: Home—3212 Salisbury Rd., Jamestown, NY 14701.

CAREER: Malden Schools, Malden, MA, teacher, 1954-55; Amerikan Kiz Koleji, Izmir, Turkey, teacher, 1955-58; Amherst public school system, Amherst, NY, teacher, 1968-88; Institute of Children's Literature, instructor, 1988—.

MEMBER: American Society of Journalists and Authors, Society of Children's Book Writers and Illustrators.

WRITINGS:

A Beautiful Pearl, Whitman, 1990.
Charles de Gaulle, Dillon/Macmillan, 1991.
Theodore Roosevelt Takes Charge, Whitman, 1992.
Joseph Stalin, Dillon/Macmillan, 1992.

Also contributor to newspapers and periodicals, including *Christian Science Monitor, USA Today,* and *Sail.*

WORK IN PROGRESS: A biography of Margaret Sanger; researching the life of Grace Murray Hopper, a computer "genius" and the first female rear admiral in the U.S. Navy.

SIDELIGHTS: Nancy Whitelaw was inspired to begin writing when she visited a school to observe its reading program. As a reading teacher, she was astonished to find that the children were not reading books. She watched as the children read brief stories and articles printed on little cardboard cards. When they finished they turned the cards over to answer the questions on the back. After checking their answers, they took another card and continued. "They reminded me of supermarket cashiers who read prices, record numbers, make change, and then greet the next customer," Whitelaw commented. "My disgust exploded in short angry bursts which became lines of a poem."

Whitelaw published that first poem in an educational journal and became hooked when she saw the words "by Nancy Whitelaw" in print. Quickly she "threw together" articles based on ideas which she had gathered during her years of teaching experiences and sent them to educational magazines. Thirty rejections later she decided to get help and signed up for several writing courses in adult education school. "I soaked up all the information I could get from other writers," she stated. Soon she began to sell articles not only to the educational magazines, but also to other magazine markets, such as *Christian Science Monitor, USA Today,* and *Sail.*

Spurred by her love of reading to children, Whitelaw then began writing for children. Because of her love for learning about people she is concentrating on writing biographies. "I am hooked on writing for young people," she concluded.

* * *

WHITMAN, Alice
See MARKER, Sherry

* * *

WIDDOWS, P(aul) F. 1918-

PERSONAL: Born August 5, 1918, in London, England; son of A. E. (a civil servant) and Margharita (Defries) Widdows; married April 5, 1958; wife's name, Huguette (died April 26, 1975). *Education:* Hertford College, Oxford, B.A., 1948; University of Chicago, Ph.D., 1967. *Politics:* Liberal. *Religion:* None.

ADDRESSES: Home—23 Burton Ave., Montreal, Quebec, Canada H3Z 1J6.

CAREER: Teacher of classics at schools in England, until 1951, and in Ontario and Montreal, Quebec, 1951-58; Sir George Williams University, Montreal, began as assistant professor, became professor of classics, 1958-78; Concordia University, Montreal, professor of classics, 1978-82.

WRITINGS:

TRANSLATOR

Selected Poems of Emile Nelligan, Ryerson Press, 1960.

Lucan's Civil War, Indiana University Press, 1988.
The Fables of Phaedrus, University of Texas Press, 1992.

WORK IN PROGRESS: Translating Horace's *Odes, Epodes,* and *Satires.*

* * *

WILLIAMS, Donna 1963-

PERSONAL: Born in 1963 in Australia.

ADDRESSES: Agent—A. P. Watt, 20 John St., London W1N 2DR, England.

CAREER: Writer.

WRITINGS:

Nobody Nowhere: The Extraordinary Autobiography of an Autistic, Times Books, 1992.
Somebody Somewhere, Times Books, 1994.

SIDELIGHTS: Donna Williams is author of *Nobody Nowhere: The Extraordinary Autobiography of an Autistic,* in which she tells of her lifelong battle with autism—a developmental disorder originating in infancy and characterized by self-absorption, repetitive and rigidly structured behavior, language dysfunction, and an inability to interact socially. Williams depicts in her book a world of disembodied color, pattern, and sound. At times she would madly rub her eyes and withdraw into "bright spots of fluffy color," attempting to escape what she called the "intrusive gabble" of other people. Torn between a dread of physical contact and a desire for emotional connection, Williams would often beat herself then assume a fetal position. "Hurting herself," as *New York Times Book Review* contributor Daniel Goleman relates, "or doing shocking things . . . were ways to reassure herself that she did indeed exist."

Goleman explains that books such as Williams's provide a valuable insight into an unfamiliar world, "revealing to outsiders that what may seem bizarre and unpredictable follows its own internal logic, however strange." Writing for the *Los Angeles Times Book Review,* Chris Goodrich found that Williams "proves herself to be rigorously analytical and remarkably free of self-pity, despite a life fraught with fear, pain, and misunderstanding." *Nobody Nowhere* was written by Williams in her efforts to better understand her world. Only upon the advice of two therapists familiar with autism did Williams decide to publish her writings. Goleman noted that the work provides "a fascinating testimony to an intelligence undimmed by mental turmoil," while Goodrich proclaimed that "*Nobody Nowhere* is as brave a book as you'll ever read."

Williams told *CA:* "Autism is not a 'mental disorder' anymore than it is a communication, social, perceptual, or neurological disorder. It is a pervasive development disorder (PDD) affecting many areas of development. It is *not* a mental illness, nor is it synonymous with mental retardation."

BIOGRAPHICAL/CRITICAL SOURCES:

BOOKS

Williams, Donna, *Nobody Nowhere: The Extraordinary Autobiography of an Autistic,* Times Books, 1992.

PERIODICALS

Los Angeles Times Book Review, November 15, 1992, p. 6.
Maclean's, November 9, 1992, p. 102.
New York Times Book Review, February 21, 1993, p. 16.
USA Today, November 11, 1992, p. D1.

* * *

WILLIAMS, R(obert) J(oseph) P(aton) 1926-

PERSONAL: Born February 25, 1926, in Wallasey, England; son of Ernest Ivor (a customs officer) and Alice (a homemaker; maiden name, Roberts) Williams; married Jelly Klara Buchli (a translator), July 19, 1952; children: Timothy Ivor, John Matthew. *Education:* Merton College, Oxford, B.A., 1948, D.Phil., 1950. *Politics:* Liberal. *Religion:* None. *Avocational Interests:* "Walking in the high hills."

ADDRESSES: Home—115 Victoria Rd., Oxford OX2 7QG, England. *Office*—Wadham College, Oxford University, Oxford OX1 3QR, England.

CAREER: Oxford University, Oxford, England, junior research fellow at Merton College, 1951-55, fellow of Wadham College, 1955—, university lecturer, 1955-72, reader in chemistry, 1972-74, Royal Society Napier Research Professor, 1974-91, honorary fellow of Merton College, 1989, senior research fellow of Wadham College, 1991—. California Institute of Technology, Buchman Memorial Lecturer, 1972; Princeton University, distinguished visiting lecturer, 1976; Indiana University—Bloomington, Frank C. Mathers Lecturer, 1978; University of Toronto, distinguished visiting lecturer, 1980; University of Zurich, Commemoration Lecturer at Biochemistry Institute, 1981; Royal Society, Bakerian Lecturer, 1981; University of Newfoundland, distinguished visiting lecturer, 1983; Dalhousie University, Walter J. Chute Lecturer, 1984; University of Norwich, Katritsky Lecturer, 1986; Pennsylvania State University, Chermeda Lecturer, 1986; University of Lund, Sunner Memorial Lecturer, 1986; Swedish Academy, A. Scheele Memorial Lecturer, 1986; University of Sussex, Alan Johnson Memorial Lecturer, 1987;

University of London, Drummond Lecturer in Biology, 1988, visiting professor at Royal Free Hospital, 1991—, Pewterers Lecturer, Institute of Neurology, 1992; University of Southern California, Stauffer Lecturer, 1990; Massachusetts Institute of Technology, Arthur D. Little Lecturer, 1991; University of Nottingham, Jesse Boot Lecturer, 1993; consultant to Unilever and Interox (Laporte).

MEMBER: Royal Society (fellow), Royal Chemical Society (president of Dalton Division, 1991-93), British Association for the Advancement of Science (president of Chemistry Section, 1985-86), Biochemical Society, National Trust, Biophysical Society, Royal Society of Science (Belgium; foreign member), Royal Swedish Academy of Science (foreign member), Lisbon Academy of Science (foreign member), Czechoslovakian Academy of Science (foreign member).

AWARDS, HONORS: Rotary International fellow in Uppsala, Sweden, 1950; Commonwealth fellow at Harvard Medical School, 1956-66; Tilden Medal, Chemical Society, 1970; Biochemical Society, Keilen Medal, 1972, Sir Frederick Gowland Hopkins Medal, 1989; Liversidge Medal, Royal Society of Chemistry, 1979; Hughes Medal, Royal Society, 1979; D.Sc., University of Liege, 1980; CLaire Brylants Medal, University of Louvain, 1980; Sir Hans Krebs Medal, European Biochemical Societies, 1985; D.Sc., University of Leicester, 1985; Copenhagen's Linderstrom-Lang Medal, 1986; Heyrovsky Medal, International Union of Biochemistry, 1988; D.Sc., University of East Anglia, 1992, and University of Keele, 1993.

WRITINGS:

(With C. S. G. Phillips) *Inorganic Chemistry,* two volumes, Oxford University Press, 1966.
(With R. E. Dwek, R. Richards, and I. D. Campbell) *NMR in Biology,* Academic Press, 1977.
(With J. J. R. Frausto da Silva) *New Trends in Bioinorganic Chemistry,* Academic Press, 1978.
(With J. R. R. Frausto da Silva) *The Biological Chemistry of the Elements,* Oxford University Press, 1991.

Contributor of more than five hundred articles to scientific journals. Editor, *European Journal of Biochemistry, Biochemica Biophysica Acta, Inorganic Biochemistry,* and *Structure and Bonding.*

SIDELIGHTS: R. J. P. Williams told *CA:* "I was a founder member of the Oxford Enzyme Group, which has devised many new methods using nuclear magnetic resonance (NMR) for the study of *in vitro* and *in vivo* biological systems. My major contributions concern metal ions and their function in biological systems. I proposed the general hypothesis of proton-driven adenosine triphosphate (ATP) formation, the Irving-Williams sequence of stability constants, the use of solvent gradients in chroma-

tography, and the entatic state of metals within proteins. Recently I have been engaged in the use of NMR in the study of metal/protein interactions, the analyses of the function of minerals in biology, and the way in which space is used in biological systems to enhance functional significance. A particular ongoing development is the analysis of mobility within proteins both in catalysis and signalling."

*   *   *

WILSON, John (Anthony) Burgess   1917-1993
(Anthony Burgess, Joseph Kell)

OBITUARY NOTICE—See index for *CA* sketch: Born February 25, 1917, in Moss Side, Manchester, England; died of cancer, November 25 (one source says 22), 1993, in London, England. Educator and writer. Wilson, a prolific author who wrote primarily under the name Anthony Burgess, was best known for his bleak 1963 work *A Clockwork Orange.* Set in a drug-laden society of the future, the novel revolves around Alex, a brutally violent gang leader, and examines themes of conformity and freedom. The subsequent film adaptation, directed by Stanley Kubrick in 1971, met with critical censure over its violence and eventually was removed from theaters. Wilson embarked on his literary career in the mid-1950s, after serving in the Education Corps of the British Army during the 1940s and later lecturing for the Ministry of Education and supervising a British grammar school. He published his first book, *Time for a Tiger,* in 1956 and began writing books in quick succession after 1959. In all he produced approximately sixty works—including novels, film scripts, plays, translations, and essays. Among his titles are *Inside Mr. Enderby* and *One Hand Clapping,* both under the pseudonym Joseph Kell; *English Literature: A Survey for Students,* under the name John Burgess Wilson; *This Man and Music; The End of the World News; The Kingdom of the Wicked; You've Had—You've Time; A Dead Man in Deptford; The Land Where the Ice Cream Grows;* and *Homage to Qwert Yuiop.* Wilson also composed numerous choral works, concertos, and operas. Beginning in the 1970s, he taught at such institutions as the University of North Carolina, and Princeton and Columbia universities.

OBITUARIES AND OTHER SOURCES:

BOOKS

Who's Who in the World, 11th edition, Marquis, 1992.

PERIODICALS

Chicago Tribune, November 26, 1993, section 3, p. 6; November 28, 1993, section 2, p. 8.
Los Angeles Times, November 26, 1993, p. A44.
New York Times, November 26, 1993, p. B23.

Times (London), November 26, 1993, p. 23.
Washington Post, November 26, 1993, p. C6.

*   *   *

WILSON, Louis E. 1939-

PERSONAL: Born March 1, 1939, in Longview, TX; son of Essie S. (a street maintenance worker) and Rebecca (a factory worker and domestic) Wilson; divorced; children: Bennett McKenzie, Mark Robert Kenneth. *Education:* Received B.A. and M.A. degrees; received Ph.D. from University of California, Los Angeles.

ADDRESSES: Office—Department of Afro-American Studies, Smith College, Northampton, MA 01063.

CAREER: Smith College, Northampton, MA, professor of Afro-American studies and head of department.

WRITINGS:

The Krobo People of Ghana to 1892, Ohio University Press, 1992.
To See a World (elementary school textbook), Houghton, 1993.
America Will Be (elementary school textbook), Houghton, 1993.
Across the Centuries (elementary school textbook), Houghton, 1993.
I Know a Place (elementary school textbook), Houghton, 1993.

WORK IN PROGRESS: African Americans and Indians in the American Revolution from Rhode Island; Free Blacks in Rhode Island: Two Narratives.

*   *   *

WISDOM, (Arthur) John (Terence Dibben) 1904-1993

OBITUARY NOTICE—See index for *CA* sketch: Born September 12, 1904, in London, England; died December 9, 1993, in Cambridge, England. Educator, philosopher, and author. Wisdom was described in a London *Times* obituary as "the only philosopher at Cambridge who came near to being leader of a school of thought" since Ludwig Wittgenstein. A professor of philosophy at St. Andrews University and then, beginning in 1934, at Cambridge University, Wisdom developed the ability to present eloquently and entertainingly his philosophical discourse, which made him a popular and influential lecturer. Of his writings, it was generally felt that his earliest works, such as 1931's *Interpretation and Analysis in Relation to Bentham's Theory of Definition,* were much stronger than his

later offerings. Though he retired from Cambridge in 1968 to spend a few years teaching at the University of Oregon, he eventually returned to Cambridge as a fellow of Trinity College. Wisdom's other writings included *Problems of Mind and Matter, Philosophy and Psycho-Analysis,* and *Paradox and Discovery.*

OBITUARIES AND OTHER SOURCES:

BOOKS

Who's Who, 146th edition, St. Martin's, 1994.

PERIODICALS

Times (London), December 13, 1993, p. 17.

*   *   *

WOLF, Stewart (George, Jr.) 1914-

PERSONAL: Born January 12, 1914, in Baltimore, MD; son of Stewart George (a manufacturer) and Angeline (Griffing) Wolf; married Virginia Danforth; children: Stewart George III, Angeline Gloria, Thomas Danforth. *Education:* Attended Yale University, 1931-33; Johns Hopkins University, A.B., 1934, M.D., 1938. *Politics:* Independent. *Religion:* Protestant.

ADDRESSES: Home and office—R.D.1, Box 1120G, Totts Gap Rd., Bangor, PA 18013.

CAREER: Cornell-New York Hospital, New York City, intern, 1938-39, resident, 1939-42; National Research Council fellow, 1941-42; Harvard-Boston City Hospital, Boston, MA, neurology fellow, 1942-43; Cornell University Medical College, New York City, assistant professor, 1946-49, associate professor of medicine, 1949-52; University of Oklahoma, Oklahoma City, professor of medicine, physiology, neurology, and psychiatry in the School of Medicine, 1952-69, regent's professor, 1969—, head of neuroscience section at Oklahoma Medical Research Foundation, 1952-69; University of Texas, Medical Branch, Galveston, professor of medicine and physiology, and director of Marine Biomedical Institute, 1970—. Totts Gap Medical Research Laboratories, director, 1958—; consultant to Will Rogers Veterans Administration Hospital, 1952-69. Affiliated with Regents National Library of Medicine, 1965-69, chairperson, 1969. Oklahoma Symphony Society, president, 1954-59. *Military service:* U.S. Army, Medical Corps; served during World War II in the Southwest Pacific; became major.

MEMBER: Pan American Medical Association, Academy of Behavioral Medicine Research, American Academy of Neurology, American Association for the Advancement of Science, American Association for the History of Medicine, American Clinical and Climatological

Association (vice-president, 1964; president, 1975-76; member of council, 1977-80), American College of Clinical Pharmacology and Chemotherapy (president, 1966-67), American College of Physicians (fellow), American Federation for Clinical Research (president, 1952-53), American Gastroenterological Association (president, 1969-70), American Heart Association, American Medical Association, American Osler Society, American Pavlovian Society (president, 1967), American Physiological Society, American Psychosomatic Society (president, 1961-62), American Society for Clinical Investigation, American Therapeutic Society (member of council, 1967-70), American Thoracic Society, Association of American Medical Colleges, Association of American Physicians, Harvey Society, Society for Experimental Biology and Medicine, Society for Neuroscience, Southern Society for Clinical Research, Central Society for Clinical Research, Philosophical Society of Texas, New York Academy of Sciences, Galveston County Medical Society, College of Physicians of Philadelphia (fellow).

AWARDS, HONORS: Honorary degree from University of Goteborg, Sweden, 1968.

WRITINGS:

(With H. G. Wolff) *Human Gastric Function: An Experimental Study of a Man and His Stomach,* Oxford University Press, 1943, 2nd edition, 1947.
(With Wolff) *Pain,* C.C Thomas, 1948, 2nd edition, 1958.
(With T. H. Holmes, H. Goodell, and Wolff) *The Human Colon: An Experimental Study Based on Direct Observation of Four Fistulous Subjects,* Paul Hoeber, 1951.
(With Wolff) *Headaches: Their Nature and Treatment,* Little, Brown, 1953.
(With P. V. Cardon, Jr., E. M. Shepard, and Wolff) *Life Stress and Essential Hypertension: A Study of Circulatory Adjustments in Man,* Williams & Wilkins, 1955.
An Evaluation of Therapeutic Drugs: With Special Reference to the Tranquilizing Drugs, Mental Hospital Service, American Psychiatric Association, 1957.
The Stomach, Oxford University Press, 1965.
(Editor of revision, with Goodell) H. G. Wolff, *Stress and Disease,* 2nd edition, C.C Thomas, 1968.
(Editor) *The Artery and the Process of Arteriosclerosis: Pathogenesis,* Plenum, 1971.
(Editor) *The Artery and the Process of Arteriosclerosis: Measurement and Modification,* Plenum, 1971.
(Editor with N. T. Werthessen) *Smooth Muscle of the Artery,* Plenum, 1975.
(With Goodell) *Behavioral Science in Clinical Medicine,* C. C Thomas, 1975.
(Editor with B. B. Berle) *Dilemmas in Diabetes,* Plenum, 1975.
(Editor with Berle) *The Biology of the Schizophrenic Process,* Plenum, 1976.

(Editor with Berle) *The Limits of Medicine: The Doctor's Job in the Coming Era,* Plenum, 1978.
(With J. G. Bruhn) *The Roseto Story: An Anatomy of Health,* University of Oklahoma Press, 1978.
(With Bruhn and Goodell) *Occupational Health as Human Ecology,* C. C Thomas, 1978.
(Editor) *Abdominal Diagnosis,* Lea & Febiger, 1979.
(Editor with Werthessen) *The Dynamics of Arterial Flow,* Plenum, 1979.
(Editor with Berle) *The Technological Imperative in Medicine,* Plenum, 1980.
Social Environment and Health, University of Washington Press, 1980.
(Editor with A. Murray) *The Composition and Function of Cell Membranes,* Plenum, 1980.
(Editor with H. Epstein) *Genetic Analysis of the X Chromosome: Studies of Duchenne Muscular Dystrophy and Related Disorders,* Plenum, 1982.
(Editor with L. I. Charash, A. Kutscher, and others) *Psychosocial Aspects of Muscular Dystrophy and Allied Diseases,* C. C Thomas, 1983.
(Editor with R. C. Strohman) *Gene Expression in Muscle,* Plenum, 1985.
(Editor with A. J. Finestone) *Occupational Stress: Health and Performance at Work,* PSG Publishing, 1986.
(With Bruhn, B. Egolf, and others) *The Power of Clan: The Influence of Human Relationship in Heart Disease,* Transaction Books, 1993.

Contributor to medical journals. Editor-in-chief, *Integrative Physiological and Behavioral Science,* 1990—; member of editorial board of a dozen journals.

WORK IN PROGRESS: The Doctors and Their Teachers, an analysis of medical education and practice; *The Brain's Control of the Heart.*

*   *   *

WOLFE, Art 1952-

PERSONAL: Born September 12, 1952, in Seattle, WA; son of Richard (a photographer and printer) and Elinor (a printer) Wolfe. *Education:* University of Washington, Seattle, degrees in art education and painting, 1975.

ADDRESSES: Agent—Bruce McGaw Graphics, 230 Fifth Ave., New York, NY, 10001.

CAREER: Photographer and painter. Works have appeared in exhibitions, including at the Frye Art Museum, Seattle, WA, and at Silver Image Gallery, Seattle, 1991.

WRITINGS:

The Imagery of Art Wolfe (monograph), Arpel Graphics, 1985.

The Sierra Club Alaska Postcard Collection: A Portfolio, Sierra Club Books, 1989.

Light on the Land (part of "Earthsong Collection" series), edited by Art Davidson, Beyond Words Publishing, 1991.

The Art of Nature Photography, text by Martha Hill, Crown, 1993.

PHOTOGRAPHER; NONFICTION

Allan Lobb, *Indian Baskets of the Northwest Coast,* drawings by Barbara Paxson, Graphic Arts Center Publishing, 1978.

(With Wilbur Mills) T. H. Watkins, *Vanishing Arctic: Alaska's National Wildlife Refuge,* introduction by Edward Hoagland, Aperture Foundation/Wilderness Society, 1988.

Art Davidson, *Alakshak, The Great Country,* foreword by Galen Rowell, Sierra Club Books, 1989.

Douglas H. Chadwick, *The Kingdom: Wildlife in North America,* Sierra Club Books, 1990.

Owls, Their Life and Behavior: A Photographic Study of the North American Species, text by Julio de la Torre, foreword by Roger Tory Peterson, Crown, 1990.

Chadwick, *Kingdom: Wildlife in North America,* Sierra Club Books, 1990.

Gary Kowalski, *The Souls of Animals,* Stillpoint Publishing, 1991.

Martin, *Masters of Disguise: A Natural History of Chameleons,* foreword by Ron Tremper, Facts on File, 1992.

Bears, Their Life and Behavior: A Photographic Study of the North American Species, text by William Ashworth, Crown, 1992.

Penguins, Puffins, and Auks, Their Lives and Behavior: A Photographic Study of the North American and Antarctic Species, text by Ashworth, Crown, 1993.

Contributor of photographs to periodicals, including *National Geographic, Smithsonian, Natural History, Time, Newsweek,* and *Outdoor Photographer.* Contributor of photographs to books, including *Mountains of North America,* Sierra Club Books; *America's Wildlife Sampler,* National Wildlife Federation; *The Wonder of Birds,* National Geographic Society; *America, Land of Wildlife,* National Wildlife Federation; and *Nature's Wonderlands,* National Geographic Society.

PHOTOGRAPHER; CHILDREN'S NONFICTION

James Martin, *Chameleons: Dragons in the Trees,* Crown, 1990.

Martin, *Hiding Out: Camouflage in the Wild,* Crown, 1993.

WORK IN PROGRESS: "A comprehensive look at biodiversity in the animal kingdom."

BIOGRAPHICAL/CRITICAL SOURCES:

PERIODICALS

American Photographer, October, 1986.

*   *   *

WOLIN, Steven J. 1940-

PERSONAL: Born October 31, 1940, in New York, NY; son of Hyman and Harriette Wolin; married Sybil Walter (a developmental psychologist), May 7, 1964; children: Jessica, Benjamin. *Education:* Brown University, A.B., 1962; Yeshiva University, M.D., 1966.

ADDRESSES: Home—3210 Newark St. NW, Washington, DC 20008. *Office*—5410 Connecticut Ave. NW, Washington, DC 20015; and Division of Research, Department of Psychiatry, George Washington University Medical Center, 2300 I St. NW, Room 613, Washington, DC 20037.

CAREER: Jewish Hospital of Brooklyn, Brooklyn, NY, intern in medicine and pediatrics, 1966-67; Bronx Municipal Hospital, Bronx, NY, resident in psychiatry, 1967-70; George Washington University, Washington, DC, clinical instructor, 1971-72, assistant clinical professor, 1972-78, associate clinical professor, 1978-83, clinical professor of psychiatry and medicine, 1983—, instructor in family therapy, 1980—, director of family therapy training. Diplomate, National Board of Medical Examiners, 1967, and American Board of Psychiatry and Neurology, 1972; private practice of psychiatry, 1970—. University of Judaism, visiting professor, 1991-92. National Council on Alcoholism, member of Criteria Committee on the Diagnosis of Alcoholism, 1971-73; consultant to National Clearinghouse for Alcohol Information. Home and School Institute, member of board of directors, 1980-86. U.S. Public Health Service, clinical associate, Alcohol, Drug Abuse, and Mental Health Administration, and National Institute for Alcohol Abuse and Alcoholism, 1970-72, became lieutenant commander.

MEMBER: World Psychiatric Association (transcultural section), American Psychiatric Association (fellow), American Association of Marriage and Family Therapy, American Society on Addiction Medicine (chairperson of Family and Generational Issues Committee, 1988-91), American Family Therapy Association, Society for the Study of Psychiatry and Culture, National Association for Children of Alcoholics (member of board of directors, 1992-93), District of Columbia Medical Society, Washington Area Children of Alcoholics Association (member of board of directors, 1987-91), Washington Psychiatric Society.

AWARDS, HONORS: Grants from National Institute for Alcohol Abuse and Alcoholism, 1974-77, 1977-80, and 1981-83, Still Water Foundation, 1984-90, and Whizin Foundation, 1992-93; shared award for distinguished contribution to family systems research from American Family Therapy Association, 1991.

WRITINGS:

(With P. Steinglass, L. A. Bennett, and D. Reiss) *The Alcoholic Family,* Basic Books, 1987.
(With wife, Sybil Wolin) *The Resilient Self: How Survivors of Troubled Families Rise Above Adversity,* Villard Books, 1993.

Work represented in books, including *Alcohol Intoxication and Withdrawal,* edited by M. M. Gross, Plenum, 1975; *Family Transitions: Continuity and Change Over the Life Cycle,* edited by C. Falicov, Guilford, 1988; and *Alcohol and the Family,* edited by R. L. Collins, K. E. Leonard, and J. S. Searles, Guilford, 1990. Contributor of about forty articles to medical and counseling journals. Member of editorial review board, *Alcohol Health and Research World,* 1981-86; advisory editor, *Journal of Family Dynamics of Addiction,* 1990—.

WORK IN PROGRESS: Survivor's Pride: Resilience in Youth at Risk, an eight-part video series, for the Attainment Company.

* * *

WOLIN, Sybil

PERSONAL: Married Steven J. Wolin (a psychiatrist and university professor), May 7, 1964. *Education:* Skidmore College, B.A., 1962; New York University, M.A., 1964; University of Maryland at College Park, Ph.D., 1987.

ADDRESSES: Home—3210 Newark St. NW, Washington, DC 20008. *Office*—5410 Connecticut Ave. NW, Washington, DC 20015.

CAREER: Junior high school English teacher in Merrick, NY, 1962-63; high school English teacher in New Rochelle, NY, 1964-69; New York State Youth Board, East Harlem Youth Employment Center, New York City, remedial reading teacher, 1969-70; Tri-Services Center, Rockville, MD, education specialist, 1975-79; private practice of educational diagnostics, remediation, and advocacy, 1979-91; University of Judaism, Los Angeles, CA, adjunct professor, 1992-93; Project Resilience, Washington, DC, writer and co-director. Adult education teacher in New Rochelle, 1969-70; consultant to Parent Education Advocacy Training Center.

MEMBER: Orton Dyslexia Society, Montgomery County Association for Children With Learning Disabilities, Phi Kappa Phi.

WRITINGS:

(With husband Steven J. Wolin) *The Resilient Self: How Survivors of Troubled Families Rise above Adversity,* Villard Books, 1993.

Contributor to *Family Dynamics of Addiction.*

* * *

WOLTERS, Richard A. 1920-1993

OBITUARY NOTICE—See index for *CA* sketch: Born February 8, 1920, in Philadelphia, PA; died of a heart attack, October 9, 1993, in Hanover, VA. Author, photographer, and chemist. Wolters was best known for his expertise in the training of hunting dogs, as demonstrated in such books as *Gun Dog, Family Dog, Water Dog,* and *Game Dog.* After a five-year stint as a chemical engineer working on rockets, Wolters became a freelance photographer, lending his skills to *Science Illustrated, Business Week,* and other publications. He had an avid interest in the outdoors, participating in such activities as parachuting, gliding, and piloting ultralight aircraft. He was honored on several occasions by the Dog Writers Association of America. Wolters' other books include *Beau from Both Ends of His Leash, Art and Technique of Soaring,* and *Once upon a Thermal.*

OBITUARIES AND OTHER SOURCES:

Writers Directory: 1992-1994, St. James Press, 1991.

PERIODICALS

New York Times, October 14, 1993, p. B10.

* * *

WOOD, Dennis (Michael) 1947-

PERSONAL: Born July 3, 1947, in West Bromwich, Staffordshire, England; son of Bernard (a manager) and Hilda (a homemaker; maiden name, Brown) Wood; married Katherine Anne Scholey (a management consultant), August 9, 1969; children: Orlando Benedict, Francis Alexander. *Education:* King's College, London, B.A. (with first class honors), 1969; St. John's College, Cambridge, Ph.D., 1972. *Avocational Interests:* Music, fly fishing, Roman archaeology, languages.

ADDRESSES: Home—12 Selly Wick Dr., Selly Park, Birmingham B29 7TH, England. *Office*—Department of

French Studies, School of Modern Languages, University of Birmingham, Edgbaston, Birmingham B15 2TT, England.

CAREER: University of Birmingham, Birmingham, England, lecturer, 1972-86, senior lecturer, 1986-89, reader in French literature, 1989—, member of board of management, Institute for Advanced Research. Universite Paul Valery, exchange lecturer, 1977.

MEMBER: Society for French Studies, Association Benjamin Constant, Association Suisse des Amis de Mme. de Charriere.

AWARDS, HONORS: Grants from Dutch Pro Musis Foundation, 1978, Swiss Pro Helvetia Foundation, 1981, 1993, British Academy, 1981, 1992, French Government, 1981, and Leverhulme Trust (for Germany and Switzerland), 1986.

WRITINGS:

(Editor) Isabelle de Charriere and Belle de Zuylen, *Oeuvres completes,* G. A. van Oorschot (Amsterdam), Volume VIII: *Romans, contes et nouvelles I, 1763-1797,* 1980, Volume IX: *Romans, contes et nouvelles II, 1798-1806,* 1981.
Constant: "Adolphe," Cambridge University Press, 1987.
(Editor with Ceri Crossley) *Annales Benjamin Constant 7: Constant in Britain/Constant et la Grande-Bretagne,* [Paris], 1987.
Benjamin Constant: A Biography, Routledge & Kegan Paul, 1993.
(Editor with C. P. Courtney) Benjamin Constant, *Correspondence generale,* Max Niemeyer Verlag (Tuebingen), Volume II: *1793-1794,* 1994, Volume III: *1795-1805,* in press.
(Editor and author of introduction and notes) Benjamin Constant, *Oeuvres completes,* Volume III: *Ecrits litteraires,* 1994.
The Novels of Isabelle de Charriere (1740-1805), Edwin Mellen Press, 1994.

Work represented in anthologies, including *Representations of Belief: Essays in Memory of C. V. Banks,* edited by Elizabeth Fallaize, Ron Hallmark, and Ian Pickup, Birmingham Modern Language Publications, 1991. Contributor to periodicals.

WORK IN PROGRESS: Editing Benjamin Constant, *Correspondence generale,* for Max Niemeyer Verlag (Tubingen), publication of Volume IV expected in 1996, Volume V, 1997; research on eighteenth- and nineteenth-century French literature and on the French novel.

SIDELIGHTS: Dennis Wood told *CA:* "After work on the novels of Isabelle de Charriere, I edited her novels and correspondence. Interest in her work led me to carry out research on her friendship with the more famous novelist and political writer Benjamin Constant. I have published a study of Constant's *Adolphe,* a biography of him, and more than twenty articles on Constant and his work, based on archival research in Europe. I am currently editing his complete correspondence with Dr. C. P. Courtney of Christ's College, Cambridge. We foresee perhaps fifteen volumes of letters, published within the framework of the complete edition in progress."

*   *   *

WOODMAN, Allen 1954-

PERSONAL: Born December 21, 1954, in Montgomery, AL; son of Frank Angelo (a designer) and Inez (a nurse and artist; maiden name, Holman) Woodman; married Jane Armstrong (a writer and teacher). *Education:* Huntingdon College, B.A., 1976; Florida State University, M.A., 1983, Ph.D., 1986.

ADDRESSES: Home—P.O. Box 22310, Flagstaff, AZ 86002. *Office*—Box 6032, English Department, Northern Arizona University, Flagstaff, AZ 86011.

CAREER: Northern Arizona University, Flagstaff, AZ, associate professor of English, 1986—.

MEMBER: Authors Guild, Society of Children's Book Writers and Illustrators, PEN West, Associated Writing Programs, Poets and Writers.

AWARDS, HONORS: Creative writing fellowship in fiction, Arizona Commission on the Arts, 1992; stories have been cited in *Best American Short Stories* and *The Pushcart Prize* series.

WRITINGS:

The Shoebox of Desire and Other Tales, Swallow's Tale Press, 1987, revised edition, Livingston University Press, 1994.
All-You-Can-Eat, Alabama (novel), Apalachee Press, 1994.

Work represented in anthologies, including *Best American Short Stories The Pushcart Prize.* Contributor to periodicals, including *The North American Review, Pennywhistle Press, Flash Fiction, Epoch, Carolina Quarterly, Apalachee Quarterly,* and *The California Quarterly.*

FOR CHILDREN

(With David Kirby) *The Cows Are Going to Paris,* Boyds Mills/St. Martin's Press, 1991.
(With Kirby) *The Bear Who Came to Stay,* Bradbury Press, 1994.

WORK IN PROGRESS: A collection of stories, *The Appliances of Loss,* Livingston University Press, 1994; two children's books; a novel; a screenplay.

*   *   *

WOODWARD, John Forster
See WOODWARD, Sandy

*   *   *

WOODWARD, Sandy 1932-

PERSONAL: Born John Forster Woodward, May 1, 1932, in Penzance (some sources say Marazion), Cornwall, England; son of Tom (a banker) and Mabel Blewis Madge (Gale) Woodward; married Charlotte Mary McMurtrie, April 9, 1960; children: one son, one daughter. *Education:* Attended Britannia Royal Navy College, 1946-50. *Avocational Interests:* Sailing, philately, skiing, desktop computers.

ADDRESSES: Office—c/o The Naval Secretary, Ministry of Defence, Old Admiralty Building, Whitehall SW1A 2BE, England.

CAREER: Has served in various posts in the British Royal Navy since 1946, including early training in cruisers and destroyers of the Home Fleet, 1950-53, submarine specialist, 1953-1971, and commanding officer of three submarines and one destroyer, 1960-77; senior training and headquarters positions since 1971, including British Ministry of Defence, the Royal College of Defence Studies, and Director of Naval Plans, 1978-81. Senior Task Group Commander in the South Atlantic Ocean during the Falklands campaign, 1982; Flag Officer, Submarines, and North Atlantic Treaty Organization (NATO) Commander, Submarines, in the Eastern Atlantic, 1983-84. British Ministry of Defence, Deputy Chief of Defence Staff (Commitments), 1985-87, Commander-in-Chief, Naval Home Command, and Flag Aide-de-Camp to the Queen, 1987-89. Management consultant, 1989—.

MEMBER: Royal Naval Sailing Association.

AWARDS, HONORS: South Atlantic Campaign Medal; Knight Commander of the Order of Bath, 1982; Knight Grand Cross of the British Empire, 1989.

WRITINGS:

(With Patrick Robinson) *One Hundred Days: The Memoirs of the Falklands Battle Group Commander,* foreword by Margaret Thatcher, Naval Institute Press, 1992.

SIDELIGHTS: Sandy Woodward, known fully as Admiral Sir John Forster Woodward, was recognized for his achievements years before the publication of his well-received book. The admiral's leadership of the British naval forces during the Falkland Islands conflict in 1982 catapulted him into the international spotlight. *One Hundred Days: The Memoirs of the Falklands Battle Group Commander* details this eventful period. The small archipelago off the coast of Argentina had been held for generations by England, but a surprise invasion by Argentina in the spring of 1982 touched off a small yet vicious war, one that tested the mettle of the entire British military system. The hostilities lasted just over three months, and Britain emerged victorious despite suffering severe losses among all its forces.

One Hundred Days was co-written with Patrick Robinson, who had previously authored works on thoroughbred racing, the America's Cup yacht race, and rowing. While the volume details the decisive actions Woodward took in the war in the South Atlantic that crowned his decades-long naval career, it is primarily concerned with the thoughts, ideas, and feelings that lay behind the action. In an example of the dramatic accounts of the strife detailed within the memoir, Woodward relates his decision to give orders to a Royal Navy nuclear submarine to attack an enemy ship, the General Belgrano. This was a risky maneuver because the cruiser was not in the immediate zone of war and Woodward had no authority to give such orders. Fortunately, the admiral's intuition was correct and his superiors supported his action: the successful sinking of the Argentine cruiser was a decisive moment in the war, resulting in the retreat of the enemy navy and smoothing the way for the landing of British amphibious forces on the Islands. Kenneth J. Hagan of the *New York Times Book Review* praised *One Hundred Days* as a "fascinating, smoothly written memoir."

BIOGRAPHICAL/CRITICAL SOURCES:

PERIODICALS

New York Times Book Review, June 14, 1992, p. 22.
Observer (London), February 16, 1992, p. 58.
Spectator, March 7, 1992, p. 34.
Times Literary Supplement, April 17, 1992, p. 11.

*   *   *

WRIGHT, Cliff 1963-

PERSONAL: Born October 24, 1963, in Newhaven, England; son of Ron (a construction site manager) and Nora (a homemaker; maiden name, Eager) Wright. *Education:* University of Brighton, B.A. (honors), 1986.

ADDRESSES: Home and office—"Greenways," Pevensey Rd., Newhaven, East Sussex BN9 9TU, England.

CAREER: Children's book writer and illustrator.

MEMBER: Greenpeace.

WRITINGS:

SELF-ILLUSTRATED PICTURE BOOKS

When the World Sleeps, Hutchinson, 1989.
Crumbs!, Hutchinson, 1990.
The Tangleweed Troll, Gollancz, 1993.

WORK IN PROGRESS: Researching English and American badgers for a fourth picture book, as yet untitled, completion expected in 1993.

SIDELIGHTS: Cliff Wright commented: "I began writing seriously whilst at college, studying illustration. I have always been most enthusiastic about developing my own ideas rather than illustrating someone else's—so the college projects which encompassed writing with pictures interested me most. Therefore, on leaving college I had a very generalized portfolio with no particular direction, although it did contain some ideas and wasn't just a collection of artwork. From that and the response from some publishers I quickly decided that writing/illustration for children was made for me."

Wright commented that his first book, *When the World Sleeps,* "started its life with too many words. It was obviously necessary to edit severely, and eventually I came to the conclusion that the story could be told with just pictures, encouraging kids to make up their own stories—although a great many publishers were concerned at this idea of a wordless picture book. As part of my own learning process, however, I have come to realize that it is essential to 'go with what you believe in,' and at last, two and a half years after it was conceived, *When the World Sleeps* was accepted for publication.

"I think it's important to develop and stretch your own capabilities, so with each successive project I have tried to introduce something different. With *Crumbs!* I hope this can be seen with the introduction of onomatopoeic words and a greater emphasis on my figurative drawing. In the third picture book, *The Tangleweed Troll,* I have tried to further the drawing still with regard to expression and movement and to develop a stronger story line—in this case every kid's desire to venture beyond his own backyard."

*   *   *

WYATT, Wesley Butler
   See TORME, Mel(vin Howard)

Y-Z

YAMADA, Nanako 1939-

PERSONAL: Born March 27, 1939, in Harubin, Manchuria; daughter of Takeshi (a physician) and Noriko (Taniyama) Narita; married Ryuji Yamada (a physicist), 1960; children: Seiji, Kouji. *Education:* Tokyo Women's Christian College, A.A., 1959; Northern Illinois University, B.A., 1985, M.A., 1989.

ADDRESSES: Home—1651 White Pines Court, Naperville, IL 60563.

CAREER: College of DuPage, Glen Ellyn, IL, instructor in Japanese language, 1990—; Northern Illinois University, De Kalb, IL, instructor in Japanese language, 1991—; free-lance art historian.

MEMBER: Association of Teachers of Japanese.

WRITINGS:

(With Helen Merritt) *Guide to Modern Japanese Woodblock Prints, 1900-1975,* University of Hawaii Press, 1992.

Author of *Takehisa Yumeji,* a script for Naperville Cable Television, 1991. Contributor to *Woman's Art Journal.*

WORK IN PROGRESS: Research on Japanese modern woodblock print frontispieces, 1890-1910; research on woodblock prints and Takehisa Yumeji.

SIDELIGHTS: Nanako Yamada told *CA:* "Even though the United States and Japan have become very close countries through the development of transportation, issues of trade, discussions in politics, and cultural exchanges, the modern Japanese arts are not yet well-known in this country. there is little written material about Japanese art history available in English.

"Although born and raised on the Asian continent, I have lived about half of my life in North America. I received my early education in Japan, then moved to the United States, where I raised two sons. After they matured, I returned to school and completed my B.A. and M.A. degrees.

"Through all my studies, the Japanese arts have remained my greatest interest. I am happy that through my writings I can share information about Japanese art that was not primarily available in English. In fact, I feel that researching, writing, and introducing Japanese art to the English-speaking world is my duty for the rest of my life."

* * *

YOUNG, Gavin (David) 1928-

PERSONAL: Born April 24, 1928, in London, England; son of Gavin David (an army officer) and Daphne (Forestier-Walker) Young. *Education:* Attended Rugby School; Trinity College, Oxford, M.A., 1950. *Avocational Interests:* Reading, travelling in remote places, music, talking late.

ADDRESSES: Home—c/o Weil, 49 Earls Court Rd., London W8 6EE, England.

Agent—Aitken, Stone & Wylie Ltd., 29 Fernshaw Rd., London SW10 0TA, England.

CAREER: Affiliated with Desert Locust Control, 1954-56; *Observer,* London, foreign correspondent covering wars and other events in Algeria, Cuba, Nagaland, the Congo, the Middle East, Kurdistan, Yemen, Bangladesh, Angola, Vietnam, and Cambodia, 1959-62, 1964-66, and 1968-90, correspondent in New York City, 1962-63, correspondent in Paris, 1967; freelance travel writer, 1977—. *Military service:* British National Service, lieutenant in the Welsh Guards, 1946-48.

MEMBER: Travellers Club (London), Cavalry and Guards club (London), Brooks's (London), Beefsteak (London), Groucho (London), Foreign Correspondents' (Hong Kong).

AWARDS, HONORS: International Journalist of the Year citation, IPC National Press Awards, 1971, for on-the-spot coverage of the Indo-Pakistan War and the birth of Bangladesh; Thomas Cook Travel Book Award, Book Trust, 1992, for *In Search of Conrad.*

WRITINGS:

NONFICTION

Return to the Marshes, Collins, 1977.
Iraq: Land of Two Rivers, Collins, 1979.
Slow Boats to China, Hutchinson, 1981, published in United States as *Halfway Around the World: An Improbable Journey,* Random House, 1981.
Slow Boats Home, Hutchinson, 1985, Random House, 1986.
Worlds Apart, Hutchinson, 1987.
Beyond Lion Rock: The Story of Cathay Pacific Airways, Hutchinson, 1988.
In Search of Conrad, Hutchinson, 1991.
Sleepers and Shadows: A Journey through America's Past, Hutchinson, in press.

Contributor to periodicals.

SIDELIGHTS: Gavin Young was a foreign correspondent for the London *Observer* for three decades; he covered wars and revolutions all over the world before he retired from his post in 1990. During the late 1970s he began penning travel books as well, starting with *Return to the Marshes.* He is best known, however, for *Halfway Around the World: An Improbable Journey, Slow Boats Home,* and *In Search of Conrad*—a book that garnered him the Thomas Cook Travel Book Award in 1992.

Halfway Around the World chronicles Young's trip from Piraeus, Greece, to Canton, China, primarily by boat. This proved a difficult task; as Jonathan Yardley explained in the *Washington Post Book World:* "Travel by ship . . . isn't what it used to be just a quarter-century ago; in fact, Young discovered, it is 'moribund.' " Young had to change his plans and travel by plane or train on three occasions, but for the most part, he arranged passage on whatever form of water craft he could. In the course of his journey, he boarded such diverse vehicles as cargo boats, Saudi ocean liners, and Indian dhows. He also experienced some dangerous moments: a dhow he was on nearly capsized in a storm, and near the Philippines his vessel was boarded by pirates who took his watch and his jacket. Some critics were not enthusiastic with Young's prose style in *Halfway Around the World,* but Yardley conceded that the author "takes the reader to exotic and faraway places; he offers enough tension and ennui to remind the reader that prolonged travel can be dangerous and/or boring; he keeps the reader interested in the seemingly simple yet eternally aggravating problem of getting from Point A to Point B." Jonathan Raban, a fellow travel writer, offered praise for *Halfway Around the World* in the *New York Review of Books,* noting that "Young is marvelous at building up the small, self-contained community of a boat at sea: it is his great good place, and his writing works over its construction lovingly."

Young followed *Halfway Around the World* with *Slow Boats Home,* a tale of his journey, again by boat, from Hong Kong, China, back to his native England. He visited places such as Samoa, Tonga, and rounded Cape Horn, the southernmost tip of South America before ending his trip in Plymouth. Geoffrey Moorhouse, a reviewer for the London *Times* enjoyed *Slow Boats Home,* declaring that "it is good to find the old-fashioned virtues of description and narrative so splendidly employed by one whose major interest is not himself, but what and whom he discovers wherever he goes."

Beginning when he was an adolescent, and throughout his long career, Young has been enamored of the works of author Joseph Conrad. Eventually the travel writer decided to follow the routes Conrad took during years that Conrad himself spent as a merchant sailor. Young published his discoveries in the 1991 book *In Search of Conrad.* In this volume, Young even discusses finding the grave of Augustine Podmore Williams, the real-life inspiration for the title character of Conrad's novel *Lord Jim.* "Williams's grave is just one stop on a search that takes Young from Singapore to Bangkok, from northern Java to the east coast of Borneo and down again through the hidden reefs of the Makassar Strait," observed David Crane in the *Spectator.* Tim Heald in the London *Times* hailed *In Search of Conrad* as "a marvellous piece of armchair escapism and thoroughly seductive" and asserted that Young "is relentless in his combing of archives, his grave-by grave examination of cemeteries, his badgering of ship's captains; and his knowledge of the Conrad oeuvre is compendious." Peter Kemp, reviewing Young's book along with several works of criticism about Conrad in the *Times Literary Supplement,* concluded that "in its reminder of the breadth of experience—the span of differing societies, crowded with a diverse diaspora of people— from which Conrad drew material for his writings, Young's work constitutes a rebuke to the pedantic narrowness and ideological *idees fixes* that constrict the critical books assembled here."

BIOGRAPHICAL/CRITICAL SOURCES:

PERIODICALS

New York Review of Books, January 21, 1982, pp. 46-47.

New York Times Book Review, January 3, 1982, p. 10.
Spectator, November 2, 1991, p. 45.
Times (London), July 11, 1985, November 16, 1991, p. 47.
Times Literary Supplement, November 27, 1981, p. 1386;
    November 15, 1991, p. 3.
Village Voice, February 10, 1982, pp. 52-53.
Washington Post Book World, October 7, 1981, p. B1.

*　　*　　*

YOUNG, J(ohn) Michael 1944-

PERSONAL: Born January 5, 1944, in Waterloo, IA; son of Robert James (a retail executive) and Lou Belle (a homemaker; maiden name, LaBarre) Young; married Carolyn Bryan (a high school teacher), January 26, 1963; children: Timothy Jason, Anne-Michelle, Christopher Bryan.

ADDRESSES: Home—803 Highland Dr., Lawrence, KS 66044. *Office*—Department of Philosophy, University of Kansas, Lawrence, KS 66045.

CAREER: University of Kansas, Lawrence, assistant professor, 1969-75, associate professor, 1975-82, professor of philosophy, 1982—. State University of New York at Stony Brook, visiting associate professor, 1979-80.

WRITINGS:

(Editor and translator) *Immanuel Kant: Lectures in Logic,* Cambridge University Press, 1992.

*　　*　　*

YOUNG, Philip
See STEWARD, Samuel M(orris)

*　　*　　*

YOUNG-EISENDRATH, Polly 1947-

PERSONAL: Born February 4, 1947; daughter of Ercil (a factory worker) and Frances (a homemaker) Young; married Richard Rickert, 1969 (divorced, 1974); married Edward Epstein (a clinical social worker and administrator), 1985; children: (first marriage) Arne (stepson), Amber, Colin; (second marriage) Noah (stepson). *Education:* Attended Institute de Touraine, 1967-68; Ohio University, A.B. (summa cum laude), 1969; Goddard College, M.A., 1974; Washington University, St. Louis, MO, M.S.W., 1977, Ph.D., 1980.

ADDRESSES: Home—350 Balligomingo Rd., Gulph Mills, PA 19428. *Office*—Clinical Associates West, 252

Radnor-Chester Rd., Radnor, PA 19087; and 204S Kirkbride, Institute of Pennsylvania Hospital, 111 North 49th St., Philadelphia, PA 19139. *Agent*—Beth Vesel, Sanford J. Greenburger Associates, Inc., 55 Fifth Ave., 15th Floor, New York, NY 10003.

CAREER: New York Bell Telephone, Personnel Assessment Center, New York City, research assistant, 1966, special assistant, 1967; Richardson Foundation, Greensboro, NC, coordinator of internship program for North Carolina Fellows Program, 1969-70; Guilford Technical Institute and Community College, Jamestown, NC, instructor in English and social sciences, 1970-73; Goddard Graduate Program, Washington, D.C., assistant regional director, 1974-75; Lindenwood Colleges, St. Louis, MO, instructor, 1975-76, associate director of Lindenwood 4, 1975-76, national program coordinator for College for Individualized Education, 1976-77, administrator of Master's Program in Art Therapy and Counseling Psychology, 1977-78; Washington University, St. Louis, instructor in counseling and social work and supervisor of Counseling Program at George Warren Brown School of Social Work, 1978-79; Bryn Mawr College, Bryn Mawr, PA, assistant professor of social work and social research, 1980-86; Clinical Associates West, chief psychologist, Jungian analyst, and president, 1986—. Bryn Mawr College, visiting lecturer in human development, 1986-89; lecturer at University of Pennsylvania, West Chester University, and Clarke Institute of Psychiatry; public speaker. C. G. Jung Center of Philadelphia, member of executive committee, 1986—; Institute of Pennsylvania Hospital, research psychologist, 1989—; C. G. Jung Foundation of the Delaware Valley, member of executive committee, 1990—; C. G. Jung Institute of Pittsburgh, member of board of directors; Round Table Associates for Analytical Psychology in the Delaware Valley, member.

MEMBER: International Association for Analytical Psychology, American Psychological Association, National Association of Social Workers, Pennsylvania Psychological Association, New York Association for Analytical Psychology, Philadelphia Association of Jungian Analysts (founding member), Philadelphia Society for Psychoanalytic Psychology, Phi Beta Kappa, Phi Kappa Phi, Mortar Board.

AWARDS, HONORS: Grant from Carol O'Donnell Foundation, 1992.

WRITINGS:

Hags and Heroes: A Feminist Approach to Jungian Psychotherapy with Couples, Inner City Press (Toronto), 1984.

(Editor with J. Hall) *The Book of the Self: Person, Pretext, Process,* New York University Press, 1987.

(With R. Wiedemann) *Female Authority: Empowering Women through Psychotherapy,* Guilford, 1987.

(With Hall) *Jung's Self Psychology: A Constructivist Perspective,* Guilford, 1991.

You're Not What I Expected: Learning to Love the Opposite Sex, Morrow, 1993.

The Cambridge Companion to Jung, Cambridge University Press, 1994.

Work represented in anthologies, including *Christianity, Patriarchy, and Abuse,* edited by C. Bohn, Pioneer Press (Philadelphia, PA), 1988; *To Be a Woman: Birth of the Conscious Feminine,* edited by C. Zweig, J. P. Tarcher, 1990; and *Gender and Soul in Psychotherapy,* edited by N. Schwartz-Salant and M. Stein, Chiron, 1991. Contributor of articles and reviews to journals in the behavioral sciences. Member of editorial board, *Harvest: Journal for Jungian Studies.*

WORK IN PROGRESS: Research on optimal experiences of adolescent inpatients at the Institute of Pennsylvania Hospital.

SIDELIGHTS: Polly Young-Eisendrath told *CA:* "Perhaps more than anything else, my writing is driven by my desire to understand. Whether I am writing a piece for a general audience or editing an academic book aimed at professionals in psychology or psychoanalysis, I am trying to understand something for myself.

"Because I work as a Jungian psychoanalyst and have the privilege of hearing people's life stories, I have little interest in fiction. Rarely is it as captivating or as bizarre as reality. Having spent thousands upon thousands of hours listening to life stories, I am perplexed and curious about how we claim to know the truth. How do we know that our memories represent reality? Why do people return again and again to the assumptions about life from which they suffer most? Why is the emotionally laden image such a powerful force in the human psyche?

"These kinds of questions take the form of philosophical inquiry for me, against a background of sociocultural context. I therefore find myself synthesizing psychology, feminism, gender studies, neuroscience, philosophy of mind, mythology, and psychoanalysis in most of what I write. My greatest challenge is to put things simply. Life appears to me as a vast complexity, and even supposedly simple truths (like we are born, we age, we die) are colored by emotional meanings and by language and culture to make them multi-toned and multi-layered. In writing I have come to doubt that simplicity is a virtue."

ZAPPA, Francis Vincent, Jr. 1940-1993 (Frank Zappa)

OBITUARY NOTICE—See index for *CA* sketch: Born December 21, 1940, in Baltimore, MD; died of prostate cancer, December 4, 1993, in Los Angeles, CA. Musician, composer, and political activist. Zappa, one of the most influential rock musicians, was "rock's most committed iconoclast," according to the *New York Times.* His bands, the Mothers of Invention and Zappa, debuted numerous talented musicians, and the record labels he founded signed a number of out-of-the-mainstream acts, including Alice Cooper and Captain Beefheart. Zappa's music ranged from doo-wop to psychedelia to Dadaist free-form and spotlighted his sometimes scatological and often satirical lyrics. His orchestral compositions have been performed by the Los Angeles Philharmonic orchestra and the Lyons Opera Ballet of France and have been conducted by Zubin Mehta (who once called Zappa "one of the few rock musicians who knows my language") and Pierre Boulez.

During the 1980s, Zappa was staunchly opposed to the type of music censorship proposed by the Parents Music Resource Center (PMRC); speaking frankly on the topic before a congressional panel, Zappa described the PMRC as a bunch of "bored housewives" whose actions were analogous to "treating dandruff by decapitation." Zappa was also a respected businessman, founding an international business consulting firm, "Why Not?," and hosting an interview program on cable television's Financial News Network. In 1989 he was invited by Czechoslovakia's President Vaclav Havel, a long-time fan of Zappa's, to serve as that country's representative to the West concerning trade and tourism. Zappa released his autobiography, *The Real Frank Zappa Book,* in 1989.

OBITUARIES AND OTHER SOURCES:

Who's Who in America, 48th edition, Marquis, 1994.

PERIODICALS

Chicago Tribune, December 7, 1993, p. 13.
Los Angeles Times, December 6, 1993, p. A1.
New York Times, December 7, 1993, p. B12.
Times (London), December 7, 1993, p. 21.

*   *   *

ZAPPA, Frank
See ZAPPA, Francis Vincent, Jr.

ZWIBAK, Jacques   1902-1994
(Andrei Sedych)

OBITUARY NOTICE—See index for *CA* sketch: Born August 14, 1902, in Pheodosia, Russia (near Odessa, now in the Ukraine); immigrated to the United States, 1942; naturalized citizen, 1947; died January 8, 1994, in Manhattan, NY. Journalist and author. Zwibak, who wrote under the pseudonym Andrei Sedych, was best known for his affiliation with New York City's Russian-language newspaper, *Novoye Russkoye Slova*—first as a contributor stationed in Europe, then as its managing editor and editor-in-chief in New York. Founded in 1910, *Novoye Russkoye Slova* ("New Russian World") claimed to be the world's oldest daily paper printed in Russian, predating both *Pravda* and *Izvestia.* In the 1920s Zwibak, then living in Paris, began contributing articles to the newspaper; he continued to write for *Novoye Russkoye Slova* on a freelance basis when he immigrated to the United States in 1942, finally joining its staff full-time in 1967. As the paper's editor-in-chief from 1973 to 1988, Zwibak encouraged the writing of articles that could help Russian-speaking people who had just arrived in America. He also the authored books of fiction and nonfiction, including *Sumasshedshii sharmanshchik* ("The Crazy Organ Grinder"), *Tol'ko o liudiakh* ("Only about People"), and *This Land of Israel.*

OBITUARIES AND OTHER SOURCES:

PERIODICALS

New York Times, January 9, 1994, p. 30.